MOON HANDBOOKS

COASTAL CALIFORNIA

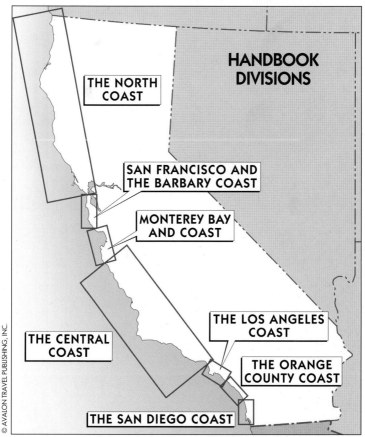

HANDBOOK DIVISIONS

THE NORTH COAST

SAN FRANCISCO AND THE BARBARY COAST

MONTEREY BAY AND COAST

THE LOS ANGELES COAST

THE CENTRAL COAST

THE ORANGE COUNTY COAST

THE SAN DIEGO COAST

MAP SYMBOLS

═══════	Divided Highway ▬▬▬	★	Point of Interest
══════	Primary Road ▬▬▬	•	Accommodation
──────	Secondary Road ══	▼	Restaurant/Bar
╌╌╌╌╌╌	Unpaved Road	▪	Other Location
─ ─ ─ ─	Trail ⋯⋯⋯	(ba)	BART Station
⬡	U.S. Interstate ⬤	▲	State Park
⬡	U.S. Highway	Λ	Campground
◯	State Highway	⛷	Ski Area
▢	County Road	⛳	Golf Course
◉	State Capital	▲	Mountain
○	City	✚	Unique Natural Feature
○	Town	⬚	Dry Lake
✕	International Airport	▨	Seasonal Lake
✕	Airfield/Airstrip		Swamp

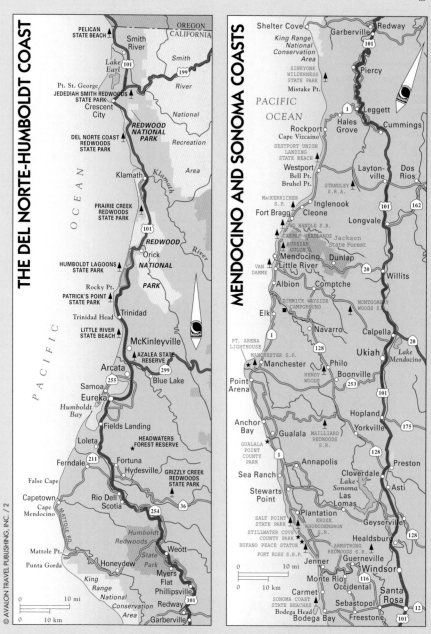

THE DEL NORTE-HUMBOLDT COAST

OREGON
CALIFORNIA

PELICAN
STATE BEACH
Smith
River

Lake
Earl
101
Smith

Smith
199
River

Pt. St. George
JEDEDIAH SMITH REDWOODS
STATE PARK
Crescent
City

REDWOOD
NATIONAL
PARK
National

DEL NORTE COAST
REDWOODS STATE PARK
Recreation

Klamath
Klamath
Area

River

O
PRAIRIE CREEK
REDWOODS
STATE PARK
101

C

REDWOOD

NATIONAL
Orick

HUMBOLDT LAGOONS
STATE PARK

E

PARK

Rocky Pt.
PATRICK'S POINT
STATE PARK

Trinidad Head
Trinidad

A

LITTLE RIVER
STATE BEACH

McKinleyville

N

AZALEA STATE
RESERVE
299

Arcata
Blue Lake
255

Samoa
Eureka

P

Humboldt
Bay

Fields Landing

A

Loleta

HEADWATERS
FOREST RESERVE

C

Ferndale
211
Fortuna
Hydesville
GRIZZLY CREEK
REDWOODS
STATE PARK

I

False Cape

36

F

Capetown
Cape
Mendocino
Rio Dell
Scotia
254

I

Mattole Pt.
Punta Gorda
Honeydew
Humboldt
Redwoods
State
Park
Weott

C
Myers
Flat
Phillipsville
King
Range
National
Conservation
Area
Redway
101

Garberville

© AVALON TRAVEL PUBLISHING, INC. / 2

0   10 mi
0   10 km

MENDOCINO AND SONOMA COASTS

Shelter Cove
Garberville
Redway

King Range
National
Conservation
Area
101

SINKYONE
WILDERNESS
STATE PARK
Mistake Pt.
Piercy

PACIFIC
OCEAN

1
Leggett
Cummings

Rockport
Cape Vizcaino
Hales
Grove

SESTPORT UNION
LANDING
STATE BEACH
Layton-
ville
Dos
Rios

Westport
Bell Pt.
Bruhel Pt.
STANDLEY
S.R.A.
101
162

MACKERRICHER
S.P.
Inglenook
Longvale

Fort Bragg
Cleone

JUG HANDLE S.R.
Jackson

CASPAR HEADLANDS
RUSSIAN
GULCH
Caspar
State Forest

Mendocino
Little River
Dunlap

VAN
DAMME
20
Willits

Albion
Comptche

DIMMICK WAYSIDE
CAMPGROUND
MONTGOMERY
WOODS S.R.

Elk
Navarro
Calpella
20

PT. ARENA
LIGHTHOUSE

1

MANCHESTER S.P.
Manchester
Philo
Ukiah
Lake
Mendocino

128
Boonville

Point
Arena

HENDY
WOODS
253

Anchor
Bay
Gualala
Hopland

MAILLIARD
REDWOODS
S.R.
Yorkville
175

GUALALA
POINT
COUNTY
PARK
1
Annapolis
128
Preston

Sea Ranch
Cloverdale
Lake
Sonoma
Asti

Stewarts
Point
Las
Lomas

SALT POINT
STATE PARK
Plantation
KRUSE
RHODODENDRON
S.R.
Geyserville
128

STILLWATER COVE
COUNTY PARK
BUFANO PEACE STATUE
FORT ROSS S.H.P.
Jenner
ARMSTRONG
REDWOODS S.R.
Healdsburg
Guerneville
Windsor

Monte Rio
116
Occidental
Santa
Rosa

Carmet
Sebastopol
12

SONOMA COAST
STATE BEACHES
Bodega Head
Bodega Bay
Freestone
101

0   10 mi
0   10 km

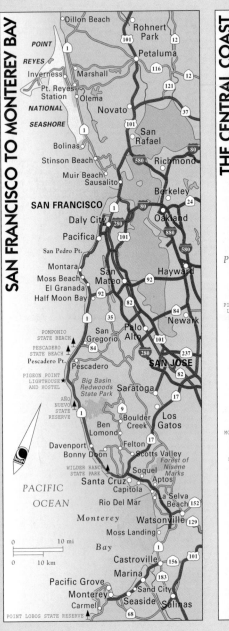

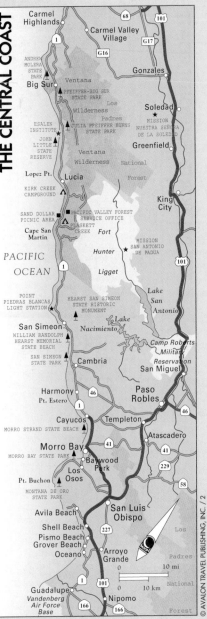

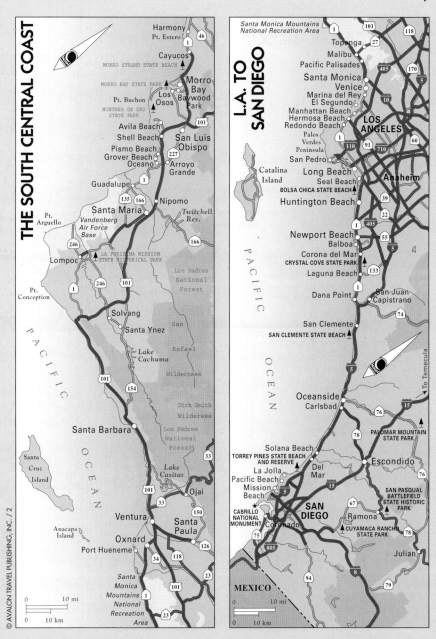

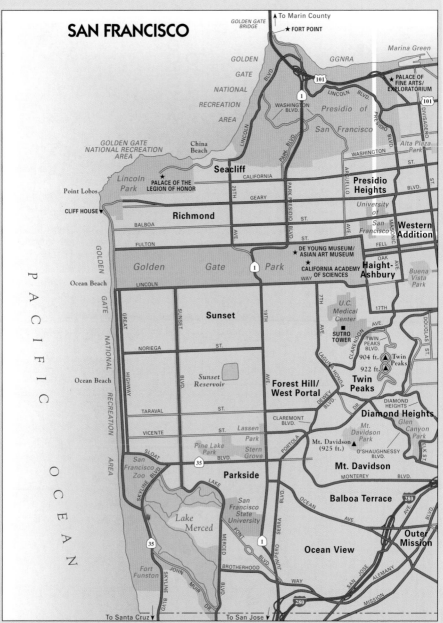

SAN FRANCISCO

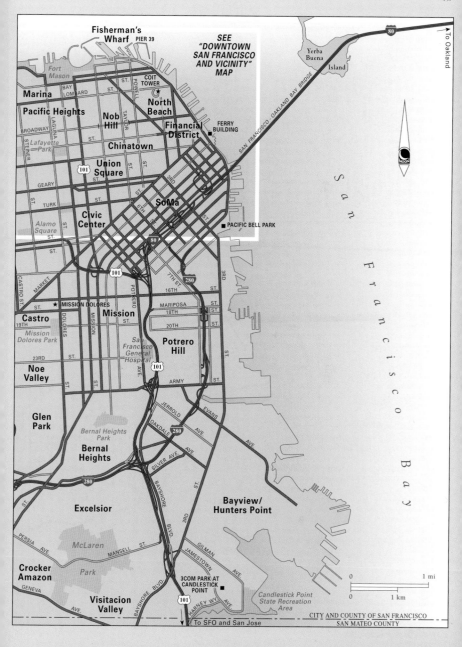

Fisherman's Wharf PIER 39

SEE "DOWNTOWN SAN FRANCISCO AND VICINITY" MAP

Yerba Buena Island

To Oakland

Fort Mason

Marina

Pacific Heights

BAY ST. LOMBARD ST.

COIT TOWER

North Beach

San Francisco Oakland Bay Bridge

POWELL ST.

TAYLOR ST.

Nob Hill

Financial District

FERRY BUILDING

BROADWAY

LAGUNA

STEINER

Lafayette Park

Chinatown

101

Union Square

GEARY

3RD

ST.

San Francisco Bay

TURK ST.

SoMa

6TH ST.

Civic Center

Alamo Square ST.

80

PACIFIC BELL PARK

CASTRO ST.

MARKET

101

280

7TH ST.

3RD

16TH ST.

MISSION DOLORES

POTRERO

MARIPOSA ST.

DOLORES ST.

Castro

19TH

Mission Dolores Park

Mission

MISSION ST.

18TH ST.

20TH ST.

Potrero Hill

23RD ST.

San Francisco General Hospital

101

Noe Valley

ARMY ST.

Glen Park

JERROLD

EVANS

Bernal Heights Park

OAKDALE 280

AVE.

AVE.

Bernal Heights

SILVER AVE.

280

BAYSHORE

ST.

3RD

Bayview/ Hunters Point

Excelsior

MANSELL ST.

McLaren Park

PERSIA AVE.

JAMESTOWN

GILMAN

AVE.

Crocker Amazon

BAYSHORE BLVD.

BLVD.

3COM PARK AT CANDLESTICK POINT

Candlestick Point State Recreation Area

GENEVA

Visitacion Valley

AVE.

101

HARNEY WY.

To SFO and San Jose

CITY AND COUNTY OF SAN FRANCISCO
SAN MATEO COUNTY

N
MOON

0   1 mi
0   1 km

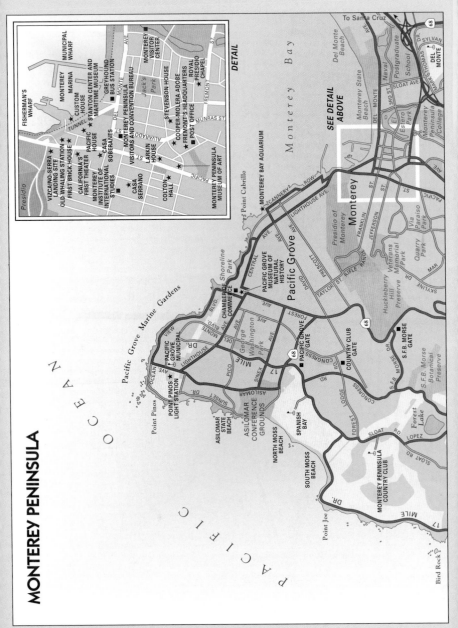

MONTEREY PENINSULA

DETAIL

- FISHERMAN'S WHARF
- MONTEREY MARINA
- MONTEREY MUNICIPAL WHARF
- VIZCAINO-SERRA LANDING SITE ★
- OLD WHALING STATION ★
- FIRST BRICK HOUSE ★
- CALIFORNIA'S FIRST THEATER ★
- MONTEREY INSTITUTE OF INTERNATIONAL STUDIES
- CUSTOM HOUSE ★
- PACIFIC HOUSE ★
- CASA SOBERANES ★
- STANTON CENTER AND MARITIME MUSEUM ■
- GREYHOUND BUS STATION ■
- MONTEREY VISITOR CENTER ■
- MONTEREY VISITORS AND CONVENTION BUREAU ■
- COOPER-MOLERA ADOBE ★
- FREMONT'S HEADQUARTERS ★
- POST OFFICE ■
- ROYAL PRESIDIO CHAPEL ★
- STEVENSON HOUSE ★
- LARKIN HOUSE ★
- CASA SERRANO ★
- COLTON HALL ★
- MONTEREY PENINSULA MUSEUM OF ART ■

Jack's Park

Presidio

MUNRAS ST

TUNNEL

ALVARADO

DEL MONTE

PACIFIC

FREMONT ST

AVE

Monterey Bay

SEE DETAIL ABOVE

To Santa Cruz

Del Monte Beach

Monterey State Beach

Del Monte Beach

Naval Postgraduate School

Monterey Peninsula College

68

SYLVAN

DEL MONTE

MARK THOMAS DR

3RD ST

SLOAT AVE

El Estero Park

Monterey

Point Cabrillo

MONTEREY BAY AQUARIUM ■

CANNERY ROW

LIGHTHOUSE AVE

Presidio of Monterey

Franklin ST

Jefferson

Via Paraiso Park

Quarry Park

PACIFIC ST

SKYLINE DR

MAR

Veterans Memorial Park

Huckleberry Hill Preserve

TAYLOR ST

PRESCOTT

DAVID

RIFLE RANGE

S.F.B. MORSE GATE ■

S.F.B. Morse Botanical Preserve

Pacific Grove

PACIFIC GROVE MUSEUM OF NATURAL HISTORY ★

Shoreline Park

CENTRAL AVE

VIEW

OCEAN VIEW BLVD

PACIFIC GROVE MUNICIPAL

CHAMBER OF COMMERCE ■

DEL MONTE BLVD

FOREST AVE

Pacific Grove Marine Gardens

LIGHTHOUSE AVE

SUNSET DR

PINE AVE

George Washington Park

FOREST

PICO

SINEX

MILE 17

ASILOMAR AVE

PACIFIC GROVE GATE ■

CONGRESS

68

COUNTRY CLUB GATE ■

RD

Point Pinos

POINT PINOS LIGHT STATION ★

ASILOMAR STATE BEACH

ASILOMAR CONFERENCE GROUNDS

NORTH MOSS BEACH

SPANISH BAY

S.F.B. MORSE DR

LODGE RD

CONGRESS

FOREST

SLOAT RD

LOPEZ RD

Forest Lake

SOUTH MOSS BEACH

MONTEREY PENINSULA COUNTRY CLUB

SLOAT RD

17 MILE DR

Point Joe

Bird Rock

O C E A N

P A C I F I C

© AVALON TRAVEL PUBLISHING, INC.

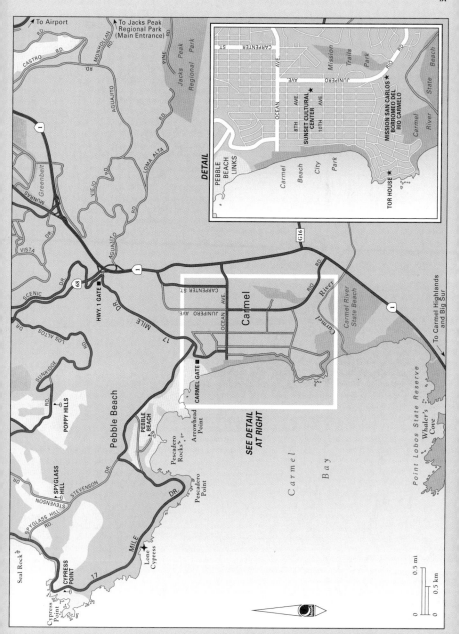

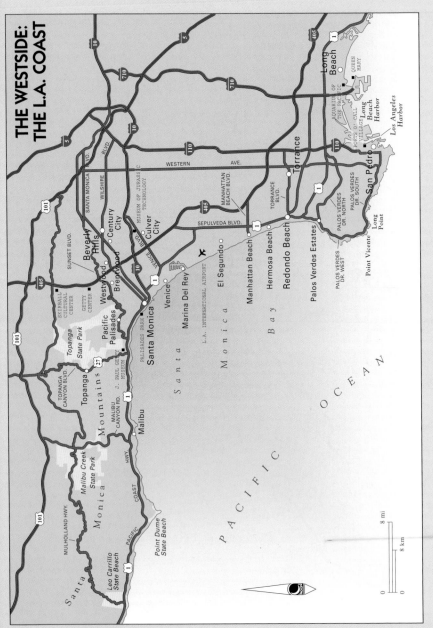

THE WESTSIDE:
THE L.A. COAST

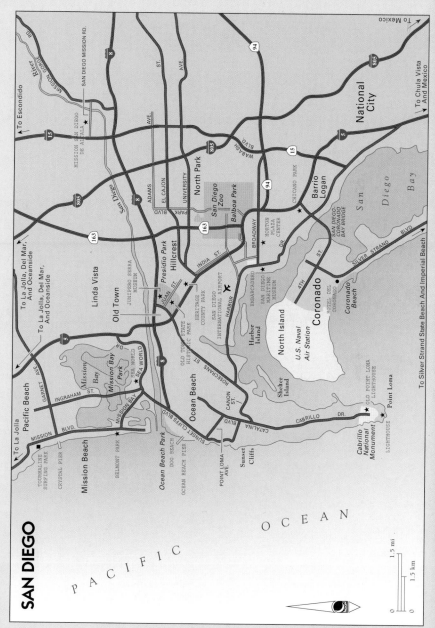

SAN DIEGO

To Mexico

National City

To Chula Vista And Mexico

To Escondido

SAN DIEGO MISSION RD.

MISSION GORGE RD.

River

To Jolla, Del Mar, And Oceanside

To La Jolla, Del Mar, And Oceanside

MISSION SAN DIEGO DE ALCALA

ST.

AVE.

AVE.

WABASH BLVD.

North Park

San Diego Zoo

Balboa Park

CHICANO PARK

Barrio Logan

ADAMS

EL CAJON

UNIVERSITY

PARK BLVD.

Presidio Park

Hillcrest

INDIA ST.

Linda Vista

Old Town

JUNIPERO SERRA MUSEUM

JUAN ST.

BROADWAY

HORTON PLAZA CENTER

HARBOR DR.

EMBARCADERO

SAN DIEGO MARITIME MUSEUM

SAN DIEGO CORONADO BAY BRIDGE

4TH ST.

SILVER STRAND

San Diego Bay

To La Jolla

Pacific Beach

GARNET AVE.

INGRAHAM ST.

Mission Bay

Mission Bay Park

SEA WORLD DR.

MISSION BAY

MISSION BLVD.

SEA WORLD

Ocean Beach

HERITAGE COUNTY PARK

OLD TOWN STATE HISTORIC PARK

SAN DIEGO INTERNATIONAL AIRPORT

ROSECRANS ST.

Harbor Island

Shelter Island

North Island

U.S. Naval Air Station

Coronado

HOTEL DEL CORONADO

Coronado Beach

SILVER STRAND BLVD.

To Silver Strand State Beach And Imperial Beach

TOURMALINE SURFING PARK

CRYSTAL PIER

Mission Beach

BELMONT PARK

MISSION BLVD.

Ocean Beach Park

SUNSET CLIFFS BLVD.

DOG BEACH

OCEAN BEACH PIER

CANON ST.

POINT LOMA AVE.

Sunset Cliffs

CATALINA BLVD.

CABRILLO DR.

Cabrillo National Monument

OLD POINT LOMA LIGHTHOUSE

LIGHTHOUSE

Point Loma

PACIFIC OCEAN

1.5 mi

1.5 km

0

0

© AVALON TRAVEL PUBLISHING, INC.

MOON HANDBOOKS

COASTAL CALIFORNIA

FIRST EDITION

KIM WEIR

**AVALON
TRAVEL**
publishing

MOON HANDBOOKS:
COASTAL CALIFORNIA
FIRST EDITION

Kim Weir

Published by
Avalon Travel Publishing, Inc.
5855 Beaudry St.
Emeryville, CA 94608, USA

© Text and photographs copyright Kim Weir, 2000.
All rights reserved.
© Illustrations and maps copyright
Avalon Travel Publishing, Inc., 2000. All rights reserved.

Some photos and illustrations are used by permission
and are the property of the original copyright owners.

ISBN: 1-56691-178-8
ISSN: 1531-1325

Editors: Steve Fahringer, Ellen Cavalli
Map Editor: Mike Ferguson
Production & Design: Carey Wilson, David Hurst
Cartography: Chris Folks, Mike Morgenfeld
Index: Leslie Miller

Front cover photo: © Marc Romanelli/ImageBank © 2000

All photos by Kim Weir unless otherwise noted.
All illustrations by Bob Race unless otherwise noted.

Distributed in the United States and Canada by Publishers Group West

Printed in U.S.A. by R. R. Donnelley

Please send all comments,
corrections, additions,
amendments, and critiques to:

**MOON HANDBOOKS:
COASTAL CALIFORNIA
AVALON TRAVEL PUBLISHING, INC.
5855 BEAUDRY ST.
EMERYVILLE, CA 94608, USA
e-mail: info@travelmatters.com
www.moon.com**

Printing History
First edition—October 2000

5 4 3 2 1 0

*I love to sail forbidden seas, and
land on barbarous coasts.*
—HERMAN MELVILLE

CONTENTS

SPECIAL TOPICS

MONTEREY BAY AND COAST . . . . 243~314

SPECIAL TOPICS

THE CENTRAL COAST . . . . 315~391
A Contrary Coast

SPECIAL TOPICS

SPECIAL TOPICS

MAP LIST

ACCOMMODATIONS RATINGS

Accommodations in this book are rated by price category, based on double-occupancy, high-season rates. Categories used are:

Budget. . . . . $35 and under
Inexpensive $35-60
Moderate $60-85
Expensive $85-110
Premium $110-150
Luxury . . . . $150 and up

ABBREVIATIONS

AAA—American Automobile
    Association
Ave.—Avenue
AYH—American Youth Hostel
B&B—bed and breakfast inn
Dr.—Drive
F—Fahrenheit

HI—Hostelling International
Hwy.—Highway
Ln.—Lane
Mt.—Mount
Pt.—Point
Rd.—Road
Rt.—Route

RV—recreational vehicle
St.—Street
TDD—Telecommunications
    Device for the Deaf
TTY—teletype
UC—University of California

EXPRESS YOURSELF

Not on just any topic, though. This being California, most things change faster than traffic lights. Because of this unfortunate fact of life in the fast lane of travel writing, comments, corrections, inadvertent omissions, and update information are always greatly appreciated. Though every effort was made to keep all current facts corralled and accounted for, it's no doubt true that *something* (most likely, a variety of things) will already be inaccurate by the time the printer's ink squirts onto the paper at press time.

Just remember this: whatever you divulge may indeed end up in print—so think twice before sending too much information about your favorite hole-in-the-wall restaurant, cheap hotel, or "secret" world's-best swimming hole or hot springs. Once such information falls into the hands of a travel writer, it probably won't be a secret for long. Address all correspondence to:

> *Moon Handbooks: Coastal California*
> C/o Avalon Travel Publishing
> 5855 Beaudry Street
> Emeryville, CA 94608
> E-mail: info@travelmatters.com
> (Please put Moon Coastal California in subject line.)

ACKNOWLEDGMENTS

I am endlessly grateful to my editor, Steve Fahringer, who is not only a scholar and a gentleman but also ace juggler, stand-up comic, diplomat in training, and all-around world-class word wrangler. I can't imagine a better boatman for this semi-civilized sail up and down California's "barbarous coasts." May we weigh anchor again together on many more trips. My gratitude, too, to Editorial Director Pauli Galin, who guides our peculiar meanderings from the safety of shore.

Always at the top of my thank you list, too, is Bill Newlin, publisher at Avalon Travel Publishing. I'm still appreciative of his original efforts to "make it work" so I might complete my longer-term task—telling the entire California story in travel book form. As Walt Whitman would say: "Oh Captain! my Captain! Our fearful trip is done." Like its predecessors, this book has weathered the rack. Let's hope we'll all still be cheering after the next book is made, and the next one after that.

The crew is so large. As always, I reserve a special category of gratitude for the many Moon Travel Handbook authors who helped me learn the ropes, particularly now-departed Joe Bisignani ("Mr. Hawaii"), Jane King, Steve Metzger, and Bob Nilsen. I offer my appreciation, too, to Ed Aust, Taran March, and Tim Moriarty for their contributions to this book's editorial content.

This time out, I extend my heartfelt thanks to Pat Reilly, my assistant on *San Francisco Handbook* and Supremely Reliable First Mate on the Southern California chapters of this book. Pat, a talented wordsmith in her own right, has a real job at San Francisco's own *Wired* magazine—one that pays considerably better than this one does—so I'm particularly grateful for her enthusiasm, good-natured determination, and graciousness in the midst of all the hard work it takes to make an easy read. Her own original writing is pretty darned seaworthy, too, and perhaps in the future we'll find enough time—and space—to give more of her own words a sail.

My thanks also to those who helped turn the words in this book into the coast-worthy craft you now hold in your hands. It's a bit confusing to correctly call the roll—and to give appropriate credit where it is due—now that Moon's administrative (and part of its editorial) staff are subsumed within the greater whole of Avalon Travel Publishing, in Emeryville. But at last report the hard-working bookmakers, of both the editorial and production persuasions, were still in the Chico office, bravely flailing away at the immense tasks before them.

Snapping off a few dozen rolls of fascinating photographs would be the best way to express my gratitude to the production crew. Words will have to suffice at the moment, though I promise to dust off the old Pentax next time I hit the road. Thanks to layout artists Dave Hurst and Carey Wilson, for their keen sense of balance, design, and overall visual aesthetics as well as patient attention paid to all those picayune graphic details. Special thanks to Chris Folks, for such fine work on the maps, and to Bob Race for his artistic contributions and dedication in organizing all of the book's graphic elements.

A hearty "Welcome Back" to Associate Publisher Donna Galassi—long-running Moon marketing inspiration and a friendly face from the good ol' days. After having worked her magic at both Foghorn and John Muir, now that all three companies are sailing together, under one mast, into new sales territory it's particularly appropriate, and pleasing, to have Donna at the helm once again. Many thanks also to Marketing Director Amanda Bleakley, as well as all those promotion and sales wizards—Mary Beth Pugh, Keith Arsenault, Stacy Johnson, Joelle Herr, Alannah Kern, and Sonia Clerc—for doing everything possible to help us all make a living in this business.

And let's not forget the webbies, including Matt Orendorff, Avalon's electronic media manager, and Mark Evrard, web designer, for keeping it all coming soon to a website near you.

My special thanks to photographer friends and sympathizers who have contributed their work to this work, including Todd Clark, Wes Dempsey, Dave Hurst, Tom Myers, Bob Nilsen, Aislinn Race, not to mention the California Department of Parks and Recreation. I extend extra gratitude to photographer Marc Romanelli, for this book's cover shot.

Reaching back into my past, I am still indebted to many of my environmental studies instructors at the University of California at Santa Barbara and to my biology professors at California State University, Chico—

particularly Doug Alexander, Wes Dempsey, Roger Lederer, Rob Schlising, and Tom Rodgers—for teaching me to *see* the living world. As I recall, that subject was never included on any class syllabus.

Arriving in the present, I also extend my heartfelt thanks to Fred Sater, media relations manager for the California Division of Tourism. I appreciate his personal encouragement and support, not to mention that refreshing sense of humor. I am also grateful for so many gracious introductions to travel industry pros at chambers of commerce and visitors bureaus throughout California. Their contributions and thoughtful suggestions have greatly improved this book's practical focus and (I hope) its overall usefulness.

—*Kim Weir*

BOB RACE

COASTING CALIFORNIA

California is a myth—a myth in the sense of a traditional tale told to impart truth and wisdom, and in the fanciful sense of some extravagant storybook fiction. Californians happen to like the quirky character of the state they're in. Whether or not they realize it, California as myth is exactly why they're here—because in California, even contradictions mean nothing. In California, almost everything is true and untrue at the same time. In California, people can pick and choose from among the choices offered, as if in a supermarket, or create their own truth. Attracted to this endless sense of creative possibilities—California's most universal creed, the source of the ingenuity and inventiveness the state is so famous for—people here are only too happy to shed the yoke of tradition, and traditional expectations, that kept them in harness elsewhere.

Californians tend to think life itself is a California invention, but "lifestyle" definitely is: people come to California to have one. Coming to California, novelist Stanley Elkin observes, "is a choice one makes, a blow one strikes for hope.

No one ever wakes up one day and says, 'I must move to Missouri.' No one chooses to find happiness in Oklahoma or Connecticut." And according to historian Kevin Starr, "California isn't a place—it's a need." Once arrived in California, according to the myth, the only reason to carry around the baggage of one's previous life is because one chooses to.

But it would be naive to assume that this natural expansiveness, this permission to be here now, is somehow new in California. It may be literally as old as the hills, a resource almost as tangible as the deep veins of gold that instantly transformed the region into a nation-state. Native peoples, the first and original laid-back Californians, seemed to understand this. Busy with the day-to-day necessities of survival, they nonetheless held the place in awe and managed to honor the untouchable earth spirits responsible for creation. The last remembered line of an ancient Ohlone dancing song—"dancing on the brink of the world"—somehow says it all about California. And particularly the California coastline.

FINDING THE GOLDEN SHORE

Native peoples had many explanations for how the land and life in California came to be. Yet it's a stranger-than-fiction fact that California as a concept was concocted in Europe, by a Spanish soldier turned romance writer.

The rocky-shored island paradise of California, according to the fictional 1510 *Las Sergas de Esplandían* ("The Exploits of Esplandian") by Garcí Ordóñez de Montalvo, overflowing with gold, gems, and pearls, was inhabited by griffins and other fantastic creatures, and "peopled by black women, with no men among them, for they lived in the fashion of Amazons" under the great Queen Calafia's rule. This imaginary wonderland, "on the right hand of the Indies, . . . an island called California, very near to the Terrestrial Paradise," fired the European imagination.

Equally inspired by the land now known as California, the Spanish attached the name to this particular place. Just how and when this came about is not precisely known. In 1864 Edward Everett Hale, author of *The Man Without a Country*, contended in the pages of the *Atlantic Monthly* that an early Spanish explorer associated the terrain of present-day Baja California with the California imagined by Montalvo. No one is certain whether that explorer was Fortún Jiménez, member of a Cortés expedition that

landed in Baja in 1533, or Francisco de Bolaños, who in 1541 explored both sides of the Baja Peninsula. But when Cabrillo, in 1542, and others attached the name California to territorial claims from Baja California north to Alaska, they did so as if its use were already well established.

USING~AND ENJOYING~ THIS BOOK

The California coastline is quite long, a narrow ribbon of rock, sand, and sandstone that meanders for more than 1,200 miles. Because of the coastline's length and this book's coastal focus, its contents had to be organized in a fairly linear fashion. As a result, this book "travels" in a fairly straightforward fashion, from north to south; working backward through the text, it "goes" south to north.

Yet this is not a linear book—because traveling in California is not a linear experience, or doesn't need to be. Meandering from place to place is by far the best way to enjoy the Golden State. So use this book to see how best to wander—and move both up and down the coast. Organized by region, city, and general area, this book was designed to make it easy to plan any trip, moving in whatever direction. Study the table of contents, flip through the chapters, and see for yourself.

THE LAND: AN ISLAND IN SPACE AND TIME

California's isolated, sometimes isolationist human history has been shaped more by the land itself than by any other fact. That early European explorers conceived of the territory as an island is a fitting irony, since in many ways—particularly geographically, but also in the evolutionary development of plant and animal life—California was, and still is, an island in both space and time.

The third-largest state in the nation, California spans 10 degrees of latitude. With a meandering 1,264-mile-long coastline, the state's western boundary is formed by the Pacific Ocean. Along most of California's great length, just landward from the sea, are the rumpled and eroded moun-

tains which are known collectively as the Coast Ranges.

Equally impressive in California's 158,693-square-mile territory is the Sierra Nevada range, which curves like a 500-mile-long spine along the state's central-eastern edge. Inland from the Coast Ranges and to the north of California's great central valley are the state's northernmost mountains, including the many distinct, wayward ranges of the Klamaths—mountains many geologists believe were originally a northwesterly extension of the Sierra Nevada. Just east of the Klamath Mountains is the southern extension of the volcanic Cascade Range, which includes Mount Shasta and Lassen Peak.

The 6,000-foot granite Castle Crags loom over I-5 north of Redding.

This great partial ring of mountains around California's heartland (with ragged eastern peaks reaching elevations of 14,000 feet and higher) as well as the vast primeval forests that once almost suffocated lower slopes, have always influenced the state's major weather patterns—and have also created a nearly impenetrable natural barrier for otherwise freely migrating plant and animal species, including human beings.

But if sky-high rugged rocks, thickets of forest, and rain-swollen rivers blocked migration to the north and east, physical barriers of a more barren nature have also slowed movement into California. To the south, the dry chaparral of the east-west Transverse Ranges and the northwest-southeast-trending Peninsular Ranges impeded northern and inland movement for most life forms. The most enduring impediment, however, is California's great southeastern expanse of desert—including both the Mojave and Colorado Deserts—and the associated desert mountains and high-desert plateaus. Here, only the strong and well-adapted survive.

CALIFORNIA QUAKING AND CONTINENTAL DRIFT

Perched along the Pacific Ring of Fire, California is known for its violent volcanic nature and for its earthquakes. Native peoples have always explained the fiery, earth-shaking temperament of the land in terms of a variety of myths and legends, but the theory of plate tectonics is now the most widely accepted scientific creation story. According to this theory, the earth's crust is divided into 20 or so major solid rock (or lithospheric) "plates" upon which both land and sea ride. The interactions of these plates are ultimately responsible for all earth movement, from continental drift and landform creation to volcanic explosions and earthquakes.

Most of California teeters on the western edge of the vast North American Plate. The adjacent Pacific Plate, which first collided with what is now California about 250 million years ago, grinds slowly but steadily northward along a line more or less defined by the famous San Andreas Fault (responsible for the massive 1906 San Francisco earthquake and fire as well as the more recent shake-up in 1989). Plate movement itself is usually imperceptible: at the rate things are going, within 10 million years Los Angeles will slide north to become San Francisco's next-door neighbor. But the steady friction and tension generated between the two plates sometimes creates special events. Every so often sudden, jolting slippage occurs between the North American and Pacific Plates in California—either along the San Andreas or some other fault line near the plate border—and one of the state's famous earthquakes occurs. Though most don't amount to much, an average of 15,000 earthquakes occur in California every year.

A still newer theory augments the plate tectonics creation story, suggesting a much more fluid local landscape—that California and the rest of the West literally "go with the flow," in particular the movement of hot, molten rock beneath the earth's crust. "Flow" theory explains the appearance of earthquake faults where they shouldn't be, scientists say, and also explains certain deformations in the continental crust. According to calculations published in the May 1996 edition of the journal *Nature,* the Sierra Nevada currently flows at the rate of one inch every three years.

CALIFORNIA'S COASTLINE

California's Coast Ranges are the largest and longest landform, extending an average of 50 miles in width and—from Southern California's Transverse Ranges north to the Oregon border—about 400 miles in length. The sedimentary Franciscan formation that comprises these

"That same prehistoric look. The look of always," Henry Miller said of Big Sur. "Nature smiling at herself in the mirror of eternity."

rounded, deeply eroded mountains began as sand and gravel washed down from the continental slope that accumulated in the ocean offshore; starting 150 million years ago, intense folding and faulting of the earth's surface gradually elevated them to mountain status. Among the many earthquake faults associated with the Coast Ranges is the famous San Andreas Fault, which crosses the southern portion of these mountains—angling northwestward from the desert—and, from San Francisco north, continues north on the seaward side of the mountains before plunging to sea at Point Arena.

Just south of the Coast Ranges is the physical boundary for greater Los Angeles—the unusual east-west-trending Santa Monica, San Gabriel, and San Bernardino Mountains, notable segments of the unusual and rugged east-west-trending Transverse Ranges that separate the southstate from the rest of California. The range actually extends westward, offshore, to form some of California's Channel Islands—Anacapa, San Miguel, Santa Cruz, and Santa Rosa. As measured on a geologic scale, the Los Angeles area is something of a new kid on the tectonic block, first rising out of the ocean 100-160 million years ago and then slipping back under water before bursting forth to stay with the help of massive igneous extrusions. The present-day landscape is of more recent origin, however, since even six million years ago the Palos Verdes peninsula was still an island in the Channel Islands chain and the ocean lapped the shores of Glendale.

Yet another mountain chain also shapes the Southern California landscape—the northwest-southeast-trending Peninsular Ranges, actually an extension of the Baja Peninsula, which appear as flat-topped marine terraces from San Diego and Orange County north to Palos Verdes, Long Beach, and Santa Monica Bay. Southern California's San Clemente Island, San Nicolas Island, and Santa Catalina Island are actually extensions of the Peninsular Ranges.

For travelers, though, California's coastline is most easily understood as either "north" or "south." The north coast is characterized by rugged, rocky shores, a tendency that extends south to Big Sur. California's northern coastline is challenging and inhospitable, with few sandy beaches and even fewer natural harbors. Along with northern ruggedness, even a few straggling redwoods extend as far south as Big Sur. Then, somewhere near Point Conception just north of Santa Barbara, the coast's attitude begins to change and Northern California starts to become Southern California, with balmier weather, calm seas, and broad, sandy beaches.

All along the coast, however, the land itself is quite unstable, with a habit of sliding out from under whole hillsides, houses, highways, and hiking trails at the slightest provocation—like rainfall.

FROM FIRE TO ICE: THE CALIFORNIA CLIMATE

California's much-ballyhooed "Mediterranean" climate is at least partially a myth. Because of extremes in landforms, in addition to various microclimatic effects, there are radical climatic differences within the state—sometimes even within a limited geographic area. But California as a whole does share most of the classic characteristics of Mediterranean climates: abundant sunny days year-round, a cool-weather coast, dry summers, and rainy winters. California, in fact, is the only region in North America where summer drought and rainy winters are typical.

Between the coast and the mountains immediately inland, where most of the state's people live, temperatures—though cooler in the north and warmer to the south—are fairly mild and uniform year-round. Because of the state's latitudinal gradation, rain also falls in accordance with this north-south shift: an average of 74 inches falls annually in Crescent City, 19-22 inches in San Francisco, and less than 10 inches in San Diego. When warm, moist ocean air blows inland over the cool California Current circulating clockwise above the equator, seasonal fog is typical along the California coast. Summer, in other words, is often cooler along the coast than autumn. (Just ask those shivering tourists who arrive in San Francisco every June wearing Bermuda shorts and sandals.)

Inland, where the marine air influence often literally evaporates, temperature extremes are typical. The clear, dry days of summer are often hot, particularly in the central valley and the deserts. (With occasional freak temperatures above 130° Fahrenheit, Death Valley is aptly named.) In winter, substantial precipitation arrives in Northern California—especially in the northwest "rain belt" and in the northern Sierra Nevada—with major storms expected from October to May. California's northern mountains "collect" most Pacific Ocean moisture as rain; in the High Sierra, the average winter snowpack is between 300 and 400 inches. Wrung out like sponges by the time they pass over the Sierra Nevada and other inland mountains, clouds have little rain or snow for the eastern-slope rainshadow.

Since the 1970s, California's climate patterns have been increasingly atypical—which may be normal, or may be early local indications of global warming. The reason no one knows for sure is because the state's "average" weather patterns were largely defined between the 1930s and the 1970s, a period of unusually stable weather conditions, it now appears. Complicating the question further is new scientific research suggesting that California's climate has been characterized, since ancient times, by alternating cycles of very wet and very dry weather—200- to 500-year cycles. Epic droughts have been traced to the Middle Ages, and just 300 years ago California experienced a drought lasting 80-100 years. California's last century and a half, it turns out, represents one of the wettest periods in the past 2,500 years.

The increasing scientific consensus is that global warming is indeed having a major impact on California weather. Since the late 1970s, El Niño "events" have increased noticeably, bringing warmer offshore waters and heavy storms in California and the Southwest. But in other years—drought times for California—"La Niña" occurs, with colder offshore waters and storms tracking into the Pacific Northwest. Being whipsawed between periods of torrential rains and flooding (yet subnormal snowpack) and devastating drought seems to be California's future—a future almost certain to feature disrupted water supplies, even without a 100-year drought.

CALIFORNIA FLORA:
BLOOMING AT THE BRINK

"In California," observed writer Joaquin Miller, "things name themselves, or rather Nature names them, and that name is visibly written on the face of things and every man may understand who can read." When explorers and settlers first stumbled upon California's living natural wonders, they didn't "read" landforms or indigenous plants and animals in the same way native peoples did, but they were quite busy nonetheless attaching new names (and eventually Latin terminology) to everything in sight. From the most delicate ephemeral wildflowers to California's two types of towering redwoods, from butterflies and birds to pronghorns, bighorn sheep, and the various subspecies of grizzly bear, the unusual and unique nature of most of the territory's life forms was astonishing. California's geographical isolation—as well as its dramatic extremes in landforms and localized climates—was (and still is) largely responsible for the phenomenal natural divergence and diversity found here.

Former President Ronald Reagan, while still governor of California and embroiled in a battle over expanding redwood parks, unwittingly expressed the old-and-in-the-way attitude about the state's resources with his now-famous gaffe, widely quoted as: "If you've seen one redwood, you've seen 'em all." (What Reagan actually said was: "A tree is a tree—how many more do you need to look at?") But his philosophy, however expressed, is the key to understanding what has happened to California's trees, other native flora, and animal species.

Even today, the variety of California's native plantlife is amazing. Nearly 5,200 species of plants are at home in the Golden State—symbolized by the orange glow of the California poppy—and more than 30% of these trees, shrubs, wildflowers, and grasses are endemic. (By comparison, only 13% of plantlife in the northeastern U.S., and one percent of flora in the British Isles, are endemic species.) In fact, California has greater species diversity than the combined totals of the central and northeastern U.S. and adjacent Canada—an area almost 10 times greater in size.

But to state that so many plant species survive in California is not to say that they thrive. The economic and physical impacts of settlement have greatly stressed the state's vegetative wealth since the days of the gold rush, when the first full-scale assaults on California forests, wetlands, grasslands, and riparian and oak woodlands were launched. The rate of exploitation of the state's 380 distinct natural communities has been relentless ever since. Half of the state's natural terrestrial environments and 40% of its aquatic communities are endangered, rare, or threatened.

Some of the state's most notable natural attractions are its unique trees—entire forests nearly toppled at the edge of extinction. California's *Sequoiadendron giganteum,* or giant sequoia, grows only in limited surviving stands in the Sierra Nevada—saved as much by the brittleness of its wood as by the public outcry of John Muir and other enlightened 19th-century voices. But the state's remaining virgin forests of *Sequoia sempervirens,* the "ever-living" coast redwoods, are still threatened by clear-cutting, a practice that also eliminates the habitat of other species. The same conservation-versus-economic expediency argument also rages over the fate of the few remaining old-growth outposts of other popular timber trees. And decades of fire suppression, logging, grazing, and recreational development in California's vast forests of ponderosa pines, combined with increasing air pollution and the state's recent drought, have led to insect infestations, tree disease, and death—and a tinder-dry, fuel-rich landscape more vulnerable than ever to uncontrollable fires. Even trees without notable economic value are threatened by compromises imposed by civilization. Among these are the ancient bristlecone pines near the California-Nevada border—the oldest living things on earth, some individuals more than 4,000 years old—now threatened by Los Angeles smog, and the gnarled yet graceful valley oak. An "indicator plant" for the state's most fertile loamy soils, even the grizzled veteran oaks not plowed under by agriculture or subdivision development are now failing to reproduce successfully.

And while the disappearance of trees is easily observed even by human eyes, other rare and unusual plants found only in California disappear, or bloom at the brink of extinction, with little apparent public concern. A subtle but perfectly adapted native perennial grass, for example, or an ephemeral herb with a spring blossom so tiny most people don't even notice it, are just as endangered by humankind's long-standing laissez-faire attitude toward the world we share with all life.

Only fairly recently, with so much of natural California already gone for good, have public attitudes begun to change. No matter what Ronald Reagan says, and despite the very real economic tradeoffs sometimes involved, most Californians—and usually the state's voters—strongly support conservation, preservation, and park expansion proposals whenever these issues arise. Yet urban and suburban sprawl and commercial development continue unabated throughout California, with little evidence that the general public connects its personal and political choices with a sense of shared responsibility for the state's continued environmental decline.

Coastal Flora

Most famous on California's north coast are its surviving stands of coast redwoods, *Sequoia sempervirens,* which flourished throughout the Northern Hemisphere 60 million years ago. The native population of these redwoods—relatives of the less commercially attractive Sierra big trees in and near Yosemite—has been reduced through logging and agriculture to isolated groves of virgin trees on the north coast. Redwoods also straggle south along the coast as far as Big Sur, though southern trees are considerably reduced in size and stature.

Also associated with fog- and rain-adapted north coast flora are Douglas and lowland firs, Sitka spruce, cedar, and yew trees; along streams and rivers are deciduous trees including alders, maples, and sycamores. In addition to native rhododendron species, the north coast is also noted for its wide variety of wild berries. As elsewhere in California, foothill woodland areas feature scattered oaks and conifers in open grasslands. Wildflowers can be stunning in spring, deep in the dark woods as well as in open coastal areas.

California's central coast region, particularly near Monterey, exhibits tremendous botanic di-

California poppies

versity. Among notable plant species is the unusually fast-growing Monterey pine, an endemic tree surviving in native groves only on hills and slopes near Monterey, Cambria, and Año Nuevo, as well as on Guadalupe and Cedros Islands off the coast of Baja, Mexico. It's now a common landscaping tree—and the world's most widely cultivated tree, grown commercially for its wood and pulp throughout the world. The unusual Monterey cypress is a relict, a specialized tree that can't survive beyond the Monterey Peninsula. The soft green Sargent cypress is more common, ranging south to Santa Barbara along the coast and inland. The Macnab cypress is found only on poor serpentine soil, as are Bishop pines, which favor swamps and the slopes from "Huckleberry Hill" near Monterey south to the San Luis Range near Point Buchon and Santa Barbara County.

Coastal redwoods thrive near Santa Cruz and south through Big Sur. Not as lusty as those on the north coast, these redwoods often keep company with Douglas fir, pines, and a dense understory of shade-loving shrubs. Other central coast trees include the Sitka spruce and beach pines. A fairly common inland tree is the chaparral-loving knobcone pine, with its tenaciously closed "fire-climax" cones. Other regional trees include the California wax myrtle, the aromatic California laurel or "bay" tree, the California nutmeg, the tan oak (and many other oaks), plus alders, big-leaf maples, and occasional madrones. Eucalyptus trees thrive in the coastal locales where they've been introduced.

Almost all native species are under siege in Southern California. In many ways the region has created, and is still creating, a new ecology, one dominated by introduced species of both plants and animals. Prominent among local plant immigrants are L.A.'s palm trees, none of which grow naturally, though native palms do flourish near Palm Springs and elsewhere in the low desert. Though as elsewhere in California native grasses were long ago replaced by introduced European species, the L.A. landscape's native oaks, sycamores, alders, and shrubs are now far outnumbered by introduced species—camellias, azaleas, ferns, and exotic tropical and semitropical tree and shrub varieties—that thrive in the mild Mediterranean climate.

CALIFORNIA FAUNA: A LONELY HOWL IN THE WILDERNESS

The Golden State's native wildlife is also quite diverse and unique. Of the 748 known species of vertebrate animals in California, 38% of freshwater fish, 29% of amphibians, and nine percent of mammals are endemic species; invertebrate variation is equally impressive. But with the disappearance of quite specific natural habitats, many of these animals are also endangered or threatened.

One notable exception is the intelligent and endlessly adaptable coyote, which—rather than be shoved out of its traditional territory even by suburban housing subdivisions—seems quite willing to put up with human incursions, so long as there are garbage cans to forage in, swimming pools to drink from, and adequate alleys of escape. Yet even the coyote's lonely late-night howl is like a cry for help in an unfriendly wilderness.

The rapid slide toward extinction among California's wild things is perhaps best symbolized by the grizzly bear, which once roamed from the mountains to the sea, though the wolf, too, has long since vanished from the landscape. The Sierra Nevada bighorn sheep, the San Joaquin kit fox, the desert tortoise, and the California condor—most surviving birds maintained now as part of a zoo-based captive breeding program—are among many species now endangered. Upward of 550 bird species have been recorded in California, and more than half of these breed here. But the vast flocks of migratory birds (so abundant they once darkened the midday sky) have been thinned out considerably, here and elsewhere, by the demise of native wetlands and by toxins.

The fate of the state's once-fabled fisheries is equally instructive. With 90% of salmon spawning grounds now gone because of the damming of rivers and streams, California's commitment to compensatory measures—fish hatcheries and ladders, for example—somehow misses the point. Now that humans are in charge of natural selection, the fish themselves are no longer wild, no longer stream-smart; many can't even find their way back to the fisheries where they hatched out (in sterile stainless steel trays). California's once-fabled marine fisheries are also in dire straits because of the combined effects of overfishing, pollution, and habitat degradation, a subject of only very recent political concern.

However, some California animals almost wiped out by hunters, habitat elimination, and contamination are starting out on the comeback trail. Included among these are native elk and the antelope-like pronghorn populations, each numbering near 500,000 before European and American settlement. Also recovering in California is the native population of desert bighorn sheep, though the Sierra bighorn is on the verge of extinction. Among marine mammals almost hunted into oblivion but now thriving in California's offshore ocean environments are the northern elephant seal and the sea otter. And in 1994 the California gray whale was removed from the federal endangered species list—the first marine creature ever "delisted"—because its current population of 21,000 or so is as high, historically speaking, as it ever was.

Until recently, California's predators—always relatively fewer in number, pouncing from the top of the food chain—fared almost as poorly as their prey, preyed upon themselves by farmers, ranchers, loggers, and hunters. Though the grand grizzly hasn't been seen in California for more than a century, California's black bear is still around—though increasingly tracked and hunted by timber interests (for the damage the bears inflict on seedling trees) and poachers out to make a fast buck on gall bladders popular in Asian pharmacology. Of California's native wildcats, only the mountain lion and the spotted, smaller bobcat survive. The last of the state's jaguars was hunted down near Palm Springs in 1860.

Coastal Birdlife

Seabirds are the most obvious seashore fauna. A surprising variety can be spotted along the shore: gulls, terns, cormorants, egrets, and brown pelicans. Many of the birds common along California's north coast can be found farther south as well. You'll see long-billed curlews, ashy petrels nesting on cliffs, surf divers like grebes and scooters, and various gulls. Pure white California gulls are seen only in winter here (they nest inland), but yellow-billed western gulls and the scarlet-billed, white-headed Heermann's gulls are common seaside scavengers. Look for the hyperactive, self-important sandpipers along the shore, along with dowitchers, plovers, godwits, and avocets. Killdeers—so named for their "ki-dee" cry—lure people and other potential predators away from their clutches of eggs by feigning serious injury.

Mallards, pintails, widgeons, shovelers, and coots are common waterfowl, though Canada geese, snow geese, sandhill cranes, and other species fly through during fall and winter migrations. Great blue herons are nearly as common along inland rivers as they are near the sea. If unseen, mourning doves can still be heard (a soft cooing), usually near water or in farm country. Families of California quail scurry across remote paths and quiet roadways, sadly oblivious to the dangers of traffic.

Great horned owls, keen-eyed nocturnal hunters with characteristic tufted "ears," usually live in wooded, hilly, or mountainous countryside. Their evening cries are eerie. Magnificent ravens, which seem to dominate the terrain as well as the native mythology of the Pacific Northwest, are quite territorial, preferring to live inland at higher foothill and mountain elevations. The American kestrel or sparrow hawk can often be spotted in open woodlands and meadows or near grazing lands. More common is the redtailed hawk, usually seen perched on telephone poles, power lines, or fences along the road— getting a good view of the countryside before snaring rabbits, ground squirrels, or field mice (though they're not above picking up an occasional roadkill).

Least appreciated among the birds of prey are the common redheaded turkey vultures. Most often spotted in spring and summer, alone or in groups, they circle above dead or dying animals until dinner's ripe. (Strictly carrion eaters, they prefer putrid flesh.) Though grotesque to humans, their featherless heads are a fine ecological adaptation: bacteria and parasites that might attach themselves as the birds feast are quickly killed by constant exposure to sunlight. And, should any toxic bacteria be swallowed, the vulture's digestive tract kills them off. Technically on the comeback trail in its natural territory, just inland from the central coast—though most are in captive breeding programs—is the massive California condor, the mythic thunderbird of Native American lore.

In rugged coastal canyons are some (but not many) golden eagles, a threatened species wrongly accused by ranchers and tale-spinners of attacking deer and livestock. Even rarer are endangered bald eagles, usually found near water —remote lakes, marshes, large rivers—primarily in inaccessible river canyons.

Most vividly illustrating L.A.'s re-creation of itself as urban tropical forest in the animal kingdom are the impressive flocks of feral parakeets, representing several species and all domestic escapees or their descendants, which thrive throughout fruitful Los Angeles. Local ornithologists estimate that at least 2,000 feral parrots are at home in Los Angeles, 1,000 in and around Pasadena alone. San Francisco also has extremely vocal escaped parakeet and parrot populations.

Brown Pelicans

The ungainly looking, web-footed brown pelicans—most noticeable perched on pilings or near piers in and around harbors—are actually incredibly graceful when diving for their dinners. A squadron of 25 or more pelicans "gone fishin'" first glide above the water then, one by one, plunge dramatically to the sea. Brown pelicans are a back-from-the-brink success story, their numbers increasing dramatically since DDT (highly concentrated in fish) was banned. California's pelican platoons are often accompanied by greedy gulls, somehow convinced they can snatch fish from the fleshy pelican pouches if they just try harder.

California Gray Whales

A close-up view of the California gray whale, the state's official (and largest) mammal, is a life-changing experience. As those dark, massive, white-barnacled heads shoot up out of the ocean to suck air, spray with the force of a firehose blasts skyward from blowholes. Watch the annual migration of the gray whale all along the California coast—from "whale vistas" on land or by boat.

Despite the fascination they hold for Californians, little is actually known about the gray whale. Once endangered by whaling—as so many whale species still are—the grays are now swimming steadily along the comeback trail. Categorized as baleen whales, which dine on plankton and other small aquatic animals sifted through hundreds of fringed, hornlike baleen plates, gray whales were once land mammals that went back to sea. In the process of evolution, they traded their fore and hind legs for fins and tail flukes. Despite their fishlike appearance, these are true mammals: warm-blooded, air-breathing creatures who nourish their young with milk.

Adult gray whales weigh 20-40 tons, not counting a few hundred pounds of parasitic barnacles. Calves weigh in at a hefty 1,500 pounds at birth and can expect to live for 30 to 60 years. They feed almost endlessly from April to October in the arctic seas between Alaska and Siberia, sucking up sediment and edible creatures on the bottom of shallow seas, then squeezing the excess water and silt out their baleen filters. Fat and sassy with an extra 6-12 inches of blubber on board, early in October they head south on their 6,000-mile journey to the warmer waters of Baja in Mexico.

Pregnant females leave first, traveling alone or in small groups. Larger groups make up the rear guard, with the older males and nonpregnant females engaging in highly competitive courtship and mating rituals along the way—quite a show for human voyeurs. The rear guard becomes the frontline on the way home: males, newly pregnant females, and young gray whales head north from February to June. Cows and calves migrate later, between March and July.

Seals, Sea Lions, and Sharks

Common in these parts is the California sea lion; the females are the barking "seals" popular in aquatic amusement parks. True seals don't have external ears, and the gregarious, fearless creatures swimming in shallow ocean waters or lolling on rocky jetties and docks usually do. Also here are northern or Steller's sea lions —which roar instead of bark and are usually lighter in color. Chunky harbor seals (no earflaps, usually with

great white shark

PAUL B. JOHNSON/CALIFORNIA DEPT. OF FISH AND GAME

ELEPHANT SEALS AND AÑO NUEVO

About 20 miles north of Santa Cruz and just across the San Mateo County line is 4,000-acre Año Nuevo State Reserve. At first glance, the windswept and cold seaward stretch of Año Nuevo seems almost desolate, inhospitable to life. This is far from the truth, however. Año Nuevo is the only place in the world where people can get off their bikes or the bus or get out of their cars and walk out among aggressive, wild northern elephant seals in their natural habitat— a species once hunted to the edge of extinction. Especially impressive is that first glimpse of hundreds of these huge seals nestled like World War II torpedoes among the sand dunes. The pendulous proboscis of a "smiling" two- to three-ton alpha bull dangles down like a firehose, so the name is apt.

For more information about Año Nuevo and the annual elephant seal migrations, see South from San Francisco in the San Francisco chapter.

California Sea Otters

Sea otters frolic north along the coast to Jenner and vicinity in Sonoma County, and south to Cambria (and beyond). Watching otters eat is quite entertaining; to really see the show, binoculars are usually necessary. Carrying softball-sized rocks in their paws, sea otters dive deep to dislodge abalone, mussels, and other shellfish, then return to the surface and leisurely smash the shells and dine while floating on their backs, "rafting" at anchor in forests of seaweed. The playful sea creatures feed heartily, each otter consuming about two and a half tons of seafood per year—much to the dismay of commercial shellfish interests.

Yet the California sea otter population, listed as a threatened species under the federal Endangered Species Act yet recently making a strong comeback, is dwindling again—and scientists aren't quite sure why. Infectious disease, coastal pollution—which also contaminates food supplies—and entrapment in wire fishing pots are all suspected reasons.

In centuries past, an estimated one-time population of almost 16,000 sea otters along the California coast was decimated by eager fur hunters. A single otter pelt was worth upward of $1,700 in 1910, when it was generally believed that sea otters were extinct here. But a small pod survived off the coast near Carmel, a secret well guarded by biologists until the Big Sur Highway opened in 1938. Until recently, the sea otters seemed to be making a comeback; their range had expanded widely up and down the coast. Much to the chagrin of the south coast commercial shellfish industry, sea otters had even started moving south past Point Conception—into shellfish waters. Even so, the number of sea otters is declining. In 1995, the U.S. Fish and Wildlife Service counted 2,377. By 1998, the population had dropped to 1,937— and some 200 dead otters washed ashore on central coast beaches, for reasons unknown.

spotted coats) more commonly haul out on sandy beaches, since they're awkward on land. Less common but rapidly increasing in numbers along the California coast—viewable at the Año Nuevo rookery during the winter mating and birthing season—are the massive northern elephant seals, the largest pinnipeds (fin-footed mammals) in the Western Hemisphere. One look at the two- or three-ton, 18-foot-long males explains the creatures' common name: their long, trunklike noses serve no real purpose beyond sexual identification, as far as humans can tell.

A wide variety of harmless sharks are common, particularly in astonishingly productive Monterey Bay, the Farrallon Islands, the Channel Islands, and other areas with abundant food supplies. Occasionally, 20-foot-long great white sharks congregate, too, to feed on sea otters, seals, and sea lions. Unprovoked attacks on humans do occur—to surfers more often than scuba divers—but are very rare. The best protection is avoiding ocean areas where great whites are common; don't go into the water alone and never where these sharks have been recently sighted.

Tidepool Life

The twice-daily ebb of ocean tides reveals an otherwise hidden world. Tidepools below rocky headlands are nature's aquariums, sheltering abalone, anemones, barnacles, mussels, hermit crabs, starfish, sea snails, sea slugs, and tiny fish. Distinct zones of marine life are defined by the tides. The highest, or "splash," zone is friendly to creatures naturally protected by shells from desiccation, including black turban snails and hermit crabs. The intertidal zones (high and low) protect spiny sea urchins and the harmless sea anemone. The "minus tide" or surf zone—farthest from shore and almost always underwater—is home to hazardous-to-human-health stingrays (particularly in late summer, watch where you step) and jellyfish.

For those who enjoy eating mussels—steamed in butter, herbs, white wine, or even fried—find them on rocky sea coasts. People pry them off underwater rocks with tire irons, pickaxes, even screwdrivers. Keep these bivalves alive in buckets of cool, fresh seawater until you're ready to eat 'em. But *no* mussel collecting is allowed during the annual "red tide" (roughly May-Oct., but variable from year to year), when tiny red plankton proliferate. These plankton are fine food for mussels and other bivalves but are toxic to humans. (The red tide is less of a problem for clams, but to be on the safe side, just eat the white meat during the annual mussel quarantine.) For current regulations and cautions, contact Fish and Game (see Coastal Recreation, below) or local sporting goods shops.

THE HISTORY OF THE GOLDEN DREAM

Europeans generally get credit for having "discovered" America, including the mythic land of California. But a dusty travel log tucked away in Chinese archives in Shenshi Province, discovered in the 19th century by an American missionary, suggests that the Chinese discovered California, in about 217 B.C. According to this saga, a storm-tossed Chinese ship—misdirected by its own compass, apparently rendered nonfunctional after a cockroach got wedged under the needle—sailed stubbornly for 100 days in the direction of what was supposed to be mainland China. (The navigator, Hee-li, reportedly ignored the protests of his crew, who pointed out that the sun was setting on the wrong horizon.) Stepping out into towering forests surrounding an almost endless inlet at the edge of the endless ocean, these unwitting adventurers reported meetings with red-skinned peoples—and giant red-barked trees.

Conventional continental settlement theory holds that the first true immigrants to the North American continent also came from Asia—crossing a broad plain across the Bering Strait, a "bridge" that existed until the end of the ice age. Archaeologists agree that the earliest Americans arrived more than 11,500 years ago, more or less in synch with geologists' belief that the Bering bridge disappeared about 14,000 years ago. Circumstantial support for this conclusion has also come from striking similarities—in blood type, teeth, and language—existing between early Americans and Asians, particularly the northern Chinese. But recent discoveries have thrown all previous American migration theories into doubt.

In 1986, French scientists working in Brazil discovered an ancient rock shelter containing stone tools, other artifacts, and charcoal that was at first carbon-dated at approximately 32,000 years old. (A subsequent announcement, that the discovery was actually more than 45,000 years old, shocked archaeologists and was widely discredited.) Wall paintings suggest that cave art developed in the Americas at about the same time it did in Europe, Asia, and Africa. Preliminary evidence of very early human habitation (possibly as long ago as 33,000 years) has also been found in Chile. Subsequent Chilean finds at Monte Verde, dated authoritatively to 10,900 to 11,200 years ago, were announced in 1997—setting off a flurry of searches for still earlier sites of human habitation.

So the question is: if migration to the Americas was via the Bering Strait, and so long ago, why hasn't any similar evidence been discovered in North America? The mummified, mat-wrapped body of an elderly man discovered in 1940 in Spirit Cave near Fallon, Nevada, has subsequently been dated as 9,415 years old—making this the only Paleonoid (more than 8,500 years old) ever found in North America; the body was particularly well preserved by the desert climate. And a human skull dated as 9,800 years old has been discovered on Canada's Prince of Wales Island. But both of these finds are thought to bolster the Bering Straits land bridge theory—as does the Monte Verde discovery in Chile, if the first American arrivals were fishing people who worked their way down the continental coastline to settle, first, in South America. Some suggest that signs of earlier human habitation in North America have been erased by climatic factors, or by glaciation. But no one really knows. One thing is certain: most archaeologists would rather be buried alive in a dig than be forced to dust off and reexamine the previously discredited "Thor Heyerdahl theory" of American settlement: that the first immigrants sailed across the Pacific, landed in South America, and then migrated northward.

CALIFORNIA'S FIRST PEOPLE

However and whenever they first arrived in California, the territory's first immigrants gradually created civilizations quite appropriate to the land they had landed in. "Tribes" like those typical elsewhere in North America did not exist in California, primarily because the political unity necessary for survival elsewhere was largely irrelevant here. Populations of California native peoples are better understood as ethnic or kinship or community groups united by common experience and shared territory.

Though no census takers were abroad in the land at the time, the presettlement population of what is now California (about 500 groups speaking 130 dialects) is estimated at about 250,000—a density four to eight times greater than early people living anywhere else in the United States. Before their almost overnight decimation—from settlement, and attendant disease, cultural disintegration, and violence—California's native peoples found the living fairly easy. The cornucopia of fish, birds, and game, in addition to almost endlessly edible plantlife, meant that hunting and gathering was not the strict struggle for survival it was elsewhere on the continent. Since abundance in all things was the rule, at least in nondesert areas, trade between tribal groups (for nonlocal favorite foods such as acorns, pine nuts, or seafood and for nonlocal woods or other prized items) was not uncommon. Plants and animals of the natural world were respected by native peoples as kindred spirits, and a deep nature mysticism was the underlying philosophy of most religious traditions and associated myths and legends.

Most California peoples were essentially non-violent, engaging in war or armed conflict only for revenge; bows and arrows, spears, and harpoons were used in hunting. The development of basketry, in general the highest art of native populations, was also quite pragmatic; baskets of specific shapes and sizes were used to gather and to store foods and for cooking in. Homes, boats, and clothing were made of the most appropriate local materials, from slabs of redwood bark and animal hides to tule reeds.

Time was not particularly important to California's first immigrants. No one kept track of passing years, and most groups didn't even have a word for "year." They paid attention, however, to the passage of the moons and seasons—the natural rhythm of life. Many native peoples were seminomadic, moving in summer into cooler mountain regions where game, roots, and berries were most abundant, and then meandering down into the foothills and valleys in autumn to collect acorns, the staff of life for most tribes, and to take shelter from winter storms.

But there was nowhere to hide from the whirling clouds of change that started sweeping into California with the arrival of early explorers and missionaries, or from the foreign flood that came when the myth of California gold became a reality. Some native peoples went out fighting: the 19th-century Modoc War was one of the last major Indian wars in the United States. And others just waited until the end of their world arrived. Most famous in this category was Ishi, the "last wild man in America" and believed to be the last of his people, captured in an Oroville slaughterhouse corral in 1911. Working as a janitor as a ward of the University of California until his death five years later from tuberculosis, Ishi walked from the Stone Age into the industrial age with dignity and without fear.

FOREIGNERS PLANT THEIR FLAGS

The first of California's official explorers were the Spanish. Though Hernán Cortés discovered a land he called California in the 1530s, Juan Rodríguez Cabrillo—actually a Portuguese, João

Rodrigues Cabrilho—first sailed the coast of Alta California ("upper," as opposed to "lower" or Baja California, which then included all of Mexico) and rode at anchor off its shores.

But the first European to actually set foot on California soil was the English pirate Sir Francis Drake, who in 1579 came ashore somewhere along the coast (exactly where is still disputed, though popular opinion suggests Point Reyes) and whose maps—like others of the day—reflected his belief that the territory was indeed an island. Upon his return to England, Drake's story of discovery served primarily to stimulate Spain's territorial appetites. Though Sebastián Vizcaíno entered Monterey Bay in 1602 (18 years before the Pilgrims arrived at Plymouth), it wasn't until 1746 that even the Spanish realized California wasn't an island. It wasn't until 1769 and 1770 that San Francisco Bay was discovered by Gaspar de Portolá and the settlements of San Diego and Monterey were founded.

Though the Spanish failed to find California's mythical gold, between 1769 and 1823 they did manage to establish 21 missions (sometimes with associated presidios) along El Camino Real or "The Royal Road" from San Diego to Sonoma, most of these on or near the coast. And from these busy mission ranch outposts, maintained by the free labor of "heathen" natives, Spain grew and manufactured great wealth.

But even at its zenith, Spain's supremacy in California was tenuous. The territory was vast and relatively unpopulated. Even massive land grants—a practice continued under later Mexican rule—did little to allay colonial fears of successful outside incursions. Russian imperialism, spreading east into Siberia and Central Asia, and then to Alaska and an 1812 outpost at Fort Ross on the north coast, seemed a clear and present danger—and perhaps actually would have been, if the Russians' agricultural and other enterprises hadn't ultimately failed. And enterprising Americans, at first just a few fur trappers and traders, were soon in the neighborhood.

As things happened, the challenge to Spain's authority came from its own transplanted population. Inspired by the news in 1822 that an independent government had been formed in Baja California's Mexico City, young California-born Spanish ("Californios") and independence-

seeking resident Spaniards declared Alta California part of the new Mexican empire. By March 1825, when California proper officially became a territory of the Republic of Mexico, the new leadership had already achieved several goals, including secularizing the missions and "freeing" the associated native neophytes (not officially achieved until 1833), which in practice meant that most became servants elsewhere. The Californios also established an independent military and judiciary, opened the territory's ports to trade, and levied taxes.

During the short period of Mexican rule, the American presence was already prominent. Since even Spain regularly failed to send supply ships, Yankee traders were always welcome in California. In no time at all, Americans had organized and dominated the territory's business sector, established successful ranches and farms, married into local families, and become prominent citizens. California, as a possible political conquest, was becoming increasingly attractive to the United States.

Gen. John C. Frémont, officially on a scientific expedition but perhaps acting under secret orders from Washington (Frémont would never say), had been stirring things up in California since 1844—engaging in a few skirmishes with the locals or provoking conflicts between Californios and American citizens in California. Though the U.S. declared war on Mexico on May 13, 1846, Frémont and his men apparently were unaware of that turn of events and took over the town of Sonoma for a short time in mid-June, raising the secessionist flag of the independent—but very short-lived—Bear Flag Republic.

With Californios never mustering much resistance to the American warriors, Commodore John C. Sloat sailed unchallenged into Monterey Bay on July 7, 1848, raised the Stars and Stripes above the Custom House in town, and claimed California for the United States. Within two days, the flag flew in both San Francisco and Sonoma, but it took some time to end the statewide skirmishes. It took even longer for official Americanization—and statehood—to proceed. The state constitution established, among other things, California as a "free" state (but only to prevent the unfair use of slave labor in the mines). This upset the balance of congres-

Gen. John C. Frémont declared California independent of Mexico and raised the flag of the short-lived Bear Flag Republic over the town of Sonoma.

sional power in the nation's anti-slavery conflict and indirectly precipitated the Civil War. Written in Monterey, the new state's constitution was adopted in October 1849 and ratified by voters in November.

GOLD IN THEM THAR HILLS

California's legendary gold was real, as it turned out. And the Americans found it—but quite by accident. The day James Marshall, who was building a lumber mill on the American River for John Sutter, discovered flecks of shiny yellow metal in the mill's tailrace seemed otherwise quite ordinary. But that day, January 24, 1848, changed everything—in California and in the world.

As fortune seekers worldwide succumbed to gold fever and swarmed into Northern California's Sierra Nevada foothills in 1849, modern-day California began creating itself. In the no-holds-barred search for personal freedom and material satisfaction (better yet, unlimited wealth), something even then recognizable as California's human character was also taking shape: the belief that anything is possible, for anyone, no matter what one's previous circumstances would suggest. Almost everyone wanted to entertain that belief. Karl Marx was of the opinion that the California gold rush was directly responsible for delaying the Russian revolution. New gold dreamers—all colors and creeds—came to California, by land and by sea, to take a chance on themselves and their luck. The luckiest ones, though, were the merchants and businesspeople who cashed in on California's dream by mining the miners.

Because of the discovery of gold, California skipped the economically exploitive U.S. territorial phase typical of other western states. With almost endless, indisputable capital at hand, Californians thumbed their noses at the Eastern financial establishment almost from the start: they could exploit the wealth of the far West themselves. And exploit it they did—mining not only the earth, but also the state's forests, fields, and water wealth. Wild California would never again be the same.

Almost overnight, "civilized" California became an economic sensation. The state was essentially admitted to the union on its own terms—because California was quite willing to go its own way and remain an independent entity otherwise. The city of San Francisco grew from a sleepy enclave of 500 souls to a hectic, hell-bent business and financial center of more than 25,000 by 1850. Other cities built on a foundation of prosperous trade included the inland supply port of Sacramento. Agriculture, at first important for feeding the state's mushrooming population of fortune hunters, soon became a de facto gold mine in its own right. Commerce expanded even more rapidly with the completion of the California-initiated transcontinental railroad and with the advent of other early communications breakthroughs such as the telegraph. California's dreams of prosperity became self-fulfilling prophecies. And as California went, so went the nation.

SOUTHERN CALIFORNIA'S GOLDEN AGE

There was gold in Southern California, too—and it was actually discovered first, at Placerita Canyon not far north of Mission San Fernando. But the subsequent discovery at Sutter's Mill soon dwarfed Southern California's gold rush-era mining finds. The bonanza here came from inflated beef prices and otherwise supplying the booming northstate gold fields. The boom went bust in the mid-1850s, and depression came to California. Only the arrival of the railroads awakened Southern California from its social and economic slumber. Lured by well-promoted tales and photographs of the salubrious sunny climate—a place where oranges grew in people's backyards, where even roses bloomed in winter—migrants arrived by the trainloads, particularly from the Midwest, throughout the 1880s. Soon agriculture, with orchards and fields of crops stretching to every horizon, became Southern California's economic strength. Real estate developments and grand hotels, often built on land owned by the railroad barons, soon boomed as well. In the late 1800s oil was discovered throughout the greater Los Angeles basin, creating still more regional wealth.

As a land with little annual rainfall, its vast underground aquifers already well on the way to depletion because of agricultural irrigation and urban use, by the early 1900s Los Angeles was quickly running out of water. Yet the inventiveness of self-taught water engineer William Mulholland, soon an international celebrity, eliminated any prospect of enforced limits on growth. When the floodgates of the famed Los Angeles Aqueduct first opened, to great public acclaim, in 1913, Southern California had made its first monumental step toward eliminating the very idea of limits. Mulholland's engineering miracle, which successfully tapped into Owens Valley water supplies that originated 250 miles to the north, also tapped into the southstate's social imagination. In no time at all the "desert" was in full bloom, landscaped with lush lawns, ferns, roses, and palm trees and populated by happy, healthy families frolicking in the sunshine.

That image, translated to the world's imagination via Hollywood's movie industry in the 1920s and subsequent years, essentially created the Southern California of today. Massive growth followed World War II, when Los Angeles began to create itself as an industrial and technological superpower—one soon beset by traffic, pollution, and social problems befitting its size.

DREAMING THE NEW GOLD DREAM

California as the land of opportunity—always a magnet for innovation, never particularly respectful of stifling and stodgy tradition—has dictated terms to the rest of the country throughout its modern history. Even with the gradual arrival of what the rest of the world could finally recognize as civilization, which included the predictable phenomenon of personal wealth translated into political power, California's commitment to prosperity and change—sometimes for its own sake—has never waned.

From the founding of the Automobile Club of Southern California in 1900 to the construction of Yosemite's Hetch Hetchy Dam (to slake San Francisco thirst) in 1923; from the establishment of the first Hollywood movie studio in 1911 to the 1927 transmission, from San Francisco, of the first television picture; from the completion in 1940 of the world's first freeway to the opening of Disneyland in 1955; from the 1960s' Free Speech Movement, the rise of Black Power in the wake of the Watts riots in 1965, and the successes of César E. Chávez's United Farm Workers Union to the Beat poets, San Francisco's Summer of Love, and the oozing up of New Age consciousness; from California's rise as leader in the development of nuclear weapons and defense technology to the creation of the microchip and personal computer and dot-com companies: California history is a chronicle of incredible change, a relentless double-time march into the new.

"All that is constant about the California of my childhood," writes Sacramento native Joan Didion in an essay from *Slouching Towards Bethlehem,* "is the rate at which it disappears."

PRACTICAL CALIFORNIA COAST

California, and coastal California in particular, is crowded—both with people trying to live the myth on a permanent basis and with those who come to visit, to re-create themselves on the standard two-week vacation plan. Summer, when school's out, is generally when the Golden State is most crowded, though this pattern is changing rapidly now that year-round schools and off-season travel are becoming common. Another trend: "mini-vacations," with workaholic Californians and other Westerners opting for one- to several-day respites spread throughout the year rather than traditional once-a-year holidays. It was once a truism that great bargains, in accommodations and transport particularly, were widely available during California's nonsummer travel season. Given changing travel patterns, this is no longer entirely true. Early spring and autumn are among the best times to tour the Northern California coastline, for example, and sunny winters along the Southern California coast—a great escape from dreary weather elsewhere—can be sublime.

Spontaneous travel, or following one's whims wherever they may lead, was once feasible in California. Unfortunately, given the immense popularity of particular destinations, those days are long gone. Particularly for those traveling on the cheap and for travelers with special needs or specific desires, some of the surprises encountered during impulsive adventuring may be unpleasant. If the availability of specific types of lodgings (including campgrounds) or eateries, or if transport details, prices, hours, and other factors are important for a pleasant trip, the best bet is calling ahead to check details and/or to make reservations. (Everything changes rapidly in California.) For a good overview of what to see and do in advance of a planned trip, including practical suggestions beyond those in this guide, also contact the chambers of commerce and/or visitor centers listed. Other good sources for local and regional information are bookstores, libraries, sporting goods and outdoor supply stores, and local, state, and federal government offices.

COASTAL RECREATION

Despite predominantly private ownership in some areas and limited public access to the coast and forest lands in others, there's always something to do along the California coast—walking, hiking, backpacking (even in winter, in Southern California), beachcombing, biking, canoeing and kayaking, fishing, sailing and sailboarding, scuba diving (many of the state's coastal parks are also considered "underwater parks"), surfing, tidepooling, whitewater rafting, or whalewatching.

Particularly along California's north coast there are almost endless possibilities for whitewater rafting adventures. Kayaking, canoeing, even tubing are popular—and reasonably safe—along some rivers. Without a doubt the best guide on the subject is *California White Water* by Jim Cassady and Fryar Calhoun, a very detailed and helpful introduction to California watersheds, including those rivers that run to the sea. But whitewater beginners should not go it alone on unfamiliar waters. For information about guided trips and licensed river guide companies, contact national forest offices and chambers of commerce.

Ocean swimming is great fun, but dangerous in some areas; *never* swim alone, and pay attention to posted warnings about undertows and heavy surf. North coast rivers offer good swimming holes, but swimming in the ocean isn't recommended—the water is cold, the coast rugged and ruthless, currents and undertows often treacherous—but determined surfers in wetsuits are increasingly common. Ocean swimming is problematic along many stretches of the central coast, too; beaches near Santa Cruz offer the safest swimming, but cold water, fog, and overcast weather can dampen swimmers' enthusiasm during the central coast summer. Expect the classic California beach scene—broad white-sand beaches, bikini-clad skaters, volleyball nets on every horizon—only in Southern California, which is defined geographically as the Santa Barbara area south.

Perfect for the less ambitious ocean fans is a casual stroll down the beach with an eye out for gifts from the sea. The best places to troll for treasures are isolated beaches far from towns; eagle-eyed locals get out and about regularly, especially after storms. While exploring tidepools, locally common along the central and north coasts, refrain from taking or turning over rocks, which provide protective habitat for sea critters (the animals, too, don't like being molested). Since low tide is the time to "do" the coast, coast-walkers, beachcombers, and clammers need a current tide table, useful for a range of about 100 coastal miles and available at local sporting goods stores and dive shops.

You can also fish for something, somehow, year-round. Salmon and trout fishing attract seasonal crowds along the north coast, and deep-sea fishing is popular just about everywhere. Particularly in Southern California, pier fishing—with adults and children alike casting their lines off public piers—is still a popular pastime, despite increasing ocean pollution problems in urban areas. For a fairly dry, hands-on sport, try clamming at low tide; in general the best clamming grounds are in the north, in places including Bodega Harbor and "the flats" of Humboldt Bay near Eureka and Arcata. Inquire at local tackle and sporting goods shops for current regulations, or contact state Fish and Game (see below). Many rules are enforced to protect threatened species, and others are for *human* well-

being. There's an annual quarantine on mussels, for example, usually from May through October, to prevent nerve paralysis caused by the seasonal "red tide."

Bicycling offers great recreational opportunity in some coastal areas—particularly rural areas with roads near or parallel to major coastal routes—but major headaches in others. In many places along the north and central coasts, Hwy. 1 is treacherously narrow, a paved roller coaster ride advisable only for experienced cyclists. And in Southern California it becomes a high-speed (sometimes stop-and-go) freeway. A good guide, if you're plan to tour the coast route by bike, is *Bicycling the Pacific Coast* by Tom Kirkendall and Vicky Spring. Inquire locally about mountain-biking opportunities.

And where do people go to re-create themselves in the great outdoors? To Northern and Southern California's vast public playgrounds—almost endless local, regional, and state parks as well as national parks and forest lands. For more information on the national parks, national forests, and other state- and federally owned lands (including Bureau of Land Management wilderness areas) mentioned in this book, contact each directly.

National Parks Information and Fees

For those planning to travel extensively in national parks in California and elsewhere in the U.S., a one-year Golden Eagle Passport pro-

clamming on
Tomales Bay

TOM MYERS PHOTOGRAPHY

whalewatching at Westport Union Landing

vides unlimited park access (not counting camping fees) for the holder and family, for the new price of $50. Though the Golden Eagle pass has recently doubled in price, it can still be worth it in California, where fees at certain national parks have recently increased; admission to Yosemite is now $20, for example. Those age 62 or older qualify for the $10 Golden Age Passport, which provides free access to national parks, monuments, and recreation areas, and a 50% discount on RV fees. Disabled travelers are eligible for the $10 Golden Access Passport, with the same privileges. You can buy all three special passes at individual national parks or obtain them in advance, along with visitor information, from: **U.S. National Park Service,** National Public Inquiries Office, U.S. Department of the Interior, 1849 C St., P.O. Box 37127, Washington, DC 20013, www.nps.gov. For regional national parks information covering California, Nevada, and Arizona, contact: **Western Region Information Office,** U.S. National Park Service, Fort Mason, Bldg. 201, San Francisco, CA 94123, tel. (415) 556-0560 (recorded) or (415) 556-0561.

Campgrounds in some national parks in California—including, off the Southern California coast, Channel Islands—can be reserved (with MasterCard or Visa) through the **National Park Reservation Service,** reservations.nps.gov, or by calling toll-free (800) 365-2267 (365-CAMP) at least eight weeks in advance. The total cost includes both the actual camping fee plus an $8-9 reservations fee. From California, call 7 a.m.-7 p.m. (10 a.m.-10 p.m. Eastern time). If you'll also be heading into the Sierra Nevada to **Yosemite,** make campground reservations via the Internet (see address above) or by calling toll-free (800) 436-7275 (436-PARK). And to cancel your reservations, call toll-free (800) 388-2733. To make national park camping reservations from outside the U.S., call (619) 452-8787.

To support the protection of U.S. national parks and their natural heritage, contact the nonprofit **National Parks and Conservation Association** (NPCA), 1776 Massachusetts Ave. NW, Washington, DC 20036, tel. (202) 223-6722, fax (202) 659-0650, www.npca.org/home/npca. Both as a public service and fundraiser, the NPCA publishes a number of comprehensive regional "overview" guides to U.S. national parks —Alaska, the Pacific, the Pacific Northwest, the Southwest included—that cost less than $10 each, plus shipping and handling. To order one or more titles, call toll-free (800) 395-7275.

National Forests
and Other Federal Lands

For general information about U.S. national forests, including wilderness areas and campgrounds, contact: **U.S. Forest Service,** U.S. Department of Agriculture, Publications, P.O. Box 96090, Washington, DC 20090, tel. (202) 205-1760. For a wealth of information via the Internet, try www.fs.fed.us. For information specifically concerning national forests and wilderness areas in California, and for maps, contact: **U.S. Forest Service, Pacific Southwest Region,** 630 Sansome St., San Francisco, CA 94111, tel. (415) 705-2870. Additional Northern and Southern California regional offices are mentioned elsewhere in this guide.

TOM MYERS PHOTOGRAPHY

Some U.S. Forest Service and Army Corps of Engineers campgrounds in Northern California can be reserved through ReserveAmerica's **National Recreation Reservation Service** (with MasterCard or Visa) at www.reserveusa.com, or call toll-free (877) 444-6777 (TDD: 877-833-6777), a service available 5 a.m.-9 p.m. (8 a.m.-midnight Eastern time) from April 1 through Labor Day and otherwise 7 a.m.-4 p.m. (10 a.m.-7 p.m. Eastern time). From outside the U.S., call (518) 885-3639. Reservations for individual campsites can be made up to eight months in advance, and for group camps up to 360 days in advance. Along with the actual costs of camping, expect to pay a per-reservation service fee of $8-9 for individual campsites (more for group sites). In addition to its first-come, first-camped campgrounds, in some areas the U.S. Forest Service offers the opportunity for "dispersed camping," meaning that you can set up minimal-impact campsites in various undeveloped areas. For detailed current recreation, camping, and other information, contact specific national forests mentioned elsewhere in this book.

Anyone planning to camp extensively in national forest campgrounds should consider buying U.S. Forest Service "camp stamps" (at national forest headquarters or at ranger district stations) in denominations of 50 cents, $1, $2, $3, $5, and $10. These prepaid camping coupons amount to a 15% discount on the going rate. (Many national forest campgrounds are first-come, first-camped; without a reserved campsite, even camp stamps won't guarantee one.) Senior adults, disabled people, and those with national Golden Age and Golden Access recreation passports pay only half the standard fee at any campground and can buy camp stamps at half the regular rate as well.

For wannabe archaeologists, the U.S. Forest Service offers the opportunity to volunteer on archaeological digs through its **Passport in Time** program—certainly one way to make up for stingy federal budgets. To receive the project's newsletter, which announces upcoming projects in various national forests, contact: Passport in Time Clearinghouse, P.O. Box 31805, Tucson, AZ 85751.

Some California public lands are managed by the **U.S. Bureau of Land Management** (BLM). For general information, contact: U.S. Bureau of Land Management, Public Affairs Office, 1849 C St. NW, LS 406, Washington, DC 20240, tel. (202) 452-5125, www.blm.gov. For information specifically related to California, contact: **California BLM,** 2800 Cottage Way, Room W1824, Sacramento, CA 95825, tel. (916) 978-4400, www.ca.blm.gov. If you plan to camp on BLM lands, be sure to request a current *California Visitor Map,* which includes campgrounds and other features; the BLM also allows "dispersed camping" in some areas (ask for details).

For information on national wildlife reserves and other protected federal lands, contact: **U.S. Fish and Wildlife Service,** Division of Refuges, 4401 N. Fairfax Dr., Room 640, Arlington, VA 22203, toll-free tel. (800) 344-9453, www.fws.gov.

California State Parks

Though the situation is destined to change by fiscal year 2000-2001 (see California Cuts State Park Fees), at last report day-use fees for admission to California state parks ranged from free (rare) to $5-7 per vehicle, with extra fees charged for dogs (if allowed), extra vehicles, and other circumstances. In highly congested areas, state parks charge no day-use fee but do charge a parking fee—making it more attractive to park elsewhere and walk or take a bus. For information on special assistance available for individuals with disabilities or other special needs, contact individual parks—which make every effort to be accommodating, in most cases.

Annual passes (nontransferable), which you can buy at most state parks and at the State Parks Store in Sacramento (see below), are $75 for day use, $50 for boat use, and $125 for both boat and day use. Annual admission passes for walk-in and "bicycle-in" users are $30 for adults, $15 for children ages 6 through 17. Golden Bear passes, for seniors age 62 and older with limited incomes and for certain others who receive public assistance, are $5 per year and allow day-use access to all state parks and off-road vehicle areas except Hearst/San Simeon, Sutter's Fort, and the California State Railroad Museum. For details on income eligibility and other requirements, call (916) 653-4000. "Limited use" Golden Bear passes, for seniors age 62 and older, allow free parking at state parks during the nonpeak park season (usually Labor Day through Memorial

CALIFORNIA CUTS STATE PARK FEES

In recent years California's state parks have struggled just to survive, challenged both by budget cuts and relentlessly escalating visitor use. Fee increases—and new types of fees—were adopted as part of the park system's survival strategy.

But suddenly the state's coffers are overflowing, as a result of economic boom times, and the state park system has a powerful new friend in Sacramento. In May 2000 Governor Gray Davis proposed a radical reduction in most visitor fees now charged at California state parks—a move designed, he announced at a press conference, "to make sure our parks are accessible to all Californians."

These across-the-board fee cuts mean that day-use and most other park fees will be reduced by half. The governor's proposal was approved by State legislature, so beginning July 1, 2000 admission and day-use fees at historic sites, museums, and 109 of the state's parks were reduced 50% (rounded to the nearest dollar).

The price of admission to the **California State Railroad Museum** in Sacramento, for example, dropped from the current $6 adults, $3 children to $3 adults, children free (age 16 and under). Day-use fees at most state parks were $5-6, and have been reduced to $2-3. Camping fees and day-use fees at the remaining state parks—primarily urban beaches and busy recreational reservoirs—will drop beginning on January 1, 2001.

Camping fees will be reduced primarily by eliminating extra fees now charged for premium, peak season, and weekend camping reservations. Current camping fees—now $24 per night, on average, all fees considered—will drop to $12 for most people. Fees for trail camps and "hike and bike" camps, now $3 per person, will be just $1. Where applicable fees for state cabin rentals, now $20-30 per night, will be reduced by half to $10-15.

Fees for most tours now offered at California state parks will remain the same. One notable exception in the governor's new state parks fee plan is **Hearst Castle**, where tour fees were reduced from $14 adults, $8 children to $10 adults, $5 children (age 16 and under) beginning August 1, 2000.

Annual fees for certain passes—parking and boat passes in particular—have been eliminated, and the Annual Day Use Parking Pass has been cut from $75 to $35. Prices for special state parks passes—the Golden Bear Pass, the Disabled Discount Pass, and the Disabled Veteran/POW Pass—will stay the same.

For more information about the state park system, see California State Parks elsewhere in this chapter or try the website, www.cal-parks.ca.gov. Individual state parks, lakes, and beaches are listed in this book under relevant regional chapters, and general information is listed below.

Day) and are $20 per year; they can be purchased in person at most state parks. Senior discounts for state park day use ($1 off) and camping ($2 off, but only if the discount is requested while making reservations) are also offered. Special state park discounts and passes are also offered for the disabled and disabled veterans/POWs (prisoners of war). For more information, contact state park headquarters (see below).

Detailed information about California's state parks, beaches, and recreation areas—with or without corporate sponsorship—is presented throughout this guide. To obtain a complete parks listing, including available facilities, campground reservation forms, and other information, contact: **California State Parks,** Public Information, P.O. Box 942896, Sacramento, CA 94296, tel. (916) 653-6995 (recorded, with an endless multiple-choice menu), www.cal-parks .ca.gov. For a catalog of state park merchandise, including books and videos, T-shirts and tote bags, contact the **California State Parks Store** at the same address, or call (916) 653-4000. To place merchandise orders, call toll-free (800) 777-0369. Most publications can also be found at staffed state parks, though not necessarily at state beaches.

State park publications include the *Official Guide to California State Parks* map and facilities listing, which includes all campgrounds, available free with admission to most state parks but available by mail, at last report, for $2; send check or money order to the attention of the Publications Section. Also available, and free: a complete parks and recreation publications list (which includes a mail order form). Other publications include the annual magazines *Events and Programs at California State Parks,* chock-full of educational and entertaining things to do, and *California Escapes,* a reasonably detailed regional rundown on all state parks.

For information about the state parks' Junior Ranger Program—many parks offer individual programs emphasizing both the state's natural and cultural heritage—call individual state parks. For general information, call (916) 653-8959. Also available through the state parks department is an annually updated "Sno-Park" guide to parking without penalty while cross-country

---

COASTWALKING: THE CALIFORNIA COASTAL TRAIL

Californians love their Pacific Ocean coastline. Love of the coast has inspired fierce battles over the years concerning just what does, and what does not, belong there. Among the things most Californians would agree belong along the coast are hiking trails—the reason for the existence of the nonprofit educational group **Coastwalk,** which sponsors group walks along the **California Coastal Trail** to introduce people to the wonders of the coast.

The California Coastal Trail seems to be an idea whose time has come. Now a Millennium Legacy Trail, honored at special White House ceremony in October 1999 recognizing 50 unique trails in the U.S., Washington, D.C., Puerto Rico, and the Virgin Islands, in March 2000 the California Coastal Trail also received a special $10,000 Millennium Trails Grant from American Express.

Yet in some places, the trail is still just an idea. It doesn't yet exist everywhere along the California coastline—and changing that fact is the other primary purpose of this unique organization. Since 1983, Coastwalk's mission has been to establish a border-to-border California Coastal Trail as well as preserve the coastal environment.

Guided four- to six-day coastwalking trips offered in 1999, typically covering 5-10 miles each day, included in the far north the Del Norte coastline, Redwood National Park in Humboldt County, the rugged Mendocino shoreline, the "Lost Coast" of Sonoma County, and Marin County. In central California, coastwalks were offered near San Francisco Bay, along the San Mateo and Santa Cruz coasts, in Monterey and San Luis Obispo Counties, and along the Santa Barbara and Ventura coasts. Southern California coastwalks in 1999 covered Los Angeles (the Santa Monica Mountains) and Catalina Island, Orange County, and San Diego County. Always popular, too, is the eight-day Lost Coast Backpack in Humboldt and Mendocino Counties.

Accommodations, arranged as part of the trip by Coastwalk, include state park campgrounds and hostels with hot showers. "Chuckwagon" dinners, prepared by volunteers, are also provided; bring your own supplies for breakfast and lunch. All gear—you'll be encouraged to travel light—is shuttled from site to site each night, so you need carry only the essentials as you walk: water bottle, lunch, camera, and jacket.

At last report daily coastwalk fees were $39 adults, $21 full-time students, and $16 children ages 12 and under—all in all a very reasonable price for a unique vacation.

For more information and to join Coastwalk—volunteers are always needed—contact Richard Nichols, Coastwalk, 1389 Cooper Rd., Sebastopol, CA 95472, tel. (707) 829-6689 or toll-free (800) 550-6854, www .californiacoastaltrail.org or www.coastwalk.org /coastwalk.

along the coast of Sonoma County

skiing or otherwise playing in the snow; for a current Sno-Park listing, write in care of the program at the state parks' address listed above or call (916) 324-1222 (automated hotline). Sno-Park permits (required) cost $3 per day or $20 for the entire season, Nov. 1-May 30; you can also buy them at REI and other sporting goods stores and at any AAA office in California. Another winter-season resource, free to AAA members, is the annual *Winter Sports Guide* for California, which lists prices and other current information for all downhill and cross-country ski areas.

California state parks offer excellent campgrounds. In addition to developed "family" campsites, which usually include a table, fire ring or outdoor stove, plus running water, flush toilets, and hot showers (RV hookups, if available, are extra), some state campgrounds also offer more primitive "walk-in" or environmental campgrounds and very simple hiker-biker campsites. Group campgrounds are also available (and reservable) at many state parks. If you plan to camp over the Memorial or Labor Day weekends, or the July 4th holiday, be sure to make reservations as early as possible.

Make campground reservations at California state parks (with MasterCard or Visa) through **ReserveAmerica,** www.reserveamerica.com, or call toll-free (800) 444-7275 (444-PARK) weekdays 8 a.m.-5 p.m. For TDD reservations, call toll-free (800) 274-7275 (274-PARK). And to cancel state park campground reservations, from the U.S. call toll-free (800) 695-2269. To make reservations from Canada or elsewhere outside the U.S., call (619) 638-5883. As in other camping situations, before calling to make reservations, know the park and campground name, how you'll be camping (tent or RV), how many nights, and how many people and vehicles. In addition to the actual camping fee, which can vary from $6-12 for more primitive campsites (without showers and/or flush toilets) to $12-28 for developed campsites, there is an $8-9 reservations fee. Sites with hookups cost slightly more. An extra $1 is charged in peak camping season (which varies by park), and an additional $1 per night is charged for peak-season Friday and Saturday nights. You can make camping reservations up to seven months in advance. Certain campsites, including some primitive en-

vironmental and hiker/biker sites, can be reserved only through the relevant state park.

To support the state's strapped park system, contact the nonprofit **California State Parks Foundation,** 800 College Ave., P.O. Box 548, Kentfield, CA 94914, tel. (415) 258-9975, fax (415) 258-9930, www.calparks.org. Through memberships and contributions, the foundation has financed about $100 million in park preservation and improvement projects in the past several decades. Volunteers are welcome to contribute sweat equity, too.

Other State Recreation Resources

For general information and fishing and hunting regulations, usually also available at sporting goods stores and bait shops where licenses and permits are sold, call the **California Department of Fish and Game** (DFG) in Sacramento at (916) 653-7664. For license information, call (916) 227-2244, www.dfg.ca.gov. For additional sportfishing information, call toll-free (800) 275-3474 (800-ASK-FISH). The DFG also offers special programs—including **Becoming an Outdoors-Woman** workshops that teach outdoor skills from flyfishing, hunting, and reading maps and compasses to backpacking, canoeing, and kayaking. For details on this particular program, call (916) 657-4333 or see the website.

For environmental and recreational netheads, the California Resources Agency's CERES website, aka the California Environmental Resources Evaluation System at ceres.ca.gov, offers an immense amount of additional information, from reports and updates on rare and endangered species to current boating regulations. The database is composed of federal, state, regional, and local agency information as well as a multitude of data and details from state and national environmental organizations—from REINAS, or the Real-time Environmental Information Network and Analysis System at the University of California at Santa Cruz, The Nature Conservancy, and NASA's Imaging Radar Home Page. Check it out.

Worth it for inveterate wildlife voyeurs is the recently revised *California Wildlife Viewing Guide* (Falcon Press, 1997), produced in conjunction with 15 state, federal, and local agencies in addition to Ducks Unlimited and the Wetlands Action Alliance. About 200 wildlife viewing sites are listed—most of these in Northern California. Look for the *California Wildlife Viewing Guide* at local bookstores, or order a copy by calling toll-free (800) 582-2665. With the sale of each book, $1 is contributed to California Watchable Wildlife Project nature tourism programs.

To support California's beleaguered native plantlife, join, volunteer with, and otherwise contribute to the **California Native Plant Society** (CNPS), 1722 J St., Ste. 17, Sacramento, CA 95814, tel. (916) 447-2677, fax (916) 447-2727, www.cnps.org. In various areas of the state, local CNPS chapters sponsor plant and habitat restoration projects. The organization also publishes some excellent books. Groups including the **Sierra Club, Audubon Society,** and **The Nature Conservancy** also sponsor hikes, backpack trips, birdwatching treks, backcountry excursions, and volunteer "working weekends" in all areas of California; call local or regional contact numbers (in the telephone book) or watch local newspapers for activity announcements.

STAYING~AND EATING~ ALONG THE COAST

Camping Out

Because of many recent years of drought and painful lessons learned about extreme fire danger near suburban and urban areas, all California national forests, most national parks, and many state parks now ban all backcountry fires—with the exception of controlled burns (under park supervision), increasingly used to thin understory vegetation to prevent uncontrollable wildfires. Some areas even prohibit portable campstoves, so be sure to check current conditions and all camping and hiking or backpacking regulations before setting out.

To increase your odds of landing a campsite where and when you want one, make reservations (where accepted). For details on reserving campsites at both national and state parks in Northern California, see relevant listings under Coastal Recreation, immediately above, and listings for specific parks elsewhere in this book. Without reservations, seek out "low-profile" campgrounds during the peak camping season—summer and often spring and fall weekends in most parts of Northern California—or

plan for off-season camping. Some areas also offer undeveloped, environmental, or dispersed "open camping" not requiring reservations; contact relevant jurisdictions above for information and regulations.

Private campgrounds are also available throughout Northern California, some of these included in the current *Campbook for California and Nevada,* available at no charge to members of the American Automobile Association (AAA), which lists (by city or locale) a wide variety of private, state, and federal campgrounds. Far more comprehensive is Tom Stienstra's *California Camping: The Complete Guide* (Foghorn Outdoors), available in most California bookstores. Or contact **California Travel Parks Association,** tel. (530) 823-1076, fax (530) 823-5883, www.campgrounds.com/ctpa, which features a great online campground directory. Request a complimentary copy of the association's annual *California RV and Campground Guide* from any member campground, or order one by mail—send $4 if you live in the U.S., $7 if outside the U.S.—by writing to: ESG Mail Service, P.O. Box 5578, Auburn, CA 95604.

For a Cheap Stay: Hostels, YMCAs, YWCAs

Among the best bargains around, for travelers of all ages, are the **Hostelling International-American Youth Hostels** (HI-AYH) scattered all along the California coastline—in major urban areas, at various scenic spots along the coast, in the redwoods, and in other appealing locations. Most are listed separately throughout this guide, but the list continually expands (and contracts); the annual HI-AYH *Hostelling North America* guide, available free with membership (or for $6.95 plus tax at most hostels), includes updated listings. Most affiliated hostels offer separate dormitory-style accommodations for men and women (and private couple or family rooms, if available), communal kitchens or low-cost food service, and/or other common facilities. Some provide storage lockers, loaner bikes, even hot tubs. At most hostels, the maximum stay is three nights; most are also closed during the day, which forces hostelers to get out and about and see the sights. Fees are typically $10-16 for HI-AYH members, usually several dollars more for nonmembers. Since most hostels are quite popular, especially during summer, reservations—usually secured with one night's advance payment—are essential. Contact individual hostels for details (or see listings elsewhere in this book), since reservation requirements vary. Guests are expected to bring sleeping bags, sleepsacks, or sheets, though sheets or sleepsacks are sometimes available; mattresses, pillows, and blankets are provided.

For membership details and more information about hostelling in the U.S. and abroad, contact: Hostelling International-American Youth Hostels, 733 15th St. NW, Ste. 840, Washington, DC 20005, tel. (202) 783-6161, fax (202) 783-6171, www.hiayh.org. For more information on Northern California hostels, contact the **HI-AYH Golden Gate Council,** 425 Divisadero St., Ste. 307, San Francisco, CA 94117, tel. (415) 863-1444 or (415) 701-1320, fax (415) 863-3865, www.norcalhostels.org, and the **HI-AYH Central California Council,** P.O. Box 3645, Merced, CA 95344, tel. (209) 383-0686, www.hostelweb.com/central-california. For information on Southern California hostels, contact the **HI-AYH Los Angeles Council,** 1434 Second St., Santa Monica, CA 90401, tel. (310) 393-6263, fax (310) 393-1769, www.hostelweb.com/losangeles, headquartered at the Santa Monica hostel, and the **HI-AYH San Diego Council,** 437 J St., Ste. 301, San Diego, CA 92101, tel. (619) 338-9981, fax (619) 525-1533, www.hostelweb.com/sandiego.

You'll find other reputable hostels in California, some independent and some affiliated with other hostel "chains" or umbrella organizations (such as the Banana Bungalow group, now well represented in Southern California). For current comprehensive U.S. listings of these private hostels, contact: **BakPak Travelers Guide,** 670 West End Ave., Ste. 1B, New York, NY 10025, tel. (718) 626-1988, fax (718) 626-2132, bakpakguide.com, and **Hostel Handbook of the U.S. and Canada,** c/o Jim Williams, 722 St. Nicholas Ave., New York, NY 10031. Copies of both these guides are also usually available at affiliated hostels.

Particularly in urban areas, the **Young Men's Christian Association** (YMCA) often offers housing, showers, and other facilities for young men (over age 18 only in some areas, if unaccompanied by parent or guardian), sometimes also for women and families. **Young Women's Christian Association** (YWCA) institutions offer housing for women only. Life being what it is these days, though, many of these institutions are primarily shelters for the destitute and the homeless; don't steal their beds unless absolutely necessary. For more information, contact: **Y's Way International,** 224 E. 47th St., New York, NY 10017, tel. (212) 308-2899 (Mon.-Fri. 9 a.m.-5 p.m. Eastern time), or contact local YMCA outposts. Another low-cost alternative in summer is on-campus housing at state colleges and universities; for current information, contact individual campuses (the student housing office).

Modern "Motor Hotels": Motels and Hotels

California, the spiritual home of highway and freeway living, is also the birthplace of the motel, the word a contraction for "motor hotels." Motels have been here longer than anywhere else, so they've had plenty of time to clone themselves. As a general precaution, when checking into a truly cheap motel, ask to see the room before signing in (and paying); some places look much more appealing from the outside than from the inside. Midrange and high-priced motels and hotels are generally okay, however. In addition to the standard California sales tax, many cities and counties—particularly near major tourism destinations—add a "bed tax" of 5-18% (or higher). To find out the actual price you'll be paying, ask before making reservations or signing in. Unless otherwise stated, rates listed in this guide do not include state sales tax or local bed taxes.

Predictably reliable on the cheaper end of the accommodations scale, though there can be considerable variation in quality and service from place to place, are a variety of budget chains fairly common throughout California. Particularly popular is **Motel 6,** a perennial budget favorite. To receive a copy of the current motel directory, from the U.S. and Canada call toll-free (800) 466-8356, which is also Motel 6's central reservations service, or try the website at www.motel6.com. (To make central reservations from outside the U.S., call (817) 355-5502; reserve by fax from Europe and the United Kingdom at 32-2-753-5858.) You can also make reservations, by phone or fax, at individual motels, some listed elsewhere in this book. Other inexpensive to moderately priced motels are often found clustered in the general vicinity of Motel 6, these including **Comfort Inn,** toll-free tel. (800) 228-5150, www.comfortinn.com; **Days Inn,** toll-free tel. (800) 329-7466, www.daysinn.com; **Econo Lodge,** toll-free tel. (800) 553-2666, www.econolodge.com; **Rodeway Inn,** toll-free tel. (800) 228-2000, www.rodewayinn.com; and **Super 8 Motels,** toll-free tel. (800) 800-8000, www.super8.com. You can also pick up a current accommodations directory at any affiliated motel.

You'll find endless other motel and hotel chains in California, most of these more expensive—but not always, given seasonal bargain rates and special discounts offered to seniors, AAA members, and other groups. "Kids stay free," free breakfast for families, and other special promotions can also make more expensive accommodations competitive. Always reliable for quality, but with considerable variation in price and level of luxury, are **Best Western** motel and hotel affiliates, toll-free tel. (800) 780-7234 in the U.S., www.bestwestern.com. Each is independently owned and managed, and some are listed in this guide. The **Four Seasons,** www.fshr.com, and **Ritz-Carlton,** www.ritzcarlton.com, hotel and resort chains top most people's "all-time favorite" lists of luxurious places to stay in California when money is no object.

For members of the American Automobile Association (AAA), the current *Tourbook for California and Nevada* (free) includes an impressive number of rated motels, hotels, and resorts, from inexpensive to top of the line, sometimes also recommended restaurants, for nearly every community and city in both Southern and Northern California. Nationwide, AAA members can also benefit from the association's reservations service, toll-free tel. (800) 272-2155; with one call, you can also request tour books and attractions information for any destination. Other travel groups or associations offer good deals and useful services, too.

Bargain Room Rates and Bed and Breakfasts

Even if you don't belong to a special group or association, you can still benefit from "bulk-buying" power, particularly in large cities—which is a special boon if you're making last-minute plans or are otherwise having little luck on your own. Various room brokers or "consolidators" buy up blocks of rooms from hoteliers at greatly discounted rates and then broker them through their own reservations services. In many cases, brokers still have bargain-priced rooms available—at discounted rates of 40-65%—when popular hotels are otherwise sold out. For great hotel deals try **Hotel Discounts,** toll-free tel. (800) 715-7666, www.hoteldiscount.com. Particularly helpful for online reservations is the discounted **USA Hotel Guide,** toll-free tel. (888) 729-7705, www.usahotelguide.com. For other bargain hotel prices in Northern and Southern California, including some medium- and high-priced spreads in San Francisco and Los Angeles, contact **Hotel Reservations Network,** toll-free tel. (800) 715-7666, www.180096hotel.com, and **Room Exchange,** toll-free tel. (800) 846-7000, www.hotelrooms.com.

Another hot trend, particularly in Northern California's most scenic coastal locales, is the bed-and-breakfast phenomenon. Many bed-and-breakfast guides and listings are available in bookstores, and some recommended B&Bs are listed in this book. Unlike the European tradition, with bed and breakfasts a low-cost yet comfortable lodging alternative, in California these inns are actually a burgeoning small-business phenomenon—usually quite pricey, in the $100-150+ range (occasionally less expensive), often more of a "special weekend getaway" for exhausted city people than a mainstream accommodations option. In some areas, though, where motel and hotel rooms are on the high end, bed and breakfasts can be quite competitive.

For more information on what's available in all parts of California, including private home stays, contact **Bed and Breakfast California,** P.O. Box 282910, San Francisco, CA 94128, tel. (650) 696-1690 or toll-free (800) 872-4500, fax (650) 696-1699, www.bbintl.com, affiliated with Bed and Breakfast International, the longest-running bed-and-breakfast reservation service in the United States. Or contact the **California Association of Bed and Breakfast Inns,** 2715 Porter St., Soquel, CA 95073, tel. (831) 462-9191, fax (831) 462-0402, www.cabbi.com.

The Land of Fruits and Nuts and California Cuisine

One of the best things about traveling in California is the food: they don't call the Golden State the land of fruits and nuts for nothing. In agricultural and rural areas, local "farm trails" or winery guides are often available—ask at local chambers of commerce and visitor centers—and following the seasonal produce trails offers visitors the unique pleasure of gathering (sometimes picking their own) fresh fruits, nuts, and vegetables direct from the growers.

This fresher, direct-to-you produce phenomenon is also quite common in most urban areas, where regular farmers' markets are *the* place to go for fresh, organic, often exotic local produce and farm products. Many of the most popular Northern California farmers' markets are listed elsewhere in this book—but ask around wherever you are, since new ones pop up constantly. For a reasonably comprehensive current listing of California Certified Farmers' Markets (meaning certified as locally grown), contact: **California Federation of Certified Farmers' Markets,** P.O. Box 1813, Davis, CA 95617, tel. (707) 753-9999, fax (707) 756-1853, farmersmarket .ucdavis.edu.

Threaded with freeways and accessible on-ramp, off-ramp commercial strips, particularly in urban areas, Northern California has more than its fair share of fast-food eateries and all-night quik-stop outlets. (Since they're so easy to find, none are listed in this guide.) Most cities and communities also have locally popular cafés and fairly inexpensive restaurants worth seeking out; many are listed here, but also ask around. Genuinely inexpensive eateries often refuse to take credit cards, so always bring some cash along just in case.

The northstate is also famous for its "California cuisine," which once typically meant consuming tastebud-tantalizing, very expensive food in very small portions—almost a cliché—while oohing and aahing over the presentation throughout the meal. But the fiscally frugal early 1990s restrained at least some of California's excesses, and even the best restaurants now offer less pretentious menus and slimmed-down prices. The state's culinary creativity is quite real, and worth pursuing (sans pretense) in many areas. Talented chefs, who have migrated up and down the coast from Los Angeles and San Francisco as well as from France and Italy, usually prefer locally grown produce, dairy products, meats, and herbs and spices as basic ingredients. To really "do" the cuisine scene, wash it all down with some fine California wine.

OTHER PRACTICAL FACTS

Conduct and Custom: Smoking, Drinking, and General Truths

Smoking is a major social sin in California, often against the law in public buildings and on public transport, with regulations particularly stringent in urban areas. People sometimes get violent over other people's smoking, so smokers need to be respectful of others' "space" and smoke outdoors when possible. Smoking has been banned outright in all California restaurants and bars, and smoking is not allowed on public airplane flights, though nervous fliers can usually smoke somewhere inside—or outside—airline terminals. Many bed and breakfasts in California are either entirely nonsmoking or restrict smoking to decks, porches, or dens; if this is an issue, inquire by calling ahead. Hotels and motels, most commonly in major urban areas or popular tourist destinations, increasingly offer non-smoking rooms (or entire floors). Ask in advance.

The legal age for buying and drinking alcohol in California is 21. Though Californians tend to (as they say) "party hearty," public drunkenness is not well tolerated. Drunken driving—which means operating an automobile (even a bicycle, technically) while under the influence—is definitely against the law. California is increasingly no-nonsense about the use of illegal drugs, too, from marijuana to cocaine, crack, and heroin. Doing time in local jails or state prisons is not the best way to do California.

English is the official language in California, and even English-speaking visitors from other countries have little trouble understanding California's "dialect" once they acclimate to the accents and slang expressions. (Californians tend to be very creative in their language.) When unsure what someone means by some peculiar phrase, ask for a translation into standard English. Particularly in urban areas, many languages are commonly spoken, and—even in English—

the accents are many. You can usually obtain at least some foreign-language brochures, maps, and other information from city visitor centers and popular tourist destinations. (If this is a major concern, inquire in advance.)

Californians are generally casual, in dress as well as etiquette. If any standard applies in most situations, it's common courtesy—still in style, generally speaking, even in California. Though "anything goes" just about anywhere, elegant restaurants usually require appropriately dressy attire for women, jacket and tie for men. (Shirts and shoes—pants or skirt too, usually—are required in any California restaurant.)

By law, public buildings in California are wheelchair-accessible, or at least partially so. The same is true of most major hotels and tourist attractions, which may offer both rooms and restrooms with complete wheelchair accessibility; some also have wheelchairs, walkers, and other mobility aids available for temporary use. Even national and state parks, increasingly, are attempting to make some sights and campgrounds more accessible for those with physical disabilities; to make special arrangements, inquire in advance. But private buildings, from restaurants to bed and breakfasts, may not be so accommodating. Those with special needs should definitely ask specific questions in advance.

Conduct and Custom: Tipping

For services rendered in the service trade, a tip is usually expected. Some say the word is derived from the Latin *stips,* for stipend or gift. Some say it's an 18th-century English acronym for "to ensure promptness," though "to ensure personal service" seems more to the point in these times. In expensive restaurants or for large groups, an automatic tip or gratuity may be included in the bill—an accepted practice in many countries but a source of irritation for many U.S. diners, who would prefer to personally evaluate the quality of service received. Otherwise, 15-20% of the before-tax total tab is the standard gratuity, and 10% the minimal acknowledgment, for those in the service trade—waitresses and waiters, barbers, hairdressers, and taxi drivers. In fine-dining circumstances, wine stewards should be acknowledged personally, at the rate of $2-5 per bottle, and the maitre d' as well, with $5 or $10. In very casual buffet-style joints, leave

$1 each for the people who clear the dishes and pour your coffee after the meal. In bars, leave $1 per drink, or 15% of the bill if you run a tab. At airports, tip skycaps $1 per bag (more if they transport your baggage any distance); tip more generously for extra assistance, such as helping wheelchair passengers or mothers with infants and small children to their gates.

At hotels, a desk clerk or concierge does not require a tip unless that person fulfills a specific request, such as snagging tickets for a sold-out concert or theater performance, in which case generosity is certainly appropriate. For baggage handlers curbside, a $1 tip is adequate; a tip of at

BEING HERE: RIGHT ATTITUDE

Whenever you arrive and wherever you go, one thing to bring along is the right attitude—bad attitude, strangely enough, being a particular problem among American travelers (including Californians) visiting California. One reason visitors become annoyed and obnoxious is because, often without realizing it, they started their trip with high, sometimes fantasy-based expectations—akin, perhaps, to being magically cured of all limitations at a Lourdes-like way station along life's freeway—and, once arrived in California, reality disappoints. Even the Golden State has traffic jams, parking problems, rude service people, and lowlifes only too happy to make off with a good time by stealing one's pocketbook—or car. Be prepared.

Visitors also bring along no-fun baggage when they go to new places and compare whatever they find with what they left behind "back home." This is disrespectful. The surest way to enjoy California is to remain open-minded about whatever you may see, hear, do, or experience. It's fine to laugh (to one's self) at California's contradictions and cultural self-consciousness—even Californians do it—but try to view new places, from sophisticated San Francisco to the most isolated and economically depressed backwater, from the perspective of the people who live and work there. Better yet, strike up conversations with locals and ask questions whenever possible. These experiences invariably become the best surprises of all—because people, places, and things in California are often not quite what they first appear to be.

least $1 per bag is appropriate for bell staff transporting luggage from the lobby to your room or from your room to the lobby. For valet parking, tip the attendant $2-3 (more if you have a very expensive car). Tip the hotel doorman if he helps with baggage or hails a cab for you. And tip swimming pool or health club personnel as appropriate for extra personal service. Unless one stays in a hotel or motel for several days, the standard practice is not to tip the housekeeper, though you can if you wish; some guests leave $1-2 each morning for the housekeeper and $1 each evening for turn-down service.

Visas for Foreign Visitors

A foreign visitor to the U.S. is required to carry a current passport and a visitor's visa plus proof of intent to leave (usually a return airplane ticket is adequate; find passport information on the Web at travel.state.gov). Also, it's wise to carry proof of one's citizenship, such as a driver's license and/or birth certificate. To be on the safe side, photocopy your legal documents and carry the photocopies separately from the originals. To obtain a U.S. visa (most visitors qualify for a B-2 or "pleasure tourist" visa, valid for up to six months), contact the nearest U.S. embassy or consulate. Should you lose the Form I-94 (proof of arrival/departure) attached to your visa, contact the nearest local U.S. **Immigration and Naturalization Service** (INS) office. Contact the INS also for a visa extension (good for a maximum of six months). To work or study in the U.S., special visas are required; contact the nearest U.S. embassy or consulate for current information. To replace a passport lost while in the U.S., contact the nearest embassy for your country. Canadian citizens entering the U.S. from Canada or Mexico do not need either a passport or visa, nor do Mexican citizens possessing a Form I-186. (Canadians under age 18 do need to carry written consent from a parent or guardian.)

Tracking Time

California, within the Pacific time zone (two hours behind Chicago, three hours behind New York) is on daylight saving time (a helps-with-harvest agricultural holdover), which means clocks are set ahead one hour from the first Sunday in April until the last Sunday in October. During the rest of the year, when it's noon in California, it's 10 a.m.

in Hawaii, 8 p.m. in London, midnight in Moscow, and 4 a.m. (the next day) in Hong Kong.

Business Hours, Banking, Money

Standard business hours in California (holidays excepted) are Monday through Friday 9 a.m.-5 p.m., though many businesses open at 8 a.m. or 10 a.m. and/or stay open until 6 p.m. or later. Traditional banking hours—10 a.m. until 3 p.m.—are not necessarily the rule in California these days. Particularly in cities, banks may open at 9 a.m. and stay open until 5 or 6 p.m., and may offer extended walk-up or drive-up window hours. Many banks and savings and loans also offer Saturday hours (usually 9 a.m.-1 p.m.) as well as 24-hour automated teller machine (ATM) service; you'll even find ATMs at most theme parks and, increasingly, inside most grocery stores. Before traveling in California, contact your bank for a list of California branches or affiliated institutions.

For the most part, traveling in California is expensive. Depending on your plans, figure out how much money you'll need—then bring more. Most banks will not cash checks (or issue cash via ATMs) for anyone without an account (or an account with some affiliated institution). Major credit cards (especially Visa and MasterCard) are almost universally accepted in California, except at inexpensive motels and restaurants. Credit cards have become a travel essential, since they are often mandatory for buying airline tickets, renting cars, or as a "security deposit" on bicycle, outdoor equipment, and other rentals. The safest way to bring cash is by carrying traveler's checks. American Express traveler's checks are the most widely recognized and accepted.

Domestic (U.S.) travelers who run short of money, and who are without credit lines on their credit cards, can ask family or friends to send a postal money order (buyable and cashable at any U.S. Postal Service post office); ask your bank to wire money to an affiliated California bank (probably for a slight fee); or have money wired office-to-office via Western Union, toll-free tel. (800) 325-6000 (800-225-5227 for credit-card money transfers; 800-325-4045 for assistance in Spanish). Use the local phone book to find Western Union offices. In each case, the surcharge depends upon the amount sent.

International travelers should avoid the necessity of wiring for money if at all possible. With a Visa, MasterCard, or American Express card, cash advances are easily available; get details about affiliated U.S. banks before leaving home, however. If you must arrange for cash to be sent from home, a cable transfer from your bank (check on corresponding California banks before leaving), a Western Union money wire, or a bank draft or international money order are all possible. Make sure you (and your sender) know the accurate address for the recipient bank, to avoid obvious nightmarish complications. In a pinch, consulates may intervene and request money from home (or your home bank) at your request—deducting their cost from funds received.

Measurements, Mail, Communications

Despite persistent efforts to wean Americans from the old ways, California and the rest of the union still abide by the British system of weights and measures (see measurements chart in the back of this book). Electrical outlets in California (and the rest of the U.S.) carry current at 117 volts, 60 cycles (Hertz) a/c; foreign electrical appliances require a converter and plug adapter.

Large cities have large post offices, usually in multiple locations. Even without a full-fledged post office, most outback California communities have at least some official outpost of the U.S. Postal Service, usually open weekdays 8 a.m.-5 p.m., for sending letters and packages and for receiving general delivery mail. At last report, basic postal rates within the U.S., which may soon increase, were 20 cents for postcards, 33 cents for letter mail (the first ounce). Rates for international mail from the U.S. were 50 cents for postcards, 60 cents for letters (the first half-ounce), except to Canada and Mexico. The postal code for any address in California is CA. For mail sent and received within the U.S., knowing and using the relevant five- or nine-digit zip code is important. Mail can be directed to any particular post office c/o "General Delivery," but the correct address and zip code for the post office receiving

WHAT TO BRING

Generally speaking, bring what you'll really need—but as little of it as possible. A good rule of thumb: select everything absolutely necessary for your travels, then take along only half. Remember, you'll be bringing back all sorts of interesting tokens of your trip, so leave space. Remember, too, that camera equipment is heavy; bring only what you'll really use. (Try carrying your packed luggage around for 15 or 20 minutes if you need motivation to lighten the load.) Standard luggage is adequate for most travelers, especially those traveling by bus or car. For those planning to be without personal wheels, and therefore destined to cover more ground on foot, a backpack—or convertible backpack-suitcase—may be more useful, since you can also carry the load on your back as needed. For any traveler, a daypack may also come in handy, for use on day hikes and outings, and as an extra bag for toting home travel trinkets.

In characteristically casual California, clothing should be sensible and comfortable. Natural and certain high-tech fibers are preferable because they "breathe" in California's variable climate. Cotton is the most fundamental California fiber—quite versatile,

too, when layered to meet one's changing needs. Shorts, jeans, T-shirts, and sandals or sport shoes are the standard tourist uniform (swimming suits at the beach). Dark or bright colors, knits, and durable clothing will keep you presentable longer than more frivolous fashions, though laundry services and coin-operated laundromats are widely available. Even for summer travel—and especially along the coast—always bring a sweater or light jacket, since summer fog can cool daytime temperatures, and evenings can be cool in coastal or foothill areas. A heavier jacket is advisable in winter, and quality cold-weather gear for winter in the mountains. Northern California's rainy season usually begins in October or November and continues into March or April (sometimes June), so pack raingear accordingly. Rain in Southern California is a more rarified phenomenon, but not entirely absent, so bring at least a lightweight waterproofed parka and/or umbrella if heading to the southstate in winter.

Those planning to participate in California-style high life should pack dress clothes, of course, but the most universally necessary thing to bring is a decent (preferably broken-in) pair of walking shoes.

such mail is important—especially in cities, where there are multiple post offices. (For zip codes and associated post office information, refer to the local phone book, call toll-free 800-332-9631, or go to www.usps.com.) To claim general delivery mail, current photo identification is required; unclaimed mail will be returned to the sender after languishing for two to four weeks. At larger post offices, **International Express Mail** is available, with delivery to major world cities in 48-72 hours.

Telephone communication is easy in California (always carry change in your pocket in case you need to make an emergency call). Local calls are often free (or inexpensive) from many motel and hotel rooms, but long-distance calls will cost you. Some hotels add a per-call surcharge even to direct-dialed or credit card calls, however, due and payable when you check out. And the anything-goes aspect of deregulation has also resulted in a spate of for-profit "telephone companies" that generate most of their income through exorbitant rates charged through the hotels, motels, and miscellaneous pay telephones they serve. Using your own long-distance carrier (usually with a personal phone card) is typically a better deal. If in doubt about what long-distance services are available on a given phone system, what rates they charge, and whether a hotel or motel surcharge will be added to your bill, ask *before* making your phone call(s). Collect and person-to-person operator-assisted calls are usually more expensive than direct-dial and telephone company (such as AT&T or Sprint) credit-card calls, but in some cases they could save you a bundle.

Telephone communication in California has been further complicated, almost overnight, by a mushrooming number of area codes, those three-digit parenthetical regional prefixes preceding seven-digit local telephone numbers. This chaotic change in California, as elsewhere, is directly related to the proliferating numbers of people, phones, fax machines, pagers, and online computer connections. Between about 1990 and 2000, every telephone area code in California has "split" (usually into two, the previous code plus a new one) at least once, and some more than once. This book has made every effort to keep up with area code changes, and has noted upcoming changes that were known at the time of publication, but it's likely that a few new area codes will present themselves nonetheless. When in doubt, call the local operator and check it out.

IN THE KNOW: SERVICES AND INFORMATION

Entertainment, Events, Holidays

Not even the sky's the limit on entertainment in California, and particularly along the coast. From air shows to harvest fairs and rodeos, from symphony to opera, from rock 'n' roll to avant-garde clubs and theater, from strip shows (male and female) to ringside seats at ladies' mud-wrestling contests, from high-stakes bingo games to horse racing—anything goes in the Golden State. Many communities offer a wide variety of special, often quite unusual, annual events; many of these are listed by region or city elsewhere in this guide.

Official holidays, especially during the warm-weather travel season and the Thanksgiving-Christmas-New Year holiday season, are often the most congested and popular (read: expensive) times to travel or stay in California. Yet this is not always true; great holiday-season bargains in accommodations are sometimes available at swank hotels that primarily cater to businesspeople. Though most tourist destinations are usually jumping, banks and many businesses close on the following major holidays: New Year's Day (January 1); Martin Luther King Jr. Day (the third Monday in January); Presidents' Day (the third Monday in February); Memorial Day (the last Monday in May); Independence Day (July 4); Labor Day (the first Monday in September); Veterans Day (November 11); Thanksgiving (the fourth Thursday in November); and Christmas (December 25). A brand new holiday in California, still in the process of being officially recognized, is César Chávez Day in late March, honoring the farm labor leader.

Basic Services

Except for some very lonely areas, even backwater areas of Northern California aren't particularly primitive. And even in bustling, well-populated Southern California, where all services are abundantly available, it definitely helps to know where they are specifically located.

Gasoline, basic groceries, laundries of some sort, and even video rentals are available just about anywhere. Outback areas are not likely to have parts for exotic sports cars, however, or 24-hour pharmacies, hospitals, garages, natural foods stores, or full-service supermarkets, so attend to any special needs or problems *before* leaving the cities. It's often cheaper, too, to stock up on most supplies, including outdoor equipment and groceries, in urban areas.

Shopping: Something for Every Style
Most stores are open during standard business hours (weekdays 8 a.m.-5 p.m. or 9 a.m.-5 p.m.) and often longer, sometimes seven days a week, because of the trend toward two-income families and ever-reduced leisure time. This trend is particularly noticeable in cities, where shops and department stores are often open until 9 p.m. or later, and where many grocery stores are open 24 hours.

Shopping malls—almost self-sustaining cities in California, with everything from clothing and major appliances to restaurants and entertainment—are the standard California trend, but cities large and small with viable downtown shopping districts often offer greater variety and uniqueness in goods and services. Also particularly popular in California are flea markets and arts-and-crafts fairs, the former usually held on weekends, the latter best for handcrafted items and often associated with the Thanksgiving-through-Christmas shopping season and/or festivals and special events. California assesses a 7.25% state sales tax on all nonfood items sold in the state, and many municipalities levy additional sales tax.

General Information
Visitors can receive free California travel-planning information by writing the **California Division of Tourism,** P.O. Box 1499, Dept. 61, Sacramento, CA 95812-1499, or by calling toll-free (800) 462-2543, extension 61. Or try the Internet site, gocalif.ca.gov, which also includes an accommodations reservation service. California's tourism office publishes a veritable gold rush of useful travel information, including the annual *California Official State Visitors Guide* and *California Celebrations*. Particularly useful for outdoor enthusiasts is the new 16-page *California*

Outdoor Recreation guide. The quarterly *California Travel Ideas* magazine is distributed free at agricultural inspection stations at the state's borders. For travel industry professionals, the *California Travel and Incentive Planner's Guide* is also available.

Most of these California tourism publications, in addition to regional and local publications, are also available at the various roadside volunteer-staffed **California Welcome Centers,** a burgeoning trend. The first official welcome center was unveiled in 1995 in Kingsburg, in the San Joaquin Valley, and the next four—in Rohnert Park, just south of Santa Rosa; in Anderson, just south of Redding; in Oakhurst in the gold country, on the way to Yosemite National Park; and at Pier 39 on San Francisco's Fisherman's Wharf—were also in Northern California. There are others in Northern California, too, including the fairly new one in Arcata. Southern California welcome centers include those in Barstow and Los Angeles. To date most welcome centers aren't well located to offer assistance to coastal travelers—Arcata and Pier 39 being notable exceptions—but eventually the network will include virtually all areas of California; along major highways and freeways, watch for signs with the "traveling bear logo," pointing the way to state welcome centers.

Most major cities and visitor destinations in Northern and Southern California also have very good visitor information bureaus and visitor centers, listed elsewhere in this book. Many offer accommodations reservations and other services; some offer information and maps in foreign languages. Chambers of commerce can be useful, too. In less populated areas, stopping by chambers of commerce is something of a hit-or-miss proposition, since office hours may be minimal; the best bet is calling ahead for information. Asking locals—people at gas stations, cafés, grocery stores, and official government outposts—is often the best way to get information about where to go, why, when, and how. Slick city magazines, good daily newspapers, and California-style weekly news and entertainment tabloids are other good sources of information.

Special Information for the Disabled
Twin Peaks Press, P.O. Box 129, Vancouver, WA 98666, tel. (360) 694-2462, or toll-free (800)

637-2256 for orders only, publishes particularly helpful books, including *Wheelchair Vagabond, Travel for the Disabled,* and *Directory of Travel Agencies for the Disabled.* Also useful is the *Travelin' Talk Directory* put out by **Travelin' Talk,** P.O. Box 3534, Clarksville, TN 37043, tel. (615) 552-6670, a network of disabled people available "to help travelers in any way they can." Membership is only $10, a bargain by any standard, since by joining up you suddenly have a vast network of allies in otherwise strange places who are all too happy to tell you what's what. Also helpful: **Mobility International USA,** P.O. Box 10767, Eugene, OR 97440, tel. and TDD (541) 343-1284, fax (541) 343-6812, www.miusa .org, which provides two-way international leadership exchanges. Disabled people who want to go to Europe to study theater, for example, or British citizens who want to come to California for Elderhostel programs—anything beyond traditional leisure travel—should call here first. The individual annual membership fee is $25 for individuals, $35 for organizations.

Special Information for Seniors

Senior adults can benefit from a great many bargains and discounts. A good source of information is the *Travel Tips for Older Americans* pamphlet published by the U.S. Government Printing Office, tel. (202) 275-3648, www.gpo.gov, available for $1.25. (Order it online at www.pueblo .gsa.gov/travel.) The federal government's Golden Age Passport offers free admission to national parks and monuments and half-price discounts for federal campsites and other recreational services; state parks also offer senior discounts. (For detailed information, see appropriate recreation listings under Coastal Recreation, above.) Discounts are also frequently offered to seniors at major tourist attractions and sights as well as for many arts, cultural, and entertainment destinations and events. Another benefit of experience is eligibility for the international **Elderhostel** program, 75 Federal St., Boston, MA 02110, tel. (617) 426-7788 or toll-free (877) 426-8056, www.elderhostel.org, which offers a variety of fairly reasonable one-week residential programs in California.

For information on travel discounts, trip planning, tours, and other membership benefits of the U.S.'s largest senior citizen organization,

contact the **American Association of Retired Persons** (AARP), 601 E St. NW, Washington, DC 20049, tel. (202) 434-2277 or toll-free (800) 227-7737, www.aarp.org. Despite the name, anyone age 50 and older—retired or not—is eligible for membership. Other membership-benefit programs for seniors include the **National Council of Senior Citizens,** 8403 Colesville Rd., Ste. 1200, Silver Springs, MD 20910, tel. (301) 578-8800, fax (301) 578-8999, www.ncscinc.org.

Not Getting Lost: Good Maps

The best all-around maps for California, either in the city or out in the countryside, are those produced by the **American Automobile Association,** which is regionally organized as the California State Automobile Association (CSAA) in Northern and Central California, and as the Automobile Club of Southern California in the southstate. The AAA maps are available at any local AAA office, and the price is right (free, but for members only). In addition to its California state map and Southern California map, AAA provides urban maps for most major cities, plus regional maps with at least some backcountry routes marked (these latter maps don't necessarily show the entire picture, however; when in doubt about unusual routes, ask locally before setting out). For more information about AAA membership, in Northern California contact the **California State Automobile Association;** the main office address is 150 Van Ness Ave., P.O. Box 1860, San Francisco, CA 94101-1860, tel. (415) 565-2012 or (415) 565-2468, www.csaa.org, but there are also regional offices throughout the northstate. Members can also order maps, tour books, and other services online. In Southern California, contact the **Automobile Club of Southern California,** 2601 S. Figueroa St., Los Angeles, CA 90007, tel. (213) 741-3686, www.aaa-calif.com. For AAA membership information, from anywhere in the U.S. call toll-free (800) 222-4357, from anywhere in the world try www.aaa.com.

The best maps money can buy, excellent for general and very detailed travel in California, are the **Thomas Bros. Maps,** typically referred to as "Thomas guides." For the big picture, particularly useful is the *California Road Atlas & Driver's Guide,* but various other, very detailed spiral-bound book-style maps in the Thomas guide street atlas series—San Francisco, Metropolitan Bay Area, Monterey County, Los Angeles, Orange County—are the standard block-by-block references, continually updated, as they have been since 1915. Thomas guides are available at any decent travel-oriented bookstore, or contact the company directly. In Southern California, you'll find a major Thomas Bros. Maps store at 603 W. Seventh St., Los Angeles, CA 90017, tel. (213) 627-4018; the map factory and other store is in Orange County, at 17731 Cowan in Irvine, tel. (949) 863-1984, fax (949) 852-9189, www.thomas.com. (You can also order maps online.) If you find yourself in San Francisco, stop by Thomas Bros. Maps, 550 Jackson St., tel. (415) 981-7520. Or order any map by calling, from anywhere in California, toll-free (800) 899-6277.

When it comes to backcountry travel—where maps quickly become either your best friend or archenemy—the going isn't nearly as easy. U.S. Geological Survey quadrangle maps in most cases are reliable for showing the contours of the terrain, but U.S. Forest Service and wilderness maps—supposedly the maps of record for finding one's way through the woods and the wilds—are often woefully out of date, with new and old logging roads (as well as disappearing or changed trail routes) confusing the situation considerably. In California, losing oneself in the wilderness is a very real, literal possibility. In addition to topo maps (carry a compass to orient yourself by landforms if all else fails) and official U.S. maps, backcountry travelers would be wise to invest in privately published guidebooks and current route or trail guides for wilderness areas; the Sierra Club and Wilderness Press publish both. Before setting out, compare all available maps and other information to spot any possible route discrepancies, then ask national forest or parks personnel for clarification. If you're lucky, you'll find someone who knows what's going on where you want to go.

Aside from well-stocked outdoor stores, the primary California source for quad maps is: **U.S. Geological Survey,** 345 Middlefield Rd., Menlo Park, CA 94025, tel. (650) 853-8300 (ask for the mapping division); an index and catalog of published California maps is available upon request. Or try the USGS website, info.er.usgs.gov, or call toll-free (888) 275-8747. Also contact the U.S. Forest Service and U.S. National Park Service (see Coastal Recreation, above). The best bet for wilderness maps and guides is **Wilderness Press,** 1200 Fifth St., Berkeley, CA 94710, tel. (510) 558-1666 or toll-free (800) 443-7227 (for orders), fax (510) 558-1696, www.wildernesspress.com. Most Wilderness Press titles are available in California bookstores.

SURVIVING: HEALTH AND SAFETY

Emergencies, Medical Care, and General Health

In most places in Northern or Southern California, call 911 in any emergency; in medical emergencies, life support personnel and ambulances will be dispatched. To make sure health care services will be readily provided, health insurance coverage is almost mandatory; carry proof of coverage while traveling in California. In urban areas and in many rural areas, 24-hour walk-in health care services are readily available, though hospital emergency rooms are the place to go in case of life-threatening circumstances.

To avoid most health and medical problems, use common sense. Eat sensibly, avoid unsafe drinking water, bring along any necessary prescription pills—and pack an extra pair of glasses or contacts, just in case. Sunglasses, especially for those unaccustomed to sunshine, as well as sunscreen and a broad-brimmed hat can help prevent sunburn, sunstroke, and heat prostration. Drink plenty of liquids, too, especially when exercising and/or in hot weather.

No vaccinations are usually necessary for traveling in California, though here as elsewhere very young children and seniors should obtain vaccinations against annually variable forms of the flu virus; exposure, especially in crowded urban areas and during the winter disease season, is a likelihood.

As in other areas of the United States and the world, the AIDS (Acquired Immune Deficiency Syndrome) virus and other sexually transmitted diseases are a concern. In mythic "anything goes" California, avoiding promiscuous or unprotected sex is the best way to avoid the danger of contracting the AIDS virus and venereal disease—though AIDS is also transmitted via shared drug needles and contaminated blood transfusions. (All medical blood supplies in California are screened for evidence of the virus.) Sexually speaking, "safe sex" is the preventive key phrase, under any circumstances beyond the strictly monogamous. This means always using condoms in sexual intercourse; oral sex only with some sort of barrier precaution; and no sharing sex toys.

City Safety

Though California's wilderness once posed a major threat to human survival, in most respects the backcountry is safer than the urban jungle of modern cities. Tourism officials don't talk about it much, but crimes against persons and property are a reality in California (though the state's overall crime rate has dropped sharply in recent years). To avoid harm, bring along your street smarts. The best overall personal crime prevention includes carrying only small amounts of cash (inconspicuously, in a money belt or against-the-body money pouch); labeling (and locking) all luggage; keeping valuables under lock and key (and, in automobiles, out of sight); being aware of people and events, and knowing where you are, at all times; and avoiding dangerous, lonely, and unlighted areas after nightfall, particularly late at night and when traveling alone. If you're not sure what neighborhoods are considered dangerous or unsafe, ask locals or hotel or motel personnel—or at the police station, if necessary.

Women traveling alone—not generally advisable, because of the unfortunate fact of misogyny in the modern world—need to take special care to avoid harm. For any independent traveler, self-defense classes (and/or a training course for carrying and using Mace) might be a worthwhile investment, if only to increase one's sense of personal power in case of a confrontation with criminals. Being assertive and confident, and acting as if you know where you are going (even when you don't), are also among the best deterrents to predators. Carry enough money for a phone call—or bus or taxi ride—and a whistle. When in doubt, don't hesitate to use it, and to yell and scream for help.

General Outdoor Safety

The most basic rule is, know what you're doing and where you're going. Next most basic: whatever you do—from swimming or surfing to hiking and backpacking—don't do it alone. For any outdoor activity, be prepared. Check with local park or national forest service officials on weather, trail, and general conditions before setting out. Correct, properly functioning equipment is as important in backpacking as it is in hang gliding, mountain climbing, mountain biking, and sailing. (When in doubt, check it out.)

Among the basics to bring along for almost any outdoor activity: a hat, sunscreen, and lip balm (to protect against the sun in summer, against heat loss, reflective sun, and the elements in winter); a whistle, compass, and mylar "space blanket" in case you become lost or stranded; insect repellent; a butane lighter or waterproof matches; a multipurpose Swiss Army-type knife; nylon rope; a flashlight; and a basic first-aid kit (including bandages, ointments and salves, antiseptics, pain relievers such as aspirin, and any necessary prescription medicines). Hikers, backpackers, and other outdoor adventurers should bring plenty of water—or water purification tablets or pump-style water purifiers for long trips—at least minimal fishing gear, good hiking shoes or boots, extra socks and shoelaces, "layerable" clothing adequate for all temperatures, and a waterproof poncho or large plastic garbage bag. (Even if thunderstorms are unlikely, any sort of packable and wearable plastic bag can keep you dry until you reach shelter.) The necessity for other outdoor equipment, from campstoves to sleeping bags and tents, depends on where you'll be going and what you'll be doing.

Poison Oak

Poison oak (actually a shrublike sumac) is a perennial trailside hazard in California, especially in lowland foothill areas and mixed forests; it exudes oily chemicals that cause a strong allergic reaction in many people, even with only brief contact. (Always be careful what you're burning around the campfire, too; smoke from poison oak, when inhaled, can inflame the lungs and create a life-threatening situation in no time flat.) The best way to avoid the painful, itchy, often long-lasting rashes associated with poison oak is to avoid contact with the plant—in all seasons—and to immediately wash one's skin or clothes if you even suspect a brush with it. (Its leaves a bright, glossy green in spring and summer, red or yellow in fall, poison oak can be a problem even in winter—when this mean-spirited deciduous shrub loses its leaves.) Learn to identify it during any time of year.

Once afflicted with poison oak, never scratch, because the oozing sores just spread the rash. Very good new products on the market include Tecnu's **Poison Oak-n-Ivy Armor** "pre-exposure lotion," produced by Tec Laboratories, Inc., of Albany, Oregon, toll-free tel. (800) 482-4464 (800-ITCHING). Apply it before potential exposure to protect yourself. Another excellent product, quite helpful if you do tangle with poison oak, is Tecnu's **Poison Oak-n-Ivy Cleanser,** the idea being to get the toxic oils off your skin as soon as possible, within hours of initial exposure or just after the rash appears. The cleanser—which smells suspiciously like kerosene—also helps eliminate the itching, remarkably well. (But do *not* apply after oozing begins.) Various drying, cortisone-based lotions, oatmeal baths, and other treatments can help control discomfort if the rash progresses to the oozing stage, but the rash itself goes away only in its own good time.

poison oak

Lyme Disease and Ticks
Even if you favor shorts for summer hiking, you had better plan on long pants, long-sleeved shirts, even insect repellent. The weather may be mild, but there's an increasing risk—particularly in California coastal and foothill areas, as in other states—that you'll contract Lyme disease, transmitted by ticks that thrive in moist lowland climates.

A new ailment on the West Coast, Lyme disease is named after the place of its 1975 discovery in Old Lyme, Connecticut. Already the most common vector-transmitted disease in the nation, Lyme is caused by spirochetes transmitted through blood, urine, and other body fluids. Research indicates it has often been wrongly diagnosed; sufferers were thought to have afflictions such as rheumatoid arthritis. Temporary paralysis, arthritic pains in the hands or arm and leg joints, swollen hands, fever, fatigue, nausea,

headaches, swollen glands, and heart palpitations are among the typical symptoms. Sometimes an unusually circular red rash appears first, between three and 30 days after the tick bite. Untreated, Lyme disease can mean a lifetime of suffering, even danger to unborn children. Treatment, once Lyme disease is discovered through blood tests, is simple and 100% effective if recognized early: tetracycline and other drugs halt the arthritic degeneration and most symptoms. Long-delayed treatment, even with extremely high doses of antibiotics, is only about 50% effective.

Outdoor prudence, coupled with an awareness of possible Lyme symptoms even months later, are the watchwords when it comes to Lyme disease. Take precautions against tick bite: the sooner ticks are found and removed, the better your chances of avoiding the disease. Tuck your pants into your boots, wear long-sleeved shirts, and use insect repellent around all clothing openings as well as on your neck and all exposed skin. Run a full-body "tick check" daily, especially checking hidden areas such as the hair and scalp. Consider leaving dogs at home if heading for Lyme country; ticks they pick up can spread the disease through your human family.

Use gloves and tweezers to remove ticks from yourself or your animals—never crush the critters with your fingers!—and wash your hands and the bitten area afterward. Better yet, smother

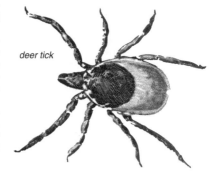

deer tick

imbedded ticks with petroleum jelly first; deprived of oxygen, they start to pull out of the skin in about a half hour, making it easy to pluck them off without tearing them in two and leaving the head imbedded.

GETTING HERE, GETTING AROUND

By Bicycle

Many parts of coastal California are not much fun for cyclists. Scenic highways may be narrow and congested, and cities are car country. Cycling on public roadways here usually means contending with a frightening amount of car traffic; brightly colored bicycle clothing and accessories, reflective tape, good lights, and other safety precautions are mandatory. And always wear a helmet. For those who choose this part of the world or bicycle touring, make the trip with help from books such as *Bicycling the Pacific Coast* (The Mountaineers) by Tom Kirkendall and Vicky Spring. Yet there are less congested areas, and good local bike paths here and there, for more timid recreational bikers; rental bike shops abound, particularly in beach areas. For those who hanker after a little two-wheel backroads sightseeing, certain areas along the central and north coasts and throughout the Sonoma and Napa County "wine countries" are still sublime for recreational cycling and touring. Very reasonable, for a guided bike tour, are some of the winter California trips offered by the nonprofit **The Wayfarers, Inc.,** P.O. Box 15671, Washington, DC 20003, tel. (201) 796-9344, fax (201) 796-0130, www.biketouring.org.

Various good regional cycling guides are available, though serious local bike shops—those frequented by cycling enthusiasts, not just sales outlets—and bike clubs are probably the best local information sources for local and regional rides as well as special cycling events. For upcoming events, other germane information, and referrals on good publications, contact: **California Association of Bicycling Organizations** (CABO), P.O. Box 26864, Dublin, CA 94568. The **Adventure Cycling Association,** P.O. Box 8308, Missoula, MT 59807, tel. (406) 721-1776 or toll-free (800) 755-2453, fax (406) 721-8754, www.adv-cycling.org, is a nonprofit national organization that researches long-distance bike routes and organizes tours for members. Its maps, guidebooks, route suggestions, and *Cyclist's Yellow Pages* can be helpful. For mountain biking information via the Internet, also try the **International Mountain Bicycling Association** at www.greatoutdoors.com/imba.

By Bus

Most destinations in Northern California are reachable by bus, either by major carrier, by "alternative" carrier, or in various combinations of long-distance and local bus lines. And if you can't get *exactly* where you want to go by bus, you can usually get close.

Greyhound is the universal bus service. Obtain a current U.S. route map by mail (see below), but check with local Greyhound offices for more detailed local route information and for information about "casino service" to Reno and other local specials. Greyhound offers discounts for senior adults and disabled travelers, and children under age 12 ride free when accompanied by a fare-paying adult (one child per adult, half fare for additional children). The **Ameripass** offers unlimited travel with on-off stops for various periods of time, but it is usually more economical for long-distance trips with few stopovers. International travelers should inquire about the **International Ameripass.** For more information, in the U.S. contact Greyhound Bus Lines, Inc., at toll-free tel. (800) 232-2222, www.greyhound.com.

Then there are alternative bus options, most notably **Green Tortoise,** the hippest trip on wheels for budget travelers, combining long-distance travel with communal sightseeing. Sign on for a westbound cross-country tour to get to California, an eastbound trip to get away—seeing some of the most spectacular sights in the U.S. along the languid, looping way. As the motto emblazoned on the back of the bus says: "Arrive inspired, not dog tired." Unlike your typical bus ride, on Green Tortoise trips you bring your sleeping bag—the buses are converted sleeping coaches, and the booths and couches convert into beds come nightfall. And you won't need to stop for meals, since healthy gourmet fare (at a cost of about $10 a day) is usually included in the freight; sometimes the food charge is optional, meaning you can bring your own. Green Tortoise also offers a weekly three-day **California**

Coast Tour, with departures from both Los Angeles and San Francisco, making it easy—and fairly entertaining—to get from one end of the state to the other. From San Francisco, you can also get to Southern California on the Green Tortoise **Death Valley National Park** tour; dropoffs can be arranged in either Bakersfield or Mojave, and Greyhound can get you to Los Angeles. For more information, contact: Green Tortoise Adventure Travel, 494 Broadway, San Francisco, CA 94133, tel. (415) 956-7500 or, from anywhere in the U.S. and Canada, toll-free tel. (800) 867-8647, www.greentortoise.com.

By Train

An unusually enjoyable way to travel the length of the West Coast to California, or to arrive here after a trip west over the Sierra Nevada or across the great desert, is by train. Travel along the coast (from Los Angeles north) on Amtrak's immensely popular and recently spiffed up **Coast Starlight,** which now features more comfortable tilt-back seats, a parlor car with library and games, and California-style fare in its dining cars. (From the south, the two-way route continues north to Oakland, across the bay from San Francisco, and eventually continues all the way to Seattle.) If you'll eventually arrive in Southern California via the scenic coastal route, from grand Union Station near downtown L.A. you can head east to New Orleans on the **Sunset Limited,** to San Antonio on the **Texas Eagle,** and to Chicago on the **Desert Wind** and the **Southwest Chief.** On Amtrak's coastal route between San Diego and San Luis Obispo, the San Diegan trains have been replaced by gleaming new double-decker **Pacific Coastliner** trains; amenities include upgraded food service (including local wines) and outlets for laptop computers.

For **Amtrak** train travel routes (including some jogs between cities in California by Amtrak bus), current price information, and reservations, contact a travel agent or call Amtrak at toll-free tel. (800) 872-7245 (USA RAIL), www.amtrak.com. For the hearing impaired, Amtrak's toll-free TTY number is (800) 523-6590 or 91.

A good deal for international travelers (even though the U.S. rail system is much more limited than most nations') and ambitious domestic travelers is the Amtrak 30-day **Explore America** pass—allowing unlimited on-off travel within various regions for a set fee—at last report $158 for any one region, $198 for any two regions, and $278 for the entire country (prices are $50 higher in summer). Up to two children ages 2-15 can travel with an adult for half fare, and students and seniors (62 and older) qualify for 15% discounts. Buy these passes outside the U.S. or through U.S. travel agents (passport required); contact Amtrak for current details. Other discounts are available for members of the active military, veterans, and disabled travelers.

By Automobile

This being California, almost everyone gets around by car. Urban freeway driving in California, because of congestion and Californians' no-nonsense get-on-with-it driving styles, can inspire panic even in nonlocal native drivers. If this is a problem, plan your trip to skirt the worst congestion—by taking back roads and older highways, if possible, or by trying neighborhood routes—but only if you know something about the neighborhoods. Alternatively, plan to arrive in San Francisco, other Bay Area destinations, Los Angeles, San Diego, and other urban locales well after the day's peak freeway commute traffic, usually any time after 7 or 8 p.m.

A good investment for anyone traveling for any length of time in California is a membership in the American Automobile Association (see above) since—among many other benefits, including excellent maps and trip-planning assistance—a AAA card entitles the bearer to no-cost emergency roadside service, including five gallons of free gas and at least limited towing, if necessary.

In mid-2000, gas prices were hovering near $2 per gallon—shockingly expensive in the opinion of most Californians but a real bargain by European standards. Gasoline in California is typically more expensive than elsewhere in the U.S., up to 40 cents per gallon more, only in part because of California's new cleaner-burning "reformulated" fuels, the world's cleanest gasoline. The effect of using the new gasoline is roughly equivalent to the effect of taking 3.5 million cars off the road on any given day—or sucking about three million pounds of toxins and particulate matter out of the air. The clean fuels are designed to reduce vehicle emissions and improve air quality, which seems to be working,

CALIFORNIA ON WHEELS

California's public officials, at least in urban areas, continue to make every effort to offer viable alternatives to automobile travel, but Golden State residents and their cars are almost inseparable. Part of the Western myth, after all, is the freedom to move, to go anywhere at the drop of a hat. Given the state's vast size and the great distances between destinations—and despite widespread awareness about the evils of air pollution, global warming, and excess energy consumption—California's love affair with wheels is a basic fact of life.

So, what's a visitor to do?

Those who arrive by air and prefer to travel by public transportation can reach most areas of California—with careful advance planning—by train and/or bus. (See relevant regional chapters for specific information.) Travelers can also tour by bicycle, an option most feasible for the very fit and flexible, requiring conscientious back-roads route mapping and careful planning.

Most people who arrive without their own wheels, however, soon choose to rent some, either a car or, for longer trips to more obscure destinations, a recreational vehicle.

All major national car rental agencies are well represented in big cities, where most California visitors first arrive, both at airports and downtown. Lower-cost statewide and local agencies are also abundant and usually reliable. Consult the telephone book yellow pages for a complete listing (and also consult the Internet). If in doubt about a given company, contact local visitor bureaus and chambers of commerce. And if you'll be arriving during the holidays or at other peak travel times, it's prudent to reserve rental vehicles well in advance.

Flat rate (daily or weekly) and unlimited mileage rentals are generally the best deal, since a California-style day trip can easily pass the 300-mile mark. When planning a trip or trips to outlying areas, it is usually much less expensive to start from—and return your rental vehicle to—agencies located in major urban areas. Renting a car in a small, remote city with the idea of ending your adventure back in a big city may make perfect sense; but the associated "drop-off fee"—essentially an inconvenience penalty imposed by the rental company, concerned about getting that car back in their shop—can range to $500 and more, a definite drawback.

Recreational vehicles (RVs), including four-wheel drives and pickup trucks with campers, are substantially more expensive to rent than cars and are usually available only through specialized agencies and RV sales dealers.

Compared to European rates, California vehicle rentals are expensive. Once comfortable with one's vehicle and familiar with California driving customs and laws, a special bonus for European and other international travelers is the price of gasoline—still remarkably inexpensive in the U.S., averaging around $2 per gallon these days, though Californians have recently been surprised by gas price increases. Even so, for the time being, at least, travel by car remains cheaper here (at least in terms of personal costs) than almost anywhere else in the world.

---

but a new concern is that clean fuel residues (particularly from the additive MTBE) are polluting California's water. Though MTBE will soon be banned, the Golden State's pollution solutions are, clearly, ideas that still need work.

To check on current **California road conditions** before setting out—always a good idea in a state with so much ongoing road construction and such variable regional weather—call **Caltrans** (California Department of Transportation) from anywhere in California at toll-free (800) 427-7623, and from outside California at (916) 445-7623. The road-condition phone numbers are accessible from touch-tone and pay phones as well as cellular phones. Or check road conditions for your entire trip route on the regularly updated Caltrans website, www.dot.ca.gov.

Though every municipality has its own peculiar laws about everything from parking to skateboarding or roller skating on sidewalks, there are basic rules everyone is expected to know and follow—especially drivers. Get a complete set of regulations from the state motor vehicles department, which has an office in all major cities and many medium-sized ones. Or contact **California Department of Motor Vehicles,** 2415 First Ave., P.O. Box 942869, Sacramento, CA 94269, www.dmv.ca.gov. Foreign visitors planning to drive should obtain an **International Driver's License** before leaving home (they're not available here); licensed U.S. drivers from other states can legally drive in California for 30 consecutive days without having to obtain a California driver's license. Disabled travelers heading for California can get special handicapped-space parking permits, good for 90 days, by requesting applications in advance from the DMV and having them signed by their doctors (there is an application fee). If you'll be renting a car, ask the rental car agency to forward a form to you when you make reservations.

Among driving rules, the most basic is observing the posted speed limit. Though many California drivers ignore any and all speed limits, it's at their own peril should the California Highway Patrol be anywhere in the vicinity. The statewide speed limit for open highway driving varies, typically posted as somewhere between 55 and 70 miles per hour; freeway speeds can vary at different points along the same route. Speed limits for cities and residential neighborhoods are sometimes substantially slower. Another avoidable traffic ticket is *not* indulging in what is colloquially known as the "California stop," slowing down and then rolling right through stop signs without first making a complete stop.

Once arrived at your destination, pay attention to parking notices, tow-away warnings, and curb color: red means no parking under any circumstances; yellow means limited stops only (usually for freight delivery); green means very limited parking; and blue means parking for the disabled only. In hilly areas—mandatory in San Francisco—always turn your front wheels *into* the curb (to keep your car from becoming a rollaway runaway) and set the emergency brake.

Driving while under the influence of alcohol or drugs is a very serious offense in California—aside from being a danger to one's own health and safety, not to mention those of innocent fellow drivers and pedestrians. Don't drink (or do drugs) and drive.

By Rental Car

Renting a car—or a recreational vehicle—in California usually won't come cheap. Rates have been accelerating, so to speak, in recent years, especially when consumers put the kibosh on mileage caps. Turns out people really liked the idea of unlimited "free" mileage. So now the average car rental price is just above $50 a day

(lower for subcompacts, higher for roadhogs). Still, bargains are sometimes available through small local agencies. Among national agencies, National and Alamo often offer the lowest prices. But in many cases, with weekly rentals and various group-association (AAA, AARP, etc.) and credit-card discounts ranging from 10-40%, you'll usually do just as well with other major rental car agencies. According to *Consumer Reports,* in 1996 **Hertz, Avis,** and **National** were rated highest by customers for clean cars, quick and courteous service, and speedy checkout.

Beware the increasingly intense pressure, once you arrive to pick up your rental car, to persuade you to buy additional insurance coverage. In some companies, rental car agents receive a commission for every insurance policy they sell, needed or not, which is why the person on the other side of the counter is so motivated (sometimes pushy and downright intimidating). Feel free to complain to management if you dislike such treatment—and to take your business elsewhere. This highly touted insurance coverage is coverage you probably don't need, from collision damage waivers—now outlawed in some states, but not in California—to liability insurance, which you probably don't need unless you have no car insurance at all (in which case it's illegal to drive in California). Some people do carry additional rental-car collision or liability insurance on their personal insurance policies—talk to your agent about this—but even that is already covered, at least domestically, if you pay for your rental car with a gold or platinum MasterCard or Visa. The same is true for American Express for domestic travelers, though American Express recently rescinded such coverage on overseas car rentals; it's possible that Visa and MasterCard will soon follow suit. (Check your personal insurance and credit-card coverage before dealing with the rental car agencies.) And bring personal proof of car insurance, though you'll rarely be asked for it. In short—buyer beware.

For current information on options and prices for rental cars in Northern California, Southern California, and elsewhere in the U.S., contact **Alamo,** toll-free tel. (800) 327-9633, www.alamo.com.; **Avis,** toll-free (800) 831-2847, www.avis.com; **Budget,** toll-free worldwide (800) 527-0700, www.budget.com; **Dollar,** toll-free (800) 800-4000, www.dollar.com; **Enterprise,** toll-free (800) 736-

8222, www.enterprise.com; **Hertz,** toll-free worldwide (800) 654-3131, www.hertz.com; **National,** toll-free (800) 227-7368, www.nationalcar.com; and **Thrifty,** toll-free (800) 847-4389, www.thrifty.com. You can also make rental car arrangements online, either directly through individual home pages or through virtual travel agencies and reservations systems such as **Travelocity,** www.travelocity.com, and **The Trip,** www.thetrip.com.

Though some rental agencies also handle recreational vehicle (RV) rentals, travelers may be able to get better deals by renting directly from local RV dealers. For suggestions, contact area visitor bureaus—and consult the local telephone book.

By Airplane

Airfares change and bargains come and go so quickly in competitive California that the best way to keep abreast of the situation is through a travel agent. Or via the Internet, where major U.S. airlines regularly offer great deals—discounts of up to 90% (typically not *quite* that good). Popular sites include **American Airlines,** www.aa.com; **Continental,** www.flycontinental.com; **Delta,** www.delta-air.com; **Northwest,** www.nwa.com; **TWA,** www.twa.com; **United,** www.ual.com; and **US Airways,** www.usairways.com. Also look up the people's favorite, **Southwest,** at www.iflyswa.com. Have your credit card handy. To find additional websites, know your computer—or call any airline's toll-free "800" number and ask. Fueling travel agents' fears that online airline ticket sales will doom them (and independent online agencies) is the news that three airlines—Continental, Delta, and Northwest—plan to launch their own "independent" online travel service.

But the online agencies may be able to fight back: **Travelzoo,** www.travelzoo.com, searches the 20 major airline websites for the deep-discounted fares and posts them, so you don't have to spend hours looking for the best deals.

Another good information source for domestic and international flight fares: the travel advertisements in the weekend travel sections of major urban newspapers. Super Saver fares (booked well in advance) can save fliers 30-70% and more. Peak travel times in and out of California being the summer and the midwinter holiday season, book flights well in advance for June-August and December travel. The best bargains in airfares are usually available from January to early May.

Bargain airfares are often available for international travelers, especially in spring and autumn. Charter flights are also good bargains, the only disadvantage usually being inflexible departure and return-flight dates. Most flights from Europe to the U.S. arrive in New York; from there, other transcontinental travel options are available. Reduced-fare flights on major airlines from Europe abound.

Keep in mind, too, if you're flying, that airlines are getting increasingly strict about how much baggage you're allowed to bring with you. They mean business with those prominent "sizer boxes" now on display in every airport. Only two pieces of carry-on luggage are allowed on most carriers—some now allow only one—and each must fit in the box. Most airlines allow three pieces of luggage total per passenger. (Fortunately for parents, diaper bags, fold-up strollers, and—at least sometimes—infant carrier seats don't count.) So if you are philosophically opposed to the concept of traveling light, bring two massive suitcases—and check them through—in addition to your carry-on. Some airlines, including American, charge extra for more than two checked bags per person. Contact each airline directly for current baggage guidelines.

BOB RACE

THE NORTH COAST
LAND OF MAGIC

Fog created California's north coast, and still defines it. Fog is everywhere, endless, eternal, *there*. Even on blazing, almost blinding days of sunshine when the veil lifts, the fog is still present somehow, because life here has been made by it. Stands of sky-scraping coast redwoods need fog to live. So do many other native north coast plants, uniquely adapted to uniformly damp conditions. The visual obscurity characteristic of the coast also benefits animals, providing a consistent, year-round supply of drinking water and, for creatures vulnerable to predators, additional protective cover.

Fog even seems to have political consequences. As elsewhere in the northstate, the secessionist spirit is alive and well on the north coast, but the fog makes it seem fuzzy, and the

See color maps of the north coast
at front of book.

urge is taken less seriously here than it is elsewhere. When, in the mid-1970s, for example, some Mendocino County citizens banded together to form their own state (they called it Northern California), the response from Sacramento was off-the-cuff and casual: "The county's departure, if it ever goes, would scarcely be noticed, at least not until the fog lifted."

People often find fog disquieting, depressing. Some almost fear it. If only momentarily, in fog we become spatially and spiritually bewildered. Our vision seems vague; we hear things. We fall prey to illusions; we hallucinate: trees walk, rocks smile, birds talk, rivers laugh, the ocean sings, someone unseen brushes our cheek. All of a sudden, we don't know where we are and haven't the foggiest notion where we're going. Life as we know it has changed. We have changed.

According to meteorologists, dense coastal fog occurs along this cool-weather coast as a result of shoreward breezes carrying warm, moist oceanic air over colder offshore waters. The air's moisture condenses into fog, which rolls in over the coastal mountains in cloudlike waves. As the marine air moves inland and is warmed by the sun, it reabsorbs its own moisture and the fog dissipates.

But science doesn't really explain fog at all—not fog as change, as creator, as fashioner of fantastic forms, as shape-shifting summoner of strange sounds, or protector of the primeval purpose. Fog, in the mythic sense, is magic.

THE LANDSCAPE

North Coast Landforms

California's northern coastline has few sandy beaches, even fewer natural harbors. Land's end is rugged and inhospitable, with surging surf

---

NORTH COAST AREA CODES ARE A'CHANGIN'

In late December 2000, and then again in October of the following year, parts of Northern California will suffer yet another change in telephone area codes—the direct result of residents' red-hot relationship with communications technology and the proliferating numbers of cellular phones, fax machines, and online computer connections that go with it.

The old 707 area, which covered much of the northern part of the Bay Area and the Wine Country, as well as the entire north coast, will get two new codes—369 and 627—in late December 2000. In affected areas to the south—including Dixon, Rio Vista, Vacaville, Fairfield, Suisun City, Benicia, and Vallejo—you can use either 707 or 369 beginning December 2000, but you must use 369 by June 2001. The second phase, introducing the 627 code, affects Cloverdale, Geyserville, Healdsburg, Sea Ranch, Bodega Bay, Guerneville, Forestville, Sebastopol, Santa Rosa, Calistoga, St. Helena, Rohnert Park, Sonoma, Yountville, and Napa. "Permissive dialing"—meaning you can use either area code—begins in October 2001, but 627 will be mandatory by April 2002.

In addition to these changes in telephone area codes, it's likely that more will occur during the useful life of this book. If you have trouble using any area codes listed in this book, dial 0 and ask the operator for current information.

---

and treacherous undertows. Because of this—and because of zero-visibility coastal fog—shipwrecks are part of the region's lore. Bits and pieces of hundreds of ships have washed up on these unsympathetic shores.

Offshore west of Eureka, some 4,000 feet below the surface, is a formation known as the Mendocino Ridge. In 1994, researchers from Oregon State University discovered 100 miles of extensive beach deposits near the now-sunken ridge, which itself is a feature of the Mendocino Fault Zone. (The meeting here of the Pacific and Gorda tectonic plates with the North American continent creates the Mendocino Triple Junction—one of the most active earthquake zones in the world.) These scientists now speculate that when the ridge was young, some three to five million years ago, it had risen as a 200-mile-long east-west "fold" of islands offshore from what is now San Francisco. These islands profoundly changed the regions' climate—deflecting the cool California Current to the west, and allowing warm, subtropical waters from Mexico to surge north along the coast—before receding. This, researchers say, would explain evidence that California's coastal climate was once quite warm—a trend that ended rather abruptly about three million years ago.

The region's major features on land are the Coast Ranges, consecutive ridges angling north to Eureka, where they meet up with the westward edge of the Klamath Mountains. Geologically, the Coast Ranges (with few peaks higher than 8,000 feet) are composed of once-oceanic, uplifted, and relatively "soft" Franciscan Complex sedimentary rock. The deep soils covering the bedrock were produced over eons by humidity (gentle but constant enough to crumble rock) and, augmented by forest humus, are generally protected from erosion by the ancient forests themselves. The thick coastal soil gives these mountains their gently rounded shape. When saturated with water, and especially when atop typically weathered bedrock, coastal hillsides have a tendency to slide. Landslides are even more common in areas where extensive logging or other removal of natural vegetation occurs, since intact native plant communities make good use of soil moisture.

Federal Wild and Scenic River status has finally been extended to the north coast's Eel,

Klamath, Smith, and Trinity Rivers, protecting them from dam projects, other water-diversion schemes, and logging within their immediate watersheds. The Smith, the state's last undammed river, is now protected as a national recreation area. Other major north coast rivers include the Garcia, Mad, Navarro, Noyo, and Russian.

North Coast Climate

The north coast has a Mediterranean climate cooled in summer by the arctic California Current. Heavy rainfall, 80-160 inches per year, and winter's endless overcast days compete with thick fog the rest of the year. The sun is most likely to make its chilly appearance during early spring, but September usually brings balmy weather. Often at the end of February, "false spring" comes and stays for a week or more. North coastal temperatures are moderate year-round, but can *feel* cold anytime, due to bone-chilling fog and moist air whisked ashore by steady ocean breezes.

A rarity along the southern Sonoma County coast but nonetheless widely observed is an offshore floating mirage resembling Oz's Emerald City, with towers, minarets, the whole show. This strange-but-true phenomenon is vaguely attributed to "climatic conditions." Also rare is the earthquake-related phenomenon of tsunamis, or giant coast-crushing waves. Radiocarbon dating of Native American cultural remains (which happen to coincide with dates of major Cascadia earthquakes) suggest that ancient tsunamis were so powerful they tossed canoes into the tops of trees. The most recent tsunami came in 1964, when a 13-foot wave generated by an 8.5-magnitude earthquake in Alaska smashed ashore in Crescent City on the Northern California coast, killing 11 people and destroying much of the town.

FLORA AND FAUNA: REDWOODS, ROOSEVELT ELK

North Coast Flora

In one of his more famous gaffes as governor of California, Ronald Reagan reportedly once cut redwood trees with the old saw, "If you've seen one, you've seen 'em all." (Reagan was misquoted, actually. What he said was, "A tree is a tree—how many more do you need to look at?") Despite Reagan's opinion on the subject, the north coast is noted for its deep, dark, and devastatingly beautiful forests of tall coastal redwoods, or *Sequoia sempervirens*—sadly, a tree most often appreciated as construction timber for suburban sun decks. Another regional tree with commercial value is the Douglas fir, *Pseudotsuga menziesii,* faster growing than redwood and often replanted by foresters on clear-cut lands. Still another is the yew, whose bark contains components that have been used to treat breast cancer.

Yews, Sitka spruces, cedars, and lowland firs reach to the coast. Maples, sycamores, and alders add contrast and color in mixed streamside forests. Foothill woodlands—scattered oaks and conifers in a sea of grasses and spring wildflowers—are common north of San Francisco. Introduced groves of Australian eucalyptus trees—planted now primarily as windbreaks, though at one time intended as timber trees—are common along the Sonoma County coast, inland, and up into Mendocino County.

Coastal shrublands have no true chaparral but share some of the same species: fragrant California laurel (bay) trees, scrub oak, dogwood, ceanothus, and purple sage. The least favorite shrub here, as elsewhere in California, is poison oak, usually found in shaded areas. Among the most beautiful coastal "shrubs"—sometimes growing to tree size—are the native rhododendron species, both the western azalea and the California rose bay.

Red elderberries, blackberries, salmonberries, raspberries, huckleberries, and gooseberries all grow wild along the north coast. Wildflowers are abundant, primarily in spring. Unusual are the creeping beach primroses, beach peas, and sea rockets on beaches and sandy dunes. Beneath redwoods grow delicate fairy lanterns, oxalis, and trillium.

North Coast Fauna

Deer are common all along the north coast. Protected colonies of Roosevelt elk can be seen far to the north in Redwood National Park. Smaller north coast mammals include dusky-footed woodrats and nocturnal "pack rats," which nest in trees and rarely travel more than 50 feet in any direction. More common are those gregarious

ICE AGE SURVIVORS: COAST REDWOODS

Though they once numbered an estimated two million, California's native population of coast redwood trees has been reduced through logging and agriculture to isolated groves of virgin trees. The tallest trees in the state but only the fourth oldest, *Sequoia sempervirens* are nonetheless ancient. Well established here when dinosaurs roamed the earth, redwood predecessors flourished throughout the Northern Hemisphere 60 million years ago. Isolated from the rest of their kind by thick ice sheets a million years ago, the redwoods made their last stand in California.

The elders among today's surviving coast redwoods are at least 2,200 years old. These trees thrive in low, foggy areas protected from fierce offshore winds. Vulnerable to both wind and soil erosion, shallow-rooted redwoods tend to topple over during severe storms. Redwoods have no need for deep taproots since fog collects on their needle-like leaves, then drips down the trunk or directly onto the ground, where the equivalent of up to 50 inches of rainfall annually is absorbed by hundreds of square feet of surface roots.

Unlike the stately, individualistic Sierra big trees or *Sequoiadendron giganteum,* the comparatively scrawny coast redwoods reach up to the sky in dense, dark-green clusters—creating living, breathing cathedrals lit by filtered flames of sun or shrouded in foggy silence. The north coast's native peoples religiously avoided inner forest areas, the abode of spirits (some ancestral). But in the modern world, the sacred has become profane. A single coast redwood provides enough lumber for hundreds of hot tubs, patio decks, and wine vats, or a couple of dozen family cabins, or a hefty school complex. Aside from its attractive reddish color, pungent fragrance, and water- and fire-resistance, redwood is also decay-, insect-, and fungus-resistant—and all the more attractive for construction.

Yet coast redwoods never really die. Left to their own devices, redwoods are capable of regenerating themselves without seeds. New young trees shoot up from stumps or from roots around the base of the old tree, forming gigantic woodland fairy rings in second- or third-growth forests. And each of these trees, when mature, can generate its own genetically identical offspring. Sometimes a large, straight limb from a fallen tree will sprout, sending up a straight line of trees. In heavily logged or otherwise traumatized forest areas, tiny winged redwood seeds find room to take root, sprout, and eventually flourish, blending into a forest with stump-regenerated trees.

Coast redwoods never really die but regenerate in many ways.

CALIFORNIA DEPARTMENT OF PARKS AND RECREATION

STORY WITHOUT END:
THE POLITICS OF HARVESTING REDWOODS

Along the north coast, the politics of logging are as universally explosive as the issue of offshore drilling. The battle to preserve redwoods, especially the remaining first-growth stands, has been going on for decades. So strong are the economic forces in support of logging and related industry that without the untiring efforts of the private Save-the-Redwoods League, Sierra Club, and other environmental organizations, most of the coast redwood groves now protected from commercial "harvesting" would be long gone. The fact that Redwood National Park north of Eureka was established at all, even if late, is something of a miracle. And the recent battle over the old-growth Headwaters Forest echoes all the wars that came before.

Environmentalists adamantly oppose the accelerating practice of clearcutting, the wholesale denuding of hillsides and entire watersheds in the name of efficiency and quick profits. "Tree huggers" have argued for years that anything other than sustained yield timber harvesting—cutting no more timber than is grown each year—not only destroys the environment by eliminating forests, wildlife habitat, and fisheries but ultimately destroys the industry itself. Someday, they've been saying for several decades, the forests will be gone and so will logging and lumber mill jobs. "Someday" has arrived. The timber business has harvested its own industry into oblivion.

The failure of both the 1990 "Green" and Forests Forever initiatives, statewide ballot propositions in favor of forest protection, has only served to increase local furor. Earth First! and other activist groups subsequently took on Pacific Lumber Company and other timber firms—taking the battle into the forests and surrounding communities, as in 1990's "Redwood Summer." Timbermen and truckers have themselves taken to the streets defending their traditional livelihoods with community parades and other events accented by yellow solidarity ribbons. The fight has become so intense, philosophically, that the Laytonville school board was publicly pressured to ban The Lorax by Dr. Seuss because of the book's anti-clearcutting sentiments. (The book banning failed, ultimately.)

A further blow to business as usual came with a 1990s admission by the California Board of Forestry that the state has allowed timber companies to cut down so many mature trees—old growth and otherwise—that there now looms a serious "timber gap," a substantial reduction in future forest harvests. The "statewide emergency" is due to "past failure" to regulate industrial timberlands and "has resulted in long-term overharvesting, drastically reducing both the productive capability of the land and maintenance of adequate wildlife habitat." This new crisis has further shocked the California timber industry, long accustomed to the board's regulatory sympathies.

Mill workers process an old giant.

TOM MYERS PHOTOGRAPHY

The most recent chapter in the redwood wars began when the north coast's Pacific Lumber Company (PALCO) was acquired in a junk bond-financed deal by Maxxam Corporation. The original PALCO was well regarded by environmentalists as a responsible, sustained-yield logger, but with Maxxam CEO Charles Hurwitz at the helm, PALCO began clearcutting on its 202,000 acres in Humboldt County, for the first time in its history—to pay the price of Hurwitz's purchase. Among PALCO's holdings: the 60,000-acre Headwaters Forest, the largest remaining stand of privately owned old-growth redwoods in the world.

When the PALCO chain saws threatened to fell the roadless 3,000-acre Headwaters Grove at the heart of the vast old-growth redwood forest, environmentalist activists went to war with Hurwitz. For more than 10 years, Earth First! and other environmental groups stopped at nothing—public protests, guerrilla theater, tree-sitting, lawsuits—to prevent the harvesting of the Headwaters Forest. After years of forest warfare and hot tempers in nearby north coast communities, a deal brokered in 1998 by U.S. Senator Dianne Feinstein seemed destined to provide the political solution. Feinstein's compromise allowed the federal and state governments to pur-chase the core Headwaters acreage and a surrounding watershed buffer—a total of 7,500 acres—and required a "habitat conservation plan" for the remaining PALCO acreage, in an attempt to balance logging and wildlife protection.

But Hurwitz balked. The federal funding authorization was set to expire, negotiations were stalled, and the Headwaters' future looked grim. Yet on March 1, 1999—with just *seven minutes* left on the funding clock—the deal was struck and signed, and the Headwaters Forest became public property—for a hefty price tag of $480 million.

After the dramatic conclusion to the Headwaters conflict, most area residents were relieved. At least some of the Headwaters Forest is now preserved, the state and federal governments will regulate logging and wildlife habitat protection on the remaining acreage, and PALCO loggers can return to work.

Some environmentalists, though, say it was a bad deal—not going far enough to protect the Headwaters ecosystem as a viable whole. They are particularly concerned about the probable loss of several pristine old-growth groves, and the threat to the coho salmon run due to damage to the Elk River watershed. They promise further court battles. The saga continues.

California gray squirrels, which feast on patches of ice plant, wild strawberries, other fruit seeds, nuts, and grasses. When surprised, black-tailed jackrabbits scurry frantically through foothill brush areas, which are also inhabited by brush rabbits or cottontail "bunnies." Raccoons and skunks are common. So are long-tailed weasels, though people rarely see them. Aquatic land mammals include muskrats or "marsh rabbits" and the vegetarian beaver.

Here, as elsewhere in California, gray foxes are common; those characteristically clever red foxes are less so. From more remote areas, particularly at dusk or dawn, comes the lonely howl of coyotes. Bobcats (truly "wildcats" when cornered) are fairly abundant but rarely seen, though mating squalls can be heard in midwinter. Fairly rare are mountain lions, which usually discover people before anyone discovers them. Black bears, found even at sea level though they range up into higher elevations, usually won't attack humans unless frightened or protecting their cubs.

A common nonnative Californian along the coast is the nocturnal opossum, the only native U.S. marsupial. Also nonnative, and preferring the cover of night for their ferocious forays through the world, are wild pigs—an aggressive cross between domesticated and imported wild European hogs. But the wildest (and largest) north coast land mammal is Bigfoot, or Sasquatch, that half-man, half-beast of lore, first reported by native peoples but rarely seen.

Anadromous Fish

North coast salmon, steelhead, and American shad are all anadromous, living in the sea but returning to freshwater streams to reproduce. Salmon and steelhead generally start their spawning runs up north coastal rivers between mid-November and late February (often earlier and later for steelhead), with distinct migration times between watersheds. There are five separate species of Pacific salmon along the coast, but nearly all are of the king and silver varieties. Unlike salmon, steelhead (large, ocean-going rainbow trout) don't die after reproducing and can spawn up to six times in a lifetime.

HISTORY: TIMBER AND TOURISM

A Portuguese sailor first sighted Cape Mendocino in 1543, but explorers avoided setting foot on the foreboding, darkly forested coastline because of the lack of natural harbors. According to some historians, Sir Francis Drake dropped anchor at Point Reyes in 1579, a landing most likely pivotal in convincing the Spanish to extend their mission chain from Mexico up the California coast to Sonoma.

But after Drake's "discovery" of the north coast, it took nearly three centuries for substantial settlement to occur. Misery was the common experience of early explorers. The intrepid Jedediah Smith nearly starved while trailblazing through the redwoods, called "a miserable forest prison" by other unlucky adventurers. The Russians arrived on California's north coast in the early 1800s to slaughter sea otters for fashionable fur coats and hats. Their Fort Ross complex on the coast north of the Russian River (now a fine state historic park) was built entirely of redwood. After the otters were all but obliterated, the Russians departed. So desperate for building materials and furniture was Sacramento's founder John Sutter that he traveled all the way up the coast to Fort Ross, purchasing (and dismantling) entire buildings for the lumber and carting off rooms full of Fort Ross furnishings and tools.

With the California gold rush of 1849 and the sudden onslaught of prospectors throughout the territory came new exploratory determination. The first settlements in California's far north, including the coastal towns of Eureka and Trinidad, started out as mining pack stations for inland gold mines. Then came redwood logging, a particularly hazardous undertaking in the early days, from felling to loading finished lumber onto schooners anchored off the rocky shoreline. (Most of the original logging towns and lumber "ports" have long since vanished.) Tourism had a respectable early start, too, particularly with the advent of drive-thru redwood trees and take-home knickknacks.

Now that the "harvesting" of the region's vast virgin redwood forests is all but complete, tourism will increasingly become a mainstay. Redwoods in isolated protected groves, a few redwood state parks, and Redwood National Park, not to mention the spectacular coastline, offer ample opportunity for increased tourism.

The Economy: North Coast Green

Depending upon the year, who's running for office, and whom you talk to, illicit marijuana growing pumps somewhere between $110 and $600 million into the north coast's economy each year. According to NORML, the National Organization for the Reform of Marijuana Laws, California leads the nation in pot production with an annual crop estimated at $2.55 billion. Traditionally, though, the lumber business has been the reigning industry, booming and busting along with construction and the dollar. Fluctuations in demand mean frequent unemployment and localized economic depressions.

Agriculture—sheep and cattle ranching, dairy farming, and commercial fishing—is less important overall, but dominant in certain areas. Recreation and tourism, especially "green" tourism, along with related small businesses and service industries, are growing in importance. Locals tend to view these inevitable incursions of "outsiders" as both a blessing and curse. There's begrudging gratitude for the money visitors spend yet at times also thinly disguised disgust for the urban manners and mores, not to mention increasing development and higher prices, that come with it.

REDWOOD NATIONAL PARK AND VICINITY

Pointing north to Oregon like a broken finger is Redwood National Park, California's finest temple to tree hugging. Although well-traveled Hwy. 101 passes through the park, away from the highway much of the park is remote and often empty of worshippers. Those visitors just passing through to the Trees of Mystery are likely unaware that they're witnessing a miracle—forests being raised (albeit slowly) from the dead. Redwood National Park is complete, yet unfinished. Standing in the shadow and sunlight of an old-growth redwood grove, mindful only of the fullness of life, is like stepping up to an altar. But elsewhere in the park—out back toward the alley, looking like remnants of some satanic rite—are shameful scars of sticks and scabbed-over earth, the result of opportunistic clear-cutting during the political wrangling that accompanied the park's formation. Today, these areas are still in the early stages of healing. Yet Redwood National Park features some magnificent groves of virgin old-growth redwood. Three of the world's 10 tallest trees grow here—one of the reasons for UNESCO's 1982 declaration of the area as a World Heritage Site, the first on the Pacific coast. Redwood National Park is also an international Man in the Biosphere Reserve.

Other people call it other things. When the sawdust finally settled after the struggle to establish this national park—the costliest of them all, with a total nonadministrative price tag of $1.4 billion—no one was happy. Despite the park's acquisitions to date, purists protest that not enough additional acres of old-growth redwoods have been preserved. Philistines are dismayed that there is so little commercial development here, so few gift shops and souvenir stands. And some locals are still unhappy that prime timber stands are now out of the loggers' reach, and that the prosperity promised somewhere just down the skid roads of Redwood National Park never arrived—or, more accurately, never matched expectations.

Though federal and state lands within the boundaries of Redwood National Park are technically under separate jurisdictions, as a practical matter the national park and its three associated state parks—the **Prairie Creek Redwoods, Del Norte Coast Redwoods,** and **Jedediah Smith Redwoods State Parks**—are cooperatively managed. In general, the visiting weather is best in late spring and early autumn. August and September are the busiest times here (the salmon fishing rush), but September after Labor Day offers fewer crowds and usually less fog.

PARK FLORA AND FAUNA

Some of the lush terrain included within the borders of Redwood National Park is so strange that filmmaker George Lucas managed to convince much of the world it was extraterrestrial in his *Return of the Jedi*. The park's dominant redwood forests host more than 1,000 species of plants and animals. Sitka spruce, firs, and pines grow on the coast. Leather-leaved salal bushes, salmonberries, and huckleberries control the forest's understory. Rhododendrons and azaleas bloom in May and June, followed by flowering carpets of oxalis or redwood sorrel, whose tiny leaves fold up like umbrellas when sunlight filters down to the forest floor. Mushrooms, various ferns, lacy bleeding hearts, and other delicate wildflowers also flourish here. In the meadows and along coastal prairies are alders, bigleaf maples, hazels, and blackberries.

Roosevelt elk, or wapiti, survive only here and in Washington's Olympic National Park, though they once roamed from the San Joaquin Valley north to Mt. Shasta. Black bears, mountain lions, bobcats, deer, beavers, raccoons, and porcupines are fairly common. Offshore are gray whales, seals, sea lions, porpoises, and sea otters, and you'll find creatures large and small in the tidepools. Trout and salmon are abundant in all three of the park's rivers.

The park is also home to 300 species of birds, including Pacific Flyway migrants, gulls, cormorants, rare brown pelicans, raptors, and songbirds. Redwood-loving birders listen for the mysterious marbled murrelet, a rare black-and-white seabird often seen but seldom heard and

Roosevelt elk

CALIFORNIA DEPARTMENT OF PARKS AND RECREATION

believed to nest in the treetops. If it can be established unequivocally that murrelets nest in old-growth forests (like the now-famous spotted owl), then their habitat will have to be protected from logging.

THE POLITICS OF PARK PRESERVATION

Before settlement, the land here was home to the Yurok, Tolowa, and Chilula peoples. These native residents thrived on an acorn-based diet supplemented by abundant deer, salmon, shellfish, berries, seaweed, and the occasional beached whale. The settlers who later arrived appreciated the landscape not as an intricate web of life, but as a resource ripe for harvest.

Logging in areas now included within Redwood National Park began in the 1850s but peaked after World War II, when annual harvests of more than one million board feet were the rule. By the early 1960s, the redwoods' days were clearly numbered. Lumber mills were closing and only 300,000 of the state's original two million acres of pristine coast redwood forest remained. Just one-sixth of that total was protected, thanks to persistent urging and financial contributions from the Save-the-Redwoods League, the Sierra Club, and other environmental organizations. As demands for redwood lumber increased, it was also increasingly clear that the time to save the remaining old-growth redwoods

and their watersheds was now—or never.

One Park, Two Compromises

The establishment of Redwood National Park by Congress in 1968 consolidated various federal, state, and private holdings along the coastline from Crescent City south to the Redwood Creek watershed near Trinidad. The park totaled only 58,000 acres, half of which was already protected within the Prairie Creek, Del Norte, and Jedediah Smith Redwoods State Parks. Included were only a small portion of the Mill Creek (Del Norte Redwoods) area and less than half of the important Redwood Creek watershed (including the Tall Trees Grove). This unsatisfactory settlement cost almost $200 million, more than the U.S. government had ever spent on land acquisition in one place.

In August 1969, President Richard Nixon, former president Lyndon B. Johnson and his wife, Lady Bird, California governor Ronald Reagan, and other bigwigs bunched together for dignified dedication ceremonies in the Lady Bird Johnson Grove. But even then, the shortsightedness of the compromise was all too obvious; bulldozers and logging trucks were making clear-cut hay on the ridgetops and unprotected watersheds beyond. Reagan didn't believe in regulating the timber companies.

With devastation of even the protected groves imminent due to the law of gravity—the onrushing impact of rain-driven erosion from clear-cut sites on areas downhill and downstream—environmentalists initiated another long round of legal-and-otherwise challenges. "Think big" U.S. Congressmember Phil Burton of San Francisco proposed an additional acquisition of 74,000 acres, countered by the National Park Service's think-small suggestion of just 21,500 acres. A final compromise, this one engineered by the Carter administration in 1978, added a total of 48,000 acres of new parklands (much of it already clear-cut and in desperate need of rehabilitation) at a cost of $300 million more, not to mention $33 million for resurrecting the destroyed slopes of Redwood Creek or the millions set aside to compensate out-of-work lumber-industry workers. In addition, the compromise included a political coup of sorts, giving the National Park Service regulatory authority in a 30,000-acre Park Protection Zone upstream from Redwood National Park proper.

The Park Today

The rehabilitation of clear-cut lands remains a top park priority—more important than recreational development. But because of the immensity of the task and the slow healing process, Redwood National Park will probably not be "finished" for decades.

For good war stories from the environmental camp, read the Sierra Club's *The Last Redwoods and the Parkland of Prairie Creek,* by Edgar and Peggy Wayburn, and the definitive *The Fight to Save the Redwoods,* by historian Susan Schrepfer. The logging industry position can be read any day of the week on the devastated slopes around the park, especially in Six Rivers National Forest.

SEEING AND DOING REDWOOD NATIONAL PARK

The main thing to do in Redwood National Park is simply *be* here. Sadly, "being here" to many area visitors means little more than pulling into the parking lot near the 49-foot-tall Paul Bunyan and Babe the Blue Ox at Klamath's Trees of Mystery, buying big-trees trinkets, or stopping for a slab or two at roadside redwood burl stands in Orick.

Though fishing, kayaking, surfing, and rafting are increasingly popular, nature study and hiking are the park's main recreational offerings. For those seeking views with the least amount of effort, take a drive along Howland Hill Rd. (one-lane dirt road) through some of the finest trees in Jedediah Smith Redwoods State Park. (Howland Hill Rd. transects the park and can be reached via South Fork Rd. off Hwy. 199 just east of the park or via Elk Valley Rd. south of Crescent City.) Or try a sunny picnic on the upland prairie overlooking the redwoods and ocean, reached via one-lane Bald Hills Rd., eight miles or more inland from Hwy. 101.

Park Hiking Trails

The together-but-separate nature of the park's interwoven state and federal jurisdictions makes everything confusing, including figuring out the park's trail system (such as it is). Pick up a copy of the joint *Trails* brochure published by the Redwood Natural History Association available at any of the state or national park information centers and offices in the area. *Trails* divides the collective system north and south, provides corresponding regional trail maps, describes the general sights along each trail, and classifies each by length and degree of difficulty. Fifty cents well spent.

Among the must-do walks is the easy and short self-guided nature trail on the old logging road to **Lady Bird Johnson Grove.** Near the grove at the overlook is an educational logging rehabilitation display comprised of acres of visual aids—devastated redwood land clear-cut in 1965 and 1970 next to a forest selectively logged at the end of World War II. At the parking lot two miles up steep Bald Hills Rd. (watch for logging trucks) you'll find a picnic area and restrooms.

The traditional route for true tree huggers, though, is the long (but also easy) 11.5-mile roundtrip hike (at least five hours one-way, overnight camping possible with permit) along **Redwood Creek Trail** to the famous **Tall Trees Grove.** The grove's **Howard Libby Redwood** was once 368 feet tall and claimed the title of the world's tallest tree. But in 1999, a storm blew off the top 10 feet, and the tree lost its tallest-tree crown, as it were, to another redwood (unmarked, for its own protection) in Montgomery Woods State Reserve in Mendocino County. The easy way to reach the grove involves taking a shuttle from the information center near Orick;

buses leave four times a day in summer, otherwise thrice-daily (small fee). For those shuttled in, the guided tour includes a ranger-led discussion of logging damage and reforestation techniques. Another possibility is coming in via the shuttle, then walking back out on the longer trail.

The longest and most memorable trek in Redwood National Park is the 30-mile-long **Coastal Trail,** which runs almost the park's entire length (hikable in sections) from near Endert's Beach south of Crescent City through Del Norte Redwoods State Park (and past the HI-AYH hostel there), inland around the mouth of the Klamath River, then south along Flint Ridge, Gold Bluffs Beach, and Fern Canyon in Prairie Creek Redwoods State Park. From there, a summers-only spur continues south along the beach to the information center.

If the entire coast route is too much, the **Flint Ridge Trail** section from the east end of Alder Camp Rd. to the ocean (primitive camping) is wild and wonderful, passing beavers and beaver dams at Marshall Pond. Easy and exquisite is the short **Fern Canyon Trail,** just off the Coastal Trail in Prairie Creek Redwoods State Park; it's less than a mile roundtrip through a 60-foot-high "canyon" of ferns laced up the sides of Home Creek's narrow ravine. To get there by car, take Davison Rd. from near Rolf's west over the one-lane bridge—watch for cattle being herded home—for six miles to the Gold Bluffs Beach Campground, then continue 1.5 miles to the parking lot. Even better is the four-mile hike west on the **James Irvine Trail** from the visitor center (or via the **Miners Ridge Trail,** which connects to Irvine by means of the **Clintonia Trail).** However you get there, the trip is worth it for the jeweled greenery—sword, deer, five-fingered, chain, bracken, lady, and licorice ferns—clinging to the canyon's ribs along the chuckling stream.

The **Revelation Trail,** just south of the visitor center in Prairie Creek Redwoods State Park, is a short self-guided nature trail for blind and sighted people, with rope and wood handrails the entire length and "touchable" sights. Trailside features are described on signs, in brochures also printed in Braille, and on cassette tapes available at the visitor center. Also special, rarely visited, and especially rich in rhododendrons is the short **Brown Creek Trail,** east of Hwy. 101 and north of the Prairie Creek visitor center.

JEDEDIAH SMITH REDWOODS STATE PARK

This is one of the most beautiful places on earth—and almost unvisited. Few people come inland even a few miles from Hwy. 101 near Crescent City.

Once Tolowa tribal territory, the Smith River, which flows through the park, was crossed by mountain man Jedediah Smith on June 20, 1828, after his grueling cross-country effort to reach the Pacific. The subsequent arrival of trappers, miners, loggers, fishermen, and farmers led to changes in the landscape and the rapid destruction of native populations. Yet this 10,000-acre stand of old-growth redwoods, Douglas fir, pines, maples, and meadows seems almost unscathed.

Historic **Howland Hill Rd.,** once a redwood-paved thoroughfare, is now graveled and meanders like a summer river through the quiet groves. The **National Tribute Grove,** a 5,000-acre memorial to veterans of World Wars I and II, is the park's largest. Tiny **Stout Grove** includes the area's largest measured redwoods. For an easy two-mile loop, walk both the **Simpson** and **Peterson Trails** through primeval redwoods and ferns. Even shorter is the combined walk along the **Leiffer** and **Ellsworth Trails,** something of a Jedediah Smith sampler. The 30-minute **Stout Grove Trail** offers trees and access to some of the Smith River's excellent summer swimming holes (complete with sandy beaches). Take the **Hiouchi Trail** for rhododendrons and huckleberries. More ambitious are hikes along both forks of the **Boy Scout Tree** and **Little Bald Hills Trails.** Also among the Smith River redwoods are excellent developed campsites. For more information about Jedediah Smith Redwoods State Park, contact the **Redwood National and State Parks Information Center,** 1111 Second St., Crescent City, CA 95531, tel. (707) 464-6101.

DEL NORTE COAST REDWOODS STATE PARK

Del Norte is a dense and foggy coastal rainforest comprised of 6,400 acres of redwoods, meadows, beaches, and tidepools. It's so wet here in winter that the developed campgrounds close. The **Damnation Creek Trail,** crossing Hwy. 1, leads through magnificent old-growth *Sequoias,* spruce, Oregon grape, and seasonal wildflowers to a tiny beach with offshore sea stacks and tidepools. Or, take the **Coastal Trail** from Wilson Creek to the bluffs. Easier is the short walk to the north coast's finest tidepools (and the Nickel Creek Primitive Camp) at the end of **Enderts Beach Trail,** accessible from Enderts Beach Rd. south of Crescent City. To see the park's second-growth redwoods, and for exceptional birdwatching, take the almost four-mile **Hobbs Wall Trail.** Beyond Del Norte Coast Redwoods as the highway descends to Crescent City is the **Rellim Demonstration Forest,** which offers a well-maintained self-guided nature trail and a comfortable lodge for fireplace-warming after your hike. For more information about Del Norte Redwoods State Park, contact the **Redwood National and State Parks Information Center,** 1111 Second St., Crescent City, CA 95531, tel. (707) 464-6101.

KLAMATH AND VICINITY

This area was once the traditional fishing and hunting territory of the Yurok people. But when settlers arrived, the Yuroks were doomed; the native people were hunted by miners for sport, their villages burned, their fisheries ruined.

In 1964, when 40 inches of rain fell within 24 hours in the Eel and Klamath River basins, the entire town of Klamath was washed away—and not as easily replaced as the gilt grizzlies on the remnants of the Douglas Memorial Bridge outside town. The grizzlies' gold cement den mates, frequently defaced by graffiti artists, decorate the new Klamath River Bridge.

The 263-mile-long Klamath River—California's second largest—drains 8,000 square miles and is fed by more than 300 tributaries, including the Salmon, Scott, and Trinity Rivers. It's also one of the world's finest fishing streams. Anglers line the Klamath—and until 1999, when the practice was banned, also waded out into the river's mouth—from late spring into winter for the salmon run—though fishing for cutthroat trout downstream from town is good year-round.

Among the sights along the primarily unpaved **Coastal Drive,** which starts on the south side of the Klamath River—great views on a sunny day—is a World War II-vintage early-warning radar station cleverly disguised as a farmhouse (complete with false windows and dormers) and barn.

In late June, Klamath's **Salmon Festival** attracts mostly locals for an unforgettable salmon barbecue, traditional Yurok dances, singing, basketry displays (not for sale), stick games, and logging skills contests.

Trees of Mystery

The site of old Klamath is now overgrown with blackberries. New Klamath is dominated by the Trees of Mystery, 5500 Hwy. 101, tel. (707) 482-2251 or toll-free (800) 638-3389, made famous by Robert Ripley's *Believe It or Not!.* Chain-sawed redwood characters are the featured attraction along Mystery's Trail of Tall Tales. The free **End of the Trail Indian Museum** is worth some time, though, with its end-of-the-line artifacts from everywhere in the U.S. and Canada.

Paul Bunyan and Babe the Blue Ox at Trees of Mystery in Klamath

Just south of Klamath is the **Tour-Thru-Tree,** 430 Hwy. 169, tel. (707) 482-5971, this one chainsawed in 1976. To get there, take the Terwer Valley exit off Hwy. 101 and go east a quarter mile on Hwy. 169. The tree is open year-round. Admission is $2 per car, 50 cents for walk-ins and bike-ins.

PRAIRIE CREEK REDWOODS STATE PARK

An almost dangerous feature at Prairie Creek is the permanent and photogenic herd of Roosevelt elk usually grazing in the meadow area right along Hwy. 101. Whether or not a loaded logging truck is tailgating, drivers tend to screech to a halt at the mere sight of these magnificent creatures—which, despite their technically wild status and correspondingly unpredictable behavior, have that bemused and bored look of animals all too familiar with humankind. A separate herd of elk grazes in the coastal meadows along 11-mile **Gold Bluffs Beach,** also noted for its excellent whalewatching, sand dunes carpeted in wild strawberries, and a primitive campground with solar showers.

Elsewhere in 14,000-acre Prairie Creek Redwoods State Park, heavy winter rainfall and thick summer fog produce rainforest lushness. Redwoods rub elbows with 200-foot-tall Sitka spruce, Douglas fir, and Western hemlock above an amazing array of shrubs, ferns, and groundcover, not to mention 800 varieties of flowers and 500 different kinds of mushrooms. **Fern Canyon** is unforgettable. Also particularly worthwhile at Prairie Creek: beachcombing, surf fishing, nature walks and photography, picnicking, and camping.

Near the visitor center/museum are some fine family campsites with flush toilets and hot showers. The more primitive beach campsites are first-come, first-camped, as are the adjacent hike-and-bike sites. Walk-in campsites are available at **Butler Creek Primitive Camp.** Register first with the office at Prairie Creek.

The park day-use fee is $5. For more information on Prairie Creek Redwoods State Park, stop by the visitor center here or other park visitor centers, or contact the **Redwood National and State Parks Information Center,** 1111 Second St., Crescent City, CA 95531, tel. (707) 464-6101.

PRACTICAL REDWOOD NATIONAL PARK

Public Camping at Redwood National Park
Each of the three state parks in the area offers developed family-type camping, with hot showers and such ($12-16 basic fee). Disposal stations for RVs are available but hookups are not. These campgrounds are popular in summer, so advance reservations are advised; call ReserveAmerica, toll-free (800) 444-7275. Though the Del Norte Campground is closed off-season due to very wet conditions (sometimes washouts), winter drop-in camping at the other campgrounds is usually no problem.

Primitive sites are also available at **Nickel Creek,** at Endert's Beach; **Flint Ridge,** west of Klamath; **DeMartin,** between Damnation and Wilson Creeks along the Coastal Trail; and along the **Redwood Creek Trail.** Obtain the required permits at information centers or at park headquarters in Crescent City. Primitive camping at the national park sites is free, though there is a small fee for environmental campsites within the state parks.

Private Camping at Redwood National Park
Riverwoods Campgrounds, 1661 W. Klamath Beach Rd. in Klamath (take the Klamath Beach Rd. exit from Hwy. 101), tel. (707) 482-5591, offers shaded grassy sites with full hookups, hot showers, a beer and tackle shop, and river access. At the north end of the Klamath River Bridge is the **Camper Corral,** tel. (707) 482-5741, offering 100 pull-through sites, most with full hookups and about half with cable TV. Other amenities include hot showers, a laundromat, rec hall, shuffleboard courts, and other recreation facilities. The **Chinook RV Resort,** 17465 Hwy. 101 S, tel. (707) 482-3511, is another fisherpeople's favorite.

Hostel and Motel Stays in Redwood National Park
Accommodation prices in and around Orick—the first outpost of civilization north of the park's excellent **Orick Redwood Visitor Center** at the mouth of Redwood Creek—are reasonable, partly because Redwood National Park is too far

north for most visitors, but also because it's foggy here during peak tourist season. Most people follow the sun. Choice in area motels is meager, but **Rolf's Motel,** next to Rolf's Park Café in Orick, tel. (707) 488-3841, is certainly convenient. Inexpensive. The **Orick Motel and RV Park,** 121381 Hwy. 101, tel. (707) 488-3501, has rooms (Budget, but often full), tent spaces, and RV hookups.

Also within national park boundaries but right on the coast—about 12 miles south of Crescent City at the Hwy. 101 junction with Wilson Creek Rd.—is the fabulous HI-AYH **Redwood Hostel,** 14480 Hwy. 101 N, tel. (707) 482-8265, known locally as the DeMartin House. This is the grandly restored one-time home of one of Del Norte County's pioneer families. The 30-bed hostel is perfect even for small group retreats, with a dining room, small dorm rooms, a common room cozied up with a woodstove, outdoor redwood decks with fine views, and good kitchen facilities. The hostel is wheelchair accessible. Couple and family rooms are available with adequate advance notice. The rate is $13 per night, members and nonmembers alike. Advance reservations are advisable in summer.

The **Motel Trees,** 15495 Hwy. 101 S (across from Trees of Mystery) in Klamath, tel. (707) 482-3152, offers amenities including a tennis court, in-room color TV with movies, and an adjacent restaurant. Inexpensive. The historic **Klamath Inn** (formerly the Requa Inn) in Requa at 451 Requa Rd., tel. (707) 482-1425 or toll-free (888) 788-1706, is an English-style country inn first opened in 1885. Some rooms have great views. Moderate. The inn's **dining room** is open to guests and nonguests alike. Reservations advised.

Eating in Redwood National Park

Most people camp, and bring their own provisions—Crescent City the last best supply stop if you're heading south into the park, and the Eureka-Arcata area if moseying north.

Best bet for a fascinating meal in Orick, not to mention friendly people, is **Rolf's Park Café,** 123664 Hwy. 101, tel. (707) 488-3841, on the highway north of Orick proper (take the Fern Canyon exit). Tables are set in the solarium and (weather permitting) outside on the deck. Rolf Rheinschmidt is known for his exotic dinner spe-

cialties, like wild turkey, elk and buffalo steaks, wild boar and bear roasts, even antelope sausage, plus chicken and pasta dishes, vegetarian dishes, and forest fare like fiddlehead ferns and wild mushrooms. Rolf also cooks up some great breakfasts, including the house specialty German Farmers Omelette, and memorable lunches featuring such things as clam chowder and grilled German sausage sandwiches. Great place. Other possibilities include the basic diner fare and good cream pies at the **Palm Cafe** in Orick, 121130 Hwy. 101, tel. (707) 488-3381, or a quick grocery stop at the **Orick Market,** 121175 Hwy. 101, tel. (707) 488-3501.

Redwood National Park
Visitor Information

In addition to the national park proper, three state parks—Prairie Creek, Del Norte, and Jedediah Smith, all covered above—are included within the larger park boundaries, protecting more redwoods (160,000 acres total for the four parks) and offering additional recreation and camping possibilities. Distinct though they are, the state and national parks are managed cooperatively. The centralized information source for all the parks is: **Redwood National and State Parks Information Center,** 1111 Second St. (at K St.), Crescent City, CA 95531, tel. (707) 464-6101, www.nps.gov/redw/. The center's telephone number includes recorded information on each of the individual parks in the system, and you can also reach a human being during office hours. There is no fee for admission to Redwood National Park, but the day-use fee for each state park is $5. This and other park visitor centers are closed on Thanksgiving, Christmas, and New Year's Day.

In addition to the main visitor center in Crescent City, several other visitor centers are available. The **Orick Redwood National Park Information Center,** near Orick at the old lumber mill site at the mouth of Redwood Creek (north of Freshwater Lagoon and west of the highway), tel. (707) 464-6101, ext. 5265, is an imposing, excellent interpretive museum. The enthusiastic staff is very helpful. Open mid-June to Labor Day, daily 8 a.m.-7 p.m., and the rest of the year, daily 9 a.m.-5 p.m. Pick up a map for the park's 200-mile trail system. Sharing the same building is the **Orick Chamber of Commerce,** P.O. Box

234, Orick, CA 95555, tel. (707) 488-2885.

Another good visitor center is **Hiouchi,** on Hwy. 199 at Jedediah Smith Redwoods State Park, tel. (707) 464-6101, ext. 5067, which features among other exhibits a handmade traditional canoe, constructed on-site. Ask here, too, about the Smith River National Recreation Area, as well as park-sponsored activities and events. Open mid-June to Labor Day, daily 8 a.m.-7 p.m.; the rest of the year, daily 8 a.m.-5 p.m.

The **Prairie Creek Visitor Center,** 127011 Newton B. Drury Scenic Parkway in Prairie Creek State Park, tel. (707) 464-6101, ext. 5301, is usually open 8 a.m.-dusk in summer and 9 a.m.-5 p.m. in winter. It features a museum with natural history exhibits, as well as a nature store.

Intrepid outdoorspeople may also want to visit California's only completely undammed river system—the three-fork Smith River and its tributaries, the focal points of the 305,337-acre **Smith River National Recreation Area** that abuts Jedediah Smith Redwoods State Park. Also worth exploring are the nearly one million acres of **Six Rivers National Forest.** For information on both, contact **Six Rivers National Forest Headquarters,** 1330 Bayshore Way in Eureka, tel. (707) 442-1721, or **Smith River NRA—Gasquet Ranger District** in Gasquet on Hwy. 199, tel. (707) 457-3131.

Park Transportation

Most people drive—and the immense size of the park makes a personal vehicle quite handy. **Greyhound,** 1603 Fourth St. in Eureka, tel. (707) 442-0370, or 500 E. Harding in Crescent City, tel. (707) 464-2807, stops on its way between those two cities at the Shoreline Deli just south of Orick, at Paul's Cannery in Klamath, and at the AYH hostel north of Klamath. To fly into the area, nearest is the **Eureka-Arcata Airport** in McKinleyville, 3561 Boeing Ave., tel. (707) 839-1906. Rental cars are available there.

NEAR REDWOOD NATIONAL PARK

CRESCENT CITY AND VICINITY

Most of the world's Easter lilies, that ultimate modern-day symbol of resurrection, are grown north of Crescent City, the only incorporated city in Del Norte County. A proud if historically downtrodden town laid out in 1853 along the crescent moon harbor, Crescent City is a grim weather-beaten gray, pounded so long by storms it has become one with the fog. Grim, too, is life for prisoners locked up just outside town at **Pelican Bay State Prison,** the state's largest maximum-security prison. The prison primes the community's economic pump with some $40 million per year and was the focus of California senator Barry Keene's Name That Prison contest. Among the unselected but otherwise superior suggestions from clever north coast minds: The Big Trees Big House, Camp Runamok, Dungeness Dungeon, Saint Dismos State (a reference to the patron saint of prisoners), and Slammer-by-the-Sea.

Crescent City still suffers from the 1964 tsunami that tore the town off its moorings after the big Alaska earthquake, as well as a freak typhoon with 80-mile-per-hour winds that hit in 1972. Life goes on, however; the once devastated and denuded waterfront is now an attractive local park and convention center. Crabbing from the public **Citizens' Wharf,** built at Crescent Harbor with entirely local resources and volunteer labor when government rebuilding assistance fell through, is especially good. The French-design harbor breakwater is unique, a system of interlocking, 25-ton concrete "tetrapods."

In February, the town hosts its annual **Crab Races** and community dinner. Crescent City's **July 4th** festivities include everything from cribbage and kite flying to sandcastle sculpting. At Smith River just north, the local **Easter in July Lily Festival** celebrates the lily bloom, the festivities including sunrise church services, a lily float contest, and food and crafts booths decked out with you-know-what. Also fun the last weekend in July is the two-mile **Gasquet Raft Race** on the Smith River, with contestants limited to rafts and other crafts paddled only by hand. (The local pronunciation is "GAS-key," in the same vein as "Del-NORT" County.)

Seeing and Doing Crescent City

See the **Battery Point Lighthouse** near town. Weather and tides permitting, walk out to it on a path more than 100 years old and visit the island museum, tel. (707) 464-3089, open Wed.-Sun. 10 a.m.-4 p.m. (small donation). Decommissioned in 1953, though it was 12 more years before they turned the light out, the Battery Point Lighthouse was restored in 1981 by Craig Miller, with local donations of materials. The Del Norte Historical Society has operated the light as a private navigational aid since 1982. Spend some time in the **Del Norte County Historical Society Museum,** 577 H St., tel. (707) 464-3922, to appreciate its collection of Native American artifacts, quilts and kitchenware, and logging and mining paraphernalia. Open Mon.-Sat. 10 a.m.-4 p.m. (admission by donation). Also at the museum is the first-order lens—over 18 feet tall—taken from the lighthouse on St. George Reef. Stop by the historic **McNulty House** nearby, 710 H St., tel. (707) 464-5186, to take in exhibits of antiques, old clocks, and works of area artists.

If poking into the actual ocean isn't enough for you, **Ocean World,** 304 Hwy. 101 S, tel. (707) 464-3522, is a small-town aquarium exhibiting sharks, stingrays, octopi, sea lions, and other marine life. Open daily year-round, 8 a.m.-8 p.m. in summer season, and 8 a.m.-5 p.m. in the off-season. Admission is $5.95 general, $3.95 ages 3-10, and free for tots (under three).

Camping in Crescent City

Nothing in Crescent City beats camping at Jedediah Smith Redwoods State Park, though four national park or national forest campgrounds lie northeast of town near Gasquet, others are to the southeast via Southfork Rd., and still more are scattered through the Smith River/Six Rivers region.

Options in town include the **Harbor RV Anchorage,** 159 Starfish Way, tel. (707) 464-1724, right on the beach at the north end of town; the **Bayside RV Park,** 750 Hwy. 101 S, tel. (707) 464-9482 or toll-free (800) 446-9482; and the **Crescent City Redwoods KOA,** 4241 Hwy. 101 N, tel. (707) 464-5744 or toll-free (800) 562-5754. Another possibility is the **Village Camper Inn RV Park,** 1543 Parkway Dr., tel. (707) 464-3544 or toll-free (800) 470-3544. You can also park the Winnie at the **Del Norte County Fairgrounds,** 421 Hwy. 101 N, tel. (707) 464-9556,

where facilities include showers and a covered driving range ($8-10 per night).

Other Crescent City Stays

Motel rates in Crescent City drop markedly in winter. The **Crescent City Travelodge,** 353 L St., tel. (707) 464-6124 or toll-free (800) 578-7878, offers 27 rooms, in-room TV (with HBO, ESPN, and CNN), a sauna, and complimentary continental breakfast. Inexpensive-Moderate. The **Super 8,** 685 Hwy. 101 S, (707) 464-4111 or toll-free (800) 800-8000, offers in-room coffee makers, cable TV with HBO, a coin-op laundry, and fax service (incoming faxes free). Moderate.

The **Pacific Motor Hotel,** north of town at 440 Hwy. 101 N, tel. (707) 464-4141, features both a sauna and indoor hot tub. Moderate. **Quality Inn,** 725 Hwy. 101 N, tel. (707) 464-6106, also offers a sauna and hot tub, as well as complimentary breakfast. Moderate. The **Curly Redwood Lodge,** 701 Hwy. 101 S (a half mile south of town on the highway, near the marina), tel. (707) 464-2137, fax (707) 464-1655, has large rooms, color TV with cable, and coffee available in the lobby. Moderate.

Just south of town and also across from the marina is the top-of-the-line **Best Western Northwoods Inn,** 655 Hwy. 101 S, tel. (707) 464-9771 or toll-free (800) 557-3396. Amenities here include in-room hair dryers and coffee makers, along with a guest laundry and spa. On-site restaurant, free breakfast. Moderate-Expensive.

Eating in Crescent City

Standard grocery chains, like Safeway, exist in Crescent City. Better, though, is a stop (and plant tour) at the north coast's noted **Rumiano Cheese Company,** 511 Ninth St. (at E St.), tel. (707) 465-1535, open Mon.-Sat. 8:30 a.m.-3:30 p.m.

Many restaurants here don't take credit cards, so bring cash. Basic for breakfast is **Glen's Bakery & Restaurant,** 722 Third St., tel. (707) 464-2914, where you can get a mean bowl of clam chowder, fresh fish dishes, and good baked goods. The **China Hut Restaurant,** 928 Ninth St., tel. (707) 464-4921, serves Cantonese, Mandarin, and Szechuan cuisine. Beer lovers will want to try **Jefferson State Brewery,** 400 Front St., tel. (707) 464-1139, with handcrafted ales and decent food. Open Sun.-Thurs. 11 a.m.-11 p.m., Fri.-Sat. 11 a.m.-midnight. For seafood, head for the **Beachcomber Restaurant,** on

the Ship Ashore north of Crescent City

Hwy. 101 at South Beach, tel. (707) 464-2205, right on the beach.

Just shy of the Oregon border is the town of Smith River and the **Best Western Ship Ashore Resort,** 12370 Hwy. 101 N, tel. (707) 487-3141 or toll-free (800) 487-3141 (Moderate-Expensive), and its popular steak and seafood restaurant, the **Captain's Galley.** The bizarre Ship Ashore Museum and Gift Shop by the highway—a 160-foot-long ship beached in the parking lot—clues diners in to the turnoff.

Crescent City Information and Services

The **Crescent City-Del Norte County Chamber of Commerce Visitor Center** is at 1001 Front St., tel. (707) 464-3174 or toll-free (800) 343-8300. For web information, try the **Del Norte County website,** www.delnorte.org. **Greyhound,** 500 E. Harding St., tel. (707) 464-2807, has two buses heading north and two heading south daily. The **post office** is at 751 Second St. (at H), tel. (707) 464-2151. The **public library** is at 190 Price Mall, tel. (707) 464-9793. For medical care and emergencies, contact **Sutter Coast Hospital,** 800 E. Washington Blvd., tel. (707) 464-8511 (information) or (707) 464-8888 (emergency room).

SOUTH FROM REDWOOD NATIONAL PARK

Humboldt Lagoons State Park

The community of **Big Lagoon** just off the highway north of Patrick's Point is also the site of Big Lagoon County Park with its dirty sand beaches and camping. Humboldt Lagoons State Park includes Big Lagoon itself (and the miles-long barrier beach separating it from the sea) and three others, a total of 1,500 beachfront acres best for beachcombing, boating, fishing, surfing, and windsurfing (swimming only for the hardy or foolhardy).

Next north is freshwater **Dry Lagoon,** five miles of sandy beach and heavy surf particularly popular with agate fanciers and black jade hunters. Camp beside this marshy lagoon at one of six environmental campsites: outhouse, no water, no dogs. Ocean fishing is possible in winter only, but there's no fishing at Dry Lagoon, which lives up to its name most of the year. **Stone Lagoon** two miles north is prettier but smaller, with boat-in primitive campsites. A half mile farther north is part-private, part-public **Freshwater Lagoon,** planted with trout for seasonal fishing (no official camping here, though RVs are a permanent fixture along the highway). The **Harry A. Merlo State Recreation Area,** 800-plus acres named for a noted Louisiana-Pacific executive, entwines throughout the lagoon area.

Boat-in and hike-in campsites are $7 ($5 extra vehicle). There is no day-use fee. The small **Humboldt Lagoons Visitors Center** is at Stone Lagoon, open summers only. For more information and to reserve campsites, contact **Humboldt Lagoons State Park,** 15336 Hwy. 101, Trinidad, CA 95570, tel. (707) 488-2041.

DISCOVERING "OLD TOWN" TRINIDAD

A booming supply town of 3,000 in the early 1850s and later a whaling port, Trinidad is now a tiny coastal village recognized as the oldest incorporated town on California's north coast. Impressive **Trinidad Head** looms over the small bay, with a white granite cross at the summit replacing the first monument placed there by Bodega y Cuadra for Spain's Charles III.

The **Trinidad Memorial Lighthouse** on Main St. was the village's original light tower and was relocated to town as a fishermen's memorial. It features a giant two-ton fog bell. The **Trinidad Museum**, 529-B Trinity St., tel. (707) 677-3883, offers displays about the region's natural and cultural history. It's open in summer, Fri.-Sun. noon-5 p.m. Humboldt State University's **Fred Telonicher Marine Laboratory**, 570 Ewing St., tel. (707) 826-3671, has an aquarium open to the public, as well as a touch tank for getting intimate with intertidal invertebrates. It's open year-round, weekdays 9 a.m.-5 p.m., and also weekends 10 a.m.-5 p.m. when school is in session.

Besides solitary beachcombing on **Trinidad State Beach** (day-use only, good for moonstones and driftwood), surfing at rugged **Luffenholtz Beach** two miles south of town, and breathtaking scenery, the area's claim to fame is salmon fishing. Commercial and sport-fishing boats, skiffs, and tackle shops line Trinidad Bay.

For more information on the area, contact: **Trinidad Chamber of Commerce**, Main St. and Patrick's Point Dr., P.O. Box 356, Trinidad, CA 95570, tel. (707) 677-1610.

Staying in Trinidad

For the most reasonable accommodations, head north on Patrick's Point Dr. to the state park and its excellent camping (see below). Nice for cabins (most have kitchens) is the recently refurbished **Bishop Pine Lodge**, 1481 Patrick's Point Dr., tel. (707) 677-3314, fax (707) 677-3444, also featuring two-bedroom units and cottages with hot tubs. Playground area, well-equipped exercise room. Moderate-Expensive. Another possibility is the **Shadow Lodge**, 687 Patrick's Point Dr., tel. (707) 677-0532, offering cottages furnished with antiques. Moderate-Expensive. In town, across from the lighthouse, the **Trinidad Bay Bed and Breakfast**, 560 Edwards St., tel. (707) 677-0840, fax (707) 677-9245, www.trinidadbaybnb.com, is a Cape Cod-style home circa 1950. It offers two standard rooms and two suites, all with king or queen beds and private baths (one suite with fireplace). Closed Dec.-January. Premium-Luxury. About five miles north of Trinidad proper and adjacent to the state park is the **Lost Whale Bed and Breakfast Inn**, 3452 Patrick's Point Dr., tel. (707) 677-3425 or toll-free (800) 677-7859, fax (707) 677-0284, www.lostwhaleinn.com, a contemporary Cape Cod with eight guest rooms (all with private bath), full breakfast, hot tub, and afternoon refreshments. Luxury. Ask about the **Farmhouse**, a two-bedroom house on five acres, also available for rent. Nearby is the relatively new and tastefully decorated **Turtle Rocks Inn B&B**, 3392 Patrick's Point Dr., tel. (707) 677-3707, www.turtlerocksinn.com, which offers six guest rooms on three oceanfront acres. Each room has a private bath, private deck, and modern amenities. Rates include a gourmet hot breakfast. Premium-Luxury (lower rates in the off-season).

Eating in Trinidad

In April or May each year, the town hosts a massive **crab feed** at Town Hall. Otherwise, *the* place to eat in Trinidad is the very relaxed and rustic **Seascape Restaurant** (once the Dock Cafe) at the harbor, tel. (707) 677-3762, which serves hearty breakfasts, excellent omelettes, and seafood specialties (good early-bird specials). Open 7 a.m.-9 p.m. daily. Reservations are a good idea at dinner. Also here, just north of town, is the excellent **Larrupin Cafe**, 1658 Patrick's Point Dr., tel. (707) 677-0230, a friendly and fine place noted for things like barbecued cracked crab, barbecued oysters, steamed mussels, and chicken breast wrapped up with artichokes and cream cheese in phyllo dough. Or try the mesquite-grilled portobello mushroom on slices of Spanish cheeses and potato bread. Excellent desserts, too. No credit cards. Other dining choices include the **Trinidad Bay Eatery & Gallery**, at Trinity and Parker, tel. (707) 677-3777, open Wed.-Sun. for breakfast and lunch, and **Merryman's Dinner House**, 100 Moonstone Beach Rd., tel. (707) 677-3111, noted for its sunsets as well as its food.

Patrick's Point State Park

The Yuroks who for centuries seasonally inhabited this area believed that the spirit of the porpoises came to live at modern-day Patrick's Point State Park just before people populated the world—and that the seven offshore sea stacks that stretch north to south like a spine were the last earthly abode of the immortals. Most impressive of these rugged monuments is **Ceremonial Rock,** nicknamed "stairway to the stars" by fond rock climbers. But both here and just north at Big Lagoon, you'll be in the right place for those "fungus among us" jokes. During the rainy season, duff from spruce trees produces delicious mushrooms—also fantastically fatal ones, so be sure you're an expert (or in the company of one) before you go rooting through forest detritus for dinner.

Old trails once walked by native peoples lead to and beyond rocky **Patrick's Point,** one of the finest whalewatching sites along the coast. "Patrick" was Patrick Beegan, the area's first white settler and a warrior after Indian scalps. Stroll the two-mile **Rim Trail** for the views, but stay back from the hazardous cliff edge. Sea lions are common on the park's southern offshore rocks near **Palmer's Point.** The short trail scrambling north from near the campground (steep going) leads to long, sandy, and aptly named **Agate Beach,** noted for its many-colored, glasslike stones.

For all its natural wonders, Patrick's Point is also fine for people (good picnicking). Except for mushroomers and whalewatchers, best visiting weather is late spring, early summer, and fall. **Whalewatching** from Ceremonial Rock or Patrick's Point (weekend ranger programs offered in January and February) is best from November to January but also good on the whales' return trip, February to May. Dress warmly and bring binoculars. Call the park for current whale-watching information. The **museum** here features natural history and native cultural exhibits. The park's day-use fee is $6.

Patrick's Point has three developed campgrounds: **Agate Beach, Abalone,** and **Penn Creek** (west of the meadows), with 123 naturally sheltered tent or trailer sites and hot showers ($16 per night). In addition, there are two group camps, 20 hike-and-bike campsites, a cabin ($55), and a yurt ($55). ReserveAmerica reservations, tel. toll-free (800) 444-7275, are mandatory during the summer. For more information, contact: Patrick's Point State Park, Trinidad, CA 95570, tel. (707) 677-3570.

Down the Coast

South of Trinidad is **Little River State Beach,** where Josiah Gregg and company arrived from Weaverville in December 1849, exhausted and near starvation. Little River has broad sandy beaches backed by dunes, and offers clamming in season, good surf fishing, and picnicking. For more information, call Patrick's Point State Beach at (707) 677-3570. Adjacent just south, reached from Hwy. 101 via Clam Beach Dr., is **Clam Beach County Park,** a good place for collecting agates and moonstones; camping is available for $5 a night.

The next wide-spot-in-the-road is **McKinleyville,** something of an Arcata suburb "where horses still have the right of way." Stop in for pub grub and a frothy pint of Black Bear Stout at **Six Rivers Brewing Co.,** 1300 Central Ave., tel. (707) 839-7580. The town lies adjacent to the Azalea State Reserve and offers good whalewatching from **McKinleyville Vista Point.** For more information on the area, contact: **McKinleyville Chamber of Commerce,** 2196 Central Ave., McKinleyville, CA 95519, tel. (707) 839-2449.

ARCATA AND VICINITY

Arcata is Eureka's alter-ego, no more resigned to the status quo than the sky here is blue. In 1996, Arcata made national news when a majority of Green Party candidates was elected to the city council. Far-from-the-mainstream publications are available even at the visitor center. In addition to Arcata's world-famous **Cross-Country Kinetic Sculpture Race** on Memorial Day weekend (see accompanying special topic), popular annual events include the **April Fools Income Tax Annual Auction,** a benefit for the North Coast Environmental Center, and the **North Country Fair,** one of the West Coast's premier craft fairs. A relaxed and liberal town, Arcata is determined to make a difference.

It would be easy to assume that the genesis of this backwoods grass-roots activism is the presence of academia, namely Humboldt State University, the only university on the north coast. But the beginnings of the Arcata *attitude* go back much

further. When Arcata was still a frontier trading post known as Union Town, 24-year-old writer Bret Harte set the tone. An unknown underling on Arcata's *The Northern Californian* between 1858 and 1860, an outraged Harte—temporarily in charge while his editor was out of town—wrote a scathing editorial about the notorious Indian Island massacre of Wiyot villagers by settlers and was summarily run out of town, shoved along on his way to fame and fortune. Besides activism, general community creativity, and education, farming and fishing are growing concerns. Appropriately enough, the popular semipro baseball team here is called the Humboldt Crabs.

SEEING AND DOING ARCATA

Humboldt State University

The presence of the university keeps things in Arcata lively. Humboldt State, east of town on Fickle Hill near 14th St. and Grant Ave., tel. (707) 826-3011, emphasizes the study of forestry, fisheries and wildlife management, and oceanography. On campus, worthwhile sights include the **arboretum, fish hatchery,** and **art gallery.**

Off campus, the **HSU Natural History Museum,** 1315 G St., tel. (707) 826-4479, features local natural history displays, an impressive fossil collection, and lots of hands-on exploration. Open Tues.-Sat. 10 a.m.-4 p.m. Admission is free (donations appreciated).

Arcata Plaza

Arcata's downtown plaza, with its memorial statue of President McKinley and out-of-place palm trees, is custom-made for watching people come and go from surrounding cafés and shops, or for resting up after a tour of local Victorian homes—if you don't mind hangin' out with the hang-out crowd. Several of the historic buildings framing the plaza are worth a look, including the **Jacoby Storehouse** on the south side, a stone-and-brick beauty with iron shutters (now housing woodwork, glass, and other fine local crafts), and the quite pleasant **Hotel Arcata.**

City, County, and State Parks

Arcata's pretty 20-acre **Redwood Park** is off Park (head east on 11th Street). Just beyond is the 600-acre **Arcata Community Forest,** with its educational **Historic Logging Trail,** hiking and mountain-biking trails, and picnicking. For more information and maps, contact or stop by the city Environmental Services Department, in City Hall at 736 F St., tel. (707) 822-8184. To get to **Mad River County Park,** with its good ocean fishing and beach, take Alliance Rd. from K St. to Spear Ave., turn left onto Upper Bay Rd., then left again.

Azalea State Reserve, a 30-acre preserve just north of Arcata on North Bank Rd. (Hwy. 200), is famous for its cascading, fragrant pink-white western azalea blooms (usually best around Memorial Day) and other wildflowers, all in the company of competing rhododendrons. Good steelhead fishing can be found in the area along North Bank Rd. near Hwy. 299's Mad River bridge. For more information, call Patrick's Point State Park at (707) 677-3570.

Arcata Bay and Marsh

Walk along Arcata Bay to appreciate the impromptu scrap wood sculptures sometimes in bloom. The most fascinating bayside sights, though, are at the Arcata Marsh and Wildlife Preserve at the foot of I Street. This was one of the first wildlife preserves in the U.S. to be created from an old landfill dump and "enhanced" by treated sewage water. The aesthetic settling ponds offer excellent birdwatching. For more information, stop by or call the **Arcata Marsh Interpretive Center,** 600 S. G St., tel. (707) 826-2359; open daily 1-5 p.m. The Redwood Region Audubon Society, tel. (707) 826-7031, offers guided walks of the preserve at 8:30 a.m. on

---

A MOVING TRIBUTE TO "FORM OVER SUBSTANCE"

If you're in the area for Memorial Day weekend, don't miss Arcata's sight-of-all-sights—the exuberant 38-mile, three-day trans-bay **World Championship Great Arcata to Ferndale Cross-Country Kinetic Sculpture Race.** Founded in 1969 by Ferndale artists Hobart Brown and Jack Mays, the race is a moving display of "form over substance." It's an almost-anything-goes tribute to unbridled imagination, but it does have a few

KINETIC SCULPTURE MUSEUM

rules. The mobile "sculptures" must be people-powered (though it is legal to get an assist from water, wind, or gravity), amphibious, and inspired by the event's high moral and ethical standards—"cheating is a privilege, not a right." (Kinetic cops patrol the course and interpret the rules.) Otherwise, anything goes—and rolls, floats, and flounders, through sand, saltwater, and swamp slime—in this ultimate endurance contest, also known at the Triathlon of the Art World.

Coming in first, even dragging in last, is not the point of this race. The contest's most coveted award is the Aurea Mediocritas, for the entry finishing closest to dead center—because, as the founders explain, winning and losing are both extremes, therefore "perfection lies somewhere in the middle." However, losing has its virtues, too, so the much-coveted Loser Award has been reinstated. Even spectators are part of the competition, thanks to the Most Worthy Fanatical Spectator Award.

Favorite entries have included Brown's own floating bus-boat, the ever-popular Pencilhead Express, the man-eating Hammerhead Cadillac, and the Chicken-and-Egg Mobile. Some race survivors are on display at the sculpture museum in Ferndale. Prerace festivities include the **Kinetic Kickoff Party** and the **Rutabaga Queen Pageant** at Eureka's Ritz Club. For information about the race, call Hobart Galleries in Ferndale at (707) 786-9259.

Saturday mornings, leaving from the end of I St., and Friends of the Arcata Marsh offers guided walks Saturday at 2 p.m., leaving from the interpretive center. Birders can call the Birdbox hot line, tel. (707) 822-5666, for information on recent sightings.

The Lanphere-Christensen Dunes Preserve
Just east of Arcata, on the Samoa Peninsula near the Mad River Slough, is the 300-acre Lanphere-Christensen Dunes Preserve, managed by the U.S. Fish and Wildlife Service. It's open to the public by permit, obtained from the office at 6800 Lanphere Rd., tel. (707) 822-6378. No camping is permitted.

Noted for its many well-preserved plant communities—from vernal pools to salt marsh to forest—and first purchased and protected in the 1940s by the Lanpheres, biologists at the university, the area is unique for another reason. At this latitude, the northern and southern dune floras overlap, meaning rare and typical plantlife from both are present as well as more than 200 species of birds and other animals. The best dune wildflowers come in June, but every season has its attractions. From April to September, bring mosquito repellent. Rain gear is wise during the rest of the year, and always wear soft-soled shoes.

Friends of the Dunes, in Manila, leads nature tours at the dunes and sponsors environmental projects there. Tours begin at the Pacific Union School parking lot, 3001 Janes Road. For more information and to receive the organization's quarterly *Dunesberry* newsletter, call (707) 444-1397.

STAYING IN ARCATA

The **Mad River Rapids RV Park,** 3501 Janes Rd. (north of town at the Giuntoli Ln./Janes Rd. exit), tel. (707) 822-7275 or toll-free (800) 822-7776, is a beautiful, full-service park offering sites with full hookups and cable TV, a heated pool and spa, restrooms, showers, a laundry, minimart, game room, and fish-cleaning station. Each site has a patio, picnic table, and lawn.

Quite decent, and right on the plaza, is the refurbished and welcoming 1915 **Hotel Arcata,** 708 Ninth St., tel. (707) 826-0217 or toll-free

(800) 344-1221, fax (707) 826-1737. Moderate. The modest **Fairwinds Motel,** 1674 G St., tel. (707) 822-0568, offers easy access to campus. Inexpensive-Moderate.

Many motels are fairly inconveniently located along Valley West Blvd., off Hwy. 101 north of town; take the Giuntoli Ln./Janes Rd. exit and turn right. These include: **North Coast Inn,** 4975 Valley West, tel. (707) 822-4861 (Premium); **Super 8,** 4887 Valley West, tel. (707) 822-8888 or toll-free (800) 800-8000 (Inexpensive); **Best Western Arcata Inn,** 4827 Valley West, tel. (707) 826-0313 or toll-free (888) 646-6514 (Moderate); **Motel 6,** 4755 Valley West, tel. (707) 822-7061 or toll-free (800) 466-8356 (Inexpensive); **Comfort Inn,** 4701 Valley West, tel. (707) 826-2827 or toll-free (800) 228-5150, with an indoor heated pool and spa (Moderate-Expensive); and the newish **Howard Johnson Express Inn,** 4700 Valley West Blvd., tel. (707) 826-9660 or toll-free (800) 446-4656, also with an indoor heated pool and spa (Moderate-Expensive). Across the highway is the **Quality Inn Mad River,** 3535 Janes Rd., tel. (707) 822-0409 or toll-free (800) 221-2222 (Expensive-Premium), which has an outdoor heated pool and jacuzzi, tennis court, fitness and game rooms, and laundry facilities, and is adjacent to the Mad River Saloon & Eatery.

If you'd prefer a B&B, try the **Lady Anne,** 902 14th St., tel. (707) 822-2797, which features five rooms (some with fireplaces, all with abundant antiques and plush guest robes) in an 1888 Queen Anne Victorian, plus full breakfast and bicycles to borrow. Expensive.

EATING IN ARCATA

First stop for those just passing through should be **Arcata Co-op,** Eighth and I Streets, tel. (707) 822-5947, a natural-foods store with an abundance of organic everything, open 9 a.m.-9 p.m. (until 8 p.m. on Sunday). Healthy groceries, vitamins, and health-care products, as well as a juice bar and deli/cafe, are also available at **Wildberries Marketplace,** at the top of G St. (at 13th), tel. (707) 822-0095. Wildberries is also the site of the **Arcata Certified Farmers' Market,** held June-Oct. on Tuesday, 3-6 p.m. The **Arcata Plaza Certified Farmers' Market** is held

May-Oct. on Saturday, 9 a.m.-1 p.m., at the Arcata Plaza (Eighth and G Streets). For details on both, call (707) 441-9999.

On the Lighter Side

Los Bagels, 1061 I St., tel. (707) 822-3150, is a popular student hangout offering mostly coffee and bagels and bread items served up with a Nicaraguan flair. The **Wildflower Cafe and Bakery,** 1604 G St., tel. (707) 822-0360, has fresh bakery items, veggie food, homemade soups and salads, and "macrobiotic night" every Wednesday. Open Mon.-Sat. for breakfast, lunch, and dinner, and Sunday for brunch.

Café Mokka, 495 J St. (at Fifth), tel. (707) 822-2228, has decadent, incredibly good pastries, good coffee, and excellent espresso (as well as private outdoor hot tubs and sauna cabins for rent out back). Another good java joint is **Muddy Waters Coffee Co.** at 1603 G Street. But don't miss **Sacred Grounds Organic Coffee Roasters,** 686 F St., tel. (707) 822-0690.

Something More Substantial

Abruzzi, 791 Eighth St. (in Jacoby's Storehouse, facing the plaza), tel. (707) 826-2345, is a slice of real Italiana here in the foggy north. Fresh daily are the baguettes, breadsticks, and tomato-onion-and-fennel-seed bread, Humboldt-grown veggies and seafood specialties. Good calzones, wonderful pastas. And do try the 14-layer torte. Upstairs, the **Plaza Grill,** tel. (707) 826-0860, offers steak, seafood, salads—even gumbo—along with great views of Humboldt Bay. **Folie Douce,** 1551 G St., between 15th and 16th, tel. (707) 822-1042, is regionally famous for its exotic and stylish wood fire-baked pizzas—everything from Thai chicken to goat cheese and wild mushroom. Reservations wise.

For a chopsticks fix, head to **Hunan Plaza,** 761 Eighth St. (on the plaza), tel. (707) 822-6105, offering Chinese food for lunch and dinner daily, with a separate vegetarian section on the menu. Or try the **New Fortune Restaurant,** at 14th and G Streets, tel. (707) 822-3993, open for lunch and dinner daily.

For homegrown brew and good basic food (a bit heavy on the grease) to go with it, try the **Humboldt Brewery,** 856 10th St., tel. (707) 826-2739, also a hot local nightspot attracting bigname blues, country, and folk talent. Open Mon.-Wed. 11:30 a.m.-11 p.m., Thurs.-Sat. 11:30 a.m.-1 a.m. Closed Sunday.

ARCATA INFORMATION AND SERVICES

The helpful **Arcata Chamber of Commerce** is in the new California Welcome Center at 1635 Heindon Rd., Arcata 95521, tel. (707) 822-3619, open weekdays 10 a.m.-5 p.m. in tourist season, and 10 a.m.-3 p.m. in winter (hours may be expanded; call for current schedule). Among the free publications available here are the *Tour Arcata's Architectural Past* brochure, *Arcata Outdoors,* and the free *Welcome to Arcata* map, in addition to a tidal wave of free local newsletters and newspapers. The very good annual *Humboldt Visitor* and the monthly *North Coast View* are particularly worthwhile for travelers. The Arcata **BLM office** is nearby at 1695 Heindon Rd., tel. (707) 825-2300, a worthwhile stop for information on exploring Samoa Dunes or camping in the King Range.

Arcata & Mad River Transit System, tel. (707) 822-3775, bases its buses at the Transit Center, 925 E St. (between Ninth and 10th). Fare is 80 cents for adults, 25 cents for seniors 65 and up and children 3-6 (extended to age 17 in summer). The Transit Center is also the local stop for **Greyhound,** same local phone or toll-free (800) 231-2222, which offers service to and from Eureka as well as points north.

EUREKA

When James T. Ryan slogged ashore here from his whaling ship in May of 1850, shouting (so the story goes) *Eureka!* ("I have found it"), what he found was California's largest natural bay north of San Francisco. Russian-American Fur Company hunters actually entered Humboldt Bay first in 1806, but the area's official discovery came in 1849 when a party led by Josiah Gregg came overland that winter seeking the mouth of the Trinity River (once thought to empty into the ocean). Gregg died in the unfriendly forests on the return trip to San Francisco, but the reports of his half-starved companions led to Eureka's establishment on "Trinity Bay" as a trading post and port serving the far northern inland gold camps.

While better than other north coast harbors, Humboldt Bay was still less than ideal. The approach across the sand bar was treacherous, and dozens of ships foundered in heavy storms or fog—a trend that continued well into this century. In 1917, the cruiser USS *Milwaukee,* flagship of the Pacific fleet, arrived to rescue a grounded submarine and ended up winching itself onto the beach, where it sat until World War II (when it was scrapped and recycled). But ever-imaginative Eureka has managed to turn even abandoned boats into a community resource. Before the Humboldt Bay Nuclear Power Plant was built here in 1963, the city got most of its energy from the generators of the salvaged Russian tanker *Donbass III,* towed into the bay and beached in 1946.

Oddly expansive and naked today, huge Humboldt Bay was once a piddling puddle at the edge of the endless redwood forest. Early loggers stripped the land closest to town first, but the bare Eureka hills were soon dotted with reincarnated redwoods—the buildings of pioneer industry, and the stately Victorians that still reflect the community's cultural roots.

No matter how vibrant the colors of the old homes here, at times it seems nothing can dispel the fog in these parts. When the fog does finally lift, in wet years the rains come, washing away hillsides and closing roads, trapping the locals behind what they refer to as the Redwood Curtain. That sense of being isolated from the rest of the human world—something harried visitors from more urban locales long for—and the need to transform life into something other than *gray* may explain why there are more artists and performers per capita in Humboldt County than anywhere else in the state. Sunshine is where one finds it, after all.

SEEING AND DOING EUREKA

Humboldt Bay

Eureka's 10-mile-long Humboldt Bay was named for the German naturalist Baron Alexander von Humboldt. So it's fitting that the extensive, if almost unknown and largely neglected, **Humboldt Bay National Wildlife Refuge** was established on the

---

BLUE OX MILLWORKS

Not really a tourist attraction but endlessly compelling is Eureka's time-honored Blue Ox Millworks complex, located at the foot of X St., tel. (707) 444-3457 or toll-free (800) 248-4259 (for tour reservations). The antithesis of all things high-tech, the Blue Ox pays hands-on homage to the beauty of craftsmanship, and particularly the craft of old-fashioned woodworking. In this going concern—a de facto living history environment, the only mill of its kind remaining in the U.S.— the machines date from 1850 to the 1940s. There's an aromatic whirl of sawing, chipping, turning, grinding, and sanding as custom orders are filled. Customers include the National Park Service—which once ordered 400 custom planters for the White House—and endless couples in the midst of Victorian restorations. Victorian replication is the specialty here, though the Blue Ox can duplicate or restore just about anything. Mill tours—visiting the main shop, sawmill, moulding plant, blacksmith shop, "logging skid camp," and more—occur Mon.-Sat. (usually closed Sunday) 9 a.m.-4 p.m. Weekday tours are usually more action-packed, if you want to see the craftsmen at work, and Saturday tours are more personally guided.

edge of the bay's South Jetty to protect the black brant, a small migratory goose, and more than 200 other bird species. (Some 36,000 black brants showed up in 1951; fewer than 1,000 come now, but their numbers are increasing.) The refuge headquarters, tel. (707) 733-5406, is on Beatrice Flat, 10 miles south of Eureka off Hwy. 101, between Loleta and Fields Landing. Plans are in the works for developing an interpretive center, hiking trails, and birdwatching blinds, and for obtaining an additional 6,000 acres of area wetlands, including portions of Indian Island (an egret rookery surrounded now by commercial and industrial development), Sand Islands, Jacoby Creek, and Eureka Slough on North Humboldt Bay.

Other harbor life includes sea lions, harbor seals, porpoises, and gray whales (seen offshore in winter and early spring). To get a look from the bay, take the **Humboldt Bay Harbor Cruise** (see Eureka Transportation and Tours, below). Human wildlife includes fishing crews, sailors, and the Humboldt State University crew teams out rowing at dusk (the best bird's-eye view is from the Cafe Marina on Woodley Island).

Fields Landing, where the last Northern California whaling station operated until 1951, is the bay's deep-water port, the place to watch large fishing boats unload their daily catch; the rest of the fleet docks at the end of Commercial St. in downtown Eureka. Field's Landing is also the place to pick up fresh Dungeness crab, usually available from Christmas to February or March. Stop when the flag's flying at **Botchie's Crab Stand,** 6670 Fields Landing Dr. just off Hwy. 101, tel. (707) 442-4134, where *only* the hand-picked best of the day's catch is for sale.

The **Samoa Bridge** connects the city of Eureka with the narrow peninsula extending south from Ar-

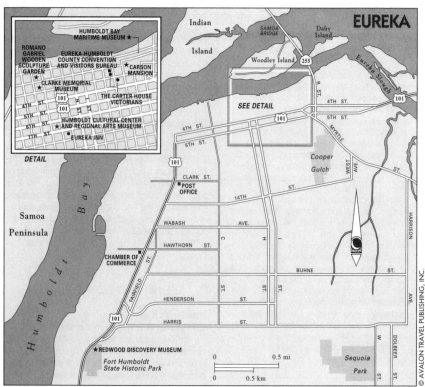

has an indoor heated pool, sauna, jacuzzi, and cable TV with HBO.

Expensive: The **Best Western Thunderbird Inn,** 232 W. Fifth St. (at Broadway), tel. (707) 443-2234 or toll-free (800) 521-6996, features large rooms, a large outdoor pool, a whirlpool, and a rec room. The large and attractive **Doubletree Hotel,** 1929 Fourth St. (between T and V Streets), tel. (707) 445-0844 or toll-free (800) 222-8733, features amenities such as a swimming pool and spa, laundry and valet service, and an excellent restaurant (Pacific Grill & Smokehouse). The **Best Western Bayshore Inn,** 3500 Broadway (Hwy. 101), tel. (707) 268-8005 or toll-free (888) 268-8005, offers an indoor/outdoor pool and spa, jacuzzi suites, and a Marie Callender's restaurant. **Quality Inn Eureka,** 1209 Fourth St. (between M and N Streets), tel. (707) 443-1601 or toll-free (800) 772-1622, features an outdoor heated pool and an indoor sauna and jacuzzi.

Two Noteworthy Lodgings

Very "old Eureka" is the excellent **Eureka Inn,** 518 Seventh St. (at F St.), tel. (707) 442-6441 or toll-free (800) 862-4906, fax (707) 442-1663, www.eurekainn.com. First opened in 1922, this imposing 1920s Tudor-style hotel is listed on the National Register of Historic Places. Among the luminaries who have wandered its halls and dined at its famous **Rib Room**—the locals' favorite seafood-and-steak restaurant—are Sir Winston Churchill, Bobby Kennedy, Mickey Mantle, Steven Spielberg, Ronald Reagan, and Shirley Temple. In addition to its spectacular clear-heart redwood interiors, the Eureka Inn features abundant amenities, including a sauna, whirlpool, year-round heated pool, three restaurants (including the **Bristol Rose Café**), three bars, "live hot jazz," a shoe-shine stand, and free transportation to and from the airport. Expensive-Luxury. Or stay at the Eureka Inn's associated **Downtowner Motor Inn,** where rates are lower. Inexpensive.

Definitely "new Eureka" but also emanating more contemporary Victorian charms are **The Carter House Victorians,** 301 L St., tel. (707) 444-8062, (707) 445-1390, or toll-free (800) 404-1390, fax (707) 444-8067, www.carterhouse.com. What has become known at The Carter House is actually a complex of four properties—The Hotel

Carter, The Carter House Inn, The Carter Cottage, and Bell Cottage—under unified management. The hotel and inn are vintage-1980s facsimiles, while the later cottages are renovations of the original 19th-century structures.

It all began with the 1981 construction of three-story **The Carter House,** built of fine rustic redwood following the very authentic (and very exacting) original design specifications of Carson Mansion architects Samuel and Joseph Newsom. Structurally, The Carter House is a stately re-creation of an 1884 "stick" Victorian home built in San Francisco and lost in the 1906 earthquake and fire. But otherwise it's quite modern, with very un-Victorian sunny rooms and suites (one with fireplace and whirlpool) and an uncluttered, almost contemporary air. That Carter House synthesis of "contemporary good taste with the elegance of a bygone era" extends also to still more luxurious **The Carter Hotel** across the street, and to the two inviting cottages. Homey **Bell Cottage** features three rooms and shared common areas, perfect for a small group traveling together. Romantic and sunny, **The Carter Cottage** is also known as "the love shack." Rates at any of The Carter House Victorians—Premium-Luxury—include luxurious amenities and a breathtaking full breakfast, evening wine and hors d'oeuvres, and before-bed cookies and tea. The outstanding restaurant here, **Restaurant 301,** is a 1998 recipient of the coveted *Wine Spectator* magazine Grand Award. Restaurant 301 is supported by the extensive, organic **301 Gardens**—guests can help harvest vegetables, fruits, and herbs before dinner—and the **301 Wineshop.** Quite special, too, are the **Winemakers Dinners at Restaurant 301.** To get you there in style, at last report Mark Carter's 1958 Bentley was still available for limo service to and from the airport.

Eureka Bed and Breakfasts

Eureka's showplace inn, a destination in its own right for connoisseurs of high-Victorian style, is the award-winning **Abigail's Elegant Victorian Mansion,** 1406 C St., tel. (707) 444-3144, fax (707) 442-5594, www.eureka-california.com. This elegant Victorian mansion offers more than four comfortable rooms (two shared baths and a Finnish sauna), fabulous breakfasts, and vintage auto tours. Guided by the inn's irrepressible innkeepers, Doug ("Jeeves") and Lily Vieyra, visitors could easily spend an entire day just touring *this* eclectic place, which is a spectacular de facto museum of authentic Victorian substance and style. Old movies and music add yet another delightful dimension to a stay here. And once you're done inside, don't miss the Victorian flower garden. Expensive-Luxury.

The 1905 **Cornelius Daly Inn,** 1125 H St., tel. (707) 445-3638 or toll-free (800) 321-9656, offers three antiques-furnished rooms (two share a bath) and two suites in a 1905 colonial revival. Guests enjoy a spectacular full breakfast, afternoon tea, phones, TV, a library, and gardens with a fish pond. But don't miss the third-floor Christmas Ballroom. Expensive-Premium.

A Weaver's Inn, 1440 B St., tel. (707) 443-8119 or toll-free (800) 992-8119, is an impressive 1883 Queen Anne Victorian featuring three rooms (two share a bath) and one suite, antiques, cottage gardens, and full breakfast. Two rooms have fireplaces, one has a two-seat soaking tub. Moderate-Premium.

The **Old Town Bed and Breakfast Inn,** 1521 Third St., tel. (707) 445-3951 or toll-free (800) 331-5098, occupies a redwood home built in 1871. The hot tub came later. Expensive-Luxury. **Upstairs at the Waterfront,** 102 F St., tel. (707) 443-9190, offers just two rooms, each with full bath and bay view. A restaurant and bar are downstairs. Premium-Luxury. The **Campton House,** 305 M St. in Old Town, tel. (707) 443-1601 or toll-free (800) 772-1622, is managed by the Quality Inn Eureka. The 1911 Arts & Crafts-style house features redwood interiors and abundant antiques. Guests can use the pool, sauna, and jacuzzi at the Quality Inn. Rates include continental breakfast and afternoon tea. Expensive.

EATING IN EUREKA

Casual Fare

Eureka hosts two certified farmers' markets, both held June-October. Fresh veggies, fruit, and other local products abound at the **Eureka Old Town Certified Farmers' Market,** Second and F Streets, held on Tuesday 10 a.m.-1 p.m. The **Eureka Certified Farmers' Market** at the Eureka Mall, Harris and Central, is held Thursday 10 a.m.-1 p.m. For details on both, call (707) 441-9999.

For just about the best bagels anywhere, try **Los Bagels,** 403 Second St. (at E), tel. (707) 442-8525, open daily for breakfast and lunch. (The original Los Bagels is in Arcata.) The **Eureka Baking Company,** 3562 Broadway (Hwy. 101), tel. (707) 445-8997, is wonderful for croissants, muffins, sourdough baguettes, and other fresh-baked fare. **Ramone's Bakery & Cafe,** 209 E St., tel. (707) 445-2923, is excellent for pastries and fresh breads, not to mention espresso and other good coffees. A great choice, too, for fresh-ground coffees (by the pound or by the cup) is **Humboldt Bay Coffee Company,** 211 F St., tel. (707) 444-3969, which offers live music on Friday and Saturday nights and outdoor seating in good weather. Another good stop for soup and sandwiches—and quite possibly the best ice cream anywhere on the north coast—is **Bon Boniere Ice Cream Parlor,** 215 F St. in Old Town, tel. (707) 268-0122.

The **Lost Coast Brewery,** 617 Fourth St., tel. (707) 445-4480, is the place to go for locally handcrafted ales like Alley Cat Amber and 8-Ball Stout, as well as good pub fare (served until midnight).

The **Sweetriver Grill & Bar** at the Bayshore Mall, 3300 Broadway, tel. (707) 444-9704, serves everything from omelettes and decent appetizers to sandwiches, burgers, and cowboy-size dinners, but the Sunday brunch is perhaps most impressive. Friday and Saturday nights feature stand-up comedy.

More Good Choices

Justifiably famous for its tomato and spinach pies, calzones, and other straightforward selections—one slice of the Sicilian pizza makes a meal—**Tomaso's,** 216 E St. (between Second and Third), tel. (707) 445-0100, is open for lunch and dinner weekdays and Saturday. Expect a wait, which will be worth it. For decent pasta and quiet atmosphere, try **Mazzotti's Ristorante Italiano,** 305 F St., tel. (707) 445-1912. Mexican food is the cuisine of choice at **Chapala,** 201 Second St., tel. (707) 443-9514. Best bet for steaks is **O.H.'s Town House** at Sixth and Summer, tel. (707) 443-4652. For Chinese food, try **Shanghai Low,** 1835 Fourth St., tel. (707) 443-8191; **Gonsea,** 2335 Fourth St., tel. (707) 444-8899; or **Kwan's Cafe,** 29 Fifth St., tel. (707) 443-3651.

The locals' long-time choice for fine dining is the **Rib Room** at the Eureka Inn, Seventh and F Streets, tel. (707) 442-6441, noted for its steaks, seafood, and great wine list. For breakfast or lunch, try the inn's **Bristol Rose Café.**

Real-Deal Seafood

Eureka's fishermen's wharf is the real thing, not a tourist trap like San Francisco's. The **Eureka Seafood Grotto** at Sixth and Broadway, tel. (707) 443-2075, is the locals' choice for seafood. The retail outlet for Eureka's fisheries as well, the Grotto is a tremendous place to slide into seafood stupor, with immense quantities of everything, all quite reasonable. The "Eureka-style" clam chowder is justifiably famous (get a quart to go), though the seafood chef sandwiches (grilled oyster, shrimp, or crab meat) and lunch and dinner specials are also excellent. Order up a plate of clams and cutlets. The **Cafe Marina** on Woodley Island, tel. (707) 443-2233, is another popular fish house (open daily for breakfast, lunch, and dinner), as are the **Café Waterfront,** 102 F St., tel. (707) 443-9190, and the **Sea Grill,** 316 E St., tel. (707) 443-7187.

The only place to buy fresh crab is **Botchie's Crab Stand,** 6670 Fields Landing Dr., at Fields Landing off Hwy. 101, open for business when the white flag (with orange crab) is flying. Crab season usually runs Dec.-March, weather permitting.

Samoa Cookhouse

At least once in a lifetime, everyone should eat at the **Samoa Cookhouse** on the Samoa Peninsula, tel. (707) 442-1659 ("open after 0600" but no reservations taken). All major credit cards are accepted, and there's a gift shop next door. The Samoa is a bona fide loggers' cookhouse oozing redwood-rugged ambience. The phrase "all you can eat" takes on new meaning here: portions are gargantuan. Good ol' American food—platters of thickly sliced ham, beef, turkey, and spare ribs (choices change daily), plus potatoes, vegetables, fresh-baked bread—is passed around among the checkered oilcloth-covered tables. Soup and salad are included, not to mention homemade apple pie for dessert. Hearty breakfasts and lunch, too. Come early on weekends, particularly in summer, and be prepared to wait an hour or so. To get there, head west from

Eureka over the Samoa Bridge, turn left, then left again at the town of Samoa (follow the signs).

Restaurant 301

The Hotel Carter's elegant and small **Restaurant 301,** 301 L St., tel. (707) 444-8062, is open nightly for candlelight, classical music, and quality dining. In fact, Restaurant 301 has become something of an international dining destination, since it won *Wine Spectator* magazine's coveted Grand Award in 1998. Fewer than 100 restaurants in the world have been so honored. According to *Wine Spectator,* Restaurant 301 is a "wine-and-food oasis . . . where a superb wine list is complemented by the culinary talent of Chef Rodger Babel." Menus here are created from fresh, local ingredients, from Humboldt Bay seafood to the fresh vegetables, fruits, and herbs harvested daily from the restaurant's own extensive organic gardens. Entrées might include marinated and grilled quail breast medallions with fresh corn waffles, pecan-crusted Pacific salmon, or fennel-roasted sturgeon. The exceptional wine list features "unusually fine and reasonably priced wines," including treasured California wines and rare French wines. The cellar here boasts more than 23,000 bottles. Reservations are a must. The Hotel Carter also offers a famous four-course breakfast. To take the experience home with you, pick up a copy of the *Carter House Cookbook,* available for sale at the hotel.

EVENTFUL, ARTFUL, ENTERTAINING EUREKA

Come in January for the unique **Almost-Annual Humboldt Pun-Off,** a delightful display of tasteless humor, benefit for Easter Seals (immensely popular, so get your tickets early). March brings **A Taste of Main Street** and the **Redwood Coast Dixieland Jazz Festival.** Fog or no fog, almost everybody crawls out in April for the annual **Rhododendron Festival.** In May comes the famous **Kinetic Sculpture Race,** starting in nearby Arcata. From June to August, count on **Summer Concerts in the Park,** at Clarke Plaza in Old Town. At the top of the lengthy regional calendar of July 4 events is the annual **Humboldt Bay Festival.** Later in July, rodeo fans can head north to the annual **Orick Rodeo** or east to the **Fortuna Rodeo.**

In July and August, the **Humboldt Arts Festival** keeps the area jumping with concerts, plays, exhibits, even special museum displays. August is hot for history, what with **Fort Humboldt Days** living history and **Steam-Up** (the monthly cranking up of ancient logging locomotives) at Fort Humboldt State Park and the **Civil War Days** reenactments in Fortuna. The annual **Humboldt County Fair** also comes in August, held in Ferndale. But there's also **Blues by the Bay.** In September, come for the **Festival on the Bay** and **Sights, Sounds & Tastes of Humboldt.** In December, the **Eureka Inn Christmas Celebration** is quite the shindig. But so is the **Trucker's Christmas Convoy** parade. For a detailed events calendar, contact local visitor bureaus.

Eureka was recently listed as number one in John Villani's *The 100 Best Small Art Towns in America.* For information about what's happening at the Humboldt Arts Council's **Cultural Center,** stop by at 636 F St., or call (707) 442-0278. Or try **The Ink People Center for the Arts,** 411 12th St., tel. (707) 442-8413. Both can fill you in on local arts events, including what's what at local galleries.

Good bets for live music include **The Ritz Club,** 240 F St. in Old Town, tel. (707) 445-8577; **Club West,** 535 Fifth St. (at G St.), tel. (707) 444-2582; and the **Palm Lounge** at the Eureka Inn. The **Eureka Symphony Orchestra,** 1437 Russ St., tel. (707) 444-2889, presents several concerts each year; call for schedule and ticket information.

PRACTICAL EUREKA

Eureka Information and Services

The **Eureka Chamber of Commerce,** 2112 Broadway, Eureka, CA 95501, tel. (707) 442-3738 or toll-free (800) 356-6381, www.eurekachamber.com, is the best stop for visitor information. Pick up Old Town information (including a listing of local antique shops) and the free Victorian walking tour guide. (*Really* taking the Victorian tour, though, means getting some exercise, since Eureka boasts well over 100 well-preserved Victorian buildings and homes, and more than 1,000 "architecturally significant" structures.) Or stop by the **Eureka Main Street Information Bureau,** 123 F St. #6, tel. (707) 442-9054. The **Eureka-Humboldt County Convention and Visitors Bureau,** 1034 Second St., tel. (707) 443-5097, toll-free (800) 338-7352 (in California), or toll-free (800) 346-3482 (outside California), www.redwoodvisitor.org, is the central source for countywide visitor information.

Eureka's main **post office** is at 337 W. Clark St., tel. (707) 442-1768, though a convenient downtown branch is located at the corner of Fifth and H Streets, tel. (707) 442-1828. **Eureka General Hospital,** 2200 Harrison Ave., tel. (707) 445-5111, offers 24-hour emergency medical care (tel. 707-441-4409). The local **California Department of Fish and Game** office is at 619 Second St., tel. (707) 445-6493, and provides regulations and licenses. Main headquarters for **Six Rivers National Forest** is at 1330 Bayshore Way, tel. (707) 442-1721, a good place to stop for camping information and forest maps ($4). The regional **California Department of Parks and Recreation** office is at 3431 Fort Ave., tel. (707) 445-6547.

Eureka Transportation and Tours

Get around town on **Eureka Transit,** 133 V St. (catch most buses at Fifth and D Streets), tel. (707) 443-0826, which runs Mon.-Saturday. The V St. station is actually headquarters for **Humboldt Transit,** same phone, which serves the area from Scotia north to Trinidad (including bicycle transport—call for details), weekdays only. Catch it along Hwy. 101. **Greyhound,** 1603 Fourth St. (at P St.), tel. (707) 442-0370, runs north to Crescent City and beyond, also south on Hwy. 101 to San Francisco. To fly into the area, the **Eureka-Arcata Airport** actually lies north of Arcata, in McKinleyville, at 3561 Boeing Ave., tel. (707) 839-1906. Rental cars are available there.

Tour the bay on **Humboldt Bay Harbor Cruises'** MV *Madaket* (once the Eureka-Samoa ferry) from the foot of C St.; call (707) 445-1910 for information. The **Eureka Chamber of Commerce,** 2112 Broadway, tel. (707) 442-3738, offers a five-hour history and sightseeing tour (Victorians, Fort Humboldt, the park and zoo, Clarke Museum, Samoa Cookhouse, the bay cruise, and more) on Tuesday and Thursday from mid-June to mid-September. Guided city tours are also offered by **Pride Enterprises Tours,** tel. (707) 445-2117 or toll-free (800) 400-1849.

EEL RIVER COUNTRY

Just south of Eureka is the Victorian village of Ferndale, well worth an excursion. Staying on Hwy. 101 leads to Fortuna and the long, meandering, and scenic highway route that winds past many redwood groves and riverbank beaches alongside the aptly named Eel River all the way to Leggett. At Leggett Hwy. 1 reclaims its independent identity and jogs seaward, just south of terrain known as The Lost Coast—see The Lost (and Found) Coast, below—slipping through Westport and Rockport on the way south to Fort Bragg and Mendocino (see Mendocino and the Mendocino Coast, below).

FERNDALE AND VICINITY

Ferndale (pop. 1,400) is a perfect rendition of a Victorian village, the kind of place Disney architects would create if they needed a new movie set. Ferndale, however, is the real thing, a thriving small town where people take turns shuttling the kids to Future Farmers of America and 4-H meetings, argue about education at PTA meetings or ice-cream socials, and gossip on street corners.

The town was first settled in 1864 by Danish immigrants; at that time, the delta plain was heavily forested. The Danes were followed by Portuguese and Italians. Today, quaint and quiet Ferndale values its streets of colorfully restored Victorians.

Seeing and Doing Ferndale
Lovers of Victoriana, take the walking tour; for a free guide to historic buildings (almost everything here qualifies), pick up the souvenir edition of the *Ferndale Enterprise* at the Kinetic Sculpture Museum or at most main street shops, or contact the **Ferndale Chamber of Commerce,** P.O. Box 325, Ferndale, CA 95536, tel. (707) 786-4477, www.victorianferndale.org/chamber.

Most of the historic commercial buildings are concentrated on three-block-long Main St., including the Roman-Renaissance **Six Rivers National Bank** building at 394 Main, originally the Ferndale Bank. The **Kinetic Sculpture Museum,** 580 Main St. (no phone, but inquire at Hobart Galleries, tel. 707-786-9259), displays a decidedly eclectic collection of survivors of the annual kinetic sculpture race, as well as works in progress. The Kinetic Sculpture Museum is usually open weekdays 10 a.m.-5 p.m., shorter hours on weekends. Worth a stop, too, is the 1892-vintage **Golden Gait Mercantile,** 421 Main St., tel. (707) 786-4891, a squeaky-floored emporium of oddities and useful daily items, from sassafras tea and traditional patent medicines to

Ferndale's
Gingerbread Mansion

butter churns, bushel (and peck) baskets, and treadle sewing machines. There's a museum on the second floor.

While touring the town—probably the best-preserved Victorian village in the state—travelers will be relieved to find that Ferndale has public restrooms (next to the post office on Main). Once off Main, most people head first to the famous **Gingerbread Mansion,** a Victorian built in a combination of Queen Anne, Eastlake, and stick styles. Tucked into its formal English gardens at 400 Berding and virtually dripping with its own frosting, the Gingerbread is one of the most photographed and painted buildings in Northern California.

In order to fully appreciate the town, take a quick visit to the **Ferndale Museum,** 515 Shaw Ave. (just off Main at the corner of Third), tel. (707) 786-4466. This small museum also includes an Oral History Library, written histories, and old *Ferndale Enterprise* newspaper archives on microfilm. The museum is open Wed.-Sat. (also Tuesday in summer) 11 a.m.-4 p.m., Sunday 1-4 p.m. Small admission.

Centerville County Park at the end of Ocean is small (pass **Portuguese Hall** on the way) but provides access to the 10 miles of beaches between False Cape and the Eel River lagoon: good beachcombing, driftwood picking, and smelt fishing in summer. On the way to 110-acre **Russ Park** (trails, forest, birdwatching) in the opposite direction, pass **Danish Hall** (built in the late 1800s, still used for community events); Ferndale's **pioneer cemetery;** and the former **Old Methodist Church,** built in 1871, at the corner of Berding.

Eventful Ferndale

In March, come for the big **Foggy Bottoms Milk Run,** when whole families and serious runners alike participate in a footrace around the farm and back to Main Street. The Portuguese **Holy Ghost Festival** is in May, with a parade, dancing, feasts. Also in May is the annual **Tour of the Unknown Coast Bicycle Ride,** which starts at the county fairgrounds and can be ridden in 10- to 100-mile increments. On Memorial Day, the **Kinetic Sculpture Race** from Arcata ends on Main St., the surviving sculptures proudly paraded through town. Some also take up residence at the Kinetic Sculpture Museum here

(for more information about the race, see Arcata and Vicinity). The annual **Scandinavian Festival** is celebrated in late June. In August, the **Humboldt County Fair** and horse races come to the fairgrounds.

On the third Thursday in September, the **Taste of Humboldt** brings a food and music sampler to Main Street. In December, come for the town's month-long **Victorian Christmas** celebrations, which include lighting up the world's tallest living Christmas tree (the 165-foot Sitka spruce on Main), a lighted-tractor parade, and the arrival of Santa Claus by horse and carriage.

Practical Ferndale

Camp at the handsome **Humboldt County Fairgrounds,** 1250 Fifth (off Van Ness), tel. (707) 786-9511 or (707) 786-1306, available for tent camping and RVs.

In the B&B department, the most notable local star is the unabashedly luxurious 1899 **Gingerbread Mansion Inn,** 400 Berding St., tel. (707) 786-4000 or toll-free (800) 952-4136, gingerbreadmansion.com, which offers 11 uniquely decorated, antique-rich rooms in a refurbished 1899 Victorian mansion. Amenities include a generous full breakfast and an afternoon tea. Premium-Luxury. Others include the **Victorian Inn,** 400 Ocean Ave., tel. (707) 786-4949 or toll-free (888) 589-1808, fax (707) 786-4558, a-victorian-inn.com, a 12-room B&B in a nicely restored 1890 Victorian, full breakfast (Expensive-Premium); **Grandmother's House,** 861 Howard St., tel. (707) 786-9704, a three-bedroom 1901 Victorian (Moderate); and the **Bartlett House,** 483 Shaw St., tel. (707) 786-4010, an 1899 Victorian cottage with two guestrooms, both with private bath, as well as a woodstove in the parlor, down comforters on the beds, and full breakfast (Expensive). Still being restored to its original glory as a "butterfat palace" is the **Queen of Harts,** 831 Main St., tel. (707) 786-9716 or toll-free (800) 469-1632, an 1885 Italianate Victorian with five rooms, each with private bath (with shower and clawfoot tub) and period furniture, full breakfast and afternoon tea included (Expensive-Premium). Another fine Ferndale bed and breakfast is the **Shaw House,** 703 Main St., tel. (707) 786-9958 or toll-free (800) 557-7429, an 1854 Carpenter Gothic Victorian with eight rooms, all with private bath, full breakfast included (Moderate-Premium).

Motels in town include the **Francis Creek Inn,** 577 Main St., tel. (707) 786-9611 (Inexpensive); the **Fern Motel,** 332 Ocean Ave., tel. (707) 786-5000 (Moderate); and **Ruriko's Ferndale Motel,** 632 Main St., tel. (707) 786-9471 (Inexpensive).

Picnickers can stop in at the **Ferndale Meat Company,** 376 Main, tel. (707) 786-4501, to pick up handmade smoked sausages and other meats from the two-story stone smokehouse, as well as cheeses and other surprises. For a sit-down meal, try immensely popular **Curley's Grill,** 460 Main St., tel. (707) 786-9696, open daily for lunch and dinner, and the small **Stage Door Café,** 451 Main, tel. (707) 786-4675, open for breakfast and lunch. Other possibilities include the **Victorian Inn** restaurant, 400 Ocean St., tel. (707) 786-4442, which is open for breakfast, lunch, and dinner and features a popular sushi and oyster bar, and **The Ivanhoe,** 315 Main St., tel. (707) 786-9000, offering Italian cuisine for dinner Tues.-Sun.

Fernbridge

Between Eureka and Ferndale near the Eel River is Fernbridge, the name for both a community and a stately seven-arch Romanesque bridge called "the queen of bridges" up here in the north. Caltrans once nearly started a local armed rebellion when it announced plans to tear the bridge down. Fernbridge is home to the **Humboldt Creamery,** 572 Fernbridge Dr., tel. (707) 725-6182, as well as **Angelina Inn,** 281 Fernbridge Dr., tel. (707) 725-3153, locally loved for its Italian dinners and prime rib, steaks, and seafood. Open daily for dinner, full bar, live music on weekends.

Loleta

Dairies account for nearly half of Humboldt County's agricultural income. Since the pasturelands near Loleta are among the richest in the world, it's only natural that the region's first creamery was established here in 1888. Because of difficult shipping logistics, much of the milk produced here is processed into butter, cheese, and dried-milk products. Big doin's here is the **Loleta Antique Show** in October, not to mention **Swauger Station Days** in July. For more information about these and other events, contact the **Loleta Chamber of Commerce,** P.O. Box 327, Loleta, CA 95551.

Loleta today is still a bucolic village of wood-frames and old brick buildings. Most of the action in town is at the award-winning **Loleta Cheese Factory,** 252 Loleta Dr., Loleta, CA 95551, tel. (707) 733-5470 or toll-free (800) 995-0453, famed for its natural Jersey milk cheeses, tasting room, and retail sales of cheese and wine. Step inside to sample and buy cheese right out of the display case. The company's famous creamy jack cheese comes in garlic, green chili, caraway, jalapeño, and smoked salmon variations. The cheddars also tease the palate—try the salami or smoked salmon versions. Watch the cheesemaking, too. The Loleta Cheese Factory is open Mon.-Fri. 9 a.m.-5 p.m., Saturday 9 a.m.-4 p.m., Sunday noon-4 p.m. Write to request a mail-order catalog.

If you decide to spend the night, try the four-room **Southport Landing Bed and Breakfast,** 444 Phelan Rd., tel. (707) 733-5915. This 1890s colonial revival mansion overlooks the Humboldt Bay National Wildlife Refuge. Guests have use of kayaks, bicycles, pool table, and a nature library. Rates include full breakfast and evening beverages/hors d'oeuvres. Expensive-Premium.

FORTUNA AND HIGHWAY 36

The largest city in southern Humboldt County, Fortuna (pop. around 10,000) was originally called Springville and established in 1875. Logging is still the major industry in these parts. Come in March for a big **Daffodil Show;** in July for the long-running **Fortuna Rodeo** and parade; in October for the **Apple Harvest Festival;** or in December for the **Christmas Music Festival.**

The **Fortuna Depot Museum,** 4 Park St., tel. (707) 725-7645, occupies the old 1893 rail depot and houses a collection of area artifacts from the local railroad, logging, and fishing industries. It's open in summer, daily 10 a.m.-4:30 p.m.; the rest of the year, Wed.-Sun. noon-4:30 p.m. Admission is free (donations appreciated).

Overnighters can choose from the **Best Western Country Inn,** 2025 Riverwalk Dr., tel. (707) 725-6822 or toll-free (800) 679-7511, with an indoor heated pool and jacuzzi (Moderate-Expensive); the **Fortuna Motor Lodge,** 275 12th St., tel. (707) 725-6993 (Inexpensive); the **Fortuna Super 8,** 1805 Alamar Way, tel. (707)

725-2888 or toll-free (800) 800-8000 (Moderate); or the **Holiday Inn Express,** 1859 Alamar Way, tel. (707) 725-5500 or toll-free (800) 465-4329 (Moderate). There's also a **KOA** RV campground in town at 2189 Riverwalk Dr., tel. (707) 725-3359 or toll-free (800) 562-0532.

For fresh regional produce, show up for the **Fortuna Certified Farmers' Market,** tel. (707) 768-3342, held May-Oct. at 10th and L Streets, on Tuesday, 3:30-6 p.m. Otherwise, **Clendenen's Cider Works,** 96 12th St. (next to the freeway), tel. (707) 725-2123, open daily Aug.-Feb., is *the* place for half-gallons of homemade apple cider and fresh local produce. The **Eel River Brewing Company,** 1777 Alamar Way, tel. (707) 725-2739, offers around half a dozen homemade beers, including Ravensbrau Porter and Climax Amber. To go with the brew, you can order from a fine menu of steaks and seafoods, pastas, and burgers. Justifiably popular with locals, and quite a find, is **Savannah's Steak & Seafood** (next to Safeway in the shopping center), 703 S. Fortuna Blvd., tel. (707) 725-7056.

For more information about Fortuna and vicinity, contact the **Fortuna Chamber of Commerce,** 735 14th St., Fortuna, CA 95540, tel. (707) 725-3959.

Van Duzen County Park

Humboldt's largest county park, Van Duzen harbors four groves of nearly undisturbed redwoods along the Van Duzen River east from Hwy. 101 via Hwy. 36. Georgia-Pacific donated these groves, as well as Cheatham Grove farther west, to the Nature Conservancy in 1969, a very large corporate conservation gift. The land was subsequently deeded to the county and the Save-the-Redwoods League. You can hike, swim, fish, picnic, and camp at both **Pamplin** and **Swimmer's Delight** groves. **Humboldt Grove** is pristine old-growth forest open only for hiking. **Redwood Grove** was severely damaged by windstorms in 1978, but hikers can still walk the old roads. Day-use fee. For more information, contact: Humboldt County Department of Public Works, Parks and Recreation Division, 1106 Second St., Eureka, CA 95501, tel. (707) 445-7651.

Grizzly Creek Redwoods State Park

Gone but not forgotten is the now-extinct California grizzly bear, exterminated here by the late 1860s. The smallest of all the redwood parks, Grizzly Creek Redwoods State Park, 35 miles southeast of Eureka, was once a stagecoach stop. It's surrounded by mostly undeveloped forests along the Van Duzen River (visited now by an occasional black bear), among which are a few redwood groves. The main things to do: hike the short trails, swim, and fish for salmon, steelhead, and trout in winter when the river's raging. Grizzly Creek also has a natural history museum inside the restored stage stop.

The campground here (30 campsites, 30 picnic sites) is open year-round. Most campsites cost $12-16. ReserveAmerica reservations, toll-free tel. (800) 444-7275, are a good idea late May-early September. Make sure to bring quarters for the hot showers. Grizzly Creek also features environmental campsites ($7-9). The park day-use fee is $5 per car. For more information, contact: Grizzly Creek Redwoods State Park, 16939 Hwy. 36, Carlotta, CA 95528, tel. (707) 777-3683.

SCOTIA AND VICINITY

Scotia is a neat-as-a-pin town perfumed by the scents of apple pie, family barbecues, and redwood sawdust. A company town built to last from redwood and founded on solid economic ground created by sustained-yield logging, picture-perfect Scotia is one of California's last wholly owned company towns. Generations of children of Pacific Lumber Company (PALCO) loggers happily grew up in Scotia, then went to work in the mills, or went away to college on PALCO-paid scholarships before returning to work as middle managers in the mill offices.

Scotia's serenity has been obliterated, to a large degree, by major economic and political events. One round of trouble started in 1985, when PALCO was taken over in a Michael Milken-related stock raid by the Maxxam Group. Environmentalists loudly mourned the passing of the old PALCO—friend of the Save-the-Redwoods League, sympathetic to conservationist thought, and opposed to clear-cutting as a forestry practice. Maxxam's Charles Hurwitz began his tenure at PALCO by clear-cutting old-growth redwoods on the company's land. When Hurwitz directed his chainsaws toward the Headwaters Grove—in the midst of PALCO's 60,000-acre Headwaters Forest, one of the last privately held stands of virgin redwoods left in the country—it sparked an environmental and political battle that has taken a decade to resolve, to less than unanimous satisfaction. (For more details, see the special topic Story Without End: The Politics of Harvesting Redwoods.) The agreement, among PALCO and the federal and state governments, saved the core groves of redwoods—for which PALCO received a hefty sum from the taxpayers—but left PALCO free to harvest the rest of its holdings, under what environmentalists contend are token environmental restrictions.

As if such stresses weren't enough, the town's business district was lost in April 1992, when fires started by a massive north coast earthquake destroyed the entire business district and damaged many area homes. (The mill was saved.) The quake's total regional price tag: somewhere in the neighborhood of $61 million.

The big event in Scotia is taking a tour of the **Pacific Lumber Company redwood sawmill,** 125 Main St., tel. (707) 764-2222, the largest in the world. Visitors are welcome to observe the operation on the company's self-guided Mill B tour (free). Also stop by the **Scotia Museum** and visitor center on Main St., tel. (707) 764-2222, ext. 247, housed in a stylized Greek temple built of redwood, with logs taking the place of fluted columns. (Formerly a bank, the building's sprouting redwood burl once had to be pruned regularly.) Open summers only.

About five miles south of town is the company's **demonstration forest,** open daily in summer (also free), and a picnic area with restrooms. **Rio Dell** across the Eel River is a residential community, its main claim to fame being good fossil hunting on the shale-and-sandstone Scotia Bluffs along the banks of the Eel.

The town holds a **Wildwood Days** festival in August. The **Rio Dell/Scotia Chamber of Commerce** is at 715 Wildwood Ave., Rio Dell, CA 95562, tel. (707) 764-3436.

Staying and Eating in Scotia

While in Scotia, consider a stop or a stay at the spruced-up **Scotia Inn,** 100 Main St. (at Mill), tel. (707) 764-5683, fax (707) 764-1707, www.scotiainn.com, a classic 1923 redwood bed and breakfast-style hotel with a very good restaurant—the **Redwood Room,** serving American and international fare—plus separate café and several bars, one known as the **Steak and Potato Pub.** The inn has eight rooms and two suites, all with private baths (one with a hot tub and whirlpool). Continental breakfast included. Expensive-Luxury. **Cinnamon Jack's Bakery,** 341 Wildwood, tel. (707) 764-5858, is a coffee shop locally famous for its cinnamon rolls and muffins.

HEADING FOR HEADWATERS

So intense was public interest in visiting the 7,500-acre Headwaters Grove after its 1999 purchase by California and the U.S. that state officials decided to limit initial access. Only those willing to hike a rugged 10 miles got an early look.

Botanists fear that tourism will threaten the fragile old-growth redwood ecosystem. No trail leads into the reserve's 3,000-acre core, but visitors can drive to the north edge of the forest, just south of Eureka, via Elk River Rd., then hike in some five miles along an abandoned logging road to reach an overlook into the unperturbed heart of the Headlands. Limited visitor access is also available from southeast of Fortuna. That logging-road route, via Newburg and Felt Springs Roads, leads to a 10-vehicle parking area at Salmon Pass. Guided hikes are also offered.

For current information on Headwaters access and guided hikes, contact the **U.S. Bureau of Land Management's Arcata Field Office,** 1695 Heindon Rd. in Arcata, tel. (707) 825-2300, fax (707) 825-2301, www.ca.blm.gov. The website includes basic maps of the area.

For background information on the battle to protect the Headwaters Grove, updates on current skirmishes, and details on other regional environmental issues, contact: **Environmental Protection Information Center (EPIC),** P.O. Box 397, Garberville, CA 95542, tel. (707) 923-2931, fax (707) 923-4210, www.wildcalifornia.org.

HUMBOLDT REDWOODS STATE PARK

This is the redwood heart of Humboldt County, where more than 40% of the world's redwoods remain. The Save-the-Redwoods League and the state have added to the park's holdings grove by grove. Most of these "dedicated groves," named in honor of those who gave to save the trees, and many of the park's developed campgrounds are along the state-park section of the Avenue of the Giants parkway.

Humboldt Redwoods State Park is one of the largest state parks in Northern California, with more than 51,000 acres of almost unfrequented redwood groves, mixed conifers, and oaks. The park offers 35 miles of hiking and backpacking trails, plus 30 miles of old logging roads—and surprising solitude so close to a freeway. Down on the flats are the deepest and darkest stands of virgin redwoods, including Rockefeller Forest, the world's largest stand of stately survivors. The rolling uplands include grass-brushed hills with mixed forest. Calypso orchids and lilies are plentiful in spring, and wild blackberries and huckleberries ripen July-September.

As is typical of the north coast, heavy rainfall and sometimes dangerously high river conditions are predictable Nov.-April. But the rampaging Eel River shrinks to garter snake size by May or June, its emerald water fringed by white sand beaches good for swimming, tubing, fishing, and for watching the annual lamprey migration. The wild and scenic stretches of the Eel are also known for early-in-the-year whitewater rafting and kayaking.

Humboldt Big Trees

At almost 13,000 acres, **Rockefeller Forest** is the main grove here and among the most valuable virgin stands of redwood remaining on the north coast (and yes, it was donated by the John D. Rockefeller family). In **Founder's Grove,** the Founder's Tree was once erroneously known as the World's Tallest Tree; the park's Dyerville Giant is—or was—actually the park's tallest at 362 feet, when last measured in 1972 (the Giant toppled over in a 1991 storm and now lies on the forest floor), and even taller trees reach skyward in Redwood National Park north of Orick. But the Founder's Tree and Dyerville Giant are two mindful monuments to the grandeur of the natural world. After exploring Founder's Grove, consider the nearby **Immortal Tree,** which has withstood almost every imaginable onslaught from both nature and humanity—a testament to this tree's tenacity, and perhaps the forest's.

Not the largest tree or most martyred but a notable one nevertheless is the *Metasequoia,* which you can see near Weott (and south down the highway at Richardson Grove State Park). It's a dawn redwood native to China, kissing cousin of both species of California redwoods.

AVENUE OF THE GIANTS

This scenic 33-mile drive on the old highway, a narrow asphalt ribbon braiding together the eastern edge of Humboldt Redwoods, the Eel River, and Hwy. 101, weaves past and through some of the largest groves of the largest remaining redwoods in Humboldt and Del Norte Counties. Get off the bike (the avenue's very nice for cycling, but wear bright clothing) or out of the car and picnic, take a short walk, and just *appreciate* these grand old giants.

The part-private, part-public Avenue is dotted with commercial attractions—tourist traps offering redwood knickknacks and trinkets manufactured overseas and trees transformed into walk-in or drive-through freaks of nature. But the curio shops and commercial trappings barely distract from the fragrant grandeur of the dim, dignified forest itself, sunlit in faint slivers and carpeted with oxalis and ferns.

Among the tiny towns dwarfed still more by the giants along the Avenue are **Redcrest, Meyers Flat,** and **Phillipsville.** In Redcrest you'll find the **Eternal Tree House,** 26510 Avenue of the Giants, tel. (707) 722-4262 (gift shop) or (707) 722-4247 (café), a 20-foot room inside a living tree. Meyers Flat boasts one of the state's oldest tourist attractions, the **Shrine Drive-Thru-Tree & Gift Shop,** 13078 Avenue of the Giants, tel. (707) 943-3154. Wagon-train travelers heading up and down the Pacific coast once pulled *their* vehicles through it. The tree stands 275 feet tall, measures 21 feet in diameter, and people can see the sky if standing inside the eight-foot-wide tree tunnel. Food is available at the **Drive-Thru-Tree Cafe,** tel. (707) 943-1665. Phillipsville is home to the **Chimney Tree,** tel. (707) 923-2265, open 8 a.m.-8 p.m. from May to mid-October, and the Tolkienesque **Hobbitown U.S.A.** (currently closed, but ask at the Chimney Tree about possible reopening).

TOM MYERS PHOTOGRAPHY

Humboldt Redwoods

Camping at Humboldt Redwoods

Camping is easy at Humboldt Redwoods, which offers hundreds of campsites and four picnic areas. **Burlington Campground** near Weott is fully developed (hot showers, restrooms, tables—the works for outdoor living), $12-16. Ditto for the **Albee Creek Campground** not far to the south, and **Hidden Springs Campground** near Miranda. All three of these campgrounds are popular, so make advance reservations in summer through ReserveAmerica, toll-free tel. (800) 444-7275.

Unusual at Humboldt Redwoods State Park are five backcountry backpackers' camps, reservable in advance (first-come) at park headquarters. These camps each have piped spring water (but no fires are allowed, so bring a campstove). Only one of the five—**Bull Creek Trail Camp**—is easily reached by nonhikers. Closest to the road but an uphill climb are **Johnson Trail Camp,** a collection of four backwoods cabins used from the 1920s to 1950s by "tie hacks" (railroad tie makers), and the **Whiskey Flat Trail Camp,** a tent camp named for the Prohibition moonshine still once tucked among these massive old-growth redwoods. **Grasshopper Trail Camp** is among the grasshoppers and deer on the meadow's edge below Grasshopper Peak (great view from the fire lookout at the top), and **Hanson Ridge Trail Camp** is tucked among firs and ferns.

In addition to the outback pleasures of these backcountry camps, the park features two walk-in environmental campgrounds: **Baxter** and **Hamilton Barn** (pick apples in the old orchard), both with convenient yet secluded campsites ($7-11; sign up at park headquarters, where you can get the particulars). Group camps and horse camps are also available. Should all the state facilities be full, the area also includes a number of private campgrounds and RV parks.

Practical Humboldt Redwoods

The day-use fee at Humboldt Redwoods is $5 per car. For maps and more information about the park, stop by or contact: Humboldt Redwoods State Park headquarters (at the Burlington Campground), P.O. Box 100, Weott, CA 95571, tel. (707) 946-2409. The **Humboldt Redwoods Interpretive Association Visitor Center,** between headquarters and Burlington Campground, tel. (707) 946-2263, is open daily 9 a.m.-5 p.m. (until 8 p.m. in July and August) and offers excellent natural history exhibits. In summer, park rangers offer guided nature walks, campfire programs, and Junior Ranger activities for kids.

Staying near Humboldt Redwoods

Very pleasant is a stay at the **Myers Country Inn,** 12913 Avenue of the Giants, Myers Flat, tel. (707) 943-3259, www.myersinn.com, an 1860-vintage two-story California-style hotel now functioning as a stylish country-style 10-room bed and breakfast. Amenities include private baths, separate entrances, a fireplace in the lobby, and complimentary continental breakfast. Premium.

Determined noncampers can find motels in the area. The **Miranda Gardens Resort,** 6766 Avenue of the Giants, Miranda, tel. (707) 943-3011, is tops in the motel department, offering rustic yet comfortable single or duplex cabins—some with two bedrooms, some with kitchens, several with fireplaces, one with spa. Moderate-Luxury. The **Whispering Pines Lodge,** next to the Eel River, 6582 Avenue of the Giants, Miranda, tel. (707) 943-3182, offers a rec room with fireplace and pool table, a heated pool, and lawn games. Expensive. The **Madrona Motel,** 2907 Avenue of the Giants, Phillipsville, tel. (707) 943-1708, is a clean and pleasant '50s-feeling place, some units with kitchens. Inexpensive.

Eating near Humboldt Redwoods

Great for a quick all-American meal, from biscuits and gravy to homemade pies, the place is the **Eternal Treehouse Café,** 26510 Avenue of the Giants in Redcrest, tel. (707) 722-4247, open daily for breakfast, lunch, and dinner. For American and international cuisine and fine wines, head toward Myers Flat and **Knight's Restaurant,** 12866 Avenue of the Giants, tel. (707) 943-3411. Two worthwhile dinner houses within driving distance are the **Scotia Inn** to the north in Scotia, at Main and Mill Streets, tel. (707) 764-5683, owned—like the rest of the town—by the Pacific Lumber Company, and the very English **Benbow Inn,** 445 Lake Benbow Dr. (south along the freeway), tel. (707) 923-2124 or toll-free (800) 355-3301.

GARBERVILLE

A former sheep ranching town, Garberville is *not* an outlaw enclave paved in $100 bills by pot-growing Mercedes Benz owners, as media mythology would have it. The town was once considered the sinsemilla cultivation capital of the world, an honor most locals are fed up with. The general belief today is that the big-time Rambo-style growers have gone elsewhere. But don't expect people here to share their knowledge *or* opinions on the subject, pro or con. With annual CAMP (Campaign Against Marijuana Production) invasions throughout the surrounding countryside, discretion is the rule of tongue when outsiders show up.

Not far north of Garberville is **M. Lockwood Memorial Park,** a popular rafting departure point also offering good fishing. Two small southerly outposts of Humboldt Redwood State Park are just north of Redway; **Whittemore Grove** and **Holbrook Grove** are both dark, cool glens perfect for picnicking and short hikes.

In June, the annual **Rodeo in the Redwoods** is the big to-do in these parts, followed in July or early August by the West Coast's largest and usually most impressive reggae festival—the **Reggae on the River** concert—which attracts top talent from Jamaica and America. For concert information, contact the **Mateel Community Center,** 59 Rusk Ln. in Redway, tel. (707) 923-3368.

Staying in Garberville

Just about everything in Garberville is on Business 101, called Redwood Drive. The 76-room **Best Western Humboldt House Inn,** 701 Redwood Dr., tel. (707) 923-2771 or toll-free (800) 528-1234, has rooms with air-conditioning, color TV, movies, and phones. Some rooms have kitchens. Other extras here include a coin-op laundry, heated pool, whirlpool, and complimentary continental breakfast. Moderate.

The smaller **Sherwood Forest Motel,** 814 Redwood Dr., tel. (707) 923-2721, is quite a find, with all the amenities found at the more expensive Humboldt House. Moderate.

Eating in Garberville

For farm-fresh fruit, veggies, and herbs, show up at the **Garberville-South Humboldt Certified Farmers' Market,** held June-Oct. at Locust and Church on Friday, 11 a.m.-3 p.m. For details, call (707) 923-2613. The locally famous **Woodrose Café,** 911 Redwood, tel. (707) 923-3191, is beloved for its fine omelettes, good vegetarian sandwiches, and like fare, everything locally and/or organically grown. Open daily for breakfast, for lunch only on weekdays. A good choice for wheatbread-and-sprouts-style Sunday champagne brunch. For straight-ahead Italian food and pizza, not to mention impressive quantities of Mexican and American fare, try **Sicilito's,** 445 Conger St. (behind the Humboldt House Inn), tel. (707) 923-2814, open Fri.-Tues. for lunch and dinner, and Wed.-Thurs. for dinner only. For fresh fish in season and good family-style Italian and American fare, the place is the **Waterwheel Restaurant,** 924 Redwood Dr., tel. (707) 923-2031, open daily for breakfast, lunch, and dinner.

Just northwest of Garberville, across the highway in Redway, is the **Mateel Cafe,** 3344 Redwood Dr., tel. (707) 923-2030, a fine-food mecca that lures folks even from San Francisco. With a

French chef and an owner who is a nutritionist, you can count on gourmet fare done right—everything from Thai tofu to seafood linguine and stone-baked pizza. Vegans, carnivores, low-protein or high-protein dieters—all will find something to satisfy and delight them on the eclectic menu. And check out that Jazzbo Room. Open Mon.-Sat. for lunch and dinner.

Garberville Information and Services

The **Garberville-Redway Chamber of Commerce,** 773 Redwood Dr., P.O. Box 445, Garberville, CA 95542, tel. (707) 923-2613 or toll-free (800) 923-2613, is open daily 9 a.m.-5 p.m. in summer, and weekdays 9 a.m.-5 p.m. in winter. The **Greyhound** station is at 432 Church St., tel. (707) 923-3388; open daily 8 a.m.-6 p.m., with departures north and south daily. The **post office** is at 368 Sprowel Creek Rd., off Redwood Dr., tel. (707) 923-2652, and the coin-op **Garberville Laundromat** is at 663 Redwood, tel. (707) 923-9242 (open daily 8 a.m.-9 p.m.).

BENBOW TO LEGGETT

Benbow Inn

Also open year-round is the elegant four-story Tudor-style Benbow Inn, 445 Lake Benbow Dr., tel. (707) 923-2124 or toll-free (800) 355-3301, fax (707) 923-2122, www.benbowinn.com. Designed by architect Albert Farr, the Benbow Inn first opened its doors in 1926 and over the years has welcomed travelers including Herbert Hoover, Charles Laughton, and Eleanor Roosevelt. A National Historic Landmark, the inn has been restored to a very English attitude. Complimentary scones and tea are served in the lobby every afternoon at 3 p.m., and the dining room serves staples like steak-and-kidney pie for dinner. Full bar. Premium-Luxury, but ask about off-season specials.

Benbow Lake State Recreation Area

This state recreation area in the midst of open woodlands just south of Garberville is aptly named only in the summer, when a temporary dam goes up on the Eel River's south fork to create Benbow Lake. The lake itself is great for swimming, sailing, canoeing, and windsurfing, with pleasant picnicking and hiking in the hills

SHAKESPEARE AT BENBOW LAKE

nearby. No fishing. It's also the scene of several summertime events, including the annual **Jazz on the Lake** festival, **Shakespeare at Benbow Lake,** and the **Summer Arts Fair.**

The lake may disappear at summer's end, but the campground remains open all year. It's popular in summer, so reserve campsites ($12-21) in advance through ReserveAmerica, toll-free tel. (800) 444-7275. For more information, contact Benbow Lake State Recreation Area, Garberville, CA 95440, tel. (707) 923-3238.

In addition to the state facilities, RVers can try the private **Benbow Valley RV Resort & Golf Course,** 7000 Benbow Dr., Garberville, CA 95440, tel. (707) 923-2777, which offers 112 sites with full hookups, as well as a golf course.

Richardson Grove
State Park and Vicinity

Richardson Grove, south of Lake Benbow, with more than 800 acres of fine redwoods, was named for 1920s California governor Friend W. Richardson, a noted conservationist of the day. Richardson Grove is popular and crowded in summer, though few people hike the backcountry trails. Picnic near the river or camp at any of three developed campgrounds (one is open all year). ReserveAmerica reservations are advisable in summer. Developed campsites are $12-16, and the park's day-use fee is $5. Hike-and-bike campsites are also available. A few cabins at Richardson Grove are also available for rent; for details, call (707) 247-3415. The **Seven Parks Natural History Association,** 1600 Hwy. 101, #8 in the visitor center at Richardson Grove Lodge, offers a variety of redwood-country publications. For more information, contact: Richardson Grove State Park, P.O. Box E, Garberville, CA 95542, tel. (707) 247-3318 (recorded) or (707) 247-3319.

Just south of Richardson Grove in **Piercy,** the **Hartsook Country Inn,** 900 Hwy. 101, tel. (707) 247-3305, boasts an impressive selection of cabins (Moderate-Expensive) and **Keith's,** a fine-dining restaurant, tel. (707) 247-3346. Just south of Piercy along the Eel River is 400-acre **Reynolds Wayside Camp,** offering picnicking and 50 unimproved campsites.

Smithe Redwoods and Confusion Hill

Four miles north of Leggett on Hwy. 101, the lovely Frank and Bess Smithe Grove of redwoods at **Smithe Redwoods State Reserve** can be reached only from the west side of the highway, though most of the 665-acre park's protected trees are to the east. A quarter-mile hike here, once a private resort with cabins and restaurant, will take you to a 60-foot waterfall. For more information, contact Standish-Hickey State Recreation Area (see address below).

Nearby is the **Confusion Hill Fun Center,** tel. (707) 925-6456, one of those places where gravity is defied and water runs uphill, etc. You can also take the kids on a train ride through the redwoods and view the world's largest redwood chainsaw sculpture. A logging museum, petting zoo, gift shop, and snack bar round out the facilities.

Standish-Hickey State Recreation Area

One mile north of Leggett, this 1,000-acre forest supports second-growth coast redwoods, firs, bigleaf maples, oaks, and alders. It's also thick with ferns and, in spring, water-loving wildflowers. Camp at any of the three campgrounds here (reservations through ReserveAmerica necessary in summer) or at one of the hike-and-bike campsites, then go fishing, swimming, or on a hike to the 225-foot-tall **Miles Standish Tree,** a massive mature redwood that somehow escaped the loggers. The trail to the tree continues on to a waterfall. The **Mill Creek** trail is a steeper, rugged five-mile loop. For more information, contact: Standish-Hickey State Recreation Area, 69350 Hwy. 101 #2, Leggett, CA 95585, tel. (707) 925-6482.

Drive-Thru-Tree Park

Leggett's "big attraction" is as schlocky as it sounds, but for some reason humans just love driving through trees. They carved this car-sized hole in the tree in the 1930s, and for a small fee people can "drive thru" it (RVs won't make it). For more information, call (707) 925-6363 or (707) 925-6446.

THE LOST (AND FOUND) COAST

Dust off the backpack, get new laces for those hiking boots. This is the place. California's isolated "Lost Coast," virtually uninhabited and more remote than any other stretch of coastline in the Lower 48, has been found. Here steep mountains soar like bald eagles—their domes tufted with chaparral, a few redwoods tucked behind the ears—and sink their grassy, rock-knuckled talons into the surf raging on black-sand beaches. Local people, of course, snort over the very idea that this splendid stretch of unfriendly coast was ever lost in the first place, even if area highways were intentionally routed away from it. *They* knew it was here. And others have known, too, for at least 3,000 years.

Finding a Lost Culture

Much of the Lost Coast is included in two major public preserves: the **King Range National Conservation Area** in Humboldt County, and the **Sinkyone Wilderness State Park** in Mendocino County. Central to the decade-long battle over expanding the Sinkyone Wilderness, which since 1987 has doubled to include 17 more miles of Mendocino coast, was the fate of 75-acre Sally Bell Grove along Little Jackass Creek. The prolonged political skirmish between former property owner Georgia-Pacific (which planned to clear-cut the area) and various private and public agencies focused first on the value of these thousand-year-old trees to posterity. But the war was also over preserving reminders of a lost culture.

Archaeologists believe that a site in the middle of Sally Bell was occupied by proto-Yukian people 3,000 to 8,000 years ago. Chipped-stone tools, stonecutting implements, milling tools, the remains of two houses, and charcoal from long-ago campfires have been discovered at the site. Since those ancient days, for at least 2,500 years up until a century ago, the Sinkyone and Mattole peoples lived permanently along this vast seaside stretch, though other groups came here seasonally when the valleys inland roasted in 100-degree heat. The living was easy, with abundant seafood a dietary staple.

The beaches fringing the King Range were sacred to the Mattole. Descendants talk about the legendary wreck of a Spanish ship along the coast from which the Mattole retrieved triangular gold coins for their children to play with. The coins were lost, however, when their caves along the coast collapsed after the 1906 earthquake. Ancient shell mounds or middens (protected by the Archaeological Resources Protection Act) still dot the seashore. Archaeologists with the U.S. Bureau of Land Management are active throughout the area each summer, and volunteers can occasionally join in on digs. More intriguing, though, is work now underway to establish the nation's first Native American-owned wilderness park, on uplands adjacent to Sinkyone, as a retreat for reestablishing traditional culture. For details, see the accompanying sidebar on the Intertribal Sinkyone Wilderness Park.

Getting There (and Not Getting Lost)

Visiting the Lost Coast requires first getting there, something of a challenge. Roads here are not for the faint of heart nor for those with unreliable vehicles. Unpaved roads are rough and rugged even under the best weather conditions; some wags refer to driving the area as "car hiking." Though Lost Coast road signs usually disappear as fast as they go up (the locals' way of sending a message), existing signs that state Steep Grade—Narrow Road: Campers and Trailers Not Advised roughly translate as "Prepare to drive off the end of the earth, then dive blindly into a fogbank."

From Humboldt Redwoods State Park, take Bull Creek Rd. west through the park and over the rugged mountains down to Honeydew. There turn north on Mattole Rd. and continue north to Petrolia, near the north end of the King Range National Conservation Area. Lost Coast hikers "going the distance" south along the King Range beaches to Shelter Cove often start outside Petrolia, near the squat old lighthouse (reached via Lighthouse Road). Arrange a shuttle system, with pickup at Shelter Cove, to keep it a one-way trip.

The easiest path to the sea is steep, narrow, and serpentine Shelter Cove Rd., which ends up at the hamlet of Shelter Cove, roughly midway down the Lost Coast; from Garberville, take Frontage Rd. one mile to Redway, and go west 26 miles on Briceland/Shelter Cove Road. Off of this road, you can turn north on wild Wilder Ridge Rd., which connects with Mattole Rd. near Honeydew, or turn south on either Briceland Rd. or Chemise Mountain Rd. to reach Sinkyone Wilderness (the last nine miles are unpaved, 4WD-only in winter and never suitable for RVs or trailers). At Four Corners junction, you can take Bear Harbor Rd. down to the ocean at Needle Rock and Bear Harbor, or head south on Usal Rd., which eventually joins Hwy. 1.

From the south, reach Sinkyone Wilderness via Usal Rd., which turns north off Hwy. 1 a few miles north of Rockport (watch carefully—it's easy to miss, especially heading north).

Practical Lost Coast

It's rainy and very wet here from October to April; the area receives 100 to 200 inches of rain annually. The land itself is unstable, with landslides common during the rainy season. Fog is common much of the rest of the year. So in any season, come prepared to get wet. But dress in layers, since in mid-summer it can also get quite warm—in the 80s to 90s—and windy as well.

To hike or backpack the Lost Coast, bring proper shoes. For coastwalking (often through sand but also over rocks), lightweight but sturdy shoes with good ankle support and nonslip tread are best. For hiking the inland backcountry—more grassland than forest due to the thin mountain soil, but also supporting chaparral, mixed stands of conifers and oaks, and omnipresent poison oak—heavy-duty hiking boots are wise. Also bring current maps of the area since hikers here are on their own, sometimes (though not always) trekking for days without meeting another human soul. Ticks, rattlesnakes, and bears can all be problematic here, and if you're planning to hike the beach, bring a tide table (some sections are impassable at high tides). Given the area's remoteness and rugged road conditions, come with a full tank of gas and bring adequate emergency supplies, food, and drinking water.

Mountain bikers will be in heaven here, provided they have strong legs, since "what goes down, must come up."

If you'd rather sightsee from sea, whale-watching charters along the Lost Coast can be arranged through **King Salmon Charters,** 1875 Buhne Dr. #67, Eureka, CA 95503, tel. (707) 442-3474.

KING RANGE NATIONAL CONSERVATION AREA

The northern reaches of the Lost Coast stretch 35 miles from south of the Mattole River to Whale Gulch. Much of the BLM's King Range National Conservation Area, a total of about 60,000 acres of rugged coastal mountains jutting up at 45-degree angles from rocky headlands, is being considered for federal wilderness protection. Despite the fact that most beaches are already closed to motorized vehicles, rebel offroaders are becoming a problem.

Most people come here to "beach backpack," hiking north to south in deference to prevailing winds. The trailhead begins near the mouth of the Mattole River. Get there from Mattole Rd. near Petrolia via Lighthouse Rd., then head south on foot. After about three miles, you'll come to the red-nippled relic of the Punta Gorda light station; the rocks nearby harbor a seabird colony and a rookery for Steller's sea lions. It's possible to continue hiking all the way south to Shelter Cove, a two- or three-day trip one-way (five days roundtrip), but a longer trek for those heading on to Sinkyone.

The trail saunters along miles of sandy beaches, around some tremendous tidepools, and up onto headlands to bypass craggy coves where streams flow to the sea. In wintry weather, this makes for quite the wild walk (check conditions before setting out); in any season, watch for rattlesnakes on rocks or draped over driftwood. Between self-protective downward glances, look around to appreciate some of the impressive shipwrecks scattered along the way. Also just offshore (in proper season) are gray whales, killer whales, porpoises, and harbor seals. Inland, forming an almost animate wall of resistance, are the mountains, their severity thinly disguised by redwoods and Douglas fir, forest meadows, chaparral scrub, and spring wildflowers. Make camp on high ground well back from the restless ocean, and always adhere to the backpacker's credo: if you pack it in, pack it out.

The 16-mile **King's Crest Trail** starts near Horse Mountain Camp and offers spectacular ocean views on rare sunny days, as does the **Chemise Mountain Trail.** Another fine inland hike is the **Buck Creek Trail** from Saddle Mountain, a challenging near-vertical descent through the fog to the beach. (Before taking the challenge, consider the comments scratched by survivors into the government's signs: "It's a real mother both ways" and "This hill will kill you.") Four primitive BLM campgrounds dot the King Range along both main access roads. It's five miles from Four Corners via Chemise Mountain Rd. to **Wailaki Camp,** picnic tables and 16 campsites on Bear Creek's south fork. (From Wailaki Camp, it's a steep 3.5-mile scramble down to the wooden bench below, another half mile to the mouth of Chemise Creek and the beach.) A bit farther is **Nadelos Camp,** with 14 sites. The smaller **Tolkan** and the very pretty, very private **Horse Mountain Camp** are on King Ranch Road.

The camping fee for the various campgrounds is $5-8 per night, and the day-use fee is $1 per day. Permits are required for building fires and using campstoves in the backcountry. All organized groups also need BLM permits. For more information, contact: **King Range National Conservation Area,** U.S. Bureau of Land Management, 1695 Heindon Rd., Arcata, CA 95521, tel. (707) 825-2300, www.ca.blm.gov/arcata/king _range.html; or the **BLM Ukiah Field Office,** 2550 N. State St., Ukiah, CA 95482, tel. (707) 468-4000.

SINKYONE WILDERNESS STATE PARK

Sinking into Sinkyone is like blinking away all known life in order to finally *see.* Named for the Sinkyone people, who refused to abandon their traditional culture and hire on elsewhere as day laborers, this place somehow still honors that indomitable spirit.

More rugged than even the King Range, at Sinkyone Wilderness State Park jagged peaks plunge into untouched tidepools where sea lions and seals play. Unafraid here, wildlife sputters, flutters, or leaps forth at every opportunity. The land seems lusher, greener, with dark virgin forests of redwoods and mixed conifers, rich grassland meadows, waterfalls, fern grottos. The one thing trekkers won't find (yet) among these 7,367 wild acres is a vast trail system. Many miles of the coast are accessible to hikers, and much of the rest of the 40-mile main trail system includes a north/south trail and some logging roads. The trail system connects with trails in the King Range National Conservation Area around the Wailaki area, but you can't reach Sinkyone from Shelter Cove by hiking south along the coast.

Sinkyone Wilderness State Park is always open for day use. The park also offers limited camping at more than 22 scattered and primitive environmental campsites, rarely full. To get oriented, stop by the park's **visitor center** at **Needle Rock Ranch House,** named for an impressive sea stack offshore just beyond the black-sand beach. (Take shelter in the cottage in bad weather—rooms here are now available for rent—otherwise camp under alders and firs nearby.) **Jones Beach** features a secluded cove and an acre of eucalyptus trees at an abandoned homestead (steep trail). Easier to get to is **Stream Side Camp,** two campsites in a wooded creekside glen, with a third perched atop a nearby knoll (with great ocean views, fog permitting). Farther inland is **Low Bridge Camp,** by a stream 1.5 miles from the visitor center.

Beautifully rugged **Bear Harbor** in the Orchard Creek meadow was once a lumber port serving northern Mendocino and southern Humboldt counties. All that's left of the nine-mile-long railroad spur that served the area from the mid-1880s until 1906 is a short rusted section of narrow-gauge track. Fuchsias cascade over the small stone dam. (In late summer, harvest a few apples from the homestead's abandoned orchard before the deer do.)

Energized after the beach trails with no place else to go, hike unpaved Usal Rd., which runs north to south and passes through Bear Harbor. Most cars can't make it past the gully in the road just over a mile south of Bear Harbor, but it's an easy walk from there to Bear Harbor campsites (excellent beach also). Other camp possibilities include a secluded seaside campground at Usal Creek, and two backpackers' camps at Jackass and Little Jackass Creeks.

Campsites are first-come, first-camped ($11 May-Sept., $7 Oct.-April), and the day-use fee is $3 per car in peak season, $2 in the off-season. Solitude seekers, please note that Sinkyone is particularly crowded on summer holiday weekends. For more information, contact: **Sinkyone Wilderness State Park,** P.O. Box 245, Whitethorn, CA 95589, tel. (707) 986-7711 (recorded), or the regional state parks office at **Richardson Grove State Park,** 1600 Hwy. 101 #8, Garberville, CA 95542, tel. (707) 247-3319. You can also pick up a park map at the **Humboldt Redwoods State Park Visitor Center,** on the Avenue of the Giants in Weott, north of Garberville.

LOST (AND FOUND) TOWNS

People in **Briceland** once made a living as bark peelers. There was a plant here built for the purpose of extracting tannic acid from the bark of the tan oak. The spot called **Whitethorn** near the headwaters of the Mattole River was once a busy stage station, then a loud lumber camp with five working sawmills. East of Honeydew is old **Ettersburg,** now posted as **Divorce Flat** and first homesteaded in 1894 by apple grower Alfter Etter.

Honeydew (population two after 5 p.m.) was named for the sweet-tasting aphid dew beneath cottonwoods down by the river. There's a gas

ALMOST LOST LAND: THE INTERTRIBAL SINKYONE WILDERNESS PARK

A side note to the recent expansion of **Sinkyone Wilderness State Park** is how it got expanded, an intriguing tale of life in the modern world. At the end of a complex series of events beginning in the mid-1970s—which included at times almost violent confrontations between logging company employees and protesters—the San Francisco-based Trust for Public Land in 1986 successfully negotiated with Georgia-Pacific to buy 7,100 acres of land appraised at $10.2 million. Seventeen miles of coastline (and 2,900 acres) were deeded by the Trust to the state park system; today the California Coastal Trail runs through it. The state contributed $2.8 million to the pot, but the public received land valued at $5.5 million. Another player in the game, the Save-the-Redwoods League, contributed $1 million and received protective custody of 400 acres of virgin redwoods, including the 75-acre Sally Bell Grove.

In addition, the California Coastal Conservancy lent $1.1 million to the Trust for Public Land to help develop a land-management and marketing plan for timber harvesting and other activities on the remaining 3,900 acres—that plan to be jointly developed by the Coastal Conservancy, interested environmental groups, the Mendocino County Board of Supervisors, and the International Woodworkers Union.

In a particularly unique twist, Native Americans also participated. By 1996—after some contentious public hearings—it was decided that they would have their own park. Working with the Trust for Public Land and the Coastal Conservancy to establish the first American Indian-owned wilderness park, a consortium of some 10 tribal groups finally gained approval for establishing the 3,900-acre **Intertribal Sinkyone Wilderness Park**—the first in the United States to be managed "in traditional ways"—in the uplands of tan oak, second-growth Douglas fir and redwood, and scrubby ceanothus, coyote bush, and berries adjacent to the Sinkyone State Wilderness Park.

A key element of the land-management plan requires the restoration of habitats damaged by logging, though limited logging—to guarantee a sustainable, mature forest—will be allowed. Unusual, though, will be the reestablishment of traditional Native American culture. Though no one will be allowed to live permanently within the intertribal wilderness, plans call for the construction of four villages—built only of traditional materials, in traditional ways—that will be available for rituals, retreats, and other cultural activities. Native groups from around the U.S. and the world are particularly interested in this project—seeing in it a possible model for cultural preservation that can be adopted elsewhere.

For current information about the Intertribal Sinkyone Wilderness Park, contact the nonprofit **Intertribal Sinkyone Wilderness Council,** 190 Ford Rd. #333, Ukiah, CA 95482, tel. (707) 463-6745, fax (707) 462-2088.

station/general store/post office in Honeydew, tel. (707) 629-3310, usually but not necessarily open Mon.-Sat. 9 a.m.-6 p.m., Sunday 10 a.m.-5 p.m. Head-turning from here, though, are the roadside views of Kings Peak and its rugged range. Perfect for picnicking is the **A.W. Way County Park** in the Mattole River valley, loveliest in spring when the wild irises bloom. Nearby is the **"Lost Coast" Mattole River Resort,** 42354 Mattole Rd., tel. (707) 629-3445, which offers housekeeping cottages. Inexpensive.

Fishing is good on the Mattole River between Honeydew and eucalyptus-sheltered **Petrolia,** named for California's first commercial oil well, drilled three miles east of here in the 1860s. Just south of downtown Petrolia is a great place to eat—the **Hideaway** bar and grill, 451 Conklin Creek Rd. (at the Mattole River bridge), tel. (707) 629-3533. It doesn't look like much from the outside, but inside the locals gather for convivial conversation over glasses of Sierra Nevada Pale Ale on tap. The food is good, too. Petrolia also has a well-stocked general store, a gas station, and the deluxe, country-style **Lost Inn** in "downtown" Petrolia, P.O. Box 107, Petrolia, CA 95558, tel. (707) 629-3394, actually a huge two-room suite in the front section of the family home (private entrance through a trellised opening and a private yard and garden). Inside you'll find a queen bed and a futon sleeper couch, a kitchenette, and a large glassed-in front porch perfect for capturing winter sun. An adjoining bedroom can also be rented—a perfect set-up for two couples traveling together. Guests enjoy fresh fruit and vegetables in season. Well-behaved pets are okay on the porch. Rates include full breakfast. Expensive.

Farther north, past the Mattole River lagoon and the road leading to the abandoned Punta Gorda Lighthouse, past the automated light tower atop Cape Ridge (built to replace the 16-sided pyramid tower built there in 1868), and past Cape Mendocino and Scottish-looking farm country lies the very Victorian town of Ferndale, just south of Eureka. As you come down to town, you'll get a great aerial view of the Eel River delta.

The big city on this lost side of the world, though, is **Shelter Cove,** a privately owned enclave within the King Range National Conservation Area once home to the Sinkyone and a major collecting point for the Pomos' clamshell money.

Today, this is the place for soaking up some wilderness within range of humanity, for whale-watching, beachcombing, skin diving, and sportfishing. Declared one of the nation's premier fly-in dining destinations by *Private Pilot* magazine, the remote **Cove Restaurant**—at the northern end of a runway, off Lower Pacific Dr. at 210 Wave Dr., tel. (707) 986-1197—is open Thurs.-Sun. for lunch and dinner. From well-prepared steaks and burgers to fresh fish and shellfish, just about everything's great. **Mario's,** at the marina, tel. (707) 986-1199, is open nightly for dinner and Fri.-Sun. for lunch. The **Shelter Cove Beachcomber Inn,** 7272 Shelter Cove Rd., tel. (707) 986-7733 or toll-free (800) 718-4789 (call between 9 a.m. and 7 p.m. or write), offers secluded rooms with brass beds, private baths, and kitchens, and has a general store. Particularly popular with pilots who can park their planes nearby, the Victorian-style **Ocean Inn Bed and Breakfast** on a bluff overlooking the ocean at 148 Dolphin Dr., tel. (707) 986-7161, features two large and three small ocean-view suites, all with the comforts of home. Moderate-Expensive, but ask about winter packages. The **Shelter Cove RV Campground,** 492 Machi Rd., tel. (707) 986-7474, offers 100 RV sites (tent campers welcome) plus boat launch services and rentals, and a market and deli. Budget. For more information on Shelter Cove, call the **Shelter Cove Information Bureau** at (707) 986-7069, or try the on-line **Shelter Cove Business Directory** at www.sojourner2000.com.

TO MENDOCINO

Travelers heading southwest from Leggett can continue south on scenic Hwy. 1. This route hugs the coast and passes easily missed Usal Rd.—the southern access road to Sinkyone Wilderness; for details, see The Lost (and Found) Coast, above—and the small coastal town of Westport.

Fort Bragg, farther south, is a major highway junction. From there, Hwy. 20 heads east through the forest and over the coastal mountains on a winding route to **Willits,** on Hwy. 101. There travelers can turn north, or turn south and head back toward the wine country. Drive carefully along Hwy. 20, especially in wet weather.

Westport and Rockport

Blink-and-you-miss-it Westport anchors itself around a couple of 90-degree bends in the highway, along a pristine stretch of coast near Westport-Union Landing State Beach. You have to slow down for the turns anyway, so pull over and explore. You may decide to stay awhile. It's not a bad base camp for travelers heading north to the Sinkyone Wilderness. Farther north, tiny Rockport is closer to the Usal Rd. turnoff to Sinkyone, but it's up a gulch away from the sea and generally not as welcoming for visitors as Westport.

The **DeHaven Valley Farm,** 39247 N. Hwy. 1, Westport, tel. (707) 961-1660, www.dehaven-valley-farm.com, is a large 1885-vintage Victorian farmhouse with a total of eight "view" rooms and cottages (two share a bath, five have fireplaces), full breakfast (dinner available in their restaurant). Expensive-Premium. Urbane accommodations are available at the cozy **Howard Creek Ranch** bed and breakfast, 40501 N. Hwy. 1 (near the south end of Usal Rd., north of Westport), tel. (707) 964-6725, fax (707) 964-1603, www.howardcreekranch.com, a New England-style farmhouse and outlying cabins on 40 acres. Most of the 12 rooms, suites, and cabins (including one built around a boat) have private baths. Amenities include gorgeous gardens, a pool, sauna, and wood-heated hot tub. Full, hearty breakfast. Moderate-Luxury.

MENDOCINO AND THE MENDOCINO COAST

People just love Mendocino. They love it for a variety of reasons. Some are smitten by the town's Cape Cod architecture, admittedly a bit odd on the California side of the continent. The seaside saltbox look of the 19th-century wood-frame homes here, explained by the fact that the original settlers were predominantly lumbermen from Maine, is one of the reasons the entire town is included on the National Register of Historic Places. Others love Mendocino for its openly artistic attitude. Of course, almost everyone loves the town's spectacular setting at the mouth of Big River—and at the edge of one of the most sublime coastlines in California.

Everybody loves Mendocino—and as a result, people tend to love Mendocino to death, at least in summer. Not even 1,000 people live here, yet the community is usually clogged with people, pets, and parked cars. Mendocino-area rental homes are inhabited in summer and at other "peak" times, but in the dead of winter, locals can barely find a neighbor to talk to. Besides, almost no one who actually *lives* here can afford to now. Exactly when it was that things

a Mendocino home and garden

TOM MYERS PHOTOGRAPHY

started to change for the worse—well, that depends on whom you talk to.

The Arts and "Culture Vultures"

In the 1950s, when nearby forests had been logged over, the lumbermill was gone, and the once bad and bawdy doghole port of Mendocino City was fading fast, the artists arrived. Living out the idea of making this coastal backwater home were prominent San Francisco painters like Dorr Bothwell, Emmy Lou Packard, and Bill Zacha, who founded the still-strong Mendocino Art Center in 1959. Soon all the arts were in full bloom on these blustery bluffs, and the town had come alive. But even back then, as *Johnny Belinda* film crews rolled through Mendocino streets and James Dean showed up for the filming of *East of Eden,* old-timers and retirees could see what was coming. The town's possibilities could very well destroy it.

In the decades since, the costs of living and doing business in Mendocino have gotten so high that most of Mendocino's artists have long since crawled out of town with their creative tails between their legs—pushed out, locals say, by the more affluent "culture vultures" who consume other people's creativity. Though many fine artists, craftspeople, performers, and writers (including Alice Walker) work throughout Mendocino County, most art, crafts, and consumables sold in Mendocino shops are imported from elsewhere. Even finding a local place to park is nearly impossible in Mendocino, a town too beautiful for its own good.

Mendocino at its Best

Thankfully, in postage-stamp-size Mendocino, cars are an unnecessary headache. You can stroll from one end of town to the other and back again—twice—without breaking a sweat. So leave your car parked at the village lodging of your choice. If you're staying elsewhere, take the bus. Or hike here, or ride a bike. Mendocino is at its best when seen on foot or from the seat of a bike. Note, however, that street addresses in Mendocino can be either three digits or five digits, all in the same block. Fortunately, the town is small and beautiful. So just find the street you need by name and wander along it until you find what you're looking for.

To stroll the streets of Mendocino or explore the headlands at the moodiest, most renewing time, come when most people don't—in November or January. This is the season when Mendocino is still itself, and seems to slip back to a time before this New Englandesque village was even an idea. A sense of that self blasts in from the bleak headlands, come winter, blowing rural reality back into town. In winter you can meet the community—the fishermen, fourth-generation loggers, first-generation marijuana farmers, apple and sheep ranchers, artists and craftspeople, even city-fleeing innkeepers and shopkeepers as they, too, come out of hiding.

The Mendocino Coast: Greater Mendocino

Given Mendocino's proximity to, and dependence on, a number of nearby coastal communities, any visit to Mendocino also includes the coastline for about 10 miles in either direction. The Mendocino Coast business, arts, and entertainment communities are so intertwined that they share a single visitors bureau.

Not counting Garberville, **Fort Bragg** north of Mendocino is the last community of any size before Eureka. Mendocino's working-class sister city to the north was named after a fort built there in 1855 for protection against hostile natives. Unpretentious home now to working (and unemployed) loggers and millworkers, an active fishing fleet, and many of Mendocino's working artists and much of their work, friendly Fort Bragg offers an array of relatively urban services and amenities not found in the smaller Mendocino. Just north of Fort Bragg is tiny **Cleone,** and at the south end of Fort Bragg is **Noyo Harbor,** with its bustling fishing fleet. Approximately halfway between Mendocino and Fort Bragg lies the little hamlet of **Caspar,** which makes Mendocino look like the big city.

Just a few miles south of Mendocino, near Van Damme State Park, is **Little River,** a tiny burg boasting its own post office but most famous for the long-running Little River Inn. A bit farther south is **Albion,** a miniscule coastal hamlet straddling the mouth of the Albion River—a natural harbor supporting a small fishing fleet. From just south of Albion and inland via Hwy. 128 is appealing **Anderson Valley** and its de facto capital **Boonville.**

SEEING AND DOING MENDOCINO

Ford House and Kelley House

Start your Mendocino explorations at the state park's Ford House **interpretive center,** near the public restrooms on the seaward side of Main, tel. (707) 937-5397. The center features a model of Mendocino as it looked 100 years ago, historical photos, exhibits on lumbering and the Pomo Indians, wildflower displays, local art, lots of brochures, free apple cider, and a store selling books and postcards. It's open year-round, daily 11 a.m.-4 p.m. (longer hours if volunteers are available).

Across the street, sedately settled into its old-fashioned gardens, is the 1861 Kelley House (entrance around the front at 45007 Albion), tel. (707) 937-5791, now housing the Mendocino region's historical society museum and library. In addition to taking in the exhibits of pioneer artifacts and historical photos, sign up for a guided walking tour of Mendocino (nominal fee) with **Mendocino Historical Research, Inc.,** which maintains and operates Kelley House as a historical research facility. The museum is open June-Sept., daily 1-4 p.m. (small admission).

Mendocino Art Center

When you're ready to head off around town, a good first destination is the nonprofit Mendocino Art Center, 45200 Little Lake Rd. (between Williams and Kasten), tel. (707) 937-5818 or toll-free (800) 653-3328, fax (707) 937-1764, www. mendocinoartcenter.com, open daily 10 a.m.-5 p.m. Though not without its occasional political problems (like most community-involved organizations worth their salt), this place is a wonder— a genuine *center* for countywide arts awareness and artistic expression. The organization sponsors apprenticeships in ceramics, textiles, and weaving, as well as fine arts programs; maintains an art library and a satellite center in Fort Bragg; and publishes its own free *Arts and Entertainment* magazine, which lists almost every upcoming event in the county. Whatever artistic endeavor is happening in Mendocino County, someone at the center knows about it.

Check out **The Gallery** and **The Showcase** here for exhibits of member artists plus special fine arts and crafts shows. The center also hous-

es three large studios, with the emphasis on textiles and fiber arts, ceramics, and fine arts, respectively. Since the belief here is that art should be accessible to everyone, the art center sponsors weekend art classes Sept.-June, and in summer offers three-week workshops. Very reasonable (shared) accommodations are available in center-sponsored apartments with kitchenettes; if that's not feasible, the art center staff will help with other arrangements.

Mendocino Art Galleries

The number of art galleries in and around Mendocino is staggering. Some seem strictly oriented to the tourist trade while others are more sophisticated.

A veritable fine furniture and woodworking emporium in town is the three-story **Highlight Gallery,** 45052 Main, tel. (707) 937-3132, which also displays handwoven textiles. The **William Zimmer Gallery,** Ukiah and Kasten, tel. (707) 937-5121, offers a large, eclectic collection of highly imaginative, contemporary fine arts and crafts. **Panache Gallery,** 10400 Kasten, tel. (707) 937-1234, specializes in fine art, glassware, and gold jewelry (a second location on Main St. stocks sterling silver jewelry). **Gallery One,** at Hwy. 1 and Main, tel. (707) 937-5154, features fine painting, photography, and works in a variety of other media.

Unique Mendocino Businesses

Despite its small size, Mendocino is stuffed with shops and stores, enough to keep shopping addicts happy for an entire weekend. **Alphonso's Mercantile,** 520 Main St. (between Kasten and Osborne), is a classical music store and smokeshop (even though Alphonso doesn't smoke anymore) with a million-dollar view of the coast. Music lovers should stroll into **Lark in the Morning,** 10460 Kasten St., tel. (707) 937-5275, with its trove of hand drums, unique stringed instruments, and even accordions. If you forgot to pack some summer reading, plan to spend some quality time at the **Gallery Bookshop & Bookwinkle's Children's Books** at Main and Kasten Streets, tel. (707) 937-2215, www.gallerybooks.com, a truly impressive independent bookstore.

Wind & Weather, in the Albion St. water tower (at Kasten), sells all kinds of devices bearing some sort of meteorological relevance—from rain gauges to anemometers to weathervanes, wind chimes, and sundials. Much of the stuff is downright fun. For a complete catalog, call toll-free (800) 922-9463. Also fascinating and very Mendocino is **Mendosa's Merchandise and Market,** 10501 Lansing (at Little Lake), tel. (707) 937-5879, one of those rare *real* hardware stores long gone from most California communities. Quite the contrast but equally wonderful (with its "food for people, not for profit" slogan) is the collectively run **Corners of the Mouth** natural food store, 45015 Ukiah (between Ford and Lansing), tel. (707) 937-5345.

Venerable **Dick's Place,** 45070 Main St., tel. (707) 937-5643, with few concessions to the changing times, is still Mendocino's real bar. Inside, the locals drink beer, plug the jukebox (lots of good Patsy Cline), and play darts. Outside, the bar's sign (a distinctly un-P.C. neon 50s-style martini glass grandfathered in under local anti-neon ordinances) is visible from miles away through the regularly dense coastal fog. Next door, and a sign of changing times, is the **Fetzer Wine Tasting Room,** tel. (707) 937-6191, open daily 10 a.m.-6 p.m.

Other Points of Interest

One of Mendocino's earliest buildings (1852) is its joss house, the **Temple of Kwan Ti,** a half block west of Kasten on Albion (between Kasten and Woodward), tel. (707) 937-4506 or (707) 937-5123, open to the public by appointment only. Though the old wooden temple boasts a bright red, well-maintained paint job, you can't help but get the feeling that the whole thing might well collapse in a strong wind.

Make sure to drop by **Crown Hall,** 45285 Ukiah St. (toward the west end), to see what's going on. The intimate theater hosts everything from local comedy troupes and community plays to big-name touring bands.

SEEING AND DOING FORT BRAGG

Skunk Train

Fort Bragg is the western terminus of the California and Western Railroad's Skunk Train, a sightseeing railroad that winds inland along the redwood-thick and rugged Noyo River gulch and over the mountains to Willits, about 40 track

miles away. The train stops at Northspur, the half-way point, where a little tourist village offers food booths, souvenir stands, and restrooms. You can return to Fort Bragg from here, a half-day roundtrip, or continue on the rest of the way to Willits for a full-day roundtrip. In addition to the Northspur stop, other short unscheduled stops are sometimes made along the way to drop off mail, medicine, and supplies to remote communities along the river. Assuming that brutal winter storms and landslides haven't obliterated the tracks or the dozens of snaking high-wire trestles recently, the ride offers some cliff-hanging nonoceanic scenery and on-board camaraderie. In Willits, the end of the line is the historic Willits railroad station, a small marvel of redwood craftsmanship.

The railroad's "Old No. 45" steam engine, Super Skunk diesel locomotives, or Skunk Motorcars (resembling city-style trolley cars), chug out from the station at Laurel St. in Fort Bragg. In summer, Old No. 45 (a 1924 2-8-2 Baldwin Mikado) runs as far as Northspur and back five days a week; in April, May, and October, it's used on a more limited, weekends-only schedule. The rest of the time, either the Skunks or Super Skunks are used.

The fare is $35 full-day, $27 half-day or one-way for adults; $18 and $14, respectively, for children 3-11. For current schedule information and advance reservations (highly recommended, especially to secure a place on one of the steam-engine runs), contact: **The Skunk Train,** tel.

(707) 964-6371 or toll-free (800) 777-5865, www.skunktrain.com.

Mendocino Coast Botanical Gardens

The nonprofit 47-acre Mendocino Coast Botanical Gardens, 18220 N. Hwy. 1 (two miles south of downtown), tel. (707) 964-4352, www.gardenbythesea.org, features native plant communities as well as formal plantings of rhododendrons, azaleas, fuchsias, and other regional favorites. Also here—in addition to some smashing views of the crashing coast—are a native plant nursery, picnic tables, the fine **Gardens Grill** restaurant, and summertime music concerts. Special events and workshops are offered, too. Wheelchair accessible. The gardens are open daily 9 a.m.-5 p.m. March-Oct., and 9 a.m.-4 p.m. the rest of the year. Admission is $6 general, $5 seniors (60 and up), $3 youths (ages 13-17), and $1 children (ages 6-12).

Historical Fort Bragg

For the local version of redwood logging history, as told through photos, artifacts, and tree-mining memorabilia, stop by the **Guest House Museum,** 343 N. Main St., tel. (707) 961-2840, in an attractive 1892 redwood mansion that was once used as a guest house for friends and customers of local Union Pacific Lumber execs. Small admission. The only remaining **fort building** from the original Fort Bragg stands a block east of the Guest House on Franklin Street.

Current Lumber Operations

Public tours of Georgia-Pacific's Fort Bragg mill are no longer offered, but you can explore the **Georgia Pacific Tree Nursery,** 90 W. Redwood Ave., tel. (707) 964-5651, where you'll have the opportunity to commune with four million seedlings, take a stroll along the nature trail, and picnic—all for free. It's open daily 8 a.m.-4 p.m. April-October. After November 1, the youngsters here take root in nearby forests, and a new nursery population takes their place.

Noyo Harbor

Fort Bragg's tiny fishing port lies at the south end of town, at the mouth of the Noyo River. It's a safe harbor for fisherfolk during stormy seas and shelters several fish restaurants popular with tourists, but fairly ho-hum in terms of cuisine and ambience. Don't miss Noyo's **Salmon Barbecue** festivities every July. It's a must-attend event for delicious fresh salmon and an intimate encounter with the local populace. Good folks, good food, big tradition.

Other Fort Bragg Attractions

People think first of Mendocino when they think of art galleries, but Fort Bragg has at least as many—and more of the "working artist" variety. Not to be missed is the nonprofit **Northcoast Artists Collaborative Gallery,** 362 N. Main St., tel. (707) 964-8266, with everything from wearable art (weavings and handpainted silk scarves)

the Skunk Train

TOM MYERS PHOTOGRAPHY

Fishing is the way of life in Noyo Harbor.

and handcrafted jewelry to original art, prints, pottery, photographs, and greeting cards made by member artists. A very impressive enterprise. Also drop by the **Fort Bragg Center for the Arts,** 337 N. Franklin St., tel. (707) 964-0807, to see what's going on. The center is within Fort Bragg's **Gallery District**—between Main and Franklin, and Redwood and Fir—so while you're in the area, see what else looks interesting. North Franklin St. between Laurel and Redwood boasts a number of **antique shops.**

Also unique in Fort Bragg is **Adirondack Design,** 350 Cypress St., P.O. Box 656, Fort Bragg, CA 95437, tel. (707) 964-4940 or toll-free (888) 643-3003 (orders only), www.adirondackdesign.com. Founded by a group known as Parents and Friends, Inc., Adirondack Design provides jobs and services for the area's developmentally disabled adults. And what a job this crew does—crafting a high-quality line of redwood garden furniture and accessories, everything from Adirondack chairs, loveseats, rockers, and swings to garden benches and planters, cold frames, and a charming "bird chalet." Adirondack even produces a small footbridge.

MENDOCINO AREA PARKS AND RECREATION

Mendocino Headlands State Park
Start exploring the area's spectacular state parks in Mendocino proper. About the only reason

there aren't shopping malls or condos and resort hotels between the town of Mendocino and its sea-stacked sandstone coast was the political creativity of William Penn Mott, the state's former director of Parks and Recreation. Mott quietly acquired the land for what is now Mendocino Headlands State Park by trading Boise Cascade some equally valuable timberlands in nearby Jackson State Forest.

The headlands and beach are subtle, more a monument to sand sculpture than an all-out ode to hard rock. The impressive stacks here and elsewhere are all that remain of sandstone headlands after eons of ocean erosion. Curving seaward around the town from Big River to the northern end of Heeser Dr., the park includes a three-mile hiking trail, a small beach along the mouth of Big River (trailheads and parking on Hwy. 1, just north of the bridge), sandstone bluffs, the area's notorious wave tunnels, offshore islands and narrows, and good tidepools. *The* peak experience from the headlands is whalewatching. (Whether watching the waves or whales, stand back from the bluff's edge. Sandstone is notoriously unstable, and the ragged rocks and wicked waves below are at best indifferent to human welfare.) For a map and more information, get oriented at Ford House or contact: Mendocino State Parks, P.O. Box 440, Mendocino, CA 95460, tel. (707) 937-5804. You can easily walk here from town—it's an invigorating and spectacular stroll away. Pick up the path at the west end of Main Street.

Van Damme State Park

This small state park just south of Mendocino is not famous but is one of the finer things about this stretch of the coast. The excellent and convenient camping here midway between Mendocino and Albion is secondary. This 1,831-acre, five-mile-long preserve around Little River's watershed points out to sea. Squeezed into a lush ravine of second-growth mixed redwood forest, Van Damme's pride is its **Fern Canyon Trail**, a 2.5-mile hiking and bicycling trail weaving across Little River through red alders, redwoods, ferns—western sword ferns, deer ferns, bird's foot ferns, and five-finger ferns, among others—and past mossy rocks, pools, and streamside herds of horsetails. A new 1.5-mile trail offers a self-guided tour of the coho salmon's life cycle.

Though the Fern Canyon Trail is easy, the going gets tougher at the east end as the path climbs the canyon and connects with the loop trail to Van Damme's **Pygmy Forest,** a gnarly thicket bonsaied by nature. What makes the pygmy forest pygmy? Beneath the thin layer of darker topsoil underfoot is *podzol* (Russian for "colored soil")—albino-gray soil as acidic as vinegar. Iron and other elements leached from the podzol collect below in a reddish hardpan layer impossible for tree roots (even moisture, for that matter) to penetrate. Similar fairy forests are common throughout coastal shelf plant communities between Salt Point State Park and Fort Bragg, an area sometimes referred to as the Mendocino White Plains. It is possible to drive most of the way to this green grove of miniatures via Airport Rd. just south of the park, and the forest is wheelchair accessible. A short self-guided discovery trail here loops through dwarfed Bolander pine (a coastal relative of the Sierra Nevada's looming lodgepole), Bishop pine, Mendocino pygmy cypress (found only between Anchor Bay and Fort Bragg), and dwarf manzanita. Also noteworthy are the spring-blooming rhododendrons, which love acidic soils and here dwarf the trees.

Van Damme's tiny beach is a popular launch point for scuba divers and is usually safe for swimming, though no lifeguards are on duty. (The 1996 addition of Spring Ranch added more beach, and some spectacular tidepools.) The redwood-sheltered campground area is protected from winds but not its own popularity; you'll need reservations April 1-October 11. A small group camp is also available.

After breakfast, stop by the visitor center and **museum** in the impressive Depression-era Civilian Conservation Corps rec hall built from hand-split timbers. Or take the short **Bog Trail** loop from the visitor center to see (and smell) the skunk cabbage and other marsh-loving life. For more information, contact the regional state parks office (see above) or Van Damme State Park, tel. (707) 937-5804. Reserve campsites ($16) in advance through ReserveAmerica, toll-free tel. (800) 444-7275. The park's day-use fee is $5.

Russian Gulch State Park

Just north of Mendocino on the site of another

Fern Canyon Trail

TOM MYERS PHOTOGRAPHY

days-past doghole port, Russian Gulch State Park is 1,200 acres of diverse redwood forests in a canyon thick with rhododendrons, azaleas, berry bushes, and ferns; coastal headlands painted in spring with wildflowers; and a broad bay with tidepools and sandy beach, perfect for scuba diving. Especially fabulous during a strong spring storm is the flower-lined cauldron of **Devil's Punch Bowl** in the middle of a meadow on the northern headlands. A portion of this 200-foot wave tunnel collapsed, forming an inland blowhole, but the devil's brew won't blast through unless the sea bubbles and boils.

Russian Gulch is a peaceable kingdom, though, perfect for birdwatching, whalewatching, and watching steelhead in their spawning waters. After a picnic on the headlands, take a half-day hike upcanyon. Make it a nine-mile loop by combining the southern trails to reach 36-foot **Russian Gulch Falls** (best in spring), then loop back to camp on the North Trail. (One of these trail links, the five-mile **Canyon Trail,** is also designated as a biking trail.) The far northern **Boundary Trail** is for hikers and horse-backers, running from the horse camp on the eastern edge of the park to the campground.

Camping at Russian Gulch is itself an attraction, with 30 family campsites ($16) tucked into the forested canyon; amenities include barbecue grills, picnic tables, food lockers, hot showers, and restrooms with laundry tubs. The separate group camp accommodates about 40 people. (This close to the coast, campers often sleep under a blanket of fog, so come prepared for wet conditions.) Reserve campsites in advance through ReserveAmerica, toll-free tel. (800) 444-7275. For more information, contact the Mendocino State Parks headquarters here, tel. (707) 937-5804. The day-use fee is $5.

Caspar Headlands
State Beach and Reserve

Just north of Russian Gulch, and reached via Pt. Cabrillo Dr., are the Caspar Headlands, hemmed in by housing. Miles of beaches are open to the public, though, from sunrise to sunset—perfect for whalewatching. The headlands are accessible only by permit. A particular point of interest is the historic 300-acre **Point Cabrillo Light Station and Preserve.** The big news lately is that 19th-century technology replaced

that of the 20th-century in 1998, thanks to the restoration efforts of dedicated volunteers. The light station's original Fresnel lens once again casts its light seaward. Though access to buildings is not allowed during restoration, which continues, guided walks of the area are offered May-Sept. on Sunday at 11 a.m.

For details about headlands access, call (707) 937-5804. For information on whalewatching weekends and guided 1.5-mile walks at the preserve, call (707) 937-0816 or try www.pointcabrillo.org.

Jug Handle State Reserve

For serious naturalists, the "ecological staircase" hike at this reserve just north of Caspar is well worth a few hours of wandering. The staircase itself is a series of uplifted marine terraces, each 100 feet higher than the last, crafted by nature. The fascination here is the *change* associated with each step up the earth ladder, expressed by distinctive plants that also slowly change the environment.

The first terrace was a sand and gravel beach in its infancy, some 100,000 years ago, and is now home to salt-tolerant and wind-resistant wildflowers. (Underwater just offshore is an embryonic new terrace in the very slow process of being born from the sea.) A conifer forest of Sitka spruce, Bishop pine, fir, and hemlock dominates the second terrace, redwoods and Douglas fir the third. Jug Handle is an example of Mendocino's amazing ecological place in the scheme of things, since the area is essentially a biological borderline for many tree species. Metaphorically speaking, Alaska meets Mexico when Sitka spruce and Bishop pine grow side by side. The phenomenon of the hardpan-hampered Mendocino pygmy forest starts on the third step, transitioning back into old-dune pine forests, then more pygmy forest on the fourth step. At the top of the stairs on the final half-million-year-old step, are more pygmy trees, these giving ground to redwoods.

The only way to get to the staircase trail is by heading west from the parking lot to Jug Handle Bay, then east again on the trails as marked, hiking under the highway. The trail was in some disrepair recently, so heads up. For more information about Jug Handle State Preserve, contact the Mendocino area state parks headquarters at Russian Gulch State Park, tel. (707) 937-5804, open Mon.-Fri. 8 a.m.-4:30 p.m.

Jackson State Forest

Bordering Jug Handle Reserve on the east is this 46,000-acre demonstration forest named after Jacob Green Jackson, founder of the Caspar Lumber Company. Extending east along the South Fork of the Noyo River and Hwy. 20, the Jackson Forest (logged since the 1850s) has picnic and camping areas, and almost unlimited trails for biking, hiking, and horseback riding. The forest is accessible at various points east off Hwy. 1 and along Hwy. 20; a forest map is necessary to get around. For more information (and a map), contact: **California Department of Forestry**, 802 N. Main St., P.O. Box 1185, Fort Bragg, CA 95437, tel. (707) 964-5674.

Mendocino Woodland
State Park and Outdoor Center

Entwined with Jackson State Forest about nine miles east of Mendocino is this woodsy 1930s camp facility—actually three separate facilities and some 200 separate buildings constructed by federal Works Progress Administration and Civilian Conservation Corps workers. Available for group retreats, each of the three rustic camps includes a well-equipped kitchen, a dining hall complete with stone fireplace, cabins, and spacious bathroom and shower facilities with both hot and cold running water. For more information, contact the nonprofit **Mendocino Woodlands Camp Association**, P.O. Box 267, Mendocino, CA 95460, tel. (707) 937-5755, www.mcn.org/1/woodlands.

MacKerricher State Park

This gorgeous stretch of ocean and forested coastal prairie starts three miles north of Fort Bragg and continues northward for seven miles. Down on the beach, you can stroll for hours past white-sand beaches, black-sand beaches, remote dunes, sheer cliffs and headlands, offshore islands, pounding surf, rocky outcroppings, and abundant tidepools. Or you can stay up atop the low bluff paralleling the shore, where you'll revel in great ocean views and, in spring, an abundance of delicate, butterfly-speckled wildflowers—baby blue eyes, sea pinks, buttercups, and wild iris.

The park's usage is de facto separated into two areas: the tourist area (crowded) and the locals' areas (desolate). Tourist usage centers around the park's little **Lake Cleone**, a fishable freshwater lagoon near the campground and picnic area. Nearby are a picturesque crescent beach pounded by a thundering shore break, and the **Laguna Point** day-use area (wheelchair accessible), a popular place for watching whales offshore and harbor seals onshore. (Another good local spot for whalewatching is **Todd's Point**, south of the Noyo Bridge, then west on Ocean View). That's the tourist's MacKerricher. Not bad.

Which leaves the locals and savvy passersby to enjoy in blissful, meditative solitude the extensive areas to the south and north, which are connected to the lake/campground area by the eight-mile-long **Old Haul Road**. Once used by logging trucks, the now-abandoned haul road parallels the shore from **Pudding Creek Beach** in the south to **Ten Mile River** in the north. Only a short stretch of the road is open to vehicles, so it's a great path for bicyclists and joggers. North of the campground area, the asphalt road gradually deteriorates until it gets buried completely by the deserted and exquisitely lovely Ten Mile Dunes; if you venture up the coast this far, you'll likely have it all to yourself. South of the campground, the road passes a few vacation homes and a gravel plant before ending up just past a parking lot and a phalanx of beachfront tourist motels. (If you wander far enough south, you'll end up at Fort Bragg's **Glass Beach** just north of town, where if you're lucky you might find a Japanese fishing float or an occasional something from a shipwreck.) Either way, you'll get magnificent ocean views and plenty of solitude.

The fine campgrounds at MacKerricher are woven into open woods of beach, Monterey, and Bishop pines. Campsites are abundant ($16, no hookups), and amenities include picnic tables, food lockers, fire rings, full bathrooms, and hot showers. It's a popular place, so reservations are wise; call ReserveAmerica toll-free, tel. (800) 444-7275. No day-use fee. For more information, call MacKerricher at (707) 964-9112 or the Mendocino state parks headquarters at (707) 937-5804.

kayaking in MacKerricher State Park

TOM MYERS PHOTOGRAPHY

Canoeing, Kayaking, Diving, and Bicycling

For sightseeing afloat practically in Mendocino, catch a canoe (or kayak) from among the **Catch a Canoe and Bikes Too!** fleet, at the Stanford Inn by the Sea (on the south bank of Big River), 44850 Comptche-Ukiah Rd., tel. (707) 937-0273 or toll-free (800) 320-2453. Birders especially will enjoy the serene estuarine tour of Big River. Catch a Canoe also rents bicycles and can offer tips on the best area rides. **Dive Crazy Adventures** in Albion, tel. (707) 937-3079, also offers kayaks and tours, dive charters, and other adventures. **North Coast Divers Supply,** 19275 S. Harbor Dr. in Fort Bragg, tel. (707) 961-1143, offers diving supplies and expertise. **Lost Coast Adventures,** tel. (707) 937-2434, offers Sea-Cave Tours at Van Damme State Park in sit-on-top ocean kayaks. At last report **free, ranger-guided canoe trips** (for age 6 and older) were still offered in summer at **Navarro River Redwoods State Park** south of Mendocino. For details, call (707) 937-5804.

Near Fort Bragg, MacKerricher's Haul Rd. is a cycle path par excellence. Rent mountain bikes, 10-speeds, and two-seaters at **Fort Bragg Cyclery,** 579 S. Franklin St., tel. (707) 964-3509.

Horseback Riding and Llama Treks

Ricochet Ridge Ranch, 24201 N. Hwy. 1, located north of Fort Bragg in Cleone, across the highway from the entrance to MacKerricher State Park, tel. (707) 964-7669, offers a daily horse-back trail ride along the beach at MacKerricher, as well as other rides (English/Western) by advance arrangement. **Back Kountry Trailrides,** about 14 miles east of Fort Bragg, tel. (707) 964-2700, www.bktrailrides.com, offers guided rides along redwood trails. For a guided llama trip, contact **Llama Treks,** tel. (707) 964-7120, www.lodgingandllamas.com.

EXCURSION INLAND: ANDERSON VALLEY

South of Little River and Albion., Hwy. 128 snakes southwest through the Anderson Valley, a route that leads ultimately to Cloverdale and the northern fringe of the Sonoma County wine country. In addition to several appealing parks, the Anderson Valley boasts some excellent wineries—**Greenwood Ridge** (home to the annual California Wine Tasting Championships), **Navarro, Husch, Roederer, Scharffenberger,** and **Handley Cellars** among them, outposts of the new north coast economy. The valley also boasts seasonal roadside produce stands and the intriguing small town of **Boonville,** home to the exceptional **Boonville Hotel,** tel. (707) 895-2210, www.boonvillehotel.com; the rabble-rousing *Anderson Valley Advertiser,* one of the state's most intriguing newspapers; and the refreshingly noncommercial **Mendocino County Fair and Apple Show,** held in mid-September.

For more information on the Anderson Valley area, contact the **Anderson Valley Chamber of Commerce,** P.O. Box 275, Boonville, CA 95414, tel. (707) 895-2379, or the **Greater Ukiah Chamber of Commerce,** 200 S. School St., Ukiah, CA 95482, tel. (707) 462-4705.

STAYING IN AND NEAR MENDOCINO

The battle of the bed and breakfasts in and around Mendocino is just one aspect of the continuing local war over commercial and residential development. The conversion of homes to bed-and-breakfast establishments means fewer housing options for people who live here, but a moratorium on B&Bs means higher prices for visitor accommodations. Most people here agree on one thing: only developers want to see large-scale housing or recreation developments in the area.

Avoid contributing to the problem altogether by camping. There are almost endless choices among the state parks nearby, and some very enjoyable, very reasonable alternatives inland along Hwy. 128 toward Ukiah. More than 2,000 commercial guest rooms are available in and around Mendocino, but that doesn't mean there's room at the inn (or motel) for spontaneous travelers. Usually people can find last-minute lodgings of some sort in Fort Bragg, though the general rule here is plan ahead or risk sleeping in your car or nestled up against your bicycle in the cold fog.

To stay in style in Mendocino, there are some great places to choose from. Advance reservations are absolutely necessary at most places on most weekends and during summer, preferably at least one month in advance (longer for greater choice). Most bed and breakfasts require a two-night minimum stay on weekends (three-night for holiday weekends) and an advance deposit.

A number of the inns listed below, in both Mendocino and Fort Bragg, are members of the **Mendocino Coast Innkeepers Association,** P.O. Box 1141, Mendocino, CA 95460, and if one inn is full, it's possible that another can be accommodating. (Request a current brochure for full information.) **Mendocino Coast Reservations,** 1000 Main St., P.O. Box 1143, Mendocino, CA 95460, tel. (707) 937-1000, (707) 937-5033, or toll-free (800) 262-7801, www.mendocinovacations.com, offers 60 or so fully furnished rentals by the weekend, week, or month, from cottages and cabins to homes and family reunion-sized retreats.

Mendocino Hotel
The grand 1878 **Mendocino Hotel & Garden Suites,** 45080 Main St., tel. (707) 937-0511 or toll-free (800) 548-0513, fax (707) 937-0513, www.mendocinohotel.com, is one of those Mendocino experiences everyone should try at least once. All 51 of its meticulous rooms and suites— 24 Victorian rooms and two suites in the historic building, and 25 one- and two-story garden rooms and suites—are furnished in American and European antiques; many have fireplaces or wood-burning stoves and views of Mendocino Bay or the one-acre gardens, plus such not-like-home little luxuries as heated towel racks, fresh flowers from someone else's garden, and chocolate truffles on the pillow at bedtime. The hotel's parlor (note the 18th-century sculpted steel fireplace) is infused with informal Victorian coziness, more casual than the crystal-studded dining room. Victorian rooms with in-room washbasins and shared baths (across the hall) are Moderate. Other rooms are Premium-Luxury— but inquire about off-season specials, which can be quite attractive.

Bed and Breakfasts in the Village
Selecting "the best" bed and breakfasts in an area like Mendocino is like asking parents which of their children they love best. A new star in town, and amazingly elegant even for Mendocino, is **The Whitegate Inn,** 499 Howard St., tel. (707) 937-4892 or toll-free (800) 531-7282, fax (707) 937-1131, www.whitegateinn.com. This classic Victorian itself served as a star vehicle— in the classic *The Russians Are Coming* as well as Julia Roberts's *Dying Young* and Bette Davis's *Strangers*. But visitors don't stay strangers for long, once they step past that white gate and succumb to the Whitegate's charms— particularly if exquisite style and gourmet breakfasts served on bone china add up to the perfect escape. The entire inn, including the seven guest rooms, is impeccably decorated in French, Italian, and Victorian antiques. Amenities include fireplaces, European featherbeds and toiletries, down comforters, TVs, and clock radios—not to

mention fresh-baked cookies and bedtime chocolates. Breakfast is also a sumptuous experience, with specialties such as pecan-and-date pancakes, eggs Florentine, and—everyone's favorite—caramel apple French toast. But don't forget to smell the roses, and all the other flowers in the spectacular cottage garden.

The charming **MacCallum House,** 45020 Albion St., tel. (707) 937-0289 or toll-free (800) 609-0492, www.maccallumhouse.com, is the town's most venerable bed and breakfast. This 1882 Victorian and its barn rooms and garden cottages, lovingly restored, still have a friendly quilts-and-steamer-trunk feel—like a fantasy weekend visit to Grandma's farm, if Grandma had some sense of style. MacCallum House features a total of 19 rooms, all with private baths. Six are in the main house, some of these named after members of the MacCallum family; the master bedroom features a fabulous mahogany sleigh bed. Another six are in the barn, including the very special Upper Barn Loft. Of the seven cottages, the Gazebo Playhouse is most affordable, and the Greenhouse Cottage is wheelchair accessible. Rates include a creative continental breakfast. Expensive-Luxury, but ask about the Winter Whale Watch Special and other packages. Also on the premises are the excellent **MacCallum House Restaurant** and the **Grey Whale Bar & Café,** tel. (707) 937-5763, www.maccallumhousedining.com, owned and overseen by Chef Alan Kantor, a graduate of the Culinary Institute of America. Both serve regional cuisine (seasonally changing menu), including fresh seafood and shellfish, meats and poultry, organic produce, and north coast wines. And don't miss the house-made ice creams. Reservations recommended.

The fine **Joshua Grindle Inn,** 44800 Little Lake Rd., tel. (707) 937-4143 or toll-free (800) 474-6353, www.joshgrin.com, is a New England country-style inn with 10 exquisite rooms furnished with Early Americana. The historic main building, surrounded with stunning cypress, was built in 1879 by local banker Joshua Grindle. All have private bathrooms; most feature wood-burning fireplaces or woodstoves; and some have deep soak tubs or other special features. Particularly inviting, for a little extra privacy, are the two large rooms in the converted water tower out back and the two "saltbox cottage" rooms.

Rates include a sumptuous full breakfast. (To take the experience home with you, for future nourishment, buy a copy of *Mendocino Mornings: A Collection of Breakfast Delights from the Joshua Grindle Inn.*) Premium-Luxury, but ask about the inn's various off-season packages, including the Off the Treadmill; Bed, Breakfast & Beaujolais; Grindle and Gardens Getaway; Mendocino Music Festival; and A Country Christmas specials. Joshua Grindle also offers an ocean-view guesthouse, located near the Point Cabrillo Light Station, north of Russian Gulch State Park.

For something more contemporary and "country," try the **Agate Cove Inn,** just north of downtown at 11201 N. Lansing St., tel. (707) 937-0551 or toll-free (800) 527-3111, fax (707) 937-0550, www.agatecove.com, which offers two rooms in an 1860s farmhouse (built by Mathias Brinzing, founder of Mendocino's first brewery) and a cluster of eight cottages, all on an acre and a half of beautifully landscaped grounds. Most rooms have fireplaces and ocean views; all have private baths, country decor, and beds with Scandia down comforters. Enjoy a fabulous full country breakfast (cooked on an antique woodstove) of omelettes or other entrées with country sausage or ham, homebaked breads, jams and jellies, and coffee or tea. Premium-Luxury. The **Sea Rock Bed and Breakfast Inn,** 11101 Lansing St., tel. (707) 937-0926 or toll-free (800) 906-0926, www.searock.com, is also a collection of country cottages and guest rooms, most of these with Franklin fireplaces; a few have kitchens, and all have private bath, queen bed, cable TV, and VCR. Breakfast buffet served in the lobby. Premium-Luxury.

The John Dougherty House Bed & Breakfast, 571 Ukiah St., tel. (707) 937-5266 or toll-free (800) 486-2104, www.jdhouse.com, is a Mendocino classic. This 1867 Saltbox, surrounded by English gardens and filled with Early American antiques, is included on the town's historic house tour. Its two light, airy suites and six rooms all have private baths, and some have spa tubs and woodstoves. There's also a charming cabin in the garden. Bountiful hot breakfast. Premium-Luxury.

The **Blue Heron Inn,** 10390 Kasten St., tel. (707) 937-4323, www.theblueheron.com, is a small charmer in the European country tradition and just a half-block from the ocean. Two of the inn's lovely and stylish upstairs rooms share a bath; the other has a private bath. Great ocean views from the deck. Expensive. Downstairs is the popular **Moosse Café,** open for lunch (brunch on Sunday) and dinner daily.

Also in town is the **Sea Gull Inn B&B,** 44960 Albion St., tel. (707) 937-5204 or toll-free (888) 937-5204, www.mcn.org/a/seagull/, where an overnight can be quite reasonable (particularly in The Shed). Inexpensive-Luxury. The **Headlands Inn,** at the corner of Albion and Howard Streets, tel. (707) 937-4431, fax (707) 937-0421, www.mcn.org/b/headlands/, is a fully restored 1868 Victorian saltbox with six rooms, each with antiques, private bath, and fireplace. In-room extras include fresh flowers, fruit, and a city newspaper. Two parlors, an English-style garden, and complimentary full breakfast, afternoon tea, and refreshments round out the amenities. Premium-Luxury.

The **Mendocino Village Inn Bed and Breakfast,** 44860 Main, tel. (707) 937-0246 or toll-free (800) 882-7029, www.mendocinoinn. com, is a New England-style Victorian circa 1882, with 10 guest rooms (two share a bath), many with fireplace or woodstove. The two attic rooms share a bath and are quite affordable. Full breakfast. Moderate-Luxury. Guests also have full spa privileges at the affiliated and adjacent **Sweetwater Spa & Inn,** 44840 Main St., tel. (707) 937-4076 or toll-free (800) 300-4140, www.sweetwaterspa.com, which offers rooms and cottages in an 1870 Victorian elsewhere in the village, also south of Mendocino in Little River. All rooms except one have private baths; most have woodstoves or fireplaces. Moderate-Luxury. Night owls, ask about the Sweetwater's special "late night" accommodations—available 11 p.m.-11 a.m. only, and including a double bed, private bath, sauna, and hot tub. Moderate.

Stanford Inn by the Sea

How organic can you get? To find out, head for the comfortably luxurious yet outdoorsy Stanford Inn by the Sea (known in a previous incarnation as the Big River Lodge), 44850 Comptche-Ukiah Rd. (at Hwy. 1, on the south bank of Big River), tel. (707) 937-5615 or toll-free (800) 331-8884, fax (707) 937-0305, www.stanfordinn.com. This is an elegant but friendly lodge in the country tradition, with big gardens. But here, the working certified organic garden and farm—Big River Nurseries—dominate the setting. The swimming pool, sauna, and spa are enclosed in one of the farm's greenhouses. The on-site **The Ravens** restaurant is strictly (and deliciously) vegetarian and/or vegan, even serving organic wines. The inn may be organic, but it's not overly fussy—pets are welcome, for a fee, and "guest-friendly" dogs, cats, llamas, and swans are available for those who arrive petless. The Stanford Inn also provides exercise facilities and complimentary mountain bikes; canoe and kayak rentals are available.

The 33 guest rooms and suites are inviting and outdoorsy, paneled in pine and redwood, and decked out with big four-poster or sleigh beds and decent reading lights. Each features a wood-burning fireplace or Irish Waterford stove, as well as house plants and original local art. Amenities include in-room coffee makers and refrigerators, TV with cable and Cinemax, and stereos with CD players (on-site CD library, or bring your own). Luxury, complimentary gourmet breakfast included, but ask about the Stanford Inn's Health Kick and other special packages.

Bed and Breakfasts near the Village

Heading north, the **Brewery Gulch Inn,** 9350 N. Hwy. 1, tel. (707) 937-4752, fax (707) 937-1736, www.redwoodinn.net, is a pre-Victorian farmhouse in a farmlike setting surrounded by gardens, orchards, open pastureland, and coastal forests. The 10-acre spread is sheltered from harsh winds and sometimes even sidesteps the fog. Small and intimate (just five rooms, two with shared bath), the inn boasts appealing features including a stone fireplace, French doors, a deck, and hearty breakfasts. From the hollow here, it's a 10-minute walk to Mendocino along the bluffs. Moderate-Luxury.

Or head south. Rachel Binah is a creative cook and caterer also noted for her **Rachel's Inn,** 8200 N. Hwy. 1, tel. (707) 937-0088 or toll-free (800) 347-9252, www.rachelsinn.com, with five rooms in the Victorian farmhouse and four suites in the adjacent barn. Just north of Van Damme State Park, the inn abuts an undeveloped strip of the park just two miles south of Mendocino. Each room has its own bathroom, a big bed, fresh flowers and personal amenities, plus individual charm: a view of the ocean or gardens, a balcony, or a fireplace. If you rent all or a combination of rooms for a casual conference or family gathering, special dinners can be arranged. Any day of the week, a good full breakfast is served in the dining room. Premium-Luxury.

Across the highway is **Glendeven,** 8221 N. Hwy. 1, tel. (707) 937-0083 or toll-free (800) 822-4536, fax (707) 937-6108, www.glendeven.com, a part-inn, part-art gallery featuring quilted paper and other textile works, abstract art, and handcrafted furniture. Declared one of the 10 best inns in the U.S. by *Country Inns* magazine, Glendeven's charms start with the New England Federalist farmhouse, continue into the secluded and luxurious Carriage House, and also surround the Stevenscroft annex. Many rooms and suites feature fireplaces and ocean views. Not to mention every imaginable amenity and sumptuous breakfast. Premium-Luxury.

South of Mendocino are several other options. Notable among them is **Cypress Cove** on Chapman Point, 45200 Chapman Dr., tel. (707) 937-1456 or toll-free (800) 942-6300, www.cypresscove.com—quite the place to get away from it all. The property's two luxury suites look out on Mendocino and the bay. Amenities include queen beds, fireplaces, and two-person jacuzzi tubs. Among the plush extras: in-room coffee, tea, brandy, chocolate, fresh flowers, and bathrobes. One suite has a full kitchen, the other a kitchenette. Luxury.

In Little River, the folksy **The Inn at Schoolhouse Creek,** 7051 N. Hwy. 1, tel. (707) 937-5525 or toll-free (800) 731-5525, www.binnb.com, features restored 1930s country-style garden cottages looking downslope to the ocean. All have a fireplace, private bath, and a TV and VCR. Rates include full breakfast, access to the welcoming lodge (books, games, and breakfast), and a chance to jump into that hot tub.

Farther south and right along the highway is the beautiful **Albion River Inn,** 3790 N. Hwy. 1, Albion, tel. (707) 937-1919 or toll-free (800) 479-7944, www.albionriverinn.com, offering 22 rooms in blufftop cottages, each one unique. Fireplaces, decks, and ocean views are par for the course here, and the inn's elegant and très-

gourmet restaurant draws locals south from Mendocino and Fort Bragg. Rates include full breakfast, wine, coffee and tea, and morning newspaper. Luxury.

The unusually charismatic **Fensalden Inn,** seven miles south of Mendocino and then inland, at 33810 Navarro Ridge Rd., Albion, tel. (707) 937-4042 or toll-free (800) 959-3850, www.fensalden.com, is a restored two-story stage station circa 1880, still straddling the ridgetop among open fields and forests. Under new ownership, the eight charming rooms feature exquisite antiques; all have fireplaces. For the more rustically inclined, there's also a Rustic Bungalow. Hors d'oeuvres, wine, and full breakfast are complimentary. Premium-Luxury.

Little River Inn

In "downtown" Little River, the classic stay is the family-owned **Little River Inn,** just south of Van Damme State Park at 7751 N. Hwy. 1, tel. (707) 937-5942 or toll-free (888) 466-5683, fax (707) 937-3944, www.littleriverinn.com, originally just one rambling old mansion built by lumberman Silas Coombs in the area's characteristic Maine style. (To get the whole story, buy a copy of *The Finn, the Twin, and the Inn: A History of the Little River Inn and Its Families.*) The Little River Inn has grown over the years. In addition to its classic fireplace cottages and updated lodging annex, it also includes new romantic luxury suites just up the hill—complete with gigantic jacuzzi tubs, wood-burning fireplaces, view decks and patios, and every imaginable amenity.

The inn also offers an 18-hole golf course—the only one on the Mendocino Coast—and tennis facilities. (For tee times, call 707-937-5667.) In addition to full meeting and small-conference facilities, new is **The Third Court** day spa, with a full menu of men's and women's body and facial massages, skin treatments, and hair and nail care. (For spa reservations, call 707-937-3099.) The old inn itself is still a slice of Victorian gingerbread. Upstairs are two small and affordable rooms—and really the best, in terms of period charm: quilt-padded attic accommodations illuminated by tiny seaward-spying dome windows. The Little River Inn is a wonderful place, all the way around. Expensive-Luxury (but inquire about specials and packages). Two-night minimum stay on weekends, three-night on holiday weekends.

Tucked in behind appealing **Ole's Whale Watch Bar** (good bar menu) is the Little River Inn's **Garden Dining Room.** The restaurant serves great food, including simple and excellent white-tablecloth breakfasts with Swedish pancakes, absolutely perfect eggs, and fresh-squeezed orange or grapefruit juice. The inn's restaurant is just about the only room in sight without an ocean view, but it does feature many windows—these opening out into lush and inviting gardens.

Heritage House

South of Little River proper, the **Heritage House,** 5200 N. Hwy. 1, tel. (707) 937-5885 or toll-free (800) 235-5885, was once a safe harbor for that notorious gangster Baby Face Nelson, though things are quite civilized and serene these days. Heritage House itself is an old Maine-style farmhouse (now the inn's dining room, kitchen, and office) and the center of a large complex of antique-rich luxury cottages and suites—the best ones looking out to sea. Premium-Luxury. Another major attraction is the exceptional yet reasonably relaxed **Heritage House Restaurant,** with its stunning domed dining room, open nightly for dinner—except when the entire establishment is shut down in winter, usually from Thanksgiving through Christmas and again January 2 to President's Day in February. The gardens (and garden shop) at Heritage House are also quite impressive

STAYING IN FORT BRAGG

Fort Bragg Bed and Breakfasts

The boxy, weathered, clear-heart redwood **Grey Whale Inn,** 615 Main St., tel. (707) 964-0640 or toll-free (800) 382-7244, fax (707) 964-4408, www.greywhaleinn.com, was once the community hospital. If you're one of those people who don't think they like bed and breakfasts—under any circumstances—this place could be the cure for what ails you. The two-story whale of an inn offers peace and privacy, very wide hallways, 14 individually decorated rooms and suites (some quite large) with myriad amenities, a base-

ment pool table and rec room, fireplace, and an award-winning breakfast buffet of hot dish, cereals, coffeecakes, fresh fruits and juices, yogurt or cheese, and good coffee. (And if you don't feel too sociable in the morning, load up a tray in the breakfast room and take breakfast back to bed with you.) A truly exceptional stay—and some of the rooms are quite affordable. Expensive-Luxury. From here it's an easy walk to the *Skunk Train* depot and downtown, to Glass Beach, and to area restaurants.

For fans of Victoriana, a particularly inviting local bed and breakfast is the 1886 **Weller House Inn,** 524 Stewart St., tel. (707) 964-4415 or toll-free (877) 893-5537, fax (707) 964-4198, www.wellerhouse.com—the only Mendocino Coast inn listed on the National Register of Historic Places. The seven Victorian guest rooms all have private baths; some have a fireplace or woodstove, jacuzzi tub, or clawfoot bathtub. "Very full" breakfast is served in the 900-square-foot ballroom, completely paneled in exquisite old redwood. Expensive-Luxury.

The two-story **Noyo River Lodge,** 500 Casa del Noyo Dr., tel. (707) 964-8045 or toll-free (800) 628-1126, www.mcn.org/a/noyoriver, is a redwood Craftsman-style mansion (circa 1868) on a hill with harbor and ocean views, rooms and suites with private baths (some with fireplaces), a restaurant and lounge, big soaking tubs, skylights, and gardens. Premium. The **Avalon House,** 561 Stewart St., tel. (707) 964-5555 or toll-free (800) 964-5556, is a 1905 Craftsman with six rooms (three with in-room spas, three with fireplaces). Moderate-Premium. The newly restored **Old Coast Hotel,** 101 N. Franklin St., tel. (707) 961-4488, has 16 rooms and a hot tub; its adjoining bar and grill is a pleasant place for dinner or a cocktail. Expensive-Luxury.

Other B&B possibilities include the **Pudding Creek Inn Bed and Breakfast,** 700 N. Main St., tel. (707) 964-9529 or toll-free (800) 227-9529, actually two 1884 Victorians connected by a garden court. The 10 rooms all have private baths, and two have fireplaces. Full breakfast buffet. Closed most of January. Moderate-Premium. Near everything, too, is the **Glass Beach Bed and Breakfast Inn,** 726 N. Main, tel. (707) 964-6774, with nine rooms (four have fireplaces), a hot tub, and full breakfast in the dining room. Expensive-Premium.

South of Fort Bragg, just north of Caspar, and across from the state park is **Annie's Jughandle Beach B&B**, 32980 Gibney Lane (at Hwy. 1), tel. (707) 964-1415 or toll-free (800) 964-9957, with five rooms with private baths and fireplaces, as well as a hot tub, ocean views, and excellent breakfasts. Expensive-Luxury.

Fort Bragg Motels and Lodges

Mendocino has most of the bed and breakfasts, but Fort Bragg has the motels—in general the most reasonable accommodations option around besides camping. Most places have cheaper off-season rates, from November through March or April. Pick up a current listing of area motels at the chamber office (see Mendocino Coast Information and Services, below).

The **Anchor Lodge** in Noyo (office in The Wharf Restaurant), 780 N. Harbor Dr., tel. (707) 964-4283, has 19 rooms. Inexpensive-Expensive. The **Fort Bragg Motel** is at 763 N. Main St., tel. (707) 964-4787 or toll-free (800) 253-9972. Inexpensive-Expensive. The **Surf Motel** is at 1220 S. Main St. (just south of the Noyo River Bridge), tel. (707) 964-5361 or toll-free (800) 339-5361, fax (707) 964-3187, www.surfmotel-fortbragg.com. Moderate-Expensive. The **Surrey Inn** is just north of the bridge at 888 S. Main, tel. (707) 964-4003 or toll-free (800) 206-9833. Inexpensive-Moderate. **Harbor Lite Lodge**, 120 N. Harbor Dr., tel. (707) 964-0221 or toll-free (800) 643-2700, overlooks Noyo Harbor from just off the highway. Moderate-Expensive.

You'll find a cluster of places on the beach side of the highway, just north of town past the Pudding Creek trestle. These places provide easy access to the Haul Road and beach. Try the very friendly **Beachcomber Motel**, 1111 N. Main St., tel. (707) 964-2402 or toll-free (800) 400-7873, www.thebeachcombermotel.com (Moderate-Luxury), which sometimes welcomes pets, or the **Surf 'n Sand Lodge**, 1131 N. Main (Hwy. 1), tel. (707) 964-9383 or toll-free (800) 964-0184 (Moderate-Luxury). Across the highway is the newish **Beach House Inn**, 100 Pudding Creek Rd., tel. (707) 961-1700 or toll-free (888) 559-9992, www.beachinn.com. Moderate-Expensive.

EATING IN MENDOCINO

Mendocino Basics

For the **Mendocino Certified Farmers' Market,** which runs May-Oct., show up on Friday, noon-2 p.m., at Howard and Main Streets; for details, call (707) 937-2728. Otherwise stock up on natural foods, for here or to go, at **Corners of the Mouth,** 45015 Ukiah St., tel. (707) 937-5345, and get general groceries at **Mendosa's,** 10501 Lansing St., tel. (707) 937-5879.

For a hefty slice of pizza or quiche, a bowl of homemade soup, or just a good Danish and a cafe latte, head for the **Mendocino Bakery,** 10485 Lansing, tel. (707) 937-0836. It's the locals' coffee house of choice and offers outdoor seating when the weather's nice. Open 7:30 a.m.-7 p.m. weekdays, 8:00 a.m.-7 p.m. weekends. The **Mendo Juice Joint,** on Ukiah a half block east of Lansing, tel. (707) 937-4033, specializes in fresh juices, smoothies, and healthy snacks.

Mendo Burgers, 10483 Lansing, tel. (707) 937-1111, is open 11 a.m.-7:30 p.m. and serves beef-, turkey-, fish-, and veggie-burgers. For that sweet tooth, try the famous ice cream (including quarter-pounder cones) at the **Mendocino Ice Cream Company,** 45090 Main, tel. (707) 937-5884; and the definitely decadent chocolates at **Mendocino Chocolate Company,** 10483 Lansing, tel. (707) 937-1107.

Simple and Good

Herbivorous visitors will be right at home at **Lu's Kitchen,** 45013 Ukiah St., tel. (707) 937-4939, which serves "organic cross-cultural vegetarian cuisine" in a casual atmosphere. Look for salads, quesadillas, and burritos in the $4-7 range.

One of the best views in town is from the big deck at the **Mendocino Café,** 10451 Lansing St., tel. (707) 937-2422 or (707) 937-6141, which has a great menu of Pacific Rim-inspired cuisine (try the Thai burrito) and a good beer selection. Another place for great views—but in a slightly more upscale atmosphere—is the **Bay View Cafe,** 45040 Main St. (upstairs), tel. (707) 937-4197, which enjoys unobstructed views of the coast from its bay-window-lined, second-story perch.

Cafe Beaujolais

No one should come anywhere near Mendocino without planning to eat at least one meal at the noted Cafe Beaujolais, 961 Ukiah St., tel. (707) 937-5614. The fresh-flower decor inside and on the

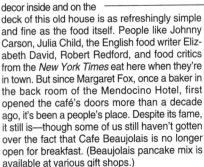

4323, featuring an eclectic menu of north coast fare—and sumptuous chocolate desserts reminiscent of its original local incarnation as the Chocolate Moosse Café. Open for lunch and dinner daily, and brunch on Sunday.

deck of this old house is as refreshingly simple and fine as the food itself. People like Johnny Carson, Julia Child, the English food writer Elizabeth David, Robert Redford, and food critics from the *New York Times* eat here when they're in town. But since Margaret Fox, once a baker in the back room of the Mendocino Hotel, first opened the café's doors more than a decade ago, it's been a people's place. Despite its fame, it still is—though some of us still haven't gotten over the fact that Cafe Beaujolais is no longer open for breakfast. (Beaujolais pancake mix is available at various gift shops.)

Dinner is a fixed-price French-and-California-cuisine affair featuring such things as local smoked salmon and roast duck with a purée of apples and turnips, still more decadent desserts, and an almost endless and excellent California wine list. Cafe Beaujolais is open nightly 5:45-9 p.m. Reservations are necessary, and they may be booked weeks ahead. Call before you arrive in town. Bring cash or personal checks; no credit cards accepted. The restaurant's bakery, called The Brickery, produces breads and pizzas from a wood-fired brick oven. It's open daily, 11 a.m. to 4 or 5 p.m.

Other Worthy Restaurants

Neighbor to the much-more-famous Cafe Beaujolais is **955 Ukiah St.**, tel. (707) 937-1955, difficult to find in the fog despite its numerically straightforward attitude. (The entrance is 100 feet off the street around a few corners.) The dining room itself is a former art studio, and dinners feature excellent fresh seafood, unforgettable bread sticks, and Navarro and Husch wines from the Anderson Valley. Open Wed.-Sun. from 6 p.m. Also quite good in town is the **MacCallum House Restaurant**, 45020 Albion, tel. (707) 937-5763, open nightly for dinner, and the **Moosse Café**, 390 Kasten St., tel. (707) 937-

For prime rib, steaks, and seafood in a semi-formal Victorian setting, consider the crystal-and-Oriental-carpet ambience of the **Mendocino Hotel**, 45080 Main St., tel. (707) 937-0511. The hotel's Garden Court restaurant and bar (the ceiling almost one immense skylight to keep the garden going) serves more casual lunch fare, good salads, sandwiches, and specials. Open daily for breakfast, lunch, and dinner.

EATING NEAR MENDOCINO

You can always find a good meal at the **Little River Inn**, which is particularly noted for its breakfasts and brunches but also offers fine American-classic dinners emphasizing steak and seafood. Another restaurant in town well worth seeking out is the inauspicious and elegantly simple **Little River Restaurant** (unaffiliated with the Little River Inn), 7750 N. Hwy. 1 (tucked away behind the post office), tel. (707) 937-4945. Don't miss it. Only 14 people can squeeze in here at any one time, but what they sit down to is a perfect meal, soup through excellent dessert, with entrées like roast lamb in mustard sauce. Reservations essential, especially on weekends. For fine dining, another top area destination is the **Heritage House Restaurant**, 5200 Hwy. 1 south of Little River, tel. (707) 937-5885, with its seasonally changing menu of superb north coast cuisine.

At the intimately elegant **Ledford House**, 3000 N. Hwy. 1 (south of "downtown" Albion), tel. (707) 937-0282, even vegetarians can try the excellent soups because none are made with meat bases. Entrées include pasta picks like ravioli stuffed with ricotta cheese in sorrel cream sauce, and some definitely nonstandard seafood and meat specialties.

EATING IN FORT BRAGG

Finding a meal in Fort Bragg is a more relaxed task than in Mendocino, with less confusion from the madding crowds. Most restaurants are casual. For farm-fresh everything, show up for the **Fort Bragg Certified Farmers' Market,** held May-Oct. on Wednesday, 3:30-6 p.m., at Laurel and Franklin. Call (707) 964-0536 for details. For something unusual to take home as a memento, stop by Carol Hall's **Hot Pepper Jelly Company,** 330 N. Main, tel. (707) 961-1422 or toll-free (800) 892-4823, an inviting shop that sells some intriguing jams and jellies, fruit syrups, mustards, herb vinegars, and unusual food-related gift items. For a sweet treat, **Goody's,** 144 N. Franklin St., tel. (707) 964-7800, is the town's old-time malt shop and soda fountain, complete with checkerboard counter (open weekdays and Saturdays). Another possibility is the **Mendocino Chocolate Company,** 542 N. Main St., tel. (707) 964-8800 or toll-free (800) 722-1107 (for orders), which serves up everything from edible seashells and Mendocino toffee to an amazing array of truffles and chews—including Fort Bragg 2x4s (peanut butter-flavored fudge "veneered" with dark chocolate) and Mr. Peanut Coastal Clusters. Though this is headquarters, there's another company outlet in Mendocino.

Breakfast and Lunch

The venerable **Egghead Omelettes of Oz,** 326 N. Main St., tel. (707) 964-5005, is a cheerful diner with booths, the whole place decorated in a Wizard of Oz theme. (Follow the Yellow Brick Road through the kitchen to the restrooms out back.) On the menu are unforgettable fried potatoes and omelettes with endless combinations for fillings, including avocado and crab. Good sandwiches at lunch. Open daily 7 a.m.-2 p.m. For picnic fixin's or a special gift for that hard-to-please carnivore, just north is the **Round Man's Smoke House,** 412 N. Main, toll-free tel. (800) 545-2935, which specializes in all kinds of meateater's delights, from smoked chinook or pepper salmon and salmon jerky to Canadian bacon and turkey apple sausage; Round Man's also sells some delightful cheeses.

Around the corner is the charming **Headlands Coffeehouse,** 120 E. Laurel St., tel. (707) 964-1987, an artsy place with an interesting crowd of locals, all the usual espresso drinks, delicious healthy food (for breakfast, try the Belgian waffle with fruit and yogurt—slurp!), and regular live acoustic music. Also a best bet for coffee, bakery items, and simple lunch is the **Thanksgiving Coffee Café,** 120 Main St., tel. (707) 964-5767, open daily 7:30 a.m.-4 p.m.

At lunch, locals line up for the Dagwood-style sandwiches at **David's Deli,** 450 S. Franklin St., tel. (707) 964-1946, but breakfast here is pretty special, too. For a unique atmosphere, head just south of town to the Mendocino Coast Botanical Gardens, where you can dine with garden views at the **Gardens Grill,** 18220 N. Hwy. 1, tel. (707) 964-7474. It's open for lunch Mon.-Sat., for dinner Thurs.-Sat., and for Sunday brunch.

American-Style Fare

When locals want a special dinner, they often head to the **Rendezvous Inn & Restaurant,** just down the street from the Grey Whale Inn at 647 N. Main St., tel. (707) 964-8142 or toll-free (800) 491-8142. This gorgeous homey bungalow with warm wood interiors serves marvelous crab cakes, jambalaya, vegetarian pasta and "beggar's purses," civet of venison, and other unusual entrées, starting from the freshest local ingredients. Open Wed.-Sun. for dinner. Upstairs are several guest rooms, each with private bath (Moderate-Expensive). Another good choice is **The Restaurant,** 418 N. Main St., tel. (707) 964-9800, where the California-style fare might include delectable entrées such as poached halibut, calimari, scallops, shrimp, steak, and quail. Open for lunch and dinner (call for current schedule) and Sunday brunch. Children's menu. Reservations wise.

Fort Bragg's favorite fancy seafood restaurant, open for dinner only, is **The Cliff House,** just south of the Harbor Bridge, 1011 S. Main St., tel. (707) 961-0255. Overlooking the jetty and the harbor, The Cliff House serves wonderful seafood and pastas—try the smoked salmon ravioli—and steaks, along with specialties including chicken mushroom Dijon and pepper steak. On Friday and Saturday night, prime rib is also on the menu.

In a little less rarified atmosphere, good food is also available at **North Coast Brewing Co. Taproom and Restaurant,** 444 N. Main, tel. (707) 964-3400, a brewpub and grill pouring award-winning handmade ales to accompany pub grub (including Route 66 chili), pastas, steaks, seafood, and Cajun-inspired dishes. On a sunny day, the outside beer garden—a genuine garden, quite appealing—can't be beat. Beer lovers take note: North Coast is among the crème de la crème of North American microbreweries, consistently producing brews that always satisfy and frequently astonish even the pickiest connoisseurs. All the offerings are outstanding, but don't miss the unique Belgian-style Pranqster or the positively evil Rasputin imperial stout. Open noon-11 p.m. daily except Monday. Across the street (at 455 N. Main) is the brewery itself, tel. (707) 964-2739, www.ncoast-brewing .com, offering free tours on weekdays, along with some memorable memorabilia and gift items.

Relatively new in town but promising is **Mendo Bistro,** 301 Main (at Redwood, upstairs in the Company Store), tel. (707) 964-4974. Here you pick a meat or seafood entrée and a style of preparation, then get it served just the way you like it. Prices are low. The restaurant at the restored **Old Coast Hotel,** 101 N. Franklin, tel. (707) 961-4488, is another possibility, with a steak and seafood menu. Open for lunch and dinner daily.

Ethnic Cuisine

Yes, Fort Bragg has outstanding ethnic food. **Viraporn's,** on S. Main St. at Chestnut (across the street from PayLess), tel. (707) 964-7931, serves great Thai food, while **Samraat,** 546 S. Main St., tel. (707) 964-0386, specializes in the tastes of India. Both of these restaurants, humble as they may appear from the outside, are worth seeking out.

Just north of town in Cleone, the legendary **Purple Rose,** 24300 N. Hwy. 1, tel. (707) 964-6507, prepares delicious and locally famous Mexican food in a bright, spacious, and casual atmosphere. The veggie burrito here is a work of culinary art. Open Wed.-Sun. for dinner. (Within walking distance from the campgrounds at MacKerricher State Park, the Purple Rose makes the perfect break from roasted weenies and marshmallows.) Mexican fare is also available in town at **El Sombrero,** 223 N. Franklin, tel. (707) 964-5780.

For Italian, everyone's favorite is **D'Aurelio's,** 438 S. Franklin St., tel. (707) 964-4227, which offers outstanding pizzas, calzones, and the like in a comfortable, casual atmosphere. Another possibility is **Bernillo's,** 220 E. Redwood Ave., tel. (707) 964-9314.

Fishing for Food in Noyo

Noyo Harbor is where the tourists go for fish. True, you'll find a "school" of inexpensive seafood eateries here amid the comings and goings of fishing boats. But none of the restaurants are memorable for either cuisine or decor. If you don't need the "down on the docks" atmosphere, you'll probably do better satisfying your seafood cravings at one of the "American-style" restaurants listed above.

That said, **The Wharf,** 780 N. Harbor Dr., tel. (707) 964-4283, serves a creamy clam chowder and crispy-outside-tender-inside fried clams, and the prime rib sandwich here is nothing to throw a crabpot at. For dinner, specialties include seafood and steak. The specialty at the plastic-tableclothed **Cap'n Flint's,** 32250 N. Harbor, tel. (707) 964-9447, is shrimp won tons with cream cheese filling. Open 11 a.m.-8:30 p.m. **El Mexicano,** 701 N. Harbor Dr., tel. (707) 964-7164, serves up authentic Mexican food, down to the fresh-daily tortillas. Open daily 10 a.m.-8:30 p.m.

EVENTFUL, ARTFUL MENDOCINO COAST

For most people, just being here along the Mendocino coast is entertainment enough. But if that's too quiet for you, the **Caspar Inn** between

Mendocino and Fort Bragg, tel. (707) 964-5565, is a venerable rock 'n' roll hotspot; this boisterous roadhouse-style tavern draws packed houses for dancing to big-name touring bands.

Mendocino Coast Festivals and Events

New in 2000 was the **Mendocino Wine & Crab Days** event, held from the last weekend in January through the first week in February. Down the coast, come February, is the annual **Gualala Chocolate Festival.** Everyone celebrates the return of the California gray whale. The **Mendocino Whale Festival,** on the first weekend in March, celebrates the annual cetacean migration with wine and clam-chowder tastings, art exhibits, music and concerts, and other special events. The **Fort Bragg Whale Festival,** held the third weekend in March, happily coincides with the arrival of spring. Festivities include chowder tasting and beer tasting (the latter courtesy of Fort Bragg's own North Coast Brewing Company), a "whale run," doll show, car show, lighthouse tours, and more. On both weekends, **whalewatching tours** are offered from Noyo Harbor, and **whalewatch talks** are offered at area state parks. In late April, come to Fort Bragg for the **John Druecker Memorial Rhododendron Show**—the granddaddy of all rhodie shows.

On the first weekend in May, Mendocino's **Annual Historic House & Building Tour** offers a self-guided tour of the town's historic treasures. In late May, Fort Bragg puts on its impressive annual **Memorial Day Quilt Show.** The **Spring Garden Tour** in mid-June, sponsored by the Mendocino Art Center, includes some of the most spectacular gardens in and near Mendocino.

On or around July 4th, Fort Bragg hosts the **World's Largest Salmon Barbecue** down at Noyo Harbor. And Mendocino holds its old-fashioned **Fourth of July Parade.** Starting in mid-July, Mendocino hosts the noted, two-week **Mendocino Music Festival,** tel. (707) 937-2044, www.mcn.org/a/music. At this gala event, held in a 600-seat tent set up next to the Ford House, the local Symphony of the Redwoods joins with talented players from Bay Area orchestras to perform classical works that might include symphonies, opera, and chamber music, as well as less highbrow fare. At Greenwood Ridge Vineyards in the Anderson Valley, come

in late July for the annual **California Wine Tasting Championships.**

Usually held the first weekend in August is the Mendocino Art Center's **Summer Art Fair.** Come to Fort Bragg in August for its **Kow Chip Bingo** tournament—pretty self-explanatory, even if you've never played bingo this way before. (Moo.) Also in August is the Mendocino Coast Botanical Gardens' **Art in the Gardens** event. Come in mid-August for the annual **Coast Pomo Indian Days.** Fort Bragg's biggest party every year is **Paul Bunyan Days,** held over Labor Day weekend and offering a logging competition, parade, and crafts fair. The following September weekend, the **Winesong!** winetasting and auction takes place at the Mendocino Coast Botanical Gardens.

Come in early November for the **Mushroom Festival** and display at Mendocino's Ford House, and Thanksgiving weekend for the **Thanksgiving Art Festival** at the Mendocino Art Center and, down the coast, the **Gualala Arts Studio Tour.**

December brings the **Mendocino Christmas Festival,** which includes tree lighting, candlelight inn tours, and other festivities. In Fort Bragg, the yuletide spirit extends to special programs by the Symphony of the Redwoods, the Gloriana Theater Company, and Warehouse Repertory—and the **Holiday Gift Show** at the restored Union Lumber Company Store, not to mention the **Hometown Christmas & Lighted Truck Parade.** This particular community party includes music, tree lighting, and truck lighting—a yuletide parade of logging trucks and big rigs all lit up for the holidays.

Mendocino Coast Arts

On the first Friday evening of the month, don't miss Fort Bragg's **First Friday** local gallery and shop "event," 5:30-8:30 p.m., sponsored by the Fort Bragg Center for the Arts. For the latest on other art events, stop by the Fort Bragg center or the Mendocino Art Center.

At home in Mendocino is the **Mendocino Theatre Company,** 45200 Little Lake Rd., tel. (707) 937-4477 or (707) 937-2718, which begins its performance season in March. An eclectic mix of one-night or short-run acts—anything from local school plays to comedy troupes to touring worldbeat bands—are presented at Mendocino's

Crown Hall, 45285 Ukiah St. (down at the west end), a delightfully intimate venue with reasonably good acoustics as well.

Fort Bragg is also quite theatrical. The **Gloriana Opera Company,** 721 N. Franklin St., tel. (707) 964-7469, offers a six-week run in summer and special events throughout the year. The **Footlighters Little Theatre,** 248 E. Laurel St., tel. (707) 964-3806, features Gay Nineties melodrama; performances occur Wednesday and Saturday from Memorial Day through Labor Day. Fort Bragg's **Warehouse Repertory Theater,** 319-A N. Main St., tel. (707) 961-2942 (admin.) or (707) 961-2940 (box office), www.warehouserep.com, the regional repertory company, sponsors the annual **Mendocino Shakespeare Festival.**

Fort Bragg is also home to the fine **Symphony of the Redwoods,** tel. (707) 964-0898, which presents several major concerts each year along the Mendocino coast, leading up to its season-capping performance in mid-July at the annual Mendocino Music Festival.

MENDOCINO COAST INFORMATION AND SERVICES

The **Fort Bragg-Mendocino Coast Chamber of Commerce,** 332 N. Main St., P.O. Box 1141, Fort Bragg, CA 95437, tel. (707) 961-6300 or toll-free (800) 726-2780, fax (707) 964-2056, www.mendocinocoast.com, is an incredible resource. It's open Mon.-Tues. and Thurs.-Fri. 9 a.m.-5 p.m., Saturday 11 a.m.-4 p.m. (closed Wednesday and Sunday). Among the free literature published by the chamber is the regularly updated *Mendocino* brochure and map (mostly a shop listing), the *Walking Tour of Historic Fort Bragg* guide, and the new *Something to Bragg About* brochure. Also available here and elsewhere is the free annual *Mendocino Visitor* tabloid, the coast guide to state parks, the *Guide to the Recreational Trails of Mendocino County,* and the Mendocino Art Center's publications.

For an "advance packet" of information, send a self-addressed, stamped, legal-size envelope.

For books on the region—and just plain great books—plan to spend some quality time in **Gallery Bookshop & Bookwinkle's Children's Books** in Mendocino at Main and Kasten Streets, tel. (707) 937-2215, www.gallerybooks.com, a truly impressive independent bookstore.

To get properly oriented along the Mendocino coast, a travel essential is Bob Lorentzen's *The Hiker's Hip Pocket Guide to the Mendocino Coast,* which keys off the white milepost markers along Hwy. 1 from the Gualala River north. The book provides abundant information about undeveloped public lands along the southern Mendocino coast, such as the state's Schooner Gulch and Whiskey Shoals Beach. Also worthwhile to carry anywhere along the coast, though a bit unwieldy, is the *California Coastal Resource Guide* by the California Coastal Commission, published by the University of California Press.

The **Fort Bragg post office** is at 203 N. Franklin, tel. (707) 964-2302, open weekdays 8:30 a.m.-5 p.m. The **Mendocino post office** is at 10500 Ford St., tel. (707) 937-5282; open weekdays 8:30 a.m.-4:30 p.m. The **Mendocino Coast District Hospital,** 700 River Dr., tel. (707) 961-1234, offers 24-hour emergency services.

Mendocino Coast Transportation
The **Mendocino Transit Authority** (MTA), based in Ukiah, tel. (707) 462-1422, runs one bus each weekday between Ukiah and Gualala via the Navarro River bridge. At the bridge, you can transfer to or from the smaller vans of **Mendocino Stage,** tel. (707) 964-0167, which run weekdays between Fort Bragg and Navarro, with stops in Mendocino. The MTA also makes roundtrips between Point Arena and Santa Rosa. Connect with **Greyhound** in Ukiah.

Near Little River, a few miles inland from the coast, is the **Little River Airport,** the closest airfield to Mendocino. Private pilots flying into the airport can get a ride into Little River or Mendocino by calling Mendocino Stage.

THE SOUTHERN MENDOCINO COAST

The coast south from Mendocino is marvelously lonely in places, still a little greener (and wetter) than Sonoma County but with similar crescent coves and pocket beaches—one after the next, like a string of pearls. If the official distinction matters, the Gualala River forms the boundary between Sonoma and Mendocino Counties.

SOUTH FROM MENDOCINO

Greater Elk

The tiny town of Elk perches on pastoral coastal bluffs. Elk was once a lumber-loading port known as Greenwood, hence **Greenwood Creek Beach State Park** across from the store, with good picnicking among the bluff pines. The park is also a popular push-off point for sea kayakers.

A genuine area institution is the **Elk Cove Inn**, 6300 S. Hwy. 1, tel. (707) 877-3321 or toll-free (800) 275-2967, www.elkcoveinn.com, where you get a spectacular view of the cove below from the inn's romantic gazebo. The Elk Cove Inn offers six fine rooms in the main 1883 Victorian, which features an upper-level parlor and private sundeck, plus four ocean-view cottages overlooking the cove. Fairly new at the Elk Cove Inn—and truly spectacular, just the thing for an extra-special weekend—are its four ocean-view luxury suites, housed in the new Craftsman-style annex. These sophisticated suites are certainly a fitting tribute to the era of craftsmanship, with a keen sense of style and every imaginable comfort, down to the fireplaces, spa tubs, California king beds with both down and regular comforters, and mini-kitchens complete with microwave, small fridge, and coffee/cappuccino maker. Floors in the bathroom feature heated floor tiles. Inn rates include full breakfast, served in a delightful, cheerful, ocean-view breakfast room with intimate tables. Expensive-Luxury, but inquire about off-season and midweek specials (particularly midweek stays Feb.-May). The Elk Cove Inn also boasts a beer and wine bar—and a full bar, including a menu of 25 different martinis.

The **Greenwood Pier Inn**, 5928 S. Hwy. 1, tel. (707) 877-9997 or (707) 877-3423, fax (707) 877-3439, www.greenwoodpierinn.com, is a complex of upscale cottages perched at the edge of the cliffs above the sea. Both the eclectic cottages and cottage-gardenlike grounds are beautifully designed, with pleasant nooks, crannies, art, and surprise delights, all of which foster a homey, romantic ambience. Most feature wood-burning fireplaces or woodstoves, and some also have in-room spa tubs. Continental breakfast is delivered to your room. Premium-Luxury. Other amenities include the cliffside hot tub, in-room massage and facials (extra), and the on-site **Greenwood Pier Café** (for more, see below).

The all-redwood Craftsman-style 1916 **Harbor House**, 5600 S. Hwy. 1, tel. (707) 877-3203 or toll-free (800) 720-7474, www.theharborhouseinn.com, is a sophisticated bed and breakfast noted for its stylish, classic accommodations (recently refurbished) and fine dining. Rates include full breakfast and fabulous four-course dinner (see below) plus access to a private strip of beach. Luxury.

Considerably more relaxed but equally charming are the cottages at **Griffin House at Greenwood Cove,** 5910 S. Hwy. 1, tel. (707) 877-3422, www.griffinn.com. The "house" is now **Bridget Dolan's Irish Pub & Dinner House,** serving pub grub and "very, very veg" specials. Out back are the flower gardens and cozy 1920s cottages, all quite fresh and inviting. Three feature sun decks and ocean views, and all have private baths (most with clawfoot tubs) and woodstoves. One includes a full kitchen, and is a best bet for families. A hearty full breakfast is served in your room. Expensive-Luxury. The **Sandpiper House Inn,** 5520 S. Hwy. 1, tel. (707) 877-3587 or toll-free (800) 894-9016, is a 1916 Victorian Craftsman offering five rooms (three with fireplaces) and gourmet full breakfast. Premium-Luxury.

If you're just passing through and looking for a bite to eat, note that the nondescript store beside the highway—the **Elk Store,** 6101 Hwy. 1, tel. (707) 877-3411—whips up some of the best deli sandwiches in the known universe, and also carries gourmet cheeses and an impressive selection of wines and microbrews. It's a must-stop if you're planning a picnic. Other possibilities include the **Roadhouse Cafe,** 6061 S. Hwy. 1, tel. (707) 877-3285, open Fri.-Sun. for breakfast and lunch (Thursday, too, in summer) and Fri.-Sat. for dinner, and the casual **Greenwood Pier Café** at the Greenwood Pier Inn, tel. (707) 877-9997, where the house-baked breads and fresh garden veggies and herbs make even a simple meal quite delightful. Open daily mid-May through October for breakfast, lunch, and dinner, Fri.-Mon. in the off-season. *The* place for fine dining in Elk is the elegant **Harbor House Inn,** 5600 Hwy. 1, tel. (707) 877-3203, beloved for its four-course meals emphasizing Sonoma County seafood, meats, poultry, and produce, à la Tuscany or Provence. Open for dinner daily, at least most of the year. Beer and wine. No credit cards. Limited seating, and advance reservations required—and be sure to request a window table.

Manchester State Park

This 5,272-acre park just north of Point Arena and the burg of Manchester is foggy in summer and cold in winter, but it presents dedicated beachcombers with a long stretch of sandy shore and dunes dotted with driftwood. Five miles of beaches stretch south to Pt. Arena. A lagoon offers good birding, and excellent salmon and steelhead fishing in both Brush and Alder Creeks. Also interesting here is the opportunity for some walk-in environmental camping, about a mile past the parking area. (Making an overnight even more thrilling is the knowledge that here at Manchester is where the San Andreas Fault plunges into the sea.) Once here, it's first-come, first-camped, with an opportunity to personally experience those predictable summer northeasterlies as they whistle through your tent. For more information about Manchester and a camping map, contact the Mendocino state parks office, tel. (707) 937-5804, or call the park directly at (707) 882-2463. More private and protected is the **KOA** campground at 44300 Kinney Ln. (adjacent to the park office), tel. (707) 882-2375.

POINT ARENA

Remote Point Arena, "discovered" by Capt. George Vancouver in 1792, is a popular spot for whalewatching. Though it's noticeably quiet here today, Point Arena was the busiest port between San Francisco and Eureka in the 1870s. When the local pier was wiped out by rogue waves in 1983, the already depressed local fishing and logging economy took yet another dive. But today Point Arena has a new pier—folks can fish here without a license—and a new economic boon: the sea urchin harvest, to satisfy the Japanese taste for *uni.*

"New" too is the **Arena theater,** 214 Main St., tel. (707) 882-3456 or (707) 882-3020, a 1927-vintage vaudeville theater, fully refurbished and open for concerts and stage productions as well as foreign, "art," and mainstream films.

Point Arena Lighthouse

A monument to the area's historically impressive ship graveyard, the Coast Guard's six-story, automated 380,000-candlepower lighthouse north of town is open to visitors (limited hours, small donation requested). Built in 1908, this lighthouse was the first in the U.S. constructed of steel-reinforced concrete; it replaced the original brick tower that had come tumbling down two years earlier. The adjacent **museum** tells tales of the hapless ships that floated their last here.

To help protect the lighthouse and preserve public access—no government support has been available—local volunteer lighthouse keepers maintain and rent out "vacation rental homes" (U.S. government-issue houses abandoned by the Coast Guard)—a good deal for families. For more information and reservations, contact **Point Arena Lighthouse Keepers, Inc.,** 45500 Lighthouse Rd., P.O. Box 11, Point Arena, CA 95468, tel. (707) 882-2777, www.mcn.org/1/palight.

Practical Point Arena

Besides the lighthouse cottages mentioned above, more conventional digs are also available in town. **La Bou's Sea Shell Inn,** 135 Main, tel. (707) 882-2000, has decent rooms with cable TV, phones, and morning coffee. Inexpensive. The **Coast Guard House Historic Inn,** 695 Arena Cove, tel. (707) 882-2442 or toll-free (800) 524-9320, is a 1901 Cape Cod with six guest rooms (two share a bath), queen or double beds, and an expanded continental breakfast. Premium-Luxury.

Don't miss dinner at **Pangaea,** 250 Main St., tel. (707) 882-3001. This self-proclaimed "café" boasts an arty, elegant interior and advertises its fare as "eclectic cuisine: global, local, organic." What that means exactly varies from night to night, but might include such mouthwatering temptations as pan-roasted Chilean sea bass with anise-scented black beans, or mahimahi with Lebanese couscous tabouleh, lentils, greens, and a cumin-scented lemony tahini sauce. Outrageous. Otherwise, try **The Galley,** 790 Port St., tel. (707) 882-2189, a safe bet for breakfast, lunch, or dinner daily.

The hippest coffee house in town is currently **Holy Grounds,** 245 Main St., tel. (707) 882-9502, which features organic espresso drinks, smoothies and juices as well as light pastries, sandwiches, wraps, and the like. Look for occasional open-mike nights.

GUALALA AND VICINITY

Though people in the area generally say whatever they please, Gualala is supposedly pronounced Wah-LA-la, the word itself Spanish for the Pomos' *wala'li* or "meeting place of the waters." These days Gualala and vicinity is also known as the north coast's "banana belt," due to its relatively temperate, fog-free climate. Crossing the Gualala River means crossing into Sonoma County. Between Gualala and Sea Ranch is **Del Mar Landing,** an ecological reserve of virgin coastline with rugged offshore rocks, tidepools, and harbor seals. Get there on the trail running south from Gualala Point Regional Park, a "gift" from Sea Ranch developers, or via Sea Ranch trails.

Practical Gualala

Life in this old lumber town still centers on the 1903 **Gualala Hotel,** 39301 S. Hwy. 1, tel. (707) 884-3441, a loud and lively bar and restaurant where haute cuisine is hearty food: chicken, steak, fried shrimp, spaghetti. Open for dinner 6-9 p.m., weekends 5-10 p.m. (For fine dining, see below—or head to St. Orres.) The hotel also offers 19 renovated rooms. Nearby are the **Seacliff Hotel,** 39140 S. Hwy. 1, tel. (707) 884-1213, offering in-room spas, fireplaces, and ocean views (Premium-Luxury), and the equally pleasant, contemporary **Breakers Inn,** 39300 S. Hwy. 1, tel. (707) 884-3200 or toll-free (800) 273-2537,

fax (707) 884-3400, www.breakersinn.com, featuring similar amenities and large private decks overlooking the sea (Premium-Luxury). The contemporary **Gualala Country Inn,** 47955 Center St. (at Hwy. 1), tel. (707) 884-4343 or toll-free (800) 564-4466, fax (707) 884-1018, www.gualala.com, offers in-room spas, fireplaces, and ocean views. Expensive-Premium.

North of town is the **Old Milano Hotel,** 38300 S. Hwy. 1, tel. (707) 884-3256, fax (707) 884-4249, a fine Victorian-style bed and breakfast listed on the National Register of Historic Places. Six rooms share two baths, but seven others (including six cottages) have private baths. One room features the canopied bed where Cathy (Merle Oberon) lay before Heathcliff (Laurence Olivier) carried her to the window for one last look at the moors. The unique "caboose" cottage not far from the main house has a woodstove, terrace, and observation cupola, and the Iris Cottage features ocean views. Rates include a full breakfast and use of the hot tub. Moderate-Luxury. The Old Milano also serves delightful dinners in its Victorian dining room.

Campers can head to **Gualala Point Regional Park,** just south of town, tel. (707) 785-2377 or (707) 527-2041, which offers coastal access and camping ($15 per night, no hookups). The park day-use fee is $3. For more amenities, try privately operated **Gualala River Redwood Park,** 46001 Gualala Rd., (707) 884-3533, in the redwoods on the north beach of the Gualala River, one mile east of town off Old Stage Road. It offers 120 sites with full hookups for $22-25 a night. Amenities include coin-op showers and restrooms.

The fine-dining restaurant of choice in Gualala these days is the **Oceansong Pacific Grille,** 39350 S. Hwy. 1, tel. (707) 884-1041, which enjoys a splendid location overlooking the beach and Gualala River. Since the kitchen has been under the direction of Swiss chef René Fueg, the restaurant has earned rave reviews from *Culinary Trends* magazine and locals alike. Seafood is one specialty, but you'll also find steaks, pastas, rack of lamb, and other entrées, all expertly done. The Frugal Thursday specials are particularly popular. For "downhome gourmet," try **The Food Company** just north of town at Robinsons Reef Rd., tel. (707) 884-1800, a combination café, deli, and bakery serving up fresh, wholesome fare. Sit outside on the sunporch or in the garden area, or pack your goodies to go. Open daily for breakfast, lunch, and dinner. To stock up on fresh local produce for the road, plan to arrive for the **Gualala Certified Farmers' Market,** held May-Oct. on Saturday, 3-5 p.m., at the Gualala Community Center. For information, call (707) 882-2474.

Saint Orres

North of Gualala is a local landmark—the ornate onion-domed inn and restaurant of St. Orres, 36601 S. Hwy. 1, tel. (707) 884-3303 or (707) 884-3335 (restaurant), fax (707) 884-1840, www.saintorres.com. Some rock 'n' roll-literate wits refer to a sit-down dinner here as "sitting in the dacha of the bay." Dazzling in all its Russian-style redwood and stained-glass glory, St. Orres is also a great place to stay. For peace, quiet, and total relaxation, nothing beats an overnight in one of the 11 handcrafted redwood cabins (some rather rustic) scattered through the forest, or in one of the eight lodge rooms (shared bathrooms). Come morning, breakfast is delivered to the door in a basket. Moderate-Luxury.

Even if they don't stay here, people come from miles around to eat at St. Orres, known for its creative French-style fare. The fixed-price dinners ($30, not including appetizers or desserts) feature such things as a salad of greens and edible flowers from the garden, cold strawberry soup, puff pastry with goat cheese and prosciutto, venison with blackberries, wild boar, Sonoma County quail, salmon and very fresh seafood in season, eggplant terrine, and grilled vegetable tart. Wonderful desserts, and good wines (beer and wine only). No credit cards. Before dinner, sit outside and watch the sun set. Reservations are a must, a month or more in advance.

Anchor Bay

For those who can afford it, a stay at the **Whale Watch Inn,** 35100 S. Hwy. 1, tel. (707) 884-3667 or toll-free (800) 942-1342, www.whale-watch.com, is just this side of coastal condo heaven. Perched on the cliffs overlooking Anchor Bay (north of Gualala), the Whale Watch is the kind of place where decadence and decency both reign and Debussy pours out over the intercom. The contemporary, romantic, sometimes surprisingly formal rooms offer amenities such as fireplaces, fresh flowers, decks, and whirlpool tubs; some have kitchens. Attendants bring breakfast to the door. Reservations are a good idea. Luxury.

Just up the road is the **North Coast Country Inn,** 34591 S. Hwy. 1, tel. (707) 884-4537, offering redwood in the rustic mode with antiques and ocean views, a library, fireplaces, kitchens, and private decks. Other amenities include an antique store, gazebo, hot tub, and full breakfast. The six rooms all have private bath. Luxury.

Abalone divers and visitors on a budget favor **Anchor Bay Campground,** down in a beachfront gulch just north of Anchor Bay village, tel. (707) 884-4222. The small campground fills up often in spring and summer; reservations are accepted up to one year in advance. Rates start at $25 per night. Electrical hookups are extra; hot showers available.

In Anchor Bay village, services include a market and wine shop, as well as the **Fish Rock Cafe,** tel. (707) 884-1639, serving burgers, soups, salads, sandwiches (including veggie varieties), and Northern California microbrews. The café is open for lunch and dinner daily.

THE SONOMA COAST

Northern California beaches are different from the gentler, kinder sandy beaches of the south-state. The coast here is wild. In stark contrast to the softly rounded hillsides landward, the Sonoma County coast presents a dramatically rugged face and an aggressive personality: undertows, swirling offshore eddies, riptides, and deadly "sleeper" or "rogue" waves. It pays to pay attention along the Sonoma coast. Since 1950, more than 70 people have been killed here by sleepers, waves that come out of nowhere to wallop the unaware, then drag them into the surf and out to sea.

October is generally the worst month of the year for dangerous surf, but it is also one of the best months to visit; in September and October the summertime shroud of fog usually lifts and the sea sparkles. Except on weekends, by autumn most Bay Area and tourist traffic has dried up like the area's seasonal streams, and it's possible to be alone with the wild things.

SEA RANCH TO TIMBER COVE

Sea Ranch

Almost since its inception, controversy has been the middle name of this 5,200-acre sheep ranch-cum-exclusive vacation home subdivision. No one could have imagined the ranch's significance in finally resolving long-fought battles over California coastal access and coastal protection. It was here in the 1970s that much of the war over beach access took place, ending with the establishment of the California Coastal Commission.

Sea Ranch architects get rave reviews for their simple, boxlike, high-priced condominiums and homes, which emulate weather-beaten local barns. The much-applauded cluster development design allowed "open space" for the aesthetic well-being of residents and passersby alike, but provided no way to get to the 10 miles of state-owned coastline without trespassing.

In 1972, Proposition 20 theoretically opened access, but the *reality* of beach access through Sea Ranch was achieved only in late 1985, when four of the six public trails across the property

were ceremoniously, officially dedicated. But here, the public-access victory is only partial; Sea Ranch charges a day-use fee. Make it worth your while. From the access at Walk-On Beach, you can link up with the Bluff Top Trail that winds along the wild coastline to Gualala Point Regional Park some miles to the north.

On the northern edge of the spread is the gnomish stone and stained-glass **Sea Ranch Chapel** designed by noted architect James Hubbell. Inside it's serene as a redwood forest. From the outside, the cedar-roofed chapel looks like an abstract artist's interpretation of a mushroom, perhaps a wave, maybe even a UFO from the Ice Age. What is it? Nice for meditation or prayer, if the door's unlocked.

Those who salivate over Sea Ranch and can afford the rates might consider an overnight stay (or maybe just a meal) at the 20-room **Sea Ranch Lodge,** 60 Seawalk Dr., tel. (707) 785-2371 or toll-free (800) 732-7262, fax (707) 785-2917, www.searanchlodge.com. Its pretty and plush accommodations look out over the Pacific, and some rooms have fireplaces and private hot tubs. Other amenities include pools, saunas, and an 18-hole links-style golf course (tel. 707-785-2468). Luxury, though ask about specials in the Premium range. Vacation home rentals are also available. Inquire at the lodge for current info, or call **Sea Ranch Escape** toll-free at (888) 732-7262 or **Rams Head Realty** toll-free at (800) 785-3455.

Stewarts Point

Heading south toward Salt Point, stop at the weather-beaten **Stewarts Point Store,** just to appreciate the 120-plus years of tradition the Richardson family has stuffed into every nook and cranny. You can buy almost anything, from canned goods and fresh vegetables to rubber boots and camp lanterns (and if they don't have it, they'll order it). Not for sale are items creating the store's ambience: the abalone shells and stuffed fish hanging from the ceiling, horse collars, oxen yoke, turn-of-the-century fish traps, and an 1888 Studebaker baby buggy.

Big news in Stewarts Point in 1996 was the completion of the 144-acre **Odiyan Buddhist**

Center, the largest Tibetan Buddhist center in the Western hemisphere. This complex, the cultivated center of 1,100 acres on Tin Barn Rd., includes six copper-domed major temples, a 113-foot gold stupa (a traditional monument to enlightenment), four libraries of sacred texts, 800 prayer flags, 1,242 prayer wheels, 200,000 clay offerings, 6,000 rose bushes, and 200,000 new trees, and is the brainchild of exiled Tibetan lama Tarthang Tulku, founder of the Nyingma Institute in Berkeley and both Dharma Publishing and Dharma Press. The main building, the three-tiered Odiyan Temple, resembles a three-dimensional mandala—symbolizing balance and order.

Salt Point State Park

This 3,500-acre park is most often compared to Point Lobos on the Monterey Peninsula, thanks to its dramatic outcroppings, tidepools and coves (this is one of the state's first official underwater preserves), wave-sculpted sandstone, lonely wind-whipped headlands, and highlands including a pygmy forest of stunted cypress, pines, and redwoods.

Though most people visit only the seaward side of the park—to dive or to examine the park's honeycombed *tafuni* rock (sculpted sandstone)—the best real hiking is across the road within the park's inland extension (pick up a map to the park when you enter).

Among Salt Point's other attractions are the dunes and several old Pomo village sites. In season, berrying, fishing, and mushrooming are favorite activities. Park rangers lead hikes and sponsor other occasional programs on weekends, and are also available to answer questions during the seasonal migration of the gray whales. The platform at Sentinal Rock is a great perch for whalewatching.

Among its other superlatives, Salt Point is also prime for camping. The park has tent and RV campsites ($16) with hot showers, as well as walk-in, bike-in, and environmental campsites. Make reservations, at least during the summer high season, through ReserveAmerica, toll-free tel. (800) 444-7275. Pleasant picnicking here, too. Day-use fee: $5 per carload (dogs $1 extra). For more information, contact: Salt Point State Park, 25050 Hwy. 1, Jenner, CA 95450, tel. (707) 847-3221 or (707) 865-2391.

Kruse Rhododendron Preserve

Adjoining Salt Point State Park, the seasonally astounding Kruse Rhododendron Preserve is an almost-natural wonder. Nowhere else on earth does *Rhododendron californicum* grow to such heights and in such profusion, in such perfect harmony—under a canopy of redwoods. Here at the 317-acre preserve, unplanted and uncultivated native rhododendrons up to 30 feet tall thrive in well-lit yet cool second-growth groves of coast redwood, Douglas fir, tan oak, and madrone. (Lumbermen downed the virgin forest, unintentionally benefiting the rhododendrons, which need cool, moist conditions but more sunshine than denser stands of redwoods offer.) The dominant shrub is the *Rhododendron macrophyllum,* or California rosebay, common throughout the Pacific Northwest. Also here is the *Rhododendron occidentale,* or western azalea, with its cream-colored flowers.

Most people say the best time to cruise into Kruse is in April or May, when the rhododendrons' spectacular pink bloom is at its finest. (Peak blooming time varies from year to year, so call ahead for current guestimates.) Another sublime time to come is a bit earlier in spring (between sweet-smelling rainstorms), when the rhododendron buds just start to show color and the tiny woods orchids, violets, and trilliums still bloom among the Irish-green ferns and mossy redwood stumps. But come anytime; the song of each season has its own magic note.

To get here from Hwy. 1, head east a short distance via Kruse Ranch Road. Coming in via the backwoods route from Cazadero is an adventure in itself, especially if the necessary signs have been taken down (again) by locals. To try it, better call ahead first for precise directions. Facilities at the preserve are appropriately minimal but include picnic tables and outhouses. For bloom predictions, preserve conditions, and other information, contact Salt Point State Park (see above).

Timber Cove

Hard to miss even in the fog, the landmark eight-story **Benjamin Bufano *Peace* sculpture** looms over Timber Cove Inn and the surrounding countryside. Once a "doghole port" for lumber schooners, like most craggy north coast indentations, Timber Cove is now a haven for the reasonably affluent. But ordinary people can stop for a look at Bufano's last, unfinished work. From the hotel parking lot, walk seaward and look up into the face of *Peace,* reigning over land and sea. The **Timber Cove Inn,** 21780 N. Hwy. 1, tel. (707) 847-3231 or toll-free (800) 987-8319, fax (707) 847-3704, offers fairly luxurious accommodations on a 26-acre point jutting out into the Pacific. Some rooms have private hot tubs, some have lofts, and most have fireplaces. Premium-Luxury.

For exceptional luxury, try the unusually fine outback accommodations available at **Timberhill Ranch Country Inn,** 35755 Hauser Bridge Rd., Cazadero, www.timberhillranch.com, about four miles inland from the highway near Salt Point and the Kruse Reserve. At press time, Timberhill was under new ownership, with renovations underway. It's scheduled to reopen in fall 2001. For information on the new owners and a sneak preview of Timberhill's super-deluxe future, visit the website. Luxury.

FORT ROSS STATE HISTORIC PARK

A large village of the Kashia Pomo people once stood here. After the Russian-American Fur Company (Czar Alexander I and President James Madison were both company officers) established its fur-trapping settlements at Bodega Bay, the firm turned its attention northward to what, in the spring of 1812, became **Fort Ross,** imperial Russia's farthest outpost. Here the Russians grew grains and vegetables to supply Alaskan colonists as well as Californios, manufactured a wide variety of products, and trapped sea otters to satisfy the voracious demand for fine furs. With pelts priced at $700 each, no trapping technique went untried. One of the most effective: grabbing a sea otter pup and using its distress calls to lure otherwise wary adults into range.

The Russians' success here and elsewhere in California led to the virtual extinction of the sea otter. Combined with devastating agricultural losses, this brought serious economic problems to the region. Commercial shipbuilding was attempted but also failed. The Russians got out from under this morass only by leaving, after selling Fort Ross and all its contents to John Sutter. Sutter (who agreed to the $30,000 price

but never made a payment) carried off most of the equipment, furnishings, tools, and whatever else he could use to improve his own fort. Sutter's empire building eventually required James Marshall to head up the American River to build a sawmill. Marshall's discovery of gold led to Sutter's instant ruin but also to the almost overnight Americanization of California.

The First Fort

The weathered redwood fortress perched on these lonely headlands, surrounded by gloomy cypress groves, was home to Russian traders and trappers for 40 years. The original 14-foot-high stockade featured corner lookouts and 40 cannons. Inside the compound were barracks, a jail, the commandant's house, warehouses, and workshops. At the fort and just outside its walls, the industrious Russians and their work crews produced household goods plus saddles, bridles, even 200-ton ships and prefabricated houses.

Perhaps due to the Russian Orthodox belief that only God is perfect, the fort was constructed with no right angles. Its Greek Orthodox chapel was the only building here destroyed by the 1906 San Francisco earthquake. It was rebuilt, then lost again to arson in 1970, though it's since been reconstructed from the original blueprints (fetched from Moscow). Outside the stockade was a bustling town of Aleut hunters' redwood huts, with a windmill and various outbuildings and shops. When the Russians at Fort Ross finally prepared to leave their failed American empire, the Pomo held a mourning ceremony to mark their departure—a testament to the visitors' amicable long-term relations with the native peoples.

The Reconstructed Fort and Other Attractions

A good place to start exploring Fort Ross is at its million-dollar **visitor center** and museum, which includes a good introductory slide program (shown throughout the day in the auditorium), as well as Pomo artifacts and basketry, other historic displays, period furnishings, and a gift shop. The free **audio tour** of the fort is itself entertaining (balalaika music, hymns, and Princess Helena Rotchev—namesake of Mt. St. Helena near Calistoga—playing Mozart on the piano).

The fort's only remaining original building (now restored) is the commandant's quarters.

the Greek Orthodox
Church at Fort Ross

BOB RACE

Other reconstructed buildings include the barracks—furnished as if Russians would sail up and bed down any minute—an artisans' center, and the armory.

The park's boundaries also encompass a beach, the ridgetop redwoods behind the fort, and other lands to the north and east. Thanks to the Coastwalk organization, hiking access (including a handicapped-accessible trail) has been added to the Black Ranch Park area south of the fort. Ask at the visitor center for current hiking information.

Practical Fort Ross

Just 12 miles north of Jenner along Hwy. 1, Fort Ross is open to the public 10 a.m.-4:30 p.m. daily (except major holidays), $6 per car. Autophobes, get here via **Mendocino Transit** buses daily from the north, tel. (707) 462-1422, or **Sonoma County Transit** from Jenner, tel. (707) 576-7433 or toll-free (800) 345-7433 in Sonoma County.

On **Living History Day** in July or August, the colony here suddenly comes back to life circa 1836. History buffs can have fun questioning repertory company volunteers to see if they know their stuff.

For those who want to rough it, first-come, first-served primitive camping is possible at **Fort Ross Reef State Campground,** tucked into a ravine just south of the fort (20 campsites, no dogs). For more information, contact: Fort Ross State Historic Park, 19005 Hwy. 1, Jenner, CA 95450, tel. (707) 847-3286 or (707) 865-2391.

Those who want to "smooth it" can instead try **Fort Ross Lodge,** 20705 Hwy. 1, Jenner, CA 95450, tel. (707) 847-3333 or toll-free (800) 968-4537, which offers all modern amenities and great ocean views. Moderate-Luxury.

EXCURSION INLAND: RUSSIAN RIVER RESORT AREA

Most people think of the Russian River as the cluster of rustic redwood-cloistered resort villages stretching from Jenner-by-the-Sea east along Hwy. 116 to Guerneville, the region once a popular resort area for well-to-do San Franciscans. The Russian River's original recreational appeal dried up many decades ago, as faster transportation and better roads took people elsewhere. Lured by low rents and the area's strange spiritual aura, back-to-the-landers started arriving in the late 1960s. The newest waves of Russian River immigrants are the relatively affluent, bringing more urbane ways and much-needed money to renovate and revitalize the area. Today's colorful cultural mix, including loggers, gays, sheep ranchers, farmers, hippies, and retirees, is surprisingly simpatico despite occasional outbreaks of intolerance. For all their apparent differences, people who manage to survive here share some common traits: they're good-humored, self-sufficient, and stubborn. After the devastating winter floods that regularly inundate the area, for example, locals accept the raging river's most recent rampage and set out, as a community, to make things right.

It's a mistake, though, to view the Russian River as strictly a Jenner-to-Guerneville phenomenon. The river's headwaters are far to the north, just southeast of Willits, though it's not much of a river until it reaches Cloverdale. Roughly paralleling Hwy. 101 inland, this slow, sidewinding waterway—called Shabaikai or Misallaako ("Long Snake") by Native Americans, and Slavianka ("Charming One") by early Russian fur traders—uncoils slowly through Sonoma County's northern wine country, and multiple small wineries cluster like grapes. To find them—representing the Alexander Valley, Chalk Hill, Dry Creek Valley, Green Valley, and Russian River Valley appellations—pick up a free map and brochure at local chamber of commerce offices. Or contact **Russian River Wine Road**, P.O. Box 46, Healdsburg, CA 95448, tel. (707) 433-4374 or toll-free (800) 723-6336, www.wineroad.com. Come on the first weekend in March for the annual **Russian River Wine Road Barrel Tasting,** the big annual event at all member wineries.

Contact the **Russian River Chamber of Commerce,** 16209 First St., P.O. Box 331, Guerneville, CA 95446, tel. (707) 869-9000, www.russianriver.com, for a current listing of resort-area lodgings, restaurants, and upcoming events. The chamber has a complete business directory of gay-oriented establishments, available for reference. Stop off at **King's Sport & Tackle,** 16258 Main St. in downtown Guerneville, tel. (707) 869-2156, for current fishing information and supplies.

Jenner

Perched like a sleepy sentinel on the steep, curvaceous hills overlooking the Pacific Ocean and the mouth of the Russian River, Jenner is primarily a pleasant collection of seaside shanties committed to watching the tourists roll by. If you, too, are just passing through, consider a meal stop at the locally popular **River's End,** 11051 Hwy. 1 in Jenner, tel. (707) 865-2484 or (707) 869-3252. Also in Jenner is **Sizzling Tandoor,** 9960 Hwy. 1 (on the south side of the Russian River bridge at Willow Creek Rd.), tel. (707) 865-0625, serving mouthwatering East Indian fare.

South of Jenner and north of Goat Rock, at the

mouth of the Russian River, a large population of harbor seals has established itself, attracting considerable human attention. Unlike sea lions, which amble along on flippers, harbor seals wriggle like inchworms until in the water, where their mobility instantly improves. On weekends, volunteer naturalists (members of Stewards of Slavianka) show up to answer questions, lend binoculars for a close-up look, and protect the seals from unleashed dogs and too-curious tourists. Do keep your distance. When panicked, harbor seals will protect themselves by biting. Some carry diseases difficult to treat in humans—which is why sailors of old used to cut off a limb if it was seal-bitten.

"Pupping season" starts in March and continues into June. During these months, harbor seals and their young become vulnerable to more predators, since they give birth on land. Some worry that Jenner's large seal colony will attract other enthusiastic observers, like sharks and killer whales. Not known to attack humans (though no one will guarantee that), killer whales also consider harbor seals a delicacy. To avoid predators, harbor seals swim upriver as far as Monte Rio while fishing for their own prey: salmon and steelhead.

SONOMA COAST STATE BEACHES

For the most part, the spectacular coastline between Jenner and Bodega Bay is owned by the state. The collective Sonoma Coast State Beaches represent some 13 coastal miles of pointy-headed offshore rock formations or "sea stacks," natural arches, and a series of secluded beaches and small coves with terrific tidepools. Don't even think about swimming here (though diving is possible in certain areas), since the cold water, heavy surf, undertows, and sleeper waves all add up to danger. But for beachcombing, ocean fishing, a stroll, or a jog—perfect. Rangers offer weekend whalewatching programs from mid-December through mid-April.

Sonoma Coast Beach Areas

Sprinkled like garnish between the various state beaches from Jenner to Bodega Bay are a variety of **public beaches,** including Blind, Shell, Goat Rock, Marshall Gulch, Schoolhouse, Carmet,

Arched Rock, Coleman, and Miwok Beaches. **Shell Beach** in the north is best for beachcombing and seaside strolls, with some tremendous tidepools and good fishing. It's a spectacularly snaky road from Hwy. 1 down to dramatic Goat Rock, popular **Goat Rock Beach,** and the dunes just east. The craggy goat itself is an impressive promontory but illegal to climb around on: more than a dozen people have drowned in recent years, swept off the rocks by surging surf. In the **Willow Creek** area, near the mouth of the Russian River on the east side of Hwy. 1, are hiking trails and simple campground facilities; this area is popular with local birdwatchers. For a great hike, take the three-mile **Dr. David Joseph Trail,** starting at the Pomo Canyon Campground just off Willow Creek Rd., south of the mouth of the Russian River (for campground details, see below). The route threads through the redwoods into the ferns, then on through the oak woodlands and grassland scrub down to the Pacific ocean at Shell Beach.

Duncans Landing, midway to Bodega Bay, is also referred to as **Death Rock;** a former offshore lumber-loading spot during the redwood harvesting heyday, today it's one of the most dangerous spots along the Sonoma coast. Plan a picture-perfect picnic near **Rock Point** on the headland (tables available). **Portuguese Beach,** best for rock fishing and surf fishing, is a sandy beach surrounded by rocky headlands. First of the beaches north of Bodega Bay is **Salmon Creek Beach,** part of which becomes a lagoon when sand shuts the creek's mouth. (If you must swim, try the lagoon here.)

Practical Sonoma Coast Beaches

Along this stretch are plentiful pulloffs for parking cars, with access to beach trails and spectacular views. The day-use fee for the Sonoma Coast State Beaches is $5. Camp at **Wright's Beach,** with 30 developed campsites (but no showers) just back from the beach ($20); or **Bodega Dunes,** a half mile south of Salmon Creek, with 98 developed sites secluded among the cypress-dotted dunes, hot showers, an RV sanitation station, and a campfire center ($16). Developed Sonoma Coast campsites are reservable in advance through ReserveAmerica, toll-free tel. (800) 444-7275. Primitive walk-in camping is available April-Nov. at 11-site **Willow Creek**

Campground along the banks of the Russian River (first-come, first-camped, $10); no dogs. Register at the trailhead, up Willow Creek Rd. (turn right at the Sizzling Tandoor restaurant). The walk-in **Pomo Canyon Campground** (also $10) is reached via the same route. About five minutes after turning off Hwy. 1, you'll reach the gravel parking lot marked Pomo Canyon Campground. From here, two trails run into the redwoods to the 21 walk-in sites, which feature a picnic table, fire grill, and leveled tent site.

For current conditions and other information on the Sonoma Coast State Beaches, call the Bodega Dunes campground at (707) 875-3483, or contact the **Salmon Creek Ranger Station,** 3095 Hwy. 1 (just north of town), Bodega Bay, CA 94923, tel. (707) 875-2603.

BODEGA BAY AND VICINITY

Alfred Hitchcock considered this quaint coastal fishing village and the inland town of Bodega perfect for filming *The Birds,* with its rather ominous suggestion that one day nature will avenge itself. But people come to Bodega Bay and vicinity to avoid thinking about such things. They come to explore the headlands, to whalewatch, to kayak, to beachcomb and tidepool, to catch and eat seafood (including local Dungeness crab), to peek into the increasing numbers of galleries and gift shops, and to *relax.* Bodega Bay's **Fisherman's Festival and Blessing of the Fleet** in April attracts upward of 25,000 people for a Mardi Gras-style boat parade, kite-flying championships, bathtub and foot races, art shows, and a barbecue. Ochlophobes, steer clear. Or come in late August for the **Bodega Bay Seafood, Art & Wine Festival,** a benefit for the Chanslor Wetlands Wildlife Project.

Just wandering through town and along the harbor is fascinating. While keeping an eye on the sky for any sign of feathered terrorists, watch the chartered "party boats" and fishing fleet at the harbor—particularly at six each evening, daily catch arrives at the Tides Wharf. Bodega, just inland, is where visitors go to reimagine scenes from Hitchcock's movie, most particularly **St. Teresa of Avila Church** and **Potter Schoolhouse.**

Most people don't know, though, that Hitchcock's story was based on actual events of Au-

Bodega Harbor

BOB RACE

gust 18, 1961, though they occurred in Capitola, Rio Del Mar, and other towns on Monterey Bay, farther south. That night, tens of thousands of crazed shearwaters slammed into doors, windows, and hapless people; the next morning these birds, both dead and dying, stank of anchovies. In 1995, researchers at the Institute of Marine Sciences at UC Santa Cruz suggested that a lethal "bloom" of a natural toxin produced by algae—domoic acid—present in Monterey Bay anchovies was probably responsible for the birds' bizarre behavior. Toxic amounts of domoic acid cause amnesia, brain damage, and dementia.

Near Bodega Bay and stretching north to Jenner are the slivers of collectively managed **Sonoma Coast State Beaches,** which include **Bodega Head** and **Bodega Dunes** near the bay itself. Inland are a variety of small spots-in-the-road, some little more than a restaurant or boarded-up gas station at a crossroads, all connected to Bodega Bay by scenic roller-coaster roads. Not far south of town in Marin County is **Dillon Beach,** known for its tidepools. Keep going south via Hwy. 1 to the sensational **Point Reyes National Seashore.**

For more information on Bodega Bay and environs, stop by the **Bodega Bay Area Visitor Information Center,** 850 Hwy. 1, P.O. Box 146, Bodega Bay, CA 94923, tel. (707) 875-3866, www.bodegabay.com. Or call the **Bodega Bay Area Chamber of Commerce** at (707) 875-3422.

Children's Bell Tower

Beyond Bodega Head, the bay, and the beautiful landscape, one of the few sights in Bodega Bay is the Children's Bell Tower, next to the Community Center on the west side of Hwy. 1, about a mile and a half north of the visitor center. The monument was inspired by a heart-rending story splashed across the front pages of the world's newspapers in 1994, when seven-year-old Nicholas Green of Bodega Bay was shot and killed while traveling with his family in Italy. His parents, Maggie and Reg Green, decided to donate Nicholas's organs to needy Italian recipients—a decision all but unheard of in Italy, and one that moved Italians and Americans alike.

Bay Area sculptor Bruce Hasson conceived and designed the bell tower as a memorial to Nicholas and the courage of his parents. Donated bells of all types—130 in all—came in from all over Italy. The centerpiece bell was cast by the Marinelli foundry, which has made bells for the papacy for 1,000 years; this bell is inscribed with the names of Nicholas and the seven Italians who were given a second chance at life thanks to the donation. In the words of Nicholas's father, when the memorial was dedicated in 1996, "We've tried to create a place of pilgrimage, a place where any parent can come for solace or inspiration, a place that reminds us of the fragility and preciousness of young life. . . ."

Bodega Coast Recreation

All popular along and near the Bodega Bay coast: birdwatching, collecting driftwood, tidepooling, surf and rock fishing, hiking, bicycling the area's strikingly scenic backroads, sea kayaking, and whalewatching. Best yet, all these activities are free.

For good swimmers, free-diving for abalone (use of scuba gear for the purpose is illegal) is a special treat. Diving season is April 1 through the end of June, then August 1 through November, assuming the abalone population is adequate for harvest. Abalone divers are required to get a California fishing license with an additional abalone stamp and carry a shell gauge (minimum size is seven inches across at the shell's broadest point) and a legal abalone iron; they can take no more than four abalone. According to new information about these creatures' lifestyles, abalone move to-ward the shore in winter, farther out to sea in summer. So it's no wonder that "shore picking" at low tide is dismal.

Bodega Area Camping

Camp at Bodega Dunes just north of the harbor, at smaller Wrights Beach on the way to Jenner, or at primitive Willow Creek Campground near Goat Rock. (For more information on these state park campgrounds, see Sonoma Coast State Beaches below). **Doran Beach County Park** to the south has first-come, first-camped primitive outdoor accommodations. Day-use fee is $3. Camping is $15 per night for the first vehicle and $5 per additional vehicle, plus $1 per dog. For information, contact the park at P.O. Box 372, Bodega Bay, CA 94923, tel. (707) 875-3540, or call regional park headquarters at (707) 527-2041. Another possibility is the private **Porto Bodega Fisherman's Marina and RV Park,** 1500 Bay Flat Rd., tel. (707) 875-2354.

Bodega Bay Motels and Inns

In town, the hotspot is the fairly pricey **Bodega Bay Lodge & Spa,** 103 Hwy. 1 (off the highway at Doran Beach Rd.), tel. (707) 875-3525 or toll-free (800) 368-2468, www.woodsidehotels.com, which offers full luxury amenities, including an ocean-view pool, spa, fitness center, and exceptional The Duck Club restaurant. Luxury. It's also adjacent to the **Bodega Harbour Golf Links,** 21301 Heron Dr., tel. (707) 875-3538, an 18-hole Scottish links-style course designed by Robert Trent Jones Jr.

Another possibility is the **Inn at the Tides,** 800 Hwy. 1, tel. (707) 875-2751 or toll-free (800) 541-7788, fax (707) 875-3285, www.innatthetides.com. Rates include full amenities (pool, sauna, whirlpool, TV and movies, and many rooms with fireplaces), great views, and continental breakfast. Premium. The Inn at the Tides also features a casual in-house restaurant—see below—and the very good Sonoma-style continental **Bay View** restaurant, and sponsors a **Dinner with the Winemaker** series of monthly dinners and winetastings. Also nice is the **Bodega Coast Inn,** 521 Hwy. 1, tel. (707) 875-2217 or toll-free (800) 346-6999, www.bodegacoastinn.com (Premium), and the old-fashioned, small **Bodega Harbor Inn,** 1345 Bodega Ave., tel. (707) 875-3594 (Moderate-Luxury), which also rents out cottages and houses.

BODEGA HEAD

Hulking Bodega Head protects Bodega Bay from the heavy seas, a visible chunk of the Pacific plate and also bulwark for the area's state beaches. Good whalewatching from here. Nearby is the University of California at Davis's **Bodega Marine Lab,** 2099 Westside Rd., tel. (707) 875-2211, a marine biology research center open to the public every Friday. Hike on and around the head on well-worn footpaths, or head out for an invigorating walk via hiking trails to **Bodega Dunes.** Five miles of hiking and horseback riding trails twist through the dunes themselves (access at the north end of the bay, via W. Bay Road). To get to Bodega Head, take Westside Rd. and follow the signs past **Westside Park.**

Doran County Park, on the south side of the bay, tel. (707) 875-3540, looks bleak, but its windswept beaches and dunes provide safe harbor for diverse wildlife and hardy plants. Swim at these protected beaches; also good clamming. Small day-use fee. Or visit the water-filled sump once destined for the nuclear age—called "hole in the head" and "the world's most expensive duckpond" by bemused locals. With Hitchcock's nature-vengeance theme in mind, we can only shudder at what might have been if PG&E had built its proposed nuclear power plant here, just four miles from the San Andreas Fault.

People often knock at the door of the Queen Anne Victorian **Bay Hill Mansion,** 3919 Bay Hill Rd., P.O. Box 567, tel. (707) 875-3577 or toll-free (800) 526-5927, www.bayhillmansion.com, to ask if it was featured in *The Birds.* (It wasn't.) But you can pretend. Five comfortable rooms (some share bath), great views of Bodega Bay. Luxury.

Nearby Lodgings
Visitors seeking the ultimate in pampering should head south of town six miles on Hwy. 1 to **Sonoma Coast Villa,** 16702 Hwy. 1 (two miles north of Valley Ford), tel. (707) 876-9818 or toll-free (888) 404-2255, fax (707) 876-9856, www.scvilla.com, a plush country estate offering complete spa services. Indulge yourself with a massage, a moor mud body treatment, a seaweed mud body mask, or an herbal body wrap, then enjoy a Mediterranean-inspired dinner, featuring fresh local produce (some right from the Villa's own organic garden) and the finest Sonoma County wines. Other amenities include a swimming pool and jacuzzi, pool table, putting green, wood-burning fireplaces, beautiful Italian slate floors, stocked refrigerators (Sonoma county wines, soft drinks), organic in-room coffee, and unique furnishings throughout. Rates include full country breakfast. Luxury.

In Valley Ford, eight miles south of Bodega Bay, the **Inn at Valley Ford,** 14395 Hwy. 1, tel. (707) 876-3182, is a cozy coast bed and breakfast with old-fashioned garden, fireplace, and antique-stuffed rooms. Private or shared bath. Rates include breakfast (with homemade breads). Moderate-Expensive. Another option in Valley Ford is the **Valley Ford Hotel,** 14415 Hwy. 1, tel. (707) 876-3600 or toll-free (800) 696-6679. The seven-room inn dates from 1864 but was renovated in 1990. Rates include full breakfast. Moderate-Expensive.

The **Chanslor Guest Ranch,** 2660 Hwy. 1 (just north of Bodega Bay), tel. (707) 875-2721, is a working horse and sheep spread that also boards people. Suites available, including one with two private balconies and a whirlpool tub. Rates include continental breakfast. Horseback riding costs extra. Moderate-Premium.

Eating in Bodega Bay
Get fresh fish and chips, even hot seafood to go, at popular **Lucas Wharf Deli and Fish Mar-**

ket, 595 Hwy. 1 (on the pier at the harbor), tel. (707) 875-3562. Or pick up a delicious seafood sandwich and microbrew, and take it out to one of the benches and tables overlooking a working dock. The adjacent sit-down **Lucas Wharf Restaurant and Bar,** tel. (707) 875-3522, is open for lunch and dinner daily and is known for its pastas and steaks as well as seafood. Great clam chowder, fisherman's stew, and sourdough bread. A bit more spiffy (and a *lot* more pricey) is the recently renovated **The Tides Wharf Restaurant,** 835 Hwy. 1 (just north of Lucas Wharf), tel. (707) 875-3652, which also overlooks the bay (and has its own dock and video arcade) and was featured as a backdrop in *The Birds.* The Tides is popular for breakfast, and you can count on fresh seafood at lunch and dinner. Open daily; there's a fresh fish market and bait shop here, too. The finest dining in town, though, is available at **The Duck Club** at the Bodega Bay Lodge, 103 Hwy. 1, tel. (707) 875-3525, famous for its Sonoma County cuisine—everything from Petaluma duck with orange sauce and Hagemann Ranch filet mignon to grilled Pacific salmon with sweet mustard glaze. Open daily for breakfast and dinner (picnic lunch available).

The **Breakers Cafe,** 1400 Hwy. 1, tel. (707) 875-2513, is another option for breakfast (waffles, Benedicts, omelettes, breakfast burritos), lunch (good sandwiches like portobello mushroom or cold shrimp and crab), and dinner (pastas, soups, salads, steaks). The wholesome **Sandpiper Dockside Café & Restaurant,** 1410 Bay Flat Rd. (take Eastshore Dr. off Hwy. 1 and go straight at the stop sign), tel. (707) 875-2278, is a casual locals' place open daily for breakfast, lunch, and dinner. The **Whaler's Inn,** 1805 Hwy. 1, tel. (707) 875-2829, is the town's "country kitchen," open daily for breakfast, lunch, and dinner, and serving fresh American-style specialties, from seafood and chicken-fried steak to barbecued ribs. No checks or credit cards.

Eating beyond Bodega Bay
To drive somewhere in order to totally enjoy sitting down again, head south on Hwy. 1 to Valley Ford, the town made famous by Christo's *Running Fence.* The frumpy white frame building is **Dinucci's,** 14485 Valley Ford Rd., tel. (707) 876-3260, a fantastically fun watering hole and

dinner house. Study the massive rosewood bar inside, shipped around Cape Horn, while waiting for a table (folks are allowed to linger over meals). The walls in the bar are almost papered in decades-old political posters, old newspaper clippings, and an eclectic collection of light-hearted local memorabilia. The dim barroom lighting reflects off the hundreds of abalone shells decorating the ceiling. Dinucci's boisterous family-style dining room has close-together, sometimes shared (it's either that or keep waiting) checkerboard-clothed tables and a very friendly serving staff. Dinner starts with antipasto, a vat of very good homemade minestrone, fresh bread, and salad, followed by seafood or pasta entrées and desserts. For $15 or so, after eating here people can barely walk to their cars.

If you're heading north, try to be hungry when you get to Jenner. Just on the south side of the Russian River Bridge in Bridgehaven is **Sizzling Tandoor,** 9960 Hwy. 1 (at Willow Creek Rd.), tel. (707) 865-0625, where you can dine on superb Indian food at tables inside or out. Open for lunch and dinner daily.

POINT REYES NATIONAL SEASHORE

Some 65,000 acres of fog-shrouded lagoons, lowland marshes, sandy beaches, coastal dunes, and ridgetop forests, Point Reyes National Seashore also features windy headlands and steep, unstable, colorful cliffs, populations of tule elk and grazing cattle, and a wonderful lighthouse all too popular for winter whalewatching. A dramatically dislocated triangular wedge of land with its apex jutting out into the Pacific Ocean, Point Reyes is also land in motion: this is earthquake country. Separated from mainland Marin County by slitlike Tomales Bay, the Point Reyes Peninsula is also sliced off at about the same spot by the San Andreas Fault. When that fault shook loose in 1906—instantly thrusting the peninsula 16 feet farther north—the city of San Francisco came tumbling down.

Geologists were long baffled by the fact that the craggy granite outcroppings of Point Reyes were identical to rock formations in the Tehachapi Mountains some 310 miles south. But the theory of plate tectonics and continental drift provided the answer. The Point Reyes Peninsula rides high on the eastern edge of the Pacific Plate, which moves about three inches to the northwest each year, grinding against the slower-moving North American Plate. The two meet in the high-stress, many-faulted rift zone of the Olema Valley, an undefined line "visible" in landforms and weather patterns. In summer, for example, fog may chill the coastal headlands and beaches while the sun shines east of Inverness Ridge.

Seasonally, dogs are specifically restricted at Point Reyes—and people must also restrain themselves—because the northern elephant seals have returned to area beaches and established a breeding colony. To protect the elephant seals during the winter breeding and pupping season, no dogs are allowed on South Beach and beaches to the south Nov.-April. Only leashed dogs are allowed on North Beach, Kehoe Beach, and the southern part of Limantour Beach. Contact the park office for current details.

To be fully informed about what's going on in and around Point Reyes while visiting, a good free companion is the quarterly tabloid *Coastal* *Traveler,* published by the area's Pulitzer Prize-winning *Point Reyes Light* newspaper and available at area shops and businesses. For advance or additional information, contact the **West Marin Chamber of Commerce,** P.O. Box 1045, Point Reyes Station, CA 94956, tel. (415) 663-9232.

SEEING AND DOING POINT REYES

Get oriented at the park's barnlike **Bear Valley Visitor Center,** tel. (415) 663-1092, just off Bear Valley Rd. (off Hwy. 1 near Olema), which, in addition to natural history and fine arts exhibits, includes a seismograph for monitoring the earth's movements. Near the picnic tables at the visitor center is the short **Earthquake Trail** loop (wheelchair accessible), which demonstrates the San Andreas seismic drama, from sag ponds and shifts in natural boundary lines to the old Shafter Ranch barn, a corner of which slid off its foundations during the 1906 San Francisco earthquake. Also near the Bear Valley Visitor Center are the short, self-guided **Woodpecker Nature Trail;** the **Morgan Horse Ranch,** where the Park Service breeds and trains its mounts; and **Kule Loklo,** an architectural re-creation of a Coast Miwok community. (When Sir Francis Drake purportedly arrived at Point Reyes in the late 1500s, he found more than 100 such villages on the peninsula.) The best time to see Kule Loklo is during July's Annual Native American Celebration, when this outdoor exhibit, complete with sweathouse, thatched and redwood bark dwellings, and dancing lodge, comes to life with Miwok basketmakers, wood- and stonecarvers, and native singing and dancing.

Limantour Estero near Drakes Estero and Drakes Beach is great for birdwatching; **McClures Beach** is best for tidepooling; and both **North Beach** and **South Beach** north of Point Reyes proper offer good beachcombing but treacherous swimming. Protected **Drakes Beach** and **Limantour Beach** along the crescent of Drakes Bay are safe for swimming.

For astounding views when the fog lifts above the ship graveyard offshore, head out to Point

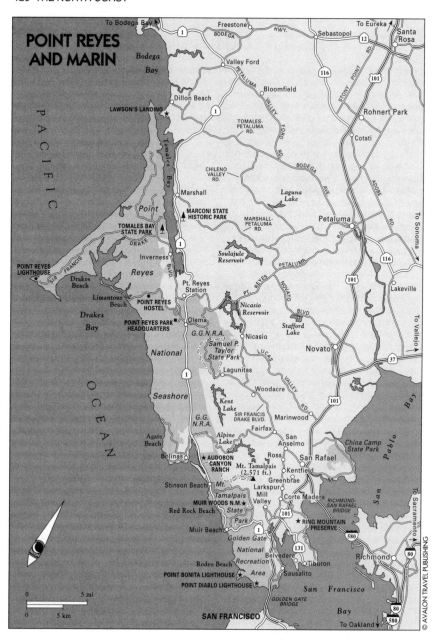

POINT REYES
AND MARIN

PACIFIC

To Bodega Bay
Freestone
Freestone
BODEGA
HWY.
To Eureka
Santa
Rosa
12
Bodega
Bay
Valley Ford
1
Sebastopol
116
101
Bloomfield
Rohnert Park
Dillon Beach
1
TOMALES-
PETALUMA
RD.
Cotati
LAWSON'S LANDING
CHILENO
VALLEY
RD.
BODEGA
AVE.
Laguna
Lake
To Sonoma
Marshall
MARCONI STATE
HISTORIC PARK
MARSHALL-
PETALUMA
RD.
Petaluma
Point
PETALUMA
116
TOMALES BAY
STATE PARK
DRAKE
Soulajule
Reservoir
101
POINT REYES
LIGHTHOUSE
Inverness
PT. REYES
NOVATO
BLVD.
Lakeville
SIR FRANCIS
Reyes
Drakes
Beach
Pt. Reyes
Station
Nicasio
Reservoir
To Vallejo
Limantour
Beach
POINT REYES
HOSTEL
Stafford
Lake
Drakes
Bay
POINT REYES PARK
HEADQUARTERS
Olema
G.G.N.R.A.
Nicasio
Novato
National
Samuel P.
Taylor
State Park
LUCAS
37
Seashore
Lagunitas
VALLEY
Woodacre
101
Kent
Lake
SIR FRANCIS
DRAKE BLVD.
Marinwood
RD.
G.G.
N.R.A.
Agate
Beach
Alpine
Lake
Fairfax
San
Anselmo
China Camp
State Park
San
Pablo
Bay
Bolinas
AUDUBON
CANYON
RANCH
Ross
San Rafael
To Sacramento
Mt. Tamalpais
(2,571 ft.)
Kentfield
Stinson Beach
Mt.
Tamalpais
Greenbrae
Larkspur
RICHMOND-
SAN RAFAEL
BRIDGE
MUIR WOODS N.M.
State
Corte Madera
Mill
Valley
580
Red Rock Beach
Park
101
RING MOUNTAIN
PRESERVE
Muir Beach
1
Golden Gate
National
Recreation
131
Richmond
80
Rodeo Beach
Belvedere
POINT BONITA LIGHTHOUSE
Area
Tiburon
Sausalito
POINT DIABLO LIGHTHOUSE
San Francisco
80
0   5 mi
0   5 km
GOLDEN GATE
BRIDGE
SAN FRANCISCO
Bay
580
To Oakland

Reyes proper and the **Point Reyes Lighthouse and Visitor Center,** tel. (415) 669-1534 (open daily 9 a.m.-5 p.m. during whalewatching season, more limited hours at other times). The Chimney Rock Trail is wonderful for spring and summer wildflowers and, if you head west, is also a roundabout way to reach the lighthouse. On all Point Reyes hikes, carry water, wear proper walking shoes, and dress for sudden, unpredictable weather changes.

To experience the sound and fury of Coast Creek hurling itself into the Pacific via the "sea tunnel" at the **Arch Rock Overlook,** dress warmly, wear raingear and slip-proof shoes, and come (via the popular Bear Valley Trail) during a storm. For safety's sake, stay well back from the spectacle, and don't attempt to walk through the tunnel under any circumstances—though people often do in calm weather.

To make the most of a full moon at Point Reyes, head to the **Wildcat Beach Overlook** via the Bear Valley Trail from the visitor center, then south via the Coast Trail to the area overlooking the beach, **Alamere Falls** (most spectacular after

THE MYSTERY OF SIR FRANCIS DRAKE

Though named by Sebastián Vizcaíno in 1603 while he was passing the rocky headlands on the 12th day of Christmas, or the Feast of the Three Kings, Point Reyes was actually explored earlier by the privateer Sir Francis Drake. Tired of pursuing Spanish ships around the world, he beached the *Pelican* (later known as the *Golden Hinde*) and came ashore at "a fit and convenient harbour" somewhere in California in June 1579. Naming the land Nova Albion, here he made repairs, rested his tired crew, and claimed the area for Queen Elizabeth I with "a plate of brasse, fast nailed to a great and firme post." This much most historians agree on. The rest of the story is contentious at best.

Where exactly did Drake land? Since the main estuary at Point Reyes is named after Drake, as is the bay, the simple answer is that he came ashore here, some 20 nautical miles north of San Francisco. But some contend that Drake actually landed at Bolinas Lagoon or explored San Francisco Bay and landed near Point San Quentin or Novato, near an old Olompali village site where a 1567 English silver sixpence was discovered in 1974. A more recent quest for remnants of Drake's visitation centers on Bodega Bay. Others say he stumbled ashore on Goleta Beach near Santa Barbara, where five cast-iron British cannons similar to those missing from the *Golden Hinde* were unearthed in the 1980s. But 70 pieces of antique Ming porcelain have been found near Point Reyes—proof

enough, say true believers of the Point Reyes theory, since four chests of Chinese porcelain, which Drake stole from the Spanish, never arrived in England. (Unbelievers counter that the porcelain washed ashore instead from the wreckage of the *San Agustin* off Drakes Bay.)

Other related questions remain unanswered. Is the infamous brass plate found on a beach near Point San Quentin in 1936 genuine or a clever forgery? After years of controversy, in the 1970s the British Museum declared the corroded placard an "undoubted fake" despite the olde English ring of its language, and metallurgists say the plate is no more than 100 years old. (To judge for yourself, the brass plate is on permanent display at UC Berkeley's Bancroft Library.)

What became of Drake's journal, which supposedly documented this journey as well as Drake's discovery of the Northwest Passage? What happened to the gold, gems, and silver Drake stole from the Spanish ship *Cacafuego* and others, estimated in today's currency values as worth $50 million? Some say no treasure was buried along the California coast, that Drake would have jettisoned cannons, china, and other goods instead to lighten his ship's load. Drake, they say, took all his loot back to England, where he and his crew became millionaires, and the queen retired some of the national debt and started the East India Company. Others, however, are still looking.

fishing on
Drake's Beach

TOM MYERS PHOTOGRAPHY

heavy rains), and the southern stretch of Drakes Bay. An alternate route to Alamere Falls, about one mile south of Wildcat Camp, is via the Palomarin Trail from Bolinas or the Five Brooks Trail. For the best panoramic vista of Drakes Bay, take the Bear Valley, Sky, then Woodward Valley Trails to the bay (alternatively, take the Coast Trail from Coast Camp to the Woodward Valley Trail), then climb up the small hill overlooking the bay, just northwest of the trail.

The **Randall Spur Trail,** created by the Civilian Conservation Corps, connects the Bolinas Ridge Trail with the various Inverness Ridge and Olema Valley trails—making Point Reyes's southern stretches more accessible for day hikers. Worth a stop on the way to the Palomarin trailhead in south Point Reyes is the **Point Reyes Bird Observatory,** tel. (415) 868-1221, established in 1965 as the first bird observatory in the country. Though it's a full-fledged research facility, the Palomarin observatory is open to the public, with educational classes (call ahead for information), interpretive exhibits, and a nature trail. To get here by car, take the unmarked turnoff to Bolinas (near highway marker 17.00 at the north end of Bolinas Lagoon), continue two miles or so to Mesa Rd., then turn right and continue four miles to the observatory's bird-banding station.

These days, visitors can also horse around in Point Reyes, thanks to guided tours offered by **Five Brooks Ranch,** tel. (415) 663-1570, www.fivebrooks.com. The two-hour Fir Top Trail Ride is $50 per person, though one-hour and

six-hours ride, overnight pack trips, and brief pony rides for the kids are also available.

Point Reyes Whalewatching
Whalewatching, particularly fine from the lighthouse, is immensely popular at Point Reyes and best from about Christmas through January, when whales pass from one to five miles offshore. (Come on a weekday to avoid the crowds.) A hundred or more whale sightings per day is fairly typical here, though a 307-step descent to the lighthouse must be negotiated first. You'll also get good views from the platform at the top of the stairs. The parking lot at the Point Reyes Lighthouse is fairly small, so in peak season, whalewatchers will have to park at Drakes Beach near the park entrance and take a shuttle bus to the lighthouse; the fee is $2.50 general, kids 12 and under free. National Park Service naturalists provide whale facts and whalewatching tips in January from 10 a.m.-4 p.m. daily, both at the lighthouse and the small information center near the viewing platform. For more information about Point Reyes whalewatching, including the complete shuttle schedule and special naturalist programs, call (415) 663-1092 or (415) 669-1534. (For more information on the migration of the gray whales, see previous chapter.) The lighthouse is open to the public for self-guided and ranger-led tours Thurs.-Monday. Otherwise, the Point Reyes Lighthouse Visitor Center is open 10 a.m.-5 p.m., and the steps down to the lighthouse open 10 a.m.-4:30 p.m. (closed in the

event of high winds). Since hours may change, call to verify before setting out.

Not far from the lighthouse is the **Point Reyes Historic Lifeboat Station,** established in 1889 with a "surfcar" (like a tiny submarine) pulled through the surf on a cable, hand-pulled surfboats, and a Lyle gun and breeches buoy. The facility is open infrequently and is available for educational programs on marine biology and maritime history. For more information, call (415) 663-1092.

Point Reyes Information

For information about Point Reyes, including current trail maps, and to obtain permits for camping and backpacking, stop by any of the park's three visitor centers: **Bear Valley Visitor Center** at the park's Bear Valley entrance; **Kenneth C. Patrick Visitor Center** at Drakes Beach; or **Point Reyes Lighthouse Visitor Center.** Or contact: Point Reyes National Seashore, Point Reyes, CA 94956, tel. (415) 663-1092.

For information about the year-round schedule of excellent classes and field seminars held at Point Reyes (most offered for credit through Dominican College, some offered cooperatively through the Elderhostel program), contact: **Point Reyes Field Seminars,** Point Reyes, CA 94956, tel. (415) 663-1200, and ask for the current seminar catalog.

A very good guidebook to the area is *Point Reyes—Secret Places & Magic Moments* by Phil Arnot. Also by Arnot (and Elvira Monroe): *Exploring Point Reyes: A Guide to Point Reyes National Seashore.*

For information about what's going on in Point Reyes and surrounding communities, pick up a copy of the Pulitzer Prize-winning **Point Reyes Light,** which made a name for itself with investigative reporting on the area's former Synanon cult. For information about area practicalities, see Staying in Western Marin and Eating Well in Western Marin below.

THE FARALLON ISLANDS

Visible from Point Reyes on a clear day are the Farallon Islands to the southwest. Protected as the Farallon National Wildlife Refuge, the largest seabird rookery south of Alaska, these islands are one of the five most ecologically productive marine environments on earth and now part of an international UNESCO Biosphere Reserve. Some 948 square nautical miles of ocean from Bodega Head to Rocky Point are included in the Gulf of the Farallones National Marine Sanctuary. These rugged granite islands 27 miles west of San Francisco are actually the above-sea-level presence of the Farallones Escarpment, which parallels the coast from the tip of Point Reyes to south of the Golden Gate. The natural but rare phenomenon of upwelling around the islands, with warm offshore winds drawing cold, nutrient-rich ocean water to the surface in spring, creates the phenomenal algae and plankton populations that support the feeding frenzies and breeding successes of animals farther up the food chain.

But during recent centuries, life has been almost undone at the Farallones. In the 1800s, "eggers" exploited the rookeries here to provide miners and San Franciscans with fresh eggs at breakfast. The islands have also survived assaults from sealers, whalers, gill netters, bombers, ocean oil slicks, and radioactive waste dumping.

In the summer, more than 250,000 breeding birds—from tufted puffins and petrels to auklets and murres—consider the Farallones home. Seals (including the once-almost-extinct northern elephant seal) and sea lions also breed here, and gray and humpback whales as well as northern fur seals are often spotted in the area. The nonprofit, member-supported **Point Reyes Bird Observatory,** 4990 Shoreline Hwy. (Hwy. 1), Stinson Beach, CA 94970, tel. (415) 868-1221, staffs a scientific study center at the Farallones (in addition to its center at Point Reyes), but otherwise people are not allowed on the islands—though the Oceanic Society—based at Fort Mason in San Francisco, tel. (415) 474-3385—sponsors educational expeditions around the Farallon Islands June-Nov. and during the winter whalewatching season. (Bring binoculars.) The public is welcome, however, at the Point Reyes Bird Observatory's Palomarin Field Station, tel. (415) 868-0655, at the end of Mesa Rd. near Bolinas, to observe bird banding. The station is open daily May-Nov. and on Wednesday, Saturday, and Sunday the rest of the year; call for hours and to make reservations for groups of five or more people.

For more information about the Farallon Islands and the surrounding marine sanctuary, contact: Gulf of the Farallones National Marine Sanctuary, tel. (415) 561-6622.

GOLDEN GATE NATIONAL RECREATION AREA AND VICINITY

Beginning immediately adjacent to Point Reyes near Olema is the Golden Gate National Recreation Area (GGNRA), which wraps itself around various state and local parks inland, then extends southeast across the Marin Headlands and the Golden Gate Bridge to include the Presidio and a thin coastal strip running south to Fort Funston. The GGNRA also includes two notable tourist attractions in San Francisco Bay: Angel Island and Alcatraz. Most notable is the dramatic natural beauty of the Marin Headlands—sea-chiseled chilly cliffs, protected valleys, and grassy wind-combed hills rich with wildlife and wildflowers, all opening out to the bay and the Pacific Ocean. Protected at first by the Nature Conservancy until coming under national management in 1972, the vast Marin Headlands feature trails for days of good hiking and backpacking (stop by headquarters for a current trail map). Backcountry and group camps are scattered across the area.

Aside from the GGNRA's natural beauty, here also is historic scenery, from the 1877 Point Bonita Lighthouse to four military installations—Forts Barry, Cronkhite, Baker, and Funston—that protected the Bay Area beginning in the 1870s and continuing through World War II.

For more information about the GGNRA, contact: **Golden Gate National Recreation Area,** Building 201, Fort Mason, San Francisco, CA 94123, tel. (415) 556-0560. Or stop for maps and other information at the **Marin Headlands GGNRA Visitor Center** at Fort Barry (near Rodeo Lagoon and Fort Cronkhite), tel. (415) 331-1540, open daily 8:30 a.m.-4:30 p.m.; or the **Muir Woods Visitor Center** at Muir Woods, tel. (415) 388-2595 or (415) 388-2596. Pick up trail maps and events calendars, and ask about backcountry camping at the visitor centers.

Several guidebooks published by the non-profit Golden Gate National Parks Association (tel. 415-561-3000 or 415-657-2757) are well worth buying—including the 96-page *Park Guide* ($9.95), which covers every feature of the recreation area.

Tomales Bay State Park

Among the half-moon beaches and secret coves along the steep cliffs and shores of Tomales Bay are those protected within fragments of Tomales Bay State Park. One section is just north of Inverness, via Pierce Point Rd. off Sir Francis Drake Blvd., and others are scattered along Hwy. 1 north of Point Reyes Station on the east side of the bay. One of the prime picnic spots at Tomales Bay is **Heart's Desire Beach,** popular for family picnicking and swimming, and usually empty on weekdays (parking $5 per vehicle). The warm, usually sunny, and surf-free inland beaches here are the main attraction, but hiking the forested eastern slope of Inverness Ridge is also worth it—especially in early spring, when trees, young ferns, and wildflowers burst forth from their winter dormancy. Unique is the park's fine virgin forest of Bishop pines. Walk-in campsites are available. For views and a great hiking trail, get directions to Inverness Ridge from Tomales Bay State Park personnel. The southern grasslands section of Tomales Bay, now included in the GGNRA after the federal purchase of the 250-acre Martinelli Ranch, is prime turf for hiking (best in March for wildflowers) and birdwatching. The trailhead and parking area is just off Hwy. 1, about 1.5 miles north of Point Reyes Station.

Along the eastern edge of Tomales Bay, the **Marconi Conference Center,** 18500 Hwy. 1, Marshall, CA 94940, tel. (415) 663-9020, occupies the 1914 Marconi Hotel once owned by Guglielmo Marconi, inventor of the wireless. This one-time communications center facility—taken over by the U.S. Navy during World War I, later operated by RCA, and more recently home to the much-praised then pilloried Synanon alcohol and drug abuse program—is now a state-owned conference center operated on the model of Asilomar on the Monterey Peninsula.

For more information about the park, contact: Tomales Bay State Park, Star Rte., Inverness, CA 94937, tel. (415) 669-1140.

Samuel P. Taylor State Park

East of Point Reyes National Seashore and hemmed in by the Golden Gate National Recreation Area is Samuel P. Taylor State Park, 2,600 acres of redwoods, mixed forests, and upcountry chaparral reached via Sir Francis Drake Boulevard. The park offers an extensive hiking and horseback trail system, a paved bicycle path running east-west, no-frills camping (including hiker/biker camps), picnicking, and swimming. For more information, contact: Samuel P. Taylor State Park, 8889 Sir Francis Drake Blvd., P.O. Box 251, Lagunitas, CA 94938, tel. (415) 488-9897 or (415) 893-1580.

East of Samuel Taylor near Nicasio is the vast Skywalker Ranch owned by Lucasfilms and George Lucas, film- and mythmaker in the tradition of mythologist Joseph Campbell and his Hero With a Thousand Faces. The public is not welcome. (And for the record, Lucas Valley Rd., connecting Nicasio and Marinwood, was named long before Lucas bought property here.) Lucasfilms is also destined to inhabit parts of San Francisco's Presidio within the GGNRA.

Bolinas Lagoon and Audubon Canyon Ranch
Well worth a visit is the Bolinas Lagoon, as serene as a Japanese nature print, especially in spring, when only the breeze or an occasional waterfowl fracas ruffles the glassy blue smoothness of this long mirror of water surrounded by a crescent-moon sandspit. Reflected above is wooded Bolinas Ridge, the northwestern extension of Mount Tamalpais. In autumn, the lagoon is much busier, temporary home to thousands of waterfowl migrating south along the Pacific Flyway as well as the salmon offshore waiting for a ferocious winter storm to break open a pathway through the sandbars blocking their migratory path. At minus tide any time of year, the surf side of the sandspit offers good beachcombing.

Facing out into the Bolinas Lagoon several miles north of Stinson Beach is the Audubon Canyon Ranch, a protected canyon offering a safe haven and rookery for great blue herons and common egrets in particular, though more than 50 other species of water birds arrive here each year. By quietly climbing up the canyon slopes during the March-July nesting season, visitors can look down into egret and heron nests high atop the redwoods in Schwartz Grove and observe the day-to-day life of parent birds and their young. Other hiking trails lead to other discoveries; picnic facilities also available.

The white Victorian farmhouse here serves as ranch headquarters and bookstore/visitor center, and participants in weekend seminar programs bed down in the bunkhouse, which features wind-powered toilets (God's truth) and solar-heated water. (Bring your own bedding, food, and other necessities.) The ranch is wheelchair accessible and generally open to the public mid-March through mid-July only on weekends and holidays, 10 a.m.-4 p.m., admission free, though donations are always appreciated. Large groups can make tour arrangements for weekdays, though the ranch is always closed Mondays. For more information, contact: Audubon Canyon Ranch, 4900 Shoreline Hwy. (Hwy. 1), Stinson Beach, CA 94970, tel. (415) 868-9244.

Mount Tamalpais State Park
Though the park also stretches downslope to the sea, take in the views of Marin County, San Francisco Bay, and the Pacific Ocean from the highest points of Mount Tamalpais. This long-loved mountain isn't particularly tall (elevation 2,600 feet), but even when foggy mists swirl everywhere below, the sun usually shines atop Mount Tam. And the state park here has it all: redwoods and ferns, hillsides thick with wildflowers, 200 miles of hiking trails with spectacular views (plus access to Muir Woods), beaches and headlands, also camping and picnicking. The best way to get here is via Hwy. 1, then via the Panoramic Hwy., winding up past Pan Toll Ranger Station and park headquarters (stop for information and a map) to near the summit. From the parking lot, it's a quarter-mile hike up a steep dirt road to the fire lookout on top of Mount Tam.

The best way to explore Mount Tamalpais is on foot. Take the loop trail around the top. For the more ambitious, head downslope to the sea and the busy public beaches at Stinson Beach, still noted for its annual Dipsea Race held on the last Sunday in August, a tradition since 1904. Rugged cross-country runners cross the still more rugged terrain from Mill Valley to the sea at Stinson Beach; the last stretch down the footpath is known as the Dipsea Trail. Or hike into the park from Marin Municipal Water District lands on the east (for information, call the Sky Oaks Ranger Station in Fairfax, tel. 415-459-5267) and head upslope, via the Cataract Trail from just off Bolinas Rd. outside of Fairfax and past

Alpine Lake—something of a steep climb but worth it for the waterfalls, most dramatic in winter and early spring but sublime for pool-sitting in summer.

Via the Matt Davis Trail, or the Bootjack Camp or Pan Toll Ranger Station routes, hike to the charming old (1904) **West Point Inn,** 1000 Panoramic Hwy., tel. (415) 388-9955, for a glass of lemonade and a rest in the porch shade. Four miles away is the **Tourist Club,** 30 Ridge Ave., tel. (415) 388-9987, a 1912 chalet where overnight stays are available only to members and their families, but hikers arriving via the Sun, Redwood, or Panoramic Trails can get snacks, cold imported beer, sodas, and juices. (To cheat for the beer, park at the end of Ridge Ave., which intersects the Panoramic Hwy., and hike the quarter-mile down the driveway.) Open daily, great views of Muir Woods from the deck. More accessible for a picnic or snack stop (bring your own) is Mount Tam's Greek-style **Mountain Theater,** a 5,000-seat outdoor amphitheater on Ridgecrest Blvd., the site each spring of a major musical stage production.

Mount Tamalpais State Park (admission free, though parking may cost you) is open daily from 7 a.m. to sunset. Limited primitive camping and other accommodations are available (see Staying in Western Marin, below). For more information, contact park headquarters at 801 Panoramic Hwy., Mill Valley, CA 94941, tel. (415) 388-2070. For current information on Mount Tam's Mountain Theater productions, contact the **Mountain Play Association,** 177 E. Blithedale, Mill Valley, CA 94941, tel. (415) 383-1100 or (415) 383-0155.

Muir Woods National Monument

Muir Woods is peaceful and serene but quite a popular place—not necessarily the best destination for getting away from them all. Lush redwood canyon country surrounds Redwood Creek within the boundaries of Mount Tamalpais State Park, with a short trail system meandering alongside the stream, up to the ridgetops, and into the monument's main Cathedral and Bohemian redwood groves. For an easy, introductory stroll, the Muir Woods Nature Trail wanders through the flatlands, identifying the characteristic trees and shrubs. Fascinating at Muir Woods, the first national monument in the U.S., are the dawn redwood from China and the park's albino redwood, the shoots from this freak of nature completely chlorophyll-free. But to avoid the crowds imported in all those tour buses clogging the parking lot, get away from the visitor center and the trails near the parking lot. Muir Woods is open daily 8 a.m.-sunset, $2 day-use fee, no picnicking or camping. No dogs. For more information, contact: Muir Woods National Monument, Mill Valley, CA 94941, tel. (415) 388-2595 or (415) 388-2596.

Fort Barry

Just north of Point Bonita, Fort Barry includes an intact 1950s missile launch site and underground bunkers not usually open to the public; one of the bunkers is still home to a Nike Hercules missile. "Guardians of the Gate" military-history tours, offered twice-monthly by park personnel, tel. (415) 331-1540, include the various batteries in the area and end at the Nike site.

Also at Fort Barry: an **AYH youth hostel,** Building 941, tel. (415) 331-2777; the **Headlands Center for the Arts,** Bldg. 144, tel. (415) 331-2787, which explores the relationship of art and the environment (studio space for artists is provided, and public programs include lectures, installations, exhibits, and performances); and the **Marin Headlands Visitor Center,** tel. (415) 331-1540, open to the public 8:30 a.m.-4:30 p.m. daily and offering hands-on natural science exhibits, and educational and historical displays.

Point Bonita Lighthouse

The Point Bonita Lighthouse (call 415-331-1540 for hours and tour information) was one of the first lighthouses ever built on the West Coast and is still operating. Technically, though, this isn't really a lighthouse—there's no house, just the French-import 1855 Fresnel lens with protective glass, walls, and roof, with gargoyle-like American eagles guarding the light. Getting here is as thrilling as being here—meandering along the half-mile footpath to the rocky point through hand-dug tunnels and across the swaying footbridge, in the middle of nowhere yet in full view of San Francisco. Especially enjoyable are the sunset and full-moon tours conducted by GGNRA rangers. The tours and admission to the lighthouse are free. For seaside barbecues, head to the picnic area at Battery Wallace near Point Bonita.

Fort Cronkhite

Just north of the Visitor Center is Fort Cronkhite, home of the **California Marine Mammal Center,** 1044 Fort Cronkhite (just above Cronkhite Beach), Sausalito, CA 94965-2610, tel. (415) 289-7325. Established in 1975, this hospital for wild animals returns its "patients," once fit, to their native marine environments. The center, with more than 400 active volunteers and popular hands-on environmental education programs for children, is open to the public daily 10 a.m.-4 p.m. Wheelchair accessible. (New members and financial contributions always welcome.) Also at Fort Cronkhite: the **Pacific Environment and Resources Center,** tel. (415) 332-8200, which offers teacher training, special elementary and secondary school programs, and exhibits on local and global environmental issues.

Other Marin GGNRA Sights

The hands-on **Bay Area Discovery Museum** at East Fort Baker, tel. (415) 487-4398, is designed for children ages 2-12 and their families. It offers a great variety of special programs year-round—"In the Dream Time" children's art workshops, for example. Open Wed.-Sun. 10 a.m.-5 p.m. Two miles north of Muir Beach is the **Slide Ranch** demonstration farm and family-oriented environmental education center, 2025 Hwy. 1, tel. (415) 381-6155, which offers special events (such as "Family Farm Day") year-round. Reservations are required for all events.

Hawk Hill

For views of the Golden Gate Bridge, San Francisco Bay, and the San Francisco skyline—not to mention exceptional birding opportunities—head to Hawk Hill (abandoned Battery 129, reached via Conzelman Rd.) on the north side of the Golden Gate above the bridge. Come in the fall (with binoculars and fog-worthy clothing) to appreciate the incredible numbers of birds of prey congregating here—100 or more each day representing 20 or so species. In spring, bring your kite. Any time of year, this is a great vantage point for watching huge cargo ships and other vessels make their way through the Golden Gate. For more information, call the Marin Headlands Visitor Center at Fort Barry, tel. (415) 331-1540.

Alcatraz: "The Rock"

Part of the GGNRA is infamous Alcatraz, one-time military outpost, then island prison and federal hellhole—"The Rock"—for hard-core criminals. Among the notorious bad guys incarcerated here were mobsters Al Capone, "Machine Gun" Kelley, and Mickey Cohen, not to mention Robert Stroud, the "Birdman of Alcatraz"—who, despite the romance of his popular myth, never kept birds on The Rock. Closed in the 1960s, then occupied for two years by Native Americans who hoped to reacquire the property for a cultural heritage center, Alcatraz Island and its prison facilities are now open for tours; see Touring the Real Rock in the San Francisco chapter. Ferries operated by the Blue & Gold Fleet at San Francisco's Pier 39, tel. (415) 773-1188 (recorded schedule) or (415) 705-5555 (information and advance ticket purchase), shuttle visitors out to The Rock and back. For general information, call the GGNRA office in San Francisco, tel. (415) 556-0560.

Angel Island State Park

Still sometimes called the "Ellis Island of the West," a century ago Angel Island was the door through which Asian immigrants passed on their way to America. Japanese and other "enemy aliens" were imprisoned here during World War II, when the island's facilities served as a detention center. Explore the West Garrison Civil War barracks and buildings at the 1863 site of Camp Reynolds—built and occupied by Union troops determined to foil the Confederacy's plans to invade the bay and then the gold country. Among the buildings, the largest surviving collection of Civil War structures in the nation, note the cannons still aimed to sea (but never used in the war because Confederate troops never showed up). On weekends, volunteers in the park's living history program—with the help of apparently willing visitors—fire off the cannons, just in case the South rises again.

Though most visitors never get past the sun and sand at Ayala Cove (where the Cove Cafe offers lunch, coffee, and beer), also worth a stop are the 1899 Chinese Immigration Center, quarantine central for new Asian arrivals, and World War II-era Fort McDowell on the island's east side near the Civil War battlements. Often

Angel Island State Park, once the Ellis Island of the West

CALIFORNIA DEPARTMENT OF PARKS AND RECREATION

sunny in summer when the rest of the Bay Area is shivering in the fog, outdoorsy types consider Angel Island's hiking trails its chief attraction. On a clear day, the view from the top of Angel Island's Mount Livermore is spectacular—with three bridges and almost the entire Bay Area seemingly within reach. The intrepid can even camp on Angel Island, which features nine hike-in environmental campsites. Call park headquarters for information and reservations. The **Tiburon-Angel Island State Park Ferry,** berthed at the pier on Main St. in Tiburon, tel. (415) 435-2131, is available to island-bound hikers, bikers, and backpackers daily during summer (and often into autumn, weather permitting), but only on weekends during the rest of the year. The **Blue & Gold Fleet,** tel. (415) 773-1188, also offers Angel Island runs from San Francisco's Pier 41.

For more information about island hikes and docent-led tours of historic sites, also current ferry schedules, contact: **Angel Island State Park headquarters,** 1455 E. Francis Blvd., San Rafael, CA 94501, or P.O. Box 866, Tiburon, CA 94920, tel. (415) 435-1915. For information on tram tours of the island, as well as mountain-bike and kayak rentals there, call (415) 897-0715. For information about island tours for the disabled and about fundraising and other volunteer work to continue the island's restoration, contact: **Angel Island Association,** P.O. Box 866, Tiburon, CA 94920, tel. (415) 435-3522.

STAYING IN WESTERN MARIN

Point Reyes Hostel

Best bet for noncamping budget travelers is **HI-AYH Point Reyes Hostel** on Limantour Rd., P.O. Box 247, Point Reyes Station, CA 94956, tel. (415) 663-8811. Pluses here include the well-equipped kitchen (get food on the way). Advance reservations advisable, particularly on weekends. To get here: from Point Reyes Station, take Seashore west from Hwy. 1, then follow Bear Valley Rd. to Limantour Rd. and continue on Limantour for six miles. Budget. For information on getting to Point Reyes on public transit, call the hostel or Golden Gate Transit, tel. (415) 923-2000. The hostel's office hours are 7:30-9:30 a.m. and 4:30-9:30 p.m. daily. Considerably closer to urban Marin but also an excellent choice is the hostel within the Golden Gate National Recreation Area. For information, see Staying in Sausalito, below.

Point Reyes Camping

So popular that each has a one-day limit, the four primitive walk-in campgrounds at Point Reyes National Seashore are perfect for backpackers, since each is within an easy day's hike of the main trailhead and each other. Call (415) 663-1092 for information; permits required (available at park headquarters on Bear Valley Rd. just west of Olema). Stop, also, to pick up maps and wilderness permits. The office is open weekdays 9 a.m.-5 p.m., weekends 8 a.m.-5 p.m.

Popular Coast Camp is most easily accessible from the parking lot at the end of Limantour Rd. and makes a good base for exploring the Limantour Estero and Sculptured Beach. Wildcat Camp is a group camp popular with Boy Scouts and others in Point Reyes's lake district (best swimming in Bass and Crystal Lakes). Glen Camp is tucked into the hills between Wildcat Camp and Bear Valley, and Sky Camp, perched on the western slopes of Mount Wittenberg, looks down over Drakes Bay and Point Reyes.

Other area camping options include the backpack and group camps of GGNRA, tel. (415) 331-1540; the state campground at Samuel P. Taylor State Park, tel. (415) 488-9897; and the 18 primitive campsites plus backpack camps

---

STEEP RAVINE: RUGGED AND INEXPENSIVE

The state's quite reasonable **Steep Ravine Environmental Cabins** on Rocky Point in Mount Tamalpais State Park, looking out to sea from near Stinson Beach, are small redwood-rustic homes-away-from-home with just the basics: platform beds (bring your own sleeping bag and pad), woodstoves, separate restrooms with pit toilets. But such a deal: $30 per cabin per night (each sleeps five) and an almost-private beach below in a spectacularly romantic setting. Before the state wrested custody of these marvelous cabins from the powerful Bay Area politicians and other clout-encumbered citizens who held long-term leases, photographer Dorothea Lange wrote about staying here in *To a Cabin,* co-authored by Margaretta K. Mitchell. Even the walk down to the bottom of Steep Ravine Canyon is inspiring, Lange noted, with "room for only those in need of sea and sky and infinity." One cabin (there are only 10) is wheelchair accessible; none have electricity, but they do have outside running water. Bring your own provisions. To reserve (up to eight weeks in advance), contact ReserveAmerica, toll-free tel. (800) 444-7275, and request an application form. You can also make reservations online; point your browser to www.cal-parks.ca.gov.

---

and group camp at Mount Tamalpais State Park, tel. (415) 388-2070.

Inns in Western Marin

Even those without wheels can explore the seaward coast of Marin County in comfort and fine style—by hiking or walking the whole way from the Golden Gate Bridge with little more than a day pack and staying along the bay at a combination of hostels, campgrounds, hotels and motels, and the area's very nice bed-and-breakfast inns. (How far to go each day and where to stay depends upon time and money available.)

For area lodging referrals and information, also contact **Point Reyes Lodging,** tel. (415) 663-1872 or toll-free (800) 539-1872; or **Inns of Point Reyes,** tel. (415) 663-1420.

Classic **Ten Inverness Way,** 10 Inverness Way (on the town's block-long main street), tel. (415) 669-1648, is comfortable and cozy. Rooms feature excellent beds, handmade quilts, and private baths; there's a stone fireplace in the living room, wonderful full breakfast, private hot tub. Premium-Luxury.

In a woodsy canyon just outside town, **Blackthorne Inn,** 266 Vallejo Ave. in Inverness Park, tel. (415) 663-8621, www.blackthorneinn.com, offers simple Japanese-style furnishings in four-level "treehouse" accommodations with decks, all splitting off the vertically spiraling staircase. Good buffet breakfast, hot tub available. The peak experience here is a stay in the Eagle's Nest, the aptly named octagonal, glass-walled room at the top of the stairs. Luxury.

Also in Inverness Park, consider **Holly Tree Inn & Cottages,** 3 Silverhills Rd., tel. (415) 663-1554 or toll-free (800) 663-1554, which offers four rooms in the inn, plus a cottage (all Premium-Luxury), as well as the off-site **Sea Star Cottage** and **Vision Cottage** (both Luxury).

Up on Inverness Ridge is **The Ark,** tel. (415) 663-9338 or toll-free (800) 808-9338, a rustic cabin with bedroom, sleeping loft, woodstove, and kitchen. Luxury. Other cottages available through the Ark's same telephone numbers include woodsy **Rosemary Cottage,** which has a woodstove and hot tub (Premium-Luxury); and **Fir Tree Cottage,** a spacious two-bedroom house perfect for families or two couples (Luxury).

Fairwinds Farm, 82 Drakes Summit, tel. (415) 663-9454, is a fairly modern Early American cottage on five acres with forest, garden, and pond, a good family setup with two beds in the bedroom, a double bed in the loft, and queen sofa bed in the living room. Full kitchen (breakfast fixings supplied, plus snacks, even a popcorn popper), fireplace, hot tub, deck. Playhouse for children, barnyard animals, too. Expensive-Premium. Near Tomales Bay, **Marsh Cottage**, 12642 Sir Francis Drake Blvd., tel. (415) 669-7168, features a fireplace and a fine view, plus kitchen with breakfast supplies. Premium.

Farther south, **Roundstone Farm**, 9940 Sir Francis Drake Blvd., Olema, tel. (415) 663-1020, is an American country-style cedar farmhouse on a 10-acre horse ranch, rooms with private baths, fireplaces, European armoires, down comforters. Premium. Also quite nice is **Bear Valley Inn**, 88 Bear Valley Rd., Olema, tel. (415) 663-1777, a restored two-story Victorian ranch house with three country-style guest rooms upstairs, woodstove and oak flooring in the parlor. Rates are available with or without full breakfast. Expensive-Premium.

For nostalgia with all the modern amenities (try to get a room away from the highway), the 1988 **Point Reyes Seashore Lodge**, 10021 Hwy. 1 (in Olema), tel. (415) 663-9000, is an elegant re-creation of a turn-of-the-century country lodge, a three-story cedar building with three two-story suites and 18 rooms, all with down comforters, telephones, and private baths, many with whirlpool tubs and fireplaces, most with a private deck or patio. Continental breakfast. Premium-Luxury.

The place for a genuine West Marin-style stay is a very modern facsimile historic hotel, a superb 1989 replica of the original **U.S. Hotel**, 26985 Hwy. 1, Tomales, tel. (707) 878-2742, a bed and breakfast with a hands-off hotel style, just eight rooms with private baths, continental breakfast served in the second-floor lobby. Expensive-Premium. The top bed-and-breakfast choice in Bolinas is **White House Inn**, 118 Kale Rd., tel. (415) 868-0279, a New England-style inn with two guest rooms sharing two bathrooms in the hall, continental breakfast. Premium.

The original 1912 **Mountain Home Inn** restaurant, 810 Panoramic Hwy. (on Mount Tamalpais), Mill Valley, tel. (415) 381-9000, has been transformed into an elegant three-story woodsy hotel with upstairs restaurant and bar. Fabulous views. Some of the rooms have fireplaces or jacuzzis. Rates include breakfast in bed. Premium-Luxury.

When Sir Francis Drake steered the Pelican to shore near here in 1579, he claimed everything in sight on behalf of Elizabeth I, Queen of England. For a taste of more modern true Brit on your way down from Mount Tam, stop at the **Pelican Inn**, 10 Pacific Way (Hwy. 1 at Muir Beach Rd.), Muir Beach, tel. (415) 383-6000. This is a very British Tudor-style country inn, a replica of a 16th-century farmhouse, where guests sit out on the lawn with pint of bitter in hand on sunny days or, when the fog rolls in, warm up around the bar's fireplace with some afternoon tea or mulled cider or wine. Hearty pub fare includes meat pies, stews, burgers, homemade breads, various dinner entrées. Restaurant and pub open 11 a.m.-11 p.m. daily except Monday. Not authentically old (built in 1979), the Pelican is still authentic: the leaded-glass windows and brass trinkets, even the oak bar and refectory tables come from England. There's usually a months-long waiting list for the seven rooms here. Luxury.

EATING IN WESTERN MARIN

Marshall, Point Reyes Station, Olema

Popular in Marshall, along the east side of Tomales Bay north of Point Reyes Station via Hwy. 1, is **Tony's Seafood**, 18863 Hwy. 1, tel. (415) 663-1107. The food's quite fresh: they clean the crabs and oysters right out front.

Famous for its Pulitzer Prize-winning newspaper, the not-yet-too-yuppie cow town of Point Reyes Station is also noted for the mooing clock atop the sheriff's substation at Fourth and C. The bovine bellow, a technical creation of Lucasfilm staff, actually emanates—like clockwork, at noon and 6 p.m.—from loudspeakers atop the Old Western Saloon at Second and Main Streets. For "udderly divine" bakery items, from French pastries, bran muffins, and scones to cookies, stop by **Bovine Bakery**, 11315 Hwy. 1 (Main St.), tel. (415) 663-9420. The **Station House Cafe**, 11180 Main (at Third St.), tel. (415) 663-1515, is the local hotspot, a cheerful country café serving breakfast, lunch, and dinner daily but particularly wonderful for breakfast, especially on foggy or rainy days.

Both a good restaurant and lodging stop, the **Olema Inn**, at Hwy. 1 and Sir Francis Drake Blvd. in Olema, tel. (415) 663-9559, is a grandmotherly kind of place serving basic good food and soups as well as California-style cuisine. Open for dinner Fri.-Sat. at 6 p.m. and for lunch and dinner during the summer. For plain ol' American food, head for **Olema Farmhouse**, 10005 Hwy. 1 in Olema, tel. (415) 663-1264: good burgers and hefty sandwiches, daily fresh fish specials.

Inverness and Vicinity

After a relaxed afternoon spent reading in **Jack Mason Museum and Inverness Public Library** on Park Ave. (open limited hours, tel. 415-669-1288 or 415-669-1099), head out Sir Francis Drake Blvd. from Inverness to **Johnson's Oyster Company**, tel. (415) 669-1149, for a tour and some farm-fresh oysters. Open Tues.-Sun. 8 a.m.-4 p.m.; free admission. **Barnaby's by the Bay**, 12938 Sir Francis Drake (at the Golden Hinde Inn just north of Inverness), tel. (415) 669-1114, open for lunch and dinner (closed Wednesday), has daily pasta and fresh fish specials, barbecued oysters, clam chowder, and crab cioppino.

Back in Inverness, **Gray Whale Pub & Pizzeria**, 12781 Sir Francis Drake, tel. (415) 669-1244, is the place for pizza, also salads, good desserts, and espresso in a pub atmosphere. Open 9 a.m.-9 p.m. daily. Or, try one of the town's two popular restaurants: **Manka's** at the Inverness Lodge (call for directions), tel. (415) 669-1034, which serves rustic American-style fare (marvelous rooms upstairs, two cabins also available), or **Vladimir's Czechoslovak Restaurant & Bar**, 12785 Sir Francis Drake, tel. (415) 669-1021, which serves good Eastern European food in an authentically boisterous atmosphere. (Yell across the room if you want dessert; that's what everyone else does.)

Bolinas

Bolinas is noted for the locals' Bolinas Border Patrol, an unofficial group dedicated to keeping outsiders out by taking down road signs. Once *in* Bolinas, however long that may take you, the gravel beach here is clean and usually uncrowded. The colorfully painted **Bolinas People's Store**, 14 Wharf Rd., tel. (415) 868-1433, is a good stop for snacks and picnic fixings. **Bolinas Bay Bakery & Cafe**, 20 Wharf Rd., tel. (415) 868-0211, is a popular breakfast and lunch stop famous for its cinnamon rolls, croissants, breads, and other fresh bakery items. **The Shop Cafe**, 46 Wharf Rd., tel. (415) 868-9984, is comfortable and cozy on a foggy or rainy day. (At lunch, try the black bean soup.) When you're ready for a casual pint of Anchor Steam, belly up to the bar at **Smiley's Schooner Saloon**, 41 Wharf Rd., tel. (415) 868-1311, a classic dive bar that's as local as it gets. Mind your manners and have some fun.

SAUSALITO

Sausalito is a community by land and by sea, a hillside hamlet far surpassed in eccentricity by the highly creative hodgepodge of houseboaters also anchored here. Though, for a time, mysterious midnight throbbings from the deep kept Sausalito's houseboat community awake night after summer night—with some locals even speculating that these nocturnal noises came from a top-secret CIA weapon being tested underwater in Richardson Bay—it eventually turned out that the racket was simply due to romance. Singing toadfish have become to Sausalito what swallows are to Capistrano, migrating into Richardson Bay from the shallows each summer for their annual mating song—comparable, collectively, to the sound of a squadron of low-flying B-17 bombers. People here have adapted to this almost indescribable language of love, and now welcome these bulging-eyed, bubble-lipped lovers back to the bay every year with their Humming Toadfish Festival, a celebration conducted by residents dressed up as sea monsters and clowns, playing kazoos.

Aside from the pleasures of just being here, stop in Sausalito at the U.S. Army Corps of Engineers' **San Francisco Bay Model**, 2100 Bridgeway, tel. (415) 332-3870, a working 1.5-acre facsimile of the Bay and Delta built by the Corps to study currents, tides, salinity, and other natural features. We should all be grateful that the ever-industrious Corps realized it couldn't build a better bay even with access to all the bulldozers, landfill, and riprap in the world and settled, instead, for just making a toy version.

Interpretive audio tours are available in English, Russian, German, Japanese, French, and Spanish. Guided group tours (10 or more people) can be arranged by calling (415) 332-3871 at least four weeks in advance. Open in summer Tues.-Fri. 9 a.m.-4 p.m., weekends and holidays 10 a.m.-5 p.m.; the rest of the year, Tues.-Sat. 9 a.m.-4 p.m. Free.

Also in Sausalito: the **Institute of Noetic Sciences,** 475 Gate 5 Rd., tel. (415) 331-5650, an organization of mostly mainstream scientists dedicated to exploring the more mysterious machinations of the human mind—that foggy frontier at the edge of the California cosmos concerned with biofeedback, mental telepathy, telekinesis, altered states of consciousness, and mental imagery in physical healing. Among Sausalito's armada of houseboat residents and bayside shops is **Heath Ceramics Outlet,** 400 Gate 5 Rd., tel. (415) 332-3732, open daily 10 a.m.-5 p.m., a wonderful array of seconds and overstocks for fine dishware fans.

Sausalito (or San Francisco, from Crissy Field via the Golden Gate Bridge) is a perfect place to start a serious Bay Area bike tour. For a 20-mile trip, head north along the paved bike path (Bay Trail), following the green "bike route" signs along the left arm of Richardson Bay to fairly new Bayfront Park in Mill Valley. Continue north to (busy and narrow) E. Blithedale Ave., and follow it east two miles or so to less-busy Tiburon Boulevard. From that thoroughfare, jog south along the bay on Greenwood Cove Rd., picking up the two-mile Tiburon Bike Path at its end. To make it a complete circle, take a ferry from Tiburon past Angel Island and Alcatraz to Fisherman's Wharf in San Francisco. From here, head back via the Bay Trail, up the grade (fairly steep) to the Golden Gate Bridge and over the bay, then back into Sausalito via the Bridgeway Bike Path.

Easier bike trips from Sausalito include the several-mile trip into Mill Valley, via the bike path past the houseboats and mudflats and marshes to Bayfront Park (picnic tables and benches available). Then backtrack to Miller Ave. and roll into town, right into the midst of a pleasant plaza-style shopping district. To get to Tiburon, from Bayfront Park follow the route described above.

For more information about Sausalito attractions and practicalities, contact: **Sausalito Chamber of Commerce,** 29 Caledonia St., Sausalito, CA 94965, tel. (415) 331-7262, open weekdays 9 a.m.-5 p.m.

Staying in Sausalito

Best bet for budget travelers in eastern Marin County is the **HI-AYH Marin Headlands Hostel,** in Building 941 at Fort Barry in Sausalito, tel. (415) 331-2777, www.norcalhostels.org, urban enough—just five minutes from the Golden Gate Bridge—but also rural, 103 beds in a 1907 building in an otherwise abandoned fort in the midst of Golden Gate National Recreation Area. Basic dorm-style accommodations with hot showers (family room available by advance reservation), but facilities also include a great kitchen, dining room, common room with fireplace, even laundry facilities, game room, tennis court, and bike storage. Quite popular in summer and on good-weather weekends, so reservations advised. Budget (extra fee for linen rental, or bring a sleeping bag). To get here: if coming from San Francisco, take the Alexander Ave. exit just north of the Golden Gate Bridge (if southbound toward the bridge, take the second Sausalito exit), then follow the signs into GGNRA and on to the hostel.

To spend considerably more for a nice stay in the same general neighborhood, the recently refurbished Spanish-style **Hotel Sausalito,** 16 El Portal, tel. (415) 332-0700 or toll-free (888) 442-0700, offers 16 Victorian-style rooms and continental breakfast. Premium-Luxury. Practically next door and right on the water is the **Inn Above Tide,** 30 El Portal, tel. (415) 332-9535 or toll-free (800) 893-8433, a luxurious boutique hotel with just 30 rooms. Great views of the city and bay. Luxury. Another possibility is Sausalito's most mythic hotel, **Casa Madrona,** 801 Bridgeway Blvd., tel. (415) 332-0502 or toll-free (800) 567-9524, both its historic (vintage 1885) and modern sections built into the hillside and connecting by quaint pathways. Newer rooms are plusher, generally speaking, but all are unique and inviting; some have spectacular views of the bay and some have fireplaces. The cottages are the epitome of privacy. Buffet breakfast. Luxury. Perched on the hillside above town, the **Alta Mira Hotel,** 125 Bulkley Ave., tel. (415) 332-1350, offers rooms with a view in a magnificent Spanish-Colonial inn; also separate cottages. Moderate-Luxury.

Eating in Sausalito
Fred's Place, 1917 Bridgeway in Sausalito, tel. (415) 332-4575, is a surprising local institution, a no-frills coffee shop where 500 or more people compete all day for Fred's 30 seats. Serving unpretentious food à la American grill—with an excellent Monterey Jack omelette and other standards plus Polish sausage and bratwurst, fresh-squeezed orange juice—Fred's is the place, for millionaires and houseboaters alike. People even wait outside in the rain to get in. Open only for breakfast and lunch, weekdays 6:30 a.m.-2:30 p.m., weekends 7 a.m.-3 p.m., no checks or credit cards.

But the **Casa Madrona Hotel** restaurant, 801 Bridgeway, tel. (415) 331-5888, offers the best food around, at breakfast, lunch (weekdays only), and dinner, Marin-style California cuisine using only the freshest available ingredients. For fine fare away from the tourist throngs, try tiny **Sushi Ran,** 107 Caledonia St., tel. (415) 332-3620. For great views, alfresco dining, and a full menu of margaritas, consider popular **Margaritaville,** 1200 Bridgeway, tel. (415) 331-3226, offering casual atmosphere and great California-style Mexican food daily for lunch and dinner (if you like it hot, try the exquisite Camarones à la Diabla). Other popular Sausalito restaurants include the **Spinnaker,** 100 Spinnaker, tel. (415) 332-1500, and **Horizons,** 558 Bridgeway, tel. (415) 331-3232—both upscale, on-the-water places specializing in great seafood.

SAN FRANCISCO CONVENTION AND VISITORS BUREAU/MICHAEL MOESON

SAN FRANCISCO AND THE BARBARY COAST
LIFE ON THE EDGE

"When I was a child growing up in Salinas we called San Francisco 'The City,'" California native John Steinbeck once observed. "Of course it was the only city we knew but I still think of it as The City as does everyone else who has ever associated with it."

San Francisco is The City, a distinction it wears with detached certitude. San Francisco has been The City since the days of the gold rush, when the world rushed in through the Golden Gate in a frenzied pursuit of both actual and alchemical riches. It remained The City forever after: when San Francisco started, however reluctantly, to abandon its Barbary Coast ways

---

See color maps of San Francisco and of the surrounding coast at front of book

---

and conceive of itself as a civilized place; when San Francisco fell down and incinerated itself in the great earthquake of 1906; when San Francisco flew up from its ashes, fully fledged, after reinventing itself; and when San Francisco set about reinventing almost everything else with its rolling social revolutions. Among those the world noticed this century, the Beatniks or "Beats" of the 1940s and '50s publicly shook the suburbs of American complacency, but the 1960s and San Francisco's Summer of Love caused the strongest social quake, part of the chaos of new consciousness that quickly changed the shape of everything.

Among its many attributes, perhaps most striking is The City's ability, still, to be all things to all people—and to simultaneously contradict itself and its own truths. San Francisco is a point of beginning. Depending upon where one starts, it is also the ultimate place to arrive. San Francisco is a comedy. And San Francisco is tragedy.

As writer Richard Rodriquez observes: "San Francisco has taken some heightened pleasure from the circus of final things. . . . San Francisco can support both comic and tragic conclusions because the city is geographically *in extremis,* a metaphor for the farthest flung possibility, a metaphor for the end of the line." But even that depends upon point of view. As Rodriquez also points out, "To speak of San Francisco as land's end is to read the map from one direction only—as Europeans would read or as the East Coast has always read it." To the people living on these hills before California's colonialization, before the gold rush, even before there was a San Francisco, the land they lived on represented the center, surrounded on three sides by water. To Mexicans extending their territorial reach, it was north. To Russian fur hunters escaping the frigid shores of Alaska, it was south. And to its many generations of Asian immigrants, surely San Francisco represented the Far East.

The precise place The City occupies in the world's imagination is irrelevant to compass points. If San Francisco is anywhere specific, it is certainly at the edge: the cutting edge of cultural combinations, the gilt edge of international commerce, the razor's edge of raw reality. And life on the edge is rarely boring.

THE LAND: NATURAL SAN FRANCISCO

Imagine San Francisco before its bridges were built: a captive city, stranded on an unstable, stubbed toe of a peninsula, one by turns twitching under the storm-driven assault of wind and water, then chilled by bone-cold fog.

The city and county of San Francisco—the two are one, duality in unity—sit on their own appendage of California earth, a political conglomeration totaling 46.4 square miles. Creating San Francisco's western edge is the Pacific Ocean, its waters cooled by strong Alaskan currents, its rough offshore rocks offering treachery to unwary sea travelers. On its eastern edge is San Francisco Bay, one of the world's most impressive natural harbors, with deep protected waters and 496 square miles of surface area.

(As vast as it is, these days the bay is only 75% of its pre-gold rush size, since its shoreline has been filled in and extended to create more land.) Connecting the two sides, and creating San Francisco's rough-and-tumble northern edge, is the three-mile-long strait known as the Golden Gate. Straddled by the world-renowned Golden Gate Bridge, this mile-wide river of sea water cuts the widest gap in the rounded Coast Ranges for a thousand miles, yet is so small that its landforms almost hide the bay that balloons inland.

Spaniards named what is now considered San Francisco Las Lomitas, or "little hills," for the landscape's most notable feature. Perhaps to create a romantic comparison with Rome, popular local mythology holds that The City was built on seven hills—Lone Mountain, Mt. Davidson, Nob Hill, Russian Hill, Telegraph Hill, and the Twin Peaks, none higher than 1,000 feet in elevation. There are actually more than 40 hills in San Francisco, all part and parcel of California's Coast Ranges, which run north and south along the state's coastline, sheltering inland valleys from the fog and winds that regularly visit San Francisco.

City on a Fault Line

The City has been shaped as much by natural forces as by historical happenstance. Its most spectacular event involved both. More than any other occurrence, San Francisco's 1906 earthquake—estimated now to have registered 8.25 on the Richter scale—woke up residents, and the world, to the fact that The City was built on very shaky ground. California's famous, 650-mile-long San Andreas Fault, as it is now known, slips just seaward of San Francisco. In the jargon of tectonic plate theory, The City sits on the North American Plate, a huge slab of earth floating on the planet's molten core, along the San Andreas earthquake fault line. Just west is the Pacific Plate. When earth-shaking pressure builds, sooner or later something has to give. In San Francisco, as elsewhere in California, a rumble and a roar and split-second motion announces an earthquake—and the fact that an interlocking section of the earth's crust has separated, a movement that may or may not be visible on the earth's surface. San Francisco's most recent major quake, on October 17, 1989, reminded us that The City's earthquake history is far from a finished chapter.

City in a Fog

San Francisco's second most famous physical feature is its weather—mild and Mediterranean but with quite perverse fog patterns, especially surprising to first-time summer visitors. When people expect sunny skies and warm temperatures, San Francisco offers instead gray and white mists, moist clouds seemingly filled with knife-sharp points of ice when driven by the wind.

Poets traditionally call forth all nine muses to honor the mysteries of fog. Scientists are much more succinct. Summer heat in California's central valley regions creates a low-pressure weather system, while cooler ocean temperatures create higher atmospheric pressure. Moving toward equilibrium, the cool and moist coastal air is drawn inland through the "mouth" of the Golden Gate and over adjacent hills, like a behemoth's belly breath. Then, as the land cools, the mists evaporate. So even during the peak fog months of July and August, wool-coat weather dissipates by midafternoon—only to roll back in shortly after sundown. Due to microclimates created by hills, certain San Francisco neighborhoods—like the Mission District, Noe Valley, and Potrero Hill—may be quite sunny and warm when the rest of the city still shivers in the fog.

San Francisco Weather

The coast's strong high-pressure system tends to moderate San Francisco weather year-round: expect average daytime temperatures of 54-65° F in summer, 48-59° F in winter. (Usually reliable is the adage that for every 10 miles you travel inland from the city, temperatures will increase by 10 degrees.) September and October are the warmest months, with balmy days near 70 degrees. The local weather pattern also prevents major rainstorms from May through October. Despite the water-rich imagery associated with the San Francisco Bay Area, the region is actually semiarid, with annual (nondrought) rainfall averaging 19-20 inches. Snow is a very rare phenomenon in the region.

HISTORY AND CULTURE: HUMAN SAN FRANCISCO

At its most basic, the recorded history of San Francisco is a story of conquest and curiosity.

The region's original inhabitants, however, were generally content with the abundant riches the land provided quite naturally. Descendants of mysterious nomads who first crossed the Bering Strait from Asia to the North American continent some 20,000 or more years ago, California's native peoples were culturally distinct. The language groups—"tribes" doesn't serve to describe California Indians—living north of the Golden Gate were classified by anthropologists as the Coast Miwok people. Though the barren and desolate site of San Francisco attracted few residents, the dominant native population throughout the greater Bay Area was called Costanoan ("coast people") or Ohlone by the Spanish, though the people called themselves Ramaytush.

In precolonial days, the region was the most densely populated on the continent north of Mexico, with a population of 10,000 people living in 30 or more permanent villages. Though each village considered itself unique, separated from others by customs and local dialect, the Ohlone intermarried and traded with other tribes and shared many cultural characteristics. Though dependent on shellfish as a dietary staple, the Ohlone also migrated inland in summer and fall to hunt game, fish, and collect acorns, which were valued throughout California for making bread and mush. Thousands of years of undisturbed cultural success created a gentle, gracious, unwarlike society—a culture that quickly passed away with the arrival of California's explorers and colonizers.

Early Explorations

Discoveries of dusty manuscripts, ancient stone anchors, and old coins now suggest that Chinese ships were the first foreign vessels to explore California's coastline, arriving centuries before Columbus bumbled into the new world. The Portuguese explorer Juan Cabrillo (João Cabrilho) was the coast's first official surveyor, though on his 1542 voyage he failed to discover the Golden Gate and the spectacular bay behind it. In 1579 the English pirate Sir Francis Drake took the first foreign step onto California soil, quite possibly near San Francisco, and claimed the land for Queen Elizabeth I. (Where exactly Drake landed is a subject of ongoing controversy and confusion. For a further discussion, see Point Reyes National Seashore.)

And even Drake failed to see the Golden Gate and its precious natural harbor, perhaps due to the subtle subterfuge of landforms and fog.

The Arrival of Spain,
Mexico, Russia, and America

In 1769, some 200 years after Drake, a Spanish scouting party led by Gaspar de Portolá discovered San Francisco Bay by accident while searching for Monterey Bay farther south. After Monterey was secured, Capt. Juan Bautista de Anza was assigned the task of colonizing this new territorial prize. With 35 families plus a lieutenant and a Franciscan priest, de Anza set out on a grueling trip from Sonora, Mexico, arriving on the peninsula's tip on June 27, 1776, just one week before the American Revolution. The first order of business was establishing a military fortress, the Presidio, at the present site of Fort Mason. And the second was establishing a church and mission outpost, about one mile south, on the shores of a small lake or lagoon named in honor of Nuestra Seño-ra de los Dolores (Our Lady of Sorrows). Though the mission church was dedicated to Saint Francis of Assisi, it became known as Mission Dolores—and the name "San Francisco" was instead attached to the spectacular bay and the eventual city that grew up on its shores.

Though Spain, then Mexico, officially secured the California territory, underscoring ownership by means of vast government land grants to retired military and civilian families, the colonial claim was somewhat tenuous. By the 1830s, Americans were already the predominant residents of the settlement at Yerba Buena Cove (at the foot of what is now Telegraph Hill), the earliest version of San Francisco. Yerba Buena was first a trading post established by William Anthony Richardson, an Englishman who married the Presidio commandant's daughter. In the early 1800s, Russian fur hunters established themselves just north along the coast, at the settlement of Fort Ross. They sailed south to trade. English, French, and American

A well-supplied prospector heads for mining camp.

trading ships were also regular visitors. By the 1840s, Yankees were arriving by both land and sea in ever greater numbers, spurred on by the nation's expansionist mood and the political dogma of "Manifest Destiny!" The official annexation of the California territory to the United States, when it came in mid-1846, was almost anticlimactic. After the 13-man force at the Presidio surrendered peacefully to the Americans, the citizens quickly changed the name of Yerba Buena to that of the bay, San Francisco—a shrewd business move, intended to attract still more trade.

The World Rushes In:
The Gold Rush and the Barbary Coast

Events of early 1848 made the name change all but irrelevant. San Francisco could hardly help attracting more business, and more businesses of every stripe, once word arrived that gold had been discovered on the American River in the foothills east of Sacramento. Before the gold rush, San Francisco was a sleepy port town with a population of 800, but within months it swelled to a city of nearly 25,000, as gold seekers arrived by the shipload from all over the globe. Those who arrived early and lit out for the gold-fields in 1848 had the best opportunity to harvest California gold. Most of the fortune hunters, however, arrived in '49, thus the term "forty-niners" to describe this phenomenal human migration.

As cosmopolitan as the overnight city of San Francisco was, with its surprisingly well-educated, liberal, and (not so surprisingly) young population, it was hardly civilized. By 1849 the ratio of men to women was about 10 to one, and saloons, gambling halls, and the notorious red-light district—known as the Barbary Coast—were the social mainstays of this rootless, risk-taking population. Though early San Francisco was primarily a tent city, fire was a constant scourge. The city started to build itself then burned to the ground six times by 1852, when San Francisco was recognized as the fourth largest port of entry in the United States. And though eccentricity and bad behavior were widely tolerated, unrestrained gang crime and murder became so commonplace that businessmen formed Committees of Vigilance to create some semblance of social order—by taking the law into their own hands and jailing, hanging, and running undesirables out of town.

More Barbarians and Big Spenders

By the late 1850s, the sources for most of California's surface gold had been picked clean. Ongoing harvesting of the state's most precious metal had become a corporate affair, an economic change made possible by the development of new technologies. The days of individualistic gold fever had subsided, and fortune hunters who remained in California turned their efforts to more long-lasting development of wealth, often in agriculture and business.

The city, though temporarily slowed by the economic depression that arrived with the end of the gold rush, was the most businesslike of them all. A recognizable city and a major financial center, no sooner had San Francisco calmed down and turned its attentions to nurturing civic pride than another boom arrived—this time silver, discovered in the Nevada territory's Comstock Lode. Silver mining required capital, heavy equipment, and organized mining technology; this was a strictly corporate raid on the earth's riches, with San Francisco and its bankers, businesses, and citizenry the main beneficiaries. Led by the silver rush "Bonanza Kings," the city's nouveau riche built themselves a residential empire atop Nob Hill and set about creating more cultured institutions.

Confident California, led by San Francisco, believed the future held nothing but greater growth, greater wealth. That was certainly the case for the "Big Four," Sacramento businessmen who financed Theodore Judah's dream of a transcontinental railroad, a development almost everyone believed would lead to an extended boom in the state's economy. Soon at home atop Nob Hill with the city's other nabobs, Charles Crocker, Mark Hopkins, Collis Huntington, and Leland Stanford also set out to establish some political machinery—the Southern Pacific Railway—to generate power and influence to match their wealth.

Bad Times and Bigotry

But the transcontinental railroad did little to help California, or San Francisco, at least initially. As naysayers had predicted, the ease of shipping goods by rail all but destroyed California's neophyte industrial base, since the state was soon glutted with lower-cost manufactured goods from the East Coast. A drought in 1869—a major setback for agricultural production—and an 1871 stock market crash made matters that much worse.

Legions of the unemployed, which included terminated railroad workers all over the West, rose up in rage throughout the 1870s and 1880s. They attacked not those who had enriched themselves at the expense of the general populace but "outsiders," specifically the Chinese who had labored long and hard at many a thankless task since the days of the gold rush. Mob violence and the torching of businesses and entire Chinese communities, in San Francisco and elsewhere, wasn't enough to satisfy such open racist hatred. Politicians too bowed to anti-Chinese sentiment, passing a series of discriminatory laws that forbade the Chinese from owning land, voting, and testifying in court, and levying a special tax against Chinese shrimp fishermen.

A near-final bigoted blow was the federal government's 1882 Oriental Exclusion Act, which essentially ended legal Asian immigration until it was repealed during World War II. San Francisco's Chinese community, for the most part working men denied the opportunity to reunite with their families, was further damaged by the Geary Act of 1892, which declared that all Chinese had to carry proper identification or face deportation. The failure of American society to support traditional Chinese culture led to rampant crime, gambling, and prostitution—acceptable diversions of the day for bachelors—and a lawless reign of terror by competing tongs who fought to control the profits. Only the gradual Americanization of the Chinese, which minimized tong influence, and the disastrous events during the spring of 1906 could change the reality of Chinatown. But the year 1906 changed everything in San Francisco.

The World Ends: Earthquake and Fire

By the early 1900s, San Francisco had entered its "gilded age," a complacent period when the city was busy enjoying its new cosmopolitan status. San Francisco had become the largest and finest city west of Chicago. The rich happily compounded their wealth in downtown high-rises and at home on Nob Hill and in other resplendent neighborhoods. The expanding middle class built rows of new Victorian homes, "painted ladies" that writer Tom Wolfe would later call "those endless staggers of bay windows," on hills far removed from the low life of the Barbary Coast, Chinatown, and the newest red-light district, The Tenderloin. But the working classes still smoldered in squalid tenements south of Market Street. Corruption ruled, politically, during the heyday of the "paint eaters"—politicians so greedy they'd even eat the paint off buildings. The cynical reporter and writer Ambrose Bierce, sniffing at the status quo, called San Francisco the "moral penal colony of the world." But the city's famous graft trials, a public political circus that resulted in 3,000 indictments but shockingly little jail time, came later.

Whatever was going on in the city, legal and otherwise, came to an abrupt halt on the morning of April 18, 1906, when a massive earthquake hit. Now estimated to have registered 8.25 on the Richter scale, the quake created huge fissures in the ground, broke water and gas mains all over the city, and caused chimneys and other unstable construction to come tumbling down. The better neighborhoods, including the city's Victorian row houses, suffered little damage. Downtown, however, was devastated. City Hall, a shoddy construction job allowed by scamming politicians and their contractor cohorts, crumbled into nothing. Though a central hospital also fell, burying doctors, nurses, and patients alike, the overall death toll from the earthquake itself was fairly small. Sadly for San Francisco, one of the fatalities was the city fire chief, whose foresight might have prevented the conflagration soon to follow.

More than 50 fires started that morning alone, racing through the low-rent neighborhoods south of Market, then into downtown, raging out of control. The flames were unchecked for four days, burning through downtown, parts of the Mission District, and also demolishing Chinatown, North Beach, Nob Hill, Telegraph Hill, and Russian Hill. The mansions along the eastern edge of Van Ness were dynamited to create an impromptu firebreak, finally stopping the firestorm.

When it was all over, the official tally of dead or missing stood at 674, though more recent research suggests the death toll was more than 3,000, since the Chinese weren't counted. The entire city center was destroyed, along with three-fourths of the city's businesses and residences. With half of its 450,000 population now homeless, San Francisco was a tent city once again. But it was an optimistic tent city, bolstered by relief and rebuilding funds sent from around the world. As reconstruction began, San Francisco also set out to clean house politically.

Modern Times

By 1912, with San Francisco more or less back on its feet, Mayor James "Sunny Jim" Rolph, who always sported a fresh flower in his lapel, seemed to symbolize the city's new era. Rolph presided over the construction of some of San Francisco's finest public statements about itself. These included the new city hall and Civic Center, as well as the 1915 world's fair and the Panama-Pacific International Exposition, a spectacular 600-acre temporary city designed by Bernard Maybeck to reflect the "mortality of grandeur and the vanity of human wishes." Though the exposition was intended to celebrate the opening of the Panama Canal, it was San Francisco's grand announcement to the world that it had not only survived but thrived in the aftermath of its earlier earthquake and fire.

During the Great Depression, San Francisco continued to defy the commonplace, dancing at the edge of unreal expectations. Two seemingly impossible spans, the Golden Gate Bridge and the Bay Bridge, were built in the 1930s. San Francisco also built the world's largest man-made island, Treasure Island, which hosted the Golden Gate International Exposition in 1939 before becoming a U.S. Navy facility. (In 1997, the Navy abandoned ship and ceded the island to the city of San Francisco; now it's a venue for occasional concerts and a regular flea market.)

No matter how spectacular its statements to the world, San Francisco had trouble at home. The 1929 stock market crash and the onset of the Depression reignited long-simmering labor strife, especially in the city's port. Four longshoremen competed for every available job along the waterfront, and members of the company-controlled Longshoremen's Association demanded kickbacks for jobs that were offered. Harry Bridges reorganized the International Longshoremen's Association, and backed by the Teamsters Union, his pro-union strike successfully closed down the waterfront. On "Bloody Thursday," July 5, 1934, 800 strikers battled with National Guard troops called in to quell a riot started by union busters. Two men were shot and killed by police, another 100 were injured, and the subsequent all-city strike—the largest general strike in U.S. history—ultimately involved most city businesses as well as the waterfront unions. More so than elsewhere on the West Coast, labor unions are still strong in San Francisco.

Other social and philosophical revolutions, for iconoclasts and oddballs alike, either got their start in San Francisco or received abundant support once arrived here. First came the 1950s-era Beatniks or "Beats"—poets, freethinkers, and jazz aficionados rebelling against the suburbanization of the American mind. The Beats were followed in short order by the 1960s, the Summer of Love, psychedelics, and rock groups like the legendary Grateful Dead. More substantial, in the '60s, the Free Speech Movement heated up across the bay in Berkeley, not to mention anti-Vietnam War protests and the rise of the Black Panther Party. Since then, San Francisco has managed to make its place at, or near, the forefront of almost every change in social awareness, from women's rights to gay pride. And in the 1980s and '90s, San Franciscans went all out for baby boomer and Gen X consumerism; young urban professionals have been setting the style for quite some time. But there are other styles, other trends. You name it, San Francisco probably has it.

SEEING SAN FRANCISCO: COASTING THE PACIFIC

Coastal travelers might start a San Francisco tour at the Golden Gate Bridge, which stretches between San Francisco and Marin County and dramatically spans the Golden Gate, the entry to San Francisco Bay. Just beyond the bridge Highway 1 splits off from Highway 101 and dashes south through the Presidio of San Francisco, just one highlight of Golden Gate National Recreation Area. The national park also hugs much of the coastline heading south, all the way to Pacifica. Notable features along the way include the Cliff House, Fort Funston, and Thornton Beach—not to mention San Francisco's famed Golden Gate Park.

GOLDEN GATE NATIONAL RECREATION AREA

One of the city's unexpected treasures, in San Francisco the Golden Gate National Recreation Area (GGNRA) starts in the north amid the pilings of the Golden Gate Bridge. Along the coast the park also follows a narrow strip of land adjacent to Hwy. 1, taking in the Cliff House, Fort Funston, Thornton Beach, and other milestones before reaching Sweeney Ridge near Pacifica. The GGNRA also includes Alcatraz Island, one of the nation's most infamous prison sites, and state-administered Angel Island, "Ellis Island of the West" to the Chinese and other immigrant groups. In late 1995, the historic Presidio—1,480 acres of forest, coastal bluffs, military outposts, and residences adjacent to the Golden Gate Bridge—was converted from military to domestic purposes and formally included in the GGNRA. Vast tracts of the southern and western Marin County headlands, north of the bridge, are also included within GGNRA boundaries, making this park a true urban wonder. Much of the credit for creating the GGNRA, the world's largest urban park, goes to the late congressman Phillip Burton. Established in 1972, the recreation area as currently envisioned includes more than 36,000 acres in a cooperative patchwork of land holdings exceeding 114 square miles. The GGNRA is also the most popular of the national parks, drawing more than 20 million visitors each year.

One major attraction of the GGNRA is the opportunity for hiking—both **urban hiking** on the San Francisco side, and **wilderness hiking** throughout the Marin Headlands. Get oriented to the recreation area's trails at any visitor center (see below), look up the National Park Service website at www.nps.gov/prsf, or sign on for any of the GGNRA's excellent guided hikes and explorations. The schedule changes constantly. A particularly spectacular section of the GGNRA's trail system is the 2.5-mile trek from the St. Francis Yacht Club to Fort Point and the Golden Gate Bridge. This walk is part of the still-in-progress **San Francisco Bay Trail,** a 450-mile shoreline trail system that will one day ring the entire bay and traverse nine Bay Area counties. Ambitious hikers can follow the GGNRA's **Coastal Trail** from San Francisco to Point Reyes National Seashore in Marin County. Once on the north side of the Golden Gate, possibilities for long hikes and backpacking trips are almost endless.

San Francisco-Side GGNRA Sights

The GGNRA includes the beaches and coastal bluffs along San Francisco's entire western edge (and both south and north), as well as seaside trails and walking and running paths along the new highway and seawall between Sloat Blvd. and the western border of Golden Gate Park.

The original Cliff House near Seal Rocks was one of San Francisco's first tourist lures, its original diversions a bit on the licentious side. That version, converted by Adolph Sutro into a family-style resort, burned to the ground in 1894 and was soon replaced by a splendid Victorian palace and an adjacent bathhouse, also fire victims. Ruins of the old **Sutro Baths** are still visible among the rocks just north. Aptly named **Seal Rocks** offshore attract vocal sea lions.

The current **Cliff House,** across the highway from Sutro Heights Park, dates from 1908 and still attracts locals and tourists alike. The views are spectacular, which explains the success of the building's Cliff House Restaurant, tel. (415) 386-3330, as well as the building's Phineas T. Barnacle pub-style deli and the Ben Butler Room bar. The stairway outdoors leads down the cliff to the GGNRA **Cliff House Visitor Center,** tel. (415) 556-8642, a good stop for information, free or low-cost publications and maps, and books. Open daily 10 a.m.-5 p.m. Also down below just behind the Cliff House is the **Musée Méchanique,** tel. (415) 386-1170, a delightful and dusty collection of penny arcade amusements (most cost a quarter)—from nickelodeons

and coin-eating music boxes to fortune-telling machines—and the odd **Camera Obscura & Hologram Gallery.** The gallery's "camera" is actually a slow revolving lens that reflects images onto a parabolic screen—with a particularly thrilling fractured-light image at sunset.

Wandering northward from Cliff House, Point Lobos Ave. and then El Camino del Mar lead to San Francisco's **Point Lobos,** the city's westernmost point. There's an overlook, to take in the view. Nearby is the **USS *San Francisco* Memorial,** part of the city's namesake ship. Also nearby is **Fort Miley,** which features a 4-H "adventure ropes" course. But the most spectacular thing in sight (on a clear day) is the postcard-pretty peek at the Golden Gate Bridge. You can even get there from here, on foot, via the **Coastal Trail,** a spectacular city hike that skirts Lincoln Park and the California Palace of the Legion of Honor before passing through the Seacliff neighborhood, then flanking the Presidio. From Fort Point at the foot of the Golden Gate, the truly intrepid can keep on trekking—straight north across the bridge to Marin County, or east past the yacht harbors to Fort Mason and the overwhelming attractions of Fisherman's Wharf.

For some slower sightseeing, backtrack to the Presidio's hiking trails and other attractions. The GGNRA's **Presidio Visitor Center,** 102 Montgomery St. (that's a *different* Montgomery St. than the one downtown), tel. (415) 561-4323, can point you in the right direction. It's open year-round, daily 9 a.m.-5 p.m. One possible detour: the **Presidio Army Museum** at Lincoln and Funston, tel. (415) 561-4331.

Or spend time exploring the coast. At low tide, the fleet of foot can beach walk (and climb) from the Golden Gate Bridge to **Baker Beach** and farther (looking back at the bridge for a seagull's-eye view). Though many flock here precisely because it is a de facto nude beach, the very naked sunbathers at Baker Beach usually hide out in the rock-secluded coves beyond the family-oriented stretch of public sand. Near Baker Beach is the miniature **Battery Lowell A. Chamberlin** "museum," a historic gun hold, home to the six-inch disappearing rifle. Weapons aficionados will want to explore more thoroughly the multitude of gun batteries farther north along the trail, near Fort Point.

WALKING ON WATER ACROSS THAT GOLDEN GATE

Nothing is as San Francisco as the city's astounding **Golden Gate Bridge,** a bright, red-orange fairy pathway up into the fog, a double-necked lyre plucked by the wind to send its surreal song spiraling skyward. The bridge stands today as testimony to the vision of political madmen and poets, almost always the progenitors of major achievements. San Francisco's own **Emperor Norton**—a gold rush-era British merchant originally known as Joshua A. Norton, who went bankrupt in the land of instant wealth but soon reinvented himself as "Norton I, Emperor of the United States and Protector of Mexico"—was the first lunatic to suggest that the vast, turbulent, and troublesome waters of the Golden Gate could be spanned by a bridge. The poet and engineer **Joseph Baermann Strauss,** a titan of a man barely five feet tall, seconded the insanity, and in 1917 he left Chicago for San Francisco, plans and models in hand, to start the 13-year lobbying campaign.

All practical doubts aside, San Francisco at large was aghast at the idea of defacing the natural majesty of the Golden Gate with a manmade monument; more than 2,000 lawsuits were filed in an effort to stop bridge construction. California's love of progress won out in the end, however, and construction of the graceful bridge, designed by architect Irwin F. Morrow, began in 1933. As Strauss himself remarked later: "It took two decades and 200 million words to convince the people that the bridge was feasible; then only four years and $35 million to put the concrete and steel together."

Building the Golden Gate Bridge was no simple task, rather, an accomplishment akin to a magical feat. Some 80,000 miles of wire were spun into the bridge's suspension cables, a sufficient length to encircle the earth (at the equator) three times, and enough concrete to create a very wide sidewalk between the country's West and East coasts was poured into the anchoring piers. Sinking the southern support pier offshore was a particular challenge, with 60-mile-an-hour tidal surges and 15-foot swells at times threatening to upend the (seasick) workers' floating trestle. Once the art-deco towers were in place, the *real* fun began—those acrobats in overalls, most earning less than $1 an hour, working in empty space to span the gap. Safety was a serious issue with Strauss and his assistant, Clifford Paine. Due to their diligence, 19 men fell but landed in safety nets instead of in the morgue, earning them honorary membership in the "Halfway to Hell Club." But just weeks before construction was completed, a scaffolding collapsed, its jagged edges tearing through the safety net and taking nine men down with it.

When the Golden Gate Bridge was finished in 1937, the world was astonished. Some 200,000 people walked across the virgin roadbed that day, just to introduce themselves to this gracious steel wonder. At that time, the bridge was the world's longest and tallest suspension structure—with a single-span,

the Golden
Gate Bridge

SAN JOSE CONVENTION AND VISITORS BUREAU

between-towers distance of 4,200 feet—and boasted the highest high-rises west of New York's Empire State Building. Its total length was 1.7 miles, and its 746-foot-tall towers were equivalent in total height to 65-story buildings. Even now, the bridge's grace is much more than aesthetic. As a suspension bridge, the Golden Gate moves with the action of the immediate neighborhood. It has rarely been closed for reasons of safety or necessary repairs, though it *was* closed, in 1960, so French President Charles de Gaulle could make a solo crossing. Even in treacherous winds, the bridge can safely sway as much as 28 feet in either direction, though standing on a slightly swinging bridge of such monstrous dimensions is an indescribably odd sensation.

Perhaps the best thing about the Golden Gate Bridge, even after all these years, is that people can still enjoy it, up close and very personally. Though the bridge toll is $3 per car (heading south), for pedestrians it's a free trip either way. The hike is ambitious, about two miles one-way. For those who don't suffer from vertigo, this is an inspiring and invigorating experience, as close to walking on water as most of us will ever get. (But it's not necessarily a life-enhancing experience for the seriously depressed or suicidal. The lure of the leap has proved too tempting for more than 900 people.) Parking is available at either end of the bridge.

Though the Golden Gate Bridge is the Bay Area's most royal span, credit for San Francisco's propulsion into the modern world of commerce and crazy traffic actually goes to the **Bay Bridge** spanning San Francisco Bay between downtown San Francisco and Oakland/Berkeley. Completed in 1936, and built atop piers sunk into the deepest deeps ever bridged, the Bay Bridge cost $80 million to complete, at that time the most expensive structure ever built. And in recent history, the Bay Bridge has made front-page and nightly news headlines. The whole world watched in horror when part of the bridge collapsed amid the torqued tensions of the 1989 earthquake, a pre-rush-hour event. There were deaths and injuries, but fewer casualties than if the quake had come during peak commuter traffic. Despite the quake, the bridge still remained structurally sound, and the more critically necessary repairs have been made. A new span for the Bay Bridge is in the planning stages.

For More Information

For information on the GGNRA included elsewhere in this chapter, see also The Presidio and Fort Point in this section; The Avenues, immediately below; and Fort Mason and Touring the Real Rock under Seeing San Francisco: Coasting the Bay. For more information on the Marin County sections of the GGNRA, see Point Reyes National Seashore and Angel Island State Park in the preceding chapter.

For current information about GGNRA features and activities, contact: **Golden Gate National Recreation Area,** Fort Mason, Building 201, tel. (415) 556-0560, www.nps.gov/goga. To check on local conditions, events, and programs, you can also call the GGNRA's other visitor centers: **Cliff House,** tel. (415) 556-8642; **Fort Point,** tel. (415) 556-1693; **Marin Headlands,** tel. (415) 331-1540; **Muir Woods,** tel. (415) 388-2596; and **Presidio,** tel. (415) 561-4323.

For a set of maps of the entire San Francisco Bay Trail ($10.95) or detailed maps of specific trail sections ($1.50 each), contact the **San Francisco Bay Trail Project,** c/o the Association of Bay Area Governments, tel. (510) 464-7900, or order the maps online at www.abag.org. About 215 of the Bay Trail's 450 total miles of trails are completed, with planning and/or construction of the rest underway. Call the Association to volunteer trail-building labor or materials, to help with fundraising, or to lead guided walks along sections of the Bay Trail.

Also of interest to area hikers: the **Bay Area Ridge Trail,** a 400-mile ridgetop route that one day will skirt the entire bay, connecting 75 parks. For information, contact the **Bay Area Ridge Trail Council,** 26 O'Farrell St., tel. (415) 391-9300, www.ridgetrail.org. You can order a book about the trail ($14.95) by calling the office.

THE AVENUES

Richmond District and Vicinity

Originally called San Francisco's Great Sand Waste, then the city's cemetery district—before the bones were dug up and shipped south to Colma in 1914—today the Richmond District is a middle-class ethnic sandwich, built upon Golden Gate Park and topped by Lincoln Park and the

THE PRESIDIO AND FORT POINT

A national historic landmark and historic military installation, San Francisco's **Presidio** is the nation's newest national park. In 1994, Congress closed the Presidio to the Sixth Army Command, and the Golden Gate National Recreation Area (GGNRA) gained 1,446 acres of the multimillion-dollar real estate. Among other proposals for putting the buildings here to good public use, it's quite possible that 23 acres on the Presidio's eastern border will house studios for filmmaker George Lucas's Industrial Light & Magic, as well as facilities for other Lucas enterprises, on the site of the old Letterman Army Hospital.

The Presidio lies directly south of the Golden Gate Bridge along the northwest tip of the San Francisco Peninsula, bordered by the Marina and Pacific Heights districts to the east and Richmond and Presidio heights to the south. To the west and north, a coastal strip of the Golden Gate National Recreation Area frames the Presidio, which boasts some 70 miles of paths and trails of its own winding along cliffs and through eucalyptus groves and coastal flora. The 1,600 buildings here, most of them eclectic blends of Victorian and Spanish-revival styles, have housed the U.S. Army since 1847.

Founded by the Spanish in 1776 as one of two original settlements in San Francisco, the Presidio had a militaristic history even then, for the area commands a strategic view of San Francisco Bay and the Pacific Ocean. The Spanish garrison ruled the peninsula for the first 50 years of the city's history, chasing off Russian whalers and trappers by means of the two cannons now guarding the entrance to the Officer's Club. After 1847, when Americans took over, the Presidio became a staging center for the Indian wars, a never-used outpost during the Civil War, and more recently, headquarters for the Sixth Army Command, which fought in the Pacific during World War II.

Today the Presidio is open to the public, and visitors may drive around and admire the neat-as-a-pin streets with their white, two-story wood Victorians and faultless lawns or trace the base's history at the **Presidio Army Museum** (one of the oldest buildings, originally the hospital) located near the corner of Lincoln Blvd. and Funston Ave., tel. (415) 561-4131. Pick up a map there showing the Presidio's hiking trails, including a six-mile historic walk and two ecology trails. Museum hours are Wed.-Sun. 12 p.m.-4 p.m., admission free.

Ranger-led GGNRA guided tours include the **Natural History of the Presidio,** an exploratory lesson in

Presidio. White Russians were the first residents, fleeing Russia after the 1917 revolution, but just about everyone else followed. A stroll down **Clement Street,** past its multiethnic eateries and shops, should bring you up to speed on the subject of cultural diversity.

The area between Arguello and Park Presidio, colloquially called "New Chinatown," is noted for its good, largely untouristed Asian eateries and shops. Russian-Americans still park themselves on the playground benches at pretty **Mountain Lake Park** near the Presidio. And the gold-painted onion domes of the Russian Orthodox **Russian Holy Virgin Cathedral of the Church in Exile,** 6210 Geary Blvd., along with the Byzantine-Roman Jewish Reform **Temple Emanu-El** at Arguello and Lake (technically in Pacific Heights), offer inspiring architectural reminders of earlier days.

Highlights of the Richmond District include the **University of San Francisco** atop Lone Mountain, an institution founded by the Jesuits in

1855, complete with spectacular **St. Ignatius** church, and the **Neptune Society Columbarium,** 1 Loraine Ct. (just off Anza near Stanyan), tel. (415) 221-1838, the final resting place of old San Francisco families including the newspaper Hearsts and department store Magnins. With its ornate neoclassical and copper-roofed rotunda, the Columbarium offers astounding acoustics, best appreciated from the upper floors. The building is open to the public weekdays 9 a.m.-5 p.m., weekends 10 a.m.-2 p.m.

Seacliff, an exclusive seaside neighborhood nestled between the Presidio and Lincoln Park, is the once-rural community where famed California photographer **Ansel Adams** was raised. West of Seacliff, **Land's End** is the city's most rugged coastline, reached via footpath from Lincoln Park and the Golden Gate National Recreation Area. **China Beach,** just below Seacliff, was probably named for Chinese immigrants trying to evade Angel Island internment by jumping ship, all a result of the Exclusion Act in effect

the San Francisco Peninsula's geology, geography, and plant and animal life, featuring an enchanted forest and the city's last free-flowing stream; **Presidio Main Post Historical Walks;** and the **Mountain Lake to Fort Point Hike.**

For more information about the Presidio and scheduled events and activities, look up the National Park Service's website at www.nps.gov/prsf, or call the **Presidio Visitor Center,** at tel. (415) 561-4323.

More businesslike in design but in many respects more interesting than the Presidio, **Fort Point** off Lincoln Blvd. is nestled directly underneath the southern tip of the Golden Gate Bridge and worth donning a few extra layers to visit. Officially the Fort Point National Historic Site since 1968, the quadrangular red-brick behemoth was modeled after South Carolina's Fort Sumter and completed in 1861 to guard the bay during the Civil War. However, the fort was never given the chance to test its mettle, as a grass-roots plot hatched by Confederate sympathizers in San Francisco to undermine the Yankee cause died for lack of funds and manpower, and the more palpable threat that the Confederate cruiser *Shenandoah* would blast its way into the bay was foiled by the war ending before the ship ever arrived.

Nonetheless, military strategists had the right idea situating the fort on the site of the old Spanish adobe-brick outpost of Castillo de San Joaquin, and through the years the fort-that-could was used as a garrison and general catchall for the Presidio, including a stint during WW I as barracks for unmarried officers. During the 1930s, when the Golden Gate Bridge was in its design phase, the fort narrowly missed being scrapped but was saved by the bridge's chief design engineer, Joseph B. Strauss, who considered the fort's demolition a waste of good masonry and designed the somewhat triumphal arch that now soars above it.

Fort Point these days enjoys a useful retirement as a historical museum, open daily 10-5, admission free. While the wind howls in the girders overhead, park rangers clad in Civil War regalia (many wearing long johns underneath) lead hourly tours, 11 a.m.-4 p.m., through the park's honeycomb of corridors, staircases, and gun ports. Cannon muster is solemnly observed at 1:30 and 2:30 p.m., and two slide shows are also offered, at 11:30 a.m. and again at 3:30 p.m. A fairly recent addition is the excellent exhibit and tribute to black American soldiers. At the bookstore, pick up some Confederate money and other military memorabilia. For more information about tours and special events, call Fort Point at (415) 556-1693.

—Taran March

---

from the 1880s to World War II. During the Civil War, this was the westernmost point of the nation's antislavery "Underground Railroad." You can swim here—facilities include a lifeguard station plus changing rooms, showers, restrooms—but the water's brisk. Northeast is **Baker Beach,** considered the city's best nude beach.

California Palace of the Legion of Honor

The area's main attraction, though, just beyond Lincoln Park's Municipal Golf Course, is the **California Palace of the Legion of Honor,** on Legion of Honor Drive (enter off 34th and Clement), tel. (415) 750-3600 (office) or (415) 863-3330 (visitor hot line), www.famsf.org. Established by French-born Alma de Bretteville Spreckels, wife of the city's sugar king, this handsome hilltop palace was built in honor of American soldiers killed in France during World War I. It's a 1920 French neoclassic, from the colonnades and triumphal arch to the outdoor equestrian bronzes. Intentionally incongruous, placed out near the parking lot in an otherwise serene setting, is George Segal's testimony to the depths of human terror and terrorism: the barbed wire and barely living bodies of *The Holocaust.* Also here are bronze castings from Rodin, including *The Thinker* and *The Shades* outdoors, just part of the Legion's collection of more than 70 Rodin originals. Inside, the permanent collection was originally exclusively French, but now includes the M.H. de Young Museum's European collection—an awesome eight-century sweep from El Greco, Rembrandt, and Rubens to Renoir, Cézanne, Degas, Monet, and Manet. Take a docent-led tour for a deeper appreciation of other features, including the Legion's period rooms.

Special events include films, lectures, and painting and music programs, the latter including Rodin Gallery pipe organ concerts as well as chamber music, jazz, and historical instrument concerts in the Florence Gould Theater. The Legion of Honor also features a pleasant café and a gift shop. Museum hours are Tues.-Sun. 9:30 a.m.-5 p.m., and until 8:45 p.m. on the first Saturday of every month. Admission is $7 adults, $5 seniors, $4 youths 12-17, free for everyone on the second Wednesday of each month. Admission may be higher during some visiting exhibitions.

The fit and fresh-air loving can get here on foot along the meandering **Coastal Trail**—follow it north from the Cliff House or south from the Golden Gate Bridge.

Sunset District

Most of San Francisco's neighborhoods are residential, streets of private retreat that aren't all that exciting except to those who live there. The Sunset District, stretching to the sea from south of Golden Gate Park, is one example, the southern section of the city's "Avenues." In summertime, the fog here at the edge of the continent is usually unrelenting, so visitors often shiver and shuffle off, muttering that in a place called "Sunset" one should be able to see it. (To appreciate the neighborhood name, come anytime *but* summer.) For beach access and often gray-day seaside recreation, from surfing and surf fishing to cycling, walking, and jogging (there's a paved path), follow the **Great Highway** south from Cliff House and stop anywhere along the way.

Stanyan Street, at the edge of the Haight and east of Golden Gate Park, offers odd and attractive shops, as does the stretch of **Ninth Avenue** near Irving and Judah. Just south of the park at its eastern edge is the **University of California at San Francisco Medical Center** atop Mt. Sutro, the small eucalyptus forest here reached via cobblestone Edgewood Ave. or, for the exercise, the Farnsworth Steps. From here, look down on the colorful Haight or north for a bird's-eye view of the **Richmond District,** the rest of the city's Avenues.

Stern Grove, at Sloat Blvd. and 19th Ave., is a wooded valley beloved for its Sunday concerts. Just off Sloat is the main gate to the **San Francisco Zoo,** which offers an Insect Zoo, a Children's Zoo, and the usual caged collection of primates, lions, tigers, and bears. (Mealtime for the big cats, at the Lion House at 2 p.m. every day except Monday, is quite a viewing treat.) Large **Lake Merced** just south, accessible via Skyline Blvd. (Hwy. 35) or Lake Merced Blvd., was once a tidal lagoon. These days it's a freshwater lake popular for canoeing, kayaking, non-motorized boating (rent boats at the Boat House on Harding), fishing (largemouth bass and trout), or just getting some fresh air.

The Lake Merced area offers one of the newer sections of the **Bay Area Ridge Trail,** a hiking route (signed with blue markers at major turning points and intersections) that one day will total 400 miles and connect 75 parks in nine Bay Area counties. Farther south still is **Fort Funston,** a one-time military installation on barren cliffs, a favorite spot for hang gliders and a good place to take Fido for an outing (dogs can be off-leash along most of the beach here). East of Lake Merced are **San Francisco State University,** one of the state university system's best—noted for its **Sutro Library** and **American Poetry Archives**— and the community of **Ingleside,** home of the 26-foot-tall sundial.

GOLDEN GATE PARK

Yet another of San Francisco's impossible dreams successfully accomplished, Golden Gate Park was once a vast expanse of sand dunes. A wasteland by urban, and urbane, standards, locals got the idea that it could be a park—and a grand park, to rival the Bois de Boulogne in Paris. Frederick Law Olmsted, who designed New York's Central Park, was asked to build it. He took one look and scoffed, saying essentially that it couldn't be done. Olmsted was wrong, as it turned out, and eventually he had the grace to admit it. William Hammond Hall, designer and chief engineer, and Scottish gardener John McLaren, the park's green-thumbed godfather, achieved the unlikely with more than a bit of West Coast ingenuity. Hall constructed a behemoth breakwater on the 1,000-acre park's west end, to block the stinging sea winds and salt spray, and started anchoring the sand by planting barley, then nitrogen-fixing lupine, then grasses. Careful grading and berming, helped along in time by windrows, further deflected the fierceness of ocean-blown storms.

"Uncle John" McLaren, Hall's successor, set about re-creating the land on a deeper level. He trucked in humus and manure to further transform sand into soil, and got busy planting more than one million trees. And that was just the beginning. In and around walkways, benches, and

AISUNN RACE

*in the Japanese
Tea Garden*

major park features, there were shrubs to plant, flowerbeds to establish, and pristine lawns to nurture. McLaren kept at it for some 55 years, dedicating his life to creating a park for the everlasting enjoyment of the citizenry. He bravely did battle with politicians, often beating them at their own games, to nurture and preserve "his" park for posterity. He fought with groundskeepers who tried to keep people off the lush lawns, and he attempted to hide despised-on-principle statues and other graven images with bushes and shrubs. In the end he lost this last battle; after McLaren died, the city erected a statue in his honor.

McLaren's Legacy

Much of the park's appeal is its astounding array of natural attractions. The botanic diversity alone, much of it exotic, somehow reflects San Francisco's multicultural consciousness—also transplanted from elsewhere, also now as natural as the sun, the moon, the salt winds, and the tides.

The dramatic **Victorian Conservatory of Flowers** on John F. Kennedy Drive, tel. (415) 641-7978, was imported from Europe and assembled here in 1878. A showcase jungle of tropical plants also noted for its seasonal botanic displays, the Conservatory was heavily damaged in a December 1995 storm and has been closed pending reconstruction. Call for an update.

The 55-acre **Strybing Arboretum and Botanical Gardens,** Ninth Ave. at Lincoln Way, tel. (415) 661-1316, features more than 7,000 different species, including many exotic and rare plants. Noted here is the collection of Australian and New Zealand plant life, along with exotics from Africa, the Americas, and Asia. Several gardens are landscaped by theme, such as the Mexican Cloud Forest and the California Redwood Grove. The serene Japanese Moon-Viewing Garden is a worthy respite when the Japanese Tea Garden is choked with tourists. Quite a delight, too, is the Fragrance Garden—a collection of culinary and medicinal herbs easily appreciated by aroma and texture, labeled also in Braille. Any plant lover will enjoy time spent in the small store. The arboretum is open weekdays 8 a.m.-4:30 p.m., weekends 10 a.m.-5 p.m.; admission is free, donations appreciated. Guided tours are offered on weekday afternoons and twice a day on weekends; call for tour times and meeting places. Next door is the **San Francisco County Fair Building,** site of the annual "fair"—in San Francisco, it's a flower show only—and home to the **Helen Crocker Russell Library,** containing some 18,000 volumes on horticulture and plants.

The **Japanese Tea Garden** on Tea Garden Dr. (off Martin Luther King Jr. Dr.), tel. (415) 752-4227 (admission information) or (415) 752-1171 (gift shop), a striking and suitable backdrop to the Asian Art Museum, is an enduring attraction, started (and maintained until the family's World War II internment) by full-time Japanese gardener Maokota Hagiwara and his family. Both a lovingly landscaped garden and tea house concession—the Hagiwaras invented the fortune cookie, first served here, though Chinatown later claimed this innovation as an old-country tradition—the Tea Garden is so popular that to enjoy even a few moments of the intended serenity, visitors should arrive early on a weekday morning or come on a rainy day. The large bronze "Buddha Who Sits Through Sun and Rain Without Shelter," cast in Japan in 1790, will surely welcome an off-day visitor. The Japanese Tea Garden is most enchanting in April, when the cherry trees are in bloom. Open daily March-Dec. 8:30 a.m.-6 p.m., Jan.-Feb. 8:30 a.m.-dusk. The tea house opens at 10 a.m. Admission is $3.50 adults, $1.25 seniors and children 6-12.

Also especially notable for spring floral color in Golden Gate Park: the **Queen Wilhelmina Tulip Garden** on the park's western edge, near the restored (northern) **Dutch Windmill**, and the **John McLaren Rhododendron Dell** near the Conservatory of Flowers. The very English **Shakespeare Garden,** beyond the Academy of Sciences, is unusual any time of year, since all the plants and flowers here are those mentioned in the Bard's works. Poignant and sobering is the expansive **National AIDS Memorial Grove,** at the east end of the park between Middle Drive East and Bowling Green Drive. Regardless of whether or not you personally know anyone with AIDS, this is a good place to wander among the groves of redwoods and dogwoods, quietly contemplating the fragility of life and your place in it. The grove is maintained by volunteers; to volunteer, or for more information, call (415) 750-8340.

Even the **San Francisco Zoo,** 1 Zoo Rd. (Sloat Blvd. at 45th Ave.), tel. (415) 753-7080, has its botanical attractions. The main reason to come, though, is to commune with the 1,000 or so animals in captivity. The zoo is open 365 days a year, 10 a.m.-5 p.m.; admission is $9 adults, $6 youths 12-17 and seniors 65 and over, $3 children 3-11, free on the first Wednesday of every month.

M.H. de Young Memorial Museum

Though plans have been bandied about for years to move both this museum and its incorporated Asian Art Museum downtown, both are currently still housed here in the park. Now merged administratively with the California Palace of the Legion of Honor into the jointly operated Fine Arts Museums of San Francisco, the de Young Museum, 75 Tea Garden Dr. (at Ninth Ave.), tel. (415) 750-3600, www.thinker.org or www.famsf.org, is one of the city's major visual arts venues. The museum, with its Spanish-style architecture, honors San Francisco newspaper publisher M.H. de Young.

The de Young's specialty is American art, from British colonial into contemporary times, and the collection here is one of the finest anywhere. Examine the exhibits of period paintings, sculpture, and decorative and domestic arts; the 20th-century American realist paintings are almost as intriguing as the textile and modern graphic arts collections. Also included in the de Young's permanent collection are traditional arts of the Americas, Africa, and Oceania. Come, too, for changing special exhibits, like "San Francisco's Old Chinatown: Photographs by Arnold Genthe."

Admission (which includes access to the Asian Art Museum) is $7 adults, $5 seniors, $4 youths 12-17 (free for everyone on the first Wednesday of each month). Call about docent-led tours. Open Tues.-Sun. 9:30 a.m.-5 p.m., and until 8:45 p.m. on the first Wednesday of each month. For current information on exhibits, call (415)

the M.H. de Young Museum

AISLINN RACE

863-3330; for information on becoming a museum member, call (415) 750-3636.

Asian Art Museum

Scheduled to move to the site of the old downtown library in 2001, the astounding Asian Art Museum, 75 Tea Garden Dr. (at Ninth Ave.), tel. (415) 379-8801, www.asianart.org, currently shares a wing and the admission charge with the de Young Museum. The museum got its start in 1966 when the late U.S. diplomat Avery Brundage donated his collection to the city. Since then it has expanded greatly. Today, in addition to its vast collections of Chinese and Japanese art, the museum holds masterpieces from some 40 other Asian cultures, including India, Tibet, Nepal, Mongolia, Korea, and Iran. The total collection—more than 12,000 objects in all, spanning 6,000 years of history—is so large that only about 10% can be displayed at any one time. Among the treasures here: the oldest known dated sculpture of Buddha, from China, circa A.D. 338 in Western time; earthenware animals from the Tang Dynasty; and an astounding array of jade artifacts. Special changing exhibits are presented periodically; call for current exhibit schedule.

The Asian Art Museum is open Tues.-Sun. 9:30 a.m.-5 p.m., except on the first Wednesday of each month, when it's open 10 a.m.-8:45 p.m. Admission (which includes access to the adjacent M.H. de Young Museum) is $7 adults, $5 seniors, $4 youths 12-17 (free for everyone on the first Wednesday of each month). Admission is sometimes higher during special exhibitions. Call for information about docent-led tours.

THE CITYPASS

The money-saving **CityPass** provides admission to six of San Francisco's top attractions—the Exploratorium, California Palace of the Legion of Honor, de Young Museum, Museum of Modern Art, California Academy of Sciences/Steinhart Aquarium, and a San Francisco Bay Cruise—for a price, at last report, half of what the individual admissions would cost: $27.75 adults, $19.75 seniors, $17.25 youths 12-17. It's good for seven days and is available at any of the participating attractions or any of the city's visitor information centers.

California Academy of Sciences

At home on the park's Music Concourse (between Martin Luther King Jr. and John F. Kennedy Drives), tel. (415) 750-7145, www.calacademy.org, the California Academy of Sciences is a multifaceted scientific institution, the oldest in the West, founded in 1853 to survey and study the vast resources of California and vicinity. In the academy's courtyard, note the intertwining whales in the fountain. These were sculpted by Robert Howard and originally served as the centerpiece of the San Francisco Building during the Golden Gate International Exposition of 1939-40.

Natural History Museum: Dioramas and exhibits include **Wild California,** the **African Hall** (with a surprisingly realistic waterhole), and **Life Through Time,** which offers a 3.5 billion-year journey into the speculative experience of early life on earth. At the **Hohfeld Earth & Space Hall,** the neon solar system tells the story of the universe and the natural forces that have shaped—and still shape—the earth. Especially popular with children is **Earthquake,** a "you are there" experience that simulates two of the city's famous earthquakes. The **Wattis Hall of Human Cultures** specializes in anthropology and features one of the broadest Native American museum collections in Northern California, with an emphasis on cultures in both North America and South America. The **Far Side of Science Gallery** includes 159 original Gary Larson cartoons, offering a hilarious perspective on humanity's scientific research. The **Gem and Mineral Hall** contains some real gems, like a 1,350-pound quartz crystal from Arkansas.

Morrison Planetarium: This 65-foot dome simulates the night sky and its astronomical phenomena; Sky Shows are offered daily, at 2 p.m. on weekdays, and hourly from 11 a.m.-4 p.m. on weekends. The associated Earth & Space Hall features a moon rock, a meteorite, and other exhibits. Admission (over and above Academy admission) is $2.50 adults, $1.25 seniors/youths, children under six free. For more information, call (415) 750-7141. But the planetarium is most noted for its weekend evening **Laserium** shows, tel. (415) 750-7138, where blue beams from a krypton/argon gas laser slice the air to the rhythm of whatever's on the stereo—classical music as well as rock. Tickets are $7 adults, and are available through BASS (tel. 415-478-2277) or at the Academy one-half hour before show time.

Steinhart Aquarium: The oldest aquarium in North America, the 1923 Steinhart Aquarium allows visitors to commune with the world's most diverse live fish collection, including representatives of around 600 different species (including fish, marine invertebrates, and other sea life). The stunning glass-walled, 100,000-gallon Fish Roundabout here puts visitors right in the swim of things, as if they were standing in the center of the open ocean; it's especially fun at feeding time (daily at 2 p.m.). Altogether there are 189 exhibits here, but some of the most dramatic include: Sharks of the Tropics; the Penguin Environment, featuring an entire breeding colony of black-footed penguins; and The Swamp, featuring tropical critters like alligators, crocodiles, snakes, lizards, and frogs. Fun for some hands-on wet and wild exploring is California Tidepool.

The Academy of Sciences, tel. (415) 221-5100 or (415) 750-7145 (24-hour recorded information), is open daily 10 a.m.-5 p.m. (extended hours from Memorial Day weekend through Labor Day). Admission is free the first Wednesday of the month (when hours are extended until 8:45 p.m.), otherwise $8.50 adults; $5.50 youths 12-17, seniors, and students with ID; and $2 children ages 4-11.

Park Activities, Events, and Information
Kennedy Drive from 19th Ave. to Stanyan is closed to automobile traffic every Sunday; enjoy a walk, bike ride, or rollerblade (bicycle and rollerblade rentals on Stanyan). **Friends of Recreation and Parks,** tel. (415) 750-5105, offers free guided tours throughout the park May-October. But even more active sports fans won't be disappointed. Golden Gate Park action includes archery, baseball and basketball, boating and rowing, fly-casting, football, horseback riding and horseshoes, lawn bowling, model yacht sailing—there's a special lake for just that purpose—plus polo, roller skating, soccer, and tennis. In addition to the exceptional Children's Playground, there are two other kiddie play areas.

Free **Golden Gate Band Concerts** are offered at 2 p.m. on Sunday and holidays at the park's Music Concourse. The **Midsummer Music Festival** in Stern Grove, Sloat Blvd. at 19th Ave., is another fun, and free, park program. Scheduled on consecutive Sundays from mid-June through August, it's quite popular, so come as

SAN FRANCISCO AS EVENT

Even more kaleidoscopic than the city's arts scene, San Francisco events include an almost endless combination of the appropriate, inappropriate, absurd, inspired, and sublime. Museums, theaters, neighborhood groups, and other cultural institutions usually offer their own annual events calendars. Even most shopping centers sponsor a surprising array of entertainment and events.

Among the city's most famous events are the two-week **San Francisco International Film Festival** in late April, featuring more than 100 films and videos from some 30 different countries; the mid-May **Bay to Breakers** race, when some 100,000 participants—many decked out in hilarious and/or scandalous costumes—hoof it from the Embarcadero out to Ocean Beach; and late May's **Carnaval San Francisco,** featuring an uninhibited parade with samba bands, dancers, floats, and hundreds of thousands of revelers. Typically in June, coinciding with the **San Francisco International Lesbian and Gay Film Festival,** comes the annual **Lesbian-Gay-Bisexual-Transgender Freedom Day Parade and Celebration,** one huge gay-pride party usually led by Dykes on Bikes and including cross-dressing cowboys (or girls), gay bands and majorettes, cheerleaders, and everyone and everything else.

Among the city's most intriguing events otherwise are galas such as the February 14 **Valentine's Day Sex Tour** at the San Francisco Zoo, where people let their animal passions run wild; the April 1 **St. Stupid's Day Parade,** a no-holds-barred celebration of foibles and foolishness; and the annual **Bay Area Robot Olympics** at the Exploratorium in September. Consult local newspapers for more complete information on what's going on when you're in town.

early as possible. (For exact dates and program information, call the park office, listed below.) A variety of other special events are regularly scheduled in Golden Gate Park, including **A la Carte, a la Park,** San Francisco's "largest outdoor dining event." This gala gourmet fest, with themed pavilions, showcases the wares of Bay Area restaurants and Sonoma County wineries, the talents of celebrity chefs, and a wide variety of entertainment. It's a benefit for the San Francisco Shakespeare Festival, which offers an annual schedule of free public performances in August. A la Carte, a la Park is usually scheduled in late summer, over the three-day Labor Day weekend. Call (415) 458-1988 for information.

To save money on visits to multiple park attractions, purchase a **Golden Gate Explorer Pass** for $14 at the park office, downtown at the visitors information center at Hallidie Plaza, or at TIX Bay Area in Union Square, tel. (415) 433-7827. For more information about park events and activities (maps are $2.50; other items are free), contact the **San Francisco Recreation and Park Department** office (which is also Golden Gate Park headquarters) in ivy-covered **McLaren Lodge,** 501 Stanyan (at Fulton, on the park's east side), tel. (415) 831-2700, open

weekdays 8 a.m.-5 p.m. The park's official website is www.civiccenter.ci.sf.ca.us/recpark/.

Light meals and snacks are available at various concessions or at **Cafe de Young** inside the de Young Museum; at the Academy of Sciences; and at the **Japanese Tea Garden Teahouse** (fortune cookies and tea). There is also great choice in restaurants near the intersection of Ninth Ave. and Irving, or along Haight and Stanyan Streets.

To reach the museums and tea garden via public transportation, board a westbound #5-Fulton bus on Market St., climbing off at Fulton and Eighth Avenue. After 6 p.m. and on Sunday and holidays, take #21-Hayes to Fulton and Sixth. Call (415) 673-MUNI for other routes and schedule information.

SEEING SAN FRANCISCO: DOWNTOWN AND OTHER DISTRICTS

In other times, San Francisco neighborhoods and districts had such distinct ethnic and cultural or functional identities that they served as separate cities within a city. It wasn't uncommon for people to be born and grow up, to work, to raise families, and to die in their own insular neighborhoods, absolutely unfamiliar with the rest of San Francisco.

For the most part, those days are long past. Since its inception, the city has transformed itself, beginning as a sleepy mission town, then a lawless gold-rush capital that gradually gained respectability and recognition as the West Coast's most sophisticated cultural and trade center. The process continues. The city's neighborhoods continue to reinvent themselves, and California's accelerated economic and social mobility also erase old boundaries. Just where one part of town ends and another begins is a favorite San Francisco topic of disagreement.

For more information about city attractions, see Delights and Diversions below. For complete practical information, including how to get around town and where to stay and eat, see the concluding sections of this chapter.

AROUND UNION SQUARE

Named after Civil War-era rallies held here in support of Union forces (California eventually spurned the Confederacy), San Francisco's Union Square is parking central for downtown shoppers, since the square also serves as the roof of the multilevel parking garage directly below. (Other garages within walking distance include the Sutter-Stockton Garage to the north, the Ellis-O'Farrell Garage two blocks south, and, across Market, the huge and inexpensive Fifth & Mission Garage.)

The landmark **Westin St. Francis Hotel** flanks Union Square on the west, its bar a time-honored retreat from nearby major stores like **Saks Fifth Avenue, Tiffany, Bullock & Jones, Macy's,** and **Neiman-Marcus** (which also has its own popular **Rotunda** restaurant for après-shop dropping; open for lunch and afternoon tea).

Immediately east of Union Square along Post,

THE San Francisco BOOK

DOWNTOWN SAN FRANCISCO AND VICINITY

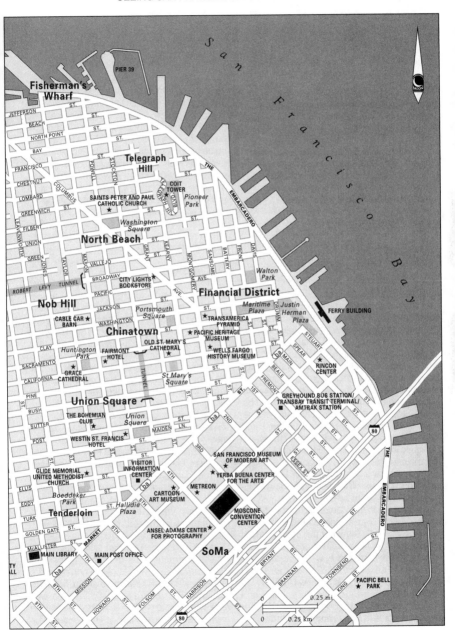

DEFINING DOWNTOWN

In San Francisco, "downtown" is a general reference to the city's hustle-bustle heart. Knowing just where it starts and ends is largely irrelevant, so long as you understand that it includes Union Square, much of Market St., and the Civic Center government and arts buildings. The Financial District and the Waterfront are also included. Six or seven blocks directly west of the Civic Center is the Alamo Square Historic District, one among other enclaves of gentrified Victorian neighborhoods in the otherwise down-and-out Western Addition, which also includes Japantown. Though purists will no doubt quibble, for reasons of proximity these are included with downtown. And while more "uptown" parts of the South of Market Area (SoMa) are essentially downtown too, as are Nob Hill and Chinatown, those areas are covered in more depth elsewhere below.

Maiden Ln., and Geary, you'll find an unabashed selection of expensive and fashionable stores, from **Cartier, Dunhill,** and **Wilkes Bashford** to **NikeTown USA, Eddie Bauer,** and **Brooks Brothers.** Or dress yourself up at **Ralph Lauren, Versace, Chanel, Laura Ashley,** and several other designer emporiums. **Gumps** at 135 Post is the elegant specialist in one-of-a-kind and rare wares, where even the furniture is art. Don't miss a stroll down traffic-free, two-block **Maiden Lane,** a one-time red-light district stretching between Stockton and Kearny, chock-full of sidewalk cafés and shops. Here stands the Circle Gallery building, most ogled for its architecture. Designed in 1949 by Frank Lloyd Wright, with its spiral interior this building is an obvious prototype for his more famous Guggenheim Museum in New York. **Crocker Galleria,** at Post and Montgomery, offers still more shopping.

Heading south from Union Square on Stockton, between O'Farrell and Market, you'll pass the famous **F.A.O. Schwarz** (full of adult-priced toys and still fun for kids); **Planet Hollywood;** and the **Virgin Megastore,** where music lovers can find just about anything to add to their CD collection. At Market St. is the new **Old Navy,** as well as a cheap thrill for shoppers—the eight-story circular escalator ride up to **Nordstrom** and other stores at **San Francisco Centre,** Fifth

and Market, which was built in the late 1980s with the hope of attracting suburbanites and squeezing out the homeless.

Just down a ways from the theater district and skirting The Tenderloin at 561 Geary (between Taylor and Jones) is the odd **Blue Lamp** bar—note the blue lamp, a classic of neo-neon art. Once just a hard-drinkers' dive, now the Blue Lamp is a campy, hipsters', hard-drinkers' dive, most interesting late at night when the neighborhood gets a bit scary. But the real reason to come here is live music, just-starting band badness. Just a few blocks away, near Union Square at 333 Geary (between Powell and Mason), is another world entirely—**Lefty O'Doul's,** a hofbrau-style deli and old-time bar stuffed to the ceiling with baseball memorabilia. Lefty was a local hero, a big leaguer who came back to manage the minor-league San Francisco Seals before the Giants came to town.

The Tenderloin

Stretching between Union Square and the Civic Center is The Tenderloin, definitely a poor choice for a casual stroll by tourists and other innocents. A down-and-out pocket of poverty pocked these days by the city signposts of human misery—drug dealing, prostitution, pornography, and violent crime—the densely populated Tenderloin earned its name around the turn of the century, when police assigned to patrol its mean streets received additional hazard pay—and, some say, substantial protection money and kickbacks. (The extra cash allowed them to dine on the choicest cuts of meat.) The Tenderloin's historic boundaries are Post, Market, Van Ness, and Powell. In reality, however, the city's designated theater district (with accompanying cafés and nightspots), many newly gentrified hotels, even the St. Francis Hotel and most Civic Center attractions fall within this no-man's land, which is especially a no-woman's land. More realistic, better-safe-than-sorry boundaries are Larkin, Mason, O'Farrell, and Market, with an extra caution also for some streets south of Market (especially Sixth) as far as Howard. As a general rule, perimeters are safer than core areas, but since this is San Francisco's highest crime area, with rape, mugging, and other assaults at an all-time high, for tenderfeet no part of The Tenderloin is considered safe—even during daylight hours. Ask local shopkeepers and restaurant or hotel personnel about the safety of specific destinations, if in doubt, and travel in groups when you do venture any distance into The Tenderloin.

But the area has its beauty, too, often most apparent through the celebrations and ministries of the Reverend Cecil Williams and congregation at the renowned **Glide Memorial United Methodist Church,** which rises up at 330 Ellis (at Taylor), tel. (415) 771-6300, www.glide.org. Glide sponsors children's assistance and other community programs, from basic survival and AIDS care to the Computers and You program, which helps the economically disadvantaged learn computer skills. The Glide Ensemble choir sings an uplifting mix of gospel, freedom songs, and rock at its celebrations, held each Sunday at 9 and 11 a.m.

And some neighborhoods are cleaning up considerably, the indirect influence of commercial redevelopment and the influx of large numbers of Asian immigrants, many from Cambodia, Laos, and Vietnam. The annual **Tet Festival** celebrates the Vietnamese New Year. The Tenderloin also supports a small but growing arts community, as the 'Loin is one of the few remaining pockets of affordable housing in San Francisco. Among the neighborhood's many bars, the **Edinburgh Castle** at 950 Geary (between Polk and Larkin), tel. (415) 885-4074, stands out, drawing an interesting crowd of Scottish expatriates and young urbanites. The pub special-izes in single malt Scotch, lager, and some of the best fish 'n' chips in the city.

MARKET STREET AND THE FINANCIAL DISTRICT

The Financial District features San Francisco's tallest, most phallic buildings, perhaps suggesting something profound about the psychology of the global capitalist thrust. When rolling into town on the river of traffic, via the Golden Gate Bridge or, especially, Oakland's Bay Bridge, this compact concentration of law offices, insurance buildings, investment companies, banks, brokerages, and high-brow businesses rises up from the sparkling waters like some fantastic illusion, the greenback-packed Emerald City of the West Coast. Even if wandering on foot and temporarily lost, to get back downtown one merely looks up and heads off toward the big buildings.

The actual boundaries of the Financial District, built upon what was once water (Yerba Buena Cove), are rather vague, dependent upon both personal opinion and that constant urban flux of form and function. In general, the district includes the entire area from the north side of Market St. to the Montgomery St. corridor, north to the Jackson Square Historic District. Market Street is anchored near the bay by the concrete square of **Justin Herman Plaza** and its either-loved-or-hated **Vaillancourt Fountain,** said to be a parody of the now-demolished freeway it once faced.

the Transamerica
Building: once
outrageous, now a
landmark

AISLINN RACE

SAN FRANCISCO ON STAGE

Geary Street near both Mason and Taylor is the official center of the theater district, and the 400 block of Geary serves as the epicenter of the mainstream theater scene. These days the concentration of upscale Union Square hotels downtown roughly duplicates the theater district boundaries. With so many fine theaters scattered throughout the city, it's something of a New York affectation to insist on that designation downtown. But San Francisco, a city that has loved its dramatic song and dance since Gold Rush days, definitely insists. Poetry readings, lectures, opera, and Shakespeare were integral to the 1800s arts scene. Superstar entertainers of the era made their mark here, from spiderdancer Lola Montez and her child protégé Lotta Crabtree to Lillie Langtry, opera star Luisa Tetrazzini, actress Helena Modjeska, and actor Edwin Booth. Today, out-of-towners flock to big musicals like *Phantom of the Opera* and evergreens like the murder mystery *Shear Madness*. Luckily, the best shows are often less crowded. Most shows begin at 8 p.m., and the majority of theaters are closed on Monday.

Theater Information

Finding information on what's going on in the theater is not a difficult task. Listings are printed in the *San Francisco Bay Guardian,* the *SF Weekly,* and the Sunday edition of the *San Francisco Chronicle.* Or check out the arts online at www.citysearch7.com. And wherever you find it, pick up a free copy of *Stagebill* magazine, www.stagebill.com, for its current and comprehensive show schedules.

Getting Tickets

Theater tickets can be purchased in advance or for half price on the day of the performance at **TIX Bay Area,** on Stockton St. at Union Square, tel. (415) 433-7827, www.tix.com. Payment is cash only, no credit card reservations. A full-service BASS ticket outlet as well, TIX also handles advance full-price tickets to many Bay Area events (open Tues.-Sat. noon-7:30 p.m.). You can get a catalog for ordering advance tickets at half price by calling **TIX by Mail,** at (415) 430-1140. To charge BASS arts and entertainment tickets by phone or to listen to recorded calendar listings, call (415) 478-2277 (BASS). Order full-price tickets in advance with a $2.50 service charge from Ticketmaster, tel. (415) 421-8497 or

toll-free (800) 755-4000, www.ticketmaster.com.

Other ticket box offices include: **City Box Office,** tel. (415) 392-4400; **Entertainment Ticketfinder,** tel. (650) 756-1414 or toll-free (800) 523-1515; and **St. Francis Theatre and Sports Tickets,** a service of the Westin St. Francis Hotel, tel. (415) 362-3500, or www.premiertickets.com.

Theater District Venues

For Broadway shows, the **Curran Theatre,** 445 Geary (between Mason and Taylor), tel. (415) 551-2000 (information), tel. (415) 478-2277 (BASS) for tickets, is the long-running standard. The repertory **American Conservatory Theater** (ACT), tel. (415) 834-3200 or (415) 749-2228 (box office), performs its big-name-headliner contemporary comedies and dramas in the venerable **Geary Theatre,** 415 Geary (at Mason).

Other neighborhood venues include the **Mason Street Theatre,** tel. (415) 982-5463, at 340 Mason (near Geary); the **Cable Car Theatre,** tel. (415) 255-9772, at 430 Mason (between Post and Geary); the **Golden Gate Theatre,** tel. (415) 551-2000, at 1 Taylor (at Golden Gate), longtime home of the Pulitzer Prize- and Tony-award-winning *Rent;* and the **Marines Memorial Theater,** tel. (415) 551-2000, at 609 Sutter (at Mason). All are good bets for off-Broadway shows. Unusual small theaters include the **Theatre on the Square,** tel. (415) 433-9300, sharing space with the Kensington Park Hotel at 450 Post (between Powell and Mason), and the **Plush Room Cabaret,** tel. (415) 885-2115, inside the York Hotel at 940 Sutter (at Leavenworth).

Performance Spaces Elsewhere

San Francisco is also home to a number of small, innovative theaters and theater troupes, including **Magic Theatre, Cowell Theater,** and **Young Performers Theatre** at Fort Mason, and the **Asian American Theatre** in the Richmond District, mentioned in more detail in The Avenues section of this chapter. The **Actors Theatre of San Francisco,** 533 Sutter (between Powell and Mason), tel. (415) 296-9179, usually offers unusual plays. Also popular for progressive dramatic theater is SoMa's **Climate Theatre,** 252 Ninth St. (at Folsom), tel. (415) 978-2345. Another innovator in the realm of performance art is **Theater Artaud,** 450 Florida St. (at 17th), tel. (415) 621-7797. **Theatre Rhinoceros,** 2926 16th

St. (between Mission and S. Van Ness), tel. (415) 861-5079, is America's oldest gay and lesbian theater company, est. 1978.

The long-running **Eureka Theatre Company,** 215 Jackson (between Front and Battery), tel. (415) 788-7469 (box office and information), is noted for its provocative, politically astute presentations. **Intersection for the Arts,** 446 Valencia St. (between 15th and 16th), tel. (415) 626-2787 (administration) or (415) 626-3311 (box office), the city's oldest alternative arts center, presents everything from experimental dramas to performance and visual art and dance. One-time "new talent" like Robin Williams, Whoopi Goldberg, and Sam Shepard are all Intersection alumni. **George Coates Performance Works,** 110 McAllister (at Leavenworth), tel. (415) 863-8520 (administration) or (415) 863-4130 (box office), offers innovative multimedia theater presentations in a re-purposed neo-Gothic cathedral.

—*Pat Reilly and Kim Weir*

Embarcadero Center

Above and behind the plaza is the astounding and Orwellian Embarcadero Center complex, the high-class heart of the Golden Gateway redevelopment project. Here is the somewhat surreal **Hyatt Regency Hotel,** noted for its 17-story indoor atrium and bizarre keyboard-like exterior, as well as the **Park Hyatt Hotel.** But the main focus is the center's four-part shopping complex, **Embarcadero One** through **Embarcadero Four,** stretching along four city blocks between Clay and Sacramento. Inside, maps and information kiosks can help the disoriented. Atop One Embarcadero is San Francisco's equivalent to the Empire State Building observation desk, here called **SkyDeck,** tel. (415) 772-0590 or toll-free (888) 737-5933. This attraction couples basic bird's-eye viewing with art and artifact exhibits, interactive touch screens providing historical and cultural information about the city, and free docent "tours." SkyDeck is open year-round (except major holidays), daily 9:30 a.m.-9 p.m.; admission is $7 adults, $4 seniors/students, $3.50 children 5-12. Wheelchair accessible.

For a hands-on lesson in the **World of Economics,** including the chance to pretend you're president of the U.S. or head of the Fed, stop by the lobby of the **Federal Reserve Bank,** 101 Market (at Spear), tel. (415) 974-2000, open weekdays 9 a.m.-4:30 p.m., to play with the computer games and displays. The **World of Oil** in the Chevron USA Building, 555 Market (at Second), tel. (415) 894-4895, open weekdays 9 a.m.-3:30 p.m., is a small museum with industry-oriented facts, including a computerized "Energy Learning Center." **Robert Frost Plaza,** at the intersection of Market and California, is a reminder that New England's poet was a San Francisco homeboy.

Heading up California St., stop at the **Bank of California** building at 400 California (between Sansome and Battery), tel. (415) 445-0200, for a tour through its basement **Museum of the Money of the American West,** everything from gold nuggets and U.S. Mint mementos to dueling pistols. The **Wells Fargo History Museum,** in Wells Fargo Bank at 420 Montgomery (near California), tel. (415) 396-2619, features an old Concord Stagecoach; a re-created early Wells Fargo office; samples of gold, gold scales, and gold-mining tools; and a hands-on telegraph exhibit, complete with telegraph key and Morse code books. It's open Mon.-Fri. 9 a.m.-5 p.m.; admission free. **Bank of America** at California and Kearny also has historical exhibits. In the 1905 **Merchants Exchange** building at California and Montgomery, the bygone boat-business days are remembered with ship models and William Coulter marine paintings. For a look at more modern mercantile action, climb to the visitors gallery for an insider's view of the action at the **Pacific Stock Exchange** at Pine and Sansome, the largest in America outside New York City.

People were outraged over the architecture of the **Transamerica Pyramid** at Montgomery and Washington, the city's tallest building, when it was completed in 1972. But now everyone has adjusted to its strange winged-spire architecture. Until recently it was possible to ride up to the 27th floor, to the "viewing area," for breathtaking sunny-day views of Coit Tower, the Golden Gate Bridge, and Alcatraz. These days, you'll get only as far as the lobby and the popular new **Virtual Observation Deck,** with its four monitors con-

THE BAWDY BARBARY COAST

Designated these days as the **Jackson Square Historical District**, the section of town stretching into North Beach across Washington St. was once called the Barbary Coast, famous since the gold rush as the world's most depraved human hellhole. Pacific Street was the main thoroughfare, a stretch of bad-boy bawdy houses, saloons, dance halls, and worse—like the "cowyards," where hundreds of prostitutes performed onstage with animals or in narrow cribs stacked as high as four stories. Words like "Mickey Finn," "Shanghaied," and "hoodlum" were coined here. Local moral wrath couldn't stop the barbarity of the Barbary Coast—and even the earthquake of 1906 spared the area, much to everyone's astonishment. Somewhat settled down by the Roaring '20s, when it was known as the International Settlement, the Barbary Coast didn't shed its barbarians entirely until the 1950s. Today it's quite tame, an oddly gentrified collection of quaint brick buildings.

nected to cameras mounted at the very tip of the Pyramid's spire. What's fun here is the chance to zoom, tilt, and pan the cameras for some fairly unusual views. Back down on the ground, head for Transamerica Center's **Redwood Park** on Friday lunch hours in summer for "Music in the Park" concerts.

CIVIC CENTER AND VICINITY

Smack dab in the center of the sleaze zone is San Francisco's major hub of government, the Civic Center, built on the one-time site of the Yerba Buena Cemetery. (See cautions mentioned under The Tenderloin above, which also apply to almost any section of downtown Market St. after dark.) A sublime example of America's beaux arts architecture, the center's **City Hall,** 401 Van Ness (at Polk), tel. (415) 554-4858, www.ci.sf.ca.us/cityhall, was modeled after St. Peter's Basilica at the Vatican, in the belle epoque style, complete with dome and majestic staircase. Renaissance-style sculptures state the city's dreams—the not necessarily incongruous collection of Wisdom, the Arts, Learning, Truth, Industry, and Labor over the Van

Ness Ave. entrance, and Commerce, Navigation, California Wealth, and San Francisco above the doors on Polk Street. After sustaining severe damage in the 1989 earthquake, the building was repaired and meticulously refurbished, and its interior stylishly redone, on the watch of equally stylish Mayor Willie Brown, a project with a price tag of several hundred million dollars. Former state senator Quentin Kopp, never a Brown fan, has called this the "Taj Mahal" of public works projects. See it yourself—free 45-minute tours are available daily.

The **War Memorial Opera House,** 301 Van Ness (at Grove), tel. (415) 865-2000, www.sf-opera.com, is the classical venue for the San Francisco Ballet Company as well as the San Francisco Opera, the place for society folk to see and be seen during the September to December opera season. Twin to the opera house, connected by extravagant iron gates, is the **Veterans Memorial Building.** The **Louise M. Davies Hall** at Van Ness and Grove, which features North America's largest concert hall organ, is the permanent venue for the **San Francisco Symphony.** If in the neighborhood, performing arts aficionados should definitely head west one block to the weekdays-only **San Francisco Performing Arts Library and Museum** at Grove and Gough.

San Francisco's **Main Library,** 100 Larkin (at Grove), tel. (415) 557-4400, is worth a browse, especially for the free Internet access offered at computer stations throughout the library. Free volunteer-led City Guides tours are headquartered here, tel. (415) 557-4266, and some depart from here. Civic Center Plaza, across Polk from the library, is home to many of the area's homeless, and also forms the garden roof for the underground **Brooks Hall** exhibit center and parking garage. **United Nations Plaza** stretches between Market St. and the Federal Building at McAllister (between Seventh and Eighth), commemorating the U.N.'s charter meeting in 1945 at the War Memorial Opera House. On Wednesday and Sunday, the plaza bustles with buyers and sellers of fish and unusual fruits and vegetables when the **Heart of the City Farmer's Market** is in bloom.

Across Market St., technically in SoMa but allied in spirit with the Civic Center, is the stunningly refurbished former San Francisco Post

Office and **U.S. Courthouse,** at Seventh and Mission. This gorgeous 1905 granite masterpiece, full of marble and mosaic floors and ceilings, was damaged in the 1989 earthquake, but it's now back and better than ever after a $91-million earthquake retrofit and rehabilitation. The post office is gone, replaced by an atrium, but the courts are back in session here. The third-floor courtroom is particularly impressive.

In addition to the area's many cafés, restaurants, and nightspots, the **California Culinary Academy,** 625 Polk St. (at Turk), tel. (415) 771-3500 or toll-free (800) 229-2433, is noted for its 16-month chef's training course in Italian, French, and nouvelle cuisine. For the curious, the academy is also an exceptionally good place to eat wonderful food at reasonable prices. The academy operates a bakery and café, the basement **Tavern on the Tenderloin** buffet, tel. (415) 771-3536, and the somewhat more formal **Careme Room,** tel. (415) 771-3535, a glass-walled dining hall where you can watch what goes on in the kitchen. Call for hours and reservation policies, which vary.

WESTERN ADDITION

These central city blocks west of Van Ness Ave. and south of Pacific Heights are certainly diverse. Settled in turn by Jewish, Japanese, and African Americans, the neighborhood's historical associations are with the Fillmore's jazz and blues bars, which hosted greats like John Coltrane and Billie Holiday in the 1950s and '60s.

The area is remarkable architecturally because so many of its 19th-century Victorians survived the 1906 earthquake, though some subsequently declined into subdivided apartments or were knocked down by the wrecking ball of redevelopment. The Western Addition's remaining Victorian enclaves are rapidly becoming gentrified. The most notable—and most photographed—example is Steiner St. facing **Alamo Square** (other pretty "painted ladies" with facelifts stretch for several blocks in all directions), though countrylike **Cottage Row** just east of Fillmore St. between Sutter and Bush is equally enchanting.

Today most of the Western Addition is home to working-class families, though the area south of Geary, considered "The Fillmore," was long composed almost exclusively of heavy-crime, low-income housing projects. Many of those boxy projects have been demolished, and redevelopment here is generally improving the aesthetics of the neighborhood.

The Western Addition's intriguing shops, restaurants, and cultural attractions reflect the neighborhood's roots. For an exceptional selection of African-American literature, check out **Marcus Books,** 1712 Fillmore (at Post), tel. (415) 346-4222, which also hosts occasional readings. Until quite recently, on Sunday mornings jazz emanated from **St. John Coltrane's African Orthodox Church** on Divisadero at Oak, a tiny storefront ministry devoted to celebrating the life of St. John Coltrane. Sadly, due to rapidly rising rents, the congregation has been forced to find a new church. For current information and church updates, check out www.saintjohncoltrane.org. Fancy dressing like a member of Run DMC? You'll find one of the country's biggest selections of Adidas clothing at **Harput's,** 1527 Fillmore (between Ellis and Geary), tel. (415) 923-9300. And **Jack's Record Cellar** 254 Scott St. (at Page), tel. (415) 431-3047, is the perfect place to browse through obscure jazz and blues records.

Fillmore Street also creates the western border of **Japantown,** or Nihonmachi, an area encompassing the neighborhoods north of Geary, south of Pine, and stretching east to Octavia. This very American variation on Japanese community includes the old-style, open-air **Buchanan Mall** between Post and Sutter, and the more modern and ambitious **Japan Center,** a three-block-long concrete mall on Geary between Fillmore and Laguna. It's inaccessibly ugly from the outside, in the American tradition, but offers intriguing attractions inside, like karaoke bars and the **Kabuki Hot Springs,** tel. (415) 922-6000, a communal bathhouse on the ground floor.

Lined with boutiques selling clothing from small labels, sidewalk restaurants, and oddball furniture stores, **Hayes Street** between Franklin and Laguna is an oasis of funky charm. Stroll over to **560 Hayes,** 560 Hayes St. (at Laguna), tel. (415) 861-7993, for an excellent selection of 1960s and '70s evening wear, including vintage items from top designers like Chanel and Gucci. Find vintage timepieces and watches at **Zeitgeist Timepieces and Jewelry,** 437 Hayes St. (between Gough and Octavia), tel. (415) 864-0185.

HAIGHT-ASHBURY

Aging hippies, random hipsters, and the hopelessly curious of all ages are still attracted to San Francisco's Haight-Ashbury, once a commercial district for adjacent Golden Gate Park and a solid family neighborhood in the vicinity of Haight Street. The Golden Gate's block-wide Panhandle (which certainly resembles one on a map) was intended as the park's carriage entrance, helped along toward the desired ambience by neighboring Victorian-age Queen Annes. Once abandoned by the middle class, however, Haight-Ashbury declined into the cheap-rent paradise surrounded by parklands that became "Hashbury," "hippies," and headquarters for the 1967 Summer of Love.

Drawn here by the drum song of the coming-of-age Aquarian Age, some 200,000 young people lived in subdivided Victorian crash pads, on the streets, and in the parks that summer, culturally recognizable by long hair, scruffy jeans, tie-dyed T-shirts, granny glasses, peace signs, beads, and the flowers-in-your-hair style of flowing skirts and velvet dresses. Essential, too, at that time: underground newspapers and unrestrained radio, black-lights and psychedelia, incense, anything that came from India (like gurus), acid and mescaline, hashish, waterpipes, marijuana and multicolored rolling papers, harmonicas, tambourines, guitars, and bongo drums. A Volkswagen van was helpful, too, so loads of people could caravan off to anti-Vietnam War rallies, to wherever it was the Grateful Dead or Jefferson Airplane were playing (for free, usually), or to Fillmore West and Winterland, where Bill Graham staged so many concerts. It was all fairly innocent, at first, an innocence that didn't last. By late 1967, cultural predators had arrived: the tourists, the national media, and serious drug pushers and pimps. Love proved to be fragile. Most true believers headed back to the land, and Haight-Ashbury became increasingly violent and dangerous, especially for the young

runaways who arrived (and still arrive) to stake a misguided claim for personal freedom.

"The Haight" today is considerably cleaner, its Victorian neighborhoods spruced up but not exactly gentrified. The classic Haight-Ashbury head shops are long gone, runaway hippies replaced by runaway punks panhandling for quarters (or worse). But Haight St. and vicinity is still hip, still socially and politically aware, still worth a stroll. The parkside Upper Haight stretch has more than its share of funky cafés, coffee shops, oddball bars and clubs, boutiques, and secondhand stores. If this all seems stodgy, amble on down to the Lower Haight in the Western Addition, an area fast becoming the city's new avant-garde district.

Seeing and Doing Haight-Ashbury

Aside from the commercial versions, there are a few significant countercultural sights in the Upper Haight, like the old Victorian **Dead House** at 710 Ashbury (near Waller), where the Grateful Dead lived and played their still-living music (and possibly where the term "deadheads" first emerged for the Dead's fanatic fans), and the **Jefferson Airplane's** old pad at 2400 Fulton (on the eastern edge of Golden Gate Park at Willard). Definitely worth a stop, for organic juice and granola, art to meditate by, and New Age computer networking, is **The Red Victorian** at 1665 Haight (near Belvedere), tel. (415) 864-1978, www.redvic.com, also a fascinating bed-and-breakfast complex that successfully honors The Haight's original innocence. Do climb on up the steep paths into nearby **Buena Vista Park,** a shocking tangle of anarchistically enchanted forest, just for the through-the-trees views.

Otherwise, the scene here is wherever you can find it. **Bound Together,** 1369 Haight St. (at Masonic), tel. (415) 431-8355, is a collective bookstore featuring a somewhat anarchistic collection: books on leftist politics, conspiracy theories, the occult, and sexuality. **Pipe Dreams,** 1376 Haight (at Masonic), tel. (415) 431-3553, is one place to go for Grateful Dead memorabilia and quaint drug paraphernalia, like water pipes and "bongs," but **Distractions,** 1552 Haight (between Clayton and Ashbury), tel. (415) 252-8751, is truest to the form; in addition to the Dead selection, you can also snoop through head shop supplies, an ample variety of Tarot cards, and Guatemalan clothing imports.

Style is another Haight St. specialty. Though secondhand clothing stores here tend to feature higher prices than elsewhere, three of the best are **Wasteland,** 1660 Haight (at Belvedere), tel. (415) 863-3150; the **Buffalo Exchange,** 1555 Haight (between Clayton and Ashbury), tel. (415) 431-7733; and **Aardvarks,** 1501 Haight (at Ashbury), tel. (415) 621-3141. For old-style music bargains—and actual albums, including a thousand hard-to-find ones—head to **Recycled Records,** 1377 Haight (at Masonic), tel. (415) 626-4075. For thousands of used CDs and tapes, try **Reckless Records,** 1401 Haight (at Masonic), tel. (415) 431-3434. Housed in a former bowling alley, **Amoeba Music,** 1855 Haight (between Stanyan and Shrader), tel. (415) 831-1200, is huge and offers an encyclopedic collection of new and used sounds.

Shops of interest in the Lower Haight include: **Zebra Records,** 475 Haight (near Webster), tel. (415) 626-9145, a DJ supply store that's the place to find cutting-edge hip hop, acid jazz, and Latin House; the **Naked Eye,** 533 Haight (between Fillmore and Steiner), tel. (415) 864-2985, which specializes in impossible-to-find videos; and **Used Rubber U.S.A.,** 597 Haight (at Steiner), tel. (415) 626-7855, which makes durable, hip, high-style handbags out of otherwise unrecycled car tires (a bit expensive). Well respected in the neighborhood for more organic personal decoration is **Erno's Tattoo Parlor,** 252 Fillmore (between Haight and Waller), tel. (415) 861-9206. Shop the Lower Haight, too, for stylish used clothing stores with good pickings, low prices, and zero crowds.

MISSION DISTRICT

Vibrant and culturally electric, the Mission District is one of San Francisco's most exciting neighborhoods. The fact that most tourists never discover the area's pleasures is a sad commentary on our times. To the same extent people fear that which seems foreign in America—a nation created by foreigners—they miss out on the experience of life as it is. And the country becomes even more hell-bent on mandating social homogenization despite ideals and rhetoric to the contrary.

On any given day in the Mission District, especially if it's sunny, the neighborhood is busy with the business of life. The largely Hispanic population—Colombian, Guatemalan, Mexican, Nicaraguan, Peruvian, Panamanian, Puerto Rican, Salvadorean—crowds the streets and congregates on corners. Whether Mission residents are out strolling with their children or shopping in the many bakeries, produce stores, and meat markets, the community's cultural energy is unmatched by any other city neighborhood—with the possible exception of Chinatown early in the morning. This remains true, even now, though gentrification has also arrived in the Mission.

Even with onrushing gentrification, the Mission's ungentrified modern attitude and still relatively low rents have also created a haven for artists, writers, social activists, and politicos. The Latino arts scene is among the city's most powerful and original. This is one of San Francisco's newest New Bohemias, a cultural crazy quilt where artists and assorted oddballs are not only tolerated but encouraged. Businesses catering to this emerging artistic consciousness are becoming prominent along Valencia St., already considered home by the city's lesbian community.

Technically, the Mission District extends south from near the Civic Center to the vicinity of Cesar Chavez (Army). Dolores or Church St. (or thereabouts) marks the western edge, Alabama St. the eastern. Mission Street, the main thoroughfare (BART stations at 16th and 24th), is lined with discount stores and pawnshops. Main commercial areas include 16th St. between Mission and Dolores, 24th St. between Valencia and York, and Valencia St.—the bohemian center of social life, lined with coffeehouses, bars, bookstores, performance art venues, and establishments serving the lesbian and women's community. For the latest word on feminist and lesbian art shows, readings, performances, and other events, stop by the nonprofit **Women's Building,** 3543 18th St. (just off Valencia), tel. (415) 431-1180.

Mission Dolores

The city's oldest structure, completed in 1791, Mission San Francisco de Asis at Dolores and 16th Streets, tel. (415) 621-8203, open daily 9 a.m.-4:30 p.m., is the sixth mission established in California by the Franciscan fathers. A donation

Mission Dolores

AISLINN RACE

of $2 or more is appreciated. (The best time to arrive, to avoid busloads of tourists and the crush of schoolchildren studying California history, is before 10 a.m.) Founded earlier, in 1776, the modest chapel and outbuildings came to be known as Mission Dolores, the name derived from a nearby lagoon and creek, Arroyo de Nuestra Señora de los Dolores, or "stream of our lady of sorrows."

And how apt the new shingle proved to be, in many ways. In the peaceful cemetery within the mission's walled compound is the "Grotto of Lourdes," the unmarked grave of more than 5,000 Ohlone and others among the native workforce. Most died of measles and other introduced diseases in the early 1800s, the rest from other varieties of devastation. After California became a state, the first U.S. Indian agent came to town to take a census of the Native American population. It was an easy count, since there was only one, a man named Pedro Alcantara who was still grieving for a missing son. Near the grotto are the vine-entwined tombstones of pioneers and prominent citizens, like California's first governor under Mexican rule, Don Luis Antonio Arguello, and San Francisco's first mayor, Don Francisco de Haro.

The sturdy mission chapel—the small humble structure, not the soaring basilica adjacent—survived the 1906 earthquake due largely to its four-foot-thick adobe walls. Inside, the painted ceilings are an artistic echo of the Ohlone, whose original designs were painted with vegetable dyes. And the simple altar offers stark contrast to the grandeur next door. For a peek at the collection of mission artifacts and memorabilia, visit the small museum.

Mission District Murals
The entire Mission District is vividly alive, with aromas and sounds competing everywhere with color. And nothing in the Mission District is quite as colorful as its mural art. More than 200 murals dot the neighborhood, ranging from brilliantly colored homages to work, families, and spiritual flight to boldly political attacks on the status quo.

Start with some **"BART art,"** at the 24th St. station, where Michael Rios' columns of humanoids lift up the rails. Another, particularly impressive set, is eight blocks down, off 24th St. on the fences and garage doors along **Balmy Alley,** and also at **Flynn Elementary School** at Precita and Harrison. At 14th and Natoma is a mural honoring Frida Kahlo, artist and wife of Diego Rivera.

Walking tours of the neighborhood murals (with well-informed guides) are led by the **Precita Eyes Mural Arts Center,** a charming gallery at 2981 24th St. (at Harrison), tel. (415) 285-2287, www.precitaeyes.org. The tours are offered every Saturday at 11 a.m. and 1:30 p.m., Sunday at 1:30 p.m.; $7 general, $4 seniors, $1 youths 18 and under. Call for information on the center's many other tours.

Other good art stops in the area include the nonprofit **Galeria de la Raza,** 2857 24th St. (at

Bryant), tel. (415) 826-8009, featuring some exciting, straight-ahead political art attacks; the affiliated **Studio 24** gift shop adjacent, with everything from books and clothing to religious icons and Day of the Dead dolls; and the **Mission Cultural Center for Latino Arts,** 2868 Mission (between 24th and 25th Streets), tel. (415) 821-1155, a community cultural and sociopolitical center that can supply you with more information on area artworks.

Potrero Hill

East of the Mission District proper and southeast of the SoMa scene is gentrifying (at least on the north side) Noe Valley-like Potrero Hill, known for its roller-coaster road rides (a favorite spot for filming TV and movie chase scenes) and the world-famous **Anchor Brewing Company** microbrewery, 1705 Mariposa St. (at 17th), tel. (415) 863-8350, makers of Anchor Steam beer. Join a free weekday tour and see how San Francisco's famous beer is brewed. If you drive to Potrero Hill, detour to the "Poor Man's Lombard" at 20th and Vermont, which has earned the dubious honor of being the city's second twistiest street. This snakelike thoroughfare is not festooned with well-landscaped sidewalks and flowerbeds, but instead an odd assortment of abandoned furniture, beer bottles, and trash. Not yet socially transformed is the south side of the hill, which is close to **Bayview-Hunters Point;** these once-industrialized neighborhoods were left behind when World War II-era shipbuilding ceased and are now ravaged by poverty, drugs, and violence.

Levi Strauss & Co. Factory

If you're curious about how the West's most historic britches evolved, stop by Levi Strauss & Co., 250 Valencia St. (between Clinton Park and Brosnan), tel. (415) 565-9100, for a free tour (Tuesday and Wednesday only, at 9 a.m., 11 a.m., and 1:30 p.m., reservations required—and make them well in advance). This, Levi's oldest factory, was built in 1906 after the company's original waterfront plant was destroyed by earthquake and fire. The company is the world's largest clothing manufacturer, and most of its factories are fully automated. But at this site you can hear the riveting story of how Levi's 501's

were originally made, and see it, too. Skilled workers cut, stitch, and assemble the button-fly jeans, as in the earlier days of the empire that Bavarian immigrant Levi Strauss built. During the boom days of the California gold rush, miners needed very rugged pants, something that wouldn't bust out at the seams. Strauss stitched up his first creations from tent canvas; when he ran out of that, he switched to sturdy brown cotton "denim" from Nimes, France. Levi's characteristic pocket rivets came along in the 1870s, but "blue jeans" weren't a reality until the next decade, when indigo blue dye was developed. After the tour, you can shop in the on-site company store.

Mission District Shopping

Clothes Contact, 473 Valencia (just north of 16th), tel. (415) 621-3212, sells fashionable vintage clothing for $8 per pound. (Consumer alert: those big suede jackets in the back weigh more than you might imagine.) Worth poking into, too, is the **Community Thrift Store,** 623-625 Valencia (between 17th and 18th), tel. (415) 861-4910, a fundraising venture for the gay and lesbian Tavern Guild. It's an expansive, inexpensive, and well-organized place, with a book selection rivaling most used bookstores. (The motto here is "out of the closet, into the store.") Cooperatively run **Modern Times Bookstore,** 888 Valencia (between 19th and 20th), tel. (415) 282-9246, is the source for progressive, radical, and Third World literature, magazines, and tapes.

If you're down on your luck, head up to **Lady Luck Candle Shop,** 311 Valencia (at 14th), tel. (415) 621-0358, a small store selling some pretty big juju, everything from high-test magic candles and religious potions (like St. John the Conqueror Spray) to Lucky Mojo Oil and Hold Your Man essential oil. **Good Vibrations,** 1210 Valencia (at 23rd), tel. (415) 974-8980, home of the vibrator museum, is a clean, user-friendly, liberated shop where women (and some men) come for adult toys, and to peruse the selection of in-print erotica, including history and literature.

More common in the Mission District are neighborhood-style antique and secondhand stores of every stripe. Bargains abound, without the inflated prices typical of trendier, more tourist-traveled areas.

CASTRO STREET AND VICINITY

The very idea is enough to make America's righteous religious right explode in an apoplectic fit, but the simple truth is that San Francisco's Castro St. is one of the safest neighborhoods in the entire city—and that's not necessarily a reference to sex practices.

San Francisco's tight-knit, well-established community of lesbian women and gay men represents roughly 15% of the city's population and 35% of its registered voters. Locally, nationally, and internationally, the Castro District epitomizes out-of-the-closet living. (There's nothing in this world like the Castro's Gay Freedom Day Parade—usually headed by hundreds of women on motorcycles, the famous Dykes on Bikes—and no neighborhood throws a better street party.) People here are committed to protecting their own and creating safe neighborhoods. What this means, for visitors straight or gay, is that there is a response—people get out of their cars, or rush out of restaurants, clubs, and apartment buildings—at the slightest sign that something is amiss.

Who ever would have guessed that a serious revival of community values in the U.S. would start in the Castro?

Actually, there have been many indications. And there are many reasons. The developing cultural and political influence of the Castro District became apparent in 1977, when openly gay Harvey Milk was elected to the San Francisco Board of Supervisors. But genuine acceptance seemed distant—never more so than in 1978, when both Milk and Mayor George Moscone were assassinated by conservative political rival Dan White, who had resigned his board seat and wanted it back. White's "diminished capacity" defense argument, which claimed that his habitual consumption of high-sugar junk food had altered his brain chemistry—the "Twinkie" defense—became a national scandal but ultimately proved successful. He was sentenced to a seven-year prison term.

The community's tragedies kept on coming, hitting even closer to home. Somewhat notorious in its adolescence as a safe haven for freestyle lifestyles, including casual human relationships and quickie sex, the Castro District was devastated by the initial impact of the AIDS epidemic. The community has been stricken by the tragic human consequences of an undiscriminating virus. But otherwise meaningless human loss has served only to strengthen the community's humanity. Just as, after Milk's assassination, greater numbers of community activists came forward to serve in positions of political influence, Castro District organizations like the Shanti Project, Open Hand, and the Names Project have extended both heart and hand to end the suffering. And fierce, in-your-face activists from groups like Act Up, Queer Nation, and Bad Cop No Donut have taken the message to the nation's streets.

So, while Castro District community values are strong and getting stronger, the ambience is not exactly apple-pie Americana. People with pierced body parts (some easily visible, some not) and dressed in motorcycle jackets still stroll in and out of leather bars. Its shops also can be somewhat unusual, like **Does Your Mother Know,** a seriously homoerotic greeting card shop on 18th St. near Castro.

Seeing and Doing the Castro

The neighborhood's business district, both avantgarde and gentrified Victorian, is small, stretching for three blocks along Castro St. between Market and 19th, and a short distance in each direction from 18th and Castro. This area is all included, geographically, in what was once recognizable as **Eureka Valley.** (Parking can be a problem, once you've arrived, so take the Muni Metro and climb off at the Castro St. Station.) Some people also include the gentrifying **Noe Valley** (with its upscale 24th St. shopping district) in the general Castro stream of consciousness, but the technical dividing line is near the crest of Castro St. at 22nd Street. Keep driving on Upper Market St., and you'll wind up into the city's geographic center. Though the ascent is actually easier from Haight-Ashbury (from Twin Peaks Blvd. just off 17th—see a good road map), either way you'll arrive at or near the top of **Twin Peaks,** with its terraced neighborhoods, astounding views, and some of the city's best stairway walks. More challenging is the short but steep hike to the top of Corona Heights Park (at Roosevelt), also noted for the very good **Josephine D. Randall Junior Museum,** 199

Museum Way (at Roosevelt), tel. (415) 554-9600, a youth-oriented natural sciences, arts, and activities center open Tues.-Sat. 10 a.m.-5 p.m. Admission free; donations welcome.

Down below, **A Different Light,** 489 Castro St. (between Market and 18th Streets), tel. (415) 431-0891, is the city's best gay and lesbian bookstore, with literature by and for. Readings and other events are occasionally offered; call for current information. Truly classic and quite traditional is the handsome and authentic art deco **Castro Theater,** 429 Castro (at Market), tel. (415) 621-6120, built in 1923. San Francisco's only true movie palace, the Castro is still a favorite city venue for classic movies and film festivals. Another highlight is the massive house Wurlitzer organ, which can make seeing a film at the Castro a truly exhilarating experience. **Cliff's Variety,** 479 Castro (at 18th), tel. (415) 431-5365, is another classic, a wonderfully old-fashioned hardware store where you can buy almost anything, from power saws to Play-doh. Retro kitsch **Uncle Mame,** 2241 Market (between Noe and Sanchez), tel. (415) 626-1953, is another Castro gem. Packed to the rafters with 1950s, '60s and '70s pop culture ephemera, this is the place to shop for vintage board games, lunch boxes, and Barbies.

Also stop by **The Names Project,** 2362 Market (between 16th and 17th), tel. (415) 863-1966, a museum-like memorial to those felled by AIDS. It's also the original home of the famous AIDS Memorial Quilt, each section created by friends and family of someone who died of the disease. Adjacent (in the same building) is **Under One Roof,** tel. (415) 252-9430, a cool and classy little gift shop with Act Up votive candles, artwork, T-shirts, and more. All money earned goes to support some 50 AIDS service organizations.

SOUTH OF MARKET (SoMa)

Known by old-timers as "south of the slot," a reference to a neighborhood sans cable cars, San Francisco's South of Market area was a working- and middle-class residential area—until all its homes were incinerated in the firestorm following the great earthquake of 1906. Rebuilt early in the century with warehouses, factories, train yards, and port businesses at **China Basin,**

these days the area has gone trendy. In the style of New York's SoHo (South of Houston), this semi-industrial stretch of the city now goes by the moniker "SoMa."

As is usually the case, the vanguard of gentrification was the artistic community: the dancers, musicians, sculptors, photographers, painters, and graphic designers who require low rents and room to create. Rehabilitating old warehouses and industrial sheds here into studios and performance spaces solved all but strictly creative problems. Then came the attractively inexpensive factory outlet stores, followed by eclectic cafés and nightclubs. The Yerba Buena Gardens redevelopment project sealed the neighborhood's fate, bringing big-time tourist attractions including the Moscone Convention Center, the San Francisco Museum of Modern Art, the Yerba Buena Center for the Arts, and The Rooftop at Yerba Buena Gardens, a multi-facility arts and entertainment complex.

Now the city's newest luxury hotel, the 30-story **W San Francisco,** towers over Third and Howard. Sony's futuristic new Metreon holds down Fourth and Mission. Even near the once-abandoned waterfront just south of the traditional Financial District boundaries, avant-garde construction like **Number One Market Street,** which incorporates the old Southern Pacific Building, and **Rincon Center,** which encompasses the preserved Depression-era mural art of the Rincon Annex Post Office, have added a new look to once down-and-out areas. More massive high-rises are on the way, and land values are shooting up in areas where previously only the neighborhood homeless did that. The starving artists have long since moved on to the Lower Haight and the Mission District, and in SoMa, the strictly eccentric is now becoming more self-consciously so.

San Francisco Museum of Modern Art

SoMa's transformation is largely due to the arrival of the San Francisco Museum of Modern Art (SFMOMA), 151 Third St. (between Mission and Howard), tel. (415) 357-4000, which moved from its cramped quarters on the third and fourth floors of the War Memorial. Many consider the modern, Swiss-designed building to be a work of art in itself. Love it or hate it, you're not likely to miss the soaring cylindrical skylight and assertive red brick of the new $60-million structure rising above the gritty streets south of Market.

The museum's permanent collection includes minor works by Georgia O'Keeffe, Pablo Picasso, Salvador Dali, Henri Matisse, and some outstanding paintings by Jackson Pollock. Mexican painters Frida Kahlo and her husband, Diego Rivera, are represented, as are the works of many Californian artists, including assembler Bruce Connor and sculptor Bruce Arneson. The museum also hosts excellent temporary exhibitions showcasing world-renowned individual artists. There's a hip little café, the **Cafe Museo,** tel. (415) 357-4500, and the **SFMOMA Museum Store,** well stocked with art books and postcards.

The Museum of Modern Art is open 11 a.m.-6 p.m. daily except Wednesday. Additionally, it's open until 9 p.m. on Thursday, and opens at 10 a.m. instead of 11 a.m. from Memorial Day weekend through Labor Day. The museum is closed on July 4th, Thanksgiving, Christmas, and New Year's Day. Admission is $8 adults, $5 seniors, and $4 students with ID (children under 12 free). Admission is free for everyone on the first Tuesday of each month, and half price Thursday 6-9 p.m. Admission charge is sometimes higher during special exhibitions.

Yerba Buena Center for the Arts

Opposite the museum on the west side of Third St. is the Yerba Buena Center for the Arts, 701 Mission St. (at Third), tel. (415) 978-2700 or (415) 978-2787 (ticket office), www.yerbabuenaarts.org, a gallery and theater complex devoted to showcasing the works of experimental, marginalized, and emerging artists. A YBC classic was the exhibition of a century of drawings for tattoos, *Pierced Hearts and True Love,* featuring drawings by prominent tattoo artists Sailor Jerry and Ed Hardy. A five-acre downtown park surrounds the complex, where a waterfall dedicated to the memory of Martin Luther King Jr. reads: "We will not be satisfied until 'justice rolls down like a river and righteousness like a mighty stream.'" Amen. The Center for the Arts galleries are open 11 a.m.-6 p.m. daily except Monday (until 8 p.m. on the first Thursday of each month). Admission is $5 adults, $3 seniors/students; children 12 and under free. Everyone gets in free on the first Thursday of every month, 6-8 p.m.

The Rooftop at Yerba Buena Gardens

Cleverly built atop the Moscone Center along Fourth, Howard, and Folsom Streets, this park-cum-entertainment complex is the latest addition to the Yerba Buena Gardens redevelopment project. It holds a 1906 carousel, a full-size indoor ice rink with city-skyline views, a bowling center, and **Zeum,** tel. (415) 777-3727, an interactive art and technology center for children ages 8-18. Hours are Wed.-Fri. noon-6 p.m., Sat.-Sun. 11 a.m.-5 p.m., and admission is $7 adults, $5 youths ages 5-18. The **Ice Skating Center,** tel. (415) 777-3727, is open for public skating daily, 1-5 p.m. Admission is $6 adults and $4.50 seniors and children ($2.50 skate rental).

Metreon

Anchoring the corner of Fourth and Mission Streets like a sleek spacecraft, the block-long, four-story-tall **Metreon,** tel. (415) 537-3400, www.metreon.com, is the latest icon of pop culture to land in San Francisco's SoMa district. The Sony Entertainment-sponsored mall features a 15-screen cinema complex, a 600-seat IMAX theatre with 2-D and 3-D capability, and fashion-forward shopping options including a Sony Style store and MicrosoftSF.

Interactive exhibits include **Where the Wild Things Are,** based on Maurice Sendak's magical children's book; an interactive 3-D show titled **The Way Things Work,** based on David Macaulay's book of the same name; and **Airtight Garage,** a futuristic gaming area based on the images of French graphic artist Jean "Mobius" Giraud. The mall's food court features offshoots of several popular local restaurants: LongLife Noodle Co., Buckhorn, Sanraku, and Firewood Café, gathered under the umbrella "a taste of San Francisco." Technically admission to Metreon is free, but doing anything will cost you. For a family of four the "all attractions" option is a bit pricey at $20 per person (children age 2 and under free), and even that doesn't include Airtight Garage games, movie or IMAX admission, restaurants, or shopping. There are multiple options, though; for admission prices, hours, and other current information, see the website or call Metreon at (415) 537-3400.

Other SoMa Sights

Across from the Moscone Center, the **Ansel Adams Center for Photography,** 250 Fourth St.

(between Howard and Folsom), tel. (415) 495-7000 or (415) 495-7242, is a major presence in San Francisco's art scene, with five galleries dedicated to the photographic art, one set aside exclusively for Adams's own internationally renowned black-and-white works. Open daily 11 a.m.-5 p.m. (until 8 p.m. on the first Thursday of every month). Admission is $5 adults, $3 students, $2 seniors/youths.

Less serious is the **Cartoon Art Museum,** 814 Mission (between Fourth and Fifth Streets), tel. (415) 227-8666, which chronicles the history of the in-print giggle, from cartoon sketches and finished art to toys and videos. Open Wed.-Fri. 11 a.m.-5 p.m., Saturday 10 a.m.-5 p.m., Sunday 1-5 p.m. Admission is $5 adults, $3 seniors/students, $1 children.

The **California Historical Society Museum,** 678 Mission St. (between Second and Third Streets), tel. (415) 357-1848, displays rare historical photographs and includes exhibits on early California movers and shakers (both human

---

CLEAN UP YOUR ACT AT BRAINWASH

No doubt the cleanest scene among SoMa's hot spots is BrainWash at 1122 Folsom, tel. (415) 861-FOOD, (415) 431-WASH, or www.brain-wash.com, a combination café, smart bar, nightclub, and laundromat in a reformed warehouse. The brainchild of UC Berkeley and Free Speech Movement alumna Susan Schindler, BrainWash ain't heavy, just semi-industrial, from the beamed ceilings and neon to the concrete floor. The decor here includes café tables corralled by steel office chairs with original decoupage artwork on the seats. (Admit it—haven't you always wanted to sit on Albert Einstein's face?) BrainWash also features a small counter/bar area, and bathrooms for either "Readers" (lined with *Dirty Laundry Comics* wallpaper) or "Writers" (with walls and ceiling of green chalkboard, chalk provided for generating brainwashable graffiti). Since literary urges know no boundaries in terms of gender, of course both are open to both basic sexes. And others.

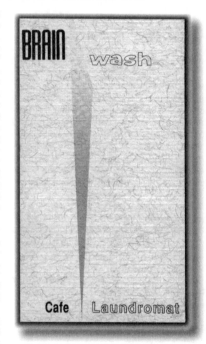

The small café at BrainWash offers quick, simple fare—salads, spinach and feta turnovers, pizza, and decent sandwiches (vegetarian and otherwise)—plus pastries and decadent pies, cakes, and cookies. Try a BrainWash Brownie, either double chocolate or double espresso. There's liquid espresso too, of course, plus cappuccinos and lattes, fresh unfiltered fruit or carrot juice, teas, beer, and wine.

Behind the café (and glass wall) is the BrainWash washhouse, a high-tech herd of washers and dryers ($1.50 per load for a regular wash load, $3.50 for a jumbo washer, and a quarter for 10 minutes of dryer time). Ask about the laundromat's wash-and-fold and dry-cleaning services. The whole shebang here is open daily 8 a.m.-12 a.m. (until 1 a.m. on Friday and Saturday nights). "Last call" for washers is 10 p.m. nightly. Call ahead to make sure, but live music is usually scheduled after 9 p.m. on Tues.-Thurs. and Friday or Saturday nights, jukebox available otherwise. BrainWash also sponsors community events, such as the "Take the Dirty Shirt Off Your Back" benefit for the STOP AIDS Project. The place can also be rented for private parties.

So come on down, almost anytime, for some Clorox and croissants.

and geologic), Western art of California, and frontier manuscripts. The museum bookstore features a great selection of books by California authors. The museum and bookstore are open Tues.-Sat. 11 a.m.-5 p.m. Small admission.

Actually closer to the waterfront and Financial District, the **Jewish Community Museum,** 121 Steuart St. (at Mission), tel. (415) 543-8880, features changing, usually exceptional exhibits on Jewish art, culture, and history. (The museum is scheduled to move to the Yerba Buena Gardens area in 2000, so call before going.) The **Telephone Pioneers Communications Museum,** 140 New Montgomery (at Natoma), tel. (415) 542-0182, offers electronic miscellany and telephone memorabilia dating to the 1870s.

SoMa Shopping

Shop-and-drop types, please note: serious bargains are available throughout SoMa's garment district. The garment industry is the city's largest, doing a wholesale business of $5 billion annually. Most of the manufacturing factories are between Second and 11th Streets, and many have off-price retail outlets for their own wares. But you won't necessarily shop in comfort, since some don't have dressing rooms and others are as jam-packed as the post office at tax time. Major merchandise marts, mostly for wholesalers, are clustered along Kansas and Townsend Streets. Some retail discount outlets for clothing, jewelry, and accessories are here, too, also along Brannan St. between Third and Sixth Streets. If at all possible, come any day but Saturday, and always be careful where you park. The parking cops are serious about ticketing violators.

Yerba Buena Square, 899 Howard St. (at Fifth), tel. (415) 543-1275, is an off-price factory mall. **Tower Outlet,** 660 Third St. (at Townsend), tel. (415) 957-9660, offers discounted CDs and tapes. Some of the best places have to be hunted down, however. **Esprit Direct,** 499 Illinois (at 16th), tel. (415) 957-2500, is a warehouse-sized store offering discounts on San Francisco's hippest women's and children's wear. (Try lunch—weekdays only—at **42 Degrees,** tucked behind the outlet at 235 16th St., tel. 415-777-5558.) Neighborhood anchor **Gunne Sax,** 35 Stanford Alley (between Second and Third, Brannan and Townsend), tel. (415) 495-3326, has a huge selection of more than 25,000 garments (including dress-up dresses); the best bargains

are way in the back. Nearby, at the border of South Park, **Jeremy's** 2 South Park (at Second), tel. (415) 882-4929, sells hip designer clothes for one-third or more off retail. Consumer alert: because some of the items are returns, be sure to check garments for snags or other signs of wear before buying. **Harper Greer,** 580 Fourth St. (between Bryant and Brannan), tel. (415) 543-4066, offers wholesale-priced fashions for women size 14 and larger.

Since shopping outlets open, close, and change names or locations at a remarkable rate, consult the "Style" section of the Sunday *San Francisco Examiner and Chronicle,* which lists discount centers and factory outlets.

SoMa Nightlife

Many SoMa restaurants (see Eating in San Francisco below) do double-duty as bars and club venues. You won't go far before finding something going on. The classic for people who wear ties even after work is **Julie's Supper Club,** 1123 Folsom (at Seventh), tel. (415) 861-0707, though **Hamburger Mary's,** 1582 Folsom St. (at 12th), tel. (415) 626-5767, has achieved an almost mythic status among the alternative crowd.

Catch touring and local rock bands at **Slim's,** 333 11th St. (between Folsom and Harrison), tel. (415) 522-0333, the cutting edge for indie rockers; pretty steep cover. Before braving the line, fill up across the street at the **20 Tank Brewery,** 316 11th (at Folsom), tel. (415) 255-9455, a lively brewpub run by the same microbrewery folks who brewed up Triple Rock in Berkeley.

The **Caribbean Zone,** 55 Natoma (between First and Second, Mission and Howard), tel. (415) 541-9465, has a mezzanine cocktail lounge created from an airplane fuselage, so you can sit and down a few with porthole-window television screens and sound effects simulate takeoff (and crash landings). Artistically and genetically expansive, in a punkish sort of way, is the **DNA Lounge,** 375 11th St. (between Harrison and Folsom), tel. (415) 626-1409, serving up dancing nightly after 9 p.m., cover on weekends.

But don't miss the **Paradise Lounge,** 1501 Folsom St. (at 11th), tel. (415) 861-6906, marvelously mazelike and sporting several bars, four separate live stages, and an upstairs pool hall. Upstairs is **Above Paradise,** featuring more music—often acoustic—and occasional poetry readings. Next door is the **Transmission The-**

AN OPEN-MINDED GUIDE
TO NIGHTCLUBBING IN SAN FRANCISCO

First, ask the basic questions: Who am I? What am I doing here? Where do I belong? To go nightclubbing in San Francisco, at least *ask* the questions. The answers don't really matter; your political, social, sexual, and musical preferences will be matched somewhere. Techno, disco, new wave, house, fusion, industrial, world beat—whatever it is you're into, it's out there, just part of the creative carnival world of San Francisco nightclubbing. Everything goes, especially cultural taboos, leaving only free-wheeling imaginations and an unadulterated desire to do one thing and only one thing—dance with total abandon. In the city, heteros, gays, lesbians, blacks, whites, Asians, and Latinos all writhe together, unified in a place where all prejudice drops away: the dance floor.

The hottest dance clubs come and go considerably faster than the Muni buses do, so the key to finding the hippest, most happening spot is to ask around. Ask people who look like they should know, such as young fashion junkies working in trendy clothing shops, used-record stores, or other abodes of pretentious cool. If you're seeking one of those infamous "warehouse" parties, then look for small invitational flyers tacked to telephone poles or posted in the above-mentioned and other likely places (particularly in the Haight, lower Haight, and Castro neighborhoods). The flyers announce a party and list a phone number to call. When you call up—ooh, the intrigue—you'll get directions to that night's secret dance locale. Warning: these roving, nonlicensed dance clubs tend to put on quite crowded parties, very expensive to boot.

Throbbing together with hundreds of other euphorics, experiencing ecstasy en masse, may be the closest we'll ever really get to living in one united world. Still, San Francisco nightclub virgins tend to avoid their initiation, somehow intimidated by the frenzied cosmic collision of electrifying lights, thumping dance tunes, and sweat-drenched bodies. But be not afraid. There are answers to even the three most common worries:

Worry: I can't dance. *Answer:* It wouldn't matter even if you could. The dance floors are so crowded, at best it's possible only to bounce up and down.

Worry: I'm straight (or gay) and the crowd seems to be predominantly gay (or straight). *Answer:* Since the limits of gender and sexuality are hopelessly blurred in San Francisco, and since nobody would care even if they weren't, just dump your angst and dance.

Worry: I'm afraid I'll look like a fool (feel out of place, be outclassed, fall down, throw up, whatever). *Answer:* As we said, nobody cares. You're totally anonymous, being one of more than 728,000 people in town. And no matter what you do, nobody will notice, since narcissism in San Francisco's clubs is at least as deep as the Grand Canyon.

—Tim Moriarty

---

atre, tel. (415) 621-4410, an 800-seat venue for live music and performing arts built in an old auto shop. And all of this adventure for a reasonable cover charge.

Since SoMa in the 1970s was a nighttime playground for the bad-boys-in-black-leather set, the gay bar scene here is still going strong. The original gay bar is **The Stud,** 399 Ninth St. (at Harrison), tel. (415) 252-7883, formerly a leather bar, now a dance bar. For dancing in the gay, country-western style, try the **Rawhide II,** 280 Seventh St. (at Folsom), tel. (415) 621-1197. But the hottest younger-set gay nightclub in the neighborhood, some say in the entire city, is the **Endup** ("you always end up at the Endup"), 401 Sixth St. (at Harrison), tel. (415) 357-0827, famous for serious dancing—"hot bodies," too,

according to an informed source—and, for cooling down, its large outdoor deck. Saturday nights are lesbian.

Other SoMa clubs to explore (if you dare) include: **El Bobo,** 1539 Folsom (between 11th and 12th), tel. (415) 861-6822, an elegant supper club open late for nightcaps and midnight munchies; the mostly lesbian **CoCo Club,** 139 Eighth St. (between Mission and Howard), tel. (415) 626-2337; **Covered Wagon Saloon,** 917 Folsom (between Fifth and Sixth), tel. (415) 974-1585, favored by bike messengers; **Holy Cow,** 1535 Folsom (between 11th and 12th), tel. (415) 621-6087; the **Hotel Utah Saloon,** 500 Fourth St. (at Bryant), tel.(415) 421-8308, featuring eclectic live music; and the dance club **1015 Folsom,** 1015 Folsom (at Sixth), tel. (415) 431-1200.

SEEING SAN FRANCISCO: COASTING THE BAY

San Francisco's waterfront stretches some six miles along the wide, seawall-straddling **Embarcadero,** which runs from China Basin south of the Bay Bridge to Fisherman's Wharf in the

north. Remnants of bygone booming port days, the docks and wharfs here are today devoted as much to tourism as to maritime commerce. The area is much improved, aesthetically, now that the elevated, view-blocking Embarcadero Freeway is gone (it was razed after being damaged in the 1989 earthquake). Today the Embarcadero is lined with nonnative Canary Island palm trees—a landscaping strategy that initially angered botanical purists who dismissed the trees as being "too L.A."

Rising up at the foot of Second St. is the new **Pacific Bell Park,** www.sfgiants.com, which replaced 3Com Park (better known by its original name—Candlestick Park) as the home of the San Francisco Giants in April 2000. Pac Bell Park sits right on the waterfront and seats 42,000 fans, offering sweeping views of the bay and the city skyline. Designed by Hellmuth, Obata & Kassabaum architect Joe Spear, the fellow responsible for Coors Field in Denver and Camden Yards in Baltimore, the park aims to combine the feel of an old-time ballpark with modern amenities. Quite modern is the potential traffic nightmare of 40,000 fans trying to drive and find parking downtown, so smart fans may find that public transportation—including BART and ferries from surrounding Bay Area communities—is a better option. The ballpark is a fairly short walk from downtown.

In China Basin is **South Beach Marina Pier,** a public fishing pier with a good skyline view of the South Beach Marina. Next along the Embarcadero are various new developments also housing restaurants, including **Bayside Village** and the world-renowned drug rehabilitation program **Delancey Street.** Next is **Hills Plaza,** a fairly new commercial-and-apartment development with a garden plaza, incorporating the shell of the old Hills Brothers Coffee building.

Across from the updated 1889 Audiffred Building at 1 Mission is city-within-the-city **Rincon Center,** incorporating the former Rincon Annex Post Office, which was saved for its classic New Deal mural art. Note, too, the **36,075-pound**

SPORTING SAN FRANCISCO

As of April 2000, the **San Francisco Giants** major-league baseball team plays ball on the bay at the city's new 42,000-seat Pacific Bell Park, tel. (415) 468-3700, www.sfgiants.com. (To betray the city's baseball heritage, zip across the bay to the Network Associates Coliseum and the Oakland A's games, tel. 510-430-8020, www.oaklandathletics.com.) Still at home at 3Com Park—once known as Candlestick Park— are the **San Francisco 49ers,** NFL footballers made famous by their numerous Super Bowl victories. For 49er tickets and information, call (415) 656-4900 or check www.sf49ers.com.

San Franciscans are big on participatory sports. Some of the city's most eclectic competitive events reflect this fact, including the famous *San Francisco Examiner* **Bay to Breakers** race in May, tel. (415) 777-7770, which attracts 100,000-plus runners, joggers, and walkers, most wearing quite creative costumes—and occasionally nothing at all. It's a phenomenon that must be experienced to be believed. (Request registration forms well in advance.)

San Francisco's outdoor and other recreational opportunities seem limited only by one's imagination (and income): hot-air ballooning, beachcombing, bicycling, birdwatching, boating, bowling, camping, canoeing, kayaking, hang-gliding, hiking, horseshoes, fishing, golf, tennis, sailing, swimming, surfing, parasailing, rowing, rock climbing, running, windsurfing. Golden Gate National Recreational Area and Golden Gate Park are major community recreation resources.

For a current rundown on sports events and recreational opportunities, or for information on specific activities, consult the helpful folks at the San Francisco Convention & Visitors Bureau (see Useful Information under Just the Facts).

brass screw from a World War II tanker at 100 Spear St., introducing the waterfront exhibits inside. More than elsewhere in the city, except perhaps Nob Hill, the ironies of Financial District art are indeed striking.

At the foot of Market St. is the **Ferry Building,** completed in 1898. Formerly the city's transportation center, the Ferry Building today is largely office space, including the **World Trade Center.** But the building still features its 661-foot arcaded facade, triumphal entrance arch, and temple-style clock tower echoing the Giralda tower of Spain's Seville cathedral. During commute hours, the area bustles with suits disembarking ferries from Marin. Hop one of the high-speed boats to Sausalito for lunch and you'll get there in about half an hour. Boats leave frequently daily, with extended hours in summer. Tickets $1.35-4.70 one-way.

The **Waterfront Promenade** stretches from the new Giants ballpark to the **San Francisco Maritime National Historic Park** at the foot of Hyde Street. The promenade, built in stages over the last few years, replaces the waterfront's old piers 14 through 22. Named **Herb Caen Way** (complete with three dots) in 1996, for the late *San Francisco Chronicle* columnist, the seawall walkway features grand views of the bay. It's a favorite spot for midday runners and office brownbaggers; literary types enjoy the poems embedded in the sidewalk.

Just south of Broadway is the city's only new pier since the 1930s; 845-foot-long **Pier 7** is an elegant public-access promenade for dawdlers and fisherfolk, complete with iron-and-wood benches, iron railings, and flanking colonnades of lampposts, the better for taking in the nighttime skyline.

FISHERMAN'S WHARF

San Francisco's fishing industry and other port-related businesses were once integral to the city's cultural and economic life. Fisherman's Wharf, which extends from Pier 39 to the municipal pier just past Aquatic Park, was originally the focus of this waterfront commerce. Early on, Chinese fishermen pulled ashore their catch here, to be followed in time by Italian fishermen who took over the territory. After World War II, however, the city's fishing industry declined dramatically, the result of both accelerated pollution of San Francisco Bay and decades of overfishing. Today, Fisherman's Wharf has largely become a carnival-style diversion for tourists. Nevertheless, beyond the shopping centers, arcade amusements, and oddball museums, a small fishing fleet struggles to survive.

Pier 39

At Beach St. and Embarcadero, Pier 39 offers schlock par excellence. If you don't mind jostling with the schools of tourists like some sort of biped sardine, you're sure to find *something* here that interests you. But this place really isn't about San Francisco—it's about shopping and

The hundreds of sea lions at Pier 39 have become an attraction in their own right.

STEVE FAHRINGER

otherwise spending your vacation wad. And you could have done that at home.

Shopping possibilities include the **Disney Store,** selling licensed Disney merchandise; the **Warner Bros. Studio Store,** selling meep-meeps, cwazy wabbits, and the like; the **NFL Shop,** offering official 49er jerseys and other pigskin paraphernalia; the **City Store,** selling actual bits of San Francisco—old street signs, old bits of cable-car cable, old bricks from Lombard St.—all to benefit San Francisco social-services programs; and **Mel Fisher's Sunken Treasure Museum Store,** displaying artifacts collected by Fisher on his shipwreck dives.

At **Turbo Ride Simulation Theatre,** tel. (415) 392-8872, you'll be thrown around in your spastic, hydraulically controlled seat in perfect time with what's happening on the big screen before you; think armchair Indiana Jones (and three similar adventure scenarios). Open daily. Summer hours are Sun.-Thurs. 10 a.m.-9:30 p.m., Friday 10 a.m.-11 p.m.; Saturday 10 a.m.-midnight. The rest of the year, it's open Sun.-Thurs. 10:30 a.m.-8:30 p.m., Fri.-Sat. 10 a.m.-10 p.m. Admission is $8 general, $5 seniors/children under 12. And at **UnderWater World,** tel. (415) 623-5300, you can travel through a 300-foot-long acrylic tube on a moving walkway, looking out on schools of glittering anchovies, stingrays, leopard sharks, and other sea creatures swimming through the 700,000-gallon Pier 39 Aquarium. UnderWater World is open daily 10 a.m.-6 p.m.; extended summer hours. Admission is $12.95 adults, $9.95 seniors, $6.50 children 3-11.

No, you won't lack for attractions to take your money at Pier 39. But for free you can spend time watching the lolling **sea lions** out on the docks, a fairly recent invasion force. The docks

TOURING THE REAL ROCK

Visiting Alcatraz is like touring the dark side of the American dream, like peering into democracy's private demon hold. At Alcatraz, freedom is a fantasy. If crime is a universal option—and everyone behind bars at Alcatraz exercised it—then all who once inhabited this desolate island prison were certainly equal. Yet all who lived on The Rock were also equal in other ways—in their utter isolation, in their human desperation, in their hopelessness.

Former prison guard Frank Heaney, born and raised in Berkeley, is now a consultant for the Blue & Gold Fleet's exclusive Alcatraz tour. When he started work as a correctional officer at age 21, Heaney found himself standing guard over some of America's most notorious felons, including George "Machine Gun" Kelly, Alvin "Creepy" Karpis, and Robert "The Birdman of Alcatraz" Stroud. Heaney soon realized that the terrifying reality of prison life was a far cry from Hollywood's James Cagney version.

The job was psychologically demanding, yet often boring. There was terror in the air, too. Inmates vowed—and attempted—to "break him." But he ignored both death threats and too-friendly comments on his youthful appeal. Guards were prohibited from conversing with the inmates—one more aspect of the criminals' endless isolation—but Heaney eventually got to know Machine Gun Kelly, whom he remembers as articulate and intellectual, "more like a bank president than a bank robber." Creepy Karpis, Ma Barker's right-hand man and the only man ever personally arrested by FBI Director J. Edgar Hoover, was little more than a braggart. And though the Birdman was considered seriously psychotic and spent most of his 54 prison years in solitary confinement, Heaney found him to be "untrustworthy" but rational and extremely intelligent. Many of Heaney's favorite stories are collected in his book *Inside the Walls of Alcatraz,* published by Bull Publishing and available at Pier 39 and the National Park Store gift shop.

Others who remember The Rock, both guards and inmates, are included on the **Alcatraz Cellhouse Tour,** an "inside" audio journey through prison history provided by the Golden Gate National Park Association and offered along with Blue & Gold Fleet tours to Alcatraz.

Among them is Jim Quillen, former inmate, who on the day we visit is here in person. He leans against the rusted iron doors of Cell Block A. His pained eyes scan the pocked walls and empty cells, each barely adequate as an open-air closet. Quillen spent the best years of his life on Alcatraz. "Ten years and one day," he says in a soft voice. "The tourists see the architecture, the history—all I see are ghosts. I can point to the exact spots where my friends have killed themselves, been murdered, gone completely insane."

once served as a marina full of pleasure boats—until the sea lions started making themselves at home. It turned out to be a futile effort trying to chase them off, so the powers that be decided to abandon the marina idea and let the pinnipeds (up to 600 of them in the peak Jan.-Feb. herring season) have their way, becoming a full-time tourist attraction. Score: Sea Lions 1, Yachties 0.

Most shops at the pier are open daily 10:30 a.m.-8:30 p.m. Hours are longer in summer. For more information, call (415) 981-7437, or look up www.pier39.com online. Also here are the **Blue & Gold Fleet** ferries to Alcatraz and elsewhere around the bay.

Along Jefferson Street

A culinary treat on the Wharf, especially in December or at other times during the mid-November-to-June season, is fresh **Dungeness crab.** You can pick out your own, live or already cooked, from the vendor stands, or head for any of the more famous Italian-style seafood restaurants here: **Alioto's, Castagliona's, Sabella's,** or the excellent and locally favored **Scoma's,** hidden slightly away from the tourist hordes on Pier 47 (near the intersection of Jones and Jefferson), tel. (415) 771-4383.

If you're in the mood for still more entertainment, Fisherman's Wharf offers a wacky variety. **Ripley's *Believe It Or Not!* Museum,** 175 Jefferson St. (near Taylor), tel. (415) 771-6188, features both bizarre and beautiful items—including a two-headed cow, a shrunken head, and other grotesqueries—collected during Robert L. Ripley's global travels. Open Sun.-Thurs. 10 a.m.-10 p.m., Fri.-Sat. 10 a.m.-midnight. Admission $8.50 adults, $7 children and seniors.

That's the main reason to visit Alcatraz—to explore this lonely, hard, wind-whipped island of exile. The ghosts here need human companionship.

There is plenty else to do, too, including the ranger-guided walk around the island, courtesy of the Golden Gate National Recreation Area (GGNRA), and poking one's nose into other buildings, other times. National park personnel also offer lectures and occasional special programs. Or take an **Evening on Alcatraz** tour, to see the sun set on the city from the island. For current information, contact the Golden Gate National Recreation Area at (415) 556-0560 or www.nps.gov/goga, stop by the **GGNRA Visitors Center** at the Cliff House in San Francisco (tel. (415) 556-8643), or contact the nonprofit, education-oriented Golden Gate National Park Association, tel. (415) 561-3000. (For more information about the recreation area in general, see that section elsewhere in this chapter and also Point Reyes National Seashore.)

If you're coming to Alcatraz, contact the **Blue & Gold Fleet,** Pier 41, Fisherman's Wharf, tel. (415) 773-1188, www.blueandgoldfleet.com, for general information. To make charge-by-phone ticket reservations—advisable, well in advance, since the tour is quite popular, attracting more than one million people each year—call (415) 705-5555, or make reservations through the Blue & Gold Fleet's website (with seven days' advance notice). At last report, roundtrip fare with audio was $12.25 per adult, $7 per child, plus a $2.25-per-ticket reservation surcharge if you re-serve your ticket by phone/Internet; there's also a $1 day-use fee in addition to the ferry price. (Be sure to be there 30 minutes early, since no refunds or exchanges are allowed if you miss the boat.) The entire audio-guided walking tour takes more than two hours, so be sure to allow yourself adequate time. (The audiotape is available in English, Japanese, German, French, Italian, and Spanish.) If at all possible, try to get booked on one of the early tours, so you can see the cellblocks and Alcatraz Island in solitude, before the rest of humanity arrives. Pack a picnic (though snacks and beverages are available), and bring all the camera and video equipment you can carry; no holds barred on photography. Wear good walking shoes, as well as warm clothes (layers best), since it can be brutally cold on Alcatraz in the fog or when the wind whips up.

In the past, the island's ruggedness made it difficult to impossible for those with limited mobility, with moderate to strenuous climbing and limited access for wheelchairs and strollers. Now wheelchair users and others with limited mobility who can't "do" the Alcatraz tour on foot can take SEAT (Sustainable Easy Access Transport) up the 12% grade hill one-quarter mile to the prison. Contact the Blue & Gold Fleet information line for details.

If you're not coming to Alcatraz in the immediate future, you can still take a comprehensive virtual tour, on the web at www.nps.gov/alcatraz/tours.

—Tim Moriarty and Kim Weir

Around Ghirardelli Square

You can also shop till you drop at elegant **Ghirardelli Square,** 900 North Point (Beach and Larkin), tel. (415) 775-5500, a complex of 50-plus shops and restaurants where you can get one of the best hot fudge sundaes anywhere, or **The Cannery,** 2801 Leavenworth (at Beach), tel. (415) 771-3112, another huge theme shopping center, this one offering outdoor street artist performances as well as the **Museum of the City of San Francisco,** tel. (415) 928-0289; **Cobb's Comedy Club,** tel. (415) 928-4320; and **Quiet Storm,** tel. (415) 771-2929, a jazz club also serving Pacific Rim cuisine. Beer lovers will be in hops heaven at The Cannery, checking out the offerings of **Beach Street Brewhouse,** tel. (415) 775-5110, offering its own housemade beers, and **Jack's Cannery Bar,** tel. (415) 931-6400, a restaurant and bar featuring 83 different beers on tap. Time-honored for imports and the occasional bargain is the nearby **Cost Plus,** 2552 Taylor (at North Point).

Quieter, less commercial pleasures are also available along Fisherman's Wharf—a stroll through **Aquatic Park** perhaps, or fishing out on **Municipal Pier.**

San Francisco
Maritime National Historical Park

Historic ships and a first-rate maritime museum make up the core of this national park on the west end of Fisherman's Wharf. To get oriented, first stop by the park's **National Maritime Museum of San Francisco** in Aquatic Park at Beach and Polk, tel. (415) 556-3002, open daily 10 a.m.-5 p.m., free admission. The double-decker building itself looks like an art deco ocean liner. Washed ashore inside are some excellent displays, from model ships and figureheads to historic photos and exhibits on fishing boats, ferries, and demonstrations of the sailor's arts. The affiliated **J. Porter Shaw Library,** tel. (415) 556-9870, housed along with the park's administrative offices west of Fisherman's Wharf in Building E at Fort Mason (a reasonable walk away along a bike/pedestrian path), holds most of the Bay Area's documented boat history, including oral histories, logbooks, photographs, and shipbuilding plans.

Not easy to miss at the foot of Hyde St. are the **Hyde Street Pier Historic Ships,** tel. (415) 556-3002 or (415) 556-6435, an always-in-progress collection that is also part of the national park. Admission $5 adults, $2 youths 12-17, free for children. Here you can clamber across the decks and crawl through the colorfully cluttered holds of some of America's most historic ships.

The Hyde Street fleet's flagship is the three-masted 1886 ***Balclutha,*** a veteran of twice-annual trips between California and the British Isles via Cape Horn. Others include the side-wheel ***Eureka*** (the world's largest passenger ferry in her day, built to ferry trains), the ocean-going tugboat ***Hercules,*** the British-built, gold rush-era paddlewheel tug ***Eppleton Hall,*** the scow schooner ***Alma,*** and the three-masted lumber schooner ***C.A. Thayer.*** Also among the collection, but berthed at Pier 45, is the **U.S.S. *Pampanito,*** a tight-quarters Balao-class World War II submarine that destroyed or damaged many Japanese vessels and also participated in the tragic sinking of the Japanese *Kachidoki Maru* and *Rayuyo Maru,* which were carrying Australian and British prisoners of war.

Tagging along on a ranger-led tour (complete with "living history" adventures in summer) is the best way to get your feet wet at this national park. Call for tour schedule (guided tours are usually offered daily). But self-guided tours are available anytime the pier is open, which is daily 9:30 a.m.-5 p.m. year-round (until 5:30 p.m. in summer); closed Thanksgiving, Christmas, and New Year's Day. Special activities give you the chance to sing sea chanteys, raise sails, watch the crews "lay aloft," or participate in the Dead Horse Ceremony—wherein the crowds heave a horse doll overboard and shout "May the sharks have his body, and the devil have his soul!"

SS *Jeremiah O'Brien*

Berthed at Pier 45 in summer, Pier 32 the rest of the year, this massive 441-foot-long World War II Liberty Ship made 11 crossings from England to the beaches of Normandy to support the Allied invasion. In 1994, it returned to Normandy for the 50th anniversary of D day. The ship is still powered by its original engines. In fact, the engine-room scenes in the movie *Titanic* were filmed here.

The historic ship is open for self-guided tours year-round, daily 10 a.m.-7 p.m.; admission is $5 adults, $4 seniors/military, $3 children. In addition, the ship makes several day-long cruises each year; you can come along for $100 per person. For more information or for cruise schedule and reservations, call (415) 441-3101.

FORT MASON

Headquarters for the Golden Gate National Recreation Area, Fort Mason is also home to **Fort Mason Center,** a complex of one-time military storage buildings at Marina Blvd. and Buchanan St., now hosting surprisingly contemporary nonprofit arts, humanities, educational, environmental, and recreational organizations and associations.

Since the 1970s, this shoreline wasteland has been transformed into an innovative multicultural community events center—perhaps the country's premier model of the impossible, successfully accomplished. Several pavilions and the Conference Center host larger group events, though smaller galleries, theaters, and offices predominate. The variety of rotating art exhibits, independent theater performances, poetry readings, lectures and workshops, and special-interest classes offered here is truly staggering.

Expansion plans include the establishment of a marine ecology center, another theater, more exhibit space, and another good-food-great-view restaurant. All in all, it's not surprising that Fort Mason is being studied by the Presidio's national park transition team, and even by other nations, as a supreme example of how urban eyesores can be transformed into national treasures.

Fort Mason Museums

The **San Francisco African American Historical & Cultural Society,** in Building C, Room 165, tel. (415) 441-0640, is a cultural and resource center featuring a library, museum (small admission), speaker's bureau, and monthly lecture series. Open Wed.-Sun. noon-5 p.m.

The **Mexican Museum,** Building D, tel. (415) 202-9700 or (415) 441-0404, www.folkart.com/~latitude/museums, is devoted exclusively to exhibitions of, and educational programs about, Mexican-American and Mexican art. Its permanent collection includes 9,000 items from five periods, including pre-Hispanic and contemporary Mexican art, and rotating exhibits attract much public attention. The changing exhibits typically focus on one particular artist or on a theme, such as "100 Years of Chroma Art Calendars." Open Wed.-Sun. 11 a.m.-5 p.m.; admission $4 adults, $3 students and seniors. The Museum plans to move downtown to the Yerba Buena Center in the not-too-distant future, so call or check with the website before setting out.

Exhibits at the **Museo ItaloAmericano,** in Building C, tel. (415) 673-2200, foster an appreciation of Italian art and culture. Open Wed.-Sun. noon-5 p.m. Small admission. Definitely worth a detour is the **San Francisco Craft & Folk Art Museum,** Building A-North, tel. (415) 775-0990, www.sfcraftandfolk.org, which features rotating exhibits of American and international folk art. Open Tues.-Fri. and Sunday 11 a.m.-5 p.m.; Saturday 10 a.m.-5 p.m. Free on Saturday, 10 a.m.-noon, otherwise there's a small admission fee.

In addition to any free hours listed above, all of the museums at the center are free (and open until 7 p.m.) on the first Wednesday of every month.

Fort Mason Performing Arts

Fort Mason Center's 440-seat **Cowell Theater,** tel. (415) 441-3400, is a performance space that hosts events ranging from the acclaimed Solo Mio Festival and the New Pickle Circus to guest speakers such as Spalding Gray and unusual video, musical, and theatrical presentations. Among its showstoppers is the **Magic Theatre,** Building D, tel. (415) 441-8001 (business office) or (415) 441-8822 (box office), which is internationally recognized as an outstanding American playwrights' theater, performing original plays by the likes of Sam Shepard and Michael McClure as well as innovative new writers.

Other Fort Mason performing arts groups include the **Performing Arts Workshop,** Building C, tel. (415) 673-2634, and the **Young Performers' Theatre,** Building C, tel. (415) 346-5550, both for young people. The **Blue Bear School of American Music,** Building D, tel. (415) 673-3600, offers lessons and workshops in rock, pop, jazz, blues, and other genres. **Bay Area Theatresports** (BATS) is an improv comedy group that performs at the **Bayfront Theater,** Building B, tel. (415) 474-8935, and **World Arts West,** Building D, tel. (415) 474-3914, promotes and produces world music and dance festivals.

Fort Mason Visual Arts

The **Fort Mason Art Campus** of the City College of San Francisco, Building B, tel. (415) 561-1840, is the place for instruction in fine arts and crafts. Works of students and faculty are showcased at the **Coffee Gallery,** in the Building B lobby, tel. (415) 561-1840. The 10-and-under set should head to the **San Francisco Children's Art Center,** Building C, tel. (415) 771-0292. One of the most intriguing galleries here is the **San Francisco Museum of Modern Art Rental Gallery,** Building A-North, tel. (415) 441-4777, representing more than 1,300 artists and offering, in addition to rotating exhibits, the opportunity to rent as well as buy works on display.

Fort Mason Environmental Organizations

The **Endangered Species Project,** Building E, tel. (415) 921-3140, works to protect wildlife and habitat and to prevent illegal poaching and trade of endangered animals. **Friends of the River,** Building C, tel. (415) 771-0400, supports efforts to protect and restore the West's waterways and riparian areas. The **Fund for Animals,** Building C, tel. (415) 474-4020, is an animal-rights organization. The **Oceanic Society,** Building E, tel. (415) 441-1106, offers environmental education programs including whalewatching trips, cruises to the Farallon Islands, and coral-reef and rainforest expeditions. The **Resource Renewal Institute,** Pier 1 North, tel. (415) 928-3774, promotes integrated environmental planning—"Green Plans"—at every level of government, both domestically and internationally. The **Tuolumne River Preservation Trust,** Building C, tel. (415) 292-3531, focuses its efforts on protecting and preserving the Tuolumne River watershed.

Glorious Grazing

No one will ever starve here, since one of the country's best vegetarian restaurants, the San Francisco Zen Center's **Greens,** is in Building A-North, tel. (415) 771-6222. It's open Mon.-Sat. for lunch and dinner and Sunday for brunch. The restaurant also offers **Greens-To-Go** take-out lunches Tues.-Sun.; call (415) 771-6330.

Other Fort Mason Services and Information

Book Bay Bookstore, Building C-South, tel. (415) 771-1076, is run by friends of the San Francisco Public Library. Book sales are regularly held to benefit the city's public-library system.

For more complete information on Fort Mason, including a copy of the monthly *Fort Mason Calendar of Events,* contact the **Fort Mason Foundation,** Building A, Fort Mason Center, tel. (415) 441-3400, www.fortmason.org, open daily 9 a.m.-5 p.m. For **recorded information** 24 hours a day, call (415) 979-3010. To order tickets for any Fort Mason events, call the **Fort Mason box office** at (415) 441-3687.

MARINA DISTRICT

The neat pastel homes of the respectable Marina District, tucked in between Fort Mason and the Presidio, disguise the fact that the entire area is essentially unstable. Built on landfill, in an area once largely bay marsh, the Mediterranean-style Marina was previously the 63-acre site of the Panama-Pacific International Exposition of 1915—San Francisco's statement to the world that it had been reborn from the ashes of the 1906 earthquake and fire. So it was ironic, and fitting, that the fireboat *Phoenix* extinguished many of the fires that blazed here following the 1989 earthquake, which caused disproportionately heavy damage in this district.

The Marina's main attractions are those that surround it—primarily the neighborhood stretch of San Francisco's astounding shoreline Golden Gate National Recreation Area, which includes the **Fort Mason** complex of galleries, museums, theaters, and nonprofit cultural and conservation organizations. (For more information, see Golden Gate National Recreation Area and Fort Mason above.) If you're in the neighborhood and find yourself near the yacht harbor, do wander out to see (and hear) the park's wonderful **Wave Organ** just east of the yacht club on Bay Street. Built of pieces from an old graveyard, the pipes are powered by sea magic. (The siren song is loudest at high tide.) Then wander west toward the Golden Gate Bridge on the **Golden Gate Promenade,** which meanders the three-plus miles from Aquatic Park and along the Marina Green—popular with kite fliers, well-dressed dog walkers, and the area's many exercise freaks—to Civil War-era **Fort Point.** (Be prepared for wind and fog.) The truly ambitious can take a hike across the bridge itself, an awesome experience.

Exhausted by nature, retreat to more sheltered attractions near the Presidio, including the remnants of the spectacular Panama-Pacific International Exhibition of 1915, the Bernard Maybeck-designed **Palace of Fine Arts,** and the indescribable **Exploratorium** inside, fun for children of all ages and a first-rate science museum. (For more area information, see The Presidio and Fort Point.) The Marina also boasts its own version of Cow Hollow's chic Union Street shopping and eating district: **Chestnut Street.**

Exploratorium: Sophisticated Child's Play

Scientific American considers this the "best science museum in the world." *Good Housekeeping* says it's the "number one science museum in the U.S." It's definitely worth spending some time here. Inside the Palace of Fine Arts, 3601 Lyon St. (at Bay), tel. (415) 397-5673, www.exploratorium.edu, the Exploratorium is billed as a museum of science, art, and human perception, and ostensibly designed for children. But this is no mass-marketed media assault on the senses, no mindless theatrical homage to simple fantasy. The truth is, adults also adore the Exploratorium, a wonderfully intelligent playground built around the mysterious natural laws of the universe.

The Exploratorium was founded in 1969 by physicist and educator Dr. Frank Oppenheimer, the original "Explainer" (as opposed to "teacher"), whose research career was abruptly ended during the blacklisting McCarthy era. Brother of J. Robert Oppenheimer (father of the atomic bomb), Frank Oppenheimer's scientific legacy was nonetheless abundant.

"Explaining science and technology without props," said Oppenheimer, "is like attempting to tell what it is like to swim without ever letting a person near the water." The Exploratorium was the original interactive science museum and influenced the establishment of hundreds of other such museums in the U.S. and abroad. Its 650-some three-dimensional exhibits delve into 13 broad subject areas: animal behavior, language, vision, sound and hearing, touch, heat and temperature, electricity, light, color, motion, patterns, waves and resonance, and weather. Everything can be experienced—from a touch-sensitive plant that shrinks from a child's probing hand, to strategically angled mirrors that create infinite reflections of the viewer; from tactile computerized fingerpainting to the wave-activated voice of the San Francisco Bay, as brought to you by the "Wave Organ." The extra special **Tactile Dome,** tel. (415) 561-0362 (reservations recommended), provides a pitch-black environment in which your vision is of no use, but your sense of touch gets a real workout.

Stock up on educational toys, games, experiments, and oddities at the Exploratorium Store. Especially worth purchasing, for teachers and brave parents alike, is the Exploratorium Science Snackbook, which includes instructions on building home or classroom versions of more than 100 Exploratorium exhibits.

The Exploratorium is open in summer daily 10 a.m.-6 p.m. (Wednesday until 9 p.m.). The rest of the year, hours are Tues.-Sun. 10 a.m.-5 p.m. (Wednesday until 9 p.m.). On the first Wednesday of each month, admission is free. Otherwise it's $9 adults, $7 seniors/students with ID, $5 youths 6-17, and $2.50 children 3-5. Admission to the Tactile Dome is $12 per person, which includes museum admission.

SEEING SAN FRANCISCO: NEAR THE BAY

A total tour of San Francisco has to include a spin through the north-of-downtown neighborhoods near or overlooking the bay, including Nob Hill, Chinatown, North Beach, and Telegraph Hill. All are easily accessible from the Embarcadero and other points along the waterfront, so walk if possible. Parking can be impossible.

COW HOLLOW AND PACIFIC HEIGHTS

Separating the Marina District from high-flying Pacific Heights is the low-lying neighborhood of Cow Hollow, a one-time dairy farm community now noted for its chic **Union Street** shopping district—an almost endless string of bars, cafés, coffeehouses, bookstores, and boutiques stretching between Van Ness and Steiner. Other chic areas have included upper **Fillmore Street** near the Heights (and near the still-surviving 1960s icon, the **Fillmore** concert hall, at Geary and Fillmore), and outer **Sacramento Street** near Presidio Avenue. **Pacific Heights** proper is the hilltop home pasture for the city's well-shod blue bloods. Its striking streets, Victorian homes, and general architectural wealth are well worth a stroll (for personal guidance, see Walking Tours, under Delights and Diversions, below). Especially noteworthy here is the **Haas-Lilienthal House,** 2007 Franklin (at Jackson), tel. (415) 441-3004, a handsome and huge Queen Anne Victorian, a survivor of the 1906 earthquake and the city's only fully furnished Victorian open for regular public tours. Tours are conducted Wednesday and Sunday; call for times. Admission is $5 adults, $3 seniors and children.

In the Cow Hollow neighborhood, don't miss the unusual 1861 **Octagon House,** 2645 Gough (at Union), tel. (415) 441-7512, owned by the National Society of Colonial Dames of America; it's now restored and fully furnished in colonial and federal period antiques. Open only on the second and fourth Thursday and the second Sunday of each month (closed in January and on holidays). Call to request special tour times. Donations greatly appreciated.

NOB HILL

Snide San Franciscans say "Snob Hill" when referring to cable car-crisscrossed Nob Hill. The official neighborhood name is purported to be short for "Nabob Hill," a reference to this highrent district's nouveau riche roots. Robert Louis Stevenson called it the "hill of palaces," referring to the grand late-1800s mansions of San Francisco's economic elite, California's railroad barons most prominent among them. Known colloquially as the "Big Four," Charles Crocker, Mark Hopkins, Collis Huntington, and Leland Stanford were accompanied by two of the "Irish Big Four" or "Bonanza Kings" (James Fair and James Flood, Nevada silver lords) as they made their acquisitive economic and cultural march into San Francisco and across the rest of California.

Of the original homes of these magnates, only one stands today—James Flood's bearish, square Connecticut brownstone, now the exclusive **Pacific-Union Club** (the "P-U," in local vernacular) at 1000 California Street. The rest of the collection was demolished by the great earthquake and fire of 1906. But some of the city's finest hotels, not to mention an exquisite Protestant place of worship, have taken their place around rather formal **Huntington Park.** Huntington's central memorial status atop Nob Hill is appropriate enough, since skinflint Collis P. Huntington was the brains of the Big Four gang and his comparatively simple home once stood here.

Facing the square from the corner of California and Taylor is the charming, surprisingly unique red-brick **Huntington Hotel** and its exceptional **Big Four** bar and restaurant. The **Mark Hopkins Hotel** ("the Mark," as it's known around town) was built on the spot of Hopkins' original ornate Victorian, at 1 Nob Hill (corner of California and Mason). Take the elevator up to the **Top of the Mark,** the bar with a view that inspired the city's song, "I Left My Heart in San Francisco," and perhaps its singer, Tony Bennett, as well. Straight across the street, facing

Mason between California and Sacramento, is the famed **Fairmont Hotel,** an architectural extravaganza built "atop Nob Hill" by James Fair's daughter Tessie (the lobby recognizable to American TV addicts as the one in the short-lived series *Hotel*). Inside, the Tiki-inspired Tonga Room is straight out of *Hawaii Five-O*. Kick back, enjoy a frozen cocktail, and soak in the strange ambience. Simulated rainstorms interrupt the tropical calm every half hour.

The **Stanford Court Hotel** at California and Powell, one of the world's finest, occupies the land where Leland Stanford's mansion once stood. For an artistic rendering of local nabobery, stop for a peek at the Stanford's lobby murals.

The Bohemian Club on the corner of Taylor and Post is a social club started by some of California's true bohemians, from Jack London, Joaquin Miller, and John Muir to Ambrose Bierce, Ina Coolbrith, and George Sterling. Though for old-time's sake some artists are invited to join, these days this very exclusive all-male club has a rank and file composed primarily of businessmen, financiers, and politicians. In July each year, these modern American bohemians retreat to the Russian River and their equally private Bohemian Grove all-male enclave for a week of fun and frolic.

Nob Hill's Invention
and the Cable Car Barn

Not just material wealth and spiritual high spirits are flaunted atop Nob Hill. Technical innovation is, too, and quite rightly, since this is where Andrew Hallidie launched the inaugural run of his famous cable cars, down Clay Street. A free stop at the **Cable Car Barn,** 1201 Mason (at Washington), tel. (415) 474-1887, open daily 10 a.m.-5 p.m. (until 6 p.m. during the summer), tells the story. No temple to tourist somnambulism, this is powerhouse central for the entire cable car system, energized solely by the kinetic energy of the cables. Electric motors turn the giant sheaves (pulleys) to whip the (underground) looped steel cables around town and power the cars. The idea is at once complex and simple. Feeding cable around corners is a bit tricky; to see how it works, hike down to a basement window and observe. But the "drive" mechanism is straightforward. Each cable car has two operators, someone working the grip, the other the brake. To "power up," heading uphill, the car's "grip" slides through the slot in the street to grab onto the cable, and the cable does the rest. Heading downhill, resisting gravity, the brake gets quite a workout. Also here: a display of historic cable cars and a gift shop.

HOBNOBBING WITH SPIRIT: GRACE CATHEDRAL

At the former site of Charles Crocker's mansion is Grace Cathedral, facing Huntington Park from Taylor St., an explosion of medieval Gothic enthusiasm inspired by the Notre Dame in Paris. Since the lot *was* cleared for construction by a very California earthquake, Grace Cathedral is built not of carefully crafted stone but steel-reinforced concrete.

Most famous here, architecturally, are the cathedral doors, cast from Lorenzo Ghiberti's Gates of Paradise from the Cathedral Baptistry in Florence, Italy. The glowing rose window is circa 1970 and comes from Chartres. Also from Chartres: Grace Cathedral's spiritual **Labyrinth,** a roll-up replica of an archetypal meditative journey in the Christian tradition. Since Grace is a "house of prayer for all people," anyone can walk the Labyrinth's three-fold path, just part of the cathedral's multifaceted **Veriditas** program. The Labyrinth is open to the public during church hours weekdays and Sunday 7 a.m.-

6 p.m., Saturday 8 a.m.-6 p.m. Music is another major attraction at Grace Cathedral, from the choral evensongs to pipe organ, carillon, and chamber music concerts. Mother church for California's Episcopal Diocese, Grace Cathedral hosts endless unusual events, including St. Francis Day in October, which honors St. Francis of Assisi—the city's patron saint—and the interconnectedness of all creation. At this celebration, all God's creatures, large and small—from elephants and police horses to dressed-up housepets, not to mention the women walking on stilts—show up to be blessed. For more information about Grace Cathedral's current calendar of odd and exhilarating events, call (415) 749-6300. And while you're in the neighborhood, take a peek into the modern **California Masonic Memorial Temple** at 1111 California, with its tiny scale model of King Solomon's Temple and colorful mosaic monument to Freemasonry.

CHINATOWN

The best time to explore Chinatown is at the crack of dawn, when crowded neighborhoods and narrow alleys explode into hustle and bustle, and when the scents, sounds, and sometimes surreal colors compete with the energy of sunrise. Due to the realities of gold rush-era life and, later, the Chinese Exclusion Act of 1882, this very American variation on a Cantonese market town was for too long an isolated, almost all-male frontier enclave with the predictable vices—a trend reversed only in the 1960s, when more relaxed immigration laws allowed the possibility of families and children. The ambitious and the educated have already moved on to the suburbs, so Chinatown today—outside of Harlem in New York, the country's most densely populated neighborhood—is home to the elderly poor and immigrants who can't speak English. It's still the largest community of Chinese anywhere outside China. And it's still a cultural and spiritual home for the Bay Area's expanding Chinese community. Even those who have left come back, if only for a great meal and a Chinese-language movie.

To get oriented, keep in mind that Stockton St. is the main thoroughfare. Grant Avenue, however, is where most tourists start, perhaps enticed away from Grant's endless upscale shops and galleries by the somewhat garish green-tiled Chinatown Gate at Bush, a 1969 gift from the Republic of China. As you wander north, notice the street-sign calligraphy, the red-painted, dragon-wrapped lampposts, and the increasingly unusual roofscapes. Grant goes the distance between Market St. and modern-day Pier 39. This happens to be San Francisco's oldest street and was little more than a rutted path in 1834, when it was dubbed Calle de la Fundación (Foundation St. or "street of the founding") by the ragtag residents of the Yerba Buena pueblo. By the mid-19th century, the street's name had been changed to Dupont, in honor of an American admiral—a change that also recognized the abrupt changing of California's political guard. But by the end of the 1800s, "Du Pon Gai" had become so synonymous with unsavory activities that downtown merchants decided on another name change, this time borrowing a bit of prestige from Ulysses S. Grant, the nation's 18th president and the Civil War's conquering general. Despite the color on Grant, the in-between streets (Sacramento, Clay, Washington, Jackson, and Pacific) and the fascinating interconnecting alleys between them represent the heart of Chinatown.

Since traffic is horrendous, parking all but impossible, and many streets almost too narrow to navigate even sans vehicle, walking is the best way to see the sights. If you haven't time to wander aimlessly, taking a guided tour is the best way to get to know the neighborhood.

The Chinatown Gate was a gift from the Republic of China.

AISLINN RACE

Seeing and Doing Chinatown

At the corner of Grant and California is **Old Saint Mary's Cathedral,** the city's Catholic cathedral from the early 1850s to 1891, still standing even after a gutting by fire in 1906. On Saint Mary's clock tower is sound maternal advice for any age: "Son, Observe the time and fly from evil." (Saint Mary has a square, too, a restful stop just east and south of California St., where there's a Bufano sculpture of Dr. Sun Yat-sen, the Republic of China's founder.) Also at the Grant/California intersection is the **Ma-Tsu Temple of the United States of America,** with shrines to Buddha and other popular deities.

Packed with restaurants and tourist shops, Grant Ave. between California and Broadway is always bustling. Of particular interest is the unusual and aptly named **Li Po Bar** at 916 Grant, a former opium den and watering hole honoring the memory of China's notoriously romantic poet, a wine-loving warrior who drowned while embracing the moon—a moon mirage, as it turned out, reflected up from a river.

The **Chinese Historical Society of America,** 644 Broadway (between Stockton and Grant), Ste. 402, tel. (415) 391-1188, is the nation's only museum specifically dedicated to preserving Chinese-American history. Chinese contributions to California culture are particularly emphasized. Some unusual artifacts in the museum's huge collection: gold-rush paraphernalia, including a "tiger fork" from Weaverville's tong war, and an old handwritten copy of Chinatown's phone book. Open Monday 1-4 p.m., Tues.-Fri. 10:30 a.m.-4 p.m.; closed weekends and major holidays. Admission is free, but donations are appreciated.

The **Pacific Heritage Museum,** 608 Commercial (between Montgomery and Kearny, Sacramento and Clay), tel. (415) 399-1124, is housed in the city's renovated brick 1875 U.S. Mint building. The museum features free rotating exhibits of Asian art and other treasures; open Tues.-Sat. 10 a.m.-4 p.m. To place it all in the larger context of California's Wild West history, head around the corner to the **Wells Fargo History Museum,** 420 Montgomery, tel. (415) 396-2619.

Portsmouth Square—people still say "square," though technically it's been a plaza since the 1920s—on Kearny between Clay and Washington is Chinatown's backyard. Here you'll get an astounding look at everyday local life, from the city's omnipresent panhandlers to early-morning tai chi to all-male afternoons of checkers, *go,* and gossip—life's lasting entertainments for Chinatown's aging bachelors. Across Kearny on the third floor of the Financial District Holiday Inn is the **Chinese Culture Center,** 750 Kearny (between Clay and Washington), tel. (415) 986-1822, which has a small gallery and gift shop but otherwise caters mostly to meeting the needs of the local community.

The further actions and attractions of Chinatown's heart are increasingly subtle, from the Washington St. herb and herbalist shops to Ross Alley's garment factories and its fortune cookie company, where you can buy some instant fortune, fresh off the press—keeping in mind, of course, that fortune cookies are an all-American invention. Intriguing, at 743 Washington, is the oldest Asian-style building in the neighborhood, the three-tiered 1909 "temple" once home to the Chinatown Telephone Exchange, now the **Bank of Canton.** But even **Bank of America,** at 701 Grant, is dressed in keeping with its cultural surroundings, with benevolent gold dragons on its columns and doors, and some 60 dragons on its facade. Also putting on the dog is **Citibank** at 845 Grant, guarded by grimacing temple dogs.

Both Jackson and Washington Streets are best bets for finding small and authentic neighborhood restaurants. **Stockton Street,** especially between Broadway and Sacramento and especially on a Saturday afternoon, is where Chinatown shops. Between Sacramento and Washington, **Waverly Place** is referred to as the "street of painted balconies," for fairly obvious reasons. There are three temples here, open to respectful visitors (donations appreciated, picture-taking usually not). **Norras Temple** at 109 Waverly is affiliated with the Buddhist Association of America, lion dancing and all, while the fourth-floor **Tien Hau Temple** at 123 Waverly primarily honors the Queen of Heaven, she who protects sojourners and seafarers as well as writers, actors, and prostitutes. The **Jeng Sen Buddhism and Taoism Association,** 146 Waverly, perhaps offers the best general introduction to Chinese religious tolerance, with a brief printed explanation (in English) of both belief systems.

For a delightfully detailed and intimate self-guided tour through the neighborhood, bring along a copy of Shirley Fong-Torres's *San Francisco Chinatown: A Walking Tour,* which includes some rarely recognized sights, such as the **Cameron House,** 920 Sacramento, a youth center named in honor of Donaldina Cameron (1869-1968), who helped young Chinese slave girls escape poverty and prostitution. Fong-Torres's marvelous and readable guide to San Francisco's Chinese community also covers history, cultural beliefs, festivals, religion and philosophy, herbal medicine (doctors and pharmacists are now licensed for these traditional practices by the state of California), and Chinese tea. It includes a very good introduction to Chinese food—from ingredients, cookware, and techniques to menus and restaurant recommendations.

Shopping Chinatown

To a greater extent than, say, Oakland's Chinatown, most shops here are aware of—and cater to—the tourist trade. But once you have some idea what you're looking for, bargains are available. Along Grant Ave., a definite must for gourmet cooks and other kitchen habitués is the **Wok Shop,** 718 Grant (between Sacramento and Clay), tel. (415) 989-3797, the specialized one-stop shopping trip for anything essential to Chinese cooking (and other types of cooking as well). The **Ten Ren Tea Company,** 949 Grant (at Jackson), tel. (415) 362-0656 or toll-free (800) 543-2885, features more than 50 varieties of teas, the prices dependent on quality and (for blends) content. There's a private area in back where you can arrange for instruction in the fine art of a proper tea ceremony. (Notice, on the wall, a photo of former president George Bush, who didn't quite get it right when he tried it.) For unusual gifts, silk shirts, high-quality linens and such, **Far East Fashions,** 953 Grant, tel. (415) 362-0986 or (415) 362-8171, is a good choice.

Finally, musicians and nonmusicians alike shouldn't miss Clara Hsu's **Clarion Music Center,** 816 Sacramento St. (at Waverly Place), tel. (415) 391-1317 or toll-free (888) 343-5374, a treasure trove full of African drums, Chinese gongs, Tibetan singing bowls, Indian sitars, Native American flutes, Bolivian panpipes, Australian didjeridoos, and other exotic instruments from every corner of the world. The store also offers lessons, workshops, and concerts to promote awareness of world musical culture. Open Mon.-Fri. 11 a.m.-6 p.m., Saturday 9 a.m.-5 p.m.

NORTH BEACH AND VICINITY

For one thing, there isn't any beach in North Beach. In the 1870s, the arm of San Francisco Bay that gave the neighborhood its name was filled in, creating more land for the growing city. And though beatniks and bohemians once brought a measure of fame to this Italian-American quarter of the city, they're all gone now, priced out of the neighborhood.

Nowadays, North Beach is almost choking on its abundance—of eateries, coffeehouses, tourist traps, and shops. Forget trying to find a parking place; public transit is the best way to get around.

Adding to neighborhood stresses and strains—

NORTH BEACH BOHEMIA

Quite a number of American poets and writers grubbed out some kind of start in North Beach: Gregory Corso, Lawrence Ferlinghetti, Allen Ginsberg, Bob Kaufman, Jack Kerouac, Gary Snyder, Kenneth Rexroth. By the 1940s, North Beach as "New Bohemia" was a local reality. It became a long-running national myth.

Otherwise sound-asleep America of the 1950s secretly loved the idea of the alienated, manic "beat generation," a phrase coined by Jack Kerouac in *On the Road.* The Beats seemed to be everything no one else was allowed to be—mostly, free. Free to drink coffee or cheap wine and talk all day; free to indulge in art, music, poetry, prose, and more sensual thrills just about any time; free to be angry and scruffy and lost in the forbidden fog of marijuana while bopping along to be-bop. But Allen Ginsberg's raging *Howl and Other Poems,* published by Ferlinghetti and City Lights, brought the wolf of censorship—an ungrateful growl that began with the seizure of inbound books by U.S. Customs and got louder when city police filed obscenity charges. The national notoriety of an extended trial, and Ginsberg's ultimate literary acquittal, brought busloads of Gray Line tourists. And the Beats moved on, though some of the cultural institutions they founded are still going strong.

and to the high costs of surviving—is the influx of Asian business and the monumental increase in Hong Kong-money property investment, both marching into North Beach from Chinatown. Old and new neighborhood residents tend to ignore each other as much as possible, in that great American melting-pot tradition. (Before the Italians called North Beach their home turf, the Irish did. And before the Irish lived here, Chileans did. In all fairness, Fisherman's Wharf was Chinese before the Italians moved in. And of course Native Americans inhabited the entire state before the Spanish, the Mexicans, the Russians, and the Americans.) Like the city itself, life here makes for a fascinating sociology experiment.

What with territorial incursions from Chinatown, the historical boundaries of North Beach increasingly clash with the actual. Basically, the entire valley between Russian Hill and Telegraph Hill is properly considered North Beach. The northern boundary stopped just short of Fisherman's Wharf, now pushed back by rampant commercial development, and Broadway was the southern boundary—a thoroughfare and area sometimes referred to as the "Marco Polo Zone" because it once represented the official end of Chinatown and the beginning of San Francisco's Little Italy. The neighborhood's spine is diagonally running Columbus Ave., which begins at the Transamerica Pyramid at the edge of the Financial District and ends at The Cannery near Fisherman's Wharf. Columbus Avenue between Filbert and Broadway is the still-beating Italian heart of modern North Beach.

Seeing and Doing North Beach

Piazzalike **Washington Square,** between Powell and Stockton, Union and Filbert, is the centerpiece of North Beach, though, as the late *San Francisco Chronicle* columnist Herb Caen once pointed out, it "isn't on Washington St., isn't a square (it's five-sided) and doesn't contain a statue of Washington but of Benjamin Franklin." (In terms of cultural consistency, this also explains the statue of Robert Louis Stevenson in Chinatown's Portsmouth Square.) There's a time capsule beneath old Ben; when the original treasures (mostly temperance tracts on the evils of alcohol) were unearthed in 1979, they were replaced with 20th-century cultural values, including a bottle of wine, a pair of Levi's, and a poem by Lawrence Fer-

linghetti. In keeping with more modern times, Washington Square also features a statue dedicated to the city's firemen, yet another contribution by eccentric little old Lillie Hitchcock Coit. **Saints Peter and Paul Catholic Church** fronts the square at 666 Filbert, its twin towers lighting up the whole neighborhood come nightfall. Noted for its rococo interior and accompanying graphic statuary of injured saints and souls burning in hell, the Saints also offers daily mass in Italian and (on Sunday) in Chinese.

Two blocks northeast of Washington Square is the **North Beach Playground,** where boccie ball is still the neighborhood game of choice, just as October's **Columbus Day Parade** and accompanying festivities still make the biggest North Beach party. Just two blocks west of the square are the stairs leading to the top of **Telegraph Hill,** identifiable by **Coit Tower,** Lillie Coit's most heartfelt memorial to the firefighters. (More on that below.)

For an overview of the area's history, stop by the free **North Beach Museum,** 1435 Stockton St. (near Green, on the mezzanine of Bayview Bank), tel. (415) 626-7070, open Mon.-Thurs. 9 a.m.-5 p.m. and Friday until 6 p.m., which displays a great collection of old North Beach photos and artifacts in occasionally changing exhibits.

The North Beach "experience" is the neighborhood itself—the coffeehouses, the restaurants, the intriguing and odd little shops. No visit is complete without a stop at Lawrence Ferlinghetti's **City Lights Bookstore,** 261 Columbus (between Broadway and Pacific), tel. (415) 362-8193, on the neighborhood's most literary alley. City Lights is the nation's first all-paperback bookstore and a rambling ode to the best of the small presses; its poetry and other literary programs still feed the souls of those who need more nourishment than what commercial bestsellers can offer. A superb small museum, **Lyle Tuttle's Tattoo Museum and Shop,** is a few blocks up the way at 841 Columbus, tel. (415) 775-4991.

You can shop till you drop in this part of town. And much of what you'll find has something to do with food. For Italian ceramics, **Biordi Italian Imports,** 412 Columbus (near Vallejo), tel. (415) 392-8096, has a fabulous selection of art intended for the table (but almost too beautiful to use). For a price—and just about everything is pricey—the folks here will ship your treasures, too.

While you're wandering, you can easily put together a picnic for a timeout in Washington Square. Italian delicatessen and meat market **Prudente & Company,** 1460 Grant (at Union), tel. (415) 421-0757, is the place to stop for traditionally cured pancetta and prosciutto. Head to landmark **Molinari's,** 373 Columbus (between Broadway and Green), tel. (415) 421-2337, for cheeses, sausages, and savory salads, or to the Italian and French **Victoria Pastry Co.,** 1362 Stockton St. (at Vallejo), tel. (415) 781-2015, for cookies, cakes, and unbelievable pastries. Other good bakery stops nearby include **Liguria Bakery,** 1700 Stockton (at Filbert), tel. (415) 421-3786, famous for its focaccia, and the **Italian French Baking Co. of San Francisco,** 1501 Grant (at Union), tel. (415) 421-3796, known for its French bread. If you didn't load up on reading material at City Lights—for after you stuff yourself but before falling asleep in the square—stop by **Cavalli Italian Book Store,** 1441 Stockton (between Vallejo and Green), tel. (415) 421-4219, for Italian newspapers, magazines, and books.

North Beach Hangouts

Caffe Greco, 423 Columbus (between Vallejo and Green), tel. (415) 397-6261, is the best of the neighborhood's newish coffeehouses. But for that classic beatnik bonhomie, head to what was once the heart of New Bohemia, the surviving **Caffe Trieste,** 601 Vallejo (at Grant), tel. (415) 392-6739. Drop by anytime for opera and Italian folk songs on the jukebox, or come on Saturday afternoon for jazz, opera, or other concerts. Also-been-there-forever **Vesuvio Cafe,** 255 Columbus Ave. (at Broadway), tel. (415) 362-3370, across Kerouac Alley from the City Lights bookstore (look for the mural with volcanoes and peace symbols), is most appreciated for its upstairs balcony section, historically a magnet for working and wannabe writers (and everyone else, too). It was a favorite haunt of Ginsberg and Kerouac, as well as an in-town favorite for Welsh poet Dylan Thomas. And Francis Ford Coppola reportedly sat down at a back table to work on *The Godfather.* A painting depicts *Homo beatnikus,* and there's even an advertisement for a do-it-yourself beatnik makeover (kit including sunglasses, a black beret, and poem).

Another righteous place to hide is **Tosca,** 242 Columbus (between Broadway and Pacific), tel.

(415) 391-1244, a late-night landmark with gaudy walls and comfortable Naugahyde booths where the hissing of the espresso machine competes with Puccini on the jukebox. Writers of all varieties still migrate here, sometimes to play pool in back. But you must behave yourself: Bob Dylan and Allen Ginsberg got thrown out of here for being unruly. **Cafe Malvina,** 1600 Stockton (at Union), tel. (415) 391-1290, is a good bet, too, especially for early-morning pastries with your coffee.

Serious social history students should also peek into the **Condor Cafe,** Columbus (at Broadway), tel. (415) 781-8222, the one-time Condor Club made famous by stripper Carol Doda and her silicone-enhanced mammaries, and now a run-of-the-mill sports bar. Still, the place offers a memory of the neighborhood's sleazier heyday. Other neighborhood perversion palaces, survivors of the same peep-show mentality, are becoming fewer and farther between, and in any event aren't really all that interesting.

Telegraph Hill and Coit Tower

The best way to get to Telegraph Hill—whether just for the view, to appreciate the city's hanging gardens, or to visit Coit Tower—is to climb the hill yourself, starting up the very steep stairs at Kearny and Filbert or ascending more gradually from the east, via either the Greenwich or Filbert steps. Following Telegraph Hill Blvd. as it winds its way from Lombard, from the west, is troublesome for drivers. Parking up top is scarce; especially on weekends you might sit for hours while you wait—just to park, mind you. A reasonable alternative is taking the #39-Coit bus.

Lillie Hitchcock Coit had a fetish for firemen. As a child, she was saved from a fire that claimed two of her playmates. As a teenager, she spent much of her time with members of San Francisco's all-volunteer Knickerbocker Engine Company No. 5, usually tagging along on fire calls and eventually becoming the team's official mascot; she was even allowed to play poker and smoke cigars with the boys. Started in 1929, financed by a Coit bequest, and completed in 1933, Coit Tower was to be a lasting memorial to the firemen. Some people say its shape resembles the nozzle of a firehose, others suggest more sexual symbolism, but the official story is that the design by Arthur Brown was intended to look "equally artistic" from any direction. Coit

COIT TOWER'S REVOLUTIONARY ART

Aside from its architectural oddity, another reason to visit Coit Tower is to appreciate the marvelous Depression-era Social Realist interior mural art in the lobby, recently restored and as striking as ever. (At

AISLINN RACE

Whatever its symbolism, Coit Tower offers great views and houses a striking collection of Depression-era frescoes.

last report, seven of the 27 total frescoes, those on the second floor and along the narrow stairway, weren't available for general public viewing, since quarters are so close that scrapes from handbags and shoes are almost inevitable. You can see these murals on the Saturday guided tour.) Even in liberal San Francisco, many of these murals have been controversial, depicting as they do the drudgery, sometimes despair, behind the idyllic facade of modern California life—particularly as seen in the lives of the state's agricultural and industrial workforce. Financed through Franklin Roosevelt's New Deal-era Public Works Art Project, some 25 local artists set out in 1934 to paint Coit Tower's interior with frescoes, the same year that Diego Rivera's revolutionary renderings of Lenin and other un-American icons created such a scandal at New York's Rockefeller Center that the great Mexican painter's work was destroyed.

In tandem with tensions produced by a serious local dock worker's strike, some in San Francisco almost exploded when it was discovered that the new art in Coit Tower wasn't entirely politically benign, that some of it suggested something less than total support for pro-capitalist ideology. In various scenes, one person is carrying *Das Kapital* by Karl Marx, and another is reading a copy of the Communist-party *Daily Worker;* grim-faced "militant unemployed" march forward into the future; women wash clothes by hand within sight of Shasta Dam; slogans oppose both hunger and fascism; and a chauffeured limousine is clearly contrasted with a Model T Ford in Steinbeck's Joad-family style. Even a hammer and sickle made it onto the walls. Unlike New York, even after an outraged vigilante committee threatened to chisel away Coit Tower's artistic offenses, San Francisco ultimately allowed it all to stay—everything, that is, except the hammer and sickle.

Tower was closed to the public for many years, due to damage caused by vandalism and water leakage. After a major interior renovation, the tower is now open in all its original glory, so come decide for yourself what the tower symbolizes. Or just come for the view. From atop the 180-foot tower, which gets extra lift from its site on top of Telegraph Hill, you get a magnificent 360-degree view of the entire Bay Area.

Coin-op telescopes allow you to get an even closer look. Coit Tower, tel. (415) 362-0808, is open daily 10 a.m.-5 p.m., until 9 p.m. in summer. Admission is free, technically, but there is a charge for the elevator ride to the top: $3.75 adults, $2.50 seniors, $1.50 children ages 6-12.

Another Telegraph Hill delight: the intimate gardens along the eastern steps. The **Filbert Steps** stairway gardens are lines with trees, ivy, and garden flowers, with a few terraces and benches nearby. Below Montgomery St., the Filbert stairway becomes a bit doddering—unpainted tired wood that leads to enchanting Napier Ln., one of San Francisco's last wooden-plank streets and a Victorian survivor of the city's 1906 devastation. (Below Napier, the stairway continues on to Sansome Street.) The brick-paved **Greenwich Steps** wander down to the cliff-hanging Julius' Castle restaurant, then continue down to the right, appearing to be private stairs to the side yard, weaving past flower gardens and old houses to reach Sansome. If you go up one way, be sure to come down the other.

Russian Hill

Also one of San Francisco's rarer pleasures is a stroll around Russian Hill, named for the belief that Russian sea otter hunters picked this place to bury their dead. One of the city's early bohemian neighborhoods and a preferred haunt for writers and other connoisseurs of quiet beauty, Russian Hill today is an enclave of the wealthy. But anyone can wander the neighborhood. If you come from North Beach, head up—it's definitely up—Vallejo St., where the sidewalks and the street eventually give way to stairs. Take a break at **Ina Coolbrith Park** at Taylor, named in honor of California's first poet laureate, a woman remarkable for many accomplishments. A member of one of Jim Beckwourth's westward wagon trains, she was the first American child to enter California by wagon. After an unhappy marriage, Coolbrith came to San Francisco, where she wrote poetry and created California's early literary circle. Many men fell in love with her, the ranks of the hopelessly smitten including Ambrose Bierce, Bret Harte, and Mark Twain. (She refused to marry any of them.) Librarian for both the Bohemian Club and the Oakland Free Library, at the latter Coolbrith took 12-year-old Jack London under her wing; her tutelage and reading suggestions were London's only formal education. Up past the confusion of lanes at Russian Hill's first summit is **Florence Street,** which heads south, and still more stairs, these leading down to Broadway (the original Broadway, which shows why the city eventually burrowed a new Broadway under the hill). Coolbrith's last home on Russian Hill still stands at 1067 Broadway.

To see the second summit—technically the park at Greenwich and Hyde—and some of the reasons why TV and movie chase scenes are frequently filmed here, wander west and climb aboard the Hyde-Powell cable car. Worth exploration on the way up: Green St., Macondray Ln. just north of Jones (which eventually takes you down to Taylor Street), and **Filbert Street,** San Francisco's steepest driveable hill, a 31.5-degree grade. (To test that thesis yourself, go very slowly.) Just over the summit, as you stare straight toward Fisherman's Wharf, is another wonder of road engineering: the one-block stretch of Lombard St. between Hyde and Leavenworth, known as the **Crookedest Street in the World.** People do drive down this snake-shaped cobblestone path, a major tourist draw, but it's much more pleasant as a walk.

DELIGHTS AND DIVERSIONS

WALKING TOURS

San Francisco is a walking city par excellence. With enough time and inclination, exploring the hills, stairways, and odd little neighborhood nooks and crannies is the most rewarding way to get to know one's way around. Helpful for getting started are the free neighborhood walking-tour pamphlets (Pacific Heights, Union Square, Chinatown, Fisherman's Wharf, the Barbary Coast Trail, and more) available at the Convention & Visitors Bureau Information Center downstairs at Hallidie Plaza (Powell and Market Streets), tel. (415) 391-2000.

Even with substantially less time, there are excellent options. A variety of local nonprofit organizations offer free or low-cost walking tours. Commercial tours—many unusual—are also available, most ranging in price from $15 to $40 per person, more for all-day tours.

Free and Inexpensive Walking Tours

Gold-rush-era San Francisco is the theme behind the city's **Barbary Coast Trail,** a four-mile self-guided walking tour from Mission St. to Aquatic Park, marked by 150 bronze plaques embedded in the sidewalk along the way. Among the 20 historic sites en route are the oldest Asian temple in North America, the western terminus of the Pony Express, and the Hyde Street historic ships. Two different guides to the trail are sold at the Hallidie Plaza visitor information center (Powell and Market).

The **City Guides** walking tours offered by Friends of the San Francisco Public Library, headquartered at the main San Francisco Public Library (Larkin and Grove), include many worthwhile neighborhood prowls. Call (415) 557-4266 for a recorded schedule of upcoming walks (what, where, and when) or try www.walking-tours.com/CityGuides. Most walks include local architecture, culture, and history, though the emphasis—Art Deco Marina, Pacific Heights Mansions, Cityscapes and Roof Mansions, the Gold Rush City, Victorian San Francisco, Haight-Ashbury, Mission Murals, Japantown—can be surprising.

City Guides are free, but donations are definitely appreciated.

Pacific Heights Walks are sponsored by the **Foundation for San Francisco's Architectural Heritage,** headquartered in the historic Haas-Lilienthal House at 2007 Franklin St. (between Washington and Jackson), tel. (415) 441-3000 (office) or (415) 441-3004 (recorded information), and offer a look at the exteriors of splendid pre-World War I mansions in eastern Pacific Heights.

Friends of Recreation and Parks, headquartered at McLaren Lodge in Golden Gate Park, Stanyan and Fell Streets, tel. (415) 263-0991 (for upcoming hike schedule), offers guided flora, fauna, and history walks through the park May-Oct., Saturday at 11 a.m. and Sunday at 11 a.m. and 2 p.m. Group tours are also available.

Precita Eyes Mural Arts Center, at 2981 24th St. (at Harrison), tel. (415) 285-2287, www.precitaeyes.org, offers fascinating two-hour mural walks through the Mission District on Saturday starting at 11 a.m. and 1:30 p.m., and Sunday at 1:30 p.m. Admission is $7 adults, $4 seniors, $1 youths 18 and under. Call for information on the center's many other tours. In addition to its self-guided Mission murals tour, the **Mexican Museum** at Fort Mason, tel. (415) 441-0404 (recorded) or (415) 202-9700, sponsors docent-led tours of San Francisco's Diego Rivera murals. The **Chinese Culture Center,** 750 Kearny (between Clay and Washington), tel. (415) 986-1822, offers both a culinary and a cultural heritage walking tour of Chinatown. (See Useful Information below for more about this organization).

The San Francisco Symphony Volunteer Council, San Francisco Opera Guild, and San Francisco Ballet Auxiliary combine their services to offer a walking tour of the three **San Francisco Performing Arts Center** facilities: Davies Symphony Hall, the War Memorial Opera House, and Herbst Theatre. The tour takes about an hour and 15 minutes; costs $5 adults, $3 seniors/students; and is offered every Monday, hourly from 10 a.m. to 2 p.m. Purchase your ticket at the Davies Symphony Hall box office (main foyer) 10 minutes before tour time. For more information, call (415) 552-8338.

Commercial Walking Tours

Helen's Walk Tours, P.O. Box 9164, Berkeley, CA 94709, tel. (510) 524-4544, offers entertaining walking tours, with a personal touch provided by personable Helen Rendon, tour guide and part-time actress. Tour groups usually meet "under the clock" at the St. Francis Hotel (Helen's the one with the wonderfully dramatic hat) before setting off on an entertaining two-hour tour of Victorian Mansions, North Beach (want to know where Marilyn Monroe married Joe DiMaggio?), or Chinatown. Other options: combine parts of two tours into a half-day Grand Tour, or, if enough time and interested people are available, request other neighborhood tours. Make reservations for any tour at least one day in advance.

Dashiell Hammett Literary Tours, tel. (510) 287-9540, are led by Don Herron, author of *The Literary World of San Francisco and its Environs.* The half-day tours wander through downtown streets and alleys, on the trail of both the writer and his detective story hero, Sam Spade. They're usually offered May-Aug., and other literary themes can be arranged. Shelley Campbell's **Footnotes Literary Walk,** tel. (415) 381-0713 or (415) 721-1763 (recorded), takes guests on a stroll through North Beach, past the former haunts of great writers.

Roger's Custom Tours, tel. (650) 742-9611, offers unusual adventures and custom tours of San Francisco tailored to your specifications. German spoken.

The personable Jay Gifford leads a **Victorian Home Walk Tour** (including a scenic bus trolley ride) through Cow Hollow and Pacific Heights, exploring distinctive Queen Anne, Edwardian, and Italianate architecture in the neighborhoods. You'll see the interior of a Queen Anne and the locations used for *Mrs. Doubtfire* and *Party of Five.* While also enjoying spectacular views of the city, bay, and gardens, you'll learn to differentiate architectural styles. Tours meet at 11 a.m. daily in the lobby of the St. Francis Hotel on Union Square and last about two and a half hours. For reservations and information, call (415) 252-9485 or visit www.victorianwalk.com.

Cruisin' the Castro, historical tours of San Francisco's gay mecca, tel. (415) 550-8110, www.webcastro.com/castrotour, are led by local historian Trevor Hailey and offer unique insight into how San Francisco's gay community has shaped the city's political, social, and cultural development. Everyone is welcome; reservations are required. Tours are offered Tues.-Sat., starting at 10 a.m. at Harvey Milk Plaza, continuing through the community's galleries, shops, and cultural sights, then ending at the Names Project (original home of the AIDS Memorial Quilt) around 2 p.m. Brunch included.

San Francisco's coffeehouse culture is the focus of **Javawalk,** tel. (415) 673-9255, www.javawalk.com, a stroll through North Beach haunts starting at 334 Grant Ave., Saturday at 10 a.m.

OTHER CITY TOURS

Tours by Land

Gray Line, tel. (415) 558-9400 or toll-free (800) 826-0202, www.grayline.com, is the city's largest tour operator, commandeering an impressive fleet of standard-brand buses and red, London-style double-deckers. The company offers a variety of narrated tours touching on the basics, in San Francisco proper and beyond. Unlike most other companies, Gray Line offers its city tour in multiple languages: Japanese, Korean, German, French, Italian, and Spanish. Much more personal is the **Great Pacific Tour Company,** 518 Octavia St. (at Hayes), tel. (415) 626-4499, www.greatpacifictour.com, which runs 13-passenger minivans on four different tours, including half-day city tours. **Tower Tours,** 77 Jefferson (at Pier 43^{1}/$_{2}$), tel. (415) 434-8687, is affiliated with Blue & Gold Fleet and also offers city tours; all tours leave from their office at Fisherman's Wharf. **Quality Tours,** 5003 Palmetto Ave., Pacifica, tel. (650) 994-5054, www.qualitytours.com, does a San Francisco architecture tour and a "whole enchilada" tour in a luxury seven-passenger Chevy suburban. **Three Babes and a Bus Nightclub Tours,** tel. (415) 552-CLUB, www.threebabes.com, caters to visiting night owls, who hop the bus and party at the city's hottest nightspots with the charming hostesses. Many firms create personalized, special-interest tours with reasonable advance notice; contact the Convention & Visitors Bureau for a complete listing.

Though both are better known for their ferry tours, both the Blue & Gold Fleet and the Red &

White Fleet (see below) also offer land tours to various Northern California attractions.

Tours by Sea

The **Blue & Gold Fleet** is based at Piers 39 and 41, tel. (415) 705-8200 (business office), (415) 773-1188 (recorded schedule), or (415) 705-5555 (information and advance ticket purchase), www.blueandgoldfleet.com. Blue & Gold offers a narrated year-round (weather permitting) **Golden Gate Bay Cruise** that leaves from Pier 39, passes under the Golden Gate Bridge, cruises by Sausalito and Angel Island, and loops back around Alcatraz. The trip takes about an hour. Fare: $17 adults, $13 seniors over 62 and youths 12-18, $9 children 5-11. The justifiably popular **Alcatraz Tour** takes you out to the infamous former prison (see the special topic Touring the Real Rock for more information). Fare is $12.25 adults with a self-guided audio tour, or $8.75 adults without the audio. Day-use fee on the rock is $1. (Also available is an evening "Alcatraz After Hours" tour, $19.75 adults, which includes a narrated guided tour.) Blue & Gold ferries also can take you to **Sausalito, Tiburon, Oakland, Alameda, Vallejo,** and **Angel Island.**

The **Red & White Fleet,** at Pier 43¹/2, tel. (415) 447-0597 or toll-free (800) 229-2784 (in California), www.redandwhite.com, offers one-hour, multilingual Bay Cruise tours that loop out under the Golden Gate and return past Sausal-ito, Angel Island, and Alcatraz ($17 adults, $13 seniors/youths, $9 kids 5-11, not including the $1 day-use fee). Other offerings include weekend Blues Cruises in summer; an excursion across the bay to Alameda to tour the aircraft carrier USS *Hornet;* and a variety of land tours in Northern California.

Hornblower Cruises and Events, tel. (415) 788-8866, www.hornblowercruises.com, has boats at Pier 33 and elsewhere around the bay. The company offers big-boat on-the-bay dining adventures, from extravagant nightly dinner dances and weekday lunches to Saturday and Sunday champagne brunch. Occasional special events, from whodunit murder mystery dinners to jazz cocktail cruises, can be especially fun. And Hornblower's Monte Carlo Cruises feature casual Las Vegas-style casino gaming tables (proceeds go to charity) on dinner cruises aboard the M/V *Monte Carlo.*

Oceanic Society Expeditions, based at Fort Mason, tel. (415) 474-3385, www.oceanic-society.org, offers a variety of seagoing natural history trips, including winter whalewatching excursions, usually late Dec.-April, and Farallon Islands nature trips, June-November. Reservations are required. Oceanic Society trips are multifaceted. For example, only scientific researchers and trusted volunteers are allowed on the cold granite Farallon Islands, but the Society's excursion to the islands takes you as close as most people ever get. The Farallons, 27 miles from the Golden

THE RED AND WHITE FLEET

cruising the Bay

Gate, are a national wildlife refuge within the Gulf of the Farallones National Marine Sanctuary, which itself is part of UNESCO's Central California Coast Biosphere Reserve. The nutrient-rich coastal waters around the islands are vital to the world's fisheries, to the health of sea mammal populations, and to the success of the breeding seabird colonies here. Some quarter million birds breed here, among them tufted puffins and rhinoceros auklets (bring a hat). The Oceanic Society trip to the islands takes eight hours, shoving off at 8:30 a.m. (Saturday, Sunday, and select Fridays) from Fort Mason. The 63-foot Oceanic Society boat carries 49 passengers and a naturalist. Contact the nonprofit Oceanic Society for other excursion options.

SAN FRANCISCO PERFORMING ARTS

San Francisco's performing arts scene offers everything from the classics to the contemporary, kitsch, and downright crazed. Find out what's going on by picking up local publications or calling the San Francisco Convention & Visitors Bureau information hot lines (see Useful Information, below). Tickets for major events and performances are available through the relevant box offices, mentioned below.

Low-income arts lovers, or those deciding to "do" the town on a last-minute whim, aren't necessarily out of luck. **TIX Bay Area,** on Stockton St. at Union Square, tel. (415) 433-7827, www.

POETIC AMUSEMENTS

There's probably only one thing better than reading a good poem in a quiet room by yourself. And that's listening to an impassioned poet reading a poem out loud in a small coffee-scented café full of attentive writers, lawyers, bikers, teachers, computer programmers, divinity students, musicians, secretaries, drug addicts, cooks, and assorted oddball others who all love poetry and are hanging onto every word being juggled by the poet behind the microphone. The only thing better than *that* is to read your own poems at an open-mike poetry reading.

One of the wonderful things about San Francisco and vicinity is that this kind of poetic melee takes place in some café, club, or bookstore almost every night, for those who know where to look. No one revels in the right to free speech like Bay Area denizens, and open poetry readings are as popular as stand-up comedy in many cafés and clubs, with sign-up lists at the door. Bring your own poetry, or just kick back and listen to some amazing musings.

The following suggested venues will get you started. Since schedules for local poetic license programs do change, it's prudent to call or otherwise check it out before setting out. Current open readings and other events are listed in the monthly tabloid *Poetry Flash,* P.O. Box 4172, Berkeley, CA 94704, tel. (510) 525-5476, the Bay Area's definitive poetry review and literary calendar, available free at many bookstores and cafés.

OPEN-MIKE POETRY READINGS IN SAN FRANCISCO

Café du Nord 2170 Market St., tel. (415) 861-5016, Sunday at 5 p.m.

Elbo Room, 647 Valencia (at 17th)., tel. (415) 552-7788, Friday at 9 p.m.

Paradise Lounge, 1501 Folsom St. (at 11th) tel. (415) 861-6906, Sunday at 8 p.m. (upstairs).

Keane's 3300 Club, 3300 Mission St. (at 29th), tel. (415) 826-6886, poetry readings on the second and fourth Tuesdays of each month since 1993.

IN THE EAST BAY

Diesel–A Bookstore, 5433 College (between Lawton and Hudson) in Oakland's Rockridge district, tel. (510) 653-9965, hosts fiction, nonfiction, and poetry readings three times a week.

La Val's Pizza and Subterranean Theatre, 1834 Euclid Ave. (at Hearst) in Berkeley, tel. (510) 843-5617, housed poetry readings and Free Speech Movement gatherings in the 1960s. Poetry readings Tuesdays at 7:30 p.m.

—Ed Aust

THEATER AS CIRCUS

Worth seeing whenever the group is in town is the much-loved, always arresting, and far from silent **San Francisco Mime Troupe**, 855 Treat Ave. (between 21st and 22nd), tel. (415) 285-1717, a decades-old institution true to the classic Greek and Roman tradition of theatrical farce—politically sophisticated street theater noted for its complex simplicity. In addition to boasting actor Peter Coyote and the late rock impresario Bill Graham as organizational alumni, and inspiring the establishment of one-time troupe member Luis Valdez's El Teatro Campesino, the Mime Troupe was repeatedly banned and arrested in its formative years. In 1966, the state Senate Un-American Activities Committee charged the group with the crime of making lewd performances, the same year troupe members were arrested in North Beach for singing Christmas carols without a permit. More recently, the Mime Troupe has won a Tony Award and three Obies.

A tad more family-oriented, "the kind of circus parents might want their kids to run away to," according to NPR's Jane Pauley, is the **Pickle Family Circus,** another exceptional city-based theater troupe, which performs at Fort Mason's Cowell Theatre, tel. (415) 441-3400.

Bizarre cabaret-style **"Beach Blanket Babylon,"** playing at Club Fugazi, 678 Green St. (between Powell and Columbus) in North Beach, tel. (415) 421-4222, is the longest-running musical revue in theatrical history. The story line is always evolving. Snow White, who seems to be seeking love in all the wrong places, encounters characters who strut straight off the front pages of the tabloids.

---

tix.com, offers day-of-performance tickets to local shows at half price. Payment is cash only, no credit card reservations. Along with being a full-service BASS ticket outlet, TIX also handles advance full-price tickets to many Bay Area events. Open Tues.-Sat. noon-7:30 p.m. You can get a catalog for ordering advance tickets at half price by calling **TIX by Mail** at (415) 430-1140. To charge BASS arts and entertainment tickets by phone or to listen to recorded calendar listings, call (415) 478-2277 (BASS). Another helpful information source: KUSF 90.3 FM's **Alternative Music and Entertainment News (AMEN)** information line, tel. (415) 221-2636.

Other ticket box offices include: **City Box Office,** tel. (415) 392-4400, **Entertainment Ticketfinder,** tel. (650) 756-1414 or toll-free (800) 523-1515, and **St. Francis Theatre and Sports Tickets,** a service of the Westin St. Francis Hotel, tel. (415) 362-3500, www.premiertickets.com.

STAYING IN SAN FRANCISCO

San Francisco is an expensive city, for the most part. A first-time visitor's first impression might be that no one is welcome here unless they show up in a Rolls Royce. The normal system of price categories used throughout this book isn't too useful here, either, when probably 90% of the lodgings fall into the "Luxury" category. To counterbalance this, price ranges for Luxury accommodations have been provided where possible.

Mind you, this is for the "standard" room, two persons, one bed, in peak summer season. (Many offer off-season and weekend deals; always ask about specials before booking.) Most also have higher-priced suites, and if you feel the need to drop $500 or $1,000 (or more) per night on a suite, you'll find plenty of places in town that will be more than happy to accommodate you. If you can afford these prices ("tariffs," actually), you'll not be disappointed. And some of the city's four- and five-star hotels also rank among its most historic, survivors—at least in part—of the great 1906 earthquake and fire.

That said, a little looking will uncover plenty of accommodations suitable for the rest of us. San Francisco offers two hostels affiliated with Hostelling International (American Youth Hostels), in addition to other hostels and inexpensive options. Other than the hostels, some dirt-cheap fleabags can be found, but they're often in seedy areas; budget travelers with city savvy, street smarts, and well-honed self-preservation skills might consider these establishments, but women

© AVALON TRAVEL PUBLISHING, INC.

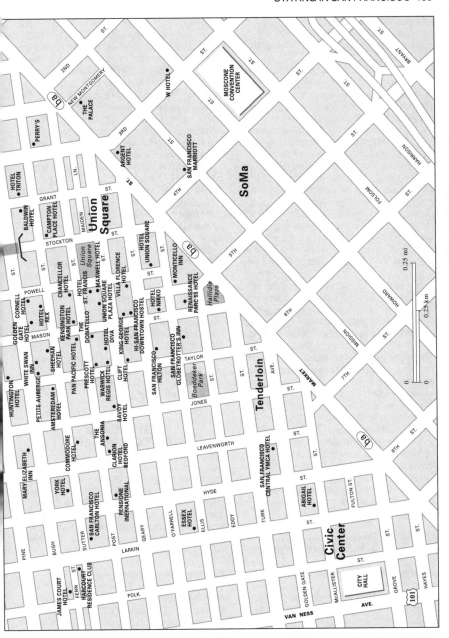

traveling solo should avoid them. (In the context of truly low-budget accommodations, "European-style" generally means "the bathrooms are in the hallway.")

City-style motels offer another world of possibilities. Some reasonably priced ones are scattered throughout the city, though Lombard St. (west of Van Ness) is the place to go for overwhelming concentrations of motel choice. The city also supports a wide variety of bed and breakfast inns, with ambiences ranging from Haight-Ashbury-style funk to very proper Victoriana.

In general, San Francisco offers great choices in the midrange hotel market, including a number of "boutique" hotels. Many of these attractive and intimate hotels—old-timers and aging grand dames now renovated and redecorated for the modern carriage trade—are well located, near visitor attractions and public transit. Lack of convenient off-street parking is rarely a drawback, since most offer some sort of valet parking arrangement. Very good to exceptional restaurants—and room service—are often associated with boutique hotels. When travel is slow, most notably in winter, off-season and package deals can make these small hotels (and others) genuine bargains. Do check around before signing in. Also check at the visitors center on Market St., since some establishments offer special coupons and other seasonal inducements. Many boutique and fine hotels also offer substantial discounts to business travelers and to members of major "travel-interested" groups, including the American Automobile Association (AAA) and the American Association of Retired People (AARP). The visitor center is located at Benjamin Swig Pavilion on the lower level of Hallidie Plaza at Market and Powell Streets. Open weekdays 9 a.m.-5:30 p.m., Saturday until 3 p.m., Sunday 10 a.m.-2 p.m. Or call (415) 391-2000. You can also call (415) 391-2001 24 hours a day for a recorded message listing daily events and activities.

Reservation Services

If you're unable to make an accommodations choice well in advance, or if you'd rather let someone else do the detail work, contact a local reservations service.

San Francisco Reservations, 22 Second St., Fourth Floor, San Francisco, CA 94105, tel. (415) 227-1500 or toll-free (800) 677-1550, offers a no-fee reservations service for more than 200

hotels, most of these in San Francisco, and keeps current on discounts, specials, and packages. The company offers preferred rates for business travelers at some of the city's finest hotels, including many of the boutiques. With one call, you can also take advantage of their free best-deal airline ticketing and car rental reservations service. Reservation lines are open daily 7 a.m.-11 p.m. If you have access to a computer, you can make reservations (three or more days in advance) through S.F. Reservations' website at www.hotelres.com.

Discount Hotel Rates/California Reservations, 165 Eighth St., Ste. 201, San Francisco, CA 94103, tel. (415) 252-1107 or toll-free (800) 576-0003, also no-fee, represents more than 200 hotels in San Francisco and beyond. Subject to room availability, the firm offers rates at quality hotels for 10-50% less than posted rates.

Bed & Breakfast California, P.O. Box 282910, San Francisco, CA 94128-2910, tel. (650) 696-1690 or toll-free (800) 872-4500, offers referrals to a wide range of California bed and breakfasts—everything from houseboat and home stays to impressive Victorians and country-style inns—especially in San Francisco, the Napa-Sonoma wine country, and the Monterey Peninsula. Rates: $70-200 per night (with two-night minimum). Similar, and often without the mandatory two-night stay, is **Bed and Breakfast San Francisco,** P.O. Box 420009, tel. (415) 899-0060 or toll-free (800) 452-8249, www.bbsf.com.

HOSTELS AND OTHER CHEAP SLEEPS

San Francisco is full of shoestring-priced hostels renting dorm-style bunks for around $12-20 per person per night. Many also have higher-priced private rooms. Some hostels are open to everybody; others, as noted below, are open only to international travelers. Most have group kitchen facilities, laundry facilities, and helpful staff to give you hot tips on seeing the city.

Hostelling International

The **San Francisco Fisherman's Wharf HI-AYH Hostel** is just west of the wharf at Fort Mason, Bldg. 240, tel. (415) 771-3645, fax (415) 771-1468, www.norcalhostels.org. It's a local institution—located on a hill overlooking the bay and occupying part of the city's urban national park, the Golden Gate National Recreation Area. Close to the "Bikecentennial" bike route and the cultural attractions of the Fort Mason complex, the hostel is within an easy stroll of Fisherman's Wharf and Ghirardelli Square, as well as Chinatown and downtown (you could take the cable car).

The hostel itself is one of HI-AYH's largest—and finest—offering a total of 160 beds in clean rooms; one chore a day expected. Popular with all age groups and families, amenities include lots of lounge space, a big kitchen, plenty of food storage, laundry facilities, and pay lockers for baggage. No lockout or curfew. Family rooms are available, as is parking, and it's wheelchair accessible. The ride board here is helpful for travelers without wheels. Guests can also participate in hostel-sponsored hikes, tours, and bike rides. Reservations are essential for groups and advisable for others—especially in summer, when this place is jumping. Rates include linen and free breakfast; 14-day maximum, no minimum stay. To reserve by mail, send one night's deposit (address above) at least three weeks in advance; by phone or fax, call at least 48 hours in advance and confirm with a major credit card (Visa, Mastercard).

Near all the downtown and theater district hubbub is the **HI-San Francisco Downtown Hostel,** 312 Mason St. (between Geary and O'Farrell), tel. (415) 788-5604, fax (415) 788-3023, www.hiayh.org, another good choice for budget travelers. This hotel-style hostel offers double and triple rooms—most share a bathroom—and amenities from kitchen to baggage storage and vending machines. Laundry facilities are nearby. The desk is essentially open for check-in 24 hours; no lockout, no curfew, no chores. Family rooms available. Groups welcome, by reservation only, and reservations for summer stays are essential for everyone and should be made at least 30 days in advance. Reserve by phone or fax with Visa or MasterCard. Rates include linens, but bring your own towel. Ask about the best nearby parking.

Other Hostels

The excellent **Green Tortoise Guest House,** 494 Broadway, tel. (415) 834-1000, fax (415) 956-4900, www.greentortoise.com, sits on the corner of Broadway and Kearny, where Chinatown runs into North Beach. It offers a kitchen,

laundry, sauna, free internet access, and complimentary breakfast. No curfew.

The **Interclub Globe Hostel,** 10 Hallam Place (south of Market near the Greyhound station, just off Folsom), tel. (415) 431-0540, is a fairly large, lively place with clean four-bed hotel rooms, a private sundeck, community lounge, pool table, café, and laundry room. The Globe is specifically for foreign guests, usually students, but these can also include Americans who present passports with stamps verifying their own international travels. Open 24 hours, no curfew. Also in the area and strictly for international travelers ("operated by students for students" and affiliated with the American Association of International Hostels) are two other SoMa budget outposts: the **European Guest House,** 761 Minna (between Eighth and Ninth Streets), tel. (415) 861-6634, and the affiliated **San Francisco International Student Center,** 1188 Folsom (near BrainWash), tel. (415) 487-1463 or (415) 255-8800, both offering dorm-style accommodations and basic amenities.

North of Market, the **San Francisco Globetrotter's Inn,** 225 Ellis St. (at Mason, one block west of Powell), tel. (415) 346-5786 (or (415) 673-4048 to reach guests), offers daily and weekly rates. In the Chinatown area, the lively **Pacific Tradewinds Guest House,** 680 Sacramento St., tel. (415) 433-7970, is in a prime spot near the Transamerica Pyramid. The hostel offers eight-bed rooms or larger dorm rooms, and rates include free tea and coffee all day, use of a fully equipped kitchen, Internet access, free maps, laundry service, fax service, long-term storage, and (I quote) "an extremely friendly, helpful, and good-looking staff." No curfew. You can make arrangements to stay through their website at www.hostels.com/pt.

A good budget bet in the Mission District is the **San Francisco International Guest House,** 2976 23rd St. (at Harrison), tel. (415) 641-1411, an uncrowded Victorian popular with Europeans. Accommodations include two- to four-bed dorm rooms, as well as four couples rooms; five day minimum stay. It's geared toward longer-term stays and usually full.

Boardinghouses

The **Mary Elizabeth Inn,** 1040 Bush (between Jones and Leavenworth), tel. (415) 673-6768, is a women's residence, part of a mission program sponsored by the United Methodist Church.

Tourists are welcome when space is available. Facilities include private rooms (shared baths) with linen service, laundry facilities, a sundeck and solarium, and two meals daily (except Sunday). Weekly rate: $155. An even better bet, though, for a longer visit in San Francisco is the **Harcourt Residence Club**, 1105 Larkin, tel. (415) 673-7720, where a stay includes two meals a day, Sunday brunch, and access to TV. Unlike most other residence hotels, this one attracts international students—a younger clientele. Weekly rates: $150-250 per person.

INEXPENSIVE HOTELS

Close to Nob Hill is the very nice **James Court Hotel**, 1353 Bush St. (between Polk and Larkin),

tel. (415) 771-2409, with European-style accommodations and basic amenities plus kitchen. Some rooms have kitchenettes and some have private baths. All have color cable TV and phone. Amenities include complimentary coffee and coin laundry.

Perhaps the epitome of San Francisco's casual, low-cost European-style stays is the **Adelaide Inn**, 5 Isadora Duncan Ct., (in the theater district, off Taylor between Geary and Post), tel. (415) 441-2261. Reservations are advisable for the 18 rooms with shared baths. Rates include continental breakfast. Inexpensive-Moderate. Also in the area, **The Ansonia**, 711 Post, tel. (415) 673-2670, is a real find. This small hotel has a friendly staff, comfortable lobby, nice rooms, a laundry, and breakfast and dinner (except on Sunday). Inexpensive-Moderate (de-

SOME HIP SAN FRANCISCO STAYS

Every city has its style, reflected in how things appear, of course, but mostly in how they feel. The following establishments offer just a sample of that inimitable San Francisco attitude.

The Phoenix Inn at 601 Eddy St. (on the corner of Eddy and Larkin at the edge of the Tenderloin), tel. (415) 776-1380 or toll-free (800) 248-9466, www .sftrips.com, is more than just a 1950s motel resurrected with flamingo pink and turquoise paint. It's a subtle see-and-be-seen art scene, first attracting rock 'n' roll stars and now attracting almost everybody—*the* place in San Francisco to spy on members of the cultural elite. This is, for example, the only place Sonic Youth ever stays in San Francisco. Just-plain-famous folks like Keanu Reeves and Ben Harper can also be spied from time to time. Like the trendy, on-site California-style restaurant, **Backflip**, even the heated swimming pool here is famous, due to its Francis Forlenza mural, "My Fifteen Minutes—Tumbling Waves," the center of a big state-sponsored stink over whether it violated health and safety codes (since public pool bottoms are supposed to be white). "That's how it is up at Eddy and Larkin, where the limos are always parkin'," according to the inn's complimentary *Phoenix Fun Book*, a cartoon-style coloring book history illustrated by *Bay Guardian* artist Lloyd Dangle. (Also as a service for guests, the Phoenix sporadically publishes its own hippest-of-the-hip guide to San Francisco, *Beyond Fisherman's Wharf*.)

Accommodations at the Phoenix—the inn named

for the city's mythic ability to rise from its own ashes, as after the 1906 earthquake—are glass-fronted, uncluttered, pool-facing '50s motel rooms upscaled to ultramodern, yet not particularly ostentatious, with handmade bamboo furniture, tropical plants, and original local art on the walls. Phoenix services include complimentary continental breakfast (room service also available), the "Phoenix Movie Channel" on in-room cable—with 15 different made-in-San Francisco movies (plus a film library with 20 "band on the road" films)—and a complete massage service, including Swedish, Esalen, Shiatsu, even poolside massage. In addition to concierge services, the Phoenix also offers blackout curtains, an on-call voice doctor (for lead vocalists with scratchy throats), and free VIP passes to SoMa's underground dance clubs. Regular rates: $89-109, and $139 for each of the three suites, including the Tour Manager Suites. Ask about deals, including the "special winter rate" for regular customers (subject to availability), with the fourth night free.

Awesomely hip, too, is the playful **Hotel Triton** on Grant, in the heart of the city's downtown gallery district. The one-time Beverly Plaza Hotel just across from the Chinatown Gateway has been reimagined and reinvented by Bill Klimpton, the man who started the boutique hotel trend in town in 1980. The Triton's artsy ambience is startling and entertaining, boldly announcing itself in the lobby with sculpted purple, teal, and gold columns, odd tassle-headed, gold brocade "dervish" chairs, and mythic Neptunian

pending upon the bathroom arrangement). Student rates for one month or longer.

MODERATE TO PREMIUM HOTELS

A budget gem in the Chinatown area, the **Obrero Hotel,** 1208 Stockton, tel. (415) 989-3960, offers just a dozen cheery bed-and-breakfast rooms with bathrooms down the hall. Full breakfast included. Inexpensive-Moderate. Another best bet is the **Grant Plaza Hotel,** 465 Grant Ave. (between Pine and Bush), tel. (415) 434-3883 or toll-free (800) 472-6899, where amenities include private baths with hair dryers, telephones with voice mail, and color TV. Group rates available. Inexpensive-Moderate. Unpretentious and reasonably priced (private bathrooms) is the **Union Square Plaza Hotel,** 432 Geary (between Powell and Mason), tel. (415) 776-7585. Expensive.

A few blocks north of the Civic Center between Hyde and Larkin, in a borderline bad neighborhood, is the justifiably popular **Essex Hotel,** 684 Ellis St., tel. (415) 474-4664 or toll-free (800) 443-7739 in California, (800) 453-7739 from elsewhere in the country. The hotel offers small rooms with private baths and telephones; some have TV. Free coffee. It's especially popular in summer—when rates are slightly higher—with foreign tourists, particularly Germans. Moderate-Expensive. Weekly rates, too.

Noteworthy for its antiques, comfort, and fresh flowers, is the small **Golden Gate Hotel,** 775 Bush St. (between Powell and Mason), tel. (415) 392-3702 or toll-free (800) 835-1118. Sixteen of the rooms have private bath; the other seven,

---

imagery on the walls. Rooms are comfortable and contemporary, with custom-designed geometric mahogany furniture, sponge-painted or diamond-patterned walls, original artwork by Chris Kidd, and unusual tilework in the bathrooms. Each guest room reflects one of three basic configurations: a king-size bed with camelback upholstered headboards, similar double beds, or oversized daybeds that double as a couch. Imaginative guest suites include the kaleidoscopic J. Garcia suite, furnished with swirls of colorful fabrics and a self-portrait of Jerry next to the bed. All rooms include soundproof windows, same-day valet/laundry service, room service, color TV with remote (also cable and movie channels), in-room fax, voice mail, and two-line phones with long cords and dataports. Basic rates: $159-179, $229-305 for deluxe rooms and suites. A nice feature of this and other Klimpton-owned hotels, too, is the fully stocked honor bar—unusual in that items are quite reasonably priced. For more information or reservations, contact: Hotel Triton, 342 Grant Ave., San Francisco, CA 94108, tel. (415) 394-0500 or toll-free (800) 433-6611, www.hotel-tritonsf.com.

Affordable style is apparent and available at other small San Francisco hotels, including Klimpton's Prescott Hotel, home to Wolfgang Puck's Postrio Restaurant. But there's nothing else in town quite like Haight-Ashbury's **Red Victorian Bed and Breakfast Inn,** a genuine blast from San Francisco's past. This 1904 survivor is red, all right, and it's a bed and breakfast—but except for the architecture, it's not very Victorian. The style is early-to-late Summer of Love. Downstairs is the Global Village Bazaar, a New Age shopper's paradise. (The Global Family also offers a coffee house, computer networking services, meditation room, and gallery of meditative art with calligraphic paintings to help you program yourself, subliminally and otherwise, with proper consciousness.) Everything is casual and cool—just two blocks from Golden Gate Park and its many attractions.

Upstairs, the Red Victorian's 18 guest rooms range from modest to decadent, with sinks in all rooms; some have private baths, others share. (If you stay in a room that shares the Aquarium Bathroom, you'll be able to answer the question: "What happens to the goldfish when you flush the toilet?") The Summer of Love Room features genuine '60s posters on the walls and a tie-dyed canopy over the bed. The Peace Room has an unusual skylight, though the Skylight Room beats the band for exotica. Or get back to nature in the Japanese Tea Garden Room, the Conservatory, or the Redwood Forest Room. Expanded continental breakfast (with granola and fresh bakery selections) and afternoon popcorn hour are included in the rates, which range from $75-120 (with specials if you stay over three days, two-night minimum on weekends). Spanish, German, and French spoken. No smoking, no pets, and leave your angst outside on the sidewalk. Well-behaved children under parental supervision are welcome. Make reservations for a summer stay well in advance. For more information, contact: The Red Victorian Bed and Breakfast Inn, 1665 Haight St., San Francisco, CA 94117, tel. (415) 864-1978, www.redvic.com.

with shared bath, are less expensive. Rates include complimentary breakfast and afternoon tea. Moderate-Expensive. **Pensione International,** 875 Post St., tel. (415) 775-3344, lies at the gentrifying edge of the Tenderloin just east of Hyde St. and offers attractive rooms with either shared or private bath. Breakfast included. Moderate-Expensive.

Located right across from the Chinatown gate just off Union Square, the bright and comfortable **Baldwin Hotel,** 321 Grant Ave. (between Sutter and Bush), tel. (415) 781-2220 or toll-free (800) 622-5394, www.baldwinhotel.com, offers comfortable, newly renovated guest rooms with TV and telephones with modem hookups. Expensive-Premium.

A relative of the Phoenix Inn, the new **Abigail Hotel,** 246 McAllister St., tel. (415) 861-9728 or toll-free (800) 243-6510, www.sftrips.com, offers spruce British-style charm and antiques, even down comforters, all just a hop, skip, and a jump from City Hall, the Civic Auditorium, and nearby arts venues. The on-site vegan restaurant, Millennium, is purportedly superb. Discounts for artists, government employees, and groups; other deals when the town slows down. Weekly and monthly rates also available. Continental breakfast included. Expensive-Premium.

Styled after a 1920s luxury liner, the **Commodore Hotel,** 825 Sutter St., tel. (415) 923-6800 or toll-free (800) 338-6848, www.sftrips.com, is a fun place to stay downtown. All of the rooms are spacious, with modern bathrooms and data ports on the phones. Downstairs, the **Titanic Café** serves California-style breakfast and lunch, and the Commodore's **Red Room** is a plush cocktail lounge decorated with rich red velvets, pearlized vinyl, and red tile. Expensive-Premium.

Nearby, and also between the theater district and Nob Hill, the newly refurbished 1909 **Amsterdam Hotel,** 749 Taylor St. (between Bush and Sutter), tel. (415) 673-3277 or toll-free (800) 637-3444, features an attractive Victorian lobby and clean, comfortable, spacious rooms, all with contemporary private bathrooms. All rooms have color cable TV, radio, and direct-dial phones. Rates include complimentary breakfast. Expensive-Premium.

Near Union Square, the **Sheehan Hotel,** 620 Sutter St. (at Mason), tel. (415) 775-6500 or toll-free (800) 848-1529 in the U.S. and Canada, is a

real find—a surprisingly elegant take on economical downtown accommodations. Rooms have cable TV and phones; some have private baths, others have European-style shared baths (these the bargains). Other facilities include an Olympic-size lap pool, a fitness and exercise room, and a downstairs tearoom and wine bar. The hotel is close to shopping, art, BART, and other public transportation. Discount parking is available. Rates include continental breakfast, and children under 12 stay free with parent(s). Moderate-Premium.

Quite charming, between Union Square and Nob Hill, is the **Cornell Hotel,** 715 Bush St. (at Powell), tel. (415) 421-3154 or toll-free (800) 232-9698, where rates include breakfast and all rooms are nonsmoking. Expensive-Premium.

BOUTIQUE HOTELS

San Francisco's bouquet of European-style boutique hotels is becoming so large that it's impossible to fit the flowers in any one container. In addition to those mentioned above, the following sampling offers an idea of the wide variety available. Most of the city's intimate and stylish small hotels are included in the annual San Francisco Convention & Visitors Bureau Lodging Guide, listed among all other accommodations options, by area, and not otherwise distinguished from more mainstream hostelries. Two clues to spotting a possible "boutique": the number of rooms (usually 75 to 150, rarely over 200) and prices in the Premium or Luxury category.

Near Union Square and Nob Hill

The 111-room **Hotel Diva,** 440 Geary (between Mason and Taylor, right across from the Curran and Geary Theaters), tel. (415) 885-0200 or toll-free (800) 553-1900, is a chrome-faced contemporary Italian classic, awarded "Best Hotel Design" honors by *Interiors* magazine. Special features include a complete business center—with computers, modems, you name it—daily newspaper, complimentary breakfast delivered to your door, meeting facilities, and a 24-hour fitness center. Monday through Friday, Diva offers complimentary limousine service to downtown. Premium-Luxury ($159-199 for standard rooms, $179-219 suites).

Cable cars roll right by the six-floor **Hotel Union Square,** 114 Powell St., tel. (415) 397-3000 or toll-free (800) 553-1900, one of the city's original boutiques, with an art deco lobby and 131 rooms decorated in a blend of contemporary California and old-brick San Francisco. Multiple amenities, including continental breakfast and on-site parking. Wonderful rooftop suites with gardens. Premium.

The one-time Elks Lodge #3 is now the 87-room **Kensington Park Hotel,** 450 Post St., tel. (415) 788-6400 or toll-free (800) 553-1900, just steps from Union Square. Its parlor lobby still sports the original handpainted Gothic ceiling and warm Queen Anne floral decor. Guests enjoy all the amenities, including financial district limo service, a fitness center, complimentary continental breakfast, and afternoon tea and sherry. Premium-Luxury ($175-205). (Inquire about hotel/theater packages, since Theatre On The Square is also located here.)

The century-old **King George Hotel,** 334 Mason (at Geary), www.kinggeorge.com, is a cozy and charming stop near Geary St. theaters and Union Square. Breakfast and afternoon tea served daily in the traditional English **Windsor Tearoom.** Ask about seasonal discounts and other specials, with rates as low as $85. Moderate-Premium.

Fairly reasonable, near the theater scene, is the cheerful and colorful **Clarion Hotel Bedford,** 761 Post St., tel. (415) 673-6040 or toll-free (800) 252-7466, a 17-story 1929 hotel featuring florals and pastels. There's a café adjacent, but don't miss the tiny mahogany-paneled Wedgwood Bar just off the lobby, decorated with china gifts from Lord Wedgwood. Luxury ($179-199). Another good choice in the vicinity is the restored art deco **Maxwell Hotel,** 386 Geary, tel. (415) 986-2000, or toll-free (888) 734-6299. Luxury (rates run $155-205, though specials can drive the price as low as $119). Also close to the theaters is the 1913 **Savoy Hotel,** 580 Geary, tel. (415) 441-2700 or toll-free (800) 227-4223, a taste of French provincial with period engravings, imported furnishings, and goose down featherbeds and pillows. Amenities include complimentary afternoon sherry and tea. Premium-Luxury ($149-229). Downstairs is the Brasserie Savoy.

Closer to Nob Hill and Chinatown is the nine-floor **Hotel Juliana,** 590 Bush St., tel. (415) 392-2540 or toll-free (800) 372-8800 in California,

(800) 328-3880 elsewhere in the United States. The 107 rooms and suites have in-room coffee makers, hair dryers, and irons and ironing boards. Other amenities include complimentary evening wine, morning limo service to the Financial District (just a few blocks away), and the on-site **Oritalia** restaurant (MediterrAsian). Premium-Luxury (singles and doubles $179, suites $235; great deals in the low season).

Also within an easy stroll of Nob Hill: the elegant art deco **York Hotel,** 940 Sutter St., tel. (415) 885-6800 or toll-free (800) 808-9675 in the U.S. and Canada, used as the setting for Alfred Hitchcock's *Vertigo.* The York offers the usual three-star comforts, including limousine service and complimentary breakfast. Expensive-Premium.

The **Villa Florence Hotel,** 225 Powell St., tel. (415) 397-7700 or toll-free (888) 501-4909 in California, (800) 553-4411 elsewhere in the U.S., www.villaflorence.com, features a 16th-century Tuscany/Italian Renaissance theme, and American-style European ambience. The colorful and comfortable guest rooms feature soundproofed walls and windows—a good idea above the cable cars and so close to Union Square—as well as in-room coffeemakers and all basic amenities. The hotel has a beauty salon and features the adjacent (and outstanding) NorCal-NorItal **Kuleto's Restaurant** and antipasto bar, tel. (415) 397-7720. Premium-Luxury ($155-215).

For an all-American historical theme, consider the **Monticello Inn,** 127 Ellis (between Powell and Cyril Magnin), tel. (415) 392-8800 or toll-free (800) 669-7777, www.monticelloinn.com. Its cool colonial-style lobby holds Chippendale reproductions and a wood-burning fireplace. Rooms feature early-American decor, soundproofed walls and windows, refrigerators, honor bars, phones with data ports and voice mail, and other amenities. Complimentary continental breakfast is served in the lobby. Premium-Luxury ($115-175). The inn's adjacent **Puccini & Pinetti,** tel. (415) 392-5500, is a highly regarded Cal-Italian restaurant well patronized by theatergoers.

Between Union Square and Nob Hill is **Hotel Rex,** 562 Sutter (between Powell and Mason), tel. (415) 433-4434 or toll-free (800) 433-4434, www.sftrips.com, furnished in 1930s style and "dedicated to the arts and literary world." Rates include a complimentary evening glass of wine.

Premium-Luxury (as high as $250). Also reasonable by boutique hotel standards is the **San Francisco Carlton Hotel,** 1075 Sutter (at Larkin), tel. (415) 673-0242 or toll-free (800) 922-7586, www.carltonhotel.com, placed on *Condé Nast Traveler's* 1999 Gold List and offering 165 comfortable rooms with Queen Anne-style chairs and pleasant decor, as well as the on-site Oak Room Grille. Expensive-Luxury ($115-175).

Moving into San Francisco's trend-setting strata, the gleeful **Hotel Triton,** 342 Grant Ave., tel. (415) 394-0500 or toll-free (800) 433-6611, is the talk of the town—and other towns as well—attracting celebrities galore as well as comparisons to New York's Paramount and Royalton Hotels. (For more information, see special topic Some Hip San Francisco Stays.)

The city has more classical class, of course. The four-star **Prescott Hotel,** 545 Post St. (between Taylor and Mason), tel. (415) 563-0303 or toll-free (800) 283-7322, www.prescotthotel.com, elegantly combines earthy Americana—most notable in the lobby—with the feel of a British men's club. Rooms and suites come complete with paisley motif, overstuffed furniture, and every imaginable amenity—from honor bar and terry robes to shoe shines and evening wine and cheeses. Not to mention room service courtesy of Wolfgang Puck's downstairs **Postrio** restaurant, where hotel guests also receive preferred dining reservations (if rooms are also reserved well in advance). Services for guests on the Executive Club Level include express check-in (and check-out), continental breakfast, hors d'oeuvres from Postrio, personal concierge service, and even stationary bicycles and rowers delivered to your room on request. Luxury ($185-215, suites run $235-255).

Among other exceptional small hostelries in the vicinity of Union Square is the wheelchair-accessible, 80-room **Warwick Regis Hotel,** 490 Geary St., tel. (415) 928-7900 or toll-free (800) 827-3447 in the U.S. and Canada, www.warwickregis.com, furnished with French and English antiques and offering exceptional service. Amenities include hair dryers and small refrigerators in every room, plus cable TV, complimentary morning newspaper, and on-site café and bar. Premium-Luxury ($135-205). Another best bet, and a bargain for the quality, is the **Chancellor Hotel,** 433 Powell (on Union Square), tel. (415) 362-2004 or toll-free (800) 428-4748, www.chancellorhotel.com, offering elegant rooms within walking distance of just about everything. (Or hop the cable car.) Expensive-Luxury ($100-230). Truly exceptional is **The Donatello,** 501 Post St. (at Mason, a block west of Union Square), tel. (415) 441-7100 or toll-free (800) 227-3184 in the U.S. and Canada, noteworthy for its four-star amenities and its restaurant, **Zingari** (tel. 415-885-8850). Luxury ($189-210). Quite refined, too, with the feel of a fine residential hotel, is **Campton Place Hotel,** 340 Stockton St. (just north of Union Square), tel. (415) 781-5555 or toll-free (800) 235-4300 in California, (800) 426-3135 in U.S. and Canada. The hotel has all the amenities, including the superb, critically acclaimed (and AAA five diamond) **Campton Place Restaurant** featuring impeccable contemporary American cuisine (tel. 415-955-5555). Luxury ($230-345).

Other Areas

The Embarcadero YMCA south of Market near the Ferry Building now shares the waterfront building with the **Harbor Court Hotel,** 165 Steuart St. (at Mission), tel. (415) 882-1300 or toll-free (800) 346-0555, www.harborcourthotel.com, a fairly phenomenal transformation at the edge of the financial district—not to mention near Pac Bell Bell Park—and a perfect setup for Giants fans and business travelers. The building's Florentine exterior has been beautifully preserved, as have the building's original arches, columns, and vaulted ceilings. Inside, the theme is oversized, Old World creature comfort. The plush rooms are rich with amenities, including TV, radio, direct-dial phones with extra-long cords, and complimentary beverages. The penthouse features a Louis XVI-style bed and 18-foot ceilings. Business travelers will appreciate the hotel's business center, financial district limo service, and same-day valet laundry service. And to work off the stress of that business meeting, head right next door to the renovated multilevel YMCA, where recreational facilities include basketball courts, aerobics classes, an Olympic-size pool, whirlpool, steam room, dry sauna, and even stationary bicycles with a view. Rates include complimentary continental breakfast and valet parking. Luxury ($220 for a Bay view room, $205 Courtyard room, specials as low as $175). Affiliated Victorian saloon-style Harry Denton's Bar & Grill here has predictably good food and becomes a lively dance club/bar scene after 10 p.m.

Adjacent and also worthwhile is the **Hotel Griffon,** 155 Steuart St. (at Mission), tel. (415) 495-2100 or toll-free (800) 321-2201 in the U.S. and Canada, www.hotelgriffon.com, with amenities like continental breakfast, complimentary morning newspaper, and a fitness center. Luxury ($220-270).

Two blocks from Pier 39 at Fisherman's Wharf, the **Tuscan Inn,** 425 North Point, tel. (415) 561-1100 or toll-free (800) 648-4626, though part of the Best Western hotel chain, has been reinvented by hotelier Bill Kimpton. The hotel features an Italianate lobby with fireplace, a central garden court, and 221 rooms and suites with modern amenities. Rates include morning coffee, tea, and biscotti, and a daily wine hour by the lobby fireplace. Premium-Luxury ($118-228). Just off the lobby is a convenient Italian trattoria, **Cafe Pescatore,** specializing in fresh fish and seafood, pastas, and pizzas (baked in a wood-burning oven) at lunch and dinner. Open for breakfast also.

Near Civic Center cultural attractions is the exceptional small **Inn at the Opera,** 333 Fulton, tel. (415) 863-8400 or toll-free (800) 325-2708, featuring complimentary breakfast and morning newspaper, in-room cookies and apples, free shoeshine service, available limousine service, and an excellent on-site restaurant, **Ovation.** The guest list often includes bigname theater people. Rooms were immaculately refurbished in 1999. Premium-Luxury (singles $140, doubles $180).

In Pacific Heights, west of Van Ness and south of Lombard, the **Sherman House,** 2160 Green St. (between Fillmore and Webster), tel. (415) 563-3600, is among the city's finest small, exclusive hotels. Once the mansion of Leander Sherman, it now attracts inordinate percentages of celebrities and stars. The ambience here, including the intimate dining room, exudes 19th-century French opulence. Luxury ($305-415). In the same neighborhood is a somewhat cheaper option for a "boutique stay": the **Laurel Inn,** 444 Presidio Avenue (at California), tel. (415) 567-8467 or toll-free (800) 552-8735, www.the-laurelinn.com. Comfortable if a bit trendy—in 1960's style—and within walking distance of the Presidio, the Laurel features 49 rooms, eigh-

teen with kitchenettes. Ask about their pet-friendly policy. Premium ($120-150).

TOP OF THE LINE HOTELS

In addition to the fine hotels mentioned above, San Francisco offers an impressive selection of large, four- and five-star superdeluxe hotels. The air in these establishments is rarefied indeed. (Sometimes the airs, too.) Many, however, do offer seasonal specials. Business-oriented hotels often feature lower weekend rates.

The Ritz
Peek into **The Ritz-Carlton, San Francisco,** 600 Stockton (between California and Pine), tel. (415) 296-7465 or toll-free (800) 241-3333, www.ritzcarlton.com, to see what a great facelift an old lady can get for $140 million. Quite impressive. And many consider the hotel's Dining Room at The Ritz-Carlton among the city's finest eateries. (For more information, see Puttin' on the Ritz.) Luxury (singles and doubles run $335-385, suites $525-3,500).

The Palace
Equally awesome—and another popular destination these days for City Guides and other walking tours—is that grande dame of San Francisco hostelries, the recently renovated and resplendent 1909 **Sheraton Palace Hotel,** 2 New Montgomery St. (downtown at Market), tel. (415) 512-1111 or toll-free (800) 325-3535, www.sf-palace.com. Wander in, under the metal grill-work awning at the New Montgomery entrance, across the polished marble sunburst on the foyer floor, and sit a spell in the lobby to appreciate the more subtle aspects of this $150 million renovation. Then mosey into the central Garden Court restaurant. The wonderful lighting here is provided, during the day, by the (cleaned and restored) 1800s atrium skylight, one of the world's largest leaded-glass creations; some 70,000 panes of glass arch over the entire room. It's a best bet for Sunday brunch. Note, too, the 10 (yes, 10) 700-pound crystal chandeliers. The Pied Piper Bar, with its famous Maxfield Parrish mural, is a Palace fixture, and adjoins **Maxfield's** restaurant. Tours of the hotel are available; call for schedules and information.

PUTTIN' ON THE RITZ

Serious visiting fans of San Francisco, at least those with serious cash, tend to equate their long-running romance with a stay on Nob Hill, home base for most of the city's ritzier hotels. And what could be ritzier than the Ritz?

The Ritz-Carlton, San Francisco, 600 Stockton at California St., tel. (415) 296-7465 or toll-free (800) 241-3333, www.ritzcarlton.com, is a local landmark, San Francisco's finest remaining example of neoclassical architecture. At the financial district's former western edge, and hailed in 1909 as a "temple of commerce," until 1973 the building served as West Coast headquarters for the Metropolitan Life Insurance Company. Expanded and revised five times since, San Francisco's Ritz has been open for business as a hotel only since 1991. After painstaking restoration (four years and $140 million worth), this nine-story grande dame still offers some odd architectural homage to its past. Witness the terra-cotta tableau over the entrance: the angelic allegorical figure ("Insurance") is protecting the American family. (Ponder the meaning of the lion's heads and winged hourglasses on your own.)

The Ritz offers a total of 336 rooms and suites, most with grand views. Amenities on the top two floors ("The Ritz-Carlton Club") include private lounge, continuous complimentary meals, and Dom Perignon and Beluga caviar every evening. All rooms, however, feature Italian marble bathrooms, in-room safes, and every modern comfort, plus access to the fitness center (indoor swimming pool, whirlpool, training room, separate men's and women's steam rooms and saunas, massage, and more). Services include the usual long list plus morning newspaper, child care, VCR and video library, car rental, and multilingual staff. Rates run $335-385 for rooms, $525-3,500 for suites. (When available, the Ritz-Carlton's "Summer Escape" package includes a deluxe guest room, continental breakfast, valet parking, and unlimited use of the fitness center.) The Ritz-Carlton also provides full conference facilities. **The Courtyard** restaurant here offers the city's only alfresco dining in a hotel setting—like eating breakfast, lunch, or dinner on someone else's well-tended garden patio. (Come on Sunday for brunch—and jazz.) Adjacent, indoors, is somewhat casual **The Restaurant.** More formal, serving neoclassical cuisine, is **The Dining Room.**

In addition to plush accommodations (rooms still have high ceilings), the Palace offers complete conference and meeting facilities, a business center, and a rooftop fitness center. The swimming pool up there, under a modern vaulted skylight, is especially enjoyable at sunset; spa services include a poolside whirlpool and dry sauna. Luxury (rooms $255-320, suites $760-2,800).

The St. Francis

Another beloved San Francisco institution is the **Westin St. Francis Hotel,** 335 Powell St. (between Post and Geary, directly across from Union Square), tel. (415) 397-7000 or toll-free (800) 228-3000, www.westin.com, a recently restored landmark recognized by the National Trust for Historic Preservation as one of the Historic Hotels of America. When the first St. Francis opened in 1849 at Clay and Dupont (Grant), it was considered the only hostelry at which ladies were safe, and was also celebrated as the first "to introduce bedsheets to the city." But San Francisco's finest was destroyed by fire four years later. By the early 1900s, reincarnation was imminent when a group of local businessmen declared their intention to rebuild the St. Francis as "a caravansary worthy of standing at the threshold of the Occident, representative of California hospitality." No expense was spared on the stylish 12-story hotel overlooking Union Square—partially opened but still under construction when the April 18, 1906, earthquake and fire hit town. Damaged but not destroyed, the restored St. Francis opened in November 1907; over the entrance was an electrically lighted image of a phoenix rising from the city's ashes. Successfully resurrected, the elegant and innovative hotel attracted royalty, international political and military leaders, theatrical stars, and literati.

But even simpler folk have long been informed, entertained, and welcomed by the St. Francis. People keep an eye on the number of unfurled flags in front of the St. Francis, for example, knowing that these herald the nationalities of visiting dignitaries. And every longtime San

Franciscan knows that any shiny old coins in their pockets most likely came from the St. Francis; the hotel's long-standing practice of washing coins—to prevent them from soiling ladies' white gloves—continues to this day. Meeting friends "under the clock" means the Magneta Clock in the hotel's Powell St. lobby, this "master clock" from Saxony a fixture since the early 1900s.

Both the Tower and Powell St. lobbies were freshened up by 1991 restorations. Highlights include three 40-foot trompe l'oeil murals by Carlo Marchiori depicting turn-of-the-century San Francisco, new inlaid marble floors and central carpet, and gold-leaf laminate applied to the ornate woodwork in the Powell St. lobby. Restoration of the original building's Colusa sandstone facade was finished in 1997.

After additions and renovations, the St. Francis today offers 1,200 luxury guest rooms and suites (request a suite brochure if you hanker to stay in the General MacArthur suite, the Queen Elizabeth II suite, or the Ron and Nancy Reagan suite), plus fitness and full meeting and conference facilities, a 1,500-square-foot ballroom, five restaurants (including elegant Victor's atop the St. Francis Tower), shopping arcade, valet parking. Luxury (rooms $255-320, suites $760-2,800).

Others Downtown

The **Clift Hotel,** 495 Geary St. (at Taylor), tel. (415) 775-4700 or toll-free (800) 652-5438, www.clifthotel.com, is a five-star midsize hotel offering every imaginable comfort and service, including free Financial District limo service, transportation to and from the airport (for a fee), and a good on-site restaurant. Luxury ($240-1,260).

Also within easy reach of downtown doings is the sleek, modern, four-star **Pan Pacific Hotel,** 500 Post St. (at Mason, one block west of Union Square), tel. (415) 771-8600, toll-free (800) 533-6465 or (800) 327-8585, www.panpac.com. The business-oriented Pan Pacific offers three phones with call waiting in each room, personal computers delivered to your room upon request, notary public and business services, and Rolls Royce shuttle service to the Financial District. It's also luxurious; bathrooms, for example, feature floor-to-ceiling Breccia marble, artwork, a mini-screen TV, and a telephone. Luxury ($199-309). "The Pampering Weekend" special starts at $139

and includes breakfast in your room or at the third-floor **Pacific** restaurant (California-fusion cuisine), tel. (415) 929-2087.

Other worthy downtown possibilities include the contemporary Japanese-style **Hotel Nikko,** 222 Mason, tel. (415) 394-1111 or toll-free (800) 645-5687, www.nikkohotels.com, which boasts a glass-enclosed rooftop pool (Luxury—$195-255).

The exquisite **Mandarin Oriental San Francisco,** 222 Sansome, tel. (415) 276-9888, (415) 885-0999, or toll-free (800) 622-0404, www.mandarin-oriental.com, is housed in the top 11 floors of the California First Interstate Building in the financial district. The 160 rooms boast great views (even from the bathrooms) and all the amenities, including wonderful **Silks** restaurant, tel. (415) 986-2020. Luxury (rooms $295-520, suites $800-1,650).

Other comfortable hotel choices near the financial district and the booming new media companies south of Market include the superstylish, granite-faced **W Hotel,** 181 Third St. (at Howard), tel. (415) 777-5300 or toll-free (877) 946-8357, www.whotels.com, which is as sleek as its next-door neighbor, the San Francisco Museum of Modern Art. This business-oriented hotel also offers boutique touches: plush down comforters and Aveda bath products in all rooms. Downstairs, the XYZ restaurant and bar serves creative fusion cuisine. Luxury (starting at $175). Also in the area, near the Moscone Center, is the **Argent Hotel,** 50 Third St., tel. (415) 974-6400 or toll-free (877) 222-6699, www.destinationtravel.com (Luxury—starting at $220).

Nob Hill

Some of the city's finest hotels cluster atop Nob Hill. Since judgment always depends upon personal taste, despite official ratings it's all but impossible to say which is "the best." Take your pick.

Across from Grace Cathedral and Huntington Park, the **Huntington Hotel,** 1075 California St. (at Taylor), tel. (415) 474-5400 or toll-free (800) 652-1539 in California, (800) 227-4683 from elsewhere in the U.S., www.huntingtonhotel.com, is the last surviving family-owned fine hotel in the neighborhood. It's a beauty, a destination in and of itself. Every room and suite (onetime residential apartments) has been individually designed and decorated, and every service is a personal gesture. Stop in just to appreciate the elegant lobby restoration. Dark and clubby, and open daily for breakfast, lunch, and dinner, the **Big Four Restaurant** off the lobby pays pleasant homage to the good ol' days of Wild West railroad barons—and often serves wild game entrées along with tamer continental contemporary cuisine. Luxury ($190-260).

Top-of-the-line, too, is the romantic, turn-of-the-20th-century **Fairmont Hotel,** 950 Mason St. (at California), tel. (415) 772-5000 or toll-free (800) 527-4727, www.fairmont.com, noted for its genuine grandeur and grace. The Fairmont offers 596 rooms (small to large) and suites, all expected amenities, and several on-site restaurants. For a panoramic Bay Area view at Sunday brunch, the place to go is the hotel's **Crown Room** atop the hotel's Tower section. Locally loved, too, however, are the hotel's **Mason's,** for steak and seafood (also open for breakfast), and the Tiki-inspired **Tonga Room,** which specializes in Chinese and Polynesian cuisine and features a simulated tropical rainstorm every half hour. The Fairmont also offers full conference and business facilities (20 meeting rooms) and the Nob Hill Club (extra fee) for fitness enthusiasts. Luxury ($229 and up).

The five-star **Renaissance Stanford Court Hotel,** 905 California St. (at Powell), tel. (415) 989-3500 or toll-free (800) 468-3571, www.renaissancehotels.com, boasts a 120-foot-long, sepia-toned lobby mural honoring San Francisco's historic diversity. On the west wall, for example, are panels depicting the hotel's predecessor, the original Leland Stanford Mansion, with railroad barons and other wealthy Nob Hill nabobs on one side, Victorian-era African Americans on the other. Other panels depict the long-running economic exploitation of California places and peoples, from Russian whaling and fur trading, redwood logging, and the California gold rush (with Native Americans and the Chinese looking on) to the 1906 earthquake and fire framed by the construction of the transcontinental railroad and California's Latinization, as represented by Mission Dolores. Stop in and see it; this is indeed the story of Northern California, if perhaps a bit romanticized.

The hotel itself is romantic, recognized by the National Trust for Historic Preservation as one of the Historic Hotels of America. The Stanford Court features a decidedly European ambience,

from the carriage entrance (with beaux arts fountain and stained-glass dome) to guest rooms decked out in 19th-century artwork, antiques, and reproductions (not to mention modern comforts like heated towel racks in the marble bathrooms and dictionaries on the writing desks). Opulent touches in the lobby include Baccarat chandeliers, Carrara marble floor, oriental carpets, original artwork, and an 1806 antique grandfather clock once owned by Napoleon Bonaparte. Guest services include complimentary stretch limo service, both for business and pleasure. Luxury ($235-315). Even if you don't stay, consider a meal (breakfast, lunch, and dinner daily, plus weekend brunch) at the hotel's Mediterranean-inspired restaurant, **Fournou's Ovens,** tel. (415) 989-1910 for reservations, considered one of San Francisco's best.

Don't forget the Mark Hopkins Hotel, now the **Mark Hopkins Inter-Continental,** 1 Nob Hill (California and Mason), tel. (415) 392-3434 or toll-free (800) 327-0200, www.interconti.com, another refined Old California old-timer. Hobnobbing with the best of them atop Nob Hill, the Mark Hopkins features 391 elegant guest rooms (many with great views) and all the amenities, not to mention the fabled **Top of the Mark** sky room, still San Francisco's favorite sky-high romantic bar scene. The French-California **Nob Hill Restaurant** is open daily for breakfast, lunch, and dinner. Luxury ($220-340).

CITY-STYLE BED AND BREAKFASTS

With most of San Francisco's European-style and boutique hotels offering breakfast and other homey touches, and many of the city's bed and breakfasts offering standard hotel services (like concierge, bellman, valet/laundry, and room service), it's truly difficult to understand the difference.

The eight-room **Chateau Tivoli** townhouse, 1057 Steiner St., tel. (415) 776-5462 or toll-free (800) 228-1647, is an 1892 Queen Anne landmark with an astounding visual presence. "Colorful" just doesn't do justice as a description of this Alamo Square painted lady. The Tivoli's eccentric exterior architectural style is electrified by 18 historic colors of paint, plus gold leaf. Painstaking restoration is apparent inside, too, from the very Victorian, period-furnished parlors

 *You'll find a number of bed-and-breakfast inns near historic Alamo Square*

SAN FRANCISCO CONVENTION AND VISITORS BUREAU/CAROL SIMOWITZ

to exquisite, individually decorated guest rooms, each reflecting at least a portion of the city's unusual social history. (Imagine, under one roof: Enrico Caruso, Aimee Crocker, Isadora Duncan, Joaquin Miller, Jack London, opera singer Luisa Tettrazini, and Mark Twain. Somehow, it is imaginable, since the mansion was once the residence of the city's pre-earthquake Tivoli Opera.) Chateau Tivoli offers nine rooms and suites, all but two with private baths, two with fireplaces. Premium-Luxury ($110-250).

One-time home to Archbishop Patrick Riordan, the **Archbishop's Mansion,** 1000 Fulton St. (at Steiner), tel. (415) 563-7872 or toll-free (800) 543-5820, is also exquisitely restored, offering comfortable rooms and suites in a French Victorian mood. Some rooms have fireplaces and in-room spas, and all have phones and TV. Continental breakfast. Luxury ($159-419). The **Alamo Square Inn,** 719 Scott St., tel. (415) 922-2055 or toll-free (800) 345-9888, www.alamoinn.com, is another neighborhood possibility, offering rooms and suites in an 1895 Queen Anne and an 1896 Tudor Revival. Expensive-Premium.

Petite Auberge, 863 Bush St. (near Nob Hill and Union Square), tel. (415) 928-6000, is an elegant French country inn right downtown, featuring Pierre Deux fabrics, terra-cotta tile, oak furniture, and lace curtains. All 26 guest rooms here have private bathrooms; 16 have fireplaces. The "Petite Suite" has its own entrance and deck, a king-size bed, fireplace, and jacuzzi. Premium-Luxury ($110-225). Two doors down is the affiliated **White Swan Inn,** 845 Bush, tel. (415) 775-1755, with parlor, library, and 26 rooms (private baths, fireplaces, wet bars) decorated with English-style decorum, from the mahogany antiques and rich fabrics to floral-print wallpapers. Premium-Luxury ($145-250). Both these inns serve full breakfast (with the morning paper), afternoon tea, and homemade cookies, and provide little amenities like thick terry bathrobes. All rooms have TV and telephone.

Close to the Presidio and Fort Mason in Cow Hollow is the **Edward II Inn,** 3155 Scott St. (at Lombard), tel. (415) 922-3000 or toll-free (800) 473-2846, an English-style country hotel and pub offering 24 rooms and six suites, all with color TV and phone, some with shared bathrooms. The suites have in-room whirlpool baths. A complimentary continental breakfast is served. Moderate-Expensive.

Peaceful and pleasant amid the hubbub of North Beach is the stylish and artsy 15-room **Hotel Bohème,** 444 Columbus Ave., tel. (415) 433-9111, offering continental charm all the way to breakfast, which is served either indoors or out on the patio. On-site restaurant, too. Premium (a good deal). Also in North Beach is the French country **Washington Square Inn,** 1660 Stockton St., tel. (415) 981-4220 or toll-free (800) 388-0220, featuring 15 rooms (most with private bath), continental breakfast, and afternoon tea. Premium-Luxury ($125-210).

Near Lafayette Park in Pacific Heights and something of a cause célèbre is **The Mansions,** 2220 Sacramento St., tel. (415) 929-9444 or toll-free (800) 826-9398, www.themansions.com, an elegant bed-and-breakfast-style hotel composed of two adjacent historic mansions filled with art. The 28 rooms and suites here are opulent and feature telephones, private bathrooms, and numerous amenities. Stroll the Bufano sculpture gardens, play billiards, or attend nightly music concerts or magic shows. Full breakfast is served every morning, in the dining area or in your room, and dinners are also available. Premium-Luxury ($139-250).

Not a B&B per se, but providing as intimate a lodging experience as you'll get, **Dockside Boat & Bed,** Pier 39, tel. (415) 392-5526 or toll-free (800) 436-2574, www.boatandbed.com, con-tracts a stable of luxury yachts, both motor and sail, on which guests can spend the night. Guys, get a clue: You can't get much more romantic than moonlight champagne with your lovely in-amorata—lying on deck, admiring the city lights, and listening to the water lap, lap, lapping against the hull. Luxury ($165-270).

EATING IN SAN FRANCISCO

San Franciscans love to eat. For a true San Franciscan, eating—and eating well—competes for first place among life's purest pleasures, right up there with the arts, exercising, and earning money. (There may be a few others.) Finding new and novel neighborhood eateries, and knowing which among the many fine dining es-tablishments are currently at the top of the trend-setters' culinary A-list, are points of pride for long-time residents. Fortunately, San Francis-cans also enjoy sharing information and opin-ions—including their restaurant preferences. So the best way to find out where to eat, and why, is simply to ask. The following listings, which rough-ly follow the geographic drift of this chapter's Seeing San Francisco sections, should help fine-food aficionados get started, and will certainly keep everyone else from starving.

THE AVENUES: RICHMOND, SEACLIFF, SUNSET

A fixture in the midst of the Golden Gate Na-tional Recreation Area and a favorite hangout at the edge of the continent, the current incar-nation of the **Cliff House,** 1090 Point Lobos Ave. (at Upper Great Hwy.), tel. (415) 386-3330, is also a decent place to eat. Sunsets are superb, the seafood sublime. As close to fancy as it gets here is **Upstairs at the Cliff House,** an Old San Francisco-style dining room. Decidedly more casual at this cliff-hanging complex are both the **Seafood and Beverage Company** and the **Phineas T. Barnacle** pub.

Heading south down the beachfront, on the opposite side of Great Hwy. is the **Beach Chalet Brewery and Restaurant,** 1000 Great Hwy. (between Fulton and Lincoln), tel. (415) 386-8439. This delightful renovation, upstairs (above a visitor center and City Store outlet) in the old 1925 Willis Polk-designed building, features wall-to-wall windows looking out on the surf (a great spot to watch the sunset), as well as creative California cuisine and a long list of housemade microbrews. The atmosphere is casual—don't come in your bathing suit, but you won't need the dinner jacket—and the service is friendly. Open daily for lunch and dinner.

Moving inland, exceptional ethnic fare is a specialty of Richmond District restaurants. The 100-plus eateries lining Clement St.—among them Asian, South American, Mexican, Italian, and even Russian restaurants and delis—are representative of the district's culinary and cul-tural mix.

Notable in the city's "new Chinatown," the modern **Fountain Court,** 354 Clement St. (at Fifth Ave.), tel. (415) 668-1100, is a wonderful, in-expensive stop for northern-style dim sum and other Shanghai specialties. One of the few San Francisco restaurants serving spicy, sweet Sin-gapore-style fare is **Straits Cafe,** 3300 Geary (at Parker), tel. (415) 668-1783, a light, airy, white-walled rendition complete with interior palm trees. For delicious (and cheap) Taiwanese food, head to the **Taiwan Restaurant,** 445 Clement (at Sixth), tel. (415) 387-1789, which serves great dumplings.

Good for Indonesian fare is **Jakarta,** 615 Bal-boa St. (between Seventh and Eighth Avenues), tel. (415) 387-5225, another airy and bright place featuring an extensive menu of unusually well-done dishes, plus an eye-catching array of arti-facts, musical instruments, and shadow puppets. Some say that the romantic **Khan Toke Thai House,** 5937 Geary (at 23rd Ave.), tel. (415) 668-6654, is San Francisco's best Southeast Asian restaurant (and a good deal). Open daily for dinner only, reservations accepted. Another reliable neighborhood choice is **Bangkok Cafe,** 2845 Geary (at Collins), tel. (415) 346-8821.

For the whole Moroccan experience, including a belly dancer on some nights, try **El Mansour,** 3121 Clement (near 32nd Ave.), tel. (415) 751-2312. A bit more grand, **Kasra Persian & Mediterranean Cuisine,** 349 Clement (at Fifth Ave.), tel. (415) 752-1101, is a very good choice for all kinds of shish kabobs.

Tiny, welcoming **Cafe Maisonnette,** 315 Eighth Ave., tel. (415) 387-7992, specializes in country-French cuisine. People rave about the rack of lamb. Monthly changing menu. **Café Riggio,** 4112 Geary (between Fifth and Sixth Avenues), tel. (415) 221-2114, is much appreciated for its antipasti, world-class calamari, and homemade cannoli for dessert.

Clement Street Bar & Grill, 708 Clement (at Eighth Ave.), tel. (415) 386-2200, serves a mostly American menu featuring vegetarian fare, grilled seafood, and California-style pastas. Farther up Geary toward the beach, **Bill's Place,** 2315 Clement (between 24th and 25th Avenues), tel. (415) 221-5262, is an eclectic burger joint with presidential portraits on the walls and a Japanese-style garden. The culinary creations here are named in honor of local celebrities. Guess what you get when you order a Carol Doda burger: two beefy patties with an olive sticking out smack dab in the middle of each. **Tia Margarita,** 300 19th Ave. (at Clement), tel. (415) 752-9274, is a long-running family café serving American-style Mexican food.

Things are more than a bit gentrified in Presidio Heights. Just a few blocks south of the Presidio is the **Magic Flute Garden Ristorante,** 3673 Sacramento (between Locust and Spruce), tel. (415) 922-1225, which offers Italian and other continental specialties in a sunny French country atmosphere. Folks also sing the praises of nearby **Tuba Garden,** 3634 Sacramento (between Locust and Spruce), tel. (415) 921-8822, a cozy Victorian open just for lunch and brunch, serving up Belgian waffles, homemade blintzes, and eggs Benedict.

Out at the edge of the Sunset District, assemble everything for a memorable picnic from the delis and shops along Taraval. Or check out the diverse ethnic neighborhood eateries. **Leon's Bar-BQ,** in an oceanside shack at 2800 Sloat Blvd. (at 46th Ave.), tel. (415) 681-3071, is a

great stop for chicken and ribs. (Leon's has outposts in the Fillmore and at Fisherman's Wharf.) **Brother's Pizza,** 3627 Taraval (near 46th Ave.), tel. (415) 753-6004, isn't much to look at, but the pizzas (try the pesto special), pastas, and calzone overcome that first impression in a big hurry. The colorful, always crowded **Casa Aguila,** 1240 Noriega (between 19th and 20th Avenues), tel. (415) 661-5593, specializes in authentic Mexican fare from Cuernavaca and offers lots of food for the money. **El Toreador Fonda Mejicana,** 50 W. Portal (between Ulloa and Vicente), tel. (415) 566-2673, is a homey place serving traditional Central and Southern Mexican food. Just down the way on the buzzing West Portal retail strip, **Cafe for All Seasons,** 150 W. Portal (between Vicente and 14th Ave.), tel. (415) 665-0900, is a popular stop for hungry shoppers. The California-American menu emphasizes light pastas, grilled fish, and big salads.

UNION SQUARE AND NOB HILL

A well-kept secret, perhaps downtown's best breakfast spot, is **Dottie's True Blue Cafe,** 522 Jones St., tel. (415) 885-2767, a genuine all-American coffee shop serving every imaginable American standard plus new cuisine, such as (at lunch) grilled eggplant sandwiches. Open daily for breakfast and lunch only, 7 a.m.-2 p.m. But those in the know say you haven't "done" the city until you've ordered breakfast—specifically, the 18 Swedish pancakes—at **Sears Fine Foods,** 439 Powell (at Post), tel. (415) 986-1160, a funky, friendly old-time San Francisco café.

Another area classic, if for other reasons, is **John's Grill,** 63 Ellis (just off Powell), tel. (415) 986-3274 or (415) 986-0069, with a neat neon sign outside and *Maltese Falcon* memorabilia just about everywhere inside. (In the book, this is where Sam Spade ate his lamb chops.) Named a National Literary Landmark by the Friends of Libraries, USA, this informal eatery ode to Dashiell Hammett serves good continental-style American fare, plus large helpings of Hammett hero worship, especially upstairs in Hammett's Den and the Maltese Falcon Room. Open Mon.-Sat. for lunch and dinner; Sunday for dinner only. Live jazz nightly.

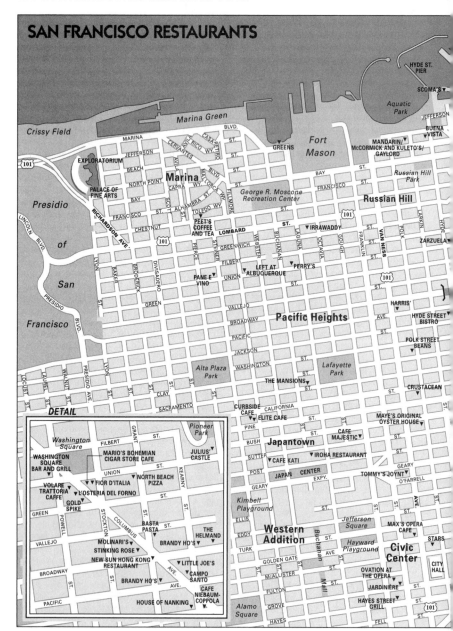

SAN FRANCISCO RESTAURANTS

HYDE ST. PIER

SCOMA'S ▼

Aquatic Park

JEFFERSON

BUENA VISTA ▼

Crissy Field

Marina Green

MARINA BLVD.

GREENS ▼

Fort Mason

MANDARIN ▼
McCORMICK AND KULETO'S/
GAYLORD

JEFFERSON

CERVANTES

CASA RITO

AVILA RICO WY.

BEACH

EXPLORATORIUM

PALACE OF FINE ARTS

NORTH POINT

BAY

CAPRA WY.

Marina

George R. Moscone Recreation Center

BAY

FRANCISCO

Russian Hill Park

Russian Hill

Presidio

FRANCISCO

CHESTNUT

SCOTT

ALHAMBRA

TOLEDO WY.

PEET'S COFFEE AND TEA

LOMBARD

STEINER

GREENWICH

IRRAWADDY ▼

LARKIN

POLK

HYDE

ZARZUELA ▼

of

PIERCE

FILBERT

UNION

LEFT AT ALBUQUERQUE ▼

PERRY'S ▼

San

BAKER

BRODERICK

DIVISADERO

GREEN

VALLEJO

HARRIS' ▼

HYDE STREET BISTRO ▼

Francisco

LYON

BROADWAY

PACIFIC

Pacific Heights

POLK STREET BEANS ▼

JACKSON

LOCUST

LAUREL

WALNUT

PRESIDIO AVE.

CLAY

Alta Plaza Park

WASHINGTON

Lafayette Park

CRUSTACEAN ▼

SACRAMENTO

THE MANSIONS ▼

CURBSIDE CAFE ▼
ELITE CAFE ▼

CALIFORNIA

MAYE'S ORIGINAL OYSTER HOUSE ▼

PINE

BUSH

Japantown

CAFE MAJESTIC ▼

DETAIL

Washington Square

Pioneer Park

FILBERT ST.

GRANT ST.

JULIUS' CASTLE ▼

SUTTER

POST

CAFE KATI ▼

IROHA RESTAURANT ▼

GEARY

WASHINGTON SQUARE BAR AND GRILL

MARIO'S BOHEMIAN CIGAR STORE CAFE

KEARNY

NORTH BEACH PIZZA ▼

JAPAN CENTER

TOMMY'S JOYNT ▼

O'FARRELL

VOLARE TRATTORIA CAFFE ▼

L'OSTERIA DEL FORNO ▼

FIOR D'ITALIA ▼

UNION

Kimbell Playground

GEARY EXPY.

GOLD SPIKE ▼

STOCKTON

COLUMBUS

ELLIS

Jefferson Square

MAX'S OPERA CAFE ▼

GREEN

POWELL

BASTA PASTA ▼

EDDY

Western Addition

STARS ▼

VALLEJO

MOLINARI'S ▼

STINKING ROSE ▼

THE HELMAND ▼

BRANDY HO'S ▼

TURK

Hayward Playground

Civic Center

CITY HALL

BROADWAY

NEW SUN HONG KONG RESTAURANT ▼

LITTLE JOE'S ▼

GOLDEN GATE AVE.

OVATION AT THE OPERA ▼

BRANDY HO'S ▼

CAMPO SANTO ▼

McALLISTER

JARDINIÈRE ▼

PACIFIC

CAFE NIEBAUM-COPPOLA ▼

HOUSE OF NANKING ▼

FULTON

GROVE

Alamo Square

HAYES

HAYES STREET GRILL ▼

FELL

© AVALON TRAVEL PUBLISHING, INC.

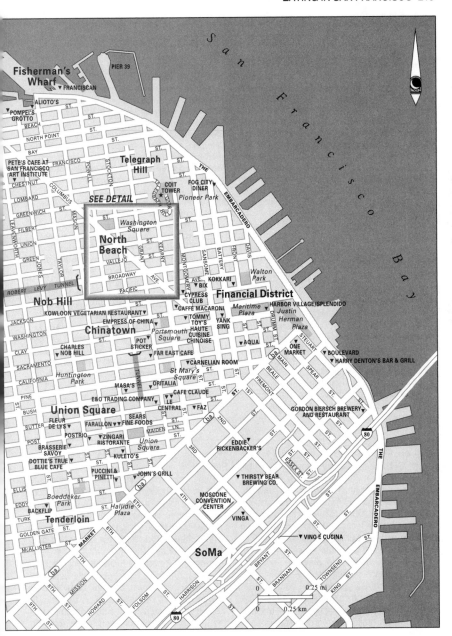

COCKTAIL TIME

Sometimes you just need to cast out the flannel shirt and Dr. Martens and join what used to be known as the "jet set" to toast the high life. The following establishments offer a sample of that old San Francisco sparkle.

Entering the magnificent art-deco **Redwood Room,** 495 Geary St. (at Taylor) at the Clift Hotel, tel. (415) 775-4700, in the heart of the theater district and just two blocks from bustling Union Square, makes you feel like you've been transported to an earlier era. Romantic lighting, gleaming redwood walls, and a baby grand appeal to WASPy types and businesspeople in search of a quiet drink. And the drinks, especially martinis, are top-notch.

The **Tonga Room** at 950 Mason St. (between California and Sacramento), tel. (415) 772-5278, opened its exotic doors in 1945 inside the Fairmont Hotel—the lobby recognizable by American TV addicts as the one in the short-lived series Hotel—to bring the Pacific Islander theme to San Francisco. Polynesian decor and thatch-roofed huts surround a deep blue lake, where simulated tropical rainstorms hit every half hour. The lethal Bora Bora Horror tops the list of intriguing frozen cocktails, combining rum, banana liqueur, and Grand Marnier with a huge slice of pineapple. Rum also features in the Hurricane, lava bowl, and the Zombie. Happy hour offers the most economical visit possible. Normally pricey drinks cost $5, and you can graze on a buffet of edible treats (egg rolls, pot stickers, and dim sum) while listening to the house band's forgettable elevator music.

The drinkery at the **Top of the Mark,** 999 California St. (at Mason), tel. (415) 392-3434, is the city's most famous view lounge, an ideal place to take friends and dazzle them with the lights of San Francisco. Large windows take in a panorama of San Francisco's landmarks, from the Twin Peaks Tower to the Transamerica Pyramid and the Golden Gate Bridge. There's live music every night, and given the ritzy setting, a $7-10 cover charge doesn't seem all that steep. Classic cocktails—Manhattans, sidecars, and Martinis–are the libations of choice. The bar food is upscale and excellently prepared, with selections ranging from a Mediterranean platter to Beluga caviar.

The word "cocktail" practically whispers from behind the ruby red silk curtains at the glamorous **Starlight Room** at 450 Powell St. (between Post and Sutter), tel. (415) 395-8595, perched on the 21st floor of the 1928 Sir Francis Drake Hotel. Polished mahogany fixtures, luxurious furnishings, and a 360-degree view of the city make the Starlight Room one of the nicest cocktail experiences going. The spacious bar embraces the retro swing theme, and a mahogany dance floor and live music by Harry Denton's Starlight Orchestra attract young swing fans and older couples from out on the town. Light supper options range from pan-roasted crab cakes to oysters on the half-shell. All of this dazzle is surprisingly affordable, with a small evening cover charge and cocktails from $7-10.

—Pat Reilly

For excellent seafood, dive into the French provincial **Brasserie Savoy** at the Savoy Hotel, 580 Geary St. (at Jones), tel. (415) 441-8080, open for breakfast (until noon), dinner, and late supper. Gallic stodgy? Mais, non! How about a "Lobster Martini"? Or a fish soup described as "haunting" by one local food writer (perhaps she had one too many Lobster Martinis?).

Farallon, 450 Post (near Powell), tel. (415) 956-6969, might be the place in town for seafood. And the unique Pat Kuleto-designed interior might make you feel like you're under the sea, in an octopus's garden, perhaps. Look for such intriguing specialties as truffled mashed potatoes with crab and sea urchin sauce, or

ginger-steamed salmon. Open for lunch Mon.-Sat. and for dinner nightly.

Two blocks from Union Square, **Oritalia,** 586 Bush St. (at Stockton), tel. (415) 782-8122, offers an eclectic menu mixing Asian, American, and Mediterranean cuisine. Try the signature tuna tartar on sticky rice cakes, perhaps, or the potato gnocchi with Maine lobster and asparagus. Open daily for dinner.

Puccini & Pinetti, 129 Ellis (at Cyril Magnin), tel. (415) 392-5500, is a beautifully designed Cal-Italian restaurant popular with theater crowds. Menu highlights include bruschetta with arugula and roasted garlic, smoked salmon pizzas, and risotto with charred leeks and wild mushrooms. Prices are surprisingly reasonable—most entrées run $10-15. Open for lunch and dinner.

Worth searching for downtown is **Cafe Claude,** 7 Claude Ln. (between Grant and Kearny, Bush and Sutter, just off Bush), tel. (415) 392-3505, an uncanny incarnation of a genuine French café, from the paper table covers to the café au lait served in bowls. Good food, plus live jazz four nights a week.

A good choice downtown for pasta is **Kuleto's,** 221 Powell St., tel. (415) 397-7720, a comfortable trattoria-style Italian restaurant and bar at the Villa Florence Hotel. It's popular for power lunching and dinner, and it's also open for peaceful, pleasant breakfasts.

Better yet, though, is **Zingari Ristorante,** 501 Post St. (at Mason, in the Donatello hotel), tel. (415) 885-8850, justifiably famous for its Northern Italian regional dishes. This premiere San Francisco restaurant, where the separate dining rooms are small and intimate, and dressing up is de rigueur, puts on a show as good as, or better than, almost anything else in the neighborhood.

People should at least pop into Wolfgang Puck's **Postrio,** 545 Post St. (at Mason, inside the Prescott Hotel), tel. (415) 776-7825, www.postrio.com, to appreciate the exquisite ribbon-patterned dining room designs by Pat Kuleto. The food here is exceptional, with most entrées representing Puck's interpretations of San Francisco classics. Since the restaurant is open for breakfast, lunch, and dinner, try Hangtown fry and some house-made pastries at breakfast, perhaps a pizza fresh from the wood-burning oven or Dungeness crab with spicy curry risotto at lunch. Dinner is an adventure. Great desserts. Make reservations well in advance, or hope for a cancellation.

Famous among local foodies, not to mention its long-standing national and international fan club, is **Masa's,** 648 Bush St. (at the Hotel Vintage Court), tel. (415) 989-7154, one of the city's finest dinner restaurants and considered by many to be the best French restaurant in the United States. Masa's serves French cuisine with a fresh California regional touch and a Spanish aesthetic. Reservations accepted three weeks in advance. Very expensive.

Fleur de Lys, 777 Sutter (between Jones and Taylor), tel. (415) 673-7779, is another local legend—a fine French restaurant that also transcends the traditional. Nothing is too heavy or overdone. Everything is elegant and expensive. Open Mon.-Sat. for dinner. Reservations. Also on Sutter is the **E&O Trading Company,** 314 Sutter (between Stockton and Grant), tel. (415) 693-0303, which serves up Pacific Rim cuisine with flavors borrowed from all over Southeast Asia: small plates include Naan breads, satays, and Vietnamese rice paper rolls. The Dragon Bar offers tropical cocktails like Mai Tais and Singapore Slings, as well as house-made microbrews. An odd combination, perhaps, but it seems to work.

On Nob Hill, **Charles Nob Hill,** 1250 Jones St., tel. (415) 771-5400, is a neighborhood French restaurant featuring specialties like Hudson Valley foie gras and Sonoma duck. Open for dinner Tues.-Saturday. Some of the city's finest hotels, on Nob Hill and elsewhere, also serve some of the city's finest food.

THE FINANCIAL DISTRICT AND EMBARCADERO

Harry Denton's Bar & Grill, 161 Steuart St. (across from Rincon Center, inside the Harbor Court Hotel), tel. (415) 882-1333, is a great bar, restaurant (hearty American cuisine), and club, usually crowded as a sardine can after 5 p.m. The food is excellent. To hold a conversation, sink into a booth in the narrow dining room above the bar scene; to take in the great scenery, head for the back room (which doubles as a dance floor Thurs.-Sat. nights). Harry Denton's is open weekdays for lunch and nightly for dinner. Nearby **Boulevard,** 1 Mission St. (at Steuart), (415) 543-6084, is a Franco-American bistro serving American classics—ribs, pork chops, mashed 'taters—in an art nouveau atmosphere. Nice views.

In the seafood swim of things, **Aqua,** 252 California St., tel. (415) 956-9662, is making a global splash among well-heeled foodies

nationwide. Entrées include basil-grilled lobster, lobster potato gnocchi, and black-mussel soufflé. Open weekdays for lunch, Mon.-Sat. for dinner.

At **Delancey Street Restaurant,** 600 Embarcadero, tel. (415) 512-5179, the restaurant staff is comprised of Delancey's drug, alcohol, and crime rehabilitees. The daily changing menu at this radical chic, sociopolitically progressive place is ethnic American—everything from matzo ball soup to pot roast. And there's a great view of Alcatraz from the outdoor dining area. Open for lunch, afternoon tea, and dinner.

On the 52nd floor of the Bank of America building, the **Carnelian Room,** 555 California St. (between Kearny and Montgomery), tel. (415) 433-7500, is the closest you'll get to dining in an airplane above the city. On a clear night, you can see all the way to Detroit. The menu is upscale American, with specialties including Dungeness crab cakes, rack of lamb, and Grand Marnier soufflé. **Yank Sing,** 427 Battery, tel. (415) 781-1111, is popular with the Financial District crowd and noteworthy for the shrimp dumplings in the shapes of goldfish and rabbits. (There's another Yank Sing at 49 Stevenson St. between First and Second Streets, tel. 415-541-4949.)

A good choice for Cantonese food is Hong Kong-style **Harbor Village,** 4 Embarcadero Center (at the corner of Clay and Drumm), tel. (415) 781-8833, serving everything from dim sum to Imperial banquets. Open daily for lunch and dinner. Straight upstairs (on the Promenade level), behind those old olive-wood doors, is splendid **Splendido,** tel. (415) 982-3222, a contemporary Mediterranean-style retreat for Italian-food fanatics. Everything here is fresh and housemade, from the breads and seafood soups to the pastas and unusual pizzas. Exceptional entrées include grilled swordfish and guinea hens roasted in the restaurant's wood-burning oven. Good wine list; save some space for dessert. Open for lunch and dinner daily; the bar serves appetizers until closing (midnight). Alfresco dining available in summer.

CIVIC CENTER AND VICINITY

Backflip, 601 Eddy (near Larkin), tel. (415) 771-3547, serves up California cuisine in an aquatically inspired setting that sits poolside at the Phoenix Hotel, another beacon of style in the seedy Tenderloin. Fountains and lots of blue have you thinking "fish" from the get-go, and sure enough, seafood is the specialty here. At night, the house turns into a nightclub with DJ dancing.

North along Polk Gulch (roughly paralleling fairly level Polk St., from Post to Broadway) are abundant cafés, coffeehouses, and avant-garde junque and clothing shops. Worthwhile eateries include **Polk Street Beans,** 1733 Polk (at Clay), tel. (415) 776-9292, a funky Eurostyle coffeehouse serving good soups and sandwiches, and **Maye's Original Oyster House,** 1233 Polk, tel. (415) 474-7674, a remarkably reasonable Italian-style seafood restaurant that's been in business in San Francisco since 1867.

Tucked inside the Inn at the Opera, **Ovation at the Opera,** 333 Fulton St. (between Gough and Franklin), tel. (415) 305-8842 or (415) 553-8100, is a class act noted as much for its romantic charms as its fine French-Continental cuisine—a fitting finale for opera fans who have plenty of cash left to fan (this place is on the expensive side). Open nightly for dinner (until 10:30 or 11 p.m. Friday and Saturday nights).

Max's Opera Cafe, 601 Van Ness, tel. (415) 771-7300, also pitches itself to the neighborhood's more theatrical standards. Like Max's enterprises elsewhere, you can count on being served huge helpings of tantalizing all-American standards. At least at dinner, you can also count on the wait staff bursting into song—maybe opera, maybe a Broadway show tune. Open daily for lunch and dinner, until late (1 a.m.) on Friday and Saturday nights for the post-theater crowds.

Also by the Opera House is the elegant and superlative **Jardinière,** 300 Grove St. (at Franklin), tel. (415) 861-5555, a French restaurant created by the city's top restaurant designer and one of its top chefs. Open for lunch weekdays and for dinner nightly (late-night menu available after 10:30 p.m.).

The **Hayes Street Grill,** 320 Hayes (at Franklin), tel. (415) 863-5545, is a busy bistro serving some of the best seafood in town. Open weekdays for lunch, Mon.-Sat. for dinner.

Sometimes more like a moveable feast for fashion, judging from all the suits and suited skirts, the **Zuni Cafe,** 1658 Market (at Gough), tel. (415) 552-2522, is an immensely popular restaurant and watering hole noted for its Italian-French country fare in a Southwestern ambience. (Expensive.) Still yuppie central, even after all these years, is somewhat immodest, barn-sized **Stars,** 555 Golden Gate Ave. (between Van Ness and Polk), tel. (415) 861-7827. It's strictly reservations-only beyond the bar.

At Chelsea Square, **Crustacean,** 1475 Polk St. (at California), tel. (415) 776-2722, is another one of those cutting-edge eateries enjoyable for ambience as well as actual eats. This place serves exceptional Euro-Asian cuisine (specialty: roast crab) and looks like a fantasy home to those particularly crunchy critters, with underwater murals and giant seahorses, not to mention handblown glass fixtures and a 17-foot wave sculpture. Open for dinners only, nightly after 5 p.m.; valet parking, full bar, extensive wine list. Reservations preferred.

Near Japan Center, **Cafe Kati,** 1963 Sutter (near Fillmore), tel. (415) 775-7313, is one of those casual neighborhood places serving surprisingly good food. **Iroha Restaurant,** 1728 Buchanan (at Post), tel. (415) 922-0321, is a great inexpensive stop for noodles and Japanese standards.

HAIGHT-ASHBURY AND VICINITY

On any afternoon, most of the restaurants and cafés lining the Haight will be filled to the gills with young hipsters chowing down on brunch specials or self-medicating with food to cure party-related hangovers.

Campy as all get out, what with those murals and all, **Cha Cha Cha,** 1805 Haight St. (at Shrader), tel. (415) 386-5758, is just a hop or skip from Golden Gate Park. A hip tapas bar, it features unforgettable entrées such as grilled chicken paillard in mustard sauce, shrimp in spicy Cajun sauce, and New Zealand mussels in marinara, so it's one of the most popular places around, so it's sometimes hard to find a place to park yourself.

Love the Haight: you can fill up at hippie-ish prices (cheap!) at several places that serve all-day breakfasts or pizza by the slice. For monstrously generous omelettes and a hearty side of potatoes, slide on into **All You Knead,** 1466 Haight (between Ashbury and Masonic), tel. (415) 552-4550. You'll get just that. Always popular for pizza is **Cybelle's,** with two neighborhood outlets: one at 1535 Haight St. (near Ashbury), tel. (415) 552-4200; the other at 203 Parnassus (at Stanyan), tel. (415) 665-8088. When East Coast transplants get homesick, they escape to **Escape from New York Pizza,** 1737 Haight (between Cole and Shrader), tel. (415) 668-5577. (There's another Escape at 508 Castro, at 18th, tel. 415-252-1515.)

In the Haight's heyday, **Magnolia Pub & Brewery,** 1398 Haight (at Masonic), tel. (415) 864-7468, was occupied by the Drugstore Café and later by Magnolia Thunderpussy's, a way-cool dessert-delivery business. The place has retained much of its bohemian charm with colorful murals and sweeping psychedelic signs out front. The menu offers a twist on traditional pub fare—mussels steamed in India Pale Ale, mushroom risotto cakes, along with regular old burgers and house-cut fries. The formidable house-made beer list includes Pale Ales, Porters, and more offbeat selections like the Old Thunderpussy Barleywine, a tribute to the brewpub's most famous tenant.

The area referred to as "the lower Haight" is an avant-garde enclave sandwiched between seedy Western Addition and the Webster St. public housing, with nary a tourist attraction in sight. Without the homeless, runaways, and drug dealers notable in the upper Haight, this several-block area has become a fairly happy haven for artists and low-end wannabes, as well as the cafés, bars, and restaurants they inhabit. (Great people-watching.) **Kate's Kitchen,** 471 Haight (at Fillmore) tel. (415) 626-3984, is a small storefront diner where the emphasis is on down-home American food like buttermilk pancakes and scallion-cheese biscuits. A bit more boisterous, with sunny-day sidewalk tables, is the **Horse Shoe Coffee House,** 566 Haight (between Fillmore and Steiner), tel. (415) 626-8852, which also offers high-octane coffee and Internet access.

Most of the neighborhood's bars serve fairly decent food during the day and into the evening; try **Mad Dog in the Fog,** 530 Haight (between Steiner and Fillmore), tel. (415) 626-7279, a rowdy English-style pub, or just across the street, painfully hip **Noc Noc,** 557 Haight, tel. (415) 861-5811. Particularly off the wall, in the spirit of the neighborhood, is **Spaghetti Western,** 576 Haight, tel. (415) 864-8461, an earring-heavy reinterpretation of our collective cowboy heritage. Lots of food for the money.

THE MISSION DISTRICT AND THE CASTRO

The Mission District is known for its open-air markets. One of the best is **La Victoria Mexican Bakery & Grocery,** 2937 24th St. (at Alabama), tel. (415) 550-9292. Buy some homemade tamales, fruit, and a few *churros* (Mexican sugar-dipped doughnuts) and have a feast at the children's park (between Bryant and York on 24th) while studying the murals. Other ethnic bakeries worth poking into for impromptu picnic fixings include **Pan Lido Salvadoreno,** 3147 22nd St. (at Capp), tel. (415) 282-3350, and **Pan Lido Bakery,** 5216 Mission (at Niagra), tel. (415) 333-2140. An ethnic change-up, serving great sandwiches, is **Lucca Ravioli Company,** 1100 Valencia (at 22nd St.), tel. (415) 647-5581.

Among the Mission's inexpensive neighborhood joints is the justifiably famous **Taqueria Can-Cun,** 2288 Mission (at 19th), tel. (415) 252-9560, which serves jumbo-size veggie burritos, handmade tortilla chips, and scorching salsa. There are two other locations: 10 blocks south on Mission (near Valencia) and at Sixth and Market. **Fina Estampa,** 2374 Mission St. (between 19th and 20th), tel. (415) 824-4437, is a nondescript Peruvian outpost featuring exceptional seafood, chicken, and beef entrées (humongous portions) and good service. At **La Rondalla,** 901 Valencia (at 20th), tel. (415) 647-7474, mariachi bands play while you eat. At **Pancho Villa Taqueria,** 3071 16th (between Mission and Valencia), tel. (415) 864-8840, you'll be hard-pressed to find anything over seven bucks. And the portions are huge, including the grand dinner plates of grilled shrimp. At **Los Jarritos,** 901 S. Van Ness Ave. (at 20th), tel. (415) 648-8383, the "little jars" add color to an already colorful menu of Jalisco specialties.

The line between the Mission and Castro Districts, like distinct geographical and sociopolitical divisions elsewhere in the city, is often blurred. **Pozole,** 2337 Market St., tel. (415) 626-2666, has an almost religious south-of-the-border folk feel, what with the candlelit shrines, skull masks, and festive colors. But the food here isn't a literal cultural interpretation—especially comforting when one recalls that *pozole* originally was human flesh specially prepared as fight fuel for Aztec warriors.

The **Flying Saucer,** 1000 Guerrero (at 22nd), tel. (415) 641-9955, where the daily-changing menu is beamed over onto the wall, is a happy landing for mostly French culinary creativity—like an interplanetary marriage between Berkeley's Chez Panisse and the Zuni Cafe in a neighborhood burger stand. Three nightly seatings.

One more stop along the Mission's restaurant row (Valencia between 16th and 24th Streets) is the bustling **Slanted Door,** 584 Valencia (at 17th), tel. (415) 861-8032, where the food is healthy, eclectic, and surprisingly reasonable. People flock from all over the city, so make a reservation or be prepared to wait. Menu changes weekly. Another popular spot for Vietnamese is **Saigon Saigon,** 1132 Valencia (at 22nd), tel. (415) 206-9635, serving an astounding array of dishes, from majestic rolls and barbecued quail to Buddha's delight (vegetarian). Open for lunch on weekdays, for dinner nightly.

Both restaurant and tapas bar, **Esperpento,** 3295 22nd St. (at Valencia), tel. (415) 282-8867, is a great place for delectable Catalonian entrées, as well as tasty and sophisticated Spanish finger foods. Fairly inexpensive. Open Mon.-Sat. for lunch and dinner. **Cafe Nidal,** 2491 Mission (at 18th), tel. (415) 285-4334, is a long-standing neighborhood stop for falafel and other inexpensive Middle Eastern specialties. **Cafe Istanbul,** 525 Valencia (between 16th and 17th), tel. (415) 863-8854, occasionally has belly dancers.

A neighborhood classic in the retro diner genre is **Boogaloos,** 3296 22nd St. (at Valencia), tel. (415) 824-3211, famous for huge breakfasts, slacker crowds, and its signature dish, the Temple o' Spuds. **Cafe Ethiopia,** 878 Valencia (at 20th), tel. (415) 285-2728, offers all the usual espresso drinks plus Ethiopian cuisine, including poultry, beef, and vegetarian dishes from mild to spicy hot. Hugely popular and excellent value for the money, **Ti Couz,** 3108 16th St. (at Valencia), tel. (415) 252-7373, specializes in crepes—stuffed with everything from spinach to salmon to berries.

For real cheap eats in the Castro, head to **Hot 'n' Hunky,** 4039 18th St., tel. (415) 621-6365, for locally famous burgers and renowned French fries, not to mention excessive neon and Marilyn Monroe memorabilia. Very Castro is **Cafe Flore,** 2298 Market St. (at Noe), tel. (415) 621-8579, a popular gay hangout and café serving up omelettes and crepes, salads and good sandwiches, and current information about what's going on in the neighborhood. (Great for people-watching, especially out on the plant-populated patio.)

Missed by most tourists but popular for brunch is the **Patio Cafe,** 531 Castro (near 18th), tel. (415) 621-4640, a romantic hideaway where diners sit outside in a sunny, glass-domed patio sheltered from the wind. Another popular Castro destination is the **Bagdad Cafe,** 2295 Market St. (at 16th), tel. (415) 621-4434, offering a healthy take on American-style fare, plus great salads. Nearby, and wonderful for succulent seafood, is the **Anchor Oyster Bar,** 579 Castro (between 18th and 19th), tel. (415) 431-3990.

It's Tops, 1801 Market (at McCoppin), tel. (415) 431-6395, looks like a classic American greasy spoon—the decor hasn't changed since 1945—but the surprise is just how good the pancakes and other breakfast selections are. **Sparky's 24-Hour Diner,** 242 Church St. (between Market and 15th), tel. (415) 626-8666, got lost somewhere in the 1950s, style-wise, but the breakfast omelettes, burgers, and salads are certainly up to modern expectations.

The atmosphere at suave, contemporary **2223 Market** (at Noe), tel. (415) 431-0692, is cozy, and the food is down-home American. Excellent garlic mashed potatoes and onion rings.

SOUTH OF MARKET (SoMa)

San Francisco's answer to New York City's SoHo, the South of Market area, or SoMa, is post-hippie, post-hip, post-just about everything. Anything goes. Reality here ranges from streetpeople chic and chichi supper clubs to only-those-in-the-know-know-where-it's-at dance clubs. An exploration of the neighborhood reveals the same stunning cultural contrast as those encampments of the homeless in front of the White House. Many areas here are considered unsafe after dark—stay with a group.

Head toward the bay down Second to reach the delightful South Park neighborhood, home to photo studios and shops serving the multimedia and advertising industries, as well as trendy coffeehouses, restaurants, and the postage-stamp-size greensward of South Park itself (bordered by Bryant and Brannan, Second and Third). The design-and-dine crowd is attracted in spades by South Park's **Infusion,** 555 Second St. (at Brannan), tel. (415) 543-2282, a busy, chic restaurant beloved for its innovative, spicy menu and fruit-infused vodka drinks. **Ristorante Ecco,** 101 South Park, tel. (415) 495-3291, is a trattoria-style California/Italian place with yellow sponge-painted walls; it's popular with the young professional crowd. Great desserts. Straight across the park is Ecco's slightly older sibling, the **South Park Cafe,** 108 South Park, tel. (415) 495-7275, an intimate French-style bistro whipping up espresso and croissants in the morning and more elaborate creations at lunch and dinner. Open daily.

After exploring Moscone Center and Yerba Buena Gardens, drop in for a cold one at **Thirsty Bear Brewing Co.,** 661 Howard (at Third), tel. (415) 974-0905, where you can enjoy one of the seven housemade microbrews and outstanding Spanish and Catalan dishes. Marked by the huge tomato hanging outside, no-fuss **Vino e Cucina,** 489 Third St. (at Bryant), tel. (415) 543-6962, offers fine Italian cuisine scene, including pastas, pizzas, and unusual specials. Exceptional **Fringale,** 570 Fourth St. (between Bryant and Brannan), tel. (415) 543-0573, is a bright and contemporary French/American bistro serving excellent food at remarkably reasonable prices—a place well worth looking for. Open for lunch weekdays and for dinner Mon.-Saturday.

Continuing southwest through the district, you'll find good and pretty cheap, fast-as-your-laundry-cycle fare at **BrainWash,** 1122 Folsom (between Seventh and Eighth), tel. (415) 861-3663 (see the special topic Clean Up Your Act at BrainWash). It's by one of the area's sociocultural flagships, **Julie's Supper Club,** 1123 Folsom, tel. (415) 861-0707, a restaurant and nightclub/bar known for its combination of space-age-meets-the-'50s supper-club style and Old West saloon atmosphere. Not to mention the famous martinis.

For spice and great atmosphere, **India Garden,** 1261 Folsom (at Ninth), tel. (415) 626-2798, is well worth poking into for wonderful nans (flatbreads) and *kulchas* baked in a tandoor oven.

Although most folks come for the fresh-brewed beer, the **20 Tank Brewery,** 316 11th St. (at Folsom), tel. (415) 255-9455, also serves respectable bar food. You can fill up on a plate of nachos, a tasty sandwich, or a bowl of chili—and almost nothing's over five bucks. For those stirred to the soul by the world burger beat, the top stop is **Hamburger Mary's,** 1582 Folsom (at 12th), tel. (415) 626-1985 (reservations) or (415) 626-5767 (information), a cleaned-up bikers' bar easily mistaken for a downhome junque store. For deliciously spicy Thai food at bargain prices, you won't go wrong at **Manora's Thai Cuisine,** 1600 Folsom (at 12th), tel. (415) 861-6224, with a menu featuring well-prepared seafood and curries. Night owls like to come here because before hitting the nearby clubs.

Also a possibility (if only for the great view of the railroad tracks) is **42 Degrees,** 235 16th St. (at Illinois, along the waterfront in China Basin), tel. (415) 777-5558, serving "nouvelle Mediterranean" food. The menu offers cuisine from southern France, Italy, Spain, and Greece—all regions at 42° north latitude. This is one of the trendiest spots around, so sometimes you wait awhile. Open weekdays for lunch and Wed.-Sat. for dinner.

FISHERMAN'S WHARF AND GHIRARDELLI SQUARE

Fisherman's Wharf is both tourist central and seafood central. Most locals wouldn't be caught dead eating at one of the Wharf's many seafood restaurants—but that doesn't mean the food isn't good here. Pick of the litter is probably **Scoma's,** on Pier 47 (walk down the pier from the intersection of Jefferson and Jones Streets), tel. (415) 771-4383. It's just off the beaten path (on the lightly pummeled path) and therefore a tad quieter and more relaxing than the others—or at least it seems so. The others would include: **A. Sabella's,** 2766 Taylor St. (at Jefferson), tel. (415) 771-4416; **Alioto's,** 8 Fisherman's Wharf (at Jefferson), tel. (415) 673-0183; the **Franciscan,** Pier 43 1/2, The Embarcadero, tel. (415)

GHIRARDELLI SQUARE

Tourist district it may be, but Ghirardelli Square houses some fine restaurants.

362-7733; **Pompei's Grotto,** 340 Jefferson St. (near Jones), tel. (415) 776-9265; and a large number of places at Pier 39. You can get a decent bowl of clam chowder and a slab of sourdough bread at any of them.

Ghirardelli Square, 900 North Point (at Larkin), though technically part of the same Fisherman's Wharf tourist area, houses some fine restaurants patronized by locals even in broad daylight. The **Mandarin,** tel. (415) 673-8812, was the city's first truly palatial Chinese restaurant and the first to serve up spicy Szechuan and Hunan dishes. The food here is still great. Stop by at lunch for off-the-menu dim sum (including green onion pie, spring rolls with yellow chives, and sesame shrimp rolls), served 11:30 a.m.-3:30 p.m. daily, or come later for dinner. You won't go wrong for seafood at **McCormick and Kuleto's,** tel. (415) 929-1730, which features its own Crab Cake Lounge and 30 to 50 fresh specialties every day. Another much-loved Ghirardelli Square eatery is **Gaylord,** tel. (415) 771-8822, serving astounding Northern Indian specialties with a side of East Indies decor.

Elsewhere in the area, the Victorian-style **Buena Vista,** 2675 Hyde St. (at Beach), tel. (415) 474-5044, is notorious as the tourist bar that introduced Irish coffee. It's a great spot to share a table for breakfast or light lunch, and the waterfront views are almost free.

THE MARINA DISTRICT, COW HOLLOW, AND PACIFIC HEIGHTS

Perhaps San Francisco's most famous, most fabulous vegetarian restaurant is **Greens,** at Building A, Fort Mason (enter at Buchanan and Marina), tel. (415) 771-6222, where the hearty fare proves for all time that meat is an unnecessary ingredient for fine dining—and where the views are plenty appetizing, too. Open for lunch and dinner Tues.-Sat., and for brunch on Sunday; reservations always advised. The bakery counter is open Tues.-Sun. from 10 a.m. to mid- or late afternoon.

Left at Albuquerque, 2140 Union St. (at Fillmore in Cow Hollow), tel. (415) 749-6700, offers Southwestern ambience and an energetic, dining-and-drinking clientele. Modern-day Malcolm Lowrys could spend the rest of their tormented days here, sampling from among 100-plus types of tequila. (Stick with the 100% blue agave reposados.) Good food, too. Open daily for lunch and dinner.

Pane e Vino, 3011 Steiner St. (at Union), tel. (415) 346-2111, is a justifiably popular neighborhood trattoria that's unpretentious and unwavering in its dedication to serving up grand, deceptively simple pastas. If you tire of privacy, head over to **Perry's,** 1944 Union (between Buchanan and Laguna), tel. (415) 922-9022, one of the city's ultimate see-and-be-seen scenes and a great burger stop.

Irrawaddy, 1769 Lombard St. (between Octavia and Laguna), tel. (415) 931-2830, is a good spot for Burmese cuisine. **Curbside Cafe,** 2417 California, tel. (415) 929-9030, specializes in flavorful delights from all over—France, Morocco, Mexico, and the Caribbean (the crab cakes are justifiably famous). **Lhasa Moon,** 2420 Lombard (at Scott), tel. (415) 674-9898, offers excellent, authentic Tibetan cuisine Thurs.-Fri. for lunch, and Tues.-Sun. for dinner.

Elite Cafe, 2049 Fillmore (between Pine and California), tel. (415) 346-8668, is a clubby pub serving Cajun and Creole food in a dark, handsome room. It's somehow appropriate to the neighborhood. **The Mansions,** 2220 Sacramento (between Laguna and Buchanan), tel. (415) 929-9444, serves wonderful food in a Victorian dining room, complete with unusual entertainment. Be sure to reserve in advance.

For people of modest means planning a special night out, **Chateau Suzanne,** 1449 Lombard, tel. (415) 771-9326, is a good choice, serving healthy and absolutely elegant French-Chinese entrées. Open Tues.-Sat. for dinner only; reservations advised.

Close to Japantown and adjacent to the Majestic Hotel (a one-time family mansion), the **Cafe Majestic,** 1500 Sutter St. (at Gough), tel. (415) 776-6400, is widely regarded as one of San Francisco's most romantic restaurants. The setting radiates old-world charm: ornate Edwardian decor, pale green and apricot decor with potted palms. It's sedate, yet far from stuffy and serves plentiful breakfasts on weekdays and brunch on weekends. Listen to a live classical pianist Fri.-Sat. nights and at Sunday brunch. Lunch is served Tues.-Fri., dinner nightly. Reservations are wise.

East of Pacific Heights, right on the stretch of Hwy. 101 that surface-streets its way through the city en route to the Golden Gate Bridge, is **Harris',** 2100 Van Ness Ave. (at Pacific), tel. (415) 673-1888, the city's best steakhouse, and unabashedly so. This is the place to come for a martini and a steak: T-bones, ribeyes, and filet mignon all star on a beefy menu. Open for dinner daily.

CHINATOWN

To find the best restaurants in Chinatown, go where the Chinese go. Some of these places may look a bit shabby, at least on the outside, and may not take reservations—or credit cards. But since the prices at small family-run enterprises are remarkably low, don't fret about leaving that plastic at home.

Very popular, and always packed, the **House of Nanking,** 919 Kearny (between Jackson and Columbus), tel. (415) 421-1429, has a great location at the foot of Chinatown on the North Beach border. To fit into this tiny restaurant, diners often sit elbow to elbow, but the excellent food and reasonable prices make it well worth the wait.

For spicy Mandarin and the best pot stickers in town, try the **Pot Sticker,** 150 Waverly Place, tel. (415) 397-9985, open daily for lunch and dinner. Another possibility is the tiny turn-of-the-20th-century **Hang Ah Tea Room,** 1 Pagoda Place (off Sacramento St.), tel. (415) 982-5686, specializing in Cantonese entrées and lunchtime dim sum. Inexpensive and locally infamous, due largely to the rude waiter routine of Edsel Ford Wong (now deceased), is three-story **Sam Woh,** 813 Washington St. (at Grant), tel. (415) 982-0596, where you can get good noodles, jook (rice gruel), and Chinese-style doughnuts (for dunking in your gruel).

Empress of China, 838 Grant Ave. (between Washington and Clay), tel. (415) 434-1345, offers a wide-ranging Chinese menu, elegant atmosphere, and great views of Chinatown and Telegraph Hill. They've been in business for three decades, so you know they're doing something right. Open daily for lunch and dinner.

Vegetarians will appreciate **Kowloon Vegetarian Restaurant,** 909 Grant Ave., tel. (415) 362-9888, which serves more than 80 meatless selections, including 20 types of vegetarian dim sum and entrées like sweet and sour or curried (faux) pork (with soybean and gluten substituting for meat). Open daily 9 a.m.-9 p.m.

JACKSON SQUARE, NORTH BEACH, AND RUSSIAN HILL

In and Around Jackson Square

"Like the Flintstones on acid," one local food fan says of the almost indescribable style of the **Cypress Club,** 500 Jackson St. (at Montgomery), tel. (415) 296-8555. This popular restaurant near the Financial District is named after the nightclub in Raymond Chandler's *The Big Sleep.* Snide types say: "Très L.A." Others have called doing lunch or dinner here "like sitting under a table" (those huge columns could be table legs) or "like going to a very expensive, very garish, catered carnival." You enter through a copper door, then push past the blood-red velvet speakeasy curtain. Curvaceous copper sectional "pillows," something like overblown landscaping berms, frame the dining room and

separate the booths. At table, you sink into plush burgundy mohair seats or pull up a clunky chair, then relax under the familiarity of the WPA-style Bay Area mural wrapping the walls near the ceiling. (Finally, something seems familiar.) Then you notice the odd polka-dotted light fixtures. If the atmosphere is stimulating, so is the food—simple French cuisine reinvented with fresh local ingredients. Matching the decor, desserts are tantalizing "architectural constructs." The wine list is remarkable—and safe, since the 14,000-bottle wine cellar is downstairs in an earthquake-proof room. The Cypress Club is open daily for dinner, Mon.-Sat. for lunch, and Sunday for brunch.

If that's not enough otherworldly ambience, head around the corner and down an alley to **Bix,** 56 Gold St. (between Jackson and Pacific, Montgomery and Sansome), tel. (415) 433-6300, a small supper club and bar with the feel of a 1940s-style film noir hideout. At Kearny and Columbus, you'll find movie-magnate-turned-winemaker Francis Ford Coppola's **Cafe Niebaum-Coppola,** 916 Kearny St., tel. (415) 291-1700, which offers an Italian menu and a good wine bar (serving, among other selections, Coppola's own vintages).

One of the country's best Greek restaurants is **Kokkari,** 200 Jackson St. (at Front), tel. (415) 981-0983. Open weekdays for lunch and Mon.-Sat. for dinner. While in the Montgomery-Washington Tower, **Tommy Toy's Haute Cuisine Chinoise,** 655 Montgomery St. (between Washington and Clay), tel. (415) 397-4888, serves up classical Chinese cuisine with traditional French touches, called "Frenchinoise" by Tommy Toy himself. The restaurant itself is impressive enough; it's patterned after the reading room of the Empress Dowager of the Ching Dynasty, and the rich decor includes priceless Asian art and antiques. Open for dinner nightly and for lunch on weekdays; reservations always advisable.

North Beach Proper

Farther north in North Beach proper, you'll find an almost endless selection of cafés and restaurants. Historically, this is the perfect out-of-the-way area to eat, drink good coffee, or just while away the hours. These days, North Beach is a somewhat odd blend of San Francisco's Beatera bohemian nostalgia, new-world Asian attitudes, and other ethnic culinary accents. An example of the "new" North Beach: the **New Sun Hong Kong Restaurant,** 606 Broadway (at the sometimes-harmonic, very cosmopolitan cultural convergence of Grant, Broadway, and Columbus), tel. (415) 956-3338. Outside, marking the building, is a three-story-tall mural depicting the North Beach jazz tradition. But this is a very Chinatown eatery, open from early morning to late at night and specializing in hot pots and earthy, homey, San Francisco-style Chinese fare.

Also here are some of old San Francisco's most traditional traditions. The **Washington Square Bar and Grill,** 1707 Powell St. (at Union), tel. (415) 982-8123, is an immensely popular social stopoff for the city's cognoscenti—a place that also serves outstanding food with your conversation. The live jazz, too, is often worth writing home about. The venerable **Fior D'Italia,** 601 Union St. (at Stockton), tel. (415) 986-1886, established in 1886, is legendary for its ambience—including the Tony Bennett Room and the Godfather Room—and its historic ability to attract highbrow Italians from around the globe.

"Follow your nose" to the **Stinking Rose,** 325 Columbus (between Broadway and Vallejo), tel. (415) 781-7673, an exceptionally popular Italian restaurant where all the food is heavily doused in garlic. For exceptional food with a more elevated perspective, a dress-up restaurant on Telegraph Hill is appropriately romantic: **Julius' Castle,** 1541 Montgomery St. (north of Union), tel. (415) 392-2222, for French and Italian, and beautiful views of the city. Not that far away (along the Embarcadero), renowned for its fine food and flair, is the one and only **Fog City Diner,** 1300 Battery St. (at Lombard), tel. (415) 982-2000. Though this is the original gourmet grazing pasture, Fog City has its imitators around the world.

But the real North Beach is elsewhere. **Campo Santo,** 240 Columbus Ave. (between Pacific and Broadway), tel. (415) 433-9623, is yet another cultural change-up: Latin American kitsch kicking up its heels with campy Day of the Dead decor. The food is lively, too, from mahimahi tacos to crab quesadillas. Open Mon.-Sat. from lunchtime through dinner (until 10 p.m.). For genuine neighborhood tradition, head to stand-up **Molinari's,** 373 Columbus (between Broadway and Green), tel. (415) 421-2337, a fixture since 1907. It's a good deli stop for fresh pastas, homemade sauces, hearty sandwiches, and tasty sweet treats. Or stop off for a meatball sandwich or cappuccino at landmark **Mario's Bohemian Cigar Store Cafe,** 566 Columbus (near Washington Square), tel. (415) 362-0536. The inexpensive sandwiches, frittata, and cannelloni here are the main menu attraction, but folks also come to sip cappuccino or Campari while watching the world whirl by, or while watching each other watching. Sorry, they don't sell cigars.

"Rain or shine, there's always a line" at very-San Francisco **Little Joe's,** 523 Broadway (between Kearny and Columbus), tel. (415) 433-4343, a boisterous bistro where the Italian food is authentic, the atmosphere happy, and everyone hale and hearty. The open kitchen is another main attraction. For faster service, belly up to a counter stool and watch the chefs at work.

Volare Trattoria Caffe, 561 Columbus (between Union and Green), tel. (415) 362-2774, offers superb Sicilian cuisine—try the exceptional calimari in tomato-garlic sauce. Owner Giovanni Zocca plants himself outside on Friday and Saturday nights and sings the restaurant's theme tune, "Volare, volare, volare, ho ho ho." Just up the street is **L'Osteria del Forno,** 519 Columbus, tel. (415) 982-1124, a tiny storefront trattoria with six tables. This place is a great budget bet for its wonderful Italian flatbread sandwiches.

For pizza, the place to go is **North Beach Pizza,** 1499 Grant (at Union), tel. (415) 433-2444, where there's always a line, and it's always worth standing in. Heading down toward the Financial District, **Caffe Macaroni,** 59 Columbus (between Washington and Jackson), tel. (415) 956-9737, is also a true blue—well, red, white, and green—pasta house in the Tuscany tradition: intimate, aromatic, and friendly.

Exceptional for Afghan fare is **The Helmand,** 430 Broadway (between Kearny and Montgomery), tel. (415) 362-0641. Here linguistics majors can enjoy ordering such dishes as *dwopiaza, bowlani,* and *sabzi challow.* Most entrées are oriented around lamb and beef, but vegetarian entrées are available and are separated out on the menu, making for easy selection.

Russian Hill
The **Hyde Street Bistro,** 1521 Hyde St. (between Jackson and Pacific), tel. (415) 292-4415, is one of those sophisticated little places where San Franciscans hide out during tourist season. It's quiet, not too trendy, and serves good French cuisine. Appreciate the breadsticks.

Ristorante Milano, 1448 Pacific Ave. (between Hyde and Larkin), tel. (415) 673-2961, is a happy, hopping little Italian restaurant with pastas—do try the lasagna—fresh fish, and sometimes surprising specials.

Not far away and a real deal for foodies who don't care one whit about the frills is **Pete's Cafe at San Francisco Art Institute,** 800 Chestnut St. (at Jones), tel. (415) 749-4567, where you can get a great lunch for $5 or less, along with one of the city's best bay views. The atmosphere is arty and existential, with paper plates and plastic utensils just to remind you that this is for students. Everything is fresh and wholesome: Southwestern black bean/vegetable stew, white bean and escarole soup, even house-roasted turkey sandwiches. Good breakfasts, too. Open in summer Mon.-Fri. 9 a.m.-2 p.m., and during the school year Mon.-Fri. 8 a.m.-9 p.m., Saturday 9 a.m.-2 p.m. (hours can vary; it's best to call ahead).

PRACTICAL SAN FRANCISCO

USEFUL INFORMATION

The clearinghouse for current visitor information is the **San Francisco Convention & Visitors Bureau,** 900 Market St. (at Powell, downstairs—below street level—outside the BART station at Hallidie Plaza), P.O. Box 429097, San Francisco, CA 94142-9097, tel. (415) 391-2000, www.sfvisitor.org. Here you can pick up official visitor pamphlets, maps, booklets, and brochures about local businesses, including current accommodations bargains and various coupon offers. Multilingual staffers are available to answer questions. The Visitor Information Center is open for walk-ins weekdays 9 a.m.-5 p.m., Sat.-Sun. 9 a.m.-3 p.m.; closed Thanksgiving, Christmas, and New Year's Day.

If you can't make it to the Visitor Information Center or are planning your trip in advance and need information, you have a couple of options. To find out what's going on in town, from entertainment and arts attractions to major professional sports events, you can call the city's free, 24-hour visitor hot line, available in five languages. To get the news in English, call (415) 391-2001; in French, tel. (415) 391-2003; in German, tel. (415) 391-2004; in Japanese, tel. (415) 391-2101; and in Spanish, tel. (415) 391-2122. The information is updated weekly. You can also write to the SFCVB to request current information on accommodations, events, and other travel planning particulars. For $3 postage and handling, you can get a copy of the SFCVB's semiannual *The San Francisco Book,* which contains thorough information about sights, activities, arts, entertainment, recreation, shopping venues, and restaurants, as well as a detailed map. (And then some.) If you'll be in town awhile, it's worth the money to request in advance.

Where-San Francisco is a slick, free magazine full of useful information on accommodations, dining, shopping, and nightlife. It's available at the Hallidie Square visitor center and else-

PREPARING FOR SAN FRANCISCO

San Francisco's weather can upset even the best-laid plans for a frolic in the summertime California sun. For one thing, there may not be any sun. In summer, when most visitors arrive, San Francisco is enjoying its citywide natural air-conditioning system, called "fog." When California's inland areas are basting in blast-furnace heat, people here might be wearing a down jacket to go walking on the beach. (Sometimes it does get hot—and "hot" by San Francisco standards refers to anything above 80° F) Especially during the summer, weather extremes even in the course of a single day are normal, so pack accordingly. Bring warm clothing (at least one sweater or jacket for cool mornings and evenings), in addition to the optimist's choice of shorts and sandals, and plan to dress in layers so you'll be prepared for anything. The weather in late spring and early autumn is usually sublime—balmy, often fog-free—so at those times you should bring two pairs of shorts (but don't forget that sweater, just in case). It rarely rains May-Oct.; raingear is prudent at other times.

Most buildings in San Francisco and most public-transit facilities should be accessible to people in wheelchairs and those with other physical limitations; many hotels, restaurants, and entertainment venues will make special accommodations, given some advance notice.

All of San Francisco's (and California's) public buildings and restaurants are nonsmoking. Most motels and hotels have nonsmoking rooms, and many have entire floors of nonsmoking rooms and suites.

Unless otherwise stated on a restaurant menu, restaurants do not include a gratuity in the bill. The standard tip for the wait staff is 15% of the total tab, though truly exceptional service may merit 20%. The average tip for taxi drivers is 15%. It's also customary to tip airport baggage handlers and hotel porters ($1 per bag, one way, is an acceptable standard), parking valets, and other service staff. When in doubt about how much to tip, just ask someone.

where around town. You can also order a subscription ($30/year) by contacting: Where Magazine, 74 New Montgomery St., Ste. 320, San Francisco, CA 94105, tel. (415) 546-6101.

Even more real: the **San Francisco Bay Guardian** and **SF Weekly** tabloid newspapers, available free almost everywhere around town. The Guardian's motto (with a hat tip to Wilbur Storey and the 1861 *Chicago Times,* as interpreted by Editor/Publisher Bruce Brugmann), "It is a newspaper's duty to print the news and raise hell," is certainly comforting in these times and also generates some decent news/feature reading, along with comprehensive arts, entertainment, and events listings. The Guardian also publishes **FYI San Francisco,** a tourist-oriented guide to the city with some of the same punchy, irreverent writing. It's free and widely available around town. The *Weekly* also offers what's-happening coverage and—to its everlasting credit—Rob Brezsny's "Free Will Astrology" column.

While roaming the city, look for other special-interest and neighborhood-scope publications. The **San Francisco Bay Times** is a fairly substantive gay and lesbian biweekly. For comprehensive events information, pick up a copy of the **Bay Area Reporter.** Widely read throughout the Sunset and Richmond Districts is **The Independent.** Other popular papers include the award-winning, hell-raising, **Street Sheet,** published by the Coalition on Homelessness in San Francisco and distributed by the homeless on San Francisco's streets; the **New Mission News;** and the **Noe Valley Voice.**

The city's major dailies are universally available at newsstands and in coin-op vending racks. The morning paper is the **San Francisco Chronicle,** and the afternoon/evening paper is the **San Francisco Examiner.** In late 1999, the *Chronicle* was sold to the Hearst Corporation, and the new owners said they would try to sell off the *Examiner.* Because the two papers have been linked in a federally approved joint operating agreement since the 1960s, the sale must be accepted by the Justice Department before it's final. But at present, the *Examiner* and *Chronicle* share printing facilities (and classified ads) and also combine forces every week to produce the humongous Sunday paper. That edition's pink "Datebook" section is packed with readable reviews, letters from sometimes demanding or de-

mented Bay Area readers, and the most comprehensive listing of everything going on in the coming week. San Francisco's major non-English and ethnic newspapers include the **Chinese Times,** the **Irish Herald,** and the African-American community's **Sun Reporter.**

If you don't feel obliged to buy what you need to read, the newish, high-tech, and highly controversial **San Francisco Main Library,** downtown at 100 Larkin (at Grove), tel. (415) 557-4400, is a good place to start becoming familiar with the local public-library system. For better or worse, the old card catalogs are gone—replaced by a computerized system—and the computers here offer free Internet access. But many users decry the seemingly low percentage of space in the expensive, expansive building actually devoted to stacks of books. A complete listing of neighborhood branch libraries is offered in the white pages of the local phone book, under "Government Pages—SF City & County —Libraries."

Other Helpful Information Contacts

For current **weather information,** call (415) 936-1212. For current San Francisco **time,** call that old-time favorite POPCORN (767-8900). For current **road conditions** anywhere in California, call toll-free (800) 427-7623. The free **DOC** (Directory On Call) service, tel. (415) 808-5000, offers a prerecorded summary of local news, sports, stocks, entertainment, and weather information.

For special assistance and information on the city's disabled services, contact the **Mayor's Office of Community Development** (Attn.: Disability Coordinator), 25 Van Ness Ave., Ste. 700, San Francisco, CA 94102, tel. (415) 252-3100, or the helpful local **Easter Seal Society,** 6221 Geary Blvd., tel. (415) 752-4888. To understand the ins and outs of disabled access to local public transit, request a copy of the **Muni Access Guide** from Muni Accessible Services Program, 949 Presidio Ave., San Francisco, CA 94115, tel. (415) 923-6142 weekdays or (415) 673-6864 anytime.

Emergency Assistance: Safety and Health

In any emergency, get to a telephone and dial 911—the universal emergency number in California. Depending upon the emergency, police,

STAYING SAFE

San Francisco is a reasonably safe city. Definitely unsafe areas, especially at night, include The Tenderloin, some areas south of Market St., parts of the Western Addition, and parts of the Mission District (including, at night, BART stops). For the most part, drug-related gang violence is confined to severely impoverished areas. The increased number of homeless people and panhandlers, particularly notable downtown, is distressing, certainly, but most of these people are harmless lost souls.

Definitely not harmless is the national crime craze known as "carjacking." As the scenario usually goes, you're sitting in your car at an intersection or at a parking garage when an armed stranger suddenly appears and demands that you get out. Though there have been highly publicized cases involving successful driver heroism, the best advice is, don't try it. If a criminal demands that you get out of your car or give up your car keys, do it. Losing a car is better than losing your life. Though there is no sure-fire prevention for carjacking, locking all car doors and rolling up windows is often suggested. Another good idea: avoid dubious or unfamiliar neighborhoods.

If your own vehicle isn't safe, keep in mind that no place is absolutely safe. And sadly, in general it still holds true that female travelers are safest if they confine themselves to main thoroughfares. As elsewhere in America, women are particularly vulnerable to assaults of every kind. At night, women traveling solo, or even with a friend or two, should stick to bustling, yuppie-happy areas like Fisherman's Wharf and Union Street. The definitely street-savvy, though, can get around fairly well in SoMa and other nightlife areas, especially in groups or by keeping to streets with plenty of benign human traffic. (You can usually tell by looking.)

---

fire, and/or ambulance personnel will be dispatched. Runaways can call home free, anytime, no questions asked, by dialing the **California Youth Crisis Line,** toll-free tel. (800) 843-5200. Other 24-hour crisis and emergency hot lines include: **Helpline,** 772-HELP; **Rape Crisis** (operated by Women Against Rape, or WAR), tel. (415) 647-7273, the number to call in the event of any violent assault; **Suicide Prevention,** tel. (415) 781-0500; **Drug Line,** tel. (415) 834-1144 or (415) 362-3400; **Alcoholics Anonymous,** tel. (415) 621-1326; **Narcotics Anonymous,** tel. (415) 621-8600; and **Poison Control,** toll-free tel. (800) 876-4766.

The San Francisco Police Department (general information line: 415-553-0123) sponsors several Japanese-style kobans—police ministation neighborhood kiosks—where you can get law-enforcement assistance if you're lucky enough to be nearby when they're open. The Hallidie Plaza Koban is in the tourist-thick cable-car zone at Market and Powell; open Tues.-Sat. 10 a.m.-6 p.m. The Chinatown Koban is on Grant between Washington and Jackson; open daily 1-9 p.m. The Japantown Koban is at Post and Buchanan; open Mon.-Fri. 11 a.m.-7 p.m.

San Francisco General Hospital, 1001 Potrero Ave. (at 22nd St., on Potrero Hill), tel. (415) 206-8000 (911 or 415-206-8111 for emergencies), provides 24-hour medical emergency and trauma care services. Another possibility is **UCSF Medical Center,** 505 Parnassus Ave. (at Third Ave.), tel. (415) 476-1000. (The UCSF dental clinic is at 707 Parnassus, tel. (415) 476-1891 or (415) 476-5814 for emergencies.) Convenient for most visitors is **Saint Francis Memorial Hospital** on Nob Hill, 900 Hyde St., tel. (415) 353-6000, which offers no-appointment-needed clinic and urgent-care medical services as well as a **Center for Sports Medicine,** tel. (415) 353-6400, and a physician referral service, toll-free tel. (800) 333-1355.

For nonemergency referrals, call the **San Francisco Medical Society,** tel. (415) 561-0853, or the **San Francisco Dental Society,** tel. (415) 421-1435.

Post Offices, Banks, Currency Exchanges, Et Cetera

San Francisco's main post office is the Rincon Annex, 180 Steuart St. (just off the Embarcadero, south of Market), San Francisco, CA 94105. It's open weekdays 7 a.m.-6 p.m., Saturday 9 a.m.-2 p.m. For help in figuring out local zip code assignments, and for general information and current postal rates, call toll-free (800) 275-8777 or log on to www.usps.gov. Regional post offices are also scattered throughout San

Francisco neighborhoods. Some branches are open extended hours, such as 7 a.m.-6 p.m. weekdays, or with limited services some Saturday hours, and some have after-hours open lobbies, so customers can purchase stamps via vending machines. Public mailboxes, for posting stamped mail, are available in every area. Stamps are also for sale in major hotels (usually in the gift shop) and, increasingly, even in major grocery stores.

Branches of major national and international banks are available in San Francisco; most offer automated cash-advance facilities, often accessible through various member systems. Getting mugged while banking is a potential disadvantage of getting cash from an automated teller. Always be aware of who is nearby and what they're doing; if possible, have a companion or two with you. If the situation doesn't feel "right," move to another location—or do your banking inside.

Most currency exchange outlets are either downtown or at the San Francisco International Airport (SFO). **Bank of America Foreign Currency Services,** 345 Montgomery St., tel. (415) 622-2451, is open Mon.-Fri. 9 a.m.-6 p.m. Another possibility is the Bank of America at the Powell St. cable car turnaround, 1 Powell (at Market), tel. (415) 622-4498 (same hours). **Thomas Cook Currency Services, Inc.,** 75 Geary, tel. (415) 362-6271 or toll-free (800) 287-7362, is open weekdays 9 a.m.-5 p.m., Saturday 10 a.m.-4 p.m. (Another location is at 1 Powell Street.) To exchange currency at the airport, head for the International Terminal, where **Bank of America,** tel. (650) 615-4700, offers currency exchange for both in- and out-bound travelers daily 7 a.m.-11 p.m.

For cardmembers, the **American Express Travel Agency** is another possibility for check cashing, traveler's-check transactions, and currency exchange. There are three San Francisco offices: 455 Market (at First), 560 California St. (between Kearny and Montgomery), and 333 Jefferson (at Jones); tel. (415) 536-2600 for all. In Northern California, the American Automobile Association (AAA) is known as the California State Automobile Association (CSAA), and the San Francisco office is near the Civic Center at 150 Van Ness Ave., tel. (415) 565-2012. The CSAA office is open weekdays for all member inquiries and almost endless services, including no-fee traveler's checks, free maps and travel information, and travel agency services.

San Francisco's major hotels, and most of the midrange boutique hotels, have a fax number and fax facilities; some offer other communications services. For telex and telegrams, you can pop into one of the many **Western Union** branches throughout the city.

TRANSPORTATION: GETTING TO AND FROM TOWN

At least on pleasure trips, Californians and other Westerners typically drive into San Francisco. The city is reached from the north via Hwy. 101 across the fabled Golden Gate Bridge ($3 toll to get into the city, no cost to get out); from the east via I-80 from Oakland/Berkeley across the increasingly choked-with-traffic Bay Bridge ($2 toll to get into the city, no cost to get out); and from the south (from the coast or from San Jose and other South Bay/peninsula communities) via Hwy. 1, Hwy. 101, or I-280/19th Avenue. Whichever way you come and go, avoid peak morning (7-9 a.m.) and afternoon/evening (4-6 p.m.) rush hours at all costs. The Bay Area's traffic congestion is truly horrendous.

Major Bay Area Airports

About 15 miles south of the city via Hwy. 101, **San Francisco International Airport** (SFO), tel. (650) 876-2377 (general information) or (650) 877-0227 (parking information), perches on a point of land at the edge of the bay. (That's one of the thrills here: taking off and landing just above the water.) Each of the three terminals—North, Central (or International), and South—has two levels, the lower for arrivals, the upper for departures. San Francisco's is the fifth busiest airport in the U.S. and seventh busiest in the world; its 80 gates handle some 32 million passengers per year. More than 40 major scheduled carriers (and smaller ones, including air charters) serve SFO. There's protected parking for 7,000 cars, best for short-term car storage.

San Francisco International has its quirks. For one thing, its odd horseshoe shape often makes for a long walk for transferring passengers; the "people movers" help somewhat, but people seem to avoid the second-floor intraterminal bus. (In all fairness, though, since SFO is primarily an origin/destination airport, for most travelers this isn't a problem.) And with such a high volume of air traffic—an average of 1,260 flights per day—delays are all too common, especially when fog rolls in and stays.

People complain, too, that the airport always seems to be under major construction. A multi-billion-dollar expansion project is underway, which at some point will result in a new international terminal. If you've got some time to kill, check out the permanent "Images of Mexico" cultural display, with masks and such, in the South Terminal connector (beyond the security check) and the outstanding changing exhibits along United's North Terminal connector. Or you can make use of the AT&T Communications Center, upstairs in the International Terminal; it's open 8 a.m.-10 p.m. and offers special phone facilities to allow callers to pay the attendants (multilingual) in cash, as well as a six-person conference room set up for teleconferencing (fax, too). Other airport facilities include restaurants (the Bay View Restaurant in the South Terminal, the North Beach Deli in the North), the South Terminal's California Marketplace (where you can get some wine and smoked fish or crab to go with that sourdough bread you're packing), and the North Terminal's Author's Bookstore, which prominently features titles by Bay Area and California writers.

Due to its excellent service record and relatively lower volume, many travelers prefer flying into and out of efficient, well-run **Oakland International Airport** just across the bay, tel. (510) 577-4000. It's fairly easy to reach from downtown San Francisco on either public transit or one of the convenient shuttle services.

Airport Shuttles

If flying into and out of SFO, avoid driving if at all possible. Airport shuttles are abundant, fairly inexpensive, and generally reliable. Most companies offer at-your-door pick-up service if you're heading to the airport (advance reservations usually required) and—coming from the airport—take you right where you're going. The usual one-way fare, depending upon the company, is around $15 per person for SFO/San Francisco service. (Inquire about prices for other shuttle options.)

TAKING A TAXI

Taxis from SFO to San Francisco cost around $30. Standard San Francisco taxi fare, which also applies to around-town trips, is $2.50 for the first mile, $1.80 per additional mile (plus tip, usually 15%). Among the 24-hour taxi companies available:

DeSoto Cab Co . . . . . . tel. (415) 673-1414
Luxor Cab . . . . tel. (415) 282-4141
Veteran's Taxicab
  Company . . . . tel. (415) 552-1300
Yellow Cab . . . . tel. (415) 626-2345

The blue-and-gold **SuperShuttle** fleet has some 100 vans coming and going all the time, tel. (415) 659-2547. When you arrive at SFO, the company's shuttle vans (no reservation needed) to the city are available at the outer island on the upper level of all terminals. To arrange a trip to the airport, call and make your pick-up reservation at least a day in advance. (And be ready when the shuttle arrives—they're usually on time.) Group, convention, and charter shuttles are also available, and you can pay on board with a major credit card. (Exact fare depends on where you start and end.)

SFO Airporter, tel. (415) 641-3100, offers nonstop runs every 20 minutes between the airport and the Financial District or Union Square. No reservations are required in either direction. **City Express Shuttle** in Oakland, tel. (510) 638-8830, offers daily shuttle service between the city of San Francisco and Oakland International Airport. **Bayporter Express, Inc.,** tel. (415) 656-2929, (415) 467-1800, or toll-free (800) 287-6783 (from inside the airport), specializes in shuttle service between most Bay Area suburban communities and SFO, and offers hourly door-to-door service between any location in San Francisco and the Oakland Airport. **Marin Airporter** in Larkspur, tel. (415) 461-4222, provides service every half hour from various Marin communities to SFO daily, 4:30 a.m.-11 p.m., and from SFO to Marin County daily, 5:30 a.m.-midnight.

San Mateo County Transit (SamTrans), toll-free tel. (800) 660-4287, offers extensive peninsula public transit, including express and regular buses from SFO to San Francisco. It's cheap, too (about $1). Buses leave the airport every 30 minutes from very early morning to just after midnight; call for exact schedule. The express buses limit passengers to carry-on luggage only, so heavily laden travelers will have to take one of the regular buses—a 10-minute-longer ride.

Buses and Trains

The **Transbay Terminal,** 425 Mission St. (just south of Market St. between First and Fremont), tel. (415) 495-1551 or (415) 495-1569, is the city's regional transportation hub. An information center on the second floor has displays, maps, and fee-free phone lines for relevant transit systems. Bus companies based here include **Greyhound,** tel. (415) 495-1569, with buses coming and going at all hours; **Golden Gate Transit,** tel. (415) 455-2000, offering buses to and from Marin County and vicinity; **AC Transit,** tel. (415) 817-1717, which serves the East Bay; and **San Mateo County Transit** (SamTrans), toll-free tel. (800) 660-4287, which runs as far south as Palo Alto. Shuttle buses here also take passengers across the bay to the Amtrak station at 245 Second St. in Oakland's Jack London Square, tel. (510) 238-4306 or toll-free (800) USA-RAIL, www.amtrak.com, where you can make train connections both north and south.

Primarily a regional commute service, **Cal-Train,** toll-free tel. (800) 660-4287 within Northern California, runs south to Palo Alto and the Amtrak station in San Jose, where you can get a bus connection to Santa Cruz. The San Francisco CalTrain depot is at Fourth and Townsend Streets.

Bay Area Ferries

Since the city is surrounded on three sides by water, ferry travel is an unusual (and unusually practical) San Francisco travel option. Before the construction of the Golden Gate Bridge in 1937, it was the only way to travel to the city from the North and East Bay areas. Nowadays, the ferries function both as viable commuter and tourist transit services. (See Delights and Diversions for more about ferry tours and other oceangoing entertainment.)

The **Blue & Gold Fleet,** tel. (415) 773-1188 (recorded schedule) or (415) 705-5555 (reservations and information), based at Fisherman's Wharf, Piers 39 and 41, offers roundtrip service daily between San Francisco (either the Ferry Building or Pier 41) and Oakland (Jack London Square), Alameda (Gateway Center), Sausalito, Tiburon, Angel Island, and Vallejo (via high-speed catamaran). The company also offers bay cruises, tours of Alcatraz, an "Island Hop" tour to both Alcatraz and Angel Island, and various land tours (Muir Woods, Yosemite, Monterey/Carmel, Wine Country).

Golden Gate Ferries, headquartered in the Ferry Building at the foot of Market St., tel. (415) 923-2000, specializes in runs to and from Sausalito (adults $4.70) and more frequent large-ferry (725-passenger capacity) trips to and from Larkspur. Family rates available, and disabled passengers and seniors (over age 65) travel at half fare.

Red & White Fleet at Fisherman's Wharf, Pier 43½, tel. (415) 447-0597 or toll-free (800) 229-2784, offers bay cruises and various land tours, as well as a commuter run to Richmond.

TRANSPORTATION: GETTING AROUND TOWN

San Francisco drivers are among the craziest in California. Whether they're actually demented, just distracted, insanely rude, or perhaps intentionally driving to a different drummer, walkers beware. The white lines of a pedestrian crosswalk seem to serve as sights, making people easier targets. Even drivers must adopt a heads-up attitude. In many areas, streets are narrow and/or incredibly steep. Finding a parking place requires psychic skills. So, while many people drive into and out of the Bay Area's big little city, if at all possible many use public transit to get around town.

But some people really want to drive in San Francisco. Others don't want to, but need to, due to the demands of their schedules. A possible compromise: if you have a car but can't stand the thought of driving it through the urban jungle yourself, hire a driver. You can hire a chauffeur, and even arrange private sightseeing tours and other outings, through companies like **WeDriveU, Inc.,** 60 E. Third Ave. in San Mateo, tel. (650) 579-5800 or toll-free (800) 773-7483. Other local limousine companies may be willing to hire-out just a city-savvy driver; call and ask.

Those maniacal bicycle delivery folks manage to daredevil their way through downtown traffic, but note their bandages—despite protective gear. For normal people, cycling is a no-go proposition downtown and on heavy-traffic thoroughfares. Bring a bike to enjoy the Golden Gate National Recreation Area and other local parks, though it may be easier to rent one. Rental outlets around Golden Gate Park include **Lincoln Cyclery,** 772 Stanyan (near Waller), tel. (415) 221-2415; **Start to Finish Bicycles,** 672 Stanyan (near Page), tel. (415) 750-4760; and **Avenue Cyclery,** 756 Stanyan, tel. (415) 387-3155. In Golden Gate Park, you can rent a bike, rollerblades, or a pedal-powered surrey at **Golden Gate Park Bike & Skate,** 3038 Fulton, tel. (415) 668-1117.

Car Rental Agencies

Some of the least expensive car rental agencies have the most imaginative names. Near the airport in South San Francisco, **Bob Leech's Auto Rental** 435 S. Airport Blvd., tel. (650) 583-3844, specializes in new Toyotas, from $25 per day with 150 fee-free miles. (You must carry a valid major credit card and be at least 23 years old; call for a ride from the airport.) Downtown, family-owned **Reliable Rent-A-Car,** 349 Mason, tel. (415) 928-4414, rents new cars with free pick-up and return for a starting rate of $19 per day ("any car, any time"). That all-American innovation, **Rent-A-Wreck,** 2955 Third St., tel. (415) 282-6293, rents out midsize used cars for around $29 per day with 150 free miles, or $159 per week with 700 free miles.

The more well-known national car rental agencies have desks at the airport, and at other locations. Their rates are usually higher than those of the independents and vary by vehicle make and model, length of rental, day of the week (sometimes season), and total mileage. Special coupon savings or substantial discounts through credit card company or other group affiliations can lower the cost considerably. If price really matters, check around. Consult the telephone book for all local locations of the companies listed below.

Agencies with offices downtown include: **Avis Rent-A-Car,** 675 Post St., tel. (415) 885-5011 or toll-free (800) 831-2847; **Budget Rent-A-Car,** 321 Mason, tel. (415) 775-5800 or toll-free (800) 527-0700; **Dollar Rent-A-Car,** 364 O'Farrell (opposite the Hilton Hotel), tel. (415) 771-5301 or toll-free (800) 800-4000; **Enterprise,** 1133 Van Ness Ave., tel. (415) 441-3369 or toll-free (800) 736-8222; **Hertz,** 433 Mason, tel. (415) 771-2200 or toll-free (800) 654-3131; and **Thrifty Rent-A-Car,** 520 Mason (at Post), tel. (415) 788-8111 or toll-free (800) 367-2277.

For a transportation thrill, all you wannabe easy riders can rent a Harley-Davidson or BMW motorcycle from **Dubbelju Tours & Service,** 271 Clara St., tel. (415) 495-2774. Rates start at $92 a day and include insurance, 100 free miles, and road service. Weekly and winter rates available. Open Mon.-Fri. 9 a.m.-noon and 4-6 p.m., Saturday 9-noon, or by appointment. German spoken.

Parking Regulations and Curb Colors

If you're driving, it pays to know the local parking regulations as well as rules of the road—it'll cost you if you don't.

PARKING AND PARKING GARAGES

If you're driving, you'll need to park. You also need to find parking, all but impossible in North Beach, the Haight, and other popular neighborhoods. San Franciscans have their pet parking theories and other wily tricks—some even consider the challenge of finding parking a sport, or at least a game of chance. But it's not so fun for visitors, who usually find it challenging enough just to find their way around. It's wise to park your car (and leave it parked, to the extent possible), then get around by public transit. Valet parking is available (for a price, usually at least $15 per day) at major and midsize hotels, and at or near major attractions, including shopping districts.

Call ahead to inquire about availability, rates, and hours at major public parking garages, which include: **Fisherman's Wharf,** 665 Beach (at Hyde), tel. (415) 673-5197; **Fifth and Mission Garage,** 833 Mission St., tel. (415) 982-8522; **Downtown,** Mason and Ellis, tel. (415) 771-1400 (ask for the garage); **Moscone Center,** 255 Third St., tel. (415) 777-2782; **Chinatown,** 733 Kearny (underground, near Portsmith Square), tel. (415) 982-6353; and **Union Street,** 1550 Union, tel. (415) 673-5728. For general information on city-owned garages, call (415) 554-9805.

And good luck.

Curbing your wheels is the law when parking on San Francisco's hilly streets. What this means: turn your wheels toward the street when parked facing uphill (so your car will roll into the curb if your brakes and/or transmission don't hold), and turn them toward the curb when facing downhill.

Also, pay close attention to painted curb colors; the city parking cops take violations seriously. Red curbs mean absolutely no stopping or parking. Yellow means loading zone (for vehicles with commercial plates only), half-hour time limit; yellow-and-black means loading zone for trucks with commercial plates only, half-hour limit; and green-yellow-and-black means taxi zone. Green indicates a 10-minute parking limit for any vehicle, and white means five minutes only, effective during the operating hours of the adjacent business. As elsewhere in the state, blue indicates parking reserved for vehicles with a California disabled placard or plate displayed. Pay attention, too, to posted street-cleaning parking limits, to time-limited parking lanes (open at rush hour to commuter traffic), and avoid even a quick-park at bus stops or in front of fire hydrants. Any violation will cost $25 or more, and the police can tow your car—which will cost you $100 or so (plus daily impound fees) to retrieve.

Public Transportation: Muni
The city's multifaceted San Francisco Municipal Railway, or Muni, headquartered at 949 Presidio Ave., tel. (415) 673-MUNI weekdays 7 a.m.-5 p.m., Sat.-Sun. 9 a.m.-5 p.m., is still the locals' public transit mainstay. One of the nation's oldest publicly owned transportation systems, Muni is far from feeble, managing to move almost 250 million people each year. Yet even small glitches can wreak havoc when so many people depend on the system; heated criticism regularly crops up on local talk-radio shows and in the Letters to the Editor sections of local newspapers.

The city's buses, light-rail electric subway-and-surface streetcars, electric trolleys, and world-renowned cable cars are all provided by Muni. It costs $2 to ride the cable car. (It's odd that people stand in long lines at the Powell and Market turnaround, since it actually makes much more sense—no waiting, unless there's absolutely no space available—to grab on at Union Square or other spots en route.) Otherwise, regular Muni fare is $1 ($0.35 for seniors

HISTORIC TRANSPORTATION: RIDING THE CABLE CARS

With or without those Rice-a-Roni ads, Muni's cable cars are a genuine San Francisco treat. (Don't allow yourself to be herded onto one of those rubber-tired motorized facsimiles that tend to cluster at Union Square, Fisherman's Wharf, and elsewhere. They are not cable cars, just lures for confused tourists.) San Francisco's cable cars are a national historic landmark, a system called "Hallidie's Folly" in honor of inventor Andrew S. Hallidie when these antiques made their debut on August 2, 1873. The only vehicles of their kind in the world, cable cars were created with the city's challenging vertical grades in mind. They are "powered" by an underground cable in perpetual motion, and by each car's grip-and-release mechanism. Even though maximum speed is about nine mph, that can seem plenty fast when the car snaps around an S-curve. (They aren't kidding when they advise riders to hold onto their seats.) After a complete $67.5 million system overhaul in the early 1980s, 26 "single-enders" now moan and groan along the two Powell St. routes, and 11 "double-enders" make the "swoop loop" along California Street. (New cars are occasionally added to the city's collection.) To get a vivid education in how cable cars work, visit the reconstructed Cable Car Barn and Museum on Nob Hill.

SAN JOSE CONVENTION AND VISITORS BUREAU

cable cars: a time-honored way to climb the city's steep streets

and youths, children under 5 free), exact coins required, and includes free transfers valid for two changes of vehicle in any direction within a two-hour period. If you'll be making lots of trips around town, pick up a multitrip discount Muni Passport (which includes cable car transit), available for sale at the Muni office, the Convention & Visitors Bureau information center downtown, Union Square's TIX box office, the City Hall information booth, and the Cable Car Museum. A one-day pass costs $6, a three-day pass $10, a seven-day pass $15, and a monthly pass $35.

Muni route information is published in the local telephone book yellow pages, or call for route verification (phone number listed above). Better yet, for a thorough orientation, check out one of the various Muni publications, most of which are available wherever Muni Passports are sold (and usually at the Transbay Terminal). A good overview and introduction is provided (free) by the *Muni Access Guide* pamphlet and the useful, seasonally updated *TimeTables,* which list current route and time information for all Muni transit. Especially useful for travelers is Muni's *Tours of Discovery* brochure, which lists popular destinations and possible tours with suggested transit routes (including travel time) and optional transfers and side trips. But the best all-around guide, easy to carry in pocket or purse, is the official annual *Muni Street & Transit Map* ($2), available at bookstores and grocery stores in addition to the usual outlets. The Muni map explains and illustrates major routes, access points, frequency of service, and also shows BART and Muni Metro subway stops, along with the Cal-Train route into San Francisco. As a city map, it's a good investment, too.

San Francisco's Muni buses are powered by internal-combustion engines, and each is identified by a number and an area or street name (such as #7 Haight or #29 Sunset). Similarly numbered local trolleys or streetcars are actually electrically operated buses, drawing power from overhead lines, and are most notable downtown and along the steepest routes. The summers-only Historic Trolley Festival is actually a do-it-yourself party, achieved by climbing aboard Muni's international fleet of vintage electric streetcars

(F-Market) that start at the Transbay Terminal and run along Market St. to and from Castro.

The Muni Metro refers to the five-line system of streetcars or light-rail vehicles, often strung together into trains of up to four cars, that run underground along Market St. and radiate out into the neighborhoods. Metro routes are identified by letters in conjunction with point of destination (J-Church, K-Ingleside, L-Taraval, M-Oceanview, and N-Judah).

Public Transportation: BART

The Bay Area's space-age, 95-mile Bay Area Rapid Transit, or BART, system headquartered in Oakland, tel. (510) 464-6000 or (650) 992-2278 (transit information), calls itself "the tourist attraction that gets people to the other tourist attractions." Fair enough. Heck, it is pretty thrilling to zip across to Oakland and Berkeley underwater in the Transbay Tube. And at least as far as it goes, BART is a good get-around alternative for people who would rather not drive. Currently, there isn't much BART service on the San Francisco side of the Bay, with 10 BART stations in San Francisco, the line ending at Colma. Some day in the not-too-distant future, a line will extend south to the airport; work is underway and is expected to be completed in 2001. But the system can take you to Oakland/Berkeley, then north to Richmond, south to Fremont, or east to Pittsburg or Pleasanton. (BART Express buses extend transit service to other East Bay communities.)

Helpful publications include the annual *All About BART* (with fares, travel times, and other details), *Fun Goes Farther on BART,* and the *BART & Buses* BART guide to connections with the bus system. BART trains operate Mon.-Fri. 4 a.m.-midnight, Saturday 6 a.m.-midnight, and Sunday 8 a.m.-midnight. Exact fare depends upon your destination, but it'll be $4.75 or less. For a special $3.90 "excursion fare," you can tour the whole system; just don't walk through the computerized exits, or you'll have to pay again before you get back on. Tickets are dispensed at machines based at each station. (Change machines, for coins or dollar bills, are nearby.) If you don't have a current Muni map, you can get your bearings at each station's color-keyed wall maps, which show destinations and routes.

SOUTH FROM SAN FRANCISCO

The unstable wave-whipped coast south of San Francisco is all buff-colored bluffs and sandy beaches faced with rough rocks. Often foggy in summer, the coastline in winter is crowded with bird- and whalewatchers. But from late summer into autumn, the weather is usually good and the crowds minimal, making this the perfect time for a superb escape. Though wetsuit-clad surfers brave the snarling swells even in gale-force winds, swimming is dangerous even on serene sunny days due to treacherous undertows. Many of the region's beaches are officially accessible as state beaches or local beach parks; others are state-owned and undeveloped, or privately owned. Almost 20 miles of this 51-mile-long coastline are included as part of the San Mateo Coast State Beaches, starting with Daly City's **Thornton Beach** (popular for fishing and picnicking) in the north and ending with tiny **Bean Hollow State Beach** just north of Año Nuevo in the south. Though campgrounds are available inland, seaside public camping is possible only at Half Moon Bay State Beach, tel. (650) 726-8820. For more beach information, call **San Mateo State Beaches,** (650) 726-8819. For more information on public-transit access to the San Mateo coast, call SamTrans toll-free at (800) 660-4287.

FROM PACIFICA SOUTH

Pacifica: California's Fog Capital

The self-proclaimed Fog Capital of California, Pacifica is sometimes a dreary place. But the locals make up for the opaque skies with *attitude.* Come here in late September for the annual **Pacific Coast Fog Fest,** which features a Fog Calling Contest (almost everyone's a winner), the Phineas Fogg Balloon Races, high-octane alcoholic "fogcutters" (if drinking, *don't* drive off into the fog), plus a fog fashion show. When the weather's sunny, the town offers superb coastal views. And good food abounds here—fog or shine. For more information on the town or the Fog Fest, call the **Pacifica Chamber of Commerce** at (650) 355-4122.

At **Sharp Park State Beach** along Beach Blvd. (reached from Hwy. 1 via Paloma Ave., Clarendon Rd., or streets in between) is the **Pacifica Pier,** popular for fishing and winter whalewatching. Migrating gray whales are attracted to the abundant plankton at the end of the community's sewage outfall pipe (the treatment plant is the building with the Spanish arches). Some old salts here say the great grays swim so close to the pier you can smell the fish on their breath.

Farther south is sort-of-secluded **Rockaway Beach,** a striking black-sand beach in a small rectangular cove where the coast has backed away from the rocky bluffs. Hotels and restaurants cluster beyond the rock-reinforced parking lot.

South from Pacifica

Long and narrow **Montara State Beach** offers hiking and rock-and-sand beachcombing. The state's tiny **Gray Whale Cove Beach** here is a concession-operated clothing-optional beach, open for all-over tans only to those 18 and over; for information, call (650) 728-5336. Just south of Montara proper is the cypress-strewn **Moss Beach** area, named for the delicate sea mosses that drape shoreline rocks at low tide.

Best for exploration Nov.-Jan. are the 30 acres of tidepools at the **James V. Fitzgerald Marine Reserve** (open daily from sunrise to sunset), which stretches south from Montara Point to Pillar Point and Princeton-by-the-Sea. At high tide, the Fitzgerald Reserve looks like any old sandy beach with a low shelf of black rocks emerging along the shore, but when the ocean rolls back, these broad rock terraces and their impressive tidepools are exposed. For area state park information, call (415) 330-6300; for information on low-tide prime time at the Fitzgerald Reserve, call (650) 728-3584; for more about docent-led guided tours of the reserve, call Coyote Point Museum, (650) 342-7755.

Nearby, along Hwy. 1 in Montara, are **McNee Ranch State Park** and Montara Mountain, with hiking trails and great views of the Pacific. Next south is **El Granada,** an unremarkable town except for the remarkable music showcased by the **Bach Dancing & Dynamite Society,** 311 Mirada Rd. (technically in Miramar), tel. (650) 726-4143, the longest-running venue for jazz greats in the Bay Area. Begun in 1958 when jazz fanatic Pete Douglas started letting jazz musicians hang out at his house and jam, public concerts blast off every Sunday (except around Christmas and New Year's) in a baroque beatnik beach house. The family lives downstairs; upstairs at "the Bach" is the concert hall and deck, though guests are free to amble down to the beach and back at all times. Admission isn't charged, but a contribution of $10-15 or so is the usual going rate for Sunday concerts. The Dancing & Dynamite Society has become so popular that Friday night candlelight dinner concerts cosponsored by local businesses or other supporters are also offered (reservations and advance payment required). For a small fee, anyone can join the society and receive a newsletter and calendar of coming attractions.

Staying Along the South Coast
Inexpensive and incredibly pleasant for a coast overnight is **HI-AYH Point Montara Lighthouse Hostel,** on Hwy. 1 at 16th St., Montara, tel. (650) 728-7177, www.norcalhostels.org. It's quite popular, so reservations are advisable. Dorm-style bunks, and couple and family rooms are available in the wheelchair-accessible annex. Budget. Also, motels—not many are inexpensive—pop up here and there along the coast.

The charming **Goose and Turrets Bed and Breakfast,** 835 George St., Montara, tel. (650) 728-5451, fax (650) 728-0141, is a huge 1908 Italian-style seaside villa that dates back to the Bay Area's early bohemian days, when the adventurous and/or artistic rode the Ocean Shore Railroad from San Francisco to the arts colony and beach here. The five guest rooms are just part of the pleasure of this 6,000-square-foot home, which features great windows on its west wall. All rooms have private bathrooms and little luxuries; three rooms have fireplaces, German down comforters, and English towel warmers. French spoken; find the Goose and Turrets on the web at www.montara.com/goose.html. Breakfast is a four-course feast; tea and treats are served in the afternoon. Expensive-Premium.

The English-style **Seal Cove Inn,** 221 Cypress Ave., Moss Beach, tel. (650) 728-4114, is another find—an elegant and romantic inn overlooking the Fitzgerald Marine Reserve. The 10 guest rooms here feature wood-burning fireplaces, refrigerators, TVs, and ocean views; some have a private deck. For small group meetings, there's even a conference room. Luxury.

Eating Along the South Coast
Traditional in Moss Beach is the straightforward Italian fare at **Dan's Place,** on Virginia Ave. overlooking the Fitzgerald Reserve, tel. (650) 728-3343; open for lunch and dinner. The old **Moss Beach Distillery** in Moss Beach, 140 Beach Way (at Ocean), tel. (650) 728-5595, is now a romantic cliffside restaurant, very good for seafood, ribs, lamb, and veal. Open for lunch and dinner. **Barbara's Fish Trap,** 281 Capistrano Rd. in Princeton-by-the-Sea, tel. (650) 728-7049, open daily for lunch and dinner, offers great Half Moon

*the popular
Point Montara
Lighthouse Hostel*

Bay views, fishnet kitsch decor, and fish selections that are a cut above the usual. Try the garlic prawns.

HALF MOON BAY

Known until the turn of the century as Spanishtown, Half Moon Bay was a farm community settled by Italians and Portuguese, and specializing in artichokes and Brussels sprouts. Down and out during the early 1900s, things picked up during Prohibition when the area became a safe harbor for Canadian rumrunners. Fast becoming a fashionable Bay Area residential suburb, Half Moon Bay is famous for its pumpkins and offers a rustic Main St. with shops, restaurants, and inns, plus pseudo-Cape Cod cluster developments along Highway 1. In 1999, Half Moon Bay's commercial ship-to-shore radiotelegraph station, the nation's last, tapped out its final Morse code transmission. Just a few miles south of Half Moon Bay off Pillar Point and legendary among extreme surfers is **Mavericks,** home of the world's baddest wave. When surf's up here, during wild winter storms, Mavericks creates mean and icy 35-foot waves—mean enough to break bones and boards.

Nearby **Burleigh Murray Ranch State Park** is still largely undeveloped, but the former 1,300-acre dairy ranch is now open to the public for day use. You can take a hike up the old ranch road, which winds up through sycamores and alders along Mill Creek. About a mile from the trailhead is the ranch's most notable feature, the only known example of an English bank barn in California. This century-old structure relied on simple but ingenious design, utilizing slope ("bank") and gravity to feed livestock most efficiently. Especially for those who can't remember even the basics of farm life, other outbuildings also deserve a peek. To get here, turn east on Higgins-Purisima Rd. from Hwy. 1 just south of Half Moon Bay. It's about two miles to the parking area (marked, on the left).

A Portuguese **Chamarita** parade and barbecue are held here seven weeks after Easter. Over the July 4th weekend, the community's **Coastside County Fair and Rodeo** takes place. But the biggest annual event in these parts is the popular **Half Moon Bay Art and Pumpkin**

Festival in October, where pumpkin-carving and pumpkin pie-eating contests as well as the Great Pumpkin Parade take center stage. For a complete list of area events and other information, contact the **Half Moon Bay/Coastside Chamber of Commerce,** 520 Kelly Ave., Half Moon Bay, CA 94019, tel. (650) 726-5202 or (650) 726-8380.

Practical Half Moon Bay

At **Half Moon Bay State Beach** campground (open year-round, hot showers and all), reservations are usually required March-Oct. to guarantee a tent or RV campsite. Unreserved space is often available on nonweekend autumn days. For reservations, call **ReserveAmerica,** toll-free (800) 444-7275.

Motels in Half Moon Bay tend to be on the pricey side. A nice midrange choice is **Harbor View Inn,** 51 Alhambra Ave. (four miles north of town in El Granada), tel. (650) 726-2329. Expensive. The upscale **Half Moon Bay Lodge,** 2400 S. Hwy. 1 (about 2.5 miles south of the Hwy. 92 junction), tel. (650) 726-9000, has a pool, jacuzzi, fitness center, some rooms with fireplaces and some with golf course views. Luxury.

The in thing in Half Moon Bay is inns, many of which offer reduced midweek rates. Much loved is the **Mill Rose Inn** bed and breakfast, 615 Mill St. (in "old town"), tel. (650) 726-7673, (650) 726-8750, or toll-free (800) 829-1794, a romantic Victorian with frills like fireplaces, a spa, English gardens, and excellent breakfasts. Luxury. Another local favorite is the restored **San Benito House** country inn, 356 Main St., tel. (650) 726-3425, with 12 rooms on the upper floor (two share a bath), plus a sauna, redwood deck with flowers and firepit, and a downstairs restaurant and saloon. Moderate-Premium. The **Old Thyme Inn,** 779 Main St., tel. (650) 726-1616 or toll-free (800) 720-4277, has some rooms with two-person whirlpools. For special occasions or extra privacy, book the Garden Suite, which features a private entrance. The atmosphere here is very English, in a casually elegant style. Rooms are individually decorated, and some feature fireplaces and/or in-room whirlpool tubs. Especially delightful for gardeners is the herb garden here, boasting more than 80 varieties (true aficionados are allowed to take cuttings). Expect such treats as homemade scones and marmalade, or possibly even French cherry flan. Expensive-Luxury.

Another historic local favorite is the **Zaballa House,** 324 Main St. (right next door to the San Benito House), tel. (650) 726-9123. It's Half Moon Bay's oldest surviving building (circa 1859) and now features nine standard guest rooms and three private-entrance suites, all with private bath. Several rooms have two-person whirlpool tubs and/or fireplaces. Ask about the "resident ghost" in Room 6. Expensive-Luxury.

The contemporary **Cypress Inn,** 407 Mirada Rd. (three miles north of Hwy. 92, just off Hwy. 1; exit at Medio Ave.), Miramar, tel. (650) 726-6002 or toll-free (800) 832-3224, is right on the beach and just a few doors down from the Bach Dynamite & Dancing Society. The inn's motto is "in celebration of nature and folk art," and the distinctive rooms—each with an ocean view and private deck, fireplace, and luxurious private bath—do live up to it, whether you stay in the Rain, Wind, Sea, Sky, Star, Sun, or Moon rooms. For a special treat, head up into the Clouds (the penthouse). Gourmet breakfasts, afternoon tea, winetasting, and hors d'oeuvres included. Massage is available by appointment. Luxury. North of Half Moon Bay, **Pillar Point Inn** 380 Capistrano Rd., El Granada, tel. (650) 728-7377, overlooks the harbor in Princeton-by-the-Sea. All rooms have fireplaces and other modern amenities. Luxury.

The **Half Moon Bay Bakery,** 514 Main, tel. (650) 726-4841, is also a stop on the local historic walking tour. The bakery still uses its original 19th-century brick oven and offers sandwiches, salads, and pastries over the counter. Other popular eateries include the **Pasta Moon** café, 315 Main St., tel. (650) 726-5125, and the **San Benito House** restaurant, 356 Main (at Mill), tel. (650) 726-3425, noted for its French and Northern Italian country cuisine at dinner. Simpler but excellent lunches (including sandwich selections on homemade breads) also served. Open Thurs.-Sun. only; excellent Sunday brunch. Call for reservations.

FROM SAN GREGORIO SOUTH

On the coast just west of tiny San Gregorio is **San Gregorio State Beach,** with the area's characteristic bluffs, a mile-long sandy beach, and a sandbar at the mouth of San Gregorio Creek. San Gregorio proper is little more than a spot in the road, but the back-roads route via Stage Rd. from here to Pescadero is pastoral and peaceful.

Inland Pescadero ("Fishing Place") was named for the creek's once-teeming trout, not for any fishing traditions on the part of the town's Portuguese settlers. Both **Pomponio** and **Pescadero State Beaches** offer small estuaries for same-named creeks. The 584-acre **Pescadero Marsh Natural Preserve** is a successful blue heron rookery, as well as a feeding and nesting area for more than 200 other bird species. (To birdwatch—best in winter—park at **Pescadero State Beach** near the bridge and walk via the Sequoia Audubon Trail, which starts below the bridge.) Rocky-shored **Bean Hollow State Beach,** a half-mile hike in, is better for tidepooling than beachcombing, though it has picnic tables and a short stretch of sand.

For a longer coast walk, head south to the **Año Nuevo** reserve. (Año Nuevo Point was named by Vizcaíno and crew shortly after New Year's Day in 1602.) The rare northern elephant seals who clamber ashore here are an item only in winter and spring, but stop here any time of year for a picnic and a stroll along Año Nuevo's three-mile-long beach.

Coastal Accommodations

The cheap place to stay in the area is **AYH Pigeon Point Lighthouse Hostel,** five miles south of the turnoff to Pescadero and just off Hwy. 1 via Pigeon Point Rd., tel. (650) 879-0633, www.norcalhostels.org. The hostel's basic but adequate facilities include bunk and family rooms, plus an on-the-cliffs hot tub. Good tidepooling nearby. Budget. Reservations are usually essential.

If the hostel is full, the campground at **Butano State Park,** tel. (650) 879-2040, probably will be too—at least on Fridays, Saturdays, and holidays May-September. Reached from Pescadero via Cloverdale Rd. (or from near Gazos Beach via Gazos Creek Rd.), the park offers 21 family campsites, 19 walk-in sites, and a handful of backcountry trail camps. During the high season, reserve main campsites through **ReserveAmerica,** toll-free tel. (800) 444-7275. The rest of the year, it's usually first-come, first-camped.

The deluxe place to camp in the area is **Costanoa Lodge and Camp,** 2001 Rossi Rd., Pescadero, tel. (650) 879-1100, a "boutique campground" and lodge built by Joie de Vivre Hotels, the San Francisco boutique-hotels specialist. Look for furnished tent cabins, as well as traditional cabins and a 40-room lodge, on this 40-acre spread. Moderate-Luxury.

Hard to beat for an overnight in Pescadero are the six cottages at **Estancia del Mar,** 460 Pigeon Point Rd., tel. (650) 879-1500, fax (650) 712-8688, e-mail: estanciadm@aol.com. Located 500 yards from the surf, each attractive cottage sleeps four and includes custom-tiled bathroom, fully equipped kitchen, wood-burning stove, and stereo/CD player/radio and VCR. Linens and towels are provided. Kids and pets welcome. Luxury, with multinight discounts.

Another option is the Spanish-style **Rancho San Gregorio** bed and breakfast, 5086 La Honda Rd., San Gregorio, tel. (650) 747-0810 or (650) 747-0722, a best bet featuring just four attractive rooms (three have woodstoves; all have private baths). Many of the veggies and fruits served at breakfast are home-grown. Great hiking nearby. Expensive-Premium. Or head south along the coast. About nine miles north of Santa Cruz, the **New Davenport Bed and Breakfast Inn,** 31 Davenport Ave. (Hwy. 1), tel. (831) 425-1818, (831) 426-4122, or toll-free (800) 870-1817, is a colorful ocean-view hideaway (rooms above the restaurant) with artist owners and beach access. Moderate-Premium.

Coastal Fare

In Pescadero, down-home **Duarte's Tavern,** 202 Stage Rd., tel. (650) 879-0464, is most noted for its artichoke soup and delicious olallieberry pie, not to mention the ever-changing fresh fish specials scrawled across the menu chalkboard. Open daily for breakfast, lunch, and dinner; reservations wise (especially in summer) for dinner and Sunday brunch. Near Pescadero is **Phipps Ranch,** where berries, dried beans, baby lettuce, squash, and other local produce are available in season. (San Mateo County's farm trails map lists other regional produce stands.)

Down the coast toward Santa Cruz, the **New Davenport Cash Store & Restaurant,** tel. (831) 426-4122, is a store, arts and crafts gallery, and inexpensive eatery with healthy food (whole grains, salads, soups) in the Americanized Mexican tradition. Great desserts. There are bed-and-breakfast rooms upstairs.

AÑO NUEVO STATE RESERVE

About 20 miles north of Santa Cruz and just across the county line is the 4,000-acre Año Nuevo State Reserve, breeding ground and rookery for sea lions and seals—particularly the unusual (and once nearly extinct) northern elephant seals. The pendulous proboscis of a "smiling" two- to three-ton alpha bull dangles down like a firehose, so the name is apt.

At first glance, the windswept and cold seaward stretch of Año Nuevo seems almost desolate, inhospitable to life. This is far from the truth, however. Año Nuevo is the only place in the world where people can get off their bikes or the bus or get out of their cars and walk out among aggressive, wild northern elephant seals in their natural habitat. Especially impressive is that first glimpse of hundreds of these huge seals nestled like World War II torpedoes among the sand dunes. A large number of other animal and plant species also consider this area home; to better appreciate the ecologically fascinating animal and plantlife of the entire area, read *The Natural History of Año Nuevo,* by Burney J. Le Boeuf and Stephanie Kaza.

Survival of the Northern Elephant Seal

Hunted almost to extinction for their oil-rich blubber, northern elephant seals numbered only 20-100 at the turn-of-the-20th-century. All these survivors lived on Isla de Guadalupe off the west coast of Baja California, Mexico. Their descendants eventually began migrating north to California. In the 1950s, a few arrived at Año Nuevo Island, attracted to its rocky safety. The first pup was born on the island in the 1960s. By 1975, the mainland dunes had slowly been colonized by seals crowded off the island rookery, and the first pup was born onshore. By 1988, 800 northern elephant seals were born on the mainland, part of a total known population of more than 80,000 and an apparent ecological success story. (Only time will tell, though, since the species' genetic diversity has been eliminated by their swim at the brink of extinction.) Though Año

*the northern
elephant seal*

BOB NILSEN

Nuevo was the first northern elephant seal rookery to be established on the California mainland, northern elephant seals are now establishing colonies elsewhere along the state coastline.

The Año Nuevo Mating Season

Male northern elephant seals start arriving in December. Who arrives first and who remains dominant among the males during the long mating season is important because the alpha bull gets to breed with most of the females. Since the males are biologically committed to conserving their energy for sex, they spend much of their time lying about as if dead, in or out of the water, often not even breathing for stretches of up to a half-hour. Not too exciting for spectators. But when two males battle each other for the "alpha" title, the bellowing, often bloody nose-to-nose battles are something to see. Arching up with heads back and canine teeth ready to tear flesh, the males bellow and bark and bang their chests together.

In January, the females start to arrive, ready to bear offspring conceived the previous year. They give birth to their pups within the first few days of their arrival. The males continue to wage war, the successful alpha bull now frantically trying to protect his harem of 50 or so females from marauders. For every two pounds in body weight a pup gains, its mother loses a pound. Within 28 days, she loses about half her weight, then, almost shriveled, she leaves. Her pup, about 60 pounds at birth, weighs 300-500 pounds a month later. Although inseminated by the bull before

leaving the rookery, the emaciated female is in no condition for another pregnancy, so "conception" is actually delayed for several months, allowing the female to feed and regain her strength. Then, after an eight-month gestation period, the cycle starts all over again.

Año Nuevo Etiquette

The Marine Mammal Act of 1972 prohibits people from harassing or otherwise disturbing these magnificent sea mammals, so be respectful. While walking among the elephant seals, remember that the seemingly sluglike creatures *are* wild beasts and can move as fast as any human across the sand, though for shorter distances. For this reason, keeping a 20-foot minimum distance between you and the seals (especially during the macho mating season) is important. No food or drinks are allowed on the reserve, and nothing in the reserve may be disturbed. The first males often begin to arrive in November before the official docent-led tours begin, so it's possible to tour the area unsupervised. Visit the dunes without a tour guide in spring and summer also, when many elephant seals return here to molt.

The reserve's "equal access boardwalk" across the sand makes it possible for physically challenged individuals to see the seals.

Information and Tours

Official 2.5-hour guided tours of Año Nuevo begin in December and continue through March, rain or shine, though January and February are the

GOING COASTAL

From south of Half Moon Bay to Santa Cruz, people will be able to go coastal in perpetuity, thanks in large part to the recent land acquisition efforts of the Peninsula Open Space Trust (POST). Thousands and thousands of acres on and near the coast are now protected from the possibility of development; some parcels are under the jurisdiction of the California Department of Parks and Recreation or other agencies, and many are open to the public (or soon will be) for day use.

Among these is **Cowell Ranch Beach** just south of Half Moon Bay, tel. (650) 726-8819, where a half-mile trail leads out to the point, and stairs trail down to a well-protected sandy beach.

Gazos Creek Beach, tel. (650) 879-2025, with its abundant tidepools, is now included within Año Nuevo State Reserve. The reserve also includes the 2,914 acres of **Cascade Ranch,** which adjoins Big Basin and Butano State Parks. Only a dream in years past, it's now possible to hike from the redwoods to the sea via the associated **Whitehouse Ridge Trail.** The result of one of the largest land deals ever negotiated by POST, one day the hiking and equestrian trails within the 5,638-acre Cloverdale Coastal Ranch south of Half Moon Bay will also be included in the new coastal parks landscape.

Just north of Santa Cruz, the 2,305-acre **Gray Whale Ranch** now part of **Wilder Ranch State Park,** tel. (650) 426-0505, was donated by the Save-the-Redwoods League and the Packard Foundation. A key wildlife corridor, the new ranch lands offer hiking and mountain-biking trails.

prime months and reservations are necessary. The reserve is open 8 a.m.-sunset; day-use parking fee $5 (hike-ins and bike-ins free, but you still must pick up a free day-use permit). Tour tickets ($4 plus surcharge for credit card reservations) are available only through ReserveAmerica's Año Nuevo and Hearst Castle reservations line, toll-free tel. (800) 444-4445. Reservations cannot be made before November 1. To take a chance on no-shows, arrive at Año Nuevo before scheduled tours and get on the waiting list. For wheelchair access reservations, beginning December 1 call (650) 879-2033, 1-4 p.m. only, on Monday, Wednesday, and Friday.

Organized bus excursions, which include walking tour tickets, are available through **San Mateo Transit,** 945 California Dr., Burlingame, CA 94010, toll-free tel. (800) 660-4287 or (650) 508-6441 (call after November 1 for reservations), and **Santa Cruz Metro** (see Santa Cruz—Getting Around above). The AYH Pigeon Point Hostel, near Año Nuevo, sometimes has extra tickets for hostelers. For more information, contact: Año Nuevo State Reserve, New Year's Creek Rd., Pescadero, CA 94060, tel. (650) 879-2027 (24-hour recorded information) or (650) 879-2025 (reserve office, open weekdays 8:30 a.m.-4 p.m.), www.anonuevo.org. The website offers links to other information, including the annual **Sealabration,** behind-the-scenes open-ended guided walks offered by the San Mateo Coast Natural History Association, and the experimental solar-powered elephant seal camera that observes the seals on an hourly basis.

MONTEREY BAY AND COAST

ONE BAY, MANY WORLDS

The only remembered line of the long-lost Ohlone people's song of world renewal, "dancing on the brink of the world," has a particularly haunting resonance around Monterey Bay. Here, in the unfriendly fog and ghostly cypress along the untamed coast, the native "coast people" once danced. Like the area's vanished dancers, Monterey Bay is a mystery: everything seen, heard, tasted, and touched only hints at what remains hidden.

The first mystery is magnificent Monterey Bay itself, almost 60 miles long and 13 miles wide. Its offshore canyons, grander than Arizona's Grand Canyon, are the area's most impressive (if un-

See color maps of Monterey Peninsula and the surrounding coast at front of book.

seen) feature: the bay's largest submarine valley dips to 10,000 feet, and the adjacent tidal mud-flats teem with life.

A second mystery is how two cities as different as Santa Cruz and Monterey could both take root and thrive on the shores of Monterey Bay.

Working- and dot-com-class Santa Cruz has the slightly seedy Boardwalk, sandy beaches, good swimming, surfers, and—helped along by the presence of UC Santa Cruz—an intelligent and open-minded social scene. Nearby are the redwoods, waterfalls, and mountain-to-sea hiking trails of Big Basin, California's first state park, plus the Año Nuevo coastal area, until recently the world's only mainland mating ground for the two-ton northern elephant seal. The monied Monterey Peninsula to the south is fringed by shifting sand dunes and some of the state's most ruggedly wild coastline. Near Monterey is peace-

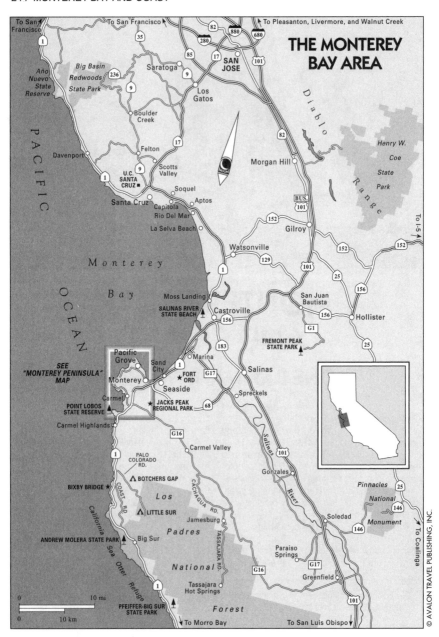

ful Pacific Grove (where alcohol has been legal only since the 1960s), Carmel-by-the-Sea (where Clint Eastwood once made everybody's day as mayor), and inland Carmel Valley (a tennis pro playground abounding in shopping centers). The Carmel Highlands hug the coast on the way south to Big Sur.

Just inland is the agriculturally rich Salinas Valley, boyhood stomping grounds of John Steinbeck. Steinbeck's focus on Depression-era farm workers unleashed great local wrath—all but forgotten and almost forgiven since his fame has subsequently benefited area tourism. Not far north, right on the San Andreas Fault, is Mission San Juan Bautista, where Jimmy Stewart and Kim Novak conquered his fear of heights in Alfred Hitchcock's *Vertigo.* Also in the neighborhood is Gilroy, self-proclaimed garlic capital of the world. South of Salinas and east of Soledad is Pinnacles National Monument, a fascinating volcanic jumble and almost "the peak" for experienced rock climbers.

MONTEREY BAY
BY LAND AND BY SEA

Much of the redwood country from San Francisco to Big Sur resembles the boulder-strewn, rough-and-tumble north coast. Here the Pacific Ocean is far from peaceful; posted warnings about dangerous swimming conditions and un-

dertows are no joke. Inland, the San Andreas Fault menaces, veering inland from the eastern side of the Coast Ranges through the Salinas Valley and on to the San Francisco Bay Area.

The Monterey Peninsula
Steinbeck captured the mood of the Monterey Peninsula in *Tortilla Flats*—"The wind . . . drove the fog across the pale moon like a thin wash of watercolor. . . . The treetops in the wind talked huskily, told fortunes and foretold deaths." The peninsula juts into the ocean 115 miles south of San Francisco and forms the southern border of Monterey Bay. The north shore sweeps in a crescent toward Santa Cruz and the Santa Cruz Mountains; east is the oak- and pine-covered Santa Lucia Range, rising in front of the barren Gabilan ("Sparrow Hawk") Mountains beloved by Steinbeck. Northward are the ecologically delicate Monterey Bay Dunes, now threatened by off-road vehicles and development. To the south, the piney hills near Point Pinos and Asilomar overlook rocky crags and coves dotted with wind-sculpted trees; farther south, beyond Carmel and the Pebble Beach golf mecca, is Point Lobos, said to be Robert Louis Stevenson's inspiration for Spyglass Hill in *Treasure Island.*

Monterey "Canyon"
Discovered in 1890 by George Davidson, Monterey Bay's submerged valley teems with sealife:

dramatically beautiful Point Lobos

CALIFORNIA DEPARTMENT OF PARKS AND RECREATION

bioluminescent fish glowing vivid blue to red, squid, tiny rare octopi, tentacle-shedding jellyfish, and myriad microscopic plants and animals. This is one of the most biologically prolific spots on the planet. Swaying with the ocean's motion, dense kelp thickets are home to sea lions, seals, sea otters, and giant Garibaldi "goldfish." Opal-eyed perch in schools of hundreds swim by leopard sharks and bottom fish. In the understory near the rocky ocean floor live abalones, anemones, crabs, sea urchins, and starfish.

Students of Monterey Canyon geology quibble over the origins of this unusual underwater valley. Computer-generated models of canyon creation suggest that the land once used to be near Bakersfield and was carved out by the Colorado River; later it shifted westward due to plate tectonics. More conventional speculation focuses on the creative forces of both the Sacramento and San Joaquin Rivers, which perhaps once emptied at Elkhorn Slough, Monterey Canyon's principal "head."

However Monterey Canyon came to be, it is now centerpiece of the 5,312-square-mile **Monterey Bay National Marine Sanctuary** which extends some 400 miles along the coast, from San Francisco's Golden Gate in the north to San Simeon in the south. Established in 1992 after a 15-year political struggle, this federally sanctioned preserve is now protected from offshore oil drilling, dumping of hazardous materials, the killing of marine mammals or birds, jet skis, and aircraft flying lower than 1,000 feet. As an indirect result of its federal protection, Monterey Bay now boasts a total of 18 marine research facilities.

Monterey Bay Climate

The legendary California beach scene is almost a fantasy here—almost but not quite. Sunshine warms the sands (between storms) from fall to early spring, but count on fog from late spring well into summer. Throughout the Monterey Bay area, it's often foggy and damp, though clear summer afternoons can get hot; the warmest months along the coast are August, September, and October. (Sunglasses, suntan lotion, and hats are prudent, but always bring a sweater.) Inland, expect hotter weather in summer, colder in winter. Rain is possible as early as October, though big storms don't usually roll in until December.

MONTEREY BAY HISTORY: CALIFORNIA FIRSTS

Cabrillo spotted Point Pinos and Monterey Bay in 1542. Sixty years later, Vizcaíno sailed into the bay and named it for the viceroy of Mexico, the count of Monte-Rey. A century later came Portolá and Father Crespi, who, later joined by Father Junípero Serra, founded both Monterey's presidio and the mission at Carmel. Monterey would later boast the state's first capital, first government building, first federal court, first newspaper, and—though other towns also claim the honor—first theater.

The quiet redwood groves near Santa Cruz remained undisturbed by civilization until the arrival of Portolá's expedition in 1769. The sickly Spaniards made camp in the Rancho de Osos section of what is now Big Basin, experiencing an almost miraculous recovery in the valley they called Cañada de Salud (Canyon of Health). A Spanish garrison and mission were soon established on the north end of Monterey Bay.

By the end of the 1700s, the entire central California coast was solidly Spanish, with missions, pueblos, and military bases or presidios holding the territory for the king of Spain. With the Mexican revolution, Californio loyalty went with the new administration closer to home. But the people here carried on their Spanish cultural heritage despite the secularization of the missions, the increasing influence of cattle ranches, and the foreign flood (primarily American) that threatened existing California tradition. Along the rugged central coast just south of the boisterous and booming gold rush port of San Francisco, the influence of this new wave of "outsiders" was felt only later and locally, primarily near Monterey and Salinas.

Monterey: Capital of Alta California

In addition to being the main port city for both Alta and Baja California, from 1775 to 1845 Monterey was the capital of Alta California—and naturally enough, the center of much political intrigue and scheming. Spared the devastating earthquakes that plagued other areas, Monterey had its own bad times, which included being burned and ransacked by the French pirate Hippolyte Bouchard in 1818. In 1822, Spanish rule ended in California. In 1845, Monterey lost part of its political prestige when Los Angeles temporarily became the territory's capital city. When the rancheros surrendered to Commodore Sloat in July 1846, the area became officially American, though the town's distinctive Spanish tranquility remained relatively undisturbed until the arrival of farmers, fishing fleets, fish canneries, and whalers. California's first constitution was drawn up in Monterey, at Colton Hall, in 1849.

Santa Cruz and
the Bad Boys of Branciforte

Santa Cruz, the site of Misión Exaltación de la Santa Cruz and a military garrison on the north end of Monterey Bay, got its start in 1791. But the 1797 establishment of Branciforte—a "model colony" financed by the Spanish government just across the San Lorenzo River—made life hard for the mission fathers. The rowdy, quasi-criminal culture of Branciforte so intrigued the native peoples that Santa Cruz men of the cloth had to use leg irons to keep the Ohlone home. And things just got worse. In 1818, the threat of pirates at nearby Monterey sent the mission folk into the hills, with the understanding that Branciforte's bad boys would pack up the mission's valuables and cart them inland for safekeeping. Instead, they looted the place and drank all the sacramental wine. The mission was eventually abandoned, then demolished by an earthquake in 1857. A small port city grew up around the plaza and borrowed the mission's name—Santa Cruz—while Branciforte, a smuggler's haven, continued to flourish until the late 1800s.

MONTEREY BAY TRANSPORTATION

Getting There by Bus or Train

Greyhound bus connections are fairly good to the Monterey Bay area, especially from major cities north and south, with service to Santa Cruz, Monterey, Salinas, San Luis Obispo, and Santa Barbara (and points in between) supplemented by local transit lines.

Amtrak's **Coast Starlight** runs from Los Angeles to Seattle with central coast stops in Oxnard, Santa Barbara, San Luis Obispo, and Salinas. For information and reservations, call Amtrak toll-free at (800) 872-7245, www.amtrak.com.

The Coast Starlight connects in L.A. and Oakland with other Amtrak trains, and it connects in San Jose with the San Francisco-San Jose **Caltrain,** tel. (650) 508-6200 or toll-free (800) 660-4287 (in the service area).

Getting There by Air

Flying is considerably more expensive. Commuter flights connect central coast cities with major urban areas. The **San Jose Airport,** the closest major airport in the north and not far from Santa Cruz, is served by commuter and major airlines. The **Monterey Peninsula Airport,** 200 Fred Kane Dr. #200, tel. (831) 648-7000, fax (831) 373-2542, offers direct and connecting flights from all domestic and foreign locales—primarily connecting flights, because this is a fairly small airport. **United Airlines/United Express,** toll-free tel. (800) 241-6522, and **American/American Eagle Airlines,** tel. (805) 541-1010, have the highest local profile, but also contact **Delta/Skywest** and **US Airways.** You can fly directly into Monterey from San Francisco, Los Angeles, or Phoenix.

The newest peninsula airport is the **Marina Municipal Airport,** north of Monterey proper on Neeson Rd. in Marina, tel. (831) 582-0102. To get to Monterey from the airports in San Jose or San Francisco—or vice-versa—you can take **Monterey-Salinas Airbus,** based at Marina Municipal Airport, 791 Neeson Rd., Marina, tel. (831) 883-2871. The buses shuttle back and forth up to 10 times daily.

Getting There by Car

This being California, most people drive cars, zipping close to the central coast on north-south Interstate 5 in the eastern San Joaquin (then cutting over by highway) or traveling the historic El Camino Real (the "Royal Road" of the mission days), now modern Hwy. 101, which connects San Jose and points north with the Monterey Peninsula, Salinas, San Luis Obispo, Santa Barbara, and Los Angeles. Almost any route to the Monterey Bay area is faster than scenic Hwy. 1 along the coast. But they don't call it number one for nothing. This hilly, treacherously twisting, mostly two-lane coast route offers spectacular scenery and lots of it, particularly along the Big Sur stretch between the Monterey Peninsula and San Luis Obispo. Driving the Big Sur route—plan carefully for walking or biking it—takes presence of mind as well as plenty of time. If possible, travel this section of Hwy. 1 from north to south to better take advantage of view-offering turnouts. Hwy. 1 between Carmel and Morro Bay is occasionally closed during winter due to landslides; call toll-free (800) 427-7623 for current road conditions.

From the San Francisco Bay area, the preferred local route to Santa Cruz (and the only main alternative to Hwy. 1) is to take I-280 or 880 south to San Jose, then hop over the hills on the congested and treacherously twisting Hwy. 17. Near Monterey, two-lane Hwy. 156 connects Highways 1 and 101 north of Monterey; Hwy. 68 makes the same connection between Monterey and Salinas. Take Laureles Canyon Rd.

(G20) for a shortcut to Carmel Valley from Hwy. 68; Carmel Valley Rd. (G16) is the "back way" to head south from the Monterey Peninsula—scenic but slow.

Getting Around
Bicycles are viable transportation. You can even hike and walk throughout the area without difficulty. Both the Monterey and Santa Cruz areas are served by good local bus systems, which in addition to Greyhound and other bus lines offer some between-city connections; in Monterey call **Monterey-Salinas Transit** at (831) 899-2555 or (831) 899-2558, and in Santa Cruz call the **Santa Cruz Metropolitan Transit District** at (831) 425-8600.

SANTA CRUZ AND VICINITY

Still in tune with its gracefully aging Boardwalk, Santa Cruz is a middle-class tourist town enlightened and enlivened by retirees and the local University of California campus. Though it's getting harder, here people can exist even if they don't have lots of money—quite a different world from the affluent, fairly staid Monterey Peninsula.

The Santa Cruz attitude has little to do with its name, taken from a nearby stream called Arroyo de Santa Cruz ("Holy Cross Creek") by Portolá. No, the town's relaxed good cheer must be karmic compensation for the morose mission days and the brutishness of nearby Branciforte. The Gay Nineties were happier here than anywhere else in Northern California, with trainloads of Bay Area vacationers in their finest summer whites stepping out to enjoy the Santa Cruz waterfront, the Sea Beach Hotel, and the landmark Boardwalk and amusement park. The young and young-at-heart headed straight for the amusement park, with its fine merry-go-round, classic wooden roller coaster, pleasure pier, natatorium (indoor pool), and dancehall casino. Meanwhile, more decadent fun lovers visited the ship anchored offshore to gamble or engage the services of prostitutes.

Santa Cruz still welcomes millions of visitors each year, yet somehow manages to retain its dignity—except when embroiled in hot local political debates or when inundated by college students during the annual rites of spring. A tourist

town it may be, but some of the best things to do here are free: watching the sunset from East or West Cliff Drives, beachcombing, bike riding (excellent local bike lanes), swimming, surfing, and sunbathing.

The "People's Republic of Santa Cruz"
Old-timers weren't ready for the changes in community consciousness that arrived in Santa Cruz along with the idyllic UC Santa Cruz campus in the 1960s. More outsiders came when back-to-the-landers fled San Francisco's Haight Ashbury for the hills near here, and when Silicon Valley electronics wizards started moving in. The city's boardwalk-and-beach hedonism may be legendary, but so were the Santa Cruz City Council's foreign policy decisions opposing contra aid, proclaiming the city a "free port" for Nicaragua, and calling for the divestiture of investments in South Africa.

Though there's always some argument, the city's progressive politics are now firmly entrenched, as are other "dancing-on-the-brink" attitudes. The People's Republic of Santa Cruz is also a way station for the spiritually weary, with its own unique evangelical crusade for higher consciousness. Dreams and dreamers run the show.

The Santa Cruz Story
The charming Santa Cruz blend of innocence and sleaze has roots in local history. The area's

earliest residents were the Ohlone people, who avoided the sacred redwood forests and subsisted on seafood, small game, acorns, and other foods gathered in woodland areas. Then came the mission and missionaries, a Spanish military garrison, and the den-of-thieves culture of Branciforte; the latter community posed an active threat to the holy fathers' attempted good works among the heathens. Misión Exaltación de la Santa Cruz declined, was abandoned, then collapsed following an earthquake in 1857.

A small trading town, borrowing the mission's name, grew up around the old mission plaza in the 1840s to supply whalers with fruits and vegetables. Nearby Branciforte became a smugglers' haven, hosting bullfight festivals and illicit activities until 1867. But the "education" and excitement imported by foreigners proved to be too much for the Ohlone; the only traces of their culture today are burial grounds. Branciforte disappeared, too, absorbed as a suburb when loggers and "bark strippers" (those who extracted tannin from tan oaks for processing leather) arrived to harvest the forests during the gold rush.

By the late 1800s, Santa Cruz was well established as a resort town. Logging continued, however. In the early 20th century, the local lumber industry was ready to log even majestic Big Basin. But those plans were thwarted by the active intervention of the Sempervirens Club, which successfully established California's first state park.

Greater Santa Cruz

Just east of Santa Cruz, along the south-facing coast here, are the towns of Soquel, Capitola, and Aptos—the Santa Cruz "burbs." High-rent **Soquel**, once a booming lumber town and the place where Portolá and his men were all but stricken by their first sight of coastal redwoods, is now noted for antiques and oaks.

The wharf in **Capitola** has stood since 1857, when the area was known as Soquel Landing. The name "Camp Capitola" was an expression of Soquel locals' desire to be the state capital—the closest they ever came. The city was, however, the state's first seaside resort. Nowadays, Capitola is big on art galleries and fine craft shops—take a stroll along Capitola Ave. from the trestle to the creek—but it's still most famous for its begonias. The year's big event is the **Begonia Festival,** usually held early in September. Stop by **Antonelli Bros. Begonia Gardens,** 2545 Capitola Rd., tel. (831) 475-5222, to see a 10,000-square-foot greenhouse display of begonias, best in August and September.

Aptos, on the other side of the freeway, is more or less the same community as Capitola but home to Cabrillo College and the **World's Shortest Parade,** usually sponsored on the July 4th weekend by the Aptos Ladies' Tuesday Evening Society.

Heading north on Hwy. 9 from Santa Cruz will take you through the Santa Cruz Mountains

---

CRUISIN' SANTA CRUZ WINERIES

The coastal mountains near Santa Cruz are well known for their redwoods. But since the late 1800s, they have also been known for their vineyards. Regional winemaking is back, helped along since 1981 by the official federal recognition of the Santa Cruz Mountain appellation for wine grapes grown in the region defined by Half Moon Bay in the north and Mount Madonna in the south. More than 40 wineries now produce Santa Cruz Mountain wines.

The eclectic **Bonny Doon Vineyard,** north of Santa Cruz at 10 Pine Flat Rd., tel. (831) 425-4518, www.bonnydoonvineyard.com, specializes in Rhône and Italian varietals, though wine lovers and critics are also smitten with the winery's worldly, witty, and wildly footnoted newsletter (also available online). Open 11 a.m.-5 p.m. daily for tastings, except major holidays.

Nearby in Felton is the award-winning and historic **Hallcrest Vineyards,** 379 Felton Empire Rd. (call for directions), tel. (831) 335-4441, noted for its cabernet sauvignon, chardonnay, merlot, and zinfandel. Hallcrest is also home to **The Organic Wine Works,** producing the nation's first certified organic wines. Made from certified organically grown grapes, the winemaking process is also organic, without the use of sulfites. Open daily 11 a.m.-5:30 p.m. Also in Felton and open only by appointment is the small **Zayante Vineyards,** 420 Old Mount Rd., tel. (831) 335-7992.

For more information about Santa Cruz area wineries, including a current wineries map, contact: **Santa Cruz Mountains Winegrowers Association,** 7605 Old Dominion Ct., Ste. A, Aptos, CA 95003, tel. (831) 479-9463, www.wines.com/santa_cruz_mountains.

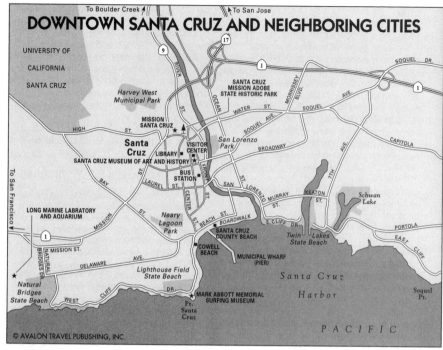

and the towns of Felton, Ben Lomond, and Boulder Creek, before winding down the other side of the mountains into Saratoga on the flank of Silicon Valley. This route is the gateway to several beautiful redwood state parks, including Henry Cowell, Fall Creek, Big Basin, and Castle Rock.

THE BOARDWALK

Santa Cruz Beach Boardwalk

The Boardwalk may be old, but it's certainly lively, with a million visitors per year. This is the West Coast's answer to Atlantic City. The original wood planking is now paved over with asphalt, stretching from 400 Beach St. for a half mile along one of Northern California's finest swimming beaches. A relatively recent multimillion-dollar face lift didn't diminish the Boardwalk's charms one iota. Open daily from Memorial Day to Labor Day each year, otherwise just on weekends, the Boardwalk's amusement park atmosphere is authentic, with 27 carnival rides, odd shops and eateries, good-time arcades, even a big-band ballroom. Ride the **Sky Glider** to get a good aerial view of the Boardwalk and beach scene.

None other than the *New York Times* has declared the 1924 **Giant Dipper** roller coaster here one of the nation's 10 best. A gleaming white wooden rocker 'n' roller, the Dipper's quite a sight any time, but it's truly impressive when lit up at night. The 1911 **Charles Looff carousel,** one of a handful of Looff creations still operating in the U.S., has 70 handcrafted horses, two chariots, and a circa 1894 Ruth Band pipe organ—all now lovingly restored to the merry-go-round's original glory. (Both the Dipper and the carousel are national historic landmarks.)

New rides feature more terror, of course. The bright lights and unusual views offered by the Italian-made **Typhoon** are just part of the joys of being suspended upside down in midair. The **Hurricane** is the Boardwalk's modern high-tech roller coaster, providing a two-minute thrill ride

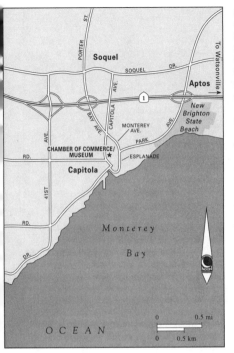

with a maximum gravitational force of 4.7 Gs, and a banking angle of 80 degrees. There's only one other of its kind in the U.S., on the east coast. Also state of the art in adrenaline inducement at the Boardwalk is the **Wave Jammer**—not to mention **Chaos, Crazy Surf, Tsunami,** and **Whirl Wind.**

The antique fun technologies in the penny arcades at the Boardwalk's west end cost a bit more these days, but it could be worth it to Measure the Thrill of Your Kisses or Find Your Ideal Mate. Playing miniature golf at the new, two-story, $5.2-million **Neptune's Kingdom** amusement center—housed in the Boardwalk's original "plunge" building or natatorium, that era well illustrated by the impressive display of historical photography in the "historium" here—is a nautically themed adventure in special effects, with an erupting volcano, firing cannons, and talking pirates. It's the perfect diversion for the video-game generation and their awestruck parents. Though the rest of the Boardwalk's attractions

are seasonal, Neptune's Kingdom and the arcade are open daily year-round. Nearby is the esteemed **Cocoanut Grove** casino and ballroom, a dignified old dancehall that still swings with nostalgic tunes from the 1930s and '40s at special shindigs. Sunday brunch in the Grove's Sun Room, with its Victorian-modern decor and galleria-style retracting glass roof, is a big event.

To fully appreciate the Boardwalk then and now, pick up the *Walking Tour of the Historical Santa Cruz Boardwalk* brochure, as well as a current attractions map/listing. Both will help you locate yourself, then and now. Annual Santa Cruz events held at the Boardwalk include the **Clam Chowder Cook-Off and Festival** in late February; the **Beach Street Haunted House** at Beach and Cliff Streets throughout October; the **Brussels Sprout Festival** in mid-October (plenty of food for people who like brussels sprouts, and special sporting events like the Sprout Toss and Sprout Putt for people who don't); and the **Santa Cruz Christmas Craft and Gift Festival** held at the Cocoanut Grove during Thanksgiving weekend (Fri.-Sunday). On Friday nights in summer, starting in June, come for free **Summertime, Summer Nights** concerts, starring groups like the Drifters and the Shirelles.

Admission to the Boardwalk is free, though enjoying its amusements is not. The best deal is the all-day ride ticket, $19.95 at last report. Season passes are available. Height, age, and chaperone requirements are enforced. During **1907 Nights,** however, on certain Monday and Tuesday evenings in summer, ride prices revert to 1907 equivalents—50 cents per ride. For current complete information, contact the **Santa Cruz Seaside Company,** 400 Beach St., Santa Cruz, CA 95060-5491, tel. (831) 423-5590, www.beachboardwalk.com. While you're at it, inquire about special vacation packages, including accommodations at the Holiday Inn, the Sea & Sand Inn, or the Carousel Motel.

For current Boardwalk hours, call (831) 426-7433. For information on special Boardwalk activities, call (831) 423-5590. To find out what's happening at the Cocoanut Grove, call (831) 423-2053.

Santa Cruz Wharf

The pier at the western end of Santa Cruz Beach, once a good place to buy cheap, fresh

*Santa Cruz
Beach Boardwalk*

TOM MYERS PHOTOGRAPHY

fish, did booming business during the state's steamship heyday. Today, the place is packed instead with tourists, and most fish markets, restaurants, and shops charge a pretty penny. Still, the wharf's worth a sunset stroll. (Peer down into the fenced-off "holes" to watch the sea lions.) A few commercial fishing boats still haul their catch of salmon and cod ashore in summer, doubling as whalewatching tour boats in winter. Worth a look, too, are the kiosk displays on wharf and fishing history.

OTHER SANTA CRUZ SIGHTS

Historic Homes Walking Tour

If over- or underwhelmed by the Boardwalk, take the Santa Cruz walking tour. This expedition is a lot quicker than it used to be, with so many of the city's unusual Victorians—with frilly wedding-cake furbelows and "witch's hat" towers on the Queen Annes—now departed to that great Historical Register in the Sky, after the 1989 earthquake. But some grande dames remain. To find them, stop by the visitors center and pick up a copy of the *Historic Santa Cruz Walking Tours and Museum Guide* brochure. Most houses are private homes or businesses, so don't trespass.

To find out more about area history, stop by the Santa Cruz Museum of Art and History. In particular, the museum staff can fill you in on regional historical sites under their care, including the Davenport Jail (1917), up the coast in Davenport, and the Evergreen Cemetery (est. 1850) at Evergreen and Coral Streets, one of the oldest Protestant cemeteries in California. Next door to the museum is the visitors center.

Santa Cruz Museum of Art and History

A sure sign that downtown Santa Cruz is almost done digging out from the rubble of the devastating 1989 earthquake is the Museum of Art and History at the McPherson Center, 705 Front St. (Front and Cooper), tel. (831) 429-1964, www.santacruzmah.org. Traveling exhibits and local artists get prominent play at the art galleries, and changing history exhibits include themes such as 1999's *Picks, Plows, and Potatoes: The Santa Cruz Region During the Gold Rush*. Open Tues.-Sun. noon-5 p.m. (until 7 p.m. on Friday), small admission. Adjacent to the museum is The Octagon, an eight-sided 1882 brick building relocated here, now the museum store. Inside is an intriguing collection of gift and art items—including, at least sometimes, the marvelously whimsical work (including greeting cards) by Santa Cruz artist James Carl Aschbacher.

Santa Cruz Mission
Adobe State Historic Park

Restored and open to the public is the Santa Cruz Mission Adobe, a state historical park just off Mission Plaza at 144 School St., tel. (831) 425-5849. This is one of the county's last remaining original adobes, built by and for Native Americans "employed" at Mission Santa Cruz. Later a 17-unit "home for new citizens," only seven units remain, these now comprising a California history museum circa the 1840s. Restored rooms illustrate the reality of how Native American, Californio, and Irish-American families once lived. Call for current information about guided tours and "living history" demonstrations (usually offered on Sundays, the latter just in March). School groups welcome—Thursday and Friday—by advance reservation only. But plan a picnic here anytime (bring your own water). The park is open Thurs.-Sun. 10 a.m.-4 p.m.; admission is $5 family or $2 adults, $1 seniors and children.

Mission Santa Cruz

Nearby, at 126 High St., is what's left of the original mission: just a memory, really. The chosen original site of the **Misión de Exaltación de la Santa Cruz** was at High and Emmet Streets, too close to the San Lorenzo River, as it turned out. The move to higher ground left only the garden at the lower level. The original Santa Cruz mission complex was finished in 1794 but was completely destroyed by earthquakes in the mid-19th century. The replica church, scaled down by two-thirds and built in 1931 on the upper level, seems to have lost more than just stature. It's open Tues.-Sat. 10 a.m.-4 p.m., Sunday 10 a.m.-2 p.m.; call (831) 426-5686 for more information.

Santa Cruz Surfing Museum

Cowabunga! Instead of a ribbon-cutting ceremony, they snipped a hot-pink surfer's leash when they opened the world's first surfing museum here in May 1986. This historical exhibit reaches back to the 1930s and features displays like the evolution of surfboards—including the Model T of boards, a 15-foot redwood plank weighing 100 pounds—and an experimental Jack O'Neill wetsuit made of nylon and foam, the forerunner to the Neoprene "shortjohn." Some say two Polynesian princes introduced surfing to Santa Cruz in 1885. True or not, by 1912 local posters announced the surfing exploits of Olympic swimmer and "Father of Surfing," Duke Kahanamoku.

The museum's location on the ground floor of the brick lighthouse on W. Cliff Dr. northwest of town near Steamer's Ln., prime surf turf, seems the most fitting place for official homage to life in pursuit of the perfect wave. The lighthouse was built by the family of Mark Abbott, a surfer killed nearby. The museum is open daily (except Tuesday) noon-4 p.m.; admission is free. For more information, call (831) 420-6289.

Santa Cruz Harley-Davidson Museum

The local Harley-Davidson shop, 1148 Soquel Ave., tel. (831) 421-9600, www.santacruz-harley.com, is something of a "destination dealership." Among the exquisitely restored Harleys on display is an H-D bicycle, first introduced in

Santa Cruz
Surfing Museum

TOM MYERS PHOTOGRAPHY

1917, a 1929 JDH two-cam twin, and a stylish 1930 VL. Historical photos, posters, and memorabilia round out the collection, which is available for public viewing Tues.-Sunday.

Santa Cruz Mystery Spot

The much bumpersticker-ballyhooed Mystery Spot is a place where "every law of gravitation has gone haywire." Or has it? Trees, people, even the Spot's rustic shack and furnishings seem spellbound by "the force"—though people wearing slick-soled shoes seem to have the hardest time staying with the mysterious program. Hard-core tourists tend to love this place— Mom or Dad or the kids can *literally* climb the walls—but others leave wondering why they spent the small fee to get in.

The Mystery Spot is at 465 Mystery Spot Rd., tel. (831) 423-8897. To get there, follow Market St. north from Water St. for a few miles; Market becomes Branciforte, and Mystery Spot Rd. branches left off Branciforte—you can't miss it. Open daily 9 a.m.-8 p.m. in summer, and 9 a.m.-5 p.m. in winter.

Spiritual/Supernatural Attractions

Perhaps more interesting even than the Mystery Spot are two other oddball attractions, these located at the **Santa Cruz Memorial Park & Funeral Home,** 3301 Paul Sweet Rd., tel. (831) 426-1601. Here you'll find displays attempting to rekindle the controversy over the **Shroud of Turin**—that renowned piece of linen purported to show Christ's after-death visage—by challenging the conclusions of carbon tests declaring the shroud a fake, as well as a life-sized wax interpretation of *The Last Supper.*

An interpretation of Da Vinci's famous painting in life-sized wax figures, *The Last Supper* is the original work of two Katherine Struberghs (mother and daughter) from Los Angeles. The women spared themselves no trial or trouble in this endeavor. (Each hair on every wax head was implanted by hand—that task alone requiring eight months.) But after some 40 years' residence at the Santa Cruz Art League, Jesus and his disciples were in a sad state of disrepair. That was before the funeral home and local Oddfellows Lodge took on the task of financing something of a resurrection. The job involved patching the cracks in the figures' heads, washing and setting

their hair and beards, replacing fingers (and fingernails and toenails), and polishing their glass eyeballs.

Visitors can see both attractions Mon.-Fri. by appointment.

UC Santa Cruz

When the doors of UC Santa Cruz opened in the 1960s, few California students could gain admission to the close-knit, redwood-cloistered campus on the hill. The selection process (complete with essay) was weighted in favor of unusual abilities, aptitudes, and attitudes—to recruit students not likely to thrive within the traditional university structure. So many children of movie stars and other members of California's monied upper classes attended UC Santa Cruz at one time that it was often playfully dubbed California's public finishing school. With grandiose plans of attracting an enrollment of 27,000 one day, the university's student body has so far remained relatively small (around 11,000 currently), though growth is on the agenda.

On a clear day, the view of Monterey Bay (and of whales passing offshore in winter and spring) from the top of the hill on the 2,000-acre campus is marvelous. Once the Henry Cowell Ranch, the University of California regents set about transforming the redwood-forested rangeland here into California's educational Camelot in 1961. They hired some of the state's finest architects, whose designs ranged from modern Mediterranean to "Italian hill village" (Kresge College). The official explanation for the Santa Cruz "college cluster" concept was to avoid the depersonalization common to large UC campuses, but another reason was alluded to when then-Governor Ronald Reagan declared the campus "riot-proof."

To truly appreciate this place, wander the campus hiking trails and paths (but not alone). Some of the old converted ranch buildings are also worth noting: the lime kilns, blacksmith's shop, cookhouse, horse barn, bull barn, slaughterhouse, cookhouse, workers' cabins, cooperage. For information and guided campus tours, stop by the wood-and-stone Cook House near the entrance. You can also obtain information by writing to UCSC Admissions Office, Cook House, Santa Cruz, CA 95064, or by calling (831) 459-4008.

The Long Marine Laboratory and Aquarium, just off Delaware Ave. near Natural Bridges State Beach on the western edge of town, is open to the public Tues.-Sun. 1-4 p.m. Tours of this UC Santa Cruz facility, including the **Seymour Marine Discovery Center,** are available. Adjacent is the state's new 18,000-square-foot **Marine Wildlife Veterinary Care and Research Center,** the nation's largest and most advanced. For aquarium information, try www.natsci.ucsc.edu/ims/ or call (831) 459-2883. The marine facilities here are rapidly expanding, too. Currently under construction are the Oil Seabird/Raptor Center, the Center for Ocean Health, and the National Marine Fisheries Service Santa Cruz.

AT THE BEACH

Beaches in Town

Most of the outdoor "action" most of the time happens at local beaches; swimming, surfing, and fishing are all big, as are tamer pastimes like beachcombing, sandcastle-building, and sunbathing. The in-town **Santa Cruz Beach** at the Boardwalk, with fine white sand and towel-to-towel baking bodies in summer, is "the scene"—especially for outsiders from San Jose, locals say. For more privacy, head east to the mouth of the San Lorenzo River. Southwest of the pier, **Cowell Beach** is a surfing beach, where Huey Lewis and the News filmed one of their music videos. Just before **Lighthouse Field State**

Beach on W. Cliff is the Santa Cruz Surfing Museum, an eclectic lighthouse collection of surf's-up memorabilia keeping watch over the hotdoggers in churning Steamer Lane.

Natural Bridges State Beach, farther southwest at the end of W. Cliff Dr., attracts the mythic monarch butterflies each year from October to May. Though Pacific Grove near Monterey proudly proclaims itself *the* destination of choice for these regal insects, Santa Cruz people claim they get the most monarchs. Sadly, generations of people walking across the sandstone "natural bridge" here finally caused the center arch to collapse. Leathery green fields of Brussels sprouts fringe the fragile sandy cliffs. For information on guided butterfly walks and tidepool tours, stop by the visitor center or call (831) 423-4609. Come in February for the annual **Migration Festival,** a park fundraiser co-sponsored by Friends of Santa Cruz State Parks. The parking fee at Natural Bridges is $6 per car; walk-ins and bike-ins are free.

Locals' Beaches

Near the city museum, along E. Cliff Dr., are **Tyrell Park** and more inaccessible sandy beaches. **Twin Lakes Beach** near the Santa Cruz Yacht Harbor, on the eastern extension of E. Cliff before it becomes Portolá, is a popular locals' beach, usually quite warm. Beyond the Santa Cruz Yacht Harbor, various small, locally popular beaches line E. Cliff Dr.; the unofficially named **26th St. Beach** (at the end of 26th St.,

beach-fishing

naturally enough) is probably tops among them. Hot for local surfing is the **Pleasure Point,** E. Cliff at Pleasure Point Drive.

Beaches North of Town

Davenport Beach, at Davenport Landing up the coast toward Año Nuevo, is a hot spot for sailboarders and often relatively uncrowded. **Red White and Blue Beach,** just south of Davenport, tel. (831) 423-6332, is a popular, privately operated nude beach (too popular, some say: women shouldn't go alone); $5 per person day use for the privilege of an all-over tan. Camping also available. Nearby is **Bonny Doon Beach,** up the coast from Santa Cruz at the intersection of Hwy. 1 and Bonny Doon Rd., south of Davenport. It's free but even wilder for sunbathing sans swimsuit. Popular with surfers.

Beaches East and South of Town

About six miles down the coast from Santa Cruz City Beach and just south of the Capitola suburbs is **New Brighton State Beach,** 1500 Park Ave., Capitola, tel. (831) 464-6330. Its 65 often-sunny acres are protected by wooded headlands that offer nature trails, good birdwatching, and a dazzling nighttime view of Monterey Bay.

Several miles farther south, two-mile-long **Seacliff State Beach,** Park Dr., Aptos, tel. (831) 685-6442 (recorded information) or (831) 685-6444 (visitor center), is so popular you may not be able to stop. It's nice for pelican-watching, hiking, fossil appreciating, swimming, and sunbathing. The wheelchair-accessible pier here reaches out to the pink concrete carcass of the doomed WW I-vintage *Palo Alto,* sunk here after seeing no wartime action, and now a long-abandoned amusement pier. Birds live in the prow these days, and people enjoy the pier's more mundane pleasures: people-watching, fishing (no license required), and strolling. Guided walks are occasionally offered; call the visitor center for schedules and reservations.

As the name suggests, **Rio del Mar** beach is where Aptos Creek meets the sea. Here you'll find restrooms, miles of sand, and limited parking. It's free.

OUT ON THE WATER

Sailing Santa Cruz and the Bay

For an unusual view of the Boardwalk and the bay, take a boat ride. One of the best going—definitely not just any boat—is the *Chardonnay II,* a 70-foot ultra-light sailing yacht offering special-emphasis cruises such as winetasting (usually on Saturdays), marine ecology (usually on Sun-

WILDER RANCH STATE PARK

Open to the public since mid-1989, Wilder Ranch State Park is best summed up as "a California coastal dairy-farm museum," a remnant of the days when dairies were more important to the local economy than tourists. Before it was a dairy farm, this was the main rancho supplying Mission Santa Cruz. Though damaged by the 1989 earthquake, the old Victorian ranch house is open again, decked out in period furnishings. The grounds also include an elaborate 1890s stable, a dairy barn, and a bunkhouse-workshop with water-driven machinery. Seasoned vehicles and farm equipment, from a 1916 Dodge touring sedan to seed spreaders and road graders, are scattered throughout the grounds.

Almost more appealing, though, are the park's miles of coastline and thousands of acres of forest, creeks, and canyons. To help visitors take in the landscape, Wilder Ranch features 34 miles of hiking, biking, and equestrian trails.

General ranch tours, led by docents dressed in period attire, are offered every Saturday and Sunday, usually at 1 p.m. Historical games are played on the lawn—hoop 'n' stick, bubbles, stilts—on weekends as well. A variety of other history- and natural history-oriented events are sponsored throughout the year, from demonstrations on making corn-husk dolls or quilts to mastering cowboy-style roping, plus guided hikes and bird walks. Usually on the first Saturday in May is the park's **annual open house,** a full day of old-fashioned family fun (and fundraising, for future park restoration work).

Wilder Ranch is two miles north of Santa Cruz on the west side of Hwy. 1 (1401 Coast Rd., about a mile past the stoplight at Western Dr.), tel. (831) 423-9703 or (831) 426-0505, and is open for day-use only ($6 per car). To get here by bus, take Santa Cruz Metro No. 40 and ask the driver to drop you at the ranch.

days), whalewatching (winter and spring)—even a Wednesday night Boat Race Cruise in the company of almost every other boat from the Santa Cruz Yacht Harbor. At last report, per-person fare for most scheduled trips was $39.95. For more information and to make reservations (required), call **Chardonnay Sailing Charters** at (831) 423-1213 or inquire online at www.chardonnay.com.

Other boat and charter companies at or near the city's yacht harbor include **Pacific Yachting,** 790 Mariner Park Way, tel. (831) 423-7245, which offers similar boat rides on smaller yachts as well as sailing lessons and a six-day seagoing instruction vacation. Probably the best deal going, though, is through the University of California at Santa Cruz Sailing Club and the university's office of Physical Education, tel. (831) 459-2531. In summer, UCSC sailing and boating courses are open to the public. If you qualify for membership—by enrolling in the alumni association and buying a current UCSC recreation card—you can use the boats all year. The local **Coast Guard Auxiliary,** 432 Oxford Way, tel. (831) 423-7119, also offers sailing, boating skills, seamanship, and coastal navigation courses.

Other Ocean Adventures

For more traditional boat tours, whalewatching trips, and fishing charters, contact **Stagnaro's Fishing Trips** at the municipal wharf, tel. (831) 427-2334, or **Shamrock Charters** at the yacht harbor, tel. (831) 476-2648.

Kayaking is great sport in these parts. **Venture Quest,** 125 Beach St., tel. (831) 427-2267, and at the municipal wharf, tel. (831) 425-8445, sells kayaks and accessories, and offers lessons and guided tours. **Kayak Connection** at the Santa Cruz Yacht Harbor, 413 Lake Ave., tel. (831) 479-1121, also rents and sells equipment, in addition to offering guided birdwatching, fishing, and moonlight tours.

Several full-service dive shops in town can provide complete current information on local diving conditions as well as instruction, rentals, and sales. Try **Aqua Safaris Scuba Center,** 6898 Soquel Ave., tel. (831) 479-4386; **Adventure Sports Unlimited,** 303 Potrero St., tel. (831) 458-3648; or **Ocean Odyssey,** 860 17th Ave., tel. (831) 475-3483.

Club Ed, on Cowell Beach (right side of Santa Cruz Wharf, in front of the WestCoast Santa Cruz Hotel, tel. (831) 459-9283 or toll-free (800) 287-7873, rents surfboards, boogieboards, skimboards, and sailboards, and offers lessons in riding all of the above. Find out more about their surf camps on the web at www.club-ed.com.

SANTA CRUZ CAMPING

Camping at the Beach

Best for nearby tent camping is **New Brighton State Beach,** 1500 Park Ave. in Capitola, tel. (831) 464-6330. "New Bright" features 115 developed campsites (especially nice ones on the cliffs), some sheltered picnic tables, and a small beach. It's a good base camp for the entire Santa Cruz area; you can get here via local bus—take No. 58 or the "Park Avenue" route. This area was once called China Beach or China Cove, after the Chinese fishermen who built a village here in the 1870s. Campsites are $17-18 April 1-Oct. 31, $14 off-season. The campground is popular, so reserve for summer at least six months ahead.

Near Aptos, **Seacliff State Beach,** tel. (831) 685-6442 or (831) 685-6444, has a better beach than New Brighton, but camping is a disappointment; the 24 sites, just for RVs, are $28-29 April 1-Oct. 31, $25 off-season, including hookups.

For more information about the area's beach parks, contact the state parks office in Santa Cruz, 600 Ocean St., tel. (831) 429-2850. For campground reservations, call ReserveAmerica toll-free at (800) 444-7275.

Camping in the Redwoods

Big Basin Redwoods State Park, 21600 Big Basin Hwy., Boulder Creek, tel. (831) 338-8860 for information, offers 190 campsites, many with trailer hookups, some tents-only walk-ins ($14-18). Reserve through ReserveAmerica, toll-free tel. (800) 444-7275. The park also boasts 36 year-round "tent cabins," each with two double beds, a camp lamp, and a woodstove. Tent cabins sleep four comfortably but can house up to eight. Rates from July 1-Aug. 31 are $44 per night on weekends (two-night minimum) and $42 midweek. The rest of the year, the rate is $40 per night. (Add $10 for linens-and-blanket rental in lieu of sleeping bags, and $1 if you bring the family dog.) For cabin reservations, call toll-free (800) 874-8368.

Henry Cowell Redwoods State Park, just north of the UC campus on Hwy. 9 in Felton, tel. (831) 335-4598 (administration) or (831) 438-2396 (campground), offers 150 sites, 105 of them "developed." Sites in the developed areas are quite civilized, with amenities including hot showers, flush toilets, tables, barbecues, and cupboards ($14-18). Reserve through ReserveAmerica, toll-free tel. (800) 444-7275.

Sites at both Big Basin and Henry Cowell Redwoods State Parks are sometimes available at the last minute, even in summer and on warm-season weekends. But make reservations—up to seven months in advance—to guarantee a space.

Camping Elsewhere

Private campgrounds and trailer parks are always a possibility; a complete current listing is available at the local chamber of commerce. Possibilities include **Cotillion Gardens,** 300 Old Big Trees Rd., Felton, CA 95018, tel. (831) 335-7669; **Carbonero Creek,** 917 Disc Dr., Scotts Valley, CA 95066, tel. (831) 438-1288; and the **Santa Cruz KOA,** 1186 San Andreas Rd., Watsonville, CA 95076, tel. (831) 722-0551 or (831) 722-2377.

STAYING IN SANTA CRUZ

HI-AYH Santa Cruz Hostel

The Santa Cruz Hostel, 321 Main St., Santa Cruz, CA 95061, tel. (831) 423-8304, fax (831) 429-8541, www.hi-santacruz.org, occupies a group of historic cottages downtown. The hostel is open year-round, is wheelchair accessible, and features an on-site cyclery, fireplace, barbecue, lockers, and a rose and herb garden. The fee is $13 for members, $16 for nonmembers, with family rooms and limited parking available (extra fee for both). Reservations strongly suggested. For other area hostels, see South From San Francisco in the previous chapter.

Santa Cruz Motels and Hotels

As a general rule, motels closer to the freeway are cheaper, while those on the river are seedier. There are some fairly inexpensive motels near the beach (some with kitchens, jacuzzis, pools, cable TV, etc.). Off-season rates in Santa Cruz are usually quite reasonable, but prices can sometimes mysteriously increase in summer and on weekends and holidays—so ask before you sign in.

Inexpensive: The **Sandpiper Lodge,** 111 Ocean, tel. (831) 429-8244, is a small motel with rooms and suites. Rates include complimentary continental breakfast.

Moderate: The **Pacific Inn,** 330 Ocean St., tel. (831) 425-3722, fax (831) 425-4983, has 36 rooms and a heated pool and spa. The attractive **Comfort Inn Santa Cruz,** 110 Plymouth St., tel. (831) 426-6224, fax (831) 426-0923, offers 63 rooms with in-room coffee and refrigerators, color TVs and VCRs, and a heated pool and spa. Suites are available. Rates include continental breakfast. Quite reasonably priced are smaller rooms at the **Beach View Inn,** just a block from the beach at 50 Front St., tel. (831) 426-3575, fax (831) 421-9218. Decent too are the **Best Western Inn,** 126 Plymouth, tel. (831) 425-4717, fax (831) 425-0643, and the **Best Western Torch-Lite Inn,** 500 Riverside Ave., tel. (831) 426-7575, fax (831) 460-1470, where smaller rooms fall into the Moderate category.

Expensive: The **Best Western All Suites Inn,** 500 Ocean St., tel. (831) 458-9898, (831) 426-8333, or toll-free (800) 528-1234, fax (831) 429-1903, offers rooms with in-room whirlpools and microwaves, some gas fireplaces, an indoor heated pool, lap pool, and sauna, and other amenities. Also quite pleasant is the **Sunset Inn,** 2424 Mission St., tel. (831) 423-7500, fax (831) 423-7500, where extras include free local phone calls and breakfast.

Luxury: For value, nothing in the motel/hotel category beats **Chaminade at Santa Cruz** up on the hill and overlooking Monterey Bay at 1 Chaminade Ln. (just off Paul Sweet Rd.), tel. (831) 475-5600 or toll-free (800) 283-6569, fax (831) 476-4948, www.chaminade.com. Occupying the old Chaminade Brothers Seminary and Monastery, this quiet resort and conference center offers a wealth of business amenities—but also personal perks, such as a health club (with massage, and men's and women's "therapy pools"), jogging track, heated pool, saunas, and whirlpools. Lighted tennis courts, too. Newly refurbished rooms and suites are scattered around the 80-acre grounds in 11 "villas" that include shared parlors with refrigerators, wet bars, and conference tables. Rooms feature king or queen beds, in-room coffee, irons and ironing boards, and two direct-line phones. Valet parking and airport transportation are available. Chaminade also boasts two good restaurants and a bar (with meal service), all open to the general public.

Adjacent to the wharf and across from Santa Cruz Beach Boardwalk, the imposing **West-Coast Santa Cruz Hotel,** 175 W. Cliff Dr., tel. (831) 426-4330 or toll-free (800) 426-0670 (reservations), fax (831) 427-2025, www.westcoast-santacruz.com, is right on the beach (the only beachfront hotel in Santa Cruz) and has 163 rooms and suites with balconies and patios, modern amenities, satellite TV, heated pool, and whirlpool.

Santa Cruz Bed and Breakfasts

Legendary is the been-there-forever local landmark, the **Babbling Brook Inn,** 1025 Laurel St., tel. (831) 427-2437 or toll-free (800) 866-1131, fax (831) 427-2457, www.cacoastalinns.com. Once a log cabin, this place was added to and otherwise spruced up by the Countess Florenzo de Chandler. All 14 rooms and suites are quite romantic, with private bathrooms, phone, and TV. Most are decorated to suggest the works of Old World artists and poets, from Cezanne and Monet to Tennyson. Most also feature a fireplace, private deck, and outside entrance. Two have whirlpool bathtubs. Full breakfast and afternoon wine and cheese (or tea and cookies) are included. Also here: a babbling brook, waterfalls, and a garden gazebo. Premium-Luxury.

Other Santa Cruz inns tend to cluster near the ocean. The 1910 **Darling House** seaside mansion at 314 W. Cliff Dr., tel. (831) 458-1958 or toll-free (800) 458-1988, www.infopoint.com/sc/lodging/darling, is an elegant 1910 Spanish Revival mansion designed by architect William Weeks. In addition to spectacular ocean views, Darling House offers eight rooms (two with private baths, two with fireplaces), telephones, and TV on request. Hot tub in the backyard, robes provided. If you loved *The Ghost and Mrs. Muir,* you'll particularly enjoy the Pacific Ocean Room here—complete with telescope. Rates include breakfast and evening beverages. Expensive-Luxury.

Another good choice is the **Cliff Crest Bed and Breakfast Inn,** just blocks from downtown and Main Beach at 407 Cliff St., tel. (831) 427-2609, fax (831) 427-2710, www.cliffcrestinn.com,

---

COMPASSION FLOWER INN: HIGH-CLASS JOINT

One of the loveliest new B&Bs in Santa Cruz is actually the nation's first "BB&B," the first "bed, bud, and breakfast" in the United States. And "bud" in this case is not a marketing slogan for beer but a reference to high quality marijuana.

The **Compassion Flower Inn** opened in March 2000 with the express purpose of being a hemp-and medical marijuana-friendly bed and breakfast. " The establishment is "named for both the beauty of the passion flower and the compassion of the medical marijuana movement" to which the owners have dedicated themselves.

If you come, don't expect to find some tie-dyed weed-happy scene reminiscent of San Francisco's Haight-Ashbury during the Summer of Love. The proprietors have impeccably restored this gothic revival Victorian, at a cost of a half-million dollars. Tastefully and creatively decorated with antiques, hand-painted furniture, and custom tilework, the Compassion Flower Inn instead harks back to its historical roots as the onetime home of Judge Edgar Spalsbury, who made regular trips to a pharmacy downtown to buy opium as a pain medication for his tuberculosis.

Rooms range from the fairly simple **Hemp Room** and **Passionflower Room,** "twin" accommodations tucked under the eaves (these two share a bath), to the first-floor, fully wheelchair accessible **Canabliss Room** and the elegant **Lover's Suite.** Particularly striking in the suite is its bathroom, where exquisite tiled hemp designs wrap the two-person sunken tub.

Rates include full organic breakfast, including fresh-baked bread, and are $125-175 (Premium-Luxury). For all rooms, there is a two-night minimum stay.

For more information or to make reservations, contact: Compassion Flower Inn, 216 Laurel St., Santa Cruz, CA 95060, tel. (831) 466-0420, www.compassionflowerinn.com.

a Queen Anne by the beach and Boardwalk. Full breakfast is served in the solarium. Expensive-Luxury. The **Chateau Victorian,** 118 First St., tel. (831) 458-9458, www. chateauvictorian.com, offers rooms with queen-sized beds, private tiled bathrooms and wood-burning fireplaces. Local Santa Cruz Mountains wines are served, as are generous continental breakfasts. Premium.

For more bed-and-breakfast choices in the greater Santa Cruz area, see listings below.

STAYING NEAR SANTA CRUZ

Staying in Ben Lomond
For a bed-and-breakfast stay in Ben Lomond, consider the lovely and woodsy **Fairview Manor,** 245 Fairview Ave., tel. (831) 336-3355 or toll-free (800) 553-8840, www.fairviewmanor.com, which features five rooms with private baths as well as a big deck overlooking the San Lorenzo River. Premium. Or try the 1879 Victorian **Chateau des Fleurs,** 7995 Hwy. 9, tel. (831) 336-8943 or toll-free (800) 291-9966, www.chateaudefleurs.com, a bed and breakfast offering three rooms with private baths, along with a full breakfast. Expensive-Premium.

Staying in Soquel
The **Blue Spruce Inn,** 2815 S. Main St., tel. (831) 464-1137 or toll-free (800) 559-1137, www.bluespruce.com, is a romantic 1875 Victorian farmhouse just a few miles from downtown Santa Cruz. Its six rooms all feature private baths and entrances, queen-sized featherbeds, and unique antique room decor color-keyed to the handmade Lancaster County quilts. Five rooms have private spas; two have gas fireplaces. Great breakfasts. Expensive-Premium.

Staying in Capitola
A long-standing local jewel is the **Capitola Venetian Hotel,** 1500 Wharf Rd., tel. (831) 476-6471 or toll-free (800) 332-2780, www.capitolavenetian.com—California's first condominium complex, built in the 1920s. These clustered Mediterranean-style stucco apartments are relaxed and relaxing, close to the beach. All have separate living rooms, kitchens with stoves, in-room coffee, and telephones with voice mail and data ports; some have balconies, ocean views,

and fireplaces. Premium-Luxury (but Moderate-Premium in the off-season).

Almost legendary almost overnight, Capitola's **Inn at Depot Hill,** 250 Monterey Ave., tel. (831) 462-3376 or toll-free (800) 572-2632, fax (831) 462-3697, www.cacoastalinns.com, is a luxurious bed and breakfast (essentially a small luxury hotel) housed in the one-time railroad depot. Each of the eight rooms features its own unique design motif, keyed from international themes (the Delft Room, Stratford-on-Avon, the Paris Room, and Portofino, for example), as well as a private garden and entrance, fireplace, telephone with modem/fax capability, and state-of-the-art TV/VCR and stereo system. The private white-marble bathrooms feature bathrobes, hair dryers, and other little luxuries. Bathrooms have double showers, so two isn't necessarily a crowd. The pure linen bedsheets are handwashed and hand-ironed daily. Rates include full breakfast, afternoon tea or wine, and after-dinner dessert. Off-street parking is provided. Luxury.

Staying in Aptos
The apartment-style **Rio Sands Motel,** 116 Aptos Beach Dr., tel. (831) 688-3207 or toll-free (800) 826-2077, fax (831) 688-6107, www.riosands. com, has a heated pool, spa, and decent rooms not far from the beach. The "kitchen suites" feature full kitchens and a separate sitting room, and sleep up to four. "Super rooms" sleep up to six and include a refrigerator and microwave. All rooms have two TVs. Extras include the large heated pool, spa, picnic area with barbecue pits, and expanded continental breakfast. The peak-season rates are Premium, with real deals available in winter.

Also a pleasant surprise is the **Best Western Seacliff Inn,** just off the highway at 7500 Old Dominion Court, tel. (831) 688-7300 or toll-free (800) 367-2003. It's a cut or two above the usual motel, and an easy stroll to the beach. The rooms are large and comfortable, with private balconies, clustering village-style around a large outdoor pool and jacuzzi area. Suites have in-room spas. But the best surprise of all is the restaurant, **Severino's,** tel. (831) 688-8987, which serves good food both inside the dining room and outside by the koi pond. Great "sunset dinner" specials are served Sun.-Thurs. 5-6:30 p.m. Luxury.

On the coast just north of Manresa State

Beach is the condo-style **Seascape Resort Monterey Bay,** 1 Seascape Resort Dr., tel. (831) 688-6800 or toll-free (800) 929-7727, fax (831) 685-0615, www.seascaperesort.com. Choices here include tasteful studios and one- and two-bedroom villas. Restaurant, golf course, tennis courts, and on-site fitness and spa facilities. Two-night minimum stay, late May through September. Luxury.

For a bed-and-breakfast stay, consider the elegant Southern-style **Mangels House Bed & Breakfast Inn,** 570 Aptos Creek Rd., tel. (831) 688-7982 or toll-free (800) 320-7401, a landmark 1886 Italianate Victorian mansion on four secluded acres at the edge of Forest of Nisene Marks State Park. One room has a fireplace; some have balconies and shared bathrooms. The best thing, though, is the location—adjacent to the State Park and primo hiking. Premium-Luxury.

Nice, too, and also near the park, is the **Bayview Hotel Bed and Breakfast Inn,** 8041 Soquel Dr., tel. (831) 688-8654 or toll-free (800) 422-9843, www.cacoastalinns.com, an 1878 Italianate Victorian hotel with 11 elegant rooms, all with private baths and some with fireplaces and two-person tubs. Downstairs is The White Magnolia restaurant, for good food California-style. Expensive-Luxury.

Another possibility is the **Inn at Manresa Beach,** 1258 San Andreas Rd., La Selva Beach, tel. (831) 728-1000 or toll-free (888) 523-2244, www.indevelopment.com, built in 1897 as a replica of Abraham Lincoln's home in Springfield, Illinois. One grass and two clay courts are available for tennis, and guests can also play badminton, croquet, or volleyball on the lawn. The eight rooms and suites here feature king or queen beds, fireplaces, private bathrooms (most with two-person spa tubs), two-line phones, and cable TV, VCR, and stereo. From here amid the strawberry and calla lily fields, it's an easy walk to both Manresa and Sand Dollar State Beaches. Luxury.

EATING IN SANTA CRUZ

Farm Trails and Farmers' Markets

To do Santa Cruz area farm trails, pick up a copy of the *Country Crossroads* map and brochure, a joint venture with Santa Clara County row-crop farmers and orchardists. It's the essential guide for hunting down strawberries, raspberries, apples, and homegrown veggies of all kinds. Or head for the local farmers' markets. The **Santa Cruz Community Certified Farmers' Market,** tel. (831) 335-7443, is held downtown at Lincoln and Cedar every Wednesday 2:30-6:30 p.m.

Near the Beach in Santa Cruz

Unforgettable for breakfast or lunch is funky **Aldo's,** 616 Atlantic Ave. (at the west end of the yacht harbor), tel. (831) 426-3736. The breakfast menu features various egg and omelette combinations. Best of all, though, is the raisin toast, made with Aldo's homemade *fugasa* bread. Eat outdoors on the old picnic tables covered with checkered plastic tablecloths to enjoy the sun, sea air, and seagulls. At lunch and dinner, look for homemade pastas and fresh fish.

The Boardwalk alone features about 20 restaurants and food stands. The best Sunday brunch experience around is also here, at the historic **Cocoanut Grove,** 400 Beach, tel. (831) 423-2053, a veritable feast for the eyes as well as the stomach. In good weather, you'll enjoy the "sunny" atmosphere created by the sunroof. Nearby, along streets near the beach and Boardwalk, are a variety of restaurants, everything from authentic and casual ethnic eateries to sit-down dining establishments. Head to the municipal wharf to see what's new in the fresh-off-the-boat seafood department.

INDIA JOZE

A noted local institution is India Joze, 1001 Center St., tel. (831) 427-3554, featuring unusual and imaginative dishes from Indonesia, east India, and Asia daily, as well as fine pastries. Open Mon.-Sat. for lunch and dinner, Sunday for brunch and dinner. Reservations strongly suggested. When the offshore squid population is healthy, India Joze is also the home of (or at least the inspiration for) the August **International Calamari Festival,** a month-long feast featuring 80-plus international dishes served up at the restaurant and other locations, plus a squid-kissing booth, the Squid Olympics, sometimes even sermons on squid sal(i)vation.

For romantic California-style and continental cuisine, the place is **Casablanca Restaurant,** 101 Main St. (at Beach), tel. (831) 426-9063, open for dinner nightly and brunch on Sunday. A lively newcomer for worldly American—and a surprising selection of vegetarian options—is **Blacks Beach Café,** E. Cliff at 15th, tel. (831) 475-2233, open Tues.-Sun. for dinner, on weekends for brunch.

Veggie Fare and Other Cheap Eats

The Crepe Place, 1134 Soquel Ave., tel. (831) 429-6994, offers inexpensive breakfasts, dessert crepes (and every other kind), good but unpretentious lunches, and dinners into the wee hours—a great place for late-night dining. Open daily for lunch and dinner, on weekends for brunch. The **Saturn Cafe,** 1230 Mission, tel. (831) 429-8505, has inexpensive and wonderful vegetarian meals for lunch, dinner, and beyond. Open daily for lunch and dinner, and until late for desserts and coffee.

For "natural fast foods," don't miss **Dharma's,** in Capitola at 4250 Capitola Rd., tel. (831) 462-1717, where you can savor a Brahma Burger, Dharma Dog, or Nuclear Sub sandwich (baked tofu, guacamole, cheese, lettuce, olives, pickle, and secret sauce on a roll).

The **Santa Cruz Brewing Co. and Front Street Pub,** 516 Front St., tel. (831) 429-8838, is a local microbrewery (tours available) featuring perennial favorites like Lighthouse Amber, Lighthouse Lager, Pacific Porter, and handcrafted seasonal brews—14 different beers in all—plus homemade root beer. The **Seabright Brewery** brewpub, 519 Seabright Ave., Ste. 107, tel. (831) 426-2739, is popular for its Seabright Amber and Pelican Pale—not to mention casual dining out on the patio. If you're heading toward Boulder Creek, beer fans, stop by the **Boulder Creek Brewery and Cafe,** 13040 Hwy. 9, tel. (831) 338-7882.

The **Santa Cruz Coffee Roasting Company** at the Palomar Inn, 1330 Pacific Ave., tel. (831) 459-0100, serves excellent coffee and a bistro-style café menu. Not far away and absolutely wonderful is **Zoccoli's Delicatessen,** 1534 Pacific Ave., tel. (831) 423-1711, where it's typical to see people lining up for sandwiches, salads, and genuine "good deal" lunch specials, usually under $5. Fresh homemade pastas. Open Mon.-Sat. 9 a.m.-5:30 p.m.

Best Bets Downtown

El Palomar at the Pacific Garden Mall, 1336 Pacific Ave., tel. (831) 425-7575, is a winner for relaxed Mexican—especially seafood—and for about a decade now has been just about everybody's choice for "best" south-of-the-border fare. Open daily for breakfast, lunch, and dinner. Full bar. (At the yacht harbor, there's **Café El Palomar,** 2222 E. Cliff Dr., tel. 831-462-4248, open 7 a.m.-5 p.m. daily.) The **Cooper Street Café** at the back of the McPherson Center, Cooper and Front Streets, tel. (831) 423-4925, is a good choice for a tasty and reasonably priced lunch—serving everything from soup and salads to quiche and pastas. Open Tues.-Sun. from 11 a.m. to 9 or 11 p.m. (until just 6 p.m. on Sunday). Sit outside on the patio in nice weather, where there's live jazz on weekend afternoons.

Quite stylish for European-style fare is the **Pearl Alley Bistro & Café,** 110 Pearl Alley, tel. (831) 429-8070, open daily for lunch (until 5 p.m.) and dinner. Full bar.

The Whole Earth Restaurant

A visit to Santa Cruz wouldn't be complete without feasting at the **Whole Earth Restaurant,** on the UC Santa Cruz campus (Redwood Blvd. next to the library), tel. (831) 426-8255. A quiet, comfortable place, this very fine organic eatery was the inspiration and training ground for Sharon Cadwallader's well-known *Whole Earth Cookbook* and its sequel. After all these years, the food is still good and still reasonable. Happy hour Friday 4:30-6:30 p.m., live music during the school year.

Chaminade

The old Chaminade Brothers Seminary and Monastery, 1 Chaminade Ln. (just off Paul Sweet Rd.), tel. (831) 475-5600, www.chaminade.com, fell into the hands of developers and is now Chaminade Executive Conference Center and Resort. As part of the deal, the new owners had to include a public restaurant in their development plans. The **Sunset Dining Room at Chaminade** is the place to come on Friday nights for what is no doubt the best seafood buffet in Santa Cruz County—15 types of fish and seafood, an outdoor grill, and a spectacular view of Monterey Bay. It's worth every penny of the (fairly high) price. The Sunset Room also serves appetizing breakfast, lunch, and dinner buffets, and a popular Sunday brunch. Outdoor dining is available, weather permitting. Open daily; reservations wise. You can also sign on for a stay here (see Staying in Santa Cruz above).

EATING NEAR SANTA CRUZ

Eating in Soquel
The **Little Tampico,** 2605 Main St., tel. (831) 475-4700, isn't exactly inexpensive. A real bargain here, though, is the specialty "Otila's Plate": a mini-taco, enchilada, tostada, and taquito, plus rice and beans. Another good choice: nachos with everything. (Various Tampico restaurant relatives dot the county, too.) Another popular Mexican restaurant in town is **Tortilla Flats,** 4616 Soquel Dr., tel. (831) 476-1754. Open daily for lunch, dinner, and Sunday brunch.

If it's Italian you crave, try **Aragona's,** 2591 Main St., tel. (831) 462-5100, which serves house-made pastas and gourmet pizzas in a garden-like setting looking out on Soquel Creek. Open daily for lunch and dinner.

Eating in Capitola
Dharma's Natural Foods Restaurant, a Santa Cruz institution now at home at 4250 Capitola Rd., tel. (831) 462-1717, is purported to be the oldest completely vegetarian restaurant in the country. Open daily for breakfast, lunch, and dinner. Also classic in Capitola is **Mr. Toots Coffeehouse** upstairs at 221-A Esplanade, tel. (831) 475-3679, where you can get a cup of joe until late, and **Pizza-My-Heart,** 209-A Esplanade, tel. (831) 475-5714.

Casual in more upscale style and unbeatable for pastries and decadent desserts is **Gayle's Bakery and Rosticceria,** 504 Bay Ave., tel. (831) 462-1200. The "rosticceria" has a wonderful selection of salads and homemade pastas, soups, sandwiches, pizza, spit-roasted meats—even "dinners-to-go" and heat-and-serve casseroles. But the aromas drifting in from Gayle's Bakery are the real draw. The bakery's breakfast pastries include various cheese Danishes, croissants, chocolatine, lemon tea bread, muffins, pecan rolls, apple-nut turnovers, and such specialties as a Schnecken ring smothered in walnuts. The apple crumb and ollalieberry pies

are unforgettable, not to mention the praline cheesecake or the two-dozen cakes—chocolate mousse, hasselnuss, raspberry, poppyseed, mocha . . . (All pies and cakes are also served by the slice.) For decadence-to-go, try Grand Marnier truffles, florentines, éclairs, or Napoleons.

Gayle's also sells more than two-dozen types of fresh-baked bread. The Capitola sourdough bread and sour baguette would be good for picnics, as would a two-pound loaf of the excellent Pain de Compagne. Gayle's is open daily 7 a.m.-7 p.m. (If you're heading back toward the Bay or San Jose the back way via Corralitos, stop by the **Corralitos Market and Sausage Co.,** 569 Corralitos Rd. via Freedom Blvd., Watsonville, tel. 831-722-2633, for homemade sausages, smoke-cured ham and turkey breast, or other specialty meats—all great with Gayle's breads.)

Near the beach, on or near the Esplanade, you'll find an endless variety of eateries. Among them, **Sea Bonne,** 231 Esplanade, tel. (831) 462-1350, is one of the area's better restaurants, serving up imaginative seafood and romantic views. Open for dinner nightly. Reservations wise. **Margaritaville,** 221 Esplanade, tel. (831) 476-2263, serves upscale Mexican fare and margaritas. Open for lunch and dinner daily and for brunch on weekends. The **Paradise Beach Grill,** 215 Esplanade, tel. (831) 476-4900, offers California cuisine as well as a variety of international dishes. Great views. Open for lunch and dinner daily. Also going for the California cuisine is **Zelda's on the Beach,** 203 Esplanade, tel. (831) 475-4900, which features an affordable lobster special on Thursday night.

The most famous restaurant in Capitola is the **Shadowbrook Restaurant,** 1750 Wharf Rd. (at Capitola Rd.), tel. (831) 475-1511, known for its romantic garden setting—ferns, roses, ivy outside, a Monterey pine and plants inside—and the tram ride down the hill to Soquel Creek. The Shadowbrook is open for "continental-flavored American" dinners nightly. Extensive wine list. Brunch, with choices like apple and cheddar omelettes, is served on weekends. Reservations recommended.

Eating in Aptos
The **Bittersweet Bistro,** 787 Rio Del Mar Blvd., tel. (831) 662-9799, offers Mediterranean-inspired bistro fare featuring fresh local and

organic produce—everything from Greek pizzettas and seafood puttanesca to garlic chicken
and grilled Monterey Bay king salmon. Open
Tues.-Sun. for "bistro hour" (3-6 p.m.)—half-
priced pizzettas and drink specials—and for dinner. The best place around for Thai food, locals
say, is **Bangkok West,** 2505 Cabrillo College
Dr., tel. (831) 479-8297, open daily for lunch
and dinner. For stylish and fresh Mexican, the
place is **Palapas** at Seascape Village on
Seascape Blvd., tel. (831) 662-9000, open daily
for lunch and dinner, brunch on Sunday.

For a romantic dinner, splurge at the **Cafe
Sparrow,** 8042 Soquel Dr., tel. (831) 688-6238,
which serves pricey but excellent country French
cuisine at lunch and dinner daily—a Santa Cruz
County dining destination that's actually family
friendly. Open Mon.-Sat. for lunch, daily for dinner. Extensive wine list. Or try the **White Magnolia,** downstairs at the Bayview Hotel, 8041
Soquel Dr., tel. (831) 685-1881, where everything is served up with a helping of the inn's historic 1878 charm.

EVENTFUL SANTA CRUZ

For an up-to-date quarterly calendar of city and
county events, contact the local visitors council
(see Santa Cruz Information and Services
below). Bike races have prominent local appeal,
and professional volleyball competitions are also
held year-round. Whalewatching in winter is another popular draw.

For wine lovers, mid-January features the
countywide winter **Wineries Passport Program,**
offering tours, tastings, and open houses at
Santa Cruz Mountains wineries (also held in
mid-April, mid-July, and mid-November). Also
mid-month, Santa Cruz celebrates the modest
mushroom with its annual **Fungus Fair.**

The **Santa Cruz Baroque Festival** starts in
February and continues until May, offering concerts of early music masterworks. For information, call (831) 457-9693. Head for the Boardwalk
in late February for the annual **Clam Chowder
Cook-Off.**

In late March, Felton holds its **Great Train
Robberies** festival, followed by the **Amazing
Egg Hunt** in April (usually). Come in May for
the **Santa Cruz Industrial Hemp Expo and
"Hemp Parade,"** and for **Bug Day** at Henry
Cowell Redwoods State Park. Memorial Day
weekend brings the annual **Civil War Reenact-
ment** at Roaring Camp, and the **Strawberry
Dessert Festival** in Watsonville.

Come to Aptos on July 4 for the **World's
Shortest Parade.** For a roarin' good time in
Roaring Camp, come in mid-July for the blue-
grass **Musical Saw Players Festival.** The
Shakespeare Santa Cruz festival runs mid-July
through August in an outdoor theater in the red-
woods at UCSC. The very fast annual **Santa
Cruz to Capitola Wharf-to-Wharf Race** in late

*Judging by the
eccentric array of local
events, Santa Cruz
residents have a
refreshingly strange
sense of humor.*

SANTA CRUZ CONFERENCE AND VISITORS COUNCIL

July is a major event for runners, with more than half of the usual number of applicants turned away due to its immense popularity—a popularity fueled by the added inducement of a $12,000 total prize purse. For information, call the "race hot line," tel. (831) 475-2196.

After 20-some years, the famed August **Cabrillo Music Festival** (described by *The New Yorker* as one of the most adventurous and attractive in America) is still going strong, with performances at UC Santa Cruz, Mission San Juan Bautista, and Watsonville. For information—and do make your plans well in advance—contact the Cabrillo Music Festival, 104 Walnut Ave., Ste. 206, Santa Cruz, CA 95060, tel. (831) 426-6966. To reserve tickets, call (831) 420-5260. Also in August, look for the **International Calamari Festival;** for information call India Joze restaurant at (831) 427-3554.

The first couple of weeks in September, Capitola's **Begonia Festival** includes several big events, including a sandcastle contest and nautical parade. It's followed (and nearly overshadowed) in mid-September by the city's annual **Art & Wine Festival,** which has become incredibly popular.

The second and third weekends in October, come for the countywide artists' **Open Studios,** with open-house art shows held everywhere, from private homes and studios to galleries and museums. It's wonderful exposure for artists and great pleasure for aficionados. Appropriately scary for Halloween is the **Missing Arm of William Wadell** hike through the dark woods at Big Basin State Park.

In late November, look for Felton's **Mountain Man Rendezvous** and the **Christmas Craft and Gift Festival** at the Boardwalk's Cocoanut Grove. In December, Felton sponsors its **Pioneer Christmas** festivities.

ARTFUL, ENTERTAINING SANTA CRUZ

Santa Cruz has more than its fair share of good movie theaters and film series. To get an idea of what's playing where, scan local entertainment papers and/or pick up a current copy of the free bimonthly *Santa Cruz Movie Times.*

Santa Cruz Clubs

If you're into big-band swing, check out **Cocoanut Grove** dances (call 408-423-5590 for information); tickets run $15 and up. **The Kuumbwa Jazz Center,** 320-2 Cedar St. #2, tel. (831) 427-2227, is a no-booze, no-cigarettes, under-21-welcome place with great jazz (often big names), and it's rarely packed. Most shows are Monday and Friday at 8 p.m.; ticket prices vary and often low. The **Catalyst,** 1011 Pacific Ave., tel. (831) 423-1336, is legendary for its Friday afternoon happy hour in the Atrium—seems like *everybody's* here from 5-7 p.m., drinking beer, making the scene, and sometimes tapping their toes to the house band: Wally's Swing World. The 700-seat theater (massive dance floor) hosts good local bands or national acts nightly (cover charge).

Local coffeehouses from Santa Cruz to Capitola also offer casual, relaxed, sometimes highbrow entertainment (like poetry readings). For women's music on Wednesday nights, head for the **Saturn Cafe,** 1230 Mission St., tel. (831) 429-8505.

Santa Cruz Area Performing Arts

On a smaller scale, local performing arts are always an adventure. The **Santa Cruz Chamber Players** specialize in both traditional and modern chamber music, with an emphasis on the unusual. For a performance schedule, call (831) 425-3149. The **Santa Cruz County Symphony,** 200 Seventh Ave. #225, tel. (831) 462-0553, schedules performances year-round at both the Santa Cruz Civic Auditorium and Watsonville's Mello Center.

The noted **Tandy Beal & Company** dance troupe, 740 Front St. #300B, tel. (831) 429-1324, performs locally when not touring internationally. The **Santa Cruz Ballet Theatre,** 2800 S. Rodeo Gulch Rd., Soquel, tel. (831) 479-1600, is a good bet for a year-end production of *The Nutcracker.* **Actors' Theatre,** 1001 Center St., tel. (831) 425-1003 (administration) or (831) 425-7529 (tickets and reservations), schedules live stage productions year-round. In Capitola, the Quonset hut-housed Capitola Theater is now the **Bay Shore Lyric Opera Company and Theater for the Performing Arts,** tel. (831) 462-3131.

On-Campus Performances

For information on what's going on at UCSC, pick up a copy of the quarterly **UCSC Performing Arts Calendar,** available around town, or call (831) 459-ARTS for information. (Other useful campus numbers include: Arts and Lectures, tel. 831-459-2826; Theatre Arts, tel. 831-459-2974; and the Music Department, tel. 831-459-2292). To order performance tickets by phone ($2 service charge), call the UCSC Ticket Office at (831) 459-2159.

SANTA CRUZ INFORMATION AND SERVICES

Santa Cruz Visitor Information

The best all-around source for city and county information is the **Santa Cruz County Conference and Visitors Council,** downtown at 701 Front St., Santa Cruz, CA 95060, tel. (831) 425-1234 or toll-free (800) 833-3494, fax (831) 425-1260, www.santacruzca.org, open Mon.-Sat. 9 a.m.-5 p.m., Sunday 10 a.m.-4 p.m. There's also a visitor information kiosk downtown on Ocean between Soquel and Water, staffed on weekends in summer (the printed travelers guide is available here on weekdays).

Definitely request the current accommodations, dining, and visitor guides. If you've got time to roam farther afield, also pick up a current copy of the *County Crossroads* farm trails map and ask about area wineries. Cyclists, request the *Santa Cruz County Bikeway Map.* Antiquers, ask for the current *Antiques, Arts, & Collectibles* directory for Santa Cruz and Monterey Counties, published every June—not a complete listing, by far, but certainly a good start. If you once were familiar with Santa Cruz and—post-1989 earthquake—now find yourself lost, pick up the *Downtown Santa Cruz Directory* brochure.

Useful Publications

A valuable source of performing arts information, focused on the university, is the *UCSC Performing Arts Calendar,* published quarterly and available around town. The excellent UC Santa Cruz paper, *City on a Hill,* is published only during the regular school year. *Santa Cruz Good Times* is a good, long-running free weekly with an entertainment guide and sometimes entertaining political features. The free *Student Guide* comes out seasonally, offering lots of ads and some entertaining reading about Santa Cruz.

The *Santa Cruz County Sentinel,* and the *Watsonville Register-Pajaronian,* are the traditional area papers. The **Santa Cruz Parks and Recreation Department** at Harvey West Park, 307 Church St., tel. (831) 429-3663, open weekdays 8 a.m.-noon and 1-5 p.m., usually publishes a *Summer Activity Guide* (especially useful for advance planning).

Santa Cruz Services

The Santa Cruz post office is at 850 Front St., tel. (831) 426-5200, and is open weekdays 8 a.m.-5 p.m. The **Santa Cruz Public Library** is at 224 Church St., tel. (831) 420-5700. (If you want to hobnob with the people on the hill, visit the **Dean McHenry Library** on campus, tel. 831-459-4000.) For senior information, stop by the **Senior Center,** 222 Market, tel. (831) 423-6640, or 1777 Capitola Rd., tel. (831) 462-1433.

SANTA CRUZ TRANSPORTATION

Getting Here

The **Greyhound** bus terminal is at 425 Front St., tel. (831) 423-1800, open weekdays 7:30 a.m.-8 p.m. Greyhound provides service from San Francisco to Santa Cruz, Fort Ord, and Monterey, as well as connections south to L.A. via Salinas or San Jose. From the East Bay and South Bay, take Amtrak (see below), now also offering bus connections from Salinas.

Getting Around

Bicyclists will be in hog heaven here, with everything from excellent bike lanes to locking bike racks at bus stops. But drivers, be warned: parking can be impossible, especially in summer, especially at the beach. There's a charge for parking at the Boardwalk (in lots with attendants), and metered parking elsewhere. Best bet: park elsewhere and take the shuttle. Second best: drive to the beach, unload passengers and beach paraphernalia, then park a mile or so away. By the time you walk back, your companions should be done battling for beach towel space.

You can usually find free parking on weekends in the public garage at the county government center at 701 Ocean St., conveniently also a stop for the summer weekends-only **Santa Cruz Beach Shuttle.** The shuttle—a great way to avoid parking nightmares—provides regular service between the county government center, downtown, and the wharf area, weekends only Memorial Day weekend through Labor Day. Fare is $1.

The **Santa Cruz Metro,** 230 Walnut Ave., tel. (831) 425-8600, provides superb public transit throughout the northern Monterey Bay area. The Metro has a "bike and ride" service for bicyclists who want to hitch a bus ride part way (bike racks onboard). Call for current route information, or pick up a free copy of the excellent *Headways* (which includes Spanish translations). Buses will get you anywhere you want to go in town and considerably beyond for $1 ($3 for an all-day pass), exact change only.

You can rent a car from **Enterprise Rent-A-Car,** 1025-B Water St., tel. (831) 426-7799 or toll-free (800) 325-8007; **Avis,** 630 Ocean St., tel. (831) 423-1244 or toll-free (800) 831-2847; and **Budget,** 919 Ocean St., tel. (831) 425-1808 or (800) 527-0700. **Yellow Cab** is at 131 Front St., tel. (831) 423-1234, also home to the **Santa Cruz Airporter,** tel. (831) 423-1214 or toll-free in California (800) 223-4142, which provides shuttle van service to both the San Francisco and San Jose airports as well as to *Caltrain* and the Amtrak station in San Jose (see also Getting Away below).

For some guided assistance in seeing the sights, contact **Earth, Sea and Sky Tours,** P.O. Box 1630, Aptos, CA 95001, tel. (831) 688-5544.

Getting Away

Metro buses can get you to Boulder Creek, Big Basin State Park, Ben Lomond, Felton, north coast beaches, *almost* all the way to Año Nuevo State Reserve just across the San Mateo County line, and to south coast beaches and towns. (**Monterey-Salinas Transit** from Watsonville provides good service in Monterey County.) For ridesharing out of town, check the ride board at UC Santa Cruz and local classifieds.

Another way to get out of town is via Santa Cruz Metro's **CalTrain Connector** buses to the San Jose train station—more than 10 trips daily on weekdays (fewer on weekends or holidays)—which directly connect with the CalTrain (to San Francisco) and **Amtrak** (to Oakland, Berkeley, and Sacramento). Fare is just $5. For information on the Connector, call (831) 425-8600; on *Caltrain* fares and schedules, call (650) 508-6200 or toll-free (800) 660-4287 (in the service area); on Amtrak, call toll-free (800) 872-7245 or try www.amtrak.com.

NEAR SANTA CRUZ

Just north of Santa Cruz, as the crow flies, is spectacular Big Basin Redwoods State Park, California's first state park. Other worthwhile parks near Big Basin include Henry Cowell Redwoods State Park—offering a hiking route connecting to Wilder Ranch State Park on the coast—and Castle Rock State Park, in addition to several local parks. Great for hiking near Aptos and Soquel is Forest of Nisene Marks State Park.

Heading south from Santa Cruz on Hwy. 1 on the way to Monterey or Salinas will pass through the towns of Watsonville and Moss Landing en route. Other area attractions include Gilroy, home of the immensely popular Gilroy Garlic Festival, and the historic mission town of San Juan Bautista.

BIG BASIN REDWOODS STATE PARK

California's first state park was established here, about 24 miles upcanyon from Santa Cruz. To save Big Basin's towering *Sequoia sempervirens* coast redwoods from loggers, 60-some conservationists led by Andrew P. Hill camped at the base of Slippery Rock on May 15, 1900, and formed the Sempervirens Club. Just two years later, in September 1902, 3,800 acres of primeval forest were deeded to the state, the beginning of California's state park system. Today, Big Basin Redwoods State Park includes more than 18,000 acres on the ocean-facing slopes of the Santa Cruz Mountains, and efforts to protect (and expand) the park still continue under the auspices of the Sempervirens Fund and Save-the-Redwoods League. Donations are always welcome.

Seeing and Doing Big Basin

The best time to be in Big Basin is in the fall, when the weather is perfect and most tourists have gone home. Winter and spring are also prime times, though usually rainier. Roadcuts into the park offer a peek into local geology—tilted, folded, twisted layers of thick marine sediments. Big Basin's **Nature Lodge** museum features good natural history exhibits and many fine books, including *Short Historic Tours of Big Basin* by Jennie and Denzil Verado. The carved-log seating and the covered stage at the amphitheater attract impromptu human performances (harmonica concerts, freestyle softshoe, joke routines) when no park campfires or other official events are scheduled.

Also here: more than 100 miles of hiking trails. Take the half-mile **Redwood Trail** loop to stretch your legs, and to see one of the park's most impressive stands of virgin redwoods. Or hike the more ambitious **Skyline-to-the-Sea** trail, at least an overnight trip. It's 11 miles from the basin rim to the seabird haven of Waddell Beach and adjacent **Theodore J. Hoover Natural Preserve,** a freshwater marsh. There are trail camps along the way (camping and fires allowed only in designated areas). Hikers, bring food and water, as Waddell Creek flows with reclaimed wastewater. Another popular route is the **Pine Mountain Trail.** Thanks to recent land acquisitions along the coast north of Santa Cruz, the new 1.5-mile **Whitehouse Ridge Trail** now joins Big Basin with Año Nuevo State Reserve; call ahead or inquire at either park for directions.

Most dramatic in Big Basin are the waterfalls. **Berry Creek Falls** is a particularly pleasant destination: rushing water, redwood mists, and glistening rocks fringed with delicate ferns. Nearby are **Silver Falls** and the **Golden Falls Cascade.**

THE ROARING CAMP AND BIG TREES RAILROAD

F. Norman Clark, the self-described "professional at oddities" who also owns the narrow-gauge railroad in Felton, bought the Southern Pacific rails connecting Santa Cruz and nearby Olympia, to make it possible for visitors to get to Henry Cowell Redwoods State Park and Felton (*almost* to Big Basin) by train. During logging's commercial heyday here in the 1900s, 20 or more trains passed over these tracks every day.

Today you can still visit Roaring Camp and ride the rails on one of two different trips. Hop aboard a 100-year-old steam engine and make an hour-and-fifteen-minute loop around a virgin redwood forest ($14 general, $9.50 kids 3-12), or take a 1940s-vintage passenger train from Felton down to Santa Cruz (roundtrip fare $15 general, $11 kids 3-12). The year-round calendar of special events includes October's **Harvest Faire** and the **Halloween Ghost Train,** the **Mountain Man Rendezvous** living history encampment in November, and December's **Pioneer Christmas.**

The railroad offers daily runs (usually just one train a day on nonsummer weekdays) from spring through November, and operates only on weekends and major holidays in winter. For more information, contact: Roaring Camp and Big Trees Narrow-Gauge Railroad, P.O. Box G-1, Felton, CA 95018, tel. (831) 335-4484, fax (831) 335-3509, www.roaringcamp.com.

SAN JOSE CONVENTION AND VISITORS BUREAU

Practical Big Basin

For park information, contact Big Basin Redwoods State Park, 21600 Big Basin Way, Boulder Creek, CA 95006, tel. (831) 338-8860. Big Basin has 190 campsites ($14-18) plus five group camps. Reserve all campsites through ReserveAmerica, toll-free tel. (800) 444-7275, up to seven months in advance. An unusual "outdoor" option: the park's tent cabins. For more information, see Santa Cruz Camping. To reserve backpacker campsites at the park's six trail camps ($10), contact park headquarters or call (831) 338-8861. Big Basin's day-use fee is $6 per vehicle (walk-ins and bike-ins are free), and a small fee is charged for the map/brochure showing all trails and major park features.

OTHER PARKS NEAR BIG BASIN

Henry Cowell Redwoods State Park

The Redwood Grove in the dark San Lorenzo Canyon here is the park's hub and one of the most impressive redwood groves along the central coast, with the "Neckbreaker," the "Giant," and the "Fremont Tree" all standouts. You can camp at Graham Hill, picnic near the grove, or head out on the 15-mile web of hiking and horseback trails. New in the summer of 1999 was the **U-Con Trail** connecting Henry Cowell to Wilder Ranch State Park on the coast—making it possible to hike, bike, or horseback ride from the redwoods to the ocean on an established trail. Henry Cowell has 150 campsites (see Santa Cruz Camping). For information about Henry Cowell Redwoods State Park, off Hwy. 9 in Felton, call (831) 335-4598 or (831) 438-2396 (campground).

Other Parks off Highway 9

Between Big Basin and Saratoga is **Castle Rock State Park,** 15300 Skyline Blvd., Los Gatos, tel. (408) 867-2952, an essentially undeveloped park and a hiker's paradise. Ask at Big Basin for current trail information. **Highlands County Park,** 8500 Hwy. 9 in Ben Lomond, is open daily 9 a.m.-dusk. This old estate, transformed into a park with picnic tables and nature trails, also has a sandy beach along the river. Another swimming spot is at **Ben Lomond County Park** on Mill St., which also offers shaded picnic tables and barbecue facilities. Free, open daily in summer. Closer to Big Basin is **Boulder Creek Park** on Middleton Ave. east of Hwy. 9 in Boulder Creek, also free. The swimming hole here has both shallows and deeps, plus there's a sandy beach. Other facilities include shaded picnic tables and barbecue pits.

Forest of Nisene Marks State Park

Nisene Marks is definitely a hiker's park. Named for the Danish immigrant who hiked here until the age of 96 and whose family donated the land for public use, this is an oasis of solitude. (This was also the epicenter of the 1989 earthquake that brought down much of Santa Cruz.) You'll have lots to see here, but little more than birdsong, rustling leaves, and babbling brooks to listen to. The park encompasses 10,000 acres of hefty second-growth redwoods on the steep southern range of the Santa Cruz Mountains, six creeks, lovely Maple Falls, alders, maples, and more rugged trails than anyone can hike in a day. Also here are an old mill site, abandoned trestles and railroad tracks, and logging cabins.

To get here from the coast, take the Aptos-Seacliff exit north from Hwy. 1 and turn right on Soquel Drive. At the first left after the stop sign, drive north on Aptos Creek Rd. and across the railroad tracks. (Bring water and food for day trips. No fires allowed.) The park is open daily 6 a.m.-sunset. For information and a trail map, contact: Forest of Nisene Marks State Park, Aptos Creek Rd., Aptos, CA 95003, tel. (831) 763-7063. To reserve the trail camp (a six-mile one-way hike, just six sites, primitive, $7 per night), call (831) 763-7064 or (831) 763-7121.

WATSONVILLE, GILROY, AND SAN JUAN BAUTISTA

Watsonville:
Strawberries and Mushrooms

An agriculturally rich city of over 25,000, Watsonville is the mushroom capital of the U.S., though the town calls this lovely section of the Pajaro Valley the "Strawberry Capital of the World," and "Apple City of the Ives." Get up to speed on local agricultural history at the **Agricultural History Project** at the Santa Cruz County Fairgrounds, tel. (831) 724-5898, museum exhibits and demonstrations open to the public on

Friday and Saturday noon-4 p.m. An almost mandatory stop, from May through January, is **Gizdich Ranch**, 55 Peckham Rd., tel. (831) 722-1056, www.gizdichranch.com, fabulous from late summer through fall for its fresh apples, home-made apple pies, and fresh-squeezed natural apple juices. Earlier in the season this is a "Pik-Yor-Sef" berry farm, with raspberries, olallieberries, and strawberries (usually also available in pies, fritters, and pastries). Also worth seeking in Watsonville are Mexican and Filipino eateries, many quite good, most inexpensive.

The Watsonville area boasts some fine state beaches. At **Manresa State Beach**, 1445 San Andreas Rd., tel. (831) 724-3750, stairways lead to the surf from the main parking lot and Sand Dollar Dr.; restrooms, an outdoor shower, and tent camping are available. Rural San Andreas Rd. also takes you to **Sunset State Beach**, 201 Sunset Beach Rd., tel. (831) 763-7062 or (831) 763-7063, four miles west of Watsonville in the Pajaro Dunes. Sunset offers 3.5 miles of nice sandy beaches, plus 90 campsites and 60 picnic sites, but also way too many RVs and not much privacy. Even so, after sunset the beach is open only to campers. Parking for pretty **Palm Beach** near Pajaro Dunes—a great place to find sand dollars—is near the end of Beach Street. Also here are picnic facilities, a par course, and restrooms. **Zmudowski State Beach** is near where the Pajaro River reaches the sea: good hiking and surf fishing, rarely crowded. Next, near Moss Landing, are **Salinas River State Beach**, Potrero Rd., tel. (831) 384-7695, and **Jetty State Beach**. To reserve campsites at all state beaches and parks, call ReserveAmerica toll-free at (800) 444-7275.

For the local *Country Crossroads* farm trails map, and other visitor information, contact the **Pajaro Valley Chamber of Commerce**, 444 Main St., P.O. Box 470, Watsonville, CA 95077, tel. (831) 724-3900, www.pvchamber.com.

Gilroy and Garlic

It's chic to reek in Gilroy. Will Rogers supposedly described Gilroy as "the only town in America where you can marinate a steak just by hanging it out on the clothesline." But Gilroy, the "undisputed garlic capital of the world," dedicates very few acres to growing the stinking rose these days. The legendary local garlic farms have been de-clining due to soil disease since 1979—ironically, the first year of the now-famous and phenomenally successful **Gilroy Garlic Festival**, tel. (408) 842-1625, www.gilroygarlicfestival.com, held the last full weekend in July. Other attractions in Gilroy include the **Indian Motorcycle** production facility (call 408-847-2221 to arrange factory tours) and Goldsmith Seeds Gilroy's seasonal six-acre **Field of Dreams** experimental flower seed garden (call 408-847-7333 for tour information). Downtown Gilroy has its attractions, too. The best place to start exploring them is the **Gilroy Historical Museum** at Fifth and Church, tel. (408) 848-0470, open weekdays 9 a.m.-5 p.m.

For more information about what's cookin' in and around Gilroy, contact: **Gilroy Chamber of Commerce**, 7471 Monterey St., Gilroy 95020, www.gilroy.org.

San Juan Bautista and *Vertigo*

The tiny town of San Juan Bautista is charming and charmed, as friendly as it is sunny. (People here say the weather in this pastoral valley is "salubrious." Take their word for it.) Named for John the Baptist, the 1797 Spanish mission of San Juan Bautista is central to this serene community at the foot of the Gabilan Mountains. But the historic plaza, still bordered by old adobes and now a state historic park, is the true center of San Juan—rallying point for two revolutions, onetime home of famed bandit Tiburcio Vasquez, and the theatrical setting for David Belasco's *Rose of the Rancho*. Movie fans may remember Jimmy Stewart and Kim Novak in the mission scenes from Alfred Hitchcock's *Vertigo*, which were filmed here.

In addition to history and celluloid celebrity, San Juan Bautista has galleries, antique and craft shops, and an incredible local theater troupe—**El Teatro Campesino**, established by noted playwright Luis Valdez *(Zoot Suit* and *Corridos)*. To get oriented, pick up a walking-tour brochure at the **San Juan Bautista Chamber of Commerce** office, 1 Polk St., tel. (831) 623-2454, or elsewhere around town. In June, experience mid-1800s mission days at **Early Days in San Juan Bautista**, a traditional celebration complete with horse-drawn carriages, period dress, music, and fandango. The barroom at the Plaza Hotel is even open for card games. The **Flea Market** here in August is one of the country's best. Later in the month, **San Juan Fiesta Day** is the most popular venue of the wandering **Cabrillo Music Festival.**

MOSS LANDING AND VICINITY

Near the mouth of Elkhorn Slough on the coast south of Watsonville, Moss Landing is a crazy quilt of weird shops and roadside knickknack stands, watched over by both a towering steam power plant (formerly under PG&E control and now owned by Duke Energy), built circa 1948, the second largest in the world, and a Kaiser firebrick-making plant. All of which makes for an odd-looking community.

First a Salinas Valley produce port, then a whaling harbor until 1930, modern Moss Landing is surrounded by artichoke and broccoli fields. The busy fishing harbor and adjoining slough are home to hundreds of bird and plant species, making this an important center for marinelife studies.

These days the area is also noted for its indoor recreational opportunities, with more than two-dozen antique and junque shops along Moss Landing Road. Show up on the last Sunday in July for the annual **Antique Street Fair,** which draws more than 350 antique dealers and at least 12,000 civilian antiquers.

Moss Landing Marine Laboratories

The laboratories here, at 895 Blanco Circle, tel. (831) 755-8650, are jointly operated by nine campuses of the California State Universities and Colleges system. Students and faculty study local marinelife, birds, and tidepools, but particularly Monterey Bay's spectacular underwater submarine canyons, which start where Elkhorn Slough enters the bay at Moss Landing. Stop for a visit and quick look around, but don't disturb classes or research projects. Better yet, come in spring—usually the first Sunday after Easter—for the big open house, when you can take a complete tour, explore the "touch tank" full of starfish, sea cucumbers, sponges, snails, and anemones, and see slide shows, movies, and marinelife dioramas.

Elkhorn Slough Reserve

Most people come here to hike and birdwatch, but the fish life in this coastal estuary, the second largest in California, is also phenomenal. No wonder the Ohlone people built villages here some 5,000 years ago. Wetlands like these, oozing with life and nourished by rich bay sediments, are among those natural environments most threatened by "progress." Thanks to The Nature Conservancy, the Elkhorn Slough (originally the mouth of the Salinas River, until a 1908 diversion) is now protected as a federal and state estuarine sanctuary and recognized as a National Estuarine Research Reserve—California's first. Elkhorn Slough is managed by the California Department of Fish and Game.

These meandering channels along an old, seven-mile-long river are thick with marshy grasses and wildflowers beneath a plateau of oaks and eucalyptus. In winter, an incredible variety of shorebirds (not counting migrating waterfowl) call this area home. Endangered and threatened birds, including the brown pelican, the California clapper rail, and the California least tern, thrive here. The tule elk once hunted by the Ohlone are long gone, but harbor seals bask on the mudflats, and bobcats, gray foxes, muskrats, otters, and black-tailed deer are still here. Come in fall for the annual **Monterey Bay Bird Festival.**

Though this is a private nature sanctuary, not a park, the public can visit. Some 4.5 miles of trails pass by tidal mudflats, salt marshes, and an old abandoned dairy. The reserve and visitor center, which offers a birdwatchers map/guide to the Pajaro Valley, are open Wed.-Sun. 9 a.m.-5 p.m. There's a small day-use fee to use the trails. Docent-led walks are offered year-round on Saturday and Sunday at 10 a.m. and 1 p.m. On the first Saturday of the month, there's also an Early Bird Walk at 8:30 a.m. Still, there's no better way to see the slough than from the seat of a kayak. Stop by the visitors' center at the entrance to arrange a guided tour, or contact: **Elkhorn Slough Foundation,** 1700 Elkhorn Rd., P.O. Box 267, Moss Landing, CA 95039, tel. (831) 728-2822 or (831) 728-5939, www.elkhornslough. org. Or arrange kayak tours through **Monterey Bay Kayaks,** 693 Del Monte Ave., Monterey, tel. (831) 373-5357 or (831) 633-2211, or **Kayak Connections,** tel. (831) 724-5692. For a guided tour aboard a 27-foot pontoon boat, contact **Elkhorn Slough Safari** in Moss Landing, tel. (831) 633-5555, www.elkornslough.com.

Practical Moss Landing
Time-honored people's eateries abound, particularly near the harbor. Most serve chowders and seafood and/or ethnic specials. **Moss Landing Oyster Bay Restaurant,** 413 Moss Landing Rd., tel. (831) 632-0119, is well known for its exceptional fresh seafood and house-made pastas and desserts. (Enjoy outdoor patio dining in good weather.) Quite good, right on the highway, is **The Whole Enchilada,** tel. (831) 633-3038, open for lunch and dinner daily and specializing in Mexican seafood entrées. (The "whole enchilada," by the way, is filet of red snapper wrapped in a corn tortilla and smothered in enchilada sauce and melted cheese.) The Enchilada's associated **Moss Landing Inn and Jazz Club,** tel. (831) 633-9990, is a bar featuring live jazz on Sunday 4:30-8:30 p.m.

"En route camping" for self-contained RVs is available at **Moss Landing State Beach.**

Castroville and Artichokes
The heart of Castroville is Swiss-Italian, which hardly explains the artichokes all over the place. Calling itself "Artichoke Capital of the World," Castroville grows 75% of California's artichokes, though that delicious leathery thistle grows throughout Santa Cruz and Monterey Counties. Come for the annual **Artichoke Festival** every May; call (831) 633-6545 or try www.artichike-festival.org for information. It's some party, too, re-

plete with artichokes fried, baked, mashed, boiled, and added as colorful ingredients to cookies and cakes. Nibble on french-fried artichokes with mayo dip and artichoke nut cake, sip artichoke soup, and sample steamed artichokes. Sometimes Hollywood gets in on the action: in 1947 Marilyn Monroe reigned as California's Artichoke Queen. If you miss the festival there are other artichoke options, including **Giant Artichoke Fruits and Vegetables** at 11241 Merritt St., tel. (831) 633-2778, and the **Thistle Hut,** just off Hwy. 1 at Cooper-Molera Rd., tel. (831) 633-4888. And the **Franco Restaurant,** 10639 Merritt, tel. (831) 633-2090, sponsors a Marilyn Monroe look-alike contest in June. But come by otherwise just to grab a burger—some say the best in the county—and to ogle the Marilyn memorabilia.

EXCURSION INLAND: SALINAS AND STEINBECK

A long-running Salinas tradition (since 1911) is the four-day **California Rodeo** held on the third weekend in July, one of the world's largest, with bronco busting and bull riding, roping and tying, barrel racing, and a big Western dance on Saturday night. The rowdiness here—cowboy-style, of course—rivals Mardi Gras. But lately John Steinbeck's literary legacy has been giving the rodeo a run for the money.

Salinas native John Steinbeck

PAT HATHAWAY COLLECTION

Salinas is the blue-collar birthplace of novelist John Steinbeck, who chronicled the lives and hard times of California's down-and-out. Publication of *The Grapes of Wrath* in 1939 didn't do much for the writer's popularity in and around Salinas. Vilified here as a left-winger and Salinas Valley traitor during his lifetime, Steinbeck never came back to his hometown. Yet some people here have long been trying to make it up to Steinbeck. After all, he was the first American ever to win both the Pulitzer and Nobel Prizes for literature. Efforts to establish a permanent local Steinbeck museum finally succeeded, and in summer 1998 the doors of the $10.3 million **National Steinbeck Center** opened to the public.

Billed as a "multimedia experience of literature, history, and art," the Steinbeck Center offers changing exhibits and seven themed permanent galleries—incorporating sights, sounds, and scents—to introduce Steinbeck's life, work, and times, with settings ranging from Doc Rickett's lab on Cannery Row and the replica boxcar of "ice-packed" lettuce to a (climbable) red pony in the barn. Seven theaters show clips from films derived from Steinbeck's writings. But some appreciations are strictly literal, including John Steinbeck's trusty green truck and camper Rocinante (named after Don Quixote's horse), in which the writer sojourned while researching *Travels with Charley.* The **Art of Writing Room,** with literary exhibits and all kinds of technical interactivity, explores the themes of Steinbeck's art and life. The 30,000-piece **Steinbeck Archives** are also here, open only to researchers by appointment. Quite accessible, though, are the sunny **Steinbeck Center Café** and the **museum store,** which features a good selection of books in addition to gift items. The center's new 6,500-square-foot wing, the **Salinas Valley Agricultural History and Education Center,** will showcase the Salinas Valley's agricultural heritage and is scheduled to open in late 2000.

The center is open daily 10 a.m.-5 p.m., but closed on Thanksgiving, Christmas, and New Year's Day. Admission is $7 adults, $6 seniors (over age 62) and students with ID, and $4 children ages 11-17 (under 10 free). For more information about the center and its events and activities, contact: National Steinbeck Center, 1 Main St., Salinas, CA 93901, tel. (831) 796-3833, fax (831) 796-3828, www.steinbeck.org.

In Salinas John Steinbeck is not only a museum, but an event—and a dining destination. On the first weekend in August, come for the annual **Steinbeck Festival**—four days of films, lectures, tours, and social mixers. For information, call (831) 796-3833. The Steinbeck family home—a jewel-box Victorian, located just two blocks from the National Steinbeck Center—was once described by the writer as "an immaculate and friendly house, grand enough, but not pretentious." And so it still is, though these days the Salinas Valley Guild serves up gourmet lunches for Steinbeck fans—featuring Salinas Valley produce and Monterey County wines and beer—at **Steinbeck House,** 132 Central St., Mon.-Sat. 11 a.m.-2:30 p.m. The menu changes weekly. Call (831) 424-2735 for information and reservations.

For area visitor information, contact: **Salinas Valley Chamber of Commerce,** 119 E. Alisal, P.O. Box 1170, Salinas, CA 93902, tel. (831) 424-7611, www.salinaschamber.com.

EXCURSION INLAND: PINNACLES NATIONAL MONUMENT

Exploring these barren 1,600 acres of volcanic spires and ravines is a little like rock climbing on the moon. The weird dark-red rocks are bizarrely eroded, unlike anywhere else in North America, forming gaping gorges, crumbling caverns, terrifying terraces. Rock climbers' heaven (not for beginners), this stunning old volcano offers excellent trails, too, with pebbles the size of houses to stumble over. Visitors afraid of earthquakes should know that the Pinnacles sit atop an active section of the San Andreas Fault. Spring is the best time to visit, when wildflowers brighten up the chaparral, but sunlight on the rocks throughout the day creates rainbows of colors year-round. Climbers come during the cool weather.

Though it was Teddy Roosevelt who first utilized presidential decree on behalf on the Pinnacles—protecting it as a national monument in 1906—in early 2000 President Clinton announced plans to expand the park by some 5,000 acres. Some of that acreage, when acquired, may encourage gentler, family-oriented recreation.

Hiking the Pinnacles

Rock climbing is the major attraction, for obvious reasons. But you can also hike. Of Pinnacles' existing (pre-expansion)16,000-plus acres, nearly 13,000 are protected as wilderness. Only hiking trails connect the park's east and west sides. Pinnacles has four self-guided nature trails; the **Geology Hike** and **Balconies Trail** are quite fascinating. The short **Moses Spring Trail** is one of the best. Longest is the trek up the **Chalone Peak Trail,** 11 miles roundtrip, passing fantastic rock formations (quite a view of Salinas once you get to the top of North Chalone Peak). Less ambitious is the **Condor Gulch Trail,** a two-mile easy hike into Balconies Caves from the Chalone Creek picnic area. Various interconnecting trails encourage creativity on foot. The best camping and caves, as well as the most fascinating rock formations and visitor center displays, are on the park's east side. The fit, fast, and willing can hike east to west and back in one (long) day. Easiest return trip is via the Old Pinnacles Trail, rather than the steep Juniper Canyon Trail. Pack plenty of water.

Practical Pinnacles

As lasting testament to the land's rugged nature, there are two districts in the Pinnacles—west and east—and it's not possible to get from one to the other by road. Within the monument, bicycles and cars may only be used on paved roads. If coming from the west, get visitor information at the **Chaparral Ranger Station,** reached via Hwy. 146 heading east (exit Hwy. 101 just south of Soledad). For most visitors, Pinnacles is most accessible from this route, but it's a narrow road, not recommended for campers and trailers. If coming from the east, stop by the **Bear Gulch Visitor Center,** reached via Hwy. 25 then Hwy. 146 heading west. From Hollister, it's about 34 miles south then about five miles west to the park entrance. Pinnacles is open for day use only; the vehicle entry fee is $5, valid for seven days. For additional information, contact: Pinnacles National Monument, 5000 Hwy. 146, Paicines, CA 95043, tel. (831) 389-4485, www.nps.gov/pinn/index.htm.

Good rules of thumb in the Pinnacles: carry water at all times, and watch out for poison oak, stinging nettles, and rattlesnakes. Spelunkers should bring good flashlights and helmets. Pick up guides to the area's plant life and natural history, also topo maps, at the visitor centers. Rock climbers can thumb through old guides there for climbing routes. No camping is offered (or allowed) within the park. The closest private camping is **Pinnacles Campground, Inc.** near the park's entrance on the east side, 2400 Hwy. 146, Paicines, CA 95043, tel. (831) 389-4462, www.pinncamp.com, which is quite nice—featuring flush toilets, hot showers, fire rings, picnic tables, swimming pool, some RV hookups, and group facilities. Basic supplies and some food are available at the campground's store.

MONTEREY: A NOSTALGIA, A DREAM

In his novel by the same name, John Steinbeck described Monterey's Cannery Row as "a poem, a stink, a grating noise, a quality of light, a tune, a habit, a nostalgia, a dream," also a corrugated collection of sardine canneries, restaurants, honky-tonks, whorehouses, and waterfront laboratories. The street, he said, groaned under the weight of "silver rivers of fish." People here liked his description so much that they eventually put it on a plaque and planted it in today's touristy Cannery Row, among the few Steinbeck-era buildings still standing.

Local promoters claim that the legendary writer would be proud of what the tourist dollar has wrought here, but this seems unlikely. When Steinbeck returned here in 1961 from his self-imposed exile, he noted the clean beaches, "where once they festered with fish guts and flies. The canneries which once put up a sickening stench are gone, their places filled with restaurants, antique shops, and the like. They fish for tourists now, not pilchards, and that species they are not likely to wipe out."

A City "Under Siege"

An early port for California immigrants and now a bustling tourist mecca, Monterey (literally, "The King's Wood") is trying hard to hang onto its once-cloistered charm. The recently spawned and justifiably popular Monterey Bay Aquarium is often blamed for the hopeless summer traffic snarls, though tourism throughout the Monterey Peninsula is the actual culprit. (The region's population and economy otherwise are in flux, with the recent closure of Fort Ord and its replacement with a new California State University campus, CSU Monterey Bay, in 1995.) More than a decade ago, *Creative States Quarterly* editor Raymond Mungo described Monterey as a city "under siege," asking rhetorically: "How do you describe the difference a tornado makes in a small town, or the arrival of sudden prosperity in a sleepy backwater?" How, indeed?

In peak summer months, avoid feeling under siege yourself—or worrying that you're contributing unduly to the city's siege state—by using Monterey's free WAVE public transit shuttles whenever possible.

MONTEREY BAY AQUARIUM

The fish are back on Cannery Row, at least at the west end. Doc's Western Biological Laboratory and the canneries immortalized by Steinbeck may be long gone, but Monterey now has an aquarium that the bohemian biologist would love.

a bubble window at the aquarium

MONTEREY BAY AQUARIUM, ROB LEWINE

PUTTING THE BAY ON DISPLAY

The engineering feats shoring up the amazingly "natural" exhibits in the 322,000-square-foot Monterey Aquarium are themselves impressive. Most remarkable are the aquatic displays, concrete tanks with unbreakable one-ton acrylic windows more than seven inches thick. The exhibits' "wave action" is simulated by a computer-controlled surge machine and hidden water jets. In the Nearshore Galleries, more than a half-million gallons of fresh seawater are pumped through the various aquarium tanks daily to keep these habitats healthy. During the day, six huge "organic" water filters screen out microorganisms that would otherwise cloud the water. At night, filtration shuts down and raw, unfiltered seawater flows through the exhibits—nourishing filter-feeders and also carrying in plant spores and animal larvae that settle and grow, just as they would in nature. The Outer Bay Galleries operate as a "semi-closed" system, with water from the main intake pipes heated to 68° F and recirculated through the exhibits. Wastes are removed by biological filters and ozone treatment, and a heat-recovery system recaptures energy from the water (cools it) before it is discharged into the bay.

In the event of an oil spill or other oceanic disaster, the aquarium's 16-inch intake pipes can be shut down on a moment's notice and the aquarium can operate as a "closed system" for up to two weeks.

Just down the street from Doc's legendary marine lab, the Monterey Bay Aquarium on Cannery Row is a world-class cluster of fish tanks built into the converted Hovden Cannery. Luring 2.35 million visitors in 1984, its first year, Monterey's best attraction is the brainchild of marine biologist Nancy Packard and her sister, aquarium director Julie Packard. Much help came from Hewlett-Packard computer magnate David Packard and wife Lucile Packard, who supported this nonprofit, public-education endeavor with a $55 million donation to their daughters' cause. Not coincidentally, Packard also personally designed many of the unique technological features of the major exhibits here. Through the aquarium's foundation, the facility also conducts its own research and environmental education and wildlife rescue programs. The aquarium's trustees, for example, have allocated $10 million for a five-year unmanned underwater exploration and research project in the bay's Monterey Canyon.

The philosophy of the folks at the Monterey Bay Aquarium, most simply summarized as "endorsing human interaction" with the natural world, is everywhere apparent, once inside. From a multilevel view of kelp forests in perpetual motion to face-to-face encounters with sharks and wolf eels, from petting velvety bat rays and starfish in "touch pools" to watching sea otters feed and frolic, here people can observe the native marine plants and wildlife of Monterey Bay up close and personal. More than 300,000 animals and plants representing 571 species—including fish, invertebrates, mammals, reptiles, birds, and plant life—can be seen here in environments closely approximating their natural communities. Volunteer guides, dressed in rust-colored jackets, are available throughout the aquarium and are only too happy to share their knowledge about the natural history of Monterey Bay.

Seeing and Doing the Aquarium

Just inside the aquarium's entrance, serving as an introduction to the **Nearshore Galleries**, is the 55,000-gallon split-level **Sea Otter Tank.** These sleek aquatic clowns consume 25% of their body weight in seafood daily. If they're not eating or playing with toys, they're grooming themselves—and with 600,000 hairs per square inch on their pelts, it's easy to understand why otters were so prized by furriers (and hunted almost to extinction). To spot an occasional otter or two slipping into the aquarium over the seawall, or to watch for whales, head for the outdoor observation decks nearby. The **Outdoor Tidepool** is surrounded by the aquarium itself on three sides, on the fourth by artificial rock, and is home to sea stars, anemones, small fish—and visiting sea otters and harbor seals who occasionally shimmy up the stairs for a better look at the people. Also here are telescopes for baywatching.

The three-story-tall **Giant Kelp Forest** exhibit, the aquarium's centerpiece and the first underwater forest ever successfully established as a display, offers a diver's-eye view of the undersea world. Dazzling is the only word for the nearby **Anchovies** exhibit, a cylindrical tank full of darting silver shapes demonstrating the "safety in numbers" group-mind philosophy. The 90-foot-long hourglass-shaped **Monterey Bay Habitats** display is a simulated underwater slice of sea life. Sharks roam the deep among the colorful anemones and sea slugs, bat rays glide under the pier with the salmon and mackerel, accompanied by octopi and wolf eels. The craggy-shored indoor-outdoor **Coastal Stream** exhibit has a steady rhythm all its own and provides a small spawning ground for salmon and steelhead. In the huge **Marine Mammals Gallery** are models of a 43-foot-long barnacled gray whale and her calf, killer whales, dolphins, sea lions, and seals.

Unusual among the predominantly bay-related exhibits, but popular, is the live chambered nautilus in the **Octopus and Kin** exhibit. Also exciting here, in a spine-tingling way, is watching an octopus suction its way across the window. But to really get "in touch" with native underwater life, visit the **Bat Ray Petting Pool**, the **Touch Tidepool** of starfish and anemones, and the **Kelp Lab.** Visitors can stroll through the **Sandy Shore** outdoor aviary to observe shorebirds.

New exhibits are continually added to the Monterey Bay Aquarium. The stunning and relatively new $57 million **Outer Bay Galleries** nearly doubled the aquarium's exhibit space when this new wing opened in early 1996. Devoted to marinelife "at the edge," where Monterey Bay meets the open ocean, the centerpiece exhibit is a one-million-gallon "indoor sea" housing a seven-foot sunfish, sharks, barracuda, stingrays, green sea turtles, and schooling bonito—all seen through the largest aquarium window yet built, an acrylic panel some 15 feet high, 54 feet wide, and weighing 78,000 pounds. Quite visually arresting in the **Drifters Gallery** is the orange and deep-blue **Sea Nettles** jellyfish exhibit, where one might stand and watch the show—something like a giant, pulsing lava lamp—for hours. Equally mesmerizing, on the way into the Outer Bay, is the swirling, endlessly circling stream of silvery mackerel, directly overhead. The best way to watch—you'll notice that young children, not yet socially self-conscious, figure this out immediately—is by lying flat on your back, looking up. The new **Mysteries of the Deep** exhibit studies the often bizarre creatures that inhabit the murky depths. Seldom seen

in an aquarium environment, the deep-dwelling species in this exhibit include mushroom soft coral, the predatory tunicate, the spiny king crab, and many others—a total of 40-60 species at any one time. In addition, daily video programs present live broadcasts from a remote submersible vehicle exploring the depths of Monterey Bay.

New at the Monterey Bay Aquarium in spring 2000: the **Splash Zone: Rock and Reef Homes** exhibit designed particularly for families with small children. On display here are some 50 species, from leafy sea dragons to black-footed penguins. An interactive tour leads through two different shoreline habitats. Special activities include crawl-through coral reef structures, "make a wave" waterplay, dress-up costumes, and sea creature puppets. Throughout the aquarium, also expect several rotating special exhibits each year.

Aquarium Tickets, Tours, Information, and Practicalities

Advance tickets are highly recommended, especially in summer. Tickets are available at any Northern California BASS outlet; call (510) 762-2277 or toll-free (800) 225-2277 from outside California. You can also order tickets directly from the aquarium, either via the website, www.mbayaq.org, a minimum of nine days in advance (tickets sent by mail), or by calling the aquarium directly toll-free (800) 756-3737 or, from outside California (831) 648-4888. You can also buy tickets at the aquarium on a just-show-up-and-take-your-chances basis—not advisable in summer.

The aquarium is open daily except Christmas, 10 a.m.-6 p.m. (from 9:30 a.m. in summer). At last report, admission was $15.95 for adults; $12.95 for youths ages 13-17, students with college ID, seniors, and active-duty military; $6.95 for children ages 3-12 and disabled visitors; free for tots under age three.

Free self-guided tour scripts with maps, also available in Spanish, French, German, and Japanese, are available at the aquarium's information desk, along with current "special event" details, including when exhibit feedings are scheduled. All aquarium facilities and exhibits are accessible to the disabled; an explanatory brochure is available at the information desk. Taped audio tours are available for rent (small fee). Docent-guided aquarium tours and tours of the aquarium's research and operations facilities are available, for a fee. (Guided tours for school groups are free, however.) For group tour information and reservations, call (831) 648-4860. For additional information, contact: Monterey Bay Aquarium, 886 Cannery Row, Monterey, CA 93940-1085, tel. (831) 648-4800 (general switchboard) or (831) 648-4888 (24-hour recorded information), fax (831) 644-4810. Or visit the "E-Quarium" anytime, for virtual tours and information, at www.mbayaq.org.

To avoid the worst of the human crush, come in the off-season (weekdays if at all possible). If you do come in summer, avoid the traffic jams by riding Monterey's WAVE Shuttle, which operates from late May into September.

CANNERY ROW, FISHERMAN'S WHARF

Searching for Steinbeck on Cannery Row

Today the strip is reminiscent of Steinbeck's Cannery Row only when you consider how tourists are packed in here come summertime: like sardines.

Of all the places the Nobel Prize-winning author immortalized, only "Doc's" marine lab at 800 Cannery Row still stands unchanged—a humble brown shack almost as unassuming as it was in 1948, the year marine biologist Ed Ricketts met his end quite suddenly, his car smashed by the *Del Monte Express* train just a few blocks away. Today the lab is owned and preserved as a historic site by the city, and open for guided public tours from time to time.

Wing Chong market, Steinbecked as "Lee Chong's Heavenly Flower Grocery," is across the street at 835 Cannery Row and now features a variety of shops. The fictional "La Ida Cafe" cathouse still survives, too, in actuality the most famous restaurant and salon on the Monterey Peninsula: **Kalisa's,** at 851 Cannery Row.

Inside the old Monterey Canning Co. cannery, 700 Cannery Row, wine enthusiasts can enjoy the **Monterey County Wine Country Museum,** and perhaps follow their museum visit with winetasting, either at **A Taste of Monterey,** tel. (831) 646-5446, which offers tastings of re-

gional wines as well as local produce to sample, or at **Bargetto Winery** downstairs, tel. (831) 373-4053.

Winetasting or no, adults might escort the kids to the nearby **Monterey County Youth Museum** (M.Y. Museum), 601 Wave St., tel. (831) 649-6444 or (831) 649-6446, a hands-on adventure full of interactive exhibits on science, art, and more. The museum is open Mon.-Tues. and Thurs.-Sat. 10 a.m.-5 p.m., Sunday noon-5 p.m. (closed Wednesday). Admission is $5.50.

For more information about Cannery Row, or to seriously trace Steinbeck's steps through the local landscape, check in at the Cannery Row Foundation's **Cannery Row Welcome Center,** in the green railroad car at 65 Prescott Ave., tel. (831) 372-8512 or (831) 373-1902. Guided tours of Cannery Row can also be arranged here. The free and widely available *The Official Cannery Row Visitors Guide* is well done, historically, and quite helpful.

This inconspicuous building was once Doc's marine laboratory.

Fisherman's Wharf

Tacky and tawdry, built up and beat up, Fisherman's Wharf is no longer a working wharf by any account. Still, a randy ramshackle charm more honest than Cannery Row surrounds this 1846 pier full of cheap shops, food stalls, decent restaurants, and stand-up bars indiscriminately frosted with gull guano and putrid fish scraps (the latter presumably leftovers from the 50-cent bags tourists buy to feed the sea lions). Built of stone by enslaved natives, convicts, and military deserters when Monterey was Alta California's capital, Fisherman's Wharf was originally a pier for cargo schooners. Later used by whalers and Italian-American fishing crews to unload their catch, the wharf today is bright and bustling, full of eateries and eaters. Come early in the morning to beat the crowds, then launch yourself on a summer sightseeing tour of Monterey Bay or a winter whalewatching cruise.

MONTEREY'S DISTINCTIVE ARCHITECTURE

Monterey State Historic Park's **Larkin House,** a two-story redwood frame with low shingled roof, adobe walls, and wooden balconies skirting the second floor, and the **Cooper-Molera Adobe** are both good examples of the "Monterey colonial" architectural style—a marriage of Yankee woodwork and Mexican adobe—that evolved here. Most traditional Monterey adobes have south-facing patios to absorb sun in winter and a northern veranda to catch cool summer breezes. On the first floor were the kitchen, storerooms, dining room, living room, and sometimes even a ballroom. The bedrooms on the second floor were entered from outside stairways, a tradition subsequently abandoned. Also distinctive in Monterey are the "swept gardens"—dirt courtyards surrounded by colorful flowers under pine canopies—which were an adaptation to the originally barren home sites.

That so many fine adobes remain in Monterey today is mostly due to genteel local poverty; until recently, few developers with grandiose plans came knocking on the door. For an even better look at traditional local adobes and their gardens, come to the **Monterey Historic Adobe and Garden Tour** in April, when many private adobes are open for public tours.

MONTEREY STATE HISTORIC PARK

Monterey State Historic Park, with headquarters at 20 Custom House Plaza, Monterey, CA 93940, tel. (831) 649-7118, www.mbay.net/~mshp, protects and preserves some fine historic adobes, most of which were surrounded at one time by enclosed gardens and walls draped with bougainvillea vines. Definitely worth seeing are the Cooper-Molera, Stevenson, and Larkin homes, as well as Casa Soberanes.

The park is open daily 10 a.m.-4 p.m. (until 5 p.m. in summer), and closed Christmas, Thanksgiving, and New Year's Day. All-day admission, which gets you into all buildings open to visitors, is $5 adults, $3 youths ages 12-17, and $2 children ages 6-12 (under 6 free). Guided tours of particular buildings are offered, as are general guided walking tours; schedules vary, so ask about current tour times. You can also design your own tours. Call for details. To poke around on your own, pick up the free *Path of History* self-guided walking-tour map before setting out. Available at most of the buildings, the brochure details the park's adobes as well as dozens of other historic sights near the bay and downtown. Also stop by the Monterey State Historic Park Visitor Center at the Stanton Center.

Stanton Center and the Maritime Museum

A good place to start any historic exploration is the colossal Stanton Center at 5 Custom House Plaza. Inside you'll find the new **Monterey State Historic Park Visitor Center,** a joint venture among the Monterey County Convention & Visitors Bureau, Monterey State Historic Park, and the Maritime Museum of Monterey. Staff here can answer questions about the park. They'll also direct you to the center's **theater,** which screens a 17-minute park-produced film about area history—a good way to quickly grasp the area's cultural context. Most walking tours of the park (led by state park staff) also leave from the Stanton Center. Buy guided walking tour tickets here, as well as tickets for the adjacent maritime museum. The Stanton Visitor Center is open seven days a week, 10 a.m.-5 p.m. For state historic park information, call (831) 649-7118 or try the web at www.mbay.net/~mshp. For visitor information, call (831) 648-5373.

Don't miss the Monterey History and Art Association's **Maritime Museum of Monterey,** tel. (831) 375-2553 or (831) 373-2469, which houses an ever-expanding local maritime artifact collection—compasses, bells, ship models, the original Fresnel lens from the Point Sur lighthouse, and much more—as well as the association's maritime research library, an acclaimed ship photography collection, and a scrimshaw collection. The museum's permanent exhibits, many interactive, cover local maritime history from the first explorers and cannery days to the present. Open daily 10 a.m.-5 p.m., closed Thanksgiving, Christmas, and New Year's Day. It's not technically part of the state park, so a separate admission is charged—$5 adults, $4 seniors/military, $3 youth, $2 children.

Custom House and Pacific House

On July 7, 1846, Commodore John Drake Sloat raised the Stars and Stripes here at Alvarado and Waterfront Streets, commemorating California's passage into American rule. The Custom House Building is the oldest government building on the West Coast—and quite multinational, since it has flown at one time or another the flags of Spain, Mexico, and the United States. Until 1867, customs duties from foreign ships were collected here. Today you can inspect typical 19th-century cargo and try to reason with the parrot in residence.

Once a hotel, then a military supply depot, the building at Scott and Calle Principal was called Pacific House when it housed a public tavern in 1850. Later came law offices, a newspaper, a ballroom for "dashaway" temperance dances, and various small shops. Today the newly renovated Pacific House includes an excellent museum of Native American artifacts (with special attention given to the Ohlone people) and interactive historical exhibits covering the city's Spanish whaling industry, pioneer/logging periods, California statehood, and more.

Larkin House and Others

Built of adobe and wood in 1835 by Yankee merchant Thomas Oliver Larkin, later the only U.S. consul in the territory during Mexican rule, this home at Jefferson and Calle Principal became the American consulate, then later military headquarters for Kearny, Mason, and Sherman. A fine pink Monterey adobe and the model for the local Colonial style, Larkin House is furnished with more than $6 million in antiques and period furnishings.

The home and headquarters of William Tecumseh Sherman is next door; it's now a museum focusing on both Larkin and Sherman. Around the corner at 540 Calle Principal, another Larkin building, the **House of the Four Winds,** is a small adobe built in the 1830s and named for its weathervane. The **Gutierrez Adobe,** a typical middle-class Monterey "double adobe" home at 580 and 590 Calle Principal, was built in 1841 and later donated to the state by the Monterey Foundation.

Cooper-Molera Adobe

The long, two-story Monterey colonial adobe *casa grande* ("big house") at 508 Munras Ave. was finished in pinkish plaster when constructed in 1829 by Capt. John Bautista Rogers Cooper for his young bride, Encarnación (of California's influential Vallejo clan). The 2.5-acre complex, which includes a neighboring home, two barns, and a visitor center, has been restored to its 19th-century authenticity.

Robert Louis Stevenson House

The sickly Scottish storyteller and poet lived at the French Hotel adobe boardinghouse at 530 Houston St. for several months in 1879 while courting his American love (and later wife), Fanny Osbourne. In a sunny upstairs room is the small portable desk at which he reputedly wrote *Treasure Island.* While in Monterey, Stevenson collected *Treasure* material on his convalescing coast walks and worked on "Amateur Immigrant," "The Old Pacific," "Capital," and "Vendetta of the West." He also worked as a reporter for the local newspaper—a job engineered by his friends, who, in order to keep the flat-broke Stevenson going, secretly paid the paper $2 a week to cover his wages. The restored downstairs is stuffed with period furniture. Several upstairs rooms are dedicated to Stevenson's memorabilia, paintings, and first editions. Local rumor has it that a 19th-century ghost—Stevenson's spirit, according to a previous caretaker—lives upstairs in the children's room.

Stevenson House kitchen

Casa Soberanes

This is an 1830 Mediterranean-style adobe with tile roof and cantilevered balcony, hidden by thick hedges at 336 Pacific. Home to the Soberanes family from 1860 to 1922, it was later donated to the state. Take the tour or just stop to appreciate the garden and abalone-bordered flower beds, some encircled by century-old glass bottles buried bottoms up.

California's First Theater

First a sailors' saloon and lodging house, this small 1844 weathered wood and adobe building at Scott and Pacific was built by the English sailor Jack Swan. It was commandeered by soldiers in 1848 for a makeshift theater, and later—with a lookout station added to the roof—became a whaling station. Wander through the place and take a trip into the bawdy past, complete with the requisite painting of a reclining nude over the bar, brass bar rail and cuspidor, oil lamps, ancient booze bottles, and old theatrical props and paraphernalia. A modern postcript is the garden out back.

Today, a local theatre troupe presents melodramas here year-round on Friday and Saturday nights; for information and reservations, call (831) 375-4916.

Casa del Oro

Built by Thomas Larkin at the corner of Scott and Olivier as part of his business empire, this two-story chalk and adobe building later served a number of purposes. At one time or another it was a barracks for American troops, a general store (Joseph Boston & Co.), a saloon, and a private residence. Rumors have it that this "house of gold" was once a mint, or that (when a saloon) it accepted gold dust in payment for drinks—thus the name.

Whaling Station

The old two-story adobe Whaling Station at 391 Decatur St. near the Custom House, now a private home, was a flophouse for Portuguese whalers in the 1850s. Tours are sometimes available (call the main state park number for information), and include access to the walled garden. Whale lovers, walk softly; the sidewalk in front of the house is made of whalebone.

California's First Brick House

This building nearby at 351 Decatur was started by Gallant Duncan Dickenson in 1847, built with bricks fashioned and fired in Monterey. The builder left for the goldfields before the house was finished, so the home—the first brick house built in California—and 60,000 bricks were auctioned off by the sheriff in 1851 for just over $1,000.

OTHER MONTEREY SIGHTS

Colton Hall

The Reverend Walter Colton, Monterey's first American alcalde, or local magistrate, built this impressive, pillared "Carmel Stone" structure at 351 Pacific, tel. (831) 646-5640, as a schoolhouse and public hall. Colton and Robert Semple published the first American newspaper in California here, cranking up the presses on August 15, 1846. California's constitutional convention took place here during September and October of 1849, and the state constitution was drafted upstairs in Colton Hall.

Next door is the 1854 **Monterey jail** (entrance on Dutra St.), a dreary, slot-windowed prison once home to gentleman-bandit Tiburcio Vasquez and killer Anastacio Garcia, who "went to God on a rope" pulled by his buddies.

Monterey Museum of Art

This fine Monterey Museum of Art at 559 Pacific, tel. (831) 372-7591, is near many local historic sites and offers an excellent collection of Western art, including bronze cowboy-and-horse statues by Charles M. Russell. The Fine Arts collection includes photography and Asian art and artifacts. Also here: folk art plus high-concept graphics, photography, paintings, sculpture, and other contemporary art in changing exhibits. Open Tues.-Sat. 10 a.m.-4 p.m., Sunday 1-4 p.m., closed holidays. Free, technically, but a $2 donation is requested. Associated with the art museum is the amazing **La Mirada.**

Casa Amesti and La Mirada

If you're in Monterey on a weekend, be sure to tour **Casa Amesti,** 516 Polk St., a genteel Monterey colonial stylishly updated in the 1920s by Frances Adler Elkins, a noted West Coast interior designer whose other projects included the International House at UC Berkeley and the Royal Hawaiian Hotel in Honolulu. The sensibility here is royal, relaxed, and European without the velvet and gilt—furniture upholstered in linen and cotton, the woodwork in the library painted French provincial blue. Since 1954, Casa Amesti has served as a luncheon venue for upper-crust members of the Old Capital Club, who contribute to its maintenance. But just plain folks can come have a look-see on Saturday and Sunday, 2-4 p.m. Small admission fee, children under age 12 free. For information, contact the Monterey History and Art Association, tel. (831) 372-2608.

Another impressive Monterey-style adobe also open to the public on a limited basis is **La Mirada,** the Castro Adobe and Frank Work Estate at 720 Via Mirada, tel. (831) 372-3689. Affiliated with the Monterey Museum of Art, the home is exquisite. The original adobe portion was the residence of Jose Castro, one of the most prominent citizens in California during the Mexican period. Purchased in 1919 by Gouverneur Morris—author/playwright and descendant of the same-named Revolutionary War figure—the adobe was restored and expanded, with the addition of a two-story wing and huge drawing room, to host artists and Hollywood stars.

These days, the 2.5-acre estate overlooking El Estero still reflects the elegance of a bygone era. The house itself is furnished in antiques and early California art, and the gardens are perhaps even more elegant, at least in season, with a walled rose garden (old and new varieties), traditional herb garden (medicinal, culinary, fragrant, and "beautifying" herbs), and a rhododendron garden with more than 300 camellias, azaleas, rhododendrons, and other flowering perennials and trees.

The house is open Thurs.-Sat. 11 a.m.-5 p.m., Sunday 1-4 p.m. Tours of the house are scheduled Thurs.-Sun. at 2 and 3 p.m. Tours of the gardens and galleries are offered Sat.-Sun. at 1 and 2 p.m. Small admission, but free on the first Sunday of every month.

Usually in May, **Springtime at La Mirada** features art, floral, and garden exhibits as well as gardening lectures and workshops and a ladies' bridge festival. There's no on- or off-street parking here, so park at Monterey Peninsula College and take the shuttle.

Monterey Institute of International Studies

This prestigious, private, and nonprofit graduate-level college headquartered at 425 Van Buren, tel. (831) 647-4100, specializes in foreign-language instruction. Students here prepare for careers in international business and government, and in language translation and interpretation. Fascinating and unique is the school's 200-seat auditorium, set up for simultaneous translations of up to four languages. Visitors are welcome Mon.-Fri. 8:30 a.m.-5 p.m., and most of the institute's programs—including guest lectures—are open to the public.

The Presidio

One of the nation's oldest military posts, the Presidio of Monterey is the physical focal point of most local history, though the original complex, founded by Portolá in 1770, was located in the area now defined by Webster, Fremont, Abrego, and El Estero Streets. History buffs, note the commemorative monuments of Portolá, Junípero Serra, Vizcaíno, and Commodore Sloat, plus late-in-the-game acknowledgement of native peoples. (When Lighthouse Ave. was widened through here, most of what remained of a 2,000-year-old Rumsen village was destroyed, leaving only a ceremonial rain rock, a rock mortar for grinding acorns, and an ancient burial ground marked by a tall wooden cross.) Also here: incredible panoramic views of Monterey Bay.

The **U.S. Army Museum,** in Building 113, tel. (831) 242-8414, once a tack house, is now filled with cavalry artifacts, uniforms, pistols, cannons, photos, posters, and dioramas about the history of the army and the Presidio. Call before coming; the museum had been closed for a long period, but should be reopened by now. The main gate at Pacific and Artillery Streets leads to the **Defense Language Institute,** tel. (831) 242-5000.

Pick up a copy of the Presidio's *Walk Through History* brochure at the Command Historian's Archives office in Building 274 (opposite the softball fields) to visit the earthen ruins and cannons of the **Fort Mervine** battlements; they were built by Commodore Sloat and dismantled in 1852. Fort Mervine's log huts were built during the Civil War.

The Royal Presidio Chapel

Originally established as a mission by Father Serra in June 1770, this building at 555 Church St. near Figueroa became the Royal Presidio Chapel of San Carlos Borromeo when the mission was relocated to Carmel. The chapel was rebuilt from stone in 1791, and after secularization in 1835, it became the San Carlos Cathedral, a parish church. The cathedral's interior walls are decorated with Native American and Mexican folk art. Above, the upper gable facade is the first European art made in California, a chalk-carved Virgin of Guadalupe tucked into a shell niche. To get here, turn onto Church St. just after Camino El Estero ends at Fremont—a district once known as Washerwoman's Gulch.

MONTEREY OUTDOORS

Peninsula Beaches and Parks

The 18-mile **Monterey Peninsula Recreation Trail** is a spectacular local feature—a walking and cycling path that stretches from Asilomar State Beach in Pacific Grove to Castroville. Scenic bay views are offered all along the way, as the trail saunters past landmarks including Point Pinos Lighthouse, Lovers Point, the Monterey Bay Aquarium, Cannery Row, Fisherman's Wharf, Custom House plaza, and Del Monte Beach. The 14-acre **Monterey Beach** is not very impressive (day use only), but you can stroll the rocky headlands on the peninsula's north side without interruption, traveling the Monterey Peninsula Recreation Trail past the **Pacific Grove Marine Gardens Fish Refuge** and **Asilomar State Beach**—tidepools, rugged shorelines, and thick carpets of brightly flowered (but nonnative) ice plant. For ocean swimming, head south to **Carmel River State Beach,** which includes a lagoon and bird sanctuary, or to **China Cove** at Point Lobos.

El Estero Park in town—bounded by Del Monte Ave., Fremont Blvd., and Camino El Estero—has a small horseshoe-shaped lagoon with ducks, pedalboat rentals, picnic tables, a par course, hiking and biking trails, and the **Dennis the Menace Playground,** designed by cartoonist Hank Ketcham. (Particularly fun here is the hedge maze.) Also at El Estero is the area's first **French Consulate,** built in 1830, moved here in 1931, and now the local visitor information center. The **Don Dahvee Park** on Munras Ave. (one leg of local motel row) is a secret oasis of picnic tables with a hiking/biking trail.

Jacks Peak County Park and "Monterey Jack"

The highest point on the peninsula (but not *that* high, at only 1,068 feet) and the focal point of a 525-acre regional park, Jacks Peak offers great views, good hiking and horseback trails, and picnicking, plus fascinating flora and wildlife. Named after the land's former owner—Scottish immigrant and entrepreneur David Jacks, best known for his local dairies and their "Monterey Jack" cheese—the park features 4.5 miles of marked trails, including the self-guided **Skyline**

MONTEREY PENINSULA GOLFING

Golfers from around the globe make a point of arriving on the Monterey Peninsula, clubs in tow, at some time in their lives. The undisputed golf capital of the world, the Pebble Beach area between Carmel and Pacific Grove is the most famous, largely due to "The Crosby," which is now the AT&T Pebble Beach National Pro Am Golf Tournament. Making headlines in 1999 was news that the Pebble Beach Company and its four world-class courses had been sold to an investor group—Clint Eastwood, Richard Ferris, Arnold Palmer, and Peter Ueberroth—for $820 million.

It may cost a pretty penny—the greens fee at Pebble Beach Golf Links, for example, is more than $300—but the public is welcome at private **Pebble Beach Golf Links,** the **Links at Spanish Bay, Spyglass Hill Golf Course,** the **Peter Hay Par 3,** and the **Del Monte Golf Course** (in Monterey), all affiliated with The Lodge at Pebble Beach on 17 Mile Dr., tel. (831) 624-3811, (831) 624-6611, or toll-free (800) 654-9300. Also open to the public are the **Poppy Hills Golf Course,** 3200 Lopez Rd. (just off 17 Mile Dr.), tel. (831) 624-2035; the **Pacific**

Grove Municipal Golf Links, 77 Asilomar Ave., tel. (831) 648-3177, which is great for beginners and reasonably priced ($14-35); the **Bayonet** and **Black Horse Golf Courses** on North-South at former Fort Ord, tel. (831) 373-3701; and the **Laguna Seca Golf Club** on York Rd. between Monterey and Salinas, tel. (831) 373-3701.

Though Pebble Beach is world-renowned for its golf courses and golf events, Carmel Valley and vicinity has nearly as many courses—most of them private in the country-club model, most recognizing reciprocal access agreements with other clubs. The **Rancho Cañada Golf Club,** about a mile east of Hwy. 1 via Carmel Valley Rd., tel. (831) 624-0111, is open to the public, however. As part and parcel of accommodations packages, nonmembers can golf at **Quail Lodge Resort,** 8000 Valley Greens Dr., tel. (831) 624-1581, and at **Carmel Valley Ranch,** 1 Old Ranch Rd. in Carmel, tel. (831) 625-9500 or toll-free (800) 422-7635 (main switchboard), or (831) 626-2510 (golf course), where two people can spend the night and play a round of golf for about $250 in winter, or $350 in summer.

Nature Trail. From Jacks Peak amid the Monterey pines, you'll have spectacular views of both Monterey Bay and Carmel Valley—and possibly the pleasure of spotting American kestrels or red-shouldered hawks soaring on the wind currents. The park's first 55 acres were purchased by The Nature Conservancy, and the rest were bought up with county, federal, and private funds. To get here, take Olmstead County Rd. (from Hwy. 68 near the Monterey Airport) for two miles. For more information, call (831) 484-1108 or the **Monterey County Parks Department,** tel. (831) 647-7799.

Other Adventures by Land—and Air

Monterey and vicinity is most famous, of course, as an elite golfing oasis. For information on public access to area courses, which are primarily private, see Monterey Peninsula Golfing.

Otherwise, get some fresh air and see the sights by bicycle. Either bring your own or rent one at any of several local bike-rental outfits. Or tool around on a moped, available for rent through **Monterey Moped Adventures,** 1250

Del Monte Ave., tel. (831) 373-2696, which also rents bikes—tandem bikes, bikes with child trailers, and "beach cruzers," plus the standards—and offers ample parking and easy access to the bayside bike/hike trail. Bike rentals are also the specialty of **Bay Bikes,** 640 Wave St., tel. (831) 646-9090, which charges about $22 a day for a 21-speed, fat-tire bike. Rollerbladers can rent skates here for around $15 a day. For more on bike rentals, see Monterey Transportation below.

Adrenaline junkies can get a bird's-eye view of the bay by throwing themselves out of an airplane with **Skydive Monterey Bay,** 3261 Imjin Rd., Marina, tel. (831) 384-3483 or toll-free (888) 229-5867. No experience is necessary; after a bit of instruction, you'll make a tandem jump harnessed to a veteran skydiver. Cost is $179. The company is open daily, year-round.

The *Californian*

Sample some early California history before the mast. The 145-foot **Tallship *Californian,*** the state's official tallship, occasionally offers four-hour day sails on Monterey Bay. The trip includes lunch and lectures, and the fee is $75 per person. The *Californian* also offers private charters, five-day Cadet Cruises (for ages 14-19), and three- and four-day hands-on High Sea Adventures for adults, and spends part of each year in San Francisco, Long Beach, and San Diego. Crew positions are sometimes available. The *Californian* is a re-creation of the *C.W. Lawrence,* a Revenue Service cutter built in Washington, D.C., in 1848. For current details and advance reservations, contact: **The Nautical Heritage Society,** 1064 Calle Negocio, Unit B, San Clemente, CA 92673, tel. (949) 369-6773 or toll-free (800) 432-2201 (reservations only), www.californian.org.

Other Adventures by Sea

Another way to "see" Monterey Bay is by getting right in it, by kayak. **Monterey Bay Kayaks,** 693 Del Monte Ave., tel. (831) 373-KELP, offers tours—bay tours and sunset tours, even trips into Elkhorn Slough and along the Salinas River—as well as classes and rentals of both open and closed kayaks. Wetsuits, paddling jackets, life jackets, water shoes, and a half-hour of on-land instruction are included in the basic all-day rental price of $25 for singles, $50 for doubles. **AB Seas Kayaks,** 32 Cannery Row #5, tel. (831) 647-0147, offers similar services at similar prices. **Adventures by the Sea** also offers kayak rentals and tours—in addition to bike rentals (bikes de-

livered to your hotel room and picked up again at no charge), bike trips (including a Pt. Pinos Lighthouse tour), rollerblade rentals, and custom-prepared beach parties. The company's "Land & Sea Package" includes kayaking in the morning, followed by mountain-bike touring in the afternoon ($90 for two). Offices are located at the Doubletree Hotel downtown, 201 Alvarado Mall, tel. (831) 648-7235; at 299 Cannery Row, tel. (831) 372-1807; and at Lover's Point in Pacific Grove, tel. (831) 648-7238.

Sailing enthusiasts can take to the bay under wind power on trips with **Olympic Sailing Charters,** 48 Fisherman's Wharf, tel. (831) 647-1957, which takes passengers aboard the luscious 67-foot racing sloop *Zeus.* Or try **Carrera Sailing,** 66 Fisherman's Wharf (at Randy's Fishing Trips), tel. (831) 375-0648, which employs the slightly more humble but nevertheless comfortable 30-foot sloop *Carrera.* Both companies offer sunset cruises for around $25 per person, as well as tours and private charters.

Other boating companies also offer bay tours (including cocktail cruises), winter whalewatching, and fishing trips (discount coupons often available at local visitor information centers). Good choices include **Monterey Sportfishing & Whale Watching Cruises,** 96 Fisherman's Wharf No. 1, tel. (831) 372-2203, (831) 372-3501, or toll-free (800) 200-2203; **Randy's Fishing Trips,** 66 Fisherman's Wharf #1, tel. (831) 372-7440, which also offers Point Sur fishing

Head to the harbor for a sport fishing excursion.

TOM MYERS PHOTOGRAPHY

charters; and **Chris' Fishing Trips,** 48 Fisherman's Wharf #1, tel. (831) 375-5951, which offers a fleet of four big boats, including the 70-foot *New Holiday.* For year-round marine mammal and whalewatching tours led by marine biologists, consider **Monterey Bay Whale Watch,** P.O. Box 52001, Pacific Grove, CA 93950, www.montereybaywhalewatch.com.

Another way to see the bay is to get a fish-eye view. The **Aquarius Dive Shop,** at two Monterey locations—32 Cannery Row, tel. (831) 375-6605, and 2040 Del Monte Ave., tel. (831) 375-1933—is the best place around for rentals, instruction, equipment, and repairs. Aquarius also offers guided underwater tours (specializing in photography and video) and can provide tips on worthwhile dives worldwide. For current dive conditions, call their 24-hour dive line at (831) 657-1020. **AB Seas Dive Charters,** 32 Cannery Row #5, tel. (831) 647-0147, offers twice-daily scuba trips as well as snorkeling instruction and trips. The company also rents kayaks and inflatable boats and teaches kayak-based diving.

THE SAND DUNE CITIES

The sand-dune city of **Marina** was once the service center supporting Fort Ord. The U.S. Army base is now closed, replaced by the fledgling campus of California State University at Monterey Bay, so Marina, the peninsula's most recently incorporated city (1975), also is being transformed. Marina now boasts a new municipal airport, sports arena, and state beach popular for hang-gliding and surfing. On the ground, explore the nearby dunes; they're serene in a simple, stark way, with fragile shrubs and wildflowers. Some are quite rare, so don't pick. By 2001 or 2002, the new **Fort Ord Dunes State Park,** tel. (831) 649-2836, once part of Fort Ord, will open to the public, featuring a four-mile stretch of beachfront.

Seaside and **Sand City,** to Marina's north, share "ownership" of former Fort Ord and the new CSU Monterey campus—and all three cities, the peninsula's traditionally low-rent neighborhoods, are still feuding with more affluent Monterey, Pacific Grove, and Carmel over future development plans. Opponents contend that proposed new hotels, golf courses, conference and shopping centers, and housing developments will adversely affect limited area water supplies, the adequacy of roads and other public infrastructure, and the environment.

But no one seems to object to the new **CSU Monterey** campus—the school's mascot is the sea otter—which has to date taken over some 2,000 acres at Fort Ord (of the 13,065 set aside for it) and is expected to grow to a student population of 13,000-15,000 by 2015. The emphasis at California's 21st state university campus is fairly unconventional. The focus here is on mastering subjects, rather than simply amassing course credits. Students are expected to become fluent in a second language as well as fully computer literate and to engage in community service work, along with more than a dozen other essential skills. The gym here is called instead the "wellness center." For information on 45-minute group tours of the campus, call (831) 582-3518. Also worth exploring are some 50 miles of trails open to the public—now known as **Fort Ord Public Lands,** 16,000 acres administered by the U.S. Bureau of Land Management, just about the last truly wild areas remaining on the Monterey Peninsula. Two fishable lakes and picnic areas are also available. As fun as it is to be out and about in these wide open spaces, hikers, bikers, and horseback riders should take care to stick only to authorized trails; military explosives and other hazards are found in still-restricted areas, and habitat restoration is underway. Some 35 rare and endangered species inhabit Fort Ord Public Lands. For current trail information, contact the BLM office in Hollister, tel. (831) 394-8314.

From Santa Cruz, head inland on Canyon del Rey Rd. to **Work Memorial Park** and the nearby **Frog Pond Natural Area** (entrance in the willows near the Del Rey Oaks City Hall), a seasonal freshwater marsh home to birds and the elusive inch-long Pacific tree frog. Or take Del Monte Ave. off Hwy. 1 to **Del Monte Beach,** one of the least-bothered beaches of Monterey Bay (no facilities).

Del Monte Ave. also takes you past the **U.S. Naval Post-Graduate School,** tel. (831) 656-2441, a Navy preflight training school during World War II and now a military university offering doctorates. It's housed on the grounds of the stately 1880 Spanish-style **Del Monte Hotel.**

The state's oldest large resort and queen of American watering holes for California's nouveau riche, the Del Monte was built by Charles Crocker and the rest of the railroading Big Four. Tour the grounds 8 a.m.-4:30 p.m. daily. Downstairs in the old hotel is the school's **museum,** with memorabilia from the Del Monte's heyday (open Mon.-Fri. 11 a.m.-2 p.m., closed on major holidays).

Worth stopping for in Seaside is the tranquil **Monterey Peninsula Buddhist Temple,** 1155 Noche Buena, tel. (831) 394-0119, surrounded by beautiful Asian-style gardens and carp-filled ponds. Come in May for the bonsai show.

For the present at least, accommodations are considerably less expensive here than elsewhere on the Monterey Peninsula. For example, RVers can hole up at **Marina Dunes RV Park,** 3330 Dunes Dr. in Marina, tel. (831) 384-6914, which has sites with full hookups as well as tent sites. It's just nine miles from Monterey, making it a good potential base of operations for your visit. For more information about the sand dune cities, contact: **Seaside/Sand City Chamber of Commerce,** 505 Broadway, Seaside, CA 93955, tel. (831) 394-6501.

MONTEREY CAMPING AND LOW-COST ALTERNATIVES

Monterey Area Camping

Right in downtown Monterey, RV campers can plug in at **Cypress Tree Inn,** 2227 N. Fremont St., tel. (831) 372-7586 or toll-free (800) 446-8303 (in California). Amenities include water and electric hookups, showers, restrooms, a hot tub, and sauna. Rates are $28 weekdays, $33 weekends. Also in Monterey, if you're desperate, try pitching a tent in year-round **Veterans Memorial Park** on Via del Rey adjacent to the presidio, tel. (831) 646-3865. First-come, first-camped, with rates $5 for hikers/bikers, $18 for others, including restrooms and hot showers. No hookups. (Arrive before 3 p.m. and get a permit from the attendant.)

Outside town on the way to Salinas is **Lake Laguna Seca,** at the Laguna Seca Raceway just off Hwy. 68, with 93 tent sites and 87 spots for RVs ($18-22 per night). Not recommended for light sleepers when the races are on. For information and reservations, contact: Laguna Seca County Recreation Area, P.O. Box 367, Salinas, CA 93905, tel. (831) 422-6138 (information), (831) 647-7799 (reservations), or toll-free (888) 588-2267.

For other camping options, head south to Carmel.

One Day Soon, a Hostel

Currently, Monterey has no hostel, though one is in the works. Drop by 778 Hawthorne St. to see if it has opened. For the latest information, call (831) 649-0375, or contact the HI-AYH Central California Council, P.O. Box 3645, Merced, CA 95344, tel. (209) 383-0686, www.hostelweb.com.

Asilomar

The state-owned **Asilomar Conference Center,** 800 Asilomar Ave. in Pacific Grove, tel. (831) 372-8016 or toll-free (800) 881-7708, fax (831) 372-7227, www.asilomarcenter.com, enjoys an incredibly beautiful 60-acre setting on the Pacific Ocean, complete with swimming pool, volleyball nets, and miles of beaches to stroll. When it's not completely booked with businesspeople, conferences, and other groups, it can be a reasonably priced choice for an overnight. Architect Julia Morgan designed many of the resort's pine lodges. Call ahead for reservations, up to 30 days in advance, or hope for last-minute cancellations. Moderate-Expensive, three meals a day included.

MONTEREY MOTELS AND HOTELS

Monterey is so close to the neighboring communities of Pacific Grove, Carmel, and Carmel Valley, not to mention its own sand-dune suburbs, that peninsula visitors with cars can conveniently plan to stay and eat throughout the area. Current complete listings of accommodations (including prices) and restaurants in Monterey proper are available free from the convention and visitors bureau. Discounts of 50% or more are available at many inns, hotels, and motels during off-season promotions.

Most of Monterey's many decent motels fall into the Moderate to Premium price categories, at least during summer and for major events, and offer all modern amenities. Many establishments provide complimentary breakfast and

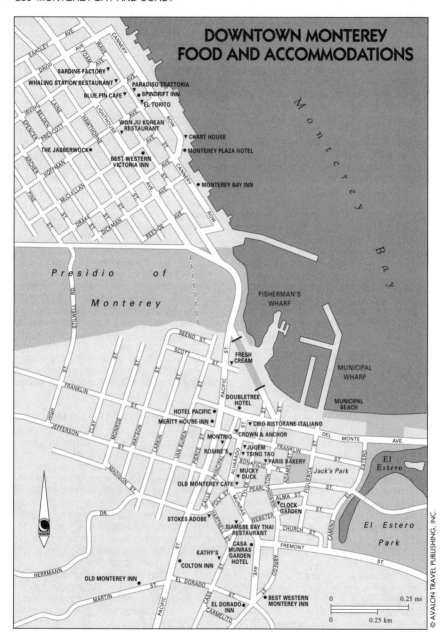

DOWNTOWN MONTEREY
FOOD AND ACCOMMODATIONS

© AVALON TRAVEL PUBLISHING, INC.

other extra services. If you're here for the Jazz Festival, plan to stay at a motel in Marina or Seaside and vicinity, or on Fremont St. (motel and fast-food row) just a block from the fairgrounds. Motels on Munras are generally pricier. Be on the lookout, especially during high season, for "floating" motel rates, wherein the price may double or triple long *after* you've made your reservation. When in doubt, request written reservation and price confirmations.

For assistance in booking midrange to high-end accommodations in and around Monterey, for individuals or groups, contact **Resort II Me Room Finders,** 2600 Garden Rd. #11, Monterey, CA 93940, tel. (831) 646-9250, (831) 642-6622, or toll-free (800) 757-5646, fax (831) 642-6641, www.resort2me.com, a firm with a good track record in matching peninsula visitors with appropriate local lodgings. Also a best bet is **Time to Coast Reservations** 1855 Gateway Blvd. #630, Concord, CA 94520, toll-free tel. (800) 555-9283, fax (925) 671-4044, www.time-tocoast.com. Monterey has other reservations and vacation rental services, and travel agents can also help arrange good-value travel packages. But feel free to shop around for bargains on your own since the entire area, from Santa Cruz south to the Monterey Peninsula, was somewhat overbuilt in the 1980s to accommodate the tourist trade.

Inexpensive and Moderate Stays

Not many motel choices in Monterey are truly inexpensive. You might try the 15-room **Driftwood Motel,** 2362 N. Fremont, tel. (831) 372-5059, where pets are possible, and the **Econo Lodge,** 2042 N. Fremont St., tel. (831) 372-5851, fax (831) 372-4228, with pool and spa, free continental breakfast, and some rooms with kitchenettes. Both are basic but pleasant, quite comfortable for anyone sticking to the family budget, and real deals in the off-season.

Most lower-priced motels fall into the Moderate category, including the **Motel 6,** 2124 N. Fremont, tel. (831) 646-8585, which is clean, has a pool, and isn't far from the downtown action—reachable on any eastbound bus (take bus No. 1). As a result, it's popular; make reservations six months or more in advance or stop by at 11 a.m. or so to check for cancellations. Another Motel 6 in the same price range (just a bit

less expensive) is just outside Monterey proper, at 100 Reservation Rd. in Marina, tel. (831) 384-1000. For any Motel 6, call toll-free (800) 466-8356 or book online at www.motel6.com.

Quite nice, quite reasonably priced, and surprisingly homey are the locally owned Comfort Inns on Munras Avenue. **Comfort Inn-Carmel Hill,** 1252 Munras Ave., tel. (831) 372-2908, fax (831) 372-7608, features just 30 cheery rooms with the usual amenities and electronic door locks. Adjacent is the **Comfort Inn-Munras,** 1262 Munras, tel. (831) 372-8088, fax (831) 373-5829. Both are Moderate-Expensive, and both are close enough—but not too close—to local attractions, especially if you're looking forward to some vigorous walking. The best thing about the location, which is quite close to Hwy. 1 and the Del Monte Shopping Center, is its walkability. Directly across the way, flanking Munras all the way back downtown to its junction with Abrego, is long, narrow **Dan Dahvee Park,** with its pleasant trees, flowers, birds—and walking paths.

Other Moderate motel options include the 15-room **El Dorado Inn,** 900 Munras, tel. (831) 373-2921; the **West Wind Lodge,** 1046 Munras Ave., tel. (831) 373-1337 or toll-free (800) 821-0805, fax (831) 372-2451, with an indoor heated pool; the very nice **Best Western Park Crest Motel,** 1100 Munras, tel. (831) 372-4576 or toll-free (800) 528-1234, fax (831) 372-2317, where rooms include in-room coffee and refrigerators and extras include TVs with free HBO, pool, hot tub, and free continental breakfast. There are also a number of good motels off Fremont.

Expensive Stays

Centrally located, near Hwy. 1 within easy reach of all area towns, is the **Bay Park Hotel,** 1425 Munras, tel. (831) 649-1020 or toll-free (800) 338-3564, fax (831) 373-4258, featuring in-room coffee makers and on-site extras including a restaurant, pool, and hot tub. The nonsmoking **Best Western Monterey Inn,** 825 Abrego, tel. (831) 373-5345 or toll-free (800) 528-1234, fax (831) 373-3246, is quite pleasant, with 80 spacious rooms, some with fireplaces, all with in-room coffee makers and refrigerators. Seasonally heated pool, hot tub.

Best bets on Fremont include the **Scottish Fairway Motel,** 2075 N. Fremont St., tel. (831) 373-5551 or toll-free (800) 373-5571, fax (831)

373-4250, where kitchens and kitchenettes are available, and the **Travelodge-Monterey/Carmel,** 2030 N. Fremont, tel. (831) 373-3381, fax (831) 649-8741.

Premium Stays

With a delightful Old World ambience, right downtown, the refurbished and fashionable **Monterey Hotel,** 406 Alvarado St., Monterey, CA 93940, tel. (831) 375-3184 or toll-free for reservations (800) 727-0960, fax (831) 373-2899, www.montereyhotel.com, comfortably combines the best features of hotels with a bed-and-breakfast feel. This graceful 1904 Victorian is classic yet contemporary. The large breakfast room downstairs is reserved for complimentary breakfast (you can watch morning news programs on the TV). Just outside the cozy lobby is a wonderful small garden where wine and cheese are served every afternoon, 5-7:30 p.m., and cookies and milk are served 8-11 p.m. Rooms and suites feature custom-made armoires (with TV sets), telephones, private baths with tub showers, antiques, queen-sized beds, and tasteful yet subtle decorating touches, all individualized. Two smaller rooms feature double beds. Every floor features an outdoor landing and deck area, and the third-floor interior landing boasts an intimate atrium parlor, lit by the skylight overhead. The only inconvenience presented by a stay at the Monterey Hotel is lack of on-site parking. But an inexpensive city lot (rarely full) is nearby. Rooms are Premium, suites are Luxury.

Offering good value in comfortable accommodations on acres of lovely landscape is the **Casa Munras Garden Hotel,** 700 Munras, tel. (831) 375-2411 or toll-free (800) 222-2446 in California, (800) 222-2558 nationwide, fax (831) 375-1365, conveniently located close to historic downtown. On-site restaurant.

Another good deal, right downtown, is the attractive and accommodating **Colton Inn,** 707 Pacific, tel. (831) 649-6500 or toll-free (800) 848-7007, fax (831) 373-6987, where extras include a sauna and sundeck. The comfortable **Doubletree Hotel at Fisherman's Wharf,** 2 Portola Plaza (adjacent to the Convention Center downtown at Pacific and Del Monte), tel. (831) 649-4511 or toll-free (800) 222-8733 (reservations), fax (831) 372-0620, boasts 380 rooms and is convenient to just about everything.

Luxury Stays

For definite bayside luxury, head for the 290-room, Craftsman-style **Monterey Plaza Hotel & Spa,** 400 Cannery Row, tel. (831) 646-1700, or toll-free (800) 334-3999 in California, (800) 631-1339 from elsewhere in the United States, fax (831) 646-5937, www.woodsidehotels.com. The Monterey Plaza's fine accommodations include Italian Empire and 18th-century Chinese furnishings, every convenience (even a complete fitness center with six Nautilus stations), and exceptional food service, including the Duck Club, one of the area's finer restaurants. The 15 Grand Suites feature a grand piano. Great on-site restaurants, rental bikes and kayaks available. Recently, the Monterey Plaza added a $6 million, 10,000-square-foot Eurostyle rooftop full-service spa and three spa-level suites. Coming soon to the nearby neighborhood is a new IMAX theater.

Also deluxe, downtown, is the contemporary, faux-adobe-style **Hotel Pacific,** 300 Pacific, tel. (831) 373-5700 or toll-free (800) 232-4141, fax (831) 373-6921, www.hotelpacific.com. All rooms are suites and feature hardwood floors, separate sitting areas, balconies or decks, fireplaces, wet bars, honor bars, in-room coffee makers, irons, ironing boards, two TVs, two phones, and terrycloth bathrobes. Tiled bathrooms have a separate shower and tub. Some rooms have a view. Continental breakfast, afternoon tea, free underground parking.

Surprisingly appealing on Cannery row is the **Spindrift Inn,** a onetime bordello at 652 Cannery Row (at Hoffman), tel. (831) 646-8900, toll-free (800) 841-1879, fax (831) 646-5342, www.spindriftinn.com. Rooms feature hardwood floors, wood-burning fireplaces, TVs with VCRs, second telephone in the tiled bathrooms with marble tubs, feather beds (many canopied) and goose-down comforters, all-cotton linens, and terry bathrobes. In the morning, continental breakfast and the newspaper of your choice is delivered to your room. With a rooftop garden and sky-high atrium, the Spindrift also offers a luxurious lobby with Oriental rugs and antiques.

The huge (575-room) **Hyatt Regency Monterey Resort and Conference Center,** 1 Old Golf Course Rd., tel. (831) 372-1234 or toll-free (800) 824-2196 or (800) 233-1234, is definitely a resort; the spacious grounds here include an 18-hole golf course, six tennis courts (extra fee for both), two pools, whirlpools, fitness center—the works. The sports bar here, **Knuckles,** offers 200 satellite channels and 11 TV monitors.

Other upscale stays include the **Monterey Bay Inn,** 242 Cannery Row, tel. (831) 373-6242 or toll-free (800) 424-6242, offering contemporary accommodations right on the bay (many view rooms with balconies). Near the Row is the **Best Western Victorian Inn,** 487 Foam St., tel. (831) 373-8000 or toll-free (800) 232-4141, where a hot tub, gas fireplaces, complimentary continental breakfast, and afternoon wine and cheese are among the amenities.

MONTEREY BED AND BREAKFASTS

Monterey's showcase country inn is the gorgeous ivy-covered 1929 English Tudor **Old Monterey Inn,** 500 Martin St., tel. (831) 375-8284 or toll-free (800) 350-2344, fax (831) 375-6730, www.oldmontereyinn.com, featuring 10 elegant rooms and suites, most with fireplaces. All have sitting areas, featherbeds, CD players, a Jacuzzi for two, and special touches such as skylights and stained glass. As if the inn itself isn't appealing enough, it is shaded by a specimen oak amid stunning gardens. Buckeye, the inn's rescued golden retriever, will probably greet you when you arrive. Marvelous full breakfasts, sunset wine hour. Luxury.

The Jabberwock, 598 Laine St., tel. (831) 372-4777 or toll-free (888) 428-7253, fax (831) 655-2946, www.jabberwockinn.com, is a seven-room "post-Victorian" with a Victorian name and an Alice-Through-the-Looking-Glass sensibility. Some rooms share baths. Rates include full breakfast (imaginative and good) plus cookies and milk at night. Premium-Luxury.

A classic in inimitable Monterey style is the historic **Merritt House Inn,** downtown at 386 Pacific St., tel. (831) 646-9686 or toll-free (800) 541-5599, fax (831) 646-5392, www.merritt-houseinn.com. The original adobe, built in 1830, features three suites with 19th-century sensibility and modern bathrooms. The 22 surrounding rooms are more contemporary. Premium-Luxury.

At the European-style **Del Monte Beach Inn,** 1110 Del Monte Ave., tel. (831) 649-4410, fax (831) 375-3818, most of the rooms share baths—which means this place is affordable for people who don't normally do B&Bs. Rates include continental breakfast. Inexpensive-Expensive.

EATING IN MONTEREY

In Monterey, eating well *and* fairly inexpensively is easier than finding low-cost lodgings. Hard to beat is picnicking at the beaches or local parks. Happy hour, at the wharf and on "the Row" and elsewhere, is a big deal in the area. In addition to cheap drinks, many bars serve good (free) food from 4-7 p.m. With an abundance of reasonably priced (and generous) breakfast places, an inexpensive alternative to three meals

haggling over fresh strawberries at the Old Monterey Marketplace Farmer's Market

a day is skipping lunch (or packing simple picnic fare), then shopping around for early-bird dinners, a mainstay at many local restaurants. Do-it-yourselfers can pick up whatever suits their culinary fancy at the open-air **Old Monterey Marketplace Certified Farmers' Market** on Alvarado St. at Pearl, held every Tuesday night 3-8 p.m. year-round (until 7 p.m. in winter). Great food, great fun. For more information, call (831) 665-8070. On Thursday, head for the **Monterey Bay Peninsula College Certified Farmers' Market,** tel. (831) 728-5060, held 2:30-6 p.m. year-round at Fremont and Phisher.

No doubt helped along by the abundance of fresh regional produce, seafood, cheese and other dairy products, poultry, and meats, the Monterey Peninsula has also become a sophisticated dining destination. Some of the area's great restaurants are listed below (in various categories), but to get a true "taste" of the Monterey Peninsula, consider dining as well in nearby Pacific Grove and Carmel.

Monterey Standards

By "standard," we mean places people can happily—and affordably—frequent. The **Old Monterey Cafe,** 489 Alvarado, tel. (831) 646-1021, serves all kinds of omelettes at breakfast plus unusual choices like calamari and eggs, lingüiça and eggs, and pigs in a blanket. Just about everything is good at lunch, too, from homemade soups, hearty shrimp Louie, and the Athenian Greek salad (with feta cheese, Greek olives, shrimp, and veggies) to the three-quarter-pound burgers and steak or calamari sandwiches. Fresh-squeezed juices; espresso and cappuccino bar. Open daily for breakfast and lunch, 7 a.m.-2:30 p.m., breakfast served until closing.

Rosine's, nearby at 434 Alvarado, tel. (831) 375-1400, is locally loved at breakfast, lunch, and dinner. In addition to good pancakes, waffles, and other standards, at breakfast here you can get veggie Benedict (with avocado, sautéed mushrooms, and tomatoes on the English muffin instead of Canadian bacon). Lunch features homemade soups, salads, sandwiches, and burgers. An array of pastas plus chicken, seafood, and steaks is on the menu at dinner, with prime rib available on Friday and Saturday nights.

Still reasonable (and delicious) is **Kathy's,** 700 Cass St., tel. (831) 647-9540. Pick any three

items for a fluffy omelette; includes home fries, cheese sauce, bran muffins, and homemade strawberry jam for around $5. Sandwiches, similarly priced, are best when eaten on the patio. Another breakfast possibility is the **Paris Bakery Café,** 271 Bonifacio Place, tel. (831) 646-1620.

For a casual lunch, dinner, or Sunday jazz brunch, the **Clock Garden,** 565 Abrego, tel. (831) 375-6100, is a popular place. Guests sit outside amid the antique clocks planted in the garden, weather permitting. Closed Sunday evening.

In Seaside, the **Fishwife Seafood Cafe,** 789 Trinity (at Fremont), tel. (831) 394-2027, offers quick and interesting seafood, pastas, and house-made desserts. (There's another Fishwife near Asilomar.) For exceptional ethnic eats, consider the Salvadoran **El Migueleño,** also in Seaside at 1066 Broadway, tel. (831) 899-2199. The house specialty, Playa Azul, combines six different kinds of seafood with ranchera sauce, white wine, and mushrooms, served with white rice and beans. For Chinese, there's **Yen Ching,** 1868 Fremont St., tel. (831) 899-7800. While you're in the general area—which also includes Marina, up the coast—scout around for other intriguing possibilities.

Back in Monterey, Thai food fanatics should try **Siamese Bay Thai Restaurant,** 131 Webster St., tel. (831) 373-1550. For Asian, two possibilities are quite close to each other—**Tsing Tao China Restaurant,** 429 Alvarado St., tel. (831) 375-3000, and **Jugem Japanese Restaurant & Sushi,** 409 Alvarado St., tel. (831) 373-6463. Both are open for lunch and dinner. Or head for **Won Ju Korean Restaurant,** 570 Lighthouse Ave., tel. (831) 656-0672.

Monterey Pubs

For fans of British pubs, the real deal in Monterey is **The Crown & Anchor,** 150 W. Franklin St., tel. (831) 649-6496, dark and inviting, with a brassy seagoing air, where the full bar features 20 beers on tap. But the food is pretty darn good, and reasonably priced—from the fish and chips or bangers and mash to spicy meatloaf, curries, cottage pie, and steak and mushroom pie. Salads and sandwiches, too, and a special menu for the "powder monkeys" (Brit sailor slang for kids). Open for lunch and dinner daily. Also consider the **London Bridge Pub,** Fisherman's Wharf #2, tel. (831) 655-2879, which specializes in authentic

British cuisine and pours more than 60 different beers to wash it down with, and the **Mucky Duck British Pub,** 479 Alvarado, tel. (831) 655-3031.

With a logo depicting a one-eyed jack doing the proverbial 12-ounce curl, **Peter B's Brewpub,** 2 Portola Plaza (in the alley behind the Doubletree Hotel), tel. (831) 649-4511, offers 10 different Carmel Brewing Co. microbrews on tap and good pub grub.

Eating at the Wharf

Named for tender squid breaded then sautéed in butter, **Abalonetti Seafood Trattoria,** 57 Fisherman's Wharf, tel. (831) 373-1851, offers relaxed lunch and dinner, primarily seafood and standard Italian fare. Fairly inexpensive, nice view. Out on the end of the secondary pier at the wharf is **Rappa's Seafood Restaurant,** Fisherman's Wharf No. 1, tel. (831) 372-7562, an oceanside oasis with outdoor dining; quite reasonable, quite good, with good early-bird dinners.

Domenico's on the Wharf, 50 Fisherman's Wharf #1, tel. (831) 372-3655, is famous for its Southern Italian accent. The menu features fresh seafood, homemade pasta, chicken, steak, and veal dishes, and a long, very California wine list. Oyster bar open from 10 a.m. daily.

But **Cafe Fina,** 47 Fisherman's Wharf #1, tel. (831) 372-5200, is probably the best bet on the wharf—very Italian, and very lively and lighthearted. On the menu you'll find everything from mesquite-barbecued fish and beef to smoked salmon on fettuccine with shallot cream sauce and a goat cheese and black olive ravioli. People go crazy over Cafe Fina's "pizzettes," little eight-inch pizzas popped hot out of the restaurant's wood-burning oven.

Eating on Cannery Row

If you're spending most of the day at the Monterey Aquarium, try the **Portola Café and Restaurant** there. Or head out onto the Row. Many of the places along Cannery Row offer early-bird dinners, so if price matters, go deal-shopping before you get hungry.

Get your margarita fix and decent Mexican fare at **El Torito,** 600 Cannery Row, tel. (831) 373-0611. For something simple, an interesting choice for "views, brews, and cues" is the **Blue Fin Café and Billiards,** 685 Cannery Row, tel. (831) 375-7000. In addition to salads, sand-

---

KALISA'S LA IDA CAFE

Legendary on the Row is that survivor of the Steinbeck era, Kalisa's, 851 Cannery Row, tel. (831) 644-9316. Billed as "A Cosmopolitan Gourmet Place," it's really an eclectic people's eatery that's reasonable for lunch and dinner (open till the wee hours on weekends) and wonderful for Sunday brunch. The coffeehouse below features deli fare and ice cream in the daytime, suppers at night; meals are sometimes served in the garden out back. The "international" fare includes Greek-style pizza, northern Thai beef salad, rock cod roulade, and fresh fish. Live entertainment on Friday and Saturday nights is varied, including anything from jazz to belly dancers or magicians.

---

wiches, and full dinners, the Blue Fin boasts a full bar emphasizing bourbons and scotches, and also serves some 40 beers, including 22 ales and lagers on tap. There's plenty to do besides eat and drink, too, thanks to 18 pool tables, snooker, foosball, darts, and shuffleboard.

Naturally enough, seafood is the predominant dinner theme along the Row. The **Chart House,** 444 Cannery Row, tel. (831) 372-3362, brings its trademark casually elegant, nautical-themed decor to the Row, serving primarily seafood, steaks, and prime rib—predictably tasty. Full bar. A bit inland but still looking to the sea for inspiration is TV chef John Pisto's casual **Whaling Station Restaurant,** 763 Wave, tel. (831) 373-3778, another locally popular dinner house offering everything from seafood and housemade pastas to mesquite-grilled Black Angus steaks. Full bar. Open daily. Pisto's newest outpost is right on the Row: **Paradiso Trattoria & Oyster Bar,** 654 Cannery Row, tel. (831) 375-4155, open daily for lunch and dinner, serving fresh California-style Mediterranean. Full bar, and an extensive Monterey County wine list.

The exceptional, semiformal **Sardine Factory,** 701 Wave St., tel. (831) 373-3775, serves California-style regional fare, from seafood and steaks to pasta and other specialties. Full bar. Open daily for dinner.

Another upscale Row restaurant going for the nautical theme is **Schooners Bistro on the Bay,** 400 Cannery Row (at the Monterey Plaza

Hotel), tel. (831) 372-2628, specializing in California cuisine at lunch and dinner. If a bistro isn't chi-chi enough for you, consider the hotel's renowned but still casual **Duck Club Restaurant,** tel. (831) 646-1706, which serves outstanding bay views and superb American regional cuisine for breakfast and dinner daily.

Stylish Dining

Fresh Cream, across from Fisherman's Wharf and upstairs at Heritage Harbor, 99 Pacific St., tel. (831) 375-9798, has wonderful French country cuisine lightened by that fresh California touch—one of the Monterey Peninsula's best restaurants, more formal than most. Great views of Monterey Bay are served, too. Expensive, but even travelers light in the pocketbook can afford dessert and coffee. Open for dinner only, menu changes daily. Call for information and reservations.

Still the contemporary dining hotspot downtown is the relaxed all-American bistro **Montrio,** 414 Calle Principal (at Franklin), tel. (831) 648-8880, *Esquire* magazine's new restaurant of the year in 1995. You might start with fire-roasted artichokes, terrine of eggplant, or Dungeness crab cakes, then continue with grilled gulf prawns, lamb tenderloins, or Black Angus New York steak. Vegetarians can dig into the oven-roasted portobello mushroom over polenta and veggie ragout. At last report, Monday was still cioppino night. Marvelous sandwiches at lunch and exquisite desserts. Full bar, great wine list. Open Mon.-Sat. for lunch, daily for dinner.

Equally stylish is the historic 1833 **Stokes Adobe,** 500 Hartnell St. (at Madison), tel. (831) 373-1110, its exteriors—including the gardens—preserving that Monterey colonial style, its interiors beautifully recast with terra cotta floors, plank ceilings, and a light, airy ambience. But the food is the thing. On the menu here is rustic, refined, and reasonably affordable California-style Mediterranean, from savory soups and salads to seafood, chicken, lamb, and beef. Small plates feature choices such as house-made mozzarella and ciabatta bread served with herbed olive oil and oven-roasted spinach gratin with mussels and herbed bread crumbs. Large plates include vegetable Napoleon of rye crepes and homemade ricotta with smoked tomato sauce, "chicken under a brick" with roasted garlic mashed potatoes and herb salad, and seared hanger steak with spinach cheese tart. Full bar, good wines. Open for lunch and dinner daily.

Other Mediterranean possibilities include **Cibo Ristorante Italiano,** 301 Alvarado, tel. (831) 649-8151, serving rustic but stylish Sicilian fare. Down the street, **Tutto Buono,** 469 Alvarado St., tel. (831) 372-1880, is another purveyor of pasta and such.

Serving up stylish "American country" fare, **Tarpy's Roadhouse** inside the historic stone Ryan Ranch homestead, three miles off Hwy. 1 on Hwy. 68 (at Canyon del Rey), tel. (831) 647-1444, is not to be confused with some cheap-eats-and-beer joint. The culinary challenge here is reinterpreting American classics—and that's no inexpensive task. Dinner includes such things as Indiana duck, Dijon-crusted lamb loin, baby back ribs, and grilled vegetables with succotash. Great desserts. Salads and sandwiches at lunch. Full bar. Open for lunch and dinner daily, brunch on Sunday.

For other high-style dining in Monterey, consider some of the choices on Cannery Row and at Fisherman's Wharf, listed above.

EVENTFUL MONTEREY

The two-week **Whalefest** celebration begins in mid-January, welcoming the migratory return of the California gray whale. Visitors have a whale of a time at free events and activities all over town, and whalewatching companies offer excursion trips. In early March, **Dixieland Monterey** brings three days of Dixie and swing to various venues around town. Mid-April, show up for the **Monterey Wine Festival,** when more than 200 wineries strut their stuff. In late April, the **Formula One International Motorcycle Races** at Laguna Seca draw a major audience. Traditionally, though, April is adobe month in Monterey, with the popular **Adobe Tour** through public and private historic buildings taking place toward the end of the month. In late May, the **Great Monterey Squid Festival** is a chic culinary indulgence for those with calamari cravings, plus arts, crafts, and entertainment.

June brings the **Great Cannery Row Sardine Festival** to Cannery Row mid-month, followed a couple of weeks later by the acclaimed

Monterey Bay Blues Festival. The **Fourth of July** celebration here is fun, with fireworks off the Coast Guard Pier. On weekends only, from late June through mid-July, is the **Monterey Bay Theatrefest** at Custom House Plaza, followed by late July's **Scottish/Irish Festival and Highland Games** at the fairgrounds.

In August, the **Monterey County Fair** comes to the fairgrounds, bringing amusement rides, livestock shows, and young faces sticky with cotton-candy residue. In early September, race car fans zoom into town for the long-running, three-day **Visa Sports Car Championships.** Come mid-September, it's time for the city's most famous event of all: the **Monterey Jazz Festival,** oldest continuous jazz fest in the nation. Not as daring as others, it nonetheless hosts legendary greats and up-and-coming talent. This is the biggest party of the year here, so get tickets and reserve rooms well in advance (four to six months). For information and tickets, contact: Monterey Jazz Festival, 2000 Fairgrounds Rd., Monterey, CA 93940, tel. (831) 373-3366 or toll-free (800) 307-3378.

In mid-November comes the **Robert Louis Stevenson Un-Birthday Party** at the Stevenson House, as well as the **Great Wine Escape Weekend,** when area wineries all hold open houses.

The **Christmas in the Adobes** yuletide tour in mid-December is another big event, with luminaria-lit historic tours of 15 adobes, each dressed up in period holiday decorations, and the festivities accompanied by music and carolers. Fee. For information, contact the Monterey State Historic Park, tel. (831) 649-7118.

MONTEREY INFORMATION

The **Monterey Visitor Center,** 401 Camino El Estero, is staffed by the Monterey County Convention & Visitors Bureau and holds reams of flyers on just about everything in and around the region. It's open April-Oct., Mon.-Sat. 9 a.m.-6 p.m., Sunday 9 a.m.-5 p.m.; Nov.-March, Mon.-Sat. 9 a.m.-5 p.m., Sunday 10 a.m.-4 p.m. The Visitor & Convention Bureau also co-sponsors the new **Monterey State Historic Park Visitor Center** at 5 Custom House Plaza, open seven days a week, 10 a.m.-5 p.m. For additional area information, including a current *Monterey County Travel & Meeting Planner,* contact: **Monterey County Convention & Visitors Bureau,** P.O. Box 1770, Monterey, CA 93942-1770, tel. (831) 649-1770, fax (831) 648-5373, www.monterey.com. For additional information and accommodations reservations, call toll-free (877) 666-8387 or try www.877monterey.com.

The **Monterey History and Art Association,** 5 Custom House Plaza, tel. (831) 372-2608, has information on the annual adobe and garden tours. For information about Monterey County parks and area hiking trails, contact **Monterey County Parks and Recreation,** P.O. Box 5279, Salinas, CA 93915, tel. (831) 647-7795 (or inquire at the **Sierra Club—Ventana chapter,** Ocean Ave. at Dolores in Carmel, tel. 831-624-8032). The **Monterey Bay National Marine Sanctuary** headquarters and information center is near the Monterey Bay Aquarium at 299 Foam St. (at D St.), tel. (831) 647-4201.

The *Monterey County Herald* is the mainline community news source. For an alternative view of things, pick up the free *Coast Weekly,* tel. (831) 394-5656, also offering entertainment and events information. Other free local publications widely available around town detail dinner specials and current activities and entertainment.

MONTEREY TRANSPORTATION

Hitching into, out of, and around the Monterey Peninsula is difficult. Even getting around by car is a problem; finding streets is confusing due to missing signs, complex traffic signals, and one-way routes. Local traffic jams can be horrendous; save yourself some headaches and avail yourself of local public transportation. Drivers, park at the 12-hour meters near Fisherman's Wharf—the cheapest lots are downtown—and walk or take the bus. For more specific parking advice, pick up the free *Smart Parking in Monterey: How to Find Affordable Legal Public Parking* brochure at area visitors centers.

Bicycling
Bicycling is another way to go. The local roads are narrow and bike paths are few, but you can get just about everywhere by bike if you're careful. Rent bikes at **Freewheeling Cycles,** 188

Webster St. (north of downtown), tel. (831) 373-3855, or **Bay Bikes,** 640 Wave St. (on Cannery Row), tel. (831) 646-9090 (also at 99-100 Pacific, tel. 831-655-8687), where you can opt for mountain bikes, touring bikes, or those four-wheel covered surreys known as "pedalinas." (Bay Bikes also has an outpost in downtown Carmel, tel. 831-625-2453.) Other bike rental firms include **Monterey Moped Adventures,** 1250 Del Monte Ave., tel. (831) 373-2696, and **Adventures by the Sea,** 299 Cannery Row, tel. (831) 372-1807, www.adventuresbythesea.com. For more about both, which also offer information on scheduled rides with the local **Velo Club Monterey,** see Monterey Outdoors above.

Buses

Once parked, from Memorial Day through Labor Day ride Monterey's **WAVE,** Waterfront Area Visitor Express, a shuttle bus system connecting the Tin Cannery shopping center (at the edge of Pacific Grove), the Monterey Bay Aquarium, Cannery Row, Fisherman's Wharf, and the town's historic downtown adobes with the downtown conference center, nearby motels and hotels, and parking garages. WAVE's Monterey-Salinas transit buses are identified by a wave logo. Buses run every 15 minutes. All-day fare (9 a.m.-6:30 p.m.) is $1 adults, 50 cents students and seniors, free to toddlers under age 5; transfers are accepted from other local buses. For more information, contact Monterey-Salinas Transit, tel. (831) 899-2555.

To get around on public buses otherwise, contact **Monterey-Salinas Transit,** 1 Ryan Ranch Rd., tel. (831) 899-2555 or (831) 424-7695 (from Salinas). "The Bus" serves the entire area, including Pacific Grove, Carmel, and Carmel Valley, from Watsonville south to Salinas. Local buses can get you just about anywhere, but some run sporadically. Pick up the free "Rider's Guide" schedule at the downtown **Transit Plaza** (where most buses stop and where Alvarado, Polk, Munras, Pearl, and Tyler Streets converge) or at motels, the chamber of commerce, and the library. The standard single-trip fare (one zone) is $1.50, exact change required, free transfers. Some longer routes traverse multiple zones and cost more. Seniors, the disabled, and children can ride for 75 cents with the transit system's courtesy card. Children under age 5

ride free. A regular adult day-pass is $3, and a super day-pass (valid on all routes and all zones) is $6; seniors and students pay half price. From late May through mid-October, bus No. 22 runs south to famous Nepenthe in Big Sur (two buses per day in each direction; $3 one-way).

Greyhound is at 1042 Del Monte Ave., tel. (831) 373-4735 or toll-free (800) 231-2222 (system-wide information and reservations), open daily 8 a.m.-10 p.m.

Amtrak Connections

Monterey-Salinas Transit buses can get you to the **Amtrak** station in Salinas, 11 Station Place, tel. (831) 422-7458 (depot) or toll-free (800) 872-7245, www.amtrak.com, for reservations and schedule information—including information on Amtrak's Thruway bus connections from Monterey and vicinity, a service included in some fares.

Other Transportation and Tours

An unusual thrill: cruising town in a facsimile Model A or Phaeton from **Rent-A-Roadster,** 229 Cannery Row, tel. (831) 647-1929. The basic rate is about $30-35 an hour, but you can arrange half-day and full-day tours, too—and head south to Big Sur and San Simeon in style.

Adventure Tours Unlimited, tel. (831) 375-2409, maintains a fleet of air-conditioned Ford vans and doubles as an airport shuttle service, with delivery and pick-up at the local airport and as far afield as San Jose, San Francisco, and Oakland. (Advance notice and reservations are required for out-of-town pick-ups.)

Ag Venture Tours, P.O. Box 2634, Monterey, CA 93942, tel. (831) 643-9463, specializes in winery tours in the Salinas Valley, Carmel Valley, and Santa Cruz Mountains (but also offers farm tours). A typical day-long tour includes tasting at three different wineries, a vineyard walk, and a picnic lunch.

Otter-Mobile Tours & Charters, based just south of town in Carmel, tel. (831) 649-4523, offers van tours of local sights ("Peninsula Highlights") as well as trips to Pt. Lobos, Big Sur, San Simeon and Hearst Castle, and wineries in the Salinas Valley. The company designs personalized tours around specific interests, from nature hikes to hunting down Steinbeck's haunts. Also based in Carmel is **Steinbeck Country Tours,** tel. (831) 659-0333.

PACIFIC GROVE AND VICINITY

Pacific Grove began in 1875 as a prim, proper tent city founded by Methodists who, Robert Louis Stevenson observed, "come to enjoy a life of teetotalism, religion, and flirtation." No boozing, waltzing, zither playing, or reading Sunday newspapers was allowed. Dedicated inebriate John Steinbeck lived here for many years, in the next century, but had to leave town to get drunk. Pacific Grove was the last "dry" town in California: alcohol has been legal here only since 1969. The first chautauqua in the western states was held here—bringing "moral attractions" to heathen Californians—and the hall where the summer meeting tents were stored still stands at 16th and Central Avenues.

Nicknamed "Butterfly City U.S.A." in honor of migrating monarchs (a big fine and/or six months in jail is the penalty for "molesting" one), Pacific Grove sparkles with Victorians and modest seacoast cottages, community pride, a rocky shoreline with wonderful tidepools, and an absolutely uncommercial Butterfly Parade in October. Also here is Asilomar, a well-known state-owned conference center with its own beautiful beach.

Pacific Grove is well served by Monterey-Salinas Transit buses (see Monterey Transportation above). For events, accommodations, restaurants, and other current information, stop by the **Pacific Grove Chamber of Commerce** at Forest and Central, P.O. Box 167, Pacific Grove, CA 93950, tel. (831) 373-3304. The **Pacific Grove Public Library,** 550 Central (at Fountain), tel. (831) 648-3160, is open Mon.-Thurs. 10 a.m.-8 p.m., Fri.-Sat. 10 a.m.-5 p.m.

SEEING AND DOING PACIFIC GROVE

From Pacific Grove, embark on the too-famous 17-Mile Drive in adjacent Pebble Beach. But better (and free), tour the surf-pounded peninsula as a populist. The city of Pacific Grove is one of few in California owning its own beaches and shores, all dedicated to public use. Less crowded and hoity-toity than the 17-Mile Drive, just as spectacular, and absolutely free is a walk, bike ride, or drive along Ocean View Boulevard. Or take the Monterey Peninsula Recreation Trail as far as you want; this path for walkers, joggers, bicyclers, skaters, and baby-stroller-pushers runs all the way from Marina to Pebble Beach. It's paved in places (right through downtown Monterey, for example), dirt in others. Or cycle from here to Carmel on the Del Monte Forest ridge via Hwy. 68 (the Holman Hwy.) for a spectacular view of the bay, surrounding mountains, and the "17-Mile" coastline to the south.

TOM MYERS PHOTOGRAPHY

Pacific Grove's surf

The "Three-Mile Drive"—or Walk

Along the Ocean View route are Berwick Park, Lovers Point, and Perkins Park; altogether, Pacific Grove boasts 13 community parks. These areas (and points in between) offer spectacular sunsets, crashing surf, craggy shorelines, swimming, sunbathing, and picnicking, plus whale-watching in season, sea otters, sea lions, seals, shorebirds, and autumn flurries of monarch butterflies. Stanford University's **Hopkins Marine Station** on Point Cabrillo (China Point) is also along the way, the crystal offshore waters and abundant marinelife attracting scientists and students from around the world. This is the first marine laboratory on the Pacific coast. (An aside for Steinbeck fans: this was the location of Chin Kee's Squid Yard in *Sweet Thursday*.) As for **Lovers Point,** the granite headland near Ocean View Blvd. and 17th St., there is considerable disagreement over whether Pacific Grove could have been *sexual* in Methodist days, when it was named. The popular local opinion, still, is

that the name actually stands for "Lovers of Jesus" Point. But conscientious researchers have established that the reference is to romance—and was, at least as far back as 1890. (For help in divining other arcane Monterey Bay Area details, pick up a copy of *Monterey County Place Names: A Geographical Dictionary,* by Donald Thomas Clark, and its companion *Santa Cruz County Place Names*.) Trysting place or no, Lovers Point is not a safe place to be during heavy weather; entirely too many people have been swept away to their deaths. Picnic at **Perkins Point,** instead, or wade or swim (safe beach). **Marine Gardens Park,** an aquatic park stretching along Ocean View, with wonderful tidepools, is a good spot for watching sea otters frolic in the seaweed just offshore.

Museum of Natural History

Pacific Grove's Museum of Natural History at 165 Forest Ave. (Forest and Central) showcases *local* wonders of nature, including sea otters,

THE MONARCH BUTTERFLIES AND BUTTERFLY TREES

Pacific Grove is the best known of the 20 or so places where monarch butterflies winter. Once partial to Monterey pine or cypress trees for perching, monarchs these days prefer eucalyptus introduced from Australia. Adults arrive in late October and early November, their distinctive orange-and-black Halloweenish wings sometimes tattered and torn after migrating thousands of miles. But they still have that urge to merge, first alighting on low shrubs, then meeting at certain local trees to socialize and sun themselves during the temperate Monterey Peninsula winter before heading north to Canada to mate in the spring and then die. Their offspring metamorphose into adult butterflies the following summer or fall and—mysteriously—make their way back to the California coast without ever having been here. Milkweed eaters, the monarchs somehow figured out this diet made them toxic to bug-loving birds—who subsequently learned to leave them alone.

Even when massed in hundreds, the butterflies may be hard to spot: with wings folded, their undersides provide neutral camouflage. But if fog-damp, monarchs will spread their wings to dry in the sun and "flash"—a priceless sight for any nature mystic.

Pacific Grove loves its monarch butterflies.

seabirds (a huge collection with more than 400 specimens), rare insects, and native plants. A fine array of Native American artifacts is on rotating display. Particularly impressive is the relief map of Monterey Bay, though youngsters will probably vote for "Sandy," the gray whale sculpture right out front. Besides the facsimile butterfly tree, the blazing feathery dried seaweed exhibit is a must-see. Many traveling exhibits visit this museum throughout the year, and the annual **Wildflower Show** on the third weekend in April is excellent. For information, call the museum at (831) 648-3116. Open Tues.-Sun. 10 a.m.-5 p.m. Admission is free (donations greatly appreciated).

Point Piños Lighthouse
Built of local granite, this is the oldest operating lighthouse on the Pacific coast. The beacon here and the mournful foghorn have been warning seagoing vessels away from the point since the 1850s. Rebuilt in 1906, the original French Fresnel lenses and prisms are still in use, though the lighthouse is now powered by electricity and a 1,000-watt lamp instead of whale oil. The lighthouse and the **U.S. Coast Guard Museum** inside are free and open Thurs.-Sun. 1-4 p.m. **Doc's Great Tidepool,** yet another Steinbeck-era footnote, is near the foot of the lighthouse.

Across from the lighthouse parking lot is fascinating **El Carmelo Cemetery,** a de facto nature preserve for deer and birds. (For more birdwatching, amble down to freshwater **Crespi Pond** near the golf course at Ocean View and Asilomar Boulevards.) The Point Piños Lighthouse is two blocks north of Lighthouse Ave. on Asilomar Boulevard. For information about the lighthouse and Coast Guard Museum, call (831) 372-4212.

Asilomar
The ladies of the Young Women's Christian Association's national Board of Directors coined this Spanish-sounding nonword from the Greek *asilo* ("refuge") and the Spanish *mar* ("sea") when they established this as a YWCA retreat in 1913. **Asilomar State Beach** has tidepools and wonderful white-sand beaches, shifting sand dunes, wind-sculpted forests, spectacular sunsets, and sea otters and gray whales offshore. Inland, many of Asilomar's original buildings (de-

signed by architect Julia Morgan, best known for Hearst's San Simeon estate) are now historical landmarks.

Primarily a conference center with meeting rooms and accommodations for groups, Asilomar is now a nonprofit unit of the California state park system. Guest or not, anyone can fly kites or build sandcastles at the beach, stop to appreciate the forest of Monterey pine and cypress, and watch for deer, raccoons, gray ground squirrels, hawks, and owls. For information, contact: Asilomar Conference Center, 800 Asilomar Blvd., P.O. Box 537, Pacific Grove, CA 93950, tel. (831) 372-

---

THE CURSE OF MONTEREY PINE PITCH CANKER

Eons ago, Monterey pines blanketed much of California's coastline. Today, only a few native stands remain in California—and within a decade at least 80% of these trees will be gone, done in by a fungus. That fungus, known as pine pitch canker, was first discovered in Alameda and Santa Cruz Counties in the mid-1980s. Since then, it has spread throughout California, via contaminated lumber and firewood, Christmas trees, infected seedlings, pruning tools, insects, birds, and wind; there is no known cure. Afflicted trees first turn brown at the tips of their branches, then erupt in pitchy spots; within the tree, water and nutrients are choked off. The open infections attract bark beetles, which bore into tree trunks and lay eggs, an invasion that hastens tree death. Usually within four years, an infected tree is completely brown and lifeless. The United Nations has declared the Monterey pine an endangered species.

Enjoy the majestic groves of Monterey pine near Monterey while they still stand, endangered as they are both by disease and further development plans. Also take care to avoid being an unwitting "carrier" for the disease; don't cart home any forest products as souvenirs. Pine pitch canker has been found in at least eight other species, including the Ponderosa pine, sugar pine, and Douglas fir, though it appears the Monterey pine is most susceptible. The California Department of Forestry is justifiably concerned that the disease will soon spread—or is already spreading—into the Sierra Nevada and California's far northern mountains.

8016 or toll-free (800) 881-7708 (reservations), fax (831) 372-7227, www.asilomarcenter.com.

The 17-Mile Drive

Technically in Pebble Beach, the best place to start off on the famed 17-Mile Drive is in Pacific Grove (or, alternatively, the Carmel Hill gate off Highway 1). Not even 17 miles long anymore since it no longer loops up to the old Del Monte Hotel, the "drive" still skirts plenty of ritzy digs in the 5,300-acre, privately owned Del Monte Forest of the four-gated town of Pebble Beach. Note the Byzantine castle of the banking/railroading Crocker family; believe it or not, the estate's private beach is heated with underground pipes.

From **Shepherd's Knoll,** there's a great panoramic view of both Monterey Bay and the Santa Cruz Mountains. **Huckleberry Hill** does have huckleberries, but botanically more fascinating is the unusual coexistence of Monterey pines, Bishop pines, and both Gowen and Monterey cypress. **Spanish Bay,** a nice place to picnic, is named for Portolá's confused land expedition from Baja in 1769; Portolá was looking for Monterey Bay, but he didn't find it until his second trip. **Point Joe** is a treacherous, turbulent convergence of conflicting ocean currents, wet and wild even on calm days. ("Joe" has been commonly mistaken by mariners as the entrance to Monterey Bay, so countless ships have gone down on these rocks.) Both **Seal Rock** and **Bird Rock** are aptly named. **Fanshell Beach** is a secluded spot good for picnics and fishing (but swimming is dangerous).

Most famous of all is the landmark **Lone Cypress**—the official (trademarked) emblem of the Monterey Peninsula—at the route's midpoint. No longer lonely, this craggy old-timer is visited by millions each year; it's now "posed" with supporting guy wires, fed and watered in summer, and recovering well from a recent termite attack. At **Pescadero Point,** note the cypress bleached ashen and ghostlike by sun, salt spray, and wind.

From Pacific Grove (or from other entrances), it won't cost you a cent to travel the 17-Mile Drive by bike—the only way to go, if you can handle some steep grades. (On weekends, cyclists must enter the drive at the Pacific Grove Gate.) By car "the drive" costs $7.75, which is refundable if you spend at least $25 on food or greens fees at The Lodge at Pebble Beach. A

map is available at any entrance. The drive is open for touring from sunrise to 30 minutes before sunset, year-round. For more information, call Pebble Beach Resort at (831) 649-8500.

Pebble Beach

Very private Pebble Beach has seven world-class golf courses made famous by Bing Crosby's namesake tournament, "The Crosby," now called the **AT&T Pebble Beach National Pro Am Golf Tournament** and held each year in late January or early February. For golfing information, see Monterey Outdoor Activities, call (831) 372-4711 or (831) 649-1533, or try www.pebblebeach.com. Also here and open to the public: jogging paths and beautiful horse trails. Just about everything else—country clubs, yacht clubs, tennis courts, swimming pools—is private (and well guarded), though the public is welcome for a price. If you're here in August, join in the **Scottish Highland Games** or see how the rich get around at the **Concours d'Élégance** classic car fest at The Lodge.

More to See and Do

Pacific Grove boasts more than 75 local art galleries, enough to keep anyone busy. The **Peninsula Potters Gallery,** 2078 Sunset Dr., tel. (831) 372-8867, is the place to appreciate the potter's art; open Mon.-Sat. 10 a.m.-4 p.m. Also worth stopping for is the **Pacific Grove Art Center,** 568 Lighthouse, tel. (831) 375-2208.

The renowned Pacific Grove **Wildflower Show** is in mid-April, with more than 600 native species (150 outdoors) in bloom at the Pacific Grove Museum of Natural History. In March or April, the **Good Old Days** celebration brings a parade, Victorian home tours, and arts and crafts galore. In late July, come for the annual **Feast of Lanterns,** a traditional boat parade and fireworks ceremony that started when Chinese fishermen lived at China Point (their village was torched in 1906).

But Pacific Grove's biggest party comes in October with **Welcome Back Monarch Day.** This native, naturalistic, and noncommercial community bash coincides with the return of the migrating monarchs and includes the **Butterfly Parade,** carnival, and bazaar, all to benefit the PTA. Not coincidentally, from October to February the most popular destination in town is the

Monarch Grove Sanctuary, on Ridge Rd. (just off Lighthouse), where docent-led tours are offered daily; for reservations, call toll-free (888) 746-6627. In December, check out **Christmas at the Inns,** when several of the local B&Bs, decorated for the holidays, hold an open house and serve refreshments.

PACIFIC GROVE HOTELS AND MOTELS

To maintain its "hometown America" aura, Pacific Grove has limited its motel development. The local chamber of commerce provides accommodations listings. Bed-and-breakfast inns are popular in Pacific Grove—see separate listings below—and these comfortable, often luxurious home lodgings compare in price to much less pleasant alternatives elsewhere on the peninsula.

Moderate Stays
Especially if the monarchs are in town, consider a stay at the **Butterfly Grove Inn,** 1073 Lighthouse Ave., tel. (831) 373-4921. Butterflies are partial to some of the trees here. The inn is quiet, with pool, spa, some kitchens and fireplaces. Choose rooms in a comfy old house or motel units. Closest to the beach are the 1930s-style cottages at **Bide-a-Wee Motel & Cottages,** 221 Asilomar Blvd., tel. (831) 372-2330. Some of the cottages have kitchenettes. Moderate-Premium. Also comfortable is woodsy **Andril Fireplace Motel & Cottages,** 569 Asilomar Blvd., tel. (831) 375-0994 (the cottages have fireplaces).

Always a best bet for a quiet stay is the well-located **Pacific Grove Motel** near Asilomar, close to the ocean and just west of 17 Mile Dr. at Lighthouse Ave. and Grove Acre, tel. (831) 372-3218 or toll-free (800) 858-8997, fax (831) 372-8842. In addition to clean rooms with refrigerators, phones, and color TV (some have attractive patios), amenities include a heated pool, hot tub, BBQ area, and playground. Very low weekday rates in winter, two-night minimum stay on weekends. Moderate-Premium. Or stay at **Asilomar,** if there's room. Asilomar has a heated pool, horseshoe pits, exercise trail, and volleyball for its guests. Cheapest are the older, rustic cottages. Some units have kitchens and fireplaces. For details, see listing above.

Premium Stays
Near Asilomar is the **Pacific Gardens Inn,** 701 Asilomar Blvd., tel. (831) 646-9414 or toll-free (800) 262-1566 in California, www.pacificgardensinn.com, where the contemporary rooms feature wood-burning fireplaces, refrigerators, TVs, and phones—even popcorn poppers and coffee makers. Suites feature full kitchens and living rooms. Complimentary continental breakfast and evening wine and cheese. Very nice. Right across from Asilomar is the all-suites **Rosedale Inn,** 775 Asilomar Blvd., tel. (831) 655-1000 or toll-free (800) 822-5606, fax (831) 655-0691, where all rooms have a ceiling fan, fireplace, large jacuzzi, wet bar, refrigerator, microwave, in-room coffee, remote-control color TV and VCR, even a hair dryer. Some suites have two or three TVs and/or a private patio.

Luxury Stays
The **Lighthouse Lodge and Suites,** 1150 and 1259 Lighthouse Ave., tel. (831) 655-2111 or toll-free (800) 858-1249, fax (831) 655-4922, www.lhls.com, are two different properties close to one another. The 31 Cape Cod-style suites feature abundant amenities—king beds and large jacuzzi tubs, plush robes, mini-kitchens with stocked honor bars—and are the most expensive. The 64 lodge rooms feature the basic motel-style comforts and are family friendly, with extras including breakfast and a complimentary poolside barbecue in the afternoon (weather permitting). Lower rates in the off-season, two-night minimum on summer weekends.

Three superswank choices in adjacent Pebble Beach are definitely beyond the reach of most people's pocketbooks. At the **Inn at Spanish Bay,** 2700 17-Mile Dr. (at the Scottish Links Golf Course), tel. (831) 647-7500, rooms are definitely deluxe, with gas-burning fireplaces, patios, and balconies with views. Amenities include beach access, a pool, saunas, whirlpools, a health club, tennis courts, and a putting green. Also an unlikely choice for most travelers is **The Lodge at Pebble Beach,** another outpost of luxury on 17-Mile Drive, tel. (831) 624-3811. (If you don't stay, peek into the *very* exclusive shops here.) A recent addition is the elegant estate-style cottages at 24-room **Casa Palmero,** near both The Lodge and the first fairway of the Pebble Beach Golf Links. For still more pampering, the **Spa at Pebble Beach** is a full-service spa facility. For reservations at any of these Pebble Beach Resort facilities, call toll-free (800) 654-9300, fax (831) 644-7958, or try www.pebble-beach.com.

PACIFIC GROVE BED AND BREAKFASTS

Victoriana is particularly popular in Pacific Grove. The most famous Victorian inn in town is the elegant **Seven Gables Inn,** 555 Ocean View Blvd., tel. (831) 372-4341, which offers ocean views from all 14 rooms and an abundance of European antiques and Victorian finery. Rates include fabulous full breakfast and afternoon tea. Luxury. Sharing the garden and offering equally exceptional, if more relaxed, Victorian style is the sibling **Grand View Inn** next door, 557 Ocean View Blvd., tel. (831) 372-4341. The view from all 10 rooms, with their antique furnishings and luxurious marble bathrooms, is indeed grand. Full breakfast, afternoon tea. Luxury.

Another Pacific Grove grande dame is the pretty-in-pink 23-room **Martine Inn,** 255 Ocean View Blvd., tel. (831) 373-3388 or toll-free (800) 852-5588, fax (831) 373-3896, www.martineinn.com, a study in Victorian refinement and propriety masquerading, on the outside, as a Mediterranean villa. Full breakfast here is served with fine china, crystal, silver, and old lace. Also enjoy wine and hors d'oeuvres in the evening, a

whirlpool, spa, game room, library, and a baby grand piano in the library. Luxury.

The lovely **Green Gables Inn,** 104 Fifth St., tel. (831) 375-2095 or toll-free (800) 722-1774, fax (831) 375-5437, is a romantic gabled Queen Anne seaside "summer house" with marvelous views, five rooms upstairs, a suite downstairs, and five rooms in the carriage house. Of these, seven feature private bathrooms. Rates include continental breakfast. The Green Gables, a Four Sisters Inn, was named the number one bed-and-breakfast inn in North America in 1997, according to the Official Hotel Guide's survey of travel agents. Premium-Luxury.

The **Gosby House Inn,** 643 Lighthouse Ave., tel. (831) 375-1287 or toll-free (800) 527-8828, fax (831) 655-9621, is another of the Four Sisters—this one a charming (and huge) Queen Anne serving up fine antiques, a restful garden, homemade food, and fresh flowers. All 20 rooms boast great bayside views, and most feature private bathrooms. Some have fireplaces, jacuzzi tubs, and TVs. Expensive-Luxury.

The 1889 **Centrella Inn,** 612 Central Ave., tel. (831) 372-3372 or toll-free (800) 233-3372, fax (831) 372-2036, www.centrellainn.com, a National Historic Landmark, offers 20 rooms plus a jacuzzi-equipped garden suite and five cottages with wood-burning fireplaces and wet bars. The cottage-style gardens are quite appealing, especially in summer. Rates include complimentary morning newspaper, full buffet breakfast, and a social hour in the afternoon

the Green Gables Inn

TOM MYERS PHOTOGRAPHY

(wine and hors d'oeuvres). Premium-Luxury.

The **Gatehouse Inn,** 225 Central Ave., tel. (831) 649-8436 or toll-free (800) 753-1881, fax (831) 648-8044, offers nine rooms in an 1884 Victorian that's strolling distance from the Monterey Bay Aquarium. Rates include gourmet full breakfast and afternoon wine and hors d'oeuvres. Premium-Luxury. Comely sister inn is the Cape Cod-style **Old St. Angela Inn,** 321 Central Ave., tel. (831) 372-3246 or toll-free (800) 748-6306, a converted 1910 country cottage featuring eight guest rooms decorated with antiques, quilts, and other homey touches. Amenities include a garden hot tub, solarium, living room with fireplace, complimentary breakfast, and afternoon wine or tea and hors d'oeuvres. Premium-Luxury. For a virtual preview of both, visit online at www.sueandlewinns.com.

The historic three-story (no elevator) **Pacific Grove Inn** is at 581 Pine (at Forest), tel. (831) 375-2825. Some rooms and suites in this 1904 Queen Anne have ocean views, most have fireplaces, and all have private baths and modern amenities like color TVs, radios, and telephones. Breakfast buffet every morning. Premium-Luxury.

But not every choice in Pacific Grove is Victorian. Perfect for aquatic sports fans—the proprietors can paddle you out to the best sea kayaking—is the **Inn at 213 Seventeen Mile Drive,** 981 Lighthouse Ave. (at 17-Mile Drive), tel. (831) 642-9514 or toll-free (800) 526-5666, fax (831) 642-9546, www.innat213-17miledr.com. Guest rooms in this restored 1928 Craftsman home and affiliated cottages feature king or queen beds and essential comforts like down comforters, TVs, and phones. All rooms have private baths. Generous buffet at breakfast, hors d'oeuvres and wine in the evening. Premium-Luxury.

EATING IN PACIFIC GROVE

Breakfast and More

You can get marvelous crepes for breakfast or lunch, as well as good waffles and homemade soups, at **Toastie's Cafe,** 702 Lighthouse Ave., tel. (831) 373-7543, open daily 7 a.m.-2 p.m. Another cheap but good choice is the **Bagel Bakery,** 201 Lighthouse Ave., tel. (831) 649-1714, where you can fill up anytime for around $5. Specialties include fresh-baked bagels, homemade soups, and a salad bar for lunch or dinner. Open Mon.-Sat. 7:30 a.m.-9 p.m., Sunday until 7 p.m. Or try the vegetarian dishes and cheesecake at **Tillie Gort's Coffee House** and art gallery at 111 Central, tel. (831) 373-0335.

For lattes, cappuccinos, espressos, or just a good cuppa joe, head to **Caravali Coffee,** 510 Lighthouse Ave., tel. (831) 655-5633; **Juice and Java,** 599 Lighthouse Ave., tel. (831) 373-8652; or the dual-purpose **Bookworks,** 667 Lighthouse Ave., tel. (831) 372-2242, where you can sample the wares in the bookstore as well as the coffeehouse.

Lunch and Dinner

Thai Bistro, 159 Central Ave., tel. (831) 372-8700, is the place to go for outstanding Thai food. Those with a fireproof palate will love the restaurant's spicy dishes, and vegetarians will appreciate the large number of meatless entrées. Open for lunch and dinner daily. (There's another Thai Bistro in Carmel Valley at 55 W. Carmel Valley Rd., tel. 831-659-5900.)

The **Crocodile Grill,** 701 Lighthouse Ave. (at Congress), tel. (831) 655-3311, offers eclectic and exotic decor along with fresh California-style Caribbean and Central-South American cuisine. Seafood is the specialty here—such things as red snapper Mardis Gras—but for dessert, don't miss the house-made Key lime cheesecake with mango syrup. Beer and wine. Open for dinner nightly except Tuesday.

Popular with locals (and a favorite of the late, great Ansel Adams) is **Pablo's,** 1184 Forest Ave., tel. (831) 646-8888, featuring *real* Mexican food, including *mariscos.* Open 11 a.m.-9 p.m. Locals say the homemade *chiles rellenos* at immensely popular **Peppers MexiCali Cafe,** 170 Forest Ave., tel. (831) 373-6892, are the best on the peninsula, but you also won't go wrong with the tamales, seafood tacos, or spicy prawns. Beer and wine served. Closed Tuesday, but otherwise open weekdays and Saturday for lunch, nightly for dinner. Also popular for seafood is the relaxed and family-friendly **Fishwife** in the Beachcomber Inn, 1996 Sunset Dr., tel. (831) 375-7107.

CARMEL AND VICINITY

Vizcaíno named the river here after Palestine's Mount Carmel, probably with the encouragement of several Carmelite friars accompanying his expedition. The name Carmel-by-the-Sea distinguishes this postcard-pretty, almost too-cute coastal village of 5,000 souls from affluent Carmel Valley 10 miles inland and Carmel Highlands just south of Point Lobos on the way to Big Sur. Everything about all the Carmels, though, says one thing quite loudly: money. Despite its bohemian beginnings, these days Carmel crankily guards its quaintness while cranking up the commercialism. (Shopping is the town's major draw.) Still free at last report are the beautiful city beaches and visits to the elegant old Carmel Mission. Almost free: tours of Robinson Jeffers's **Tor House** and fabulous **Point Lobos** just south of town.

Carmel hasn't always been so crowded or so crotchety. Open-minded artists, poets, writers, and other oddballs were the community's original movers and shakers—most of them shaken up and out of San Francisco after the 1906 earthquake. Upton Sinclair, Sinclair Lewis, Robinson Jeffers, and Jack London were some of the literary lights who once twinkled in this town. Master photographers Ansel Adams and Edward Weston were more recent residents. But, as often happens in California, land values shot up and the original bohemians were priced right out of the neighborhood.

Carmel-by-the-Sea is facing trying times. Sinclair Lewis predicted the future in 1933 when he said to Carmelites: "For God's sake, don't let the Babbits run the town. You've got every other city in the country beat." Growth—how much and what kind—is always the issue here. Tourists who come here to stroll and shop (locals sometimes refer to them as "the T-shirt and ice cream people") are both loved and hated.

In summer and on most warm-weather weekends, traffic on Hwy. 1 is backed up for a mile or more in either direction by the Carmel "crunch." Sane people take the bus, ride bikes, or walk to get here. This overly quaint community is so congested that parking is usually nonexistent. (Even if you do find a parking slot in downtown Carmel, you won't get to dawdle; parking is limited to one hour, and you'll risk a steep fine if you're late getting back.) Other scarce items in Carmel: streetlights, traffic signals, street signs, sidewalks, house numbers, mailboxes, neon signs, and jukeboxes.

SEEING AND DOING CARMEL

Out and About

To get oriented, take a walk. Carmel has a few tiny parks hidden here and there, including one especially for walkers—**Mission Trails Park,** featuring about five miles of trails winding through redwoods, willows, and wildflowers (in season). Finding it is challenging since Carmel doesn't believe in signs. To do the walk the easy way, start at the park's cleverly concealed Flanders Dr. entrance off Hatton Rd. (appreciate the **Lester Rowntree Memorial Arboretum** just inside) before strolling downhill to the Rio Rd. trailhead near the mission. Then visit the mission or head downtown. Carmel's shops and galleries alone are an easy day-long distraction for true shoppers, but local architecture is also intriguing. The area between Fifth and Eighth Sts. and Junipero and the city beach is packed with seacoast cottages, Carmel gingerbread "dollhouses," and adobe-and-post homes typical of the area.

Carmel Walks, tel. (831) 642-2700, www. carmelwalks.com, offers a great two-hour guided walk, with highlights including the town's original fairytale cottages, architecture by Bernard Maybeck and Charles S. Greene, onetime homes of the bohemians, the local doings of photographers Edward Weston and Ansel Adams, and oddities such as the house made entirely of doors and the one built from pieces of old ships. Well-behaved dogs (on leashes) are welcome, too, since the tour also visits Doris Day's pet-friendly hotel, includes tales of locally famous dogs, and notes local restaurants where dogs are permitted to dine with the family out on the patio. At last report walks—$15 per person, dogs free—were offered Tues.-Fri. at 10 a.m. and Saturday at 10 a.m. and 2 p.m. Reservations required.

CARMEL VALLEY AND PENINSULA WINERIES

Not surprising in such a moderate Mediterranean climate, vineyards do well here. So do wineries and wines, recognized as eight distinct appellations. To keep up with them all, pick up the free *Monterey Wine Country* brochure and map at area visitor centers, or contact the **Monterey County Vintners & Growers Association,** P.O. Box 1793, Monterey, CA 93942-1793, tel. (831) 375-9400, www.montereywines.org. Wine-related events well worth showing up for include the **Annual Winemakers' Celebration** in August and **The Great Wine Escape Weekend** in November. If you're short on touring time this trip, many Monterey County wines are available for tasting at **A Taste of Monterey,** 700 Cannery Row in Monterey, tel. (831) 646-5446, www.tastemonterey.com, open daily 11 a.m.-6 p.m.

The very small **Chateau Julien Winery,** 8940 Carmel Valley Rd., Carmel, CA 95923, tel. (831) 624-2600, www.chateaujulien.com, is housed in a French-style chateau and is open daily with tours on weekdays. The winery's chardonnay and merlot have both been honored as the best in the U.S. at the American Wine Championships in New York. Southwest of Carmel Valley and bordering Los Padres National Forest is the remote spring-fed "boutique" **Durney Vineyards,** owned by William Durney and his wife, screenwriter Dorothy Kingsley. The winery is not open to the public, but these organic wines are available for tasting in Carmel Valley Village at 69 W. Carmel Valley Rd., tel. (831) 659-6220 or toll-free (800) 625-8466, and are widely sold in Carmel, Monterey, and vicinity.

Bernardus Winery's tasting room, 5 W. Carmel Valley Rd., tel. (831) 659-1900, www.bernardus.com, is open 11 a.m.-5 p.m. daily. Also look around for other premium small-production wines, such as **Joullian Vineyards** (cabernet sauvignon, sauvignon blanc, merlot, zinfandel, and chardonnay). Joullian's new winery visitor center, located at 20300 Cachagua Rd., tel. (831) 659-2800, is open for tasting and sales Mon.-Fri. 11 a.m.-3 p.m., excluding holidays.

Between Greenfield and Soledad along the inland Hwy. 101 corridor are a handful of good wineries. The 1978 private reserve cabernet sauvignon of **Jekel Vineyards,** 40155 Walnut Ave., Greenfield, CA 93927, tel. (831) 674-5522 or (831) 674-5525 (tasting room), washed out Lafite-Rothschild and other international competitors in France in 1982. Tasting daily 10 a.m.-5 p.m. (appointments needed for tours or for groups of six or more). **Smith & Hook Winery-Hahn Estates** 37700 Foothill Blvd., Soledad, CA 93960, tel. (831) 678-2132, www. hahnestates.com, is known for its cabernet sauvignon—also for the amazing view across the Salinas Valley to the Gabilan Mountains. Open daily 11 a.m.-4 p.m. tours by appointment. Also in the area: **Chalone Vineyard** on Stonewall Canyon Rd. (Hwy. 146), tel. (831) 678-1717, www.chalonewinegroup.com, the county's oldest vineyard and winery, known for its estate-bottled varietals; and noted **Paraiso Springs Vineyard,** 38060 Paraiso Springs Rd., tel. (831) 678-0300, www.usawines.com/paraiso for tasting Mon.-Fri. noon-4 p.m., Sat.-Sun. 11 a.m.-5 p.m. (tours by appointment).

Farther north is small **Cloninger Cellars,** 1645 River Rd., Salinas, CA 93908, tel. (831) 675-9463, www.usawines.com/cloninger, which offers chardonnay, pinot noir, and cabernet sauvignon in its tasting room. Open for tasting Fri.-Mon. 11 a.m.-5 p.m., Tues.-Thurs. by appointment.

Also worth popping into in Salinas is **Morgan Winery,** 590 Brunken Ave., tel. (831) 751-7777, www.morganwinery.com, which has garnered a glut of gold medals and other recognition for its chardonnays. Winners here, too, are the cabernet, pinot noir, and sauvignon blanc.

True wine fanatics must make one more stop—at America's most award-winning vineyard, **Ventana Vineyards,** 2999 Monterey-Salinas Hwy. (near the Monterey Airport just outside Monterey on Hwy. 68), tel. (831) 372-7415, www.ventanawines.com. Open daily 11 a.m.-6 p.m.

Carmel Beaches

The downtown crescent of **Carmel Beach City Park** is beautiful—steeply sloping, blinding-white sands and aquamarine waters—but too cold and dangerous for swimming, and a tourist zoo in summer. (A winter sunset stroll is wonderful, though.) A better alternative is to take Scenic Rd. (or Carmelo St.) south from Santa Lucia off Rio Rd. to **Carmel River State Beach,** fringed with eucalyptus and cypress and often uncrowded (but dangerous in high surf). This is where locals go to get away. The nearby marsh is a bird sanctuary providing habitat for hawks, kingfishers, cormorants, herons, pelicans, sandpipers, snowy egrets, and sometimes flocks of migrating ducks and geese. Beyond (and almost a secret) is **Middle Beach,** a curving sandy crescent on the south side of the Carmel River and just north of **Monastery Beach** at San Jose Creek. Middle is accessible year-round by taking Ribera Rd. from Hwy. 1; in summer or fall you can also get there by walking across the dry riverbed and following the trail. Safety note: Middle Beach is hazardous for swimming and sometimes even for beachwalking, due to freak 10-foot waves. Monastery Beach is popular for scuba diving but its surf conditions are equally treacherous.

Carmel Mission

The Carmel Mission, properly called Mission Basilica San Carlos Borromeo del Rio Carmelo, is wonderful and well worth a visit. California's second mission, it was originally established at the Monterey Presidio in 1770, then moved here the following year. One-time headquarters and favorite foreign home of Father Junípero Serra, whose remains are buried at the foot of the altar in the sanctuary, the mission's magnificent vine-draped cathedral is the first thing to catch the eye. The romantic baroque stone church, one of the state's most graceful buildings, complete with four-bell Moorish tower, arched roof, and star-shaped central window, was completed in 1797.

Most of the buildings here are reconstructions, however, since the Carmel Mission fell to ruins in the 1800s. But these "new" old buildings, painstakingly rebuilt and restored in the 1930s under the direction of Sir Harry Downie, fail to suggest the size and complexity of the original bustling mission complex: an odd-shaped quadrangle with a central fountain, gardens, kitchen, carpenter and blacksmith shops, soldiers' housing, and priests' quarters. The native peoples attached to the mission—a labor force of 4,000 Christian converts—lived separately in a nearby village. More than 3,000 "mission Indians" are buried in the silent, simple cemetery. Most graves in these gardens are unmarked, but some are decorated with abalone shells. The gardens themselves, started by Downie, are fabulous: old-fashioned plant varieties, from bougainvillea to bird of paradise, fuchsias, and "tower of jewels."

The Carmel Mission has three museums. The "book museum" holds California's first unofficial library—the 600 volumes Padre Serra brought to California in 1769. The silver altar furnishings are also originals, as are the ornate vestments, Spanish and native artifacts, and other mission memorabilia. Serra's simple priest's cell is a lesson by contrast in modern materialism.

The mission is just a few blocks west of Hwy. 1 at 3080 Rio Rd., tel. (831) 624-3600 (gift shop) or (831) 624-1271 (rectory), and is open for self-guided tours Mon.-Sat. 9:30 a.m.-4:30 p.m., Sunday 10:30 a.m.-4:15 p.m. Admission is free, but donations are appreciated.

Robinson Jeffers's Tor House

A medieval-looking granite retreat on a rocky knoll above Carmel Bay, Tor House was built by family-man poet Robinson Jeffers, who hauled the huge stones up from the beach below with the help of other strong arms and horse teams. The manual labor, he said, cleared his mind and "my fingers had the art to make stone love stone." California's dark prince of poetry, Jeffers was generally aloof from the peninsula's other "seacoast bohemians." On the day he died here, January 20, 1962, it snowed—a rare event along any stretch of California's coast.

You can only begin to appreciate Tor House from the outside (it's just a short walk up from Carmel River Beach, on Ocean View Ave. between Scenic Rd. and Stewart Way). Jeffers built the three-story Hawk Tower, complete with secret passageway, for his wife, Una. The mellow redwood paneling, warm oriental rugs, and lovely gardens here soften the impact of the home's bleak tawny exterior, the overall effect somehow symbolizing Jeffers's hearth-centered life far removed from the world's insanity. Almost whimsical is the collection of 100-plus uni-

CALIFORNIA DEPARTMENT OF PARKS AND RECREATION

the poet Robinson Jeffers

corns the poet gathered. Tor House is still in-habited, so don't go snooping around. Small-group guided tours are offered Fri.-Sat., advance reservations required. Write Jeffers's Tor House, 26304 Ocean View Ave., P.O. Box 1887, Carmel, CA 93921, or call (831) 624-1813 or (831) 624-1840. You can also check them out online at www.torhouse.org. Adults $7, full-time college students $4, high school students $2. No children under 12.

STAYING IN CARMEL

Area Camping

Mary Austin's observation that "beauty is cheap here" may apply to the views, but little else in the greater Carmel area—with the exception of camping.

Carmel by the River RV Park, 27680 Schulte Rd. (off Carmel Valley Rd.), tel. (831) 624-9329, fax (831) 624-8416, is well away from it all—some 35 attractively landscaped sites right on the Carmel River, with full hookups, cable TV, laundromat, rec room, and other amenities. Budget-Inexpen-

sive. Nearby **Saddle Mountain Recreation Park,** also at the end of Schulte Rd., tel. (831) 624-1617, fax (831) 624-4470, offers both tent and RV sites, restrooms, showers, picnic tables, a swimming pool, playground, and other recreational possibil-ities—including nearby hiking trails. Budget. An-other possibility is **Veteran's Park** (see Monterey Camping and Low-Cost Alternatives above).

In the primitive-and-distant category, camp southeast of Carmel Valley at the U.S. Forest Service **White Oaks Campground,** seven sites, or **China Camp,** six sites; both are first-come, first-camped, and best suited for wilderness trekkers. Farther on you'll find **Tassajara Zen Mountain Center,** offering camping (and other accommodations) in summer by advance reser-vation—call (415) 865-1899 after April 1, or try www.sfzc.com for info—and the nearby Forest Service **Arroyo Seco Campground,** with 46 sites. Camping is also plentiful to the south in Big Sur. The Forest Service sites require pur-chase of a $5 daily (or $30 annual) Adventure Pass, available at Forest Service ranger stations and many sporting goods stores and other ven-dors. For more information on local Forest Ser-vice campgrounds, call the Monterey District of Los Padres National Forest at (831) 385-5434.

Expensive Stays

Wonderful is the only word for the historic **Pine Inn,** downtown on Ocean between Monte Verde and Lincoln, tel. (831) 624-3851 or toll-free (800) 228-3851, fax (831) 624-3030, www.pine-inn.com. This small hotel offers comfortable "Carmel Vic-torian" accommodations and fine dining at the on-site **Il Fornaio** restaurant and bakery; there's even a gazebo with rollback roof for eating al-fresco, fog permitting. Even if you don't stay, sit on the terrace, act affluent, and sip Ramos fizzes. Ex-pensive-Luxury.

The **Carmel River Inn,** 26600 Oliver Rd. (south of town on Hwy. 1 at the Carmel River Bridge), P.O. Box 221609, Carmel, CA 93922, tel. (831) 624-1575 or toll-free (800) 882-8142, fax (831) 624-0290, www.carmelriverinn.com, is a pleasant 10-acre riverside spread with a heated pool, 24 cozy family-friendly cottages and duplexes (some with wood-burning fire-places and kitchens), and 19 motel rooms. Two-night minimum stay on weekends. Pets wel-come, $25 per pet. Expensive-Luxury.

Other above-average Carmel accommodations—and there are plenty to choose from—include the **Carmel Oaks Inn,** Fifth and Mission, tel. (831) 624-5547 or toll-free (800) 266-5547, fax (831) 625-5908, attractive and convenient, a bargain by local standards, and the **Lobos Lodge,** Monte Verde and Ocean, tel. (831) 624-3874, fax (831) 624-0135.

Premium and Luxury Stays

The **Sundial Lodge,** Monte Verde and Seventh, tel. (831) 624-8578, is a cross between a small hotel and a bed and breakfast. Each of the 19 antique-furnished rooms has a private bath, TV, and telephone. Other amenities include lovely English gardens and courtyard, continental breakfast, and afternoon tea. Premium-Luxury.

The landmark 1929 **Cypress Inn,** downtown at Lincoln and Seventh, tel. (831) 624-3871 or toll-free (800) 443-7443, fax (831) 624-8216, www.cypress-inn.com, is a charming, gracious, and intimate place—another small hotel with a bed-and-breakfast sensibility, recently updated. Pets are allowed—invited, actually, since actress-owner Doris Day is an animal-rights activist. Dog beds provided. And when hotel staff places a mint on your pillow at turn-down, they'll also leave a treat for your dog or cat. How's *that* for service? Premium-Luxury. Continental breakfast.

Très Carmel, and a historic treasure, is the Mediterranean-style 1904 **La Playa Hotel,** Camino Real and Eighth, tel. (831) 624-6476 or toll-free (800) 582-8900, fax (831) 624-7966, where lush gardens surround guest rooms and cottages on the terraced hillside. Recently remodeled, rooms at La Playa feature evocative Spanish-style furnishings. The five cottages feature fireplaces, ocean-view decks, and separate living areas. Especially enjoyable when the gardens are in their glory is the on-site **Terrace Grill.** Premium-Luxury.

The luxurious **Adobe Inn,** downtown at Dolores and Eighth, tel. (831) 624-3933 or toll-free (800) 388-3933, features just about every amenity. Rooms include gas fireplaces, wet bars and refrigerators, patios or decks, color TVs, and phones; some have ocean views. Other amenities include a sauna and heated pool. Premium-Luxury.

Another option is the recently upgraded, 19-room Victorian-style **Chateau de Carmel** at Fifth and Junipero, tel. (831) 624-1900, (831) 624-8515 or toll-free (800) 325-8515, fax (831) 624-1571. Luxury.

Mission Ranch

Long the traditional place to stay, just outside town, is the Mission Ranch, 26270 Dolores (at 15th), tel. (831) 624-6436 or toll-free (800) 538-8221, fax (831) 626-4163. A quiet spread now owned by Clint Eastwood, Mission Ranch overlooks the Carmel River and features views of the Carmel River wetlands and Point Lobos. And the mission *is* nearby. With Eastwood ownership, the Victorian farmhouse and its outbuildings have had an expensive makeover, and together now resemble a Western village—a total of 31 guest rooms decorated here and there with props from Eastwood movies. Lodgings are available in the main house, the Hayloft, the Bunkhouse (which has its own living room and kitchen), and the Barn. The newer Meadow View Rooms feature, well, meadow views. Expensive-Luxury. Another attraction is the casual on-site **Restaurant at Mission Ranch,** tel. (831) 625-9040, which serves make-my-day American fare.

Bed and Breakfast Stays

Local inns offer an almost overwhelming amount of choice. (Keep in mind, what with the B&B craze, that "inn" in Carmel may be a code word for revamped motel.) Local bed-and-breakfast inns are comparable in price to most Carmel area motels, and they're usually much homier.

A Carmel classic is the ivy-draped **Stonehouse Inn,** Eighth and Monte Verde, tel. (831) 624-4569 or toll-free (877) 748-6618, www.carmelstonehouse.com, constructed by local Indians. All six rooms here are named after local luminaries, mostly writers, and all but two share bathrooms. Rates include full breakfast, wine and sherry, and hors d'oeuvres. Expensive-Luxury. The **Cobblestone Inn,** on Junipero near Eighth, tel. (831) 625-5222 or toll-free (800) 833-8836, fax (831) 625-0478, is a traditional Carmel home with a cobblestone courtyard, gas fireplaces in the guestrooms, and English country-house antiques. Rates include a full breakfast buffet, complimentary tea, and hors d'oeuvres. Expensive-Luxury.

The **Green Lantern Inn,** Eighth and Casanova, tel. (831) 624-4392, fax (831) 624-9591, offers 18 rustic multiunit cottages, some with lofts, others with fireplaces or sunset-viewing porches, not far from town or the beaches. Generous continental breakfast with fresh-squeezed juices served in the morning, wine and cheese in the afternoon. Expensive-Luxury. The Victorian **Sea View Inn,** on Camino Real between 11th and 12th, tel. (831) 624-8778, is three blocks from the beach and offers eight rooms, six with private bath, and antique-filled decor. Rates include continental breakfast as well as afternoon tea and cookies or sherry. Expensive-Premium. **The Homestead,** Lincoln and Eighth, tel. (831) 624-4119, rents rooms and cottages with private baths at easy-on-the-budget rates. Moderate-Expensive.

The pleasant **Carmel Wayfarer Inn,** Fourth Ave. at Mission St., tel. (831) 624-2711 or toll-free (800) 533-2711, fax (831) 625-1210, is now a bed and breakfast. Some rooms feature ocean views and kitchens, most have gas fireplaces. Rates include breakfast. Expensive-Premium. Most rooms at the 11-room **Vagabond House Inn,** Fourth and Dolores, tel. (831) 624-7738 or toll-free (800) 262-1262, fax (831) 626-1243, have fireplaces; some have kitchens. Continental breakfast is served in your room. Pets welcome. Expensive-Luxury.

STAYING IN CARMEL HIGHLANDS

The swank and well-known 1916 **Highlands Inn,** along Hwy. 1 four miles south of Carmel, tel. (831) 620-1234, toll-free (800) 682-4811 in California, or toll-free (800) 233-1234 (Hyatt central reservations), www.highlands-inn.com, is indeed beautiful, though many people would have to forfeit their rent or house payment to stay long. That may not be a problem much longer, though, since the Highlands Inn is now beginning to sell off its luxurious rooms and suites as timeshares—a reality not too popular with long-time guests—Quite luxurious, with some of the world's most spectacular views, some suites feature wood-burning fireplaces, double spa baths, fully equipped kitchens, and all the comforts. Luxury. Even those of more plebeian means can enjoy a stroll through the Grand Lodge to appreciate the oak woodwork, twin yellow granite fireplaces, gorgeous earth-toned carpet, leather sofas and chairs, and granite tables. Or stay for a meal. The exceptional **Pacific's Edge** features stunning sunset views and was a top-10 winner in *Wine Spectator* magazine's 1998 Reader's Choice Awards. Open for lunch, dinner, and Sunday brunch. The more casual **California Market** is open daily 7 a.m.-10 p.m.

The nearby **Tickle Pink Inn,** just south of the Highlands Inn at 155 Highlands Dr., tel. (831) 624-1244, (831) 624-1915, or toll-free (800) 635-4774, fax (831) 626-9516, www.ticklepink.com, offers equally spectacular views and 35 inviting rooms and suites, ocean-view hot tub, continental breakfast, and wine and cheese at sunset. Two-night minimum stay on weekends. Luxury.

STAYING IN CARMEL VALLEY

Robles del Rio Lodge, 200 Punta Del Monte, tel. (831) 659-3705 or toll-free (800) 883-0843, fax (831) 659-5157, www.bestlodgings.com/sites/roblesdelrio, perches atop a hill overlooking Carmel Valley and is reached via winding back roads—a bit hard to find the first time. Scheduled to reopen in summer 2000 following an extensive remodel, Robles del Rio is well worth the trip. There are pine-paneled rooms in the main lodge as well as outlying cabins. A stay here includes a fabulous continental breakfast served near the lodge fireplace—house-made muffins and pastries, fresh fruit, juices, soft-cooked eggs, and coffee. Other amenities include a pool, sauna, whirlpool, and tennis court. After its remodel, Robles del Rio will also feature a 12,000-square-foot health, wellness, and rejuvenation center. Call for current details and rates. Affiliated with the lodge is the excellent **The Ridge** restaurant, tel. (831) 659-0170.

In the meantime, a popular local tradition is the historic **Los Laureles Country Inn,** 313 W. Carmel Valley Rd., tel. (831) 659-2233 or toll-free (800) 533-4404, fax (831) 659-0481, once part of the Boronda Spanish land grant and later a Del Monte ranch. Rooms here used to be horse stables, for Muriel Vanderbilt's well-bred thoroughbreds. The inn has an excellent restaurant (American regional), pool, and conference facilities. Golf packages, too. Expensive-Luxury.

A great choice, too, is the **Carmel Valley Lodge** on Carmel Valley Rd. at Ford, tel. (831)

659-2261 or toll-free (800) 641-4646 (reservations only), fax (831) 659-4558, www.valleylodge.com. After all, who can resist "Come listen to your beard grow" as an advertising slogan? The Lodge features rooms fronting the lovely gardens plus one- and two-bedroom cottages with fireplaces and kitchens. Other amenities include a pool, sauna, hot tub, and fitness center. Dog friendly. Premium-Luxury.

But if you must see how the other one percent lives, head for the five-star **Quail Lodge Resort & Golf Club** at the Carmel Valley Golf and Country Club, 8205 Valley Greens Dr., tel. (831) 624-1581 or toll-free (800) 538-9516, fax (831) 624-3726. The lodge features elegant contemporary rooms and suites, some with fireplaces, plus access to private tennis and golf facilities and fine dining at **The Covey** restaurant. Luxury.

Pricey, too, in the same vein is **Carmel Valley Ranch Resort,** 1 Old Ranch Rd. (off Robinson Canyon Rd.), tel. (831) 625-9500 or toll-free (800) 4-CARMEL, fax (831) 624-2858, a gated resort with 100 suites, all individually decorated, with wood-burning fireplaces and private decks. Some suites feature a private outdoor hot tub. Recreation facilities include a private golf course, 12 tennis courts, pools, saunas, and whirlpools. Luxury.

Luxurious but still something of a new concept in Carmel Valley accommodations is the **Bernardus Lodge,** tel. (831) 659-3247 or toll-free (888) 648-9463, fax (831) 659-3131, www.bernardus.com, a luxury resort affiliated with the Bernardus Winery and open since August 1999. Crafted from limestone, logs, ceramic tiles, and rich interior woods, the nine village-style buildings feature 57 suites for "discriminating travelers" and offer endless luxury amenities, including a different wine-and-cheese tasting every night at turn-down, a full-service spa, and special educational forums on gardening, the culinary arts, and viticulture. On-site ballroom and restaurants. Outdoor recreation options include tennis and boccie ball, croquet, swimming, hiking and horseback riding on adjacent mountain trails, and golfing at neighboring resorts. Luxury.

Otherwise, for a super-luxury stay—and to avoid the country clubs and other "too new" places—the choice is the 330-acre **Stonepine Estate Resort,** 150 E. Carmel Valley Rd., tel.

(831) 659-2245, fax (831) 659-5160, www.stonepinecalifornia.com, once the Crocker family's summer home. A Carmel version of a French chateau, Stonepine features luxury suites in the manor house, Chateau Noel, and others in Briar Rose Cottage, the Gate House, and—for horse lovers—the Paddock House. Luxury.

For more information about Carmel Valley lodgings and restaurants, contact the Carmel Valley Chamber of Commerce, 91 W. Carmel Valley Rd., tel. (831) 659-4000.

EATING IN CARMEL

Great at Breakfast and Lunch

For a perfect omelette with home fries and homemade valley pork sausage, try **The Cottage,** on Lincoln between Ocean and Seventh, tel. (831) 625-6260. Also great for breakfast is **Katy's Place,** on the west side of Mission between Fifth and Sixth, tel. (831) 624-0199, another quaint cottage, this one boasting the largest breakfast and lunch menu on the West Coast. Great eggs Benedict. Open daily. Also cozy and crowded is **Em Le's,** Dolores and Fifth, tel. (831) 625-6780. Try the buttermilk waffles, available for lunch or dinner. The **Tuck Box** tearoom, on Dolores near Seventh, tel. (831) 624-6365, inspires you to stop, just to take a photograph. It was once famous for its pecan pie, shepherd's pie, and Welsh rarebit, as well as great cheap breakfasts. New owners have changed the menu—and prices.

More Good Food, at Lunch and Dinner

Everyone tries the **Hog's Breath Inn,** former mayor Clint Eastwood's rather famous Carmel eatery on San Carlos between Fifth and Sixth, tel. (831) 625-1044, presided over by—you guessed it—a hog's head. Though it was hibernating for a year or so following a partnership dissolution, as of May 2000 the Hog's Breath was breathing again, and probably still serving up billboard-sized images of Clint Eastwood, Dirty Harry burgers, and steak and seafood.

The **Rio Grill,** 101 Crossroads Blvd. (Hwy. 1 at Rio Rd.), tel. (831) 625-5436, is a long-running favorite for innovative Southwestern-style American fare. Everything is fresh and/or made from scratch, and many entrées are served straight from the oakwood smoker. Open for lunch and dinner daily, great Sunday brunch. Interesting, too, is inexpensive **From Scratch** restaurant at The Barnyard Shopping Center, tel. (831) 625-2448, a casual and eclectic place with local art on the walls. Open for breakfast and lunch daily, for dinner Tues.-Sat., and for brunch on Sunday.

A great choice at lunch, dinner, and weekend brunch is the **6th Avenue Grill,** on Sixth at Mission, tel. (831) 624-6562, serving California-style Mediterranean, from salads, sandwiches, and pastas at lunch to wild mushroom stew at dinner. The dinner specialty at the **Flying Fish Grill** at the Carmel Plaza shopping center, on Mission between Ocean and Seventh, tel. (831) 625-1962, is Pacific Rim seafood—from yin-yan salmon to peppered ahi tuna served with angel hair pasta. Both establishments serve beer and wine only. Another possibility for seafood is **Flaherty's,** on Sixth between Dolores and San Carlos, tel. (831) 625-1500 or (831) 624-0311, which offers just-off-the-boat-fresh catch of the day, along with great chowders and cioppino.

Fine for takeout pastries and desserts or a light French-country lunch is **Patisserie Boissiere,** on Mission between Ocean and Seventh, tel. (831) 624-5008. For good value and great food, the place is **Chez Christian Bistro & Restaurant,** on Ocean between Lincoln and Monte Verde, tel. (831) 625-4331, which offers a varied menu—everything from salads, pastas, fresh seafood, chicken, and steaks to the chef's specialty confit de canard, a classic French preparation of duck. French and California wines. Carmel boasts an outpost of **Ristorante Piatti,** too, on Sixth at Junipero, tel. (831) 625-1766, open daily for lunch and dinner. Locally popular for Italian and unpretentious is **La Dolce Vita,** on San Carlos between Seventh and Eighth, tel. (831) 624-3667, open daily for both lunch and dinner. Beer and wine.

Downtown's **China Gourmet,** on Fifth between San Carlos and Dolores, tel. (831) 624-3941, specializes in Mandarin and Szechuan cuisine, while **China Delight,** 133 Crossroads Blvd. (in the Crossroads Shopping Center), tel. (831) 624-3941, prepares Mandarin, Szechuan, and Cantonese dishes with no MSG.

Fine Dining

All the Carmels are crowded with "cuisine," some possibilities mentioned previously. Ask around if you're looking for the latest special dining experience. One of the more recent local stars is **Robert Kinkaid's Bistro,** an outpost of French-country atmosphere in the Crossroads Shopping Center, 217 Crossroads Blvd., tel. (831) 624-9626, brought to you by the chef behind Monterey's Fresh Cream. The stylish bistro fare includes such things as sautéed red snapper, roast duckling with sweet wild cherry sauce, and cassoulet à la Robert. Open for lunch on weekdays, dinner daily. Friendly **Sans Souci,** on Lincoln between Fifth and Sixth, tel. (831) 624-6220, is another fairly new French restaurant, this one serving both contemporary and classic fare. Full bar. **Crème Carmel Restaurant,** behind a liquor store on San Carlos between Ocean and Seventh, tel. (831) 624-0444, showcases the abundance of fresh local produce, herbs, seafood, and poultry with a light French touch. Nightly vegetarian plate, wonderful chocolate soufflé. Full bar. **The French Poodle,** Junipero and Fifth, tel. (831) 624-8643, still gets rave reviews for its light French cuisine, and the wine list is extensive. Those in the know say the venerable **L'Escargot,** Mission and Fourth, tel. (831) 624-4914, is one of the finest French restaurants on the peninsula.

Casanova, Fifth and Mission, tel. (831) 625-0501, serves both country-style French and Italian cuisine in a landmark local Mediterranean-style house (complete with heated garden seating for you temperature-sensitive romantics). House-made pastas here are exceptional, as are the desserts. Impressive wine list. Open daily for breakfast, lunch, and dinner. Equally popular, for its Northern Italian fare, is **Raffaello,** Mission between Ocean and Seventh, tel. (831) 624-1541, where the decor is intimate and the pasta sublime. Extensive wine list. Open for dinner nightly except Tuesday. Sophisticated yet simple too is **La Bohême,** Dolores and Seventh, tel. (831) 624-7500, a tiny, family-style place with French cuisine and European peasant fare for dinner. No reservations; call for the day's menu, or pick up the monthly calendar when you get to town. Open daily for dinner. Beer and wine. Elegant **Anton & Michel,** in the Court of the Fountains on Mission between Ocean and Seventh, tel. (831) 624-2406, isn't really that expensive considering the setting and good continental fare.

Even if you can't afford to stay there, you can probably afford to eat at the Highlands Inn, on Hwy. 1 south of Carmel. The inn's **California Market** restaurant, tel. (831) 622-5450, serves California regional dishes with fresh local ingredients. Ocean-view and deck dining, fabulous scenery. Open for breakfast, lunch, and dinner daily. In the considerably pricier category at the Highlands is the elegant and renowned **Pacific's Edge** restaurant, tel. (831) 622-5445, open for lunch, dinner, and Sunday brunch.

ENTERTAINING, EVENTFUL CARMEL

Entertaining Carmel

Sunsets from the beach or from craggy Point Lobos are entertainment enough for anyone. But the **Sierra Club** folks above the shoe store, on Ocean near Dolores, tel. (831) 624-8032, provide helpful information on hikes, sights, and occasional bike rides. Open Mon.-Sat. 12:30-4:30 p.m.

For live drama, the outdoor **Forest Theater,** Santa Rita and Mountain View, tel. (831) 626-1681, hosts light drama and musicals, Shakespeare, and concerts. (There's also an *indoor* **Forest Theater.**) The **Pacific Repertory Theatre Company** presents a variety of live stage productions at the Golden Bough Theatre, on Monte Verde between Eighth and Ninth; for information, call (831) 622-0100 (Tues.-Sat. noon-4 p.m.).

Carmel "proper" has laws prohibiting live music and leg-shaking inside the city limits. **Mission Ranch,** in the county 11 blocks out of town at 26270 Dolores, tel. (831) 625-9040, has a piano bar. Otherwise, you'll have to head into rowdy Monterey for dancing and prancing. But you can always go barhopping locally.

Eventful Carmel

June kicks off the theater season in Carmel. Right around the first of the month (or slightly before), the Pacific Repertory Theatre troupe opens its performance season, part of which is devoted to midsummer's **Carmel Shakespeare Festival.** Plays are presented at the Golden Bough Playhouse and other venues. The entire season runs through mid-October. The **Films in the Forest** theater series also gets under-

way in June at the outdoor Forest Theatre; call (831) 626-1681 for information.

Johann Sebastian Bach never knew a place like Carmel, but his spirit lives here nonetheless. From mid-July to early August, Carmel sponsors its traditionally understated **Bach Festival,** honoring J.S. and other composers of his era, with daily concerts, recitals, and lectures at the mission and elsewhere. If you're going, get your tickets *early.* For information: Carmel Bach Festival, P.O. Box 575, Carmel, CA 93921, tel. (831) 624-1521 or (831) 624-2046. Closer to performance dates, stop by the festival office at the Sunset Cultural Center, San Carlos at Ninth, from 11 a.m.-3 p.m.

At Carmel Beach, usually on a Sunday in late September or early October, the **Great Sandcastle Building Contest** gets underway. Events include "Novice" and "Advanced Sandbox." (Try getting the date from the Monterey Chamber of Commerce, as Carmel locals generally "don't know," just to keep the tourists away.) Also in October: the **Tor House Festival.** In December, the **Music for Christmas** series held at the Carmel Mission is quite nice. And special events take place from early in the month right up through Christmas eve during the **Carmel Lights Up the Season** festival.

CARMEL INFORMATION AND TRANSPORTATION

The *Carmel Pine Cone* newspaper covers local events and politics. The **Carmel Business Association** is upstairs in the Eastwood Building on San Carlos between Fifth and Sixth, P.O. Box 4444, Carmel, CA 93921, tel. (831) 624-2522. Its annual *Guide to Carmel* includes information on just about everything—from shopping hot spots to accommodations and eateries. The **Tourist Information Center,** Ocean and Mission, P.O. Box 7430, tel. (831) 624-1711, is quite helpful, and provides assistance with lodging reservations. There's also an **Information Center** at the Thunderbird Bookstore and Cafe in The Barnyard on Hwy. 1 near Rio Rd. just south of town. The **Carmel Valley Chamber of Commerce** is in the Oak Building at 71 W. Carmel Valley Rd., P.O. Box 288, Carmel Valley, CA 93924, tel. (831) 659-4000.

To get to Carmel from Monterey without car or bike, take Monterey-Salinas Transit bus No. 52 (24 hours), tel. (831) 899-2555.

POINT LOBOS

One of the crown jewels of California's state parks, Point Lobos State Reserve is a 1,250-acre coastal wonderland about four miles south of Carmel. Pack a picnic; this is the best the Monterey area has to offer. The relentless surf and wild winds have pounded these reddish shores for millennia, sculpting six miles of shallow aquamarine coves, wonderful tidepools, aptly named Bird Island, and jutting points: Granite, Coal, Chute, China, Cannery, Pinnacle, Pelican, and Lobos itself. From here, look to the sea, as Santa Cruz poet William Everson has, "standing in cypress and surrounded by cypress, watching through its witchery as the surf explodes in unbelievable beauty on the granite below." Local lore has it that Point Lobos inspired Robert Louis Stevenson's Spyglass Hill in *Treasure Island*. The muse for Robinson Jeffers's somber "Tamar" definitely lived (and lives) here.

a Point Lobos cypress

Seeing and Doing Point Lobos

From the dramatic headlands, watch for whales in winter. Many other marine mammals are year-round residents. Brown pelicans and cormorants preen themselves on offshore rocks. Here, the sea otters aren't shy: they boldly crack open abalone and dine in front of visitors. (The entire central coast area, from San Francisco south to beyond Big Sur, is protected as part of the **Monterey Bay National Marine Sanctuary.** If heading south into Big Sur country, watch offshore otter antics—best with binoculars—from highway turnouts.) Harbor seals hide in the coves.

whaler's cabin

TOM MYERS PHOTOGRAPHY

LISA ABBOTT

The languorous, loudly barking sea lions gave rise to the original Spanish name Punta de los Lobos Marinos ("Point of the Sea Wolves"). Follow the crisscrossing reserve trails for a morning walk through groves of naturally bonsaied Monterey cypress and pine, accented by colorful seasonal wildflowers (300 species, best in April). Watch for poison oak, which thrives here, too. Whaler's Cove near the picnic and parking area was once a granite quarry, then a whaler's cove—the cabin and cast-iron rendering pot are still there—and an abalone cannery. It's something of a miracle that the Point Lobos headland exists almost unscarred, as cattle grazed here for decades. Fortunately for us all, turn-of-the-last-century housing subdivision plans for Point Lobos were scuttled.

Safety First

Point Lobos is considered one of the state's "underwater parks," in recognition of its aquatic beauty. Scuba diving is popular but allowed by permit only; call (831) 624-8413 for reservations. Diver safety is a major concern of park staff. Get permits and current information about what to expect down below before easing into the water. Safety first for landlubbers, too: people aren't kidding when they mention "treacherous cliff and surf conditions" here, so think first before scrambling off in search of bigger and better tidepools. Particularly dangerous even in serene surf is the Monastery Beach area, near San Jose Creek just beyond the reserve's northern border; there's a steep offshore drop-off into submarine Carmel Canyon and unstable sand underfoot. Children should be carefully supervised, and even experienced divers and swimmers might think twice before going into the water.

Practical Point Lobos

Point Lobos is beautiful—and popular. It can be crowded in summer and sometimes on spring and fall weekends. Since only 450 people are allowed into the park at one time, plan your trip accordingly and come early in the day (or wait in long lines along Hwy. 1—not fun). Open for day use only (sunrise till sunset 9 a.m.-7 p.m. in summer, until 5 p.m. in winter), $7 per car, but free for walk-ins and bike-ins. Bikes must stay on pavement in the park—no trail riding.

You can also get to Point Lobos on Monterey-Salinas Transit's bus No. 22 (to Big Sur). From Carmel, it's a fairly easy bike ride. The weather can be cold, damp, and windy even in summer, so bring a sweater or jacket in addition to good walking shoes (and, if you have them, binoculars). The park's informative brochure is printed in five languages. Guided tours are offered daily.

To better appreciate local flora and the 200-plus species of birds spotted at Point Lobos, pick up the plant and bird lists at the ranger station. In May, the Department of Fish and Game's **Marine Resources and Marine Pollution Studies Laboratory** at Granite Canyon sponsors an open house. For more information, contact: Point Lobos State Reserve, Rt. 1 Box 62, Carmel, CA 93923, tel. (831) 624-4909.

TOM MYERS PHOTOGRAPHY

THE CENTRAL COAST

Along this swath of coastline where north becomes south, something in the air eventually transforms people into curmudgeons. The prevailing attitude is quite straightforward: *go away.* Henry Miller, one of the coast's crustiest and lustiest curmudgeons, believed the source of this sentiment was the land itself, speaking through its inhabitants. "And so it happens," he wrote from his home in Big Sur, "that whoever settles in this region tries to keep others from coming here. Something about the land makes one long to keep it intact—and strictly for oneself." And so it happens, like children denied candy or toys or the latest fashion fad, we want it all the more. The desire becomes altogether too great, and the rest of us can't stay away. In many ways the central coast's inherent inaccessibility is its greatest appeal. Yet there are other attractions, particularly farther south.

See color maps of the Central Coast at front of book.

Cruising the Central Coast

Just south of ruggedly aloof Big Sur is famous "Hearst Castle," now known formally as Hearst San Simeon State Historic Monument—the monumental 144-room monument to media magnate William Randolph Hearst, his wealth, and his whimsy, one of the state's most popular visitor attractions. Always worth a stop, next south, is the scenic coastal town of Cambria, with its lush Monterey pines, galleries, and shops considered by some the Carmel of the southern Big Sur coast.

The biggest city immediately south from San Simeon is San Luis Obispo, a convenient stop halfway between L.A. and San Francisco along Hwy. 101 and most famous for inventing both the word and the modern concept of "motel," a contraction of "motor hotel." Agriculture is big business in and around San Luis Obispo, a fact reflected in the prominent presence of the well-respected California State Polytechnic University, also known as Cal Poly or (snidely) "Cow Poly." Pick up an "Ag's My Bag" bumpersticker as a souvenir or—if you can time your trip appropriately—roll into town on a Thursday evening to enjoy the Higuera Street Farmers' Market, one of the best anywhere (cancelled only in the event of rain).

Well worth going out of your way to find is Mission San Antonio de Padua, inland from the coast and north of San Luis Obispo, located smack-dab in the middle of Fort Hunter-Liggett (security check at the base gate). Not the grandest or most spruced-up, San Antonio de Padua is perhaps the most genuinely evocative of all the California missions. Nearby Lake San Antonio is popular in winter for guided bald eagle-watching tours.

Off in the other direction, via Hwy. 58, is the Carrizo Plain Preserve, earthquake territory once sacred to the Chumash people. The native grasses and shrub lands surrounding Soda Lake offer refuge to some of the state's most endangered animal species. And if you head east from Paso Robles toward the San Joaquin Valley via Hwy. 46, you'll come to the shrine marking (almost) the spot where actor James Dean (Rebel Without a Cause, Giant, and East of Eden) died in a head-on car accident in 1955. Paso Robles itself and nearby Templeton anchor an increasingly popular—and increasingly impressive—wine region.

Morro Rock, California's little Gibraltar, spotted by Cabrillo in 1542, is the first thing people notice at Morro Bay on the coast west of San Luis Obispo. But the Morro Bay Chess Club maintains its giant outdoor chessboard downtown, and Morro Bay State Park, Montana de Oro State Park, and area beaches are also worth exploring. The one-time port towns and piers along San Luis Obispo Bay to the south also have their attractions, including the famous F. McClintock's Saloon and Dining House on Hwy. 101 in Pismo Beach, famous for its performance art, courtesy of the wait staff—who fill your glasses (without spilling, usually) pouring from a pitcher held several feet in the air—and infamous for its fried turkey nut appetizers.

Santa Maria just over the border in Santa Barbara County is most noted for its own unique culinary heritage, this one preserved since the days of the vaqueros. This is the hometown of "Santa Maria Barbecue," a complete meal that traditionally includes slabs of prime sirloin barbecued over a slow red-oak fire then sliced as

thin as paper, served with *salsa cruda,* pinquito beans, salad, toasted garlic bread, and dessert. Near town is the Guadalupe-Nipomo Dunes Preserve, a coastal wildlife and plant preserve also protecting the remains of Cecil B. DeMille's *The Ten Commandments* movie set, buried under the sand here once filming was finished.

Lompoc is noted for its blooming flower fields—this is a major seed-producing area—and is home to Vandenberg Air Force Base as well as Mission La Purisima State Historic Park four miles east of town, California's only complete mission compound.

Farther south, Solvang is a Danish-style town founded in 1911 and now a well-trod tourist destination. If you've got time, worth exploring nearby are the towns of Los Olivos and Los Alamos, center of northern Santa Barbara County's impressive wine country.

Technically speaking, Point Conception just below Vandenberg marks the spot where California turns on itself—that pivotal geographical point where Northern California becomes Southern California, where rugged and rocky coastline gives way to broad white sandy beaches. The climatic and terrain changes are unmistakable by the time you arrive in Santa Barbara, a richly endowed city noted for its gracious red-tile-roofed California Spanish-style buildings—for the most part an architectural affectation subsequent to the devastating 1925 earthquake. Attractions include the Santa Barbara County Courthouse; Mission Santa Barbara, "Queen of the Missions"; the Santa Barbara Museum of Natural History; and the Santa Barbara Botanic Gardens. Despite the presence of offshore oil wells, public beaches in the area are sublime.

Continue south from Santa Barbara to Ventura to set off on whalewatching trips and guided boat tours of California's Channel Islands National Park, often visible from Santa Barbara and vicinity.

A CONTRARY COAST

The land itself is unfriendly, at least from the human perspective. Especially in the north, the indomitable unstable terrain—with its habit of sliding out from under whole hillsides, houses, highways, and hiking trails at the slightest provocation—has made the area hard to inhabit. Despite its contrariness, the central coast, that unmistakable pivotal point between California's north and south, successfully blends both.

The Great Transition

Though the collective Coast Ranges continue south through the region, here the terrain takes on a new look. The redwoods thin out, limiting themselves to a few large groves in Big Sur country and otherwise straggling south a short distance beyond San Simeon, tucked into hidden folds in the rounded coastal mountains. Where redwood country ends, either the grasslands of the dominant coastal oak woodlands begin or the chaparral takes over, in places almost impenetrable. Even the coastline reflects the transition—the rocky rough-and-tumble shores along the Big Sur coast transform into tamer beaches and bluffs near San Simeon and points south.

Los Padres National Forest inland from the coast is similarly divided into two distinct sections. The northernmost (and largest) Monterey County section includes most of the rugged 100-mile-long Santa Lucia Range and its Ventana Wilderness. The southern stretch of Los Padres, essentially the San Luis Obispo and Santa Barbara backcountry, is often closed to hikers and backpackers during the summer due to high fire danger. This area includes the southern extension of the Santa Lucias, the La Panza Range, the Sierra Madre Mountains, also the San Rafael

Wilderness and a portion of the San Rafael Mountains. Farther south but still in Los Padres National Forest are the Santa Ynez Mountains east of Santa Barbara, angling northwest to Point Arguello near Lompoc, and part of the unusual east-west Transverse Ranges that create the geographic boundary between north-central and Southern California.

Another clue is that the north-south transition occurs here is water or, moving southward, the increasingly obvious lack of it. Though both the North and South Forks of the Little Sur River, the Big Sur River a few miles to the south, and other northern waterways flow to the sea throughout the year, as does the Cuyama River in the south (known as the Santa Maria River as it nears the ocean), most of the area's streams are seasonal. But off-season hikers, beware: even inland streams with a six-month flow are not to be dismissed during winter and spring, when deceptively dinky creekbeds can become death-dealing torrents overnight.

Major lakes throughout California's central coast region are actually water-capturing reservoirs, including Lake San Antonio, known for its winter bald eagle population, Lake Nacimiento on the other side of the mountains from San Simeon, and Santa Margarita Lake east of San Luis Obispo near the headwaters of the Salinas River. Other popular regional reservoirs include Lopez Lake southeast of San Luis Obispo and Lake Cachuma near Santa Barbara.

BIG SUR AND FALLING METEORS

The poet Robinson Jeffers described this redwood-and-rock coast as "that jagged country which nothing but a falling meteor will ever plow." It's only fitting, then, that this area was called Jeffers Country long before it became known as Big Sur. Sienna-colored sandstone and granite, surly waves, and the sundown sea come together in a never-ending dance of creation and destruction. Writer Henry Miller said Big Sur was "the face of the earth as the creator intended it to look," a point hard to argue. But Big Sur as a specific *place* is difficult to locate. It's not only a town, a valley, and a river—the entire coastline from just south of Carmel Highlands to somewhere north of San Simeon (some suggest the

southern limit is the Monterey County line) is considered Big Sur country.

Once "in" Big Sur, wherever that might be, visitors notice some genuine oddities—odd at least by California standards. Until recently most people here didn't have much money and didn't seem to care. (This is changing as the truly wealthy move in.) They built simple or unusual dwellings—redwood cabins, glass tepees and geodesic domes, even round redwood houses with the look of wine barrels ready to roll into the sea—both to fit the limited space available but also to express that elusive Big Sur sense of *style*.

Because the terrain itself is so tormented and twisted, broadcast signals rarely arrive in Big Sur.

In the days before satellite dishes there was virtually no TV; electricity and telephones with dial service have only been available in Big Sur since the 1950s, and some people along the south coast and in more remote areas still have neither.

Social life in Big Sur consists of bowling at the naval station, attending a poetry reading or the annual Big Sur Potluck Revue at the Grange Hall in the valley, driving into "town" (Monterey) for a few movie cassettes, or—for a really wild night—drinks on the deck at sunset and dancing cheek to cheek at Nepenthe. Big Sur is a very *different* California, where even the chamber of commerce urges visitors "to slow down, meditate," and "catch up with your soul."

It's almost impossible to catch up with your soul, however, when traffic is bumper-to-bumper. Appreciating Big Sur while driving or, only for the brave, bicycling in a mile-long coastline convoy is akin to honeymooning in Hades—a universal impulse but entirely the wrong ambience. As it snakes through Big Sur, California's Coast Highway (Hwy. 1), the state's first scenic highway and one of the world's most spectacular roadways, slips around the prominent ribs of the Santa Lucia Mountains, slides into dark wooded canyons, and soars across graceful bridges spanning the void. Though its existence means that a trip into Monterey no longer takes an entire day, people here nonetheless resent the highway that brings the flamed-out and frantic.

To show some respect, come to Big Sur during the week, in balmy April or early May when wildflowers burst forth, or in late September or October to avoid the thick summer fog. Though winter is generally rainy, weeks of sparkling warm weather aren't uncommon. In April, Big Sur hosts the annual **Big Sur International Marathon,** with 1,600 or more runners hugging the highway curves from the village to Carmel.

THE BIG SUR STORY

The earliest Big Sur inhabitants, the Esselen people, once occupied a 25-mile-long and 10-mile-wide stretch of coast from Point Sur to near Lucia in the south. A small group of Ohlone, the Sargenta-Ruc, lived from south of the Palo Colorado Canyon to the Big Sur River's mouth. Though most of the area's Salinan peoples lived inland in the Salinas Valley near what is now Fort Hunter-Liggett, villages were also scattered along the Big Sur coast south of Lucia. Little is known about area natives, since mission-forced intertribal marriages and introduced diseases soon obliterated them. It is known, though, that the number of Esselens in Big Sur was estimated at between 900 and 1,300 when the Spanish arrived after 1770 and that the Esselen people lived in the Big Sur Valley at least 3,000 years ago.

The Esselen people were long gone by the time the first area settlers arrived. Grizzly bears were the greatest 18th-century threat to settlement, since the terrain discouraged any type of travel and the usual wildlife predation that came with it. The name Big Sur ("Big South" in Spanish, a reference point from the Monterey perspective) comes from Rio Grande del Sur, or the Big Sur River, which flows to the sea at Point Sur. The river itself was the focal point of the 1834 Mexican land grant and the Cooper family's Rancho El Sur until 1965.

Then, in the early 1900s came the highway, a hazardous 15-year construction project between Big Sur proper and San Simeon. Hardworking Chinese laborers were recruited for the job along with less willing workers from the state's prisons. The highway was completed in 1937, though many lives and much equipment were lost to the sea. Maintaining this remote ribbon of highway and its 29 bridges is still a treacherous year-round task. Following the wild winter storms of 1982-83, for example, 42 landslides blocked the highway; the "big one" near Julia Pfeiffer Burns State Park took 19 bulldozers and more than a year to clear.

Big Sur's Semi-Civil Wars and Big Surbanization
Today only 1,300 people live in Big Sur country—just 300 more than in the early 1900s. Yet "Big Surbanization" is underway. Land not included in Los Padres National Forest and the Ventana Wilderness is largely privately owned. Plans for more hotels, restaurants, and civilized comforts for frazzled travelers continue to come up, and the eternal, wild peace Robinson Jeffers predicted would reign here forever has at last been touched by ripples of civilization. Nobody wants the character of Big Sur to change, but people can't agree on how best to save it.

As elsewhere in California, some Big Sur landowners believe that private property rights are sacrosanct, beyond the regulation of God or the government. Others argue that state and local land-use controls are adequate. Still others contend that federal intervention is necessary, possibly granting the region "scenic area" or national park status—an idea fought sawtooth and nail by most residents. The reason Big Sur is still ruggedly beautiful, they say, is because local people have kept it that way. A favorite response to the suggestion of more government involvement: "Don't Yosemitecate Big Sur." In March 1986, both of California's senators proposed that the U.S. Forest Service take primary responsibility for safeguarding Big Sur's scenic beauty—with no new logging, mining claims, or grazing privileges allowed. The final result, which limits but doesn't eliminate new development, seems to please almost everyone.

DOING BIG SUR

The ultimate activity in Big Sur is just bumming around: scrambling down to beaches to hunt for jade and peer into tidepools or scuba dive or surf where it's possible, also cycling, sightseeing, and watching the sun set. Along the coastline proper there are few long hiking trails, since

---

THE ESALEN INSTITUTE

The Esselen and Salinan peoples frequented the hot springs here, supposedly called *tok-i-tok,* "hot healing water." In 1939, Dr. H.C. Murphy (who officiated at John Steinbeck's birth in Salinas) opened Slate's Hot Springs resort on the site. The hot springs were transformed by grandson Michael Murphy into the famed Esalen Institute, where human-potential practitioners and participants including Joan Baez, Gregory Bateson, the Beatles, Jerry Brown, Carlos Castaneda, Buckminster Fuller, Aldous Huxley, Linus Pauling, B.F. Skinner, Hunter S. Thompson, and Alan Watts taught or learned in residential workshops.

Esalen is the Cadillac of New Age retreats, according to absurdist/comedian/editor Paul Krassner. Even writer Alice Kahn who, before arriving at Esalen, considered herself the "last psycho-virgin in California" and "hard-core unevolved," eventually admitted that there was something about the Esalen Institute that defied all cynicism.

Esalen's magic doesn't necessarily come cheap. The introductory "Experiencing Esalen" weekend workshop runs $485 or so, including simple but pleasant accommodations and wonderful meals ($230 if a sleeping bag is all you'll need). Five-day workshops are substantially more—in the $750-and-up range. But Esalen tries to accommodate even the less affluent with scholarships, a work-study program, senior citizen discounts, family rates, and bunk bed or sleeping bag options. You can also arrange just an overnight or weekend stay (sans enlightenment) assuming space is available.

Esalen offers more than 400 workshops each year, these "relating to our greater human capacity." Topics cover everything from the arts and creative expression to "intellectual play," from dreams to spiritual healing, from martial arts to shamanism. Equally mythic are Esalen's baths. In February 1998 a mudslide roared down the hill to demolish the previous bathhouse facilities, though an ambitious rebuilding project is now underway. The new, improved Esalen baths, scheduled to open in late 2000, will include a geothermally heated swimming pool and a handicapped-accessible hot tub and massage area. In the meantime, Esalen's "temporary baths" are available—but only to Esalen guests. When the new bath house opens, Esalen will again satisfy the California Coastal Commission's public access requirement, by allowing the general public access to the hot tubs (at the fairly unappealing hours of 1-3 a.m. daily). Call for details. The massages at Esalen are world-renowned, from $50 an hour. Nudity is big at Esalen, particularly in the hot tubs, swimming pool, and massage area, though not required.

Entrance to Esalen and its facilities is strictly by reservation only. For information on workshops and lodgings and to request a copy of Esalen's current catalog, contact: Esalen Institute, Big Sur, CA 93920, tel. (831) 667-3000, www.esalen.org. The website's online *In the Air* magazine offers a good sense of what Esalen is all about, and also includes a complete current workshop catalog (which you can download). To make workshop reservations, call (831) 667-3005 or fax completed registration forms to (831) 667-2724.

much of the terrain is treacherous and most of the rest privately owned, but the Big Sur backcountry offers good hiking and backpacking.

Ventana Wilderness

Local lore has it that a natural land bridge once connected two mountain peaks at Bottchers Gap, creating a window (or *ventana* in Spanish) until the 1906 San Francisco earthquake brought it all tumbling down. The Big Sur, Little Sur, Arroyo Seco, and Carmel Rivers all cut through this 161,000-acre area, creating dramatic canyon gorges and wildlands well worth exploring. Steep, sharp-crested ridges and serrated V-shaped valleys are clothed mostly in oaks, madrones, and dense chaparral. Redwoods grow on north-facing slopes near the fog-cooled coast, pines at higher elevations. The gnarly spiral-shaped bristlecone firs found only here are in the rockiest, most remote areas, their total range only about 12 miles wide and 55 miles long.

Most of all, the Ventana Wilderness provides a great escape from the creeping coastal traffic (a free visitor permit is required to enter), and offers great backpacking and hiking when the Sierra Nevada, Klamath Mountains, and Cascades are still snowbound—though roads here are sometimes impassible during the rainy season. Hunting, fishing, and horseback riding are also permitted. Crisscrossing Ventana Wilderness are nearly 400 miles of backcountry trails and 82 vehicle-accessible campgrounds (trailside camping possible with a permit).

The wilderness trailheads are at Big Sur Station, Carmel River, China Camp, Arroyo Seco, Memorial Park, Bottchers Gap, and Cone Peak Road. The Ventana Wilderness recreation map, available for $4 from ranger district offices, shows all roads, trails, and campgrounds. Fire-hazardous areas, routinely closed to the public after July 1 (or earlier), are coded yellow on maps.

Trail and campground traffic fluctuates from year to year, so solitude seekers should ask rangers about more remote routes and destinations. Since the devastating Marble Cone fire of 1978 (and other more recent fires), much of what once was forest is now chaparral and brushland. As natural succession progresses, dense undergrowth obliterates trails not already erased by erosion. Despite dedicated volunteer trail work, lack of federal trail maintenance has also taken its toll.

Backcountry travelers should also take care to heed fire regulations. Because of the high fire danger in peak tourist season, using a campstove or building a fire outside designated campgrounds requires a fire permit. Also, bring water—but think twice before bringing Fido along, since flea-transmitted plague is a possibility. Other bothersome realities include ticks (especially in winter and early spring), rattlesnakes, poison oak, and fast-rising rivers and streams following rainstorms.

Big Sur Hikes

The grandest views of Big Sur come from the ridges just back from the coast. A great companion is *Hiking the Big Sur Country* by Jeffrey P. Schaffer (Wilderness Press). The short but steep **Valley View Trail** from Pfeiffer-Big Sur State Park is usually uncrowded, especially midweek; there are benches up top for sitting and staring off the edge of the world. Those *serious* about coastal hiking should walk all the way from Pfeiffer-Big Sur to Salmon Creek near the southern Monterey County line. The trip from Bottchers Gap to Ventana Double Cone via **Skinner Ridge Trail** is about 16 miles one way and challenging, with a variety of possible campsites, dazzling spring wildflowers, and oak and pine forests.

Otherwise, take either the nine-mile **Pine Ridge Trail** from Big Sur or the 15-mile trail from China Camp on Chews Ridge to undeveloped Sykes Hot Springs, just 400 yards from Sykes Camp (very popular these days). Another good, fairly short *visual* hike is the trip to nearby Mount Manuel, a nine-mile roundtrip. The two-mile walk to **Pfeiffer Beach** is also worth it—miles from the highway, fringed by forest, with a wading cove and meditative monolith.

Big Sur Back Roads

For an unforgettable dry-season side trip, a true joy ride, take the **Old Coast Road** from just north of the Bixby Bridge inland to the Big Sur Valley: barren granite, a thickly forested gorge, and good views of sea and sky before the road loops back to Hwy. 1 south of Point Sur near the entrance to Andrew Molera State Park. **Palo**

Colorado Road, mostly unpaved and narrow, winds through a canyon of redwoods, ferns, and summer homes, up onto hot and dry Las Piedras Ridge, then down into the Little Sur watershed.

Marvelous for the sense of adventure as well as the views is a drive along the **Nacimiento-Fergusson Road** from the coast inland to what's left of old Jolon and the fabulous nearby mission, both included within the Fort Hunter-Liggett Military Reservation. (Taking this route is always somewhat risky, particularly on weekends, since all roads through Hunter-Liggett are closed when military exercises are underway.) Even more thrilling is driving rough-and-ready **Los Burros Road** farther south, an unmarked turnoff just south of Willow Creek and Cape San Martin that leads to the long-gone town of Manchester in the Los Burros gold mining district; an indestructible vehicle and plenty of time is required for this route, and it's often closed to traffic after winter storms.

Big Sur back roads leading to the sea are rarer and easy to miss. About one mile south of the entrance to Pfeiffer-Big Sur State Park is **Sycamore Canyon Road,** which winds its way downhill for two exciting miles before the parking lot near Pfeiffer Beach. At Willow Creek there's a road curling down from the vista point to the rocky beach below, and just south of Willow Creek a dirt road leads to Cape San Martin (good for views any day but especially fine for whalewatching).

SEEING BIG SUR

Garrapata and Point Sur State Parks

Garrapata State Park stretches north along the coast for more than four miles from Soberanes Point, where the Santa Lucia Mountains first dive into the sea. Southward, the at-first unimpressive **Point Sur** and its lighthouse beacon stand out beyond 2,879-acre Garrapata State Park and beach, the latter named after the noble wood tick and featuring a crescent of creek-veined white sand, granite arches, caves and grottos, and sea otters. Ticks or no ticks, the unofficial nude beach here is one of the best in Northern California. Winter whalewatching is usually good from high ground. On weekends in January, ranger-led whalewatch programs are held at Granite Canyon. Or, if it's not foggy, take the two-mile loop trail from the turnout for the view.

For more information about the park, call the **Big Sur Station** State Parks/U.S. Forest Service office at (831) 667-2315.

South of Garrapata and inland is private **Palo Colorado Canyon,** reached via the road of the same name. Dark and secluded even in summer, the canyon is often cut off from the rest of the world when winter storms stomp through. The name itself is Spanish for "tall redwood." About eight miles in at the end of the road is isolated **Bottchers Gap Campground,** complete with restrooms, picnic tables, and multiple

CALIFORNIA DEPARTMENT OF PARKS AND RECREATION

Point Sur lighthouse

trailheads into the Ventana Wilderness. A few miles farther south on the highway is the famous **Rainbow Bridge** (now called Bixby Creek Bridge), 260 feet high and 700 feet long, the highest single-arch bridge in the world when constructed in 1932 and still the most photographed of all Big Sur bridges.

Point Sur State Historic Park

Up atop Point Sur stands the Point Sur Lightstation, an 1889 sandstone affair still standing guard at this shipwreck site once known as the Graveyard of the Pacific. In the days when the only way to get here was on horseback, 395 wooden stair steps led to the lighthouse, originally a giant multiwick kerosene lantern surrounded by a Fresnel lens with a 16-panel prism. The Point Sur Lightstation is now computer-operated and features an electrical aero-beacon, radio-beacon, and fog "diaphone." This 34-acre area and its central rocky mound (good views and whale-watching) is now a state park, though the Coast Guard still maintains the lighthouse. Guided three-hour lighthouse walking tours ($5) are offered five or six times a week in summer, three times weekly in winter. Current tour information is posted throughout Big Sur, or call (831) 625-4419. For information about winter whalewatching programs here and at both Garrapata and Julia Pfeiffer Burns State Parks, call (831) 667-2315.

Andrew Molera State Park

Inland and up, past what remains of the pioneering Molera Ranch (part of the original Rancho El Sur), is marvelous Andrew Molera State Park, a 2,100-acre park first donated to the Nature Conservancy by Frances Molera in honor of her brother, then deeded to the state for management. There's no pavement here, just a rundown dirt parking lot and a short trail winding through sycamores, maples, and a few redwoods along the east fork of the Big Sur River to the two-mile beach and adjacent seabird-sanctuary lagoon below. (The big breakers cresting along the coast here are created by the Sur Breakers Reef.) The trail north of the river's mouth leads up a steep promontory to Garnet Beach, noted for its colorful pebbles. Except when firefighting crews are camped here and on major holiday weekends, it's usually uncrowded at Andrew Molera.

Among its other attractions, the park also features a primitive yet peaceful 10-acre walk-in campground just one-quarter mile from the parking lot (three-night limit, $3 per person, dogs allowed only with leash and proof of current rabies vaccination). For more information about the park, contact: Andrew Molera State Park, P.O. Box A, Big Sur, CA 93920, tel. (831) 667-2315.

Also at the park: **Molera Horseback Tours,** P.O. Box 111, Big Sur, CA 93920, tel. (831) 625-5486 or toll-free (800) 942-5486, which offers regularly scheduled one- to three-hour rides along the beach and through meadows and redwood groves. Guides explain the history, flora, and fauna of the area. Private rides are also available by appointment. Rates are $25-35 an hour.

Pfeiffer-Big Sur State Park

Inland on the other side of the ridge from Andrew Molera State Park is protected, sunny Big Sur Valley, a visitor-oriented settlement surrounding picnic and camping facilities at 821-acre Pfeiffer-Big Sur State Park adjoining the Ventana Wilderness. Take the one-mile nature trail or meander up through the redwoods to **Pfeiffer Falls,** a verdant, fern-lined canyon at its best in spring and early summer, then on up to **Valley View** for a look at the precipitous Big Sur River gorge below. Redwoods, sycamores, big-leaf maples, cottonwoods, and willows hug the river, giving way to oaks, chaparral, and Santa Lucia bristlecone fir at higher elevations. There's abundant poison oak, and raccoons can be particularly pesky here, like the begging birds, so keep food out of harm's way.

To hike within the Ventana Wilderness, head south on the highway one-half mile to the U.S. Forest Service office (where trails begin), tel. (831) 667-2315, for a permit and current information. About a mile south of the entrance to Pfeiffer-Big Sur is the road to Los Padres National Forest's **Pfeiffer Beach** (take the second right-hand turnoff after the park) and its cypresses, craggy caves, and mauve and white sands streaked with black. It's heaven here on a clear, calm day, but the hissing sand stings mercilessly when the weather is up. On any day, forget the idea of an ocean swim. The water's cold, the surf capricious, and the currents tricky; even expert divers need to register with rangers before jumping in. Pfeiffer Beach is open to the public 6 a.m.-sunset.

RICH THOMPSON

Venturing into one of the Big Sur River Gorge's swimming holes calls for extremely warm weather.

The outdoor amphitheater at Pfeiffer-Big Sur State Park (which hosts many of the park's educational summer campfires and interpretive programs) and lagoons were built by the Civilian Conservation Corps during the Depression. The large developed year-round campground has more than 200 campsites with picnic tables and hot showers ($16 per night). To make reservations—advisable in summer, when the park is particularly crowded, and on good-weather weekends—call ReserveAmerica, tel. (800) 444-7275. The day-use fee for short park hikes and picnicking is $5. For more information, contact: Pfeiffer-Big Sur State Park, Big Sur, CA 93920, tel. (831) 667-2315.

Urban Big Sur

Nowhere in Big Sur country are visitors really diverted from the land because big-time boutiques, gaudy gift shops, even movie theaters don't exist. But urban Big Sur starts at Big Sur Valley and stretches south past the post office and U.S. Forest Service office to Deetjen's Big Sur Inn. This "big city" part of Big Sur includes the area's most famous inns and restaurants: the Ventana Inn, Nepenthe, and Deetjen's (see Big Sur Practicalities below). Fascinating about Nepenthe is the fact that although cinematographer Orson Welles was persona non grata just down the coast at San Simeon (for his too-faithful portrayal of William Randolph Hearst in *Citizen Kane*), when he bought what was then the Trails Club Log Cabin in Big Sur for his wife Rita Hayworth in

1944, he was able to haunt Hearst from the north. Welles's place became Nepenthe ("surcease from sorrows") shortly after he sold it in 1947.

South of Deetjen's is the noted **Coast Gallery** at Lafler Canyon (named for editor Henry Lafler, a friend of Jack London), tel. (831) 667-2301, open daily 9 a.m.-5 p.m. Rebuilt from redwood water tanks in 1973, the Coast Gallery offers fine local arts and crafts, from jewelry and pottery to paintings (including watercolors by Henry Miller), sculpture, and woodcarvings. Nearby is the **Henry Miller Memorial Library,** a collection of friendly clutter about the writer and his life's work, located on the highway about one mile south of the Ventana Inn but almost hidden behind redwoods and an unassuming redwood double gate. Henry Miller lived, wrote, and painted in Big Sur 1944-1962. The library is housed not in Henry Miller's former home but in that of the late Emil White. A good friend of Miller's, White said he started the library "because I missed him." Now a community cultural arts center, the library sponsors exhibits, poetry readings, concerts, and special events throughout the year. Original art and prints, posters, and postcards are available in the gallery. Miller's books, including rare editions, are also available. In summer the library is often open daily, but year-round is always open on weekends, 11 a.m.-6 p.m., and for special events. For current information, contact: **Henry Miller Library,** Hwy. 1, Big Sur, CA 93920, tel./fax (831) 667-2574, www.henrymiller.org. Or call the county library at (831) 667-2537.

Julia Pfeiffer Burns State Park

Partington Cove is about one mile south of Partington Ridge, the impressive northern boundary of Julia Pfeiffer Burns State Park. To get down to the cove, park on the east side of the highway and head down the steep trail that starts near the fence (by the black mailbox) on the west side of the road. The branching trail leads back into the redwoods to the tiny beach at the stream's mouth, or across a wooden footbridge, through a rock tunnel hewn in the 1880s by pioneer John Partington, and on to the old dock where tan bark was once loaded onto seagoing freighters. A fine place for a smidgen of inspirational solitude.

There's a stone marker farther south at the park's official entrance, about seven miles south of Nepenthe. These spectacular 4,000 acres straddling the highway also include a large underwater park offshore. Picnic in the coast redwoods by McWay Creek (almost the southern limit of their range) or hike up into the chaparral and the Los Padres National Forest. After picnicking, take the short walk along McWay Creek (watch for poison oak) then through the tunnel under the road to **Saddle Rock** and the cliffs above **Waterfall Cove,** the only California waterfall that plunges directly into the sea. The cliffs are rugged here; it's a good place to view whales and otters. Only experienced divers, by permit, are allowed to scuba offshore.

The park also features limited year-round camping at walk-in environmental sites and group campgrounds only. For more information about the park, including winter whalewatching programs held here on weekends, contact: Julia Pfeiffer Burns State Park, Big Sur, CA 93920, tel. (831) 667-2315.

The still raw 1,400-foot-wide slash of earth just north of Julia Pfeiffer Burns State Park, which stopped traffic through Big Sur for more than a year, has earned the area's landslide-of-all-time award (so far). Heading south from the park, the highway crosses Anderson Creek and rugged Anderson Canyon, where an old collection of highway construction cabins for convicts sheltered such bohemians as Henry Miller and his friend Emil White in the 1940s. A few human residents and a new population of bald eagles now call Anderson Canyon home.

Other Nature Reserves

Just south of the Esalen Institute is the **John Little State Reserve,** 21 acres of coast open to the public for day use (frequently foggy). About five miles south of Esalen, beyond the Dolan Creek and dramatic Big Creek bridges, is the entrance to **Landels-Hill Big Creek Reserve,** more than 4,000 acres cooperatively managed by The Nature Conservancy, the Save-the-Redwoods League, and the University of California. Safe behind these rusted cast-iron gates are 11 different plant communities, at least 350 plant species, 100 varieties of birds, and 50 types of mammals. A 10-acre area is open as a public educational center, groups welcome. For more information, contact: Landels-Hill Big Creek Reserve, UC Environmental Field Program, attention John Smiley, 231 Clark Kerr Hall, Santa Cruz, CA 95064, or call (831) 667-2543.

Lucia and the New Camaldoli Hermitage

The tiny "town" of Lucia is privately owned, with gas station and a good down-home restaurant open after 7 a.m. until dark, when they shut off the generator. Try the homemade split pea soup. Different, too, is a stay in one of the 10 rustic coastal cabins at **Lucia Lodge** (Expensive-Premium). Come nightfall, kerosene lanterns provide the ambience. A simple yet spectacular spot; call (831) 667-2391 for information (no reservations).

South of Lucia (at the white cross), the road to the left leads to the New Camaldoli Hermitage, a small Benedictine monastery at the former Lucia Ranch. The sign says that the monks "regret we cannot invite you to camp, hunt, or enjoy a walk on our property" due to the hermitage's customary solitude and avoidance of "unnecessary speaking." But visitors *can* come to buy crafts and homemade fruitcake and to attend daily mass.

In addition, the hermitage is available for very serene retreats of up to several days (few outsiders can stand the no-talk rules for much longer than that), simple meals included (suggested offering $30 a day). For more information, contact: New Camaldoli Hermitage, Director of Vocations, Big Sur, CA 93920, tel. (831) 667-2456 or (831) 667-2341.

Limekiln State Park

About two miles south of Lucia is the newest Big Sur state park, open since 1995, 716 acres in an isolated and steep coastal canyon preserving some of the oldest, largest, and most vigorous redwoods in Monterey County. Named for the towering wood-fired kilns that smelted quarried limestone into powdered lime—essential for mixing cement—here in the late 1800s, Limekiln State Park offers a steep one-mile roundtrip creekside hike through redwoods to the four kilns, passing a waterfall (to the right at the first fork), pools, and cascades along the way. Day-use area for picnicking ($5 fee) and a very appealing 43-site family campground with minimal amenities but abundant ambience. To get here, take the signed turnoff (on the inland or landward side of the highway) just south of the Limekiln Canyon Bridge. For more information, contact: Limekiln State Park, 63025 Hwy. 1, Big Sur, CA 93920, tel. (831) 667-2403. See also Public Camping in Big Sur below.

Pacific Valley and Gorda

The four-mile marine terrace of Pacific Valley south of Wild Cattle Creek Bridge and north of Willow Creek offers good coastal access and jade, the closest thing to big business in these parts. **Sand Dollar Beach** is a crescent of rocky beach, perfect for picnics and hang gliding; jade hunting is particularly good at **Jade Cove,** actually a series of coves between Plaskett Point and Willow Creek under striking serpentine cliffs shaped by the sea. Take the path down to the rocky cove and look for the rare and valuable harder-than-steel blue-green nephrite jade, one of two types of true jade, though most people find only mediocre gray-green Monterey jade. (But think big: in 1971, several offshore divers dragged up an eight-foot-long, 9,000-pound boulder of solid nephrite jade valued at $180,000.)

Willow Creek (a road heads down just south of the bridge) is more accessible for jade hunters, another rocky beach with crashing surf, good rock fishing, and restrooms. From **Cape San Martin** just south (rough dirt road hidden behind the bluff, easy to miss), take in the spectacular 360-degree coastal views.

Stop by the **Pacific Valley Center** restaurant, tel. (805) 927-8655, for great homemade pie. And stop by the **U.S. Forest Service** office, also in Pacific Valley, tel. (805) 927-4211, to get wilderness and fire permits, then take the short hike to **Salmon Creek Falls,** a 75-foot cascade of crystal water just 200 yards off the highway. (From the Forest Service office, work your way up the creek, then climb along the notch behind the falls for a view from the inside out.) This is also just about the end of redwood country; there are a few lost-looking loners near the creek.

Gorda (Spanish for "fat girl," nicknamed "Sorta Gorda" by locals) south of Pacific Valley is another tiny, privately owned spot in the road, casual and friendly, gas and a general store.

PRACTICAL BIG SUR

Public Camping in Big Sur

In the accommodations category nothing but camping is truly inexpensive in Big Sur, so to travel on the cheap, make campground reservations *early* (where applicable) and stock up on groceries and sundries in Monterey up north or in San Luis Obispo to the south. The U.S. Forest Service **Bottchers Gap Campground** on Palo Colorado Canyon Rd. has primitive, walk-in tent sites (first-come, first-camped, rough road). The Forest Service **Kirk Creek Campground** is far south of urban Big Sur and just north of the intersection with Nacimiento-Fergusson Rd.: it consists of 33 first-come, first-camped sites, picnic tables, and grills all situated on a grassy seaside bluff. A great choice, $16 per night, just $4 for cyclists. (Inland, halfway to Jolon, are two small creekside campgrounds managed by Los Padres National Forest, free since there's no reliable drinking water, but popular with deer hunters.) Also Forest Service and even farther south is **Plaskett Creek Campground.**

For more information on the area's national forest campgrounds and for free visitor permits, fire permits, maps, and other information about Los Padres National Forest and the Ventana Wilderness, stop by the **Big Sur Station** State Parks/U.S. Forest Service office at Pfeiffer-Big Sur State Park, open daily 8 a.m.-4:30 p.m., tel. (831) 667-2315; the Forest Service district office farther south at **Pacific Valley,** tel. (805) 927-4211; or the **Monterey Ranger District** office at 406 S. Mildred Ave., King City, CA 93930, tel. (831) 385-5434.

For secluded camping, try **Andrew Molera State Park,** with 50 walk-in tent sites not far from the dusty parking lot, $3, or **Julia Pfeiffer Burns State Park,** almost as nice, with two separate environmental campgrounds (far from RVs). More comforts (including flush toilets and hot showers) are available at the attractive redwoods-and-river family campground at **Pfeiffer-Big Sur State Park,** 200-plus tents-only campsites plus a regular summer schedule of educational and informational programs, $16 per night. For information about any of the area's state park campgrounds, stop by the office at Pfeiffer-Big Sur State Park or call (831) 667-2315. For ReserveAmerica reservations (usually necessary May-early Sept. and on warm-weather weekends), call toll-free (800) 444-7275.

Another possibility, just south of Lucia, is the postcard-pretty **Limekiln State Park,** 63025 Hwy. 1, tel. (831) 667-2403, which takes up most of the steep canyon and offers some good hiking in addition to attractive tent and RV sites for $20-22 (no hookups, but water, hot showers, and flush toilets). For reservations, call ReserveAmerica toll-free at (800) 444-7275.

Private Camping in Big Sur

Not far from the state campgrounds at Pfeiffer-Big Sur State Park is the private riverside **Big Sur Campground,** Hwy. 1, tel. (831) 667-2322, with tent sites and RV sites including hookups at $26 and up, as well as tent cabins and cabins. Also on the Big Sur River is the **Riverside Campground,** Hwy. 1, tel. (831) 667-2414, with tent or RV sites plus cabins. The private **Ventana Camp Grounds** near the Ventana Inn, Hwy. 1, tel. (831) 667-2688, has 70 sites near a stream in a very scenic redwood setting, some RV hookups, hot showers, fireplaces, and picnic tables.

Affordable Big Sur Accommodations

Always a best bet for cabins and affordable for just plain folks is the charming **Ripplewood Resort** about a mile north of Pfeiffer-Big Sur, tel. (831) 667-2242, where the primo units, most with fireplaces and kitchens (bring your own cookware), are down by the Big Sur River (and booked months in advance for summer). Moderate-Expensive. Other options include the adobe **Glen Oaks Motel,** tel. (831) 667-2105, and the **Fernwood Resort,** tel. (831) 667-2422,

both on Hwy. 1 and both Moderate-Expensive. The **Big Sur River Inn,** on Hwy. 1 in Big Sur Valley, tel. (831) 625-5255 or toll-free (800) 548-3610, is a motel-restaurant-bar popular with locals and featuring views of the river and live music most weekends. Expensive-Luxury. The **Big Sur Lodge** nearby, just inside the park's entrance, tel. (831) 667-3100, is quiet, with pool, sauna, restaurant, and a circle of comfy cabins. Premium, but substantially lower in winter and early spring.

Deetjen's Big Sur Inn

Just south of the noted Nepenthe restaurant and the Henry Miller Library is the landward Norwegian-style Deetjen's Big Sur Inn in Castro Canyon, tel. (831) 667-2377, a rambling, ever-blooming inn with redwood rooms, the experience now listed on the National Register of Historic Places. *Very* Big Sur. The 19 eccentric, rustic rooms chock-full of bric-a-brac—one's named Chateau Fiasco, after the Bay of Pigs invasion—have no TVs, no telephones, thin walls, front doors that don't lock, fireplaces, books, and reasonably functional plumbing. Forget about trendy creature comforts. People love this place—and have, ever since it opened in the 1930s—because it has *soul*. Private or shared bath. Reservations advised because rooms are usually booked up many months in advance. Expensive-Luxury. Eating at Deetjen's is as big a treat as an overnight. Wonderfully hearty, wholesome breakfasts are served 8-11:30 a.m., and dinner starts at 6:15 p.m. Reservations are also taken for meals.

Ventana Inn & Spa

Perhaps tuned into the same philosophical frequency as Henry Miller—"There being nothing to improve on in the surroundings, the tendency is to set about improving oneself"—in the beginning, when writer Lawrence A. Spector first built this place in 1975, the Ventana Inn people didn't provide distractions like TV or tennis courts. Though it's still a hip, high-priced resort, and there are still no tennis courts, things have changed. Now the desperately undiverted *can* phone home, if need be, or watch in-room TV or videos. But the woodsy, world-class Ventana high up on the hill in Big Sur, tel. (831) 667-2331, (831) 624-4812, or toll-free (800) 628-

6500, fax (831) 667-2419, www.ventanainn.com, still offers luxurious and relaxed contemporary lodgings on 240 acres overlooking the sea, outdoor Japanese hot baths, and heated pools.

This rough-hewn and hand-built hostelry is comprised of 12 separate buildings with rooms featuring unfinished cedar interiors, parquet floors, and down-home luxuries like queen- or king-sized beds with handpainted headboards, handmade quilted spreads, and lots of pillows. All rooms are reasonably large and have in-room refrigerators; most have fireplaces. Rooms and suites with both fireplaces and hot tubs are at the top of the inn's price range. The Ventana Inn also has a library, not to mention hiking trails and hammocks. Complimentary group classes—so very *California*—include Native American tai chi, Chi Gong, guided meditation, yoga, and hiking. Complimentary continental breakfast is served (delivered to your room by request), and in the afternoon from 4 to 5:30 p.m. enjoy the complimentary wine and cheese buffet in the main lodge. Luxury, reservations usually essential. Two-night minimum on weekends. Children are discouraged at Ventana, which is not set up to entertain or otherwise look after them.

Ranked the number two of the 25 "Best Small Hotels in the World" in the 1998 *Travel & Leisure* reader survey, the Ventana Inn became the Ventana Inn & Spa with the 1999 debut of its full-service spa. For a price, expect world-class massage, wraps, facials, scrubs, and other body therapies.

If a stay here or a self-pampering spa session seem just *too rich,* try drinks-with-a-view or a bite of enticing California cuisine served in the lovely two-tiered **Cielo** restaurant overlooking the ocean, a pleasant stroll through the woods. The Ventana Inn is located 0.8 miles south of Pfeiffer-Big Sur State Park; look for the sign on the left.

Post Ranch Inn

For good reason, new Big Sur commercial development has been rare in the 1990s. If further coastal development must come, the environmentally conscious Post Ranch Inn offers the style—if not the price range—most Californians would cheer. All the upscale travel mags rave about the place, open since 1992, calling it "one of the best places to stay in the world" *(Condé*

Nast Traveler) and "the most spectacular hotel on the Pacific Coast" *(Travel & Leisure).* And with good reason, since this place is something special. Developer Myles Williams, of New Christy Minstrels folk singing fame, and architect Mickey Muennig took the Big Sur region's rugged love of the land to heart when they built the very contemporary Post Ranch Inn. They also acknowledged the community's increasing economic stratification and took other real-world problems into account, adding 24 housing units for workers (affordable housing now scarce in these parts) and donating land for Big Sur's first fire station.

Perched on a ridge overlooking the grand Pacific Ocean, the Post Ranch Inn is a carefully executed aesthetic study in nature awareness. The 30 redwood-and-glass "guest houses" are designed and built to harmonize with—almost disappear into—the hilltop landscape. The triangular "tree houses" are built on stilts, to avoid damaging the roots of the oaks with which they intertwine; the spectacular sod-roofed "ocean houses" literally blend into the ocean views; and the gracious "coast house" duplexes impersonate stand-tall coastal redwoods. Absolute privacy and understated, earth-toned luxury are the main points here. Each house includes a wood-burning fireplace, two-person spa tub in the stunning slate bathroom, a good sound system, in-room refrigerators stocked with complimentary snacks, a private deck, king-sized bed—and views. Extra amenities include plush robes, in-room coffee makers and hair dryers, even walking sticks. Priced for Hollywood entertainment execs (like Ventana, in the $300 and up range), continental breakfast is included. Luxury.

Guests can also enjoy the **Post Ranch Spa**—offering massage, wraps, and facials—and the exceptional California-style **Sierra Mar** restaurant, where the views are every bit as inviting as the daily changing menu. Full bar. Open for lunch and dinner.

The Post Ranch Inn is 30 miles south of Carmel on Hwy. 1, on the west (seaward) side of the road. As at Ventana, children are discouraged here, since the inn is not set up to entertain or otherwise look after them. For more information, contact: Post Ranch Inn, P.O. Box 219, Big Sur, CA 93920, tel. (831) 667-2200, www.postranchinn.com. For inn reservations, call toll-free

(800) 527-2200. For restaurant reservations, call (831) 667-2800.

Eating Well in Big Sur

Look for fairly inexpensive fare in and around the Big Sur Valley. Good for breakfast is the

---

NEPENTHE

Nepenthe, about a mile south of the Ventana Inn, was built almost exactly on the site of the cabin Orson Welles bought for Rita Hayworth. So it's not too surprising that the restaurant is almost as legendary as Big Sur itself. A striking multilevel structure complete with an arts and crafts center, the restaurant was named for an ancient Egyptian drug taken to help people forget. Naturally enough, the bar here does a brisk business.

As is traditional at Nepenthe, relax on the upper deck (the "gay pavilion," presided over by a sculpted bronze and redwood phoenix) with drink in hand to salute the sea and setting sun. Surreal views. The open-beamed restaurant and its outdoor above-ocean terrace isn't nearly as rowdy as all those bohemian celebrity stories would suggest. Nonetheless, thrill-seekers insist on sitting on the top deck, though there's often more room available downstairs at the health food deli and deck. The fare here is good, but not as spectacular (on a clear day) as the views. Try the homemade soups, the hefty chef's salad, any of the vegetarian selections, or the world-famous Ambrosia burger (an excellent cheeseburger on French roll with pickles and a salad for a hefty price) accompanied by a Basket o' Fries. Good pies and cakes for dessert.

To avoid the worst of the tourist traffic and to appreciate Nepenthe at its best, come later in September or October. And although Nepenthe is casual any time of year, it's not *that* casual. Local lore has it that John F. Kennedy was once turned away because he showed up barefoot. Nepenthe is open for lunch and dinner daily, with music and dancing around the hearth at night. For more information or reservations, call (831) 667-2345.

And if at the moment you can't be here in person, you can be here in spirit—much easier now that Nepenthe has an online weather camera pointing south over the back deck. To "see" what's happening along Nepenthe's coastline, try www.nepenthebigsur.com.

Ripplewood Resort just north of Pfeiffer-Big Sur near the tiny Big Sur Library, tel. (831) 667-2242, where favorites include the homemade baked goods and French toast. **Deetjen's**, tel. (831) 667-2377, is special for breakfast, wholesome and hearty fare served in the open-beamed hobbit-style dining rooms. Dinner is more formal (fireplace blazing to ward off the chill mist, classical music, two seatings, by reservation only), with entrées including steaks, fish, California country cuisine, and vegetarian dishes. Tasty home-baked pies are an after-meal specialty at the casual **Trails Head Café** at the Big Sur Lodge, tel. (831) 667-3111, overlooking the river, also known for red snapper and California-style fare. Beer and wine.

Everyone should sample the view from **Nepenthe** at least once in their lifetime. A culinary hot spot is the **Glen Oaks Restaurant** next door to the Ripplewood Resort, tel. (831) 667-2264 or (831) 667-2865, with fine music, flowers, and elegance à la Big Sur. Entrées emphasize what's local and fresh, and include crepes, good vegetarian, and seafood. Open for dinner Wed.-Mon. nights. The Glen Oaks also serves a fine Sunday brunch, with omelettes, eggs Benedict, and cornmeal hotcakes. A quarter-mile north of Palo Colorado Rd. on Hwy. 1 is the **Rocky Point Restaurant**, tel. (831) 624-2933, a reasonably well-heeled roadhouse overlooking the ocean. Open for breakfast, lunch, and dinner daily.

The finest of local fine dining is served at the area's luxury-hotel restaurants—at **Cielo** at the Ventana Inn & Spa, and **Sierra Mar** at the Post Ranch Inn—which both serve lunch and dinner daily. For information, see listings above.

Big Sur Information, Services, and Transportation

For general information about the area, contact the **Big Sur Chamber of Commerce**, P.O. Box 87, Big Sur, CA 93920, tel. (831) 667-2100. (Send a stamped, self-addressed legal-sized envelope for a free guide to Big Sur.) Combined headquarters for the state parks and U.S. Forest Seville is **Big Sur Station** on the south side of Pfeiffer-Big Sur on Hwy. 1, Big Sur, CA 93920, tel. (831) 667-2315. Open daily 8 a.m.-4:30 p.m., this is the place to go in search of forest and wilderness maps, permits, and backcountry camping and recreation information. There's a

laundromat at Pfeiffer-Big Sur State Park in the Big Sur Lodge complex.

Bicycling Big Sur can be marvelous but less than fun when fighting RVs and weekend speedsters for road space. Forewarned, fearless cyclists should plan to ride from north to south to take advantage of the tailwind. (Driving south makes sense, too, since most vistas and turnouts are seaward.) It takes *at least* five hours by car to drive the 150 miles of Hwy. 1 between Monterey and San Luis Obispo.

Hitchhiking is almost as difficult as safely riding a bicycle along this stretch of Hwy. 1, so don't count on using your thumbs for transportation. More reliable is **Monterey-Salinas Transit** Bus No. 22, which runs to and from Big Sur daily mid-April to October, stopping at Point Lobos, Garrapata State Park, the Bixby Creek Bridge, Point Sur Lightstation, Pfeiffer-Big Sur and the River Inn, Pfeiffer Beach, the Ventana Inn, and Nepenthe; call (831) 899-2555 for information.

SAN SIMEON AND VICINITY

Hearst San Simeon
State Historic Monument

This site ranks right up there with Disneyland as one of California's premier tourist attractions. Somehow that fact alone puts the place into proper perspective. Media magnate William Randolph Hearst's castle is a rich man's playground filled to overflowing with artistic diversions and other expensive toys, a monument to one man's monumental ego and equally impressive poor taste.

In real life, of course, Hearst was a wealthy and powerful man, the subject of the greatest American movie ever made, Orson Welles's 1941 *Citizen Kane.* "Pleasure," Hearst once wrote, "is worth what you can afford to pay for it." (And that attitude showed itself quite early: on his 10th birthday, little William asked for the Louvre as a present.) One scene in the movie, where Charles Foster Kane shouts across the cavernous living room at Xanadu to attract the attention of his bored young mistress, endlessly working jigsaw puzzles while she sits before a fireplace as big as the mouth of Jonah's whale, won't seem so surreal once you see San Simeon.

Designed by Berkeley architect Julia Morgan, the buildings themselves are odd yet handsome hallmarks of Spanish Renaissance architecture. The centerpiece La Casa Grande alone has 115 rooms (including a movie theater, a billiards room, two libraries, and 31 bathrooms) adorned with silk banners, fine Belgian and French tapestries, French fireplaces, European choir stalls, and ornately carved ceilings—some from continental monasteries, churches, and castles. The furnishings and art

Hearst collected from around the world complete the picture, one that includes everything but humor, grace, warmth, and understanding.

The notably self-negating nature of this rich but richly disappointed man's life is somehow fully expressed here in the country's most ostentatious and theatrical temple to obscene wealth. In contrast to Orson Welles's authentic artistic interpretation of a Hearst-like life, William Randolph's idea of hearth, home, and humanity was

on Hearst's enchanted hill

full-flown fantasy sadly separated from heart and vision.

THE CAST OF CHARACTERS

Orson Welles, his brilliant film career essentially destroyed by William Randolph Hearst's vengeful media and movie industry machinations, was probably never invited to the famous celebrity encounters staged at La Cuesta Encantada, The Enchanted Hill. Hearst's wife, who refused to divorce him despite his insistence, never socialized here either (though she did come to the castle on occasion when summoned to preside over meetings with presidents and such). But those attending Hearst's flamboyant parties, carefully orchestrated by the lord of the manor and his lady and mistress, Ziegfeld Follies showgirl Marion Davies, included characters such as Charlie Chaplin, Greta Garbo, Clark Gable, Vivien Leigh, Laurence Olivier, Shirley Temple, Mary Pickford, and Rudolph Valentino. Even Hollywood moguls like Louis B. Mayer, Jack Warner, and Darryl Zanuck got through the gates, as did garrulous professional gossips including Hedda Hopper and Louella Parsons. Celebrities from farther afield, including Winston Churchill, President Calvin Coolidge, Charles Lindbergh, and George Bernard Shaw, also helped Hearst stave off the inevitable loneliness at the top. Cary Grant, a regular at "the ranch," said it was "a great place to spend the Depression."

Among Hearst's numerous house rules (informal dress only, no dirty jokes, no drinking in excess, and—ironically—no accompaniment by anyone other than one's spouse), perhaps his most revealing was: "Never mention death." But in the movie, only on his deathbed does Charles Foster Kane finally recognize the true worth and wreckage of his life. The word he whispers at the end—remembering the only thing he had ever really loved, his little sled—almost echoes through the great halls of San Simeon: *Rosebud . . . .*

Citizen Hearst

The name San Simeon was originally given to three Mexican land grants—40,000 acres bought by mining scion George Hearst in 1865. The first millionaire Hearst owned Nevada's Comstock Lode silver mine, Ophir silver mine, and the rich Homestake gold mine in South Dakota, and staked-out territory in California's goldfields. George Hearst later expanded the family holdings to 250,000 acres (including 50 miles of coastline) for the family's "Camp Hill" Victorian retreat and cattle ranch. With his substantial wealth, he was even able to buy himself a U.S. Senate seat.

But young William Randolph had even more ambitious plans—personally and for the property. The only son of the senator and San Francisco schoolteacher, socialite, and philanthropist Phoebe Apperson, the high-rolling junior Hearst took a fraction of the family wealth and his daddy's failing *San Francisco Examiner* and created a successful yellow-journalism chain, eventually adding radio stations and movie production companies.

Putting his newfound power of propaganda to work in the political arena, Hearst (primarily for the headlines) goaded Congress into launching the Spanish-American War in 1898. But unlike his father, William Randolph was unable to buy much personal political power. Though he aspired to the presidency, he had to settle for two terms as a congressmember from New York.

Following his parents' death, Hearst decided to build a house at "the ranch," partly as a place to store his already burgeoning art collection. Architect Julia Morgan, a family favorite, signed on for the project in 1919—for her, the beginning of a 28-year architectural collaboration. Morgan and Hearst planned the ever-evolving Enchanted Hill as a Mediterranean hill town, with La Casa Grande, the main house, as the "cathedral" facing the sea. Three additional palaces were clustered in front, the whole town surrounded by lavish terraced gardens.

Julia Morgan

Julia Morgan, San Simeon's architect, supervised the execution of almost every detail of Hearst's rambling 165-room pleasure palace. This 95-pound, teetotaling, workaholic woman was UC Berkeley's first female engineering graduate (at a time when a total of two-dozen women were enrolled there) and the first woman to graduate from the École des Beaux-Arts in Paris. Her eccentric mentor Bernard Maybeck, whose California redwood homes characteristically "climb the hill" on steep lots to blend into the landscape, encouraged her career, as did John Galen Howard of New York.

Though credited only after her death for her accomplishments, Morgan deserved at least as much recognition for her work as Edith Wharton in American literature and Mary Cassatt in painting, irate architecture and art historians have pointed out. But if acclaim came late for Morgan, it was partly her preference. She loathed publicity, disdained the very idea of celebrity, and believed that architects should be like anonymous medieval masters and let the work speak for itself.

Morgan's work with Hearst departed dramatically from her belief that buildings should be unobtrusive, the cornerstone of her brilliant but equally unobtrusive career. "My style," she said to those who seemed bewildered by the contradiction, "is to please my client." Pleasing her client in this case was quite a task. Hearst arbitrarily and habitually changed his mind, all the while complaining about slow progress and high costs. And she certainly didn't do the job for money, though Hearst and her other clients paid her well. Morgan divided her substantial earnings among her staff, keeping only about $10,000 annually to cover office overhead and personal expenses.

The perennially private Morgan, who never allowed her name to be posted at construction sites, designed almost 800 buildings in California and the West, among them the original Asilomar, the Berkeley City Club, the Oakland YWCA, and the bell tower, library, social hall, and gym at Oakland's Mills College. She also designed and supervised the reconstruction of San Francisco's Fairmont Hotel following its devastation in the 1906 earthquake. Other Hearst commissions included the family's Wyntoon retreat near Mount Shasta as well as the *Los Angeles Herald-Examiner* building.

THE SET: LIGHTS, ACTION, CAMERAS

Though the family, through the Hearst Corporation, gave the white elephant San Simeon to the state in 1958 in memory of Phoebe Apperson Hearst, descendants still own most of the surrounding land (and Hearst's art). Hearst's obsession was never satisfied and the project never technically finished, but most of La Casa Grande and adjacent buildings, pools, and grand

the Gothic Library

gardens graced La Cuesta Encantada by the time major construction ceased in 1947 when Hearst became ill and moved away. He died four years later.

In spring when the hills are emerald green, from the faraway highway Hearst's castle appears as if by magic up on the hill. (Before the place opened for public tours in the 1950s, the closest view commoners could get was from the road, with the assistance of coin-operated telescopes.) One thing visitors *don't* see on the shuttle up the enchanted hill is Hearst's 2,000-acre zoo—"the largest private zoo since Noah," as Charles Foster Kane would put it—once the country's largest. The inmates have long since been dispersed, though survivors of Hearst's exotic elk, zebras, Barbary sheep, and Himalayan goat herds still roam the grounds.

There are four separate day tours of the Hearst San Simeon State Historic Monument, each taking approximately two hours, plus an evening tour of the same duration. Theoretically the San Simeon tours could all be taken in a day, but don't try it. So much Hearst in the short span of a day could be detrimental to one's well-being. A dosage of two tours per day makes the trip here worthwhile yet not overwhelming. Visitors obsessed with seeing it all should plan a two-day stay in the area or come back again some other time. Whichever tour or combination of tours you select, be sure to wear comfortable walking shoes. Lots of stairs.

Tour One is a good first-time visit, taking in the castle's main floor, one guest house, and some of the gardens—a total of 150 steps and a half mile of walking. Included on the tour is a short showing in the theater of some of Hearst's "home movies." Particularly impressive in a gloomy Gothic way is the dining room, but the billiards room and mammoth great hall, with Canova's *Venus,* are also unforgettable. All the tours include both the Greco-Roman Neptune Pool and statuary, and the indoor Roman Pool with its mosaics of lapis lazuli and gold leaf. It's hard to imagine Churchill, cigar in mouth, cavorting here in an inner tube.

Tour Two requires more walking, covering the mansion's upper floors, the libraries, kitchen, and Hearst's Gothic Suite (from which he ran his 94 separate business enterprises), with its rose-tinted windows. The delightfully lit Celestial Suite was the nonetheless depressing extramarital playground of Hearst and Marion Davies.

Tour Three covers one of the guest houses plus the "new wing" of the main house, with its 36 luxurious bedrooms, sitting rooms, and marble bathrooms furnished with fine art. This tour also includes a short film detailing the extraordinary efforts involved in building the castle.

Gardeners will be moved to tears by **Tour Four** (April-Aug. only), which includes a long stroll through the San Simeon grounds but does not go inside the castle itself. Realizing that all the rich topsoil here had to be manually carried up the hill makes the array of exotic plant life, including unusual camellias and some 6,000 rosebushes, all the more impressive—not to mention the fact that gardeners at San Simeon worked only at night because Hearst couldn't stand watching them. Also included on the fourth tour is the lower level of the elegant, 17-room Casa del Mar guest house (where Hearst spent much of his time), the recently redone underground Neptune Pool dressing rooms, the never-finished bowling alley, and Hearst's wine cellar. David Niven once remarked that, with Hearst as host, the wine flowed "like glue." Subsequently, Niven was the only guest allowed free access to the castle's wine cellar.

Evening Tours are two-hour adventures featuring the highlights of other tours—with the added benefit of allowing you to pretend to be some Hollywood celebrity, just arrived and in need of orientation. (Hearst himself handed out tour maps, since newcomers often got lost.) Docents dressed in period costume inhabit the rooms, play poker or pool, and show you around. It's worth it just to see the castle in lights. At last report, evening tours were offered on Friday and Saturday nights March-May and Sept.-Dec., but call for current details.

Features and Coming Attractions

Someone should have called upon one of Julia Morgan's architectural disciples to design San Simeon's $7 million **visitor center** at the foot of The Enchanted Hill. Far from enchanting itself, the Spanish-style stucco and tile structure is actually more reminiscent of a Taco Bell-cum-urban transportation terminal, with four separate loading docks for people trucked off on the various tours. One redeeming feature of the center, however, is the exhibition room, which offers over an hour's worth of very good information about Hearst's life and times, as well as Morgan's. Another special feature is the conservation area, where visitors can watch artisans in their monumental daily work of maintaining and preserving Hearst's monument to himself.

Adjacent to the visitor center is the Hearst Castle's giant-screened **National Geographic Theatre,** tel. (805) 927-6811, where at last report the larger-than-life *Hearst Castle—Building the Dream* and *Everest* were showing on the 70-foot by 52-foot screen. Call for current times and details (no reservations required).

San Simeon is open daily except Thanksgiving, Christmas, and New Year's Day, with the regular two-hour tours leaving the visitor center area on the hour from early morning until around dusk. Tour schedules change by season and day of the week. Reservations aren't required, but the chance of getting tickets on a drop-in, last-minute basis is small. For current schedule information and reservations, call ReserveAmerica toll-free at (800) 444-4445 (all major credit cards accepted). Wheelchair-access tours of San Simeon are offered on a different schedule; call (805) 927-2070 for reservations and information.

Admission to each of the four San Simeon day tours is $14 adults, $8 children. Evening tour rates are $25 adults, $13 children. A special brochure for international travelers (printed in Japanese, Korean, French, German, Hebrew, Italian, and Spanish) is available. With a little forethought (see Near San Simeon below), visitors can avoid eating the concession-style food here.

Christmas at the Castle is a special treat for those who come during the otherwise downtime month of December. Holiday visitors are treated to the palace in all its yuletide splendor: access to the castle's most popular features plus towering tinsel-and-twinkle Christmas trees, an exact replica of the Hearst family's traditional nativity scene, tour guides dressed in period costume—experiences once shared only by friends and celebrity guests.

For other information, write Hearst San Simeon State Historic Monument, 750 Hearst Castle Rd., San Simeon, CA 93452, or call (805) 927-2020 or (805) 927-2000, www.hearstcastle.org.

NEAR SAN SIMEON

San Simeon: The Town and Beaches

Done with the display of pompous circumstance on the hill, head for the serene sandy beaches nearby for a long coast walk to clear out the clutter. Good ocean swimming. Nude sunbathers sometimes congregate at the north end of **William Randolph Hearst Memorial State Beach** across the highway from Hearst Castle, indulging in a healthy hedonism Hearst would absolutely hate, but otherwise it's a family-style stop with good picnicking, restrooms, and a public pier popular for fishing. Day-use fee: $4.

While enjoying Hearst's memorial beach, keep in mind that in 1998 the California Coastal Commission nixed Hearst Corporation plans to build a 365-acre luxury hotel and golf resort complex on the coast near here.

Another picnicking possibility, especially for whalewatchers, is **Piedras Blancas Lighthouse** just up the coast. The lighthouse, built in 1874, is

LIFE IN HARMONY

People like to start wedded life auspiciously by getting married at the chapel in Harmony, actually a converted wine and cheese shop. Over the years, this privately owned one-time dairy town has also grown into a laid-back artsy enclave, with pottery and glass-blowers' shops, an artists' studio, gift and T-shirt shop, and restaurant (shuttered at last report). As the story goes, Harmony (population 18, more or less) got its name in the 1890s when feuding neighbors put aside their differences to build a school; when it was finished, they called it Harmony Valley Schoolhouse. The old Harmony Valley Creamery, where none other than William Randolph Hearst once stopped for provisions on the way to his castle, is now an arts and crafts complex and restaurant.

If you're curious about life in Harmony, stop by to see what's new, now that the town has changed hands. Local life has been less harmonious since 1998 when the new owner, a Hollywood developer, began to unveil his plans for a 700-acre world peace theme park here.

now automated and off-limits to the public. Wonderful tidepools and good abalone diving are characteristics of the coast near here, at **Twin Creeks Beach,** but public access may be restricted, as the area seems to be turning into a seasonal home for a northern elephant seal colony. The beaches at **San Simeon State Park** farther south near Cambria are larger and rockier. The park features three separate day-use areas popular for fishing and picnicking, 70 primitive campsites, and 134 developed campsites near San Simeon Creek off San Simeon Creek Rd. (five miles south of San Simeon on Hwy. 1). If you need to stretch your legs, take the pleasant three-mile **San Simeon Creek Trail,** starting from the Washburn Day Use Area. For park information, call (805) 927-2035 or (805) 927-2020.

The "town" of San Simeon is actually two tiny towns: the original Spanish-style, red-tile-roofed village built for Hearst employees, and "San Simeon Acres," the highway's motel row. The old **Sebastian's General Store,** tel. (805) 927-4217, in the real San Simeon is a state historic monument and a great picnic supply stop with old-time post office and more modern garden café. Quite casual and comfortable, with whaling implements on the wall. Party boats powered by **Virg's Fish'n,** tel. (805) 927-4676 or (805) 927-4677, set out from the harbor March-Oct. for fishing. Ask about whalewatching tours.

Cambria

Its borders blending into San Simeon about eight miles south of Hearst Castle, the artsy coastal town of Cambria now bears the Roman name for ancient Wales but was previously called Rosaville, San Simeon, and (seriously) Slabtown. In some ways, Cambria is becoming the Carmel of southern Big Sur, with its glut of galleries and other come-hither shops, but without the smog and crowds. Several of the area's historic buildings remain, including the 1877 Squibb-Darke home, the Brambles restaurant on Burton Dr. in Old Town to the east, and the restored Santa Rosa Catholic Church on Bridge St. (across Main, past the library and post office).

Though the cliffs and No Trespassing signs across Santa Rosa Creek tend to slow people down, **Moonstone Beach** offers miles of walking, sea otters, sunsets, and good surfing.

Just outside Cambria in Cambria Pines—if it's still standing—is Arthur Beal's beautifully bizarre **Nit Wit Ridge,** a middle-class San Simeon and a state historical monument since 1981. A multilevel, sandcastle-like cement structure lovingly built by local garbage man Art Beal (also known as Captain Nitwit and Dr. Tinkerpaw), construction started in 1928 with a one-room shack architecturally enhanced with cement, abalone shells, glass, discarded car parts, toilet seats, and beer cans, with later additions of bones, driftwood, feathers, and rock. Nit Wit Ridge is none too popular with some of the neighbors these days, however. Art Beal died in 1992 and his masterpiece has started to crumble, since the cement was made of beach sand. Ask locally if the Art Beal Foundation has had any success in raising funds for preservation—and otherwise holding back the bulldozers. To get to Nit Wit Ridge, in Cambria head south on Main St., turn left on Sheffield, left again on Cornwall, then right on Hillcrest and head uphill. If it's still standing, look but don't touch.

Something of a tragedy for Cambria, and for everyone who loves this lovely town, is news that its breathtaking stands of Monterey pines are doomed, according to the experts—victims of a virulent fungus known as pine pitch canker, expected to wipe out 80% of the trees here over the next few decades. Cambria's forest of native Monterey pines is one of only three in California, five in the world. Since worried foresters fear spread of the disease elsewhere along the coast and eventually into the Sierra Nevada, do *not* pick up pine cones or other forest souvenirs to take home with you, since you may also be transporting this plague.

PRACTICAL SAN SIMEON AND VICINITY

San Simeon and the stretch of shoreline it dominates is so close to San Luis Obispo and Morro Bay that people often make day trips here from those communities to do the castle. For San Simeon visitors who have reserved four or five tours over a several-day period or who prefer more convenient accommodations and eateries, there are some decent choices near San Simeon and Cambria. For current information about local practicalities, contact the **San Simeon Chamber of Commerce,** 250 San Simeon Ave., Ste. 3-B, P.O. Box 1, San Simeon, CA 93452, tel. (805) 927-3500, or the **Cambria Chamber of Commerce,** 767 Main, Cambria, CA 93428, tel. (805) 927-3624.

Camping near San Simeon

Most motels near San Simeon and Cambria are often stuffed with groups assembled for castle tours, so for open-air solitude, camping up or down the coast is a sensible option. (As with motels, make reservations well in advance.) Public camping is available at large **San Simeon State Park,** offering developed sites with hot showers near the beach, $16, also primitive hillside sites at the park's **Washburn** area; call (805) 927-2035 or (805) 927-2020 for information. Or camp farther south at either **Atascadero State Beach** (summer only) or mighty fine **Morro Bay State Park,** tel. (805) 772-2560. Year-round, make ReserveAmerica reservations for all three by calling toll-free (800) 444-7275.

Staying near San Simeon

The beachfront **Piedras Blancas Motel** seven miles north of Hearst's house on Hwy 1., tel.

(805) 927-4202, boasts views of the castle on sunny days and often has vacancies when places closer to San Simeon are full. Premium. Another possibility is the remote **Ragged Point Inn,** 19019 Hwy. 1 (15 miles north of San Simeon), Ragged Point, tel. (805) 927-4502. Luxury. Well south of San Simeon and Cambria, **Cayucos** also has decent, less expensive motels.

From October or November into mid-spring, even the more expensive motels in San Simeon proper feature cheaper rates. Sometimes offering great bargains in the off-season is the **Silver Surf Motel,** 9390 Castillo Dr. (the frontage road parallel to the highway), tel. (805) 927-4661 or toll-free (800) 621-3999 (reservations only), www.silversurfmotel.com. Some rooms feature ocean views, balconies, and fireplaces; all have phones, TV, and complimentary coffee and tea. Pool and spa. Moderate-Expensive. Also a bargain by San Simeon standards, and a particularly good deal in winter, is the **San Simeon Lodge,** 9520 Castillo Dr. (south of the monument), tel. (805) 927-4601, featuring basic but decent rooms (remodeled in 1997) with TV and phones. Moderate-Expensive. The nearby **El Rey Garden Inn,** 9260 Castillo Dr., tel. (805) 927-3998 or toll-free (800) 821-7914, www.elreygardeninn.com, offers something close to luxury—large rooms with amenities (TV, movies, phones), some with gas fireplaces and refrigerators. Expensive. Both also have heated swimming pools, and the good **Europa** restaurant is an added attraction at the El Rey.

Staying in Cambria

Some Cambria accommodations are less pricey—and there are plenty of places to choose from. For cabins, try the **Cambria Pines Lodge,** 2905 Burton Dr., tel. (805) 927-4200 or toll-free (800) 445-6868, where the facilities include an indoor pool, sauna, and whirlpool on a 25-acre spread. Rates include full breakfast. Moderate-Premium. The tiny **Bluebird Motel** just west of Burton Dr. at 1880 Main, tel. (805) 927-4634 or toll-free (800) 552-5434, www.bluebirdmotel.com, offers creekside rooms and suites with fireplaces, in-room refrigerators, color TV, and VCRs. Moderate-Luxury.

Other best bets include the **San Simeon Pines Seaside Resort,** 7200 Moonstone Beach Dr. (at Hwy. 1), tel. (805) 927-4648, woodsy and

right across the street from Moonstone Beach, with heated pool, nine-hole par 3 golf, playground, croquet, and shuffleboard. Some cottage units feature wood-burning fireplaces. Moderate-Expensive. The **Sand Pebbles Inn,** 6252 Moonstone Beach Dr., tel. (805) 927-5600, fax (805) 927-0393, features French country decor, views, gas fireplaces, in-room refrigerators, color TVs with video players, and hair dryers; some rooms have whirlpools. Continental breakfast and afternoon tea included. Expensive-Luxury. For more English-French country, complete with canopy beds, try the popular **Blue Dolphin Inn,** 6470 Moonstone Beach Dr., tel. (805) 927-3300. Expensive-Luxury. The small, smoke-free **White Water Inn** near Leffingwell Landing at 6790 Moonstone Beach Dr., tel. (805) 927-1066, refurbished in the mid-1990s, offers abundant amenities—VCRs and TVs, free movies, hair dryers, radios, in-room refrigerators, gas fireplaces, and continental breakfast delivered to your room—and some attractive special packages. Moderate-Premium.

For an air of English oceanside charm, consider the 60-room **Fogcatcher Inn** at 6400 Moonstone Beach Dr., tel. (805) 927-1400 or toll-free (800) 425-4121, www.moonstonemgmt.com, with many amenities plus heated pool and whirlpool. Expensive-Luxury. Sometimes a good bargain, too, by local standards is the Fogcatcher's sister **Sea Otter Inn,** 6656 Moonstone Beach Dr., tel. (805) 927-5888 or toll-free (800) 965-8347. Expensive-Premium.

Cambria Bed and Breakfasts

Cambria offers options for the bed-and-breakfast set. The fine **Blue Whale Inn,** 6736 Moonstone Beach Dr., tel. (805) 927-4647, www.bluewhaleinn.com, features six striking European country-style "mini-suites" with ocean views, separate entrances, gas fireplaces, and refrigerators. Full breakfast, afternoon refreshments. Luxury. Two-night minimum stay on weekends.

The two-story early American **J. Patrick House Bed and Breakfast Inn,** 2990 Burton Dr., tel. (805) 927-3812 or toll-free (800) 341-8258, is an intriguing log home and guest house. All rooms have private baths, most feature a wood-burning fireplace. Comfortable garden room, where breakfast and veggie hors d'oeuvres are served. Premium-Luxury. Furnished with turn-of-the-20th-century antiques is the charming two-story 1870s **Olallieberry Inn** and cottage, 2476 Main, tel. (805) 927-3222, fax (805) 927-0202, which offers nine rooms with private baths. Expensive-Luxury.

Other Cambria bed-and-breakfast choices include the three-story, seven-room **Beach House,** 6360 Moonstone Beach Dr., tel. (805) 927-3136, where all rooms feature private baths, two have fireplaces, and telescopes and binoculars are provided for watching whales, dolphins, and surfers (Premium-Luxury); and **Windrush,** down the road at 6820 Moonstone, tel. (805) 927-8844, with just two rooms, each with separate entrance and private bath (Expensive).

Eating Well near Hearst Castle

Stop at **Sebastian's General Store** in San Simeon, tel. (805) 927-4217, to stock up on picnic supplies or enjoy burgers and such in the outdoor café. If you're here in winter, keep an eye out for the migrating monarch butterflies that flutter to these cypress and eucalyptus trees.

Most restaurants are in Cambria. Great for ethnic lunch or dinner, usually including some vegetarian choices, is **Robin's** at 4095 Burton Dr., tel. (805) 927-5007. Reservations suggested on weekends, or call ahead for takeout. Try **Mustache Pete's** across the street, 4090 Burton Dr., tel. (805) 927-8589, for Italian, particularly calzones and pizzas (takeout and early-bird dinners). For Chinese, try **China Restaurant,** 1602 Main St., tel. (805) 927-6778. All-American **Linn's** at 2277 Main, tel. (805) 927-0371, is a best

bet for soups, salads, sandwiches, and specialty pot pies. Open daily (except Christmas) for breakfast, lunch, and dinner. Or try **Grandma Porte's** across the street at 2282 Main St., tel. (805) 927-8519, also open for breakfast, lunch, and dinner daily, offering American standards plus some Mexican choices.

Casual but excellent for American fare from pastas to seafood, and famous for its fresh-baked breads and pastries, is the small dinners-only **Sow's Ear** restaurant at 2248 Main St. in Cambria, tel. (805) 927-4865. Diners *can* get a good hamburger for dinner at the English-style **Brambles Dinner House,** 4005 Burton Dr. in Cambria, tel. (805) 927-4716, but even better are the homemade soups, breads, and oak-wood-broiled salmon. The Brambles is famous for its prime rib with Yorkshire pudding, excellent roast rack of lamb, and brandy ice cream for dessert. Reservations are almost essential, even at Sunday brunch.

The **Moonstone Beach Bar & Grill,** 6550 Moonstone Beach Dr., tel. (805) 927-3859, specializes in seafood and offers oceanfront dining alfresco (weather permitting) at lunch and dinner. Another possibility is the **Cambria Pines Restaurant** at the Lodge, 2905 Burton Dr., tel. (805) 927-4200, serving steak, seafood, pastas, and other upscale fare.

Canozzi's Saloon, 2226 Main, tel. (805) 927-8941, is a rusty old tavern and pool hall with odd signs and memorabilia hanging from the ceiling—*the* place for listening to live music and making the scene, Cambria-style, on Saturday night.

MORRO BAY AND VICINITY

The first thing visitors notice is the Rock, spotted by Cabrillo in 1542. Morro Reef has been a significant navigational landfall for mariners for more than three centuries and was noted in the diaries of Portolá, Crespi, and Costanso. (That wouldn't impress the native peoples, though; Chumash artifacts found here date to 4700 B.C.) Morro Rock is the last visible volcanic peak in the 21-million-year-old series of nine cones that stretch to San Luis Obispo; the chain is known as the **Seven Sisters** (one is submerged and one is out of line). Before extensive quarrying, this "Gibraltar of the Pacific" stood much higher than its current 576 feet and, until the 1930s, was an island at high tide. The height of the Rock seems reduced even more by the proximity of the three 450-foot-tall power plant smokestacks jutting from the edge of the bay like giant gun barrels, part of the scenery since 1953.

Until the rise of tourism, commercial fishing, especially for abalone and albacore, was Morro Bay's major industry. But intrepid amateurs can try clam digging for geoducks (Washington clams) or some barehanded grunion snatching during full-moon high tides from March through August. Pier fishing is also good here on the city's three T-piers, north of the Embarcadero and opposite the Rock. Morro Bay also boasts a thriving nature-oriented tourism industry—and a kitsch- and gift-shop-oriented tourism industry, perfect for shopaholics. Or watch the boats in the bay from **Tidelands Park**, at the south end of the Embarcadero, or take a ride on the *Tiger's Folly II* replica river boat. Laid-back **Baywood Park** on the bay just a few miles south of Morro Bay is a better choice for those determined to avoid the crowds.

Thanks to a few local bars and the Morro Bay Chess Club, Morro Bay also has *culture*. The star in that department is the chess club's **giant outdoor chessboard,** especially eye-catching when demonstration tournaments are under way after noon on Saturday along the Embarcadero. With each of the game's carved redwood pieces weighing between 18 and 30 pounds, playing chess here offers more than a mere mental workout. Anyone can play, by reservation, either on the giant board or on punier standard-sized chess tables along the perimeter. During the town's **Harbor Days Celebration** in October, local drama buffs in full costume *become* chess pieces. Another major event is the **Morro Bay Winter Bird Festival.** And come to Morro Bay in December for the **Christmas Parade** of lighted boats on the bay's waters.

For more information about local attractions, events, and practicalities, call the **Morro Bay Chamber of Commerce,** tel. (805) 772-4467 or toll-free (800) 231-0592.

SEEING AND DOING MORRO BAY

The entire town of Morro Bay, including Morro Rock, is a bird sanctuary and nature preserve in deference to the endangered peregrine falcons, great blue herons, and other bird species that have selected the Rock and vicinity as a rookery. The bay and adjacent mudflats create a fertile wetland, one of the most significant along the California coast for sheer number of resident bird species and one of the top 10 national birdwatching spots. Guns are banned throughout Morro Bay—the rock, the town, and the state park.

Morro Bay State Park

A multifaceted park dominating the entire bay area, Morro Bay State Park includes the sand dunes on the spit, dual Morro Strand State Beach farther north, a natural history museum, adjacent golf course, and the Los Osos Oaks State Reserve just inland from the bay on Los Osos Valley Road. The park's campgrounds and picnic areas seem like value-added bonuses.

Eucalyptus trees shade the bay near park headquarters and attract monarch butterflies after the October bloom. A more interesting first stop for most people, though, is the park's excellent **Museum of Natural History** on Country Club Dr., tel. (805) 772-2694, www.mbspmuseum.org, which emphasizes the wildlife of the headlands and adjacent aquatic environments, offers guided natural history hikes, and features fun hands-on touch pools and other nature exhibits, a good bookshop, and great views of Morro Bay below. It's open daily 10 a.m.-5 p.m., closed Thanksgiving, Christmas, and New Year's Day; free for campers, otherwise small admission.

Next, explore the mouth of **Los Osos Creek,** one of the largest natural coastal marshlands remaining in California. Wildflowers on adjacent grassy hills are most striking in spring, but their blooms, seeds, and vegetation attract birds year-round. Rent a canoe or kayak for some unforgettable eyeball-to-eyeball encounters. (Get an area bird checklist and other local birdwatching information at the museum.) Take a boat to reach the **Sand Spit Wild Area,** the pristine peninsula separating Morro Bay from the ocean (protected shell mounds, good birding), or come the long way from Montaña de Oro State Park to the south. For the adventurous: Hike the entire Morro Bay sand spit, an eight-mile roundtrip from the Sunset Terrace golf course around the inlet and over the sand dunes toward Morro Rock.

Once known separately as Morro Strand and Atascadero state beaches, the two sections of **Morro Strand State Beach** north of Morro Bay, tel. (805) 772-2560, feature several broad miles of sandy strand with small naked dunes along Estero Bay and adjacent to residential areas; the beach is popular for surfing, skin diving, surf fishing, swimming, and sunning (clam digging prohibited). Another spot of state beach, with picnic tables, pier, and playground, is in family-friendly **Cayucos** just north.

Los Osos Oaks State Reserve, southeast of the bay at the end of Los Osos Valley Rd., is a 90-acre grove acquired in 1972 to preserve one of the few old stands of coast oaks remaining in the area. These gnarled oldsters, coast live oaks, scrub oaks, and various hybrids, create an eerie impression on early morning hikes. Stay on the trail: the understory here is mostly poison oak.

The park is open for day use sunrise to sunset daily. The park's day-use fee is $6 per vehicle (camping and museum admission extra). For camping information, see below. For other park information, stop by the natural history museum (above) or call (805) 772-2560 or (805) 772-2694.

Montaña de Oro State Park
Just south of the sand spit is Montaña de Oro State Park ("Mountain of Gold"), its name par-

ticularly apt in spring when the hills are ablaze with yellow and orange wildflowers, from California poppies and yellow mustard to goldfields and fiddleneck. Any time of year, 8,000-acre Montaña de Oro is a hiker's park. The seclusion here also means abundant wildlife: sea lions, harbor seals, and sea otters at sea; gray foxes, mule deer, bobcats, and sometimes even mountain lions on land. From near **Point Buchon** (private property), the whalewatching is superb, but you can find other good vantage points along the Bluff Trail.

The area's wild beauty stretches from the seven-mile shoreline of 50-foot bluffs and tidepools, surging surf, and sandy beaches inland to Valencia Peak (great ocean views looking north to Piedras Blancas, south to Point Sal) and up Islay Creek to the waterfalls. The best tidepools are at **Corallina Cove,** though **Quarry Cove** comes in a close second. There's good tidepooling after the five-minute creekside scramble down from Hazard Canyon, also access to the entire sand spit and silent beaches. South of the **Spooner's Cove** visitor center, part of the old ranch, is an old Chumash campsite.

To get to Montaña de Oro, head west on Los Osos Valley Rd. from San Luis Obispo back roads or Hwy. 101, and then follow Pecho Valley Rd. south to the end. For basic information and to get oriented, stop by the natural history museum at Morro Bay State Park (see above) or call (805) 528-0513 or (805) 772-7434. Montaña de Oro's facilities are appropriately limited but picnic tables overlook the cove. Nearby is the valley **Islay Creek Campground,** 50 primitive, environmental, and hiker/biker sites, with pit toilets. Call for information.

PRACTICAL MORRO BAY

Morro Bay Camping
Basic beach camping is the set-up at **Morro Strand State Beach** north of the bay, 104 barren beachfront RV parking lot sites (no hookups) featuring some tent camping sites; campsites include tables, stoves, restrooms, and cold outdoor showers. Considerably more comfortable is camping at **Morro Bay State Park** near park headquarters, 135 tree-shaded campsites with tables, stoves, hot showers, restrooms, and laun-

You'll know you're in Morro Bay when you see the three 450-foot-tall power plant smokestacks dominating the landscape.

dry tubs, also RV hookups (20 sites) and sanitation station. **Montaña de Oro State Park** also offers camping at its Islay Creek Campground—50 wooded primitive (tents and RVs) and environmental sites, pit toilets only. Pre fee cuts, camping fees were $10 and up at Montaña de Oro (environmental, group, and equestrian camping) and $14-23 at Morro Strand and Morro Bay. Call each park for details. For reservable campsites, ReserveAmerica reservations, toll-free tel. (800) 444-7275, are advisable year-round; at Morro Strand reservations are taken only for summer.

Staying in Morro Bay

In addition to camping, Morro Bay offers comfy real-bed alternatives—most of these fairly reasonable. The ever-affordable **Motel 6,** about a mile from the beach at 298 Atascadero Rd. (Hwy. 1 at Hwy. 41), tel. (805) 772-5641 or toll-free (800) 466-8356 for reservations (nationwide), fax (805) 772-3233, www.motel6.com, is $56 double on summer weekends, lower at other times. Inexpensive. Much closer to the bay scene and a best bet is the tiny, two-story **Best Western Tradewinds Motel,** 225 Beach St. (at Market Ave.), tel. (805) 772-7376 or toll-free (800) 628-3500, fax (805) 772-2090, Moderate-Premium ($79 and up) in summer, though smaller rooms go for as low as $49 double in the off-season. All rooms have in-room refrigerators and coffeemakers and color TV with cable (free movies). Other midrange motel favorites include

the **Breakers Motel,** 780 Market Ave. (at Morro Bay Blvd.), tel. (805) 772-7317 or toll-free (800) 932-8899, fax (805) 772-4771, with rates from $78, and **La Serena Inn,** 990 Morro Ave., tel. (805) 772-5665 or toll-free (800) 248-1511, fax (805) 772-1044, www.laserenainn.com. Both are Moderate-Expensive.

Uptown for these parts is **The Inn at Morro Bay** a mile south of town just outside the entrance to Morro Bay State Park, tel. (805) 772-5651 or toll-free (800) 321-9566 for reservations, fax (805) 772-4779, www.innatmorrobay.com, where attractive rooms are $99 and up—bay views come at a premium, especially on summer weekends—though discounts and specials are possible. Expensive-Luxury. A less stylish but quite pleasant alternative is the small **Beachwalker Inn** motel just a block from the beach at 501 S. Ocean Ave. in Cayucos, tel. (805) 995-2133 or toll-free (800) 750-2133 for reservations, fax (805) 995-3139, www.beachwalkerinn.com, where double rooms are $85 and up in summer, as low as $65 in winter.

For more complete lodging listings, contact the local chamber of commerce.

Eating in Morro Bay

A local tradition is **Dorn's Original Breakers Cafe,** 801 Market St., tel. (805) 772-4415, with wonderful pecan waffles, buttermilk pancakes, and veggie omelettes for breakfast, an impressive Boston clam chowder and marinated seafood salads and various sandwiches at lunch.

Generous seafood dinners are served with good views of the bay.

People could drown in the aquatic ambience around Morro Bay. For more fresh fish, stop off at **Giovanni's Fish Market** right in front of the boat docks at 1001 Front St., open 9 a.m.-6 p.m. Seafood places leap out all along the Embarcadero, many of them open for lunch and dinner and many featuring early-bird dinner specials. Very good and very popular is **Rose's Landing Restaurant,** 725 Embarcadero, tel. (805) 772-4441, on the waterfront overlooking the bay. Good specials, but come early or make reservations because people pack in here like sardines, probably because the bar is shaped like a boat. Also on the waterfront: the **Great American Fish Company,** 1185 Embarcadero, tel. (805) 772-4407, which specializes in mesquite-grilled seafood. The place for sushi and such is **Harada,** 630 Embarcadero, tel. (805) 772-1410. For pasta and vegetarian selections as well as seafood, jockey for a patio table at **Hoppe's Hip Pocket Bistro,** 901 Embarcadero, tel. (805) 772-5371.

For something a bit fancier at dinner—yet still casual—consider **Hoppe's Marina Square,** overlooking the bay at 699 Embarcadero, tel. (805) 772-5371, where the steak and seafood are served with continental flair. Or head for the popular **Paradise Restaurant** at The Inn at Morro Bay near Morro Bay State Park, tel. (805) 772-2743, for fine dining American style and an inviting Sunday brunch.

SAN LUIS OBISPO AND VICINITY

Before freeway arteries pulsed with California car traffic, when trips between San Francisco and Los Angeles took at least two days, north-south travelers naturally appreciated San Luis Obispo as the most reasonable midpoint stopover. So it's not surprising that San Luis Obispo gave birth to both the concept and the word "motel," a contraction of "motor hotel."

In 1925 when the Spanish colonial **Milestone Mo-tel** (now the Motel Inn) opened, it was the first roadside hostelry to call itself a motel. A sign at the entrance told travelers how to pronounce the new word, and Pasadena architect Arthur Heineman, who designed the place, even copyrighted it.

Playwright Sam Shepard uses motels as symbols of all that is déclassé, desolate, and depressing in the United States. Vladimir Nabokov vilified motels from a continental perspective in *Lolita:* "We held in contempt the plain white-washed clapboard Kabins, with their faint sewerish smell or some other gloomy self-conscious stench and nothing to boast of. . . ." J. Edgar Hoover, former FBI director and self-styled arbiter of the nation's personal and political morality, attacked motels in 1940 as "assignation camps" and "crime camps" contributing to the downfall of America. From that perspective, then, seemingly innocent San Luis Obispo is where the downfall of America began.

Hoover's opinions aside, San Luis Obispo is a peaceful and pretty college town that has so far escaped the head-on collision with urban and suburban traffic under way in places such as Monterey and Ventura. **California State Polytechnic University** (Cal Poly) here is a major jewel in the community's crown, though the college is still snidely referred to as "Cow Poly" or "Cow Tech" in some circles. The Beef Pavilion, crops, swine, and poultry units do collectively clamor for center-stage attention on the campus just northeast of town, but the college is not just an agricultural school anymore. Cal Poly's architectural school is excellent, the largest in the country, as are the engineering and computer science departments. And since students here "learn by doing," there's almost always something fascinating doing on campus—particularly now that the impressive new $30 million **Performing Arts Center** has opened its opera house-style doors.

San Luis Obispo as a mission fortress was established in 1772 and named for the 13th-century Saint Louis, bishop of Toulouse, who also inadvertently lent his name to this California city and county in 1850. But San Luis Obispo's saintly antecedents have been overshadowed, politically speaking, by PG&E's Diablo Canyon Nuclear Power Plant. Diablo, in Spanish, means "the devil." Though some claim Diablo Canyon has tarnished the town's halo of rural serenity, most of the forward-looking folks of San Luis Obispo don't seem bothered. They assume, like the rest of us, that the devil's due won't come due anytime soon.

San Luis Obispo's rip-snortin' intercollegiate rodeo and livestock competitions in April, the notorious **Poly Royale**, is no more, since locals got a bit tired of the out-of-control crowds and partying. But there's always **La Fiesta** at the Mission Plaza Park in May, with Spanish-era music, costumes, feasting, and dancing. In July, come for the **Central Coast Renaissance Faire.** One of the West Coast's finest cycling events is the **SLO Criterium**, also in July. The biggest arts event of the year is the annual **Mozart Festival** (www.mozartfestival.com) in late July and early August. The 20 or more intimate concerts are held at the on-campus Performing Arts Center, at the mission, and in cafes, parks, and wineries throughout the area, from Arroyo Grande to San Miguel. Composers, conductors, and musicians from around the world come to town to evoke the spirit of Amadeus. Free public Mozart Akademie lectures by various distinguished visitors are part of the week's program; the **Festival Fringe** activities include free art exhibits, concerts, and poetry readings. Come in August for the **Central Coast Wine Festival,** in November for the annual **Harvest Celebration.**

For more information about attractions and events throughout the county, contact: **San Luis Obispo County Visitors and Conference Bureau,** 1041 Chorro St., Ste. E, San Luis Obispo 93401, tel. (805) 541-8000 or toll-free (800) 634-1414, fax (805) 543-1255, www.sanluisobispocounty.com. Alternatively, stop by or contact the adjacent **San Luis Obispo Chamber of Commerce and Visitor Center,** 1039 Chorro St., tel. (805) 781-2777, www.visitslo.com. The visitor center is open Tues.-Fri. 8 a.m.-5 p.m. and Sat.-Mon. 10 a.m.-5 p.m. The chamber also sells tickets for Hearst Castle tours at San Simeon up the coast, if you're thinking of heading that way and don't have reservations. For information about area arts events, contact the **San Luis Obispo County Arts Council,** tel. (805) 544-9251, www.sloartscouncil.org. For whatever else is happening here and in northern Santa Barbara County, pick up a copy of *New Times* magazine, www.newtimes-slo.com.

SEEING AND DOING SAN LUIS OBISPO

Downtown San Luis Obispo

The creekside **Mission San Luis Obispo de Tolosa** downtown, founded by Father Junípero Serra in 1772 and still central to community life, was the fifth in the chain. Originally built of tules and logs, then of five-foot-thick adobe with tiled roofs to prevent native peoples from torching the place, this isn't one of California's most intriguing missions. The stars on the parish church ceiling *are* different, though, and the mission's combination belfry and vestibule is another unique feature. The museum, once the priest's quarters, is worth a short stop for the arrowheads, baskets, Father Serra's vestments, and tangential trivia: books, portraits of mission workers, a winepress, handmade knives, and 1880s office furniture carved by the Cherokee. The mission itself, at 751 Palm St. on the edge of the downtown Mission Plaza area between Chorro and Garden and Monterey and Higuera Streets, is open 9 a.m.-5 p.m. in summer, 10 a.m.-4 p.m. otherwise (closed Easter, Thanksgiving, Christmas, and New Year's Day). Small donation requested. Call (805) 543-6850 for more information.

From the mission, San Luis Obispo's historic walking tour leads through parts of hip and homey downtown, past Victorians, adobes, and the old-time train depot. Court St. is the site of the old **Bull and Bear Pit,** an early California "sporting" arena. The **San Luis Obispo County Historical Museum** at the far end of Mission Plaza in the old Carnegie library, 696 Monterey St., tel. (805) 543-0638, open Wed.-Sun. 10 a.m.-4 p.m., houses a collection of local memorabilia, including Chumash artifacts and settlers' glassware, antique clothes, even hair wreaths, also an extensive historical photo archive and research library. Just across the street is the **San Luis Obispo Art Center.** On the other side of the public bathrooms is the historic **Murray Adobe.** The **Ah Louis Store,** 800 Palm St., is all that remains of San Luis Obispo's once-thriving Chinatown. Established in 1874, Ah Louis's store was the county's first Chinese general store and the bank, counting house, and post office for the many Chinese employed by the Southern Pacific

WORTHWHILE NORTH OF SAN LUIS OBISPO

North of San Luis Obispo proper, Santa Margarita was once a small outpost of the mission, with a chapel, grain storage, and lodging rooms. The biggest thing around today, though, is tiny **Santa Margarita Lake,** which offers camping, picnicking, and fishing. For info, call (805) 438-5485 or check www.centralcoast.com/santamargaritalake/. East via Hwy. 58 is the fascinating **Carrizo Plain Natural Area,** sometimes referred to as "California's Serengeti," much of the land now protected within a vast Nature Conservancy preserve. Though almost everything else in California has been endlessly exploited, the Carrizo Plain somehow missed out on the march of progress. The San Andreas Fault is on the plain's eastern edge, and the region is hot in summer and cold in winter. Yet the plain, once a prehistoric lake, was sacred to the Chumash, whose Great Spirits lived here—and shook the earth, when angered. Eight miles wide and 50 miles long, the Carrizo Plain preserves the last large remnant of the San Joaquin Valley's natural terrain, where sandhill cranes winter and some 600 pronghorn antelope roam native grasslands. The best time to come for a look is in late winter and early spring.

North via Hwy. 101 are **Atascadero** and **Paso Robles,** center of another notable California wine country. Still farther north on the main highway is sleepy little **San Miguel** with its fine old mission and, to the west, **Lake Nacimiento.** As the highway hums northward through the Salinas Valley, to the west lies **Lake San Antonio,** popular for bald eagle watching in winter.

Beyond Jolon, smack in the midst of Fort Hunter-Liggett, is **Mission San Antonio de Padua,** tel. (831) 385-4478, not the biggest nor most ravishingly restored mission, certainly not the most popular, but somehow the most evocative of Spanish California—well worth the detour. For a simple yet special stay less than a half-mile away, consider the **Hacienda Guest Lodge,** tel. (831) 386-2900, the original ranch house designed for William Randolph Hearst by Julia Morgan, built in 1922. Later an officers club, the Hacienda is now a combination hotel, restaurant, bar, bowling alley with snack bar, and campground. Nothing fancy, but a tremendous value. A steak dinner is $10 or so. Rooms or suites with private baths start at $46 (Inexpensive); those with shared baths are $33 (Budget). Weather and road conditions permitting, from Fort Hunter-Liggett it's possible to take the back-roads route, Nacimiento-Fergusson Rd., over the mountains to Big Sur.

Railroad between 1884 and 1894 to dig eight train tunnels through the Cuesta Mountains.

Touring the County's Bounty

The "Ag's My Bag" bumper stickers on cars and pickup trucks you'll see throughout San Luis Obispo don't lie; agriculture seems to be everybody's bag here. In San Luis Obispo County, local produce *is* local and remarkably diverse because of the mild and varied climate. Bring bags and boxes along and take home seasonal produce, everything from almonds to zucchini. To find the best of the county's bounty, pick up pamphlets at the visitor bureau or chamber offices—or attend any of the eight weekly area farmers markets.

The biggest and some say the best of these, a cross between a no-bargains-barred shopping spree and a street party, is San Luis Obispo's main event. The **San Luis Obispo Higuera Street Certified Farmers' Market,** tel. (805) 544-9570, is held in downtown San Luis Obispo every Thursday 6:30-9:30 p.m., weather permitting, along the 600-900 blocks of Higuera (between Osos and Broad Streets). Show up early to find a parking place, since the whole county comes to the city on Thursday evenings—the main reason area shops and restaurants are open late on this particular weeknight. On tap Thursday evenings: live entertainment, arts, crafts, and good food in addition to fine fresh fruits, vegetables, and flowers.

Particularly worth it, too, from late summer into early November, is the 13-mile **See Canyon apple tour** of the half-dozen 1900s-vintage orchards in the narrow canyon southwest of town. Apples grown here are not the kind usually found in supermarkets: old-time Arkansas Blacks, Splendors from Tasmania, and Gravensteins plus more modern "Jonalicious," New Zealand Galas, and the very tart Tohuku variety so popular in France. Among the most popular apple stops in See Canyon: Gopher Glen Apples, Daisy Dell Apple Ranch, and Ruda's Apples. To take the See Canyon tour: head south from San Luis Obispo on Hwy. 101 and then west on San Luis Bay Dr.; after a mile or so turn right onto See Canyon Rd., which eventually becomes Prefumo Canyon Rd.—with great views of Morro Bay— and connects farther north with Los Osos Valley Road. A left turn here leads to Morro Bay, a right back to Hwy. 101 just south of San Luis.

Touring the County's Wineries

When you're done with apples, try some fruit of the vine. Together the **Edna Valley** and **Arroyo Grande Valley** comprise yet another upstart wine region just inland from the California coast; the small wineries here were first successful with chardonnay and pinot noir grapes. **Edna Valley Vineyard,** for example, specializes in both, while **Meridian** features an exceptional Edna Valley chardonnay. Most of these regional wineries lie between San Luis Obispo and Arroyo Grande, on small agricultural holdings and

hillsides east of Hwy. 227. Come the first weekend in May for the annual **Roll Out the Barrels** winery barrel tasting and "passport" event. For a current tour map or other information, contact: **Edna Valley Arroyo Grande Valley Vintners,** 5825 Orcutt Rd., San Luis Obispo, CA 93401, tel. (805) 541-5868, fax (805) 541-3934, www.the-grid.net/vintners. Some area wineries are not vintner association members, however. For a reasonably comprehensive listing of wineries within the larger Central Coast appellation— which ranges from the southern San Francisco Bay Area to Santa Barbara—see www.villa-creek.com/region_winerys.html.

North-county wineries are also well worth looking for. Another of California's newer small winery regions lies near **Paso Robles, Templeton,** and **Atascadero,** throughout the hills and valleys both east and west of Hwy. 101, a region where cabernet, chardonnay, merlot, syrah, and zinfandel grapes do well. As in Edna Valley and Arroyo Grande, most wineries here are small, family-run operations producing 5,000 or

JAMES DEAN DIED HERE

Rebels otherwise without a cause might spend a few minutes in Cholame (sho-LAMB), 27 miles east of Paso Robles on the way to Lost Hills via hustle-bustle Hwy. 46. At the onetime intersection of Highways 41 and 46 (the exact routing of the roads has since changed), actor James Dean met death at the age of 24. The star of only three movies—*East of Eden,* his trademark *Rebel Without a Cause,* and *Giant*— Dean, heading west into the blinding sun, died instantly when his speeding silver Porsche slammed head-on into a Ford at 5:59 p.m. on September 30, 1955.

And every September 30th since 1979, members of a Southern California car club trace the route of Dean's last road trip, starting in Van Nuys, during the annual en masse migration to Cholame on the James Dean Memorial Run—just about the ultimate experience for 1950s car enthusiasts.

But in front of Cholame's postage stamp-sized post office and outside the restaurant a half mile from the actual place Dean died, there's an oddly evocative stainless-steel obelisk in his memory, paid for by a businessman from Japan. The memorial is wrapped around a lone tree and landscaped with

9,000 pounds of imported Japanese gravel, a concrete bench, and engraved bronze tablets—a pilgrimage site for fans from around the world. (Inside, Dean fans can buy memorial T-shirts, sun visors, posters, and postcards. The proceeds go toward maintaining the monument.)

Seita Ohnishi's explanation etched on the tablets reads:

This monument stands as a small token of my appreciation for the people of America. It also stands for James Dean and other American Rebels. . . . In Japan, we say his death came as suddenly as it does to cherry blossoms. The petals of early spring always fall at the height of their ephemeral brilliance. Death in youth is life that glows eternal.

But in keeping with James Dean's own favorite words—from Antoine de Saint-Exupery, "What is essential is invisible to the eye"—what was important about Dean's life is not necessarily here.

fewer bottles per year—casual and "country," as different from the now-big-business Napa and Sonoma county wine industries as well-broke cowboy boots are from Bruno Maglis. Many offer tours only with reservations, especially during the hectic autumn harvest season. Among the many possible stops: **Justin Vineyards and Winery** on Chimney Rock Rd., specializing in barrel-fermented chardonnays and known for its Isosceles, a blend of cabernet franc, cabernet sauvignon, and merlot, and the **Martin Brothers Winery** on Buena Vista Rd., known for its award-winning Italian-style cabernet sauvignon, chardonnay, and zinfandel as well as summer Opera Under the Stars and occasional jazz concerts. Come in mid-May for the **Paso Robles Wine Festival Weekend.** For current regional wineries information, contact the **Paso Robles Visitors & Conference Bureau,** 1225 Park St., Paso Robles, CA 93446, tel. (805) 238-0506 or toll-free (800) 406-4040, fax (805) 238-0527, http://pasorobleschamber.com, open weekdays and on Saturday 10 a.m.-4 p.m., and the **Paso Robles Vintners and Growers Association,** 622 12th St., tel. (805) 239-8463, fax (805) 237-6439, www.pasowine.com.

ALONG SAN LUIS OBISPO BAY

Bayside Diversions
Gentler than Big Sur's, the coastline near San Luis Obispo offers rocky terraces, sandy dunes, and a big-picture view of the Seven Sisters, vol-

canic peaks that saunter seaward from San Luis Obispo to "the rock" at Morro Bay. By car the coastal communities of Morro Bay, Avila Beach, and Pismo Beach are all less than 15 minutes away from San Luis Obispo.

The pier at **Port San Luis,** old Port Hartford and once a regular steamship stop, is now a favorite fishing spot. **Avila Beach** just east along the bay is a favorite surfers' beach town on the way to becoming trendy, its protected beaches tucked into the cove. (Try to ignore the oil tanks looming overhead.) These days Avila Beach is still recovering from Unocal Corp.'s massive "oil change" on the beach, a multi-million-dollar project that involved excavating then replacing tons of soil and sand soaked with some 420,000 gallons of petroleum, and relocating (or demolishing then replacing) many of those famously funky beach-shack Front St. businesses and other buildings. Stop by and see how clean a cleaned-up beach town can get. Less appealing but definitely private is clothing-optional **Pirate's Cove** beaches a mile south of Avila Beach (weirdos possible, so bring a friend). But before leaving Avila Beach, do the hot springs. Relaxed, funky, and family-friendly **Avila Hot Springs,** also an RV and tent-camping resort at 250 Avila Beach Dr., tel. (805) 595-2359 or toll-free (800) 332-2359 or (800) 543-2359 for reservations, www.campgrounds.com, features a large freshwater swimming pool in addition to private step-down tiled hot mineral tubs in the original 1930s bathhouse and the hot outdoor pools. (Rent inner tubes and float in the warm pool.) Spa services are also available. The more uptown and historic **Sycamore Mineral Springs Resort,** 1215 Avila Beach Dr., tel. (805) 595-7302 or toll-free (800) 234-5831 for reservations, www.smsr.com and www.sycamoresprings.com, offers pleasant motel-style hotel rooms, suites, and bed-and-breakfast stays—not to mention a swimming pool, volleyball courts, and The Gardens of Avila restaurant—in addition to hot mineral soaks, massage, facials, and other spa services. The very private lattice-screened redwood hot tubs, which rent by the hour 24 hours a day, are strategically scattered around the landscaped wooded hillside (hot tub reservations advised).

Shell Beach south of Pirate's Cove and north of Pismo Beach is a marine-terrace town with lots of antique shops and two wooden staircas-

---

HIKING THE DIABLO COAST

The 10 miles of coast north of Port San Luis is pristine and rugged, home to sea lions, pelicans, and cormorants. The presence of the **Diablo Canyon Nuclear Plant** means this entire area has long been off-limits to coastwalkers for security reasons. But now the **Pecho Coast Trail** traverses several miles of this once-lost coast, from just north of Avila Beach to Point San Luis Lighthouse and the marine terrace just beyond. Before you strap on those hiking boots, though, pick up the phone and call (805) 541-8735; the area is accessible on guided hikes only, and only by reservation.

TOURING DIABLO CANYON

Since guards at the two-unit Diablo Canyon Nuclear Power Plant control the traffic flow here near Port San Luis, don't plan on walking in for a casual look-see. Years of anti-nuclear protest have made security serious business. Trouble was Diablo's middle name for 20 years, thanks to relentless anti-nuclear energy protesters. Critics of the plant, built just a few miles from the Hosgri offshore earthquake fault, have consistently attempted to shut down construction—then, later, the on-line plants—with lawsuits and civil disobedience.

In 1997, Pacific Gas & Electric (PG&E) agreed to pay $14 million to settle charges it had deliberately underreported damage to sealife at Diablo Canyon, the indirect result of the 2.5 billion gallons of seawater sucked into the plant each day.

Despite environmentalists and anti-nuke naysayers, PG&E promotes the plant as "solid as the Rock of Gibraltar," a good neighbor until the end of time; PG&E also hopes its rock is a rock-solid investment, with its total $5.8 billion construction price tag fi-nanced through Northern California customers' utility bills. Though both are now on-line, Diablo's first nuclear reactor set a nationwide performance record during its first year of operation, producing more than eight billion kilowatt-hours of electricity while operating at capacity 93 percent of the time.

How do local people feel about Diablo Canyon? You'll find both gung-ho support and absolute opposition but primarily, in the typically apolitical American tradition, a "let's-wait-and-see" attitude prevails.

The utility's pretty, Spanish-looking **PG&E Community Center** about 12 miles south of San Luis Obispo via Hwy. 101 at 6588 Ontario Rd. (exit at San Luis Bay Dr.) in Avila Beach, tel. (805) 546-5280, open 9 a.m.-5 p.m. daily, offers simple but flashy presentations on fission nuclear energy, also three- to four-hour **overlook tours** of the plant site by bus, including stops at the marine biology lab and a simulated control room. But if you want to hear what a nuclear-meltdown siren sounds like, you'll have to make reservations.

---

es leading to the rocky coast below. Primo is shoving off from Shell Beach for ocean kayaking, an adventure easily undertaken with help from **Central Coast Kayaks** on Shell Beach Rd., tel. (805) 773-3500.

Pismo Beach and Other Bayside Communities

Shell Beach segues into **Pismo Beach** proper, once a haute destination for 1930s celebrities, now a cleaned-up, family-friendly, and fairly affordable beach community. Pismo Beach was first famous for its pismo clams, a population now nearly decimated. The Spanish *pismo* means "a place to fish," but the Chumash *pismu* means "a place where blobs of tar wash up on the beach." Since good fishing is a historical fact and, in the absence of major coastal oil spills, beach tar from here to Santa Barbara is a natural phenomenon, pick your own derivation. For more information about the area and its attractions, contact: **Pismo Beach Chamber of Commerce & Visitors Center,** 581 Dolliver, tel. (805) 773-4382, fax (805) 773-6772, www.pismocham-ber.com, open Mon.-Sat. 9 a.m.-5 p.m. and Sunday 10 a.m.-4 p.m.

The six miles of shoreline from Pismo Beach to Oceano is primarily **Pismo State Beach,** with a small dunes preserve tacked on to the southern end. Dominated by the **Oceano Dunes State Vehicular Recreation Area** dune buggy heaven, Pismo offers little for solitude-seeking beach and dune lovers beyond pier fishing. Such souls will feel considerably more comfortable at the Nature Conservancy's now extensive **Guadalupe-Nipomo Dunes Preserve** farther south (see Santa Maria and Vicinity, below) or at isolated **Point Sal State Beach,** reached from Hwy. 101 south of Santa Maria via Betteravia and Brown Roads.

Oceano and vicinity, just south of Pismo Beach, have seen wilder days. Sneaky sand dunes advanced on the town's famous dance pavilion, cottages, and wharf years ago, destroying them all. The dunes here are the highest and whitest in the state, blocked from straying farther south by the Point Sal cliffs. Inland are marshes and shallow lagoons, resting areas for mallards and teal and home during the Depression to the "Dunites," an eclectic group of artists, astrologers, loners, nudists, and writers. These days Oceano's most notable attraction is **The**

Great American Melodrama, tel. (805) 489-2499, where old-fashioned entertainment comes with dinner.

Inland from Oceano and the Pismo Beach area is **Arroyo Grande,** nothing but a stage stop in 1877, now an attractive village with Old West-style antique and other shops, some bed and breakfasts, and surrounding flower seed farms. At the Village Green near city hall, you'll see a small park and a 71-foot-long swinging bridge built in 1875. For more information, contact: **Arroyo Grande Chamber of Commerce & Visitors Center,** 800 W. Branch, tel. (805) 489-1488, fax (805) 489-2239, open weekdays 10 a.m.-5 p.m.

PRACTICAL SAN LUIS OBISPO

Camping Near San Luis Obispo

Camp at Lopez Lake about 11 miles northeast of Arroyo Grande, a pretty little reservoir also good for fishing, swimming (waterslide, too), sailing, and windsurfing. Primitive tent campsites, shaded by oaks, are $13, sites with full hookups $21. For more information, call **Lopez Lake Recreation Area** at (805) 489-8019 or (805) 489-2095, www.centralcoast.com/lakelopez. For hikers and fisherpeople, the day-use fee at Lopez Lake is $5; pets (on leashes) are $2 extra, boat launch fees are $2-4.

Beach camping is also a good bet. State park campsites are available at Morro Bay, with the best developed ones at **Morro Bay State Park** and primitive ones at **Montaña de Oro.** For details, see Morro Bay and Vicinity, above. The hot mineral tubs and pools are the main attraction at **Avila Hot Springs** on Avila Beach Dr. in Avila Beach, but you can also pitch a tent here for $18 (up to six people) or park your RV, $19 with electricity, $23 for full hookups. For more resort information see Along San Luis Obispo Bay, above.

Contact the visitors center in San Luis Obispo for more camping suggestions.

A Hostel and Affordable "Motor Hotels"

San Luis Obispo has a new HI/AYH hostel location—**Hostel Obispo,** 1617 Santa Rosa St. (Hwy. 1), San Luis Obispo, CA 93401, tel. (805) 544-4678, fax (805) 544-3142, www.hostelweb.com, with a per-bed rate of $15-17 for dorm beds, $37.50-40 for private rooms. Reservations accepted by mail or fax, with deposit (no credit cards). Extras here include laundry, bike rentals, on-site parking, and a garden and patio with barbecue. Hostel Obispo also offers group trips and hiking and biking "adventure tours." Budget.

The quite decent **Motel 6** here, 1433 Calle Joaquin (take the Los Osos Valley Rd. exit from Hwy. 101), San Luis Obispo 93401, tel. (805) 549-9595, fax (805) 544-2826, or toll-free (800) 466-8356 for reservations (nationwide), www. motel6.com, is convenient for hikers planning to head out early for the Los Osos Preserve and other Morro Bay area parks. Beyond the basics, facilities include a pool and laundry. Regular high-season weekend rates are $50, higher during major local events, lower most of the year. Inexpensive. Another, larger Motel 6 is just a stroll away, on the other side of Los Osos Valley Rd., tel. (805) 541-6992, with similar rates.

Most San Luis Obispo motels are on or near Monterey St., including the local **Super 8,** 1951 Monterey St., tel. (805) 544-7895 or toll-free (800) 800-8000 for reservations (nationwide), fax (805) 546-7895, with summer double rates $55 and up. Also quite reasonable in the neighborhood: the small **Villa Motel,** 1670 Monterey (at Grand), local tel. (805) 543-8071 or toll-free (800) 554-0059, fax (805) 549-4389, which also offers a heated pool and free breakfast. Inexpensive-Premium, with summer rates of $49 double and up, winter rates as low as $40 double. Weekly rates available. Quite inviting is the friendly Southwestern B&B-style **Adobe Inn,** 1473 Monterey, tel. (805) 549-0321 or toll-free (800) 676-1588, fax (805) 549-0383, www.adobeinns.com, with summer weekday rates $75 double, weekend rates $95, homemade breakfast included. (But off-season rates can be as low as $55—a real deal.) Moderate-Expensive.

More luxurious accommodations are available, too, particularly on Monterey St. and also on Madonna Rd.; contact the visitors bureau for a current listing. For other affordable options, head for Pismo Beach, where bargains abound—especially in the off-season.

Memorable Local "Motor Hotels" and Inns

The **Motel Inn,** San Luis Obispo's first and original "mo-tel," closed some years back for historic renovation and eventual expansion. In the meantime the next best thing is right next door—

the **Apple Farm Inn,** 2015 Monterey St., San Luis Obispo 93401, tel. (805) 544-2040 or toll-free (800) 374-3705 for reservations, fax (805) 546-9495, www.applefarm.com. Behind the locally famous **Apple Farm Restaurant** is the rest of the ranch—in this case, a quaint three-story motel with contemporary country-inn airs. Rooms feature fireplaces, four-poster beds, and other period furnishings, even armoires. Equally pleasant but less expensive are the more motel-like rooms in the **Apple Farm Trellis Court,** adjacent. Inn rooms start at $169 in the high season, dropping to $149 in winter. Motel rooms start at $119 in summer, $99 at other times. Expensive-Luxury.

The Cliffs at Shell Beach, 2757 Shell Beach Rd. in Pismo Beach 93449, tel. (805) 773-5000 or toll-free (800) 826-7827, fax (805) 773-0764, once offered the only seaside-resort accommodations in the San Luis Obispo area. The Cliffs, a hotel-style motel, sits right on the beach (actually, the cliffs above the beach). Rooms are spacious and attractive, done in day-at-the-beach colors, and feature the usual modern amenities plus in-room coffeemakers. Most have private patios and ocean views. The suites are something special, complete with in-room jacuzzis. Premium-Luxury. Regular room rates start at $130, but ask about discounts, off-season specials, and packages. Premium-Luxury. To get here from Hwy. 101: If coming from the north, exit at Shell Beach Rd.; from the south, exit at Spyglass Road. Other area options include the **Spyglass Inn,** 2705 Spyglass Dr., tel. (805) 773-4855 or toll-free (800) 824-2612, fax (805) 773-5298, www.spyglassinn.com (Expensive-Luxury), and **Cottage Inn by the Sea,** 2351 Price St., tel. (805) 773-4617 or toll-free (888) 440-8400, www.cottage-inn.com (Luxury).

Fun for bed and breakfast fans: the 13-room **Garden Street Inn,** 1212 Garden St. in San Luis Obispo, tel. (805) 545-9802 or toll-free (800) 488-2045, fax (805) 545-9403, www.gardenstreetinn.com, an 1887 Italianate Queen Anne Victorian was originally the centerpiece of the local Mission Vineyard. Rooms and suites are individually theme decorated; Valley of the Moon commemorates the life and times of Jack London, Walden is a Thoreau tribute, and Amadeus remembers Mozart. No phone, no TVs, so be prepared to truly relax. Suites include extras such as jacuzzi bath/showers, private decks, separate bedrooms. Full breakfast is served every morning, wine and cheese every evening. Expensive-Luxury. Rooms start at $100, suites at $150, with a two-night minimum stay on weekends.

For something to write home about, consider **The Madonna Inn,** 100 Madonna Rd., San Luis Obispo 93405, tel. (805) 543-3000 or toll-free (800) 543-9666, fax (805) 543-1800, www.madonnainn.com. One of the most unusual motels anywhere, the Madonna is noted for quirky "theme" rooms and suites, some with waterfalls and other dramatic elements, each one of the 109 rooms here unique. Some sample themes: the Daisy Mae Room, the Caveman Room, the Cloud Nine Suite, the Love Nest. You get the idea—immensely popular with newlyweds and couples tired of the same old anniversary celebration. This Madonna is getting a bit tired these days, too, but still, a stay here is *different.* Rooms are Premium-Luxury, with rates $127-310. Those who don't stay should satisfy their curiosity by wandering the halls and peeking into any open rooms. Men—and undaunted women—should also check out the men's bathroom off the lobby, most notable for its free-flowing waterfall urinal and seashell washbasins. Other attractions include a very good restaurant, bar, and on-site bakery.

More relaxing, in its unpretentious way, is **Sycamore Mineral Springs Resort** in Avila Beach at 1215 Avila Beach Rd. in San Luis Obispo, tel. (805) 595-7302 or toll-free (800) 234-5831, fax (805) 781-2598, www.sycamoresprings.com, or with very private rent-a-hot tubs (clothing optional) tucked into the oak-covered hillsides and available 24 hours per day. Spa services including acupressure, reflexology, polarity therapy, shiatsu, facials, and Swedish massage are also available. Motel-style rooms here, each with a private hot tub outside on the patio or deck, are $119 and up. The resort's new two-room suites, with four-poster beds, fine wood furnishings, and wet bars, marble fireplaces, and sofas, start at $209. A stay here also includes a $12 credit toward breakfast at very good, very reasonably priced California-style **The Gardens of Avila** restaurant here, which also serves lunch and dinner daily and Sunday brunch. Bed-and-breakfast rooms are also available, $169-300. Premium-Luxury.

Dining Downtown and Around

San Luis Obispo boasts more than 60 eateries, so look around—especially downtown, where delis, small cafes, and restaurants surround the plaza area. Good for breakfast is **Louisa's Place,** 964 Higuera St., tel. (805) 541-0227, a countertop-style cafe locally popular for its buckwheat pancakes and lunch specials. **Pete's Southside Cafe,** 1815 Osos St., tel. (805) 549-8133, is an outpost of the original Avila Beach Pete's all gussied up for more stylish times. But the fresh seafood is still fresh, the Mexican selections still good, and the atmosphere still bright and bustling. It's open for lunch and dinner, on Sunday for dinner only.

The **Big Sky Café,** 1121 Broad St., tel. (805) 545-5401, serves great Southwestern selections and other eclectic New American fare. Justifiably popular, too, is **Mother's Tavern,** 725 Higuera St., tel. (805) 541-3853, where the specialty is "California tavern food"—everything from burgers and steaks to pastas, salads, and sandwiches. Another hit at Mother's is the tavern's house band, the jump blues and swing band Sugar Daddy Swing Kings. So cool. The cool destination for the weekday "Happy Hour and a Half" is the old-brick **SLO Brewing Co.** downtown at 1119 Garden St. (between Higuera and Marsh Streets), tel. (805) 543-1843, open for lunch and dinner daily (just noon-5 p.m. on Sunday). Brewpub fans believe the main attractions here are the Amber Ale, Pale Ale, and Porter—and at least one seasonal brew, on tap. Live entertainment later too, most nights.

Stylin' it in San Luis Obispo might include lunch or dinner at **Cafe Roma,** in a new location at Railroad Square near the train station, 1020 Railroad Ave., tel. (805) 541-6800, open Tues.-Fri. for lunch and Tues.-Sun. for dinner. Noted for its authentic northern Italian fare, Cafe Roma is one of San Luis Obispo's most popular fine food destinations. The pastas are always good, though you won't go wrong with the Tuscan chicken or osso bucco. The wine list is also a treat, a mix of classy regional Californians and classic Italians. Also quite good, downtown next to the Fremont Theater, is **Buona Tavola,** 1037 Monterey St., tel. (805) 545-8000, also open for lunch and dinner.

A fun family-style place convenient to motel row is **Izzy Ortega's Mexican Restaurant and Cantina** next to the Holiday Inn at 1850 Monterey St., tel. (805) 543-3333, open daily 11:30 a.m. until at least 9 p.m. (bar open later). Colorful and cheerful with a party-hearty American attitude, Izzy's is one of San Luis Obispo's most popular restaurants. The food's quite good, and considerably more authentic than most Americanized Mexican. Try the shrimp or fish tacos, for example, the pork tamales, or the tasty bean soup. Entrees get more ambitious, including steak ranchero and broiled garlic shrimp. Children's menu available.

Another place to take the kids, especially if you can get them to pay: the original **F. McClintocks Saloon and Dining House,** 750 Mattie Rd. in Pismo Beach, tel. (805) 773-1892, open daily (after 3 or 4 p.m.) for dinner, and on Sunday at 9:30-9 p.m., for "ranch breakfast," early supper, and dinner (closed some major holidays). Beef—aged, "hand-cut," and then barbecued over oak wood—is the secret to the success of this kicky outpost of commercialized mom-and-pop cowboy kitsch. (The gift shop overfloweth.) Everything here is pretty good, however. The machismo challenge, typically issued by men to men, is eating the oddest menu item—fried turkey nuts—without squawking. And if you like that sort of thing, come in mid-July for the Annual Mountain Oyster Feed, held out back. But kids are more impressed by the wait staff, who pour water by holding the pitcher at least two feet above the table—and never spill a drop. And don't miss the Birthday Picture Gallery. Or mosey on over to the other area F. McClintocks locations; there's one here in SLO at 686 Higuera St., tel. (805) 541-0686, and others in Paso Robles and Arroyo Grande.

The classic surfers' fuel center in Pismo Beach is the **Splash Café,** just a block from the pier at 197 Pomeroy Ave., tel. (805) 773-4653, where you can get a bread bowl full of wonderful New England-style clam chowder for under $5. A bit more stylish for seafood is the **Olde Port Inn,** in Avila Beach at Port San Luis's Pier #3, tel. (805) 595-2515. Well worth looking for in nearby Arroyo Grande is **Massimo's,** 640 Oak Park Blvd., tel. (805) 474-9211, where northern Italian is the specialty.

And if you're heading north from the area, **Villa Creek** in Paso Robles, 1144 Pine St., tel. (805) 238-3000, specializes in early Californian, and **McPhee's Grill** at 416 Main St. in Templeton, tel. (805) 434-3204, is known for its regional American.

SANTA MARIA AND VICINITY

This onetime ranch-country hitching post on the northern fringe of Santa Barbara County is quickly growing out into its flower fields, thanks in part to the proximity of Vandenberg Air Force Base. Built on sand flats, Santa Maria has an abundance of trees, unusually wide streets—origi-

nally to more easily reverse eight-mule wagon rigs—and one of the West's best repertory theater programs.

Come in April for the annual **Santa Maria Valley Strawberry Festival** at the county fairgrounds, and the **Santa Maria Bluegrass Festival.** The "West's Best Rodeo," Santa Maria's **Elks Rodeo and Parade,** is the big event in late May or early June. The **Santa Barbara County Fair** in late July is old-fashioned family fun complete with carnival, exhibits, entertainment, and horse show. Biplanes, hot-air balloons, and sky divers all converge in September for Santa

---

IN SEARCH OF *THE TEN COMMANDMENTS*

The coastal dunes due west of Santa Maria provide habitat for California brown pelicans and the endangered least terns, though Cecil B. DeMille probably didn't think much about such things in 1923 when he built, and then buried, a dozen four-ton plaster sphinxes, four statues of Ramses the Magnificent, and an entire pharaonic city here—the original movie set for *The Ten Commandments.* Referred to as the dune that never moves, Ten Commandment Hill is now part of the **Guadalupe-Nipomo Dunes Preserve** and the first thing visitors see at the Guadalupe entrance.

This large coastal dunes preserve is part of the seemingly simple yet quite complicated and fragile Nipomo Dunes ecosystem, which stretches from Pismo Beach south to Vandenberg. Created by howling wind and enormous offshore swells, the seaward dunes are sizable parabola-shaped mounds of sharp-grained sand in almost perpetual motion. The more stable back dunes stand 200 feet tall and offer more hospitable habitat for the 18 endangered and rare endemic coastal scrub species counted to date by members of the California Native Plant Society. Among the most instantly impressive is the yellow-flowered giant coreopsis, which grows only on the Channel Islands and on the coast from Los Angeles north to the Nipomo Dunes.

Oso Flaco Lake to the north of Guadalupe is a surprising sparkling blue coastal oasis, actually a group of small lakes fringed by shrubs and surrounded by sand dunes (and the din from dune buggyists penned up just northward at the Oceano Dunes State Vehicular Recreation Area).

To the south is **Mussel Rock,** at 500 feet the tallest sand dune in California. Sit and watch the

sunset while the surf spits and sputters across the sand. Or hike to Point Sal and **Point Sal State Beach,** a wonderfully remote stretch of headlands, rocky outcroppings, and sand (the treacherous surf is unsafe for swimming) just north of Vandenberg. (To get there, head west on the Brown Rd. turnoff three miles south of Guadalupe, and then take Point Sal Road.) Good whalewatching.

Though the preserve holdings started with 3,400 acres, including the critical central section relinquished by Mobil Oil Corporation, the preserve now embraces a total of 20,000 acres owned by the Nature Conservancy and various public agencies. The San Luis Obispo-based People for Nipomo Dunes led the dunes preservation effort with the idea of creating a Nipomo Dunes National Seashore, protected federally like Point Reyes to the north. The dunes area now recognized as a National Natural Landmark.

The preserve is accessible from Hwy. 101 in Santa Maria (via Hwy. 166) or from Hwy. 1 farther west near Guadalupe. There are two preserve entrances. To reach the Guadalupe entrance, from Guadalupe continue to the west end of W. Main Street. To reach the Oso Flaco Lake entrance, from Hwy. 1 about three miles north of Guadalupe turn left onto Oso Flaco Lake Road. The Oso Flaco Lake area is handicapped accessible, with a mile-long boardwalk. The preserve is open dawn to dusk 365 days each year. No overnight camping, dogs, or four-wheel drive vehicles are allowed.

For more information, stop by the **Dunes Center,** in downtown Guadalupe at 951 Guadalupe St. (Hwy. 1), tel. (805) 343-2455, www.dunescenter.org. The center is open Friday 2-4 p.m. and on weekends noon-4 p.m.

Maria's **Air Fair.** But good times anytime are almost guaranteed by the fine **Pacific Conservatory of the Performing Arts,** which offers Shakespeare, musicals such as *Narnia* and *I Do, I Do,* and dramas such as *Amadeus* and Eugene O'Neill's *Long Day's Journey Into Night.* Performances are also held in Solvang, but the troupe's headquarters are at the local Allan Hancock College, 800 S. College Dr. in Santa Maria, www.pcpa.org, tel. (805) 922-8313 or, for tickets, toll-free (800) 727-2123.

Fairly new in the neighborhood is the two-hangar **Santa Maria Museum of Flight,** 3015 Airpark Rd., tel. (805) 922-8758, open Fri.-Sun. 9 a.m.-5 p.m. (until 4 p.m. in winter), which documents general flight history with both antique and model planes, with an emphasis on local contributions to aviation history. (Santa Maria was a basing station during World War II.) The once-secret Norden bombsight, the Fleet Model 2, and the Stinson V77-Reliant are among the treasures on display. The Early Aviation Hangar houses aircraft, memorabilia, models, and photos chronicling the years stretching between the Wright Brothers' first flights to World War II. A veritable flock of antique planes perches here in July for the **Primary Trainer Fly-In.** For broader local historical perspective, the **Santa Maria Valley Historical Museum** is downtown adjacent to the visitor bureau/chamber of commerce office at 616 S. Broadway, tel. (805) 922-3130, and is open Tues.-Sat. noon-5 p.m. A fascination here: the Barbecue Hall of Fame.

For more information about Santa Maria and vicinity, contact: **Santa Maria Visitor and Convention Bureau,** 614 S. Broadway, Santa Maria, CA 93454, tel. (805) 925-2403 or toll-free (800) 331-3779, fax (805) 928-7559, www.santa-maria.com, which offers accommodations, food, and regional wine-tour information. Also pick up a copy of the *Walk Through History* local walking tour guide. For area camping and regional recreation information, contact the **Santa Lucia Ranger District** office of the Los Padres National Forest at 1616 N. Carlotti Dr. in Santa Maria, tel. (805) 925-9538, www.r5.fs.fed.us/lospadres.

LOMPOC AND VICINITY

Probably Chumash for "shell mound," Lompoc these days is a bustling military town amid blooming flower fields, a commercial crazy-quilt patchwork of fragrant sweet peas, larkspurs, asters, poppies, marigolds, zinnias, and petunias adding vivid bloom to the city's cheeks from June through September. The local flower seed business is under pressure from foreign agricultural production, but the bloom boom is still healthy enough to make the tourists smile. At **Vandenberg Air Force Base** just west of town—home of the 30th Space Wing, and the only U.S. military installation that launches unmanned government and commercial satellites in addition to intercontinental ballistic missiles (ICBMs)—evening launches create colorful sky

Mission La Purísima is the state's largest and only complete mission complex.

trails at sunset. Free tours of Vandenberg, which might include a former space shuttle launch site, an underground missile silo, and a shipwrecked 1923 naval destroyer, are offered Wednesday at 10 a.m. (pending missions permitting). For details and reservations, call (805) 606-3595.

Another significant but subtler local presence is the area's medium security prison—until recently also a comfortable minimum security prison camp known fondly as Club Fed, historic home away from home for white-collar criminals, including Nixon-era Watergate scandal alumni Dwight Chapin, John Dean, H.R. Haldeman, and Donald Segretti. Inside trader Ivan Boesky, former San Diego Chargers running back Chuck Muncie, and convicted Soviet spy Christopher Boyce (of *The Falcon and the Snowman* fame) did some time here, too.

Mission La Purísima Concepción (see below) is the area's main attraction, but stop by the **Lompoc Museum,** 200 S. H St., tel. (805) 736-3888, open afternoons Tues.-Sun., to review the city's pioneering Prohibitionist history. And poke around town to appreciate the **Lompoc Valley Mural Project** (more than 60 and counting) and the city's unique Italian stone pines. Beach hikers can head south for miles from **Ocean Beach County Park** at Vandenberg Air Force Base, reached from Lompoc via Hwy. 246 (heading west) and then Ocean Beach Road; often windy, so come prepared. Also locally famous for beach walks, good picnics, fishing, and fabulous sunsets is isolated, windswept, and wicked-waved **Jalama Beach County Park** about five miles south of Lompoc via Hwy. 1 and Jalama Rd., site of the annual **Heavy Wind Surfing Championships** in May. Come to town in June for the annual **Lompoc Flower Festival** and associated **Valley of the Flowers Half-Marathon.**

For more information about the area, contact the **Lompoc Valley Chamber of Commerce,** 111 S. I St., Lompoc, CA 93436, tel. (805) 736-4567, www.lompoc.com, which offers a "flower drive" brochure/map (routes also available on the website), events, and practical information.

La Purísima Mission State Historic Park

The largest mission complex in the state, now situated on 1,000 unspoiled acres about four miles east of Lompoc on Hwy. 246, Misión de la Con-

cepción Purísima de María Santísima ("Mission of the Immaculate Conception of Most Holy Mary") was the 11th in California's chain of coastal missions when it was built in what is now downtown Lompoc in 1787. Almost all of the original Mission La Purísima was destroyed just before Christmas Day in 1812 by a devastating earthquake and deluge. Another traumatic year was 1824, when rebellious Chumash, angry at their exploitation by soldiers, captured the mission and held it for a month. Ten years later, the mission was essentially abandoned.

Now an impressive state historic park and California's only complete mission complex, the new La Purísima (built between 1813 and 1818) is unusual in its layout. All buildings line up like ducks in a row along El Camino Real, rather than occupying more traditional positions surrounding an interior courtyard. Also unique here is the fine Depression-era restoration work accomplished primarily by the Civilian Conservation Corps under state and national parks supervision. Completely rebuilt from the ground up with handmade adobe bricks, tiles, and dyes essentially identical to the originals, the mission's handhewn redwood timbers, doors, and furniture, even the artwork and decorative designs, also come as close to authenticity as well-disciplined architectural imagination allows.

At La Purísima, secular existence has been emphasized over the religious life. Workshops and living quarters, the soldiers' quarters, and simple cells of the padres offer a sense of the unromantic and less-than-luxurious life in mission times. More interesting, though, are the shops where the mission's work went on: the bakery, the soap and tallow factory, weaving rooms, olive press, and grain mill. The mission's museum includes an excellent collection of artifacts and historical displays. Wander along remnants of El Camino Real, past the livestock corrals, the cemetery, and the long, narrow church. (Inside, notice the abalone shells for holding holy water and the absence of benches; worshippers knelt on the adobe brick floor.)

Mission gardens, once irrigated by an ingenious water system, include scarecrow-guarded vegetables mixed with flowers and herbs, native plant gardens, even Castilian roses. The old pear orchards and vineyards have been replanted though a few ancient specimens remain.

Main mission events include the **Fiesta** in mid-May, spring and summer demonstrations of mission arts, crafts, and daily life—Purísima's **People's Days**—and the luminaria-lit **Founding Day** celebration in December (very popular, so plan; advance tickets required). The mission is open daily, from May through September 9 a.m.-6 p.m., otherwise 9 a.m.-5 p.m.; $5 per vehicle day-use fee. During the off-season, come later in the afternoon to avoid school tours and take the 90-minute recorded tour. Guided tours are available by appointment. For more information, contact: **La Purísima Mission State Historic Park,** 2295 Purisima Rd., tel. (805) 733-3713.

Point Conception

Just below Vandenberg Air Force Base is the place California turns on itself. Point Conception, an almost inaccessible elbow of land stabbing the sea about 40 miles north of Santa Barbara, is the spot where California's coastal "direction" swings from north-south to east-west, the geographical pivotal point separating temperature and climate zones, northstate from southstate. A lone wind-whipped lighthouse teeters at the edge of every mariner's nightmare, California's Cape Horn.

Inaccessible by car, Point Conception can be reached by hikers from **Jalama Beach County Park** just south of Vandenberg (from south of Lompoc, take Jalama Rd. west from Hwy. 1). Some hike along the railroad right-of-way on the plateau—illegal, of course, so you've been warned—but with equal caution one can take the more adventurous route along the beach and cliffs to commune with startled deer, seals, sea lions, and whales offshore.

Staying in Santa Maria and Lompoc

If you need to spoil yourself but don't have big enough bucks to do that in places like Carmel or Santa Barbara, consider the **Santa Maria Inn,** a half-mile south of Main St. at 801 S. Broadway, tel. (805) 928-7777 or toll-free (800) 447-3529 for reservations, fax (805) 928-5690, www.santa-mariainn.com. This historic English Tudor-style hostelry, built in 1917, is Santa Maria's pride and joy—a grande dame that once hosted California luminaries such as William Randolph Hearst and actress Marion Davies on their way to and from San Simeon and Hollywood stars including Charlie Chaplin, Mary Pickford, Douglas Fairbanks, Rudolph Valentino, Marlene Dietrich, Marilyn Monroe, John Wayne, and Jimmy Stewart. More recently, even Demi Moore. The Santa Maria Inn, renovated and redecorated in Old English style, now includes full fitness facilities in addition to the swimming pool. Rooms in the older hotel section are smaller yet more "historic"; more spacious accommodations are situated in the hotel's newer Tower. All accommodations feature abundant amenities, from color TVs with video players and hair dryers to in-room coffeemakers and refrigerators. Rooms are Expensive-Premium ($89-119) and suites are Luxury ($149-259), with discounts, specials, and golf, theater, and wine packages also available. The inn's restaurant and lounge are also local stars. Come on Sunday for the hotel's famous brunch, usually including Santa Maria-style barbecue.

For absolutely budget travelers, the best bet is camping. Near Lompoc just down the road, camp south of Vandenberg at **Jalama Beach County Park,** once the site of a Chumash village, where campsites are first-come, first-camped; for more information call (805) 736-3504. Other possibilities include **Lopez Lake** to the north and state park campsites near **Morro Bay** (for area information, see above), though there are reasonable motels in the area, most of them in Santa Maria on or near Broadway. Among these is the **Santa Maria Motel 6,** 2040 N. Preisker Ln. (Broadway at Hwy. 101), tel. (805) 928-8111 or toll-free (800) 466-8356, fax (805) 349-1219, www.motel6.com, Inexpensive ($44-48).

Motels in Lompoc are also fairly inexpensive, most of them along H Street. One choice in Lompoc is the **Best Western Vandenberg Inn,** 940 E. Ocean Ave., tel. (805) 735-7731, fax (805) 737-0012, www.bestwestern.com, with color TV with cable and in-room refrigerators, heated pool, spa, and sauna. Free breakfast. Moderate-Expensive ($70-100). Also a good value is the attractive **Inn of Lompoc,** 1122 N. H St., tel. (805) 735-7744, fax (805) 736-0421. Moderate-Expensive ($79-89).

Eating in Santa Maria, Lompoc, and Vicinity

Since the area boasts agricultural abundance, you can usually count on good pickin's at local farmers' markets. The **Santa Maria Certified**

Farmers' Market is held Wednesday 1-5 p.m. in the Mervyn's parking lot, Broadway and Main, and the **Lompoc Certified Farmers' Market** on Friday 2 p.m.-dusk on the corner of I St. and Ocean Avenue. For more information on either market, call (805) 343-2135.

Though Santa Maria is a difficult place for vegetarians to avoid feeling deprived, there are compensations—like the great Cajun fare at **Chef Rick's Ultimately Fine Foods,** in the Lucky Shopping Center at 4869 S. Bradley Rd., tel. (805) 937-9512. Or meat-eaters might want to track down some world-famous **Santa Maria-style barbecue.** Passed down from the days of the vaqueros, the meal traditionally includes delectable slabs of prime sirloin beef barbecued over a slow red-oak fire, then sliced as thin as paper—and served with the chunky *salsa cruda* people drown it in—pinquito beans (grown only in Santa Barbara County), salad, toasted garlic bread, and dessert, unquestionably the ultimate in California cowboy fare. Especially on Sunday, barbecue is the easiest meal to find in and around Santa Maria. The most authentic local version is served on weekends at local charity affairs of one sort or another, but several steakhouses serve it anytime.

The best of the Santa Maria barbecue bunch is the **Hitching Post,** open 5-9:30 p.m. at 3325 Point Sal Rd., tel. (805) 937-6151, in Casmalia, a tiny town southeast of Santa Maria more recently famous as the state's Class I toxic waste landfill. (The big sign at the landfill reads: Casmalia Toxic Dump—It's A Resource.) Back at the Hitching Post, you can watch the meat being barbecued over the oak fire from the other side of the glass wall. Though the wine selection is good—full bar, too—they say it's okay to drink the water here because it's pumped in from the Santa Maria Valley. Another best bet, just north of Santa Maria, is **Jocko's,** 125 N. Thompson St. in Nipomo, tel. (805) 929-3686, a Santa Maria-style steakhouse also known for its spicy beans, open daily.

West of Santa Maria is tiny Guadalupe, a Latino-Italian-Swiss-Filipino-Chinese colony also famous for its small and authentic ethnic eateries.

Tom's in Lompoc, 115 E. Cottage Ave., tel. (805) 736-9996, is everybody's favorite burger joint. For burgers fresh off the oak-fired barbecue pit, the place is the **Outpost,** 118 S. H St., tel.

(805) 735-1130. But, for café society, head for the **South Side Coffee Company,** 105 S. H St., tel. (805) 737-3730. And as unlikely as it may seem to find a good Japanese restaurant in these parts, don't pass up **Oki Sushi,** 1206 W. Ocean Ave., tel. (805) 735-7170.

For other dining options in the vicinity, just ask around.

SOLVANG AND VICINITY

Solvang, "sunny meadow" or "sunny valley" in Danish, was founded in 1911 by immigrants from Denmark seeking a pastoral spot to establish a folk school. This attractive representation of Denmark is now a well-trod tourist destination in the otherwise sleepy Santa Ynez Valley, complete with Scandinavian-style motels, restaurants, shops, even windmills. Recent history has also had its impact here. Though national media always put former President Ronald Reagan's Western White House in Santa Barbara, it was actually closer to Solvang, off Refugio Road. The Reagans don't live at the ranch any more. But when they did, they made quite an impression. When Ron and Nancy arrived at the Solvang polls to vote, for example, SWAT teams took over the town.

In summer and on many weekends, tourists take over the town. To appreciate the authentic taste of Denmark here—and, surprisingly, the experience is largely authentic—come some other time, in winter, spring, or fall. Come in February for the **Flying Leap Storytellers Festival,** in March for **Taste of Solvang,** in April for the **Vintners Festival.** And in September Solvang hosts **Danish Days,** a colorful community celebration honoring the old country since 1936, with authentic dress, outdoor dancing and feasts, roving entertainers, and theater. Yet there is a special compensation for those who do come in summer: **Summer Theaterfest** performances by the **Pacific Conservatory of the Performing Arts** in Solvang's 700-seat outdoor Solvang Festival Theatre. For current information, call the theatre at (805) 922-8313 or try the website, www.pcpa.org. And about four miles from the Reagan ranch, the **Circle Bar B Guest Ranch,** tel. (805) 968-1113, www.circlebarb.com, stages dinner theater productions in an old barn (now a

100-seat theater) from May into November; call for current information.

For more information on attractions and events in and around Solvang, contact: **Solvang Conference and Visitors Bureau,** P.O. Box 70, Solvang, CA 93464, toll-free tel. (800) 468-6765, www.solvangusa.com, or the **Solvang Chamber of Commerce,** P.O. Box 465, Solvang, CA 93464, tel. (805) 688-0701, www.solvangcc.com.

Seeing and Doing Solvang and Vicinity

A wander through Solvang offers thatched-roofed buildings with wooden roof storks, almost endless bakeries and gift shops, and surprises such as the **wind harp** near the **Bethania Lutheran Church,** where services are still conducted in Danish once each month. The **Wulff Windmill** on Fredensborg Canyon Rd. northwest of town is a historic landmark, once used to grind grain and pump water. For an appreciation of Danish culture, stop by the **Elverhøj Danish Heritage and Fine Arts Museum** on Elverjoy Way, tel. (805) 686-1211, an accurate representation of an 18th-century Danish farmhouse open Wed.-Sun. 1-4 p.m. Perfect for picnics: **Hans Christian Andersen Park** off Atterdag Rd., three blocks north of Mission Dr., complete with children's playground.

New in Solvang, open for tours by reservation only, is the free **Western Wear Museum,** 435 First St., tel. (805) 693-5000 or (805) 688-3388, 10 rooms of silver-screen cowboy regalia and other western wear themes; most fun for the kiddos is the "cowkids" room.

Mission Santa Inés just east of Solvang off Hwy. 246 (on Mission Dr.), tel. (805) 688-4815, www.missionsantaines.org, was established in 1804, the 19th of the state's 21 missions and the last in the region. Get a more complete story on the tour of this rosy-tan mission with its copper roof tiles, attractive bell tower, original murals, and decent museum. It's open daily; small donation requested. Bingo and such are the main attractions at the otherwise almost invisible **Santa Ynez Indian Reservation,** on the highway in Santa Ynez. More interesting for most folks is the **Santa Ynez Valley Historical Society Museum** on Sagunto St. in Santa Ynez, tel. (805) 688-7889, open Fri.-Sun. 1-4 p.m., a respectful look at local tradition. Also here is the **Parks-Janeway Carriage House,** with a restored collection of horse-drawn buggies, car-

riages, carts, and stagecoaches; at last report the carriage house was open during museum hours, and also open Tues.-Thurs. 10 a.m.-4 p.m.

Seeing and Doing the Santa Ynez Valley

Rancho San Fernando Rey near Santa Ynez is noteworthy as the birthplace of Palomino horses, one of the few "color" breeds, golden creatures descended from Arabian stock with flaxen manes and tails. Horse ranches, in fact, whether specializing in Arabians, American paints, quarter-horses, thoroughbreds, Peruvian *paso finos* or other breeds, are big business in these parts. Monty Roberts of *The Man Who Listens to Horses* fame, is headquartered in the valley at 110-acre **Flag is Up Farms,** a thoroughbred racing and training ranch and event center.

Most Santa Ynez Valley back roads offer wonderful cycling, increasing numbers of small wineries, and sublime pastoral scenery. **Santa Barbara County wineries**—a cornucopia—are becoming big business, and a major regional attraction. For more on area wineries, see Santa Barbara Wine Country later in this chapter.

Nojoqui Falls County Park, www.sbparks. com, is about six miles south of Solvang on Alisal Rd., a beautiful bike ride from town but more easily accessible from Nojoqui Pass on Hwy. 101. Some say the Chumash word *nojoqui* (nah-HO-wee) means "honeymoon," a possible reference to a tragic love story staged here in Chumash mythology. The park itself includes 84 acres of oaks, limestone cliffs, and a sparkling 168-foot vernal (spring only) waterfall, in addition to hiking trails and picnic and playground facilities.

Los Olivos, once a stage stop at the end of a narrow-gauge railroad rolling down from the north, is now a tiny Western revival town seemingly transplanted from the Mother Lode. If the town looks familiar, it may be because its main street served as a set for TV series *Mayberry RFD.* Nowadays, the county's booming boutique wine trade is quite visible from here. Well worth a stop for wine aficionados is the **Los Olivos Wine & Spirits Emporium** on Grand Ave. south of town, tel. (805) 688-4409 or toll-free (888) 729-4637 (SB-WINES), www.sbwines.com, which definitely purveys some of the area's finest. Also check out the **Wilding Museum— America's Wilderness in Art,** in town across from St. Mark's, tel. (805) 688-1082. The main attraction in nearby **Ballard** is the Ballard School, a classic little red schoolhouse still used for kindergarten classes. **Los Alamos** off Hwy. 101 northwest of Buellton is another spot in the road experiencing a Western-style wine country renaissance. From Los Alamos, take a spin through the Solomon Hills, hideout for the notorious anti-gringo *bandito* Salomon Pico, Pio Pico's cousin, a native Northern Californian and inspiration for the mythical Zorro of comic book and movie fame. Head south on Hwy. 101, and then turn left on little-traveled Alisos Canyon Rd. to Foxen Canyon Rd., which leads past the granite **Frémont-Foxen Monument** commemorating John C. Frémont's bloodless December 1846 capture of Santa Barbara (with the help of local guide Benjamin Foxen). To take in more of the area's charms, try an alternate route to Hwy. 101 between Santa Barbara and the Solvang area, the locally favorite but bustling backroads route (via Hwy. 154 just beyond Santa Ynez) over San Marcos Pass to Lake Cachuma.

PRACTICAL SOLVANG

Staying in and near Solvang

In the Solvang-Buellton area, camp off Foxen Canyon Rd. at **Zaca** ("peace and quiet" in Chumash) **Lake**, actually two natural lakes, both privately owned and surrounded by abundant plant and wildlife, great hiking trails, and good swimming. The facilities include a rustic resort, picnic areas, horseback riding, good swimming. No motor boats allowed, but visitors can rent canoes, sailboats, fishing skiffs. For more information, contact: **The Lodge,** Zaca Lake, P.O. Box 187, Los Olivos, CA 93441, tel. (805) 688-4891. To get here, take Foxen Canyon Rd. from near Los Olivos (or Zaca Station Rd. from just north of Solvang on Hwy. 101), and then turn down the marked dirt road beyond the gate.

You'll find a **Motel 6** in Buellton just off Hwy. 246 as it slides into Solvang at 333 McMurray Rd., P.O. Box 1670, Buellton 93427, tel. (805) 688-7797 or toll-free (800) 466-8356 fax (805) 686-0297, www.motel6.com, with pool, color TV, and movies. Reserve well in advance. Inexpensive-Moderate, with rooms $58-68 from mid-June through September—lower in the off-season, higher on special-event weekends. Look

around in the same general vicinity for other less expensive possibilities and along Hwy. 101, also just outside Solvang on Alisal Road. Also quite basic but right in the middle of town is the 12-room **Viking Motel,** 1506 Mission Dr., tel. (805) 688-1337, fax (805) 693-9499. Inexpensive-Premium ($42-125). The 14-room **Hamlet Motel,** 1532 Mission Dr., tel. (805) 688-4413 or toll-free (800) 253-5033, fax (805) 686-1301, is also a good deal. Inexpensive-Luxury ($50-175).

Most lodgings in Solvang proper tend to be pricier, especially in summer. Weekend rates are often higher, too. The **Best Western Kronborg Inn,** 1440 Mission Dr., tel. (805) 688-2383 or toll-free (800) 528-1234, fax (805) 688-1821, features pleasant, newly redecorated rooms, refrigerators and coffeemakers in all rooms, color TV with cable, heated pool, and spa. Some "pet rooms" available, too. Moderate-Expensive ($60-95). **Inns of California,** 1450 Mission Dr., tel. (805) 688-3210, fax (805) 688-0026, has comfortable rooms and a heated pool. Moderate-Luxury ($60-$195).

Quite appealing in that Solvang style is the **Chimney Sweep Inn,** 1564 Copenhagen Dr., tel. (805) 688-2111 or toll-free (800) 824-6444, fax (805) 688-8824, which features individually decorated rooms, loft rooms, suites, and garden cottages. Complimentary Danish bakery breakfast. And there's a spa in the gazebo. Expensive-Luxury ($90 and up). Still a great value is **Country Inn & Suites,** 1455 Mission Dr., tel. (805) 688-2018 or toll-free (800) 446-4000, fax (805) 688-1156, with attractive, spacious rooms, abundant amenities, and free country breakfast and "hospitality reception" refreshments and snacks daily. Premium ($128-148), but ask about specials. Solvang's full-service hotel is the **Solvang Royal Scandinavian Inn,** 400 Alisal Rd., tel. (805) 688-8000 or toll-free (800) 624-5572, fax (805) 688-0761, featuring large rooms and heated pool. Moderate-Luxury, with summer rates of $99 and up ($79 and up in winter). An impressive newcomer is the 40-room **Petersen Village Inn,** 1576 Mission Dr., tel. (805) 688-3121 or toll-free (800) 321-8985, fax (805) 688-5732, featuring all the amenities, including European buffet breakfast and evening dessert buffet.

For more complete listings of accommodations, contact the local chamber of commerce or visitor bureau.

Special Solvang-Area Stays

Since 1946 Solvang's 10,000-acre cattle ranch, **The Alisal Guest Ranch and Resort,** has become one of California's premier resorts—offering absolute peace and rustic luxury, with no phones, no television sets, and no radios. Though the "cottages" here are quite comfortable, the real appeal is out of doors: long hikes, wrangler-led horseback rides, tennis, horseshoes, shuffleboard, croquet, badminton, volleyball, pool, table tennis, swimming, and just lounging around the pool. The Alisal even has its own lake. But some come just for the exceptional 18-hole golf course here. And some come just to loaf in the mild climate—bestirring themselves only to head for the excellent ranch-house restaurant (breakfast and dinner are included; lunch is also available). The Alisal provides a children's program in summer. For summer, book six months in advance. Rates (two-night minimum) aren't affordable for most real cowpokes, though, at $375 and up. Luxury. For more information, contact: The Alisal Ranch, 1054 Alisal Rd., tel. (805) 688-6411 or toll-free (800) 425-4725 for reservations, fax (805) 688-2510, www.alisal.com.

Among other Solvang-area entries in the "very special stay" category is the historic Western-French **Fess Parker's Wine Country Inn** in Los Olivos, formerly the Los Olivos Grand Hotel country inn, a luxurious 21-suite turn-of-the-century hostelry with rooms named after the Western artists or French impressionists whose works decorate the walls. The hotel's elegant but casual **Vintage Room** restaurant is open for lunch and dinner daily, breakfast on weekends. Luxury. Rooms, with gas fireplaces, are $175-400 and up, but inquire about discounts and off-season specials. For more information and reservations, contact: Fess Parker's Wine Country Inn, 2860 Grand Ave., P.O. Box 849, Los Olivos, CA 93441, tel. (805) 688-7788 or toll-free (800) 446-2455, fax (805) 688-1942, www.fessparker.com.

Quite nice, too, and also smack dab in the middle of Santa Barbara County wine country, is **The Ballard Inn,** 2436 Baseline Ave., Ballard, CA 93463, tel. (805) 688-7770 or toll-free (800) 638-2466 for reservations, fax (805) 688-9560, www.ballardinn.com, a contemporary two-story country inn with 15 rooms and all the amenities. Luxury, with rates $170-250. The inn offers breakfast cooked to order, afternoon hors d'oeu-

vres, and winetasting. The inn's dinner-only **Cafe Chardonnay** serves well-prepared fish, chicken, chops and other wine-enhancing possibilities.

Eating in and near Solvang

Solvang's Danish bakeries are legendary, and many visitors manage to eat reasonably well without going much farther. The **Solvang Bakery,** 460 Alisal Rd., tel. (805) 688-4939, is one good choice. Farm-style breakfast places and pancake houses are also big around town. A solid cafe-style choice is **The Mustard Seed** ("Good Home Cookin' Naturally"), 1655 Mission Dr., tel. (805) 688-1318, a warm and casual family- and country-style place with outdoor patio, open for breakfast and lunch seven days a week, and for dinner every night but Sunday. Expect good egg "scrambles" or Danish omelettes at breakfast, sandwiches and salads at lunch, and home-style cooking at dinner (beef stew, beef liver, chicken fried steak, even a vegetarian platter) though the best deal of all is the Seed's full-meal homemade chicken pot pie, served with either soup or salad. Inexpensive choices, too, for "seedlings" (children ages 10 and under). For sophisticated Solvang fare, the place is the **Brothers Restaurant** inside the Storybook Inn, 409 First St., tel. (805) 688-9934. Always special for a fine dine is the **River Grill** at the Alisal Ranch, outside town at 1054 Alisal Rd., tel. (805) 688-7784.

Though the general consensus is that it's not as good as it used to be, now that it's become a restaurant chain, the original **Andersen's Pea Soup** is in nearby Buellton (you can't miss it on Hwy. 246, with its own Best Western motel). But Buellton won't disappoint. Best bet for breakfast, for miles around, is **Ellen's Danish Pancake House,** 272 Avenue the Flags, tel. (805) 688-5312. For Mexican, the place is **Javy's Café,** 406 E. Hwy. 246, tel. (805) 688-7758. Buellton also boasts the sequel to the original Hitching Post barbecue palace and steakhouse in Casmalia (see above), the dinner-only **Hitching Post II,** 406 E. Hwy. 246, tel. (805) 688-0676.

Other great eating possibilities are scattered throughout surrounding vineyard country. The casual French country-style **Ballard Store** restaurant in block-long Ballard closed in late 1999, alas. But there are other possibilities, including the small **Cafe Chardonnay** in the Ballard Inn, 2436 Baseline Rd., tel. (805) 688-7770, open for dinner Wed.-Sun. nights. Reservations are advisable. Or head to Los Olivos.

About five miles north of Solvang on Hwy. 154 in Los Olivos is historic **Mattei's Tavern,** tel. (805) 688-4820, once a train depot and stage stop, now a white-frame dinner house specializing in steak, seafood, and other hearty fare. It's open noon-3 p.m. for lunch too, Fri.-Sun. only. Reservations advisable. Or try the **Los Olivos Café,** 2798 Grand Ave., tel. (805) 688-7265, open daily for lunch and dinner. For something simple, stop by **Panino,** 2900 Grand Ave., tel. (805) 688-9304, for smoothies, any one of the 30-something sandwiches, and picnic supplies. Exceptional in these parts for fine dining is the elegant yet casual **Vintage Room** at Fess Parker's Wine Country Inn, 2860 Grand Ave., tel. (805) 688-7788, open for breakfast, lunch, and dinner.

As elsewhere in the Santa Ynez Valley, in Santa Ynez the tried-and-true bumps up against the new—though wine country sensibility is fast outpacing cowboy-style steak and eggs. Still going strong, though, for basic 1950s-style breakfast along with great burgers and fries is the **Longhorn Coffee Shop & Bakery,** 3687 Sagunto St., tel. (805) 688-5912. Also here is **Maverick Saloon,** tel. (805) 688-5841, kind of a country-western juke joint popular for line dancing and karaoke. At home in the same complex yet cultural and culinary worlds away is world-class **Trattoria Grappolo,** tel. (805) 688-6899, famous for its homemade pastas and wood-fired pizza. Other foodie destinations include the **Santa Ynez Feed & Grill,** 3544 Sagunto St., tel. (805) 693-5100, and **Vineyard House,** 3631 Sagunto, tel. (805) 688-2886.

Los Alamos also has its attractions, but still downhome and kicked-back, including **Charlie's,** 97 Den, tel. (805) 344-4404, and the fairly mellow biker tavern **Ghostriders,** 550 Bell, tel. (805) 344-2111.

SANTA BARBARA AND VICINITY

Santa Barbara is beautiful, rich, and proud of it. Though her past is somewhat mysterious (she goes by the name "Santa Teresa" in the works of mystery writers Ross MacDonald and Sue Grafton), her presence hints at natural luck almost as incredible as her beauty, cosmic beneficence only briefly perturbed by unavoidable misfortune. If she were a flesh-and-blood woman, she would sway down the brick sidewalks, her aristocratic nose pointed upward, a satisfied smile on her face.

But such easy grace is no accident, of course; Santa Barbara's beauty regime is strict. She insists that the facades of all buildings (including McDonald's) reflect the Spanish style she favors. Death, decay, or other disarray in her environment displeases her; the only time she curses is when she spits out the words "developer," "development," and "oil companies," these latter responsible for the 1969 oil spill that fouled 20 miles of her pristine beaches. Her most peculiar personality quirk is that she secretly believes she lives in Northern California, despite social intercourse with everything Southern Californian.

Santa Barbara is generous with her gifts, and she has everything: beautiful beaches and understated, stark chaparral slopes, colleges and universities, a celebrated arts and entertainment scene, fine restaurants (more restaurants per capita than any other U.S. city, in fact) and luxury resorts, trendy boutiques, antique shops. Though her sun shines brightest on celebrity residents—among them, in recent history, Cher, Julia Child, Michael Douglas, Jane Fonda, Kenny Loggins, Steve Martin, Priscilla Presley, and John Travolta—she magnanimously allows the middle class to bask in her glow.

But the shadow side to Santa Barbara's radiance is the basically ugly belief that she must shun any and all things unsightly. Poverty is unsightly and Santa Barbara doesn't want to see it. So her people passed laws prohibiting the homeless from sleeping in public on the sidewalks.

Santa Barbara Natural History:
Dignified But Dry

The city itself faces south, spreading back toward the dry but dignified Santa Ynes Mountains like a Spanish fan. The Channel Islands offshore protect Santa Barbara's sublime coastal bay and unruffled beaches. Despite the genuine devastation of the 1969 oil spill here, the gooey

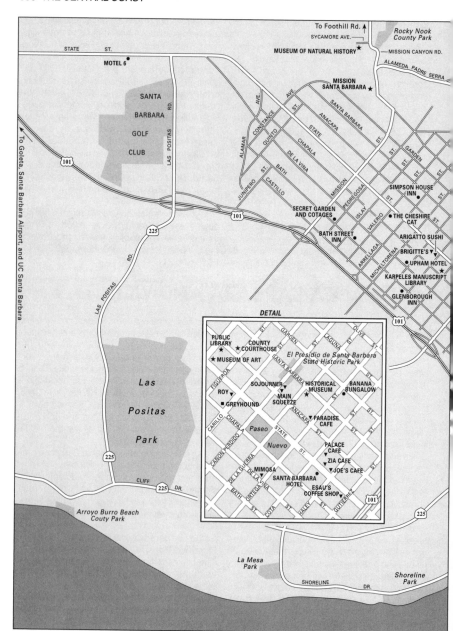

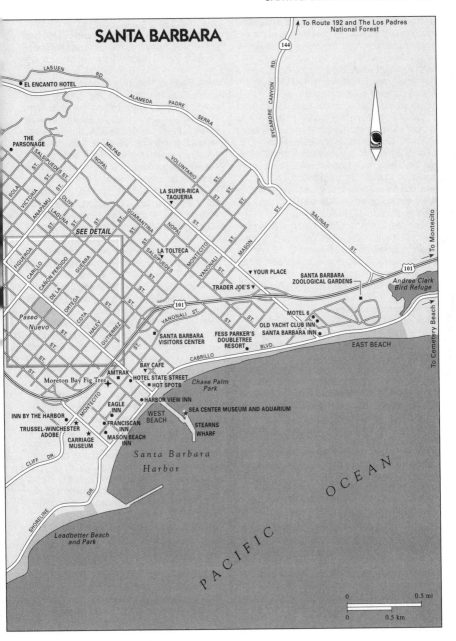

SANTA BARBARA

To Route 192 and The Los Padres
National Forest

144

LASUEN RD.

● EL ENCANTO HOTEL

ALAMEDA PADRE SERRA

SYCAMORE CANYON RD.

MOON

To Montecito

THE
PARSONAGE

SALSIPUEDES ST.
SOLAR ST.
VICTORIA ST.
ANAPAMU ST.
LAGUNA ST.
OLIVE ST.
MILPAS
NOPAL

VOLUNTARIO ST.

LA SUPER-RICA
TAQUERIA

QUARANTINA ST.

SALINAS ST.

SEE DETAIL

FIGUEROA ST.
CARILLO ST.
CANON PERDIDO
DE LA GUERRA ST.
ORTEGA ST.
COTA ST.
HALEY ST.
GUTIERREZ

NOPAL ST.
SALSIPUEDES ST.

LA TOLTECA

MONTECITO ST.
VANONALI ST.
MASON ST.

▼ YOUR PLACE

SANTA BARBARA
ZOOLOGICAL GARDENS

101

Andree Clark
Bird Refuge

TRADER JOE'S ▼

101

Paseo
Nuevo

VANONALI ST.

MOTEL 6

OLD YACHT CLUB INN
SANTA BARBARA INN

EAST BEACH

SANTA BARBARA
VISITORS CENTER

FESS PARKER'S
DOUBLETREE
RESORT

CABRILLO BLVD.

To Cemetery Beach

AMTRAK

BAY CAFE

HOTEL STATE STREET

Moreton Bay Fig Tree

HOT SPOTS

Chase Palm
Park

HARBOR VIEW INN

EAGLE
INN

SEA CENTER MUSEUM AND AQUARIUM

INN BY THE HARBOR

FRANCISCAN
INN

WEST
BEACH

STEARNS
WHARF

TRUSSEL-WINCHESTER
ADOBE

MASON BEACH
INN

MONTECITO

CARRIAGE
MUSEUM

CLIFF DR.

*Santa Barbara
Harbor*

OCEAN

SHORELINE DR.

*Leadbetter Beach
and Park*

PACIFIC

0   0.5 mi

0   0.5 km

blobs of tar on shoreline rocks and white sand are primarily natural, from Monterey shale petroleum deposits hundreds of feet thick in some areas. Near Santa Barbara, earthquake fault lines run east-west, like the mountains whose deformed rock formations hint at the intensity of underground earth movement.

The palms and eucalyptus trees, in fact *most* of the plants commonly growing along Santa Barbara streets and beaches, are introduced species. Native plants in and around Santa Barbara today include live oaks, pines, and California bay trees, also toyon, greasewood, manzanita, and other chaparral shrubs. Shadier valleys and grassy hillsides are dazzling with wildflowers in spring. About 400 species of birds are found in the Santa Barbara region.

The most common "city birds" include the western mockingbird, California jays, house finches, sparrows, and hummingbirds. At the beach, sandpipers, terns, gulls, and other seabirds are common. Migrating ducks, geese, and other waterfowl visit the city's lake refuge.

Santa Barbara History:
Basking in Gentility, Beset by Troubles

Before there even was a Santa Barbara, before the Bronze Age, an ancient Oak Grove people lived here. Then later, equally mysterious Hunting People arrived with improved technology: arrows, clubs, spearheads, and tools used for digging shellfish. These hunters and gatherers slowly merged their society with still later arrivals to become the industrious Chumash, whose few descendants today live inland and along nearby coasts.

As with many native California peoples the central focus of the Chumash was spiritual, though they nonetheless found time for their industries: boat-making, fishing, and trading with island residents across the channel. Only remnants of the rich ancient Chumash culture remain—baskets, beads, charms, and money—many of these items now in museums. Forced into Christianity by zealous Spanish missionaries, the Chumash near Santa Barbara were all but wiped out by foreign diseases, their own social and spiritual decline, and alcoholism.

Despite its aura of established comfort, Santa Barbara has suffered two major earthquakes (the first flattened the original mission), a tidal wave, direct enemy attack during World War II, an ecologically devastating offshore oil spill, and fires—many, many fires. Vizcaíno was the first to Europeanize the place. He named the channel after Saint Barbara in 1602, though the name "Santa Barbara Virgin and Martyr" didn't have much to stick to until it was later applied to the presidio in 1782 and the mission four years later.

For many years, aristocratic Spanish families basked in their own gentility here, making Santa Barbara the social capital of Alta California even if Monterey was designated the political capital. With mission secularization, Santa Barbara high society became landed gentry—but only briefly. The grand ranchos all but dried up, littered with cattle bones picked clean by condors and vultures during the devastating drought of the 1860s. Upstart Americans then snatched up the land and with it, local political power. In the late 1880s the industrialists arrived along with old money, banks, brokerage houses, and the Southern Pacific Railroad. When oil was discovered offshore in the 1890s and the first offshore oil well started pumping near Summerland in 1896, they kept coming.

No sooner had the Montecito mansions and Santa Barbara power palaces settled onto their new foundations than they were removed from those foundations—suddenly, shockingly. From the present-day perspective the earthquake of June 1925, which left the city in ruins, was the best thing that ever happened to Santa Barbara. During the city's reconstruction, a quickly formed architectural review board declared that new buildings in Santa Barbara would henceforth be Mediterranean in design and style, appropriate to the area's balmy climate and sympathetic to its Hispanic cultural heritage. The town's trademark old Spanish California adobe look—cream-colored stucco, sloping red-tile roofs, and wrought-iron grillwork—is a unified effect of fairly modern origin.

Santa Barbara had barely rebuilt itself when a Japanese submarine surfaced offshore in 1942 to attack an oil refinery nearby. Oil was the issue again in 1969, when a massive spill from an offshore oil rig blackened 20 miles of beaches in and around Santa Barbara, killing thousands of birds and destroying the local marine ecology. That event fired up ocean lovers all over California and helped launch the successful 1972

California Coastal Protection Initiative, which created the California Coastal Commission to protect the coast as well as the public's access. Starting in the 1980s, a seven-year drought forced Santa Barbara residents to drain their swimming pools and paint their dried-up lawns green. (Water conservation is a serious concern in these parts.) Then, in 1990, the devastating Painted Cave arson fire killed one person and torched 4,900 acres, racing through the chaparral near San Marcos Pass and then seaward, down into the residential canyons of Goleta and northern Santa Barbara. Sometimes change is a challenge to survival.

Yet even change-wary Santa Barbara welcomes innovation, as it did in the early 1990s when CalTrans coughed up $58 million to widen U.S. Highway 101 through the city to six lanes, remove all four freeway stoplights, and route crosstown traffic either over or under the freeway instead of across it—thus eliminating one of California's most complicated and nightmarish traffic bottlenecks. Innovation is also a byword in the local business community—increasingly high-tech, increasingly cutting-edge.

SEEING SANTA BARBARA: DOWNTOWN

Since the founding of **Mission Santa Barbara** in 1786 at the upper end of what is now Laguna St., the altar light has never been extinguished—

and that's saying something. Originally a collection of simple adobes, Santa Barbara's "Queen of the Missions" and California's 10th was named for a Roman virgin beheaded by her pagan father. The mission was subsequently all but flattened by the 1812 earthquake, the same year the town on the coastal plain below was all but swept away by a huge tidal wave. Another earthquake, in 1925, did its best to bring the mission down.

The Queen of the Missions still stands—indeed queenly, presiding over the city and sea below with two massive squared towers, arcades, and domed belfries. The dignified Ionic columns, arched entrance, and double-paneled doors add to the mission's grace. The genesis of the city's original water system is also here, an impressive network of aqueducts, filter house, and Spanish gristmill. The larger of the mission's two reservoirs, circa 1806, is still in use by the city, and the 1807 mission dam is now part of the Santa Barbara Botanic Garden just up the canyon. The **museum** tells the mission's story with history displays, photographs, and a reconstructed kitchen. Self-guided tours are offered daily 9 a.m.-5 p.m., small admission fee (children under age 12 free). For details or more information, stop by the mission at 2201 Laguna St., call (805) 682-4149, or try www.sbmission.org.

There's more historical Santa Barbara downtown, just down the hill. Get oriented at the **Santa Barbara Historical Society Museum,** 136 E. De La Guerra, tel. (805) 966-1601, an impressive

Santa Barbara's "Queen of the Missions"

NATURAL SANTA BARBARA

The best of natural Santa Barbara and vicinity is on display at the exceptional **Santa Barbara Museum of Natural History** two blocks north of the mission at 2559 Puesta Del Sol Rd., tel. (805) 682-4711, www.sbnature.org. This Spanish-style cluster of buildings and courtyards includes excellent exhibits on the Chumash and other indigenous peoples, collections of fossils, geology displays, nature exhibits (including a busy beehive), even some original Audubon lithographs. In addition to the museum's classes on every natural history topic under the sun, there's a planetarium and observatory here, tel. (805) 682-3224, offering a popular Sunday afternoon program. The museum also sponsors a year-round schedule of films and special events—including **monarch butterfly tours** in January (by reservation) and the **Wine Festival** in August. On the way in or out, stop outside near the parking lot to appreciate the 72-foot-long skeleton of a blue whale, recently restored. The natural history museum is open 9 a.m.-5 p.m. daily (from 10 a.m. on Sunday and holidays), closed Thanksgiving, Christmas, and New Year's Day. Admission is $6 adults, $5 seniors and students (ages 13-17), and $4 children age 12 and under, free on the first Sunday of every month. Nearby and perfect for an almost-country picnic is **Rocky Nook County Park.**

The 65-acre **Santa Barbara Botanic Garden,** 1212 Mission Canyon Rd., tel. (805) 682-4726, www.sbbg.org, is "dedicated to the study of California's native plants." Too many people miss this natural Santa Barbara treasure. Plants native to Santa Barbara and vicinity are the main event (don't miss the spectacular spring wildflowers) but cacti, other succulents, even redwoods are at home in the gardens here. Good gift shop—particularly popular with gardeners and plant lovers. Lectures, classes, trips, and special events are often scheduled, and docent-guided tours are offered daily at 2 p.m., also on Thursday, Saturday, and Sunday at 10:30 a.m. Best, though, is showing up when nothing's going on and just wandering the grounds—a stroll that can easily become a brisk five-mile hike. The botanic garden is open daily 9 a.m.-sunset (gift shop open until 4 p.m. in winter, 5 p.m. in summer). Small admission (under age 5 free), and once you're in docent-guided tours are free, but donations and membership support are always appreciated.

---

regional history museum featuring everything from antique toys to vaquero-style saddles within its collection of period costumes, documents, and Santa Barbara memorabilia. The museum is open Tues.-Sat. 10 a.m.-5 p.m., Sunday noon-5 p.m. Guided tours are offered; call for details. Admission is free, though nonmembers must pay for use of the historical society's associated **Gledhill Library** (call for current hours). The museum's adjacent 19th-century **Casa Covarrubias** and **Historic Adobe** also offer a peek into the past. (Museum docents can also tell you about the society's restored **Trussell-Winchester Adobe** and the 1862 Queen Anne **Fernald House,** located together at 412-414 W. Montecito St. and usually open for guided tours on Sunday only, 2-4 p.m. Nearby is the **Carriage and Western Arts Museum,** 129 Castillo St., tel. (805) 962-2353, at the north end of Pershing Park, open by donation Mon.-Sat. 9 a.m.-3 p.m. and 2-4 p.m. on Sunday.) Most of Santa Barbara's other surviving adobes, now private residences or office buildings, are included on downtown's self-guided **Red Tile Walk-**

ing Tour, outlined in the visitor guide and also available on the website.

The walking tour's traditional starting point is the **Santa Barbara County Courthouse,** a must-see destination one block from State St. at Anapamu and Anacapa, tel. (805) 962-6464, an L-shaped Spanish-Moorish castle with spacious interiors decorated with murals, mosaics, ceramic Tunisian tile, and handcarved wood, quite possibly the most beautiful public building anywhere in California. County supervisors meet in the Assembly Room, with its romantic four-wall historic mural created by a Cecil B. DeMille set designer, and sit in comfortable leather-covered, brass-studded benches and chairs under handmade iron chandeliers. The spectacular views of the city from the clock tower or the *mirador* balcony alone are worth the trip. The courthouse is open 8 a.m.-5 p.m. on weekdays, 9-5 on weekends and holidays, with free guided tours offered at 2 p.m. Mon.-Sat., also at 10:30 a.m. on Friday.

Across the street at 40 E. Anapamu St. sits the stunning Spanish-style **Santa Barbara**

Public Library, tel. (805) 962-7653, with its grand Peake-Warshaw murals and both the Faulkner Gallery and Townley Room art displays. It's open Mon.-Thurs. 10 a.m.-9 p.m., Friday and Saturday 10 a.m.-5:30 p.m., and Sunday 1-5 p.m. Well worth a stop in the other direction is the unusual **Karpeles Manuscript Library,** 21 W. Anapamu, tel. (805) 962-5322, a free museum featuring an extensive collection of both original and facsimile manuscripts—music, letters, maps, illustrations, books, treaties, and such. It's open daily 10 a.m.-4 p.m., closed Thanksgiving and Christmas.

El Presidio de Santa Barbara State Historic Park, 123 E. Cañon Perdido St. (between Anacapa and Santa Barbara Sts.), tel. (805) 966-9719, an ambitious reconstruction, is now under way. The project was undertaken by the private Santa Barbara Trust for Historic Preservation to re-create the original 1782 Presidio Real, imperial Spain's last military outpost in California. Before restoration began, all that remained of the original presidio were two crumbling adobe buildings; one, El Cuartel, is Santa Barbara's oldest building and the second oldest in the state. Started in 1961, the project was expected to be completed by the year 2000. To date two buildings have been restored and five reconstructed.

Along with history, downtown offers it own perspectives on the history of art at the **Santa Barbara Museum of Art,** 1130 State St. (between Anapamu and Figueroa), tel. (805) 963-4364, www.sbmuseart.org, an outstanding regional museum that attracts impressive traveling exhibits. The permanent collection here boasts 19th-century Impressionists including Chagall, Matisse, and Monet; O'Keeffe, Eakins, Hooper, and other major American artists; and an eclectic assortment of classical antiquities, Asian art, photography, prints, and drawings. Good bookstore and on-site cafe. The museum is open Tues.-Sat. 11 a.m.-5 p.m. (until 9 p.m. on Thursday) and Sunday noon-5 p.m. Docents guide free gallery tours at 1 p.m. Tours of special exhibitions are offered Wednesday and Saturday only, at noon. Admissions is $5 adults, $3 seniors, $2 students with ID and children ages 6-17. The museum is free to everyone, though, every Thursday and on the first Sunday of every month (under age 6 always free).

Confusing the line between real and faux history are downtown's many stylish shops—art galleries galore and **Brinkerhoff Avenue,** famous for its antiques—and, now, two shopping centers. **El Paseo,** California's first shopping center and the originator of the city's distinctive architectural "look," is a clustered two-story collection of Spanish colonial revival shops built in the early 1920s around courtyards, fountains, and gardens (enter from State St., near De La Guerra). The stylish new **Paseo Nuevo** mission-style mall, anchored by Nordstrom and The Broadway between State and Chapala Streets and Ortega and Cañon Perdido, offers upscale shops and shopping. Particularly worthwhile here is the 4,500-square-foot **Contemporary Arts Forum,** tel. (805) 966-5373, an adventurous contemporary arts gallery and exhibition space often sponsoring traveling shows, other special exhibits, and lectures.

To the benefit of visitors and residents alike, Santa Barbara is generous with public parking downtown. Park in any of 10 various lots, and the first 90 minutes is free; the incorrigibly cheap could, conceivably, move their cars from lot to lot at precise intervals and stay downtown all day for free.

SEEING SANTA BARBARA: AROUND TOWN AND BEYOND

The **Moreton Bay Fig Tree** at Chapala and Montecito Streets (where Hwy. 101 rolls by) is considered the nation's largest. Affectionately called "the old rubber tree" by some, though it produces neither rubber nor figs, this Australian native is large enough (they say) to shelter 10,000 people from the noonday sun. Street people and transient philosophers are attracted to its welcoming attitude, much to the rest of the community's chagrin.

Nearby is the Santa Barbara harbor area; the city's "bay" is little more than a curvaceous beach front. **Stearns Wharf,** tel. (805) 564-5518, at the foot of State St. and the oldest operating wharf on the West Coast, offers pier fishing, shops, restaurants. Worthwhile here is the **Sea Center Museum and Aquarium,** tel. (805) 962-0885, a branch of the Santa Barbara Museum of Natural History open daily 10 a.m.-5 p.m. The emphasis here is on the marine life of the Santa Barbara Channel, just offshore, with seawater

You'll know you've found the Santa Barbara Museum of Natural History when you spot the whale skeleton.

tank exhibits, a computer learning center, and an outdoor "touch tank" for an up-close-and-personal introduction to underwater wonders (touch-tank exhibit open noon-4 p.m. every day except Wednesday). Small admission. Also worth a stop on the wharf, if you care to learn more about California's endlessly threatened natural environments, is **The Nature Conservancy Visitor Center,** 213 Stearns Wharf, tel. (805) 962-9111, open on weekdays noon-4 p.m., on Saturday and Sunday 11 a.m.-5 p.m.

To the east of the pier is pleasant **East Beach,** buffered from busy Cabrillo Blvd. by the manicured lawns, footpaths, and bike trails of expanded **Chase Palm Park,** which stretches along the north side of Cabrillo Blvd. from Garden St. to Calle César Chávez. At the east end of East Beach is **Cemetery Beach,** a popular nude beach (one of four in the area). Also reasonably secluded is Montecito's **Butterfly Beach,** below the Four Seasons Biltmore Hotel. West of Stearns Wharf is the municipal harbor, protected by a long stone breakwater, and **West Beach.** The promising new **Santa Barbara Maritime Museum,** tel. (805) 962-8404, www.sbmm.org, is situated at the harbor entrance, in the Waterfront Center. Pending unveiling of the museum's main exhibit hall, the "preview center" is open daily 10 a.m.-4 p.m. Farther west are **Leadbetter Beach** and **Shoreline Park,** also tiny **La Mesa Park** and **Arroyo Burro Beach,** popular for swimming and surfing.

Overlooking West Beach is the **Santa Barbara Zoological Gardens,** a onetime estate at 500 Niños Dr. (off E. Cabrillo Blvd.), tel. (805) 962-6310 (recorded) or (805) 962-5339, www.santabarbarazoo.org, with more than 600 exotic animals in almost natural habitats—one of the best smaller zoos anywhere. Santa Barbara's zoo has an outstanding walk-through "aquatic aviary," a portholed Sealarium, and islands for squirrel monkeys and gibbons. Nocturnal Hall, a walk-in tropical aviary on the outside, houses nocturnal animals within. Also here: a peaceful picnic area, small botanic garden, farmyard, Wild West playground, and zany mini-trains. The zoo is open daily 10 a.m.-5 p.m., adults $7, children and seniors $5 (under age 2 free). The **Andree Clark Bird Refuge** is a landscaped 50-acre preserve of reclaimed marshland at the east end of E. Cabrillo Blvd. adjoining the zoo, with freshwater fowl, also bike trails and footpaths; if you really like to bike it, the paved **Cabrillo Bikeway** runs to the refuge from the harbor. Guided refuge tours are sometimes offered by the local Audubon Society chapter.

North and West of Santa Barbara

Just up the coast from Santa Barbara proper on a beautiful stretch of beachfront property in Goleta is the **University of California at Santa Barbara** campus. Bordered on two sides by the Pacific Ocean, miles of white-sand beaches, and a natural lagoon, the campus itself is a beauty. Noted for its comprehensive environmental studies program—one of the first of its kind in the nation—and its engineering, education, and scientific

SANTA BARBARA WINE COUNTRY

Santa Barbara County is premium wine country. The county's winemaking history reaches back more than 200 years, though small vineyards and wineries established since the 1970s and 1980s are responsible for the area's regional viticultural revival. The unusual east-west orientation of the Santa Ynez Mountains and associated valleys allows fog-laden ocean air to flow inland—creating dry summers with cool nights and warm days. Cabernet sauvignon, sauvignon blanc, pinot noir, chardonnay, and riesling are among the wine grapes that thrive here, though Rhône varietals are a new trend.

Yet when does a good thing become too much of a good thing?

This is a question asked more frequently here and elsewhere along the central coast, especially following a nearly successful local ballot initiative in fall 1998 that would have severely restricted local wine grape growers' ability to clearcut native oaks and other vegetation to plant vineyards. Environmentalists, grape growers, and county planning officials are trying to come up with a collaborative solution to this particular problem, to avoid the possibility of another public—and vitriolic—political battle.

Most of Santa Barbara County's wineries—well over 50 and counting—are scattered throughout the Santa Ynez Valley, beyond San Marcos Pass northwest of Santa Barbara and southeast of Santa Maria.

Award-winning **The Gainey Vineyard,** 3950 E. Hwy. 246, P.O. Box 910, Santa Ynez 93460, tel. (805) 688-0558, fax (805) 688-5864, is noted for its cabernets, chardonnays, and pinot noirs. The contemporary 12,000-foot winery and tasting room and adjacent picnic area is open daily 10 a.m.-5 p.m. for tours and tasting. (Very informative tours.) The vineyard also sponsors a variety of evening concerts—popular regional jazz bands and the likes of Randy Newman—which sell out fast.

Almost everyone stops at the **Fess Parker Winery,** 6200 Foxen Canyon Rd. in Los Olivos, tel. (805) 688-1545 or toll-free (800) 841-1104, fax (805) 686-1130, www.fessparker.com, open for tasting and sales daily 10 a.m.-5 p.m. (closed Thanksgiving, Christmas, and New Year's Day) and for group tours only (by arrangement). Most popular here is syrah,

which tends to sell out almost instantaneously every year, and a very good chardonnay. And anyone with a yen for the good ol' days of 1950s television will have fun in the gift shop, featuring Davy Crockett "coonskin" caps and other Fess Parker TV-star memorabilia. On most weekends Parker is available in person to autograph wine bottles. Tours and admission to the gift shop are free, but there is a fee for tastings.

Also popular in Los Olivos is **Firestone Vineyard,** 5000 Zaca Station Rd., tel. (805) 688-3940, fax (805) 686-1256, open daily 10 a.m.-5 p.m. for tasting (closed major holidays), tours also offered. Firestone was the first in the country to produce estate-grown wines. People go out of their way to pick up Firestone's award-winning cabernet sauvignon, though the winery is actually best known for Johannesburg riesling. Picnicking here is a pleasure, with picnic tables surrounding a fountain in the courtyard. Tastings and tours are free, but a fee is charged for groups of 15 or more.

Not far southeast of Santa Maria is the **Byron Vineyard and Winery,** located at 5230 Tepusquet Rd., tel. (805) 937-7288, named 1992 "Winery of the Year" by *Wine and Spirits* magazine and now owned by Robert Mondavi.

But with 50 or so member wineries in the local vintners' association—and major events such as the spring **Santa Barbara County Vintners' Festival,** the fall **Celebration of Harvest,** and other galas to help introduce them—it takes more than a few stops to fully appreciate the region. For a current winery map and guide, and for current events information, contact: **Santa Barbara County Vintners' Association,** P.O. Box 1558, Santa Ynez 93460, tel. (805) 688-0881 or toll-free tel. (800) 218-0881, fax (805) 686-5881, www.sbcountywines.com.

And the region's wineries don't begin or end in Santa Barbara County, thanks to the mild central coast climate. Small wineries also cluster farther north near San Luis Obispo—in the **Edna** and **Arroyo Grande Valleys**—and, more famously, north of San Luis Obispo near **Paso Robles** and **Templeton.** For more information, see San Luis Obispo and Vicinity, above.

instrumentation programs, the university gained national attention in the late 1960s and early '70s for anti-Vietnam War activities in the adjacent "student ghetto" of **Isla Vista,** still jam-packed with stucco apartment buildings and bustling with student-oriented businesses and activities.

Diversions in nearby **Goleta** include the **South Coast Railroad Museum,** 300 N. Los Carneros Rd., tel. (805) 964-3540, featuring a restored 1901 Southern Pacific depot, antiques and artifacts, a 300-square-foot model railroad, miniature train rides for the kiddies, and handcar rides for older kids. Open Wed.-Sun. 1-4 p.m. Next door is the historic Victorian **Stow House,** tel. (805) 964-4407, open weekends only 2-4 p.m. from February through December (museum closed on rainy days), though the grounds are open year-round. Popular local events staged at Stow House include the annual **Goleta Valley Lemon Festival** and the **Old-Time Fiddlers' Convention.** Another area attraction is the two-acre **Santa Barbara Orchid Estate,** 1250 Orchid Dr., tel. (805) 967-1284, www.sborchid.com, with more than 100 varieties on display (plants and cut flowers available for sale), an entire acre of them under glass.

Attractions along the coast north of Santa Barbara and Goleta include three spectacular state "beach" parks. Farthest north is **Gaviota State Park,** about 22 miles north of Goleta, a small beach area that also includes 3,000 associated acres of chaparral, campsites, picnic areas, hiking trails, and hike-in hot springs. Next down-coast and perhaps loveliest of all, just 12 miles north of Goleta, is breathtaking **Refugio State Beach,** a white-sand cove fringed by palm trees and protected from the pounding surf by a rocky point. Here are more campsites—just five facing the beach—plus a glorious group camp. Two miles south, connected by paved bike path to Refugio, is **El Capitan State Beach,** most popular for year-round camping. All three beaches are open daily dusk until dark for day use ($5 per vehicle fee). For current information on all three beaches, call (805) 968-1033. For campground reservations—essential in summer and on weekends, prudent any time—call ReserveAmerica at toll-free (800) 444-7275.

About 18 miles northwest of Santa Barbara, on the way to Solvang and Santa Ynez via Hwy. 154, is **Cachuma Lake,** the largest manmade lake in Southern California, a 3,200-acre, trout-stocked, oak woodland reservoir open for day use 6 a.m.-10 p.m. daily. Stop by the **Cachuma Nature Center** to get oriented. Also a county park, Cachuma is ripe for year-round recreation: boating, sailing, hiking, and swimming in pools (Memorial Day through Labor Day only). No "body contact" with the lake is allowed, since this is the city of Santa Barbara's primary water supply. Fishing is a year-round draw, as is bird-watching; more than 275 bird species have been spotted here. A major new attraction here is the two-hour **Eagle Cruise** led by the park's naturalist, offered only November to March when the bald eagles arrive for their own winter respite (fee, by reservation only). The lake has pleasant picnic areas and developed campsites for both tents and RVs, also group camps. Day use is $3.50 per vehicle, camping $12 and up. And a quarter will get you a three-minute hot shower. For more information, contact: Cachuma Lake Recreation Area, HC 58—Hwy. 154, Santa Barbara, CA 93105, tel. (805) 686-5054 (recorded) or (805) 686-5050 for information, weekend events, and Fish Watch, tel. (805) 686-5055 (voice/TDD), www.sbparks.com.

Remote **Gibraltar Reservoir** off Paradise and Camuesa Roads farther south is open for long-weekend trout fishing January through March, but reservations and permits from the city of Santa Barbara are necessary. Also worth seeing, for dedicated backroaders, is **Chumash Painted Cave State Historic Park** off Painted Cave Rd., with its characteristic black, red, and yellow pictographs. Gaze in through the iron grating now in place to discourage vandals, or call (805) 968-3294 for tour information. Parking on the road's narrow shoulder accommodates only one or two cars (definitely no trailers or RVs).

South and East of Santa Barbara

The balmy beaches, yacht harbor, and wooded estates of **Montecito,** just south of Santa Barbara, seem tailor-made for the people behind commercial trademarks such as DuPont, Fleischmann, Pillsbury, and Stetson—and they were. Especially worth seeing in Montecito is surreal **Lotusland,** created by the flamboyant and independent Madame Ganna Walska, thwarted opera singer and compulsive marrier of millionaires. Here you'll find the world's finest private collection of cycads (relatives of pine trees that look like palms), also cacti and succulents, a luxuriant fern garden lacking only prehistoric dinosaurs, an eccentric "Japanese" garden, a fantastic aloe-and-abalone-shell "forest," weeping euphorbias, 20-foot-tall elephant's feet, lily and lotus ponds, bromeliads, orchids, and roses. Casual or drop-in garden tours are not possible, but the gardens are open by reservation to those interested in horticulture or botany. Make reservations for the two-hour tours ($10 per person, no children under age 12) by contacting the Ganna Walska Lotusland Foundation, 695 Ashley Rd., Santa Barbara 93108, tel. (805) 969-3767. Because the house and gardens are in a residential area, there is an annual limit of 9,000 visitors (no drive-by lookie-loos, please; such voyeurism upsets the neighbors, and you can't see anything anyway). Beginning on or about November 15, reservations are taken for the following year—and the entire year's tours are typically booked by January 15.

The burg of **Summerland** just south along the coast is the site of California's first offshore oil drilling in the 1890s. The Spiritualists, a sect known for its séances and merriment, settled here first on former mission lands (thus the locals' derogatory nickname, "Spookville"). Most architectural evidence of Summerland's past was bulldozed during the 1925 construction of Hwy. 101 and 15 years later, when the highway became a freeway. Summerland offers a county park, a nice beach, and a boom in antique shops, restaurants, and bed-and-breakfast inns, but the town's most entertaining feature somehow disappeared in the last decade—the sign reading: Population 3,001, Feet Above Sea Level 280, Established 1870, Total: 5,151. Following Lillie Avenue east (it becomes Villa Real) leads to the **Santa Barbara Polo and Racquet Club,** where exhibitions and tournaments are scheduled on Sunday, sometimes on Saturday, spring through fall.

Carpinteria farther south on the way to Ventura was once a Chumash village. Cabrillo stumbled upon it in August of 1542, and Portolá later called it Carpinteria or "carpenter shop" because of the natives' industrious canoe-making. People say **Carpinteria State Beach,** a onetime bean field now complete with large campground and hiker/biker campsites, sports the "safest beach in the world" because the surf breaks 2,000 feet

out from shore, beyond the reef, and there's no undertow. Other local attractions include the free **Carpinteria Valley Museum of History,** 956 Maple Ave., tel. (805) 684-3112 (free, but donations appreciated). Carpinteria's main streets also boast an abundance of antique shops.

For more information about Summerland and Carpinteria, call the **Carpinteria Valley Chamber of Commerce** at (805) 684-5479 or toll-free (800) 563-6900, www.carpcofc.com.

From south of Carpinteria, Hwy. 150 leads to Lake Casitas and to Ojai, made famous as a setting for Shangri-La in the movie *Lost Horizon.* For more information on these areas and the coast south of Carpinteria, see Venturing Ventura, below.

DOING SANTA BARBARA

Eventful Santa Barbara
Come in January for the annual **Hang Gliding Festival** in Mesa Flight Park. Held in late February or early March (usually March), the four-day **Santa Barbara International Film Festival** is quite the bash, with premieres and screenings of both international and U.S. films, followed by the city's three-month theater festival. Also in March comes the **Whale Festival & Week of the Whale.** In April, Santa Barbara hosts the annual **International Orchid Show,** a major flower fest. (The Santa Barbara Orchid Fair comes in July.) Also in April: the **Santa Barbara County Vintners' Festival,** a spring wine aficionado and foodie fest, and the three-day multiethnic **Presidio Days,** Santa Barbara's annual birthday party.

A main event in May—there are many, including **Cinco de Mayo,** the **Santa Barbara Harbor Festival** (formerly the Fishermen's Festival), and the **Santa Barbara Arts and Crafts Show**—is the *I Madonnari* **Italian Street Painting Festival,** a chalk art festival, the first in the nation, named for the 16th-century Italian street painters and held at the Santa Barbara Mission courtyard. June brings the **Summer Solstice Parade,** a sometimes sunny longest-day-of-the-year lunacy including wacky floats, giant puppets, fantasy costumes and masks, dance, mime, and a festive street fair, and the **Big Dog Parade and Block Party** on State Street. Also in late June: **Semana Nautica,** a two-week summer sports festival featuring air, sea, land, pool, and adaptive sports. (The winter Semana Nautica, reduced to just a few days, comes in early February.)

Santa Barbara's **Fourth of July** includes a parade downtown, fireworks along the waterfront, and festivities all over town—including the Santa Barbara Symphony's free pops concert at the Santa Barbara Courthouse. The Santa Barbara **National Horse Show** in July is one of the top five horse events in the U.S., followed by the black-tie **Charity Hunt Ball.** Also in July: the **Chinese Festival** in Oak Park, the annual **California Outrigger Championships,** the **Old Mission Art Festival,** and the annual **Santa Barbara County Fair** in Santa Maria. August's **Old Spanish Days Fiesta** is a classy five-day celebration of the city's heritage with parades, carnival, rodeo, herds of horses, performances, other special events, and two colorful marketplaces—festive but dignified, a festival featuring plentiful freebies. Come in August also for the annual **Mariachi Festival,** the **Santa Barbara International Wine Auction,** and the annual **Kite Festival** at Shoreline Park.

The prestigious **Pacific Coast Open Polo Tournament** is held on three consecutive weekends in August. The elegant **Santa Barbara Concours d'Elegance** in September features spit-polished antique and classic cars, a winner's parade, and picnic. In late September or early October comes the **Santa Barbara International Jazz Festival and World Music Beach Party** at Stearns Wharf. In October comes the Santa Barbara Vintners' Association **Celebration of Harvest,** another foodie and wine festival, this one also featuring dancing, exhibits, and storytelling, and the **Santa Barbara Art Walk** fine arts show and sale. But don't miss the **California Avocado Festival** and the annual Goleta Lemon Festival. Santa Barbara's **National Amateur Horse Show** in November has a few days of Western events and a week of English-style riding competition in the largest amateur show in the nation. *Una Pastorella,* a re-creation of the traditional shepherd's nativity play, is staged in December inside the Presidio Chapel, and the **Yuletide Boat Parade** lights up Stearns Wharf. Also show up for **Winterfest** at the Santa Barbara Botanic Garden.

Artful, Entertaining Santa Barbara

The main arts event every March is the annual **Santa Barbara International Film Festival,** tel. (805) 963-0023, www.sbfilmfestival.org, with movie screenings at various local theaters. Local bookstores, cafes, and college campuses boast their fair share of poetry readings and other literary events; come in May for the **Santa Barbara Poetry Festival,** a regional and national poetry forum. The **Santa Barbara Writers' Conference,** which in the past has attracted popular scribes including Ray Bradbury and Amy Tan, convenes in June.

Public concerts have a long history in Santa Barbara. Native peoples greeted Portolá and company not with arrows, after all, but with "weird noises" on bowl flutes and whistles. Such tradition is perhaps why the small city of Santa Barbara offers an astounding array of arts events—including more concerts per capita than anyplace else in the country, from the classics and jazz to rock and pop.

Performances by the **Santa Barbara Symphony, tel. (805) 898-9626, www.thesymphony.org,** and Montecito's **Music Academy of the West,** tel. (805) 969-4726, www.musicacademy.org, are held throughout the year, throughout the community. The symphony holds its summer concerts at the Santa Barbara County Bowl, its regular series performances at the spectacular Arlington Center for the Performing Arts (for more on these venues, see below). The academy's eight-week summer music festival, held at various venues in Santa Barbara and at a private estate in Montecito, is one of the world's most acclaimed. The **Los Angeles Philharmonic** also performs fairly regularly in Santa Barbara, along with an ever-changing roster of world-class and regional performers. The **UC Santa Barbara Arts and Lectures** program, tel. (805) 893-2080, www.ucsb.edu, sponsors a lengthy calendar of special events, including readings and lectures, ballet, modern dance, and chamber music. If you're in the Goleta area, stop by to appreciate changing exhibits at the fine **University Art Museum,** tel. (805) 961-2951. **Santa Barbara City College** in Santa Barbara proper has a modern performing arts complex, the **Garvin Theatre,** tel. (805) 965-5935, www.sbcc.net, which stages dozens of performances each year. **La Casa de la Raza** on the city's lower east side at 601 Montecito, tel. (805) 965-8581, is the local Latino cultural center, sponsoring films, plays, lectures, and special concerts.

Santa Barbara's **Lobero Theatre,** 33 E. Cañon Perdido St., tel. (805) 963-0761, www.lobero. com, the city's first fashionable theatrical venue, was first established in 1873 in an old adobe schoolhouse. Headquartered here are the **Contemporary Music Theatre,** the **Santa Barbara Grand Opera Association,** the **Santa Barbara Dance Theater,** the **Santa Barbara Chamber Orchestra,** and the **Gilbert and Sullivan Company of Santa Barbara,** though various other groups and series—including **Sings Like Hell**— also call the Lobero home. The **Santa Barbara Civic Light Opera,** tel. (805) 962-1922, performs at the **Granada Theatre,** tel. (805) 966-2324. Another popular local venue is the sylvan **Santa Barbara County Bowl** outdoor amphitheater— cut-stone seating, revolving stage, great visibility and acoustics—which hosts a wide variety of contemporary and classical acts, usually from May through September.

But Santa Barbara's cultural gem is the Alhambra-like Arlington Theatre, also known as the **Arlington Center for the Performing Arts,** built on the site of the old Arlington Hotel at 1317 State St., tel. (805) 963-4408, a onetime 1930s movie palace where the domed ceiling still sparkles with electric stars; in its heyday there was even a cloud-making machine here. An arched passageway leads into the lobby, and the stage is flanked by two Spanish "villages," part of its architectural allure. In addition to regular Santa Barbara Symphony performances, the Arlington also hosts touring symphonies sponsored by the **Community Arts Music Association,** tel. (805) 966-4324.

For advance tickets for most local arts performances, call **State of the Arts,** toll-free tel. (800) 398-0722 or **Ticketmaster,** tel. (805) 583-8700 or toll-free (800) 765-6255.

After touring the **Santa Barbara Museum of Art,** 1130 State St., tel. (805) 963-4364, and poking into nearby galleries—the **Contemporary Arts Forum** at the Paseo Nuevo mall downtown, tel. (805) 966-5373, exhibits both established and up-and-coming artists—head to Montecito and the **Western States Museum of Photography** at the renowned **Brooks Institute of**

Photography, 1321 Alameda Padre Serra, tel. (805) 966-3888, www.brooks.edu, with its outstanding rotating exhibits plus a collection of historic shutterbug stuff. The museum is open weekdays 8 a.m.-5 p.m. daily, closed weekends and holidays. Also, on select Fridays the institute sponsors a public open house; guided campus tours can usually be arranged as well. To dabble in more artsy-craftsy fare, every sunny Sunday there's a **Beach Arts and Crafts Show** in Santa Barbara at Palm Park along Cabrillo Blvd., just east of Stearns Wharf, from 10 a.m. to dusk.

Santa Barbara hosts an amazing number of arts and crafts fairs, benefits, cat, dog, and horse shows, community festivals, and other events throughout the year. To find out what's going on while you're in town—and what might be hip or happening in local nightlife—pick up a current issue of the free *Santa Barbara Independent,* www.independent.com, published on Thursday each week and offering local news coverage and excellent arts and entertainment features, reviews, and calendar listings. The daily *Santa Barbara News-Press,* www.newspress.com, also features calendar listings and a special Friday *Scene* magazine insert.

Recreation, Tours, and Other Adventures

If it's remotely related to sky, sea, sand, or sandtrap, Santa Barbara has it. Popular local recreational pursuits vary from in-line skating, strolling, and cycling to sailing and scuba diving, from kayaking to lawn bowling, hiking and horseback riding to polo. Winter whalewatching tours, windsurfing, golf—a major regional pastime, judging from the number of world-class courses scattered throughout Santa Barbara County—and tennis also keep people out and about.

For a complete listing of boat and charter rentals, also organized tours in and around Santa Barbara, stop by local visitor centers—or consult the current phone book. An official concessionaire for trips to offshore Channel Islands National Park is Santa Barbara's own **Truth Aquatics,** 301 W. Cabrillo Blvd., tel. (805) 962-1127 or toll-free (800) 927-4688, fax (805) 564-6754, www.truthaquatics.com, an award-winning scuba diving fleet that also offers island hiking, camping, and natural history tours. If you'd rather shove off from Ventura, **Island Packer Cruises,** headquartered at 1867 Spinnaker Dr., Ventura 93001,

(805) 642-7688 (recorded), fax (805) 642-6573, www.islandpacker.com, offers fair-weather trips and winter whalewatching tours to the Channel Islands. Reservations are required for all trips which, unfortunately, can be cancelled at the last minute because of inclement weather. (For more on what to see and do offshore, see Islands in Time: Channel Islands National Park, below.) The **Santa Barbara Museum of Natural History,** tel. (805) 682-4711, also offers whalewatching tours, along with **Captain Don's Harbor Tours,** tel. (805) 969-5217.

PRACTICAL SANTA BARBARA

STAYING IN SANTA BARBARA

Santa Barbara is a popular destination year-round—a wonderful winter getaway when the rest of the nation is snowbound—but the "high season" is July and August, extending into balmy fall weekends, when warm weather coastal fog all but disappears. Most accommodation rates, fairly high any time, are highest in the summer, on weekends, and during major special events. If you plan to arrive in summer and are particular about where you'll be staying—an issue for budget travelers and families as well as the affluent—book your reservations many months, even a year, in advance. Though the practice has long been business as usual at area bed and breakfasts, increasingly even motels and hotels require a two-night minimum stay on weekends (three-night minimum on holiday weekends).

For help in sorting out the possibilities, try local no-fee booking agencies, including **Coastal Getaways,** tel. (805) 969-1258, **Central Coast Reservations,** toll-free tel. (800) 557-7898, and **Santa Barbara Hot Spots,** tel. (805) 564-1637 or toll-free (800) 793-7666.

Campgrounds, Yurts,
a Hostel, and a Monastery
Nearby **Los Padres National Forest** offers plenty of campgrounds. A complete campground listing and forest map, $2, is available at the National Forest headquarters in Goleta, 6755 Hollister Ave., Ste. 150, tel. (805) 968-6640, www.r5.fs.fed.us/lospadres; all are first-come, first-camped (no reservations taken) with a two-week maximum stay. Closer to the ocean are the three developed state beach campgrounds northwest of Santa Barbara—**Gaviota, Refugio,** and **El Capitan.** All are popular and quite nice, even for sunny winter camping (popular with snowbirds). For general information on all three, call (805) 968-1033. Reserve campsites at all three—well-worn El Capitan is especially popular year-round—through ReserveAmerica, toll-free tel. (800) 444-7275; it's first-come, first-camped from December through February. Gaviota has the smallest campground, and El Capitan and Refugio are like Siamese twins, sharing the palm-lined shoreline and a bike trail but featuring distinct identities otherwise (some campsites at Refugio are sublime, but Gaviota is most pleasant and reclusive). All offer sites with hot showers and flush toilets, some have RV hookups. Also within reasonable range of Santa Barbara is huge—262 total campsites, 126 with RV hookups—**Carpinteria State Beach** 12 miles southeast of Santa Barbara and just off Hwy. 101, local tel. (805) 684-2811 or (805) 968-3294, toll-free tel. (800) 444-7275 for reservations. Dogs (six-foot leash) are permitted at all of these state campgrounds for an extra $1 per day, but are not allowed on beaches or trails.

The biggest campground around is a bit farther away and inland via Hwy. 154: the county's very pleasant **Cachuma Lake Recreation Area,** with a total of almost 1,000 family and group campsites available on either a first-come or reservation basis, $12 and up (hookups extra). Cachuma offers tent, yurt, and RV camping. The fabric-covered yurts feature platform beds, electric lights and heating, lockable doors, and wood-framed screened windows. General camping amenities include hot showers, restrooms, fireplaces with grills, picnic tables, swimming pools (summer only), and nonswimming lake recreation opportunities. Primitive and hiker/biker campsites are less expensive. Dogs—on leashes—are welcomed, for a $1-per-day fee and current proof of rabies vaccination; pets are not allowed on trails. For current reservation information and other specifics, call (805) 686-5054 or 686-5055, www.sbparks.org.

Santa Barbara also boasts a 60-bed **Banana Bungalow Santa Barbara,** 210 E. Ortega St., tel. (805) 963-0154 or toll-free tel. (800) 346-7835, fax (805) 963-0184, www.bananabungalow.com, within an easy stroll of both the bus and train stations. Budget, with rates $16-22.

For a peaceful retreat, consider the **Mount Calvary Guest House** at 2500 Gilbraltar Rd., tel. (805) 962-9855, www.mount-calvary.org, a palatial 1940s mountaintop Spanish-style villa with incredible vistas, great hiking access, plenty of comfortable spare bedrooms, and Benedictine monks happy to serve you. Moderate. Rates are $70 per person suggested donation (all meals included, on the American plan), with both single and double rooms (singles share an adjoining bath). Individuals—no partiers, please—are welcome for personal retreats.

In addition to the yurts available at Lake Cachuma, there's also the **White Lotus Foundation,** 2500 San Marcos Pass, tel. (805) 964-1944, www.whitelotus.org, a yoga teaching institute that makes theirs available on a space available basis. Moderate ($70 couple per night).

Inexpensive-Moderate Motels and Hotels

Beyond hostels and such, finding inexpensive accommodations in Santa Barbara is a challenge. There's always Motel 6, which here isn't all that inexpensive. The **Motel 6 Santa Barbara,** 443 Corona Del Mar, tel. (805) 564-1392 or toll-free tel. (800) 466-8356 (nationwide), fax (805) 963-4687, www.motel6.com, is close to the beach and downtown, newly renovated, and small, featuring the usual basic accommodations plus color TV and HBO, phones, free local calls. Very popular; for the summer-fall season, book at least six months in advance. Moderate, with rates $63-84, depending on the season (weekends in summer and fall are highest). If there's no room here, there's another Motel 6 downtown, 3505 State St., tel. (805) 687-5400, still another north of town near Goleta, and two more south of town near Carpinteria.

The once stately old hotels at the beach end of State St. are other low-end possibilities, though these are rapidly becoming boutique hotels. Of the rest, some places look better than they are, passing trains offer unwanted wake-up calls in the middle of the night, and it's a little sleazy here after dark (pack your street smarts). A best bet for an inexpensive stay, still, is the **Hotel State Street,** 121 State St., tel. (805) 966-6586, where high-season rates for clean rooms with shared baths are $50, with private baths $90 and up, continental breakfast included. Inexpensive-Expensive.

Midrange Motels and Hotels

Most medium-priced motels here are pricey compared to similar accommodations elsewhere. But since this is Santa Barbara, who can complain? The following offer exceptional value, including good location, for the money.

Appealing and fairly affordable among Santa Barbara's burgeoning downtown boutique hotel roster is the 1926-vintage **Hotel Santa Barbara,** 533 State St. (at Cota), tel. (805) 957-9300 or toll-free (888) 259-7700, fax (805) 962-2412, www.hotelsantabarbara.com. Rooms are light, airy, and attractively decorated. An abundance of great restaurants are just a stroll away from the welcoming lobby. Expensive-Luxury ($99-209), but look for good seasonal specials.

Santa Barbara's newest downtown boutique, open since late 1999, is the very stylish Holiday Inn Express **Hotel Virginia,** just a hop and skip from the beach at 17 W. Haley St. (east of State St.), tel. (805) 963-9757 or toll-free (800) 549-1700, fax (805) 963-1747, www.hotelvirginia.com, listed on the National Register of Historic Places. Décor in this 1916-vintage, 61-room hotel emphasizes the spectacular Malibu and Catalina tilework now preserved and restored here—including the striking mosaic fountain in the lobby—and also showcases local art and artists. Rooms, decked out in a contemporary take on classic art-deco style, feature all the modern comforts, from state-of-the-art phones and data ports to hair dryers and in-room irons and ironing boards; some have balconies with wrought-iron railings and French windows. A stay includes expanded continental breakfast, with good coffee, fresh juices and fruit, locally baked goods, cereals, and yogurt. Luxury, with regular rates $159-199, though specials can drop the tab to as low as $99.

A classic in the Santa Barbara area is the historic blue-roofed **Miramar Hotel,** in Montecito at 1555 S. Jameson Ln., tel. (805) 969-2203 or toll-free (800) 322-6983 for reservations (in California), fax (805) 969-3163, www.sbmiramar.com. The Miramar was more tranquil in pre-freeway days but it's nonetheless still charming, perfect for unfussy families. Semitropical gardens and beachfront location add to the appeal. Expensive-Luxury. Regular rooms are $89 and up in summer, with cheaper, fairly spartan rooms closer to the thundering traffic, quieter ones clustered around the pool or along the 500-foot beachfront. Cottage and parlor suites with one, two, or three bedrooms (some have kitchens) start at $159. But even with a simple room you can enjoy the tennis and shuffleboard courts, the two swimming pools, the health spa, the on-site restaurants—and the beach. For burgers and such, the kids will love the **Miramar Diner,** open 11 a.m.-6 p.m. This venerable diner cum ice cream fountain, snuggled into a 1950s' Pullman car with a view, adds an element of olden-days excitement to the simple menu of burgers, sandwiches, soups, salads, and ice cream creations—especially realistic when real trains rumble by.

The attractive 53-room **Franciscan Inn,** 109 Bath St. (just south of Hwy. 101), tel. (805) 963-8845, fax (805) 564-3295, www.franciscaninn.com, offers high-season rates in the Expensive-Luxury range, $105-200, with tasteful decor and all the country-style comforts plus swimming pool and whirlpool, just a block from the beach. Almost half the rooms here have kitchenettes (extra).

Another find is **The Eagle Inn,** 232 Natoma Ave. (three blocks south of Hwy. 101, at Bath), tel. (805) 965-3586 or toll-free (800) 767-0030, fax (805) 966-1218, www.theeagleinn.com. Most rooms at this very attractive Spanish-style motel, a onetime apartment complex, are more like apartments, with full-stocked kitchens and the homey, well-kept kind of comfort that makes you want to stay longer than you'd planned. Even better is the fact that the Eagle Inn is only a block and a half from the beach. On-site laundry, cable TV, and free movies (no air conditioning). Expensive-Luxury ($89-160), with off-season and weekday rates the real deal. For summer, book rooms by mid-May.

Also quite appealing and close to the beach is the **Inn by the Harbor,** 433 W. Montecito St., tel. (805) 963-7851 or toll-free (800) 626-1986, fax (805) 962-9428, www.sbhotels.com, a classic Mediterranean-style motel. Many units have kitchens. Expensive-Luxury ($102-168). See the website for the rundown on sister motels nearby.

Another good value, a gussied-up motel done up in appealing country-French décor, well situated for a beach-oriented vacation, is the smoke-free 45-room **Country Inn by the Sea** two blocks south of Hwy. 101 at 128 Castillo St., tel. (805) 963-4471 or toll-free tel. (800) 455-4647, fax (805) 962-2633, www.countryinnbythesea.com. Most rooms come with a balcony or patio plus color TV, VCRs, free movies, and tasty continental breakfast. Extras include a small swimming pool, saunas, spa, and a nearby city park with tennis courts. Premium-Luxury ($149-209), though off-season and discounted rates drop down as low as $99.

Other good midrange possibilities include the **Coast Village Inn** in the center of Montecito at 1188 Coast Village Rd., tel. (805) 969-3266 or toll-free (800) 257-5131, fax (805) 969-7117, www.coastvillageinn.com, Premium-Luxury ($125-165, though specials drop to $89); the **El Prado Inn** downtown at 1601 State St., tel. (805) 966-0807 or toll-free (800) 669-8979, fax (805) 966-6502, www.elprado.com, Expensive-Luxury ($85-170); and the **Mason Beach Inn** just south of Hwy. 101 at 324 W. Mason St., tel. (805) 962-3203 or toll-free (800) 446-0444, fax (805) 962-1056, Expensive-Luxury ($85-195).

High-End Motels and Hotels

Lacking the history of other upscale area hotels but little else, 360-room **Fess Parker's Doubletree Resort,** previously the Red Lion Inn, is a luxurious Spanish-style resort motel across from the beach at 633 E. Cabrillo Blvd., tel. (805) 564-4333 or toll-free (800) 879-2929, fax (805) 564-4964, www.fpdtr.com. The huge resort motel, situated on 24 acres, features basketball and shuffleboard courts, a putting green, lighted tennis courts, exercise facilities, rental bikes, heated pool, sauna, and whirlpool. **Maxi's** restaurant is another mainstay. Rooms include all the usual comforts plus in-room coffeemakers, honor bars, color TV with cable and movies, and radios. Luxury. Room rates starting at $195, but inquire about specials and seasonal discounts.

Also fronting the beach, adjacent to Stearns Wharf, is the 80-room **Harbor View Inn** just west of State St. at 28 W. Cabrillo Blvd., tel. (805) 963-0780 or toll-free (800) 755-0222, fax (805) 963-7967. Very attractive rooms feature the usual deluxe amenities plus in-room coffeemakers, refrigerators, safes, and color TV with cable. In addition to the swimming pool and whirlpool, there's a heated wading pool for the kiddos and bike, rollerblade, and skate rentals. On-site restaurant. Luxury, with high-season rates $180 and up (ocean-view rooms most expensive).

Though it's really just a spiffed-up Santa Barbara beach motel, dedicated foodies are drawn to the 71-room **Santa Barbara Inn,** 901 E. Cabrillo Blvd., tel. (805) 966-2285 or toll-free (800) 231-0431, fax (805) 966-6584, www .santabarbarainn.com. That's because after filling up on the fine California-French fare at **Citronelle,** chef Michel Richard's on-site restaurant, guests can just waddle right over to their rooms—or across the street to the beach—and rest until mealtime comes around again. Rooms here are spacious and attractive, with refrigerators, coffeemakers, and color TV with cable TV. Some have kitchens, some have air conditioning. In addition to the heated pool and whirlpool, there's a sundeck on the third floor. Luxury, with regular rates $219-309; discounts and off-season specials can drop the tab considerably. Weekly and monthly rates are available.

In 1928 the little tramp himself, Charlie Chaplin, and his later scandal-plagued partner Fatty Arbuckle established the **Montecito Inn,** 1295 Coast Village Rd., tel. (805) 969-7854 or toll-free (800) 843-2017, fax (805) 969-0623, www.montecitoinn.com, as a Hollywood hideout. These days an attractive and trendy small hotel with Mediterranean provincial style, the Montecito Inn features somewhat small rooms with all the usual amenities—no air conditioning, but there are ceiling fans—plus an attractive pool and spa area out back. Seven spacious new Mediterranean-style luxury suites feature bathrooms of Italian marble plus jacuzzis; some suites have fireplaces. The inn sits close to the freeway, right in town—an easy stroll to most of Montecito's action. Luxury, with rates starting at $185.

Especially Fun for Families

The **Circle Bar B Guest Ranch** at 1800 Refugio Rd. beyond Goleta, tel. (805) 968-1113, www.circlebarb.com, is a place the kids will get excited about—a genuine ranch dedicated to horseback rides (extra) and all kids of family-appropriate fun, hiking, picnicking, and diving into the neigh-borhood swimming hole. And the dinner theater does drama down at the barn, spring through fall. Accommodations, some cabin-style, are Western-themed and quite comfortable. Luxury, with high-season rates starting at $186 double. (two-night minimum on weekends, three nights on holiday weekends). In summer, plan to book at least six weeks in advance on weekends, four weeks otherwise. The ranch is about three and a half miles inland from Refugio State Beach, via Refugio Rd., 20 miles north of Santa Barbara via Hwy. 101.

Just the basics for a camping-style stay but considerably less pricey is a stay at **Rancho Osos Stables & Guest Ranch,** 3750 Paradise Rd. in Santa Barbara, tel. (805) 683-5686 or toll-free (800) 859-3640, adjacent to the Santa Ynez River and Los Padres National Forest. Overnight options at "Western Town" include colorful tongue-and-groove pine cabins complete with beds, coffeemaker, and small refrigerator or any of 10 Conestoga covered wagons circled around the campfire. Each wagon features electricity, hardwood floors, and four Army-style cots. Inexpensive, with cabins $46 a night, wagons $27. Hot showers, bathrooms, charcoal barbecue pits, and abundant picnic tables are nearby. Hearty meals are available on weekends at the on-site Chuck Wagon and nearby Stone Lodge Kitchen.

If money is no object and you and the li'l dogies will be moseyin' north, within easy reach is the luxurious **Alisal Guest Ranch and Resort** just outside Solvang, tel. (805) 688-6411 (for details, see Solvang and Vicinity, above). Also, the 4200-square-foot ranch house at the family-owned **Cottontail Creek Ranch,** tel. (805) 995-1787, www.cottontrailcreek.com, is available 12 weeks of the year as a vacation rental.

Santa Barbara-Area Bed and Breakfasts

Santa Barbara is a B&B bonanza—that phenomenon quite rare in and around Southern California. Many local bed and breakfasts and B&B-style inns are as reasonably priced as local motels, if not more so, and most offer reduced rates, specials, or packages for off-season and/or weekday stays. Many require a two-night minimum stay on weekends and/or a three-night stay over longer holiday weekends. Here as elsewhere in California, most bed and breakfasts are smoke-free. However, you may be allowed to smoke on a terrace or patio, or on a nearby street corner.

Quite appealing and a great value by Santa Barbara standards is the **Secret Garden and Cottages,** 1908 Bath St., tel. (805) 687-2300, fax (805) 687-4576, www.secretgarden.com, a collection of craftsman-style cottages with most of the 11 rooms are named after particular birds. Weather permitting, breakfast is served in the garden. Premium-Luxury, with rates $115-225.

Near the beach is the award-winning **Old Yacht Club Inn,** 431 Corona Del Mar Dr., tel. (805) 962-1277 or toll-free (800) 549-1676 (California) or (800) 676-1676 (U.S.), fax (805) 962-3989, www.oldyachtclubinn.com, actually once a yacht club, though this homey 1912 stucco craftsman was built as a private home. Santa Barbara's first bed and breakfast, open since 1980, the Yacht Club's main house features yachting memorabilia and five rooms decorated in period furnishings of various moods. Four more rooms, all with private entrances, are available in the adjacent tile-roofed Hitchcock House. Just two blocks from the beach, the Yacht Club also provides bikes to tour the neighborhood. Fabulous breakfasts and famous Saturday night dinners (extra, by reservation). Premium-Luxury, with rates $110-190.

The gracious three-story Queen Anne **Bath Street Inn** is just south of Mission St. at 1720 Bath St., tel. (805) 682-9680 or toll-free (800) 341-2284, fax (805) 569-1281, www.travel-seek. com. Some of the 12 rooms, in the main house and summer house out back, feature fireplaces and whirlpool tubs; some also have in-room refrigerators and coffeemakers; one features a kitchen, whirlpool tub, and separate entrance. In addition to full breakfast, tea is served in the afternoon, wine in the evening. Expensive-Luxury, with rates $100-190 (20% discount Sun.-Thurs., summers and holiday weeks excepted).

Other bed and breakfast possibilities include the **Glenborough Inn,** 1327 Bath St., tel. (805) 966-0589 or toll-free (888) 966-0589, fax (805) 564-8610, www.silcom.com/~glenboro, actually a combination of five turn-of-the-century homes and cottages with 14 rooms (Expensive-Luxury, $100-380); **The Parsonage,** 1600 Olive St., tel. (805) 962-9336, fax (805) 962-9336, with six rooms in an 1892 Victorian (Premium-Luxury, $125-325); and **The Cheshire Cat,** 36 W. Vale-rio St. (at Chapala), tel. (805) 569-1610, fax (805) 682-1876, www.cheshirecat.com, a collection of houses and cottages with rooms named after characters in Alice's adventures (Premium-Luxury, $140-350).

For those uncomfortable with the forced social intimacy of most bed and breakfast inns, the historic **Upham Hotel,** 1404 De La Vina St., tel. (805) 962-0058 or toll-free (800) 727-0876, fax (805) 963-2825, www.uphamhotel.com, offers a friendly alternative. Built in 1871 by Amasa Lincoln, a Boston banker who set sail for California to build himself a New England-style inn, these days the Upham is still more hotel than bed and breakfast. This Victorian hotel features 50 rooms and garden cottages on an acre of land in the heart of town, just a stroll from State Street. The Upham's primary eccentricity is in its guest register—an incongruous celebrity collection including Richard Nixon, Aldous Huxley, and Agatha Christie. Rooms in the main building are smallish but comfortable, with nice antique touches; more contemporary, more expensive rooms and suites are situated in various outbuildings and garden cottages. The fireplace-cozy lobby resembles an English parlor. The buffet breakfast can be taken indoors, out on the wraparound veranda, or out in the garden in an Adirondack chair. Wine and cheese are served in the evening. The on-site **Louie's** restaurant is quite good. Premium-Luxury ($140 and up).

Truly exceptional among Santa Barbara's bed-and-breakfast celebrities is the landmark **Simpson House Inn,** 121 E. Arrellaga St., tel. (805) 963-7067 or toll-free (800) 676-1280 (U.S.), fax (805) 564-4811, www.simpsonhouseinn.com. Centerpiece is the uncluttered 1874 Eastlake Italianate Victorian, exquisitely restored with period furnishings, oriental rugs, and English lace. Other rooms are in a onetime barn—the 19th-century "barn suites," complete with authentic interior walls—and three separate garden cottages with stone fireplaces and English charm. The gardens here, an entire acre of horticultural adventure sculpted into various semi-private "outdoor rooms," are most charming of all. Full gourmet breakfast is served on the veranda or in the formal dining room, along with afternoon or evening hors d'oeuvres (including Santa Barbara County wines). Luxury, with rates $195-500.

Quite nice is the 16-room English country-style **Inn on Summerhill** south of Montecito at 2520 Lillie Ave. south of town in Summerland, tel. (805) 969-9998 or toll-free (800) 845-5566, fax (805) 565-9948, another award-winning bed and breakfast. This one boasts suite-style rooms with canopied beds and all the contemporary comforts—in-room refrigerators, jacuzzi tubs, color TV with cable and VCRs—plus full homemade breakfast and, come evening, hors d'oeuvres and dessert. Luxury, with rates $215 and up.

And if you're pushing farther on down the coast, a bed-and-breakfast gem along the way—particularly for fans of T.S. Eliot—is **Prufrock's Garden Inn,** 600 Linden Ave. in Carpinteria, tel. (805) 566-9696 or toll-free (877) 837-6257, fax (805) 566-9404, www.prufrocks.com. Premium-Luxury, with rates $120-250, but in the off season weekday rates can drop quite a bit.

Luxury Hotels and Resorts

If money is no object—if this is a once-in-a-lifetime visit and you want something close to guaranteed bliss—*the* place is the **Four Seasons**

THE FOUR SEASONS BILTMORE, SANTA BARBARA

You might never want to leave once you settle into the Four Seasons Biltmore.

Biltmore Hotel in the Montecito area at 1260 Channel Dr., tel. (805) 969-2261 or toll-free (800) 332-3442 (U.S.) and (800) 268-6282 (Canada), fax (805) 969-4212, www.fourseasons.com. Even *Condé Nast Traveler* says this is one of the finest resorts in the nation. The vast but intimate tile-roofed 1927 resort, designed in "Spanish ecclesiastical" style with endless other Mediterranean details by architect Reginald Johnson, just oozes luxurious old-money charm. Visitors could spend an entire stay just appreciating the craftsmanship, from the hand-made decorative Mexican tiles and the irregular mission-style *ladrillos* (tile floors) to the massive oak doors at the hotel's entrance. Endless archways, stairways, low towers, fountains, loggias, and bougainvillea-draped walkways threaded through the lush 21-acre grounds make just finding your room an architectural adventure. Yet for all its understated elegance and luxury—and its Olympic-sized swimming pool, lighted tennis courts, kids program, excellent restaurants, multilingual staff, full conference and business facilities—a stay can be almost reasonable. And for sheer extravagance, nobody beats the Biltmore's Sunday brunch. Luxury, with regular high-season rates are $290-600, with larger ocean-view rooms and cottages most expensive; inquire about special packages and off-season specials.

Or head to the **San Ysidro Ranch,** in Montecito at 900 San Ysidro Ln. (at Mountain Dr.), tel. (805) 969-5046 or toll-free (800) 368-6788, fax (805) 565-1995, www.sanysidroranch.com. The ranch is an honorable member of the Relais at Châteaux international hotel association, one of the few in the U.S., which explains its current exclusive cachet. But actor Ronald Colman owned the ranch in the 1930s, and in those rowdier years it was a popular Hollywood trysting place. One can still see why. These romantic cottages—the ultimate rooms with a view, scattered throughout some of Santa Barbara's most stunning gardens—are prized for their seclusion as well as their understated luxury. John and Jackie Kennedy honeymooned here, Laurence Olivier and Vivien Leigh were married here, and ink-stained scribes including Somerset Maugham and Sinclair Lewis hid out here to write. Winston Churchill wrote his memoirs here. Individually decorated rooms feature wood-burning fireplaces and endless little luxuries—such as in-room massage and other spa and beauty services (extra)—and the grounds include a swimming pool, wading pool, tennis courts, and stables. Horseback riding is immensely popular here. You can also golf, with privileges at the nearby Montecito Country Club. If you can't afford to stay here, a special breakfast, lunch, dinner, or spectacular Sunday brunch at the excellent California-style American **Stonehouse** restaurant at least gets you a look around (reservations highly recommended). Luxury. Cottage rooms start at $375 and luxury cottages top out at $3,750, with a two-night minimum stay on weekends, a three- or four-night minimum on holiday weekends.

Just as enchanting in its own way, and a tad less expensive, is the 10-acre hilltop **El Encanto Hotel & Garden Villas,** 1900 Lasuen Rd. (at Alameda Padre Serra), tel. (805) 687-5000 or toll-free (800) 678-8946, fax (805) 687-3903, www.nthp.org. This sprawling country inn, just a half-mile from the Santa Barbara Mission, once served as student and faculty housing for the original University of California at Santa Barbara campus; when the university headed north to Goleta in 1915, El Encanto was born. A charter member of the National Trust for Historic Preservation's Historic Hotels of America, El Encanto is a maze of tile-roofed Spanish colonial revival-style *casitas* and craftsman-style cottages tucked in among the oaks and luxuriant hillside gardens. (Don't lose the map the staff give you when you check in; you'll definitely need it to find your way around.) Over the years El Encanto has welcomed endless celebrities and dignitaries, including Franklin Delano Roosevelt. But just about anyone will feel at home in these understated yet very pleasant lodgings, decorated in French country style. Many rooms feature wood-burning fireplaces, quite cheering on rain- or fog-chilled evenings; hotel staff regularly replenish the wood supply on the porch. Some have refrigerators and kitchens. "View" rooms are higher on the hillside, some distance from the main building. A private, reclusive resort, El Encanto's amenities include a year-round solar- and gas-heated swimming pool, tennis courts and full-time tennis pro, library, and lounge. Views from the excellent on-site restaurant— open daily for breakfast, lunch, and dinner—and the hotel lobby overlook the city and the vast Pacific Ocean, a dazzling sight at sunset. Luxury, with rooms $239-419, cottage suites $379-1,200. Ask about off-season and midweek packages and specials.

EATING IN SANTA BARBARA

Farmers' Markets, Trader Joe's

The **Santa Barbara Downtown Certified Farmers' Market,** tel. (805) 962-5354, is the place to load up on premium fresh flowers, herbs, vegetables, fruits, nuts, honey, eggs, and other farm-fresh local produce. The market is held on the corner of Santa Barbara and Cota Streets every Saturday 8:30 a.m.-12:30 p.m. The **Santa Barbara Old Town Certified Farmers' Market** (same phone) convenes along the 500-600 blocks of State St. on Tuesday, 4-7:30 p.m. in summer and 3-6:30 p.m. in winter. Other area farmers' markets are held in Goleta and Carpinteria on Thursday afternoon, and in Montecito on Friday morning; call for locations and current hours.

Though Santa Barbara has its share of gourmet delis—see food listings below—it also has a **Trader Joe's,** 29 S. Milpas St., tel. (805) 564-7878, which means just about anybody can afford to put together a stylish picnic dinner for the beach.

Inexpensive and Good

Even people who can't afford to sleep in Santa Barbara can usually find a good meal here. For "gourmet tacos," Santa Barbara's most famous dining destination is **La Super-Rica Taqueria,** 622 N. Milpas, tel. (805) 963-4940, an unassuming hole-in-the-wall and long-running favorite of chef Julia Child and appreciative fellow foodies. This mom-and-pop place serves the best soft tacos around—fresh house-made corn tortillas topped with chorizo, chicken, beef, or pork—and unforgettable seafood tamales. For Santa Barbara at its best, grab a taco and a cold beer and head for the patio—or head for the beach and a sunset picnic. Also worth a takeout stop: **La Tolteca** restaurant and deli, 614-616 E. Haley, tel. (805) 963-0847, not real close to downtown but cheap—a tortilla-factory restaurant serving great homemade tamales, tostadas, tacos, and burritos (call for current hours).

Santa Barbara is a health-conscious city, and people from all walks of life tend to appreciate foods that'll do their bodies good. Been-there-forever **Sojourner,** 134 E. Cañon Perdido St., tel. (805) 965-7922, serves inexpensive vegetarian and vegan fare, from vegetable-rich homemade soups and black-bean stew to veggie lasagna. Also good for healthy and veggie basics, including juices and smoothies, is the **Main Squeeze** two doors down at 138 E. Cañon Perdido, tel. (805) 966-5365.

Super for inexpensive all-American breakfast is the people's favorite **Esau's Coffee Shop,** 403 State St., tel. (805) 965-4416, where everything is homemade, right down to the biscuits and home fries. It's open until 1 p.m. for breakfast and lunch (most people do breakfast).

The oldest place in town is reportedly **Joe's Cafe** and bar, 536 State St. (near Cota), tel. (805) 966-4638, a reasonably inexpensive local institution—marked by the eagle—that keeps shuffling around downtown. (Since Joe's is often mobbed, come at an off hour.) Check out the history on the walls while you enjoy excellent ravioli, steaks, fried chicken, sometimes-fresh swordfish, rainbow trout, and Santa Maria-style barbecue. Good pasta salads. *Big* meals, no desserts, and notoriously potent drinks. It's open for lunch and dinner daily.

Stylish Yet Affordable

Santa Barbara loves its restaurants served up with some style. The city's better restaurants also tend to cluster downtown, making many city blocks irresistible for foodies. For the best quiche in town, for example, head to **Mousse Odile,** 18 E. Cota St., tel. (805) 962-5393, actually a French deli serving breakfast, lunch, and dinner. The chocolate dessert mousse drives people wild. For California-style French bistro fare, the place is **Mimosa,** 700 De La Vina St., tel. (805) 682-2272, open for lunch weekdays only, for dinner nightly. For Thai, **Your Place,** 22 N. Milpas St., Ste. A, tel. (805) 966-5151, is a best bet. Fabulous and locally famous for sushi is **Arigato Sushi,** 11 W. Victoria St. #16, tel. (805) 965-6074.

For Southwestern, seek out the blue-corn tortillas and marvelous cheese *chiles rellenos* is the **Zia Cafe,** 532 State St., tel. (805) 962-5391, open daily for both lunch and dinner. **Roy,** 7 W.

Carillo, tel. (805) 966-5636, is famous for serving stylish and fresh California-style American at astonishingly low prices.

Fish, fish, fish—the ocean around here is still full of them, even after the Bay Cafe has had its way. The **Bay Cafe,** 131 Anacapa St., tel. (805) 963-2215, serves all kinds of charbroiled fish at dinner, from salmon to swordfish, plus the Bay's rendition of surf 'n' turf, paellas, and shrimp and other seafood pastas. At lunch, expect some of the same but also fish and chips, tostadas, crab melts, and seafood salad. Just about everything tastes better if you're sitting out on the patio. The Bay Cafe is open for lunch and dinner daily.

Fun at breakfast, lunch, and dinner is the other-era **Paradise Cafe,** 702 Anacapa St., tel. (805) 962-4416, specializing in new renditions of predominantly all-American fare—eggs and omelettes, beefy burgers, and woodfire-grilled chicken, chops, fish, and steaks. But the Paradise Cafe is most famous for its steamed mussels—fresh from the Santa Barbara Channel, scraped off the legs of offshore oil rigs—and for the fact that it serves an exceptional selection of Santa Barbara County wines. Lively bar scene. Half the town shows up on Sunday (starting at 9 a.m.) for the Paradise Café's killer breakfast/brunch. Breakfast is served only on Sunday.

Locally beloved for Cajun is the original **Cajun Kitchen,** 1924 De la Vina, Ste. A (near Mission St.), tel. (805) 965-1004. Those in the know say to show up early on Saturday morning—before everyone else gets there—for the unforgettable chile verde. There are Cajun Kitchens all over, elsewhere in town at 901 Chapala St., tel. (805) 965-1004, and also in Goleta and Carpinteria. **The Palace Cafe,** 8 E. Cota St. (at State), tel. (805) 966-3133, is Santa Barbara's other New Orleans niche, serving imaginative and exceptionally well-prepared fish, crawfish, "Cajun popcorn," and other Cajun-Creole and Caribbean fare. The menu changes nightly. It's open daily for lunch and dinner.

Busy **Brigitte's** California-style bistro at 1325 State St., tel. (805) 966-9676, serves everything one would expect—pizzas with pizzazz, refined pastas, grill specialties, grand salads—along with an impressive California wine list. For something simpler, stop by the associated bakery and deli adjacent for sandwiches, takeout salads, fresh-baked breads, and other bakery items.

Then there's always **The Patio** at the Four Seasons Biltmore, 1260 Channel Dr., tel. (805) 969-2261, open daily for breakfast, lunch, and dinner. Even if a stay at Santa Barbara's venerable Biltmore is impossible, almost anyone can swing a meal here—at least at The Patio, reasonably relaxed and quite good. A wonderful French, Mediterranean, or Italian buffet is served every evening. If money's no object, of course, the ultimate is dress-up dinner in the Biltmore's oceanview **La Marina** restaurant. Either choice offers an excuse to appreciate the lobby and explore the grounds of this 1927 Spanish-Mediterranean hotel, exquisitely restored in 1987.

Stylish Yet Affordable Nearby

For something different on the San Marcos Pass route between Santa Barbara and the Solvang area, stop at **Cold Spring Tavern,** an old stagecoach stop at 5995 Stagecoach Rd. off Hwy. 154, tel. (805) 967-0066. The evocative Old West ambience here comes with some fairly sophisticated fare—such things as charbroiled quail—along with more traditional meat, potatoes, and biscuits with gravy. It's open daily for lunch and dinner, on weekends only for breakfast.

Otherwise, beyond Santa Barbara proper and the Santa Ynez Valley (see Solvang and Vicinity, above), the place to go is Montecito. This uptown Santa Barbara suburb has its share of snazzy restaurants, many of them strung out along Coast Village Road, the main drag—also home to the Friday morning farmers' market—and many of them reasonably priced. Always a best bet is the California-style **Montecito Cafe** at the stylish Montecito Inn, 1295 Coast Village Rd., tel. (805) 969-3392, open daily for lunch and dinner. For fashionable deli and cafe fare, the place is **Tutti's,** 1209 Coast Village Rd., tel. (805) 969-5809, open daily for breakfast, lunch, and dinner. Poke around the neighborhood for other possibilities, since restaurants sometimes come and go quite quickly. Such is the nature of style.

Or try **Piatti** in Montecito at 516 San Ysidro Rd. (at E. Valley Rd.), tel. (805) 969-7520, open for lunch and dinner daily. This cheerful Italian was cooked up by the owners of Auberge du Soleil and the local San Ysidro Ranch, two of California's most prestigious resorts. But anybody can feel comfortable here, what with colorful vegetables on the walls and a sunny-patio sense of place. Sit down and celebrate the Santa Barbara good life with homemade pastas, good salads, and chicken, fish, and other entrees. Piatti is open daily for both lunch and dinner.

Pane e Vino, 1482 E. Valley Rd. in Montecito, tel. (805) 969-9274, is another popular local Italian, this one serving good Northern Italian—perfect pasta and fine chicken and fish dishes. Bread and wine, too. For something still simpler—pizzas, pasta, sandwiches, and such—head next door to Pane e Vino's kissing cousin **Via Vai,** tel. (805) 565-9393.

For fine deli and cafe fare or to pack a gourmet picnic basket, don't miss the **Pierre LaFond**

Ye Cold Spring Tavern, outside Santa Barbara, was once a stagecoach stop.

food market at 516 San Ysidro Rd. #1, tel. (805) 565-1503, where you'll find it all—and then some. There's another Pierre on State Street in downtown Santa Barbara, tel. (805) 962-1455.

Super-Fine Dining

In Santa Barbara, perennially laid-back, even fine dining is often a reasonably casual affair. Jackets are required in some dining rooms; if you're concerned about being too dressed up or down, call ahead.

Santa Barbara's all abuzz about Michel Richard's French **Citronelle** restaurant at the Santa Barbara Inn, 901 Cabrillo Blvd., tel. (805) 963-0111, coastal sibling to the famous Citrus in Los Angeles. This attractive, upbeat, and airy oceanside bistro, associated with the Santa Barbara Inn, the gussied-up motel adjacent, serves quiche Lorraine, eggs Benedict, and variations on more traditional American fare for brunch. Lunch and dinner selections include such choices as salmon fettuccine with saffron sauce, chicken ravioli, and Caesar salad with scallops. Wonderful appetizers and soups, exceptional California wine list, and unforgettable desserts— such as the famed chocolate hazelnut bar. It's open daily for lunch and dinner, for brunch on weekends, and sometimes for weekday breakfast; call for current details.

Also at the top of the local food chain is dinner-only **La Marina** at the Four Seasons Biltmore Hotel, 1260 Channel Dr., tel. (805) 969-2261. Seafood typically stars on the menu but roasted pheasant, chicken, steaks, even delectable vegetarian selections are also available. And the stylish Sunday brunch here is something to write home about.

Also exceptional is the **Stonehouse** restaurant at the San Ysidro Ranch in Montecito, 900 San Ysidro Ln., tel. (805) 969-5046, open daily for breakfast, lunch, and dinner, also serving wonderful Sunday brunch. Another, more casual possibility at the ranch is the **Plow & Angel Bistro.**

Charming and quite romantic for California-style is the **El Encanto Dining Room** at the El Encanto Hotel and Garden Villas, 1900 Lasuen Rd., tel. (805) 687-5000, though **Downey's** downtown at 1305 State St., tel. (805) 966-5006, is more innovative and consistent.

TRANSPORTATION AND INFORMATION

Santa Barbara Transportation

Many of the region's finest pleasures, including the Santa Barbara wine country and the lovely state beaches 20-plus miles north of town, can't be reached by public transit. Look in the telephone yellow pages or contact the local chamber of commerce or visitor bureau for car rental agencies.

To get around town without a car, **Santa Barbara Metropolitan Transit District** buses offer mainly commuter services but connect with most nearby destinations, including Goleta and Carpinteria. The transit center, 1020 Chapala St. at Cabrillo, is behind Greyhound. Call (805) 683-3702 for current route and fare information, or try www.sbmtd.gov. But for many people the transit district's electric **Downtown-Waterfront Shuttles,** which run along State Street between Cabrillo Blvd. (at Stearns Wharf) and Sola St., 10:15 a.m.-6 p.m., and along the Waterfront (Cabrillo Blvd.) 10 a.m.-5:45 p.m.; at last report the all-day fare was still just 25 cents. The less frequent morning and early evening service (times vary depending on the day) runs between the zoo on the east and the Arlington Theatre on the west. Also convenient in many cases is the **Santa Barbara Trolley,** tel. (805) 965-0353, which connects most of downtown's sights with destinations as far-flung as the Santa Barbara Mission and nearby botanic gardens with the waterfront, the zoo, and downtown Montecito. All routes start and end at Stearns Wharf. Pick up a current trolley schedule and route map; at last report all-day trolley fare was $3 adults, $2 children.

Greyhound, 34 W. Carrillo, tel. (805) 965-7551, offers good bus connections to and from L.A. and San Francisco. Even better than buses, though, is the opportunity Santa Barbara provides for traveling by train. The **Amtrak** station is downtown at 209 State St., tel. (805) 687-6848, with trains rolling south to Los Angeles and north to San Francisco; for current schedule and fare information, call toll-free (800) 872-7245 or try the websites, www.amtrak.com or www.amtrakwest.com.

Limited air transport is available at the **Santa Barbara Municipal Airport** just north in Goleta at 601 Firestone Rd., tel. (805) 967-7111. But you can also arrange a ride to or from LAX with **Santa Barbara Airbus,** tel. (805) 964-7759. For prepaid reservations—usually the cheapest way to go—call toll-free (800) 733-6354.

Santa Barbara Information

To request information before your trip, contact the **Santa Barbara Conference and Visitors Bureau,** 510 State St., Santa Barbara 93101, tel. (805) 966-9222, fax (805) 966-1728, www. santabarbaraca.com. For a copy of its comprehensive current visitor guide, call toll-free tel. (800) 927-4688—or download a PDF version from the website. (There's also a downtown parking map on the web.) Or stop in for visitor information when you arrive. The visitors bureau sponsors two walk-in visitor centers: the **Santa Barbara Visitor Information Center,** 1 Garden St. (at Cabrillo Blvd., across from Chase Palm Park), tel. (805) 965-3021, open Mon-Sat. 9 a.m.-5 p.m. and Sunday 10 a.m.-5 p.m., and **Hot Spots,** 36 State St., tel. (805) 564-1637 or toll-free (800) 793-7666; the lobby is open 24 hours, and there's an ATM here and a coffee machine. Among the informational offerings typically available: the current edition of the *Santa Barbara County Wineries* brochure and touring map and the *Antiques Map and Guide* for Santa Barbara, Montecito, and Summerland. Also pick up the *Red Tile Walking Tour* brochure (information and route also available on the website) and ask about bike rentals and such. People here are passionate about renting those "pedalinas," for example, for wheeling slowly along the beachfront bikepath.

The **main post office** is at 836 Anacapa, tel. (805) 564-2266 or toll-free (800) 275-8777, and the attractive **Santa Barbara Central Library** is at 40 E. Anapamu, tel. (805) 962-7653. For current entertainment and events information, pick up current copies of the weekly *Santa Barbara Independent* and the daily *Santa Barbara News-Press.* You'll find other publications around town, too.

VENTURING VENTURA

Here's a thought to ponder while fueling that gas hog for a cruise from Santa Barbara to Ventura County, Los Angeles, and beyond. Scientists from USC now predict that rising sea levels caused by global warming will create havoc along much of the Ventura County coastline in the coming 50 years, with coastal military bases, power plants, harbors, hotels, businesses, and residential areas increasingly battered and left to bail out after major storms and associated floods. Because the coastal Oxnard Plain is so level, and so near sea level, the effects of global warming will be felt there sooner than elsewhere along the California coastline. By the year 2040, they say, sea level here will be permanently two feet higher than it is today. A 10-foot increase in sea level is "highly unlikely"—except during serious storms.

Roadtrippers not yet running on empty because of fossil-fuel guilt will find much to enjoy here along the coast north of Los Angeles.

The scenic route into Los Angeles County from the north is via the Pacific Coast Highway (PCH) to Malibu, though most people take the Ventura Freeway through the San Fernando Valley—one of L.A.'s most congested freeways. A more serene if roundabout inland alternative is Hwy. 126 through Piru, Fillmore, and Santa Paula; or take the Ronald Reagan Freeway, Hwy. 118, through Simi Valley.

Ventura County highlights include artsy Ojai, home to the annual Ojai Music Festival, and very Victorian Santa Paula, inland, home to the Santa Paula Union Oil Museum. Quite appealing along the coast is Ventura, with its San Buenaventura Mission and a welcoming old-fashioned downtown, state beach, and pleasant boat harbor—headquarters for Channel Islands National Park and point of departure for most park visitors. Fun for harbor hounds, too, is nearby Oxnard, with its downtown Heritage Square and historical museums.

OJAI: SVELTE SHANGRI-LA

To the native Chumash peoples, Ojai (OH-hi) was the spiritual center of the world. Plenty of

later arrivals shared similar beliefs, which is why the Krishnamurti Foundation and Library, the Krotona Institute of Theosophy and Library, Aldous Huxley's Happy Valley School, and so many other philosophical and religious icons have centered themselves in this lovely valley. Southern California's newest religion, the quest for svelte health, is also reasonably well represented here—particularly at The Oaks at Ojai health spa downtown, sister to The Palms at Palm Springs.

The mountain-ringed Ojai Valley nests in the shadows of the Topatopa Mountains. According to local lore, Ojai means "the nest" in Chumash, though linguists say "moon" is the word's actual meaning; some residents now interpret the name of their spiritual nesting place as "valley of the nesting moon." Also according to local lore, Frank Capra set up his cameras at Dennison Grade east of town to shoot Ronald Coleman's first impressions of lush Shangri-La, the valley of eternal youth, for his 1937 film *Lost Horizons*—a film fact still in some dispute, since most of Capra's filming actually took place near Palm Springs.

But no one disputes the truth of Ojai's fabled "pink moment," that magical time close to sunset when the entire valley glows pink in the light of the waning sun—the community's most unifying spiritual event. Visitors can pay homage at least indirectly by signing on for a trip with **Pink Moment Jeep Tours,** tel. (805) 646-3227, which offers around-town tours as well as rugged backcountry jaunts.

For more information about the area, contact: **Ojai Valley Chamber of Commerce and Visitors Bureau,** 150 W. Ojai Ave., Ojai, CA 93023, tel. (805) 646-8126, www.the-ojai.org. For area hiking, camping, and other national forest information, stop by the **Ojai Ranger District Office** of Los Padres National Forest, 1190 E. Ojai Ave., tel. (805) 646-4348, www.r5.fs.fed.us/lospadres.

Seeing and Doing Ojai

Artsy and laid-back downtown Ojai is neat but nondescript, architecturally distinguished by its mission revival architecture, particularly the clock tower atop the downtown post office and the pergola fronting Libbey Park. For a brief community introduction, stop by the **Ojai Valley Museum,** 130 E. Ojai Ave., tel. (805) 646-1390. Or explore the various antique shops, art and pottery galleries, boutiques, and bookstores. A local institution is **Bart's Corner,** 302 W. Matilija, tel. (805) 646-3755, an open-air used bookstore not known for bargains but for its inimitable ambience.

Ojai's inhabitants seem to share a striking love of the land. Join in with a visit to Ojai's 275-acre **International Center for Earth Concerns** at the headwaters to Lake Casitas, tel. (805) 649-3535, www.earthconcerns.org, "a place to know and work for nature." Included here are 30 acres of botanical gardens, a parrot sanctuary, and a small retreat center. Open to the public by reservation only for birdwalks and garden and herb tours. (Pack a lunch and bring water.) For a current walk schedule and reservations, call or consult the website. Also intriguing for a stroll in nature is the **Studio in the Hills,** tel. (805) 646-2000, where "The Walk" means an arty, spirit-expanding experience walking through the chaparral.

People here also love the arts. Find out what's going on, artistically speaking, at the **Ojai Center for the Arts,** 113 S. Montgomery St., tel. (805) 646-0117, which sponsors monthly art shows and community theater. Except in July, August, and December, the **Ojai Film Society,** tel. (805) 646-8946, www.ojai,net/film, presents fine films every Sunday at 4:30 p.m. at the Ojai Playhouse. The society will also debut the first **Ojai International Film Festival** in November 2000.

As famous as The Pink Moment is Ojai's three-day **Ojai Music Festival,** "the class act of all California music festivals" since the 1940s, held either on the last weekend in May or in early June under the oaks at the Libbey Park Bowl. Along with the classics, the Ojai festival distinguishes itself by showcasing post-World War II works, including progressive and avant-garde compositions. Single-performance ticket prices are $15-65, depending on where you sit, and series tickets are $70-290. Hard wooden benches are the "good seats" (bring a cushion, or buy one); cheap-seaters get to sprawl out on the lawn behind the bowl. For current schedule information or to buy tickets, contact: **Ojai Festivals, Ltd.,** tel. (805) 646-2053, fax (805) 646-6037, www.ojaifestival.org.

But you can hear music free in summer at the **summer band concerts** held in Libbey Park every Wednesday in July and August, starting at 8 p.m. Other worthwhile local events include the big-deal **Ojai Valley Tennis Tournament** in late April, the **Ojai Garden Tour** in May, the **Ojai Valley Mexican Fiesta** in September, and the **Bowlful of Blues** festival in October.

Lake Casitas

Central to outdoor Ojai life is lovely Lake Casitas to the west off Hwy. 150, a 6,200-acre regional recreation area and reservoir most famous for its trout and bass fishing. The 1984 Olympics rowing and canoeing events were held here. Prime for camping and fun for picnicking and letting the kids let off a little steam—there are many playgrounds here—Lake Casitas has never been open for public swimming, but officials are at least considering changing that policy, much to the dismay of fisherfolk. Campgrounds and group camps here are quite nice, featuring both basic tent camping sites and full hookups for RVs. Two- or three-night minimum stays are required on weekends. Camping fees begin at $12 per campsite per day (up to six people) and climb to $22 for full hookups on a holiday weekend. Hiker/biker campsites are $2 per person. Other facilities include boat launch and docking facilities, a full-service marina, snackbar, store, and coin-operated showers. Boat rentals are available.

The lake's day-use fee is $5 per vehicle ($6 on holiday weekends), $1 extra for pets (on leashes). For general park information, contact: Lake Casitas Recreation Area, 11311 Santa Ana Rd., Ventura, CA 93001, tel. (805) 649-2233. You can reserve campsites up to several days, but no more than 90 days, in advance of your arrival.

Staying in and near Ojai

If you're not camping at Lake Casitas, consider the national forest's **Wheeler Gorge Campground** on Matilija Creek, about eight miles north of Ojai on Hwy. 33, near Wheeler Springs; for information call the Ojai ranger station, tel. (805) 646-4348; for reservations, from 7-120 days in advance, call toll-free (800) 280-2267. Another possibility is woodsy **Camp Comfort** on San Antonio Creek two miles south of town at 11969 N. Creek Rd., tel. (805) 646-2314 or (805)

654-3951 for reservations. With tent sites and some RV hookups, extras here include hot showers, laundry, and a small store.

Good choices among midrange area motels include the **Hummingbird Inn,** 1208 E. Ojai Ave., tel. (805) 646-4365 or toll-free (800) 228-3744, fax (805) 646-0625, www.hummingbird-innofojai.com, with clean rooms, a pool, and on-site spa; pets are allowed on approval. Moderate-Premium, with high-season rates $76-145. The comfortable **Best Western Casa Ojai** nearby at 1302 E. Ojai Ave., tel. (805) 646-8175 or toll-free (800) 255-8175, fax (805) 640-8247, www.bestwestern.com, also includes a pool and spa. Moderate-Premium, with rates $80-120. A real deal in the neighborhood, though, is the **Oakridge Inn** east of Lake Casitas at 780 N. Ventura Ave., tel. (805) 649-4018, fax (805) 649-4436, www.oakridgeinn.com, Inexpensive-Expensive ($55-95).

Just about the hippest place around, though, is a onetime motor court south of town, restyled into the artsy **Blue Iguana Inn,** 11794 N. Ventura Ave., tel. (805) 646-5277, fax (805) 646-8078, www.blueiguanainn.com, where you can meet Iggy the iguana yourself at the tiled mosaic fountain in the courtyard. The inn, carefully crafted in old mission style—arched designs, terra cotta tile roofs, handmade Ojai tilework—showcases the work of local artists. Expensive-Luxury, with rooms and kitchen suites $99-160.

For peeling away the pounds and inches, one place is **The Oaks at Ojai,** "the affordable spa" at 122 E. Ojai Ave., tel. (805) 646-5573 or toll-free tel. (800) 753-6257, www.oaksspa.com, where the total fitness and stress management program comes with all meals—about 750 calories per day—and a fairly hefty tab. Luxury, with rates from $145 per person.

For the most luxurious local stay, just west of town is the historic 220-acre **Ojai Valley Inn,** appropriately situated on Country Club Rd., tel. (805) 646-5511 or toll-free (800) 422-6524 (hotel), toll-free (888) 772-6524 (spa), fax (805) 646-7969, www.ojairesort.com. In 1923 the wealthy glass manufacturer Edward Drummond Libbey, whose name crops up frequently in these parts, commissioned architect Walter Neff to design the stylish Spanish colonial golf course clubhouse here. The rest of the Ojai Valley Inn, with its 18-hole golf course (now featured on the Se-

nior PGA Tour), putting green, tennis center, riding stables and "ranch," Camp Ojai for kids, and complete health spa, exercise, business, and conference facilities, has grown up around Neff's original contribution. Completely renovated and restyled in the 1980s and updated since, this Spanish-style grande dame features 207 rooms and suites, two swimming pools, two restaurants, 24-hour room service, bike rentals, and hiking and jogging trails. Luxury. Rooms start at $245, suites at $390, though discounts and off-season specials can drop the tab considerably.

Eating in Ojai

The weekly **Ojai Certified Farmers' Market,** with local baked goods and pastries in addition to the usual cornucopia of fresh produce and flowers, convenes every Sunday morning in summer 9 a.m.-1 p.m. downtown behind the Arcade, 300 E. Matilija, tel. (805) 646-4444. Put together an impromptu picnic with help from **Bill Baker's Bakery,** 457 E. Ojai Ave., tel. (805) 646-1558, which features the famed and flavorful wheat-free breads and other baked goods originally invented by Bill Baker in the 1930s. Poke around town for pizza places and cafe-style possibilities. French-influenced California-style **Suzanne's Cuisine,** 502 W. Ojai Ave., tel. (805) 640-1961, is a best bet at lunch and dinner (closed on Tuesday). Another long-standing local favorite is **Boccali's,** 3277 Ojai-Santa Paula Rd., tel. (805) 646-6116, where the vegetables accompanying the pizza and traditional Italian come from the restaurant garden.

For natural food elevated to fine dining *experience,* the place is the **Ranch House** restaurant on S. Lomita Ave., tel. (805) 646-2360. Founder Alan Hooker first came to Ojai in 1946 to hear Krishnamurti speak, and within a few years he was catering the event—and thus the original Ranch House was born. Since it moved to a spot closer to the highway, the restaurant still serves the finest, freshest natural foods anywhere, here often accompanied by rich sauces and—gasp!—real creamery butter. (Herbs still come from the restaurant's herb garden.) The Ranch House is open for dinner only Wed.-Sat., for lunch and dinner on Sunday, closed Monday and Tuesday. Expensive. To take this place home with you, pick up a copy of *California Herb Cookery: From the Ranch House Restaurant.*

Other possibilities for fine dining include the Belgian **L'Auberge,** 314 El Paseo, tel. (805) 646-2288, open for dinner Wed.-Mon. and for lunch and dinner on weekends (closed Tuesday). Or head to the Ojai Valley Inn and the **Oak Grill and Terrace,** tel. (805) 646-5511 ext. 700, open for lunch and dinner.

From Ojai

It's a quick trip from Ojai back to Santa Barbara via Hwy. 50 and then either Hwy. 192 or Hwy. 101 along the coast—the usual route, for daytrippers. For a much longer alternative road trip to Santa Barbara, head north past Wheeler Springs on Hwy. 33, up the switchbacks to Pine Mountain Summit, then drop down into Cuyama Valley; follow Hwy. 166 past the badlands burg of New Cuyama into Santa Maria. From there, dabble in Santa Barbara County's boutique wine country around Los Alamos and Los Olivos before cruising past Cachuma Lake and into Santa Barbara via Hwy. 154.

SANTA PAULA: BLAST FROM THE PAST

Like nearby Fillmore, Santa Paula is most famous for its delightful 19th-century downtown, both in its architecture and ambience. The Victorian-era buildings along well-manicured Main St., in other respects representing an antiquers' holiday, are constructed, uniquely, of weathered red brick and Sespe sandstone. Queen Anne and Victorian homes line nearby streets, blending here and there with Mediterranean and craftsman styles. Yet Santa Paula offers its historic eccentricities; on the four-sided clock tower downtown, notice the bullet holes on the clock's north face, a distinguishing feature. Even the privately owned airport here is a surprise, a relic from the heyday of open-cockpit aviation; planes in the air on any weekend here comprise an ever-changing antique plane museum.

Still surrounded by orange and lemon groves and occasional oil derricks—and so far spared the indignities of suburban sprawl—Santa Paula was built from the wealth generated by the California oil boom of the late 1800s and the subsequent success of area agriculture. The free **Santa Paula Union Oil Museum,** 1001 E Main St. (10th and Main), tel. (805) 933-0076, open Wed.-Sun. 10 a.m.-4 p.m., tells part of the story. The museum store sells copies of the Santa Paula Historical Society's "Neighborhoods and Neighbors of the Past," which tells some of the rest by guiding visitors through historic residential neighborhoods. A drive through Santa Paula's surrounding citrus groves completes the tale. Ventura County is still California's largest lemon producer (California is the largest producer in the U.S.), and Santa Paula is the industry star. Santa Paula's Limoneira Co. is the county's largest lemon grower, with 40 percent of its crop—the most perfect oval fruit—exported to Hong Kong and elsewhere in Asia, where the lemons can fetch a price of $2 each.

For more information about the area, stop by the **Santa Paula Chamber of Commerce** at the historic train depot, 200 N. 10th St. (10th and Santa Barbara Sts.), tel. (805) 525-5561.

Practical Santa Paula

Notable among Santa Paula's notable bed and breakfasts is the Spanish revival **Fern Oaks Inn,** 1025 Ojai Rd., tel. (805) 525-7747, fax (805) 933-5001, www.fernoaksinn.com, Expensive-Premium ($95-130), breakfast included. For a decent meal, try **Familia Diaz,** 245 S. 10th St., tel. (805) 525-2813, a local tradition for decades. In 1996 this cheerful restaurant, known for its homemade red *chile colorado* tamales, celebrated its 60th anniversary with a special tamale (such as shrimp) each month. But you can't go wrong with anything here, from the *carnitas, chile verde,* and *chiles rellenos* to fish dishes. Kids' menu, too. It's open daily for lunch and dinner. For fine dining, head to Ojai, a mere 20 minutes away. Or continue to Santa Barbara.

Near Santa Paula

Another of Southern California's "last best small towns" is historic **Fillmore,** east of Santa Paula via Hwy. 126, also noted for its intriguing brick-and-masonry downtown. But Fillmore sits astride the Oak Ridge earthquake fault. Right after a costly downtown spruce-up campaign, in early 1994 came the devastating Northridge earthquake. About $200 million in structural damage later—much of it to downtown buildings—Fillmore is still putting itself back together again. Family-style fun here includes rides on the

Fillmore and Western Railway, 250 Central Ave. (red caboose on the north side of city hall), tel. (805) 524-2546 or toll-free (800) 773-8724, www.fwry.com, where special-event trains include the Summer Sunset BBQ and the Spaghetti Western Dinner Train.

Directly south of Fillmore via Hwy. 23 is the affluent suburb of **Moorpark,** most famous as the first town in the U.S. to be completely powered by nuclear energy—a 1957 event that actually lasted only about an hour but which 20 million people watched on TV two weeks later, thanks to newsman Edward R. Murrow. Moorpark's nuclear adventure was an early Southern California Edison experiment that lasted just a couple of years. A small nuclear plant in the Simi Hills supplied only a part of the city's energy during most of the experiment.

VENTURA: HOMETOWN ADVENTURES

Travelers on Highway 101 are typically in such a hurry to get either to or from Santa Barbara that they miss Ventura, still one of the most pleasant surprises along the coast north of Los Angeles. Its surrounding farmlands are fast being lost to the usual California housing developments and shopping centers, but historic downtown Ventura retains both its dignity and serenity. Stopping here is like visiting an old friend's oft-described hometown, since you'll feel like you've been here before.

Fun local events include the annual **Fourth of July Street Faire** downtown, the weekend **Summer by the Sea** music, entertainment, and arts and crafts offerings every Saturday and Sunday from mid-July through August at the Ventura Pier and Promenade; and the August **California Beach Festival** at San Buenaventura Beach and the **Ventura County Fair** at Seaside Park. If you're here in early October, don't miss Southern California's own two-day **Kinetic Sculpture Race at Ventura,** www.ventura-kinetic-race.com, a people-powered artistic event to benefit the local homeless. Come in December for the **Parade of Lights** at Ventura Harbor.

For more information, contact: **Ventura Visitors and Convention Bureau,** 89 S. California St., Ste. C, Ventura, CA 93001, tel. (805) 648-2075 or toll-free (800) 333-2989, fax (805) 648-2150, www.ventura-usa.com. Among available information: local guides to antique shops and art galleries, and listings of sportfishing and whale-watching tour companies, shopping centers, local golf courses, and parks and other area recreational facilities.

Adventuring in Downtown Ventura

The centerpiece of Ventura's homey downtown Main Street business district is **Mission San Buenaventura,** 211 E. Main St., tel. (805) 643-4318, the ninth mission established in California

Mission San Buenaventura, the ninth mission established in California, was Father Junípero Serra's last.

and the last founded by Father Junípero Serra. Nearby is the very enjoyable **Ventura County Museum of History and Art,** 100 E. Main, tel. (805) 653-0323, www.vcmha.org, open Tues.-Sun. 10 a.m.-5 p.m. (closed major holidays). Beyond the excellent exhibits—the Chumash, mission-era, and California statehood exhibits of the Huntsinger Gallery, the "three-dimension portraits" of the Smith Gallery, the contemporary local art on display in the Hoffman Gallery—the museum's gift shop is unusually fine. Admission is $4 adults, $3 seniors and AAA members, $1 children (under age 6 free). Nearby, at 113 E. Main, is the small but fascinating **Albinger Archaeological Museum,** tel. (805) 648-5823 or (805) 658-4726, where an ongoing dig into one city block has unearthed artifacts from more than 3,500 years of coastal civilization; in 1974 and 1975 alone, more than 30,000 prehistoric, Chumash, Spanish, Mexican, American, and Chinese artifacts were unearthed. Admission is free. The Albinger museum is open Wed.-Sun 10 a.m.-4 p.m. in summer; call for current off-season hours.

A few blocks away is the simple **Ortega Adobe,** 215 W. Main St., tel. (805) 658-4726, the 19th-century birthplace of the Ortega chile and salsa company, the first commercial food concern of its kind in California and originator of both the chile fire-roasting and canning processes. More evocative of the days of the Mexican ranchos, however, is the two-story Monterey-style **Olivas Adobe** hacienda east of the harbor at 4200 Olivas Park Dr., tel. (805) 644-4346, once the main house of vast Rancho San Miguel. Grounds are open daily 10 a.m.-4 p.m.; the house is open weekends only 10 a.m.-4 p.m.

The visitors bureau can suggest more local attractions. But since Erle Stanley Gardner, prolific author of the Perry Mason mysteries, was once a notable local presence, consider taking the **Erle Stanley Gardner Tour** of Ventura. Suggested stops are included on the website, www.erlestanleygardner.com.

The Beach, the Pier, the Harbor

Not all of Ventura's pleasures are downtown, however—at least not right downtown. A popular surfing locale, Ventura also boasts fine two-mile-long **San Buenaventura State Beach,** within strolling distance of downtown, extended by miles and miles of beach access up and down the coast. The recently restored 1,958-foot-long **Ventura Pier,** just south of downtown and east of California St. off Harbor Blvd., reopened in 1993 after a seven-year renovation and unveiled anew in 2000 following the addition of a new octagonal extension, is the state's oldest and longest wooden pier. Still popular for fishing, the pier boasts a large restaurant, snackbar, the blowhole-like copper kinetic sculpture *Wavespout,* and lights that illuminate the beach after dark. West of the pier, at the end of Figueroa St., is **Surfer's Point,** one of the state's premiere point breaks—a good place to watch longboard surfing.

South along the coast, past the beach-scene **Seaward Avenue Business District,** is relaxed **Ventura Harbor,** just off Harbor Boulevard. For information on the Channel Islands and permitted recreational activities, see Islands in Time: Channel Islands National Park, below.

Staying in Ventura

Stylish downtown is the historic **Bella Maggiore Inn,** 67 S. California St. (on the west side of California between Main and Santa Clara), tel. (805) 652-0277 or toll-free (800) 523-8479, fax (805) 648-5670. This three-story bed and breakfast hotel, built in 1924, has a breezy Mediterranean style—with fireplace, potted palms, and Italian chandeliers in the lobby, and shuttered windows, Capuan beds, ceiling fans, and fresh flowers in the graceful guest rooms. Moderate-Luxury, with rates $75-150. Weather permitting—and it usually is—breakfast is served outside, in the lovely interior courtyard. In fact **Nona's Courtyard Cafe** here, a snazzy little Californian with a Northern Italian accent, is reason enough to stay. Breakfast can be a simple matter of coffee, pastries, and fresh fruit, or, for hearty appetites, omelettes and egg dishes. Expect good salads, sandwiches, and pastas at lunch, and chicken, fresh fish, and seafood at dinner (menu changes weekly). Nona's is open daily for breakfast, Mon.-Sat. for lunch, and Friday, Saturday, and Sunday for dinner.

Ventura's newest B&B is the **Victorian Rose,** 896 E. Main St., tel. (805) 641-1888, fax (805) 643-1335, www.victorian-rose.com, a very Gothic onetime church where the five gorgeous guest rooms all feature private baths. Full breakfast included. Expensive-Premium, $99-145.

Ventura offers a number of surprising reasonable hotels and motels; for a complete listing, ask at the visitors bureau. One good choice is the local outpost of **Country Inn & Suites,** 298 Chestnut St., tel. (805) 653-1434 or toll-free (800) 456-4000, fax (805) 648-7126, www.countryinns.com, along with all the usual amenities plus refrigerators, microwaves, wet bars, in-room coffee, remote-control color TVs with videocassette players, even hairdryers. Full country breakfast included. Expensive-Premium, with rates $89-119 (but ask about specials).

Eating in Ventura

Johnny's, 176 N. Ventura Ave., tel. (805) 648-2021, is famous for its burritos. People come from miles around just to sink their teeth into *chile verde* burritos, *chile relleno* burritos, and other intriguing possibilities. Another local draw is the **Rosarito Beach Café,** 692 E. Main St., tel. (805) 653-7343, where fresh fish is a main attraction. For more seafood at lunch or dinner, head to the harbor and the **Spinnaker Seafood Broiler,** Ventura Harbor Village, 1583 Spinnaker Dr., tel. (805) 339-0717, or the nearby **Greek at the Harbor,** tel. (805) 650-5350. Better yet is California-style **Eric Ericsson's Fish Company,** 668 Harbor Blvd., tel. (805) 643-4783.

Back downtown, consider very attractive **Nona's Courtyard Café** at the historic Bella Maggiore Inn, 67 S. California St. (see above), just the California-style Italian antidote for too much freeway-flying. Quite fine is **Jonathan's at Peirano's,** 204 E. Main St., tel. (805) 648-4853, where the style is also Mediterranean. The **71 Palm Restaurant,** 71 N. Palm St., tel. (805) 653-7222, specializes in French classics.

ISLANDS IN TIME: CHANNEL ISLANDS NATIONAL PARK

Privately owned **Santa Catalina Island** is the only truly populated island among Southern California's eight Channel Islands. Populated by humans, that is. Many of the rest are inhabited by, or surrounded by, such rare, endangered, and endemic animals and plants—various whale and seal species, the island fox, the giant coreopsis "tree" (tree sunflowers), and the Santa Cruz Island ironweed among them—that biologists describe the Channel Islands, collectively, as North America's Galápagos.

San Miguel, Anacapa, Santa Cruz, and Santa Rosa Islands are seaward extensions of the east-west-trending Transverse Ranges (Santa Monica Mountains), and Santa Barbara, San Clemente, and San Nicolas are the visible ocean outposts of the Peninsular Range. Out-there **San Nicolas** and **San Clemente Islands,** property of the U.S. Navy, have rarely been visited. San Clemente has the unfortunate history of being used for bombing runs and military target practice. In the 1950s San Nicolas, inspiration for the book *Island of the Blue Dolphins,* was a top-secret post for monitoring submarines from the U.S.S.R. Since San Nicolas still contains ancient petroglyphs of dolphins, sharks, and whales, it's entirely appropriate that this same Cold War technology is now used to track the movements of migrating whales.

Channel Islands preservation efforts first succeeded in 1938, when President Franklin D. Roosevelt protected Anacapa and Santa Barbara Islands as a national monument. The five northernmost Channel Islands are now included in Channel Islands National Park, 250,000 acres of isolated Southern California real estate set aside in 1980 by President Jimmy Carter for federal preservation. (Odd, by national park standards, is the fact that half these acres are below the ocean's surface.) With some planning, visitors can set out for **San Miguel, Santa Rosa, Santa Cruz, Anacapa,** and **Santa Barbara Islands.** Primitive camping is allowed on all five islands.

Islands in Time

The Channel Islands discovery of a complete fossilized skeleton of a pygmy or "dwarf" mammoth generated major excitement in the summer of 1994. Scientists speculate that this unusual miniature species, standing only four to six feet tall, was descended from woolly mammoths who swam here from the Southern California mainland during the Pleistocene, when the islands were "one" and just a few miles off the coast.

These islands in time reveal more surprises. For one thing, they are still on the move. Satellite measurements in the early 1990s showed that Santa Catalina, San Clemente, and San Nicolas Islands are moving northwest about one-half inch per year, and that a section of California's coastline is slowly converging with Santa Cruz and Santa Rosa islands—narrowing the Santa Barbara Channel by the same one-half inch each year.

For another, the Channel Islands provide some of the earliest North American evidence of human habitation. Prehistoric cooking pits found in conjunction with mammoth bones on Santa Rosa Island point to a neighborhood barbecue bash about 30,000-40,000 years ago.

Humans, other animals, and plant species have been introduced to the islands over the vast expanse of time; some failed, and some evolved into unique species as geographical isolation led to genetic isolation; 145 species of Channel Islands plants and animals are found nowhere else on earth.

Unusual animals found on the islands today include the island fox—a distant relative of the mainland's gray fox and about the size of a cat—various rodents, bats, and feral goats and pigs. (Of the islands' endemic mammals, the deer mouse is known to carry hantavirus.) More than 260 bird species have been spotted on and around Santa Cruz Island alone. Brown pelican rookeries and the largest U.S. colony of Xantus's murrelet and black petrels are Channel Islands highlights.

Channel Islands National Park is also a national marine sanctuary and international biosphere preserve, an ecosystem protectorate including all five islands and a six-mile area surrounding each one. During its annual migration south to Baja, Mexico, between January and March, the California gray whale appears in large numbers throughout the Channel Islands. In recent years a fairly large population of the rare and endangered blue whale, the world's largest creature, has tarried here as well. More than two dozen species of marine mammals—whales, sharks, dolphins and porpoises, various seal and sea lion species, sea otters—inhabit these waters during at least part of the year. Because of "upwelling" along California's coast and the Pacific Ocean's rich nutrient levels, vast kelp and other marine "forests" provide food

and shelter for vast numbers of animals. Island tidepools also teem with sealife.

San Miguel Island

The most westerly of the Channel Islands, 9,325-acre San Miguel in the north is most famous for the thousands and thousands of seals and sea lions—up to 30,000 in summer, the population including the once-rare northern elephant seal—that bask in the sun at Bennett Point. Also notable for hikers are its giant coreopsis "trees" and ghostly caliche forests, the latter an odd moonscape of calcified plant fossils—a natural variation on sandcasting—of up to 14,000 years old. Local landmarks include a modest memorial to Cabrillo, believed to have died here in 1583, and the ruins of the Lester Ranch of caretaker Herbert Lester, "King of San Miguel," who committed suicide here in 1942 rather than be forcibly evicted by the military. The weather here can be wicked—always windy, foggy, often rainy—so come prepared. Primitive camping, hiking, beach exploration, and ranger-led hikes are the main attractions, but be sure to stick to established trails. San Miguel was once used for bombing practice, and live ordnance is constantly being discovered beneath the island's shifting sands.

Santa Rosa Island

The national park system has owned 52,794-acre Santa Rosa since 1986. The island's main attractions aren't the usual tourist trappings, particularly some 2,000 archaeology sites (strictly off-limits) related to Chumash Indian and Chinese abalone fishing settlements. Ruthlessly wind-whipped, Santa Rosa nonetheless protects rare and endangered plants, including one of only two surviving natural stands of Torrey pines (the other is near La Jolla). Despite federal ownership overgrazing has recently a problem on Santa Rosa. In addition to primitive camping and kayak beach camping, hiking, ranger-guided hikes, and vehicle tours are Santa Rosa's main attractions.

Santa Cruz Island

In 1997, preservationists finally took complete possession of 24-mile-long, 60,645-acre Santa Cruz Island, the largest of the eight Channel Islands. Island Adventures, a private firm

blue whale

that had offered private bow-hunting trips and bed-and-breakfast overnights on the east end of Santa Cruz, was evicted and the National Park Service bought its part of the island, to the east. The Nature Conservancy owns the other 90 percent and manages it as the **Santa Cruz Island Preserve,** to date a noticeably healthier ecosystem. But park officials are restoring damaged east-end habitats, long overgrazed by sheep, goats, and feral pigs, and the historic Gherini Ranch. The ranch will eventually become the human-oriented hub of the park's five islands.

Already the park's primary draw, Santa Cruz is the most luxuriant of the Channel Islands. Two mountain ranges traverse Santa Cruz, one red, one white, and the island's picturesque Central Valley is an active earthquake zone. (According to local lore, terror created by the great California earthquake of 1812 finally convinced the native Chumash to leave Santa Cruz for life in the mainland's Franciscan missions.) This slice of the French Mediterranean right off the coast of California is the onetime ranching empire of Justinian Caire. Caire's winery here, finally closed during Prohibition, was at that time one of Southern California's largest. The Caire family's chapel and other buildings of the subsequent Santa Cruz Island Company ranch were preserved by subsequent owners, members of the Stanton family, and by The Nature Conservancy.

The island's curvaceous coastline boasts many natural harbors, bays, and popular dive spots, along with some spectacular sea caves. The landscape features 10 distinct plant communities, about 650 plant species scattered from pine forests, oak woodlands, and riparian streams and springs to meadows, sandy beaches, and dunes. The seascape features many more plant and animal communities, which makes Santa Cruz paradise for divers, kayakers, snorkelers, and tidepoolers. (Look, but don't touch.) More than 260 bird species have been spotted on and around the island, including the endemic Santa Cruz Island scrub jay, bigger and bluer than its mainland cousins. Hike, camp, and explore on the park's property. Private boaters, call The Nature Conservancy, tel. (805) 964-7839, to request permission to land on the west side of Santa Cruz.

Anacapa Island

Wind-whipped Anacapa Island is most accessible from the mainland, just 11 miles from Oxnard. Quite popular for daytrippers, 699-acre Anacapa is actually three distinct islands divided by narrow channels. **East Anacapa** is the usual human destination. On the way to Landing Cove is 80-foot-tall **Arch Rock,** an immense eroded volcanic "bridge" with a 50-foot arch, unofficial emblem of the Channel Islands since James Whistler sketched it during his stint in the U.S. Coast Guard. Once ashore it's a quick 154 steps straight up to the blufftops, where the meandering nature trail begins. Beyond the visitor center, standing vigil at the entrance to the Santa Barbara Channel, is the U.S. Coast Guard's restored, solar-powered **East End Lighthouse** and associated museum, open for public tours. (Inquire at the park's mainland visitor center for details.) If time, weather, and water conditions permit, **Landing Cove** and **Frenchy's Cove** are popular for snorkeling and swimming. Guided **kayak tours** are also popular here.

On **Middle Anacapa** the stands of giant coreopsis ("tree sunflowers") are stunning when in bloom—on a clear day, their vibrant color is visible from the mainland. Craggy **West Anacapa,** the largest of the three, is off-limits to the public, protected as a brown pelican rookery and reserve.

Santa Barbara Island

Ever fantasized about being stranded on a desert island? Want to play *Survivor*? Here's a possible destination. Unlike the lushly landscaped, socially sophisticated mainland city of the same name, 639-acre Santa Barbara Island is a piece of California in the raw. Smallest of the park's five islands, Santa Barbara has no trees, no natural beaches, and no fresh water. Its sheer cliffs rise abruptly from the sea. It's often windy and foggy in quick succession; in winter Santa Barbara's thin thatch of grass and scrub is green. Most popular with birders, divers, and kayakers, in warm weather Santa Barbara also attracts pinniped peepers, hikers, and campers. (Bring *everything*, including water.) A lonely 25 miles west of Catalina, a long, often choppy three hours from Ventura Harbor, Santa Barbara is most appreciated by avid island and/or wildlife aficionados.

Channel Islands Practicalities

For more information on the islands and permitted recreational activities, contact: **Channel Islands National Park Visitors Center,** 1901 Spinnaker Dr., Ventura, CA 93001, tel. (805) 658-5730, www.nps.gov/chis. Or sign on for an island tour (see below). The visitor center in Ventura Harbor is *the* stop for relevant books, maps, and a good general introduction to the history and natural history of the islands. For hiking permits for San Miguel Island, call (805) 658-5711.

At last report primitive park campgrounds were available on all five islands. If you're planning to camp or hike (permits required), come prepared for anything—wind, in particular—because the weather can change abruptly. For current information, inquire at the park's visitor center; for camping permits—free, though there is a $2.50 reservation fee per campsite per day—are available by calling Biospherics, Inc., at toll-free (800) 365-2267.

Channel Islands Tours and Trips

Unless you have your own boat, if you're shoving off from Ventura you'll be going via **Island Packer Cruises,** which offers the rare opportunity to get up close and personal with Channel Islands National Park, an area otherwise all but inaccessible for the average traveler. Since island access is limited, extra benefits of an Island Packer trip—some trips, anyway—include the chance to hike, snorkel, or kayak. Camping dropoffs can also be arranged. Whalewatching (January through March) is particularly popular, especially since whales, dolphins, seals, and sea lions favor the protected waters and abundant food supplies near the Channel Islands. But every season has its unique pleasures. Spring, for example, offers the chance to see wildflowers and rare endemic plants in bloom.

For current information, contact: Island Packer Tours, 1867 Spinnaker Dr., Ventura, CA 93001, tel. (805) 642-7688 (recorded) or (805) 642-1393, fax (805) 642-6573, www.island-packers.com. The company's office is adjacent to the park's visitor center in Ventura Harbor (closed Thanksgiving and Christmas). Reservations are required for all trips, but are subject to last-minute cancellation in case of big waves or bad weather. For popular weekend outings, reserve well in advance. In spring and summer,

Island Packer operates tours to—or around—all five islands. Call for specific information about "transport" services for backpackers and long-term campers.

If you're departing from Santa Barbara, the official Channel Islands trip concessionaire there is **Truth Aquatics,** 301 W. Cabrillo Blvd., Santa Barbara, CA 93101, tel. (805) 962-1127, fax (805) 564-6754, www.truthaquatics.com.

Channel Islands Aviation offers daytrip transportation, tours, and "dropoffs" to and from Santa Rosa Island (and Santa Catalina Island). For current information, contact: Channel Islands Aviation, 305 Durley Ave., Camarillo, CA 93010, tel. (805) 987-1301.

OXNARD AND VICINITY

One notices in Ventura County the immense impact of recent and continuing growth—subdivisions and commercial developments all but consuming the county's once sleepy, agricultural past. Oxnard, still known for its annual May **California Strawberry Festival,** was once known for its sugar beet, bean, and strawberry fields, along with mile after mile of citrus orchards and packing sheds. The vanishing fruit industry is memorialized at the stylized Oxnard Factory Outlet mall at Rice Ave. off Gonzales Road.

The center of civic pride downtown is impressive **Heritage Square,** a collection of immaculately restored, landmark historic local buildings and replicas now home to shops, law offices and such. A stroll away is the neoclassical **Carnegie Art Museum,** 424 S. C St., tel. (805) 385-8179, which showcases local arts and artists Thurs.-Sun (call for current hours, small admission), and the **Ventura County Gull Wings Children's Museum,** 414 W. Fourth St., tel. (805) 483-3005, www.gullwingsmuseum4kids.org, open Wed.-Sun. 1-5 p.m. (small admission). Or head for the waterfront and Oxnard's surprisingly tony **Channel Islands Harbor,** where the **Ventura County Maritime Museum** at Fisherman's Wharf, 2731 S. Victoria Ave., tel. (805) 984-6260, open daily 11 a.m.-5 p.m., offers an overview of maritime history, ship models, and ocean-themed artwork. Among the treasures collected here: a copy of the map of Anacapa Island drawn by James Whistler. Most appealing of all is **Oxnard State Beach,** broad and sandy, backed by dunes and comfortably weathered beach bungalows.

For more information about the area, contact: **Oxnard Convention & Visitors Bureau,** Heritage Square, 711 S. A St., Oxnard, CA 93030, tel. (805) 385-7545 or toll-free (800) 269-6273, www.oxnardtourism.com. For harbor information, contact: **Channel Islands Harbor Visitor Center,** 3810 W. Channel Islands Blvd., Ste. G, Oxnard, CA 93035, tel. (805) 985-4852, www.channelislandsharbor.com.

Near Oxnard: Port Hueneme

The area's military-industrial development is most notable just south of Oxnard in and around Port Hueneme (wy-NEE-mee), about 60 miles north of L.A. and 40 miles south of Santa Barbara. A Chumash word meaning "halfway" or "resting place" and previously spelled Y-neema, Wyneema, and, officially, Wynema until 1940, when the U.S. Post Office altered it, Hueneme is still sometimes pronounced "way-NAYma" by old-timers here. A major military and civilian port—the only deep water port between San Francisco and Los Angeles—Hueneme is most noted for its **Point Mugu Naval Air Weapons Station,** at last report still a survivor of U.S. defense budget cuts. The **Naval Construction Battalion Center,** "Home of the Pacific Seabees," has been at home here since 1942. If naval history fans first stop at the Ventura Road gate for a visitor pass, the free **U.S. Navy Civil Engineer Corps/Seabee Museum** on the base at Ventura Rd. and Sunkist Ave., tel. (805) 982-5165, is well worth a visit—one of the finest military museums around. Open Mon.-Sat. 9 a.m.-4 p.m., Sunday 12:30-4:30 p.m. Free. Port Hueneme also boasts a small city history museum

downtown next to the chamber of commerce, but adjacent **Grandpa,** the city's most aged downtown resident, a 375-year-old Monterey cypress, was finally recycled into walking sticks and such in 1997.

Staying in and around Oxnard

Oxnard is fairly affordable, compared to other coastal locales. For a fairly complete accommodations list, contact the visitors bureau. Very nice is the **Best Western Oxnard Inn,** 1156 S. Oxnard Blvd., tel. (805) 483-9581 or toll-free tel. (800) 469-6273, fax (805) 483-4072, www.bestwestern.com, with in-room refrigerators, microwaves, coffeemakers, and all the usual motel amenities plus swimming pool and whirlpool spa. Expensive ($89-99). A best bet for a harbor stay is the **Casa Sirena Marina Resort,** 3605 Peninsula Rd., tel. (805) 985-6311 or toll-free (800) 447-3529, fax (805) 985-4329. Expensive ($79-99), but look for off-season specials.

Eating in and around Oxnard

If you don't have time to drive area back roads in search of fresh produce, the **Oxnard Certified Farmers' Market,** tel. (805) 483-7960, is held in Downtown Plaza Park at Fifth and B Sts. on Thursday, 10 a.m.-1 p.m. The **Oxnard-Channel Islands Harbor Certified Farmers' Market,** tel. (805) 652-2089 is held on Sunday 10 a.m.-2 p.m. at the foot of Harbor Blvd. in the harbor. Otherwise, almost anyone will tell you that **The Whale's Tail** in the harbor at 3950 Blue Fin Circle, tel. (805) 985-2511, is the best place around. Also decent for seafood is **Tugs** upstairs in the Marine Emporium at 3600 S. Harbor Blvd., tel. (805) 985-8847, open for breakfast, lunch, and dinner.

MURLEEN FERGUSON CATE/CALIFORNIA DIVISION OF TOURISM

THE LOS ANGELES COAST

Scribes and small-screen prognosticators love to announce the death of Los Angeles. With every new disaster they do it again. Most recently L.A. was dead because of the nasty Northridge earthquake of 1994. The quake demolished entire neighborhoods and snapped off major freeways, thereby desecrating the city's most cherished cultural symbol—spokes in the sacred wheel of Southern California life. Just months before that, Los Angeles faced death because of raging wildfires and rampaging winter mudslides that came in their wake. Before that the city was doomed by the demise of California's defense industry, coupled with the economic and social challenge of absorbing a seemingly endless stream of illegal immigrants. Not to mention riots related to the Rodney King police brutality case, and the Watts riots almost 30 years before that. Not to mention the smog.

The apocalyptic tendencies of Los Angeles—more accurately, our determination to place Los Angeles at the center of our fascinations with

See color map of L.A. Coast at front of book.

disaster and futuristic despair—are as well-represented in literature as in real life. Consider the nuclear holocaust in Thomas Pynchon's *Gravity's Rainbow.* The earthquake in *The Last Tycoon.* The riot in *The Day of the Locust.* And little-known classics such as Marie Corelli's strange 1921 romance *Secret Power,* in which L.A. is decimated by an atomic explosion, and Ward Moore's hilarious 1947 *Greener Than You Think,* in which the city is done in by bermuda grass. Movies have also made their contribution to the cult of L.A. Apocalypse, of course, *Blade Runner* most memorably.

Even so, in recent years L.A. has suffered from entirely too much dystopia, entirely too much rumination on the subject of utopia gone wrong. Entirely too much *reality.* And reality has never been the point here. Los Angeles, after all, is both the world's foremost fantasy factory and the psychic playground for America's most childlike narcissisms.

The lesson of Los Angeles is the lesson of the movies. Big faces on the big screen reassure us that "individual lives have scope and grandeur," in the words of California writer Richard Rodriguez. "The attention L.A. lavishes on a single face is as generous a metaphor as I can find for the love of God."

From a strictly secular point of view, the sun is also generous. In Los Angeles the sun always shines, on the degenerate and deserving alike. At last report this was still true.

LAND OF ENDLESS SUNSHINE

LOS ANGELES AS PLACE

As defined by the U.S. Census Bureau, the greater Los Angeles metropolitan area encompasses Los Angeles County, including the city of Los Angeles, and urban areas of adjacent Orange, Riverside, San Bernardino, and Ventura Counties. The total population of the five-county L.A. area—well over 15 million by now, and counting—exceeds the population of every state in the union except California, New York, and Texas. Taking in a total of 34,149 square miles, greater Los Angeles—with its abundance of computers, fax machines, and cellular phones—has more telephone area codes than any other region of the country.

Even Los Angeles proper is difficult to locate precisely. Its geographical boundaries are puzzling even to people who live here, which is why Angelenos have fairly vague notions of official local lines of demarcation. The writer Dorothy

COASTING LOS ANGELES

Los Angeles is a complicated place. Yet the Los Angeles coast is not particularly perplexing. The Westside's Beverly Hills has the swank shopping districts and Brentwood the artsy new Getty Center, but coastal Los Angeles—the rest of L.A.'s Westside—has the sand. In some ways the only thing that connects the diverse communities of coastal L.A. *is* the beach, miles and miles of dazzling white sand, one of the most enduring symbols of the Southern California good life.

Santa Monica is L.A.'s beach city extraordinaire, where well-to-do-homeowners, retirees, young families, and the homeless coexist peaceably—and where everyone else on the Westside comes to play. Just north is the strung-out stretch of beach known as Malibu, where celebrities and artsy eccentrics live both on the beach and in the sylvan enclaves of Topanga Canyon. Immediately south of Santa Monica is Venice, home to aging bohemians, young hipsters, street performers, and Muscle Beach. On L.A.'s sociopolitical map coastal Westside also includes Marina del Rey, Playa del Rey, the South Bay's stylish Palos Verdes Peninsula, and the very western working-port cities of Long Beach and San Pedro. A short boat ride west leads to fabled Santa Catalina Island and the tiny tourist town of Avalon. Also visible offshore on a clear day, seeming to bob in the blue Pacific Ocean like massive pieces of driftwood, are the lonely, lovely islands of Channel Islands National Park.

ROBERT HOLMES/CALIFORNIA DIVISION OF TOURISM

"REAL" LOS ANGELES

Outsiders' interpretations of Los Angeles—what everyone thinks they know about the place—are often seriously mistaken. For all its casual friendliness, Los Angeles is actually an aloof city, self-protective. One certainly experiences that truth on the freeways—so many millions of people, so oblivious to each other, every person moving through life in his own freewheeling, independent world. For all its fabled flamboyance and sometimes shameless public shenanigans, Los Angeles is in real life a very private place. "Real" L.A. is a private, not a public, domain—which is why finding it is such a challenge for visitors. When L.A. isn't performing on its varied public stages—and L.A. in all its guises works long, hard hours—the city stays home with family and friends, or goes out to play, privately. Los Angeles tolerates its tourists as revenue enhancements—"tourist" a term that was invented here—but rarely invites them home or out on the town. Traditionally, the supremacy of individuality and the need for privacy follow Angelenos everywhere.

For all its vastness, or perhaps because of it, L.A. is also parochial and self-absorbed. "Family values" matter here because immediate family is almost all there is to anchor people in such a fast-paced, unrooted society. Even political battles in Los Angeles are largely fought on the neighborhood level. Yet such self-absorption has its price. While Southern California can't muster the political will to properly finance its public schools, libraries, and health-care services, Los Angeles is number one in the nation for plastic surgery: breast enhancements, liposuction, facelifts, nose and eyelid jobs. Fitness centers are also central to Southern California culture, as are psychiatrists and psychologists and sometimes out-there spiritual advisers.

For all its vast wealth, Los Angeles largely lacks the memorable monuments to grand ideas and idealism so typical of European and other American cities, be they cathedrals, museums, or public libraries. While exceptions to this rule can still be found downtown and in affluent communities including Beverly Hills and Pasadena, the most striking architecture in Los Angeles is private, not public. Rather than invest its billions in old-fashioned public betterment and enlightenment, L.A. spends its money on private pleasures—on great walled mansions and estates and, on a more modest scale out in the suburbs, on backyard barbecues, swimming pools, and all the other accoutrements of middle-class family living.

Parochial Los Angeles does seem improbable, given the city's social and cultural perch at the edge of both Mexico and the Pacific Rim. Yet even L.A.'s recent arrivals tend to settle into particular neighborhoods. Because of its insularity, until quite recently Los Angeles could imagine itself untouched by the multiethnic chaos that now defines it.

Rather than a melting pot, L.A. is a multicultural anthology in which every recent ethnic arrival has its own page, if not an entire separate chapter. Immigrants from more than 140 different nations live within Los Angeles County, including the largest populations of Armenians, Filipinos, and Koreans outside their respective nations and the largest U.S. populations of Cambodians, Iranians, and Japanese. Latin American immigrants—Guatemalans, Mexicans, and Salvadorans—dominate many chapters, as do third- and fourth-generation migrants from the U.S. Midwest. Still, the story lines rarely intersect.

This, says writer Richard Rodriguez, is as it has always been in Los Angeles—and in America. Thanks to Protestantism, he says, the 19th-century U.S. with its waves of new immigrants "became a country of tribes and neighborhoods more truly than a nation of solitary individuals. Then, as today, Americans trusted diversity, not uniformity." Yet, according to Rodriguez, "any immigrant kid could tell you that America exists. There *is* a culture. There is a shared accent, a shared defiance of authority, a shared skepticism about community." By extension, there is also a shared culture in Los Angeles.

A strikingly tolerant city, Los Angeles is also quite lively. National trendsetter in popular entertainment, lifestyle, style, and vocabulary, Los Angeles boasts more university graduates per capita than any other U.S. city. There are more colleges and universities here, a total of 176 at last count, than in the entire state of Massachusetts. But culture here doesn't always come with a university degree. Los Angeles is also the mural capital of the world, with a "collection" of more than 1,500 outdoor wall paintings displayed on storefronts (and sides), street corners, and alleyways throughout the county. Long characterized as culturally and intellectually vapid, Los Angeles is home to more actors, artists, dancers, filmmakers, musicians, and writers than any other city—at any time in the history of civilization.

After taking a good look around, even visitors soon realize that Los Angeles is not just a trip to Universal Studios or Disneyland anymore.

Parker once observed that Los Angeles amounted to "seventy-two suburbs in search of a city." She was correct, historically. In the latter years of the 19th century small cities sprang up throughout Los Angeles County, typically at the end of the city's famed trolley lines. Then came freeways and two-car garages and the dominance of L.A.'s automobility, trends that soon filled in the spaces between communities. Shortly after World War II the present-day tendency toward sprawl was well-established, with boundaries between L.A. the city and L.A. the county almost hopelessly blurred by exponential growth.

For the record, the present-day city of Los Angeles takes in 467 square miles, or almost one-tenth of Los Angeles County's 4,083-square-mile area; the city includes many apparently separate communities or districts such as Hollywood. Aside from the city of Los Angeles, there are numerous unincorporated areas known as Los Angeles—and 87 other incorporated cities within the county's borders—all of which are still considered "L.A." in a general sense.

Yet even the terms traditionally used to define L.A.'s relationship with itself—such as "city" or "downtown" or "suburbs"—have been largely abandoned by urban planners, who now conceive of L.A. as a series of "constellations" or urban villages comprising a metropolitan "galaxy."

Palm Trees and Feral Parakeets: Creating a New Ecology

The lushness of the Southern California landscape is as native as pink plastic lawn flamingos. Both the official city flower, the bird of paradise, and the official city tree, the Erythrina palm, are exotic imports. Except in rare areas, native plant species have long since lost out to domesticated plants in Los Angeles. Increasingly, native animal species that manage to survive in and around Los Angeles are forced to compete with humans and feral dogs and cats—even feral parakeets and parrots—for limited territory and food supplies.

In many ways Los Angeles has created, and is still creating, a new ecology, one dominated by introduced species of both plants and animals. Prominent among local plant immigrants are L.A.'s palm trees, none of which grow here naturally, though native palms do grow near Palm Springs and elsewhere in the low desert. Here as elsewhere in California native grasses were long ago

SANTA ANA WINDS

Wherever you find yourself in the Los Angeles universe, things change when the Santa Ana winds blow from the northeast off the desert, typically between November and January. The atmosphere here becomes hot and dry and unbelievably irritating. The way Raymond Chandler described it in his short story "Red Wind," the dusty, desiccating Santa Ana winds "come down through the mountain passes and curl your hair and make your nerves jump and your skin itch. On nights like that every booze party ends in a fight. Meek little wives feel the edge of the carving knife and study the backs of their husbands' necks." This notable Southern California weather phenomenon, which reverses the usual cool west-to-east air flow off the ocean, also increases the danger of late fall wildfires and plays havoc with people's allergies. But don't let a blustery Santa Ana season put you off. Desert winds do have the beneficial effect of scrubbing the air clean throughout the entire Los Angeles Basin—which is why a December or January day can offer the most glorious scenic vistas in Southern California.

replaced by introduced European species, and the L.A. landscape's native oaks, sycamores, alders, and shrubs are now outnumbered by introduced species—camellias, azaleas, ferns, and exotic tropical and semi-tropical tree and shrub varieties—that thrive in the mild Mediterranean climate. Most vividly illustrating L.A.'s re-creation of itself as urban tropical forest in the animal kingdom are the impressive flocks of feral parakeets, representing several species and all domestic escapees or their descendants, which thrive throughout fruitful Los Angeles. Local ornithologists also estimate that at least 2,000 feral parrots are at home in Los Angeles, 1,000 in and around Pasadena alone. A flock of about 400 red-crowned parrots was spotted in 1995 in the San Gabriel Valley, for example, and red-crowned and lilac-crowned parrots have been spotted in the San Fernando Valley.

DUSTY PUEBLO DAYS

In the beginning there was "Los Angeles man," a mysterious area resident whose skeleton,

*old Mexican dwelling,
late 19th century*

COURTESY AISLINN RACE

unearthed in 1936, has been dated as 7,000 years old. In more recent times, from Malibu north lived the Chumash, a fairly sophisticated seafaring people who fished and traded along the coast and throughout the Channel Islands. But the first known residents of Los Angeles proper were the native Gabrieleño people, who had been pushed west onto this arid, drought-prone plain by more aggressive Shoshonean peoples who dominated territories to the east. Sometimes known as the Yang-Na, the name of their village near what is downtown Los Angeles, the total local population has been estimated at about 5,000, scattered throughout the region in communities as large as 1,000 people. The Gabrieleño were here to welcome the first explorers to the Bahia de los Fumos or "Bay of the Fires" (or "Smokes"), so named by Portuguese explorer Juan Rodríguez Cabrillo from offshore in 1542. The "smokes" here were the Indian fires that created the landscape's notable and lingering brown haze—L.A.'s earliest smog.

But the first explorer to arrive in Los Angeles was Gaspar de Portolá, the Spanish governor of the Californias, while on his discovery mission of 1769-70. It would be 10 years before the Spanish availed themselves of the Gabrieleño's prime cottonwood- and alder-sheltered location along the river bank, one of the few spots where the Los Angeles River flowed year-round.

Los Angeles as place was officially founded in 1781, established by the Spanish as a supply center for Alta California and named after the L.A. River, which in turn was originally named after the festival of the Virgin corresponding to its date of discovery: El Pueblo de Nuestra Señora la Reina de los Angeles de Porciúncula, or "Town of Our Lady Queen of the Angels of Porciúncula." In the beginning Los Angeles was a dusty little pueblo of modest adobes scattered near the river. The city's first settlers were 44 villagers from the Spanish territory that later became Mexico's Sonora and Sinaloa Provinces—an entourage of blacks, Indians, and mestizos (people of mixed black, Indian, and Spanish ancestry) accompanied by two Spaniards. More than half of the new arrivals were children.

Though Los Angeles served as the capital of California briefly, in 1845, for the most part even the transfers of power between Spain and Mexico after Mexican independence and between Mexico and the United States after the Mexican-American War had little impact here. The Los Angeles area boasted vast ranchos and an early version of landed gentry, yet most of the Spanish missions and associated cultural enclaves were established elsewhere—along the coast, the region's primary transportation corridor. The 1849 discovery of gold near Sacramento in the north, and San Francisco's subsequent debut as California's center of wealth and power, created a temporary boom market for southstate beef but otherwise left Los Angeles to languish as a lawless frontier border town best known for murder, mayhem, and general anarchy.

In the devastating drought years of the 1860s the Spanish land grants came under American ownership, thanks to the U.S. judicial system, and cattle gave way to sheep, thanks to the great demand for wool during the Civil War era. Sheep gradually gave way to wheat and then orchards and vineyards and endless other agricultural crops as farmers discovered the profit potential of such a salubrious climate.

CITY OF DREAMS AND DREAMERS

That Los Angeles is both "city of angels" and favored social demon-hold of modern literature and cinema is, here, an acceptable contradiction. Contrast, contradiction, and irony are the lifeblood of Los Angeles. Yet it wasn't always thus. In its younger years Los Angeles seemed inspired by the idealistic, almost innocent ideas that directed its growth. Utopia preceded dystopia, at least officially.

The coming of the railroads—first linking Los Angeles to San Francisco in 1871, and then directly to the rest of the U.S. via transcontinental railroad in 1876—set the stage for L.A.'s first, and subsequently unrelenting, boom years. As boosters and boosterism promoted the benefits to personal health and wealth offered by Southern California, the mass migration began.

Yet there was a central idea behind the U.S. migration to Southern California—the belief that simple, healthful living amid gardens, orange groves, and the fellowship of good friends and neighbors could save civilization from the dehumanization and mindlessness of the industrial era. Earlier in this century, Pasadena, Riverside, and countless other Southern California communities shaped themselves from such ideals. That idea came to be symbolized throughout the U.S. by the humble orange—by Southern California's endless orange groves.

As a symbol of the Southern California dream—a regional variation of the American dream, particularly "middle-class America's desire for a home and happy marriage and healthy children," according to historian Kevin Starr—the orange as icon of the good life was crated for wholesale consumption throughout the U.S. by advertising executives employed by the California Fruit Growers Exchange (known for its trademark "Sunkist" brand). Real estate sales campaigns in general, promoted by early L.A. power brokers and landowners—railroad barons such as Henry E.

Huntington and Charles Nordhuff, and newspaper publishers such as Harrison Gray Otis of the *Los Angeles Times*—often emphasized the same theme, though the boosters' general credo was: "Big is Good, Bigger is Better, Biggest is Best." In parts of the country where winter meant blinding blizzards rather than blooming roses, the campaign wasn't a terribly hard sell.

Pasadena, in the San Gabriel Valley just east of downtown Los Angeles, would reap the richest rewards of California's orange era. Described by acclaimed turn-of-the-century astronomer George Ellery Hale as the "Athens of the West," Pasadena took root in the San Gabriel Valley Orange Association of 1875 and then grew its own golden age of arts and sciences. The arrival of the railroad in 1885 brought bushels of well-heeled easterners eager to escape to a kinder climate—the beginning of Pasadena's long-running reputation as a choice West Coast winter vacation destination. Many of Pasadena's wealthy winterers decided to stay on year-round, to soak up a full measure of sun and the scent of orange blossoms, and they soon built grand homes on the city's wide, wandering streets.

Thanks to the humble orange the arts and all aspects of culture, not just horticulture, flourished in Pasadena, which made California's greatest contributions to the Arts and Crafts movement. Pasadena's craftsman architecture—most popular from 1900 to 1940, and also fairly common elsewhere throughout Southern California—relied on an uncluttered, woodsy, nature-oriented approach that combined the sensibilities of a Swiss chalet with Japanese (sometimes Chinese) and Tudor touches. Emphasizing simplicity and harmony with nature, they stood as repudiation of all things Victorian.

Pasadena was in step with the march of progress throughout Southern California in other ways as well—most particularly with its annual Tournament of Roses Parade, the ultimate boosteristic beacon of the California good life. Where else, after all, could one find *roses* on New Year's Day?

WATER, OIL, AND AUTOS EVERYWHERE

However, Southern California's endless self-promotion was limited by the landscape's arid

SOME CLASSIC L.A. DRIVES

The Stars-to-Sea Highway

If you have an adventurous spirit and time to spare, the classic L.A. "view" tour is the "Stars-to-Sea Highway," 25-mile **Mulholland Drive** heading west from the Hollywood Fwy. (the 101) near Cahuenga Pass in the Hollywood Hills to Woodland Hills. For truly intrepid scenery seekers, the route continues out of the Santa Monica Mountains to the Pacific Ocean at Leo Carrillo State Beach and the Pacific Coast Hwy. (Hwy. 1) just east of the Ventura County line. (To do the entire route, which includes a fairly rugged unpaved section through Topanga State Park just southeast of Woodland Hills and other rough spots, a four-wheel-drive or other reasonably reliable, destruction-proof vehicle is advised.) Alternatively, take just half the trip by exiting in either direction from the San Diego Freeway (the 405) north of Brentwood near Sepulveda Pass.

Notable just east of the Hollywood Freeway is the lovely mission-style concrete "castle wall" and moat known as **Hollywood Reservoir**. Originally named Mulholland Dam when it was formally dedicated in 1925—to honor L.A.'s premier water engineer, William Mulholland, architect of the Los Angeles Aqueduct—the reservoir was quietly renamed after the St. Francis Dam disaster that soon doomed Mulholland's career and reputation. Yet Mulholland's namesake street remains unchanged.

Heading east to west, Mulholland Dr. snakes west along the ridgetops above Hollywood, offering both close-ups of some spectacular homes and breath-

taking panoramas of the endless L.A. basin and the San Fernando Valley. At night, it's all absolutely dazzling, particularly from the **Mt. Olympus Overlook** about one mile west of the **Hollywood Bowl Overlook** (at Runyon Canyon Park's northern entrance). Both daytime and nighttime views are typically better—and, in a sense, less "breathtaking"—in winter and early spring, when the smog level is low.

At the junction of Mulholland Dr. and Topanga Canyon Blvd., Mulholland Dr. becomes "Hwy." but otherwise continues to slither west across the twisting spine of the Santa Monica Mountains, slicing through suburban sprawl and wilderness along the way. Most scenic is the eight-mile "outback" section between **Las Virgenes** and **Kanan Dume Roads**, which has starred as Australia, England, and other imaginary movie locales. Following the route all the way west eventually leads to the Pacific Ocean. Plan to pack a picnic lunch (or dinner) and head for remote, picturesque **Nicholas Canyon County Beach** south of Leo Carrillo State Beach.

Cheap Thrills

Another way to start a Mulholland Drive sojourn—definitely a cheap thrill—is to begin your trip on **Dixie Canyon Ave.** just off Ventura Blvd. to the north in Sherman Oaks. At Dixie Canyon's suburban end, the road is wide and civilized, at least for a few blocks. But it soon descends wildly—hey, great views!—trying to decide, as its ruts, rattles, and rolls down the mountainside, whether it is merely a

---

nature. No matter how grand the gardens grew in Southern California, nothing could grow for long without water. And with the arrival of hordes of migrants, water was increasingly scarce. Just as Los Angeles was beginning to grow into a recognizable city, the severe Southern California drought of 1892-1904 threatened the city's fragile foothold at the edge of its own dream.

Enter William Mulholland, an Irish immigrant who came to America in 1878, a self-educated man who began his career in Los Angeles as a ditchdigger and ended it as the city's chief water engineer. As superintendent of the Los Angeles City Water Company, Mulholland was a conscientious steward of L.A.'s limited liquid resources, but even concerted conservation was

not enough. By 1903 it was clear that L.A. would either have to stop growing altogether—certainly an unacceptable conclusion among L.A.'s well-invested business boosters—or find more water.

So Mulholland and his good friend Fred Eaton, former mayor of Los Angeles, set out to find more water—in the Owens Valley on the eastern side of the Sierra Nevada about 250 miles north of Los Angeles. Mulholland quickly figured that the Owens River could supply enough water to support a city of two million souls instead of 200,000. Thus the Los Angeles Aqueduct, "the most gigantic and difficult engineering project undertaken by any American city," was created—and William Mulholland became an overnight celebrity among the engineers of academe, self-twisted and treacherous one-lane dirt road or a coyote path. (Not recommended for street cars, but definitely a possibility for off-roaders, and experienced mountain bikers.) The prospect of civilized transport, *paved road,* again presents itself at the intersection with Mulholland Drive.

Another cheap thrill starts in the Silver Lake neighborhood. From Glendale Blvd., head north on Alvarado into the hills above Echo Park to **Fargo St.**—L.A.'s steepest up-and-down thoroughfare—and create your own amusement ride. (Good brakes and steady nerves mandatory.) Adjacent **Baxter** is also good for a few gasps.

Urban adventurers with a preference for flatland might instead prefer the more thought-provoking sociological thrills associated with taking **Santa Monica Blvd., Sunset Blvd.,** or **Wilshire Blvd.** west from downtown.

On the Beach

By and large the Southern California coastal driving experience will not mirror any of those appealing escapist images used by TV car commercials to brainwash consumers. The success of the cars-are-freedom sales pitch is reflected, instead, in bumper-to-bumper traffic and the occasional sun- or celebrity-drunk yahoo determined to run others off the road. But a drive along L.A.'s stretch of the famed **Pacific Coast Hwy.** ("PCH," or Hwy. 1) can be a pleasure—especially on a nonsummer weekday—if you get out and about *early,* before the crazy people are out of bed.

But the point of driving PCH is not to escape the horrors of overpopulated urban life. The point is to immerse, wallow, or *drown* yourself in them. Since parking will be all but impossible in many coastal areas, you'll have plenty of time to work on it.

For a lightweight beach tour, begin amid the boatgroupie culture of **Marina del Rey,** the world's largest man-made harbor with associated upscale hotels and restaurants, and then work your way north through the tortured seaside eccentricities and spruced-up canals of **Venice** to open-minded **Santa Monica,** where at last report the middle-class still co-existed with the rich and famous and the occasional poor person. Heading north past **Pacific Palisades** and its swell seaside jogging park eventually leads to **Malibu,** where movie stars and other shy, affluent types apparently don't mind paying millions and millions of dollars for exclusive homes that periodically burn up in wildfires or, after the torrential rains that follow, slide down into the sea. Your reward, if you continue north to near **Ventura County,** is access to some of L.A.'s best "getaway" beaches.

A more serious—but more complicated—tour of the L.A. coastline starts in Long Beach far to the south, detouring from PCH to take in the heavy-industrial byways of sister port cities Wilmington and San Pedro on the way to the pleasant serenity of the Palos Verdes Peninsula. Once you roll down out of Rolling Hills, again stick to coastal roadways to tour the South Bay beaches and beach towns of Redondo Beach, Hermosa Beach, Manhattan Beach, and El Segundo, some quite semi-industrial. (Miniature oil derricks, even in people's backyards, are not particularly uncommon in this neck of the woods.) From El Segundo on into Playa del Rey, you can enjoy the endless aerial traffic coming and going from LAX.

---

educated immigrants everywhere, and civic boosters.

When in 1913 sweet Owens Valley water finally started flowing into the San Fernando Valley from Mulholland's ditch, an event for which 30,000-40,000 residents and a parade of dignitaries turned out, Mulholland said to the multitude: "There it is—Take it." And take it they did. They took it to transform the drought-parched landscape into a lush garden of palm trees, fruit trees, and roses that soon welcomed Hollywood—and which Hollywood soon shared with the world via the movies, attracting hundreds of thousands of new residents.

The landscape also sprouted oil wells. In 1892 Edward Doheny discovered oil at "Greasy Gulch," near what is now MacArthur Park. By 1897 there were more than 500 oil wells in and around downtown alone, although oil discoveries fanned out in all directions. Almost overnight California became the third-largest oil producing state in the nation.

Wide open spaces and abundant local fuel supplies made far-flung Los Angeles a perfect testing ground for America's latest invention—the horseless carriage. Automobiles first took to the Los Angeles streets in 1897; by 1915 about 55,000 cars populated area roadways, and by 1927 L.A. was considered a "completely motorized civilization." Ever-inventive Los Angeles established the world's first gas station in 1912; built the world's first freeway in 1939, the

Pasadena Freeway (110) from Pasadena into downtown; and installed the world's first parking meter in 1942.

HOLLYWOOD'S HEYDAY

To imagine Hollywood as a pious, prohibitionist utopia is more than most modern cinematic myth-makers could manage. Yet so it was until moviemaking came to town. Technically the southstate's moving picture industry began in 1907 in Los Angeles, which Selig Studios chose for filming the outdoor scenes for *The Count of Monte Cristo*. But the distinction between Los Angeles and Holly-wood as a film location was moot by 1911, in a sense, since in 1910 the small L.A. suburb of Hollywood sur-rendered its charter and be-came part of Los Angeles. In that same year David Wark Griffith, leading di-rector of New York's Bio-graph film company, came west to Los Angeles with his wife, Linda, and his film troupe, including 17-year-old Mary Pickford, and installed them in the Hollywood Inn on Hollywood Boulevard for the winter-spring shooting season. Between January 20 and April 6, Griffith's troupe produced 21 films in distinct southstate settings—the first films shot entirely *in* Southern Cali-fornia—including *The Thread of Destiny* at Mission San Gabriel and *Ramona* in Ventura County. Griffith's disciple Mack Sennett arrived in 1912 to begin his Keystone comedies, star ve-hicles for the English vaudevillian Charlie Chaplin.

Still, Hollywood resisted Southern Californi-a's growing general affinity for film. But before the community could mobilize much protest against the carousing, notoriously carefree movie people, they had already arrived. Within five years about 35 movie studios had relocated from the East and Midwest, creating overnight chaos on Hol-lywood's sleepy unpaved streets. But concerns about Hollywood's moral corruption proved to be no match for movie industry money, and by the Roaring '20s, Hollywood's stars glittered as national and international idols.

During the 1920s and '30s the stretch of Hol-lywood Boulevard between La Brea Avenue and Vine Street glittered with glitz, boasting magnifi-cent movie theaters, notorious nightclubs (Hol-lywood invented the Flapper style), notoriously good restaurants, chic shops, and stylish hotels. By the mid-1920s the Hollywood movie business was the fifth-largest industry in the United States, generating 90 percent of the world's films and grossing about $1.5 billion per year.

But the emerging West Coast film industry reached far beyond Hollywood, right into the heart and mind of heartland America and, quite quickly, the world. Movies appealed to the ele-mental and universal human experience; to get the drift of the story lines, one did not need an Ivy League educa-tion. Soon Hollywood—Los Angeles—both created and interpreted national aspira-tions, and modern mass cul-ture was born.

BARBIES AND BOMBERS: LOS ANGELES AFTER WORLD WAR II

For all of Southern California's earlier, more innocent glories, the modern middle-class myth of Los Angeles is largely the creation of the post-World War II era. And L.A. had rallied for the war effort in a big way, turning its entre-preneurial spirit to the task of building bigger and better aircraft and weaponry—the begin-nings of Southern California's centrality to the U.S. defense and space technology industries. It's not by accident that Hughes Aircraft, Mc-Donnell Douglas, Northrup, and Lockheed are practically neighborhood names in Los Ange-les. Though the regional aerospace industry ac-tually got its start in the first world war, during

NEON~L.A.'S SIGNATURE FLASH

If imitation is the sincerest form of flattery, just imagine how flattered Los Angeles is by the existence of Las Vegas and all that flashy neon.

The **Museum of Neon Art (MONA)** in L.A., open at its new downtown location since February of 1996, celebrates the city's love affair with neon lighting—a commercial art form that once decorated countless L.A. storefronts, theater marquees, and roof lines. The original fuel for L.A.'s signature flash was neon itself, a colorless, odorless gas that glows orangey-red when zapped by electricity, a fact of nature first discovered in France in 1898. (Other colors are created by other gases.) America's first neon signs, manufactured in France, were installed in 1923 at an L.A. Packard dealership.

Some of L.A.'s original tubular light show still shines, lighting up **Broadway** downtown, sections of **Wilshire Boulevard, Western Ave.** between Wilshire and Third St., **Alvarado St.** flanking MacArthur Park, and countless other streets. (For a fairly comprehensive map of restored Los Angeles neon, see the "neon map" on city's Department of Cultural Affairs website, www.culturela.org.) Other areas, such as **Melrose Ave.,** are at the forefront of the city's neo-neon renaissance, thanks in large part to citywide consciousness-raising credited to MONA and its founding artist Lili Lakich.

Downtown on the first floor of the Renaissance Tower, in Grand Hope Park on W. Olympic, the Museum of Neon Art (MONA) is the only permanent neon museum in the world. A stunning and electrically enigmatic likeness of the Mona Lisa—the museum's logo, designed by Lakich—marks the spot. The permanent collection at MONA includes an impressive array of classic L.A. neon and electric signs, dating from the 1920s. Changing exhibits—such as the museum's opening 1996 exhibition, *Electric Muse: A Spectrum of Neon, Electric, and Kinetic Sculpture*—emphasize neon as a contemporary art form. Head to **CityWalk** outside Universal Studios to appreciate more of the MONA collection, which includes the Richfield Eagle and the Melrose Theater sign.

For a still flashier appreciation of local lights, sign on for the museum's after-dark "Neon Cruise" L.A. bus tour, offered at least monthly, $40 per person. In addition to its neon tours, the museum offers introductory classes in neon design and technique four times each year.

The Museum of Neon Art is open Wed.-Sat. 11 a.m.-5 p.m. and Sunday noon-5 p.m. (closed Monday, Tuesday, and major holidays). On the second Thursday of every month, the museum is also open 5-8 p.m.—and at that time admission is free. Otherwise admission is $5 adults, $3.50 seniors and students (children age 12 and under free). Call for current information on docent-led tours, current exhibits, neon art classes, and "Neon Cruise" tours. The museum's entrance is on Hope (at Olympic); during regular museum hours, free parking is available in the Renaissance Tower's garage on Grand just south of Ninth Street.

For current exhibit and other information, and to make reservations for MONA's Neon Tours, contact: Museum of Neon Art (MONA), Renaissance Tower, 501 W. Olympic Blvd., tel. (213) 489-9918, fax (213) 489-9932, www.museneon.org.

MUSEUM OF NEON ART

MONA, the glowing logo of the Museum of Neon Art, was created by Lili Lakich in 1981.

SPORTING LOS ANGELES

The news in 1997 that **Los Angeles Dodgers** owner Peter O'Malley was planning to sell the city's National League baseball team, possibly to international media mogul Rupert Murdoch, was enough to send the entire region into fits of athletic apoplexy. At last report such evil deed had indeed been done, yet young boys and their fathers (and young girls and their mothers) still flock to Dodger Stadium in Chávez Ravine downtown, just off the Pasadena Freeway in Elysian Park, for the summer ritual of dugouts and Dodger 'dogs. For current info and tickets, call the Dodgers at (213) 224-1400. For the latest news about the team, in five different languages no less, try www.dodgers.com. For American League ball, head for Anaheim in Orange County and the **Anaheim Angels,** formerly the California Angels.

Big news in Los Angeles is downtown's new **Staples Center,** 1111 S. Figueroa St., toll-free tel. (877) 305-1111 for general information or (213) 742-7340 for tickets, www.staplescenter.com. Among the teams now calling the Staples Center home are the NBA's **Los Angeles Lakers,** a team still synonymous with Earvin "Magic" Johnson and Shaquille O'Neal, and the **Los Angeles Clippers.** The National Hockey League's **Los Angeles Kings** also get down at the Staples Center.

The oddest thing about sporting Los Angeles in early 2000 is that the region lacks a national football franchise, since both the Los Angeles Rams and the Los Angeles Raiders (previously and subsequently the Oakland Raiders) packed up and left town in 1995. What to do? Since Los Angeles has always lived by the "If We Build It, They Will Come" sports philosophy, local discussion now centers on where to build a new football stadium, to lure a new franchise. Local and regional boosters are salivating over the prospect of landing "the big one" for their own neighborhoods. Given the success of the Disney Company in regional sports—Disney's Mighty Ducks have made quite a splash in hockey at The Pond in Anaheim, and Disney is now part owner of the Anaheim Angels—some local wags think a new NFL expansion team here could be called the Lion Kings, perhaps housed in The Den.

While you wait for the return of the NFL, whenever and wherever that may be, there's always the Arena Football League and the **Los Angeles Avengers,** also part of the Staples Center sports stable (see above). And there's always collegiate football. The mythic L.A. teams are the **University of California at Los Angeles (UCLA) Bruins,** tel. (310) 825-2101, www.uclabruins.com (you can order tickets online) and the **University of Southern California (USC) Trojans,** tel. (213) 740-4672.

Other spectator sports abound throughout the region, from golf, tennis, beach volleyball, and surfing tournaments to thoroughbred racing; consult local newspapers for current offerings.

World War II Southern California produced one-third of America's warplanes. Military bases were also a growth industry in and around Los Angeles; after passing through on the way to war in the Pacific theater, many soldiers decided to come back to L.A. to stay—a decision that fueled massive post-war suburban growth.

Yet for all their success in putting Los Angeles on the military-industrial map, the war years wrote particularly shameful chapters of American history, including the mass incarceration of L.A.'s Japanese-American citizens and Japanese immigrants in relocation camps—an event that disenfranchised and shattered entire families and communities. Also infamous were the "zoot suit riots" of 1943, during which uniformed U.S. servicemen took it upon themselves to beat bloody any young Mexican American, black, or Filipino males they found in the general vicinity of downtown—a rampage successfully stopped only by special order of the U.S. State Department.

Los Angeles in the 1950s and 1960s was, officially, a happy, homogenized, and sunny suburban existence, birthplace of the Barbie doll, the DC-3, and the Internet. Yet certain post-war chapters of L.A. history were also dark and frightening, early shadows cast by the Cold War, including local activities of the House Un-American Activities Committee. Such events successfully launched the national political career of young Richard Nixon, born and raised in Orange County just south of Los Angeles, but ended the careers of many actors, artists, and writers as a direct result of the Hollywood blacklist.

LOS ANGELES IN THE NEW AGE

Like the rest of the nation, most of Los Angeles remained fairly comatose, culturally speaking, throughout the 1950s. But that all changed in the 1960s as Southern California established itself as a high-tech and industrial center and the world's entertainment industry capital. In the 1960s messengers from L.A.'s ever-present spiritual fringe—rogue philosophers, faith-healers, and miscellaneous other true believers well established here since the city's early days of alternative cures for consumption (tuberculosis)—stepped forward to help create California's New Age along with wild-haired surfers, dope-smoking students, and fad-happy hipsters of all socioeconomic stripes.

But L.A.'s new age was not just dope and VW vans. Los Angeles awoke to sober new truths about itself in the 1960s, following the Watts riots of 1965—a firestorm of long-repressed racial rage ignited over a seemingly insignificant incident, a six-day "incident" in which 34 people died. Sadly for Watts, the riots served primarily to end outside economic and social investment in some of L.A.'s poorest neighborhoods. In a sense, the incipient political messages of the 1960s weren't fully realized in Los Angeles until the 1970s, along with the next social sea change—the news that whites or "Anglos" were again a demographic minority in Los Angeles for the first time since the mid-1800s. Absorbing the full impact of this new reality, politically and socially, is proving to be a major challenge for Los Angeles.

The 1980s were watershed years for most of Los Angeles, especially in the years leading up to and immediately following the 1984 Olympic Games. (Los Angeles is the only city in the world to have hosted the Olympics twice; the first time was in 1932.) Suddenly Los Angeles, not New York, was the place to be—and continued to be that place, thanks to the city's newly vibrant architecture, arts, movie, music, and theater. That Los Angeles also came of age in a culinary sense, becoming one of the world's foremost destinations for fine food aficionados, also elevated the city's sense of itself.

Yet Los Angeles cannot forever evade its shadows, racism and poverty among the disenfranchised, a theme that emerged with a vengeance in the 1990s. Natural disasters grabbed their share of the headlines in these years—the Northridge earthquake, massive fires, mudslides—but social disasters had the most lasting impact. The racial rage that first ignited the Watts riots, having simmered almost silently for three decades, erupted again full force when the videotape of Rodney King being "subdued" by Los Angeles Police Department officers was broadcast around the world. After the original acquittal of the officers, full-scale rioting ensued—throughout downtown L.A., Koreatown, Hollywood, and coming perilously close to Beverly Hills and other affluent Westside addresses. The riots again proved counterproductive, setting off racial backlash and sinking affected neighborhoods into deeper poverty. The acquittal of O.J. Simpson in the subsequent racially tinged murder case reinforced a self-righteous backlash, a development that seemed to offer little hope for more enlightened relations between the races.

Yet racial tension is not a black and white issue in Los Angeles. The question is much more complicated than that, given the vast numbers of African, Middle Eastern, Eastern European, South American, and Asian immigrants now at home in the region. For example, many segments of the white, black, and even Latino communities are outspoken these days against the social and economic impacts of ongoing illegal immigration—also a racially and culturally loaded issue.

As California writer Richard Rodriguez says, the birth of a new society—any birth—is traumatic. And Los Angeles is just now, at the beginning of the 21st century, being born. Now that the city has lost its "suburban innocence," that development certainly an improvement over past obliviousness, Los Angeles is beginning to create itself. While this new Los Angeles is "forming within the terror and suspicion and fear that people have of one another," as Rodriguez says, it's "better not to like one another than not to know the stranger exists."

THE NEXT LOS ANGELES~ BACK TO THE FUTURE?

In the 1990s, two California historians have largely shaped the popular public debate over whether

L.A.'s cup is now half-full or half-empty. Mike Davis, author of *City of Quartz: Excavating the Future in Los Angeles,* views the bleak L.A. landscape of gang warfare, racial strife, and mindless mass middle-class culture through a Marxist lens, as an endless capitalist struggle with clear classes of winners and losers. Decent jobs for the working class, he says, have all but disappeared in L.A., plunging major sections of the population into the poverty that breeds despair and violence. Kevin Starr, now California's state librarian and author of *Material Dreams: Southern California Through the 1900s,* sees L.A. as "the Great Gatsby of American cities," a land still perfumed by the memory of orange blos-soms, rose gardens, and tile-roofed bungalows. Utopian Los Angeles would return, he says, if "you banish violent crime from L.A."

But both agree that the only hope for a feasible future in Los Angeles is a vigorous defense of public life and public space—libraries and parks and social institutions—and an end to the city's tendency to wall itself off from itself within private estates and gated communities.

To the extent that Los Angeles succeeds in reinventing itself, in reincarnating itself as a new and inclusive city, it will be by heading "back to the future"—toward a community-oriented sensibility that somehow got left behind in L.A.'s mad pursuit of personal dreams.

PRACTICAL LOS ANGELES

GETTING INFORMED

To receive a comprehensive and current visitors guide, the glossy *Destination Los Angeles,* and other information before coming to Los Angeles, write to: **Los Angeles Convention and Visitors Bureau (LACVB),** 633 W. Fifth St., Ste. 6000, Los Angeles 90071, tel. (213) 689-8822, fax (213) 624-1992, or call toll-free in the U.S. and Canada (800) 228-2452 (24 hours a day). To get up to speed on the Internet, the address is www.lacvb.com. Visitors can also make hotel and rental car reservations through the LACVB's toll-free number. Other publications include a variety of popular "pocket guides" and the annual magazine-style *Festivals of Los Angeles* guide. To find out what else is going on around town, call the bureau's 24-hour events hot line at (213) 689-8822; with a touch-tone phone, dial up current events information in English, French, German, Japanese, and Spanish.

Los Angeles also sponsors two separate walk-in visitor centers, both of which provide region-wide information—maps, brochures, calendars, information on foreign-language tours, shopping, dining, even listings of upcoming television tapings—much of it available in six languages, as well as multilingual personal assistance. The LACVB's **Downtown Visitor Information Center,** 685 S. Figueroa St. (between Wilshire Blvd. and Seventh St.), is open Mon.-Fri. 8 a.m.-5 p.m., and Saturday 8:30 a.m.-5 p.m. The satellite **Hollywood Visitor Information Center** is inside the historic Janes House at Janes Square, 6541 Hollywood Blvd. in Hollywood, and is open Mon.-Sat 9 a.m.-5 p.m. For visitor assistance by phone, call the LACVB at (213) 689-8822.

Local chambers of commerce and visitor information bureaus also abound up and down the Los Angeles coast; all can be quite helpful. Contact any of them—listed in this chapter—for visitor information in advance of, or during, your visit.

Local publications can be particularly helpful in introducing oneself to the wonders of Los Angeles. The local newspaper of record—California's newspaper of record, really—is the *Los Angeles Times,* distributed everywhere. Pick it up if only for the Sunday "Calendar" section, which lays out just about everything going on in town in the week ahead. The Thursday edition of the *Times* includes its "Calendar Weekend" pull-out section. Various cities also have local daily and/or weekly newspapers. Among magazines, *Los Angeles* is the slick "lifestyle" publication.

But to find out what's really hip and happenin', pick up alternative publications such as the *L.A. Weekly,* not to mention countless 'zines that come and go faster than freeway traffic, available in coffeehouses, neighborhood restaurants, bookstores, and other popular hangouts. Particularly good, wherever you might find them: *Poetry Flash* and *Art Issues.*

Otherwise, the best local source of visitor information is the local telephone book, particularly if you seek a particular product or service. Pick the closest place with the right product and/or right price, since distances in Los Angeles can turn a simple errand into an all-day adventure.

GETTING THERE: BY FREEWAY

One self-guided Los Angeles tour that few visitors ever take, at least not intentionally, is a tour of local freeways—*every* local freeway. It wouldn't take all that long, either, if one drove a few miles on each. Depending upon local traffic, of course.

No, though Angelenos love their freeways they use them strictly to get wherever they're going. They've been doing it ever since 1940.

LOS ANGELES AS DIVERSION

Unless one refuses to participate in the ongoing circus that is Los Angeles, it's almost impossible to avoid diversion here—starting with the family-focused theme parks scattered throughout Southern California. But L.A. offers much more to see and do, from exceptional museums to classic movie theaters, from live theater and concert performances to endlessly cool dance clubs. And the impressive Los Angeles parade of festivals and special community events could keep anyone entertained for a lifetime.

There are two primary approaches for experiencing Los Angeles arts and entertainment. The first is placing a major arts or entertainment performance (or community event) at the center of one's travel plans, and then planning everything else—where you'll stay and eat, what else you'll see and do—accordingly. The other is to grab a local newspaper—the *L.A. Weekly* or *New Times*, say, or the Thursday or Sunday calendar sections of the *Los Angeles Times*—and see what strikes your fancy at the moment, a style of "planning" most Angelenos exercise frequently. Or, at least for major goings-on, call the **Los Angeles Convention and Visitors Bureau** 24-hour events line at (213) 689-8822; a touch-tone menu allows callers to select from a five-language access menu, with events information available in English, French, German, Japanese, and Spanish.

And once visitors arrive by freeway, in either their personal or rental cars, they join in the same transportation rite.

Los Angeles is connected to itself and to the rest of the world by more freeways than any other city in America—a total of 16 major freeways and a large handful of lesser ones. Life on a Los Angeles freeway—any freeway—is life in the fast lane, a very fast lane. Noteworthy as the first freeway in Los Angeles, also the first freeway in the West, is the Pasadena Freeway, the 8.2-mile stretch of narrow-laned roadway still connecting Pasadena to downtown through the Arroyo Seco. The freeway's first five miles opened for business on December 30, 1940, designed for cars traveling about 45 miles per hour. Of course no one called it a freeway in those days, though people did sometimes call it a "free way." One proposed name for L.A.'s first ode to automobile, which was known as the Arroyo Seco Parkway, was "stopless motorway," a phrase that somehow failed to seize the public's imagination.

But freeways themselves did.

Many Los Angeles freeway routes actually follow old footpaths once used by deer and native peoples; the paths later became mission roads, stagecoach routes to the beach, paved roads, streetcar lines, and finally freeways. With the impressive tangle of roadway today—Los Angeles features 27 freeways, weaving in and out of each other like the strands of a giant, if loose, concrete yarn ball—it's almost impossible to imagine a footpath climbing sleepily up Sepulveda Pass, which the San Diego Freeway dominates today.

The newest freeway in Los Angeles—most likely its last—is the 17-mile, eight-lane, east-west **Century Freeway,** also known as Interstate 105 or the Glenn Anderson Freeway, that stretches between Norwalk and El Segundo near LAX. The Century parallels the Santa Monica (10) and Artesia (91) Freeways, and connects four major north-south routes: the San Diego (405), Harbor (110), Long Beach (710), and San Gabriel River (605) Freeways. An alternate route from downtown to LAX, the Century's notable features include the elevated Green Line trolley tracks down the center median, traffic sensors, closed-circuit TV cameras (so Caltrans can see why traffic has slowed), and metered on-ramps.

THE FREEWAY MAZE: UNTANGLING THE CONCRETE YARN BALL

Antelope Valley Freeway	Hwy. 14
Artesia Freeway	Hwy. 91
Corona del Mar Freeway	Hwy. 73
Foothill Freeway	I-210
Garden Grove Freeway	Hwy. 22
Gardenia Freeway	Hwy. 91
Glendale Freeway	Hwy. 2
Golden State Freeway	I-5
Harbor Freeway	I-110 ("the 110")
Hollywood Freeway	Hwy. 101 and Hwy. 170
Long Beach Freeway	I-710 ("the 710")
Marina Freeway	Hwy. 90
Orange Freeway	Hwy. 57
Pasadena Freeway	I-110 ("the 110")
Pomona Freeway	Hwy. 60
Riverside Freeway	Hwy. 91
Ronald Reagan Freeway	Hwy. 118
San Bernardino Freeway	I-10 ("the 10")
San Diego Freeway	I-405 ("the 405")
San Gabriel River	I-605
Santa Ana Freeway	I-5 and Hwy. 101
Santa Monica Freeway	I-10
Terminal Island Freeway	Hwy. 47
Ventura Freeway	Hwy. 101 and Hwy. 134

times faster, sometimes slower, depending upon local conditions. But speed is everything in L.A., another local metaphor for unlimited personal freedom. Even when 55 mph was the official speed limit here, almost no one paid any attention. And for newcomers and visitors, this can be a nerve-wracking fact of freeway life. Los Angeles drivers are typically good drivers, but people here drive fast—*very* fast, at least 70 or 75 mph when things are moving along well, though it's not uncommon for neophytes to be passed by locals zipping along at 80, 85, or 90. One must either "go with the flow," at least to an extent, to avoid the ire of fellow drivers—and to avoid becoming a traffic hazard or accident oneself—or stay in the right-hand lanes, stubbornly going the speed limit and contending with the constant distraction of cars jockeying for position as they merge on and off the freeway. Fast drivers have no problem with L.A.'s addiction to speed, but cautious drivers and slowpokes may be unnerved.

Beating the Rush

For years a local truism held that the Ventura Freeway (Hwy. 101) through the San Fernando Valley was the world's busiest roadway, and L.A.'s busiest freeway. But this was never true, it turns out, despite what the *Guinness Book of World Records* says. Because car-counting meters on the Santa Monica (I-10) and San Diego (I-405) Freeways—the actual record-breakers—were broken for almost five years, the entire world was misinformed. Most nightmarish of all is the junction of the San Diego and Santa Monica, not far north of Los Angeles International Airport.

To avoid getting stuck in L.A.'s slow (but rarely stopped-dead) rush-hour freeway traffic, on weekdays avoid being on the road between peak commute hours, 6-10 a.m. and 3-7 p.m. Plan to set out on your sightseeing excursions mid-morning, enjoying lunch and dinner in the same general vicinity before getting back on the

Also quite modern is the new elevated section—the "transitway," for buses and carpoolers only—of the Harbor Freeway (I-110) near downtown, just a few miles long but a harbinger of roadways to come, as Los Angeles builds and rebuilds its freeways to manage ever-increasing levels of traffic.

Yet other concerns tend to weave their way into local freeway lore. The area's shortest freeway—the Marina Freeway (90), not even two miles long—was originally known as the Richard M. Nixon Freeway, for example, so named in 1971 by the California Assembly. But after the Watergate debacle, the state Senate stripped Nixon of his freeway title in 1976.

Speeding Toward Freedom

The posted freeway speed in most areas of Los Angeles is 65 or 70 miles per hour (mph), some-

freeways. On weekends, avoid going in the same direction as "escape" and "return" traffic—leaving L.A. in all directions on Friday afternoons or evenings and returning late in the day on Sunday. Otherwise, get going early on weekends, and avoid stadiums and sports arenas before and after big games.

Avoiding traffic jams—knowing when to switch freeways, and when to exit freeways and take surface-street or connector road shortcuts—is

something of an art in Los Angeles. Yet even visitors can play the game with the aid of a tutor, such as the popular *L.A. Shortcuts: The Guidebook for Drivers Who Hate to Wait.* For those who prefer to avoid freeways altogether—it's possible to do that, even in Los Angeles—guides such as *Freeway Alternates* can help you do just that.

Don't ever misplace your map. Even native Los Angeles residents constantly refer to them, particularly the excellent, very detailed Thomas

---

STAY OUT OF THE WAY IN L.A.: SOME RULES OF THE ROAD

People in Los Angeles measure distance not in miles but in minutes—meaning minutes by freeway, or drive time. Angelenos also chronically underestimate drive times. This peculiar form of bragging rights ultimately implies that a *true* Angeleno could actually get from Pasadena to Santa Monica in 15 minutes, though you'll soon realize that you won't. (Angelenos also typically blame traffic when they're late—an excuse almost everyone will accept.) When taking directions from locals, then, visitors would be wise to generously pad the alleged drive time—or to double-check it, with the aid of a good map.

In keeping with their underestimation of average drive times, Los Angeles drivers also grossly underestimate their travel speed. If the posted speed limit is 65 miles per hour, most Angelenos will drive 80 or 85—and actually believe themselves when they tell the California Highway Patrol officer they were only going 60.

Angelenos typically refer to local freeways by name, not number—which can be mighty confusing for neophytes, since the Hollywood Freeway (101) is also the Ventura Freeway, the Santa Monica Freeway (I-10) is also the San Bernardino Freeway, the Golden State Freeway (I-5) is also the Santa Ana Freeway, and the faithful north-south San Diego Freeway never actually arrives in San Diego (not until after it's become I-5). When Angelenos *do* mention freeway numbers instead of names they use "the" as a fairly pointless modifier, as in "the 405" and "the 110," so when you hear such phrases you'll at least know that the topic of freeways is under discussion. Fortunately for visitors, most maps list both freeway names and numbers.

Then there are those unique L.A. words or phrases that make no sense whatsoever to innocent tourists, such as "Sigalert," even if they are listed in the *Oxford English Dictionary.* A Sigalert, according to the *OED,* is "a message broadcast on the radio giving warning of traffic congestion; a traffic jam," though technically Sigalerts apply only to tie-ups of 30 minutes or more. The word itself pays homage to L.A. radio broadcaster Loyd Sigmon, whose breaking traffic-jam bulletins of the 1950s are the stuff of local legend.

More important than local lingo, however, is a clear understanding of the local rules of the road. Los Angeles drivers never signal their intention to change lanes on the freeway, for example—a sure mark of a tourist—because doing so only allows others an opportunity to fill that particular spot of road first. Yet if someone honks, rudely cuts you off—which probably wouldn't have happened if you hadn't signaled—or tailgates for revenge, do remain calm. Don't allow that middle finger to leave the steering wheel, either, since no amount of rude driving is worth getting rammed at 70 miles per hour (or worse).

Also, never drive in front of a BMW or behind a Volvo.

Be particularly generous to L.A. drivers—give them a wide berth—if it's "pouring down rain" (as measured in actual precipitation, a tenth of an inch or less) because most Angelenos have never seen rain. Those who have tend to use wet roadways as yet another technique to increase their overall speed, through the miracle of hydroplaning. Most L.A. drivers don't know the difference between headlight high beams and low beams, either, so don't bother trying to explain the concept. In Los Angeles, headlights are either on or off. Be grateful, when it's dark outside, if the car coming toward you has them on.

Bros. maps. Almost every car in Los Angeles has a Thomas Bros. guide to Los Angeles or Los Angeles/Orange County, if not San Diego or Riverside/San Bernardino, right there in the glove compartment, easily available when the need arises. And the need *will* arise, the minute you miss your first freeway change and need to figure out if there's another way to get where you're going without doubling back (sometimes there isn't). But such detailed maps cost money, not typically worth the investment if you'll only be here a week or two. If you're a AAA member, stock up on California, Southern California, and L.A. city or regional maps either before you come or as soon as you arrive. Or buy good road maps at local visitor bureaus and travel-oriented bookstores.

Basic Freeway Facts—And Safety
Despite increasingly congested freeways, the idea of carpooling didn't really begin to catch on in L.A. until the 1990s, when "carpool only" lanes—High-Occupancy Vehicle (HOV) or "diamond lanes"—began to appear on local freeways, and when area employers started offering financial incentives to get people out of their cars. Even now, most vehicles on the road carry only one person. But HOV lanes, which require at least two occupants, are starting to work in Los Angeles—speeding up trip time in the diamond lane (usually the number one lane, closest to the freeway median) as well as the general flow of traffic. If you're driving solo on L.A.'s freeways, frustrated by a traffic slowdown, don't be tempted to dart into a diamond lane and cheat the system. Fines are stiff—close to $300, sometimes higher—and in the age of cellular phones, don't think an angry Angeleno stuck in traffic will hesitate to turn you in. Once you're pulled over by the California Highway Patrol (CHP), no excuse will get you off.

Given Los Angeles drivers' lust for speed, slower drivers—people going only 70 miles per hour, say—should stay in the center or center-right lanes if at all possible, allowing faster drivers plenty of room to move as they race toward their destinies. If you'll be traveling only a short distance on a particular freeway, and if traffic is heavy, stay in the freeway's right-hand lanes and avoid the frustration of maneuvering between lanes—assuming your upcoming exit will be to the right, of course. That's usually the case,

particularly on L.A.'s newer freeways and interchanges, but some freeways feature surprising (surprising if you don't know about them) left-hand exits or traffic "splits." So study your road map carefully before setting off into unfamiliar territory—the Thomas Bros. guides include handy freeway entry and exit maps—and watch freeway signs carefully. If you're paying attention, you'll usually have plenty of time to prepare even for left exits. Familiarizing yourself with route maps ahead of time will also help in planning an instant emergency strategy, should you miss a key exit at some point. Also allow yourself extra travel time to avoid feeling pressured, a factor that may affect your concentration.

Most traffic congestion in Los Angeles is caused by "traffic incidents," not accidents, these varying from unexpected breakdowns to flat tires. To avoid being an incident, make sure your vehicle is road-ready before setting out. But should the unexpected occur, pull off to the right to park if at all possible, turn on your emergency blinkers or "flashers," and call for help from the nearest "call box." Numbered call boxes (yet another L.A. invention), no more than a mile apart (often closer) on the right shoulder of every area freeway, are not telephones; they can be used only for automobile emergencies. Once you explain your problem and your location (relative to the box), the operator will dispatch towing assistance—a service sometimes offered free by local authorities, but AAA or other towing service coverage is always handy.

GETTING THERE: BY BUS, BOAT, TRAIN, AND PLANE

By Bus, Boat, And Train
Greyhound/Trailways is the primary commercial bus service into greater Los Angeles. Routes come from all directions—certainly wherever there's a freeway—and can deliver travelers, if not to the desired city, then at least as close as the nearest major transit center. The main L.A. Greyhound bus terminal is downtown. If you need to get to the coast and no one can meet you there—and Greyhound connections seem dubious—simply catch a local bus and complete the trip via the available mass-transit system. (Call to clarify local connections, using relevant sections

Catalina Island, part of L.A. County, lies a boat ride away.

below, once you devise your main bus route.) Alternative bus companies, including **Green Tortoise,** can also deliver travelers to Los Angeles.

Always a pleasure—harking back to Hollywood's golden era—is coming and going by train, a service provided by **Amtrak** these days. Stepping out into grand Union Station near downtown Los Angeles, where one can also make intercity train connections, is a delight even for the most jaded traveler. From Los Angeles, trains run to Santa Barbara and points farther north—a lovely trip, often following the coastline—as well as east across the desert. For Amtrak info and reservations, call toll-free (800) 872-7245, www.amtrak.com. For more information on bus and train travel, see this book's introduction.

More unusual, but not *that* unusual, is arriving in Los Angeles by boat. Most major cruise ships dock at **Los Angeles Harbor** in San Pedro, or in adjacent Long Beach. Contact your travel agent to arrange a cruise-ship cruise to Los Angeles.

By Airplane

Most visitors, if they don't arrive by car, come by air. The largest airport in the region is **Los Angeles International Airport,** most commonly known by its unfortunately suggestive international handle, "LAX" (pronounced EL-AY-EX, however), and near the coast just south of Marina del Rey and north of El Segundo, west of the San Diego Freeway (I-405). This is the airport everybody loves to hate. But few hate it enough to try another airport, why is why traffic can be so nightmarish in the general vicinity.

To avoid the crush at LAX, even locals often use other regional airports, including the **Long Beach Airport,** tel. (562) 570-2600 (recorded) or 570-2619, www.ci.long-beach.ca.us; the **John Wayne Airport** in Orange County, tel. (949) 252-5200, www.ocair.com; the **Burbank/Pasadena/Glendale Airport,** tel. (818) 840-8840, www.bur.com, in the San Fernando Valley but convenient to Hollywood, Pasadena, and downtown; and the surprisingly busy **Ontario International Airport** serving San Bernardino and Riverside, tel. (909) 988-2700 or (909) 937-1256 (Traveler's Aid of Ontario), www.lawa.org/ont.

Los Angeles International Airport

As writer Pico Iyer has observed, airports are "the new epicenters and paradigms of our dawning post-national age—not just the bus terminals of the global village but the prototypes, in some sense, for our polyglot, multicolored, user-friendly future." That's as good a general description as any for LAX, but Iyer points out that the airport is also a metaphor for L.A. itself, "a flat, spaced-out desert kind of place, highly automotive, not deeply hospitable, with little reading matter and no organizing principle."

What a welcome to L.A. Served by about 80 major airlines, Los Angeles International Airport handles about 54 million passengers each year, making this the fifth-busiest airport in the world. And while the idea seems insane, airport officials and some local politicians are pushing to expand airport business by about 60 percent by the year 2015—a likelihood none too popular with surrounding residents already beset by horrendous traffic, air pollution, and airplane noise. Since surrounding land is scarce, proposed new runways would be built out into Santa Monica Bay with an assist from massive landfill

EXCURSIONS INLAND: TOURING L.A.

Los Angeles is a sprawling, spread-out place, a city that seems to extend beyond all landward horizons. Basic issues—like deciding what to see and do in this expansive world of possibilities, and figuring out how to get there—tend to confound first-time visitors. One perfectly legitimate way to "do" L.A., then, is by signing up for guided tours, thereby delegating the details to the hired help.

Guided Tours by Car, Bus, and Hearse

To tour the lives and lifestyles of L.A.'s rich and notorious, you can always stop for the latest editions of various "Maps to the Stars' Homes" hawked by Beverly Hills area entrepreneurs. More fun, though, was the **Grave Line Tours** guided postmortem tour of local fame, an enterprise launched in 1987. "Mourners" climbed into the Cadillac hearse and cruise the streets of Hollywood, Beverly Hills, and other Los Angeles neighborhoods to find out how, when, where, and sometimes why celebrities died. Since 1999 the classic Grave Line hearse tour has been offered by **Tourland,** tel. (323) 782-9652, www.tourlandusa.com. Tourland's **Oh Heavenly Tour** revisits the sometimes tawdry and twisted pasts of local celebrities by reservation only, though standby seating is sometimes available. In addition, Tourland offers an evening **Haunted Hearse Tour,** which visits locales reportedly haunted by celebrities. The fee for each tour is $40 per person.

Architours promotes "architecture, art, and design as a cultural resource." Tours and special events emphasize culture, history, residential and public architecture, gardens and plazas, public and private art, and furniture and graphic design. For current details and reservations, contact: Architours, P.O. Box 8057, Los Angeles, CA 90008, tel. (323) 294-5821 or toll-free (888) 627-2448, fax (323) 294-5825, www.architours.com. Or try a quirky trip with **Googie Tours,** named for a defunct local coffeeshop chain, which specializes in Southern California's fast-disappearing vernacular architecture. Tour stars include bowling alleys, cocktail lounges, coffeeshops, motels, and fine-dining destinations such as the giant drive-through Donut Hole doughnut shop in La Puente. For information, contact: Googie Tours, P.O. Box 34787, Los Angeles, CA 90034, tel. (323) 980-3480.

Also fairly astonishing are the monthly guided **Mural Tours** of various areas of Los Angeles—downtown L.A., East L.A., and South-Central L.A.—well off the typical tourist track. Tours of the world's largest "street gallery" are offered jointly but in alternate months by the Mural Conservancy of Los Angeles (MCLA) and the Social and Public Art Resource Center (SPARC). Typical mural tour topics might include **A Day with East Los Streetscapers, Community Murals of Social Conscience and Activism,** and **African-American Murals.** The **Downtown Mural Tour** is quite enlightening, but visitors determined to stay within reach of ocean breezes can try **West L.A./Venice Murals** or **Murals of the South Bay.** Most tours cost $25. For more information or to make reservations, contact the **Mural Conservancy of Los Angeles Tours,** P.O. Box 5483, Sherman Oaks, CA 91413, tel. (818) 470-8864 or (323) 257-4544, www.lamurals.org. The **Social and Public Art Resource Center** (SPARC), 685 Venice Blvd., Venice, CA 90291, tel. (310) 822-9560, fax (310) 827-8717, www.sparcmurals.org, no longer offers its immensely popular mural tours, due to lack of funding, but it's still possible to organize private group tours through SPARC ($200/hour, two-hour minimum) with at least two months' advance notice.

Some of the neon lighting, dating to the 1920s, that made Los Angeles one of the world's flashiest cities is now on display at the Museum of Neon Art (MONA) downtown; you can appreciate much of the rest at CityWalk outside Universal Studios, and still more abundantly along certain city streets. To see some of L.A.'s historic local lights in their neo-natural neon environments, sign on for the museum's after-dark **Neon Cruise** guided double-deck bus tour, an event usually offered every month for a fee of $45 per person. For current information, contact: **Museum of Neon Art,** Renaissance Tower, 501 W. Olympic Blvd., Los Angeles, CA 90015, tel. (213) 489-9918, fax (213) 489-9932, www.museneon.org.

For more local arts exposure, free guided, two-hour **Metro Art Project Tours** are also offered in L.A. For details, call (213) 922-4278.

Guided Tours on Foot, by Bike, via Skateboard

Guided walking tours are available in most areas of Los Angeles; contact visitor centers for current details. Now a long-running local institution, the **Los Angeles Conservancy** offers inexpensive and informative walking tours designed to interpret L.A.'s past, present, and future. The group offers 12 regular tours—in addition to occasional special tours—emphasizing historic areas and structures. These include **Little Tokyo, Pershing Square,** and **El Pueblo de Los Angeles** as well as **Union Station, City Hall,** and other landmark buildings. The **Broadway Theaters** tour, which allows visitors inside some of L.A.'s grand old movie theaters, is one of the Conservancy's most popular. The usual Conservancy tour fee is $8. All tours, typically one or two hours, start Saturday at 10 a.m. Reservations are required; you can reserve by phone or online. The Art Deco, Broadway Theaters, and Pershing Square tours are offered every Saturday. Others—including The Biltmore Hotel, Union Station, Little Tokyo, Terra Cotta, Palaces of Finance, and Angelino Heights, in addition to miscellaneous special tours—are offered on a regular rotating schedule. No tours are offered on Thanksgiving, Christmas, or New Year's Day. For more information or reservations, contact: **Los Angeles Conservancy Tours,** 523 W. Sixth St., Ste. 1216, Los Angeles, CA 90014, tel. (213) 623-2489, fax (213) 623-3909, www.la-conservancy.org.

Combining a walking tour with quick trips on the city's metro system and unique funicular railway, historian Greg Fischer's two-hour **Angel City Tours,** tel. (310) 470-4463, offer a facts-versus-fiction historical introduction to downtown L.A.

But why walk when you can run? **Off 'N Running Tours,** toll-free tel. (800) 523-8687, offers three- to eight-mile courses for fitness walkers and runners in Santa Monica, Beverly Hills, and downtown L.A.; the $45 per person fee includes a runner's breakfast and—for L.A. memorabilia—a T-shirt. Or consider a two- to four-hour tour of Santa Monica, Venice, and Marina del Rey by bicycle or roller blades, both offered by **Perry's Beach Café and Rentals,** tel. (310) 372-3138.

Spectator sports fans, how 'bout a behind-the-scenes baseball history tour? Dodger blue is on display at guided **Dodger Stadium Tours,** tel. (323) 224-1400 (tickets also available at the stadium gift shop), which include the clubhouse, press box, bullpen, dugout, and the new 8,000-square-foot museum.

construction projects. If the idea of an endlessly bigger LAX, a $12 billion project, seems less than appealing, the only effective way travelers can express that opinion is by taking their business elsewhere—for a listing of other area airports, see above—and by further making that point in letters and phone calls to local officials. International visitors are almost destined to disembark here, however.

Even an unexpanded LAX can't help inventing and reinventing itself. These days LAX is busy improving itself yet again—adding a space-age veneer—including spiffing up its food service. The airport's Jetsonsesque "theme building" has become the otherworldly L.A. Encounter cafe, redesigned by Disney Imagineering and complete with lava lamps, a robotic maître d', and waiters in space suits. The futuristic menu, designed by local chefs John Sedlar and Patrick Glennon, includes "chocolate planetary orbs with Saturn rings" as the house dessert. But pay no attention to the restaurant's flight status video monitors—strictly fictitious, unless you're headed to Mars. Other airport food concessions include McDonald's, Wolfgang Puck's Express, the Daily Grill, and other trendy contenders.

New, too, is the Rhino Chasers pub. Reasonably healthy food, from bran muffins to green salads and other vegetables, is available everywhere. Look for a variety of international cuisines in the International Terminal.

As in most monstrously large airports, once you arrive you follow airport signs to find parking, rental car agencies, and terminals—and pray you'll get to the right places on time. Pray, too, that no one breaks into your car if you leave it in the lots here. Because rates of vandalism tend to be high in the airport's far-flung B and C parking lots—though they are patrolled regularly by security guards—LAX users often opt for one of the many private guarded lots just west of the San Diego Freeway (the 405) along Century Blvd.; various airport-area hotels also offer nonguest parking, for a price. That price—and the level of service provided—can vary greatly among private parking lots, so it pays to check out available options thoroughly.

All in all, it's much simpler to forget about driving and parking, if at all possible, and get a ride with **Super Shuttle,** tel. (213) 775-6600, (310) 782-6600, or toll-free (800) 554-3146 in Los Angeles County, www.supershuttle.com/lax. To make reservations from outside L.A. County, call (310) 782-6600. There are many, many other shuttle services, of course—even flashier limo service, as well as regular cab service—so pick a carrier licensed by the Los Angeles Dept. of Airports. Some shuttles offer discounts for senior citizens and AAA members and on prepaid round trips. Always make shuttle reservations at least 24 hours in advance. Many higher-end area hotels also offer airport shuttle service, either free or low-cost. For current LAX transit information, including public transit connections, try the websites: www.lawa.org/lax and www.quickaid.com/airports/lax.

LAX has eight domestic terminals and one international terminal, all of them connected by free shuttle buses. Restrooms, nursery rooms, basic business services, lockers, gift shops, restaurants, and bar/lounges are available in every terminal. For computerized visitor assistance in various languages, head to one of the airport's "QuickAID" touch-screen video terminals. Even better is LAX Traveler's Aid, which features a foreign language translation "link." To get away from the airport's bustle, head for the theme building or the palm-lined oasis in Terminal 5.

GETTING AROUND

Most visitors come to Los Angeles by car, or climb into a rental car immediately after arrival, and get around the way Angelenos do—via the vast web of local freeways. Once you get here by freeway you're already getting around by freeway, so for a detailed introduction to that adventure see Getting There: By Freeway, above.

By MTA

The Los Angeles Metropolitan Transit Authority provides public bus service throughout Los Angeles County, with some routes more generously staffed—and more useful to visitors—than others. The city's MTA buses are the only reliable form of mass transit for city residents without cars, including large segments of L.A.'s working poor population and the elderly. When MTA raised bus fares in the mid-1990s, protests erupted in so many quarters, particularly from various public-interest groups and community organizations, that the preexisting general fare of $1.35 (90 cents with prepaid tokens) will con-

tinue at least for a while. Monthly MTA passes still cost $42, 15-day passes $21, and weekly passes $11. (Weekly and monthly passes run Sun.-Sat. and are also good for the local Metrorail subway system). On some bus routes, off-peak individual fares are just 75 cents. In addition, MTA agreed to beef up its bus service at least a bit—adding 150 or so buses.

For information on MTA routes and fares, call (213) 626-4455 or toll-free (800) 266-6883 (800-252-9040 TTY). Sometimes it seems as if no one will ever answer the phone, however, so for detailed regional bus route and schedule information, try the website: www.mta.net. And to buy passes, it's typically easier to stop by local **MTA Customer Centers,** at various locations. See the website for a current listing of centers and other retail outlets—altogether some 750 possibilities, listed by community.

A variety of other local transit systems also serve greater Los Angeles; for current information on public transportation in Santa Monica, Long Beach, and other areas, see relevant sections below; contact local visitors bureaus; or see the MTA website, www.mta.net, which provides handy transit "links" throughout Southern California.

By Metrorail and Metrolink

Los Angeles once boasted one of the world's most far-flung and efficient public transportation systems—the Pacific Electric Red Car electric trolley system that connected nearly every suburban or coastal L.A. community with each other and with downtown. The Red Cars, in fact, were largely responsible for L.A.'s sprawling growth pattern—more so than freeways, which came much later—since trolley transport made it convenient for people to get around even without cars. When the last of the Red Car trolley system was dismantled in 1961, L.A.'s congestion and smog problems quickly reached crisis proportions.

Los Angeles is once again looking to mass-transit trains and trolleys to solve its traffic problems, though at this point things aren't working quite as well as the old Red Cars did.

Operated by the Metropolitan Transit Authority (MTA) and built with generous amounts of federal funding, the new and multifaceted Los Angeles Metrorail system serves fairly limited areas of L.A. and Southern California, though plans call for substantial regional expansion. Designed primarily for Los Angeles commuters of the professional class, it would seem, the system has suffered from cost overruns, dramatic construction delays, and the local and national humiliations of fraud and kickback allegations, federal investigations, and substantial recent funding cuts. Los Angeles itself seems almost evenly divided on the question of whether its modern mass-transit system has been worth it—and whether it will make any real difference in eliminating area traffic congestion. (Metrorail's ongoing disasters were publicly symbolized, in the mid-1990s, by the giant construction-related cave-in and sinkhole along Hollywood Boulevard.) A 1997 poll determined that, by a narrow majority, Los Angeles residents oppose the city's new subway system, including further construction, and doubt that it will ever serve parts of the city that most need it.

Metrorail's most vocal critics point out that the system was designed primarily for the convenience of more affluent commuters, that it rarely goes when many residents (and visitors) would like it to go, and that the money spent on Metrorail would have been better spent on improving the local bus system.

The MTA's **Red Line,** the city's subway, serves Union Station, downtown L.A., a short section of Wilshire Blvd., and Hollywood; the line is now on its way into the San Fernando Valley—a construction process creating considerable local consternation—and will one day extend to the ocean, according to current plans. The MTA's **Blue Line** electric trolleys run 22 miles between Long Beach and downtown L.A., passing Watts Towers and other rarely-seen-by-tourists neighborhoods along the way. The Blue Line is linked to the recently opened east-west **Green Line** that connects Norwalk to El Segundo (but not nearby LAX; you'll have to lug your luggage onto an airport bus for that trip). For that utilitarian lapse in particular—and since El Segundo is no longer a major aerospace employment hub, thanks to U.S defense downsizing—the Green Line has been dubbed the "train to nowhere" in the local press. Scoring at least one point for convenience, however, the Blue Line stops just one block from the transit mall in downtown Long Beach.

The MTA's Metrolink commuter rail system, launched in 1992, is the fastest-growing commuter rail system in the nation. Metrolink "links" cities such as San Bernardino, Riverside, Lancaster, Oxnard, and Oceanside to Los Angeles. Though the entire system is far from entirely useful even for visitors, both Metrorail and Metrolink do offer the opportunity for unusual car-free daytrips and around-town excursions.

Fares for the Metrorail system are the same as for MTA buses; for details, see By MTA, above. Fares for Metrolink trains vary according to distance traveled. For route and other information on the Metrorail Red, Blue, and Green Lines, call MTA at (213) 626-4455 or toll-free (800) 266-6883. For route and fare information for the Metrolink regional commuter trains, call toll-free (800) 371-5465.

SANTA MONICA AND VICINITY

Santa Monica is the quintessential L.A. beach town, a distinction held since the early 1900s when the original Looff "pleasure pier" was the bayside beacon for long days of Southern California-style fun in the sun. But unlike other popular L.A. tourist destinations, Santa Monica is much more than just a pretty face and a good time on the weekends—despite its place in L.A. literature as the barely disguised 1930s' "Bay City" in Raymond Chandler's *Farewell My Lovely*. These days the city is considered politically "progressive," a rarity in Southern California. That tendency has translated into rent control—recently abolished, after significant local damage in the Northridge earthquake—and a trend toward liberal politicians that's still going strong. Though he is destined to retire soon due to term limits, Santa Monica's state senator is Tom Hayden, a thoughtful politico better known as an anti-Vietnam War activist and one of the original Chicago Seven, ex-husband of actress and fitness enthusiast Jane Fonda. (The fact that Hayden ran unsuccessfully against Richard Riordan for L.A. mayor in 1997 hasn't diminished his stature here.) And Santa Monica's state Assembly member Sheila Kuehl—better known in some circles as the character Zelda Gilroy from *The Many Lives of Dobie Gillis* 1960s TV series—is California's first openly gay legislator, a Harvard Law School grad who was elected to the Assembly in 1994 and the first woman in California history to be named as speaker pro tem. The city's political tendencies have spawned, particularly among local landlords, the disparaging nickname of "People's Republic of Santa Monica"—not nearly as marketable as "The Zenith City by the Sunset Sea" of the late 19th century or the present "A Fortunate People in a Fortunate Land." By Southern California standards the community is also atypical socially—movie stars and the just plain wealthy blended with a large expatriate British population, senior citizens, middle-class and low-income families, and poverty-stricken activists, artists, and street people. As odd as it seems in these days of escalating public intolerance, most everyone here gets along most of the time.

Most of Santa Monica's initial attractions are front and center, along or near the edge of Santa Monica Bay—the bay implied in the title of that insipid yet notoriously popular TV show *Baywatch,* which has since moved on to Hawaii. The city's own strand of sand is Santa Monica State Beach. On weekends and in summer an equal draw is the associated Santa Monica Pier—now including a 1922 carousel and a carnival of fun rides. But Santa Monica offers much, much more, including the nearby pleasures of Malibu, Venice, the Santa Monica Mountains National Recreation Area, and Will Rogers State Historic Park, wacky and world-class art galleries, imaginative shopping, and an unusual range of good accommodations and great restaurants—in every price category. Beach town or no, Santa Monica has it all.

Most people arrive via the Santa Monica Freeway (I-10), though one of the city's claims to fame is its location at the Pacific Ocean end of the original Route 66. Once here, it's easy to get around via the city's Big Blue Bus. (If you're driving, bring pockets full of quarters. Local parking meters, particularly near the beach, have voracious appetites.) For current information about "Bay City," contact: **Santa Monica Visitor Center,** 1400 Ocean Ave., Santa Monica 90401, tel. (310) 393-7593, www.santamonica.com, which is in Palisades Park and open for drop-in assistance daily 10 a.m.-4 p.m. (until 5 p.m. in summer). Watch L.A.-area newspapers for Santa Monica special events, major ones scheduled on weekends and/or summer evenings, or call Santa Monica's 24-hour "Funshine Line," (310) 393-7593.

Earlier People, Earlier Republics

Gaspar de Portolá claimed what is now Santa Monica for Spain in 1769. According to local legend, Franciscan Father Juan Crespi selected the name—choosing St. Monica because the area's natural springs reminded him of the tears she shed when her son Augustine, destined to become a saint himself, turned to Christianity. But the grassy mesa was still unoccupied in 1822, when nascent Mexico rousted the Spanish. A three-way tussle over its ownership because of conflicting land-grant titles was resolved only in 1851, after California statehood: Don Francisco Sepulveda received 30,000-acre Rancho San Vicente y Santa Monica, while Ysidro Reyes and Francisco Marquez jointly gained the 6,600-acre Boca de Santa Monica, which included Santa Monica Canyon and much of the bayside coastline.

In 1872 cattleman Colonel R.S. Baker bought the Sepulveda spread and much of the Reyes-Marquez property. Just two years later Baker sold three-fourths of his land wealth to the British-born millionaire John P. Jones, the junior U.S. senator from Nevada. Jones had big ideas. Together he and Baker planned the new town of Santa Monica, which would include a wharf and interconnected trans-California railroad—to serve Jones's Nevada silver mines and other future industry. Some in Los Angeles detected a threat to their own potential prosperity and attacked the planned city of Santa Monica as an intended rival. But others lined up eagerly in 1885 to buy the city's first lots. Within months Santa Monica was booming, boasting more than 150 homes, 75 or so "tent" or temporary homes, and 1,000 citizens. With the wharf open for business and the railroad under construction, a prosperous future seemed assured.

In 1877 the city's first resort, the Santa Monica Bath House, opened for business. A full day's stagecoach ride from downtown Los Angeles, Santa Monica nonetheless beckoned as a balmy respite while the rest of L.A. scorched in the summer heat. Vacationers could enjoy the cool ocean breezes from tents pitched in Santa Monica Canyon. Hotels, restaurants, and shops soon followed; summer residents began to stay year-round. In 1887 Santa Monica voted to incorporate and become an independent city.

Yet Santa Monica's success would be some time coming. Jones lost most of his fortune—and his railroad—when silver prices plummeted. His wharf was condemned and quickly demolished.

Losing the Port but Finding No "Pier" in Tourism

The earliest incarnation of Santa Monica's pier was known in the early 1870s as "Shoo-Fly Landing," the point of departure for asphalt tar from Hancock Park's La Brea Ranch that was destined to become paved streets in San Francisco. Then came John Jones's 1875 Los An-geles and Independence railroad, its wharf and depot allowing steamers to deliver goods destined for Los Angeles via railway.

In the late 1880s the Los Angeles "port war" began. Collis Huntington, owner of Southern Pacific Railroad, wanted L.A.'s official harbor to be in Santa Monica—where he, coincidentally, owned most everything. Those who feared Huntington's monopoly in the Santa Monica area and elsewhere fought hard against his plans. Nonetheless determined that the Port of Los Angeles would be in Santa Monica, Huntington upped the ante by building California's most massive pier; his finished Santa Monica Pier measured 4,720 feet long and 130 feet wide when it opened for business in 1902. Yet Huntington lost the war, and San Pedro to the south became L.A.'s primary port city. All Santa Monica shipping stopped by 1910, and raging surf ravaged Huntington's grand pier.

But if Santa Monica failed as a center of commerce and trade, it succeeded as one of the region's preferred recreation destinations. Santa Monica's grand Arcadia Hotel, the North Beach Bath House, and the Deauville Beach Club soon signaled the city's arrival among L.A.'s monied minions. And the city's final incarnation of its earlier dreams, the Santa Monica Municipal Pier, arrived in 1912, quickly followed by the adjoining Looff "pleasure pier" in 1916. The Looff pier featured a trademark carousel, other amusements, and the enormous Blue Streak roller coaster. In July of 1924 the La Monica Ballroom opened at pier's end; it was the largest ballroom in the world, host to crowds of up to 10,000. Rather than a rough industrial port, Santa Monica became instead a sleepy seaside retreat—a serene small town largely unperturbed by progress until the 1960s and the completion of the Santa Monica Freeway, when it became easier for the world to get here.

Yet illicit entertainment did arrive, symbolized in the 1920s by offshore gambling ships. These 24-hour floating casinos were careful to remain at least three miles from shore, just beyond the state's legal jurisdiction. Water taxis ferried customers from the pier to the *Tango, Texas, Showboat,* and *Rex,* ships that could host up to 1,900 guests at a time. Offshore gambling flourished here until 1939, when the California Supreme Court declared the area between Point Dume

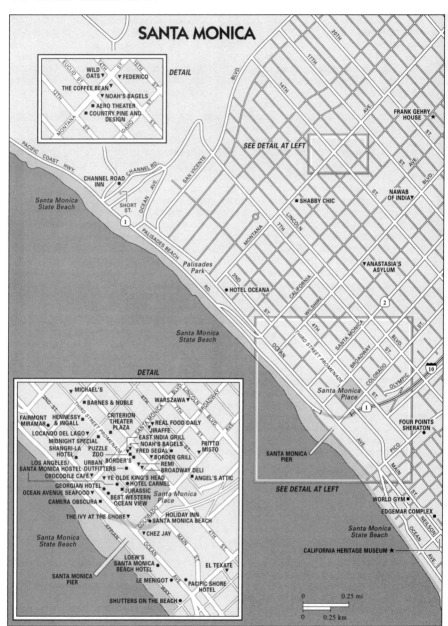

SANTA MONICA

DETAIL

EUCLID ST.
WILD OATS ▼
14TH ST.
15TH ST.
▼ FEDERICO
THE COFFEE BEAN ■
12TH ST.
▼ NOAH'S BAGELS
■ AERO THEATER
■ COUNTRY PINE AND DESIGN
MONTANA ST.
IDAHO ST.

20TH
17TH
14TH
BLVD.
AVE.

FRANK GEHRY HOUSE ★

PACIFIC COAST HWY.

CHANNEL RD.
OCEAN AVE.
SAN VICENTE

SEE DETAIL AT LEFT

CHANNEL ROAD INN

ST.
AVE.
BLVD.

NAWAB OF INDIA ▼

Santa Monica State Beach

SHORT ST.

1

PALISADES BEACH

■ SHABBY CHIC

LINCOLN

MONTANA
7TH

ST.

Palisades Park

RD.

2ND
CALIFORNIA
WILSHIRE

▼ ANASTASIA'S ASYLUM

● HOTEL OCEANA

ST.

2

Santa Monica State Beach

4TH
SANTA MONICA
BLVD.
ST.

OCEAN
ST.
Third Street Promenade
BROADWAY
COLORADO ST.
OLYMPIC

10

Santa Monica Place

1

FOUR POINTS SHERATON

SANTA MONICA PIER

PICO
MAIN ST.

SEE DETAIL AT LEFT

WORLD GYM ■

EDGEMAR COMPLEX ■

Santa Monica State Beach

CALIFORNIA HERITAGE MUSEUM ★

OCEAN
NEILSON
AVE.

DETAIL

▼ MICHAEL'S
2ND ST.
Third Street Promenade
BLVD.
LINCOLN
BROADWAY
■ BARNES & NOBLE
WARSZAWA ▼
FAIRMONT MIRAMAR
HENNESSY & INGALL
CRITERION THEATER PLAZA
▼ REAL FOOD DAILY
JIRAFFE ▼
EAST INDIA GRILL ▼
LOCANDO DEL LAGO ▼
MIDNIGHT SPECIAL
▼ NOAH'S BAGELS
FRITTO MISTO ▼
SHANGRI-LA HOTEL
PUZZLE ZOO
FRED SEGAL ■
▼ BORDER GRILL
LOS ANGELES/ SANTA MONICA HOSTEL
URBAN OUTFITTERS
■ BORDER'S
REMI ▼
BROADWAY DELI ■
CROCODILE CAFÉ ▼
YE OLDE KING'S HEAD ●
■ ANGEL'S ATTIC
GEORGIAN HOTEL ●
● HOTEL CARMEL
OCEAN AVENUE SEAFOOD ▼
JURASSIC
BEST WESTERN OCEAN VIEW
CAMERA OBSCURA ■
Santa Monica Place
THE IVY AT THE SHORE ▼
COLORADO
HOLIDAY INN ● SANTA MONICA BEACH
4TH ST.
CHEZ JAY ●
Santa Monica State Beach
ZEPHYR
OCEAN
MAIN ST.
EL TEXATE ▼
SANTA MONICA PIER
LOEW'S SANTA MONICA BEACH HOTEL
LE MERIGOT ●
AVE.
WAY
PACIFIC SHORE HOTEL
SHUTTERS ON THE BEACH ●

0   0.25 mi
0   0.25 km

© AVALON TRAVEL PUBLISHING, INC.

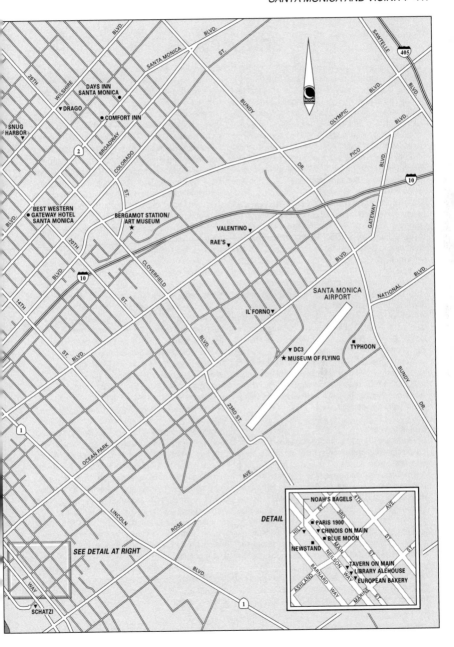

DAYS INN
SANTA MONICA

▼ DRAGO

● COMFORT INN

SNUG
HARBOR ▼

BEST WESTERN
● GATEWAY HOTEL
SANTA MONICA

BERGAMOT STATION/
ART MUSEUM ★

VALENTINO ▼

RAE'S ▼

IL FORNO ▼

SANTA MONICA
AIRPORT

TYPHOON ■

▼ DC3
★ MUSEUM OF FLYING

SEE DETAIL AT RIGHT

▼ SCHATZI

DETAIL

NOAH'S BAGELS

● PARIS 1900
▼ CHINOIS ON MAIN
■ BLUE MOON

NEWSTAND

▼ TAVERN ON MAIN
■ LIBRARY ALEHOUSE
▼ EUROPEAN BAKERY

LIFE'S A BEACH

Along with the cult of celebrity, palm trees, and fancy freeways lined with bright shiny cars, the beach is among L.A.'s most universal symbols. The beach—as in The Beach, the youthful social creation of 1950s Los Angeles—is all about sun-bleached attitude, arcane sports, superficial sexuality, and salt-water-scented steel guitar. And The Beach lives on today, with each youthful summer's new toast-brown crop happily packed into the stucco sameness of beachfront sardine cans. Pale imitations turn up in places such as Florida and Australia, but Los Angeles invented The Beach.

And so the slang phrase "Life's a Beach" takes on genuine meaning in Los Angeles County, where the sunny sands of L.A. lore now suffer a relentless assault of urban ills, all related to the southstate's relentless population growth. Too much traffic and too little parking. Garbage. Graffiti. Alcohol- and gang-related violence. Water pollution. Still a localized problem, ocean water pollution levels are generally decreasing because of improved sewage treatment facilities and greater citizen awareness about the effects of dumping toxic substances into sewers and storm drains. Yet if pollution is disappearing, in some places so is the sand—in a natural southward drift exacerbated by the construction of breakwaters and harbors and, inland, by damming the rivers and streams—and associated sediment flow—that would otherwise replenish the sand supply. These days, maintaining the bay's wide white beaches is additional engineering work.

Fun in the Sun

Santa Monica Bay, the shallow white sand-fringed coastal indentation harboring most of L.A. County's beaches, was once one of the world's richest fishing areas. Those days are gone, after a half-century's relentless flow of industrial chemicals and other toxic wastes from land to sea. But the bay is slowly getting cleaner—clean enough that, in the 1990s, even porpoises returned. According to L.A.'s **Heal the Bay**, to swim safely avoid obvious pollution "problem areas" (usually posted as no-swim areas), steer clear of all storm drains (most of which are *not* signed or otherwise identified, so heads up), and don't swim for at least three days after a rainstorm. For the latest information on the environmental health of Santa Monica Bay's beaches, contact: Heal the Bay, 2701

Ocean Park Blvd., Ste. 150, Santa Monica, CA 90405, tel. (310) 581-4188, fax (310) 581-4195, www.healthebay.org. A nonprofit coalition working to achieve fishable, swimmable, and surfable coastal waters—with pollution levels within standards set by the federal Clean Water Act—Heal the Bay publishes an **Annual Beach Report Card** for L.A. County's beaches, also available on the website, complete with maps and charts of both dry (summer) and wet weather pollution measurements. To support its work, Heal the Bay sponsors occasional fundraisers and community events and also sells T-shirts, sweatshirts, and other items. Go ahead and buy one. It's a very good cause.

But if alcohol—even beer or wine—is a central cause in your life, forget about enjoying it at the beach. It is illegal to drink alcohol on public beaches (and at city and county parks), a zero-tolerance policy that can get you booted off the beach and cost you $50 to boot if you're cited. The get-tough beach booze policy is in response to astronomical increases in alcohol-related assaults, drownings, and post-beach car wrecks. (And what lifeguards say is law at the beach. Unless you want to leave the beach earlier than planned, think twice before defying them.)

You can sunbathe, though. And swim, fairly safely where lifeguards are on duty. And surf, body surf, and boogie-board. And play very competitive beach volleyball. And picnic. Particularly north of Malibu and near the Palos Verdes Peninsula you can tide-pool. Pier and surf fishing are permitted at most piers and many public beaches. Catches include spotfin and yellowfin croakers, corbina, and barred and walleyed perch. And you can run with the grunion, which come ashore to spawn on certain nights in March, June, July, and August. When the annual grunion runs are announced in local media, hundreds of people suddenly arrive after dark, flashlights in hand, ready to gather the slippery silver fish by hand—or try to. (For more on the annual grunion run, see Grunion Run Free, So Why Can't We? in the Orange County chapter.) Or you can watch sunsets, often spectacularly colorful given L.A.'s polluted air.

Deep-sea fishing expeditions—in search of barracuda, kelp bass, bonito, halibut, mackerel, rockfish, and sheepshead—and winter whalewatching excursions depart from Paradise Cove, Santa Monica,

Marina del Rey, Redondo Beach, San Pedro, Long Beach and other spots along the coast. Contact local visitor bureaus and chambers of commerce for excursion boat suggestions.

Beach Practicalities
Beach curfews are fairly standard, with beaches usually closed to the public midnight-6 a.m.; some parking lots also close at midnight, though others close at sunset. No parking is allowed on most stretches of Pacific Coast Hwy. (PCH) 10 p.m.-6 a.m.; PCH parking is free, where you can find it. For public parking lots, available at many beaches, weekday rates range from $2 to $7 per day (rates usually higher on weekends). Pay close attention to parking signs to avoid the unhappy experience of finding that your car has been locked up for the night or, worse yet, towed and impounded. It'll be mighty expensive to get it out of car jail.

For general beach information, stop by or call the **Los Angeles County Department of Beaches and Harbors Visitor Information Center,** 4701 Admiralty Way in Marina del Rey, tel. (310) 305-9545 or (310) 305-9546, fax (310) 822-0119, http://beaches.co.la.ca.us. For questions about specific beaches, call **L.A. County Lifeguard Headquarters** at (310) 577-5700. (Be patient if you're put on hold; rescues and other beach emergencies take precedence. And these folks do get busy, particularly in summer and on balmy weekends.) For general beach weather and tides (recorded), call (310) 457-9701. For a beach-by-beach surf report, updated three times daily by L.A. County lifeguards (this is a revenue-generating service), call (900) 844-9283. Make reservations for state park and beach campgrounds along the L.A. County coast, mentioned elsewhere in this chapter, through ReserveAmerica at toll-free tel. (800) 446-7275.

and Point Vicente as "bay," not open sea, and therefore subject to state regulation.

The beachfront running south of the Santa Monica Pier to Venice Beach was Chandler's mythic if slightly sleazy "Bay City." Stretching along the pearly sand north of the pier was early L.A.'s notorious "Gold Coast," where sumptuous spreads included the fabulous beach homes of Marion Davies (mistress of William Randolph Hearst) and others of Hollywood's party-hearty set. Almost all that remains of that era is the Sand and Sea Club at 415 PCH, once servants' quarters for the Davies mansion. A few surviving Gold Coast-era mansions have been similarly reincarnated, or walled off from public view. Other old-timers hang on, or try to. Santa Monica's landmark 1926 Breakers Beach Club—more recently reborn as the Sea Castle Apartments, then vacated because of severe damage inflicted by the 1994 Northridge earthquake and miscellaneous fires—was gutted by fire in 1996. Now the Sea Castle has been reincarnated yet again as a complex of 178 luxury apartments.

AT THE BEACH

Chances are good that you'll recognize **Palisades Park,** even if you've never been there. Most people have seen it hundreds of times on TV and in the movies—the classic leisurely-L.A.-at-the-beach setting, where lovers stroll at sunset against a backdrop of swaying palms and rustling eucalyptus, and everybody's grandparents walk the poodle or gather on park benches to gossip and play friendly games of chess. This popular film location, a narrow 14-block-long strip of lawn, benches, and trees perched atop steep, eroding bluffs overlooking the Santa Monica Pier, the beach, and the Pacific Ocean, is often visitors' first stop, given the convenient location of the Santa Monica Visitor Center here. At the Senior Recreation Center, nearby at 1450 Ocean Ave., tel. (310) 458-8644, is Santa Monica's own **Camera Obscura,** a tourist attraction more popular in the 18th- and 19th-century U.S. than today. Perhaps the optical "illusion" created by a camera obscura—rendering reality so clearly—is simply too real in these days of virtual reality. (Ask for the key and see for yourself. Small fee.) An oddity that dates to Leonardo da Vinci's notebooks and 11th-century Arab scholarship, the Camera Obscura is composed of prisms, lenses, and mirrors installed in a darkened chamber that allows light in through an opening no larger than a pinhole. The camera then projects a reversed (upside-down) image of the outside world (in this case, a swath of the coastline) onto a white circular disk along the chamber's opposite wall.

Lots of fun awaits families at the revamped and extended Santa Monica Pier, especially on weekends and in the summer.

DONNA CARROLL

Once reality has been virtually established, head for the beach. The good news is, the wide strand of dazzling white sand at **Santa Monica State Beach** is one of the busiest beaches around in summer—which is bad news if you're looking for privacy. It's also bad news if the ocean is temporarily off-limits because of pollution, an ongoing storm-drain and urban-waste disposal problem generated throughout L.A. and an issue that raises the ire of residents around Santa Monica Bay. (For the possibility of wide open spaces at the beach, head north beyond Malibu or south to the world-famous weirdness of Venice Beach, where most of the action is along the Boardwalk. For general beach information and a bay pollution update, see Life's a Beach above.) A day at the beach includes the usual seeing-and-being-seen scene, sometimes a rousing round of beach volleyball, and performance artists—California clowns. Not to mention those overgrown lifeguard chairs-cum-musical instruments—let's call them "wind" instruments—installed as public art projects between the pier and Pico Boulevard. On a breezy day the aluminum pipes atop artist Douglas Hollis's 18-foot-tall *Singing Beach Chairs* catch the wind and make odd tunes.

Santa Monica Pier and Pacific Park
Santa Monica's mild-mannered municipal pier and pleasure pier survived the usual ups and downs of tourist-town life largely unscathed until the 1970s, when civic warfare raged over the fate of the dilapidated piers, then slated for de-

molition by the Santa Monica City Council. The slow work of rebuilding the past began—an effort slowed still further by 1983's disastrous storms, which dismembered major sections of the pier. Work on the municipal pier was completed in 1990, including restoration of the two-story **Hippodrome** (with its 1922 Looff carousel, featured in *The Sting* and other films), the original arcades, and the old bumper cars. Much of the rest of the pier is lined with restaurants, fast fooderies, and curio shops. Fishing, once a favorite recreational activity at the pier, is no longer recommended because of bay pollution. Special events, including weekend **music concerts,** annual **Cirque du Soleil** performances, and multiple new amusements, now attract the crowds.

At the foot of the rebuilt and expanded pier complex is the new **children's playground** designed by Moore, Rubell, and Yudell, featuring an assortment of kiddie-style carnival rides and a huge dragon's head carved from river-washed granite that "snorts" a soothing, safe mist (water).

Santa Monica's new pier extension is Pacific Park, tel. (310) 260-8744, www.pacpark.com. Pacific Park harks back to the good ol' days of California amusement piers, until now an extinct species on the West Coast. Major new attractions here include an ocean-view roller coaster—the five-story-tall **Santa Monica West Coaster**—and California's only giant ferris wheel, the **Pacific Wheel.** In addition to more pedestrian rides for the kids, a thrill for adults is the **Sig Alert** bumper-car adventure.

Other new pier attractions include the **UCLA Ocean Discovery Center,** (310) 393-6149, an interactive aquarium-style education center with tidepool and "under the pier" marine life exhibits.

Admission to both the municipal pier and Pacific Park is free, but there is a charge for various attractions. Prices for most of the new Pacific Park amusement rides are in the $1-3 range, for example. The amusement park is open daily 10 a.m.-10 p.m. in summer, with an abbreviated schedule in winter.

South Bay Bicycle Trail

What better way to see the beach, and the Los Angeles beach scene, than by bike? The South Bay Bicycle Trail, accessible at any point along the route, runs south from the white sand of Will Rogers State Beach along local beaches to Torrance, with a strategic inland detour only to bypass the harbor at Marina del Rey. Highlights along the way include the dazzling Santa Monica beach scene, wild and wacky Venice Beach, complete with rollerbladers run amok and muscle-bound Muscle Beach, and the tony trendiness of Marina del Rey's boating brigade. And the swaying palms, sun, sand, and fresh ocean air. Oh sure, a few ecstasy-assassinating intrusions await along the way, especially toward the South Bay, where the L.A. Department of Water and Power's power plant smokestacks and incessant LAX jet traffic detract from an otherwise postcard-perfect setting. But you can pull over to rest your angst at municipal piers and other key attractions, including Marina del Rey's boat harbor and the shop-happy King Harbor at the north end of Redondo Beach.

Since most people in greater Los Angeles don't make it to the beach until close to noon, early morning is a great time for a bike ride. (This being the beach side of a very urban area, avoid being on the bike path after dark.) The paved bike path runs a total distance of approximately

---

VIEW FROM THE EDGE: THE MUSEUM OF JURASSIC TECHNOLOGY

If you bring the kids, prepare for possible whining. Prepare for the fact that they'll think you tricked them. They'll think you offered an afternoon in Jurassic Park (as in ***Jurassic Park*—The Ride**) when instead, you offered them something equally amazing from "real life"—a view of the world as seen from the edge of science.

The motto of West L.A.'s strange Museum of Jurassic Technology is "nature as metaphor." This particular metaphorical interpretation of the natural world is most intriguing. Half the exhibits are real—or seem to be—and the others are highly unlikely, from the mounted horns, spore-eating ants, and fruit-stone carvings to the superstitions exhibit. An enormous hit in 1996 was the exhibit of "microminiature" creations by Soviet-Armenian violinist Hagop Sandaldjian, including likenesses of Disney's Goofy and Snow White and the Seven Dwarfs, even Pope John Paul II, all mounted on sewing needles and visible only through microscopes. Some of Sandaldjian's works are still on display in the Churchy Marrin Annex, where at last report the main exhibit was **Garden of Eden on Wheels: Selected Collections from Los Angeles Area Mobile Home and Trailer Parks.** On exhibit in the Coolidge Pavilion, opened in September 1999, is **The World is Bound with Secret Knots: The Life and Works of Athanasius Kircher, S.J., 1602-1680.**

In the opinion of Lawrence Weschler, author of *Mr. Wilson's Cabinet of Wonder,* the Jurassic rekindles one's sense of wonder while undermining "the sense of the authoritative" normally extended to museums. But the museum's curator suggests you leave even that preconception at home. Wonder is as wonder does—metaphorically speaking.

The Museum of Jurassic Technology, in a nondescript storefront in Culver City's historic Palms District, on Venice Blvd. four blocks west of Robertson Blvd. (directly across from Bagley), is open Thursday 2-8 p.m. (sometimes from noon) and Fri.-Sun. noon-6 p.m. (closed major holidays and the first Thursday in May). Suggested donation is $4 adults, $2.50 children (under age 12 free), students, and seniors). For more information, contact: Museum of Jurassic Technology, 9341 Venice Blvd., Culver City, CA 90232, tel. (310) 836-6131, fax (310) 287-2267, www.mjt.org.

20 miles; even a biking beginner can make the one-way trip in two hours or less. Start early and stop for breakfast before heading back. Bike rental establishments are available all along the beachfront bike path.

MORE SANTA MONICA ATTRACTIONS

Extremely hip Santa Monica claims its share of attractions from yesteryear, including the **Angel's Attic** museum of antique dollhouse miniatures, toys, trains, and dolls housed in a beautifully restored 19th-century Victorian at 516 Colorado Ave., tel. (310) 394-8331, open Thurs.-Sun. 12:30-4:30 p.m. Admission is $6.50 adults, $4 seniors, and $3.50 children under age 12. With reservations, you can enjoy tea, lemonade, and cookies on the veranda (for an additional $7.50 per person). The **California Heritage Museum,** 2612 Main St., tel. (310) 392-8537, open Wed.-Sun. 11 a.m.-4 p.m., is housed in an 1894 American colonial revival mansion designed by Sumner P. Hunt and later moved to the unlikely intersection of Ocean Park Ave. and Main. The home once belonged to Roy Jones, son of city founder John Jones. The first floor has been restored and furnished in typical Santa Monica style of three eras: the 1890s, the 1910s, and the 1920s. The second floor serves as a gallery for historical exhibits and shows by contemporary local artists. The city's archives are also housed here. General admission is $3, students and seniors $2.

Museum of Flying

Airplane fans and fanatics will enjoy this colorful museum, starring the *New Orleans,* the first plane to fly around the world—one of two opencockpit Douglas World Cruisers that made the trip in 1924. Douglas Aircraft Company planes are well-represented throughout, in fact, which is only fitting since the museum sits on the site of the original Douglas Aircraft Company, precursor to McDonnell Douglas. (Don't miss the original Donald Douglas boardroom on the second floor—a fabulous 22-seat round table with a built-in illuminated globe as its centerpiece.) Almost all planes here have been meticulously restored and are still flight-ready, including the

red-and-yellow checkerboard *Harvard II* T-6 trainer and the *Dago Red* P-51 Mustang, the world-record speeder clocked at 570 miles per hour in 1983. Video kiosks on the first floor, where most planes are displayed, show most of the planes in action. More history of flight awaits on the second floor, largely dedicated to Donald Douglas memorabilia. The museum's theater, film and video archives, and the Donald Douglas library are on the third floor. The museum also boasts a great little book and gift shop. While you're in the general neighborhood, tour architect Gregory Ain's **Mar Vista** futuristic housing subdivisions, built for Douglas Aircraft workers in the late 1940s, on the 3500 blocks of Meier, Moore, and Beethoven Streets. Like Douglas aircraft, some houses have survived in near-original condition.

For lunch and dinner, the adjacent, very good **DC3 Restaurant,** tel. (310) 399-2323, serves upscale food with an ethnic twist: menu options include inventive appetizers like DC3 seafood wontons, soups, salads, and entrees like blackened swordfish or Napoleon of salmon filet.

The Museum of Flying is at home in a hangar at 2772 Donald Douglas Loop N, on the north side of the Santa Monica Airport, one block south of Ocean Park Blvd. via 28th Street. The museum is open Wed.-Sun. 10 a.m.-5 p.m. At last report admission was $7 adults, $5 seniors and students with ID, and $3 for children ages 3-17. For more information, call (310) 392-8822 or check www.museumofflying.org.

Santa Monica Museum of Art

Santa Monica cool extends to its arts scene, which succeeds in being as cutting edge—or just "edge," as they say in these parts—as any in L.A. To start your personal search for edge art, try the Santa Monica Art Museum, tel. (310) 586-6488, previously at home in the Edgemar complex along Main St. and in new digs among various local edge galleries at Bergamot Station, 2525 Michigan Ave., Bldg. G-1. Also surrounded by architect's offices and working artists' studios, the museum exhibits modern and contemporary sculpture and painting by relatively unknown artists and also presents performance and video art. Call for information on current shows and events. At last report the museum was open Tues.-Sat. 11 a.m.-6 p.m. and for

Friday night "salons," closed Sunday and Monday and also Thanksgiving, Christmas, and New Year's Day. But call to verify hours, as well as current exhibit information, because the schedule is somewhat fluid. Admission is by suggested donation—$3 for most folks, $1 for artists.

Bergamot Station

Near the freeway and the intersection of 26th St. and Olympic Blvd., Bergamot Station—named for the old Red Car trolley station that stood here until the 1950s—at 2525 Michigan Ave., building G-2, tel. (310) 829-5854, is the city's latest cutting-edge arts locale. This contemporary but still fairly low-rent conglomeration of more than two dozen fine-arts galleries features almost six acres of "arts space." Not to mention new digs for the Santa Monica Museum of Art or plans for Hiro Yamagata's 35,000-square-foot **Situation,** an arts space designed to focus on "the state of being that is present only in the moment."

Bergamot Station is typically open Wed.-Sun. 11 a.m.-6 p.m. and Fri. 11 a.m.-10 p.m., but various galleries may schedule events at other times.

For a more comprehensive listing of local galleries, inquire at the visitor center—and pick up a current copy of the *L.A. Weekly.*

Frank Gehry House, Other Local Architecture

Speaking of art and artists: In what sort of home would an acclaimed local architect live? Take a drive by 1002 22nd St. (at Washington) and see for yourself. Noted for his innovative designs, Santa Monica's own Frank O. Gehry transformed this house, once a small Dutch-style cottage, into a highly unusual example of the architectural arts. Using low-cost materials such as sheet metal and chain-link fencing for which Gehry has become famous, his domestic creation was included in a *Los Angeles Magazine* article titled "Nightmare Neighbors." The Gehry House so enraged one local architecture critic that he encouraged his dog to do his "duty" on Gehry's lawn, making his own symbolic statement.

For a traditionally pleasing local architectural tour, take a look at local **John Byers** homes. A prolific architect of the late 1920s, Byers built an enclave of attractive Spanish colonial houses on lovely La Mesa Dr., just off San Vicente, in the shade of gigantic Moreton Bay fig trees planted by Santa Monica's earliest residents. Look for some of Byers's homes at 2021, 2034, 2101, 2153 and 2210 La Mesa Drive, and for his one-time office nearby at 246 26th Street.

Third Street Promenade

When you're done with the public parade on and around the pier, try this one. Santa Monica's Third Street Promenade has become one of L.A.'s hottest "destination streets," an easygoing shopping and entertainment district just blocks from the beach. A pedestrian-only adventure, Third St. between Wilshire and Broadway is an intriguing mix of old and new Santa Monica, of

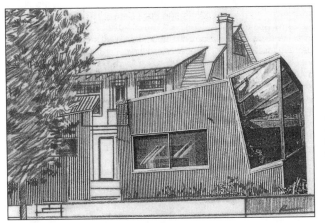

Architect Frank Gehry's house, adorned with sheet metal and chain-link fence, outraged some of his neighbors.

kitsch and chic and chain stores, all decked out with palm trees, topiary sculpture, pushcart vendors, and street entertainers. Beyond the boutiques and funky stores here, diversions and entertainment along these three blocks include great bookstores, galleries, multiplex movie theaters, coffeehouses, and good restaurants.

Start with the bookstores. Long-running **Midnight Special,** 1318 Third St. (between Arizona and Santa Monica), tel. (310) 393-2923, specializes in books and magazines and literature, politics, and poetry (regular readings scheduled). Equally revered **Hennessy & Ingall,** 1254 Third (just north of Arizona), tel. (310) 458-9074, is *the* stop for books and publications on architecture, art, and design. The chains are here, too. The neighborhood boasts a **Barnes & Noble,** 1201 Third (at Wilshire), tel. (310) 260-9110, and a **Borders** bookshop, music store, and café at 1415 Third (between Santa Monica and Broadway), tel. (310) 393-9290.

Equally fun, though, are the eccentricities of some of the truly eccentric shops—assuming they haven't been displaced by the chain-sponsored commerce rapidly increasing here. Always entertaining: the **Urban Outfitters** warehouse at 1440 Third, tel. (310) 394-1404, stark in its ersatz post-Apocalypse decor and specializing in consumer goods for nonconsumers and **Jurassic**'s museum-grade fossils at 131 Broadway (at Second). One of the most intriguing toy stores around is **Puzzle Zoo,** 1413 Third, tel. (310) 393-9201, where you might find the limited edition Goddess of the Sun Barbie and the Kasparov electronic chess partner.

Then try the eateries—**Johnny Rockets** tel. (310) 394-6362, for burgers; the more uptown **Broadway Deli** on the promenade tel. (310) 451-0616; and exceptional Italian **Remi,** tel. (310) 393-6545, sibling to New York's Remi. And the ubiquitous **Starbucks.**

At the south end of the promenade, just across Broadway, is **Santa Monica Place,** for still more shopping. This three-story enclosed Frank Gehry-designed mall has an open, breezy feel, thanks to its ocean-facing windows and skylights. Among other claims to fame—including **Ann Taylor**'s classic women's clothing, **Williams-Sonoma** housewares, and **The Body Shop**'s soaps and lotions—Santa Monica Place starred in Arnold Schwarzenegger's *Terminator 2.*

Just north of the Third St. action is **Fred Segal,** 500 Broadway (at Fifth), tel. (310) 393-2322, the hippest of hip department stores, companion to the original store on Melrose. Divided into a series of stylish boutiques for men, women, and children, this is a great people-watching place even if you'll never afford the freight. Fred Segal seems to attract affluent and hip teens and people who look like recording artists (and may well be). Look for the spectacular half-price sales each September—though even then Fred Segal is quite expensive.

Best for Third Street Promenade parking, by the way, are the various public lots along Fourth, reasonably inexpensive. But if you're just here for a quick stroll, the parking lot at Santa Monica Place is free for a stay under three hours (small flat fee in the evening).

Montana Avenue

Long considered one of Santa Monica's most stylish shopping streets, Montana Ave. between Lincoln Blvd. and 17th St. (near Brentwood north of Wilshire) is *very* Westside, an expensive blend of chic shops and nosh stops. **Federico,** 1522 Montana, tel. (310) 458-4134, is a long-running local favorite, selling Native American, Mexican, and silver jewelry. **Country Pine & Design,** 1318 Montana, tel. (310) 451-0317, is famous for its unique items for the home. **Shabby Chic,** 930 Montana, tel. (310) 453-0985, is a popular local furnishings shop. Stop at **The Coffee Bean** at 1426 Montana, tel. (310) 453-2093, for delicious coffee and baked goods. Or try the casual **Wolfgang Puck Café** at 1323 Montana Ave. (at 14th), tel. (310) 393-0290. And while you're in the neighborhood, see what's playing at the independent **Aero** theater, 1328 Montana, tel. (310) 395-4990, which starred in the movie *Get Shorty.*

Strolling Main Street

A stroll along Main always affords an intriguing introduction to the real Santa Monica and its unique cultural combination of chi-chi and cheap. Though Main stretches south from Pico Blvd. on the north to Rose Ave. in Venice Beach, particularly popular for shopping and dining is the area between Ocean Park and Rose, where the classic old-brick buildings attract both the trendy and the traditional. You'll know you've gone too far, and drifted south into eccentric Venice, once you see sculptor Jonathan Borofsky's clownish three-story-tall "ballerino" looming above Main like the crazed stage creation of some mad puppeteer—a huge ballerina's body, en pointe, crowned by a sad clown face complete with five-o'clock shadow.

Most famous along Main are some of Santa Monica's most famous restaurants, including Arnold Schwarzenegger's **Schatzi**, 3100 Main St., tel. (310) 399-4800, and Wolfgang Puck's **Chinois on Main**, 2709 Main St., tel. (310) 392-9025. But the many other main attractions include Joe Gold's **World Gym**, 2210 Main, tel. (310) 450-0080, where Arnold Schwarzenegger got serious about working out (he still drops by occasionally) and where the clients include a list of big and bulky world champs as long as your arm.

Or try **Newsstand**, 2726 Main St., tel. (310) 396-7722, boasting L.A.'s best selection of magazines and newspapers. Another hit is **Blue Moon**, 2717 Main, tel. (310) 450-7075, something of a French-styled *parfumerie* selling sunglasses on the side. **Paris 1900**, 2703 Main St., tel. (310) 396-0405, recycles the glad rags of the rich circa 1900-1930. Just down the way is cybersoul sister to Almost Paradise in Long Beach and Cyber Java in nearby Venice Beach, Santa Monica's own worldly **World Cafe**, 2820 Main, tel. (310) 392-1661 (www.worldcafela.com), where neon-lit hieroglyphics, Captain Nemo dining-room decor, and Mexican patio umbrellas set the stage for sophisticated drinks, snacks, and cyberchat.

Until recently home to the Santa Monica Museum of Art, the **Edgemar** complex along the 2400 block of Main was designed by Santa Monica architect Frank O. Gehry (Mr. Chain-Link-and-Sheet-Metal himself) and built on the site of the old Edgemar Egg Company. Poke around here to find more galleries and shops and eateries.

VENICE: WESTSIDE BOHEMIA

Abbott Kinney had a dream. That dream became a vision, a utopian plan, then an obsession. What was Abbott Kinney's dream? He built an exotic seaside resort here, patterned after the great Italian city (complete with canals), and he expected the grandeur of his creation to spark an early 20th-century American cultural renaissance and create an international image of Los Angeles as sophisticated Mediterranean city. Kinney's plans never quite succeeded. But in recent decades his vision has been revisited, as Venice has become one of L.A.'s avant-garde outposts of the arts and architecture. Yet, as in Kinney's day, the hedonistic eccentricities of Venice Beach and along its two-mile Ocean Front Walk are still the community's main attractions.

For some local events and referral information, call the **Venice Area Chamber of Commerce** at (310) 396-7016. For current visitor information, call up Venice on the Internet at www.venice.net/chamber, or contact the L.A. visitor bureau at (213) 689-8822, www.lacvb.com.

Abbott Kinney's Dream

After making his millions selling Sweet Caporal cigarettes, Abbott Kinney came to California to build his personal Venice. In 1904 Kinney bought 160 acres of marshland just south of Santa Monica for his "Venice of America" seaside resort. He drained the marsh, re-creating it as a canal-laced landscape, and then hired architect Norman F. Marsh to design Venice, patterned after its namesake Italian city. The first phase of Kinney's dream included an elaborate Italianate business district, its first first-class hotel—the St. Mark Hotel, patterned after St. Mark's Cathedral in Venice, Italy—and a grand 2,500-seat public auditorium out on the new pier.

The city's three-day opening gala, a veritable circus of enthusiasms, began on July 4, 1905. More than 40,000 potential buyers toured Venice's 19 miles of 40-foot-wide canals in gondolas imported for the occasion, like their gondoliers, from Italy. Others paraded down city streets on the backs of camels. In the auditorium out on the pier, Sarah Bernhardt performed *Camille* during a black-tie performance, backed by the Chicago Symphony Orchestra. Enthralled tourists came and went, and many bought property. Hundreds of lots at the beach along Venice's new canals were sold, some for the then-astronomical price of $2,700 each—twice the going price of Beverly Hills real estate. Yet construction was slow. A number of modest craftsman-style homes were built along Venice's canals, but not the grand rococo palaces that Kinney had envisioned.

Abbott Kinney soon concluded that most people were more interested in the pleasures of sun and surf than in high culture, and in 1907 he built a grand casino. Buoyed by that success, Venice soon featured the world's largest amusement park, with 10-cent camel rides, two roller coasters—including the famous Race through the Clouds—and a dance pavilion. He imported the Ferris wheel from Chicago's 1893 Columbian Exposition. He built an Arabian-style bathhouse with hot salt water, and a bowling alley, a skating rink, a shooting gallery, and an aquacade. Abbott Kinney's Venice became a metaphor for what L.A. would become—a unique combination of popular and classical cultures.

Yet for all its successes, large and small, Abbott Kinney's dream seemed to depend on him, personally, for its continuing existence. After he died in 1920, Venice soon hit the skids—largely because of the demise of L.A.'s electric trolley system and the increasing popularity of the automobile. (Venice's location, far from a major thoroughfare, put the resort at a competitive disadvantage for the tourist trade.) Then small oil wells and derricks dotted the landscape throughout Venice, petroleum-based goo blackened the canals and beaches, and the remaining tourists left town. Kinney's dream became a nightmare. Soon plagued by storms, fires, and political scandals, Venice residents voted in the 1920s to annex themselves to the city of Los Angeles. Most of the city's increasingly murky canals were filled in because of public health concerns. Abbott Kinney's dream died.

Of Arts and Eccentricities

In a style Abbott Kinney could never have imagined, the dream of Venice as cultural mecca did revive. Drawn to the community's relatively low rents and unique, vaguely European style—including the arched bridges over the canals—in the 1950s beatniks and other bohemians arrived to establish L.A.'s latest avant-garde enclave, quickly followed in the 1960s by Summer of Love devotees and in the 1970s by working artists. Many well-known L.A. artists have studios in Venice, lured by the (once) affordable rents, eccentric ambience, and proximity to the beach. In the 1980s Venice—certain parts of Venice—became a chi-chi address for cool-conscious Westsiders. The latter turn of events has spawned some interesting architectural styles

as well. Since building codes here are more lenient than in adjacent beach towns, architects solved the problem of postage stamp-size lots by building multilevel structures—and then sometimes finishing them with intentionally shabby exteriors to discourage burglars. Though beset in recent years by seemingly uncontrollable gang violence and other urban ills, Venice still proudly parades its eccentricities. A community where million-dollar homes stand next to run-down shanties, Venice has even cleaned up its canals.

Trouble in Bohemia

Venice has had its share of troubles in recent years. Black vs. Latino gang wars over the crack-cocaine trade broke out throughout the region—in Oakwood, Santa Monica, Mar Vista, and Culver City—in 1994, and 17 people, many of them innocent bystanders, were cut down in the crossfire. Outraged Venetians pushed for a greater L.A. police presence and protection—and got it, at least during the day, when tourists were afoot. But chaos still reigned at night. In a well-planned fit of vigilante justice, early one morning a group of ski-masked residents wielding sledgehammers demolished four permanent concrete picnic tables that had consistently attracted a bad element to the Boardwalk during the wee hours. Awakened by the racket, watching from their windows, the neighbors cheered. Subsequently, almost all of Los Angeles cheered.

Despite Venice's considerable bad press, most neighborhoods here are vital, with genuine and genuinely strong cross-cultural community connections. Most of the community is united against gangster violence. For haven't-got-a-clue visitors and tourists, however, recent local history suggests due caution. If at all in doubt about one's street savvy, stick to the well-trodden tourist path along the Venice Boardwalk—and plan to blow this pop stand well before nightfall. The after-dark scene can get mighty unsavory, not just here but elsewhere along the L.A. coast where major boulevards or freeway exit/on-ramp routes dead-end at the beach. Such strategic spots tend to attract gangsters with an eye to making a quick getaway, as necessary.

Ocean Front Walk and Venice Beach

Abbott Kinney's gaudy amusement park, the Coney Island of the West for two decades, is

local Venice flavor

long gone. But its spirit lives on. Unless the kids have led a truly sheltered suburban life—or perhaps especially if they have—they'll probably enjoy the human zoo that Venice's Ocean Front Walk, known locally as the Venice Boardwalk, has exhibited in recent years. Watch 'em watch Rastafarians and bikini-clad babes on in-line skates blithely dodge bicyclists, baby strollers, and bug-eyed tourists. Robert Gruenberg, the Venice Boardwalk's famous chainsaw juggler, hung up his gas-powered Sears Craftsman in 1994, alas. But there's plenty more circus available here—rollerskating swamis, fire-eaters, palmists, and tarot card readers along with dancers, singers, and comedians. Sidewalk merchants sell T-shirts, sunglasses, hats, clothing, jewelry, crystals, and posters along the Venice Boardwalk, which stretches for two miles along Ocean Front Walk between Ozone Ave. and Washington Street. Venice's oceanfront promenade and pier have been undergoing major renovations—a $5.5 million project scheduled for completion in summer 2000—adding new entertainment areas, lighting, and even pagodas.

Once the kids are satiated with the street performance, nudge them on to Muscle Beach, "the pit" where muscle people get pumped on open-air weightlifting. (This Muscle Beach is no real relation to the original Muscle Beach of Jack LaLanne fame, just south of the Santa Monica Pier; old-timers say it was originally known as Mussel Beach—after those well-muscled bivalves.) Among the endless snack stands, best

bet for meat lovers is **Jody Maroni's Sausage Kingdom,** 2011 Ocean Walk, tel. (310) 306-1995, famous throughout L.A. for its fabulous all-natural links—from sweet Italian to Yucatán chicken. But if the Boardwalk's crowded sidewalk cafés seem just too crowded, beat a retreat to the **Rose Cafe,** 220 Rose Ave., tel. (310) 399-0711, Venice's coolest coffeehouse, bakery, deli, and neighborhood café since almost forever. While in the neighborhood, die-hard shoppers should stop by **DNA Clothing Company,** 411 Rose, tel. (310) 399-0341, one of L.A.'s best outlet shopping spots, featuring top-drawer clothing and jeans for women and men at bargain-basement prices.

Then do the beach, which doesn't get nearly the attention—or crowds—as do the Venice Boardwalk or Santa Monica State Beach just north. Venice Beach is a *beautiful* beach, a broad belt of palm-dotted white sand stretching up coast and down and out into the surf. The huge concrete **Venice Pier** at the foot of Washington Blvd.—still closed at last report, pending reconstruction—was a fairly unromantic contemporary creation that was quite popular with skaters and pier fishers.

Other Venice Sights

Like Abbott Kinney, start with the canals and then move on to the arts. The **Venice Canals**—six survive—are just minutes east of the busy beach scene, in a fairly upscale neighborhood bordered on the south by Washington St., on the north by S. Venice Blvd., on the west by Pacific Ave., and on the east by Ocean Avenue. After decades of political battles, the surviving canals were restored in 1993. **Grand** and **Eastern** Canals run north-south, and **Carroll, Linnie, Howland,** and **Sherman** Canals run east-west. Since the neighborhood's transportation system is largely dependent on canal and footpath, only the Grand Canal—along Pacific Ave.—can be reached by road.

The Grand Lagoon, or where it once was, can be found at Windward Ave. and Main Street. Now a concrete traffic circle, this originally was where all of the canals met. A few of the original **Venice arcades,** patterned after those surrounding the Piazza San Marco in Venice, Italy, remain at St. Mark's Place, 67-71 Windward.

Yet don't wander too far. Not many blocks from the canals is the now-notorious neighborhood known as **Oakwood.** Plagued with drug and gang activity, Oakwood is known locally as the Demilitarized Zone or DMZ. While living in this neighborhood, according to L.A. artistic lore, actor Dennis Hopper was inspired to direct the film *Colors.*

More inspiring for most people are local arts venues. The **Beyond Baroque Literary Arts Center** is housed in Venice's onetime city hall, 681 Venice Blvd., tel. (310) 822-3006. Both small press-oriented bookstore and library, this is also the place for poetry readings and other local literary events. Next door, in the 1923 art-deco old Venice Police Station, is the **Social and Public Art Resource Center (SPARC),** 685 Venice Blvd., tel. (310) 822-9560, www.sparcmurals.com, where a block of jail cells has been converted into an art gallery. Yet SPARC is considerably more famous for its work in preserving and promoting mural art projects throughout Los Angeles. Stop by for some local suggestions—SPARC knows everything about public murals, and there are endless people's-art displays throughout the area, some dating to the 1960s—or sign on for one of the group's guided mural tours, an unforgettable and enlightening experience.

Come in May and meet local artists during the popular annual **Venice Art Walk,** an open studios-style arts event and silent auction that's also a primary fundraiser for the Venice Family Clinic. The Venice Art Walk is usually scheduled for the fourth Sunday in May. Or shop for art anytime. Long-running local galleries include

L.A. Louver, 45 N. Venice Blvd., tel. (310) 822-4955, famous for its representation of artists Wallace Berman, David Hockney, and Edward Kienholz, among many others.

More affordable for most folks are the arts, crafts, and antique shops along the 1200-1500 blocks of **Abbott Kinney Boulevard**—until 1990 known as W. Washington Blvd., a source of endless confusion, what with Washington Blvd. and Washington St., too. Now it's one of L.A.'s relaxed new "destination" streets. To get started, try **Toni's Arte,** 1426 Abbott Kinney Blvd., tel. (310) 399-2122. For pizza, stop by **Abbott's Pizza Company,** 1407 Abbott Kinney Blvd., tel. (310) 396-7334, famous for its funky atmosphere and killer pizzas. Abbott's even offers breakfast and dessert pizzas. Right next door is **Abbott's Habit** coffeehouse, tel. (310) 399-1171, serving the real thing by the mug or by the pound, along with bakery items.

Marina del Rey,
Playa del Rey, and Playa Vista

Undeveloped coastal wetlands until 1968, when the county of Los Angeles set about the business of draining one of the coast's last remaining wetlands and building the largest man-made small-craft harbor in the world, Marina del Rey is largely boat harbor—and boats, boats, boats. When row after row of life-at-the-beach-themed apartment houses and condominiums were built here in the late 1960s and early '70s it was only natural, given the area's proximity to LAX, that planeloads of stewardesses, stewards, and other unattached airline employees would move in to share the neighborhood with the retirees and yachties—which won Marina del Rey its reputation as preferred port for swinging singles. Redevelopment plans—allowing 22-story high-rise "residential towers," apartment buildings, and hotels while ignoring the need for new parks and other genuine public access—will likely change the character of the neighborhood yet again.

Marina del Rey offers few attractions beyond upscale hotels (including a Ritz-Carlton) and fairly corporate entertainments. For tourist kitsch there's always **Fisherman's Village,** 13755 Fiji Way, tel. (310) 823-5411, an odd replication of a New England fishing village featuring gift shops, restaurants, South Seas foliage, and a view of the Marina channel. From here, you can sign on for a dinner cruise with **Hornblower Dining Yachts,** tel. (310) 301-6000, or sportfishing and winter whalewatching tours with **Marina del Rey Sportfishing,** tel. (310) 822-3625.

According to the annual "beach pollution report card" issued by Heal the Bay, always-popular **Mother's Beach** on Palawan Way within the marina is not recommended for swimming—especially for kids—because of continuing harbor pollution. A better bet by far is **Dockweiler State Beach,** sometimes known locally as Playa del Rey, below the bluffs along the harbor's face, with little at-the-beach clutter but clean restrooms, lifeguards, and some grassy picnic areas. Dockweiler stretches from Venice south to the mouth of the harbor and beyond, on the harbor's south side. Water quality is generally good at Dockweiler, except near storm drain outlets and, south of the harbor, near the outfall for the Hyperion sewage treatment plant.

For more information about the area, contact: **Los Angeles County Dept. of Beaches and Harbors,** Visitor Information Center, 4701 Admiralty Way, Marina del Rey, tel. (310) 305-9546, www.beaches.co.la.ca.us.

Just south of Marina del Rey and east of the beach, surrounding the intersection of Lincoln and Jefferson Boulevards, is a surviving 1,000-acre section of the once-wildlife-rich **Ballona Wetlands,** owned at one time by eccentric billionaire Howard Hughes, who built his famous *Spruce Goose* here. The fate of the Ballona Wetlands—how much should be preserved or restored, how, and where—is an ongoing battle in one of L.A.'s latest development wars. **Playa Vista,** as this new city along the Westchester bluffs will be called, was slated to become the city's latest "Hollywood" if the new **Dreamworks SKG** film studio and other proposed commercial and residential developments proceeded as planned. However, progress on the project was delayed when environmentalists protested the destruction of the area's wetlands. Dreamworks subsequently pulled out of the project.

STAYING IN SANTA MONICA AND VICINITY

Santa Monica and other coastal enclaves are typically well-booked and most expensive on weekends, though midweek and seasonal specials are possible. More significant, for true budget travelers and families, is the fact that in addition to the ubiquitous luxury options, Santa Monica and other coastal communities feature a variety of hostels and other inexpensive and midrange motel options.

LOW-RENT SANTA MONICA STAYS

The best bargain around is the 200-bed Hostelling International-American Youth Hostels **Los Angeles/Santa Monica Hostel,** 1436 Second St. (between Santa Monica Blvd. and Broadway), Santa Monica, tel. (310) 393-9913, www.hiayh.org or www.hostelweb.com/losangeles. This is a budget traveler's bonanza, even though prices here are a bit higher than in other area hostels. What you get for the difference is an exceptional value, just two blocks from the beach and pier and, in the other direction, one block from the lively Third Street Promenade.

The Santa Monica International is at home in a four-story onetime town hall, an aged brick and dark wood building complete with historic common room (once a saloon), full-service travel store, laundry and kitchen, library, TV room, large open-air courtyard, bicycle storage, and lockers. Most of the rooms are dormitory style with two or four beds per room (linen rental, small extra fee), though private rooms are available for couples. Bathrooms are shared. Free airport shuttle service and organized area tours (extra) are also offered. This hostel is understandably popular, so make reservations (by phone, fax, or mail, with credit card confirmation) well in advance. Budget.

Venice, just blocks south of Santa Monica, offers other hostel-style accommodations. Also inquire at the visitor center for lower rent suggestions.

MIDRANGE SANTA MONICA STAYS

As elsewhere, midrange accommodations in Santa Monica comprise a somewhat confusing category. Most of the options listed here offer

Affordable stays are just blocks away from the beach in Santa Monica.

aters, and restaurants. Though this is largely a families-and-couples kind of place, from mid-September through May the Hotel Carmel offers college students (with IDs) a hefty rate discount. Expensive-Premium, with rates $80-155.

Up on a hill three blocks inland from the ocean is the very comfortable 309-room **Four Points Sheraton** 530 Pico Blvd., tel. (310) 399-9344 or toll-free (888) 627-8532 for central reservations, www.fourpoints.com, featuring two heated pools, in-room coffeemakers and the usual comforts, even free airport shuttle service. Premium-Luxury ($139-175), sometimes dropping to Expensive in the off season. For a similar deal close to the beach and pier, try the **Holiday Inn Santa Monica Beach,** 120 Colorado Blvd., tel. (310) 451-0676 or toll-free (800) 465-4329 for central reservations, www.holidayinn.com, with swimming pool and the usual amenities. Luxury ($159-239).

Other possibilities include the **Best Western Ocean View Hotel,** 1447 Ocean Ave., tel. (310) 458-4888, or toll-free (800) 452-4888. Premium ($139-259), but often Expensive in the off season. And the 168-room **Pacific Shore Hotel** near both the beach and Main Street at 1819 Ocean Ave., tel. (310) 451-8711 or toll-free (800) 622-8711, which features an exercise room, pool, sauna, jacuzzi, and sundeck. Some rooms have ocean views. Expensive-Luxury ($109-169).

Not near the Beach

Well away from the beach but fairly affordable—particularly in the off season—and quite comfortable is the **Best Western Gateway Hotel Santa Monica,** 1920 Santa Monica Blvd., tel. (310) 829-9100 or toll-free (800) 528-1234 (central reservations), www.bestwestern.com, which offers free beach shuttle service, full fitness facilities, and in-room video games among its many amenities. Premium ($109-139). Other possibilities in the same vicinity include the **Comfort Inn,** 2815 Santa Monica Blvd., tel. (310) 828-5517 or toll-free (800) 228-5150, www.comfortinn.com, where a stay includes free morning newspaper and breakfast and amenities include in-room coffeemakers and refrigerators plus family-size heated pool, and the **Days Inn Santa Monica,** 3007 Santa Monica Blvd., tel. (310) 829-6333 or toll-free (800) 591-5995, www.daysinn.com. Both are Expensive-Premium ($87-150).

"moderate" prices throughout the year. Yet during the off season or in slow years, and/or with the right discount or package deal, some of Santa Monica's "classic" and high-rent offerings can become quite affordable (see other listings below). It often pays to inquire. Many of the following offer student, senior citizen, AAA, and/or other discounts or specials.

Notable near the Beach

A notable deal by Santa Monica standards is the **Hotel Carmel** near the HI-AYH hostel at 201 Broadway (at Second St.), tel. (310) 451-2469, or toll-free (800) 445-8695. This is one of Santa Monica's grande dames, well-preserved and still quite attractive after all these years, with lovely lobby and basic rooms with ceiling fans-a best bet for budget-conscious families bound for the beach. The Hotel Carmel is also a jump away from the Third Street Promenade's premier people-watching and shops, movie the-

CLASSIC SANTA MONICA STAYS

Shangri-La Hotel

Santa Monica's 1939 Shangri-La Hotel, 1301 Ocean Ave. (at Arizona Ave.), tel. (310) 394-2791 or toll-free (800) 345-7829, www.shangri-la-hotel.com, is a local favorite, an art-deco ocean liner of a building looming large from a corner berth. Popular with writers and more eccentric movie stars, the Shangri-La has no pool and no bar, but this small 55-room hotel does offer evocative elegance overlooking Palisades Park, a nice continental breakfast and free morning newspaper, and afternoon tea. Most of the tasteful rooms—successfully restored to their original deco glory, but with color TVs and cable—feature full kitchens and sundecks; most have ocean views. Luxury ($145-420).

Georgian Hotel

Another art-deco gem, the historic eight-story Georgian near the pier at 1415 Ocean Ave., tel. (310) 395-9945 or toll-free (800) 538-8147, www.georgianhotel.com, was lovingly restored to its 1933 ambience in 1993. Most of the 84 rooms and suites offer ocean views, along with contemporary comforts including coffeemakers, refrigerators, honor bars, and cable TV (free movies); some have microwaves. No air conditioning, usually unnecessary here. Breakfast is served in the dining room every morning, afternoon tea and cocktails on the veranda. Lunch and dinner are also available. Luxury ($210-475).

Hotel Oceana

Another likely spot to spot the occasional off-duty celebrity is the very cool Hotel Oceana a few blocks north of Wilshire at 849 Ocean Ave. (between Montana and Idaho Aves.), tel. (310) 393-0486 or toll-free tel. (800) 777-0758, www.hoteloceana.com. Tasteful rooms overlook the courtyard pool; others offer ocean views. Basic amenities include kitchens, in-room coffeemakers, microwaves, cable TV (free movies). Air conditioning is rarely needed so close to the ocean, so the Oceana doesn't have it. Though technically this is a pretty high-rent class act, if you opt for one of the few studio apartments—and if you come in the dead of the off season, say, February—a stay here might be almost affordable, about half the usual tab; rates are higher but still more reasonable in spring and fall. Continental breakfast included. Luxury ($250-600).

Channel Road Inn Bed and Breakfast

A real find for B&B fans, the Channel Road Inn just east of Pacific Coast Highway is just a mile or two north of the Santa Monica Pier and Third St. Promenade. The inn is an inviting shingle-sided 1910 colonial revival period piece moved to this site in the 1960s and then transformed into a 14-room inn in the late 1980s. Most rooms and suites offer ocean views, some feature fireplaces, and all have private baths. Just a block from the beach, technically just beyond Santa Monica city limits, the inn also offers a friendly introduction to neighborhood life. Bikes are available if you feel like exploring, or soak up the ambience from the bayview hot tub. A good deal including full breakfast and home-baked muffins. For more information or reservations, contact: Channel Road Inn, 219 W. Channel Rd., tel. (310) 459-1920, www.channelroadinn.com. Premium to Luxury ($150-325).

MORE HIGH-RENT SANTA MONICA STAYS

Fairmont Miramar Hotel

Santa Monica's classic classy hotel is downtown's historic Miramar, "where Wilshire meets the sea," now a Fairmont, 101 Wilshire Blvd., tel. (310) 576-7777 or toll-free tel. (800) 325-3535, www.fairmont.com. Onetime private mansion and Santa Monica playground for Hollywood stars including Humphrey Bogart, Greta Garbo, and Betty Grable, the Miramar still requires an entrance; visitors drive in through impressive wrought-iron gates and circle the huge Moreton Bay fig. Time and a $33 million restoration continue to transform the Miramar. The once-palatial grounds have been subdivided by progress, and the hotel's fabled courtyard bungalows, surrounding the lush jungle, pool, and patio just beyond the bright and spacious lobby, have been replaced with 31 snazzy new ones. Yet the Miramar abides, with a sophisticated international atmosphere both rarified and relaxed. The hotel's historic charms are most apparent in the older brick Palisades wing, overlooking Palisades Park, yet rooms in the more contemporary Ocean Tower come with almost aerial views. Amenities abound, including in-room safes, coffeemakers, and honor bars, color TVs with cable (free movies), countless little luxuries, a wonderful on-site restaurant, and full fitness facilities. Luxury, with rates $249 and up.

Le Merigot Beach Hotel

Santa Monica's newest upscale hotel, just a block from the beach at 1740 Ocean Ave., Le Merigot is a contemporary take on the city's art deco sensibilities, from the potted palms and blond woods in the lobby to the day-at-the-beach pastel colors and artful furnishings in the 175 guest rooms—some with views. Yet the attitude here is European—so L.A.—and extends to the hotel's **Cézanne** restaurant, **Café Promenade,** and **Le Troquet** bar. For more information or reservations, call (310) 395-9700 or toll-free (877) 637-4468, www.lemerigotbeachhotel.com. Luxury, with rates $279-459.

Loews Santa Monica Beach Hotel

Before Shutters opened its shutters onto the Santa Monica sands, the fairly new Loews Santa Monica Beach Hotel, 1700 Ocean Ave. (between Pico and Colorado), tel. (310) 458-6700 or toll-free (800) 235-6397 (central reservations), www.loewshotels.com, had the notable distinction of being L.A.'s only beachfront hotel. Though this hotel isn't exactly *on* the beach, it's certainly close enough. The stunning contemporary lobby, colored in soft tones of seafoam green, peach, and sand and accented by potted palms and bold wrought-iron grillwork and glass, somehow evokes L.A.'s most intriguing Victorian-era architecture, downtown L.A.'s famed Bradbury Building. The same general idea—inspiring skylit enclosures—carries over to the indoor-outdoor pool area overlooking the beach. Many of the hotel's 350 rooms and 35 one- and two-bedroom suites, luxuriantly decked out and featuring the usual amenities, overlook the beach. Other attractions include complete fitness facilities (personal trainers available), the adult-supervised Splash Club for vacationing families, the sophisticated French Provincial **Lavande** restaurant, tel. (310) 576-3181, and the casual **Ocean Cafe.** Luxury, with rates $310 and up.

Shutters on the Beach

Definitely on the beach, Shutters on the Beach, 1 Pico Blvd. (just off Ocean Ave.), tel. (310) 458-0030 or toll-free (800) 334-9000, www.shuttersonthebeach.com, looms over the sand like an overgrown beachhouse—shutters and all—by design. Shutters, with its 198 rooms and suites right on the beach, was designed in the spirit of Southern California beach homes and resorts of the 1920s and 1930s. Otherwise, everything is cutting-edge contemporary, light, open, and vaguely reminiscent of plein-air watercolors. Rooms are small but attractive—note that some "partial view" rooms barely spy the sea—with the usual luxury amenities, marble bathrooms, and large jacuzzi tubs. Sliding shutter doors open onto private patios or balconies, providing the "shutters" of the hotel's name. Other pluses include two good on-site restaurants, the outstanding **One Pico,** tel. (310) 587-1717, and the casual café **Pedals,** both the **HandleBar** and an attractive lobby lounge, large pool and patio areas, spa, full fitness facilities—even a rental service for Santa Monica essentials, from bikes, in-line skates, and volleyball nets to swim fins and children's beach toys. Unfortunately for determined ocean swimmers, the hotel's beach sits at the mouth of the Pico-Kenter storm drain, with its attendant bacterial "danger" signs from time to time—so heads up if you actually brave the waters. Luxury, with rates $340 and up.

STAYING IN VENICE AND VICINITY

People's Stays: Venice Hostels

The **Cadillac Hotel,** 401 Ocean Front Walk (at Dudley), tel. (310) 399-8876, isn't the Cadillac of hotels. Venice isn't the Cadillac of beach towns, for that matter, and not a totally comfortable area after dark. But if the wild and wacky rush of Southern California humanity is your scene—people-watching from sidewalk cafés, dodging the in-line skaters and cheap trinket stalls on the way to the wide, wide expanse of white sand—then the art-deco Cadillac Hotel is one place to park yourself come nightfall. Most of the rooms (30) are private (just the basics), some with private bathrooms. Moderate-Expensive ($69-120). The remainder offer hostel-style dorm accommodations, with four beds to a room and bathrooms down the hall. Inexpensive. Other features: sundeck, sauna, gym, laundry and storage facilities, even a pool table. Free airport shuttle service.

Other nearby hostels run by InterClub include the **Venice Beach Hotel,** 25 Windward Ave., tel. (310) 392-3376, and the **Airport Hostel,** 2221 Lincoln Blvd., tel. (310) 305-0250, both of which offer dormitory-style and private rooms. Budget to Inexpensive.

Venice Beach House

The Venice Beach House is an L.A. rarity—a bed and breakfast. This one is a rarity among rarities, however, since this early 20th-century home also happens to be a graceful craftsman bungalow just steps from the beach and a block from the Venice Canals. North of Washington Blvd. and west of Pacific Blvd. on one of Venice's "walk streets" (onetime canals, long since filled in), the Venice Beach House features nine well-appointed period rooms with antiques and wicker. The Pier Suite comes with a sitting room, fireplace, king-size bed, and ocean view; smaller, less expensive garden-view rooms share bathrooms. Expensive-Luxury. For reservations, contact: Venice Beach House, 15 30th Ave., Venice 90291, tel. (310) 823-1966.

Other Venice Stays

Quite nice in Venice's motel category is the **Inn at Venice Beach** just two blocks from the beach at 327 Washington Blvd., tel. (310) 821-2557, toll-free tel. (800) 828-0688, or www.mansion-inn.com. Expensive-Premium ($99-149). Fun and funky in Venice, with spacious and attractive rooms, is the **Marina Pacific Hotel and Suites** just a block from the beach and otherwise smack-dab in the middle of everything at 1697 Pacific Ave., tel. (310) 452-1111 or toll-free (800) 421-8151, www.mphotel.com. Premium-Luxury ($119-169).

Staying in Marina del Ray

Reigning monarch of the South Bay hotel scene is **The Ritz-Carlton, Marina del Rey,** 4375 Admiralty Way, Marina del Rey, tel. (310) 823-1700 or toll-free (800) 241-3333, www.ritzcarlton.com, which here serves as scenic backdrop for yachts and yachters. The usual ritzy amenities abound, thick terrycloth robes and every other imaginable comfort, plus full fitness and business facilities. The crisp, classic decor includes French doors in most rooms, opening out onto balconies overlooking the boat harbor. Dining options include the excellent **Terrace Restaurant** and the less formal **Pool Café.** Luxury.

More fun and much more affordable for most people, though, is the **Best Western Jamaica Bay Inn** on Mother's Beach at 4175 Admiralty Way, tel. (310) 823-5333 or toll-free (888) 823-5333, www.bestwestern-jamaicabay.com, the only place around actually *on* the beach. (Because of harbor pollution, however, ocean swimming here is not advisable.) Rooms are large, with either terraces or balconies, and bathrooms are a bit small. Pleasant beachfront café. Expensive-Luxury ($89-189).

EATING IN SANTA MONICA AND VICINITY

PEOPLE'S EATS

People's Eats: Farmers' Markets
If you time things right, load up on fresh fruits, vegetables, fabulous flowers, and other essentials at the big-deal **Santa Monica Certified Farmers' Market,** held year-round at Arizona Ave. between Second and Third Sts. on Wednesday 9:30 a.m.-2 p.m. (bring quarters for area parking meters) and on Saturday 8:30 a.m.-1 p.m. Also on Saturday, there's an open-air Farmers' Market at the intersection of **Pico Blvd. and Cloverfield,** 8 a.m.-1 p.m. On Sunday there's still another, at **Victorian Heritage Square** at Ocean Park Blvd. and Main St., scheduled 9:30 a.m.-1 p.m., the fun here including pony rides and other kid's stuff.

Otherwise, for natural foods, cosmetics, and such, there's always the **Wild Oats Community Market,** 1425 Montana Ave. (at 15th St.), tel. (310) 576-4707, a link in the chain that genuine co-ops tend to disdain.

People's Eats near the Pier
A real deal for authentic Mexican is colorful **El Texate Oaxacan Restaurant,** 316 Pico Blvd. (at Fourth St.), tel. (310) 399-1115, which at first glance looks something like a surfer bar. The treasure here is the wide selection of rich mole sauces, blends of roasted chiles, seeds, nuts, and spices so perfect with chicken (start with the *coloradito,* or "little red"). Entrees include enchiladas, *chiles rellenos, empañadas,* and pizzalike *clayudas* and *memelas.* If you're not in the mood for margaritas or beer, wash everything down with *tejate*—the traditional summer drink created from cornmeal, chocolate, and walnuts. El Texate is open daily 9 a.m.-11:30 p.m. Also always a people's favorite: the colorful **Crocodile Cafe,** 101 Santa Monica Blvd. (at Ocean), tel. (310) 394-4783, the onetime site of Santa Monica's dignified old-school French Belle-Vue restaurant. The terribly hip Crocodile is so popular that it's not the best choice if you'll need to be somewhere soon. Otherwise, the fare is usually worth the wait—especially for the money. Some appetizers, such as the chicken tacos, make a meal. Or order the grilled romaine salad, dressed with yogurt and spicy pecans. Or the Santa Fe or "almost cheeseless" pizzas. And any of the Pasadena Baking Company desserts. It's open daily for lunch and dinner (until midnight). Full bar.

For an extreme stylistic alternative, a good bet for families, head for **Ye Olde King's Head Restaurant and Pub,** 116 Santa Monica Blvd. (between Ocean and Second St.), tel. (310) 451-

Head to the Third Street Promenade for a collection of eateries.

JUSTINE HILL

1402, which has been serving English specialties for more than 25 years—everything from fish and chips and bangers and mash to royal tea. Entertainment provided by warm beer and darts. It's open for lunch and dinner daily, for high tea weekdays only.

Numerous people's possibilities lie along the Third Street Promenade, an easy stroll from the beach. For an array of dining options, check out the food court at the **Criterion Theater Plaza,** 1315 Third St., where nothing on any menu is more than $12 (most choices are much less). Among the star here is **Wolfgang Puck Express,** tel. (310) 576-4770, for fast reasonably priced pastas, pizzas, and salads. This and other fast fooderies here are open daily 11 a.m.-11 p.m.

People's Eats Not near the Pier

For a very good, very inexpensive bagel breakfast, the place is ubiquitous **Noah's New York Bagels,** 1426 Santa Monica Blvd. (between 14th and 15th Sts.), tel. (310) 587-9103; there is another Noah's at 2710 Main St. (near Hill), tel. (310) 396-4339. A best bet for vegetarians, with the kitchen open into the wee hours seven days a week, is **Anastasia's Asylum,** 1028 Wilshire Blvd. (at 11th St.), tel. (310) 394-7113, a fun and funky art gallery/coffeehouse/restaurant serving tofu lasagna along with open-tonight nights. For organic vegetarian food, the place is **Real Food Daily,** 514 Santa Monica Blvd., tel. (310) 451-7544, fresh and unusually good, from *seitan* fajitas to vegetable sushi and eggless Caesar and Peruvian quinoa salads. Good desserts, too. It's open Mon.-Sat. for lunch and dinner. Exceptional vegetarian fare is available at **Nawab of India,** 1621 Wilshire Blvd. (at 17th St.), tel. (310) 829-1106, noted for its home-style Northern Indian lunch buffets (brunch buffet on weekends).

One of the best for all-American breakfast is **Rae's,** 2901 Pico Blvd. (at 29th St.), tel. (310) 828-7937, a real-deal 1950s diner where, most weekends, people are only too happy to line up and wait. (No credit cards.) Rae's is open daily for breakfast, lunch, and dinner. Or head to breakfast-anytime **Snug Harbor,** 2323 Wilshire Blvd. (between 23rd and 24th Streets), tel. (310) 828-2991, where diner standards, including the dinner salad, are more sophisticated than you'd expect. Omelettes star at breakfast—available anytime—along with fresh-squeezed orange and grapefruit juices. Snug Harbor is open for breakfast, lunch, and dinner on weekdays, for breakfast and lunch only on weekends.

Given the endless possibilities along Main, one of the better choices is among the least expensive—attractive **Tavern on Main,** 2907 Main St. (at Ashland Ave.), tel. (310) 392-2772, serving contemporary ($5) takes on all-American standards in nouveau 1930s style. If you've been frugal while wandering Main, blow a few bucks at local sweets and dessert shops, including the nearby chocoholic shrine **European Bakery,** 2915 Main, tel. (310) 581-3525, famous for creating wonderful brownie biscotti, luscious cakes, and almost everything else in sight from Valrhona chocolate. For some after-dinner cheer, the **Library Alehouse,** 2911 Main, tel. (310) 314-4855, is a veritable library of Pacific Northwest microbrews on tap, where the various "taster specials" allow you to sample five three-ounce samples. (You can also "read" on the patio.) Some might prefer splurging on a Salty Dog—grapefruit juice and vodka served margarita style in a salt-rimmed glass. The place to get 'em is the **Galley,** 2442 Main, tel. (310) 452-1934, Santa Monica's oldest surviving dark bar and surf and turf restaurant.

A bit fancy for cheap-eats freaks but quite affordable for the genre is Italian **Il Forno,** 2901 Ocean Park Blvd. (between 29th and 30th Streets), tel. (310) 450-1241, a best bet for antipasti, pastas, and pizza. It's noisy, friendly, reliable, and open weekdays only for lunch, Mon.-Sat. for dinner.

And there's a fabulous new Italian in town—**Fritto Misto,** 601 Colorado Ave. (at Sixth St.), tel. (310) 458-2829, busy, unbelievably reasonable, and well worth the long waits. Owner Robert Kerr makes his own pasta, ravioli, and sausages fresh daily. House specialties include such things as "Atomic" pasta—two seared Cajun-seasoned chicken breasts served on a bed of chile linguine and tossed with peppers and onions in a chipotle cream sauce. Not to mention some marvelous vegetarian selections. Here, you can also create your own specialty by selecting pasta, sauce, and favorite add-ins. The wine list includes boutique wines listed at half the price other restaurants charge. Such a deal! Don't miss the delectable desserts. Open for lunch and dinner.

RICHER PEOPLE'S EATS

Richer People's Eats near the Pier

Santa Monica's legendary high-class diner and sawdust-floored dive is **Chez Jay,** just steps from the pier's entrance at 1657 Ocean Ave. (between Pico and Colorado), tel. (310) 395-1741, once a favorite coastal hangout for regulars Ava Gardner, Vivien Leigh, Frank Sinatra, and Willie Shoemaker. The private booth in back is sometimes called the Kissinger Room, because Henry Kissinger often hid out there with his dates. According to local lore, this is also the place Daniel Ellsburg—working next door at the Rand Corporation think tank—passed the Vietnam War-era *Pentagon Papers* to a reporter. Things are a bit less exciting these days. Continental Chez Jay, the name alone an uncanny spoof on L.A. food snobbery, serves such things as exceptional steaks, lobster thermidor, steamed clams, and shrimp curry, most everything accompanied by the restaurant's famous side dish—baked potatoes, bananas, and sour cream. Dessert is "nonfattening homemade organic cheesecake." Chez Jay is open for lunch on weekdays, dinner nightly.

Almost always worth the dent in the pocketbook: **Ocean Avenue Seafood,** 1401 Ocean Ave. (at Santa Monica Blvd.), tel. (310) 394-5669, a stylish yet classic oyster bar and seafood restaurant featuring modern art, pastel walls, dark wood paneling, and an indoor-outdoor bar. Classics such as the New England clam chowder, crab cakes, and blackened catfish are always available—but the ever-changing list of fish and fish dishes, usually offering more than two dozen choices on any given day, keeps everyone surprised. It's open daily for lunch and dinner (brunch on Sunday).

Even more expensive is **The Ivy at the Shore,** almost facing the pier from 1541 Ocean Ave. (at Colorado), tel. (310) 393-3113. This fashionable faux beach shack, complete with bamboo, breezy patio seating (glassed-in and heated on nippy evenings), and tropical-themed bar, is notable along palm-lined Ocean. Like its stylish older sibling near West Hollywood, this Ivy specializes in California-style adaptations of no-nonsense regional Americana—crab cakes, shrimp, and other seafood specialties, Cajun

prime rib, Louisiana meatloaf, pizzas, and pastas. Simpler at lunch are the sandwiches and salads (don't forget the Maui onion rings). The Ivy's Caesar salad is famous throughout Los Angeles. Almost equally famous: delectable desserts. Ivy's is open daily for lunch and dinner (brunch on Sunday); closed major holidays.

Richer People's Eats near the Promenade

Start searching for possibilities where almost everyone else does, along the Third Street Promenade. Prime for people-watching—one of those only-in-L.A. places—is the spacious, light, and airy **Broadway Deli,** 1457 Third St. (at Broadway), tel. (310) 451-0616, where the proprietors don't do a particularly good job with traditional New York deli standards. (But hey, this is California.) The Broadway does just about everything else, though, from superb French bistro fare to reinvented American comfort food, including macaroni and cheese and killer burgers. (Not necessarily impressive: the blintzes, pastrami sandwiches, lox, and other Jewish deli standards, though they are served here.) Put together an unforgettable picnic lunch or dinner by ordering takeout from the deli counter. Or settle into a booth, and order just about anything your heart desires—from blueberry pancakes and French toast to Caesar salad, beef stew, chicken pot pie, pizza, mushroom barley soup, and tapioca crème brûlée. This is a fairly pricey place, but if you order judiciously you'll still be able to afford the gas—or plane fare—to get home. Espresso bar, fresh-baked breads and bagels, delightful desserts. Astonishing foodie shop, too, which you'll get to know well while you wait (no reservations). The Broadway Deli is open daily 7 a.m.-midnight, 8 a.m. until 1 a.m. on Friday and Saturday nights.

But don't overlook dignified yet relaxed **Remi** also near Broadway, at 1451 Third St. (near Broadway), tel. (310) 393-6545. Though cousin to New York's Remi, this restaurant's influences come all the way from Venice—the one in Italy, not the eccentric upstart just down the beach. The jaunty nautical theme here launches all kinds of classics, such as grilled quail, roasted stuffed pork chops, rack of lamb, and some stunning seafood pastas. The perfect finish for a perfect meal: the house-made tiramisu. Remi is open daily for lunch and dinner (closed for

Christmas and New Year's Day). If Remi's not possible, other choices include **Locando del Lago,** 231 Arizona Ave. (between Second and Third Sts.), tel. (310) 451-3525, noted for dishes from Lombardy. The patio is also a plus.

One block east of the Promenade and well worth the detour is the flamboyant dinners-only **Border Grill,** 1444 Fourth St. (near Broadway), tel. (310) 451-1655. The bizarre and bright faux folk art-splashed walls serve as apt accompaniment to the stunning food served here—everything the creation of chefs Mary Sue Milliken and Susan Feniger, who apply their formal training in classical French cooking to the bold flavors of coastal Mexico and Central America. You can make a meal of the appetizers, the green corn tamales, the *panuchos* and *platano empañadas* stuffed with cheese and black beans, thereby keeping the total tab almost reasonable. Then again, you'd miss the entrees—such things as grilled skirt steak marinated with garlic, cilantro and cracked pepper, served with moros, avocado-corn relish and Roma tomatoes, sautéed rock shrimp with toasted *ancho* chiles, and marinated breast of chicken served with onion-orange salsa. And for dessert, how about a slice of Oaxacan chocolate cake? Full bar. The Border Grill is open nightly for dinner (closed major holidays).

Richer People's Eats Elsewhere

Culinary stars at the Santa Monica Airport include stylish California-style **DC-3** at the Museum of Flying, 2800 Donald Douglas Loop N. (just off 28th St., south of Ocean Park Blvd.), tel. (310) 399-2323, which serves grilled seafood, chicken, and such, along with a hip and lively singles bar scene during happy hour and on weekends; live jazz some nights. The romantic runway views at sunset are thrown in for free. During the week, DC-3 provides a valuable public service for parents. While adults sit down to peaceful fixed-price dinners on Tuesday, Wednesday, and Thursday nights, the kids are whisked away, stuffed with pizza, and otherwise entertained on their own supervised museum tour. Another high-flyer at the airport is the exotic Pacific Rim **Typhoon,** 3221 Donald Douglas Loop S. (at Airport Ave.), tel. (310) 390-6565, where the "pilot's pillar" showcases the pilot's licenses of some of the famous and infamous who have flown in for the pan-Asian fare. Universal favorites include Thai coconut

chicken curry, Indonesian stir fry, and fried catfish. Up on the roof, weather permitting, is the Asian beer garden.

Main Street has its own stars, including sophisticated California-style **Röckenwaggner** inside the Edgemar complex at 2435 Main (near Pico), tel. (310) 399-6504, the perfect choice for a special weekend brunch. The marinated mushroom salad is one of Chef Hans Röckenwaggner's signature dishes, along with the smoked salmon "short stack" and other exceptional fish and seafood. Röckenwaggner's is open for weekend brunch, lunch Tues.-Fri., and dinner daily.

Warszawa, 1414 Lincoln Blvd. (between Santa Monica Blvd. and Broadway), tel. (310) 393-8831, is the only Polish restaurant in town—and a very good one. In a onetime private home, Warszawa serves hearty dinners in four cozy lace-curtained rooms. Favorite dishes here include the thick pea soup with smoked ham, roast duckling stuffed with herbs, and hunter's stew with sausage, sauerkraut, beef, bacon, and dumplings. For dessert, try the cheesecake with brown sugar crust, the rum torte, or the chocolate cream walnut cake. Warszawa is open Tues-Sun. for dinner.

Rich People's Eats

Known for its fine California cuisine, **JiRaffe,** 502 Santa Monica Blvd. (at Fifth St.), tel. (310) 917-6671, is one of the Westside's most innovative and popular restaurants. The culinary creation of two talented L.A. chefs, Josiah Citrin and Raphael Lunetta, formerly of Jackson's in West Hollywood, JiRaffe serves such things as grilled smoked pork chops with wild rice, smoked bacon, apple chutney, and cider sauce, and whitefish with zucchini and artichokes, fava beans, and sugar snap peas.

Though there's plenty of competition these days, **Chinois on Main,** 2709 Main St. (between Hill and Ashland), tel. (310) 392-9025, is still one of L.A.'s best, and most popular, restaurants. One of the oldest L.A. offspring of celebrity chef Wolfgang Puck and his partner Barbara Lazaroff, Chinois as environment reflects the China of Lazaroff's childhood imagination as painted in celadon green, fuschia, and black, with chinoiserie cranes and dragon on the walls. Carved window frames open onto an orchid garden. Chinois as eatery was originally invented by

Puck in partnership with chef Kazuto Matsusaka; most of the "Chinois Classics" are still here, including the fried catfish with ginger, the tuna tempura sashimi, and the Szechuan pancakes with stir-fried duck, mushrooms, and cilantro. But the menu has also evolved under the guidance of new chef Makoto Tanaka into something simpler and lighter, with lovely vegetable-rich lo mein with soy, honey, and black bean sauce (lunch only) and seared scallops with a sauce of red onions, red wine, cream, and butter. Chinois is noisy, expensive, and sometimes a challenge for reservations—if it's important, try weeks in advance—but it's still one of the best shows in town.

If you can't get reservations at Chinois then try **Valentino**, 3115 W. Pico Blvd. (west of Bundy Dr.), tel. (310) 829-4313, the best Italian restaurant in L.A.; respectable restaurant critics say it's the best in the entire country. This casual, chic dining destination stars lobster cannelloni and other surprising pastas, osso buco, and fish, lamb, rabbit, and veal entrées. As important as the spectacular food is Valentino's wine list, one of the best anywhere—though it did suffer something of a setback when about 20,000 bottles of wine shattered in the 1994 Northridge earthquake. Valentino is open for dinner only, Mon.-Saturday. Very expensive. Reservations mandatory.

Drago, 2628 Wilshire Blvd. (at 26th St.), tel. (310) 828-1585, is Santa Monica's other dashing, elegant Italian, showcasing variations on Sicilian country fare—pastas and risottos, grilled fish and roasted quail. Excellent wine list. It's open for lunch on weekdays, for dinner every night. Reservations required.

Michael's, 1147 Third St. (just beyond the Promenade), tel. (310) 451-0843, was Santa Monica's—and one of L.A.'s—original California cuisine scenes. Owner Michael McCarty, a Cordon Bleu chef, opened his restaurant here in 1979 at the brash age of 26—quickly "blowing L.A.'s mind" with his modern American cuisine. So many of L.A.'s great chefs and restaurant owners worked here at one time or another that in 1995 Michael's hosted a celebrity-chef reunion as a benefit for local museums—an immense success, with L.A.'s best manning personal cooking stations for the benefit of the assembled masses. The snob appeal of a meal at Michael's no longer sells as well as it once

did, even in L.A., and the astronomical prices have dropped by a third. (Still very expensive.) But the patio still beckons as one of the prettiest dining destinations in the city, and McCarty's personal contemporary art collection still enlivens the restaurant's walls. Michael's is open Mon.-Fri. for lunch, Mon.-Sat. for dinner. Reservations wise. There's another **Michael's** in New York City.

For other fine dining possibilities, consider Santa Monica's upscale hotels.

EATING IN VENICE AND VICINITY

Eating In Venice
For all practical purposes the unincorporated Venice district of L.A. is the southern extension of Santa Monica—quite convenient if you've got wheels and typically safe to explore if you stick to the main drags and don't hang out too late after nightfall.

If you're in or around Venice, the premier local people's place is the **Rose Cafe**, 220 Rose Ave. (at Main St.), tel. (310) 399-0711. Not the best restaurant in town and not one of the trendy beachfront venues, in many ways the Rose Cafe *is* Venice. This is where true Venetians hang out, along with an inordinate number of movie people at times and young execs. The style here is beach bohemian, coffee and pastries being the staff of life. For lunch and dinner, consider a salad or simple sandwich. The patio is the place to be.

Figtree's Cafe, right on the Venice Boardwalk at 429 Ocean Front Walk, tel. (310) 392-4937, is another locals' favorite for breakfast. (Get there early on weekends, by 9 a.m., and expect slow service; regulars are liable to nurse their cappuccinos and read the Sunday paper for hours.) Vegetarian dishes are a specialty. Try the wonderful polenta, the hearty French toast on thick-sliced raisin nut bread, or the satisfying Santa Fe omelette. Lunch and dinner fare includes pastas, burritos, tostadas, veggie stir fry, and fresh fish. Figtree's is open daily for breakfast, lunch, and dinner.

A best bet among more expensive Venetian venues lives with Jonathan Borofsky's Emmett Kelly-faced dancer, the sad *Ballerina Clown en pointe* above the intersection of Rose and Main. Trendy **Chaya Venice**, 110 Navy St. (at Main), tel. (310) 396-1179, stars art-deco Asian decor, eclectic Franco-Japanese-California fare, and seafood—curried crab soup, spring rolls, even a sushi bar. It's open weekdays for lunch, Sunday for brunch, nightly for dinner. Even better, though, and a real find for frugal foodies, is **Joe's,** 1023 Abbott Kinney Blvd. (between Westminster and Broadway), tel. (310) 399-5811, where the California-French seafood stars at lunch (Tues.-Fri. only), Sunday brunch, and dinner. One of L.A.'s best restaurants, serving one of L.A.'s best Sunday brunches. Also fairly inexpensive and quite good for Thai is romantic **Siamese Garden** right on Venice's Grand Canal at 301 Washington Blvd. (near Strongs Dr.), tel. (310) 821-0098, open for lunch weekdays only, for dinner nightly.

Eating in Marina del Rey

Aunt Kizzy's Back Porch in the Villa Marina Shopping Center at 4325 Glencoe Ave. (between Washington Blvd. and Mindanao Way), tel. (310) 578-1005, is not exactly what you'd expect in a Marina del Rey mini-mall. Aunt Kizzy's is a fantastic country-style soul food cafe serving hefty portions of crispy fried chicken, catfish, ribs, pork chops, and jambalaya, along with rice and red beans and Southern-style vegetables. Everything here is so good that people are willing to wait and wait to get in—and they do, with nary a complaint. Aunt Kizzy's is open daily

for lunch 11 a.m.-4 p.m., for dinner 4-10 p.m. (closed Thanksgiving and Christmas).

If you just can't wait, another possibility is **Benny's Barbecue,** 4077 Lincoln Blvd. (near Washington), tel. (310) 821-6939, a takeout stand in the marina that's locally famous for dishing out fiery barbecued ribs, lamb shanks, L.A.'s best hot links, beans, and excellent coleslaw. Also beloved in these parts: **Killer Shrimp,** 523 Washington St. (at Ocean), tel. (310) 578-2293. You like the name? You'll like the place. An unassuming storefront in an ugly mini-mall that serves one item only: killer shrimp, flown in fresh daily from Louisiana, prepared in a lively sauce of beer, butter, garlic, secret herbs and spices, and served with crusty French bread just made for dipping.

Considerably more stylish and expensive is the California-style **Cafe del Rey,** 4551 Admiralty Way (at Bali Way), tel. (310) 823-6395, where the eclectic international fare runs from the very simple—pizzas, tasty burgers, niçoise salad—to the surprisingly imaginative. The cafe is open daily for lunch and dinner, also a good choice for Sunday brunch. Another fine-dining choice, especially if you're en route to LAX, is dinner-only **The Library** at the Los Angeles Renaissance Hotel, 9620 Airport Blvd. in Inglewood, tel. (310) 337-2800, famous for its exceptionally well-prepared seafood. For a dining *experience,* the place is **The Dining Room** at the Ritz-Carlton, 4375 Admiralty Way, tel. (310) 823-1700.

UP THE COAST: NORTH OF SANTA MONICA

Heading north from Santa Monica via the Pacific Coast Hwy. (PCH, or Hwy. 1) leads to the pleasures of Ventura, Santa Barbara, and San Luis Obispo Counties and, eventually, the famous Big Sur coast. Well worth exploring on this side of the L.A. County line are some of L.A.'s favorite residential hideouts—Pacific Palisades, Topanga Canyon, and Malibu—and some of its best beaches. Seeming almost as vast as the Pacific Ocean it looms above is the Santa Monica Mountains National Recreation Area, a crazy quilt of wilderness areas and preserves interspersed with outposts of suburbia. Many recreation area highlights, detailed in Wilderness City: The Santa Monica Mountains, are easily accessible from PCH north of Santa Monica.

PACIFIC PALISADES: AN OPTIMIST'S PARADISE

Like sections of Santa Monica and Malibu, Pacific Palisades perches atop high cliffs (palisades) overlooking the Pacific Ocean. The cliffs are famous for giving way during heavy rains, encouraging expensive homes to slip off their moorings and entire hillsides to slide away to sea—mudslides that inconveniently block the Pacific Coast Highway below. Otherwise the main event in this amazingly upmarket neighborhood just north of Santa Monica is the annual **Fourth of July parade**—an event in which members of the community's long-running **Optimist Club** march down the street, in close-order drill, in their underwear. The existence of the Optimists is still central to community life, as is Swarthmore Ave., center of the low-key local business district. But Will Rogers State Historic Park is usually more celebrated—as are Gelson's grocery, a best bet for spotting local celebrities, and Mort's restaurant, *the* place to eat (celebs primarily hang on the wall). Celebrities are legion in Pacific Palisades. Ron and Nancy Reagan lived here before they moved to the White House in 1984, for example, and past mayors of Pacific Palisades include Chevy Chase, Dom DeLuise, Ted Knight, and Rita Moreno.

For current information on the area, contact: **Pacific Palisades Chamber of Commerce,** 15330 Antioch St., Pacific Palisades, tel. (310) 459-7963.

Methodists, Artists, and Optimists on Parade
Pacific Palisades began its official community life as a movie studio back lot built by Thomas Ince at the end of Sunset Blvd. in the early 1900s. The area was more thoroughly settled in the 1920s by members of the Methodist Episcopal Church who hoped to establish a western Chautauqua here. The Chautauqua was a cultural, educational, moral, and philosophical program with communal overtones, a social movement started in New York in the late 1870s. Summer Chautauqua events featuring artists, writers, and other philosophers were held in Pacific Palisades during these early years—which helps explain why local streets are largely named for former Methodist bishops, religious schools, and scholars. But interest in the Chautauqua movement soon faded, and the Methodist movers and shakers here lost their land grant in 1928.

Artists, writers, and movie stars soon arrived in their stead, a trend that lasted for two solid decades. Some of them, including Aldous Huxley, Elsa Lancaster, Charles Laughton, and Thomas Mann, emigrated to escape the threat of Nazi Germany. (Pacific Palisades reminded them of the French Riviera, it was said.) By the 1940s the community was well-established as an L.A. center for art and architecture, though affluence is the primary criterion for residence nowadays.

The Uplifters Club
Harry Haldeman—grandfather of H.R. (Bob) Haldeman, a key player in ex-President Richard

Nixon's infamous Watergate debacle—was a jovial plumbing supply businessman originally from Chicago, a man as passionate about hard liquor and Cuban cigars as conservative politics. Inspired by the example of San Francisco's exclusive Bohemian Club, in 1913 Haldeman and like-minded revelers recruited from the still-prestigious Los Angeles Athletic Club established the Uplifters Club—the name "The Lofty and Exalted Order of Uplifters" contributed by *The Wizard of Oz* author L. Frank Baum. Though the group's official motto was "to uplift art and promote good fellowship," the ability to lift up one's glass was also crucial. After Prohibition's nationwide alcohol ban went into effect in 1919, the group bought 120 acres of redwoods and eucalyptus groves in Rustic Canyon (below what would later become the Will Rogers ranch) and founded the Uplifters Ranch—a private retreat where captains of industry and a select group of talented friends could protect their sybaritic revelry from the long arm of the law.

The Uplifters' social centerpiece was its clubhouse, now part of the eight-acre **Rustic Canyon Recreation Center** and park on Latimer Road, tel. (310) 454-5734, open to the public. In its hard-drinking heyday the Spanish colonial revival clubhouse featured drinking halls, a grand ballroom, and a "library" (actually a poker parlor). Uplifting the grounds were tennis courts, a swimming pool, polo field, trapshooting range, outdoor amphitheater, and dormitories, all part of the wooded playground enjoyed by Walt Disney, Busby Berkeley, Harold Lloyd, Daryl F. Zanuck, and others among L.A.'s most privileged ranks. In 1922 members began to build rustic weekend and summer cabins on land leased from the Uplifters; many of these structures remain. The Uplifters Club dissolved more than 50 years ago but artists, writers, and actual and spiritual descendants of the Uplifters continue to live here.

To reach Rustic Canyon Recreation Center—and to take a respectful peek at this part of the Pacific Palisades past—head south from Sunset Blvd. via Brooktree Rd., which follows a tree-lined brook, to the old clubhouse at 600-700 Latimer Road. (Allow plenty of time to get lost. Both Latimer and Haldeman Roads, the Uplifters' main thoroughfares, are narrow, with no curbs or gutters, and largely unlighted at night.) A handful of cabins and lodges—all private residences, so don't trespass or otherwise be obnoxious—still stand, among them 31, 32, 34, 35, and 38 Haldeman and 1, 3, and 8 Latimer. The Marco Hellman cabin at 38 Haldeman was transplanted from *The Courtship of Miles Standish* 1923 movie set. Earl Warren, former California governor and U.S. Supreme Court justice, summered here during the 1940s and '50s.

Seeing and Doing Pacific Palisades
The most popular local attraction lies well east along Sunset, near Brentwood—**Will Rogers State Historic Park,** 1501 Will Rogers State Park Rd. (just north of Sunset Blvd.), tel. (310) 454-8212. This 187-acre ranch estate is where noted cowboy humorist and philosopher Will Rogers lived from 1924 until his death in 1935. Rogers's ranch-style home, open daily for public tours, is also a museum; don't fail to appreciate the wraparound shower on the second floor. (For more information on the Rogers park and the adjacent Topanga State Park wilderness, see Wilderness City: The Santa Monica Mountains.) The lush lawns and landscaped grounds, where the horsy set still plays polo matches on weekends, are also perfect for picnics, frisbee, and sunbathing.

Near the ocean end of Sunset is the **Self-Realization Fellowship Lake Shrine,** 17190 Sunset Blvd., tel. (310) 454-4114, which was used as a movie location before Paramahansa Yogananda, author of *Autobiography of a Yogi,* bought the 10-acre site in 1950. At the center of the shrine, dedicated to the universality of all religions and the exaltation of nature, is the picturesque, luxuriantly landscaped spring-fed lake. A small chapel shaped like a Dutch windmill, a golden-domed archway, a houseboat, and gazebos frame lake views and provide good photo ops. The shrine is open to the public for peaceful walks and meditation. Call for information.

Other Pacific Palisades sights are architectural. Most of the significant area architecture was influenced by John Entenza, editor and publisher of the trendsetting *Arts and Architecture* magazine, and his **Case Study House Project,** which encouraged prominent Southern California architects to experiment with new materials and styles. Noted "case study" houses include the landmark international-style **Eames House and Studio,** 203 Chautauqua Blvd., something like a three-dimensional Mondrian painting set in a meadow, designed by Charles Eames in 1947-49; the similar **Entenza House,** 205 Chautauqua Blvd., designed by Charles Eames and Eero Saarinen in 1949; and the international redwood-and-brick **Bailey House,** 219 Chautauqua, designed by Richard J. Neutra in 1946-48. Pacific Palisades features many other architectural gems, most of which are not visible from public streets.

Quite accessible, however, are the **Castellammare Stairways,** reached from Sunset Blvd. via Castellammare Dr., which leads up to this enclave of million-dollar homes overlooking the Pacific Ocean. Among the vertical hiking possibilities here (near Castellammare): the stairway just off Posetano Rd. that climbs to Revello Dr., and the stairway from Breve Way to Porto Marina. For sheer popularity, however, stop on the way back into Santa Monica for a run up the 200-step **Adelaide Stairway** (promoted as L.A.'s Ultimate Stairway in myriad magazine "lifestyle" articles), which starts, on the uphill end, at Fourth

the international-style Eames House

St. and Adelaide Dr. and winds down to E. Channel Road. Come during the week to avoid the hordes of fitness fanatics who turn the stairway into a human freeway on weekends.

Topanga Canyon

The equally indefinable inland and upland neighbor to Malibu is the laid-back burg of Topanga in mountainous Topanga Canyon, reached from PCH via Topanga Canyon Blvd. (Hwy. 27), increasingly a high-speed commuter thoroughfare. (The tailgaters' apparent message: Pull over or die.) Beyond the highway, the artsy community sprawls off in all directions—up tortured hillsides, down one-lane roads—within the canyon's 21-acre watershed. Famous for its mudslides, Topanga Canyon does shed water after heavy winter rains—which certainly explains the Chumash name, Topanga, roughly translated as "Mountains that Run into the Sea." Here, they often do. When hillsides aren't preoccupied with slip-sliding away, rustic cabins, lodges, standard-brand ranch homes, and more ambitious architectural adventures provide both physical and spiritual home for Topanga's people, predominantly actors, artists, musicians, poets, writers, and screenwriters. Topanga thrives on its artistic ambience and its community eccentricities—the roadside crystal stands and such—many of which hark back to the earliest inklings of the Age of Aquarius. Yet given the region's increasing suburban popularity, back-to-the-landers without 30-year-old roots would be financially challenged to plant themselves here today.

Most of Topanga the town is strung out along the highway about halfway between the San Fernando Valley and the Pacific Ocean. A popular stop for breakfast and lunch is **Willows**, 137 S. Topanga Canyon Blvd., tel. (310) 455-8788. You can also stop locally for supplies and deli sandwiches at places such as **Fernwood Market**, 446 S. Topanga Canyon Blvd., tel. (310) 455-2412, and **Froggy's Topanga Fresh Fish Market** (also a good restaurant), 1105 N. Topanga Canyon Blvd., tel. (310) 455-1728.

Some classic Topanga neighborhoods and destinations, including the **Inn of the Seventh Ray** natural-foods restaurant, tel. (310) 455-1311, are tucked in among the creekside oaks and sycamores alongside Old Topanga Canyon Rd., which eventually intersects scenic Mulhol-

land Highway. For books about the area and basic New Age supplies, stop by **The Spiral Staircase** next to the Inn of the Seventh Ray at 128 Old Topanga Canyon, tel. (310) 455-3370.

Another wonder in Topanga is **The Will Geer Theatricum Botanicum,** 1419 N. Topanga Canyon Blvd., tel. (310) 455-3723, a small, woodsy outdoor theater that remains part of the legacy of actor/philosopher Will Geer. The classically trained Geer eventually became one of the world's most beloved actors—baby boomers will remember him as Grandpa Walton on *The Waltons* TV series—yet his professional and personal lives were all but undone in the 1950s by his refusal to cooperate with the communist-hunting House Committee on Un-American Activities. "Blacklisted," or barred from working in Hollywood, Geer moved his family to Topanga Canyon and established a Shakespearean theater to showcase the talents of other blacklisted Hollywood talent. Along with theater tickets, he and his family also sold their home-grown vegetables. Will Geer's daughter, Ellen, has served as the theater's artistic director since 1979, the year after the actor's death. Call for current program information or check the theater's website at www.theatricum.com.

Easily accessible from Topanga is **Topanga State Park,** prime for hiking—in the absence of major storms and mudslides—especially in "the green months" of winter and early spring. For more information, see Wilderness City: The Santa Monica Mountains.

MALIBU: SURFING CELEBRITY

Aside from an appreciation for Malibu's clean beaches, good surf, and aquamarine waters, the one thing that unites Malibu residents is the Pacific Coast Highway, which here is a tenuous lifeline. Celebrated for its surfing, its celebrities, and its chic coastal cachet, Malibu most often makes it into the news as a disaster area for its almost predictable "natural" catastrophes, created by human incursions into an unstable, fire-adapted ecosystem. Whether or not wildfires have finished their occasional summer and fall windsprints to the sea, the rains begin—and the mudslides, which may carry houses, carports, landscaped yards, sometimes streets and entire hillsides with them. If the Pacific Coast Hwy. is closed for days at a time, be it from behemoth bouncing boulders or mudslides, people here take it in stride. Building more houses here—and continually rebuilding them—is not particularly intelligent.

Yet try telling that to people in Malibu, who moved here to get away from it all. The fact that "it" had already arrived, in the forms of crushing urban crowds and nightmarish traffic, was a prime motivating factor for Malibu's incorporation in 1990. During his one-year term as the city's "honorary mayor," actor Martin Sheen declared Malibu a nuclear-free zone and a refuge for the homeless. But since incorporation residents have drawn battle lines over growth-related issues.

Despite the definitive dot on most maps, Malibu as place has always been difficult to find. Though the star-studded Malibu Colony, the Malibu Pier, and several Malibu beaches have served as unofficial community signposts, in most people's minds "Malibu" was a rather vague regional appellation taking in the 20-plus miles of Los Angeles County coastline between Topanga Canyon and Ventura County. But now Malibu has definite city limits, and an official 20-square-mile territory, stretching north from Topanga Canyon to Leo Carrillo State Beach at the Ventura County line.

The main attractions are Malibu's beaches—more than 20 miles of them. The beaches along the Malibu coastline are still reasonably clean, despite heavy recreational use and some local pollution problems, and provide some of the best surfing and ocean swimming in Southern California. Traffic on a summer day along the Pacific Coast Highway can be brutal and parking nearly impossible, however. Plan to arrive before the noontime "rush hour"—say, by 11 a.m., if not earlier—while parking places are still available. A second highway rush usually occurs between 4 and 5 p.m., when most people head home for dinner. If you're well supplied and willing to while away some time, the good

news is that sunsets are fairly unpopulated and peaceful. Better yet, come in the off season—spring, fall, and winter—when beaches can be quite balmy and pleasant yet much less crowded. The weather is moderate year-round. Barring the occasional storm, some of the finest beach days come in winter—though some spots are crowded on weekends during whalewatching season.

For current information about the area, contact: **Malibu Chamber of Commerce,** 23805 Stuart Ranch Rd., Ste. 100, Malibu, tel. (310) 456-9025, www.malibu.org.

Landing on Malibu

Though the ocean here draws the soul, the land is more highly valued. After the native Chumash people were dispatched to nearby Franciscan missions, Malibu's history became an endless tangle of land and road-building disputes.

José Bartólome Tapía traveled to California from Sonora, Mexico, in 1775 with the de Anza expedition. In 1805 Spain granted Tapía, a farmer and the eldest of nine children, the Topanga Malibu Sequit ranch, named for three area Indian villages. The ranch thrived until Tapía died in 1824, though his wife, Doña Maria, kept it until 1848. After the death of her eldest son Doña Maria sold the ranch, for 400 pesos, to a granddaughter's husband, Leon Victor Prudhomme, a 26-year-old Frenchman. But in the transition from Mexican to American rule in 1850, records detailing the early Spanish land grant to Tapía were lost. After a long legal dispute with the California Land Commission, Prudhomme sold the ranch in 1857 to Matthew Keller, an Irishman who took advantage of the defective title and the Panic of 1857 to buy it for the outrageously low price of 10 cents per acre, or a total of less than $1,400. Keller gained undisputed legal title in 1863 and presided over the ranch's 13,300-plus acres, which produced some of California's first wines, until his death in 1881. Son Henry Keller sold the land in 1887 for $10 an acre.

Frederick Hastings Rindge, son of a Massachusetts wool merchant, inherited a $2 million estate in 1883 at the age of 26. A Harvard graduate, Rindge established a city hall, public library, a boys' school, and children's sanitarium in Cambridge before he and his wife, May, bought the Malibu rancho and moved to California. The change, Rindge believed, would improve his health. The family built a home on Ocean Ave. in Santa Monica—a day's journey by wagon from Malibu, where the primitive dirt road could be crossed only at low tide—and began to improve the isolated ranch. As detailed in Rindge's book, *Happy Days in Southern California,* published in 1898, the family built a lovely, landscaped home east of Malibu Creek, added a barn, corrals, and bunkhouses, and planted grain and lemon groves. Most of the land was set aside for cattle grazing, though. The Rindge family eventually owned the entire 24-mile stretch of coastline north of Las Flores Canyon.

The happiest days ended in 1903 thanks to the worst fire in Malibu's recorded history, probably started by squatters. Fanned by hot Santa Ana winds, the wildfire rapidly torched the entire ranch. Along with most everything else the family home was destroyed, which forced the Rindges to move into Los Angeles. Two years later Frederick Rindge died.

When Frederick Rindge died in 1905, his widow, May, began fighting what became an endless series of turf battles to protect the land from trespasses large and small—from homesteaders, squatters, railroads, and the state of California's highway-building plans. When armed guards, high fences, and dynamiting her own roads failed to stop progress, May Rindge resorted to the courts. She appealed California's plan to condemn part of her property, to build the Pacific Coast Hwy., all the way to the U.S. Supreme Court—and lost.

Celebrities and Surfing

In the midst of the daunting financial problems generated by her war against the Pacific Coast Highway, the "Queen of Malibu" May Rindge decided to lease out beachfront property, at Malibu La Costa and between Carbon Canyon and the Malibu Pier. Actress Anna Q. Nilsson signed the first lease, and the area was quickly established as a residential colony for publicity-shunning movie people. Among Malibu's first wave of celluloid

celebrities were Clara Bow, Ronald Colman, Dolores Del Rio, John Gilbert, Barbara Stanwyck, and Jack Warner. Later, Escondido, Trancas, and Zuma Beaches were opened to development, and still more movie stars moved to the area. The celebs have been coming ever since, their presence now central to the Malibu mystique. (Less celebrated citizens try not to stare but still get a thrill from spotting movie stars stopping for basic supplies at Trancas Market and other local shopping hot spots.) Luminaries of current or recent history include Johnny Carson, Ted Danson, Larry Hagman, Dustin Hoffman, Madonna, Burgess Meredith, Carroll O'Connor, Robert Redford, Steven Spielberg, and Sylvester Stallone. And Danny DeVito and Rhea Perlman, Bruce Willis and Demi Moore, and John McEnroe and Tatum O'Neal. To name a few. And not counting the colony's large numbers of artists, writers, and other talented citizens.

Malibu is also famous for its surfers, who cherish access to the coast's best breaks and beaches as much as Malibu's movie stars cherish absolute privacy—a continuing source of social tension that somehow adds to the peculiar ambience. Here, throughout the Malibu Colony, megamillion-dollar beachfront bungalows and baronial estates adopt a sober streetside decorum that rarely hints of the glass-walled glories on the private side. Building such exclusive homes in the style of townhouses—with little or no space in between to discourage both snooping and beach access—somehow just encourages public curiosity, making people ever more determined to find the few available access walkways (follow the surfers). Malibu Rd. along the waterfront is a classic example.

Malibu Pier

Start exploring Malibu at the 700-foot Malibu Pier, opened to the public with great fanfare and fireworks on July 4, 1945. The present-day pier replaced the 400-foot-long Rindge Pier, built here in 1903 so supplies could be delivered to the ranch by boat. Rindge's pier was later damaged by storms and then intentionally demolished in 1943. The pier area is particularly popular for fishing (tackle and bait available) and watching both surfers and sunsets. Surrounding the pier is Malibu Lagoon State Beach, which includes the Malibu estuary, the historic Adamson House and associated museum, and **Malibu**

Surfrider Beach, one of the West Coast's most famous surfing beaches. Largely east of the pier (it feels "south") though the best breaks are to the west ("north"), Malibu Surfrider Beach has been celebrated in countless Frankie Avalon, Annette Funicello, and *Gidget* movies. More significantly, according to local lore, Surfrider is California's 1926 surfing birthplace. In summer perfect waves roll to shore at Surfrider day after day—an accident of ocean currents, upwellings, and winds that creates heaven for surfers, kayakers, and windsurfers but hell for those who dislike overcrowded beaches. Swimming and surfing aren't recommended here, since Heal the Bay regularly "flunks" Surfrider and adjacent beaches in its annual water quality survey. But surfers still come, since they have to go where the waves are. If you want to watch, the pier offers ringside railings for surfing voyeurs.

If you hunger for a bracing after-beach breakfast, head for the **PierView Cafe and Cantina,** tel. (310) 456-6962, on the beach just east of the pier. Or head for local shopping malls. Best bets for breakfast or weekend brunch—and later meals—include **Marmalade** in the Cross Creek Plaza, tel. (310) 317-4242, and, at Malibu Colony Plaza, both casual **Coogie's,** tel. (310) 317-1444, and uptown **Granita,** tel. (310) 456-0488, the latter sea-themed culinary adventure established by Wolfgang Puck and Barbara Lazaroff.

Malibu Lagoon State Beach

Malibu Lagoon offers an opportunity for impromptu birdwatching and nature appreciation, right off the highway. One of only two estuaries remaining within the boundaries of Santa Monica Mountains National Recreation Area, this small patch of marsh at the mouth of Malibu Creek serves as a natural fish nursery—and bountiful buffet for neighborhood and migrating shorebirds. (While visiting, stay on the boardwalks.) More than 200 species of birds use Malibu Lagoon as a migratory stopover. Nearby beach areas are popular for swimming, though water at the mouth of Malibu Creek is polluted—twice monthly, the lagoon is drained—and swimming is not recommended on those days. With its offshore reefs and kelp beds, the area is also popular with skin and scuba divers.

Also well worth exploring: the adjoining **Malibu Lagoon Museum** and the grand **Adamson House.** Chances are you'll never see the inside of local movie stars' homes, so amuse yourself, while touring Adamson House, with the knowledge that most celebrities would kill to own a place like this. Former home of Rhoda and Merritt Adamson—daughter and son-in law of Frederick and May Rindge, who owned the vast Malibu Ranch in the early 1900s—this 1929 Spanish-Moorish beach house was designed by architect Stiles O. Clements, who took full advantage of the Rindge-owned Malibu Tile Company's exceptional craftsmanship. The stunning Adamson House, listed on the National Register of Historic Places, is rich with handcrafted teak, graceful wrought-iron work, and leaded-glass windows. But, inside and out, it is primarily a tile-setter's fantasy—a real-life museum-quality display of 1920s' California tilework, richly colored geometric and animal-motif patterns worked into the walkways, walls, and lavish fountains. There's even a tiled outdoor dog shower. The museum adjacent, at home in the home's seven-car garage, chronicles area history with memorabilia, art, artifacts, and photographs.

Malibu Lagoon State Beach adjoins the Malibu Pier and includes famous Malibu Surfrider Beach (see above). Adamson House and the Malibu Lagoon Museum, 23200 Pacific Coast Hwy. (Hwy. 1), are one-quarter mile west of the Malibu Pier and 13 miles west of Santa Monica. The lagoon and Adamson House grounds are technically open 24 hours, though the adjacent county parking lot ($5 fee), shared with Surfrider Beach, is open daily 8 a.m.-5 p.m. only (side-street parking available early morning and evening). Another parking lot ($6) is one block north at Cross Creek Road. Beach, lagoon, and museum access are free. Adamson House tours are $2 adults, $1 children. The Adamson House is open only for tours (one hour), usually offered Wed.-Sat. 11 a.m.-3 p.m. (last tour at 2 p.m.); the museum is open during the same hours. Reservations are required for groups of 12 or more and the museum closes on days with moderate to heavy rain—call ahead. For more information, call (310) 456-8432.

MALIBU: THE COASTLINE

Beaches North of Malibu Colony

Last stop before the Ventura County line in the north is **Leo Carrillo State Beach,** typically

WILDERNESS CITY:
THE SANTA MONICA MOUNTAINS

One of the few east-west-trending mountain ranges in the U.S., the Santa Monica Mountains extend upward from the sea as part of the Channel Islands and then eastward from Pacific Ocean beaches and tidepools to Mt. Hollywood in Griffith Park on the mainland, creating the geographical divide between the Los Angeles Basin and the San Fernando Valley.

The Santa Monica Mountains National Recreation Area, a 70,000-acre parkland pastiche created by Congress in 1978, protects much of the remaining open space in the Santa Monica Mountains—city, county, state, federal, private, and once-private lands and beaches—within a unified identity. Yet within that unity is great diversity. Maintaining separate boundaries are parks of long standing, including Malibu Creek State Park, Topanga State Park, and Will Rogers State Historic Park, various public beaches, and attractions such as Paramount Ranch, Peter Strauss Ranch, and the fairly new Streisand Center for Conservancy Studies. Thanks to the Santa Monica Mountains Conservancy and other groups and individuals, land acquisitions continue to expand this national park—and the boundaries of individual parks within it—while extending the recreation area's trail system, popular with hikers, mountain bikers, and horseback riders. At last report, hikers, bikers, and equestrians were still battling over the issue of increasing mountain bike access to back-country trails—to some an issue of overuse and abuse of trails as well as "machine-age encroachment," to others a question of equal rights for cyclists.

At the beaches summer is prime time, but the off-seasons offer at least the opportunity for solitude (and better beachcombing). Winter and spring, when the sky is blue and the hills are green, are the best seasons for exploring the mountains, which boast about 860 species of flowering plants in environments varying from grasslands, oak woodlands, and riparian sycamore and fern glades to coastal chaparral and craggy red-rock canyons. The only Mediterranean ecosystem protected by the National Park Service, the Santa Monicas have posed for TV and movie crews as Greece, Italy, France, Korea, the Wild West, and the antebellum South. Some areas are absolutely otherworldly; interplanetary film possibilities have yet to be fully explored here.

But because so much of the area is urban, surrounded by millions of people and bordered by two of the world's busiest freeways, and its attractions far-flung, finding one's way around in the Santa Monica Mountains can get complicated. To get oriented, stop by or contact the national park's visitor center and associated bookstore, open daily 9 a.m.-5 p.m., closed Thanksgiving, Christmas, and New Year's Day). Along with maps and other helpful publications, the office offers a wonderful quarterly calendar of guided walks and other events, *Outdoors in the Santa Monica Mountains National Recreation Area,* also available online.

For more information, contact: **Santa Monica Mountains National Recreation Area Visitor Center,** 401 W. Hillcrest Dr., Thousand Oaks, CA 91360, tel. (805) 370-2301, www.nps.gov/samo. To get there from the Ventura Freeway (Hwy. 101), exit at Lynn Rd. and continue north; turn east on Hillcrest; then turn left onto McCloud. The visitor center is the first driveway on the right. For information on area state parks, contact **California State Parks,** 1925 Las Virgenes Rd., Calabasas, CA 91302, tel. (818) 880-0350. Though associated state parks and beaches charge at least a nominal day-use fee, general access to national parks land is free. (For information on relevant state parks, see listings below. For state and county beaches, see Life's a Beach.) Access hours also vary. Wildfires are a major threat to the park and its urban and suburban neighbors, so no fires are allowed within most park areas. Permission to explore environmentally sensitive areas, including **Cold Creek Canyon Preserve** near Topanga State Park, are by permit only, so docent-led hikes are usually the best way to go.

Highlights of Santa Monica Mountains National Recreation Area include:

Will Rogers State Historic Park

"The more you read about politics," laureate Will Rogers once observed, "you got to admit that each party is worse than the other." America's favorite cowboy commentator, originally a rodeo trick roper, was still making a name for himself in 1928 when he and his family settled at this ranch in then-rural Pacific Palisades, just north of Santa Monica.

The unassuming 31-room home features mission-style furniture, eclectic Western decor, and some eye-catching oddities—including a stuffed calf Rogers regularly used for indoor roping practice. Museum exhibits tell the Will Rogers story, up to and including his tragic death in 1935. To make a day of it, enjoy the picnic grounds and the national park's hiking trails—including very popular Backbone Trail, now open to mountain bikers. Otherwise, the big weekend draw is the equestrian action—polo matches, a continuation of the tradition started by Rogers himself, open to the public. There's also a roping and training area for horses.

For more information, contact: Will Rogers State Historic Park, 1501 Will Rogers State Park Rd., tel. (310) 454-8212, fax (310) 459-2031. The park is open daily 8 a.m.-7 p.m. in summer, 8 a.m.-6 p.m. in other seasons. The Rogers home/museum is open 10:30 a.m.-5 p.m. daily for tours (closed Thanksgiving, Christmas, and New Year's Day). Tours run every hour on the half-hour, starting at 10:30 a.m., with the last tour at 4:30 p.m. Weather permitting, polo matches are scheduled on Saturday at 2 p.m. and Sunday at 10 a.m. Park admission is free, technically, but parking is $5 per vehicle.

Topanga State Park

Native peoples called this canyon "Topanga," meaning "the place where the mountains meet the sea." And so it is. One of the world's largest urban wildlands, Topanga State Park's 11,000-plus acres, preserved as open space, are almost all within L.A.'s city limits. Topanga is a hiker's and equestrian's park, with most fire roads now also open to mountain bikers. Most trailheads start at the old Trippet Ranch at the park's official entrance, with pleasant picnic area and self-guided nature trail. The eastern section of the aptly named Backbone Trail ambles along ridgetops and then down toward the sea, ending at Will Rogers State Historic Park—and offering, en route, some dazzling views of the Pacific Ocean and Santa Monica Bay.

To reach the park entrance, head south from the Ventura Freeway (the 101) or north from Pacific Coast Highway (Hwy. 1), exit at Topanga Canyon Blvd. and turn east onto Entrada Road. Hikers can also reach the park from Will Rogers State Historic Park. The park is open daily 8 a.m.-sunset (parking lot hours), but Topanga is actually never closed except during extreme fire danger or other emergency. Technically, park admission is free, but parking is $5. No dogs allowed. For more information, contact: Topanga State Park, 20825 Entrada Rd., Topanga 90290, tel. (310) 454-8212 or (818) 880-0350.

Malibu Creek State Park

Fans of the *M*A*S*H* television series, filmed at Malibu Creek State Park, will recognize the scenery—and enjoy posing for impromptu photos inside the junked jeep and ambulance parked in weeds along the Crags Road trail route. Much of the land now included in the park was owned by Twentieth Century Fox until the mid-1970s, so, naturally, many TV shows and movies have been filmed here over the years—and at adjacent Paramount Ranch. Free and technical rockclimbing are also popular here.

Yet trails are the real draw. The short one-mile hike to Century Lake is an easy trek for the kids. (The old *M*A*S*H* set is one mile farther.) Starting at the parking lot, head west on Crags Road to Malibu Creek. Head right at the fork to reach the visitor center, for basic information and orientation. Cross the bridge here and continue up the road; at the crest, descend to the left. Man-made Century Lake, now something of a freshwater marsh, is quite inviting to ducks and other waterfowl. If the kids are still willing, backtrack toward the bridge and then take the Gorge Trail south to Rock Pool—yet another one of those Southern California sights that seems vaguely familiar since you may have seen it before—in movies such as *Swiss Family Robinson*.

Six miles of the Backbone Trail also traverse the park. For inveterate hikers, Malibu Creek State Park also offers trail access to the city of Calabasas's **Lost Hills Park.** Other visitor draws include pleasant picnicking, a large campground, and the regional state park headquarters. The land's main claim to fame, however, is as the southernmost natural habitat of California's valley oak.

Parking lot hours are 8 a.m.-sunset, though the park itself is open 24 hours except in extreme fire danger or other emergency. Parking is $5 per vehicle. The visitor center is open limited hours, on weekends only. Call for information on nature walks and special activities. To get here: From the Ventura Freeway (the 101) in Calabasas, head south on Las Virgenes Road three miles to the Mulholland Hwy. intersection. Continue south on Las Virgenes/Malibu Canyon Rd. another quarter-mile to the park's entrance. From Pacific Coast Highway (Hwy. 1), head north almost six miles on Malibu Canyon Road to the park entrance. For more information, contact: Malibu

(continued on next page)

WILDERNESS CITY:
THE SANTA MONICA MOUNTAINS
(continued)

Creek State Park, 1925 Las Virgenes Rd., Calabasas 91302, tel. (818) 880-0367 or (818) 880-0350, fax (818) 880-6165.

Paramount Ranch

The primary set for filming the popular television series *Dr. Quinn, Medicine Woman,* Western Town at Paramount Ranch boasts an illustrious Hollywood-western history. A remnant of 2,700 acres of Rancho Las Virgenes bought by Paramount Studios in 1927, the ranch also served as studio set for *The Rifleman* and *Have Gun Will Travel* episodes, not to mention *Bat Masterson* and *The Cisco Kid.*

When the kids are done poking through the facades of Western Town, why not take a hike? Just behind Western Town is half-mile Coyote Canyon Trail. In early spring the route leads up through the wildflowers and oak woodlands to some possible picnic sites—and a good eagle's-eye view of Western Town below—before circling back down. For a more ambitious hike, set out on the park's Run Trail. A recent 320-acre addition to Paramount Ranch adds still more trail.

On weekdays, Western Town is often used for film shoots. During filming the public is welcome to observe but not to wander through the sets. The Old West sets are open to the public every weekend and on weekdays when no filming is under way. Filming or no, the ranch is open to the public daily for picnicking and hiking, 8 a.m.-sunset. Most educational, however, are the monthly Saturday-morning guided hikes (free, call for scheduled dates).

To get here: From the Ventura Freeway (the 101), exit at Kanan Road and continue south for about three-fourths of a mile. Turn left at the "Cornell Way" sign and then go to the right (Cornell Way becomes Cornell Road). The ranch entrance is another two-and-a-half miles on the right.

Celebrity Spreads: Streisand and Strauss

Wonderful as a respite from San Fernando Valley gridlock is the **Peter Strauss Ranch** near Agoura, where you can picnic on the lawn or stretch your legs on a mile-long stroll. Among newer park acquisitions is the Barbra Streisand Center for Conservancy Studies. Actress, songstress, and movie pro-

ducer Barbra Streisand donated her exclusive 22.5-acre, $15 million Malibu spread to the state in late 1993, and it's now known as **Ramirez Canyon Park,** operated by the Santa Monica Mountains Conservancy. An environmental think tank, the Streisand Center for Conservancy Studies offers occasional public tours of the center's architectural, botanical, and historical features, including two of four homes here. For both of these celebrity spreads, call the national park office for current information.

Point Mugu State Park

Here, about 10 miles south of Oxnard in Ventura County, the Santa Monica Mountains meet the sea. Many hillside areas were seriously burned in Southern California's raging 1993 wildfires, as was much of Malibu's mountainous backdrop, but the coastal chaparral and woodlands are rapidly regenerating. The rugged Boney Mountain Wilderness, a section of the Backbone Trail, and the ocean-view La Jolla Canyon Loop Trail are hiking highlights of this 13,300-acre park. To enjoy the beach, try Sycamore Cove or Thornhill Broome (the latter backed by campsites). Inquire about swimming safety. Adjacent to Point Mugu, in the north, is the national park's Rancho Sierra Vista and Satwiwa Native American Natural Area. Adjoining on the southeast is the recreation area's Circle X Ranch.

Visitor facilities include developed woodland campsites (less wooded now) at Big Sycamore Creek Campground and primitive campsites at the beach, picnic areas, restrooms, dump station, and trails for horses, hikers, and mountain bikers. For campsite reservations, especially during the peak April-Sept. season (and weekends), call ReserveAmerica, toll-free (800) 444-7275. For other visitor information, contact: Point Mugu State Park, 9000 W. Pacific Coast Hwy., Malibu 91301, tel. (818) 880-0350, (805) 488-5223 (recorded), or (805) 488-1827.

Palo Comado Canyon and
Other Recent Acquisitions

In 1993 the Santa Monica Mountains Conservancy acquired about 1,600 acres owned by entertainer Bob Hope in Palo Comado Canyon next to the Ventura County line; the deal was part of a complicated land transaction involving the Ahmanson Ranch development in the works northeast of Calabasas in nearby Las Virgenes Canyon. (Runkle Ranch, more than 4,000 acres near Simi Valley, and 339-acre Corral Canyon near Malibu are also set for acquisition.) The hiking high point of Palo Comado is 750 acres of oaks, meadows, and old movie sets at **China Flat.**

Another long-standing park priority is acquiring parcels to eventually extend popular **Backbone Trail** the entire 65-mile distance between Will Rogers State Historic Park and Point Mugu State Park. New sections of trail include **Fossil Ridge** and **Hondo Canyon,** both accessible from Mulholland Highway. The acquisition of **Zuma and Trancas Canyons,** between Mulholland Hwy./Encinal Canyon Rd. and PCH, is also a step in that direction.

The Santa Monica Mountains Conservancy and the recreation area are in the process of acquiring other new acreage. For current information on new areas open to the public, contact the national parks office.

much less crowded than the "city beaches" closer to Malibu Colony, Santa Monica, and urban points south. Named for the actor who played Pancho in *The Cisco Kid* TV series, 1,600-acre Leo Carrillo features 1.5 miles of stupendous craggy coastline and both rocky and sandy beaches—the totality perfect for surfing, sailboarding, swimming, and, at low tide, tidepooling. A popular whalewatching spot in winter, Leo Carrillo is also good for scuba diving. (Riptides are a danger occasionally.) Inland, ranger-guided hikes are regularly scheduled, and, in summer, campfire programs. Pleasant picnicking, too (there's a store here). A pretty campground, across the highway, is set among the sycamores back from the beach, and there's another nearby at North Beach. For a spectacular ocean view with minimal effort, take the short trail up the hill from near the booth at the campground entrance. Leo Carrillo State Beach, 35000 Pacific Coast Hwy. (Hwy. 1), is 25 miles west of Santa Monica and about 15 miles from "downtown" Malibu. Leo Carrillo's main entrance is just east of Mulholland Hwy.'s intersection with the highway—a great drive, if you're out exploring. Day-use parking is $6 per vehicle; call for camping fees, which vary for developed, RV (self-contained), and hike/bike sites. The beach is open daily 8 a.m.-midnight. The visitor center is open daily in summer. For more information, call (805) 488-5223. For camping reservations, a must in summer and on most weekends, call ReserveAmerica toll-free at (800) 444-7275.

Next east is one of L.A.'s best-kept secrets, rumored to be the preferred beach escape for L.A.'s lifeguards on their days off—picturesque, pristine, and remote **Nicholas Canyon County Beach,** 34000 Pacific Coast Highway. Nicholas,

a graceful quarter moon of sand curving around a small bay, is well-protected from highway noise and has no skate rentals, no snack stands—none of the usual L.A. beach chaos and clutter. Just peace, quiet, and a few kayakers and surfers. (And lifeguards and restrooms.) The **Robert H. Meyer Memorial State Beach,** next east at 33000 Pacific Coast Hwy., is actually a string of smaller state beaches tucked into a residential area: **El Pescador, La Piedra,** and **El Matador,** the lovely latter beach the most popular. As many as 10 episodes of *Baywatch* were once filmed here each year, but most people come for the dramatic cliffs, rock formations, and caves along the sandy beach. (No lifeguards but picnic tables and portable toilets. Parking lot open 8 a.m.-sunset, fee.) Nearby is **El Sol State Beach,** difficult to find.

Trancas Beach at PCH and Guernsey Ave. is another residential-area beach, most accessible by walking from **Zuma Beach.** Zuma, 30000 Pacific Coast Hwy., was the location for a multitude of 1950s and 1960s surfing movies—the likes of *Deadman's Curve, Beach Blanket Bingo,* and *Back to the Beach*—but gathered even more fame in the 1970s, thanks to singer/songwriter Neil Young's album *Zuma.* Postcard-pretty if hardly private, Zuma's appeal is as fundamental as its endless expanse of white sand, rowdy beach volleyball, and children's playground. Popular with the rowdy surfing set. For all the fun and frolic, though, think safety. Riptides here have been known to drag up to 20 people at a time straight out to sea—keeping the lifeguards plenty busy. Access to the beach, open sunrise to sunset, is free but there is a fee to park in the *huge* lot. Locals avoid even that by jockeying for highway and street parking. Full services are available (lifeguards, restrooms, snack bars, and rental shops). Just below often-packed Zuma is clean, sandy, and equally popular **Westward Beach,** reached from Pacific Coast Hwy. via Westward Beach Rd. (limited free parking along the beach road). Or, park at Zuma and walk along the beach.

Continue on Westward Beach Rd. to reach the parking lot for busy **Point Dume State Beach,** whose sand neatly segues into Westward's. Point Dume once featured a vertical "point"—a rocky peak—in addition to its seaward point, until the former was flattened for a housing development. Reaching Point Dume's secluded series of sandy pocket beaches and rocky shores, scattered below impressive cliffs, requires a little walking. Small caves and tidepools abound throughout the 35-acre **Point Dume Natural Preserve,** where the rocky west face is popular with technical climbers. A stairway and hiking trail start at Westward Beach and climb to the headlands and the **Point Dume Whale Watch,** a popular series of sites for watching the midwinter migration of California gray whales—good for views any time. Look for California brown pelicans, California sea lions, and harbor seals on offshore rocks. Though it's not condoned as a nude beach officially, historically beach-in-the-buff enthusiasts have always hiked around the point or down the stairway from the headlands to the rocky north end of **Pirate's Cove** and its stunning beach, but winter storms often block access. Point Dume is a good swimming, sunbathing, and diving beach (for experienced divers), only fair for surfing; lifeguards, very clean restrooms, outdoor showers, and a soft drink vending machine provided. Parking at Point Dume is $6.

Point Dume adjoins pretty, private **Paradise Cove Beach.** But unless you're absolutely desperate to find a place to toss down the beach towel, the parking fee alone—$15—is enough to discourage most people from trying this tiny beach near the pier on Paradise Cove Road. (If you park on PCH and walk in, it'll cost you only $5. And the Sandcastle Restaurant validates parking.) But it is a quiet, family-friendly beach with rocky bluffs, caves, and tidepools to explore. At Pacific Coast Hwy. and Escondido Rd. is coastal access (highway parking only) for residential-area **Escondido Beach,** narrow, sandy, and empty, indeed fairly well hidden. Look for the Coastal Access signs. Actual "access" begins at a gate on the ocean side of the highway, which is unlocked 6:30 a.m.-6:30 p.m. daily, just north of Geoffrey's Restaurant in the 27400 "block" of the Pacific Coast Hwy.; the beach path starts at a stairwell between two houses. No lifeguard, no services.

Then there's very narrow **Dan Blocker State Beach,** named for the big, brawny actor better known as affable Hoss Cartwright on TV's long-running *Bonanza.* Dan Blocker extends from Malibu Rd. (at Pacific Coast Hwy.) to Corral Canyon Road. Most people head for the sandier southeast end, which can be packed; beach fans can find more privacy toward the less accessible, rockier end near the mouth of Corral Creek. Highway parking only, easy beach access. Popular for surf fishing and swimmers; lifeguards in summer and on busy weekends.

For those willing to brave the movie-star-beachhouse obstacles along Malibu Rd., back in Malibu Colony both **Puerco Beach** and **Amarillo Beach** beckon (no lifeguards, bathrooms, or other services). Park on the north end of Malibu Rd., where it meets the highway, or from the highway take Webb Way south to Malibu Rd., praying all the while for a parking spot. To reach Amarillo and points east, it's easiest to walk from Puerco.

Along the coast are a few decent stops for a meal with a view, including the **Paradise Cove Beach Café** at Paradise Cove, tel. (310) 457-2503, and **Geoffrey's** near Point Dume, tel. (310) 457-1519. If your beach explorations lead you far afield, don't forget the ever-popular **Neptune's Net** on PCH about a mile north of the Ventura County line, tel. (310) 457-3095, beloved for its downhome, no-frills funk. Best bet at lunch or dinner is the steamed shellfish. Pick your own lobsters or crabs right out of the fish tanks.

Beaches South of Malibu Colony

Beyond Malibu Lagoon State Beach and Malibu Surfrider Beach near the pier (see Malibu Pier and Malibu Lagoon listings above) is a string of difficult-to-reach residential-area sandy spots: **Carbon Beach,** 22200 Pacific Coast Hwy., just west of Carbon Canyon Rd.; **La Costa Beach,** 21400 PCH; **Las Flores Beach,** 20900 PCH; and **Big Rock Beach** (look for the big rock), 20600 PCH, just north of Carbon Canyon Road.

The best way to reach all of these beaches—and watch the tides, so you don't get stranded—is by walking east from Malibu Surfrider Beach or west from Las Tunas. By contrast, rocky **Las Tunas Beach** next east, right on the highway, is very easy to reach but not all that pleasant because of the din of traffic. It's most popular with surf fishers and scuba divers; lifeguards in season, portable toilets. Bring water.

Topanga State Beach, easy to find along the 18700 "block" of Pacific Coast Hwy., a quarter-mile west of the J. Paul Getty Museum and a quarter-mile east of Topanga Canyon Blvd., is popular for swimming (if you don't mind dodging a few ocean rocks) and sunny picnics. On a clear day, from the bluffs here you can see Catalina Island. Sometimes you can also see dolphins just offshore, or passing whales. Mostly what you'll see at Topanga, though, are surfers and sailboats. The swells here are second only to those at Malibu Surfrider. The water quality is usually good, too, so in summer the beach can be quite crowded. The small parking lot ($5 fee) is usually full by 11 a.m., or try to find a spot along the highway. Lifeguards, full services. Another good possibility is **Castle Rock Beach** across the highway from the Getty Museum, a pleasant sandy beach with easy access, parking lot ($6), portable toilets, lifeguards.

Will Rogers State Beach seems to stretch forever beneath the unstable palisades of Pacific Palisades—and this strand of sand does go on some distance, since from here to Redondo Beach it is interrupted only by the boat harbor at Marina del Rey. An excellent swimming beach—particularly toward the north, where water quality is usually best—Will Rogers is uncrowded, at least compared to teeming Santa Monica State Beach just south, because of limited parking. Surfing is fair. Facilities include playgrounds, picnic tables, volleyball nets, lifeguards, restrooms, the works.

BEYOND THE BEACHES

The Getty Villa: J. Paul Getty Museum

Beyond the surf and the stars, the community's most famous attraction is now the second location for the renowned J. Paul Getty Museum, 17985 Pacific Coast Hwy. (between Sunset and Topanga Canyon Boulevards), Malibu, www.getty.edu—still closed at last report, though after remodeling it is expected to reopen in 2002 as the Getty Center's classical antiquities exhibit and restoration center. (If you can't wait, head to Brentwood and the glorious new Getty Center, tel. (310) 440-7300; see Cities on a Hill.) The museum's collection of European paintings and drawings—Goya, Cézanne, van Gogh, Rembrandt, Renoir—along with illuminated manuscripts, American and European photography, home furnishings fit for French royalty, and European sculpture, bronzes, ceramics, and glass, are now installed at the Getty Center.

The 38-gallery Getty Villa is, and will be, perfect for the Getty classics, one of the finest U.S. collections of ancient Greek and Roman art and artifacts—sculptures and figurines, vases, mosaics, and paintings. When the museum reopens, expect special exhibits of ancient Asian and Eastern European art as well.

The Getty Villa is also a classic—a re-creation of the Villa dei Papiri, an ancient Roman country house with a view of the Bay of Naples. Even the Getty gardens, the trees, shrubs, and flowers, the statuary and outdoor wall paintings, represent those at the original villa of 2,000 years ago. Villa dei Papiri, thought to have belonged to Julius Caesar's father-in-law, was buried by the volcanic rubble of Mt. Vesuvius when the mountain erupted in A.D. 79. Discovered by treasure hunters and excavated during the 18th century, the reborn villa inspired Getty; the Getty Villa, completed in 1974, was constructed from excavation drawings.

Other Malibu Attractions

Other attractions include the prestigious private **Pepperdine University** campus, 24255 Pacific Coast Hwy., tel. (310) 456-4000, a nondenominational four-year liberal arts college established in 1973 by George Pepperdine, founder of Western Auto Supply. The attractive 819-acre campus, on a hill overlooking the ocean, was designed by architect William Pereira. These days Pepperdine is particularly noted for its postgraduate law and business schools. The men's volleyball team is typically one of the best in the country—which isn't that surprising, given the number of beach volleyball nets strung up all along the Malibu coast. Pepperdine's popularity among Southern California surfers was

EXCURSIONS INLAND: CITIES ON A HILL

Two new "cities" recently risen on the hills over-looking Sepulveda Pass, just off the San Diego Free-way north of Brentwood and Bel-Air, are among L.A.'s most striking new cultural attractions. The $800 million Getty Center, one of the world's most re-markable arts facilities, opened in December 1997. Originally envisioned as a second location for the renowned J. Paul Getty Museum at home in Malibu since the 1970s, "the Getty" has become consider-ably more—starting with six huge stone building complexes and gorgeous central garden on 110 ter-raced acres offering panoramic views of the city, the sea, and surrounding mountains. The complex in-cludes a restaurant and two cafes; a 450-seat audi-torium; a 750,000-volume library; education class-rooms, programs, and interactive technologies; and sophisticated art conservation and restoration facilities.

Not far north of the Getty is the impressive $65 mil-lion Skirball Cultural Center, a three-winged mod-ernist monument of pink granite, green slate, and curving stainless steel with visitor-friendly facilities in-cluding the extraordinary Skirball Museum of Jewish History and a children's Discovery Center.

GETTY CENTER

"The Getty" is L.A.'s latest astonishment—architect Richard Meier's contemporary yet classic arts en-clave, a 25-acre complex built of imported Italian travertine marble rising like a medieval castle above both city and sea on a ridge above Brentwood. "If God had the money," observed L.A. design critic Sam Hall Kaplan years before the Getty Center even opened its doors, "this is perhaps what he would do." The architectural statement, in his view, is that "this is a cultural institution here for the ages, not a passing indulgence, not a deconstructionist exer-cise by yet another narcissistic architect."

Whether God and other architects like it or not, and whatever else the Getty Center accomplishes, it has successfully carved out and created facility space—lots of it, nearly one million square feet—to make art appreciation more central to L.A. life. (Situated right next to the San Diego Freeway, how much more central and accessible could an L.A. art mu-seum be?) It has also built the most formidable pri-vate arts program in the world, thanks in large part to the $4.1 billion J. Paul Getty Trust, an accumula-tion of cash now more than triple the oil baron's orig-inal bequest in 1976.

In addition to its stunning new museum and ever-expanding museum collection, Getty Trust projects now housed at the Getty Center include its interna-tional arts conservation and restoration institute, its high-tech art history information institute, its research institute fellowships in art history and the humanities, and its education, grant, and museum management programs. Getty Center highlights also include a 450-seat auditorium and a 750,000-volume library with reading areas and a small exhibit area.

Yet the Getty Center's centerpiece is its muse-um. Inside the two-story circular lobby are two small theaters for visitor orientation and a book and gift shop. Surrounding a central garden courtyard are the five museum pavilions—vast galleries that allow dis-play of much more of the J. Paul Getty Museum's collection, including European sculptures, illuminat-ed manuscripts from the Middles Ages and the Re-naissance, and previously unseen photographs from its collection of more than 60,000. Galleries are also highly "interactive," with audio guides, multimedia computer stations, and expanded special-audience educational programs.

Prominently on display, in the sophisticated natural light of second-floor galleries, are stars of the Getty's growing Impressionist and post-Impressionist paint-ing galaxy, including Vincent van Gogh's *Irises* and Claude Monet's *Morning, Snow Effect* and *Wheat-stacks*. Visitors may also see fairly new Renais-sance acquisitions—including Michelangelo's 1530 chalk-and-ink drawing *The Holy Family with the In-fant Baptist on the Rest on the Flight into Egypt*, bought in 1993 for $6.27 million, and Fra Bartolom-meo's *The Holy Family with the Infant St. John*, painted in 1509 and bought in 1996 for $22.5 million.

The museum's 15-room decorative arts section is a study in opulence. Here, exquisitely tarted-up rooms—with damask walls, faux marble, mirrors, and elaborately carved and painted panels—au-thentically exhibit the Getty's French furniture, ta-pestries, and other elegant domestic wares from baroque, neoclassical, Régence, rococo, and other stylistic periods.

The previous showcase of the J. Paul Getty Trust was the original J. Paul Getty Museum in Malibu, an exact replica of a Roman villa now the muse-

the entrance to the museum—open, yet weighty

um's second campus and known as the Getty Villa, closed for renovation and reconfiguration. The villa is scheduled to reopen in the year 2002 as both the Getty Trust's museum of Greek and Roman antiquities and its ancient archaeology and cultures center. Special exhibits of the ancient art and artifacts of Asia, Africa, Latin America, the Near East, and Eastern Europe will also be featured at the Getty Villa.

Robert Irwin's Central Garden

Another Getty Center attraction is the 134,000-square-foot Central Garden near the museum, designed by "real-world" L.A. artist Robert Irwin—an intentionally self-conscious human-crafted garden reflecting upon the natural world as humanity has made it. Like a sculptor using both geometric and photosynthetic elements as "clay," Irwin has created a garden shaped like a huge handheld mirror, the overall image a severe and architectural landscape in winter yet soft, scented, and sensuous in summer. The mirror's "handle," roughly paralleled by a pathway, is created by an echo-chambered stream flanked by flowering plants and a canopy of trees. At stream's end, within a circular "natural" amphitheater,

the stream becomes a shallow pool surrounded by a geometric maze of flowering azaleas—images of nature that seem to float on the water's surface. Irwin's garden won't be in full flower for at least a decade, since it will take at least that many years for the two main tree plantings—the sensuous crape myrtle and the London plane trees that will one day form a carefully clipped canopy above the stream—to achieve their intended effects. So in the meantime, just pull up one of the French cafe chairs and sit a spell. And enjoy.

The Practical Getty

Plan to spend the day, and either pack a picnic—picnic area available—or sample any of several good restaurants. You'll be in company. About 1.5 million visitors are expected to commune with the Old Masters and other elements of the Getty's art world here each year. They all arrive at the hilltop palace after a five-minute electric monorail-style tram ride up the hill from the six-story underground parking garage at the west end of Getty Center Dr., just off the San Diego Freeway (the 405) and N. Sepulveda Boulevard. The Getty Center is open to the public Tuesday and Wednesday 11 a.m.-7 p.m., Thursday and Friday 11 a.m.-9 p.m., and Saturday and Sunday 10 a.m.-6 p.m. Closed on Monday and on major holidays. Admission is free, though there is a $5 parking fee. Parking reservations are *required,* though college students with a valid current ID are exempt from that requirement, as is anyone arriving by bicycle, motorcycle, shuttle, bus, or taxi. L.A.'s MTA Bus 561 and Santa Monica's Big Blue Bus 14 stop at the Getty's entrance.

For current information on special programs, current exhibits, and reservations, contact: Getty Center, 1200 Getty Center Dr., Los Angeles, CA 90049, tel. (310) 440-7300, fax (310) 454-6633, www.getty.edu.

SKIRBALL CULTURAL CENTER

About two miles north of the Getty Center is the splendidly simple four-story Skirball Cultural Center, designed by Boston-based architect Moshe Safdie and first opened to the public in April of 1996. Various other museums and cultural monuments document the Jewish experience, but this one celebrates Jewish life—and Jewish-American life—in an effort to explain Jewish traditions, values, and vision. Yet the new Skirball center is dedicated to full participation in L.A.'s efforts to "create a new

(continued on next page)

EXCURSIONS INLAND: CITIES ON A HILL
(continued)

paradigm for its cultural institutions." Part of the point here is interpreting the American-Jewish experience as it translates to the experience of all immigrants—an effort to strengthen the fabric of American society and its institutions.

The center itself is some institution—including the Skirball Museum of Jewish History, the hands-on children's Discovery Center, an education center with classrooms, computer lab and resource center, plus auditorium, conference facilities, and a large outdoor courtyard for concerts and other events, altogether 125,000 square feet of buildings on a 15-acre site.

The 15,000-square-foot museum covers 4,000 years of Jewish history throughout the world, celebrating in particular the American-Jewish experience. (An earlier, much smaller incarnation of the museum was, until recently, housed at Hebrew Union College just south of downtown L.A.) The core permanent exhibit—*Visions and Values: Jewish Life from Antiquity to America*—includes artifacts and art from ancient Israel and around the world, an ancient mosaic from Tiberias, re-created ruins of a sixth-century synagogue, and gallery exhibits on beliefs and celebrations. Then visitors "cross the big ocean," accompanied by sounds of the sea, beginning the American Jewish experience. Particularly evocative here: the huge replica of the Statue of Liberty's torch and original benches from

Ellis Island. After more American Jewish history—including a reminder of the first Jewish arrivals in North America, who came from Brazil in the mid-1600s—exhibits integrate American Jewish accomplishments and experience with the Holocaust and the rise of present-day Israel.

The Skirball Center also offers special exhibits from time to time, including, in mid-2000, the Library of Congress exhibition (co-sponsored by the Getty Center) **Sigmund Freud: Conflict and Culture,** which explored Freud's contested legacies.

The Skirball Cultural Center is on N. Sepulveda Blvd., on the west side of the San Diego Freeway just south of Mulholland Dr.; from the 405, exit at Sepulveda and follow the signs. The museum is open Tues.-Sat. noon-5 p.m. (until 9 p.m. on Thursday), and on Sunday 11 a.m.-5 p.m. Facilities include a great on-site restaurant and gift shop. Call or see the website for current information on changing exhibits, which regularly include art and history retrospectives and also spotlight very contemporary themes. The Skirball is closed on Monday and on Thanksgiving, Christmas, and New Year's Day; call for other holiday closings. Admission is $8 adults, $6 seniors and students, free for children under age 12. For more information, contact: Skirball Cultural Center, 2701 N. Sepulveda Blvd., Los Angeles, CA 90049, tel. (310) 440-4500, fax (310) 440-4595, www.skirball.com.

---

lampooned in Garry Trudeau's *Doonesbury* cartoon strip in 1997, when it was announced that Whitewater special prosecutor Kenneth Starr would soon join the faculty here. Bigger news in most years: summer's **Malibu Strawberry Creek Music Festival** and other special performances and events held here.

Then there's the vast expanse of **Santa Monica Mountains National Recreation Area,** which dips its chaparral-covered toes into the sea all along the Malibu coastline. Many mountainous areas were severely scorched during Malibu's 1993 wildfires; the fire-adapted ecosystem is quickly recovering, but fire scars are still apparent in many areas. For more information about parks and other destinations reasonably accessible from near Malibu, see Wilderness City: Santa Monica Mountains.

Charmlee Regional County Park is a little-known but charming park overlooking the Pacific—460 acres of meadows, oak woodlands, and chaparral on bluffs up to 1,300 feet above sea level. Charmlee is stunning for spring wildflowers and a perfect spot for watching the winter migration of the gray whales, just offshore. The undeveloped park is also ideal for a simple get-off-the-highway picnic, or for hiking on trails and fire roads. It's open during daylight hours, year-round. To get here, take Encinal Canyon Rd. from Pacific Coast Hwy. north of Malibu.

STAYING NORTH OF SANTA MONICA

Malibu offers the main accommodations action north of Santa Monica. And Malibu is a bit short on inexpensive places to stay—on places to stay, period—which is just the way Malibu likes it. Beyond the area's state park campsites, the 30 fairly quaint but clean 1920s-vintage cabins of the **Topanga Ranch Motel** south of central Malibu, right across from the beach at 18711 Pacific Coast Hwy. (PCH), tel. (310) 456-5486, are among the area's more affordable options. Some units have kitchens; a few boast two bedrooms. Moderate ($60-85). The attractive 21-room **Casa Malibu Inn** right on the beach in "downtown" Malibu, 22752 PCH, tel. (310) 456-2219, features an inviting central courtyard, some rooms with kitchens and balconies. Expensive-Luxury ($95-329). Another possibility is the decent 16-room **Malibu Country Inn** motel north of Malibu proper at 6506 Westward Beach Rd. (at PCH), tel. (310) 457-9622, with a small swimming pool, in-room refrigerators and coffeemakers. Luxury ($125-250), but somewhat less expensive in the off season.

Since 1990, Malibu has boasted a seriously stylish small hotel right on the beach, complete with tilework and berber carpets—the **Malibu Beach Inn,** in the pink and snuggled onto a strip of beachfront near the pier at 22878 Pacific Coast Hwy., tel. (310) 456-6444 or toll-free (800) 462-5428, www.malibubeachinn.com. Space here is too tight for so much as a swimming pool—but who needs a pool when the wide blue Pacific Ocean is in your front yard? Rooms are reasonably spacious, with the usual luxury amenities, small private balconies, and gas fireplaces (most rooms). Perfect for just hanging out: the motel's friendly Mediterranean-style terra-cotta-tiled patio hanging out over the rocky shore. Two-night minimum stay on weekends from May through October. Luxury ($169-249).

For a still quieter, still more serene weekend stay, room to retreat is often available for individuals at the Franciscan **Serra Retreat Center,** 3401 Serra Rd., P.O. Box 127, Malibu, CA 90265, tel. (310) 456-6631, or www.sbfranciscans.org, which offers regular group retreats at this scenic remnant of the original Topanga Malibu Sequit ranch, the spot where "Queen of Malibu" May Rindge started but never completed her hilltop mansion. Premium ($90-140) suggested per-day donation, which includes three substantial meals.

EATING NORTH OF SANTA MONICA

Just north of Santa Monica in Pacific Palisades, **Gladstone's 4 Fish,** 17300 Pacific Coast Hwy. (at Sunset Blvd.), tel. (310) 454-3474, has always been one of the most popular restaurants on the Westside—not because the food was so great but because, for singles, it was such a terrific place for trolling. (After a close call in 1997, when it looked as if Gladstone's might lose its prime beachfront locale, the lease was renewed for another long run.) The wait is always long, the crowd is always noisy. But even if you eat elsewhere, have a tropical drink on the patio at sunset just to watch the attractive beach buns and bunnies.

Dinner-only **Modo Mio,** 15200 Sunset Blvd. (enter on La Cruz), tel. (310) 459-0979, is the place for dinner, a stylish yet cozy neighborhood favorite serving rustic Tuscan fare. The incredible selection of specials keeps everyone surprised. For less expensive reservations-required fare, closer to Santa Monica, *the* place is the popular Italian **Caffe Delfini,** 147 W. Channel Rd. (at Pacific Coast Highway), tel. (310) 459-8823, where seafood and pastas star—Delfini's famous seafood soup and such things as broiled shrimp with fresh tomato and basil and homemade ravioli. The restaurant also has a regular celebrity clientele. Less expensive still, perfect for pizza, is the friendly neighborhood dinner-only **Vittorio!,** 16646 Marquez Ave. (at Sunset), tel. (310) 459-3755. Inexpensive just off Pacific Coast Highway is **Marix Tex Mex Playa,** 118 Entrada Dr., tel. (310) 459-8596, the coastal cousin of West Hollywood's happiest Tex-Mex joint, famous for its fajitas. This place is open daily for breakfast, lunch, and dinner.

Not to be missed in Topanga Canyon: **Froggy's Topanga Fresh Fish Market,** 1105 N. Topanga Canyon Blvd. (Hwy. 27), tel. (310) 455-1728. Malibu's chi-chi crowd may do fish at some swank place near the beach, but everybody else comes here. This fun and funky fish palace, a Topanga Canyon classic, doesn't get by on looks or general eccentricity. The fish is the thing, and here it's done quite well. Open for dinners, Froggy's is noteworthy for its rotisserie chicken and salads but famous for chowder, shrimp, lobster, and just about anything else that's fresh and on the menu. It's open 5 p.m.-9:30 p.m., until 10 p.m. on Friday and Saturday nights, closed Thanksgiving and Christmas. This place is easiest to find when navigating by local landmarks. With that proviso, Froggy's is on Topanga Canyon Blvd. (Hwy. 27) on the San Fernando Valley side of the post office but on the Pacific Coast Highway side of Theatricum Botanicum, the very cool community theater. Also locally famous, for vegetarian and some meatier entrées: the hip and hippie-friendly **Inn of the Seventh Ray** in Topanga Canyon at 128 Old Topanga Rd., tel. (310) 455-1311, famous for its homemade bread and Sunday brunch. The inn is open daily for lunch and dinner.

Eating in Malibu

Top of the food chain in Malibu proper is gloriously garish **Granita** in the Malibu Colony Plaza mall at 23725 W. Malibu Rd., tel. (310) 456-0488, another of Wolfgang Puck and Barbara Lazaroff's progeny, sometimes puckishly referred to as Spago-by-the-Sea. The interior, with the trademark open kitchen and equally typical high decibel levels, was designed to resemble an underwater sea cave inhabited by eclectic fishlike creatures—no wilder than the imaginative California-style Mediterranean fare. Yet it almost seems barbaric to dive into so much fish and seafood, no matter how delectable, while they're watching. Usually clotted with celebrities, Granita makes it challenging for regular people to get in, particularly on weekends. Try reservations—and coming for lunch during the week. It's very expensive and open for lunch Wed.-Fri., for brunch on Saturday and Sunday, for dinner every night.

Another fine-dining destination—if you find yourself in the vicinity of Malibu and in the mood for a drive—is exquisite **Saddle Peak Lodge,** a onetime hunting lodge in the Santa Monica Mountains near Calabasas, tel. (818) 222-3888.

For fish tacos, surfers and like-minded souls roll in to the fun and funky **Reel Inn,** 18661 Pacific Coast Hwy. (at Topanga Canyon Blvd.), tel. (310) 456-8221. More sophisticated and stylish, quite good for simpler fare and takeout, is **Marmalade,** 3894 S. Cross Creek Rd. (at PCH), tel. (310) 317-4242, a simple deli cafe featuring fresh bakery items (with or without marmalade), good salads, soups, and such things as chicken pot pie. (There's another Marmalade in Santa Monica, on Montana Avenue, and one in Westlake Village.) Pricier but unpretentious is Italian **Allegria,** 22821 Pacific Coast Hwy. (just south of Cross Creek Rd.), tel. (310) 456-3132, a lively trattoria serving authentic Venetian-style pastas and pizza. Another celeb-watching hotspot, open daily for lunch and dinner. To linger over a homey Italian meal, the place is **Tra di Noi,** 3835 Cross Creek Rd., tel. (310) 456-0169.

DOWN THE COAST: THE SOUTH BAY

SOUTH BAY BEACH CITIES

The strands of sand and beach towns south of Los Angeles International Airport (LAX) comprise L.A.'s "South Bay," the southern Santa Monica Bay. This is where the Beach Boys came of age—in Manhattan Beach—and where, in nearby Hermosa Beach and Redondo Beach, Southern California's middle-American surf culture got its biggest sendoff in the 1950s and '60s. But it all started in 1907 when George Freeth, billed as "the man who could walk on water," was imported to Redondo Beach by that ceaseless land-sales promoter Henry Huntington for a special "prove it" performance. Walking the offshore waves with the help of an eight-foot, 200-pound wooden surfboard, Freeth introduced the ancient Polynesian sport of kings to the neighborhood. You can tour the entire area from a bicycle seat, thanks to the 20-mile **South Bay Bike Trail** that runs from Will Rogers State Beach (north of Santa Monica) to Torrance Beach in the south. Or you can drive. Huge public parking lots abound along the South Bay's beaches.

Rising above the southernmost reach of Santa Monica Bay is the Palos Verdes Peninsula, a collection of affluent residential enclaves that separate L.A.'s surf cities and their semi-industrial inland neighbors from San Pedro and the Port of Los Angeles, next south, and Long Beach, home port of the RMS *Queen Mary*, the new Long Beach Aquarium of the Pacific, and other attractions. Next stop south of Long Beach is Orange County.

El Segundo and Manhattan Beach

El Segundo is sometimes also described as L.A.'s own Mayberry, U.S.A., for its insular Midwestern mores. Before the end of the Cold War and the rapid decline of Southern California's defense industry, no one much minded comments about "El Stinko," a reference to Playa del Rey's 144-acre Hyperion Waste Treatment Plant and its downwind influence here. And no one complained about the huge circa-1911 Chevron oil refinery just south. (The town was named for it. El Segundo means "The Second [One]" in Spanish, since Standard Oil's first refinery—this plant was Standard before it was Chevron—opened in Richmond, near San Francisco.) And no one seemed to hear the ear-rending racket from LAX jet traffic overhead. Everyone was too busy working—at Aerospace Corp., Hughes Aircraft, Northrop, Rockwell, and TRW. Not to mention Mattel Toys. Some of those jobs have disappeared, in L.A.'s new post-defense economy, but others have taken their place. These days El Segundo—conveniently near LAX, after all—is getting serious about attracting new industry and, closer to the beach, trendier and tourism-related businesses.

Chic Manhattan Beach, just south, already riding the latter wave, doesn't have such problems—which is why restaurants and businesses along the El Segundo side of the bustling, increasingly chi-chi Rosecrans Ave. corridor shamelessly advertise their address as "Manhattan Beach." At the beach—Manhattan State Beach, a continuation of the nearly seamless broad bay strand that starts north of Santa Monica—you'll find excellent swimming, lifeguards, both clean water and sand, the works. If you're driving, you'll find free parking along Vista del Mar to Highland, metered parking along most streets, and public lots close to attractive "downtown," at both 11th and 13th Streets. There's also a metered lot at 43rd Street. For fishing, try 900-foot **Manhattan Beach Pier** at the foot of Manhattan Beach Boulevard. You can also stroll **The Strand,** which here wanders past beachfront homes as it meanders south to Hermosa Beach.

For more information about the area, contact the **City of El Segundo,** tel. (310) 607-2249, www.elsegundo.org, and the **City of Manhattan Beach,** tel. (310) 802-5000, www.ci.manhattan-beach.ca.us.

Redondo Beach and Hermosa Beach

Redondo State Beach is the hot-weather hot spot in these parts, though nothing like this old resort town's turn-of-the century heyday. Still, at times it's almost as difficult to park your beach towel as it is your car. As elsewhere along L.A.'s

South Bay, the two miles of beach here are wide and sandy. The **Redondo Beach Pier,** at the foot of Torrance Blvd., marks the beach's northern reaches. In 1988 storms and subsequent fires ravaged the 60-year-old wooden horseshoe-shaped pier, the most recent of many local pier incarnations—and the city rebuilt in grand style. Designed by Edward Beall, the new, nautically themed $11 million Redondo Beach Pier—complete with sail-like awnings—is a sturdy yet wondrous concrete creation, complete with 1,800 life-size etchings of marine life, including sharks, scuba divers, and whales. (Water quality near the pier is less than perfect, though.) **King Harbor** just north, along Harbor Drive between Horondo and Beryl Streets, is the result of a massive redevelopment that cost Redondo Beach its historic downtown, replacing it with 50 acres of high-rise apartment buildings. King Harbor has its own piers, with restaurants, shops, and such, and also offers harbor cruises, sportfishing and winter whalewatching charters, and bike and other sports equipment rentals. Not to take a back seat to Long Beach, Redondo Beach even offers gondola rides at King Harbor, through **Gondola Amore,** tel. (310) 376-6977. The best surfing is just north, at Hermosa Beach, and well south of Redondo at Torrance Beach. Be that as it may, come to Redondo in August for the annual **Surf Festival.**

Head north from Redondo to Hermosa Beach, most famous as L.A.'s best for beach volleyball, site of numerous competitions and championship matches. Hermosa Beach also features row upon row of at-the-beach apartments and the **Hermosa Beach Pier,** historically a fishing pier, which along with lower Pier Ave. had a $1.5 million facelift in early 1997 to create another L.A. "destination street." **The Strand** stroll here is quite pleasant, passing beach homes, restaurants, and shops. Not to be missed in the neighborhood is the independent **Nations! Travelstore,** 500-504 Pier Ave., tel. (310) 318-9915 or toll-free (800) 546-8060, www.nationstravelmall.com, a combination bookstore, map and supply stop, and travel agency beloved for its exceptional product selection and customer service.

Head south from Redondo to Torrance Beach and then, for top-notch surfing, stroll to Malaga Cove below the bluffs. It's easier to get to the cove from the Palos Verdes Peninsula (see below).

For more information about the area, contact: **Redondo Beach Visitors Bureau,** 200 N. Pacific Coast Hwy., tel. toll-free tel. (800) 282-0333 or 310) 374-2171, www.redondo.org, and the **Torrance Visitors Bureau,** 3400 Torrance Blvd., tel. (310) 792-2343, www.torrnet.com.

PALOS VERDES PENINSULA

If you lived in paradise, wouldn't you want to keep it that way? The upper-class and upper-middle-class communities atop Palos Verdes Peninsula are fairly exclusive, and largely proud of it—a sense of entitlement that, unfortunately, sometimes extends to local beaches. Demonstrating an international surfing phenomenon known as "localism," the feared Bay Boys of Palos Verdes—"trust-fund babies," according to a *Surfer* magazine editor—have long made it their business to keep nonlocals out of primo surf spots such as Lunada Bay, a stance that has led to verbal assaults and worse on more than one occasion, and an attitude that has led to significant lawsuits against Palos Verdes Estates. Whatever the absolute truth underlying such conflicts, it's clear that no one here wants the now-common California beach overcrowding problems and related traumas—trash, graffiti, violence—that are increasing all along the coast, particularly at the best surfing beaches.

Few such troubles perturb the Palos Verdes Peninsula, which eons ago was one of the Channel Islands. Serious social problems here include the challenge of dodging horses and riders on public streets (equestrians have the right-of-way) and coping with the noise and effluence of the wild peacock flocks in Rolling Hills Estates and Palos Verdes Estates. The peninsula is home to several of L.A.'s most affluent communities—Rolling Hills is, officially, the wealthiest town in America, and its neighbors are also at the top of the list—and what its people value most is their privacy. Yet despite ongoing surf-turf wars the peninsula's parks, other public facilities, and businesses generally welcome visitors.

Though you must meander the peninsula's winding interior roads to get a close-up view of life here, most people are satisfied with a leisurely coastal drive. And, on a clear day, the views are spectacular. Starting in the north, from Pacific

Coast Highway (Hwy. 1) head southwest on Palos Verdes Blvd., which soon becomes Palos Verdes Dr. W, then, at Hawthorne Blvd., Palos Verdes Dr. S; heading north on Palos Verdes Dr. E eventually leads to east-west Palos Verdes Dr. N, completing the blufftop "perimeter" drive. But a true coastal tour would continue east along 25th St. into San Pedro, perhaps jogging south to Paseo del Mar and then east again to the Cabrillo Marine Aquarium.

Touring the Palos Verdes Peninsula

First stop along the peninsula coast tour is in town, actually, in Palos Verdes Estates. The **Neptune Fountain** at the **Malaga Cove Plaza** was inspired by the architecture of Italy's Sorrentine Peninsula. (When in the 1960s King Neptune's anatomy was somehow dismembered, locals rallied and replaced the notable lost part with a strategic fig leaf.) Elsewhere throughout this area are architectural reminders of what the Palos Verdes Peninsula might have been, if plans made in the 1920s by banker Frank A. Vanderlip, architect Myron Hunt, and the similarly talented sons of landscape architect Frederick Law Olmsted had been fully realized. To appreciate the Olmsteds's local heritage, head to **La Venta Inn,** 796 Via del Monte, tel. (310) 373-0123, then it's off to **Malaga Cove** proper, accessible from Paseo del Mar (east of Via Arroyo), an inspiring sidetrip in its own right. Also known as **RAT Beach** (short for "Right After Torrance" Beach, not an urban wildlife reference), this top-notch surfing beach is equally popular for rock and shell collecting and tidepool exploration.

From Malaga Cove the truly adventurous can scrabble south over the rocks to the shale-cliffed scenery of **Bluff Cove,** also popular with surfers, and on to the famous surf-turf battleground of **Lunada Bay,** a six-mile roundtrip. This adventure is recommended only during pacific surf—and only at low tide, when the tide's heading out. Notable near Lunada is the 1961 wreckage of the Greek freighter *Dominator,* which failed to dominate these treacherous shores.

Back on the main road, continue south to one of L.A.'s premier winter whalewatching sights— the **Point Vicente Interpretive Center** at 31501 Palos Verdes Dr. W., tel. (310) 377-5370, where the second-floor gallery is packed with California

gray whale voyeurs from mid-December into March each year. Any time—at least on a clear day—the center offers an impressive view of Santa Catalina Island and a worthwhile introduction to area natural history. Open daily, except major holidays. Small fee.

The historic 1926 **Point Vicente Lighthouse** perches on a cliff farther down the coast at 31550 Palos Verdes Dr. W., tel. (310) 541-0334. The 67-foot-tall lighthouse is powered by a two-million-candlepower bulb, and visitors can climb the 74 steps to the top to check out the handcrafted Fresnel lens that produces the long light beam. Tours are held every second Saturday 9 a.m.-3 p.m. and by appointment for groups.

Next south is the peninsula's rather notorious **Portuguese Bend** area, where in the 1950s massive landslides doomed more than 100 homes. Things are still plenty unstable today. One of this neighborhood's most popular attractions is the small but stunning **Wayfarers Chapel,** 5755 Palos Verdes Dr. S., tel. (310) 377-1650, designed by Lloyd Wright (son of Frank Lloyd Wright) and built of glass, redwood, and Palos Verdes stone. Except during special events—weddings are understandably popular here, typically scheduled on weekends between 1 and 3 p.m.—this Swedenborgian Church chapel and lovely grounds are open daily for meditation.

For some prime-time picnicking, try nearby **Abalone Cove Shoreline Park and Ecological Preserve,** a federal reserve near Portuguese Point at 5970 Palos Verdes Dr. S., tel. (310) 377-1222, where the grassy lawn offers easy access to the rocky beach below—and to tidepools teeming with these precious, and protected, ocean creatures. Best time for abalone voyeurism is in December and January. Parking $5. Nearby **Smuggler's Cove** is a long-popular nude beach, unofficially, so a subject of local conflict.

If you're making a day of it, the best bet in Southern California for dahlia and fuchsia displays is the **South Coast Botanic Garden,** a onetime landfill at 26300 Crenshaw Blvd., tel. (310) 544-6815, where the peak dahlia bloom comes in mid-August. Also here: plant collections representing every continent except Antarctica (organized by color), some 1,600 roses, and the "Garden of the Senses."

To explore local features and natural history in more detail, sign on for one of the monthly guided hikes offered through the **Palos Verdes Peninsula Land Conservancy,** tel. (310) 541-7613, www.pvplc.org. For more information about the area, contact: **Palos Verdes Peninsula Chamber of Commerce,** tel. (310) 377-8111, www.palosverdes.com/pvpcc.

San Pedro

With its hilly streets, ocean fog, views, and military installations, San Pedro is, some local wags say, L.A.'s own little San Francisco, complete with a miniature, but much friendlier, Mission District, along Pacific Street. (It's san PEE-dro, by the way, despite California's predilection elsewhere for correct Spanish pronunciation.) That perspective is a hard sell even in this semi-industrial port city, however.

If people find themselves in San Pedro, most head to the shops, restaurants, and other tourist diversions of **Ports O' Call Village** at the end of Sixth St., tel. (310) 831-0287, a shopping mall in the style of a New England seaside village. But San Pedro has more intriguing features—including the **Port of Los Angeles** itself, which was created at a cost of $60 million between 1920 and 1940. The best way to get the big picture is on guided boat tours ($6-10) with **Spirit Cruises,** tel. (310) 548-8080, which depart from Ports O' Call. From the **World Cruise Terminal** and **Catalina Terminal** here, travelers depart on sea journeys near and far. A particularly impressive sight is soaring **Vincent Thomas Bridge,** which from the Harbor Fwy. (the 110) connects San Pedro (via Hwy. 47) to Terminal Island—Southern California's largest suspension bridge, built in 1963 (small toll on the return trip). **Terminal Island,** once known as Rattlesnake Island, was a vibrant resort destination earlier in this century, L.A.'s own Brighton Beach, complete with pleasure pier. Starting in 1906, it was also home to a close-knit village of Japanese-American fishermen and their families—an idyllic life ended forever with World War II-era Japanese internment in 1942. Terminal Island today, an uninviting diesel-scented jungle of canneries, loading cranes, and old warships, also includes a federal penitentiary.

Other significant San Pedro attractions include two seaworthy museums: the **Los Ange-**les Maritime Museum at Berth 84 (at the foot of Sixth St.), tel. (310) 548-7618, and the **S.S. Lane Victory Ship Museum** at Berth 94 (near the World Cruise Terminal), tel. (310) 519-9545, a onetime ammunition carrier, now a national historic landmark. Well worth a stop in nearby **Wilmington** are the **Banning Residence Museum,** 401 E. M St., tel. (310) 548-7777, the restored 1864 Greek revival mansion of General Phineas Banning and a major interpretive center for 19th-century L.A. history, and the **Drum Barracks Civil War Museum,** 1052 Banning Blvd., tel. (310) 548-7509, the only remaining structure from the Civil War-era Camp Drum, where 7,000 troops were based. Both museums are open only for guided tours (call for times); donations greatly appreciated.

Definitely worth a stop, especially with tots in tow, is the **Cabrillo Marine Aquarium and Museum,** 3720 Stephen White Dr., tel. (310) 548-7562, open Tues.-Fri. noon-5 p.m. and on weekends 10 a.m.-5 p.m. (open on some "holiday" Mondays, closed Thanksgiving, Christmas). It's free—suggested donation is $2 adults, $1 children, and parking is $6.50—and full of educational opportunity, thus quite popular with school groups. But anyone can be a kid here. Housed in a contemporary Frank Gehry-designed building, the Cabrillo features 38 tanks now home to an abundance of Southern California sea life. Among the most popular exhibits: the "tidal tank," a veritable room with a view of a wave, and the shark tank. Other exhibits include a "touch tank" filled with sea anemones and starfish, and a whalebone graveyard. The aquarium also offers seasonal whalewatching tours and "grunion run" programs; call for current information. From here, set out for both **Cabrillo Beach** and 1200-foot **Cabrillo Pier,** just inside the breakwater. Also worth a stop (though not open to the public) **Point Fermin Lighthouse** at the end of the breakwater at 807 Paseo del Mar—the only remaining wooden lighthouse on the Pacific Coast, shining forth here since 1874.

Budget travelers, keep in mind that San Pedro's **Point Fermin Park,** back toward the Palos Verdes Peninsula on S. Paseo del Mar, includes the **HI-AYH Los Angeles/South Bay Hostel,** 3601 S. Gaffey St., Bldg. 613, tel. (310) 831-2836. Next to Point Fermin Park is San Pedro's own "sunken city." In 1929 an entire neighborhood of exclusive homes started slipping to sea here—at the rate of 12 inches per day—and was quickly relocated to more solid ground. But the ground kept slipping, and keeps slipping. The jumble of old pavement and palm trees is a slightly surreal sight. If you get hungry and enjoy biker bars, *the* place locally is **Walker's Cafe,** almost on the sunken-city spot at 700 S. Paseo Del Mar, tel. (310) 833-3623.

The best beach around for scuba diving and pleasant scenery is San Pedro's rocky **Royal Palms State Beach** on the Palos Verdes Peninsula at the south end of Western Avenue.

For more information about the area, contact: **San Pedro Peninsula Chamber of Commerce,** 390 W. Seventh St., tel. (310) 832-7272, www.sanpedrochamber.com.

PRACTICAL SOUTH BAY

Accommodations options south of Santa Monica range from very inexpensive at-the-beach hostels to midrange motels and five-star luxury hotels.

Close to both beach and LAX is ever-popular **Barnabey's Hotel,** 3501 Sepulveda Blvd. (a half block south of Rosecrans), Manhattan Beach, tel. (310) 545-8466 or toll-free (800) 552-5285. Three-story Barnabey's is a real surprise—an ersatz 19th-century English inn with four-poster beds and an antique-rich ambience yet all the modern conveniences, including in-room coffeemakers and data ports, on-site pub, pool, and jacuzzi. Premium-Luxury ($130-200).

For other places to stay in Redondo Beach, Torrance, and elsewhere in the South Bay, contact local visitor bureaus and chambers of commerce.

To find what's new and sometimes the best in South Bay dining, explore on and around piers and coastal areas. Possibilities in Manhattan Beach include the popular Americanized Mexican **Pancho's,** 3615 Highland Ave. (at Rosecrans Ave.), tel. (310) 545-6670, where entrees start at about $7. Look for the **Wolfgang Puck Café,** tel. (310) 607-9653, and other trendy alternatives along the Rosecrans Avenue corridor separating El Segundo and Manhattan Beach. Quite impressive is California-French

style **Reed's,** 2640 N. Sepulveda Blvd. (near Marine), tel. (310) 546-3299, a shopping-center shining light. Dinner entrees about $20. Another pricey possibility is California-French **Cafe Pierre,** 317 Manhattan Beach Blvd. (at Highland Ave.), tel. (310) 545-5252. This upscale beach café is noted for outstanding bouillabaisse and grilled fish.

Great for vegetarian is **The Spot** in Hermosa Beach at 110 Second St. (at Hermosa Ave.), tel. (310) 376-2355, though the Middle Eastern **Habash Cafe,** 233 Pacific Coast Hwy. (between Second and Third Streets), tel. (310) 376-6620, offers some intriguing nonmeat alternatives at breakfast, lunch, and dinner. The onetime Diana's in Hermosa Beach has now been incorporated into the original **Hennessey's Tavern,** 8 Pier Ave., tel. (310) 372-5759, a fairly sophisticated beach pub serving suds and sandwiches and live entertainment on weekends. (You'll find Hennessey's all up and down this stretch of L.A. coastline.)

For fast-food seafood in Redondo Beach, check out **The Blue Moon Saloon,** 207 N. Harbor Dr. (near Beryl), tel. (310) 374-3411. For something a bit fancier, try popular **Chez Melange,** at the Palos Verdes Inn, 1716 Pacific Coast Hwy. (near Palos Verdes Blvd.), tel. (310) 540-1222, a Spago for just plain folks serving everything from Japanese to Cajun, open every night for dinner, on weekdays for breakfast and lunch, and on Sunday for brunch. Chez Melange has spawned two respected spin-offs in the general vicinity, too—**Depot** inside a beautifully restored train depot in Torrance at 1250 Cabrillo Ave. (at Torrance Blvd.), tel. (310) 787-7501, and the casual Cal-Asian **Gina Lee's Bistro** in Redondo Beach at 211 Palos Verdes Blvd. (between Pacific Coast Hwy. and Catalina Ave.), tel. (310) 375-4462.

Quite good in Torrance for eclectic California cuisine is **Christine,** open for weekday lunches and dinner daily at the Hillside Village, 24530 Hawthorne Blvd., tel. (310) 373-1952, but **Aioli,** 1261 Cabrillo Ave. (at Torrance Blvd.), tel. (310) 320-9200, offers options beyond the sit-down dining room—including the **Breadstix Bakery** and tapas. Aioli is open for dinner every night, for lunch on weekdays only, and for brunch on Sunday.

LONG BEACH:
IOWA BY THE BAY GOES BIG TIME

Long Beach is the second-largest city in Los Angeles County, dwarfed only by L.A. itself, and the fifth-largest in the state. The city's history follows the fairly predictable Southern California course, from coastal wilderness and rangeland suburb of Spain and Mexico to extensive Midwestern settlement. The population of transplants from Iowa was once so dominant, in fact, that "Iowa picnics" became the most memorable community social gatherings during the Great Depression. Then came turn-of-the-20th-century seaside resort and booming port, regional oil development, and the monumental Long Beach earthquake that flattened downtown in 1933—the indirect impetus for downtown's then-new art deco style. Howard Hughes, the aviator and engineer later famous as the world's most eccentric billionaire, made history here in 1947 when he took his *Spruce Goose*—the world's largest airplane—for its first and only flight.

During and since World War II, but before the post-Cold War era of military downsizing, the U.S. Navy was central to Long Beach life, given the presence of the Long Beach Naval Station, Long Beach Naval Ship Yard, and Boeing, McDonnell Douglas, and other aviation and defense-related industry. Symbol of that past was the Iowa-class USS *Missouri,* America's last active battleship, host to Japan's formal surrender at the end of World War II and later recruit for offshore duty in the Persian Gulf during Operation Desert Storm. When "Mighty Mo" was finally decommissioned here in 1992, thousands and thousands turned out for the event. Both the naval station and shipyard have since been shut down. Yet the city is determined to recover from its defense-related economic losses. The Port of Long Beach is the busiest cargo port on the West Coast, doing a brisk Pacific Rim trade, and promoting downtown and port-side tourism is also a major priority.

Long Beach is an astonishingly diverse community with large immigrant populations, recently gaining national notoriety as the first California city to adopt a uniforms-only public school dress code. Despite the city's pressing social problems, people visit Long Beach primarily because it's still apple-pie appealing, unassuming, and affordable, with clean air and coastal diversions, a spruced-up downtown, and a lively cultural scene. (Many also show up here on business; both the Long Beach Convention and Entertainment Center and the World Trade Center are downtown.) And some say there are more worthy breakfast, burger, and pie shops in Long Beach than anywhere else in L.A. County.

Though bad press from occasional outbreaks of gang warfare is a bane of Long Beach existence, visitors don't need to be overly concerned. (One area at high risk for violent crime is north of downtown, straddling the 710 between Hwy. 47 and Temple Ave., south of Pacific Coast Highway and north of Seventh St.; another, well north of downtown, stretches between Long Beach Blvd. and Orange Ave., south of South St. and north of Del Amo Boulevard.) Reasonable precautions are prudent, of course, as in any urban area.

Special annual events well worth the trip include the **Toyota Grand Prix of Long Beach** in April—an event that transforms Shoreline Drive, Seaside Way, and other downtown streets into an international raceway—the **Cajun and Zydeco Festival** in June, and the long-running **Long Beach Blues Festival** in September.

The **Long Beach Freeway,** the 710, a major shipping corridor, delivers residents, visitors, and truckers alike right into downtown and/or the port district. Newcomers, heads up: Should you see a spectacular crash on six-lane **Shoreline Drive** in Long Beach, it's not always necessary to call 911. One of Hollywood's favorite filming sites for "freeway" disasters, Shoreline is regularly shut down for film shoots—20 or more times in an average year. (Don't worry. Actual traffic is routed around the action.) But in Long Beach, it's uniquely possible to get out—and stay out—of your car altogether.

camouflaged oil wells
on a man-made island
off Long Beach

TOM MYERS PHOTOGRAPHY

Excellent public transportation includes L.A. Metrorail's **Blue Line** mass transit system, tel. (213) 626-4455 (schedules) or tel. (213) 922-6235 (information), which runs 22 miles between Long Beach and downtown L.A. At downtown's **Long Beach Transit Mall** at First St. and the Promenade, riders can connect to 36 different local bus routes and interconnect with other bus systems. For detailed regional bus route and schedule information, stop by the **Long Beach Transit Information Center,** 223 E. First St., or call Long Beach Transit, tel. (562) 591-2301, L.A.'s Metropolitan Transit Authority, tel. (562) 626-4455, and Orange County Transit District, toll-free tel. (714) 636-RIDE.

Best yet for visitors is the free **Long Beach Runabout** downtown shuttle, tel. (562) 591-2301, which ferries folks around downtown and to and from the *Queen Mary,* Shoreline Village, the convention center, hotels, restaurants, and shopping districts. If you'd prefer to get around by water but left the yacht back home, the 40-foot **Catalina Express** water taxi, toll-free tel. (800) 995-4386, connects the aquarium with Shoreline Village, the *Queen Mary,* and with the Catalina Express terminal (for the trip to Catalina Island).

For more information about Long Beach and its attractions, contact: **Long Beach Convention and Visitors Bureau,** One World Trade Center, Ste. 300, Long Beach 90831, tel. (562) 436-3645, or toll-free tel. (800) 452-7829, or www.go-longbeach.org.

SEEING AND DOING LONG BEACH

On the Waterfront in Long Beach
The visitor action in Long Beach is downtown and nearby, on the waterfront. The famed **Pike Amusement Park**—where Southern California once entertained itself on the roller coaster and boardwalk, and where W.C. Fields, Buster Keaton, and other early film-industry icons made movies—once stood near the current site of the huge Long Beach Convention and Entertainment Center. Though Hollywood subsequently stole the moviemaking spotlight, later Long Beach films have included *The Creature from the Black Lagoon, Corrina Corrina, Speed,* and the opening scenes to *Lethal Weapon.* And until quite recently TV's *Baywatch* was filmed here, too, at least in part.

Though the new **Long Beach Aquarium of the Pacific,** tel. (562) 590-3100, is the city's newest big attraction, surrounding **Rainbow Harbor** is now home port for the tallship *Californian,* toll-free tel. (800) 432-2201, www.californian.org, available for high-seas adventure sails when it's moored in Long Beach. For more boating, take a Venetian-style gondola ride through the Naples Island neighborhood with **Gondola Getaway,** tel. (562) 433-9595, where the basket of bread, cheese, and salami is provided—along with the "O Sole Mio"—but you'll have to bring your own vino. Still most famous in Long Beach, though, is the RMS *Queen Mary,* tel. (562) 435-3511, a floating cruise ship-cum-museum moored on the other side of Queensway Bridge featuring hotel rooms, restaurants, and shops. The gigantic golf ball-like geodesic dome nearby is the Queen Mary Seaport Dome, onetime home of Howard Hughes's *Spruce Goose,* now a popular movie-making soundstage.

Looking out onto the Queen, from the downtown side of the bay, is the **Shoreline Village** shopping complex at 407 Shoreline Village Dr., tel. (562) 435-4093, complete with a 1906 **Charles Looff carousel** for the kiddos.

Or head for the wide white sandy beach. Or take a beachfront bike ride. Well worth a stop at the beach is the **Long Beach Museum of Art,** 2300 E. Ocean Blvd., tel. (562) 439-2119,

www.lbma.org, where you get artistic beach views in addition to an eyeful of contemporary art, photography, and sculpture. The museum is scheduled to reopen, after renovation, in September 2000, and when it does will be open Tues.-Sun. 11 a.m.-7 p.m. Admission is $5 adults, $4 students/seniors.

Bike It or Not: Beach and Bay Overview
The paved **Shoreline Path** introduces bicyclists to Long Beach as both port and "pleasure place," weaving its way from the Los Angeles River and Shoreline Village on the west to Belmont Shore on the east, paralleling Ocean Boulevard—and the beach—for much of the way. The route starts at the port, near Shoreline Village and within view of the venerable RMS *Queen Mary.* The

---

EXCURSION INLAND:
"OUR TOWN" AND A TOWERING IMAGINATION

One of the world's finest folk art shrines, the elaborate walled complex known as **Watts Towers** at 1765 E. 107th St. in South-Central L.A., was built by Italian immigrant Simon Rodia. Working without helpers—without formal plans, for that matter, and without scaffolding, machinery, rivets, or bolts—from 1921 until 1954 Rodia labored in his free time to build what he called Nuestro Pueblo, or "Our Town." His walled town first consisted of his small home, a gazebo, a fountain, a fireplace, and a barbecue—all framed from discarded steel (old pipes and bedframes), slathered with cement, then decorated with broken bottle glass, seashells, and bits of broken tiles and dishes. Then Rodia expanded, adding the three eccentric Gothic-style spires, more fountains, a fishpond, birdbaths, even a covered porch—everything woven together with patterned pathways and elaborate arches.

Simon Rodia was not without detractors. During World War II, for example, some thought the towers were secret radio transmitters designed to aid the Japanese. Others believed the elaborate compound was a secret burial site for his wife. But Rodia's town was actually a monument to historic adventurers and explorers. One tower, for example, represents Marco Polo's ship.

Rodia, who earned his living as a mason and tile-setter, abandoned his masterpiece almost as soon as it was completed. He deeded the property to a

neighbor and then vanished from the neighborhood without telling a soul why he was inspired to build his "town," or why he was leaving. Years later, Rodia was found living in Martinez, near San Francisco. He finally told at least part of the story. "I wanted to do something for the United States," he said. "Because I was raised here, you understand, because there are nice people in this country." Rodia's monument to the vastness of human potential is now a National Historic Landmark.

The Watts Towers sustained an estimated $2 million damage in the 1994 Northridge earthquake, and repairs funded by the Federal Emergency Management Agency are now underway. Public tours of Watts Towers have been suspended temporarily because of ongoing renovation and restoration work, which in 2000 was already several years behind schedule due to the complexity of the task. The towers and some details are still visible from outside, however. At some point "outside" docent-guided group tours may resume. For more information, contact: **Watts Towers of Simon Rodia State Historic Park,** c/o City of Los Angeles Department of Cultural Affairs, 1727 E. 107th St., Los Angeles, CA 90002, www.culturela.com. Or call the community-based **Watts Towers Art Center** next door to the towers, tel. (213) 847-4646, for current tour information. The Watts Towers complex is accessible by Metrorail's Blue Line; get off at the 103rd St. stop.

path heads east along the broad, sandy beach—and those enticing semitropical "islands" offshore, actually dressed-up oil drilling platforms—while sashaying past some stately historic buildings along Ocean Boulevard, including one mansion now home to the **Long Beach Museum of Art.** End of the line is the remarkably congested **Belmont Shore** area, where the "elite retreat" cachet still holds. (One of the best respites in sight here is the Belmont Brewing Company at the foot of tiny **Belmont Pier,** beloved locally for fishing.) Beyond the beachfront homes the bike path becomes a boardwalk, for pedestrians only. Only locals get to the beach early, which makes mornings the best time for a bike ride. As is always prudent in L.A., avoid being on the bike trail after dark.

Long Beach is also as good a place as any to begin a more ambitious tour of L.A.'s **Port of Los Angeles** commercial and industrial development, a trek not advisable by bike. San Pedro is L.A.'s cruise ship central as well as departure point for many Catalina ferries and other pleasure craft. Farther west are the placid coastal pleasures of Palos Verdes and vicinity; continue north to explore a few South Bay beach towns. To explore south of Long Beach, follow Second St. in Belmont Shore to Pacific Coast Hwy. (PCH) and then continue southeast across the San Gabriel River to arrive in Orange County and Seal Beach, Huntington Beach, and Newport Beach along the coast.

Long Beach Aquarium of the Pacific

The latest star—shall we say sea star?—brightening the Long Beach waterfront is the $100 million, 120,000-square-foot Long Beach Aquarium of the Pacific. At least indirectly inspired by the phenomenal success of the Monterey Bay Aquarium, which was the first to examine local ocean ecology in such exquisite, intimate, and technologically enhanced detail, the emphasis here is on the entire Pacific Ocean, the largest body of water on earth.

The Aquarium of the Pacific features 550 species of aquatic life in three major galleries, these corresponding to the ocean's three regions: **Southern California/Baja,** the **Tropical Pacific,** and the **Northern Pacific.** The Great Hall of the Pacific—the size of a football field, to represent the Pacific's vastness—offers an overview and a preview.

The aquarium first dips into the offshore waters of Southern California and the Baja Peninsula, from underwater kelp forests to bird's- and otter's-eye views of seals and sea lions frolicking in a facsimile Catalina Island environment. The interactive Kids' Cove here teaches the kiddos about other families' habits and habitats—in this case, those of marine animal families—and allows them to hike through whale bones, "hatch" bird eggs, and hide out with the hermit crabs. Then it's a quick splash south to Baja's Sea of Cortez and its sea turtles, skates, and rays. The Northern Pacific exhibits begin in the icy Bering Sea, where puffins nest near playful sea otters. This frigid sea shares other aquatic wealth, from schooling fish to giant octopuses and Japanese spider crabs. First stop in the Tropical Pacific is a peaceful lagoon in Micronesia, which sets the stage for the stunning 35,000-gallon Deep Reef exhibit—the aquarium's largest—with its vivid panorama of tropical sea life. If you time it right, you can watch divers feed the fish. Should you need feeding yourself, dive into the aquarium's **Café Scuba,** overlooking Rainbow Harbor. And to take home some specific memento of the Pacific Ocean, see what's on sale at the **Pacific Collections** gift shop.

The Long Beach Aquarium of the Pacific is centerpiece of the $650-million Queensbay Bay redevelopment project. The largest waterfront development in California history, Queensway Bay also encompasses the Rainbow Harbor resort complex.

Just off Shoreline Drive at 100 Aquarium Way (follow the signs), the Aquarium of the Pacific is open daily 9 a.m.-6 p.m. (closed Christmas). At last report admission was $14.95 adults, $11.95 seniors (age 60 and older), and $7.95 children (ages 3-11). Group rates (for 20 or more) are available with advance reservations. For more information or to purchase advance tickets, call the aquarium at (562) 590-3100 or check the website at www.aquariumofpacific.org. The 40-foot **Catalina Express** water taxi, toll-free tel. (800) 995-4386, connects the aquarium with Shoreline Village, the *Queen Mary,* and the Catalina Express terminal (for the trip to Catalina Island).

RMS *Queen Mary*

If the kids have never been on an ocean liner, a setting right out of old romantic movies, they might enjoy exploring this one. Who knows? If they loved *Titanic* the movie, they might just love this ship. The RMS *Queen Mary*, with its sleek streamline-modern interiors, was first launched in 1936. At 1,019 feet long, this is one of the largest passenger ships ever built. More details—and some insight into luxury travel standards of yesteryear—are revealed in stateroom and other exhibits. The engine room and the bridge offer hands-on perspective on the mechanics of this massive ship. Also onboard: hotel rooms, restaurants, and shops. The adjacent **Queen Mary Seaport** offers more of Southern California's ubiquitous shopping.

At last report *Queen Mary* admission was $15 adults, $13 seniors (age 55 and older) and active members of the military (with ID), $9 children ages 4-11. Guided one-hour tours cost an additional $7 adults, $4 children. Parking is $8 per day. For more information and hotel and restaurant reservations, call (562) 435-3511, or toll-free (800) 437-2934 (hotel reservations), or check www.queenmary.com. The *Queen Mary* is open daily 10 a.m.-6 p.m.; last admission is 30 minutes before closing on Saturday, otherwise 90 minutes before closing. The *Queen Mary* is directly across the harbor from the Aquarium of the Pacific at 1126 Queen's Hwy., Pier J. From the end of the Long Beach Freeway (the 710), follow the signs. From downtown, get here via Shoreline Dr. and Queensway Bridge.

A new companion for the *Queen* is a retired Soviet submarine once capable of firing low-grade nuclear torpedoes. Commissioned in 1973 by the Soviet government, Podvodnaya Lodka B-427, also known by the code name *Scorpion*, was decommissioned in 1994. Tours of the *Scorpion*, berthed at the bow of the *Queen Mary*, are $10 adults and $9 seniors, military with I.D., and children ages 4-11. Hours are 10 a.m.-6 p.m. daily, but last admission is 30-90 minutes before closing (depending on the day). Call (562) 435-3511 for current details.

More Long Beach Attractions

The new **Museum of Latin American Art** close to downtown at 628 Alamitos Ave. (the northern extension of Shoreline Dr., south of Seventh St.), tel. (562) 437-1689, www.molaa.com, is the only U.S. museum with this exclusive artistic focus. This 1920-vintage 20,000-square-foot building houses the Robert Gumbiner Foundation collection of Latin American art, rotating contemporary exhibits, "La Galeria" gallery and store, and both performance area and research library. The museum is open Tues.-Sat. 11:30 a.m.-7:30 p.m., Sunday noon-6 p.m. Admission is $7 adults, $5 students and seniors, free for children 12 and under. Call for current exhibit information or check the museum website.

Other Long Beach museums include the free **Lifeguard Museum** at the historic Long Beach **Marine Stadium**, 5255 Appian Way, built for the 1932 Olympics, tel. (562) 570-1360, open only 10 a.m.-2 p.m. on the second Saturday of each

The RMS Queen Mary *is one of the largest passenger ships ever built.*

month. (But call first. Sometimes the lifeguard business gets too busy to indulge even history, especially during summer.) For an introduction to local history, stop by the **Historical Society of Long Beach Gallery and Research Center,** in the Breakers Building, tel. (562) 495-1210.

Amateur historians should also explore two small outposts of early Southern California still at home in Long Beach. The seven-acre remnant of **Rancho Los Alamitos,** 6400 E. Bixby Hill Rd., tel. (562) 431-3541, offers free tours of the 1800-vintage adobe, later farm buildings, and lovely gardens Wed.-Sun. 1-5 p.m. (last tour starts at 4 p.m.). **Rancho Los Cerritos,** 4600 Virginia Rd., tel. (562) 570-1755, offers weekend-only guided tours of this 1844 Monterey-style adobe home and surrounding gardens—once the center of a 27,000-acre sheep ranch—which is also open to the public Wed.-Sun. 1-5 p.m. Admission to both homes is free. Closed on holidays.

Historians of California's future should visit **Little Cambodia** along Anaheim St., the largest Cambodian settlement outside Phnom Penh. For business, restaurant, and other information, call the **Cambodian Association of America,** tel. (562) 426-6002, or the **United Cambodian Community,** tel. (562) 433-2490.

Book lovers, don't miss family-run **Acres of Books,** 240 Long Beach Blvd. (at Maple), tel. (562) 437-6980, the nation's largest selection of used books, open here since 1934 and reported to be one of writer Ray Bradbury's favorites. Another historic local business is **Bert Grimms Tattoo Studio,** 22 S. Chestnut Pl. (at Ocean), tel. (562) 432-9304, where, according to local lore, gangsters Bonnie Parker and Pretty Boy Floyd got their skin ink. Prime-time for shopping is a 15-block stretch of Second Street in Belmont Shore and downtown's Pine Avenue/Broadway district.

PRACTICAL LONG BEACH

Staying in Long Beach
In the absence of a major downtown convention, and particularly in the off-season, Long Beach-area accommodations can be a relative bargain for families and budget travelers. The best bargain anytime, complete with panoramic ocean views and surrounding sports fields, park,

and picnic areas, is the nearby 60-bed Hostelling International-American Youth Hostels **Los Angeles/South Bay Hostel** in Angel's Gate Park in San Pedro at 3601 S. Gaffey St., Bldg. 613, tel. (310) 831-8109, www.hostelweb.com, primarily dorm-style accommodations (groups welcome) though private rooms are available. The hostel features on-site kitchen and laundry, library, TV and VCR, and barbecue—and from here it's just a stroll to the beach. Dorm beds are $16 members, $18 non-members; private rooms $39 non-members, $42 members. Budget. Reservations essential in summer.

Other fairly inexpensive accommodations abound in Long Beach along or near Pacific Coast Highway. Here, though, the highway runs through some rough neighborhoods and—if you were expecting oceanfront views—doesn't get close to the coast until it reaches the Orange County line. Be that as it may, best bets include **Motel 6** on Seventh St. near California State University at Long Beach, tel. (562) 597-1311 or toll-free (800) 466-8356, www.motel6.com, with rates $54 double (Moderate), and **Super 8** across from the community hospital, tel. (562) 597-7701 with rates $66 double and up (Moderate-Expensive). Just south of PCH is the **Best Western of Long Beach,** 1725 Long Beach Blvd., tel. (562) 599-5555 or toll-free (800) 528-1234 (central reservations), www.best-western.com, where a plus is the proximity of the Metrorail Blue Line across the street. Rates start at $89 double. Expensive.

Fairly basic but good choices closer to the beach and just a few blocks from the convention center include the **Inn of Long Beach,** 185 Atlantic Ave., tel. (562) 435-3791, innoflong-beach.com, from $79 double (Moderate), and the nearby **TraveLodge Convention Center,** 80 Atlantic Ave., tel. (562) 435-2471 or toll-free (800) 578-7878, from $89 double (Expensive).

Keep in mind that high-end accommodations are sometimes quite reasonable in Long Beach, especially on weekends, during the holiday season, or with AAA, AARP, and other discounts. So inquire about discounts and packages at some of the nicest local hotels, including the **Hyatt Regency Long Beach** at Two World Trade Center (Ocean Ave. and Golden Shore St.), tel. (562) 491-1234, with rates $199-299 (Luxury); the **Renaissance Long Beach Hotel,** 111 E. Ocean

Blvd. (at Pine), tel. (562) 437-5900, with rates $145-165 (Premium-Luxury); and the **Westin Long Beach,** 333 E. Ocean Blvd., tel. (562) 436-3000, with rates $119-199 (Premium-Luxury).

For something definitely different, consider an onboard overnight at the RMS *Queen Mary,* at 1126 Queen's Hwy., Pier J., tel. (562) 435-3511, www.queenmary.com, and sleep in a 1936-vintage oceanliner cabin. Special package deals include the Catalina Getaway, Paradise Package, and the Royal Romance Package. Rates are $125-400 (Deluxe-Luxury). For more ship information, see the general travel listing for the *Queen Mary,* above.

Long Beach also offers bed and breakfast choices, including the antique-rich **Lord Mayor's Inn Bed & Breakfast,** 435 Cedar Ave. (between Fourth and Fifth Sts.), tel. (562) 436-0324, www.lordmayors.com, the onetime home of Long Beach's first mayor, Charles Windham, elected in the early 1900s. Savory cinnamon rolls come with breakfast. Rates are $85-125 (Expensive-Premium).

Eating in Long Beach: Downtown
Increasingly stylish dining and shopping star downtown on and near Pine Avenue and along Belmont Shore's Second Street. Popular and good for fresh fish and seafood downtown is the **King's Fish House Pine Avenue,** 100 W. Broadway (at Pine), tel. (562) 432-7463, open for lunch and dinner daily, for breakfast on weekends. For classy Northern Italian, the place is grand **L'Opera,** 101 Pine (at First St.), tel. (562) 491-0066, open nightly for dinner, weekdays for lunch. Among the many other choices in the neighborhood: the see-and-be-seen **Alegria Cocina Latina,** 115 Pine (at First), tel. (562) 436-3388, where tapas star but gazpacho, sandwiches, salads, and substantial dinners are also on tap (the deli opens in the morning, too, for pastries and coffee). Live music nightly, and don't miss the Flamenco show. For a contemporary culinary escape to the islands of the Caribbean, try **Cha Cha Cha,** 762 Pacific Avenue (near Eighth St.), tel. (562) 436-3900, open for lunch and dinner daily.

After dinner downtown, there's entertainment. Among downtown's most popular nightclubs: the **Blue Cafe,** 210 Promenade North (at Broadway), tel. (562) 983-7111, famous for its blues acts, bil-

liards, and low ($5-10) cover charge; **Cohiba Club,** 144 Pine (at Broadway), tel. (562) 437-7700, for dancing to DJs and live bands; and **Jillian's,** 110 Pine (near Broadway), tel. (562) 628-8866, for billiards and dancing in The Vault.

If making the scene isn't your scene, the mellowest coffeehouse around is **The Library,** 3418 E. Broadway (at Redondo Ave.), tel. (562) 433-2393, which features plush couches and good paperbacks. Also here: banana-flavored cheesecake and baseball-sized blueberry muffins. And you can always go to the movies, at the large selection of screens downtown provided by AMC's **Pine Square 16,** tel. (562) 435-1335, one of Southern California's largest cinema complexes.

Eating in Long Beach: Near Belmont Shore
A classic Long Beach dining destination is lively **Small Cafe** (formerly Russell's) near Belmont Shore, 5656 E. Second St. (near Westminster), tel. (562) 434-0226, one of the southstate's best burger establishments. Some people come strictly for the pies with the mile-high meringues, including banana, chocolate, peanut butter, and sour cream. Another all-American burger destination is **Hof's Hut,** 4828 E. Second St. (at St. Joseph), tel. (562) 439-4775, where the Hofburger is the main attraction—not counting the snorkeler's fin dangling from the stuffed shark's mouth. For fancier American-style fare, the place is **Shenandoah Cafe,** 4722 E. Second (at Park), tel. (562) 434-3469.

A bit more international is **Provençe Boulangerie,** 191 Park Ave. (at Second St.), tel. (562) 433-8281, doing a brisk business in coffee, croissants, baguettes, wonderful breads, soup, and other simple wonders. Best for Italian is genuinely friendly **Christy's Italian Cafe,** 3937 E. Broadway (at Termino Ave.), tel. (562) 433-7133. (If you're one of those cigar-sucking trendoids, the **Havana Cigar Club** is right next door.) For fabulous Indian food, the place is **Natraj,** 5262 E. Second St. (near La Verne Ave.), tel. (562) 930-0930, where the Mon.-Sat. lunch buffet and the all-you-can-eat Sunday brunch are particularly great deals. But the classic vegetarian hot spot in Belmont Shore is inexpensive **Papa Jon's Natural Market & Cafe,** 5006 E. Second St. (at Argonne Ave.), tel. (562) 439-1059, serving a great TLT—tofu, lettuce, and tomato sandwich—as well as broccoli sesame pasta, vegetable shepherd's pie, spinach lasagne, and veggie and tempeh burgers.

For eats at the beach try the **Belmont Brewing Company**, 25 39th Pl., near the end of Belmont Pier, tel. (562) 433-3891, where good food is served with respectable local brews—including the popular dark Long Beach Crude. Also near the pier, overlooking the beach near the end of Termino (behind Yankee Doodles) is **Ragazzi Ristorante,** tel. (562) 438-3773, serving a nice selection of pastas, pizzas, and chicken and fish dishes. For big-time beefeaters, **555 East** at 555 E. Ocean Blvd. (near Atlantic), tel. (562) 437-0626, bills itself as an American Steakhouse and is generally considered the best in Long Beach.

CATALINA: 22 MILES ACROSS THE SEA

Thanks to one of those schmaltzy old songs, Santa Catalina Island's original location in the American imagination as "island of romance" was "twenty-six miles across the sea," though it's actually only 22 miles from San Pedro on the mainland. But romantic it was—first famous as the private fiefdom of William Wrigley Jr., of chewing gum fame, and as onetime spring training camp for his Chicago Cubs. The western pulp writer Zane Grey, whose "pueblo" now serves as a hotel, also loved Catalina. And the roster of movie stars and celebrities who have been here at one time or another, for one reason or another, would practically fill a book. Catalina even has its own movable movie memorabilia—a herd of buffalo, woolly chocolate-colored descendants of beasts originally imported in 1924 for the filming of *The Vanishing American.*

Yet all is not nostalgic. In its own way, quaint Catalina also walks the cutting edge. To solve its ongoing water supply problems, for example, Catalina started up its own desalination plant to transform seawater into drinking water. Because unrestrained automobile traffic would clearly ruin the town, perhaps even sink the island, few cars are allowed on Catalina. Instead, if not on foot most people get around greater Avalon by golf cart—an appropriate local transportation. And most of the island is owned, and protected, by private trusts—which means that all but the most innocuous activities, such as eating and shopping, are strictly regulated. Hiking and biking are by permit only, for example, and camping in the interior is by reservation only.

Present-day Catalina, second largest of the Channel Islands at 48,438 acres, otherwise retains its charms—fresh air and mild climate, rugged open space, a healthy ocean environment—because the island is relatively unpopulated. Avalon, the island's only town, boasts barely 3,000 souls. Southern California's version of a whitewashed Mediterranean hillside village perched above a balmy bay, Avalon is brushed with bright colors and stunning tiles—the most concentrated public and private displays of 1930s' California tile work anywhere. Anchoring Avalon Bay on the north, just beyond the town's tiny bayside commercial district, is the spectacular Moorish Casino, the art-deco masterpiece built by William Wrigley, Jr., to house the first theater specifically designed for movies. Beyond Avalon the island's other primary visitor destination is remote Two Harbors, snuggled into the isthmus to the northwest.

The official island population may be miniscule but the unofficial head count can be astronomical in summer and on "event" weekends. (Avoid the crazy crowds by coming in spring or in October—on a weekday if at all possible.) If you're a people person, annual events well worth the trip over include the **Silent Film Festival** at the Casino's Avalon Theatre, a benefit for the Catalina Island Museum Society; the **Fourth of July** gala, including golf cart parade and spectacular fireworks over Avalon Bay; the **Catalina Festival of Art** in late September; the two-weekend **Catalina Jazz Trax Festival** in October; and the glitzy big-band **New Year's Eve Celebration** at the Casino Ballroom.

Crowds or no crowds, most folks manage only a daytrip—taking in the ocean wind and waves on the way and then sampling the shops and the island's main "urban" sights before climbing back on the ferry to head home. (For daytrips avoid Tuesday and Wednesday, when the cruise ships dock.) One of California's small tragedies is the fact that so few visitors realize that on a longer stay Catalina offers *solitude,* a very rare Southern California commodity, and a wealth of other worthwhile pursuits.

SEEING AND DOING CATALINA

Avalon

Avalon is fringed with palms, olive trees, and tourists. Most of the latter spend most of their time clustered along bayside Crescent Avenue, the city's main commercial strip. While you're still figuring out where else to go, the moment you step off the ferry start your impromptu Avalon "tile tour." The city's eccentric beachfront **plaza** is one huge outdoor installation of decorated geometric tiles. All along the waterfront, watch for Catalina's unique building facades, fountains, and decorative planters. Don't miss **El Encanto Market Place** and, along the beach, the **Serpentine Wall.** If a brisk but brief walk fits the agenda, head uphill to the recently restored **Wrigley Memorial.** The granddaddy of all tile destinations, though, is on the other end of town— Wrigley's **Casino** at the north end of the bay. Included in the Casino's small museum collection are dishware, pottery, and inlaid tables. Along with other interior and exterior tile work, the Casino's patio is paved with classic Catalina tiles.

Catalina Island's grand Casino was originally William J. Wrigley, Jr.'s Casino, a circular Moorish palace built for dancing (he forbade drinking and gambling) and sedately presiding over the bay since 1929. Wrigley was a stickler for detail. So perfect were the acoustics of the movie theater here—the first designed specifically for "talking pictures"—that in 1931 engineers for New York's Radio City Music Hall came to Catalina for a lesson. But the theater's glories don't stop with the sound. The art-deco murals and spectacular tile work are both by John Gabriel Beckman, onetime art director for Columbia Studios, who also painted Grauman's Chinese Theater in Hollywood. Completely refurbished in 1987, the Casino harbors other attractions—including its original **Page pipe organ,** small **art gallery,** the **Catalina Island Museum** (open daily, small donation), and a grand second-floor **ballroom.** And its view of the bay. Sadly, for impromptu types, the only way to see the entire Casino is on a guided walking tour (see below). Otherwise you can visit the museum and art gallery separately, the ballroom only during special events. For information on the weekly movie— usually well worth it, and one of the few ways to appreciate the fabulous interior of the Casino's **Avalon Theatre**—call (310) 510-0179.

If time permits, and if Avalon proper loses its appeal, head for the ocean—or the island's interior. Swimming, sunbathing, snorkeling, skindiving, sportfishing, kayaking, golfing, parasailing, sailing, bicycling, hiking, and camping are a few possible diversions. Various tours, by land or by sea, are also quite worthwhile. For suggestions on what else to do, see Catalina Hiking and Biking and Catalina Tours and Diversions, below.

Touring Two Harbors and the Interior

Welcome to The Other Catalina—the one where you really can get away from it all, especially in the winter. The most protected of Two Harbors' "two" is **Catalina Harbor,** on the island's ocean side; **Isthmus Cove,** the other, faces into the channel on Catalina's north side. Once called Union Harbor, this unassuming half-mile-wide isthmus bore witness to much of Catalina's most colorful history, starting with the mysterious temple and rites of the native Gabrieleño Indians reported by the 1602 Vizcaíno expedition. From the island's own fur trader, smuggler, bootlegger, and

Chewing-gum tycoon William Wrigley Jr. built the art deco Casino to house the first theater specifically designed for movies.

gold rush days through late 19th-century tourism, Two Harbors has maintained both its solitude and serenity, a dirt-road refuge remaining the getaway "mooring" of choice for both boaters and campers—and filmmakers. Movies filmed in and around Two Harbors include *Mutiny on the Bounty, Treasure Island, Sea Hawk, The Ten Commandments, The King of Kings, McHale's Navy,* and *MacArthur.*

The sweeping seascape is the main attraction at Two Harbors, about six miles from Catalina's western tip, whether one enjoys it on the beach, on foot, or onboard a kayak. By way of general introduction, take the short hike from the village at Isthmus Cove—where the ferries and shuttles dock—across the isthmus to Catalina Harbor. (Beware of buffalo.) In addition, from Two Harbors hikers can set out on Catalina's most westerly trails. West island campsites, camping tepees, tent cabins, rustic cabins (available mid-October to mid-April), boat-accessible yurts, the Banning House bed and breakfast, kayak and "safari" tours, and scuba and snorkeling trips are all available through a single concessionaire: Two Harbors, tel. (310) 510-2800. Also here is the **Catalina Marine Science Center** operated at Big Fisherman's Cove (near Isthmus Cove) by the University of Southern California's Institute for Marine and Coastal Studies, available for group tours by reservation.

Catalina Hiking and Biking

It's possible to tour Catalina Island's hilly backcountry terrain by bus, but, if at all possible, hiking or biking is the better way to go. The sights, sounds, and scents offered by Catalina's unique sea-bound ecosystem, including unusual plant and animal life and some astonishing 360-degree vistas, are so much more savory when discovered in solitude. You can combine almost two dozen trails—some long, some short, some scenic, some less so—to turn an island trip into a trek. Make it an overnight or multiday trip by camping at Little Harbor Campground and/or Two Harbors Cove Campground—and more remote campsites beyond. But unless you're willing to literally carry the kids, a trans-island trek may be too challenging for youngsters.

The most ambitious island bike ride starts from Avalon and traverses the entire island's hilly terrain, by road, to Two Harbors. You can bring your own bicycles across from the mainland, by arrangement with Catalina's Express, or rent bikes on the island. Again, the trek is typically too tough for the kiddos; bike rides in and around Avalon are a fun family alternative.

Hiking or biking into Catalina's interior is by permit only; bike permits ($50 per person or $75 per family per year) are required for treks beyond Avalon and vicinity. To obtain permits and other current information, call the **Santa Catalina Island Conservancy** at (310) 510-2595.

Guided hikes and other outdoor adventures are available through **Catalina Fitness Company,** tel. (310) 510-9255, and other local concerns.

Catalina Tours and Diversions

If hiking and biking seem too *vigorous* and you're without golf cart, consider taking one of Catalina's popular guided tours. Discovery Tours, toll-free tel. (800) 626-1496, operated by the island's Santa Catalina Island (SCI) Company, dominates the market—and has since 1894. For a trip to the isthmus for a picnic dinner take the **Sundown Isthmus Tour,** offered only in the warmer months. Also exciting, also seasonal, are the **Flying Fish** and **Seal Rocks** tours onboard the *Blanche W.* Among the newest tours Discovery offers is the **Undersea Tour.** If you're not a scuba diver or snorkeler, the best way to see the sea—and under the sea—surrounding Catalina Island is from a semi-submersible boat. Both the *Starlight* and *Emerald* cruise the swaying fronds of the offshore kelp forest. Passengers get up close and personal with the fish, crustaceans, and other sea creatures through the large underwater windows. As on glass bottom boat tours, on a night cruise you may also see a live ocean light show—the phenomenon of phosphorescence. Or go down all the way (to a depth of about 40 feet) in the two-person **Seamobile Submersible** yellow submarine, toll-free tel. (877) 252-6262, a trip offered June through October.

Discovery Tours for landlubbers, toll-free tel. (800) 626-1496, include the very worthwhile **Casino Walking Tour,** which pokes into the Casino Ballroom, the Avalon Theatre, and almost every other cranny of William Wrigley, Jr.'s masterpiece. To see the rest of Avalon without walking up and down all those hills, sign on for the **Avalon Scenic Tour** or the **Avalon Scenic &**

Botanical Garden Tour. The **Skyline Drive** tour offers an inland "overview," between Avalon and the Catalina Nature Center at the airport. The 28-mile, half-day **Inland Motor Tour** includes a refreshment stop at William Wrigley, Jr.'s **El Rancho Escondido** Arabian horse ranch. Tour prices start at $9 and range to $35 per person, at last report, with lower rates for children and seniors. "Combo" tours can save a few dollars. For more information or reservations, contact the SCI Company's **Discovery Tours,** tel. (310) 510-8687 or (800) 626-1496 (reservations); once on the island, stop by the Discovery Tours center across from the Green Pleasure Pier. For something more adventurous on land, the Santa Catalina Island Conservancy offers **Jeep Eco-Tours,** tel. (310) 510-2595.

Other individuals and groups also offer tours and activity-oriented attractions—including ocean rafting, scuba and "shark" diving, sportfishing, and golfing and miniature golfing. For a current list of suggestions, contact the visitor bureau (see below) or, once arrived, poke around the Green Pleasure Pier in Avalon and elsewhere along the waterfront. Or head for Two Harbors (see above), which offers its own diversions.

CATALINA PRACTICALITIES

Staying in Catalina: Camping

If you'll be here longer than a day, you'll need a place to stay. The most inexpensive option is camping. Avalon's only campground is **Hermit Gulch** just over a mile outside town, tel. (310) 510-8368, which features flush toilets and lighted restrooms, coin showers, and both tent cabins and tepees in addition to standard campsites. The most popular place "on the other side" is the large **Two Harbors Campground** at the isthmus, with flush toilets and cold showers. Teepee camping—definitely something different—is also available at Two Harbors, as are rustic cabins (off-season only) and fairly uptown "yurts" at Goat Harbor. Other "out there" developed campgrounds include palm-fringed and protected **Little Harbors Campground,** the only option along the island's south (windward) side; **Black Jack** in the pines atop Mt. Black Jack, the only inland choice; and on-the-beach **Parson's Landing** north of Two Harbors. Call tel.

(310) 510-8368 for reservations at any of these campgrounds. Reservations for and various Catalina Island Conservancy primitive boat-in "cove" campsites—including **Starlight Beach** and **Frog Rock Cove,** on the island's leeward side—are available through Two Harbors, tel. (310) 510-2800. **Descanso Beach Ocean Sports,** tel. (310) 510-1226, offers camping trips—by kayak—to remote island locales.

Staying in Catalina: Hotels and Inns

With the exception of campgrounds, most accommodation options are in Avalon. The local visitor bureau (see below) is quite helpful in arranging hotels and bed-and-breakfast inn reservations—mandatory during the island's summer season—or, request current visitor information well in advance of your trip and go it on your own. (Prices can be "fluid," especially at peak visitor times, so get a firm commitment when you reserve. Two- or three-night minimum stays on weekends, especially in summer, are the rule.) For bargain rates, come in the off-season—the best time to come anyway, in many respects—which generally runs from mid-October through mid-April. Ask about other specials and packages. The visitor bureau can also recommend local home and condominium rental agencies.

"Uptown" in Two Harbors is the **Banning House Lodge,** tel. (310) 510-2800, or (800) 785-8425, a most comfortable base camp for backcountry Catalina exploration. This comfortably rustic turn-of-the-century hunting lodge, now an 11-room bed and breakfast overlooking both harbors, has hosted Hollywood celebrities on location and, during World War II, U.S. Coast guard officers. Each room has a view and a historic theme. Warm yourself by the living room fireplace in the evenings, in the company of fellow explorers and the vacant stares of animal-head trophies. Room rates start at $119. Premium.

Most elegant in Avalon is the **The Inn on Mt. Ada,** overlooking Avalon Bay from Wrigley Rd., tel. (310) 510-2030, (800) 608-7669, www.catalina.com/mtada. One of California's most elegant bed and breakfast inns, this onetime summer estate of chewing gum magnate William Wrigley Jr., and family is a graceful Georgian colonial mansion built in 1921. Now included on the National Register of Historic Places, this six-room bed and breakfast still boasts many of its original furnishings and all the accoutrements of upper-class ease. Yet the friendliness of its new identity makes it Southern California's getaway of choice for celebrating very special events. (For weddings, anniversary celebrations, and other occasions, you can rent the entire inn.) A stay here is much less expensive—and the island itself is much less crowded—on winter weekdays. High-season rates start at $330 (two-night minimum on weekends). Premium. All meals included.

Intriguing choices in town, for different reasons, include the pretty pink **Hotel St. Lauren** on Beacon St., tel. (310) 510-2299, (800) 645-2496, www.stlauren.com, a "modern Victorian" with ample motel-style amenities, rooftop patio, and high-season rates of $142-310 (Premium-Luxury), and the actually historic **Zane Grey Pueblo Hotel** at 199 Chimes Tower Rd., tel. (310) 510-0966 or toll-free tel. (800) 378-3256. Zane Grey, American master of the romantic cowboy adventure novel, started his romance with Catalina Island in the 1920s. The island's healthy herd of bison is one Zane Grey legacy—descendants of the 14 left behind after the 1924 filming of *The Vanishing American*. Avalon's Zane Grey Pueblo is another. A rambling adobe on a hill overlooking Avalon, Grey's former home is now a bed-and-breakfast-style hotel with modern plumbing and private baths but few other concessions to modern times. The Pueblo features rooms named after Zane Grey novels, striking 1920s-style Southwestern decor, even an arrowhead-shaped swimming pool. Rates are a relative bargain at $135-165. Premium-Luxury.

Across from the beach and fairly affordable is the SCI Company's 1950s-style **Pavilion Lodge,** toll-free tel. (800) 322-3434, with rates from $109 (Premium-Luxury). Popular high-end hotels (motels without cars or parking) along bustling Crescent Ave. that sometimes offer affordable rooms in the off-season or midweek include the romantic Mediterranean-style **Hotel Villa Portofino,** tel. (310) 510-0555 or toll-free (800) 346-2326, with rates $145-295 (Premium-Luxury), and the **Hotel Metropole,** tel. (310) 510-1884, or toll-free (800) 541-8528, with high-season rates $335-395 (Luxury). Less expensive inland is the Best Western **Catalina Canyon Resort** on Country Club Dr., tel. (310) 510-0325, or toll-free (800) 253-9361 (shuttle service provided to and from town). High-season rates are $119-350 (Premium-Luxury).

For cheaper rates—and a better workout—plan to climb Avalon's hills and/or stay in older small hotels. The recently remodeled, diver-friendly **Catalina Beach House,** tel. (310) 510-1078 or toll-free (800) 974-6835, offers high-season weekend rates as low as $95, with discounts during the week and in the off-season. Moderate-Expensive. Charming and quaint, also usually best bets for low weekday rates, are the old-Catalina-style housekeeping cottages at **La Paloma,** tel. (310) 510-1505 or toll-free (800) 310-1505. High season rates are $89 and up. Expensive.

Eating in Catalina

When you're hungry, Catalina is happy to feed you. Fast fooderies and restaurants cluster along Avalon's waterfront. For pizza and Italian-style sandwiches in an eclectic college-kid atmosphere, the place is **Antonio's Pizzeria** at 230 Crescent Ave. (at Metropol), tel. (310) 510-0008. **Cafe Prego** at 603 Crescent (near Clarissa), tel. (310) 510-1218, is friendly and comfortable, a neighborhood bistro facing the bay along Avalon's main drag—just about perfect for escaping the madding crowds at dinner (in summer, lunch too). You won't go wrong with the seafood pastas or the lasagna, but you can also "go American" and get a good steak. Or head for all-American **Rick's Cafe** at 417 Crescent (at the green pier), tel. (310) 510-0333. Catalina's classic local breakfast cafe, also open for lunch, is the **Runway Cafe** way out there at the airport at 1 Buffalo Springs Rd., tel. (310) 510-2196.

The time-honored choice for fresh fish at lunch or dinner is **Armstrong's Fish Market and Seafood Restaurant** at 306 Crescent Ave., tel. (310) 510-0113. For a romantic Italian dinner, the place is **Villa Portofino** at 111 Crescent, tel. (310) 510-0508; for continental, **The Channel House** at the Metropole Marketplace, tel. (310) 510-1617.

Getting Here, Getting Oriented

For an unforgettable trip over to Catalina, take the helicopter—a 15-minute ride over via **Island Express,** tel. (310) 510-2525. Though Catalina boasts a small airport and yacht harbors, most people get here via commercial ferry. **Catalina Express** ferries, tel. (310) 519-1212 or toll-free tel. (800) 360-1212, depart from San Pedro Harbor and Long Beach. From June into September, the Express also offers a 45-minute coastal shuttle between Avalon and Two Harbors. Catalina Cruises' **Catalina Jet** passenger ships, tel. toll-free (800) 228-2546, make daily departures from Long Beach year-round. Another possibility by sea is **Catalina Passenger Service,** tel. (949) 673-5245, which sets sail from Newport Beach at the Balboa Pavilion.

For current details on transportation options, tours, special events, accommodations options and packages, and other practical information, contact: **Catalina Island Chamber of Commerce and Visitors Bureau,** P.O. Box 217, Avalon, CA 90704, tel. (310) 510-1520, www.catalina.com.

For in-depth information, the best comprehensive guidebook to Santa Catalina Island and environs is *Guide to Catalina and California's Channel Islands* by Chicki Mallan, widely available on the island, around departure points on the mainland, and in California bookstores.

THE ORANGE COAST
THE DIFFERENCE BETWEEN L.A. AND ORANGE COUNTY

Sun-kissed Southern California rivals, Orange County and Los Angeles argue endlessly about whose neighborhood is most blessed—a full-blown feud evolved into advanced social sport, sometimes nasty, sometimes hilarious.

The differences between the two are difficult to grasp for those just passing through, though. Both feature sunny neighborhoods strung together by shopping centers and stressful freeways. Both have sped through the Southern California boom-bust cycles of agriculture, oil, land development, and aerospace. Both steal their water from elsewhere. Both have sandy beaches, bad neighborhoods, good neighborhoods, all of it high-priced. Both embrace an

See color map of Orange County coast area at front of book.

idealized self-image, disregarding uglier truths. And both believe the other is missing the best of all possible worlds.

Some say the spat started in the late 1800s, when Los Angeles County was almost as large as Ohio. Tired of taxation without representation, and bitter about their second-class status, residents of the Santa Ana Valley—modern-day Orange County—staged their first anti-tax rebellion by seceding from L.A. Though often amicable, the post-break-up bickering continues to this day.

Urbane Angelenos point out that orange trees in Orange County are about as abundant as the seals at Seal Beach. (There are no seals at Seal Beach.) That high culture in Orange County is best represented by the John Wayne statue at the airport. That the entire county, in fact, is more G-rated than a Disney cartoon. That only Orange County could produce the likes of ex-President Richard Nixon, not to mention local politicians prone to stating publicly that men who support abortion rights are "women trapped in men's bodies . . . who are looking for an easy lay" as Rep. Robert K. "B-1 Bob" Dornan of Garden Grove once said. (Dornan since lost his congressional seat to a Latina, Loretta Sanchez, a subject that still rankles.) That at its best Orange County exhibits a standard-brand and superficial beauty, at its worst, vapid nouveau-riche snobbery. That the FBI has identified Orange County as the capital of white-collar crime,

and that when Orange County filed for bankruptcy in 1994, it entered the record books with the biggest municipal bankruptcy in U.S. history. That, all things considered, Orange County is little more than an emergency gasoline stop on the road to San Diego.

Indignant Orange County residents counter that people from Los Angeles are self-absorbed cultural elitists who live only to consume the latest fads in food, clothing, and thought. Behind all that anti-Orange posturing, they say, Angelenos are just

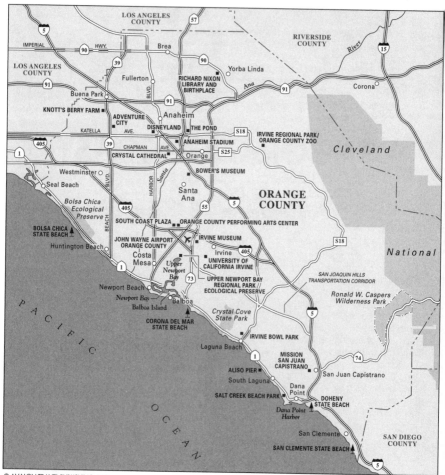

jealous—because Orange County, not L.A., now represents the quintessential Southern California lifestyle. Orange County has no smog. People in Orange County can still drop the tops on their convertibles and surf the freeways fast enough to get speeding tickets. They can go to the beach without getting caught in gang crossfire. And they aren't social hypocrites. People in Orange County, where beach-bleached blondes are the societal ideal, don't congratulate themselves on multiculturalism in the light of day and then retreat at night, in the L.A. style, to economically and ethnically segregated neighborhoods.

But according to T. Jefferson Parker in his entertaining essay "Behind the Orange Curtain," only one fundamental difference separates Los Angeles citizens from those who inhabit the Big Orange:

L.A. people all want to be someone else. Look at them, and, as Jim Harrison has written, "see the folly whirling in their eyes." The waiters all want to be novelists; the novelists all want to be screenwriters; the screenwriters all want to direct; the directors all want to produce; the producers all want to keep the other guys relegated to net participation and guild minimums.

Now take Orange Countians. We know who we are. The blandly handsome, heavily mortgaged, marathon-running, aerospace department manager, driving to work in his Taurus, does not entertain dreams of movie making. He has weapons to build, a country to defend, a family to provide for. Or take the blond mall rat, age 16, eyes aflame with consumer fever. She doesn't secretly wish to be Michelle Pfeiffer. She actually has never heard of Michelle Pfeiffer. The loose-jawed surfer dude in Huntington Beach entertains not a single thought besides the next south swell, south being to his left, he's pretty sure, if he's facing the gnardical tubes of the Pacific, which he usually is.

People in L.A., Parker explains, "want to be someone else because they're miserable; people in Orange County are content to be who they are because they're happy. It's clear. People in L.A. can't face reality. We can."

Reality is complicated, of course. Orange County is whiter and wealthier than Los Angeles, still, but L.A. voters also sent Richard Nixon and Ronald Reagan to the White House. Orange County voters are more likely than Angelenos to oppose offshore oil-drilling and to support environmental action, but these days both regions are equally lathered over the issue of illegal

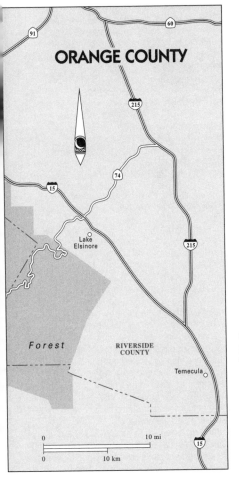

immigration. And, all denial aside, Orange County does have smog, as well as nightmarish freeway congestion. But it also has culture with a capital "C," symbolized by the spectacular Performing Arts Center adjacent (you guessed it) to its most famous shopping mall.

Born into endless summer, freed from community by freeways, and taught to believe that here, life can be all things to all people, Orange County and Los Angeles are actually very much alike. But Los Angeles is older, more experienced. Like a village elder trying to atone for the folly of youth, the City of Angels seems more willing to acknowledge the shadow side of the sunny Southern California dream and to struggle to make peace with it.

GETTING ORIENTED TO THE BIG ORANGE

Take a good look at Orange County. According to a 1976 British Broadcasting Corporation (BBC) documentary, Orange County represents "the culmination of the American dream." Those who claim to know such things contend that Orange County is also a picture postcard of America's future, an in-progress postsuburban ode to progress featuring four-star hotels, high-tech and *Fortune* 500 companies, and wave after wave of master-planned communities. Most famous in this latter category is Orange County's overnight city of Irvine (incorporated in 1971, with the slogan "Another Day in Paradise") and its University of California at Irvine campus—both developed on former agricultural holdings by the Irvine Company, the county's largest landowner.

The main feature of this futuristic postcard, though, is the general absence of "downtown," replaced in Orange County's newly developed nether regions by mini-malls and, more centrally, a shopping mall cum cultural center—the onetime lima bean field known as South Coast Plaza, among the state's top tourist draws.

Orange trees are rare in Orange County these days. Not so surf and surfers, yachts and yachters, sunny white-sand beaches, and shopping elevated to the status of art. For these attractions head to the coastal cities, which generally offer arts, entertainment, nightlife, better restaurants, and most hotels.

John Wayne, the gunslinging namesake of Orange County's airport

Less well advertised is the fact that Orange County, unlike other vast swaths of suburbanized Southern California, still offers outdoor adventure, including some sublime hikes. Unrelenting development makes the opportunity increasingly rare along the coast—with the reliable exceptions of Crystal Cove State Park and vicinity, and the Upper Newport Bay or "Back Bay"—and slightly less difficult elsewhere.

The Los Angeles-style east-west social divide also applies in Orange County, with citizens here also separated north and south. Ethnic and lower-income neighborhoods are concentrated in older inland cities, largely in the north, while new development—destined for the more affluent—is spreading ever southward, especially along the coast.

Getting oriented to inland Orange County cities makes it easier for first-time visitors to find the amusement parks (invariably near freeways). Most famous among the world's theme parks is

EVENTFUL ORANGE COUNTY

Among Orange County's more famous events is the astonishing **Pageant of the Masters** scheduled during July and August in Laguna Beach, with life imitating art imitating life in the form of *tableaux vivants,* or living pictures. The main annual events up the coast in Huntington Beach include the **Bluetorch Pro of Surfing,** (formerly known as the OP Pro) usually held in July, and the **U.S. Open of Surfing,** in August, the most well-known among the multitude of local surfing competitions. The **Orange County Fair,** held at the fairgrounds in Costa Mesa, also comes in July.

But there's always something worth doing. Come at other times throughout the year to appreciate surprising aspects of local culture and community.

Whalewatching is a major draw in winter, particularly during January and February, with excursion boats departing from Newport Beach, Dana Point, and other coastal locales. Dana Point's popular **Festival of the Whales,** complete with film festival, street fair, and concert series, is held over several consecutive weekends from mid-February into early March. Unique in February is the **Tet Festival** in Westminster's Little Saigon, celebrating the Vietnamese New Year.

According to local legend the swallows return to Mission San Juan Capistrano every year on March 19—thus the annual **Festival de los Golondrinas** or The Swallows Festival in San Juan Capistrano, with **Swallows Day** now typically scheduled for the weekend closest to that mythic date. In late March and early April comes Mission San Juan Capistrano's **Mud Slinging Festival,** during which "children of all ages" (including politicians, appropriately enough) personally participate in renewing the adobe mud facades of the mission's historic buildings.

In April comes the **Spring Garden Tour** in Laguna Beach and, at the local Sawdust Festival grounds, Laguna's annual **Art Walk.** Another big deal in April is **A Night in Fullerton,** an all-out introduction to local art galleries and other downtown attractions, complete with shuttle bus transport, not to mention the countywide **Imagination Celebration** for children, teenagers, and families. Also in April: the popular **Temecula Balloon and Wine Festival** nearby, in Riverside County's Temecula Valley.

Garden Grove's historic **Strawberry Festival** in May celebrates the bygone days of gardens and groves, when the community was known as the strawberry capital of America. Also scheduled in May: the **Anaheim Children's Festival** and, in Costa Mesa, the annual **Highland Gathering and Festival** celebrating Scottish culture. In late June comes **A Taste of Orange County** held at the Irvine Spectrum in Irvine, a three-day sampling of local cuisine, wine, and music—blues, reggae, jazz, and country-western.

The high season for Orange County arts arrives in Laguna Beach in late June and early July—the beginning of the summer's continuing events in Laguna Canyon, including the juried **Art-A-Fair** show, the alternative arts **Sawdust Festival,** and the more traditional **Festival of Arts,** which includes the annual Pageant of the Masters performances.

The annual mid-August **Pier Fest** in Huntington Beach celebrates the reconstructed Huntington Beach Pier, California's longest concrete municipal pier.

Autumn activities include the **Orange International Street Fair** in the city of Orange, the annual **Sand Castle and Sand Sculpture Contest** at Corona Del Mar State Beach, the **Tallships Festival** at the Orange County Marine Institute in Dana Point Harbor, and the **Wooden Ships Festival** in Newport Beach—all scheduled in September. The big event in October is the ghoulish, ghostly, and frightfully fun **Halloween Haunt** at Knott's Berry Farm—not recommended for children, who would probably prefer much less spooky **Camp Spooky.** Disneyland also gets into the act, with trick-or-treating at **Mickey's Halloween Treat.**

The holiday season officially begins in November, with **A Christmas Fantasy Parade** at Disneyland, the **Knott's Berry Farm Christmas Crafts Village,** and other crafts fairs. Traditional favorites in December include the **Christmas Boat Parade** in Newport Harbor and the Huntington Harbor **Cruise of Lights.**

For more information about these and other events, contact the Anaheim/Orange County Visitor and Convention Bureau, tel. (714) 765-8888, as well as local visitor bureaus.

GRUNION RUN FREE, SO WHY CAN'T WE?

It's a live sex show, yet almost innocent, even wholesome—and certainly educational. This particular procreation education usually begins after midnight. Sometimes shining small flashlights to show the way, people suddenly dash onto the beach, giggling and grabbing—for grunion, those silvery Southern California sexpots of the smelt persuasion.

Human voyeurs come down to the beach not only to watch the frenzied fish but also to catch them—literally—in the act. The hunt seems unsporting, since the grunion are, after all, deeply distracted. Without the aid of nets, window screens, kitchen sieves, and other illegal devices, however, grabbing grunion is actually a challenge. Grunion fisherfolk, optimistically armed with buckets as well as flashlights, can use only their bare hands. And grunion are slippery, like long, wriggling bars of soap. They're also rather sly. No matter what tide charts may say, grunion never show up exactly when and where they're predicted, sometimes skipping the days, hours, and locales people expect. Sometimes just a few roll in with the surf, sometimes thousands. Grunion seem to be more patient even than surfers, content to flip and flop around in the water as long as necessary, waiting for the right wave.

For many years the "grunion run," strictly a Southern California phenomenon, was thought to be some form of moonstruck romance. Much to the delight of local romantics, it was commonly believed that the fish swam ashore during spring and summer simply to fin-dance in the moonlight.

Scientists established in 1919, however, that nature was quite purposeful. The way it really works is this: After dark, near both the new and full moons but after high tide has started to recede, wave after wave of grunion surf onto local beaches. Each wave's "dance" takes 30 seconds or less. Females burrow into the sand, dorsal fin-deep, to lay their eggs (about 2,000 each) while the males circle seductively, fertilizing the roe. All parental responsibility thus discharged, the grunion catch the next wave and head back out to sea. About two weeks later, at the next moon-heightened high tide, the young'n' grunion hatch and are washed out into the big, big watery world.

Fairly remote beaches all along the coast, from Santa Barbara south, are good bets for the grunion grab. Prime possibilities in Orange County include dark stretches of beaches at or near Bolsa Chica, Huntington Beach, Laguna Beach, Dana Point, and San Clemente.

March through August are peak grunion-running periods. Grabbing grunion is against the law in April and May, however, to allow the species some spawning success. And anyone over age 16 must have a California fishing license—available at most local bait and sporting goods shops, along with tide charts, tall tales, and free advice.

Anaheim's Disneyland. In nearby Buena Park is Disneyland's predecessor, Knotts Berry Farm (original home of the boysenberry), and a multitude of lesser-known family entertainments.

Inland Orange County can also claim television evangelist and "possibility thinking" enthusiast Reverend Robert Schuller, who started the world's first drive-in ministry, a tradition still honored at the multi-million-dollar Crystal Cathedral in Garden Grove.

Former U.S. President Richard Milhous Nixon was born (and buried) in the northeastern Orange County town of Yorba Linda, site of the Richard Nixon Library and Birthplace.

And where else but in Orange County would the very airport be named after that mythic icon of God-fearing gunfighter capitalism, John Wayne?

The Orange County Coast

Orange County's 42-mile coastline arches to the southeast like a sliver of crescent moon, from the San Gabriel River and Seal Beach in the north to San Clemente and San Diego County in the south. Seal Beach suns itself on the ocean edge of what once were vast coastal wetlands—spongy salt-grass marshes that provided prime bird habitat. Then came the discovery of oil; the region's oil and housing industries devised new and better land uses. Small oil derricks still dot the landscape, as they have for some time. The major 1920s community celebration in Huntington Beach just to the south, for example, was the "Black Gold Days Festival," held over Labor Day weekend. In these times, though, Huntington Beach worships the ocean—specifically, spectacular surf, the draw for international surf competitions and associated tourist trade.

Just south of the Santa Ana River begins Newport Beach, premier yachting port for Southern California since the 1920s. Not so staid these days, now the symbolic center of Orange County's high-rolling, high-living lifestyle, the Newport Beach area embraces an upscale collection of bayside communities including Balboa Island, Lido Isle, and Corona del Mar. The next major city down coast is Laguna Beach, a low-key artists' enclave in the early 1900s but renowned today for its high-rent real estate and highly unusual ode to the arts, the Pageant of the Masters. The coast saunters south past Laguna Niguel, one of Orange County's newest cities, then Dana Point, the small yacht-harbor community named for Richard Henry Dana, Jr., author of *Two Years Before The Mast*. Taking leave of Harvard University in the 1830s, in hopes that the sea air might improve his health, Dana and shipmates came ashore here strictly for commerce—to load tanned cattle hides from the nearby mission at San Juan Capistrano. Famous for the expectation

that swallows will return (as the song goes) every year on March 19th, the mission is a worthwhile destination any day of the year.

Last stop along the Orange County coast is San Clemente, where the onetime Western White House compound of ex-President Richard M. Nixon is visible from the state beach.

Other Juicy Attractions

Without the geographic guidance of coastline or monumental mountains, inland Orange County communities tend to blend into successive freeway overpasses, underpasses, and exits. Usually first on the first-time visitor's to-do list is Disneyland just off I-5 in Anaheim, followed by Knott's Berry Farm and other family-oriented diversions nearby. Theme parks may be the main theme in these parts, but Orange County has more to offer—provided you don't try to get to or from anywhere during commute hours.

ORANGE COUNTY BASICS

Most cities in Orange County have visitor bureaus and/or chambers of commerce, many of these listed by locale below. Because Anaheim's Disneyland has been the main tourist attraction for decades, it's no accident that the best overall source for travel information is the **Anaheim/Orange County Visitor and Convention Bureau,** based at the Anaheim Convention Center, 800 W. Katella Ave., tel. (714) 765-8888. Call the **Visitor Information Hot Line,** tel. (714) 765-8888 ext. 9888, for recorded information on attractions, entertainment, and upcoming events.

For information on Orange County via the Internet, the visitor bureau's address is www.anaheimoc.org. The visitor bureau also sponsors various promotions, these sometimes including special discount coupons that come in handy. For example, a "Family Values" coupon book is available by calling the bureau at (714) 765-8888.

The newspaper of record is the *Orange County Register,* fast being outpaced by the highly competitive *Los Angeles Times,* which prints a special Orange County edition. The local *Daily Pilot,* now owned by the *Times,* is included with the *Times*'s home delivery.

Biggest and hippest of the alternative newspapers regionally has long been the *L.A. Weekly,*

SPORTING ORANGE COUNTY

Some sort of sports-franchise virus seems to be afflicting Southern California these days. Foreshadowing the Los Angeles loss—or, more appropriately, *return*—of the L.A. Raiders football team to Oakland, in 1995 Orange County lost its **Los Angeles Rams** pro football team to St. Louis. **Anaheim Stadium** still hosts **Anaheim Angels** baseball games, however. For information, call (714) 634-2000. For almost any stadium event, by the way, a popular pre- and post-game stop is **The Catch** restaurant right across the street, tel. (714) 978-3700, where fresh fish and Angus steaks are served in lively sports-bar style.

Also notable is the Disney Company's **Mighty Ducks of Anaheim** National Hockey League expansion team, tel. (714) 704-2500, part of the new NHL Pacific Division. Though some wags refer to the endeavor as the "Mighty Bucks," the Ducks nest at the area's newest sports stadium, the impressive **Arrowhead Pond of Anaheim** (known affectionately as "The Pond") across the street from the Anaheim Stadium. The Ducks' season begins in early October and runs through April.

available at hip places countywide. In late 1995 the *Weekly* launched its *O.C. Weekly,* surely a sign that Orange County's arts, entertainment, and alternative political scene has come into its own. Other interesting free magazines and newspapers include *Entertainment Today,* and *The Sun* (the latter distributed in Seal Beach and Huntington Beach). The slick-paper lifestyle magazine, written more for residents than people just passing through, is *Orange Coast.*

Transportation by Air
Though LAX is Southern California's main international airport, the smaller regionals—John Wayne, Long Beach, Burbank, and Ontario—generally offer competitive fares and fewer hassles. Depending on where you're headed, regional flights may also let you avoid the freeway trip through L.A.—nightmarish during commute hours.

Inside Orange County's spiffy expanded and remodeled **John Wayne Orange County Airport,** tel. (949) 252-5200, John Wayne himself is there to greet you. (You can't miss him.) Along with various commuter services, airlines serving John Wayne include **Alaska, America West, American, Continental, Delta, Northwest, TWA,** and **United.** And it was a big, big deal in 1994 when no-frills **Southwest** added its name to the list.

The John Wayne Airport is centrally located, technically in Santa Ana but also practically in Costa Mesa, Irvine, and Newport Beach. Easiest freeway access is from I-405. Also feasible is the Costa Mesa Freeway (Hwy. 55), which connects I-5, the latter often a horrendous transition. If traveling Newport Bay area streets, another possibility is MacArthur Blvd. (Hwy. 73) from the coast, which delivers you right to the terminals.

Most car rental agencies have outposts at John Wayne. The cheapest but not most convenient means to and from the airport is public transit, **Orange County Transportation Authority (OCTA)** buses, tel. (714) 636-RIDE (636-7433), ext. 10 for route and fare information. If you go this route be sure to leave yourself *plenty* of time. Up-market hotels (sometimes others) offer free airport shuttles. Next-best bet: a commercial shuttle service such as **SuperShuttle,**

toll-free tel. (800) 258-3826, which offers 24-hour door-to-door service.

Transportation by Train
The main Orange County stop for **Amtrak** is in the south, the striking **San Juan Capistrano Depot** in San Juan Capistrano, just west of Camino Capistrano at 26701 Vertugo St., tel. (800) 872-7245, open limited hours. Local OCTA buses (see Transportation by Bus, below) connect to Laguna Beach and San Clemente. Amtrak also stops at the pier in San Clemente—where you can catch Bus 91 south to the last stop, then take Bus 1 north along the coast. Amtrak also stops in Anaheim, Santa Ana, and Fullerton. Call Amtrak toll-free (800) 872-7245 for route, fare, and reservation information, or check www.amtrak.com.

The first Orange County link in the periwinkle-and-white **Metrolink** Southern California mass transit system is at Fullerton, where the commuter trains made their debuts in March of 1994. The trains run on weekdays only; for current fare and schedule information, call toll-free (800) 371-5465, or check www.metrolink-trains.com.

Transportation by Bus
Cars are king in Orange County, but you can get here and get around reasonably well by bus. The **Santa Ana Greyhound Station** is in the transit center just off the Santa Ana Freeway (I-5), 1000 E. Santa Ana Blvd. at Santiago, toll-free tel. (800) 231-2222. In Santa Ana call (714) 542-2215; in Anaheim, (714) 999-1256. From Santa Ana, buses connect with L.A., Riverside, and San Diego as well as Santa Barbara, San Luis Obispo, and San Francisco. Greyhound can also get you to and from the coast, with very limited service to Laguna Beach and Huntington Beach. Local public transit expands bus travel options.

Orange County Transportation Authority (OCTA) buses, tel. (714) 636-7433, ext. 10 for current schedule and fares, serve the entire county, albeit on a fairly limited basis. Daily start and end times vary by route, but on weekdays buses are available after 5 or 6 a.m. and run until 7 or 8 p.m. Weekend service starts later and ends earlier. If you're relying on buses, be sure to check current hours.

Transportation by Car

Two freeways—I-405, known as "the 405" or the San Diego Freeway in local vernacular, and I-5, known hereabouts as the Santa Ana Freeway—are Orange County's major north-south thoroughfares. Judicious use of other intersecting freeways will get you almost anywhere. Most Orange County freeways are now undergoing major reconstruction, however, to keep pace with general growth and traffic increases, so allow extra time in key locales (especially during commute hours).

Construction continues at I-5 and Hwy. 55, the Costa Mesa Freeway; the 55 runs directly into downtown Newport Beach. If coming via the 405, take Hwy. 73, the Corona del Mar Freeway, *then* the 55. For more road construction headaches, head north to the junction of Hwy. 55 and Hwy. 91. The 55 connects Santa Ana, Tustin, and Orange with Hwy. 91, the Riverside Freeway, which in Orange County runs west-east from La Palma through the Anaheim/Fullerton area and on toward Corona in Riverside County.

The most notorious local freeway construction project has an unofficial title—"the Orange Crush," in the city of Orange at the intersection of I-5, Hwy. 57, and Hwy. 22. The Garden Grove Freeway, Hwy. 22, connects the 405 to the 55 just north of Santa Ana and Tustin as well as the southern end of Hwy. 57, the Orange Freeway. The Orange runs north through Placentia to intersect Hwy. 90, the Imperial Highway, which connects Brea with Yorba Linda and Hwy. 91.

California's Pacific Coast Highway (PCH), or Hwy. 1, is Orange County's scenic route—running almost the entire length of the coastline before merging with I-5 just east of Dana Point in the south county. A multilane route most of the way, PCH is typically a slog—slowed like everything else in Southern California by too much traffic. And most people here do drive, usually one to a vehicle.

SEAL BEACH AND VICINITY

Enticed by more famous Orange County beach towns, tourists tend to miss Seal Beach—a neat-as-a-pin neighborhood with a 1950s' bohemian feel, an attractive downtown, and plenty of pom-pom palms. The beach itself is wide and sandy, offering a view of both ocean and the man-made offshore island featuring California's first offshore oil well, drilled in 1954.

Enjoy Main Street. The **Book Store,** 213 Main, tel. (562) 598-1818, is a classic in the used-book genre, an overwhelming hodgepodge of words in print. (Proprietor Nathan Cohen, a retired merchant seaman, may offer help in navigating the stacks.) With or without book in hand, stop nearby for ice cream or cappuccino; bikini shops and beach-style boutiques offer more expensive distractions. After the beach and a stroll on the pier, to stay longer take in a movie at the landmark **Bay Theatre,** tel. (562) 431-9988, known for its eclectic and arty films.

If the beach scene here gets too crowded, just south are **Surfside Beach** and **Sunset Beach,** quieter areas with public beaches and lifeguard towers. (Stroll. Bike it. Take the bus. If driving, park along either North or South Pacific Avenues, parallel to PCH.)

For a fine bike ride, the **bikeway** at Bolsa Chica State Beach, just south, begins at Warner and runs south all the way to Huntington State Beach, about five miles. Heading north by bike is not much fun, with cyclists competing with cars on PCH all the way to Belmont Shores (Long Beach).

For more information about the area, including exact dates for upcoming events, call the **Seal Beach Chamber of Commerce** at (562) 799-0179 between 10 a.m. and 2 p.m. on weekdays or check www.sealbeachchamber.com.

The Seal Beach Pier

A prime attraction, right at the end of Main Street, is the Seal Beach Pier, one of the longest along the coast (1,865 feet) and a focal point of local life since its construction in 1906. Popular these days for rock cod fishing (rental rods and bait available) and promenade-style people watching, the Seal Beach Pier boasts a colorful past. Crown jewel of the "Jewel City" amusement complex, the pier at one time sported 50 giant rainbow-making "scintillator" lamps to enhance nighttime ocean swimming. Jewel City itself featured a roller coaster shipped down from San Francisco after the 1915 World's Fair. Movie stars and special events, such as stunt fliers, also attracted the crowds.

Not everyone considered the local goings-on innocent, however. One Orange County preacher called Seal Beach "the plague spot at our doors." In 1916—when ladies were required to wear stockings while bathing in public—the wild women of Seal Beach flagrantly violated the law by painting their legs "to fool the coppers." And in the 1920s and '30s, sailors from Long Beach and bad boys from Los Angeles were known to sneak down to Seal Beach to partake of the more serious sins of illicit gambling and prostitution.

The pier itself has had wild times, too. It survived the earthquake in 1933, but not the big breakers of 1935. It survived a hurricane in 1939, but not the disastrous storms of 1983. The most recent incarnation of the Seal Beach Pier opened to the public on January 27, 1985.

Staying in Seal Beach

If you think this laid-back, blast-from-the-past beach town is the perfect place to park yourself permanently, think again. At last report Seal Beach had Orange County's highest rents. And you won't find much here in the way of budget accommodations. (Try Huntington Beach instead.) A possibility for families, though, if you can stand the kids in your room (children under 17 stay free), is the **Radisson Inn,** 600 Marina Dr., tel. (562) 493-7501, www.radisson.com, with the usual motel amenities, fitness center, pool, whirlpool, bike rentals, and rates usually $99-146. Expensive-Premium. And if the 1850s are more your style than the 1950s, consider a stay at the two-story **Seal Beach Inn and Gardens,** a stylish and secluded 23-room bed and breakfast close to the beach at 212 Fifth St., tel. (562) 493-2416 or toll-free (800) 443-3292, www.sealbeachinn.com. Guest rooms, some with kitchens, refrigerators, and whirlpool baths, are furnished with antiques and named after flowers—many of which you'll find here, part of the riot of color blooming forth from every container, cranny, and nook. There's a small swimming pool, too. Luxury, with rates $165-350, depending upon type of room.

Eating in Seal Beach

Head to the pier for bomber-size burgers and a view of the oil wells. *The* place forever—or at least since the Seal Beach Grand Old Opry House gave up the ghost—is flashy diner-style **Ruby's** at the end of the pier, tel. (562) 431-7829, where you'll find all kinds of patties, including chicken, turkey, and veggie, plus great shakes and other tasty pleasures from the past. Breakfast is a best bet, too. And if you miss it here, Ruby's is almost an institution along the coast and elsewhere in Orange County.

The most popular all-around hangout in Seal Beach is **Hennessey's Tavern,** 140 Main, tel. (562) 598-4419, one of a small chain of Irish-style pubs serving breakfast, lunch, and dinner in addition to beer, here overflowing with surfers, hippies, country music, and the scent of suntan lotion. Best bet for breakfast, though, is the homey long-running **Harbor House Cafe** on PCH (at Anderson) just south of town in Sunset Beach, tel. (562) 592-5404, open 24 hours, famous for its omelettes, almost as famous for the gallery of movie stars on knotty-pine walls.

An unusual local landmark since 1930 and still offering homage to the good ol' stunt flying days is the **Glide 'er Inn,** 1400 PCH, tel. (562) 431-3022, where the reference is to aeronautics in general, biplanes in particular. Airplane memorabilia papers the walls, model planes serve as de facto mobiles, and seafood dominates the menu.

If seafood is your passion, though, **Walt's Wharf,** 201 Main, tel. (562) 598-4433, offers greater creativity with whatever's in season—such things as oak-grilled Chilean sea bass with roasted macadamia nuts. There's an oyster bar here, too, and a good selection of imported beers. Another good choice, for seafood and prime rib, not to mention great breakfasts, is the **Kinda Lahaina Broiler,** 901 Ocean Ave., tel. (562) 596-3864.

BOLSA CHICA STATE BEACH

Stretching south three miles from Seal Beach in the north to the Huntington Beach Pier, broad, sandy Bolsa Chica State Beach is in one sense an extension of what you'll find farther south at Huntington State Beach—thousands of paved parking places, restrooms with showers, fire rings, snack stands, and all. The primary differences? This is a better bet for beginning surfers than Huntington Beach. Also, Bolsa Chica offers 50 RV campsites.

The main parking lot entrance is on PCH about 1.5 miles south of Warner Avenue. Day use (parking fee) is $6. For more information about Bolsa Chica, call (714) 848-1566. To reserve a campsite—a necessity in summer—call ReserveAmerica toll-free at (800) 444-7275 or check www.reserveamerica.com.

Bolsa Chica Ecological Reserve

In many ways more fascinating than the beach is 1100-acre Bolsa Chica Ecological Reserve across PCH. Not exactly pristine, Bolsa Chica is an on-going oilfield restoration project; some areas are not open to the public. Bolsa Chica, one of the county's few remaining wetland tracts, provides seasonal habitat for more than 200 species of waterfowl and shorebirds, including the endangered California least tern. Amigos de Bolsa Chica, a local citizens' group, is responsible for preventing the total loss of Bolsa Chica to another marina and housing development. So shake that sand out of your shoes and stroll along the 1.5-mile loop trail, just to see what a little enlightened citizen action can do. For current information on guided walks, usually offered September through April on the first Saturday of the month starting at 9 a.m., call (714) 897-7003.

HUNTINGTON BEACH AND VICINITY

SURF CITY

If you've tried to find Surf City on a California map, put an "X" right here, on the once-grungy blue-collar oil town of Huntington Beach. The city has long called itself "Surfing Capital of the World" and "Surf City." But now it's official. After some public skirmishes with Santa Cruz, that scrappy little surf city up north, Huntington Beach ended up with the Surf City trademark.

Surfers have dominated the local fauna since the 1920s. But surfing didn't become a social phenomenon even in Huntington Beach until the 1960s, when Bruce Brown of nearby Dana Point was knighted the "Fellini of foam" for *Endless Summer,* his classic surfing film, and Dick Dale, "King of the Surf Guitar," rode the same wave to the top of the pop music charts. (Dale's sound was a total Orange County creation, since even his guitar—a Fender Stratocaster—was a local invention, thanks to Leo Fender of Fullerton.) Then came the Beach Boys, who captured the national teenage imagination and catapulted surfing into the category of popular sport. But then came the Beatles. Almost overnight everyone—everyone except serious surfers—tuned into another wavelength, an entirely different cultural wave.

According to local lore, surfing was imported to Huntington Beach from Hawaii in 1907. In those days surfers were all but alone in the Orange County surf, riding 100-pound homemade red-wood boards. But wood has long since given way to polyurethane, plain canvas swim trunks to neoprene wetsuits. And "mellow" has lost out to "aggro" (aggressive attitude, in the lingo) now that conditions are crowded and surfing is a multibillion-dollar international sports and fashion industry.

THE NEW SURF CITY

About seven million people do Huntington Beach every year, most just day-tripping. It's tough to find the skurfy surf-rat bar scenes and seedy low-rent storefronts of yore, though. They're all but gone—replaced in the 1980s and '90s by a strategically redeveloped business and tourism district with a crisp California-Mediterranean style. Huntington Beach figured that spiffing up the neighborhood might attract a different crowd—people inclined to spend more money than surfers typically do, thereby increasing sales tax revenues. Subsequent downtown redevelopment involved razing seven of nine city blocks and ponying up large public subsidies for developers—investments that haven't entirely paid off yet.

From the point of view of history-minded surfers, there went the neighborhood.

But even with redevelopment, surfing is still the main event in Huntington Beach. Annual competitions include the **The Bluetorch Pro of Surfing** (formerly the OP Pro), usually held in late July, a famed stop on the Association of Surfing

Professionals world tour and the largest surfing event on the U.S. mainland. But Bluetooth qualifier events are just the prelude to August's **U.S. Open of Surfing,** part of the World Surfing Championship tour. If battling the seriously surf-crazed crowds during big-time competition is an unappealing option, you'll find many smaller, more neighborly surfing events staged throughout the year.

For more information about Huntington Beach, contact: **Huntington Beach Conference and Visitors Bureau,** 417 Main Street, tel. toll-free (800) 729-6232 (SAY-OCEAN) or tel. (714) 969-3492.

HUNTINGTON BEACH BEACHES

The city beach or **"Main Beach"** starts in the north at Goldenwest, saunters past the Huntington Beach Pier—itself a seaward extension of Main St.—and then meanders south, merging at Beach Blvd. (south of Main) with **Huntington State Beach.** The state beach stretches south another two miles to just beyond Brookhurst, at the Santa Ana River and Newport Beach border.

The pier area is Huntington's most famous and challenging surfing zone, but the state beach is the stuff of surfing movies—one of the widest, whitest expanses of sand you'll see this side of the Colorado Desert. A five-acre preserve along the river protects nesting sites for the California least tern. Across PCH from the state beach is 114-acre **Huntington Beach Wetlands,** a small preserve under the jurisdiction of the California Department of Fish and Game.

In summer, and on almost any hot-weather weekend, plan to arrive quite early to stake out territory for your beach towel. Aside from sunbathing, swimming, surfing, and just bummin' around, beaches around here are known for very serious volleyball. They're also popular for picnicking and the peaceable pursuit of surf fishing and cycling. Facilities include countless paved parking spaces, wheelchair access, restrooms with cold showers and dressing rooms, picnic tables, stores and snack stands, even fire rings for after-dark beach parties—the happening scene, especially near the pier. And the lifeguards mean it when they tell you to quit doing whatever you're doing.

For beach parties, be aware that the curfew is 11 p.m. No camping is allowed. The parking fee for both city and state beaches is $6 (avoidable if you walk). Parking lots are accessible from PCH at Magnolia, Newland, Huntington, and Main. For more beach information, call (714) 848-1566.

For surfing lessons, contact local surf shops. Most offer beginner and intermediate lessons, if not advanced. **Huntington Surf & Sport,** for example, at PCH and Warner, tel. (714) 841-4000, offers a half-day private lesson for $125, board and wetsuit included. Lessons are available daily (typically in the morning, when the surf's best), but call at least a week or two in advance for reservations.

The Huntington Beach Pier

In 1904 the city was officially christened Huntington Beach after Henry Huntington, the fellow responsible for extending the Pacific Electric Railroad out this way. But the first pier here was built in 1903, when Huntington Beach was still called Pacific City and still hoping to become the West Coast rival to Atlantic City. In 1914 the original was replaced with a concrete pier, the first ever built in the U.S.—bearing some resemblance to the brand-new pier you'll see today, opened to great public fanfare in 1992.

The Huntington Beach Pier has been torn up, by both hellacious waves and earthquakes, and then rebuilt so often that even locals get fuzzy on the history. But pier problems peaked in the 1980s. Big winter waves in early 1983 battered the end of the pier, and the End Cafe, so the pier's end was removed, rebuilt, and the whole thing reopened in 1985. January storms in 1988 finally brought the end of The End, however, when it dropped into the ocean—along with plenty of the pier itself—some 10 minutes after the proprietor closed up shop. The pier was closed, demolished, and completely rebuilt at a cost of $10.2 million.

The new, improved, pedestrian-friendly Huntington Beach Pier, 12 feet taller than the original and 1,856 feet long, is still the place for watching sunsets and daring surfers. Pier fishing is a strong local tradition. Another link in the Ruby's dining chain also sits out here. For other dining and diversions, head across PCH to Main Street.

Dwight's Snack Bar, tel. (714) 536-8083, on the beach just south of the pier, is the place to go for almost any kind of rental, including beach chairs, boogie boards, bikes, and in-line skates. (For rentals, bring a driver's license.) Just north of the pier is the **Kite Connection,** tel. (714) 536-3630, which sells and rents "sport kites." Rentals run $8-12 an hour; lessons are free. Call for information about the local **Kite Festival,** held here every spring.

SEEING SURF CITY

The International Surfing Museum

Mandatory for any serious study of local history is a visit to Huntington Beach's International Surfing Museum, 411 Olive Ave., tel. (714) 960-3483. The spruced-up 1930s' building itself offers hidden cultural history as the onetime location of Sam Lanni's acclaimed **Safari Sam's** night-club—*the* local club scene until 1985, when Sam sauntered off to hunt new challenges.

Among the oldies but goodies collected inside are vintage surfboards, of course, including Batman's board from the original movie. Also here: the cornerstone from the original 1903 pier, and the bust of Duke Kahanamoku once on display at the foot of the pier.

Famed Hawaiian swimmer and four-time Olympic winner, Kahanamoku was 20 years old in 1911 when he and his friend George Freeth surfed local beaches—introducing the sport to California, according to local lore—on the way to the 1912 Olympic games.

Especially fun among regular exhibits is the 1960s display, a rollicking reminiscence on surf-dom's lasting cultural impact. Special exhibits rotate about every three months, with themes such as "Music, Music, Music"—an amazing array of surf music albums—and "Women in Surfing," which coincided with the debut of *Wahine,* the first women's surfing magazine.

The museum is open noon-5 p.m., daily in summer and Wed.-Sun. in winter. Admission is $2 adults, $1 students, children under 6 free.

Other Huntington Beach Attractions

There *was* life before surfing, even in Huntington Beach. The best place to explore that life is the **Newland House** at 19820 Beach Blvd. (at Adams Ave.), tel. (714) 962-5777, a Victorian farmhouse included on the National Register of Historic Places. The house and gardens have been meticulously refurbished; many of the 19th-century furnishings are original family pieces. And anyone who thinks recorded music began with compact discs should be sure to check out the working Victrola here. The Newland House is open Wednesday and Thursday 2-4:30 p.m., and on weekends noon-4 p.m. Friendly, informative guides are available for tours. Small admission.

Also worth a stop, if something special's going on, is the cultural focal point of local redevelopment—the **Huntington Beach Art Center,** 538 Main, tel. (714) 374-1650, which offers gallery

THE SURFRIDERS: SURFING GOES GREEN

You'd never guess it, to watch competitive young surfers duke it out for ocean elbow room, but surfing has *traditions,* concerns much more lasting than who gets there first, fastest, or with the most finesse.

One surfing tradition is caring about coastal waters and fighting environmental decline, whether from oil and sewage spills or impending development. Surfing is increasingly an endangered species, a development directly related to human activity as well as human efforts to correct the problem. Flood-control dams upriver, for example, prevent sand from flowing to sea to replenish beaches. The coastal breakwaters and jetties built to trap existing sand have the unfortunate side effect of aggravating sand erosion—the ocean continues to suck it out to sea—while destroying waves.

But even surfers were shocked in February of 1990 when the British Petroleum-chartered oil tanker *American Trader* impaled itself on its own anchor about a mile offshore. About 400,000 gallons of oil spilled, much of it scooped up or dispersed at sea but a substantial amount washing ashore to foul 15 miles of beaches and wetlands and kill seabirds from Anaheim Bay in L.A. County to the Newport Beach peninsula. In one of those ironies of fate—since Huntington Beach is still Orange County's

main oil producer—most of the oil came ashore near Bolsa Chica and Huntington Beach. Along with the professional crews, hundreds of Orange County volunteers turned out to stop the oil and then to clean things up.

Since 1984 the Surfrider Foundation, which began in surf-happy Huntington Beach, has been on the front lines of the battle to protect the oceans and the coastline. Originally a handful of long-haired locals—the group began educating the public by spray painting storm drains with the message "Drains to Ocean," and it is still famous for its guerrilla theater—the Surfrider Foundation is now a national organization.

In addition to some notable national victories—including restoring natural dune habitat on the Outer Banks in North Carolina and, in Hawaii, successfully suing Honolulu for dumping raw sewage into Kailua Bay—the foundation is still at the forefront of the long-running local battle to forestall a housing subdivision at the Bolsa Chica wetlands.

For more information about the organization, or to join, contact: **Surfrider Foundation,** 122 S. El Camino Real #67, San Clemente, CA 92672, tel. (949) 492-8170, fax (949) 492-8142, www.surfrider.org.

---

shows, traveling exhibitions, and studio space for artists-in-residence programs, plus sponsors a multitude of community arts education programs. Gallery admission is $3.

Unlike other Orange County beach towns, at last report Huntington Beach didn't offer commercial whalewatching excursions. But you can embark from here on a **Sail Catalina** trip, tel. (714) 568-9650, the first sailing passenger service to and from Catalina Island since the late 1800s. The boat motors over in the morning, shoving off from Peters Landing, then sails back. Sunset cruises and off-season charters are also available.

STAYING IN SURF CITY

Best bet for budget travelers is the very clean **Colonial Inn Youth Hostel,** housed in a circa-1903 three-story colonial at 421 Eighth St., tel.

(714) 536-3315. Opt for a bed in one of three communal rooms ($16) or, for more privacy, check into one of 14 double rooms with twin beds ($18 per person). Curfew here is 11 p.m., but you can rent a late key.

In other options, Huntington Beach offers more reasonably priced choices than most beach towns, but most of the better motel deals are inland along Beach Boulevard. Settle in at the **Comfort Suites,** for example, 16301 Beach Blvd. (at McDonald, one block west of I-405), tel. toll-free (800) 714-4040 or (714) 841-1812, for $59 double. Inexpensive

Comfortable, reasonable, and right across the highway from the beach is the small **Sun 'n' Sands Motel,** 1102 PCH (five blocks north of the pier, between Main and Goldenwest), tel. (714) 536-2543, with the basics plus pool and free movies, cable TV. Inexpensive-Moderate, with rates $59 and up in the summer season, from $45 otherwise (kids under 12 free).

For a different beach ambience, try the neat and neighborly **Sunset Bed and Breakfast,** 16401 PCH (at 25th St.), tel. (562) 592-1666. Inexpensive-Expensive, with summer rates $45-95, winter rates $45-85.

A central feature of downtown redevelopment is the upscale **Waterfront Hilton Beach Resort,** 21000 PCH, toll-free tel. (800) 822-7873 or (714) 960-7873. Beyond the stunning lobby, with its waterfalls and tropical plants, the Mediterranean-style complex offers 12 stories of ocean-view rooms across from the beach and balmy palm landscaping, pretty pool area, tennis courts, and more. Premium-Luxury, with official rates $135 and up in summer, otherwise $115 and up, but ask about special discounts and packages.

EATING IN SURF CITY

Locals' Favorites
Some of the local surf scene's most beloved hangouts survive, much to everyone's post-redevelopment relief. **The Sugar Shack,** tel. (714) 536-0355, still stands, for example, a funky little cafe at 213½ Main, the place *everybody* goes, for more than 25 years. The Shack serves surfer-sized breakfast starting at 6 a.m., juicy burgers and such at lunch and early dinner. If it's crowded, add your name to the waiting list—cleverly attached to the tree out front.

Popular with college students and the young local surf set, is boisterous, cool, and casual **Huntington Beach Beer Company,** 201 Main (at Walnut), tel. (714) 960-5343, where the specialty is pizza baked in a wood fired oven. Sandwiches and salads are also on tap, everything washed down by brewskies such as Huntington Beach Blonde and Brick Shot Red. Quite the scene on Friday and Saturday nights.

A popular locals' choice is the **Park Bench Cafe** in Huntington Central Park, 17732 Goldenwest (at Slater), tel. (714) 842-0775, especially enjoyable on a glorious sunny day—and most famous recently for the addition of its special Canine Cuisine menu, a bone tossed to patrons also visiting the neighborhood "bark park." Doggie selections include the Hot Diggity Dog (hot dog on a bun) and the Wrangler Roundup (ground turkey patty). Humans shouldn't fear that the place has gone to the dogs, however.

Dogs and their people dine only on the perimeter of the patio, on the lawn. Breakfast and lunch are served daily except Monday (closed). Another good bet here: **Breakfast in the Park,** tel. (714) 848-0690. Huntington Central Park is on both sides of Goldenwest, between Edwards and Gothard.

For healthy vegetarian, the place is **Mother's Market and Kitchen** next to the Newland House at 19770 Beach Blvd., tel. (714) 963-6667, where breakfast, lunch, and dinner are served daily, 9 a.m.-9:30 p.m. The market here is well worth a wander, too, selling fresh produce, kitchen gadgets, and natural cosmetics.

But don't miss **Tosh's Mediterranean Cuisine and Bakery,** 16871 Beach Blvd., tel. (714) 842-3315, where you can pack a special picnic basket or sit down for marvelous Greek and Turkish fare at either lunch or dinner (seafood and vegetarian selections also available). Very good value if you're ravenous, since bread, soup, and salad are served with meals. For good sushi and such, try **Matsu Japanese Restaurant, Steakhouse, and Sushi Bar** across from the Friendship Inn at 18035 Beach Blvd. (at Talbert), tel. (714) 848-4404.

Locals' Favorites: Fancier Fare
For casual dining, head over to **Studio Café,** 300 PCH, tel. (714) 536-8775, specializing in seafood and sea views. Other local restaurants get more attention. **Baci,** 18748 Beach Blvd. (at Ellis), tel. (714) 965-1194, is quite good—some say the best, locally—for Italian, and reasonably priced as well. The very good continental **Palm Court** restaurant at the Waterfront Hilton, tel. (714) 960-7873, is also quite popular—casual during the day but dress-up dining with a view come nightfall.

Eventful, Entertaining Huntington Beach
In addition to annual surfing competitions, major events in Huntington Beach include the annual **Fourth of July Parade and Fireworks Show** and the **Pier Fest** in August. At Christmas, consider coming for the annual **Huntington Harbour "Cruise of Lights"** tour of outdoor holiday decor. Something is going on almost all the time, however; stop by the visitor center for a complete listing.

As for entertainment, if you're lucky you'll arrive when Dick Dale and the Deltones are playing paeans to the surf, somewhere in Orange County. If not, rock out on weekends at **Out of Bounds** at 21022 Brookhurst St. (at Atlanta), tel. (714) 968-9800, or head for the long-running **Longboard Restaurant and Pub,** 217 Main, tel. (714) 960-1896, to sample the bar scene. Otherwise, nightlife here has never entirely recovered since the famous Golden Bear was bulldozed into oblivion and Safari Sam's closed shop. Near-by, though, for rock 'n' dinner, there's the **Galaxy Theater,** 3503 S. Harbor in Santa Ana (just off the 405), tel. (714) 957-0600. Well worth the trip south is **The Coach House** in a semi-industrial complex off the freeway in San Juan Capistrano. (For details, see San Juan Capistrano, below.) And Newport Beach, just south of Huntington, offers nightlife galore.

For local community theater, see what's playing at the **Huntington Beach Playhouse,** 21141 Strathmore Ln., tel. (714) 375-0696.

NEWPORT BEACH AND VICINITY

Postsuburbia seems to require constant investment in the supremacy of the new. In most parts of Southern California, for example, tradition dictates that at the first sign of aging either a bulldozer or cosmetic surgeon be called in. That said, even Orange County has history. And Newport Beach is a good place to start looking for it.

History of La Puerta Nueva

After native peoples were safely corraled at the missions, the land now known as Newport Beach was originally included in the Rancho Santiago de Santa Ana, granted by the Spanish government in 1810 to Juan Peralta and Jose Antonio Yorba. In 1837 the Mexican government gave the land to Jose Sepulveda as part of his 47,000-acre Rancho San Joaquin. On early maps the upper reaches of what is now Newport Bay were identified as Bolsa de San Joaquin (Pocket or Bay of San Joaquin) or Bolsa de Guigara (Bay with High Banks). The as-yet-unformed harbor area was poetically described as Cienega de los Ranos (Frog Swamp) and Cienega de San Joaquin (San Joaquin Swamp). The modern name, La Puerta Nueva (The New Port) came in the 1870s, with the construction of a livestock/supply loading chute, wharf, and warehouse.

Now a nouveau-riche niche with a nautical theme, in the 1920s and '30s Newport Beach was the preferred seaside escape for the old-money minions from Los Angeles. (In California "old money," like all other things, is relative.) Henry E. Huntington made it all possible with the extension of the Pacific Electric Railroad to Newport Bay. And close-to-home adventure continued outward from Newport, the cat's meow being the ferryboat daytrip to Catalina Island. Once the shallow harbor was dredged, landfill islands, yachting marinas, and summer homes starting popping up all over the place.

Modern Newport Beach

Famous former residents include John Wayne, Shirley Temple, even George Burns and Gracie Allen, Roy Rogers and Dale Evans. Celebrities come and go, though. In the end the truly astounding thing about Newport Beach is the price paid here for social status, reflected most obviously in the value of both real estate and boat slips. A million or two will buy little more than a modest beach bungalow with no yard, no parking, and no rest from the daily summer struggle with nightmarish tourist traffic. Some of the luxury yachts on display in Newport Harbor carry equally phenomenal price tags. And some people would sell their very souls just for the chance to

ANAHEIM AREA VISITOR AND CONVENTION BUREAU

Newport Beach boasts some of the highest-priced real estate and yacht slips in Southern California.

drop anchor in one of the 10,000 slips here, *the* high-price, high-prestige California yacht harbor. Go figure.

Of course the *weather* is quite nice, year-round.

For those who track the ever-changing local identity of California's Hwy. 1, or Pacific Coast Hwy., as it slides south along the coast, here it's called West Coast Hwy. until it crosses the channel on the west side of the harbor at lower Newport Bay, and East Coast Hwy. on the east side. For more information on the area, contact the **Newport Beach Conference and Visitors Bureau,** 3300 W. Coast Hwy., Newport Beach, tel. toll-free (800) 942-6278 or (714) 722-1611. To explore Newport on the Web, go to www.newportbeach-cvb.com.

SEEING NEWPORT BEACH

Despite its high-priced harbor and hotels, keep in mind that Newport Beach is still more residential

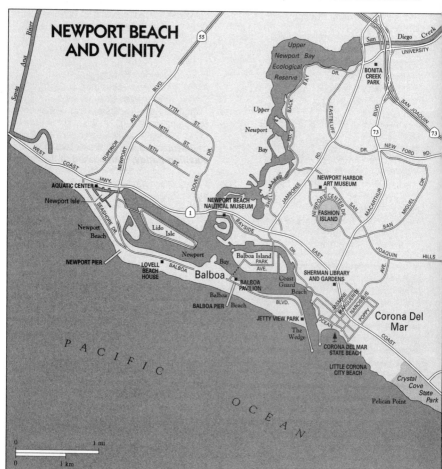

area than tourist destination. The unmistakable aroma of money, money, money is often aloft on the sea breeze, but just plain folks still find plenty to do here. Newport Beach is just so darned *pleasant*.

Hold that thought when you're trapped in traffic on Pacific Coast Highway or desperately trying to snare a parking place.

Parking is such a nightmare, particularly near the college-student scene at Newport Pier, that touring the area on foot is truly a stress-reducing

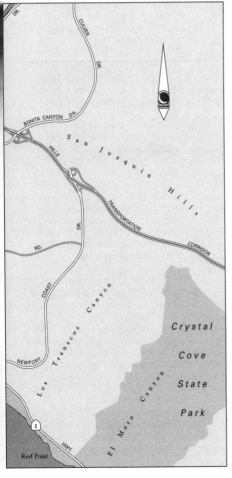

alternative. If hiking long urban distances isn't feasible, cycling might be—so bring bikes if you've got them, or plan to rent.

Exploring Newport Harbor from its watery underside isn't all that pleasurable, given the sheer numbers of boats and people. The exception to the rule is Corona del Mar State Beach, with offshore reefs worth exploring. Even better is Crystal Cove State Park between Newport and Laguna Beach, an underwater marine sanctuary with good diving. Laguna Beach is actually closer to Crystal Cove, but if you're based in Newport rent snorkeling or scuba gear (certification required for divers) at the **Aquatic Center,** 4537 W. Coast Hwy. (at Balboa), tel. (949) 650-5440.

The best way to tour Newport Harbor is by boat. Unusual is a one-hour gondola tour with **Gondola Company of Newport,** headquarters at Lido Marina Village, 3404 Via Oporto, Suite 102B, tel. (714) 675-1212.

For the classic harbor cruise—during which you'll find out just which celebrities lived where, et cetera—try **Catalina Passenger Service** and its *Pavilion Queen,* an ersatz river boat, and *Pavilion Paddy,* both docked at the Balboa Pavilion. In addition, CPS offers trips to and from Catalina Island as well as whalewatching tours. For current information call toll-free (800) 830-7744 or (949) 673-5245.

Most whalewatching and sportfishing tours also shove off from the pavilion. **Bongos Sportfishing Charters,** 2140 Newport Blvd., tel. (949) 673-2810, offers whale trips from just after Christmas through March and sportfishing year-round, as does **Newport Landing Sportfishing,** 309 Palm St., tel. (949) 675-0550. For information on private exclusive yacht charters, for total privacy and/or to accommodate large groups, contact the visitors bureau for referrals.

ON THE BALBOA PENINSULA

First and often last stop on a people's tour is the Balboa Peninsula, a long, arthritic finger of sand pointing south from **Newport Boulevard,** the seaward end of the line for the Costa Mesa (55) Freeway. You can also get here from the Coast Highway and **Balboa Boulevard.** Humanity is so well-established here, the entire harbor so sheltered from sea-driven storms, it's a surprise to discover that the peninsula is a geological newborn. The Balboa Peninsula didn't begin to exist until after 1825, a year of massive flooding that caused the Santa Ana River to suddenly change course and deposit sand and sediments in the harbor.

Newport Pier and Vicinity

The Newport Pier—about a half-mile past the highway at the ocean end of McFadden Place, between 20th and 21st Sts.—was originally McFadden's Wharf, built in 1888 to accommodate the train from Santa Ana delivering produce and steamship passengers. **Newport Beach**—the actual beach by that name—stretches both west and east from the pier (this one constructed in the 1940s), which serves as madding-crowd central in summer and on most weekends.

The most historic attraction at the Newport Pier is the **Newport Dory Fishing Fleet** adjacent. Hard at it since 1891, this is the only surviving dory fleet on the West Coast. Arrive by 10 a.m. to scoop up some of the day's catch, marketed in open-air stalls. For more information on the fleet and other aspects of Newport's harbor history, stop by the **Newport Beach Nautical Museum** at its new location in the Reuben E. Lee "river barge," 151 E. Coast Hwy., tel. (949) 673-7863, open Tues.-Sun. 10 a.m.-5 p.m.

To try your hand at the landlubber's version of the dorymen's life, consider pier fishing. **Baldy's Tackle,** 100 McFadden, has been around almost as long as the dorymen; stop by to rent fishing tackle as well as bikes. It's a five-minute walk to the end of the pier.

Balboa Pier and Vicinity

A stroll to the Balboa Pier, which juts into the ocean from Balboa's Main St., two miles to the east, takes considerably longer—especially if you dawdle along the concrete boardwalk. Accompanied by landscaped lawn, bandstand, and palm trees, the Balboa Pier is the focal point for more placid pursuits. On most days **Balboa Beach** is relatively lonely and quiet, especially on the stretch toward the jetty. Even the ocean is quieter here, since the sandy beach falls away steeply and the waves seem to arrive from nowhere.

Downcoast is the jetty, a rocky chin protecting the harbor mouth as it inhales and exhales sailboats. The angle formed between Balboa Beach and the jetty is known as **The Wedge,** internationally famous for its stupendous shore breaks, locally infamous for bone-breaking bodysurfing, surfing, and swimming. (It's dangerous. No joke.) To get the big picture, head out to **Jetty View Park** at the tip of the peninsula.

Balboa Proper

Both the pier and the **Balboa Pavilion** at 400 Main St.—originally a bathhouse cum boathouse, now de facto loading dock for boat tours—were built in 1905 by Southern California developers working overtime to attract home buyers to this otherwise desolate sandspit. (Encouraged by a generous cash donation and free railroad right-of-way, Henry E. Huntington aided their cause on July 4, 1906, when the first of his electric trolleys to Newport Beach delivered potential buyers from Los Angeles.) In the 1940s the pavilion was a big-band bandstand—home of the "Balboa" dance craze—though the nearby Rendezvous Ballroom, long gone, was the more famous venue.

Not to be missed amid the surrounding shops and schlock is the reconstructed Balboa **Fun Zone** promenade along the bay, one of the few places left anywhere with genuine arcade-era pinball machines, skee ball, and such. For electronics addicts, video games are available.

Adjacent to the pavilion is the three-car Balboa Ferry, for the trip to and from Balboa Island.

Also worth appreciating is the lovely 1930 Spanish colonial **Balboa Inn** at the foot of the pier, a hotel designed by architect Walter Hagedohn, more famous for his Union Station in Los Angeles.

A still grander presence presides at W. Ocean Front and 13th Street, back toward the Newport Pier—the concrete **Lovell Beach House.** Considered one of the finest American examples of early modern architecture, it was designed in 1926 by Rudolph M. Schindler for health enthusiast Dr. Lovell. The house is suspended above the beach by columns and cantilevers, actually five poured-concrete frames. The ground level is an outdoor living area combining a fireplace with the necessities of parking, play, and washing up. The main living area above (two stories) ponders the Pacific. Sleeping balconies, once al fresco, are now enclosed—surely in recognition of the fog-chill factor—and the roof features a sunken sunbathing deck. But Bauhaus is not *your* house, so don't bother the residents.

OFF THE BALBOA PENINSULA

Balboa Island and Vicinity

Not to be confused with Balboa Peninsula is Balboa Island just off the mainland, a buffed neighborhood of beach bungalows reached by car from W. Coast Hwy. and Marine Avenue.

If you drive, though, you won't see much, because you'll never find a place to park. A better option—and much more fun—is coming over as a pedestrian on the nearly perpetual **Balboa Island Ferries,** tel. (949) 673-1070, a service shuttling people and automobiles (maximum capacity, three cars at a time) back and forth daily since the early 1900s. The ferries ($1 fare) run daily—from 6:30 a.m. to midnight Sun.-Thurs., until 2 a.m. on Friday and Saturday nights—between Palm Ave. on the peninsula and Agate Ave. on the island.

"Agate," by the way, indicates another island oddity. Most cross streets are named for gems and stones—Jade, Topaz, Garnet, and Emerald.

Marine Ave. is the village boutiquery and business district, where one can also pursue simple pleasures—such as a world-famous "Balboa bar" (vanilla ice cream bars dipped in chocolate) from **Dad's,** or a frozen chocolate-dipped banana from **Sugar 'n' Spice.** *The* restaurant on Balboa Island is **Amelia's,** 311 Marine Ave., tel. (949) 673-6580, known for seafood, Italian specialties, and family-run atmosphere.

To eyeball James Cagney's onetime island estate, head west. That's it, just offshore at the end of Park—**Collins Isle,** sticking out from the west side of Balboa Island like a sandy little toe.

Like other private landfill islands scattered around the bay, **Lido Isle** to the harbor's far west—reached from the peninsula via Newport Boulevard and Via Lido—is an elite and elegant residential enclave where potentially public lawn areas are designated "private" community parks.

Corona Del Mar and Vicinity

Gardeners enjoy the **Sherman Library and Gardens** in Corona del Mar. Here they get a thorough education in just what will grow, and grow well, in the onetime desert of Southern California. Just south of the harbor on the mainland at 2647 E. Coast Hwy. (at MacArthur Blvd.), tel. (949) 673-2261, the Sherman honors the "Pacific Southwest" in its specialized library and two-acre garden of desert and tropical plants. More tropicals, and a koi pond, are in the modern conservatory. Also here: a wheelchair-accessible "discovery garden" for the seeing-impaired. The gardens are open 10:30 a.m.-4 p.m. daily except major holidays, the library on weekdays only. Small admission. The Tea Garden restaurant here serves light lunch fare, pastries, beverages, but is open to the public only on Saturday, Sunday, and Monday 11 a.m.-3 p.m.

Besides shops and shopping, the star attraction of Corona del Mar is half-mile-long **Corona Del Mar State Beach** at the mouth of Newport Harbor, operated by the city and framed by cliffs and the rocky jetty at the eastern harbor entrance. Offshore is crystal-clear azure ocean; underfoot, warm white sand; everywhere around, lush landscaping—the classic California postcard. It would be wonderful, too, if everyone else in Southern California weren't so determined to be here. To reach the parking lot and day-use facilities for the main beach, from the Coast Hwy. take Jasmine St. to Ocean Boulevard. Day use (parking) is $6, but for the privilege of paying it, be sure to get here early. For more information, call the visitor bureau, tel. (949) 722-1611.

Also hardly a secret is **Big Corona Beach** off Marguerite Avenue, where one can just sit and watch the boats pass. The secluded cove at **Little Corona Beach,** with its **tidepool reserve** (visit at low tide), is reached via Ocean Blvd. (at Poppy).

Other Newport Beaches

Back in Newport is the only "secret" beach around, the small **Coast Guard Beach** at the Harbor Master Coast Guard Station. Here you'll find a relatively peaceful stretch of sand, safe swimming, volleyball nets (bring your own ball), and picnic tables. Park on the street. The Coast Guard Beach is off the 1900 block of Bayside Drive. To get here from the highway, take Jamboree toward Balboa Island and then turn left onto Bayside.

"Bay beaches" include just about any accessible patches of sand fringing Newport Bay. One with lifeguards, volleyball nets, restrooms, showers, and some wind protection is on the peninsula's Bay Avenue between 18th and 19th Streets. Look for others at Montero and 10th Sts., and at the end of every street on Balboa Island.

EXCURSION INLAND:
THE BOWERS MUSEUM OF CULTURAL ART

That the largest museum in Orange County is dedicated to preserving the art and artifacts of the world's indigenous peoples is quite fitting, given the county's increasing cultural diversity.

Easily accessible from Newport Beach and reopened in 1992 after a four-year, $12 million facelift, the Bowers Museum of Cultural Art in Santa Ana is as expansive in scope as it is small in size. The appealing 1932 Spanish mission-style building downtown, complete with courtyard, was not only renovated but expanded, tripling exhibit space to more than 19,000 square feet. But the territory is still too tight for permanent display of the museum's 85,000-piece collection. So the Bowers Museum is known for its imaginative special shows, such as *African Icons of Power, Perú Before the Inca, Art of the Himalayas,* and *River of Gold: Pre-Columbian Treasures from Sitio Conte.* There's always a reason to come back.

Among permanent exhibits are *Arts of Native America*—art and artifacts from various North American cultures, including intricate beadwork from Plains cultures and exquisite Pomo basketry from Northern California—and *Realm of the Ancestors,* representations of the argonaut cultures of Southeast Asia and Pacific Oceania. Ancient stone art and ceramics of pre-Columbian Mexico and Central America are collected in *Vision of the Shaman, Song of the Priest.*

Also permanent is *California Legacies,* both tribute to Orange County's diverse cultural heritage and homage to the museum's humble beginnings as an odd collection of local memorabilia. (The museum's first show—recently repeated—was a collection of dolls donated by children.) Starting in the 1970s the Bowers Museum began to supplement its collection of regional ceramics and orange crate labels in an aggressive acquisitions program emphasizing pre-Columbian and Native American culture.

The museum's special evening and weekend events, such as "Spirits of the Rainforest" and "California Folk Art," are usually well worth the trip.

New at the Bowers Museum is the **Kidseum,** an all-kid section opened in 1995 to "promote cultural understanding among the peoples of Africa, the Americas, and the Pacific Rim." Among the Kidseum's unique attractions: the storytelling room, the theater, the art laboratory, and exhibit space for children's art from around the world.

The Bowers Museum "partnership"—the institution is owned by the city of Santa Ana, managed and governed by a private, nonprofit Board of Governors, and financed with contributions from the private sector—

Inside the Bowers Museum visitors will find an 85,000-piece collection of art and artifacts from the world's indigenous peoples, such as this human face mask.

BOWERS MUSEUM

also sponsors an impressive community education program. Unusual, too, is the Bowers's international cultural art travel program (members only).

Plan a stop at the museum shop for its unusually thoughtful array of books, jewelry, and one-of-a-kind art from around the world. Proceeds support the museum and its programs.

Practical Bowers

And do enjoy the Bowers Museum international culinary offerings. Just inside the entrance is the Southwesternesque **Topaz Cafe**, the museum's social centerpiece, serving exceptional meals and memorable desserts, everything moderately priced. Launched by local restaurant wizard David Wilhelm and Executive Chef John Sharpe, both of Barbacoa, Bistro 201, Diva, Cancun Cafe, and Zuni Grill fame, the indoor-outdoor Topaz Cafe is open for lunch Tuesday through Saturday, for dinner Tuesday through Friday, and for buffet brunch on Sunday—the latter highly recommended. Reservations are wise.

The Bowers Museum of Cultural Art, 2002 N. Main St.(Santa Ana 92706), on Main at 20th St., has free parking available in the adjacent lot (between 19th and 20th). Museum galleries are open Tues.-Fri. 10 a.m.-4 p.m., and Saturday and Sunday 10 a.m.-6 p.m. Kidseum galleries are open Saturday and Sunday 10 a.m.-4 p.m. Admission is $4 adults, $3 seniors/students, and $2 for children ages 5-12 (under 5 free). For general information call the Bowers Museum at (714) 567-3600; for membership, (714) 567-3688; for tours, (714) 567-3680; for museum store information, (714) 567-3643. For schedule information and reservations at the Topaz Cafe, call (714) 835-2002. Or check out the website at www.bowers.org.

Though the Orange, Garden Grove, and Costa Mesa Freeways converge quite close to downtown Santa Ana, the easiest way to get to the Bowers Museum from the coast is via the 55 (the Costa Mesa Freeway) then the Santa Ana Freeway (I-5). From I-5 northbound, exit at 17th St. and head west four blocks to Main and turn north (right). If for some reason you're on I-5 southbound, exit at Main and turn right. (Call to verify directions; the details may change once freeway construction in the area is completed.) By bus, OCTA routes 51, 53, and 55 will get you to the Bowers.

UPPER NEWPORT BAY ECOLOGICAL RESERVE

Visitors quickly appreciate why the Spanish called this place "Frog Swamp," since the Upper Newport Bay Ecological Reserve or "Back Bay" is a brackish salt- and fresh-water marsh complete with cattails, pickleweed, and aromatic mudflats. The most frightening fact is that this very small preserve is the largest remaining unengineered estuary in Southern California.

The Back Bay may be small but it is a marvel—an ecologically rich Pacific Flyway sanctuary that provides shelter to about 200 bird species and 20,000-30,000 birds during the year. Two endangered species, the light-footed clapper rail and Belding's savanna sparrow (found only in Southern California), can be spotted here, along with the California brown pelican, the California least tern, and the peregrine falcon.

Cut off by the Coast Hwy. on the west and surrounded by view homes perched high on the earthy diatomaceous cliffs, the Back Bay is best appreciated on foot or by bike—bike trails span the northern stretches and follow San Diego Creek—though you can see most of it by car. Auto tour access (one-way only) is off lower Jamboree Rd.; turn onto Backbay Dr. at the Hyatt Newporter and keep going. Parking areas are scattered along the route—so even if you're driving, pick a spot, park, and get out to see the sights in person.

No matter how you go, stop first at the **Newport Bay Naturalists office** on Shellmaker Island (600 Shellmaker Dr., just off Backbay Dr.), tel. (949) 640-6746, or check www.newportbay.org for maps, bird and plant checklists, and historical background.

Naturalists offer free two-hour guided **discovery walks** every Saturday and Sunday, starting at Shellmaker Island at 1 p.m. Also offered on weekends throughout the year: canoe and kayak tours, twilight cruises, an evening "owl prowl," and family campfire programs. For more information, contact the office on Shellmaker Island (see above).

From October through March Newport Bay enthusiasts also offer free walking tours, starting in the preserve's southeast corner near the intersection of Backbay and Eastbluff Drives. For

SOUTH COAST PLAZA:
SHOPPING AS THE CENTER OF EVERYTHING

Consumerism as Culture

Think of it as a theme park for consumerism, this one attracting more than 20 million visitors each year and, in 1999, raking in an estimated $12.4 billion. The most notable diversion at Orange County's South Coast Plaza mega-mall in Costa Mesa is the mall itself. Unique in the neighborhood, though, are the sociocultural segues between art, commerce, entertainment, finance, and fine dining—Orange County's foremost foray into the culture of consumerism and consumerism as culture.

This being one of the largest-grossing retail centers in the U.S., going to South Coast Plaza typically involves spending money. But rest assured that here commerce is not crass. The preferred promotional etiquette at South Coast Plaza is to refer the mall itself as a "retail center," its shoppers as "guests."

All in all, it's hard to imagine the landscape a few short decades ago, when it was just another Orange County lima bean field.

A New South Coast Plaza

As in other theme parks, the territory here is geographically subdivided. The center is three-story **South Coast Plaza at Bristol,** 3333 Bristol Street (between the 405 and Sunflower), tel. (714) 435-2000, www .southcoastplaza.com, with its multistory atriums and elegant décor and a surprising variety of shops anchored by Bullock's, Nordstrom, Macy's, Sears, and Robinsons-May. On the west end is **Jewel Court,** Orange County's version of Rodeo Drive, with upscale shops including Tiffany & Co., Emporio Armani, Louis Vuitton, Cartier, and Chanel. Centerpiece of **Carousel Court** on the mall's east end is—you guessed it—a turn-of-the-20th-century carousel, a fitting enticement for the Sesame Street General Store, Disney Store, GapKids, FAO Schwarz, and other attractions aimed at the younger set.

Then there's the single-level **South Coast Plaza Village** just east of the main mall at Sunflower and Bear Streets, where the Edwards Cinema complex is one notable diversion. Once known as Crystal Court, **South Coast Plaza at Bear,** north of the main mall at 3333 Bear Street, includes an eclectic array, from Abercrombie & Fitch and Adrienne Vittadini to Victoria's Secret. There's also a kiddie carousel here, a new feature, this one with a King Arthur theme.

South of South Coast Plaza and Bristol is the **South Coast Plaza Town Center,** sometimes referred to as The Offices, an area bisected by Anton Blvd. and Town Center Dr.—a shimmering 96-acre orchard of bank and business office towers, visual and performing-arts venues, multiplex movie theaters, and inviting eateries.

Major changes at the mall in 1999 and 2000, announced as A New South Coast Plaza, include two new anchors for South Coast Plaza at Bear—a 42,000-square-foot Crate & Barrel Home Store, the chain's West Coast flagship, and a Macy's Home store. Also new is an elevated pedestrian walkway to connect the Bear and Bristol malls. At the main mall, Robinsons-May is expanding by 50,000 square feet. And a new 300,000-square-foot symphony hall designed by renowned architect Cesar Pelli, the **Segerstrom Center for the Arts** to be located next to South Coast Repertory, is coming soon.

Consuming Culture and "California Scenario"

The neighborhood's main action may be trafficking in commerce and consumer goods, but the main attraction is art—most of it in Town Center.

Almost perfectly hidden, wedged into the courtyard created by two black-glass business towers and the adjacent public parking lot, is an understated yet powerful exploration of the California myth—***California Scenario*** by the late Isamu Noguchi. This expansive "sculpture garden" offers much more than the term typically implies, staging separate but unified California themes with stunning directness and native-son humor. *Land Use,* for example, is a long, narrow chunk of concrete-colored granite dominating the crest of a landscaped knoll. A meandering stream flows from the tall *Water Source,* past *Desert Land,* to squat, stylized *Water Use.* Funniest of all, though, is *Spirit of the Lima Bean,* 15 dignified desert-colored boulders of decomposed granite piled up to honor South Coast Plaza's primary developers and benefactors, the Segerstrom family—perhaps only incidentally paying homage to the land's previous purpose.

California Scenario is tucked away behind the Great Western Bank Building, 3200 Park Center Drive (off Anton Blvd.); parking is available in the adjacent public lot. The courtyard is open daily 8 a.m.-midnight. Appreciating Noguchi's art is absolutely free. For more information, call (714) 435-2100.

Various other public sculptures—by **Henry Moore, Joan Miró, Alexander Calder, Claire Falkenstein,** and others—are scattered throughout the Town Center area, indoors and out. If you're too rushed to see them all after doing the mall, walk over to the performing arts center on Town Center Drive—take the pedestrian bridge that spans Bristol—for the stunning first-time impact of Richard Lippold's 60-foot-tall *Fire Bird,* a spectacular vision any time but especially after dark.

Also worthwhile in the arts department is the gallery inside **Bank of America,** 555 Anton. At South Coast Plaza proper, the **Laguna Art Museum** hosts a satellite gallery inside its shop at the mall's east end. Both are free.

Consuming Culture: Performance Arts

The post-modern **Orange County Performing Arts Center** hosts the Los Angeles Philharmonic and touring companies, including the American Ballet Theatre, the Joffrey Ballet, the New York City Ballet, and the New York City Opera, though popular musicals predominate. Near-perfect acoustics are the hallmark of the center's 3,000-seat Segerstrom Hall. Incidentally, the center's $73 million tab was picked up entirely through private donations. The performing arts center is on Town Center Drive at Avenue of the Arts. Call (714) 556-2787 for current performance information (recorded) or (714) 556-2122 (administration). Or try the website, www.ocpac.org. Buy tickets for most performances through Ticketmaster, tel. (714) 740-7878: day-of-performance seats are often available.

Physically but not artistically overshadowed by the performing arts center is the Tony award-winning **South Coast Repertory Theater,** tel. (714) 957-4033, www.scr.org. For tickets, call the box office at (714) 708-5555. Started decades ago as a seat-of-the-pants repertory troupe, critical acclaim came along for South Coast Repertory with the brave decision to produce works by new playwrights, though not everything presented resembles avant-garde art. The Mainstage Theater here seats 507, the smaller Second Stage just 161, so call well in advance for current show schedule and reservations; last-minute tickets are scarce. Best bet for spur-of-the-moment attendance: matinees and midweek performances.

Eating at South Coast Plaza

There are dozens of dining options at South Coast Plaza. A best bet for families is the local **Ruby's** burgers-and-shakes outpost, at Bear Street, tel. (714) 662-7829. For a change of pace head south to the Southwestern **El Torito Grill** in Town Center at

633 Anton Blvd.(at Bristol), tel. (714) 662-0798, where specialties such as red snapper fajitas keep the crowds coming back for more. Fun for sushi is **San Kai,** all but hidden away in a nondescript minimall at 3940 S. Bristol, tel. (714) 241-7115. This relaxed and unpretentious neighborhood-style Japanese restaurant, open for lunch and dinner, comes complete with sushi bar. You won't go wrong with the California roll, but try San Kai's crunchy roll and spicy tuna handroll. Or the sautéed calamari.

Inside South Coast Plaza at Bristol, between Bullock's and the Bullock's men's store, is the **Wolfgang Puck Cafe,** tel. (714) 546-9653, a stylish but casual California cafe serving reasonably priced renditions of trademark Puck-style pizzas, pastas, and salads. In the Sears wing is the **Rainforest Café,** tel. (714) 424-9200, where the stylish casual fare comes with the ultimate in faux-environment dining. Justifiably popular is the casual **Gustaf Anders Back Pocket,** tel. (714) 668-1737.

For upper-crust pizza at lunch or before a show, the place is **Scott's Seafood Grill and Bar** at 3300 Bristol (at Anton), tel. (714) 979-2400. A Southern California link in the popular San Francisco-based chain, Scott's is considerably more famous for its seafood, its generous Sunday brunch, and its fixed-price pre-theater menu.

Popular with patrons of the arts is David Wilhelm's dramatically elegant **Diva** near the performing arts center, 600 Anton (at Bristol), tel. (714) 754-0600, serving a contemporary California menu so exciting its audience keeps coming back for encores. The signature "ahi towers" here are meant to mimic neighborhood architecture. It's open for lunch weekdays only, for dinner nightly. Jazz several nights each week. Also drawing the stylish crowds these days is **Pinot Provence,** at the Westin Hotel, 686 Anton, tel. (714) 444-5900, a slice of life from the south of France and Joachim Splichal's only Orange County restaurant.

Practical South Coast Plaza

South Coast Plaza offers a multitude of "concierge services," including stroller and wheelchair loans, package checking, valet parking, and dinner or theater reservations. For assistance, stop by the concierge desk on the mall's first level, in the center near the carousel, or call (714) 435-8571 or toll-free (800) 782-8888. To find your way around, pick up a current South Coast Plaza Directory. Also request the mall's Address Book brochure and map. For other South Coast Plaza information, try the website, www.southcoastplaza.com.

(continued on next page)

more information, call Newport Bay Naturalists at (949) 640-6746.

For restrooms and a pleasant picnic after a Back Bay adventure, head to **Bonita Creek Park** on University Dr., just one block east of the Jamboree-Eastcliff intersection.

The Back Bay is also accessible from the north. The heavily eroded, star-thistly perimeter is less aesthetic (this is, after all, primarily a judiciously preserved wetlands area) but otherwise wonderful for a meditative stroll up and down the bluffs. To get here from Highway 73: Exit at Irvine Ave. and head west about 1.5 miles, then turn left onto University Drive. Parking (street) is usually available on University.

ARTFUL, ENTERTAINING, AND EVENTFUL NEWPORT

Newport Area Arts

Marooned in a business park near Fashion Island is the **Orange County Museum of Art,** originally known as the Newport Harbor Art Museum, 850 San Clemente Dr., tel. (949) 759-1122, nationally acclaimed in the late 1980s for its contemporary California art collection and cutting-edge special exhibits. One of its recent achievements was the traveling Anne Frank exhibit, with over 600 photographs. And recently the museum's fortunes received a boost when it was announced that the Irvine Company was donating an adjoining library building for a proposed expansion project.

Particularly striking outside are this museum's red "gem," a sculpture by Jonathan Borofsky, a rusting six-foot iron cube protruding from the building, and the outdoor sculptures. Particularly striking inside are the rotating exhibits—and here, even the permanent collection rotates. The museum is open Tues.-Sun. 10 a.m.-5p.m. (closed Monday). Admission is $5 adults, $4 students/seniors, free for children under 16.

For classic or limited-run films, the place is the **Edwards Lido Cinema,** 3459 Via Lido, tel. (949) 673-8350, cozy one-screen theatre with comfortable seating. Matinee prices are $3.75 on showings before 6 p.m.

Newport Area Entertainment

To avoid the making-the-scene scene, a comfortable alternative is a coffeehouse. Something of a surprise on the peninsula is the **Alta Cafe Warehouse and Roasting Co.,** 506 31st St. (off Newport Blvd.), tel. (949) 675-0233. The fare is simple but wholesome at breakfast, lunch, and dinner, the atmosphere relaxed and moody, the coffee blends strong and witty. (The Frank Sumatra, for example, is distinguished by its "good personality.") For entertainment, blues, jazz, and folk music are on the menu. Alta Cafe is typically open 7 a.m.-11:30 p.m. p.m., until 12:30 a.m. on Friday and Saturday nights.

Best bet for jazz, though, is the **Studio Cafe** near the Balboa Pier, 100 Main St. (at Balboa), tel. (949) 675-7760, with top-flight blues or jazz on tap nightly. It also offers a dining room and full bar, so you could do worse than to just park yourself here once the sun sets. The Sunday afternoon jam session is worth a special trip.

And if you find yourself washed ashore anywhere near the Fashion Island mall, rocking out in the mall's parking lot is Orange County's outpost of the **Hard Rock Cafe,** 451 Newport Center Dr. (at San Miguel), tel. (949) 640-8844. The usual burgers and such are served, along with hygienic exposure to rock 'n' roll memorabilia as suitable for young rockers as for aging hipster parents. People also stop by to collect T-shirts and the local variation of Hard Rock's glam-rock guitar lapel pin.

Otherwise, Newport Beach is somewhat notorious as a making-the-scene scene. Hot clubs include **The Warehouse,** at 3450 Via Oporto, tel. (949) 673-4700, with dancing Thursday, Friday, and Saturday nights. On weekends there's a DJ upstairs, live band downstairs. If you eat dinner here (seafood) the dancing's free; otherwise, there's a $5 cover.

The View on the 16th floor of the Marriott in Fashion Island, 900 Newport Center, tel. (949) 640-4000, offers live jazz and dancing on Friday and Saturday nights. Overlooking the Balboa Peninsula, this is also the place to drink in the view over drinks.

Newport Area Events

The most famous local event is the annual **Newport Harbor Christmas Boat Parade** wherein more sporting members of the local yachting crowd decorate their boats in lights and sometimes outlandish decorations and then cruise the harbor. During the week before Christmas, typically, the parade circumnavigates the harbor from 6:30-8:30 p.m.—beginning and ending at Collins Island—putting on quite a show for the folks assembled in restaurants and along public beaches. (Also fun at Christmas: the outrageously beautiful—and outrageously expensive—Christmas decorations at **Roger's Gardens,** 2301 San Joaquin Hills Rd., tel. 949-640-5800.) Expect similar silliness at the theme-oriented **Character Boat Parade,** usually held in mid- to late July. The 10-day **Newport Seafest,** which includes seafaring fun as well as **A Taste of Newport,** usually begins in mid-September. Contact the visitor bureau at toll-free (800) 942-6278, www.newportbeach-cvb.com, for more information on these and other events.

STAYING IN NEWPORT BEACH

Newport Camping

It's not cheap and the ambience leaves room for improvement, but **Newport Dunes RV Park** just off Jamboree Rd. at 1131 Back Bay Dr., tel. (949) 729-3863 or toll-free (800) 288-0770, is close to the harbor action. It's also practically in the Back Bay, if you're hankering for a hike. It even has a small marina (rental boats available) and children's playground. But if you're going to play here, you'll pay: RVers and intrepid tent campers unpack themselves onto small concrete slabs—like sardines into a can—and pay $25 and up. Budget. Alternatives include state park campgrounds up and down the coast.

Lower Rent Newport Accommodations

In Newport Beach and elsewhere along the coast, you'll pay a premium for seaside location and ocean views. Ritzier hotels cluster near the airport and area malls. It's certainly no crime if travelers in search of more modest accommodation retreat to Costa Mesa, just inland from Newport.

One particularly pleasant motel on northbound Newport Boulevard (where it becomes a one-way paralleling the 55 Freeway) is less than a mile from the harbor and reasonably close to everything else—most notably the shops and restaurants at the Triangle Square complex, which is within easy walking distance. Rooms at the **Holiday Inn Express,** 2070 Newport Blvd., between 21st and Bay Ave., tel. (949) 631-6000, feature all the basics; some have microwaves and refrigerators. With the ocean so close by, who cares that it doesn't have a pool? Expensive, with standard rates starting at $99, $89 with AAA or AARP membership. The **Days Inn** adjacent, 2100 Newport Blvd., tel. (949) 642-2670, $59-89, has a pool.

One of the best deals in the entire county is just off the 405 Freeway—the **Country Side Inn and Suites,** 325 S. Bristol St. in Costa Mesa (on South Bristol at Red Hill Ave., on the west side of the street), tel. toll-free (800) 322-9992 or (714) 549-0300. This well-appointed modern motel, within easy reach of the coast and all other major Orange County attractions, has country French bed-and-breakfast style. Amenities include in-room refrigerators and color TV with videocassette players. Some rooms and studio suites feature microwaves and whirlpools. Extras include full buffet breakfast and morning newspapers, plus two swimming pools, whirlpools, exercise facilities, coin laundry. Since the Country Side here does substantial "business" business, weekend rates are lowest—a real boon for pleasure travelers—starting at $89. Weekday rates are substantially higher, but with big discounts for AAA and AARP members. Expensive-Luxury. Weekly and monthly rates are also available.

Higher Rent Newport Accommodations

The area's up-market and luxury hotels generally do double-duty as both business and pleasure destinations, thus their locations—within easy reach of corporate business parks, major malls, and John Wayne Airport. Official rates are high;

ask about specials and packages, especially for off-season weekends.

Top of the mark is the 19-story **Four Seasons Hotel Newport Beach** near Fashion Island, 690 Newport Center, tel. toll-free (800) 332-3442 or (949) 759-0808, www.fourseasons.com, rated in 1994 by *Condé Nast Traveler* readers as one of the world's finest hotels. From the outside it looks like yet another too-tall, bewindowed box. Inside, though, it's elegant yet airy, all sand-beige and pastels. And those windows let in some grand views. Along with luxury in-room amenities, facilities here include tennis courts, a huge pool, complete fitness center, and guaranteed tee times and weekend golf packages at nearby courses. The Four Seasons even offers free mountain bikes—the better to explore the Bay. Among the several restaurants here is **Pavilion,** where people dress up for the California-style American. The Four Seasons also boasts a complete business center, not to mention full conference facilities. Luxury, with rates $235-475.

Overlooking the Back Bay, **Marriott Suites Newport Beach,** 500 Bayview Circle (at Jamboree Rd.), tel. toll-free (800) 228-9290 or (949) 854-4500, www.marriott.com, is primarily an upscale business-oriented hotel, quite welcoming on weekends for pleasure travelers. Pool, saunas, fitness facilities, and rental bikes make a weekend stay more than pleasant. Standard in-room amenities are almost too much, from two color TVs and two phones (with call waiting) to wet bar and refrigerator. Premium-Luxury, with rates $139-199 (children 18 and under free).

From the outside the **Sutton Place Hotel** (formerly Le Meridien Newport Beach), 4500 MacArthur Blvd., tel. toll-free (800) 243-4141 or (949) 476-2001, www.suttonplace.com, looks something like a squared-off cruise ship, this one with big windows on every deck. Inside, it's very contemporary, very Southern California, with all the expected amenities, including tennis courts, pool, and business center. Most beloved at Sutton Place is its French restaurant **Antoine,** one of Orange County's best in any category. Premium-Luxury, with rates $118-185. While Sutton Place is technically in Newport Beach, for all practical purposes it's a South Coast Plaza/John Wayne Airport hotel. Stay here to take advantage of weekend South Coast Repertory theater and/or Pageant of the Masters packages.

More convenient to Newport Harbor is the **Hyatt Newporter,** 1107 Jamboree Rd., tel. toll-free (800) 233-1234 or (949) 729-1234, www.hyattnewporter.com, with spacious resort-style grounds and an amazing array of sports and fitness facilities—including access to the John Wayne Tennis Club. Luxury, with rates $169 and up. Lush, too, but less outdoorsy is the **Newport Beach Marriott Hotel and Tennis Club** near Fashion Island, 900 Newport Center Dr., tel. toll-free (800) 228-9290 or (714) 640-4000, www.marriot.com. The "tennis club" refers to eight lighted tennis courts (extra). Golf is also available. Luxury, with rates $169 and up.

Anyone opting for a street-side room at the appealing 1930s' Spanish-style **Balboa Inn,** by the Balboa Pier and Balboa Beach at 105 Main St., tel. (714) 675-3412, www.balboainn.com, also receives a free nightly live-jazz serenade from the Studio Cafe just across the way. The decor here is flowery country French. Each of the 34 rooms and 14 suites boasts a view of some sort (not necessarily the ocean), though the most pacifying peek at the Pacific is from the pool area. Seven rooms include an in-room spa, 10 have a fireplace. Continental breakfast is served in the lobby. Luxury, with rates from $169, from $145 in the off-season. Kareem Abdul-Jabbar once owned the place, which explains the oversized doorways and furniture in Room 220.

Newport Bed and Breakfast Inns

Newport Beach bed and breakfast inns deliver the most ocean ambience. Probably the best bet for romance—and not all that pricey if you opt for a cheaper room—is the two-story **Portofino Beach Hotel** on Balboa Peninsula just north of the pier, 2306 W. Ocean Front (at 23rd St.), tel. (949) 673-7030, www.portofinobeachhotel.com, with 15 rooms, four villas, and a "casa" that sleeps 10. The style here is upscale European, with decor running to antiques, armoires, and brass beds. Some rooms and three villas look out over the ocean; some feature skylights, fireplaces, and in-room whirlpool tubs. Luxury, with rates $159-279 (weekly rates available), and children 16 and under stay free. Breakfast is included; there's also a restaurant on the premises.

For Victorian romance with frills, flounces, and French and American antiques, try the **Doryman's Inn** nearby, a 1891 brick beauty across from the Newport Pier at 2102 W. Ocean Front, tel. (949) 675-7300. Every room features a fireplace and sunken marble jacuzzi tub, some have a four-poster bed with mirrored headboard. Besides breakfast, other goodies include a bottle of wine or champagne upon arrival, butter cookies and chocolates in the evening, a patio with a view, even a rooftop sundeck. Luxury, with rates: $175-325.

The only place to stay out on Balboa Island (adults only) is the downhome 1925 **Balboa Island Hotel,** convenient to the ferry at 127 Agate Ave., tel. (949) 675-3613. The three rooms here, two with a queen bed, one with a twin, share bathrooms. For breakfast, count on fresh fruit, muffins, and coffee. Moderate, with rates $85 in the high season, $65 otherwise.

EATING OUT À LA NEWPORT

Casual at Breakfast

You'll find no shortage of coffee-and-pastry stops in and around Newport Beach. For atmosphere à la Berkeley on Balboa Peninsula, try the **Alta Cafe Warehouse and Roasting Co.,** 506 31st St. (off Newport Blvd.), tel. (949) 675-0233. For croissants and great coffee, try **C'est Si Bon,** off the highway in Newport Beach at 149 Riverside, tel. (949) 645-0447, also in Corona del Mar at 3444 E. Coast Hwy., tel. (949) 675-0994.

As beloved in Orange County as Peet's is in Berkeley, **Diedrich's** is the native java hot spot. The closest Newport location for most folks is actually in Costa Mesa at 474 E. 17th St. (the extension of Westcliff Dr., near Irvine Ave.), tel. (949) 646-0323. There's another in Newport Beach proper at 3601 Jamboree Rd., tel. (949) 833-9143, more convenient if you're heading out to the Back Bay. Seattle-based **Starbucks Coffee** is also established here, tucked into a little shopping center at 1128 Irvine Ave., tel. (949) 650-0369, and no doubt many more places by now, but the minimalist atmosphere is more conducive to takeout than hangout.

Funky for classic American breakfast is laidback, low-key **Cappy's Cafe,** 5930 W. Coast Hwy. in Newport Beach, tel. (949) 646-4202. If you find yourself out on Balboa Island early in the day, try **Wilma's Patio,** 225 Marine, tel. (949) 675-5542. On the peninsula, consider **Britta's**

Cafe two blocks from the Balboa Pavilion at 205 Main, tel. (949) 675-8146, though **Ruby's** at the end of the Balboa Pier has its charms. (For more on Ruby's, see below.)

Consider any of the area's upscale hotels for something more elegant in the morning.

Local Classics

The 1940s-style **Ruby's** out on Balboa Pier, tel. (949) 675-7829, is the first and original in this popular chain of boogying burger joints done in red, white, and polished chrome. Sitting on the roof for al fresco breakfast is a real treat at this one. The original Ruby's is still going strong, but now there are Ruby's outposts all over Southern California.

But the best bet for *fast* fast food—fresh burgers sans ambience—is **In-N-Out Burger,** closest here at 594 19th St. in Costa Mesa, toll-free tel. (800) 786-1000, where snap-to service comes with the employee profit-sharing plan.

Food snobs pooh-pooh the place, but for inexpensive and decent seafood *everybody* goes to **The Crab Cooker,** a lobster-red presence on the peninsula at 2200 Newport Blvd., tel. (949) 673-0100. Lunch and dinner specialties include Manhattan-style clam chowder, mesquite-grilled seafood and, yes, crab. As you can tell from a glance at the shuffling crowd on the sidewalk outside, no reservations are taken here (no credit cards either); add your name to the list and then join the line. Once you land a table, appreciate the ambience. A shark chained to the ceiling presides over the close-quarters decor: formica tables with quaint plastic breadstick and condiment containers, paper plates and placemats, even disposable silverware. At last report copies of the proprietor's 45 rpm single, "I Know Why The Fishes Cry," were still available for $1. There's another Crab Cooker in Tustin, 17260 E. 17th St., tel. (714) 573-1077.

Sabatino's Sausage Company

Virtually immune to tourist traffic is Sabatino's Lido Shipyard Sausage Company, tel. (949) 723-0645, tucked in among the boat shops and warehouses at 251 Shipyard Way, Cabin D on the Lido Peninsula—itself an opposable thumb on Balboa Peninsula, accessible via Lido Park Dr. just off Lafayette Ave. in Newport Beach.

Sabatino's is open daily for lunch and dinner. Eat cafe-style outdoors, weather permitting, to fully appreciate the semi-industrial shipyard ambience, or indoors, where the atmosphere is also relaxed. Sandwiches and salads dominate the lunch menu; you can't go wrong with any Sabatino's sausage sandwich or a Caesar salad, but the Sizzling Sausage Platter is a star attraction, served with pasta and bread (best with the giardinera, or Italian-style olive relish). The wonderful Sicilian sausages here date from an 1864 Sabatino family innovation, in which fat is removed from the meat and special goat's-milk cheese added in its stead. The result? Sausages, either mild or spicy, that are quite moist and incredibly tasty. Especially at dinner Sabatino's is also popular for its pasta specialties and other traditional Italian dishes—chicken, fresh fish, and veal selections, not to mention a superb rack of lamb. But unless you're religious about vegetarianism, do *not* leave this place without taking along at least one selection from the sausage counter.

Finding Sabatino's is a bit tricky, though certainly worth the effort. From downtown Newport Beach, head south on Newport Boulevard. After crossing the Coast Highway, turn left onto Via Lido (at the first light). Turn right onto Lafayette, then left at Lido Park Drive. There's a stop sign and "Lido Peninsula" sign, though it looks as if you're driving into a residential area. Continue to the next stop sign, at Shipyard, and turn right.

Also Imaginative and Affordable

JACKshrimp, 2400 W. Coast Hwy. (near Tustin Ave.), tel. (949) 650-5577, is hot stuff, a jammin' jambalaya joint serving secret-recipe jambalaya and Louisiana-style shrimp specialties in a very casual atmosphere. Lunch is served only on Friday, 11:30 a.m.-2:30 p.m. Dinner is served nightly, Mon.-Thurs. 5:30-10 p.m., Friday and Saturday until 11, on Sunday starting at 3:30 p.m.

The Golden Truffle, 1767 Newport Blvd. (between 17th and 18th, just before the 55 Freeway begins in Costa Mesa), tel. (949) 645-9858, is as unassuming as it is exceptional, a French-Caribbean bistro serving specialties such as Chianti braised lamb shank with noodles and Caribbean prime Angus skirt steak with soul slaw and fries. The Jamaican jerk chicken salad is nothing to shake a stick at either. The menu changes seasonally, featuring 15-20 specials every night. It's open Tues.-Sat. for lunch and dinner.

For healthy Mexican, the place is **La Fogata** near the Port Theater in Corona del Mar, 3025 E. Coast Hwy., tel. (949) 673-2211. In the same neighborhood and worth it for fancy Indian fare is **Mayur,** 2931 E. Coast Hwy., tel. (949) 675-6622, featuring seafood and other specialties, such as shrimp Vindaloo, shrimp Tandoori, and chicken tikka Masala.

One of the area's best bets for Chinese is in Costa Mesa—the long-running **Mandarin Gourmet,** 1500 Adams Ave., tel. (714) 540-1937, is beloved for its traditional Peking duck, seafood dishes, and almost endless menu.

For exceptional French picnic fixings, try the **Pascal Epicerie,** tel. (949) 261-9041, adjacent to the famed restaurant of the same name on Bristol Street. For more information, see Fine Dining, below.

Higher-Priced Spreads

To dent the bankroll on behalf of the beefeater tradition, hoof it over to **Five Crowns,** 3801 Pacific Coast Hwy. (at Poppy) in Corona del Mar, tel. (949) 760-0331. This ersatz English manor is beloved by tourists and locals alike for its humongous portions of prime rib and other specialties. The filet mignon is excellent, tender enough to slice with a spoon. The tony New England-style **Yankee Tavern,** 333 Bayside Drive in Newport Beach, tel. (949) 675-5333, adds dressed-down East Coast airs. Highlights include a traditional New England boiled dinner. The rest of the menu runs to beer-battered fish and chips, turkey meat loaf, and Yankee pot roast.

Tonier but most appreciated for its spectacular seafood is **21 Ocean Front** overlooking Newport Pier at 21 Ocean Front, tel. (949) 675-2566. One of the best bets around, though, is surprisingly relaxed **Bistro 201,** 3333 W. Pacific Coast Hwy., tel. (949) 631-1551.

Fine Dining, Dressed Up and Dressed Down

Genuine gastronomic adventure awaits in Newport Beach. Head to the south of France, for example, via one of Orange County's best restaurants. Serving Provençal in a rose garden of a bistro, **Pascal** in a shopping center just off the Del Mar Freeway at 1000 N. Bristol Ave. (near Jamboree), tel. (949) 752-0107, is just about everyone's favorite unstuffy French restaurant. Specialties include seared salmon filet with watercress sauce and baby lamb rack with sweet garlic. Reservations definitely advised. Men: jacket required. You can also try Pascal to go—thanks to the dandy little take-out shop adjacent, tel. (949) 261-9041, which offers baguette sandwiches and such things as eggplant caviar, unusual salads, whole cooked chickens, and French ham and cheeses.

Another contender for favorite French restaurant is **Aubergine** on the Balboa Peninsula at 508 29th St., tel. (949) 723-4150, open Tues.-Sat. from 6 p.m. (reservations a must). Fine dining doesn't get finer than this, at a Cal-French restaurant still one of the brightest stars on the southstate's dining scene. Set in a beachside cottage, the restaurant recently reopened after a complete renovation with a stylishly understated new décor. Choice of three fixed-price menus: three course, $55; five course, $75; and the chef's nine course tasting menu for $90. And the atmosphere is unusually warm, only in part due to the neighborhood setting.

For fancy-dress California cuisine at dinner or quite special Sunday brunch, **The Pavilion** at the Four Seasons Hotel near Fashion Island at 690 Newport Center Dr. (at Santa Cruz), tel. (949) 760-4920, is hard to beat. Orange County's most popular dress-up dining spot, though, seems to be Fashion Island's **The Ritz,** 880 Newport Center Dr. (at Santa Barbara), tel. (949) 720-1800, where you can expect traditional continental fare.

EXCURSION INLAND: DISNEYLAND AND VICINITY

The Happiest Place on Earth

Anyone who has been a child or had a child since Walt Disney first opened his Magic Kingdom in 1955 already knows most everything of import about Disneyland.

In Disneyland, stories have happy endings. And every performer on the 76-acre Disney stage—from Mickey Mouse and Donald Duck to the latest batch of lovable audio-animatronic creations—smiles, waves, and then smiles some more, as a matter of company policy. They don't call this "The Happiest Place On Earth" for nothing. In Disneyland, if the hero doesn't do it single-handedly, then whiz-bang technological wizardry will save the day. In Disneyland, democracy equals capitalism. And capitalism automatically creates social justice.

In other words, Disneyland isn't real, though suburban America desperately wants to believe it is.

ROBERT HOLMES/CALIFORNIA DIVISION OF TOURISM

Check out the sight gags at Toontown, where electronics bring cartoons to almost-life.

Real or not, Disneyland is as good as it gets, if what you're looking for is a clean, well-lighted, life-sized fantasy theater showcasing Mom, Pop, apple pie, and the American flag. It's also one of the few public places in socially subdivided Southern California where families play in public. For the middle class in particular, commercial enterprises such as Disneyland, Universal Studios, and regional malls have all but taken the places of downtown plazas and neighborhood parks.

Doing Disneyland

To make a conscious journey through this cartoon version of America's collective unconscious, consider Disneyland as an oversized map of psychic symbols. This territory is divided into eight distinct "lands," each with one overall theme but multiple attractions.

And though the Walt Disney Company cancelled plans to expand Disneyland into an international mega-resort—with a Westcot theme park, 4,600 new hotel rooms, new amphitheater, and two humongous parking structures—**Disney's California Adventure,** a separate 55-acre theme park adjacent to Disneyland, has taken its place. *This* California will showcase Hollywood and the entertainment industry, the California beach scene, and outdoor California. Scheduled to open in 2001, Disney's California Adventure will also include a new hotel and other commercial features. When it does open—and the ongoing construction chaos in the neighborhood subsides—it would be fair to count this as one large new land—Californialand.

But of the lands in Disneyland proper, once "shoppe"ed out on **Main Street, U.S.A.,** from the Central Plaza wander straight ahead—through Sleeping Beauty's castle—into **Fantasyland** and then to **Mickey's Toontown,** both of these latter destinations mandatory for younger youngsters. To start exploring elsewhere, turn left to **Adventureland**—where the **Indiana Jones Adventure** still draws rave reviews and crowds—and **Frontierland/Rivers of America, Critter Country,** and **New Orleans Square.**

Turn right and you'll land in **Tomorrowland,** earning quite the visitor buzz these days. Walt Disney's original 1950s futurism had seemed terribly tired lately, considering the brave new worlds that have come along since, so Tomorrowland has had a conceptual and technical facelift. Particularly appealing is the new **Astro Orbitor,** inspired by 15th-century artist, futurist, and inventor Leonardo da Vinci. Or test drive the **Rocket Rods,** and visit **Innoventions** for a preview of futuristic technology hosted by that audianimatronic wizard Mr. Tom Morrow. Still fun is the R2D2-introduced **Star Tours,** a fantastic voyage into virtual reality with stellar special effects and more than a few interstellar surprises.

Practical Disneyland

Though hours are subject to change, in summer the park is open 9 a.m.-midnight Sunday through Friday, until 1 a.m. on Saturday night. Otherwise, Disneyland is typically open 10 a.m.-6 p.m. on weekdays and 9 a.m. to midnight on weekends.

Bring plenty of money—what you'd like to spend and then some. At last report a one-day Disneyland "unlimited passport," covering park admission plus all attractions and rides, was $41 for adults (age 10 and over), with 10-year-olds defined as adults since May 2000, and $31 for children ages 3-9. (Children under age 3 get in free.) Two- and three-day, non-transferable passports are also available. Prices typically increase at least slightly every year. Guided Disneyland tours, annual passes, and special packages are available. Members of AAA, AARP, and other organizations may also receive special discounts. (Disneyland "flex" passports, for example, recently available through participating AAA offices, covered five consecutive days—including parking—for the price of a two-day pass.) Packages and special promotions are always subject to change.

But the price of admission is only the beginning. There's parking, too, and Disneyland doesn't allow you to pack in food or beverages, so expect to spend at least $25 per person for two meals and snacks. (The food tab can go much higher.) And the total cost of Mickey Mouse ears, miscellaneous T-shirts, and other Disneyland memorabilia may floor otherwise frugal fun lovers.

And while devil-may-care types arrive in Disneyland on a whim, most people (certainly most people with small children) *plan,* and plan carefully. Considering the investment of time, money, and emotional energy a trip to Disneyland requires—and since it matters what you'll see and do, and whether you'll enjoy it—it pays to make appropriate plans, including hotel or motel reservations, well in advance. A two- or three-day stay will allow you to see and do just about everything, much less stressfully than a whiz-bang one-day whirlwind tour. But if your family can't afford the extra time or expense, do Disneyland in a day by accepting in advance that you won't accomplish everything—then set priorities.

For current information, contact **Disneyland,** 1313 Harbor Blvd., P.O. Box 3232, Anaheim, CA 92803-3232, tel. (714) 781-4565, fax (714) 781-1341, http://disney.go.com/Disneyland.

Near Disneyland

Just minutes from Disneyland in Buena Park is **Knott's Berry Farm,** the nation's first theme park. Originally famous for Cordelia Knott's fried chicken dinners and for its fresh berries—in particular Orange County's own boysenberries, a delectable cross between blackberries, raspberries, and loganberries that Walter Knott helped develop during the Depression—Knott's Berry Farm evolved into a family-run, family-friendly monument to America's pioneering spirit. It was only in 1968 that the family decided to fence the park and charge admission. Nowadays about five million people drop by each year to share the original Knott family dream. From attractions like **Ghost Town**—Walter Knott's first and original outpost of wholesome, Old West fun—and other themed areas to radical rides like **HammerHead** and the **Supreme Scream,** Knott's offers family fun for all ages. A major Southern California attraction, come October, is Knott's **Halloween Haunt,** the best adult Halloween party *anywhere,* and **Knott's Scary Farm** for the kids. Very popular, so get your tickets early.

At last report park admission was $38 adults and $28 children (ages 3-11) and seniors (age 60 and up). Or come after 4 p.m. in summer for $16.95. Knott's is open every day but Christmas—in summer 9 a.m.-midnight (until 1 a.m. Saturday night) and in winter 10 a.m.-6 p.m. Mon.-Fri., 10 a.m.-10 p.m. on Saturday, and 10 a.m.-7 p.m. Sunday, though holiday hours may differ. The entire park may close during bad weather; if in doubt, call ahead.

For more information, contact: Knott's Berry Farm, 8039 Beach Blvd., Buena Park, CA 90620, tel. (714) 220-5200 (taped information) or 220-5220 for special guest services, www.knotts.com.

Family-style amusement is a major industry in Buena Park, with various diversions strung out like Christmas lights along Beach Boulevard. One of the best is **Medieval Times,** an ersatz trip into the days of sword fights and knights in armor jousting on horseback. Show times at Medieval Times, 7662 Beach Blvd., tel. (714) 523-1100 or toll-free (800) 899-6600, www.medievaltimes.com, vary depending on the day, so call for details. Reservations and an early arrival are advisable, too, since tour groups can pack the place. Another possibility is **Wild Bill's Wild West Dinner Extravaganza,** practically next door at 7600 Beach Blvd., tel. (714) 522-4611 or, for reservations, toll-free (800) 883-1546, which offers the same family-oriented dinner and entertainment concept but with a country-western twang.

For current area information, contact: **Buena Park Convention & Visitors Office,** 6280 Manchester Blvd., Buena Park 90621, tel. (714) 562-3560 or toll-free (800) 541-3953.

EXCURSION INLAND: RICHARD NIXON LIBRARY

The Comeback Kid Comes Home

After his death in 1994, ex-President Richard Milhous Nixon finally came home—to the **Richard Nixon Library and Birthplace** in Yorba Linda. More than 40,000 people showed up to say goodbye to Orange County's most famous homeboy, including all five living U.S. presidents, heads of state, Watergate warrior G. Gordon Liddy, and immigrant Vietnamese shopkeepers from the Asia Garden Mall in nearby Westminster. For Nixon loyalists his funeral was a time of genuine grief. For his equally constant foes the day was also quite sad—because for all Nixon's brilliance in the political arena in the end he seemed a tragic figure.

The only American president ever forced by impending impeachment to resign from office, Richard M. Nixon personified the dark side of American politics yet never seemed to understand or accept any real responsibility for his fall. Those who knew him best, who were most familiar with the depths of that Nixonian darkness, have tried to understand. Some speculate that too much success, too soon, created a

Some folks raised a ruckus when Richard Nixon was honored with a postage stamp.

political persona ill-prepared to handle defeat, let alone opposition. According to former Secretary of State Henry Kissinger, Richard Nixon was "a strange mixture of calculation, deviousness, idealism, tenderness, tawdriness, courage, and daring" and a man who wanted to be remembered for his idealism. Less widely quoted is another observation from Kissinger: "Think what this man could have done if anyone had ever loved him."

Nixon's World in Nixon's Words: The Nixon Library and Birthplace

Designated a California historical landmark in January 1995, the Richard Nixon Library and Birthplace first opened on July 19, 1990. The pageantry was nothing if not patriotic, with much speechifying, red, white, and blue balloons galore, and tens of thousands of well-wishers.

The $21 million price tag was equally impressive, making this the most expensive monument yet built in honor of presidents past. Unlike other presidential museums, funded at least in part by the government and subject to some degree of federal review, Nixon's is entirely self-supporting—a fact that threatened, early on, to embroil the institution in as much controversy as the ex-president himself. Before the Nixon Library even opened its doors, critics charged that Nixon and his employees would offer only a flattering spin on his life and times.

It's true that the Nixon Library—more accurately, museum—serves primarily to glorify its namesake rather than explain, let alone criti-

cize. (With or without federal funding, the same can be said of all post-presidency memorials, however.) It's also true that the displays here are exceptionally well done, conceptually and technically. Exploring the place for yourself is well worth the side trip into Orange County's suburban hinterlands.

No matter how humbling his end, Richard Milhous Nixon's beginnings were humble indeed. He was born on January 9, 1913, in a tiny farmhouse built from a Sears Roebuck kit by his father, Frank. His mother, Hannah, named him after the English king Richard Plantagenet, "Richard the Lionhearted." (All the Nixon boys were named after English kings.)

Restored to its original simplicity at a cost of $400,000, the Nixon birthplace is definitely worth a stop after the museum tour. (On audio tape, Richard Nixon himself will guide you through.) Most of the modest furnishings are original, including the living room piano, Little Richard's violin, and the bed in which the future president was born, supplemented by a few period pieces and reproductions. The tiny kitchen comes complete with wood cooking stove, Hannah's cookbooks, and sundry everyday implements of domesticity. The attic room upstairs, shared by Richard Nixon and his three brothers, is typically off limits to visitors. But just imagine a barefoot, nine-year-old Richard Nixon scrambling upstairs to practice his accordion.

Practical Nixon Library

The Nixon Library and Birthplace is at the corner of Yorba Linda Blvd. and Eureka Avenue. For information (pre-recorded), including special exhibits and events, call (714) 993-3393; on the Internet, try www.nixonfoundation.org. Otherwise, for information write: Richard Nixon Library and Birthplace, 18001 Yorba Linda Blvd., Yorba Linda, CA 92686. (fax: 528-0544.) The museum is open Mon.-Sat. 10 a.m.-5 p.m., Sunday 11 a.m.-5 p.m. Admission is $5.95 adults, $4.95 active military, $3.95 seniors, and $2 children ages 8-11 (under 7 free). Free parking.

If you're coming by car, both Hwy. 57 (the Orange Freeway) and Hwy. 91 (the Riverside Freeway) will get you here; both are also accessible from I-5. From Newport Beach and nearby coastal areas, the best option is heading inland via Hwy. 55, which merges into Hwy. 91 (then go east.) From Hwy. 91, exit at Hwy. 90 (the Imperial Highway) and head north, exiting at Yorba Linda Blvd. and then heading west. From Hwy. 57, exit at Yorba Linda Blvd. and head east.

DOWN THE COAST: CRYSTAL COVE STATE PARK

South along the coast toward Laguna Beach is one of Orange County's genuine gems, Crystal Cove State Park, the largest remaining patch of coastal land still open to the general public. And what a patch it is—tide pools and sandy coves along more than three miles of shoreline, plus, on the other side of the highway, once-wooded El Moro Canyon in the San Joaquin Hills, a total of 2,791 acres owned until 1979 by the Irvine Company.

The beach here, open daily from 6 a.m. to sunset, is usually one of the loneliest around—a real draw when you've had enough of Orange County crowds. Offshore, to a depth of 120 feet, is one of the state's official "underwater parks," a prime scuba- and skin-diving locale. For more pedestrian aquatic explorations, study local tide tables and head for the tidepools. This low-tide adventure (don't touch) is usually better in winter, when the tides are more extreme because of the gravitational pull of both sun and moon. Access points to beach parking and facilities are at El Moro Canyon, Reef Point, Los Trancos, and Pelican Point.

Inland, some 23 miles of trails wind through the hills of El Moro Canyon, which is heaven for mountain bikers, hikers, and pikers on horseback. Climb on up, at least for the ocean views, or come along on park-sponsored interpretive walks or backcountry hikes—the latter often to places not otherwise open to the public.

Also fascinating is the *town* of **Crystal Cove,** seemingly unchanged since the 1920s and now included on the National Register of Historic Places. The 46 beachfront bungalows, originally built to house Irvine Company ranch hands, are scheduled to be made available for rent one day soon—a process delayed by the fact that current residents are (understandably) reluctant to leave their cheap oceanfront digs. Other park facilities are currently available, including fairly unobtrusive picnic areas and restrooms with showers.

The day-use fee at Crystal Cove is $6. For other park information, including if and when the cabins and campground will be available, contact: Crystal Cove State Park, 8471 Pacific Coast Hwy., Crystal Cove, tel. (949) 494-3539 or 492-0802.

LAGUNA BEACH AND VICINITY

THE ARTS, ARTISTS, AND ASSORTED OTHERS

Unlike most beach towns, laid-back Laguna Beach has tried to put a lid on the booming business of T-shirteries and other standards of the tourism trade—to little avail. It's hard to believe that this village of just under 30,000 attracts about three million tourists each year. Why do they come? Because Laguna Beach is lovely, for one thing, with a woodsy, small-town feel, white-sand beaches, and craggy coastal coves and outcroppings vaguely reminiscent of Big Sur. For another, because this artsy onetime artists colony has a quirky creative character.

Built on land never included within a land-grant rancho, since the days of early settlement Laguna Beach has gone its own way. And the town still cultivates its eccentricities. Chief among them is the odd and oddly compelling annual Pageant of the Masters presentation of *tableaux vivants,* "living pictures" allowing life to imitate art imitating life. Other oddities persist. Even in this uncharitable bottom-line age, for example, affluent Laguna Beach still tries to find room for artists, oddballs, and assorted others who don't fit the mass-produced American mold. Nonetheless, having money is almost a necessity here.

Worthy civic intentions notwithstanding, bohemians have all but been replaced by BMWs and beach resorts.

Even this latest Laguna Beach lifestyle is threatened by success. The city's population has more than doubled in the past 10 years. With the arrival of tourist season every summer, the population doubles again. On summer weekends in particular, traffic can become hopelessly snarled—in town, and up and down the highway—with parking spaces nearly as precious as local real estate. And more people are on the way. Like waves from an inland sea, new residential developments roll toward Laguna Beach from the north, south, and east.

Artistic Laguna Beach

In the 1930s Laguna Beach was hardly the typical California tourist destination. The real appeal was the possibility of escaping, from Los Angeles and vicinity in particular. Big-screen stars fleeing their own celebrity, including Charlie Chaplin and Bette Davis, and a galaxy of lesser-known artists populated little Laguna Beach. For the most part, this tiny artists' enclave was close enough to L.A. for convenience yet far enough away to avoid public curiosity and scrutiny. That trend continued over the years, even as cultural celebs became more beat, then countercultural. In the 1960s,

lovely Laguna Beach, haven for artists and other eccentrics

ANAHEIM AREA VISITOR AND CONVENTION BUREAU

for example, Timothy Leary was a common local sighting.

These days the Laguna Beach arts scene is populated in part by members of the city's large gay and lesbian community, responsible for new public housing and other support for AIDS patients. Financial pressures for local artists—those still here—are immense, however, since most are quickly being priced out of the market for both living and studio space.

THE PAGEANT OF THE MASTERS AND FESTIVAL OF THE ARTS

Especially on a first-time trip to Laguna Beach, seeing the sights should be synonymous with attending the town's simultaneous Festival of the Arts and Pageant of the Masters, held together in July and August.

The fine arts and crafts on display—all strictly local, displayed by artists and craftspeople from up and down the Orange County coast—are fine, the variety great: hand-made musical instruments, furniture, sculpture, and scrimshaw. There's even a "junior art" division.

But the pageant is unlike anything you're likely to encounter anywhere else on earth—a living, breathing tribute to the art world's old masters and ancient treasures, a carefully staged two-hour magic show that's been tickling everyone's fancy since the 1930s.

The Pageant of the Masters

The pageant's *tableaux vivants,* or living pictures, are large-scale sleight of hand or trompe d'oeil, literally, "fooling the eye." Whether the oversized artwork on display is Leonardo da Vinci's *Last Supper* (a pageant favorite), Renoir's *Grape Pickers at Lunch,* or Monet's *Women in the Garden,* on cue the costumed participants come on stage and freeze into the background frieze. Then—after the house goes dark and the stage lights come on—the entire audience gasps. Because there on stage, 50 times larger than life, is an uncanny reproduction of the real thing.

So there's really no need to traipse across the country to the Metropolitan, or cross oceans to the Louvre or Uffizi, when you can come to Laguna Beach.

It's not all high art, though. In the process of dazzling the crowds with impersonations of two- and three-dimensional reality, pageanteers also pose as sculptures, California orange-crate labels, hair combs and other jewelry, even postage stamps.

It takes endless volunteer effort—not to mention 100 gallons of makeup, 75 gallons of paint, 1000 yards of fabric, and a budget of about $800,000—to pull off this elaborate charade. Annual pageant proceeds, usually in excess of $200,000, support scholarships for high school and college students.

Pageant and Festival Practicalities

The annual arts festival and pageant take place in July and August at Irvine Bowl Park, also known as the Festival of the Arts Pageant Grounds, 650 Laguna Canyon Road. The theater is the Irvine Bowl itself, a 2500-seat theater nestled into the canyon hillside.

More than 250,000 people typically attend these events, so also plan for lodgings. If you're staying in town, walk to the festival; it's only a few blocks from Main Beach. If you're here just for the day and driving, once parked, stay parked—then, if you're also heading downtown, walk. To find a parking place, arrive very early in the day. A shuttle bus service (small fee) runs between the area's summer festivals and the parking lots along Laguna Canyon Road.

Admission to the festival itself is $5. Pageant tickets start at $10 each and are generally sold out months in advance, but if you're lucky there may be cancellations on an appropriate performance night. For current information contact: **Festival of the Arts/Pageant of the Masters,** 650 Laguna Canyon Rd., Laguna Beach, tel. (949) 497-6582 for general information, toll-free (800) 487-3378 to order tickets, or check www.pageanttickets.com.

The Sawdust Festival and Art-A-Fair

Since the 1960s the Sawdust Festival has been the "alternative" Laguna Beach arts celebration, now a major-league crafts fair held more or less concurrently across the road at 935 Laguna Canyon Rd., tel. (949) 494-3030, www.sawdustartfestival.org. These days it's an "Auld Tyme Faire," in the ever-popular Renaissance style, with mimes, strolling minstrels, and plenty of ale.

Also going on every summer: the juried Art-A-Fair festivities at 777 Laguna Canyon Rd., tel. (949) 494-4514, or check www.art-a-fair.com.

OTHER LAGUNA BEACH ARTS

More Arts Festivals
If slogging through the summer crowds seems unappealing, come some other time. Arts and crafts fairs of some sort are scheduled year-round, including the April **Art Walk Lunch** at the festival grounds (eat, then meet the artists) and the Sawdust Festival's **Winter Fantasy** from mid-November into December. During the rest of the year, crafts fairs are typically scheduled at least twice each month; call the visitors bureau at (949) 497-9229 for information.

The Laguna Art Museum
These days Laguna Beach is hardly recognizable as "SoHo by the Sea." But at the turn of the century—the last century—scores of American artists arrived here determined to paint in the open air *(en plein air)* like the French impressionists and Hudson River School. The legacy of artists of The Plein Air School, including Joseph Kleitsch, William Griffith, and Frank Cuprien, has been lasting. Which explains the fact that, while other high school football teams identify themselves as "cougars" or "chargers," for example, the big bruisers here are known as the Laguna Beach High Artists—surely enough to strike fear into the heart of any opponent.

The hot pink Laguna Art Museum, 307 Cliff Dr. (at Coast Hwy.), tel. (949) 494-6531, www.lagunaartmuseum.org, has earned renown as the only Southern California art museum to focus exclusively on American art—contemporary California art in particular, along with avant-garde special shows. After a short-lived merger with the Orange County Museum of Art, the Laguna Art Museum is once again a local institution. At last report the museum was open Tues.-Sun. 11 a.m.-5 p.m., and until 9 p.m. the first Thursday of the month (with free admission). Regular admission: $5 adults, $4 students, $3 children.

The Laguna Playhouse
Another local pleasure is the Laguna Playhouse, featuring a fine local repertory program. The playhouse, 606 Laguna Canyon Rd., tel. (949) 497-ARTS, www.lagunaplayhouse.com, often presents original work by local playwrights, sometimes as community fundraisers.

The Ballet Pacifica
Ballet Pacifica's office burned down in the 1993 Laguna Beach fire, thus the official relocation to Irvine. As far as locals are concerned, though, it's still a Laguna Beach phenomenon. The children's concert series is still staged here, at the Festival Forum Theater, 650 Laguna Canyon Rd., in September or October and in February, March, and April. Ballet Pacifica's Christmas *Nutcracker* and three other performances (October, March, and May) are staged at Irvine's Barclay Theater. For current information, call (949) 851-9930.

THE ART OF SHOPPING

Laguna Beach Galleries
Shopping is a serious local pastime, a primary local attraction. Laguna Beach is chock-full of shops, where you'll find the tackiest of tourist bric-a-brac and fine art and jewelry. Laguna Beach boasts 60-70 art galleries. Unlike special exhibits and collection displays at the local art museum, however, much of the gallery fare is far from cutting edge, in California or elsewhere. To be sure you're buying local art—to support the health and welfare of artists still managing to survive in high-rent Orange County—attend local arts and craft fairs, mentioned above. And when in doubt, don't hesitate to ask. Otherwise, to find out what's what and where it might be, pick up the current *Local Arts* guide, available in most shops.

For an introduction to Laguna Beach's Plein Air School, stop by **Redfern Gallery,** 1540 S. Coast Hwy., tel. (949) 497-3356. That's the specialty. **The Vladimir Solokov Studio Gallery** in the same complex, tel. (714) 494-3633, is a working studio specializing in bright-colored abstract and mixed media paintings. Nearby, at 1390 S. Coast, is the **Esther Wells Collection,** tel. (949) 494-2497, noted for its impressionistic watercolors (always some local art on display) as well as sculpture and jewelry.

To appreciate just how much disposable income some people have, stop by the **Sherwood**

Gallery, 460 S. Coast Hwy., tel. (949) 497-2668, with its contemporary and pop art, sculpture (some kinetic), jewelry, and unusual furnishings. The colorful "Seven Stack Suitcase Dresser" spotted on one stroll, for example, cost a mere $5,400, the "Law & Order Chess Set," $3,200.

Other Shops

Thee Foxes' Trot, 264 Forest Ave., tel. (949) 494-4997, is a good stop for bath and home-wares and a limited selection of unusual wom-en's clothing. Also good for gifts and homewares is **Areo,** 207 Ocean Ave., tel. (949) 376-0535, where some of the vases, candles, candlesticks, and jewelry are locally made (ask).

Kyber Pass, 1970 S. Coast Hwy., tel. (949) 494-5021, specializes in jewelry, clothing, and art from Afghanistan. In the this-is-kitschy category, trail's end might be **Trails West Galleries,** 1476 S. Pacific Coast Hwy., tel. (949) 494-7888, where you can find Western art (paintings and sculp-ture) and such things as cowhide-covered pi-anos. Try **Tippecanoes,** 648 S. Coast Hwy., tel. (949) 494-1200, for antique oddities and vin-tage clothing.

In the next block is **Laguna Village,** 577 S. Coast Hwy., with various arts and crafts booths—a good bet for finding local work—plus the **La-guna Village Cafe,** tel. (949) 494-6344, a good bet for a beer-and-breakers break, out on the patio overlooking the ocean. To get up to speed on local writers, almost as numerous in this town as painters and potters, stop by **Upchurch-**

Brown Booksellers, (949) 497-8373, in the Lumberyard Village.

OUTDOOR LAGUNA BEACH: BEACHES AND PARKS

Main Beach and Vicinity

Main Beach is, well, the city's main beach, dom-inating the ocean side of downtown between the Laguna Art Museum and Hotel Laguna near Park Avenue. You'll know you've arrived when you spot the imposing glassed-in lifeguard tower, something of a local landmark. Most of the year you also can't miss the pick-up basketball play-ers, almost as competitive as the volleyballers. A wooden boardwalk snakes along the beach, with its youngsters, oldsters, and rollerbladers. At this intriguing if tamer version of Muscle Beach in Venice, everybody and everything hangs out.

South of Main Beach, overseen by high-priced real estate, are Laguna's "street beaches." Sec-tions of this slim one-mile strand of sand are known by the names of intersecting streets, from **Sleepy Hollow Lane** and **Thalia** to **Oak** and **Brooks.** Farther south still is half-mile **Arch Cove,** popular for sunbathing, its section again named after relevant streets (Bluebird Canyon, Agate, Pearl, etc.).

Since the coast (actually, the beach) is clear between Laguna Beach and South Laguna, you might find a completely private cove if you're willing to walk, surf-dodge, and rock-hop the

*at the beach
in Laguna Beach*

distance—not advisable at high tide. For more on what you'll find if you're crazy enough to try it, see South Laguna Beaches and Aliso Pier, below.

Greeters Corner

While wandering toward Main Beach, take note of Greeters Corner in **Main Beach Park** at the end of Forest Avenue. The statue in front of the **Greeters Corner Restaurant**, 329 S. Coast Hwy., tel. (949) 494-0361, commemorates the town's long tradition of greeters—and, in particular, Eiler Larsen. A Danish immigrant and World War I veteran, Larsen arrived in Laguna Beach in the 1930s to serve as "the Laguna greeter," a title (and unpaid job) he held for 30 years. An organized attempt to silence Larsen failed in 1959, once a local survey established that almost 90 percent of the citizenry wanted him to stay—and to continue waving and bellowing at passing cars.

Someone has served in the role of local greeter since the late 19th century, when Laguna Beach was known as Lagona—a variation of "Lagonas," a coastal territory named in the 1500s by local native peoples. In the 1880s, for example, Portuguese fisherman Joe Lucas would holler at passing stagecoaches. At last report, the town's greeting duties fall to a fellow by the name of Number One Archer.

More Laguna Beach Beaches

North of Main Beach, atop the bluffs along Cliff Dr., is the **Heisler Park** promenade, a fine place for lolling on the lawn, picnicking, and people-watching (public restrooms are here, too). Down below are two rocky coves with nice tidepools, **Picnic Beach** at the end of Myrtle St. and **Rockpile Beach** at the end of Jasmine.

Nearby are three inlets that manage to combine the best of the beach scene with the best of beach scenery: **Shaw's Cove, Fisherman's Cove,** and **Diver's Cove.** Needless to say, the area is beloved by locals and often crowded. The path down to Shaw's Cove is on Cliff Dr. at the end of Fairview; entrances to Fisherman's and Diver's coves are close together on Cliff, in the 600 block.

Half-moon **Crescent Bay Beach** (entrance at Cliff and Circle Dr.) is quite enticing, and usually offers some privacy for sunning, swimming, and skindiving. To reach **Crescent Bay Point Park** (great views) from Cliff Dr., turn left onto the highway and left again onto Crescent Bay Drive.

Special Beaches and a "Bark Park"

Popular for bodysurfing yet quite private by Laguna Beach standards, **Victoria Beach** is a local favorite. To get here, take Victoria Drive from the highway and then turn right onto Dumond. Tiny fan-shaped **Moss Beach** at the end of Moss St. is one of the best around, well-protected for swimming, also popular for scuba diving. The three rocky fingers of **Wood's Cove** have helped create the pocket beaches here, plus providing a pounding-surf sideshow, great swimming, good scuba diving. (To get here, take the steps down from the intersection of Ocean Way and Diamond Street.) None of these beaches have public restrooms—the price of privacy—but at last report lifeguards were on duty, at least in summer.

If you bring Fido or Fifi along on this trip, you'll soon discover that dogs are not welcome at the beach (not to mention most other places). Laguna Beach offers some consolation, though. The city's Dog Park out on Laguna Canyon Road, known by locals as the Bark Park, is one of very few public areas in Orange County where people can legally let their dogs run free. (Free in this case means "loose"; it actually costs $2 to use this well-fenced pooch park.) And if you're sans beast but bored, come out to the Bark Park anyway. Watching dogs and their people at play is cheap entertainment. Laguna Beach's Bark Park is sponsored by RUFF, "Rescuing Unwanted Furry Friends."

South Laguna Beaches and Aliso Pier

Several miles south of Laguna Beach proper is the area aptly known as South Laguna. The main attraction here is **Aliso Creek Beach Park** at the mouth of Aliso Creek. In the late 1800s Helena Modjeska—the Shakespearean actress for whom Orange County's Modjeska Canyon was named—camped out with her entourage here in the coastal wilderness to beat the summer heat. Though houses are now the dominant feature of the surrounding landscape, the first thing you'll really notice is the Aliso Pier, which looks like a gargantuan arrow about to be shot out to sea. But take time to explore the small sandy coves here and the rocky tidepools beyond. For relative privacy, head south; to commune with the college-age crowd, head north.

Short, diamond-headed Aliso Pier is one of California's newest, constructed in 1972. It's also one of the state's most striking, awarded "outstanding design" status by the American Institute of Interior Designers. Only 620 feet long, the pier platform is concrete, perched atop pairs of hexagonal concrete pilings, with a upward-rising angle to help deflect the destructive force of the wild wave action that comes with heavy storms. Even the banisters are unusual (if not exactly politically correct), made of the very hard, scratch-resistant tropical wood *apatung*. And the platform's diamond shape requires extra banister—by design, to allow more elbow room for fisherfolk. At the foot of the pier is a hexagonal concession building, last stop for tackle, snacks, and a trip to the restroom.

STAYING IN LAGUNA BEACH

"Inexpensive" and "expensive" are relative terms, but it's safe to say that nothing in Laguna Beach is truly inexpensive. Here, and down the coast at the Ritz-Carlton, expensive really is expensive. If a low-rent stay is a must, hang your hat in

EXCURSION INLAND: MADAME MODJESKA *IN AMERICA*

Susan Sontag's recent novel *In America* was inspired by Orange County's own Helena Modjeska, the noted 19th-century actress who renounced her European stage career and emigrated from Poland to the United States to start a utopian farming venture with her husband. In its fictionalized facts, the book parallels Modjeska's story. A star of the Warsaw stage married to the aristocratic Count Bozenta—in revolt against his family and dreaming of his own agricultural Eden—in 1876 Modjeska and her husband arrived in California with an accomplished entourage that included Henryk Sienkiewicz, who later won the Nobel Prize for literature.

In the book, as in real life, they all settled down in what was then the Wild West of Orange County—European overlords determined to wring both civilization and crops out of the wily Mexican-American wilderness.

And in the book, as in the course of actual events, none of the privileged Poles knew beans about farming. As Modjeska would later recall in her autobiography: "The most alarming feature of this bucolic fancy was the rapid disappearance of cash and the absence of even a shadow of income."

So Helena Modjeska resumed her career—and soon became one of the most accomplished actresses on the American stage during the golden age of theater.

"It felt like, an escapade; like leaving home; like telling lies—and she would tell many lies," reflects Sontag's protagonist as she arrives in San Francisco. "She was beginning again; she was rejoining her destiny, which conferred on her the rich sensation that she had never gone astray."

As Modjeska's star ascended in America, she crisscrossed the country in her own private railroad

car and eventually played opposite Edwin Booth and Maurice Barrymore, the greatest actors of the day. She became Camille, and Ophelia. She was Nora in the premiere of Ibsen's *A Doll's House.* Yet her most famous role was Rosalind in Shakespeare's *As You Like It.*

Equally adept at besting the twists and turns of fate, in the 1880s the now wealthy Madame Modjeska and Count Bozenta returned to Orange County to build a more theatrical version of their earlier dream. The grand rambling home they built here, complete with a small stage extending out into the garden, was called Arden, as Modjeska later wrote, "because, like the Forest of Arden in *As You Like it,* everything that Shakespeare speaks of was on the spot—oak trees, running brooks, palms, snakes, even lions." She and the count lived here for 18 happy years, from 1888 to 1906.

Mountain lions still roam the Santa Ana Mountains, though they are not so common these days. And Modjeska's home still stands in a live oak grove on the banks of Santiago Creek, its original Forest of Arden—English yews, palms, white lilac, and crown of thorns—still thriving. Now a National Historic Landmark known as **Modjeska House Historical Park,** 25151 Serrano Rd. in Modjeska Canyon, about 10 miles east of Lake Forest via Santiago Canyon Rd., the estate is owned by the county of Orange. The home and gardens are open to the public only for docent-guided tours—the canyon road is narrow, the area residential, and gawkers are discouraged—which at last report were offered by advance reservation only at 10 a.m. on the second and fourth Saturday of the month. Tour fee is $5. For more information and reservations, call (949) 855-2028.

Huntington Beach, or, if heading south, try camping or a cheap motel in Dana Point or the hostel in San Clemente.

Most Laguna Beach lodging rates go up for "the season" either in mid-June or on July 1—just in time for the local arts festivals—and then dive again in mid-September. If you're willing to miss the summer arts pageantry and attendant crowds, come in early June (it can be foggy) or just about any other time. For better value, look for establishments "close to" (not on) the beach and "near" (not in) town, and request a room at the lower end of the options range.

Less Expensive Laguna Options

Both Best Westerns offer good value even in summer, better value in the off-season. To make toll-free telephone reservations at any Best Western, call (800) 780-7234 (U.S. and Canada). Closest to town is the **Best Western Laguna Brisas Spa Hotel,** 1600 S. Coast Hwy., tel. toll-free (800) 624-4442 or (949) 497-7272, www.bestwestern.com, "just 58 steps from the beach." Half the rooms have an ocean view. All rooms include huge in-room whirlpools, cable TV, free movies, and refrigerators (the latter upon request). Continental breakfast is served. You'll find a coin laundry on the premises, along with heated pool, spa, and sundeck. Premium-Luxury, with rates $149 and up from June into early September, $129 and up otherwise, kids under 12 stay free (in your room). Senior and AAA discounts available. The attractive **Best Western Laguna Reef Inn** south of town at 30806 S. Coast Hwy., tel. (949) 499-2227, is Expensive—a straight $99 in the summer for one person ($10 for each extra person, kids 10 and under free), otherwise $69 and up in the off season. Some units have kitchens, $15 extra. Continental breakfast.

In the motel category, you also can't go too far wrong at the 22-room **Best Inn,** 1404 N. Coast Hwy., tel. toll-free (800) 221-2222 for reservations, otherwise (949) 494-6464, Expensive (basic rates $99 and up from mid-June through mid-September, otherwise $79 and up). And check www.bestinn.com for special discounts for seniors, government and the military.

More Expensive, More Ambience

There's something quite comforting about the predictability of motels, but other styles of accommodation offer more *romance.* Or something.

Two moderately expensive hotels offer both beachtown ambience and convenient central location. The former Hotel San Maarten is now the **Holiday Inn Laguna Beach** across from the beach at 696 S. Coast Hwy., tel. toll-free tel. (800) 228-5691 or (949) 494-1001, www.holiday-inn.com. Breezy French Caribbean style enlivens the lobby—note the handpainted ceiling, verdant nature scenes of birds, plants, and flowers—and the tropical courtyard, with its patio and pool. Rooms don't necessarily court the same flash but are reliably "Holiday Inn." Premium-Luxury. Regular rooms run $129-159 on weekdays in summer and $179-199 on weekends; rates are $109-139 at other times, continental breakfast included. Suites with kitchenettes and microwaves (some have in-room spas) are available. Also here, a restaurant and bar, plus free parking.

The local grande dame—and the only place around with a private beach—is the recently redone landmark **Hotel Laguna,** practically on Main Beach at 425 S. Coast Hwy., tel. toll-free (800) 524-2927 (in California only) or (949) 494-1151, www.hotellaguna.com. Most rooms are modern, with ceiling fans and the basics, and some afford ocean views. Since the Hotel Laguna was Humphrey Bogart's favorite Laguna Beach hideaway, two suites—the **Bogart Suite** and **Bacall Suite**—get special treatment, complete with canopy beds. Premium-Luxury. Room rates run $110-250 in summer, $85-225 and up at other times, with free valet parking. On-site you'll find a spectacularly good seafood restaurant, **Claes Seafood, Etc.,** and **Le Bar,** for an ocean view with your cocktails.

Laguna Beach Bed and Breakfast Inns

Local bed and breakfast establishments also offer non-motel ambience. The **Carriage House Inn,** 1322 Catalina St., tel. (949) 494-8945, www.carriagehouse.com, is the historic colonial home once owned by film czar Cecil B. DeMille. In a residential neighborhood and all done up New Orleans style, the two-story Carriage House features a lushly landscaped brick courtyard and six one- and two-bedroom guest suites. All include a living room and private bathroom; all but one feature kitchens and refrigerators; some have in-room coffeemakers. Premium-Luxury. Basic rates year-round are $125-165 ($20 per additional person for the two-bedroom suites), weekly rates available. To get here: About one mile south of Laguna Beach turn east onto Cress Street, go two blocks to Catalina, then turn left.

A long-running local favorite is the Mediterranean-style **Casa Laguna Inn** bed and breakfast at 2510 S. Coast Hwy., tel. toll-free (800) 233-0449 or (949) 494-2996, www.casalaguna.com, an updated ode to 1930s' California. Paths wander past the bell tower and courtyard and throughout the terraced gardens, connecting rooms and suites. Also here are a one-bedroom cottage with private ocean view, fireplace, and full kitchen, and the two-bedroom Mission House. Rooms are small, suites are spacious; some have views; and all are tastefully furnished with antiques and overhead fans. The pool has a view. Head to the library in the morning for continental breakfast; tea is served in the afternoon, wine and hors d'oeuvres in the evening. In July and August there's a two-night minimum on weekends. Premium-Luxury. Peak weekend rates are $135-250, weekday rates $105-225. During the rest of the year, when rates run $105 and up (higher, again, on weekends), modest rooms here can be a best bet for budget romance.

Family-Friendly Aliso Creek Inn

A nice set-up for families or traveling homebodies—and a good deal for just about anybody in the off-season—is the lovely **Aliso Creek Inn** in South Laguna at 31106 S. Coast Hwy., tel. toll-free (800) 223-3309 or (949) 499-2271, www.alisocreek.com. Just a few hundred yards from the beach yet nestled into a steep-walled canyon, this relaxed 80-acre condo-style motel and resort complex offers a good selection of housekeeping units, from studios to one- and two-bedroom suites, all with kitchens, patios, sitting areas, color TV, free movies. Amenities include a pool, whirlpool, even a wading pool for the kids, not to mention the nine-hole golf course, restaurant, and bar. For those predictable practical family emergencies, there's a coin laundry. Free bonus: Aliso Creek itself, which meanders through the resort grounds on its way to the ocean. Luxury. From July 1 through Labor Day rates run $155-328. Otherwise, expect to pay $112-297. Meeting rooms are available.

High-End Hotels

If money is absolutely no object, consider heading south a short distance to Dana Point and the **Ritz-Carlton Laguna Niguel,** the south-state's most luxurious hotel resort. For information, see Dana Point and Vicinity, below.

Otherwise, if you plan to park yourself at the beach and don't care what it costs, *the* place in Laguna Beach is the light and airy **Surf & Sand Hotel** right on the beach south of town at 1555 S. Coast Hwy. (at Bluebird Canyon Dr.), tel. toll-free (800) 524-8621 for reservations or (949) 497-4477, www.jcresorts.com. Rooms in the nine-story tower have the most breathtaking views, of course, but you won't go wrong elsewhere here, since most rooms are within 30 feet of the beach and include a private balcony looking out over the surf, surfers, and heated pool. Decor is tastefully understated in a day-at-the-beach palette, with sand-colored walls and raw-silk upholstery, shuttered windows and naked wood. The fun indoor-outdoor **Splashes** restaurant sits right on the beach. The art deco lounge is a choice spot for cocktails at sunset. Luxury. Rates run $310-425 from Memorial Day through October, with a two-night minimum stay in July and on June and September weekends, and a three-day minimum in August. In other seasons prices start at $260, but if business is off you may be able to do better. Ask about specials and packages.

High-end hotels in Laguna Beach also include the fairly new, well-located, yet reasonably secluded **Inn at Laguna Beach** near Main Beach at 211 N. Coast Hwy., tel. toll-free (800) 544-4479 for reservations or (714) 497-9722, fax (714) 497-9972. Most rooms are fairly small but attractive, with abundant amenities. Many have a view, too, not to mention color TV/cable and VCRs. In-room continental breakfast is provided. Luxury. High-season rates, from July 1 through Labor Day, run $249-459. The Inn at Laguna Beach is an especially sweet deal in the off-season, when prices are $129 and up.

EATING IN LAGUNA BEACH

Beach Town Breakfast

Locals' choice for artsy minimalist breakfast is the very cool **Cafe Zinc,** 350 Ocean Ave. (at Forest), tel. (949) 494-6302, though on weekends be prepared to wait at the counter and to fight for a table. The morning repast here is as simple as a huge hot cappuccino with a muffin. The frittatas are also good, not to mention the huevos rancheros with papaya salsa. If you come late, order a salad and some homemade soup—very good here—and do lunch. No credit cards. Next door is the equally cool **Cafe Zinc Market,** where you can load up on bread and baked goods, salads, cookbooks, even sundry kitchen items.

The **Beach House Inn,** centrally situated between Main Beach and PCH behind Vacation Village at 619 Sleepy Hollow Ln., tel. (949) 494-9707, is a Laguna Beach institution. This is the onetime home of Slim Summerstone, one of the original Keystone Cops. The ambience here is quite casual, and every table offers an ocean view—definitely a fine start for any day. The Beach House is best known for its lobster, steamed clams, and fresh fish specials, yet the all-American breakfast is also a best-bet. Beloved locally for breakfast, especially al fresco, is **The Cottage,** 308 N. Coast Hwy., tel. (949) 494-3023. Another possibility is the **Laguna Village Cafe,** 577 S. Coast Hwy., tel. (949) 494-6344.

For a special see-and-be-seen Sunday brunch right on the beach, head to **Splashes** outside at the Surf & Sand Hotel, 1555 S. Coast Hwy. (at Bluebird Canyon Dr.), tel. (949) 497-4477. If it's foggy or cool, the food's just as good when served indoors.

Laguna Lunch

Many of the more upscale eateries around town also serve lunch, often a variation of the dinner menu but with smaller servings at lower prices. See the "Dining Adventure" listings below for possibilities.

Tops in the *very casual* cheap-eats fast-food category is **Taco Loco,** 640 S. Coast Hwy. (PCH between Cleo and Legion), tel. (949) 497-1635, where the ambience is asphalt-meets-the-sea-breeze and surfers scarf down fish tacos—such things as fresh lobster or mahi-mahi on blue corn tortillas—as quickly as possible. Vegetarians, don't despair. Taco Loco also serves a killer tofu burger.

For imaginative pizza, *the* place is **Z Pizza,** the original well south near Aliso Creek, 30902 S. Coast Hwy., tel. (949) 499-4949. Of course there's

a **Ruby's** here (S. Coast Hwy. at Nyes), tel. (949) 497-7829, the nostalgic diner-style choice for burgers, shakes, fries, and all those other things we all know we shouldn't eat. Ditto for **Johnny Rockets,** at 190 S. Coast Hwy., tel. (949) 497-7252.

Late in the afternoon or before dinner, stop for a drink at **Las Brisas,** 361 Cliff Dr. (N. Coast Hwy.), tel. (949) 497-5434, a place still known among old-timers as the Victor Hugo Inn. The main reason to dawdle here, though, is to drink in the views—while considering the possibility that Orange County promoters haven't overhyped the "Riviera" angle after all.

Dining Adventures, Not Too Pricey

For intimate noshing, **Ti Amo,** 31727 S. Coast Hwy., tel. (949) 499-5350, is the perfect spot perched on a bluff overlooking the sea. The place has been lavishly decorated with sponge-painted walls and rich drapes. Entrees include paella, homemade pasta, and wonderful seafood. Or, create an appetizing light meal from several selections on the appetizer menu. Reservations wise at dinner.

If you're craving pasta at dinner, try the two-story **Sorrento Grille,** 370 Glenneyre St. (near Mermaid), tel. (949) 494-8686, an American bistro and "martini bar," though some people prefer the artier, quieter **Ristorante Rumari** (dinner only) on the highway between Center and Pearl, tel. (949) 494-0400, specializing in Northern Italian and Sicilian dishes, particularly fish.

At 998 S. Coast Hwy. (just south of Thalia) **Natraj,** tel. (949) 497-9197, is the best bet for authentic Indian food—for many miles in any direction.

More Fine Dining Adventures

Five Feet refers to Laguna Beach's elevation. But this local hotspot at 328 Glenneyre, on the corner of Forest and Glenneyre, tel. (949) 497-4955, is actually more famous for fine nouvelle Chinese served up with pop art and pink neon. A must for first-timers: the catfish. It's open for dinner nightly, for lunch on Fridays only.

Tops in local hotel dining is **Claes Seafood, Etc.** at the Hotel Laguna, 425 S. Coast Hwy., tel. (949) 494-1151. The seafood, of course, is particularly spectacular. (It's also open daily for breakfast and lunch.) Or, drive south to Dana Point and **The Dining Room,** tel. (949) 240-

2000, at the Ritz-Carlton Laguna Niguel for spectacular food in an equally stunning setting (semiformal attire). The Ritz-Carlton also offers more casual fare at breakfast, lunch, and dinner in its **Terrace** restaurant, tel. (949) 240-5008—out on the terrace overlooking the ocean—and **Club Bar and Grill.** For more information, see Dana Point and Vicinity, below.

ENTERTAINING LAGUNA BEACH

To do the movies, there's an **Edwards Cinema,** 162 S. Coast Hwy., tel. (949) 497-1711. For live rock 'n' roll, or reggae—sometimes star-quality—try the comfortably seedy **Sandpiper,** 1183 S. Coast Hwy., tel. (949) 494-4694 (cover charge), a place downhome enough to also offer pinball wizardry and dart boards. At last report Monday night was reggae night at the **White House,** 340 S. Coast Hwy., tel. (949) 494-8088.

After-hours coffee haunts—such as the **Renaissance Cafe,** 234 Forest, tel. (949) 497-5282, and the **Diedrich's** nearby, tel. (949) 497-7660, in the onetime Marriner's bookstore—are otherwise the main attractions, along with local bars. For beer lovers, best bets include the lively **Laguna Beach Brewing Company,** 422 S. Coast Hwy., tel. (949) 499-2337, serving 10 different handmade brews along with decent salads and pub fare, and the more stylish **Ocean Avenue Brewery,** 237 Ocean, tel. (949) 497-3381, noted for its lagers and porters. The prettiest place in town for pounding a few with a view, though, is the **Towers Lounge** atop the Surf & Sand Hotel at 1555 S. Coast, tel. (949) 497-4477.

Gay clubs are prominent in Laguna Beach, particularly the **Boom Boom Room** and, upstairs, **Hunky's Video Bar and Grill** at the Coast Inn, 1401 S. Coast Hwy., tel. (949) 494-7588, altogether quite lively, with dance floor and two bars. Considerably more sedate is **Main Street,** a piano bar at 1460 S. Coast Hwy., tel. (949) 494-0056.

LAGUNA BEACH INFORMATION AND TRAVEL TIPS

Trip Planning and Information

Famous Laguna Beach arts festivals make the sun-loving summer beach scene that much more congested. Anyone phobic about personal space (and parking space) might consider coming for the arts festivals as a daytrip—staying elsewhere—and returning at some other time for more thorough exploration.

For more information about local attractions, contact the **Laguna Beach Visitor Bureau and Chamber of Commerce,** 252 Broadway, Laguna Beach, toll-free tel. (800) 877-1115 (prerecorded) or tel. (949) 497-9229, www.lagunabeachinfo.org.

Traffic Safety, Getting Oriented, Parking

If you plan to come or go from the east via Laguna Canyon Rd. (Hwy. 133), which connects Laguna Beach to the 405 inland—*be extra cautious.* This narrow two-lane highway has become Orange County's blood alley, its high accident rate attributed to too many people in too much of a hurry. The same caution holds for the alternative route inland, Laguna Canyon Rd. to El Toro Rd. to I-5. Aside from the coast highway, there are no other routes into Laguna Beach.

Once here, you'll need to orient yourself to Pacific Coast Highway. Laguna Beach highway addresses north of Broadway are designated "North Coast Highway"; those south of town to Crown Valley Parkway, "South Coast Highway."

Unless your vehicle is safely stored at a local motel or hotel, parking is a challenge. Metered parking (bring *lots* of quarters) is available on many streets. There are also various lots (try Ocean) where all-day parking runs around $8-10. If you're coming just for the Pageant of the Masters and associated arts festivals, *come early,* park in the large lots along Laguna Canyon Rd., and shuttle back and forth to town. Arrive by 10 a.m. and there should be no problem.

DANA POINT AND VICINITY

BEFORE THE MAST, BEFORE THE HOBIE CAT

Given the modern-day dominance of subdivisions, shopping malls, and rush-hour traffic, one might forget that, before the United States claimed the territory, pioneers from Spain and the new nation of Mexico made their homes in a much quieter California. For a glimpse into that brave old world, pick up a copy of *Two Years Before the Mast,* published in 1840 by Richard Henry Dana, Jr. On leave from his studies at Harvard University to recover from measles-related afflictions, Dana put to sea onboard the *Pilgrim,* a small square-rigged Boston brig that delivered East Coast fineries to California in exchange for tanned cowhides carted over from the mission at San Juan Capistrano and other ports. San Juan Cove—now Dana Cove, which includes Dana Point Harbor, all within Capistrano Bay—was the only safe anchorage between San Diego and Santa Barbara. When Dana returned to Boston and an eventual career as a noted maritime attorney, he recalled the cove, with its rocky harbor and striking 200-foot cliffs, as "the only romantic spot in California."

And perhaps it was. "There was grandeur in everything around," Dana said. In those days the ocean surf swept all the way in to dramatic, sculptured cliffs. Huge prehistoric vultures—California condors, carrion eaters now all but extinct, bred in zoos—launched themselves from these cliffs; birds of prey, ravens and herons, perched here as well. And long before swallows discovered the Capistrano mission, they nested in cliff crevices here.

More recently Dana Point has celebrated the grandeur of local surf, surfing, and surf-related innovations. Several times each year, when storms drove classic long-angled 30-foot waves around Dana Point from the west, hard-core surfers from far and wide assembled here to brave the "Killer Dana." Just like the local cattlehide trade, Killer Danas are history; harbor construction altered the offshore terrain. But to pay homage to those days of yore, stop by **Hobie Sports** in Lantern Bay Village, 24825 Del Prado, tel. (949) 496-2366, where rare and historic surfboards from the collection of Hobie Alter—local inventor of the foam-core surfboard and the Hobie Cat catamaran—are on display.

For more complete information about the area, contact: **Dana Point Chamber of Commerce,** 24681 La Plaza, Suite 120, Dana Point, tel. (949) 496-1555, www.danapoint-chamber.com.

SEEING AND DOING DANA POINT

A city only since 1989, Dana Point today combines boat harbor, beaches, and Boston saltbox condominium developments. This stylistic twist testifies to popular identification with Richard Henry Dana's East Coast origins yet is odd, given the area's more enduring Spanish and Mexican roots. To sample original local architectural styles, explore older streets, including Chula Vista, Ruby Lantern, Blue Lantern, El Camino Capistrano, and Santa Clara.

A Note on "Lantern" Streets

This peculiar local street-name phenomenon is not a recent affectation. In the 1920s Dana Point's "downtown" was defined by the Spanish-style plaza, and by streets intersecting Pacific Coast Highway—then known as the Roosevelt Coast Highway—and which were named for the rainbow collection of ship's lanterns that marked them, the latter inspiration attributed to Anna Walters Walker, Dana Point's first developer. Most of the original copper street lanterns are long gone, but about 15 of the originals light the newly spiffed-up plaza park.

Dana Point Harbor

The cultural focal point for Dana Point is Dana Point Harbor, tel. (949) 496-6177, where breakwater construction began in 1966. Here, about 2500 yachts bob and sway with the tides. The harbor also features a man-made island park—reached via Island Way—an inner breakwater created during the harbor's unusual cofferdam construction.

Though home port is now in Long Beach, Dana Point Harbor is a regular port for the Nautical Heritage Society's speedy topsail schooner **Californian,** the state's official tall ship. The *Californian* is a re-creation of the first U.S. cutter to patrol the Pacific coast during the bad and bawdy gold rush, the 1848 **C.W. Lawrence** (in service to the U.S. Revenue Service, precursor of the U.S. Coast Guard). Since America's revenuers now typically enlist computers instead of ships to track down scofflaws, the *Californian* is free to serve as an international goodwill ambassador—circling the Pacific Rim each year, visiting Canada, Mexico, and closer ports, as well as occasionally (such as during the 1984 Olympics) leading the Tall Ships Festival parade and embarking on other international adventures. Appropriately enough, Queen Calafia, the imagined matriarchal monarch of the island paradise of California, is enthroned as the ship's figurehead. When moored here—see the website for current information—the *Californian* offers

Dana Point: under the mast

day sails to the public and participates in other educational programs. The Nautical Heritage Society also owns the 1913 Q-Class racing sloop **Virginia,** the only yacht on the West Coast included on the National Historic Register, available for private sailing lessons. For more information, contact the **Nautical Heritage Society,** 1064 Calle Negocio, Unit B, San Clemente, CA 92673, tel. (949) 369-6773 or toll-free (800) 432-2201, http://californian.org.

Adjacent to the *Californian* is the **Orange County Marine Institute,** tel. (949) 496-2274, noted for its educational and other programs, including nighttime "bioluminescence cruises."

Other harbor diversions include kayaking, canoeing, parasailing, fishing, sportfishing, whale-watching (in winter), and tidepooling. **Dana Wharf Sportfishing** on the harbor's eastern edge, tel. (949) 496-5794, handles sportfishing trips, whalewatching and other scenic excursions, and parasailing.

Surfin' USA: Doheny State Beach

Just east of the harbor is Doheny State Beach, donated to the state in the 1930s by L.A. oil man Edward Lawrence Doheny in honor of his son, Ned. The local surf made a bigger cultural splash, though, especially when Doheny made it into the lyrics of the Beach Boys' classic "Surfin' USA."

Head to the broad white-sand beach for the usual fun. The rocky area at the harbor end draws divers and anglers. At night beach bonfires are quite popular, if not nearly as wild as they once were (alcohol consumption has been banned). With the exception of surfing, nothing is as popular here as the grunion run, typically good. (See Grunion Run Free, So Why Can't We? earlier in this chapter.) Doheny also features acres of lawn, a cool change when the sand really cooks. Worth a special stop is the **marine life museum** inside the visitor center, with its 3000-gallon native fish aquarium and tidepool "touch tank."

Bike riding is actually quite feasible in and beyond Dana Point. The **San Juan Creek Bike Trail** starts just north of the beach; dart under PCH and take the trail all the way into San Juan Capistrano. Alternatively, take the Doheny bike path south along the sand to Capistrano Beach Park and, at Beach Road, merge into the PCH bike lanes. You can ride south into San Clemente, or north as far as Laguna Beach.

Developed campsites (hot showers, picnic tables, fire rings, plus RV necessities) are tucked into the landscape; some are more sheltered than others. Day-use facilities lie to the west of San Juan Creek. The entrance to Doheny State Beach is just off PCH at 25300 Dana Point Harbor Drive; follow the signs. Day use is $5, full-facility camping $17-23. Group camps are available. For more information, call (949) 496-6171. To reserve campsites through ReserveAmerica, call (800) 444-7275.

Salt Creek Beach and Park

Almost an adjunct to the Ritz-Carlton Laguna Niguel resort, Salt Creek Beach north of Dana Point proper has long been noted for its good surfing. Two of the best "breaks" around, not often personally appreciated by Ritz-Carlton guests, include "The Point" just below the hotel and "The Beach" to the north. On windy days you'll see hang gliders surf the thermals. And on a clear day you'll see Catalina Island.

Though Salt Creek Beach technically stretches both north and south of the Ritz-Carlton, the southern strand is also referred to as **Laguna Niguel Beach.** (Land use politics in action: Most everyone thought this stretch of coastline would be incorporated into the new city of Laguna Niguel, thus the name of the beach and the hotel. Instead, the area was included in the new city of Dana Point.)

Above the beach is a seven-acre blufftop park, with vast ocean views. Here you'll find picnic tables and barbecue pits, showers, even a basketball court. A natural amphitheater created by the dramatic slope of the lawn provides a popular venue for summer performances.

Salt Point is just off the highway, with access at both Selva Rd. and Ritz-Carlton Drive.

PRACTICAL DANA POINT

Sleeping before the Mast

To mind the budget, camp at Doheny. (See Surfin' USA: Doheny State Beach, above.) A winner in the cheap-stay basic-motel contest—if you're not autophobic—is the small **Dana Marina Inn Motel,** 34111 Coast Hwy., tel. (949) 496-1300, quaintly situated on an island at the apex of local traffic flow (where PCH divides into two one-way thoroughfares, part of what defines "downtown"). Inexpensive, with rates $46 and up. Another possibility is the **Dana Villa Motel,** 34311 S. Coast Hwy. (Del Obispo and PCH), tel. (949) 496-5727. Inexpensive, with rates $55 and up.

For a few more animal comforts, the **Best Western Marina Inn,** 24800 Dana Point Harbor Drive, tel. toll-free (800) 255-6843 or (949) 496-1203, www.bestwestern.com, is a good deal anytime. Expensive-Premium, with rates $84-130.

Dana Point offers pricier places, too, including the very pleasant Victorian Cape Cod-style **Marriott's Laguna Cliffs Resort** (the former Dana Point Resort) adjacent to Doheny State Beach, just west of the highway at 25135 Park Lantern, tel. toll-free (800) 533-9748 or (949) 661-5000, www.marriott.com. The ambience here is refined casual, those rooms with a view clearly the most appealing. "Activity" amenities include two swimming pools, whirlpools, steam rooms, sauna, exercise room, lighted tennis courts, even ping pong. Luxury, with rates $155-299, though ask about specials.

Even more charming, in the bed-and-breakfast style, is the 29-room **Blue Lantern Inn,** 34343 Blue Lantern, tel. (949) 661-1304, www.foursisters.com, perched on a bluff overlooking Dana Point Harbor. Built in the fashion of a traditional Cape Cod inn, the Blue Lantern is part of a chain of ten luxurious Four Sisters inns along the coast. Each room has a fireplace, sitting area, refrigerator with soft drinks, and in-room whirlpool tub. The tower rooms offer a delicious coastal view almost any time. Full breakfast and afternoon hors d' oeuvres are served in the library. Luxury, with rates: $150-500, prices roughly correlated with "view" value. Be sure to book well in advance.

Ritz-Carlton Laguna Niguel

Just 10 miles south of Laguna Beach is Orange County's finest resort—a gem for those who can afford the price tag of pure getaway pleasure.

The Ritz-Carlton Laguna Niguel is a long, low chateau perched grandly on cliffs overlooking the ocean. The northern Monarch Bay Wing faces north toward Salt Creek Beach and an 18-hole par-70 golf course designed by Robert Trent Jones. The Dana Point Wing overlooks ocean, palm trees, and sunset scenery. Amenities here include four outdoor tennis courts, two heated pools with jacuzzi, and a complete fitness center with exercise rooms, steam room, sauna, and massage.

Once inside the lobby, guests are greeted by raw-silk wall coverings, French tapestries, Chinese horses, and art, art, art. This Ritz boasts an impressive hotel collection of American and British 19th-century art, not to mention crystal chandeliers (even in the elevators). All rooms have small private terraces, and are attractive and comfortable in the somewhat staid Ritz-Carlton style. Amenities include color TV, free movies, in-room honor bars and safes plus, in the bathrooms, hair dryers, an extra telephone, and thick terry bathrobes. As is typical at Ritz-Carlton hotels, 24-hour room service and other services are top drawer.

In the afternoon, take tea in the mahogany-paneled library. Casual meals, breakfast, lunch, and dinner, are served at the Ritz's **Terrace** cafe restaurant (outside on the terrace, overlooking the ocean). Another possibility is the **Club Grill and Bar,** which also serves live music in the evening. When cost is no object, **The Dining Room** is truly exceptional, one of the best restaurants in Orange County. And though a dressed-down dress code is otherwise strictly enforced in Dana Point and Laguna Beach, the Ritz-Carlton insists on some semblance of formality. Jackets and ties are required even in the bar, semi-formal attire in The Dining Room.

Almost more fun than exploring the hotel is traipsing around the grounds. It's not at all unusual to see cottontail rabbits boldly grazing on the lawn amid the asters and shasta daisies. (Complete garden tours are offered, with a $25 lunch attached.) **Salt Creek Beach** stretches to the north and south of the Ritz-Carlton—an easy exploratory stroll, especially from the hotel, with its easy-access ramp. If heading back uphill is daunting, hotel guests can catch a ride on the Ritz's tiny motorized tram.

The Ritz-Carlton Laguna Niguel is just off PCH at 33533 Ritz-Carlton Dr. in Dana Point, tel. toll-free (800) 241-3333 or (949) 240-2000, www.ritzcarlton.com. Luxury, with room rates $395-575 per night in summer, from $295 otherwise. Suites start at $650. Ask about specials and packages.

Dining and Entertainment before the Mast

To pack it away with style, try Sunday brunch at the Marriott's **Watercolors** restaurant (expensive), 25135 Park Lantern, tel. (949) 661-5000, noted for its views, its contemporary American cuisine, and its kids-welcome attitude. A best bet in the dinner-only category is elegant Italian **Luciana's,** south of Blue Lantern at 24312 Del Prado, tel. (949) 661-6500, most famous for its pastas.

Though the Ritz-Carlton is certainly a classier bar scene, more fun is the **Mugs Away Saloon,** 27324 Camino Capistrano in Laguna Niguel, tel. (949) 582-9716, the local answer to attitude bars everywhere. In this one, you drink, dance, and admire the bare-behinds photo collection. These Mugs Away "mugs" commemorate the bar's annual "Moon Amtrak" event, wherein patrons drop their drawers to terrorize and/or titillate train travelers.

SAN JUAN CAPISTRANO

Orange County's Mission Days

Few reminders remain of the area's first known people, named by conquistadores the "Juañeno" after the mission at San Juan Capistrano. The Juañenos' 10-month combined solar and lunar calendar—unique in California but common among the Pueblo people in the American Southwest—was one remnant of native culture that survived mission influences long enough to be noted.

Today's Orange County travelers navigate by freeway the desert landscape of cactus, sagebrush, and native grass trod by Captain Gaspar de Portolá and the first inland incursion of Spanish in 1769. Padre Fermí Francisco de Lasuén, one of the far-ranging Franciscan fathers, came in 1775 to select a mission site, San Juan Capistrano. Father Junípero Serra showed up to dedicate the mission in 1776, the same year Juan Bautista de Anza arrived with the region's first livestock. As was their custom elsewhere, missionaries soon planted gardens, orchards, and vineyards, establishing a foundation for the region's very rich agriculture.

Then began the much-romanticized era of the Californios, the California-born descendants of early Spanish and Mexican settlers. Though only one of the 20 original Spanish land grants was located here—the Yorba family's 30,000-acre Santiago de Santa Ana, which included part of the land now incorporated into the cities of Orange, Santa Ana, and Newport Beach—under Mexican rule the region was divided into six major ranchos. The holdings of the Peralta, Sepulveda, and Yorba families would later form the 93,000-acre Irvine Ranch, from which sprouted the cities of Santa Ana and Tustin and, later, the meticulously planned city of Irvine.

The Swallows of Capistrano

A schmaltzy song started it all. The 1939 Leon Rene tune "When the Swallows Come Back to Capistrano" is responsible for the excited flutter here every year on March 19, St. Joseph's Day, when tourists flock to town to welcome the return of the cliff swallows from their annual Argentina migration. Identifiable by their squared-off cleft tails and propensity for nesting under overhangs and in other protected high-altitude spots, the swallows' first official return was in 1776—the

the return of the pigeons

year the United States became a nation and the year Father Junípero Serra established the mission. Serra recorded the event in his diary.

Nowadays, though, on March 19 tourists typically far outnumber the swallows, which never did respect that particular day much anyway. (According to ornithologists, the swallows return in the spring, March 19 being close enough to the spring equinox, with "scouts" spotted quite early in March.) Modern life has created confusion for the mission's mythic swallows. Too many people and too much hubbub scare them off, for one thing. Earthquakes, and earthquake repairs, have knocked down hundreds of old swallow nests, for another, and subsequent scaffolding put up to protect the mission has discouraged still more birds. As a result visitors are as likely to see cliff swallows nesting in the high arches of the May Co. store downtown as at the mission.

All that aside, San Juan Capistrano does what it can to help the swallows do their historical duty—by setting out a buffet of ladybugs and green lacewing larvae in the rose garden in March. It also plans most of its **Fiesta de las Golondrinas,** with parade, fun runs, and people dressed up in swallow costumes, for the week framing March 19. Putting local politicians and other volunteers to good use, the festivities culminate later in the month with a "mud-slinging" contest—with the mud and straw slapped onto old adobes to help preserve them.

Though there isn't yet a song to serve as a swallow send-off, Capistrano's birds are supposed to depart on St. John's Day, October 23.

Mission San Juan Capistrano

Its crumbling church walls steadied by scaffolding and surrounded by very contemporary New World ambience, Mission San Juan Capistrano is not the most vigorous survivor of California's 21-mission chain. Yet it's impressive nonetheless. The **quadrangle,** with its storerooms and workshops for making clothing, candles, soap, and pottery, was the center of mission life. Today, exhibits, a 12-minute film, and museum displays (including the piano on which the famous swallow song was composed) tell the basic story. Most evocative, though—if you can imagine the scaffolding *desaparecido*—are the ruins of the **Great Stone Church,** built in 1797 and destroyed by an earthquake in 1812. To get an exact idea of what the old church looked like, sans the patina of time, visit the Spanish Renaissance **New Church of Mission San Juan Capistrano** on Camino Capistrano, with its stunning interior murals and artwork. Next door—draped in spectacular color when the bougainvillea is in bloom, and still in use after all these years—is the mission's original **Serra Chapel**, the only one remaining in California in which Father Serra said mass. Capistrano's chapel, constructed in 1777, is also the oldest building standing in the Golden State. Quite striking inside is the ornate "golden altar," made of cherry wood more than 300 years ago and brought here from Barcelona, Spain, in 1922. Wander the grounds, with its ancient gardens, ponds, and Native American cemetery, to complete a thoughtful tour of San Juan Capistrano, once considered "the jewel of the missions."

Mission San Juan Capistrano is on Camino Capistrano at Ortega Hwy. (Hwy. 74) and accessible either from PCH or I-5. Admission is $6 adults, $4 for seniors and children ages 3-12 (under 3 free). It's open daily 8:30 a.m.-5 p.m. Free guided tours are offered on Sunday at 1 p.m. Call (949) 248-2048 for current information.

Other Capistrano Sights, Excitements

Across from the mission's new church is another local newcomer—the postmodern mission-style **San Juan Capistrano Regional Library**, 31495 El Camino Real (at Acjachema), tel. (949) 493-1752, designed by Princeton University architect Michael Graves. The courtyard and gardens offer peaceful and private retreats for reading. Call for current hours.

Nearby is the **O'Neill Museum**, 31831 Los Rios St., tel. (949) 493-8444, a petite 19th-century Victorian with local memorabilia on display. Pick up the local **historic walking tour** map here (and at the chamber office or various area businesses) to discover San Juan Capistrano's remaining adobes and other venerable ancients. The 1894 Spanish revival **Capistrano Depot**, 26701 Verdugo, for example, is a stunning stop for **Amtrak.**

Not everything in the area is ancient. One of Orange County's hippest clubs is here—**The Coach House,** tucked into a warehouse at 33157 Camino Capistrano, tel. (949) 496-8930, known for good—sometimes great—live music

acts. For the best seats, make dinner reservations. And if you find yourself near Santa Ana, also well worth tracking down is the Coach House's sister club, **The Galaxy Theater.**

Ronald W. Caspers Wilderness Park

If the balmy beaches become boring, if you crave a little skin-searing summer heat, Caspers Wilderness Park is the place to go hiking on a hot summer's day. Most people, of course, come anytime *but* summer. Spring, when the hillsides are heavy with wildflowers, is especially appealing.

Caspers has had its share of bad press in recent years, mostly due to **mountain lion attacks** on small children. Though adults are also potential victims, the high-pitched voices and quick, preylike movements of children make them particularly vulnerable. Until someone gets a better idea about how humans and big cats can safely share a neighborhood, Caspers is open only to adults (age 18 and older). Children can picnic and camp here, however, in the company of adults, and are allowed on ranger-guided Saturday hikes. Campsites (no hookups) are particularly popular with RVers, since the terrain isn't that friendly to tents (permitted). Day use is $4 on weekends, $2 during the week, and camping is $12 per vehicle. Hikers and campers must obtain a wilderness permit (free), available here.

The entrance to Ronald W. Caspers Regional Park is at 33401 Ortega Hwy. (Hwy. 74), about eight miles from San Juan Capistrano. For more information, contact Ronald W. Caspers Wilderness Park, P.O. Box 395, San Juan Capistrano, tel. (949) 728-0235 or (949) 728-3420.

San Juan Capistrano Information

For more information on the area, contact: **San Juan Capistrano Chamber of Commerce,** 31781 Camino Capistrano, Suite 306, San Juan Capistrano, tel. (949) 493-4700, www.sanjuan-chamber.com

SAN CLEMENTE

This isn't much of a tourist town. The people of San Clemente prefer it that way—and you'll be glad, too, if peace and quiet have eluded you elsewhere. The well-guarded solitude of this red-tile-roofed Republican town was its primary appeal for ex-President Richard M. Nixon and his wife, Pat, who retreated here to La Casa Pacifica, the **Western White House,** overlooking the beach. The best view of Nixon's former estate, a palm-shrouded 25-acre compound, is from San Clemente State Beach. Otherwise, the most exciting scene around is at the San Clemente Pier adjoining the city beach, reached via Avenida Del Mar, where crewcut Marines from nearby Camp Pendleton cavort alongside civilians. For more information about the area, contact: **San Clemente Chamber of Commerce,** 1100 N. El Camino Real, tel. (949) 492-1131, www.scchamber.com.

San Clemente State Beach

Backed by craggy white sandstone bluffs and wind-warped coastal chaparral, mile-long San Clemente State Beach, with its fine white sand, is still one of the best things in town—comparatively uncrowded when every other beach in the county is overrun. Reached via various trails, the beach is popular for skin diving, surfing, and just plain sunning and swimming. Up on the landscaped bluffs are picnic areas and a developed campground with 157 sites (72 with hookups). Day use (parking) is $6; camping, $18-22 in peak season. For camping reservations, call ReserveAmerica toll-free at (800) 444-7275.

To get here, from I-5 exit at Avenida Calafia near the south side of town and follow the signs. For more information, call (949) 492-3156 or (949) 492-0802.

Rancho Mission Viejo Land Conservancy

On this 1200-acre preserve, three typically distinct ecosystems—oak woodlands, grasslands, and coastal sage scrub—come together to create a richly diverse pocket of Southern California's fast-fading natural history. To protect this heritage, the city of San Clemente, Orange County, and the Rancho Mission Viejo Company entered into a conservation agreement allowing only limited public access. Naturalist-led horseback rides (extra fee), Saturday and evening hikes (the latter in summer only), and new-moon "astronomy nights" are typically offered (small fee) by reservation only. For current information call (949) 489-9778, or check www.theconservancy.org.

Staying in San Clemente

For lone travelers, even cheaper than camping (but without the sand-in-your-shoes ambience) is the clean **San Clemente Beach AYH Hostel,** just five blocks from Amtrak and a couple of blocks from the beach in the onetime public library at 233 Avenida Granada, tel. (949) 492-2848 or toll-free (800) 444-6111; for general AYH info, check www.hiayh.org. For a bed in one of two dorm rooms (there's also a family room) and access to kitchen and laundry, expect to pay $12 (members) or $14 (nonmembers). Groups and families welcome. Otherwise, San Clemente has a surprising number of decent motels with what are, by Orange County standards, quite reasonable rates. One best bet for the basics is the small **San Clemente Beach Travelodge** close to I-5 but just a block from the state beach at 2441 S. El Camino Real, toll-free tel. (800) 843-1704 or (949) 498-5954, www.travelodge.com. Moderate-Luxury, starting at $69 in summer, $45 otherwise. Always a find where you find it is the **Country Inn & Suites,** located west of I-5 behind Pico Plaza at 35 Calle de Industrias, tel. toll-free (800) 874-0860 or (949) 498-8800, www.countrysuites.com. Expensive-Premium.

Practically on the beach is the tiny, hill-hugging **Casa Tropicana,** right across from the pier at 610 Avenida Victoria, tel. (949) 492-1234 or toll-free (800) 492-1245, www.casatropicana.com. This beachfront bed-and-breakfast hotel has a festive "tropical paradise" ambience, an attitude also animating the **Tropicana Bar & Grill** downstairs. Rooms are themed—Coral Reef, Key Largo, Out of Africa—and most feature in-room jacuzzis. Full breakfast is included, either in your room or downstairs in the restaurant. Also enjoy the loaner beach chairs and umbrellas. Premium-Luxury, with high-season rates $120-280 (weekday and off-season rates much lower). Two-night minimum on summer weekends.

Eating in San Clemente

You won't starve in San Clemente, but in general the eating-out options are less abundant than elsewhere along the coast. The **Beach Garden Cafe** across from the pier at 618 1/2 Avenida Victoria, tel. (949) 498-8145, is a best bet for breakfast.

Next door, at Casa Tropicana, is the **Tropicana Bar & Grill,** 610 Avenida Victoria, tel. (949) 498-8767, serving burgers, pasta, and salads along with live music on weekend nights. At the foot of the pier is **The Fisherman's Restaurant and Bar,** 611 Avenida Victoria, tel. (949) 498-6390, noted for its fresh seafood (changing menu) at both lunch and dinner. Other specialties include the eggplant Parmigiana and grilled vegetable sandwiches.

From San Clemente South

Before freeway traffic slithers south into San Diego County, it all becomes one with I-5. The area near the new city of Lake Forest, once known as El Toro, is where I-5 and the 405 suddenly join, condensing into the I-5 leg of the San Diego Freeway. This traffic nightmare is known as the "El Toro Y." (Heads up.) Just north of San Clemente, Pacific Coast Hwy. (Hwy. 1) also becomes one with I-5.

Driving south from San Clemente, note the daunting seven-mile freeway barrier marking the center divide—intended to deter illegal aliens heading north on foot from San Diego, as they're all too frequently killed while dashing across the freeway.

Just across the county border lies **San Onofre State Beach,** part of a larger state park complete with campground. The most imposing coastal neighbor is the **San Onofre Nuclear Power Plant,** looming at the end of the beach. Next is the massive acreage of Camp Pendleton, a fitting introduction to the dominance of military interests and inclinations in San Diego County.

TOM MYERS PHOTOGRAPHY

THE SAN DIEGO COAST

To discover San Diego County's northern coastline, exit the freeway and amble along the ocean. You can exit anywhere, of course, but for the longest coastal cruise, start just south of the Orange County border and head south to La Jolla. The street name changes in each community—becoming Carlsbad Boulevard in Carlsbad, for example, and Camino del Mar in Del Mar—so old Highway 101 is also known, prosaically, as County Road S21.

First stop for most people, just after the old highway separates from I-5, is Oceanside, with a nice pier and beach, urban adjunct to the sprawling Camp Pendleton U.S. Marine base. Just inland is Mission San Luis Rey, "King of the Missions." Farther north along the coast, just south of the county line, is San Onofre State Beach (san ON-uh-fray), technically in San Diego County but geopolitically more connected to San Clemente and other Orange County lo-

cales. An unavoidable feature of remote San Onofre is its mid-beach nuclear power plant, though the area also offers good spots for swimming and surfing.

South of Oceanside is Carlsbad, named after Karlsbad, Bohemia, for the similar mineral content in the local spring water, most famous these days as the home of Legoland. Next stop is Encinitas—including, technically, the communities of Leucadia, Cardiff-by-the-Sea, and Olivehain. Encinitas is historically famous for its flower fields—poinsettias in particular—the downtown Self-Realization Fellowship, the Quail Botanical Gardens, San Elijo State Beach (and the area's various locals' beaches), and Leucadia's galleries and shops.

For a full measure of the simpler pleasures, stop in sunny Solana Beach, just north of Del Mar. Known for its celebrities and chic shopping, Del Mar is also home to the Del Mar Thoroughbred Club summer horse races—and the beach here is dandy. Torrey Pines Road leads south from Del Mar to La Jolla. Along the way are the Torrey Pines reserve, beach, and coastal lagoon, technically still part of the city of San Diego.

See color maps of San Diego and the surrounding coast at front of book.

A thorough exploration of northern San Diego County also includes excursions inland to Escondido and vicinity, best known as home to the San Diego Wild Animal Park; the apple-pie American frontier town of Julian; and fabulous Anza-Borrego Desert State Park, most inviting in early spring.

SOUTH ALONG THE COAST

Oceanside and Vicinity

Immediately north of Carlsbad and almost a suburb of Camp Pendleton is Oceanside, with its own pier, a nice beach with largely crew-cut clientele, and an active, attractive harbor area. A local attraction is the **California Surf Museum,** tel. (760) 721-6876, www.surfmuseum.org, an eclectic, almost offhand display of surfboards with themed exhibits and zany gift shop. For more information about the area, call the **Oceanside Visitors and Conference Center** at (760) 721-1101, or look them up online at www.oceansidechamber.com.

Historic **Mission San Luis Rey de Francia,** the "King of the Missions" at 4050 Mission Avenue in San Luis Rey, tel. (760) 757-3651, was founded in 1798 but not completed until 1815; in 1893 it became a Franciscan seminary. Wander the grounds of San Luis Rey, the state's largest but one of its less visited missions, for an appreciation of early California culture—and the enduring wonder of adobe construction. Museum exhibits and displays reveal the rough reality of mission life. Mission San Luis Rey is four miles east of I-5 via Hwy. 76 (Mission Ave.) and is open Mon.-Sat. 10 a.m.-4:30 p.m., Sunday noon-4:30 p.m. for self-guided tours, closed major U.S. holidays. Admission is $4 adults, $1 children ages 8-14.

North of Camp Pendleton is **San Onofre State Beach.** The odd detail here is the **San Onofre Nuclear Power Plant,** about five miles south of San Clemente, serving as the Mason-Dixon line between north and south beaches though the two are connected by a public walkway along the seawall. The north is known for excellent surfing, the south for good swimming and bodysurfing and it's very nice "primitive" campground (for both tents and RVs, no hook-ups). It's open daily 6 a.m.-sunset. Day-use fee is $6 per vehicle, camping is extra. For more information about the beaches here, call (949) 492-4872.

Carlsbad: Bracing for the Big Time

According to local lore, Carlsbad was named after Karlsbad, Bohemia, since its "waters" had a composition identical to the mineral waters of the Ninth Spa in what is now the Czech Republic. Little wonder, then, that the spa trade was also hot here, beginning in the 1880s. You can see remnants and mementos of that era at the picturesque stone **Alt Karlsbad Haus,** now a gift shop and museum on Carlsbad Boulevard (closed at last report). Adjacent are the original wells, capped after World War II.

Present-day Carlsbad is best known as an affluent, family-friendly beach town cum San Diego bedroom community, populated by surfers, eccentrics, entrepreneurs, and high-technology firms. But this genuinely laid-back coastal escape exploded with hustle, bustle, and new business when the 128-acre **Legoland** children's theme park and affiliated resort opened here in 1999. But even now Carlsbad wows the crowds—every spring in particular, when tourists plow through surrounding **Carlsbad Ranch** flower fields tel. 760-431-0352, best for the ranunculus bloom, early March through late April, and jam into California's largest street fair, the **Carlsbad Village Faire.**

Visitors attracted to homegrown pleasures can sunbathe and swim at the beach, stroll along the seawall (Carlsbad's beach promenade), explore local lagoons, and loll around in coffeehouses and the casual, sometimes eclectic restaurants and shops collected along Carlsbad Boulevard.

Lined with **antique shops** selling heavy silver jewelry, country quilts and estate furniture, the three blocks of State Street between Oak and Beech is an oasis of retro charm. Stroll over to **Aanteek Aavenue Mall,** 2832 State Street, tel. (760) 434-8742, for an excellent variety of wares under one roof, including vintage china, glass, and jewelry. Find vintage wares at **Black Roads Antiques,** 2988 State Street, tel. (760) 729-3032.

Wind-driven winter waves tend to batter Carlsbad-area beaches, so Carlsbad State Beach and others are typically closed in winter and spring. They're also typically rockier than the southstate stereotype. Of the two local state beaches, **Carlsbad State Beach** is usually the best bet for sandy sunbathing. Farther south on Carlsbad Boulevard (at Poinsettia Lane) is **South Carlsbad State Beach,** popular for ocean swimming as well as its large blufftop campground (reservations mandatory). Then there are Carlsbad's lagoons. South of Poinsettia along the shore is the quarter-mile interpretive walkway for **Batiquitos Lagoon,** now being revivified and reconnected with the ocean. For more information, call the Batiquitos foundation at (760) 943-7583. North of downtown is the **Buena Vista Lagoon,** with an Audubon Society nature center. Call the Audubon Society at (760) 439-2473 or look up the Buena Vista chapter on www .audubon.org for information about scheduled birding and other events.

For more information about the community, contact the **Carlsbad Convention and Visitors Bureau** housed in the old Santa Fe Depot on Carlsbad Village Drive, tel. (760) 434-6093 or toll-free tel. (800) 227-5722. It's open Monday through Friday 9 a.m. to 5 p.m., Saturday and Sunday 10 a.m. to 2 p.m.

Quail Botanical Gardens

Known as "Flower Capital of the World," Encinitas is losing some floral ground to encroaching suburbia. Quail Botanical Gardens, a local horticultural star, is still going strong, however. Here you can wander 30 acres of canyon appreciating thousands of species: tropical and subtropical immigrants from Central and South America, Australia, Africa, and the Himalayas, also drought-resistant native plants.

Quail Botanical Gardens is closed the first Monday of every month, otherwise open daily 9 a.m.-5 p.m. (closed Thanksgiving, Christmas, and New Year's Day). It offers general tours (free) every Saturday at 10 a.m. and free children's tours on the first Tuesday of every month. (Group tours are offered only by appointment.) Admission is free on the first Tuesday of every month, otherwise it's $5 adults, $4 seniors, $2 children ages 5-12 (under 5 free). For plant and gift shop purchases, come between 10 a.m. and 4 p.m. daily. Quail Botanical Gardens, 230 Quail Gardens Dr., Encinitas, tel. (760) 436-3036, www.qbgardens.com, is approximately 20 miles north of San Diego between Leucadia and Encinitas Boulevards. To get here from I-5, exit at Encinitas Boulevard and head east. Turn left (north) onto Quail Gardens Drive. The gardens are on the left.

Solana Beach

Solana means "sunny spot" in Español, and Solana Beach is still fun and funky in laid-back

LEGOLAND CARLSBAD: A BIG-TIME SMALL WORLD

With over 40 rides, shows, and attractions on 128 acres of appealing parkland, Legoland Carlsbad offers a full and exciting day out for children and their families just 30 miles north of San Diego in Carlsbad.

Opened in 1999, Legoland Carlsbad is the world's second Lego-themed theme park, inspired by the original in Denmark. Like the first Legoland, this one is as expansive in scope as it is small in scale. For starters, there are fantastically detailed Lego models to admire, including 1:20 scale Lego brick reproductions of famous cities like San Francisco, Paris, and New York, each complete with moving vehicles and small-scale people scurrying about the streets. Also quite striking, and fun as educational tools, are replicas of favorite international landmarks; the Sydney Opera House, San Francisco's Alamo Square, New York's Empire State Building, and Mount Rushmore were built using over 30 million Lego bricks.

What sets Legoland apart from other California theme parks is its absence of white-knuckle rides. Rides and attractions here—including a driving school with cars, a gravity coaster, a mini excursion tour, and a DUPLO building area—appeal instead to the two-to-twelve-year-old crowd. Even the food differs from regular theme park fare, with a European twist. Expect fresh fruit, applesauce, salads, and breadsticks along with homemade pizzas, popcorn, and chicken sticks.

Legoland, 1 Lego Dr. (at Cannon Rd.), tel. (760) 918-5346, www.legolandca.com, is open daily 10 a.m. to dusk, which translates into 10 a.m.-5 p.m. in winter, 9 a.m.-9 p.m. in summer. Admission is $34 adults, $29 children (ages 3-16). Ask at the gate for special discounts for seniors (over 60). Parking, available in the adjacent lot, is $6. To get here from I-5, take the Cannon exit east.

—*Pat Reilly*

beach town style yet starting to try on civic phrases such as "chic" and "stylish." To sample the eclectic commercial side of this confusion, stroll the business district, more or less concentrated between Lomas Santa Fe Drive to the north and Via de la Valle to the south, Old Highway 101 to the west, and Cedros Avenue to the east. Still, the beach in Solana Beach is the big thing, though finding a way down to it is something of a challenge. (Hint: Look for the "pillbox.")

STAYING ALONG THE COAST

Budget travelers, head to **Motel 6.** There's one in south Carlsbad at 750 Raintree Dr., toll-free tel. (800) 466-8356 or (760) 431-0745, fax (760) 431-9207. No surprises, and the price is right, $40 single, $46 double. Inexpensive. That price gets you basic rooms with color TV and cable, plus swimming pool and proximity to the beach. (If there's no room, there are two other Motel 6 choices in Carlsbad, and another two in adjacent Oceanside.) To get here from I-5: exit west at Poinsettia Lane, turn north on Avenida Encinas, then east (right) onto Raintree.

A decent choice in Oceanside is the **Days Inn,** 3170 Vista Way, toll-free tel. (800) 458-6064 or (760) 757-2200, fax (760) 757-2389. Rooms are nothing fancy but quite pleasant, with color TV, cable, and free movies. Special diversions include a children's playground, whirlpool, and exercise room plus (for a fee) access to the adjacent 18-hole golf course and lighted tennis courts. The motel is just a few miles from the Carlsbad beach. Moderate. Rates are $69-79, with weekly and monthly rates available.

In Carlsbad, a best-bet for families is the very attractive, very popular **Best Western Beach View Lodge,** 3180 Carlsbad Blvd., Carlsbad, toll-free tel. (800) 535-5588 or (760) 729-1151, fax (760) 434-5405, where all rooms have refrigerators, some have kitchens or kitchenettes. Expensive-Premium. There's also a heated pool, whirlpool, and sauna, with rates from $80-120. (Monthly rates available in the off-season.) Pricier but right on the beach is the **Best Western Beach Terrace Inn,** on the beach at 2775 Ocean St., toll-free tel. (800) 433-5415 or (760) 729-5951, fax (760) 729-1078. Most rooms have kitchens, many have ocean views. Premium-

Luxury. Rates $119-189. Also popular and pricier still is the **Carlsbad Inn Beach Resort,** 3075 Carlsbad Blvd., toll-free tel. (800) 235-3939 or (760) 434-7020, where the Old World meets the New World under the palm trees. Luxury. Rates $169-239. For the ultimate Carlsbad stay, head for **La Costa Resort and Spa** (see below).

Right next to I-5 but otherwise perfect for a more uptown stay is the **Country Inn,** 1661 Villa Cardiff Dr., Cardiff-by-the-Sea, toll-free tel. (800) 322-9993 or (760) 944-0427, fax (760) 944-7708, a stylish Old World-style motel with a pool, whirlpool, and bed-and-breakfast amenities—full breakfast and morning newspaper, fresh fruit, and afternoon refreshments. Moderate-Premium. A great deal, with rates $82-125.

The **Ocean Inn** in Encinitas at 1444 N. Hwy. 101 (between La Costa Ave. and Leucadia Blvd.), toll-free tel. (800) 546-1598 or (760) 436-1988, fax (760) 436-3921, is a best bet for a base camp, since from here it's just a five-minute walk to the beach. Rooms come with all the motel basics plus in-room refrigerators and microwaves—bring your own cookware and utensils—and color TV, cable, and video players; some feature in-room whirlpool tubs. Other pluses: on-site laundry and rental bikes. Moderate-Expensive. Rates start at $69 single, $79 double. Closest to the beach, though, is the relaxed **Moonlight Beach Hotel,** 233 Second St., toll-free tel. (800) 323-1259 or (760) 753-0623, with large rooms and kitchenettes. Moderate. Rates $56-76.

La Costa Resort and Spa
One of California's premier resort retreats, this one is luxurious but relaxed and low-key. Almost a self-contained city, this 400-acre spread comes complete with its own movie theater. Carlsbad's La Costa features world-class spa and fitness facilities, swimming pools, tennis courts, racquetball courts, and two PGA championship 18-hole golf courses. (Inquire about special golf and tennis packages.) To keep it simple, rent bikes here and cruise on down to the beach. Luxury. Rates $175-2,300. For more information call toll-free (800) 854-5000 or (760) 438-9111, fax (760) 438-3758, or check out www.lacosta.com. To get here, drive two miles east of I-5 via La Costa Ave., and then continue north for a quarter-mile on El Camino Real.

EATING ALONG THE COAST

As might be expected, Carlsbad is rich with restaurants. Some okay choices: for southwestern, the **Coyote Bar & Grill** in the Village Faire Shopping Center at 300 Carlsbad Village Dr., tel. (760) 729-4695; for Mexican, **Fidel's Norte** near the beach scene at 3003 Carlsbad Blvd., tel. (760) 729-0903; for American, the **Pea Soup Andersen's** outpost at the Best Western Andersen's Inn, 850 Palomar Airport Rd., tel. (760) 438-7880.

For more bohemian atmosphere you can do better, though, at places such as **Kafana Coffee** at the beach, 3076 Carlsbad Blvd., tel. (760) 720-0074 which showcases live music every night in summer and on weekend nights in winter, and the **Pizza Port**, a pizza parlor cum surfer hangout at 571 Carlsbad Village Dr., tel. (760) 720-7007. For fine dining, the place is casual **Neimans** inside the grand Queen Anne mansion once owned by local "waters" promoter Gerhard Schutte, along the waterfront at 300 Carlsbad Village Dr., tel. (760) 729-4131. People come from miles around just for the Sunday brunch.

Rico's Taco Shop in the Target shopping center at 165-L S. El Camino Real in Encinitas, tel. (760) 944-7689, is a safe place to bring the kids even after a sand-in-their-shoes day at the beach—quick, casual, and quite good, if what you're looking for is health-conscious Mexican food. At lunch and dinner, the fish tacos and burritos, *carne asada* selections, and *taquitos* are hard to beat. Rico's is open daily 8 a.m.-9 p.m., closed holidays. For fancier fare, wander the **First Street** area in downtown Encinitas to see what's new and appetizing.

Ki's Juice Bar and Restaurant, 2591 S. Hwy. 101 (near Chesterfield) in Cardiff-by-the-Sea, tel. (760) 436-5236, is not strictly vegetarian—but if that's what you're looking for, this is where you'll find it. Everything here is fresh and healthy, including organic seven grain cereal and tofu scramble at breakfast and veggie stir fry, egg salad sandwiches, and Ki's salmon salad at lunch. Expect more of the same at dinner, plus pasta. Juice bar choices include fruit and ice cream smoothies—a chance to try a decent date shake—and fresh juices and blends, including orange and grapefruit, carrot and watermelon.

Ki's serves food for the soul, too—live jazz on Friday and Saturday nights (no cover with dinner). It's open Sun.-Thurs. 8 a.m.-9:30 p.m., Fri.-Sat. 8 a.m.-9 p.m., closed holidays. For a totally different take—steak and seafood and such—try the predictably good **Chart House,** nearby at 2588 S. Hwy. 101, tel. (760) 436-4044, and **The Beach House,** 2530 S. Hwy. 101, tel. (760) 753-1321.

The fare at **Solana Beach Brewery and Pizza Port,** 135 N. Hwy. 101 (at Loma Santa Fe), tel. (760) 736-0370, includes good pizza and salads—simple, straightforward flavors intended to complement the local brew. Offerings here include Beacon's Bitter, 101 Nut Brown, Rivermouth Raspberry, and Sharkbite Red Ale. If you can't decide, ask for the "taster"—four four-ounce glasses, a sample of each. While you're sampling, the kids can visit the arcade area. The place is open daily 11 a.m.-12 a.m., closed major holidays. Another possibility: wood-fired pizzas from the **California Pizza Kitchen** in the Boardwalk mall, 437 S. Hwy. 1, tel. (858) 739-0999. The pizzas are out of the ordinary—popular choices include the BBQ Chicken Pizza with Gouda cheese, onions and barbecue sauce, the Thai Chicken Pizza with spicy peanut-ginger and sesame sauce, and the Vegetarian Pizza with Japanese Eggplant. Open Mon.-Sat. 11:30-10 p.m., Sun. 11:30-9 p.m. CPK also has outposts in La Jolla, tel. (858) 675-4424, and Carmel Mountain Ranch, tel. (858) 457-4222.

Two-story **Fidel's,** 607 Valley Ave. (near Stevens) in Solana Beach, tel. (858) 755-5292, is the place for Mexican food—and lots of it. A combination plate, with rice, beans, and entrées of your choice, should satisfy even the most boisterous beach appetite (children's plates available). If at all possible, grab a table out on the patio. There's another Fidel's on Carlsbad Boulevard in Carlsbad, tel. (760) 729-0903. Fidel's is open daily 11 a.m.-9:30 p.m., sometimes later on weekends, and closed Christmas. Reservations taken only for groups of eight or more.

EXCURSIONS INLAND: ESCONDIDO AND VICINITY

Escondido: Wine and Wild Animals

Escondido, which means "hidden" in Spanish, is far from invisible these days. Center of the

AISLINN RACE

Endangered creatures such as the zebra live in simulated versions of their natural habitats at the Wild Animal Park.

vast inland territory north of San Diego and its suburbs, Escondido is home to the remarkable San Diego Wild Animal Park—where visitors "visit" Africa and Asia, and exotic animal and plantlife in open-air "natural" habitats, via monorail. Adjacent to this world tour of natural history is a monument to the hurried march of local history—the San Pasqual Battlefield State Historic Park. Here in 1846 a small band of "Californios," or California-born Mexican citizens, vanquished legendary scout Kit Carson and U.S. Army troops in one of the more infamous battles of the Mexican-American War. In more recent history Escondido has added high culture to its list of assets, with the $74 million California Center for the Arts, Escondido.

Radiating from Escondido like the spokes of a roughed-up wagon wheel are roads leading to other attractions—including the Lawrence Welk Resort, with its own theater for Broadway-style musical productions. Local vineyards and wineries are also a major draw, most particularly Deer Park Vintage Cars and Wines, famous also for its fabulous array of 1950s kitsch.

From Escondido, intrepid travelers can set out on multiple "loop" daytrips—to Palomar Mountain State Park and the Palomar Observatory and then on to Julian, for example, or to Julian via Highway 78, and then on into Anza-Borrego or Rancho Cuyamaca State Parks before looping back. For more information on Palomar Mountain State Park and the observatory, see immediately below. Julian and the surrounding area are equally accessible from San Diego, and for that reason are listed under San Diego below.

For more information on the region, contact: **San Diego North County Convention and Visitors Bureau,** 720 N. Broadway, Escondido 92025, toll-free tel. (800) 848-3336 or (760) 745-4741, fax (760) 745-4796 or www.sandiegonorth.com.

San Diego Wild Animal Park

The main modern-day attraction in San Pasqual Valley is the 2,200-acre San Diego Wild Animal Park, affiliated with the San Diego Zoo. Here, the collected endangered species are exhibited in their own wide open spaces, the separate habitats representing Asian plains, Asian marshlands and swamps, North Africa, South Africa, and East Africa. Hikers can hoof it into East Africa on the hilly one-and-three-quarter-mile **Kilimanjaro Safari Walk,** with observation platforms that allow spying on the lions and elephants below. Cages are still cages, of course, no matter how aesthetic, so what you see here is far from "natural," in any meaningful sense. But here people are penned up, too—onboard the **Wgasa Bush Line** monorail, the park's main event. The five-mile monorail ride—sit on the right side if at all possible—traverses the prairies and canyonlands. Especially during summer heat, the best time to hop aboard is early evening, when the park's creatures are up and about and eating. Even better, in summer, are the after-dark treks, when all the park's a stage—lit by sodium-vapor lamps.

The kids will probably insist on extra time at **Nairobi Village,** the center of everything, complete with "petting kraal" (remarkably toddler-tolerant sheep and goats here); the interactive **Mombasa Lagoon** exhibit; the indoor **Hidden Jungle,** with tropical creatures not typically seen; the interactive **Lorikeet Landing,** an Australian rainforest where people can feed the nectar-loving birds all day long; and the long-running **Bird Show Amphitheater,** starring birds of prey and other performers. Exotic gardens here showcase more than 3,000 botanical specimens.

The park's most exotic activity—a must for photographers—is the **photo caravan tour,** which allows shutterbugs to get up close and personal from *inside* the animal compounds,

CONDOR RIDGE: BORN TO BE WILD

The world can be a dangerous place. And no one, certainly no non-human species, can keep all attendant hazards of the civilized world out of their neighborhood. The latest local symbol of this struggle is the California condor *(Gymnogyps californianus)*, the powerful and primal vulture known to Native Americans as the thunderbird. The largest land bird in North America, until 10,000 to 12,000 years ago the California condor flew and foraged across the southern reaches of what is now the United States, from the Pacific to the Atlantic Oceans. Pre-Columbian hunters soon dispatched most of the mammoths and other large animals on whose carcasses the condor fed. By the time of early European exploration the species had retrenched along the North American coastline from British Columbia to Baja California; condors were sometimes observed feeding on beached whales. In more recent California history the California condor soared inland from the San Rafael Mountains to Sequoia National Park, protected from harm by the land's inaccessibility. Now most of the species' survivors live in protective custody—in "condorminium" cages at California zoos—because the condor's natural environment can no longer assure the bird's survival. Research suggests the precipitous recent decline of the condor was caused by lead shot and bullets, inadvertently consumed by feeding condors, in addition to the increasing incursions of civilization, in the form of power lines, antifreeze, and other hazards.

In 1987 the last wild California condors were captured and packed off as breeders for the captive breeding program, a last, fairly desperate attempt to save the species from extinction. For the coastal Chumash people—haunted by what they were witnessing—the condor round-up suggested the end of the condor, and the end of the condor signaled the end of the world, the "time of purification" when the earth would shake and all life would end then begin again.

Condor Ridge: Engaging Extinction

But the California condor hasn't yet disappeared. Though the species is still teetering on the edge of extinction, captive breeding and some success in releasing the birds into remote areas of their original range offer hope that the end of the world has been postponed. By mid-2000 85 condors had been released into the wild, and 49 were still thriving there.

To get up-close and personal with the California condor—not something likely to happen in nature—stroll through the San Diego Wild Animal Park's new **Condor Ridge** habitat.

A dozen species of rare and endangered North American animals are exhibited here, beginning with the endangered thick-billed parrots once thriving in the pines of Arizona, New Mexico, and northern Mexico. At the base of the pines here, darting among the shrubs, are western greater roadrunners. Next come the grasslands, where northern porcupines accompany the rare, steel-gray aplomado falcons. The prairies habitat is home to endangered black-footed ferrets, desert tortoises, black-tailed prairie dogs, western burrowing owls, American magpies, and western Harris hawks.

At the end of the trail is an observation deck and interpretive center concerning recovery efforts on behalf of the California condor and desert big horn sheep, the latter observed here scrambling around on steep hillsides. Several California condors can also be seen, in their six-story cage.

---

snapping shots from an open-air truck. The tours run daily, and cost between $85-105, depending on the tour. For information and reservations, call (760) 738-5049 or toll-free (800) 934-2267. Family-friendly **Roar and Snore overnight campouts** are also offered, seasonally.

The San Diego Wild Animal Park is open daily from 9 a.m., with gates closing at 4 p.m. in winter and 6 p.m. in summer (grounds close an hour later). In summer, Thursday through Sunday evenings are "Swamp Nights," with admission until 8 p.m. and the park itself open until 10 p.m.

The park is open for extended hours at other times, too, for special events. At last report admission was $21.95 adults, and $14.95 children ages 3-11 (parking extra). A "combination pass," $38.35 adults, $23.15 children, also covers one day's admission to the San Diego Zoo (to use within five days of purchase). Wheelchairs and strollers are available for rent. To get here: exit I-15 in Escondido at Via Rancho Parkway and follow the signs east; it's about six miles to the park. From I-5, exit at Highway 78 and head east to I-15; continue south on I-15, then exit east at Via Rancho Parkway. For current information (pre-recorded), call the San Diego Wild Animal Park at (760) 747-8702, TTY/TDD (760) 738-5067, or check out www.sandiegozoo.org.

San Pasqual Battlefield State Historic Park

Near the San Diego Wild Animal Park is the battlefield park, with multiple historic sights and monuments. Even with the nice visitor center here, the social and territorial skirmishes leading to California statehood don't titillate visitors as much as the animal park. The area's roadside produce stands often do, however. Keeping in mind that more than half of the U.S. avocado crop comes from San Diego County, take in more of the area's agricultural riches by meandering north toward Pauma Valley, Pala, or Fallbrook via back roads.

Escondido-Area Wineries

Just north of the Lawrence Welk Resort is **Deer Park Vintage Cars and Wines,** 29013 Champagne Blvd. (old Hwy. 395), tel. (760) 749-1666, www.deerparkwinery.com. Adults will enjoy Deer Park's local chardonnay, plus the selection of

---

LAWRENCE WELK MUSEUM

The Lawrence Welk Resort north of town, just off I-15 at 8860 Lawrence Welk Dr., Escondido, tel. (760) 749-3448, is quite contemporary and well-appointed, though in a sense it seems like something straight out of the 1950s. Most of Lawrence Welk's elderly fans come to his namesake resort to golf, swim, play tennis, just loaf, and take in a Broadway-style musical. Featuring stars from the long-running *Lawrence Welk Show,* the **Lawrence Welk Theater's** performance schedules include shows such as *Gotta Sing! Gotta Dance!, George M!, Mame,* and *A Welk Musical Christmas.* For a free look at memorabilia and a short lesson in television history, stop by the free **Lawrence Welk Museum** here. It's open daily 10:30 a.m.-5 p.m.

To get here: from I-15 northbound, exit at Deer Springs/Mountain Meadow Rd., turn right on Mountain Meadow, then left onto Champagne Boulevard. From I-15 southbound, exit at Gopher Canyon Rd., turn left (it becomes Old Castle Rd.), then right onto Champagne Boulevard.

---

award-winning red and white wines from its more famous Napa Valley winery. (Try the cabernet.) Also here are a great deli/gourmet market and very pleasant picnic area. Fun for the kids, too, is Deer Park's auto museum—spread throughout various buildings—which includes the world's largest collection of convertibles. Deer Park also displays an amazing antique radio and television collection. To take home some classic Americana, head for the gift shop. One-hour self-guided tours plus tasting are free; admission to the car museum is $6 adults, $4 seniors 55 and older, free for children under age 12. Deer Park is open daily 10 a.m.-5 p.m., until 6 p.m. in summer, closed Thanksgiving, Christmas, and New Year's Day.

The **Ferrara Winery,** 1120 W. 15th Ave. in Escondido, tel. (760) 745-7632, is a favorite wine stop. In honor of San Diego County's oldest winemaking and grape-growing family, the Ferrara enterprise has been designated a state historical point of interest. Of particular interest to travelers: the wonderful red wines, white wines, dry wines, and dessert wines. The tasting room also features fresh grape juice, wine marinades, and wine vinegars. All Ferrara grape products are crushed, aged and/or brewed, bottled, and sold only on the premises. Self-guided tours (15-20 minutes) and wine tasting are free. The tasting room is open daily 10 a.m.-5 p.m., closed Christmas Day. To get here: From I-15 exit east at Ninth Ave., turn south onto Upas, then west onto 15th.

Orfila Vineyards and Winery, 13455 San Pasqual Rd., toll-free tel. (800) 868-9463 or (760) 738-6500, orfila.com, formerly Thomas Jaeger Vineyards, is a popular stop on Gray Line and other organized tours. Orfila's wine specialties include cabernet, merlot, chardonnay, and tawny port. The very pleasant picnic area here, overlooking vineyards and valley, is the site of many weddings and other celebrations. Custom gift baskets are available at the gift shop. Tours and tastings are free for individuals; for groups (fee) reservations are required. Orfila's is open daily 10 a.m.-6 p.m. One guided tour is offered daily, at 2 p.m., but visitors can take the self-guided tour any time. The winery is closed Thanksgiving, Christmas, and New Year's Day. To get here: exit I-15 at Via Rancho Parkway. Follow the signs toward the San Diego Wild Animal Park, but turn right onto Pasqual Valley Rd. and continue one mile.

The **Bernardo Winery,** 13330 Paseo del Verano Norte, south of Escondido in the Rancho San Bernardo area, tel. (858) 487-1866, www.bernardowinery.com, is one of the oldest continuously operating wineries in Southern California. The wine-tasting room, something of a general store, also features gourmet foods, olive oil, and private-label wines. Self-guided winery tours take about 10 minutes. Lunch is served in the patio dining room daily (except Monday) 11 a.m.-3 p.m. The wine-tasting room is open daily 9 a.m.-5 p.m., gift shops 10 a.m.-5 p.m. (shops closed Monday), and closed major holidays. To get here from I-15: exit at Rancho Bernardo Rd., turn north onto Pomerado Rd., then east onto Paseo del Verano Norte (just past the Oaks North Golf Club). Continue for one-and-a-half miles.

Palomar Mountain State Park
This mile-high park at the edge of the Cleveland National Forest offers a refreshing pine-scented change from the scrubbier foothills below. Aside from the fine conifers and oaks, the park's easy hikes, meadows, fishing pond, great campground, and just general remoteness are its main attractions. Visitors ascend from Highway 76 east of Pauma Valley via the "Highway to the Stars" (County Rd. S6), built for access to the famous Mount Palomar Observatory, which is just east of the park. The park is open for day use, sunrise to sunset, $5 per car. Campsites are $14. Call for current reservation information. For more information, contact regional park headquarters: Cuyamaca Rancho State Park, 12551 State Highway 79, Descanso, tel. (760) 765-0755, look up www.cuyamaca.statepark.org, or call the park directly at (760) 742-3462 (sometimes a recorded information message).

Mount Palomar Observatory
Something of a reluctant tourist attraction, the world-famous Mount Palomar Observatory was built in 1928 to take astronomical advantage of its elevation (6,100 feet), distance from coastal fog, and absence of urban light pollution. No longer boasting the world's largest reflecting telescope, this is still a serious research facility of the California Institute of Technology (Cal Tech) in Pasadena. Visitors can view the 200-inch Hale Telescope and study deep-space photos and other memorabilia. The observatory, tel. (760)

742-2119, astro.caltech.edu/observatories/palomar/, is open daily 9 a.m.-4 p.m.

For more excitement, consider taking the **Palomar Plunge,** the lazy person's observatory tour and cycling adventure—all downhill from Mount Palomar. The half-day trek costs $75 per person, including lunch at *the* place to eat on the mountain, the vegetarian **Mother's Kitchen.** If you're not camping, the place to stay in these parts is the **Lazy H Ranch,** down the mountain in Pauma Valley, tel. (760) 742-3669. For more information, contact: **Gravity Activated Sports,** 16220 Hwy. 76, P.O. Box 683, Pauma Valley, www.gasports.com, toll-free tel. (800) 985-4427.

Staying and Eating in the Escondido Area
Among inexpensive area stays: **Super 8,** 526 W. Washington Ave. (just west of Centre City Pkwy.), tel. (760) 747-3711. Inexpensive ($45s, $55d), and **Motel 6** off the parkway at 900 N. Quince St. (at Mission), tel. (760) 745-9252, $52 s/d. Inexpensive. The very nice **Best Western Escondido,** 1700 Seven Oakes Rd. east of I-15 (exit at El Norte Pkwy.), tel. (760) 740-1700, is a very good value, with rooms $79 and up. Expensive-Premium.

The undisputed star of local lodgings is south of town in the Rancho Bernardo area—the **Rancho Bernardo Inn,** 17550 Bernardo Oaks Dr., San Diego, toll-free tel. (800) 439-7529 or (858) 675-8500, www.jcresorts.com, 265 acres of exquisite tile-roofed rooms, two restaurants, and exceptional resort facilities including a total of 108 holes of golf (45 on site), tennis college, health spa, two swimming pools, rental bikes, the works. Luxury. Rates are $239 and up. If that's too rich for you, Rancho Bernardo boasts many other nice motels and hotels, most quite reasonably priced.

If you're in a hurry, fast fooderies abound. If you're freeway flyin', other choices concentrate along Centre City Pkwy., the I-15 business loop, including the **Fireside Grill & Deli,** tel. (760) 745-1931, for steaks and such, and **The Brigantine,** tel. (760) 743-4718, for seafood.

If you're looking for finer fare, **Sirino's,** 113 W. Grand Ave. (at Broadway), tel. (760) 745-3835, is locally famous for its French classics, quite the find in downtown Escondido. Nowadays Sirino's also offers Italian-style fare: pizzas, pastas, and salads perfect for a lighter meal. Whether you go Italian or French at dinner, be sure to leave room for delectable dessert. It's open for dinner Tues.-Sat., closed major holidays. Also quite good, just across the street, is

150 Grand (fortunately, at 150 W. Grand), tel. (760) 738-6868.

The regional fine dining destination, though, is the elegant French **El Bizcocho** at the Rancho Bernardo Inn (see above), tel. (858) 675-8500.

SAN DIEGO

SAN DIEGO AS DISCOVERY

Captain Juan Rodríguez Cabrillo stepped out onto Point Loma, the tip of what is now San Diego Bay, and claimed the territory for Spain in 1542. His footfall has echoed through contemporary time as California's first and original point of discovery.

The U.S. military discovered San Diego earlier this century and settled in for a long stay, drawn by the area's sublime weather, its fine natural port, and its high-flying wide open spaces.

Despite its straitlaced military tradition, San Diego is no longer a simple social montage of battleship gray and camouflage green, no longer a predictable bastion of conservatism. New people, new high-tech industries, and new ideas have moved in.

Visitors to San Diego discover, and rediscover, a salubrious endless summer of beaches and balmy breezes along with world-class enclaves of culture and equally surprising moderate prices. They discover San Diego's relaxed, casual approach to day-to-day life and find that, here, just about anyone can feel comfortable. The oldest city in California and the state's second largest, San Diego somehow still retains a simpler, small-town sensibility—beyond the freeway traffic, that is.

THE LAY OF THE LAND

Though first-time visitors may see little beyond the harbor and the white-sand beaches of San Diego the city, San Diego the county offers much, much more in terms of diverse land forms. Almost one-third of San Diego County is publicly owned and accessible to the public, including 802-square-mile Anza-Borrego Desert State Park, an additional 700-plus square miles of federal land within Cleveland National Forest and federal Bureau of Land Management (BLM) preserves, and numerous county and city parks. Not open to the public but invaluable for creating de facto wildlife sanctuaries and "corridors" on the fringes of urban Southern California is the vast acreage included within U.S. military bases, most notably Camp Pendleton in northern San Diego County.

Inland, or eastward, from the ocean and the beaches, the San Diego landscape becomes one of lowlands and valleys—with the area's only truly "Mediterranean" climate—flanked by the western foothills of the north-south-trending Peninsular Ranges. Most of the county is included, geographically speaking, within the hilly and mountainous Peninsular Range, which reaches to just above 6,000 feet in elevation. The range's eastern slope is high desert, rapidly descending toward the low desert of the Salton Sea and surrounding sink.

San Diego's "Perfect" Climate

Just about everyone in San Diego will tell you the climate here is perfect. And so it usually is, if perfection is measured in the 60-70° F range in summer, in the mid-40s to mid-60s in winter. In late summer and fall, however, "Santa Anas" sometimes blow in-several-day events created by inland high pressure; in a reversal of the usual weather pattern, with winds blowing east, or inland, from the cool, moist coastal plain, desiccated desert winds blow west to the ocean. During strong Santa Ana conditions heat-wave mirages shimmer up and down the coastline, with temperatures reaching 100° F or higher; inland, grassland and wilderness wildfire danger becomes extreme. Milder Santa Anas, however, chase away the coastal fog and create wonderful dry weather and temperatures in the mid-80s, often sublime in October and November. What little rainfall there is along the coast and in the foothills—an average of 10-15 inches in a typical year—falls primarily from December into March.

Farther inland, the climate becomes somewhat less predictable. Mild temperatures and low rainfall predominate throughout the foothills in most years, but atop higher Peninsular Range peaks—including Cuyamaca, Laguna, and Palomar—expect cool summer temperatures and substantially more rain, even some snow, in winter. The high-desert climate just beyond the mountains is hot in summer yet cool, sometimes quite cold, in winter. Farther east the low desert begins—an environment isolated from the moderating effects of the ocean, with 100-plus summertime temperatures and mild winters. Though desert rainfall is typically negligible, in some years an astonishingly intense *chabusco* or tropical storm will dump as much as 10-16 inches of rain in a single day.

THE SAN DIEGO STORY

The first known San Diego residents, called the Diegueños by the Spanish, populated the area for thousands of years before European settlement. The Ipai people living north of the San Diego River and the Tapai people to the south shared a linguistic heritage with the Yuma. Foragers who relied on the abundance of the land—particularly the acorn harvest from oak groves and other plantlife—the Ipai and Tapai also ate fish, shellfish, and small mammals. They made pottery, unusual in California, for storing both water and food. Well-developed arts included abstract rock art painting, sand painting, and ceramic etching.

Yet the characteristic most noted by the Spanish, in the words of California's first Spanish governor, Pedro Fages, was a "natural and crusty pride," an attitude "absolutely opposed to all rational subjection and full of the spirit of independence." Some historians suggest that if the Ipai and Tapai had possessed any semblance of organized social structure, their resistance to the Spanish *conquistadores* might have succeeded—and might have sent the first explorers packing. Settlement deterred might have meant settlement denied, or at least delayed long enough for England or France to claim California and otherwise radically alter the march of modern history across the New World's western landscape.

Foothold for a Spanish California

Though they repeatedly attacked the local mission and other Spanish outposts, the Diegueños did not succeed in their insurrections. So, officially, California was discovered by Spain. Hernán Cortés spotted the land he called California in 1535, but it was Captain Juan Rodríguez Cabrillo—actually a Portuguese named João Rodrigues Cabrilho—who first sailed the California coast, in search of the mythic Straits of Anian, or the Northwest Passage, to the Spice Islands. On September 28, 1542, Cabrillo stepped out onto "The Point of California," present-day Point Loma, and named the harbor it protected San Miguel, after Saint Michael. Then, on November 10, 1602, the more adequately equipped Sebastián Vizcaíno arrived. He declared Cabrillo's records too sketchy to positively identify the area (and other areas), and two days later, on the feast day of Franciscan San Diego de Acalá, he renamed the bay after the saint and, perhaps incidentally, after his own flagship, the *San Diego*.

Settling Into Spanish California

It would be 167 years before the Spanish returned to San Diego, spurred by the territorial threat of Russians moving south from Alaska. Fearing that the Russian fur traders and settlers might soon control California's harbors, endangering Spain's hold on Mexico, King Charles insisted that royal forces move north from their Mexican bases to formally take possession of—to colonize—California, an enterprise called "The Sacred Expedition of 1769."

Five expedition parties set out, two by land and three by sea. The seafarers fared the worst. One ship never arrived, and the crews of those that did were decimated by scurvy and other diseases. The first overland party set up its bivouac—and de facto hospital for the sickened sailors they found by the bay—in what is now Old Town, thereby locating the city. The second overland party, led by Gaspár de Portolá, commander of the colonization forces and California's first governor, arrived in late June.

California's First Mission and First City

The ceremonial establishment of San Diego as Spanish colony came on July 16, 1769, when the assembled multitudes ascended the hill above their encampment. The first official European foothold in California, this "Plymouth

Rock of the West Coast" was chosen as the site for both California's first mission and its associated military presidio for its commanding views of the valley and the bay. After a solemn mass Father Junípero Serra, the "father president" of California's not-yet-founded mission chain, dedicated the site to the glory of God.

But because of the poor quality of surrounding soils, the mission failed to thrive. The Diegueño people were considered so dangerous that no one was allowed to leave the walled presidio compound surrounding the mission for any purpose without an armed military escort. Native peoples distrusted the military in equal measure, making it difficult for missionaries to attract neophytes—the workforce necessary for both the agricultural success and cultural transformation (some would say genocide) central to California mission society. So in 1774 the mission relocated about five miles up the valley—disastrously, at first, since the unprotected, unfinished mission was soon attacked and burned by 400 or so Diegueño. Things had settled down considerably by 1777, when the new mission complex was consecrated. It soon flourished, with olive, date, and pear orchards, lush gardens, vineyards, and vast herds of sheep, cattle, and horses. Mission life was good, and fairly uneventful—at least until 1812, when a powerful earthquake shattered the mission church. The modern Mission San Diego owes much of its present appearance to the reconstruction work of 1813.

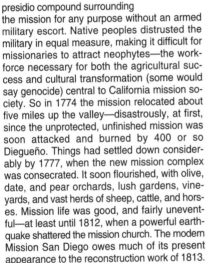

The Mission San Diego de Acalá was California's first.

A Sleepy Spanish, Mexican, and American City

Though San Diego was the first Spanish settlement in California, it wasn't the most influential. Monterey to the north soon became California's capital city and cultural center. But after the Mexican revolution, San Diego gained new prestige as de facto capital of both Alta and Baja California because of the personal preference of the governor.

Under Mexican rule, mission days ended and the oft-romanticized era of the ranchos began,

supported by brisk Yankee trade for cattle hides, known as "California bank notes." When California was finally included within United States territory after 1848, San Diego barely noticed. With the world's attention focused on booming San Francisco and the Northern California gold rush, San Diego remained a solidly Mexican town, with fiestas and bullfights and other cultural traditions in full flower. U.S. sensibilities established themselves here quite slowly, aided by stagecoach and steamer and the eventual arrival of the railroad. Otherwise business boomed and busted, along with the rest of Southern California, into

HIGH-FLYING SAN DIEGO

The development of San Diego has been shaped more by its aerial history—commingled with U.S. military history—than by any other factor.

In the early days of aviation, the industry's pioneers took flight in San Diego to take full advantage of the superb flying weather. **Charles Lindbergh,** the first man to cross the Atlantic Ocean in an airplane, is perhaps the most famous of these fanatical fly boys. In 1927 Lindbergh commissioned San Diegan T. Claude Ryan to build a plane based on Ryan's M-1 design (with wings above the fuselage). Within months, after very few test flights, "Lucky Lindy" left San Diego in his *Spirit of St. Louis*—touching down only briefly on the East Coast before flying off into the history books.

The U.S. military has had a distinguished aerial history in San Diego as well, beginning with test flights made by Glen Curtiss from Coronado's **North Island Naval Station** in 1911. Special air shows and other public events are scheduled at North Island and—at least until its recent move east—at **Miramar Naval Air Station,** the real-life Top Gun, which preceded the movie of the same name.

To get up to speed on San Diego's high-flying history, visit the **San Diego Aerospace Museum** in Balboa Park.

WAR AT THE BORDER
IN A WORLD WITHOUT BORDERS

Globalization and "the global economy," those beloved buzzwords of international business, suggest that boundaries now have little meaning in matters of capital and commerce. This unfettered flow of finance, goods, and information, this brave new world without borders, clearly serves the interests of those who possess money, material wealth, and expertise—the winners of the globalization game in all nations. But in a world without economic borders, what becomes of the losers, the left-behind? Those displaced by the global economy seem doomed to wander across national borders, legally and otherwise, in search of work. In search of survival. Their fate is largely ignored by architects of the new one-world economy.

In California, the effects of immigration have reached phenomenal—some would say mythic—proportions. According to Rubén Martínez in "The Myth of Borders," published in 1996 by the L.A. Weekly: "There is no border; no matter how many walls and infrared goggles and moats and machine-gun turrets, there is no border—just history, and history is movement across the borders we imagine out of fear."

Yet just try telling that to most Californians—of all ethnicities—who increasingly feel beseiged by "foreigners" in their own communities and who are baffled, culturally and politically, by the challenges of coping with such immense social change.

According to the federal Immigration and Naturalization Service (INS), by early 1997 the national surge in immigration totaled 24.6 million people, or 9.3 percent of the total U.S. population, the highest proportion since the 1930s. And the number of illegal immigrants nationwide had again reached five million—an increase of about 28 percent in four years, nearly the same peak levels reached before the sweeping Immigration Reform and Control Act (IRCA) amnesty program of a decade earlier.

California absorbs a disproportionate share of immigrants, legal and illegal. The Golden State now absorbs more than half of all legal immigrants annually. At least two million undocumented immigrants live in California, a number increasing by 100,000 each year. In Los Angeles County at least 40 percent of the population is foreign-born (compared to 11 percent in 1970). Latinos alone now account for over 28 percent of all California residents, and are projected to reach 50 percent—representing the majority—by the year 2040. One in four Californians is foreign-born—more than eight million people—which is a simpler yet dramatic way to represent the impact of this new turn-of-the-century immigration boom on the Golden State.

Such is the statistical background for recent chapters in California political history that have earned banner headlines in newspapers nationwide—particularly the vitriolic political battle over Proposition 187, which denied public funding for education, health care, and other public services to illegal immigrants, and the surprisingly quick political backlash that removed Republican governor Pete Wilson from office and replaced him with a Democrat, Gray Davis.

San Diego has been ground zero in California for the federal government's long-running war against illegal border crossings from adjacent Mexico.

And in the war over illegal immigration and Proposition 187, no place in California was more furious in its political fisticuffs than San Diego, sister city to Tijuana, Mexico. Tired of heavy illegal immigrant foot traffic in middle-class neighborhoods and traffic-dodging on area freeways, illegal shantytowns alongside tony suburbs, and overcrowded public schools and hospitals, conservative San Diego lost its cool. Ex-Mayor Roger Hedgecock, a radio talk show host opposed to "opening the trough for the whole Third World," helped fan the flames: "Jesus never said, 'Fork over your taxes because the government is going to take care of everyone in the world.'" To the chagrin of even Prop 187 supporters, already a bit anxious over the measure's "police state" political potential, Republican state Sen. William Craven proposed special "identification cards" for Latinos. After his office was inundated by angry protests, Craven said he meant to suggest identification cards only for individuals seeking state services.

On the other side of the fence, figuratively and sometimes literally, were anti-Prop 187 forces, including the Catholic church, college students, community activists, and the city of Tijuana, Mexico. The Tijuana City Council officially declared Gov. Pete Wilson unwelcome in its town. Tijuana newspapers promoted a weekend boycott of San Diego busi_{nesses}—underscoring just how economically interconnected the two cities, and the two nations, actually are. (The commerce issue did get some local attention, even among Prop 187 supporters; according to the Greater San Diego Chamber of Commerce, cross-border commerce generates about $2 billion a year for San Diego.) And protesting students marched into an anti-Prop 187 rally dressed as pilgrims to propose a "Mayflower Amendment" to send all European-Americans "back to Europe."

The fact is, immigration from Mexico to "El Norte" has gone on for so long—to the great benefit of California business, ever voracious for inexpensive labor—that in some regions of Mexico, particularly the impoverished north and west, the journey is now both a presumed right and rite of passage.

Disregarding the territorial claims of native peoples, in the beginning California and the rest of the U.S. Southwest *was* Mexico, the spoils of Mexico's war for independence from Spain. Though the new nation of Mexico inhabited the territory for just two decades, the "Californio" culture on both sides of what is now the U.S.-Mexican border had flourished for multiple generations. In that sense Mexican nationals and pro-immigrant activists are correct when they contend that "Anglos," a term generally referring to present-day white citizens of the U.S., illegally invaded the territory. The ultimate result of the Mexican-American War waged between 1846 and 1848 was little more than a government-funded land grab—a touchy subject in U.S.-Mexico relations to this day.

The historical argument is generally a hard sell on this side of the border, though, particularly in areas—like San Diego—inundated by illegal immigrants.

Yet legally and otherwise, these days Mexico is coming home to California. And despite endless rhetoric and get-tough federal legislation to the contrary, the U.S. government has no real desire to end illegal immigration, and actually "protects the traffic in cheap Mexican labor," argues Wade Graham in the July 1996 *Harper's* article, "Masters of the Game." The reasons, he says, "are as old as our century-long thirst for cheap labor and as recent as today's currency-market fluctuations."

The truth about illegal immigration, Graham says, is that "until such time as U.S. law barring the employment of illegal aliens is enforced—or U.S. wages drop below those of the Third World—poor foreigners will continue to come here" because politicians have "neither the political security nor the will to alter this fact."

In other words, there will continue to be war at the border in this odd new world without borders. But as things stand, that war will never be won.

---

the 20th century. In 1900, the population of the entire county was 15,000.

The American Military Moves In

San Diego's presence as a major American city coincided with the arrival of the U.S. military, the Navy in particular. The Navy's Pacific Fleet, based in National City, has long been at home on San Diego Bay. The modern military presence began almost unnoticeably, however, with the humble U.S. Naval Coaling Station built in 1907 on the bay side of Point Loma. San Diego's now-famous aircraft and aerospace industries, largely related to defense, started in 1917, with the World War I-era establishment of the North Island U.S. Naval Air Station on Coronado Island—the air base that served as the actual starting point of Charles Lindbergh's famous transatlantic solo flight in 1927. More famous in modern times, the Miramar Naval Air Station just north of San Diego inspired the macho-guy-in-the-sky movie *Top Gun*. Though there have been other cutbacks and changes, San Diego's most dramatic post-Cold War downsizing denouement came in 1996, when the Navy's Top Gun school moved to Fallon, Nevada, and Miramar became a Marine base. Camp Pendleton, once a Mexican rancho, more recently a U.S. Marine base, still dominates northern San Diego County.

Everyone Else Arrives— Legally and Otherwise

Throughout World War II the local tuna industry was an economic mainstay. In 1950 San Diego was the top fishing port in the U.S., producing about $30 million in fish. By 1960, because of stiff competition from Japanese and South American fishing fleets, that chapter in San Diego history was all but over. Maritime markets soon sailed in new directions, however, with increases in port exporting and shipbuilding.

After World War II the aircraft and defense industries also took off, the latter fueled by generous federal government funding. Until economic diversification began, fairly recently, almost 80 percent of local income was derived from defense, both directly and indirectly.

Scientific and technological research facilities also benefited, at least by regional association, along with high-tech industry and academic institutions. But the intelligentsia here is not entirely dedicated to military and industrial pursuits. La Jolla, for example, hosts the internationally renowned Salk Institute and the University of California at San Diego, with its famed Scripps Institution of Oceanography.

Retirees and tourists—both drawn by the sun, the sand, the sea, and the sublime weather—also have a notable presence in and around San Diego.

Not everything is copacetic in San Diego these days, however, and not everyone is welcome. California's current war against illegal immigrants who cross the border from Mexico is fought quite fiercely here—a fact that at first seems ironic, considering San Diego's Spanish and Mexican roots, and odd, considering the community's long-cherished "sister city" relationship with Tijuana, Mexico. Illegal immigration has always occurred here to some degree, yet in recent years San Diego has been literally and figuratively overrun—though that trend has slowed some as the immigrant war has been pushed inland by more successful deterrence here. Residents have been frightened by strangers creeping through their backyards at night, and outraged by "birthing clinics" along the U.S.-Mexico border that cater to women who want their children born as U.S. citizens. And they still fear the increase in wildfires sparked by immigrants' campfires in the tinder-dry back country.

SEEING AND DOING SAN DIEGO

As predictable as the ocean tides, tourists tend to flow toward San Diego's major attractions: Sea World, the San Diego Zoo, and, in the north county, the San Diego Wild Animal Park. But San Diego—the sunny city, the county, and the endless sky and seashore—reveals its deeper nature only to those who take time to explore its neighborhoods and less advertised attractions.

Downtown's brightest light is Balboa Park, home of the San Diego Zoo and the most impressive concentration of world-class museums in any California city. Though new freeway interchanges make it more difficult to connect with the rest of downtown, the effort is worth it. The modern downtown mainstay is Horton Plaza, a stunning and stylish shopping mall disguised as a virtual city. Adjacent is San Diego's Gaslamp District, its Victorian buildings newly gussied-up and glittering with shops, restaurants, and nightlife.

Along the bay is the Embarcadero, offering a quick visual cruise of the city's maritime heart and military soul. Across the bay, reached by ferry or bridge, is Coronado, home of the historic Hotel Del Coronado, the North Island Naval Station, and neighborhoods of military retirees. Look for some astounding public art and the largely Latino Barrio Logan on the way to Coronado and in the shadow of the soaring San Diego-Coronado Bay Bridge.

Head uptown to Old Town San Diego, a state historic park where shopping and fairly commercial diversions attract most visitor interest. Technically, though, "uptown" is centered along Washington Street in artsy Hillcrest (from First to Fifth Streets), a San Diego version of San Francisco's Castro Street; eventually Washington becomes Adams Avenue, "Antiques Row." Also worth exploring: the India Street Art Colony near Washington Street and "Little Italy," along India just north of Date Street. The Linda Vista and North Park neighborhoods, not far away, are home to San Diego's large Asian communities and to many of the city's most authentic (and least expensive) Asian restaurants.

Along the coast are San Diego's beach communities, from Ocean Beach, Mission Beach, and Pacific Beach to the distinct, and distinctly affluent, La Jolla and nearby Del Mar—all included within San Diego city limits.

BALBOA PARK

BALBOA BACKGROUND AND FOREGROUND

San Diego's cultural heart and soul, home to its renowned zoo, magnificent museums, and much of the city's thriving theater program, Balboa Park is also an architectural and horticultural masterpiece. Unimaginatively known as City Park when its original 1,400 acres of chaparral and scrub brush were set aside by the city in 1868, Balboa Park began to develop its Spanish colonial revival character in preparation for the 1915-1917 Panama-California International Exposition, a massive cultural coming-out party sponsored by the city to celebrate the completion of the Panama Canal.

The elaborate exuberance of the original buildings, intended to be temporary, can be credited to New York architect Bertram G. Goodhue, who personally designed the Fine Arts Building, the California State Building (now the Museum of Man), and the Cabrillo Bridge along El Prado—the formal entrance into the park's beaux arts center. Goodhue also set the stage for other architects.

With the arrival of World War I and San Diego's sudden centrality to the war effort, the exhibition buildings were conscripted for service. In the 1920s, as the military settled into permanent San Diego quarters, the city wisely established the precedent that makes present-day Balboa Park possible—donating the exposition buildings to various nonprofit cultural institutions.

The development of Balboa Park's cultural center continued with construction of the 1935 California-Pacific International Exposition, which added still more buildings, these by architect Richard Requa, with Aztec, Mayan, and Southwestern motifs.

Balboa Park Overview

San Diego's huge central park is lush and inviting, perfect for picnics and aimless ambling. Yet it's almost impossible to *be* aimless, given Balboa Park's astonishing array of attractions. Most visitors start at the San Diego Zoo, at the north end of the park just off Park Boulevard; the zoo can easily become a daylong adventure. Between the zoo and El Prado is the Spanish Village Art Center, tel. (619) 233-9050, studio space for artists and artisans who also sell their wares

PRACTICAL BALBOA PARK

If at all possible, spend at least two full days in Balboa Park. Entering the park is free, but the majority of its attractions—the zoo, most museums, the theater program—charge admission. The most economical option for touring the museums, typically, is the multiple-museum ticket—at last report, including admission to nine museums, $25—which is usually a bargain even if you won't be seeing them all. Most museums also offer a "free Tuesday" once each month, with some free on the first Tuesday of the month, others free on the second Tuesday, and so forth. Most museums are open daily from 10 a.m. to at least 4 p.m., but schedules can vary throughout the year; if your time in town is tight, call ahead to verify hours.

For more detailed information on the zoo, museums, and major attractions, see the listings below. For additional information on the park and its current programs and events, contact the very helpful **Balboa Park Information Center** in Balboa Park, inside the House of Hospitality at 1549 El Prado, San Diego, tel. (619) 239-0512, open daily 9 a.m.-4 p.m.

If you're coming by car, the traditional entrance to Balboa Park is from downtown, heading east via Laurel St. and over the Laurel Street Bridge (the Cabrillo Bridge) spanning Hwy. 163. Once over the bridge, the street becomes El Prado, which soon becomes the park's primary pedestrian mall. Parking is a particular challenge on summer weekends, so come early in the day; you'll discover that the first lot, at Plaza de Panama, is almost always full. Continue south to find others. The other main route into the park, much more convenient if the zoo is your first or primary destination, is via Park Boulevard. From Hwy. 163, exit at Park Blvd.; from I-5, exit at Pershing Dr. and follow the signs.

(open daily 11 a.m.-4 p.m., free). At the eastern end of El Prado begins Balboa Park's endless parade of museums. Fairly new ones, such as the Reuben H. Fleet Space Theater and Science Center, tel. (619) 233-1233, and the Museum of Photographic Arts, tel. (619) 238-7559, stand beside longtime favorites, including the San Diego Natural History Museum, tel. (619) 232-3821, the San Diego Museum of Art, tel. (619) 232-7931, and the Museum of Man, tel. (619) 239-2001. Adjacent and just north, along Old Globe Way, is the rebuilt Old Globe Theatre—the original Shakespearean venue was torched in a 1978 arson fire—and the other two theaters of the Simon Edison Centre for the Performing Arts, tel. (619) 239-2255. Another don't-miss destination: the 1915 Botanical Building, tel. (619) 239-0512, with its lotus pond and impressive collection of tropical and subtropical plants.

Attractions south of El Prado include the Japanese Friendship Garden, tel. (619) 239-0512, and the Spreckels Organ Pavilion with its 1914 Spreckels Organ featuring 4,445 pipes or 72 ranks, tel. (619) 236-5717. (Free concerts are offered year-round on Sunday afternoons at 2 p.m. and, in July and August, on Monday evenings at 8 p.m.) Still more museums farther south include the San Diego Automotive Museum, tel. (619) 231-2886, and the excellent San Diego Aerospace Museum, tel. (619) 234-8291, as well as the Centro Cultural de la Raza, tel. (619) 235-6135, "the people's cultural center."

ALONG EL PRADO

Reuben H. Fleet
Space Theater and Science Center

Two blocks south of the zoo at 1875 El Prado, just off Park Boulevard near the fountain in Plaza de Balboa, the Reuben H. Fleet Space Theater and Science Center is ever-popular—especially with more precocious kids. The main attraction here is the Omnimax theater, the world's first, which projects movies through a fish-eye lens onto the 76-foot Imax tilted dome. The space theater premieres you-could-be-there space, science, art, nature, and exploration films such as *Eyes on the Universe* and *Titanica*. (Save your neck from cyberstrain by sitting in the back.) Fun even for adults is the 9,500-square-foot sci-

ence center, with dozens of well-done interactive and hands-on exhibits—such as Chinese resonant bowls and the Bernoulli Effect beachball. Don't miss the gift shop, with an unusually good selection of books, games, and toys.

Theater admission varies, depending on the movie, but is typically $6.50-11 for adults, $5.50-9 for seniors, and $5-8 for children ages 5-15. Center admission is free on the first Tuesday of every month, otherwise it's $6.50 adults, $5 for kids. The center is open Monday and Tuesday 9:30 a.m.-5 p.m.; Wednesday, Thursday, and Sunday 9:30 a.m.-7 p.m.; and Friday and Saturday 9:30 a.m.-9 p.m. For current movie and other information, call (619) 233-1233, or look up www.rhfleet.org.

San Diego Natural History Museum

This imposing museum at 1788 El Prado chronicles the earth's wonders, among them shore ecology, seismography, and local gemstones. Of the "all natural ingredients" on exhibit, kids most savor the live insect displays along with the dinosaur skeletons and other fossils. And just inside the main entrance, swinging from a 43-foot cable, the museum's Foucault Pendulum verifies that the planet is, in fact, rotating on its axis. Special traveling exhibits, films, lectures, and nature outings—including winter whalewatching tours—are also big draws.

Museum admission is $7 adults, $6 seniors and active military, $5 children ages 6-17, free on the first Tuesday of every month. Hours sometimes vary, but the museum is typically open daily 9:30 a.m.-4:30 p.m., closed on Thanksgiving, Christmas, and New Year's Day. The San Diego Natural History Museum is located near the fountain in Plaza de Balboa, just south of the San Diego Zoo and Village Place off Park Boulevard. For more information, call (619) 232-3821, or check out www.sdnhm.org.

Museum of Photographic Arts

The Museum of Photographic Arts inside the Casa de Balboa, 1649 El Prado, focuses on both photography as art and the history of photographic arts—showcasing the works of well-known photographers such as Ansel Adams, Edward Weston, and Henri Cartier-Bresson along with those of newer artists. The museum sponsors six to eight special gallery exhibits each year, such as **New York, New York** and **Robert Frank: The Americans,** and a series on marriage, **The Model Wife.** Don't miss the museum store, with fine prints, posters, calendars, cards, and the largest selection of photography books in the western U.S. Admission is $6, free for museum members and children under age 12 accompanied by an adult. It's open daily 10 a.m.-5 p.m., closed on major holidays. For current and upcoming shows and other information, call (619) 238-7559, or check out www.mopa.org.

Museum of San Diego History

Another prominent resident of Casa de Balboa at 1649 El Prado, the history museum features rotating thematic exhibits from the San Diego Historical Society's permanent collection plus national traveling exhibits—almost always something of interest, even for the kids. Also take time to take in at least one of the historical society's other local outposts—the **Junípero Serra Museum** in Old Town, for example, or the marvelous **Villa Montezuma/Jesse Shepard House** near the Gaslamp Quarter. The Museum of San Diego History is open Tues.-Sun. 10 a.m.-4:30 p.m., closed Thanksgiving, Christmas, and New Year's Day. Admission is free on the second Tuesday of every month, otherwise $5 for adults; $4 for seniors, students, and active military; and $2 for children ages 6-17. For more information, call (619) 232-6203.

San Diego Model Railroad Museum

Down in the Casa de Balboa basement at 1649 El Prado is the San Diego Model Railroad Museum, boasting the world's largest collection of mini-gauge trains—paradise for toy train lovers. Six separate, and intricate, scale-model exhibits, including the bustling Southern Pacific/Santa Fe route over Tehachapi Pass, come complete with sound effects: bells, whistles, and screeching brakes. With any luck, maybe one of the museum's train buffs will hand over the controls. The museum is open Tues.-Fri.—and the first Tuesday of every month, when admission is free—11 a.m.-4 p.m., and on Saturday and Sunday 11 a.m.-5 p.m. Admission is free for children under age 15, otherwise $4 adults, $3 for students, seniors, and active military. For more information, call (619) 696-0199 or check out www.sdmodelrailroadm.com.

Casa de Balboa's **San Diego Hall of Champions Sports Museum,** tel. (619) 234-2544, is worth a stop for sports fans particularly interested in local heroes.

FINDING SAN DIEGO'S LATINO HERITAGE

Given the city's Spanish and Mexican cultural roots, San Diego's Latino community is not as visible to visitors as one might expect. The city's phenomenal growth in this century has been fueled primarily by crew-cut U.S. military crews and socially conservative retirees, after all, and most recently by high-tech corporados. The contributions of even San Diego's earliest "Californio" families, rooted here since early mission days, somehow got lost in the fray—including heated community response in recent years to increased illegal immigration from Mexico, San Diego's neighbor to the south. But local appreciation of Latino arts and cultures is increasing. Come in September, for example, for the month-long **Mexican Cultural Festival.**

One San Diego arts icon—now threatened by proposed freeway expansion and reconstruction plans—is **Chicano Park** beneath the San Diego-Coronado Bay Bridge in Barrio Logan. The park is primarily composed of vivid, larger-than-life murals contributed by artists from throughout California, spectacular public art "displayed" on the bridge's concrete supports.

More accessible for most visitors, however, is **El Centro Cultural de la Raza**—"The People's Cultural Center"—in San Diego's Balboa Park, regularly open Wed.-Sun. noon-5 p.m. (free) and at other times for special events. This onetime water tower, a gallery in the round since the 1960s, originally showcased Chicano, or Mexican-American, art as well as theater, dance, and literary productions. In recent years El Centro's focus has expanded to include other Central, South, and Native American cultures. Typically political, El Centro's art exhibits have earned national and international acclaim. An outgrowth of El Centro is the **Border Arts Workshop,** sponsoring art, drama, and music collaborations in venues on both sides of the U.S.-Mexico border.

San Diego Museum of Art

On the park's Plaza de Panama at 1450 El Prado, the San Diego Museum of Art is best known for its European Renaissance and Baroque paintings, including works by Goya, El Greco, Rubens, and Van Ruisdale. The collection also includes Dali, Matisse, O'Keeffe, and Toulouse-Lautrec. The cutting-edge contemporary California art in the Frederick R. Weisman Gallery alone is well worth the trip. If the kids are more experienced with computer manipulation than art appreciation, seize the opportunity to expand their horizons—by starting them off at the museum's interactive computer "gallery," the first system of its kind in the U.S. Another draw here is the sculpture garden and, for lunch, the **Sculpture Garden Cafe.**

Regular admission is $8 adults; $6 seniors, active military, and students (with ID); $3 children ages 6-17. Free admission on the third Tuesday of every month. It's open Tues.-Sun 10 a.m.-4:30 p.m. For current exhibits and other information, call (619) 232-7931 or check www.sdmart.com.

Timken Museum of Art

Just east of the San Diego Museum of Art at 1500 El Prado, near the Lotus Pond, is the Timken Museum of Art, at home in an attractive building that is Balboa Park's most noticeable architectural anomaly. The collection here is intriguing, dominated by lesser-known works of significant 18th- and 19th-century artists from both Europe and America. It's open Tues.-Sat. 10 a.m.-4:30 p.m., Sunday 1:30-4:30 p.m., closed Monday and the month of September. Admission is free, with free guided tours offered Tues.-Thurs. 10 a.m.-noon. For more information call (619) 239-5548 during regular museum hours.

Mingei International Museum of World Folk Art

After two distinguished decades in La Jolla, the marvelous Mingei Museum—where the "art of the people, by the people, and for the people comes to the people"—has made its permanent home in Balboa Park's remodeled House of Charm at 1439 El Prado since the summer of 1996, an arrangement offering six times the museum's original space. Over the years the changing exhibits here have included **Folk Toys of the World, Wearable Folk Art,** and **Kindred**

Spirits: The Eloquence of Function in American Shaker and Japanese Arts of Daily Life. Call for current exhibit information.

The House of Charm sits on the southwestern corner of the Plaza de Panama. At last report the Mingei was open Tues.-Sun. 10 a.m.-4 p.m., closed on all national holidays. Admission is $5 adults, $2 children. For more information, call (619) 239-0003 or check www.mingei.org.

San Diego Museum of Man

The grand Museum of Man, west of the Plaza de Panama at 1350 El Prado, under the California Tower, is striking enough from the outside. The anthropological collection here, one of the finest in the country, made its debut during the 1915 Balboa Park exposition. Expanded and updated over the years, exhibits chronicle human development but emphasize Mexican, Native American (particularly Southwestern), and South American societies. Egyptian artifacts are among recent acquisitions. Equally intriguing, though, is the museum's **Lifestyles and Ceremonies** exhibit, reflecting the dazzling diversity of San Diego's own society.

The San Diego Museum of Man is open daily 10 a.m.-4:30 p.m., closed Thanksgiving, Christmas, and New Year's Day. Admission is $5 adults, $4.50 military and seniors, $3 children ages 6-17, free for children under age 6. It's free for everyone on the third Tuesday of every month. For current program and other information, call (619) 239-2001 or check www.museumofman.org.

BEYOND EL PRADO

San Diego Aerospace Museum and International Aerospace Hall of Fame

These days Balboa Park's exquisite art deco Ford Building—one of the finest remaining examples of its species in the United States, trimmed at night in blue neon—houses an equally impressive and artistic display of aeronautical history makers. Local history is represented by a replica of Charles Lindbergh's *Spirit of St. Louis,* and by a glider on loan from the National Air and Space Museum, first flown in 1883 near San Diego. Especially compelling: the ersatz aircraft carrier flight deck with its World War II-vintage planes. There's much more—about 70

exhibits and other information, call (619) 234-8291 or check www.aerospacemuseum.org.

San Diego Automotive Museum

Nearby, at 2080 Pan American Plaza, this was the Palace of Transportation during Balboa Park's 1935-36 exposition. Car-loving kids of all ages will enjoy this particular garage. About 80 classics and exotics—Hollywood's cars, roadsters, and an exceptional motorcycle collection—make up the permanent collection. Special shows and events—call for current program information—are often quite fun. The gift shop, with unusual and one-of-a-kind items, is a cornucopia for car fanatics.

The San Diego Automotive Museum is open daily 10 a.m.-4:30 p.m. (until 5:30 p.m. in summer), last admission one-half hour before closing. It's closed Thanksgiving, Christmas, and New Year's Day. Admission is free on the fourth Tuesday of every month, otherwise $7 adults, $6 seniors and active military, $3 children ages 6-15, free for children under 6. For current exhibits and other information, call (619) 231-2886 or check www.sdautomuseum.org.

SAN DIEGO ZOO

The world-class San Diego Zoo sprang from very humble beginnings. Its original animals were chosen from those left behind by the Panama-California International Exposition. Now famous for its large exotic and endangered animal population and its lush, complex tropical landscape, the 100-acre San Diego Zoo is immensely popular—the city's top visitor draw, attracting more than three million people each year.

Part of the zoo's appeal is the near absence of prison-bar-style cages and pens. Most animals here—the zoo refers to them as "captivating instead of captive"—are kept in naturally landscaped, moated enclosures, very large walk-through aviaries, and other fairly innovative environments. Rarities among the zoo's 4,000 animals (800 species) include Australian koalas, the first exhibited outside Australia, New Zealand long-billed kiwis, Sichuan takins from China, wild Mongolian or Przewalski's horses—forerunners of all domesticated horses—and Komodo dragons from Indonesia. Special "guest animals"

OLD GLOBE THEATRE AND FRIENDS

First there was San Diego's Old Globe Theatre; dramatic outdoor Shakespeare productions were its original claim to fame. Now joining the 581-seat Old Globe are two more theaters in Balboa Park's performing arts center—the 225-seat **Cassius Carter Centre Stage** and the 612-seat **Lowell Davies Festival Theatre.** The performance calendar for this major-league regional repertory is full almost year-round.

The Old Globe and fellow theaters are in Balboa Park, near the Museum of Man, and reached via Park Blvd. and Old Globe Way. The regular theater season runs from January into June. The **Old Globe Festival,** showcasing Shakespeare, other classics, and modern works, both indoors and out, officially runs from July into September but summer shows can—and usually do—extend through November. No performances are scheduled on major U.S. holidays.

Advance ticket purchases are recommended. Admission varies, in the $23-42 range. For prerecorded ticket information, call (619) 239-2255. For bargain same-day tickets to these and other area theaters, as well as to music and dance events, contact the **Times Arts Tix** ticket center at Horton Plaza, tel. (619) 497-5000, or check the San Diego Performing Arts League website at www.sandiegoperforms.com.

For more information, contact the **Old Globe Theatre,** tel. (619) 231-1941, www.oldglobe.org. Call for current performance schedule and box office hours.

aircraft, with displays arranged artfully and chronologically, accompanied by helpful historical and technical facts. The gift shop here is particularly worthwhile, since proceeds support the museum and its ongoing aircraft assembly and restoration projects.

The San Diego Aerospace Museum is in the southern section of Balboa Park at 2001 Pan American Plaza, most easily reached via Park Blvd. and then President's Way. Admission is free on the fourth Tuesday of the month, otherwise $8 adults, $6 seniors, $3 "juniors" ages 6-17, and free for children under 6 and active-duty military. It's open daily 10 a.m.-4:30 p.m., closed Thanksgiving and Christmas Day. For current

include two giant pandas on loan from the People's Republic of China, Shi Shi and Bai Yun, who gave birth to a cub, Hua Mei, on August 21, 1999. The San Diego Zoo also boasts the world's largest collection of parrots and parrotlike birds.

The natural habitats—the Polar Bear Plunge, Hippo Beach, Gorilla Tropics, Tiger River, Sun Bear Forest, Pygmy Chimps at Bonobo Road, African Kopje, and Australasia—are most impressive, designed as distinct "bioclimatic zones" with characteristic combinations of plant and animal species.

The San Diego Zoo is also noteworthy for its ongoing research, starting in 1916 with the Zoological Hospital and Biological Research Institute, now known as the Center for Reproduction of Endangered Species (CRES). More than 20 years old, CRES is dedicated to managing species survival—helping endangered and threatened species to mate and produce young successfully, in captivity and in their natural habitats. The California condor captive-breeding program, artificial insemination and other reproductive research, including the "Frozen Zoo" sperm, egg, and embryo bank, and ongoing disease prevention work, are among notable CRES accomplishments.

Since we're all on this big round spaceship together, research done at the San Diego Zoo to save individual animal species, no matter how obscure, may one day save us all.

Polar Bear Plunge
The Polar Bear Plunge is one of the largest polar bear exhibits in the world and a fairly complex arctic kingdom. Chillin' here with the bears are Siberian reindeer, arctic foxes, snowy owls, and a dozen other bird species. The polar bear pond here, near the Skyfari tram station at the zoo's western end, is actually an Olympic-sized pool. The two-level underwater viewing area, with a huge five-inch-thick acrylic window, and other viewing windows allow visitors to watch the bears play all day. In a necessary concession to climatic reality, the 50-plus species of plants integrated into the environment here are not tundra natives, though these immigrants from around the world look like summertime tundra plantlife.

Hippo Beach
Quite the spectacular splash since it opened in the summer of 1995, Hippo Beach is the zoo's hippopotamus habitat. The thrill here is being able to go nose-to-nose with Funani and Jabba—and to get a fish's-eye view of these two-ton herbivores and their astonishing underwater ballets—thanks to the 105-foot-long observation window that flanks the 150,000-gallon pool. The landscape, built to resemble an African marsh, is also home to several fish and bird species. Chances are the kids will be more impressed by the nearby pod of humanized hippos—Lifeguard Mitch, Kahuna Kevin, and Sally the Surfer among the happy hoofers here—sculpted of sand and coated with 30 gallons of Elmer's glue. More fascinating for most adults: the replica of the Egyptian "Tawaret" frieze, depicting the hippo goddess of fertility and child protection.

The zoo's polar bears bring a hint of the arctic to sunny San Diego.

SAN DIEGO ZOO

Tiger River

A complex Asian rainforest with computer-controlled misting and irrigation systems to simulate 100 inches of annual rainfall, Tiger River was the zoo's first bioclimatic undertaking. Starting near the zoo's Flamingo Lagoon, wander down the ersatz dry riverbed and into the canyon below under a canopy of fig, coral, and orchid trees, flowering ginger, palms, along with 400 other exotic species of bamboo, shrubs, and ferns. First you'll encounter a false gavial, a large crocodile relation, then the slithering ropes of pythons, then the web-footed fishing cats. The reeds and cattails in the marsh are home to pygmy geese, white-breasted kingfishers, and other rainforest birds. Next are the Malayan tapirs, piglike creatures related to both the horse and rhinoceros. Then comes the rainforest royalty, the kings and queens of cats, the tigers—allowed here to play in the ponds or just lounge around in the grass. Rare white tigers and Indochinese tigers alternate in this exhibit. What you won't see is the sophisticated behind-the-scenes scene developed for this aspect of the zoo's ongoing captive-breeding efforts.

Gorilla Tropics

The rainforest extends to Gorilla Tropics, wildly popular since it opened in 1991. The gorillas—four adults and three youngsters, at last count—are central, of course, happily settled onto a hillside planted with figs, bananas, and bamboo. (Here as elsewhere in the San Diego Zoo, the animals eat and otherwise fully enjoy their environment; forests of replacement plants are always on hand.) The jungle sounds, most notable here and throughout nearby aviaries, are provided by a compact disc system with 144 speakers, cleverly camouflaged throughout the landscape.

Scripps Aviary

Just as grand as the gorilla show is a slow stroll through this huge multilevel free-flight aviary, home to hundreds of exotic African birds, including jicanas and the rare Waldrapp ibis. The sound of thunder signals imminent "rain"—in this rainforest it's provided by misting pipes. To avoid other surprises from the sky, heads up. Smaller aviaries nearby shelter carmine bee-eaters, hornbills, and softbill species.

Pygmy Chimps at Bonobo Road

Not smaller than common chimpanzees yet equally entertaining, the pygmy chimps—also known as "bonobos" in their native Zaire—may be the zoo's most clownish characters, whether playing in the oddly twisted palm forest here or making funny faces at humans on the other side of the glass. These chimps, yet another seriously threatened species, are the first ever exhibited in a U.S. zoo. Also hereabouts are Angolan colobus monkeys and Garnett's galagos, or "bush babies," both arboreal or "treetop" species; rare African crowned eagles, current captive-breeding candidates; and a baboon spider, Africa's largest tarantula.

Sun Bear Forest

In the zoo's central canyon, this ersatz corner of Malaysia is home to playful Malayan sun bears—long-clawed, pigeon-toed tree dwellers that could instead be "moon bears," since the striking gold on their chests is crescent-shaped. The smallest bears in the world, sun bears are hardly cuddly teddy-bear types. Zoologists consider them pound for pound the world's meanest, most aggressive bears. But they're also clownish and quite agile, and willing, like Winnie the Pooh, to do almost anything for honey. Also at home in this particular rainforest are dozens of lion-tailed macaques, a critically endangered species native to India. These arboreal acrobats take advantage of special rubberized monkey-proof "vines" for their impromptu performances. Note the impressive and irreplaceable 40-foot-tall ficus, the only one of its kind at the zoo. Nearby, in a small aviary, are still more exotic birds.

Children's Zoo

Though even the restrooms here are designed for four-year-olds, the Children's Zoo is immensely appealing to "kids" of all ages. Most popular are the two baby animal nurseries, where human babies peer through the glass at animal babies—these rejected by their mothers, injured, or otherwise sickly—as they are bottle-fed and reared by their human caretakers.

At the petting zoo, sheep, goats, and pot-bellied pigs are on parade. Other animals exhibited at the Children's Zoo include exotic birds, spider monkeys, tree kangaroos, small-clawed otters from Asia, lesser pandas, and the always popular—"Ooooh, mom, what's *that?*"—naked mole-rats. Zookeepers also personally present other animals, from lesser anteaters to meerkats, throughout the day.

To Do the Zoo, Think Strategically

The zoo is vast and spread out—a moderately challenging four- to five-mile hike if you're in a big hurry and determined to see it all, a potentially tiring stroll even if you're not—so study your zoo map before setting out. The white pathways indicate higher elevations, these shading into gray and then into black, the zoo's lowest elevations. With some forethought, occasional backtracking, and strategic use of the zoo's two central moving staircases, it's possible to do most of your walking on flat ground or heading downhill. The upper mesa levels are less shaded, so see these areas first, particularly during hotter autumn weather.

If all-out zoo trekking is not feasible, take the guided double-decker bus tour for a general introduction—not a bad idea anyway, considering the valuable overview, informationally, and the great view from the open-air upper deck—then walk only to the must-see attractions on your list. (Spanish-language bus tours are offered daily at noon.) Alternatively, take the Kangaroo Bus, and hop on and off all day for short-distance explorations. Get the big picture on the Skyfari aerial tram, which crosses the zoo just above the treetops, from near the Reptile House to the Horn and Hoof Mesa.

Most zoo animals are most active, and entertaining, in the mornings and late afternoon, so plan to lunch and take in various animal shows—The Wild Ones, for example, and the Wegeforth National Park Sea Lion Show—during mid-day siesta time.

Other Zoo Practicalities

The zoo is open daily from 9 a.m. to dusk, which means entrance gates close at 4 p.m. from fall through spring and at 9 p.m. in summer (visitors can stay an hour longer). General admission, which includes admission to the Children's Zoo and all shows, is $18 adults, $8 for children ages 3-11, free for age 2 and under. Deluxe admission, which includes the guided bus tour plus the two-way fare for the Skyfari aerial tram, costs $21 for adults and $11 for children 3-11. Admis-

sion is free for everyone on October 3, Founder's Day, and free for children under age 12 during the entire month of October.

Strollers, wheelchairs, and motorized scooters are available for rent on the front plaza next to the clock tower. Film is available at the nearby information booth (as are video camera rentals), but bring your own—more than you think you'll need—since it's expensive here. If you run short of cash, a real possibility if you venture into the zoo's great gift shops, you'll find an ATM in front of the Reptile House. For parking excess baggage, lockers are behind the Reptile House. To save money on meals, pack your own picnic, though snack stands and eateries abound (vegetarian fare available). Best bet for a simple sit-down meal is the **Peacock & Raven** deli just inside the entrance overlooking the peacock lagoon.

For more information, contact the San Diego Zoo, tel. (619) 234-3153 (recorded) or (619) 231-1515. To study up on the web, the address is www.sandiegozoo.org. For information on specialty walking and bus tours, call (619) 685-3264. For information on the zoo's various education programs, including lectures, workshops, and the popular parent-participation pre-schooler program, call (619) 557-3969. For information about the many benefits of membership in the Zoological Society of San Diego, which operates both the zoo and the San Diego Wild Animal Park near Escondido, call (619) 231-0251.

Fun near Balboa: Hillcrest and Vicinity

Just north of Balboa Park and its fairly traditional ambience is Hillcrest, the one San Diego neighborhood noted for its eccentricities. This conservative city's gay district, centered along Washington and University Avenues between First and Fifth, Hillcrest is also the place to sample the artsy bohemian life, San Diego-style—the small record and bookshops, eclectic art films, small theaters, and good casual restaurants. Redevelopment is the watchword here, though, as elsewhere in San Diego—so hurry, before it all gets too upscale and safely cool.

For music classics and what's new internationally, spin into **Off The Record,** 3849 Fifth Ave. (at University), tel. (619) 298-4755. Some of San Diego's best independent bookstores are located in Hillcrest, including **Grounds for Murder,** 3940 Fourth St. (at Washington), tel. (619)

299-9500, which provides a vacation's worth of whodunits; **Bountiful Books,** 3834 Fifth Ave. between University and Robinson, tel. (619) 491-0664, which boasts more than 20,000 new, used and rare titles; and **Fifth Avenue Books,** 3838 Fifth Ave. between University and Robinson, tel. (619) 291-4660, which offers collectible first editions. One of the best bookstores in town, though, is been-there-forever **Blue Door Books,** 3823 Fifth Ave. (at University), tel. (619) 298-8610, locally famous for the Lawrence Ferlinghetti poem the poet wrote in honor of the bookstore.

The **Hillcrest Theater,** 3965 Fifth Ave., tel. (619) 299-2100, showing artsy independent and foreign films, is prominent at colorful **Village Hillcrest,** a neo-retro-looking contemporary complex at Fifth and Washington. Underground public parking is available here, if you're having little luck elsewhere. For original plays, head over to tiny **Quentin Crisp Theatre,** 3704 Sixth Ave. (at Pennsylvania), tel. (619) 688-9210, which stages controversial and quirky plays like *Denial of the Fittest,* a one woman show written and performed by Judith Sloan.

For coffee and philosophical conversation, *the* place is **The Coffee Bean & Tea Leaf** at 3865 Fifth Ave. (at University), tel. (619) 298-5908. Good neighborhood eateries include, for the kids, the faux-'50s **Corvette Diner** at 3946 Fifth Ave. between University and Washington, tel. (619) 542-1001, and, more for grown-ups, fun **Kemo Sabe,** 3958 Fifth between University and Washington, tel. (619) 220-6802, with its contemporary twists on ethnic favorites. You'll also find Thai food and taco shops on and around University near Fifth.

Farther east along University, at Eighth, is the **Uptown District** complex, another emblem of neighborhood redevelopment. For an eclectic collection of antiqueries, continue east on Washington, north on Park and Mission until it becomes **Adams Avenue.**

OLD TOWN, DOWNTOWN, AND AROUND

OLD TOWN SAN DIEGO

The old adobe survivors of Old Town San Diego, the state's most popular historic park, are intertwined with—and clearly outnumbered by—a wide variety of mini-malls, gift shops, restaurants, and other commercial enterprises that now surround Old Town Plaza.

But modern consumerism didn't doom Old Town's old-timers. It was fate, in the form of a devastating fire in 1872. Most of Old Town's surviving historic buildings, among the earliest outposts of early California settlement history, are clustered in the six-block area bounded by Juan Street on the north, Congress Street on the south, Wallace Street on the west, and Twiggs Street on the east.

Walking Old Town

Highlights of an Old Town history walk include the **Seeley Stables** at Calhoun and Twiggs Sts., tel. (619) 220-5442, Old Town San Diego's transportation center until the 20th century, now a museum of horse-and-buggy rolling stock and western memorabilia. (Admission is $2 adults, $1 children.) On Mason at Calhoun is the 1829 **La Casa de Bandini,** center of the young city's social life during Mexican rule, and then after the Yankees arrived, the **Cosmopolitan Hotel.** The ground-floor rooms and walled gardens are now inhabited by a popular Mexican restaurant, **Casa de Bandini,** tel. (619) 297-8211, where strolling mariachi bands serenade diners on the patio.

A visit to adobe **La Casa de Estudillo,** tel. (619) 220-5422, on Mason Street between Calhoun and San Diego Ave., is a must. (Admission is $2 adults, $1 children and includes admission to the Seeley museum, and vice versa.) Built in 1827 by Captain José M. Estudillo, commander of the presidio, this was one of the finest homes in Mexican California. Note the leather-tied beams, and the exquisite furnishings, from the Steinway spinet pianos to the blue Duncan Phyfe sofa and elegant oriental rugs. Yet it was the courtyard, with its gardens, well, and out-door *horno* (bake oven), that served as the center of family life—still serene and meditative, at least on slower days. Family members continued to live here until 1887, after which the home gradually declined. Bought in 1905 by local mover and shaker John D. Spreckels, who restored its grandeur, the house was opened to the public in 1910—promoted as "Ramona's Marriage Place," since the small chapel here reportedly inspired the wedding scene in Helen Hunt Jackson's wildly popular 19th-century novel *Ramona.* The house was eventually deeded to the state; its current restoration began in 1969.

Also worth exploring: the 1847 **San Diego Courthouse,** the **Wells Fargo Museum,** the 1865 **Mason Street School,** and the local **Dental Museum.** Inside the tiny **San Diego Union Newspaper Building** is a once-modern marvel of the journalism trade—an ancient Blickensderfer typewriter, complete with wood carrying case.

Just outside Old Town proper is the **Mormon Battalion Visitors Center** at 2510 Juan Street, tel. (619) 298-3317, free admission, which tells the story of the longest infantry march in history. Also worth a stop for history aficionados is the two-story brick 1857 **Whaley House Museum,** 2482 San Diego Avenue, tel. (619) 298-2482, one of the few homes in the country ever declared by the U.S. government to be haunted. It served as county courthouse and government center in the 1870s. Artifacts and period memorabilia collected here include one of six "life masks" made of Abraham Lincoln. Admission $4 adults, $2 children.

Old Town Practicalities

The park itself is free, as is admission to most of its historic buildings, though a few other Old Town-area attractions charge admission. The park's historic buildings are open daily from 10 a.m. to at least 4 p.m., closed Thanksgiving, Christmas, and New Year's Day. Restaurants and some shops have extended hours.

Free Old Town walking tours depart daily at 11 a.m. and 2 p.m. from the state park office, the Robinson-Rose House, 4002 Wallace Street,

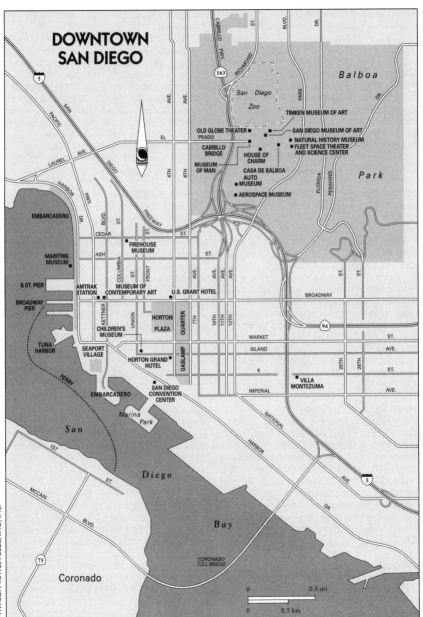

DOWNTOWN SAN DIEGO

Balboa

San Diego Zoo

TIMKEN MUSEUM OF ART

OLD GLOBE THEATER
PRADO
SAN DIEGO MUSEUM OF ART
NATURAL HISTORY MUSEUM
CABRILLO BRIDGE
HOUSE OF CHARM
FLEET SPACE THEATER AND SCIENCE CENTER
MUSEUM OF MAN
CASA DE BALBOA
AUTO MUSEUM
AEROSPACE MUSEUM

Park

EMBARCADERO

MARITIME MUSEUM

FIREHOUSE MUSEUM

CEDAR
ASH

B ST. PIER

BROADWAY PIER

AMTRAK STATION
MUSEUM OF CONTEMPORARY ART
U.S. GRANT HOTEL

BROADWAY

CHILDREN'S MUSEUM
HORTON PLAZA
QUARTER

TUNA HARBOR

SEAPORT VILLAGE
HORTON GRAND HOTEL
GASLAMP

MARKET
ISLAND
K
IMPERIAL

VILLA MONTEZUMA

EMBARCADERO

SAN DIEGO CONVENTION CENTER

Marina Park

San

Diego

Bay

CORONADO TOLL BRIDGE

Coronado

0   0.5 mi

0   0.5 km

© AVALON TRAVEL PUBLISHING, INC.

tel. (619) 220-5423—also the source for self-guided tour brochures, if you're lucky, as well as special event schedules and other current info. On the first Saturday of each month and every Wednesday, from 10 a.m.-1 p.m. in the Machado y Stewart Adobe, park staff and other local history buffs don period costumes to demonstrate various domestic arts, and next to La Casa de Bandini, the village smithy plies his trade. For more information contact: **Old Town San Diego State Historic Park,** 4002 Wallace St., San Diego, tel. (619) 220-5423.

Old Town San Diego is wedged into the shadows of two major thoroughfares, just east of I-5 and just south of I-8. From I-5, exit at Old Town Avenue. From I-8, exit at Taylor Street, head south, then turn left onto San Diego Avenue. If coming from Point Loma and vicinity, take Rosecrans Avenue east all the way to Old Town.

Parking can be a nightmare near Old Town, so if you're driving come as early as possible. In 1996 the **San Diego Trolley** extended its routes to include Old Town; taking the trolley is definitely a safe and sane alternative. For a guided get-around—a good general introduction to San Diego, with the option of hopping off at various points and catching a later trolley to continue the tour—try **Old Town Trolley Tours,** headquartered at the tiny Old Town theater on Twiggs Street. These commercial trolley tours leave (and arrive) every 30 minutes between 9 a.m.-4 p.m. Call (619) 298-8687 for more information.

Up the Hill from Old Town

Most notable in **Presidio Park,** just up the hill from Old Town via Taylor Street and Presidio Drive, is the imposing mission revival-style **Junípero Serra Museum,** 2727 Presidio Dr., tel. (619) 297-3258, built in 1929, which many visitors mistake for San Diego's mission. Run by the local historical society on behalf of the city, the Serra museum does mark the hill climbed by Father Serra and his party to lay claim to the territory, and almost marks the site of the Royal Presidio of San Diego and the original mission. Museum exhibits emphasize San Diego's Spanish period, including a fascinating furniture collection and artifacts from presidio excavations. Climb the museum tower for breathtaking panoramic views. The Junípero Serra Museum is open Fri.-Sun. 10 a.m.-4:30 p.m. Admission is $5 adults, $4 seniors, students and military, $2 children 6-17, free for kids age 6 and under.

The entire park, actually, serves as a museum, with various statues, memorials, and the Serra Cross—built in 1913 from presidio floor tiles—telling various parts of the story. The presidio site, directly below the Serra museum, is a National Historic Landmark, where excavations have been ongoing since 1965. The presidio's chapel, sundry walls, tile floors, and thresholds, even cannonballs, have been discovered.

Presidio Park is perfect for picnics, by the way, but parking is fairly limited, so consider walking up—or come anytime but on a summer weekend.

If you've got the time, worth exploring beyond Old Town proper is **Heritage Park,** tel. (619) 291-9784, up Juan Street near Kearney. Here you'll find a collection of brazenly bright Victorians saved from the wrecking ball by the Save Our Heritage Organization (SOHO). One mansion houses a B&B, another an antique store, and yet another a doll shop.

To the San Diego Mission

This isn't the most exciting or evocative of California's 21 missions, but it is the first. First founded by Father Junípero Serra in 1769, atop what is now Presidio Hill, the mission was moved to this location in 1774. The new site promised more water and improved agricultural prospects, but it didn't provide peace. Threatened by the mission's territorial incursions, in 1775 native peoples declared war—burning the mission, destroying religious paraphernalia, and killing one priest (Luis Jayme, California's first Catholic martyr, who is honored here). Wander the garden, stop by the museum, and visit the original chapel—California's first church—for a peek into the mission's past and present lives.

To get to Mission San Diego, 10818 San Diego Mission Rd., from Presidio Park, follow Presidio Dr. down the hill and bear right onto Taylor; at the first light, turn left and merge onto I-8 (heading east). Exit at Mission Gorge Rd. and turn left; turn left again onto San Diego Mission Road. The museum and gardens are open daily 9 a.m.-5 p.m. Admission is $2 adults, $1 seniors (over age 55), and 50 cents for children (under age 12). "Tote-a-tape" tours are available. For more information, call (619) 281-8449.

DOWNTOWN SAN DIEGO

Until fairly recently San Diego was known as the city with no downtown, since even residents preferred to be anywhere but. All that has changed after more than two decades of serious redevelopment work that managed to preserve and polish, rather than destroy, what remained of the area's historic character. San Diego now has a lively, people-friendly downtown that segues quite neatly into the Embarcadero and the bay.

Downtown San Diego got its start in 1867, the day Alonzo Erastus Horton strolled off a sidewheel steamer onto the "New Town" wharf, at the foot of what is now Fifth Street. Horton saw immediately that San Diego the city should be here, along the bay, not near the Old Town site chosen for security reasons by the Spanish. So Horton soon bought from the city 960 acres of "downtown" land for 27.5 cents an acre—a foolish outlay of $260 for jackrabbits, dust, and fleas, in the minds of lesser civic visionaries.

Nicknamed "Short Block Horton" for the short city blocks he laid out south of Broadway—shorter blocks made for more corner lots, which went for premium prices—Alonzo E. Horton sold so much land so fast he claimed to grow weary from handling all that money, day after day. Yet in the midst of San Diego's first real estate boom, Horton's fatigue failed to stop him. His developments in what was then known as Horton's Addition continued, with a pier, a de facto town hall, and facilities for the railroad, though his grandest accomplishment was the two-story brick Horton House hotel, built for the extravagant sum of $150,000, near the present-day U.S. Grant Hotel. There seemed to be no end to Horton's success.

Yet it did end, thanks to John D. Spreckels, the sugar magnate associated in local lore with Coronado Island. Building on Horton's original vision, Spreckels built a better pier and started developing downtown land north of Broadway—soon the most stylish business districts and neighborhoods in town.

Horton's development empire, known today as the Gaslamp Quarter, deteriorated into shabby "Stingaree," named after offshore stingrays and noted for its flophouse hotels, brothels, "pros-

titution cribs," and just general vice (with a capital V). Despite the San Diego Ladies Purity League's determination to clean things up in 1914, in preparation for the Pan-American International Exposition, the neighborhood continued its decline—a trend finally reversed in the 1970s, as San Diego got serious about redevelopment, renovation, and historic preservation.

Horton Plaza

Horton Plaza rises out of old-fashioned downtown San Diego like a Mediterranean or Middle Eastern version of the Emerald City—a jumble of odd open-air plazas, tiled courtyards and fountains, sculptures, stairways, cupolas, and towers all splashed with bold colors and draped in fluttering banners. This architectural marvel, designed by Jon Jerde and presented to the world in 1985, is clearly not your run-of-the-mill shopping mall. Yet as a mall, anchored by Nordstrom, the Broadway, Robinsons-May, and Mervyn's and stuffed to its ramparts with shops, restaurants, and movie theaters, it's a wild success. Particularly good reasons to start your downtown exploration here include the local visitor bureau's helpful **San Diego International Visitor Center,** at 11 Horton Plaza at the corner of First Avenue and F Street, tel. (619) 236-1232; the **Horton Plaza Farmers Market,** for uptown picnic fixings, good wines, and wonderful bakery goods; and the impressive **San Diego Repertory Theater Company,** with two stages here.

Horton Plaza inhabits the entire downtown "block" between Broadway and G St. and First and Fourth Avenues. The mall is regularly open Mon.-Fri. 10 a.m.-9 p.m., Saturday 10 a.m.-7 p.m., and Sunday 11 a.m.-6 p.m. (with later Saturday hours in summer and pre-Christmas). Restaurants, theaters, and some shops have extended hours. Walk here or take the trolley or bus, if at all possible, since parking in the underground lot is often nonexistent. For information on what's up, contact: Horton Plaza, 324 Horton Plaza, San Diego, tel. (800) 214-7467 or (619) 238-1596, fax (619) 239-4021. For info via the Internet, the address is www.horton-plaza.com.

The Gaslamp Quarter

Most of San Diego's venerable Victorian business buildings, constructed between the Civil War and World War I, are in the city's Gaslamp

Quarter, the downtown area just east of Horton Plaza, between Fourth and Sixth Streets and Broadway and L Street. Notorious for "nefarious activity" during decades of decline, the quarter has been undergoing a Renaissance of sorts—with historic hotels, new shops, art galleries, trendy restaurants, and nightclubs at the forefront of this particular downtown revival.

Gaslamp District highlights include the **Horton Grand Hotel,** tel. (619) 544-1886, at Island and Third, a Victorian-style creation dating from the 1980s—or the 1880s, if you count original construction dates. The Horton Grand is a recreation done in the spirit, if not the architectural truth, of two old downtown hotels otherwise doomed by redevelopment—the old Horton Grand Hotel on E Street and the Saddlery Hotel, also known as the Kahle Saddlery and even earlier, when Wyatt Earp stayed there, as the Brooklyn Hotel. (The bricks and balustrades on Fourth are from the Horton Grand, those on the other side from the Saddlery.) If you don't stay at the Horton Grand, at least wander the lobby areas and visit the small Chinese museum commemorating San Diego's vanished Chinatown.

Other neighborhood landmarks include the baroque revival-style **Louis Bank of Commerce**—known as the Golden Poppy when it served as a whorehouse—on Fifth between E and F Sts., the **Backesto Building** on Fifth at Market, and the Romanesque revival **George J. Keating Building** on F St. at Fifth.

One of Southern California's most popular hip urban events, the annual two-day food and music festival **San Diego Street Scene** takes over the Gaslamp Quarter on two consecutive days in September. To find out about other happenings in the neighborhood, call the **Gaslamp Quarter Association,** tel. (619) 233-5227.

For guided and self-guided historic tours, contact the **Gaslamp Quarter Foundation** headquarters, inside the William Heath Davis House at 410 Island (at Fourth), tel. (619) 233-4692—the office is open weekdays 10 a.m.-2 p.m., Saturday 10 a.m.-4 p.m., Sunday noon-4 p.m.—or pick up a free brochure/map at area visitor information centers. The foundation's fun self-guided audio tours can be arranged for almost any time, and guided tours leave from the Davis house every Saturday at 11 a.m. A $5 donation is requested for each tour.

Villa Montezuma

After Balboa Park it might be tough convincing the kids they want to do another museum, and, after Horton Plaza, that this old house has entertainment value. But it does. Gaudy and splendid, Villa Montezuma is one of the strangest, most opulent "High Victorians" remaining in California. Built for internationally renowned musician, writer, and spiritualist Jesse Shepard, it's something of a monument to the 1880s' theosophy movement. Shepard and his followers held musical seances and otherwise communed with the spirits here, providing an early—and elegant—example of California's historic fascination with unorthodox spiritual orthodoxy. Villa Montezuma, 1925 K St. (at 20th), is open Saturday and Sunday only, noon-4:30 p.m. Admission is $5, children 6-17 $2, free for children under age 6. For more information, call (619) 239-2211.

Children's Museum/
Museo de los Niños of San Diego

Since moving downtown from La Jolla in 1994, San Diego's children's museum has gone interactive in an even bigger way—and that's no technological toss-off. The idea here is that children need to "plug in" to the real world, not just virtual ones. Lessons in real life include **Identity/Identidad** and other bilingual exhibits, along with hand puppet shows and other performances held in conjunction with hands-on workshops. **The Box Show,** a series of boxlike exhibits dedicated to both artistic and educational ends, includes Cora's Rain House, a giant tin building nestled into a recycled-water rainforest.

The children's museum, 200 W. Island Ave. (between Front and Union Sts.), is open Tues.-Sun. 10 a.m.-4 p.m., closed Monday and major holidays. Admission is $6 for adults and children age 3 and older, $3 for seniors. For current programs, events, and other information, call (619) 233-5437.

Other Downtown Draws

Across from Horton Plaza's south side at 777 Front Street and adjacent to the haute shopping heaven is the **Paladion** shopping center, tel. (619) 232-1685. North of Horton's Plaza, along Broadway at Kettner Drive, is the 1915 **Santa Fe Train Depot,** the city's Amtrak station these days, notably overshadowed by the 34-story **1 American**

Plaza office tower. Part of the plaza is the downtown outpost of San Diego's **Museum of Contemporary Art,** 1001 Kettner Blvd. (at Broadway), tel. (619) 234-1001, www.mcasandiego.org, the museum's secondary locale housing part of the museum's 3,000 works. For more information on both museums, see La Jolla and Vicinity, below.

Farther east on Broadway, between First and Second Aves., is the grand old **Spreckels Theater,** 121 Broadway, tel. (619) 235-9500, a popular local concert venue. Across the street and one block farther is the 1910 **U.S. Grant Hotel,** 326 Broadway, tel. (619) 232-3121, San Diego's most classically elegant hostelry, commissioned by Grant's widow. The U.S. Grant was restored to its original grandeur—do stop to see the lobby—in the 1980s after a painstaking $80 million renovation.

Another time-honored presence a bit farther afield is the **Firehouse Museum,** 1572 Columbia St. (near Cedar), tel. (619) 232-3473, with fire-fighting technology representing handcart and horse-drawn engine eras as well as the earlier ages of internal combustion engines.

AROUND SAN DIEGO BAY

A superlative harbor, San Diego Bay begins at Point Loma, where Cabrillo stepped ashore. Its fairly narrow mouth is created by the "island" city of Coronado, which is connected to San Diego's South Bay area by a narrow isthmus of sand. This seemingly tenuous connection actually forms the long, protected bay.

Starting at Point Loma, major features along the bay's long inland curve include the Cabrillo National Monument, an impressive land's end complete with venerable lighthouse, whale-watching platform, excellent visitor center, bayside trails, even tidepools.

Next come Shelter Island and Harbor Island, not natural islands but onetime shoals built into bayside real estate with the help of harbor dredging.

Fronting San Diego Bay and increasingly integrated with most everyone's idea of "downtown" is the Embarcadero, a bayside walkway along Harbor Drive that winds its way past an armada of vessels—some of them tour boats and cruise ships, others converted into gift shops

and restaurants—and other harbor attractions.

Particularly noteworthy in the attractions category is the **San Diego Maritime Museum,** floating at 1492 N. Harbor Dr. the foot of Ash Street, tel. (619) 234-9153. About a half-mile south is the art deco B Street Pier, also known as the Cruise Ship Pier, local port for major cruise ship lines. Next south is the Broadway Pier, also known as the Excursion Pier, largely dedicated to sportfishing, whalewatching, and harbor tour companies. This is also the place to catch the San Diego-Coronado Ferry to Coronado Island.

Though San Diego's tuna fishing heyday is long gone, the next stop south is Tuna Harbor, headquarters for the American Tunaboat Association and also home to the very popular Fish Market restaurant and fresh-fish market. Navy ships may be tied up nearby; if so, on weekends they're usually open for tours.

Usually getting most of the neighborhood attention, though, is Seaport Village, a seafaring-themed shopping and restaurant development with turn-of-the-century style. For children and nonshoppers, the best thing here goes 'round and 'round—the 1890 Looff Broadway Flying Horses Carousel, originally stabled at Coney Island. Worth a stroll nearby is the Embarcadero Marine Park North, a grassy public park angling out into the bay.

Seaport Village ends at the San Diego Marriott Hotel and Marina, though the walkway wanders on. The striking San Diego Convention Center at the foot of Fifth, designed by Arthur Erickson and built by the Port of San Diego, is just beyond the hotel. With its fiberglass "sails" and wavelike walls, the convention center could only be confused with a choppy day at the America's Cup. South of the convention center is the Embarcadero Marina Park South and the stunning Coronado Bay Bridge. South of the bridge and east of I-5 begins the region's South Bay.

Cabrillo National Monument

Here's a bit of history with open-air flair. This breathtaking 144-acre vantage point on the ocean edge of San Diego Bay commemorates Cabrillo's exploration of the California coastline in 1542. What actually marks the spot is the Point Loma Lighthouse (no longer in operation but open to the public), a newer lighthouse, various viewpoints, plus a winter whalewatching station,

CORONADO: CROWN OF THE BAY

Across from San Diego's Embarcadero is Coronado, an "island" connected to the mainland only by a sandy isthmus and by a sky-skimming arched bridge. A separate city reached from downtown San Diego either by ferry or via the San Diego-Coronado Bay Bridge, Coronado boasts the North Island U.S. Naval Air Station—Charles Lindbergh's departure point for his famous round-the-world flight—and, on the east, the U.S. Naval Amphibious Base, home for the elite Navy SEALS.

Not too surprisingly, the military has, in a sense, created the community here, a culture that revolves around the sound and fury of naval air technology and the needs and interests of retired naval officers and their families. Well-heeled tourists and celebrities are also well attended on Coronado, however, and have been for over a century. The local roll-call of fame includes Charles Lindbergh, the Duke and Duchess of Windsor, 14 U.S. presidents, and a dizzying number of stars from both the stage and the silver screen. The list also includes Frank Baum, who wrote *The Wizard of Oz* while living here. **The Wizard of Oz House** still stands, at 1101 Star Park Circle.

Hotel del Coronado:
The Victorian Heart of Local History

The island's historic centerpiece is the astonishing Hotel del Coronado—known affectionately as the "Hotel Del" or, simply, "the Del"—one of California's grand old hotels, built in 1888, a national historic landmark. When it opened, this sprawling barn-red-and-white Victorian, with its wood shingles, turrets, and cupolas, was the largest structure outside New York City to be lighted with electricity. (Thomas Edison himself officiated at the switch-on ceremony for the hotel's first Christmas tree.) Among other movies, the 1959 comedy *Some Like It Hot,* starring Tony Curtis, Jack Lemmon, and Marilyn Monroe, was filmed at the Hotel Del.

Meander through the lobby and along dark-wood downstairs corridors, where photographs and other mementos tell the hotel's story, and stroll the gorgeous grounds. Fairly recent additions include the craftsman-style **Duchess of Windsor Cottage.** Now a meeting hall, the cottage was onetime Coronado home of Wallis Warfield Spencer—the Duchess of Windsor after King Edward abdicated the English throne to marry her.

John D. Spreckels, the sugar-refining millionaire, bought the Coronado Beach Company and its in-progress Hotel del Coronado in 1887—just as San Diego's first boom days were busting. But Spreckels, whose San Diego-area development projects included water engineering, railroads, and Coronado's unique "tent city" resort, survived even the dark days in style. The entire Spreckels family relocated here from San Francisco after the 1906 earthquake and fire; their former home is now the center of Coronado's **Glorietta Bay Inn.**

Guided tours of the Hotel del Coronado, at last report $10 per person, were being offered again starting in June 2000, following the hotel's $50 million

When it opened in 1888, the Hotel Del was the largest building outside New York City to be lighted with electricity.

COURTESY AISLINN RACE

restoration of its grand centerpiece, the Victorian building. Call the hotel at (619) 435-6611, or try www.hoteldel.com, for details and reservations.

For the entire Coronado story, stop by the free **Coronado Historical Museum** on Loma Avenue, tel. (619) 435-7242, open Wed.-Sat. 10 a.m.-4 p.m. and Sunday noon-4 p.m.

Coronado Beaches

Coronado's spectacular white-sand beaches are almost equally revered. Just oceanward from the Hotel Del is unbelievably broad **Coronado Beach**, typically uncrowded even in the summer, since most locals prefer beaches just north and south. On the island's bay side are several smaller, more protected beaches.

Silver Strand State Beach, tel. (619) 435-5184, extends the entire length of Coronado's sandy isthmus, with beaches on both sides of Silver Strand Boulevard (Hwy. 75), from near Hotel del Coronado to Imperial Beach. This popular family beach, great for swimming, was named for the small silver sea shells washed up along the shoreline. Beyond lifeguards, restrooms, and other basic services, facilities here include first-come RV campsites (self-contained only; no hook-ups), $14 per night in the summer. Silver Strand is open daily, 8 a.m.-9 p.m. in summer, until 8 p.m. during the spring, until 7 p.m. during winter. Beach use is free, though there is a parking fee (free from Labor Day through March). For more information about Silver Strand and other area state parks and beaches, contact **California State Parks, San Diego Coast District Headquarters,** 9609 Waples Street, Suite 200, San Diego 92121, tel. (619) 642-4200, fax (619) 642-4222.

Seeing and Doing Coronado

Coronado's other present-day pleasures include sun, sand, sailing, windsurfing, 15 miles of shoreline bikepaths—you can ride all the way to Imperial Beach—and specialty shopping along downtown Coronado's revitalized **Orange Avenue** and at the Seaport-Village like **Ferry Landing Marketplace.** In addition to its city pool, its 130-acre municipal golf course, its 18 parks, and its 18 public tennis courts, Coronado offers other diversions. **Gondola Cruises,** tel. (619) 429-6317, shoves off from the Loews resort on Venetian-style tours of the Coronado Cays canals. Three-hour guided **Navy base tours** of North Island Naval Air Station are offered on Fridays by Old Town Trolley Tours, tel. (619) 298-8687. Or take a **Coronado Walking Tour,** tel. (619) 435-5892 or (619) 435-5993. And you can always see what's playing at the **Coronado Playhouse** on Strand Way, tel. (619) 435-4856, or the **Lamb's Players Theatre** on Orange Ave., tel. (619) 437-0600.

Coronado also sponsors an almost endless series of special events—from the downhome **Coronado Flower Show** in Spreckels Park every spring and **Art in the Park** on the first and third Sunday of each month to a dazzling **Fourth of July** parade and fireworks. A **Coronado Christmas** is quite eventful, from the treelighting ceremonies at the Hotel Del and Santa Claus (sometimes in sunglasses) to caroling, choirs, and—reminiscent of a tradition started locally by Frank Baum—children's story hours. Coronado's Christmas **Parade of Lights,** with every boat in sight decked out in Christmas finery, is usually scheduled for one week in mid-December.

Staying on Coronado: Pricey

If planning to splurge while in the neighborhood, stay at least one night at the historic **Hotel del Coronado,** the city's crowning glory. The legendary and eclectic Queen Anne "Hotel Del" features a classic dark-wood lobby, with a still-functioning birdcage elevator and a spectacular support-free formal dining room, the latter used only on special occasions. Guest rooms in the original wooden section of the hotel, with its marvelous quirky corridors, boast all modern amenities yet a Victorian sensibility—all the more dazzling following the Hotel Del's $50 million renovation, completed in June 2000. Newer hotel units near the beach include the Ocean Towers, the California Cabanas, and the Beach House. And if you aren't sufficiently entertained by the hotel's grandeur, its Olympic-size swimming pool, tennis courts, and pristine white-sand Coronado Beach—beach chairs, umbrellas, towels, even boogie boards provided—then watch the hotel's closed-circuit TV, showing movie after movie filmed at the Hotel Del. Other amenities include wonderful on-site restaurants, from the stunningly Victorian Crown-Coronet dining room, complete with chandeliers designed by *Wizard of Oz* author Frank Baum, to the romantic Prince of Wales Grill and the new Sheerwater (formerly the Ocean Terrace), serving California coastal cuisine. (For very Victorian High Tea, head for the Palm Court on Sunday afternoon.) Not to mention various business services, shopping, complete spa services (extra), and rental bikes, sailboards, and sailboats. Luxury. Summer room rates begin at $190, with a two-night minimum on weekends, though ask about packages and off-season deals. For more

(continued on next page)

CORONADO: CROWN OF THE BAY

(continued)

information, contact: Hotel del Coronado, 1500 Orange Avenue, Coronado, CA 92118, tel. (619) 435-6611, fax (619) 522-8262, www.hoteldel.com. For reservations, call toll-free (800) 468-3533, fax (619) 522-8262, or reserve online.

Another top choice is the 15-acre **Loews Coronado Bay Resort,** 4000 Coronado Bay Rd., toll-free tel. (800) 235-6397 or (619) 424-4000, fax (619) 424-4400, www.loewshotels.com, a lovely contemporary hotel with light and airy view rooms—every room has a view, be it of the ocean, the bay, or the marina (moor your own). All the usual luxuries, on-site restaurants, fitness and business facilities, even a kid's program are provided. Rates start at $195, but ask about specials. Luxury.

Also appealing in the pricier category is the **Coronado Island Marriott Resort,** formerly Le Meridien San Diego, 16 acres fronting the bay directly across from downtown, with lush landscaping, lagoons full of fish and flamingos, tennis courts, pools, health and fitness facilities, business services, and great restaurants. Rooms, suites, and villas, all with a balcony or patio, open onto either a bay or lagoon view. Luxury. Rates start at $230, but look for off-season specials and packages. The Coronado Island Marriott is at 2000 Second St. (at Glorietta), tel. (619) 435-3000, fax (619) 435-3032, www.marriotthotels.com.

Staying on Coronado: Not So Pricey

Thankfully for just plain folks and most families,

Coronado also offers budget-friendlier choices, including the **Crown City Inn,** 520 Orange Ave. (between Fifth and Sixth), toll-free tel. (800) 422-1173 or (619) 435-3116, fax (619) 435-6750, www.crowncityinn.com. Every room at this attractive Mediterranean-style motel has a refrigerator, microwave, and coffeemaker, in-room modem hookup, ironing board and iron, plus color TV and cable with free movies. Heated pool, complimentary bikes, on-site laundry facilities. Even better, from here it's just a 10-minute walk to the beach. The **Crown City Bistro** here is open for breakfast, lunch, and dinner and provides impressive room service. Expensive-Premium, with summer rates starting at $105 ($85 in the off-season). Ask about discounts and specials.

If there's no room at that inn, **La Avenida Inn,** 1315 Orange, tel. (619) 435-3191, fax (619) 435-5024, and the **Best Western Suites Coronado Island,** 235 Orange, toll-free tel. (800) 528-1234 or (619) 437-1666, fax (619) 437-0188, are both good alternatives. Contact the local visitor center (see below) for more suggestions.

Eating on Coronado

For fresh produce and flowers, show up on Tuesday for the **Coronado Certified Farmers' Market,** tel. (619) 741-3763, held at the Ferry Market Landing, First St. and B Avenue. Microbrewery fans, you'll find Coronado's own at the **Coronado Brewing Company,** 170 Orange, tel. (619) 437-4452. For

stopping to smell the flowers at the Coronado Flower Show in Spreckels Park

CORONADO VISITOR INFORMATION

Pacific Rim-style Southwestern (reservations), the place is the **Chameleon Café,** 1301 Orange Ave., tel. (619) 437-6677. Delightful for French bistro fare is **Chez Loma,** near the history museum at 1132 Loma Ave. (at Orange), tel. (619) 435-0661.

Generally speaking, though, seafood is the thing in Coronado. For good seafood at lunch and dinner and a chance to appreciate America's Cup memorabilia, head for the **Bay Beach Cafe** at Ferry Market Landing, tel. (619) 435-4900. Another best bet for seafood—not to mention the macadamia nut pie—is **Pehoe's,** nearby at 1201 First St., tel. (619) 437-4474, with bay views, patio tables, and a good Sunday brunch. For a bit of remodeled history with your seafood and steaks, **The Chart House** is at home in the Hotel del Coronado's onetime boathouse at 1701 Strand Way, tel. (619) 435-0155 (casual, children's menu, dinner only, reservations required).

If you're prepared to spend some real money, stars of the local fine dining scene tend to cluster at Coronado's luxury hotels. The elegant **Crown-Coronet Room** at the Hotel del Coronado serves an astonishing, excellent brunch banquet on Sunday—probably enough calories to fuel the entire naval air base for a week—but the hotel also offers more contemporary style, including the **Prince of Wales Grill** and **Sheerwater,** with spacious outside terraces and gigantic fireplaces. For more information or restaurant reservations, call the hotel at (619) 435-6611. Other hotel hot spots include **Azzura Point** at Loews Coronado Bay Resort, tel. (619) 424-4000, and the charming **L'Escale** brasserie and jazzy **La Provence** at the Coronado Island Marriott, tel. (619) 522-3039.

Coronado Information and Transportation

For more information about Coronado, contact the very helpful **Coronado Visitor Information** office, 1047 B Ave., Coronado, CA 92118, tel. (619) 437-8788, fax (619) 437-6006, www.coronado.ca.us.

Getting around Coronado is fun (except on particularly hectic weekends), thanks to its walkable streets lined with trees and bungalows, its paved bikepaths, and the **Coronado 904 Shuttle,** tel. (619) 233-3004, $1 fare.

Getting to Coronado is even more fun, especially if you take the **Bay Ferry** from the Broadway Pier in San Diego to Coronado's Ferry Landing at First and B Streets. Ferries leave San Diego every hour on the hour 9 a.m.-9 p.m. Sun.-Thurs. (until 10 on weekend nights), and return from Coronado every hour on the half-hour, from 9:30 a.m.-9:30 p.m. Sun.-Thurs. (until 10:30 p.m. on weekend nights). Ferry fare is $2 (pedestrians and bicyclists only), 50 cents extra if you BYOB (bring your own bike). **San Diego Harbor Excursion water taxi,** tel. (619) 235-8294, travels to Ferry Landing Marketplace, the Hotel Del, and Le Meridien from Seaport Village on the mainland.

It's also fairly exciting to drive over. It's like riding a rainbow, gliding up and then over the soaring arch of the **San Diego-Coronado Bay Bridge** (Hwy. 75). The toll is $1 heading into Coronado—free with two or more people in the car—and free returning to the mainland.

---

tidepools (explorable at low tide), trails, and a good visitor center. There are no food concessions, however, so bring a picnic or snacks if you'll be staying awhile.

Fully appreciate the breathtaking bay views by hiking the **Bayside Trail,** an asphalt road threading through old World War II military installations, meandering east along the bay. Watch sailboats and ships, not to mention the soaring sea birds—and, on aerially active days, U.S. Navy aircraft taking off from the North Island Naval Air Station across from the trail on Coronado Island. This two-mile roundtrip (easy) begins near the lighthouse and typically takes just over one hour.

One of San Diego's best bets for **tidepooling** lies within a stone's throw of San Diego Bay, on the rocky western edge of the Point Loma Peninsula. At low tide, the tidepools near the Coast Guard station teem with ocean creatures tossed ashore at high tide—crabs, sometimes an octopus or jellyfish—and also reveal more stationary residents of the rocks, including anemones and starfish. It's okay to look, but not touch, since the tidepools are protected reserves. Ask park rangers about expected low tides. To reach the tidepools, go north from the visitor center. The first road to the left leads to the Coast Guard station and the peninsula's western shore.

Cabrillo National Monument, 1800 Cabrillo Memorial Dr. (the southern end of Cabrillo Memorial Dr., Hwy. 209), is open in winter daily 9 a.m.-5:15 p.m., though the Bayside Trail is open only 9 a.m.-4 p.m. In summer the park is open until sunset, with extended trail hours. Admission is $5 per vehicle, $2 per person entering by bicycle or on foot, and free for seniors with Golden Age Passports, the disabled, and children age 16 and under. For more information, contact: Cabrillo National Monument, tel. (619) 557-5450, www.nps.gov/cabr.

Shelter and Harbor Islands

Shelter Island's main claim to fame is as the yacht-harbor home of the America's Cup international sailing competitions, sponsored by the San Diego Yacht Club. But Shelter Island has its charms even without the America's Cup hubbub, most notably a family-friendly fishing pier, yachter's hangouts such as the Fiddler's Green and the Brigantine, and "tiki" resort hotels and restaurants noted for their Polynesian and faux-Polynesian style.

Harbor Island is another yachter's haven, this one close to the San Diego Airport and not coincidentally filled to the gills with waterfront hotels and restaurants.

San Diego Maritime Museum

Star of the show here is the three-masted *Star of India*—the oldest iron-hulled merchant ship still afloat, first launched from the Isle of Man in 1863 as the *Euterpe*. The 1904 *Medea,* a relative youngster hailing from Scotland, was quite a beauty in her day—with imported teak decks and housing, finished inside with quarter-sawn English oak. The museum's gift shop is holed up next door inside the *Berkeley,* an 1898 ferry most famous for serving as rescue ship during the 1906 San Francisco earthquake and fire.

The San Diego Maritime Museum, 1306 N. Harbor Dr., at the foot of Ash St. (the *Star of India* floats at the foot of Grape St.), is open daily 9 a.m.-8 p.m. Admission is $6 adults ($12 for an entire family), $4 seniors and children ages 13-17, $2 children ages 6-12. The museum is supported entirely by private contributions, making this a particularly good place for seafaring history buffs to make an extra donation. For more information, call (619) 234-9153.

The South Bay

National City is known for its **Naval Station San Diego,** a.k.a. the 32nd Street Naval Base, home port of the U.S. Pacific Fleet, not to mention the area's shipbuilding yards and the **National City Marine Terminal.**

The South Bay's **Chula Vista** is famous for its **ARCO Training Center** for Olympic athletes, one of only three in the U.S.—the other two dedicated to winter sports—and the **Sweetwater Marsh National Wildlife Refuge.**

Imperial Beach, in the same-named community, stars the **Imperial Beach Pier** and plenty of warm, white sand—the most essential ingredient for its fabulous **U.S. Open Sandcastle Competition** held here each year. Following the sand from Imperial Beach northwest onto the strand leads to **Silver Strand State Beach,** a superb swimming beach on the way to Coronado, justifiably popular with families. For more information on Coronado-area beaches, see Coronado: Crown of the Bay.

Southernmost, adjacent to the U.S.-Mexican border, is **Border Field State Park and Beach.** People avoid the beach here like the plague, since chronic sewage contamination from Tijuana has made swimming unsafe. And beyond the beach this otherwise serene wetlands preserve along the U.S.-Mexican border seems like a war zone, with Border Patrol helicopters slicing the air overhead in search of, and to deter, illegal immigrants. It's difficult to ignore the intensity of this daily San Diego-area drama. The state park is adjacent to the **Tijuana River National Estuarine Sanctuary National Wildlife Refuge,** with visitor center, guided walks and trails, and ongoing research facilities in Imperial Beach.

BEACH TOWNS AND BEACHES

Beyond downtown, starting north of Point Loma, are the oceanside communities of Ocean Beach, Mission Beach, and Pacific Beach. Still farther north are the fairly exclusive and expensive communities of La Jolla and Del Mar, also included within San Diego's city limits.

Ocean Beach

Strung out along Sunset Cliffs Boulevard just north of Point Loma is Ocean Beach, "O.B." in locals' lingo. Sitting just beyond the western end of the I-8 Freeway, Ocean Beach is San Diego's "farthest out" community—an unusual and unusually settled beach neighborhood with a hip (and hippie) history, an unusual collection of old-timers, surfers, young families, hipsters of all ages, and a smattering of ne'er-do-wells. To get a feel for the place, head for the **Ocean Beach Pier** (though beaches nearest the pier are sometimes unsavory) and stroll the **Newport Avenue** commercial district. Dog lovers, note that Ocean Beach's **Dog Beach** is one of only three in the county (along with Coronado and Del Mar) where canines can cavort sans leash. (Watch your step.) For more seclusion, head south to the cove beach at **Sunset Cliffs,** on the Point Loma Peninsula—popular with locals and surfers, accessible at low tide and only via slippery sandstone pathways or from the stairways at the feet of Bermuda and Santa Cruz Avenues.

Mission Beach and Mission Bay

Next stop north, beyond the San Diego River, is Mission Beach—about 17 miles of ocean beach and boardwalk plus Mission Bay, onetime wetlands refashioned, in the 1960s, into a faux bay resort area with man-made beaches, hotels, motels, marinas, and condominiums. When passing through in 1542, Cabrillo himself called it a "false bay," since the outlet led straight into the swamp.

Inland, Mission Bay Park is largely undeveloped and "natural"—meaning, in this case, undeveloped—a park popular with San Diegans looking for open space and bracing saltwater breezes for jogging, walking, biking, kite-flying, and watersports. If you're interested in the view

from the water but are without your own boat, get around via the **Harbor Hopper,** tel. (858) 488-2720, water taxi service or take a sunset cruise on the *Bahia Belle,* tel. (858) 488-0551, docked at the Bahia Hotel on West Mission Bay Drive.

Attractions along the ocean include both **South Mission** and **North Mission Beaches,** waterfront walkways, and grassy parks. The **Belmont Park** area, once an abandoned amusement park and boardwalk, now includes shops and shopping in addition to the historic **Giant Dipper** wooden rollercoaster and equally venerable **The Plunge** swimming pool.

Sea World

People either love or hate Mission Bay's Sea World, an Anheuser-Busch entertainment park with an ocean animal theme. Those who love Sea World say it offers families the chance to see unusual or endangered sea life up close and personal, a positive experience that increases environmental awareness. Those who hate it point out that with friends such as these—and with an excellent aquarium just north, in La Jolla, not to mention San Diego County's exceptional zoos—the beleaguered and endangered creatures of the sea hardly need enemies.

A recent controversy here, for example, involved the Shamu Backstage killer whale exhibit, interactive in the sense that park guests feed, pet, and participate in training Sea World's killer whales. All in all, this is the water-park equivalent of a petting zoo, animal rights activists say. They

Sea World

believe that rather than capturing, breeding, and training whales to perform tricks, Sea World should dedicate its considerable resources to making the real world safe for whales—these captive whales, for starters—and other wild things. Sea World officials respond that whale participation is "voluntary," that whales can swim away—albeit only so far as the next pool—if they wish to avoid their fans.

Of course the traditional star performers of the Sea World show, here and elsewhere, are **Shamu** the killer whale and **Baby Shamu,** actually stage names for a half-dozen or more individual whales. The aforementioned **Shamu Backstage** encounter is adjacent to Shamu Stadium; visitors view the whales through a 70-foot window in the 1.7 million gallon pool while waiting in line to touch them. And if that's not enough Shamu to-do, the kids can pose for pictures with an ersatz Shamu and Baby Shamu in two-acre **Shamu's Happy Harbor,** an active—and inter-active—playground.

Increasingly, "encounter" and "interactive" are the watchwords at Sea World, because more than anything else, people want to touch—or almost touch—animals they would never see, even at a distance, in real life.

So there's **Shark Encounter,** a three-part exhibit that permits visitors to commune with captive sharks from above, below, and "within" their habitat. A transparent acrylic tunnel allows you to "walk through" the shark tank. At **Penguin Encounter,** a moving sidewalk takes you through a glassed-in Arctic and the hundreds of emperor penguins gliding over glacierlike ice and into the water. At **Rocky Point Preserve,** visitors interact with—feed, pet, and talk to—bottlenose dolphins. Sea World also includes a **California Tide Pool** touch pool and a **Forbidden Reef**—kids love anything that's forbidden—with bat rays and moray eels.

But for those who can afford it, none of the "encounter" exhibits come close to the popularity of Sea World's **interactive dolphin program,** where an extra $125 buys you the chance to don a wetsuit, do a little dolphin training, and then take a dip in the dolphin pool.

There's more to see and do at Sea World, open daily from at least 10 a.m. to dusk, from 9 a.m. in summer (call for current summer schedule). As you might expect, the experience is expensive, with admission $40 adults, $30 children ages 3-11, plus food, high-priced mementos, and parking ($4 motorcycles, $7 cars, and $9 RVs). Behind-the-scenes tours, in addition to other educational activities and the dolphin interaction program, are available by arrangement.

Sea World is in Mission Bay; to get here from I-5, exit at Sea World Dr. and follow the signs. For more information, contact Sea World, 1720 S. Shores Rd., San Diego, tel. (619) 226-3901 for recorded information or tel. (619) 226-3815.

Pacific Beach

Hippest of all local beach towns these days is Pacific Beach or "P.B." in the local vernacular, where surf, surfers, skates, skaters, hip shops and just hangin' out define local culture. Most of the action is at the beach, at the **Lahaina Beach House** at 710 Oliver, tel. (858) 270-3888, at **Garnet Street** shops, and, after dark, at the **Society Billiard Café,** 1051 Garnet Ave., tel. (858) 272-7665, Unique here is the **Crystal Pier,** the only pier in California to include a hotel. Social historians and surf scene voyeurs can visit **Tourmaline Surfing Park** (Tourmaline St. at La Jolla Blvd.), the only stretch of local coastline dedicated exclusively to worshippers of the next wave, however grizzled they may be.

LA JOLLA AND VICINITY: SEASIDE SOPHISTICATION

Along the coast just north of Pacific Beach is the village of La Jolla, seven miles of sublime coastline that serves as San Diego's answer to the Riviera—a sophisticated red-tile-roofed Mediterranean image local commerce cultivates quite profitably, and one that attracts old-money minions as well as movie stars.

La Jolla (La HOY-yah, though people here say, simply, "the Village") means "jewel" in Spanish, or, according to local Native American tradition, "hole" or "cave." Both meanings are fitting. Hammered for eons by the relentless surf, the coastal bluffs beneath La Jolla's dazzling real estate are laced with caves, large and small, some explorable by land, some by sea. Other natural attractions are local beaches—including the infamous Windansea Beach, the top-notch but highly territorial surf scene described by Tom

Wolfe in *The Pump House Gang*—and area parks, including Torrey Pines State Reserve, sanctuary for about 6,000 very rare pine trees.

Not rare, however, is the human imperative to see, be seen, and make the scene—these, as well as shopping, are major pastimes in and around La Jolla's upmarket downtown. Any and all downtown adventures are best undertaken on foot, since finding a place to park can be all but impossible.

For more information about La Jolla, and for friendly practical assistance from the volunteer staff, contact the **La Jolla Town Council,** 7734 Herschell, La Jolla, tel. (858) 454-1444. Since La Jolla is technically part of the city of San Diego, information is also available from the International Visitor Information Center at Horton Plaza in downtown San Diego, tel. (619) 236-1232.

Along the Coast:
Ellen Browning Scripps Park and Beyond

La Jolla's aqua-blue ocean and adjacent beaches are beautiful but unbelievably popular. If personal space and peace are on your agenda, you won't find either here. Instead, head north along the coast.

Nonetheless, one of La Jolla's jewels is Ellen Browning Scripps Park overlooking La Jolla Cove, a palm-lined promenade where everyone goes to see the sea scene (and be seen). Even children regularly dip into the Scripps legacy; a wonderful local diversion is the **Children's Pool** at the park's south end, with shallow waters and a curved

beach protected by a seawall. In recent years, sea lions basking on **Shell Beach** just to the north have provided free entertainment.

South toward Pacific Beach is San Diego's surfing paradise, an area including mythic **Windansea Beach** and **Tourmaline Surfing Park,** neither particularly fun for "outsiders."

North from Children's Pool, starting offshore just south of Point La Jolla, is the **San Diego-La Jolla Underwater Park.** Most popular for skin-diving and snorkeling is northern **La Jolla Cove.** Lining La Jolla Bay north of the cove are the town's famed **La Jolla Caves** (small admission), some of them accessible by a stairway starting at the La Jolla Cave and Shell Shop on Coast Boulevard. The best **tidepools** around are along the coast north of the Scripps Pier at the Scripps Institution of Oceanography on La Jolla Shores Drive, the former site of the Scripps aquarium. **La Jolla Shores beaches,** including those below residential areas, are among the best for swimming and sunbathing, along with Torrey Pines State Beach and Del Mar Beach farther north. Between La Jolla Shores and Torrey Pines is an almost inaccessible, unauthorized nude beach known as **Black's Beach,** best reached from Torrey Pines at low tide. For more on that area, see "Torrey Pines State Reserve and Beach," below.

Museum of Contemporary Art

This 1915 Irving Gill original is the primary location of San Diego's Museum of Contemporary Art, 700 Prospect, tel. (858) 454-3541, www.mcsandiego.org. Once home to Ellen Browning Scripps, it reopened in March 1996 after a somewhat controversial two-year, $9.25 million renovation and expansion. Traveling exhibits tend toward the provocative and cutting edge—or, simply, "edge," as they say in L.A.—as do shows from the post-1950s permanent collection. (Call for current program information.) A smaller museum branch in downtown San Diego, on Kettner Blvd. at Broadway, tel. (619) 234-1001, is also well worth a stop.

Both museums are open Tues.-Sat. 10 a.m.-5 p.m., Sunday noon-5 p.m., closed Thanksgiving, Christmas, and New Year's Day. The La Jolla museum is also open Wednesday night until 8 p.m. Admission is $4 for adults, $2 for seniors (ages 65 and older), military, and students (ages 12-18), and free for children under age 12. Both museums are free on the first Tuesday and Sunday of every month.

Birch Aquarium at Scripps

The Birch Aquarium at Scripps is the public information center for the University of California's renowned Scripps Institution of Oceanography. Aquarium exhibits include a replica of Scripps Canyon, the underwater valley just off the La Jolla coast, and an abundance of re-created marine habitats—a kelp forest, for example, and aquatic homes for creatures such as the bioluminescent "flashlight fish." Exhibits in the adjacent building, collected under the banner **Exploring the Blue Planet,** delve into oceanography as science. The simulated submarine dive has major kid appeal. Another fascination: the "ocean supermarket" display of everyday items derived from the ocean.

The Birch Aquarium at Scripps, 2300 Expedition Way, tel. (858) 534-3474, is on the edge of the University of California, San Diego campus. The museum is open daily 9 a.m.-5 p.m. (last admission at 4:30 p.m.), closed on Thanksgiving and Christmas. Admission is $8.50 for adults, $7.50 for seniors (age 60 and older), $6 students, $5 for kids (ages 3-17). Parking is $3. Visit the aquarium web site at www.aquarium.ucsd.edu.

La Jolla Playhouse

The Tony Award-winning La Jolla Playhouse, 2910 La Jolla Village Dr., tel. (858) 550-1010, ac-

tually performing at two small theaters at the Mandell Weiss Center for the Performing Arts on the University of California campus, was founded in 1947 by Gregory Peck and like-minded theater buffs. By producing original musicals and plays that subsequently made a name for themselves, such as *Big River, A Walk in the Woods,* The Who's *Tommy,* and various Neil Simon works, the La Jolla Playhouse has established itself in the past decades as one of the most innovative regional theaters in the country. The theater's performance season runs from May through October. Admission varies, but tickets are typically in the $25-40 range. Call for box office hours, which change throughout the year. The Mandell Weiss Center for the Performing Arts is on the University of California campus, La Jolla Village Dr. at Revelle College Drive. For current program information, call (858) 550-1010, or visit the playhouse website at www.lajollaplayhouse.com.

Also worth a stop on campus, even if you're just passing through, is the **Stuart Collection** of

---

THE SCRIPPS LEGACY

Ellen Browning Scripps was half-sister of newspaper publisher Edward Wyllis Scripps, founder of the United Press (UP) newspaper syndicate. A respected journalist too, Ellen Browning Scripps also made millions in real estate—good fortune she shared with Southern California by founding Scripps College in Claremont and by endowing, with her brother, the Scripps Institution of Oceanography in La Jolla. Part of the genteel community of artists, writers, scientists, and just plain wealthy people that settled La Jolla at the turn of the century, she was also a patron of architecture—in particular local architect Irving J. Gill, who designed her 1915 home, now San Diego's Museum of Contemporary Art, and various public buildings there.

In a sense the Scripps family's philanthropic contributions to the community set the stage for present-day La Jolla's cultural influence, with its renowned Salk Institute and the sprawling University of California at San Diego, which now includes the Scripps Institution of Oceanography, the Scripps-affiliated Stephen Birch Aquarium-Museum, and the nationally recognized La Jolla Playhouse theater program.

outdoor art. Many of the outdoor pieces stand within an easy walk of the whimsical Theodore Geisel Library, named after the late La Jolla resident better known as Dr. Seuss.

Elsewhere Downtown and Around

Girard Avenue downtown is prime-time for La Jolla shopping. Among the multitude of cool shops here—not all of them expensive, by the way—is **Gallery Alexander,** 7850 Girard (between Wall and Silverado), tel. (858) 459-9433, with whimsical and unusual items in home furnishings, ceramics, glassware, and jewelry. Also try **Gallery Eight,** 7454 Girard, tel. (858) 454-9781.

Poke around elsewhere, too, looking for places such as **John Cole's Book Shop,** in a historic house overlooking the ocean at 780 Prospect (at Eads Ave.), tel. (858) 454-4766, and **The Artful Soul,** 1237-C Prospect St. (between Ivanhoe and Cave), tel. (858) 459-2009, locally owned and operated and quite casual, showcasing good work by about 20 local artists and artisans. Jewelry is the mainstay, each piece identified by artist, along with small gift items.

To get the big picture of La Jolla and vicinity, head to **Mount Soledad,** reached by following Nautilus Street east. From the summit of this tinder-dry hill, the area's traditional site for outdoor Easter Sunday services, at night the headlights and taillights of the traffic flow below on I-5 seem like endless dazzling strands of diamonds and rubies.

Torrey Pines State Reserve and Beach

Here's a story of endangered species that doesn't star human beings as the culprits, for a change. Protected in this small preserve are about 10,000 Torrey pines *(Pinus torreyana).* The rarest pine trees in the United States, these beautifully primeval, strange, and scraggly five-needle pines represent an Ice Age species endangered by too-specific climatic and soil needs. Get oriented at the attractive 1923 adobe-style visitor center, once a private lodge. Short and easy hiking trails wind through the semi-desert forests.

Below the heavily eroded bluffs is Torrey Pines State Beach, one of the most beautiful in San Diego County. Adjacent, technically in Del Mar, is **Los Penasquitos Lagoon,** wetlands that serve as wildlife refuge and bird sanctuary, an area almost destroyed in the 1960s by the construction of the Pacific Coast Highway route here.

Torrey Pines is north of La Jolla Village, just off N. Torrey Pines Road. To reach the preserve from I-5, exit at Genesee Ave. and head west. Turn north (right) onto N. Torrey Pines Road. To reach the beach from I-5, exit at Carmel Valley Rd. and head west. One parking lot is near the beach, another near the preserve's visitor center. Admission is free, but parking is $4 with a $1 discount for seniors. The beach is open daily, 8 a.m. to sunset; the visitor center is open 9 a.m. to sunset. For more information, contact Torrey Pines State Reserve and Beach, tel. (858) 755-2063, www.torreypine.org.

TOM MYERS PHOTOGRAPHY

Del Mar: Where the Turf Meets the Surf

For Del Mar's surf, head for **Del Mar Beach.** To watch the sunset, locals and visitors alike gather up top, on the bluffs at the end of 15th Street. For Del Mar's turf, head to the fairgrounds. Del Mar is most famous for its elegant art deco Spanish colonial **Del Mar Race Track,** "Where the Turf Meets the Surf." Recently reconstructed, the track is the place for some serious thoroughbred racing from late July into mid-September. The show here has always been something of a star-studded affair. The Del Mar Thoroughbred Club was organized in the 1930s by entertainer Bing Crosby and some of his cronies, because Crosby wanted some of the glitz and glitter of glamour racing close to his home in Rancho Santa Fe. Mostly serious gamblers and more sedate business types make up the crowd these days. But you can pony up on the ponies even in the off-season, thanks to the new age of satellite betting. Admission to the Del Mar Race Track, 2260 Jimmy Durante Blvd. (Via de la Valle Rd. at Coast Blvd.), is $4 ($7 for grandstand seats). For more information, call (619) 755-1141, or tap into current info via the Internet at www.dmtc.com.

Upscale accommodations and restaurants aren't hard to find in and around Del Mar; there are also some great deals. (For local suggestions, see Staying in San Diego, below.) Shopping opportunities also aren't hard to find, especially in upscale malls such as the Del Mar Plaza. Good deals can be found here, too. For example: relatively inexpensive for earthy natural-fiber women's wear is **Chico's,** tel. (858) 792-7080. Stop by the **Del Mar Chamber of Commerce,** 1104 Camino del Mar, tel. (858) 755-4844, for more information.

EXCURSIONS INLAND: JULIAN AND VICINITY

The Apple-Pie Old West

This slice of apple-pie Americana, easily reached from either San Diego or Escondido, really does know its apples; small orchards climb the area's hillsides. Julian sprang to life as a hill-country mining town during Southern California's gold rush in the 1890s, and then declined into near ghost-town status until the area's affinity for apple growing was actively cultivated. Since

then the town's Wild West character has been spruced up and tamed, as apples (also peaches and pears), fresh-squeezed apple cider, home-made apple pie, and the wistful American desire for simpler times have transformed tiny Julian into a major tourist draw. Bushels of visitors tumble into town during the desert's spring wildflower show, in summer, and for its **Apple Days** and **Fall Harvest Festival** celebrations—also peak seasons for local parking problems. Other main events in the fall include the **Julian Weed Show and Art Mart** and the ever-popular annual **Fiddle, Banjo, Guitar, and Mandolin Contest.** Otherwise, poking into the town's museums and peering into lace-curtained curio and gift shops are Julian's primary attractions.

Another reason to tarry here—especially for intrepid desert and high-country explorers who prefer a bed to starry nights in a sleeping bag—is the town's proximity to both Anza-Borrego Desert State Park and Cuyamaca Rancho State Park.

For current information about the community, contact the **Julian Chamber of Commerce,** 2129 Main St., Julian, tel. (760) 765-1857 or visit the chamber's website at www.julianca.com.

Julian Pioneer Museum

Just over a block south of Main at 2811 Washington St., tel. (760) 765-0227, the Julian Pioneer Museum memorializes the hardrock mining and hardscrabble living—as well as the lace curtains and high-button shoes—so prominent in this tiny town's past. This onetime brewery showcases Julian's homage to its pioneering past, with clothing, familiar household items, photographs, and stuffed samples of area wildlife. Native American artifacts are also on display. It's open from Tues.-Sun. 10 a.m.-4 p.m. from April through November, otherwise open only on weekends and national holidays (same hours) except New Year's Day, Thanksgiving, and Christmas. Admission is $1.

Eagle Mining Company

Notable at the north end of C St., tel. (760) 765-0036, is a rare opportunity to tour the inner workings of a gold mine. Dug into a mountainside, the old Eagle Mine and High Peaks Mine ceased commercial operation in 1942, but the mine tunnels and plenty of mining paraphernalia are still in place. The tour explains local gold mining history and demonstrates various mining techniques; during the school year, school tours tend to overrun the place, so come late in the day. The kids even get the chance to pan for gold—but if they find some, they have to leave it at the mine. Hourly tours are offered daily 10 a.m.-3 p.m., weather permitting, not counting time spent in "rock shop." Admission is $7 adults, $3 children ages 6-15, $1 age 5 and under.

Anza-Borrego Desert State Park

The largest state park in the contiguous United States, reaching south from the Santa Rosa Mountains almost to the Mexican border, Anza-Borrego Desert State Park consists of 600,000 acres of Colorado Desert. "Anza" refers to Juan Bautista de Anza, the Spanish captain who explored the area in 1774, establishing a viable land route from Mexico to California coastal settlements; "borrego" is Spanish for bighorn sheep. Some sights in this spectacular vastness can be appreciated from the road—the **Borrego Badlands,** the **Carrizo Badlands,** and the **Salton Sea** off in the distance—but other wonders, including **Borrego Palm Canyon, Hellhole Canyon,** and other palm oases, require the effort of a hike. In a good rain year, the park's spring wildflower bloom—usually starting in March, peaking in April—can be spectacular.

An excellent **visitor center** near park headquarters, tel. (760) 767-4205, is the best place to start an Anza-Borrego exploration. Call the park's wildflower hot line, tel. (760) 767-4684, for peak spring wildflower bloom predictions. The park is open 24 hours and admission is free (except for the Palm Canyon Trail, where hikers are charged $5 at the gate); the visitor center is open daily 9 a.m.-5 p.m. For additional information, contact the local state park headquarters at 200 Palm Canyon Drive, tel. (760) 767-5311.

Cuyamaca Rancho State Park

A high-country surprise on the edge of the desert east of San Diego, 25,000-acre Cuyamaca Rancho State Park (KWEE-uh-MACK-uh) features both lowland chaparral and fairly lush conifer and oak woodlands. As it's one of the few areas in Southern California with marked seasonal change, come for spring wildflowers, summer thunderstorms, fall colors, and, in winter, snow-dusted mountain peaks. Most of the area is designated as

wilderness; camping, nature study, and serious hiking are the park's major attractions.

The park's 110 miles of hiking and horseback riding trails (backcountry camping allowed) lead to **Cuyamaca Peak,** the park's tallest at 6,512 feet; the less challenging **Stonewall Peak,** with kind switchbacks; and also wind through meadows and oak woodlands. In recent years, mountain lion attacks have become an increasing concern—so hike in groups and otherwise heed all recommended safety precautions.

Also of note: the 1870 **Stonewall Jackson Gold Mine** at the north end of the park, not particularly impressive but providing mute testimony to the area's gold-rush era, and the park museum. Housed, along with park headquarters, in the stone **Ralph M. Dyar Homestead,** the museum emphasizes the culture of the Kumeya'ay Indians who settled the area about 7,000 years ago.

The park is open for day use from sunrise to sunset ($5 per vehicle), and at least one campground is open year-round. Call for camping reservation information (seasonal). For more information: Cuyamaca Rancho State Park, 12551 State Hwy. 79, Descanso, tel. (760) 765-0755, or visit www.cuyamaca.statepark.org.

Much of the rest of San Diego County's mountain wilderness is just to the east—the **Mount Laguna Recreation Area** in **Cleveland National Forest,** with still more hiking, camping, and picnicking potential. Though urbanites come east via I-8 and then amble north from Pine Valley via Laguna Mountain Road, the area is also accessible from Julian. Instead of following Highway 79 to Cuyamaca, turn onto the **Sunrise Highway** (County Road S1) just before Lake Cuyamaca, and keep climbing for some of the county's most spectacular desert views.

Julian Area Accommodations

Bed and breakfasts are the thing in these parts. *The* place since forever—the 1970s, actually—is the fine and funky old-time **Julian Hotel** 2023 Main Street, tel. (760) 765-0201, www.julianhotel .com, built during Julian's heyday by Albert and Margaret Robinson, freed slaves. Historical authenticity is the keynote here, since the hotel is listed on the National Register of Historic Places. Most rooms are small, with shared baths, though a one-room cottage, the honeymoon suite, and several rooms do feature private baths. Moderate-Luxury. Rates: $72-175 (two-night minimum stay on weekends).

Not part of the town's Wild West heritage but looking the part is the **Julian Lodge**, 2720 C St. (at Fourth and C, a half-block south of Main), toll-free tel. (800) 542-1420 or (760) 765-1420. This two-story wood frame hotel boasts modern amenities beneath its 19th-century charm, expressed in attractive period-style rooms (fairly small, as in the good ol' days). All rooms have cable TV but no phone; some have refrigerators and radios. A friendly fireplace beckons from downstairs in the breakfast parlor. And the conference room is not just for conferences—it turns into a good set-up for family stays, complete with a Murphy bed and rollaway cots. Moderate-Premium. Rates start at $74. Also new in the neighborhood, quite nice, and substantially more expensive is the **Orchard Hill Country Inn**, 2502 Washington St., tel. (760) 765-1700, www.orchardhill.com. Luxury. Rates are $160-265.

Shadow Mountain Ranch, beyond Julian proper at 2771 Frisius Rd., tel. (760) 765-0323, is a onetime cattle ranch and apple orchard refashioned into a country-style bed and breakfast inn. Accommodations are available in either the main house—two rooms with fireplaces and antiques—or in the ranch's four cottages, each with particular charms. Grandma's Attic is all wicker and lace, for example, and The Enchanted Cottage—atop a hill—has a potbellied stove and a view of the pines. For couples traveling together, Manzanita Cottage offers two bedrooms with separate entrances, a living room (complete with woodstove), and kitchen. Unique, though, is the Tree House, available only in the summer. Generous ranch-style breakfasts are included. Expensive-Premium. Rates are $90 and up, two-night minimum on weekends.

But if bed and breakfasts just aren't your style, plan to camp at either Cuyamaca Rancho or Anza-Borrego Desert State Parks (at least some campsites open year-round). Or beat a high-desert retreat to Borrego Springs in the midst of Anza-Borrego. **La Casa del Zorro** (see below) is the classiest act around, but another good choice is the frontier-style **Palm Canyon Resort** silhouetted against the stunning mountains at 221 Palm Canyon Dr. (near the park visitor center), Borrego Springs, toll-free tel. (800) 342-

0044 in California or (760) 767-5341. Rooms are spacious and quite attractive in subdued western style, with color TV, cable, and in-room coffeemakers and refrigerators. Also here are a swimming pool, whirlpool, and on-site restaurant and "saloon." Moderate-Premium. Rates start at $85 in the typical fall, winter, and spring travel season, at $60 in torrid summer heat. There's a Good Sam RV park here, too.

La Casa del Zorro Resort Hotel

One of those classic California desert resorts, La Casa del Zorro started out as an adobe ranch house, built in 1937. Since then, whitewashed adobe-style "casitas" have spread out over 32 tree-shaded acres. Rooms here are beautifully decorated and comfortable. Resort amenities include putting green, tennis courts, three swimming pools, rental bikes, and volleyball. (Child care can be arranged.) Two good restaurants are also part of the complex. Moderate-Luxury. Room rates start at $85 for suites; the separate two- to four-bedroom "casitas," run $375 to $950 in season (substantially lower in summer), with a two-night minimum stay on weekends. For more information: La Casa del Zorro Resort Hotel, 3845 Yaqui Pass Rd., Borrego Springs, toll-free tel. (800) 824-1844 or (760) 767-5323, www.lacasadelzorro.com.

Eating in and around Julian

Julian isn't known for its great restaurants. Popular for lunch, though, is **Mom's Apple Pies,** tel. (760) 765-2472, and for dinner, the **Julian Grill,** tel. (760) 765-0173. Except on weekends and holidays, the dining room at the craftsman-style Orchard Hill Country Inn on Washington St. north of Main, tel. (760) 765-1420, is open to nonguests (call for reservations).

If a genuinely good meal is mandatory, get ready to drive—all the way to Borrego Springs, in the middle of Anza-Borrego Desert State Park. **La Casa del Zorro Restaurant** at the resort, 3845 Yaqui Pass Rd., tel. (760) 767-5323, is the place for dress-up dinners out in the desert, as well as a more casual breakfast and lunch. Dinner entrees include chicken *cordon bleu,* prime rib, scampi, Alaskan salmon, and vegetable curry. Lighter a la carte specials and the changing early bird specials are the real deals. La Casa del Zorro also offers a feast for the spirit—Old California ambience with candlelit whitewashed walls reminiscent of 1930s Palm Springs. The restaurant is open daily 7 a.m.-3 p.m., Friday and Saturday 5-10 p.m., and on Sunday 4:30-10 p.m.

But don't miss **Dudley's Bakery**, 30218 Hwy. 78, an area institution near the junction with Hwy. 79 in Santa Ysabel, tel. (760) 765-0488 or toll-free (800) 225-3348, open daily 8 a.m.-5 p.m. Cali-

fornia history aficionados may stop in Santa Ysabel to peek into **Mission Asistencia de Santa Isabel,** a small 18th-century mission outpost reconstructed in more recent times. But everyone stops at Dudley's across the street before heading into the wilderness or back into the city. This is the place to load up on specialty breads—how about jalapeño loaf?—breakfast pastries, and other goodies. Dudley's offers deli fare, too.

ARTFUL, ENTERTAINING SAN DIEGO

San Diego is renowned for the art museums and other cultural riches collected in Balboa Park, and for both the **Old Globe Shakespeare Festival** and **La Jolla Playhouse** theater programs. The **California Ballet Company, San Diego Opera, San Diego Symphony,** and **San Diego Civic Light Opera** are also center stage on the local arts scene. And the **La Jolla Symphony,** the **La Jolla Chamber Music Society,** and other music groups are still going strong. Touring concerts and other national troupes perform both at downtown venues and at area college and university campuses—the University of California, San Diego, San Diego State University, local community colleges, and private colleges and universities, which are also good bets for guest speakers and eclectic special events. Pick up local newspapers to find out what's going on where. Local papers also publish listings of local art galleries; many are concentrated in the Gaslamp Quarter, in La Jolla, and elsewhere along the coast.

Though Balboa Park's three stages and the La Jolla Playhouse are local theatrical stars, smaller repertory groups and venues abound—including the acclaimed **Blackfriars Theatre** downtown at 121 Broadway, Ste. 203, tel. (619) 232-4088; the contemporary **San Diego Repertory Theater,** 79 Horton Plaza, tel. (619) 235-8025; and the cabaret-style **Coronado Playhouse,** 1775 Strand Way, tel. (619) 435-4856.

Mainstream movie theaters are everywhere; multiple multiplexes cluster at area malls and elsewhere. Often the most challenging cinema is served forth from smaller, sometimes historic theaters. Happening in Hillcrest, for example, is the **Hillcrest Cinemas** multiplex, 3965 Fifth

Ave., tel. (619) 299-2100, showing foreign and art films. The art-revival house **Ken Cinema** on Adams Avenue, tel. (619) 283-5909 is brought to you by the same folks. The **Sherwood Auditorium** at the Museum of Contemporary Art in La Jolla, 700 Prospect, tel. (619) 454-2594, also screens classic and foreign films.

Entertaining San Diego

San Diego *is* entertaining, from its distinctive neighborhood bar scenes and dance clubs to respectable jazz and rock venues. Again, local newspapers are the best source for what's going on while you're in town. An eclectic around-town club-scene cruise for older hipsters might include, for acoustic jazz, **Croce's** in the Gaslamp Quarter, 802 Fifth Ave., tel. (619) 233-4355; the top-flight jazz venue **Chris' Shores Grill** on the top floor of the Summer House Inn in La Jolla, 7955 La Jolla Shores Dr., tel. (858) 459-0541; and, for live rock, R&B, reggae, and whatever, the Quonset-hut-chic **Belly Up Tavern** in Solana Beach, 143 S. Cedros Ave., tel. (858) 481-9022. And there's always **Planet Hollywood** at Horton Plaza, tel. (619) 702-7827, and the also loud **Hard Rock Cafe** in La Jolla, tel. (858) 454-5101. If the arthritis and bursitis aren't giving you too much grief, consider headin' out for a country-western stomp at **In Cahootz** in Mission Valley, 5373 Mission Center Rd., tel. (619) 291-8635. Otherwise, it's safe to settle in at the bar at the **U.S. Grant Hotel** downtown, tel. (619) 232-3121, for great local blues and jazz, or soak up some classy piano-bar comfort at the **Westgate Hotel** downtown, tel. (619) 238-1818, and at **Hotel del Coronado** across the water, tel. (619) 522-8262.

EVENTFUL SAN DIEGO

With the sublime weather here, it's little wonder that so many San Diego events, among them open-air theater and street festivals, are staged outdoors. Unique or oddball local events can be the most fun, so while you're here ask around and study local newspapers. Museums, colleges, and universities also sponsor a variety of unusual activities.

Mid-December through mid- March is **whale watching** season, when California gray whales make their northern migration. And in January, catch the **San Diego Marathon** as it winds 26.2 miles down the coast from Carlsbad. The ever-popular international **Festival of Animation,** staged in La Jolla at the Museum of Contemporary Art's Sherwood Auditorium, runs from mid-January through April; the *Sick and Twisted* short-subject collection is screened after mid-night. Major San Diego spring events include the **Ocean Beach Kite Festival** in March; the **San Diego Crew Classic,** the **Downtown ArtWalk,** and the **Coronado Flower Show** in April; and the **Pacific Beach Block Party,** the Olympic-caliber **Del Mar National Horseshow,** and Old Town's **Cinco de Mayo** festivities in May.

In June, come for the **San Diego County Fair** at the fairgrounds in Del Mar, the **Mostly Mozart Festival** downtown in the Spreckels Theater, the annual **Ocean Beach Street Fair and Chili Cook-Off,** the **San Diego International Triathlon,** and the **Rock n' Roll Marathon.** Also in June, the **Twilight in the Park** summer concert series in Balboa Park begins, continuing through August. In July, the annual **San Diego Lesbian and Gay Pride Parade** is a huge draw, with a rally and festival well into the night. Also in July, **Sand Castle Days** at the Imperial Beach Pier is a big hit, fun in the sun along with serious competitive sand castle construction, along with the **Sizzling Summer Jazz Festival** on Coronado. The **Hillcrest Cityfest Street Fair** comes in August, along with the **Thundertub Regatta** at Mission Bay, part of America's Finest City Week festivities, and the immensely popular **San Diego Comic Convention** happens at the convention center. The convention pays homage to comic books, cartoon and comic art, and comic artists.

The biggest big deal in September is the Gaslamp Quarter's **Street Scene** fall food and music festival (sometimes scheduled in late August), while the **Adams Avenue Street Fair,** a right neighborly neighborhood block party, is much more laid-back. In October, when admission is free for children all month, **Zoo Founder's Day** makes a human zoo out of the San Diego Zoo. All kinds of Halloween fun—including the **Haunted Museum of Man** in Balboa Park, and an **Underwater Pumpkin Carving Contest** in La Jolla—round out the year's foremost month of fright. For animals on the march, head to El Cajon with kids in tow in November for the annual **Mother Goose Parade** or to the **Carlsbad Village Faire** in Carlsbad. Magical among the multitude of holiday events in December is **Christmas on El Prado** in Balboa Park and, along the bay downtown, the **San Diego Harbor Parade of Lights.**

OUTDOOR SAN DIEGO

The sun always shines in San Diego County, powerfully enough, most of the time, to dry up even the chance of rain. Since even San Diego's major tourist attractions are out in the open air, it's little wonder then that, here, life is lived outdoors. Recreation and sports are central to local life, which explains the area's endless variety of outdoor activities. Begin with aerial sports—skydiving, sky sailing, aerial barnstorming. Then beach combing, bicycling, birdwatching, boating—every imaginable type of boat and water sport—and even bocce ball. There's golfing—lots of it, with lush green courses spread out everywhere—and Frisbee golf in Balboa Park. And hiking. Horseback riding. Kayaking. Kite-flying. Racquetball. Recreational working-out, at the legion of local health and fitness clubs. Rock climbing. Rollerblading. Sportfishing, swimming, surfing, snorkeling, shark diving, scuba diving, sailing, and sailboarding. Tennis. Volleyball at the beaches. Waterskiing. Whale-watching. You name it, chances are San Diego does it—and has at least one outfitter offering the necessary equipment and/or service. For a current listing, contact the local visitor bureau (see Practical San Diego, below).

Recreational San Diego

Inexplicably, nonathletic types sometimes find themselves in San Diego. For them, the local

SAN DIEGO WHALEWATCHING, BY LAND AND BY SEA

California is one of the world's premier whale-watching locations. The state's long coastline and natural vantage points, good harbors and specialized sportfishing and tour fleets, make whalewatching an immensely popular year-round pursuit for residents and visitors alike.

Most impressive is the annual offshore migration of the California gray whale, until recently an endangered species. In winter, gray whales migrate south along the coast from the frigid Bering Straits to the more tropical climate of Mexico's Baja California. Most boisterous—and most entertaining to watch—is the migration south in January, when mature bulls and breeding cows cruise California waters. Their splashy mating behavior—which often includes "breaching," or leaping up out of the water before slamming back to sea—is a particular thrill on offshore whalewatching tours. By February these newly pregnant females and promiscuous male hangers-on begin their return migration, sometimes passing, en route, southbound stragglers—juveniles and immature whales of both sexes. In March gray whale cows with newborn calves start north from Mexico,

easily visible from land, typically, because of their slow pace and tendency to travel close to shore.

During the summer, blue whales and humpback whales can be observed near southern California's **Channel Islands National Park.**

Sublime and sunny San Diego, with balmy beach weather even in winter, attracts pods and pods of fair-weather whalewatchers. Prime viewpoint in winter is **Cabrillo National Monument** at the mouth of the bay, outfitted with an observation platform. (Since Cabrillo is often crowded, keep in mind that there are many other good locations along the coast.) The **Scripps Institution of Oceanography,** the **San Diego Natural History Museum,** and local **sportfishing and tour companies** all offer oceangoing whalewatching tours. Contact local visitor information centers for current details.

The California gray whale was once endangered.

love affair with aerobic exercise, buff bodies, and too-dark tans can be a bit intimidating. For the record, however, you *can* come to San Diego, have a good time, and leave the exercise to someone else. At last report there was no law—no official law, anyway—stating otherwise.

Sign on for a San Diego Bay tour, for example. **Hornblower Cruises** at the Cruise Ship Pier, 1066 N. Harbor, tel. (619) 234-8687, www.hornblower.com, offers mainstream one- and two-hour harbor tours, brunch and dinner cruises, even whalewatching trips, with rates $12 and up. The cheapest water trip around, something of a self-designed tour, is the **Coronado Ferry,** which departs from the nearby Broadway Pier, $2 each way (plus 50 cents if you bring a bike), tel. (619) 234-4111 for information and schedules.

(See Coronado: Crown of the Bay for more information.) Part with substantially more cash for a sailboat cruise, with outfits such as **Sail U.S.A.,** tel. (619) 298-6822.

You can also take a train trip—or a self-designed train-oriented nostalgia trip. Take the **San Diego Trolley** on a 30-mile route around San Diego with more than a dozen stops. Stations include Presidio Park, Balboa Park, San Diego Zoo, Coronado, Gaslamp Quarter, and Horton Plaza. The trolley costs $20 for adults, $8 for children 6-12 (free for children 5 and under), and you can hop off and on again at any point to make the complete loop. The trolley also goes east to old-hometown-style La Mesa, for example, for a visit to the **La Mesa Depot Museum** (open weekends only), tel. (619) 595-3030. A more ambitious weekend possibility: the 16-mile roundtrip backcountry boogie aboard a vintage steam- or diesel-powered train on the **San Diego**

& **Arizona Railway,** starting at **Campo Depot,** tel. (619) 478-9937 (weekends), well east of San Diego in Campo, near the Mexican border. In winter and early spring, you can also take a trip from Campo to Tecate, Mexico.

Or, how 'bout an aerial excursion? **Skysurfer Balloon Company** in Del Mar, tel. toll-free (800) 660-6809 or (619) 481-6800, for hot-air ballooning, is one good possibility. **Barnstorming Adventures, Ltd.,** tel. toll-free (800) 759-5667 or (760) 438-7680, www.barnstorming.com, is another, definitely something you can't do every day. Climb into a beautifully restored open-cockpit biplane and go for an easy 20-minute spin or a high-flying "Sunset Snuggler" tour. If you're feeling dangerous, stay out for an hour long aerial roller-coaster ride with dogfight maneuvers. Vintage plane rides start at $98 per person for 20 minutes. Flights usually depart from either Palomar Airport or Gillespie Field, only as scheduled (reservations required).

Sporting San Diego

Spectator sports are ever-popular with San Diego's armchair athletes. For pro baseball, the National League **San Diego Padres** fill the bill at Qualcomm Stadium ("the Q") at 9449 Friars Rd. in Mission Valley (intersection of I-8 and I-805) from mid-April to October. For schedule info, call (619) 283-4494; for tickets, (619) 29-PADRES. During pro football season, the stadium's stars are the **San Diego Chargers,** tel. (619) 280-2111. For Padres and Chargers home games, consider taking the **Express** bus, tel. (619) 233-3004, which picks up fans at several locations throughout the city beginning two hours before the game.

The **San Diego Sports Arena** hosts the U.S. International Hockey League **San Diego Gulls,** tel. (619) 224-4625 or (619) 224-4171, from October through April, and the rock 'em-sock 'em **San Diego Sockers** professional indoor soccer team, tel. (619) 224-GOAL, October-May.

To watch Sunday polo matches from June through October, head to Rancho Santa Fe and the **San Diego Polo Club,** tel. (858) 481-9217. In late July through mid-September, you'll find horse-racing action at the **Del Mar Race Track** in Del Mar, tel. (858) 755-1141.

SHOPPING SAN DIEGO

You're not looking very hard if you can't find something to buy in San Diego. Major malls are the obvious places to start parting with your hard-earned cash—places such as **Horton Plaza** and the nearby **Paladion** downtown, **Fashion Valley** and the **Mission Valley Center** near Hotel Circle, the huge **University Town Center** in La Jolla's Golden Triangle, and Del Mar's cunningly camouflaged **Del Mar Plaza.** The **San Diego Factory Outlet Center,** tel. (619) 690-2999, in San Ysidro, near the Mexican border, is also immensely popular. Savvy shoppers can pick up bargains at **Carlsbad Company Stores,** tel. (760) 804-9000, with bargains from Barney's New York, Kenneth Cole and The Gap, among others. The traditional bargainhunter's bonanza, however, is **Kobey's Swap Meet** at the Sports Arena parking lot, 3500 Sports Arena Blvd., tel. (619) 226-0650. Fun and funky, it's open Thurs.-Sun. 7 a.m.-3 p.m. (admission $1).

For specialty items, migrate to the most likely neighborhoods. **Hillcrest,** for example, is a good bet for trendy clothes, gifts, and good bookstores and music shops, as is **La Jolla,** also known for homewares, home fashions, and art galleries. For tourist-grade international arts and crafts and Mexican memorabilia, head for Old Town and **Bazaar del Mundo, La Esplanade,** and **Old Town Mercado.** (Do comparison shop here; some places are substantially less expensive than others.) To hunt down seafaring wares, look around on and near both **Harbor Island** and **Shelter Island.**

STAYING IN SAN DIEGO

A pleasant surprise in San Diego is the range of surprisingly decent accommodation options, from dirt cheap to definitely expensive. You'd expect to find upscale hotels, inns, and resorts along the coast, downtown, and elsewhere, but the surprise is that prime visitor areas also feature hostels, very inexpensive hotels, and reasonably priced, pleasant motels. The following suggestions are arranged by general locale. For more choices, see also Coronado: Crown of the Bay above and/or contact the local visitors bureau (see Practical San Diego, below). For bed and breakfast listings, contact the **Bed & Breakfast Guild of San Diego,** tel. (619) 523-1300, or the countywide **Bed & Breakfast Directory for San Diego,** tel. (619) 297-3130 or toll-free (800) 619-7666.

In these increasingly bargain-conscious times, pursue discounts, an effort that pays off particularly well in the September through mid-June "off season." Why summer is still prime time for vacationers to San Diego, considering the marvelous year-round climate, remains something of a mystery—but don't complain, since everyone else's shortsightedness can save you from the crowds *and* save you money. For summertime bargains, head inland; away from the moderate coastal climate, temperatures soar and prices drop. Larger hotels, resorts, and motel chains almost always offer discounts, with special deals and packages during slow periods. As elsewhere in California and the U.S., members of the American Automobile Association (AAA) and the American Association of Retired Persons (AARP) qualify for sometimes substantial discount rates at many accommodations, as do corporate customers. For major deals—savings as much as 50 percent, in some cases—consider booking even resort accommodations through **San Diego Hotel Reservations,** tel. (800) 728-3227. While making travel plans, be aware of the city's all-out conventioneering—and be flexible about trip timing, if at all possible. San Diego's success at attracting major conventions and staging major events is great for the hotel business but bad news for savvy travelers suddenly unable to get a bargain rate.

STAYING IN AND AROUND DOWNTOWN

U.S. Grant Hotel

Downtown's most dignified and time-honored presence, the landmark U.S. Grant Hotel was built in 1910 by Ulysses S. Grant, Jr., son of the former Civil War general and U.S. president. After decades of decline mid-century, the 11-story U.S. Grant reopened in 1985 after an impressive $80 million renovation. The classy classic lobby, with its Palladian columns, marble floors, crystal chandeliers, Old World art, and Chinese porcelain, sets the tone for the guest rooms. Regular rooms are somewhat small but tastefully done in Queen Anne-style mahogany, even the armoire hiding the TV (cable provided; movies available). Marble and tile bathrooms offer other modern comforts, such as terrycloth robes and handmilled soaps. Luxury. Official room rates are $185-205 and up but, with reservations at least one month in advance and special discounts (AAA members and others), can go as low as $129. Ask about off-season specials and packages, too. One of downtown's best restaurants is the **Grant Grill** here, tel. (619) 239-6806, surprisingly reasonable, serving breakfast, lunch, and dinner. Other facilities include exercise room (massage extra), business center, and conference rooms.

The U.S. Grant, downtown at 326 Broadway, inhabits an entire city block. Its formal entrance is directly across from Horton Plaza but, unless on foot, most guests enter the lobby from the parking lot (valet parking). For more information, call (619) 232-3121, or check www.grandheritage.com. For reservations, call toll-free (800) 237-5029.

More Uptown Downtown Hotels

The 19-story **Westgate Hotel** is a classic modern American study in contrast—in this case, the contrast between somewhat formal Old World luxury and the ubiquitous, thoroughly modern downtown high-rise in which it hides. The lobby sparkles with Baccarat crystal chandeliers; high tea is served every afternoon. The theme of classical opulence continues through on-site restaurants and into the antique-furnished guest rooms, where bathrooms come with Italian marble and gold-plated fixtures. From the ninth floor up, rooms come with a view, too. Luxury. Rack rates run $184-224, with considerable price flexibility depending on what's going on. Weekends are usually the best deal, with $150 the typical rate. The Westgate is at 1055 Second Ave. (at C St.), tel. (619) 238-1818, fax (619) 557-3737. For reservations, call toll-free (800) 221-3802.

If you prefer more contemporary big-hotel ambience with the usual amenities plus an indoor pool and gym, another good choice downtown is the contemporary **Embassy Suites,** 601 Pacific Hwy. (at N. Harbor Dr.), tel. (800) EMBASSY or (619) 239-2400. This is a better setup for families, too, since all suites feature a separate bedroom plus conveniences like refrigerators, hairdryers, coffeemakers, and microwaves. All rooms have city or bay views. Full breakfast, as you like it (served in the restaurant), is included, along with free cocktails. Luxury. Rates run $189-300, with various discounts and specials often available.

The **Wyndham Emerald Plaza,** formerly the Pan Pacific Hotel, also caters to the business trade, but with swimming pool, full fitness facilities, and abundant other extras, it's quite comfortable for tourists who prefer a downtown base. Luxury. Rates are generally lowest on the weekend, too, sometimes starting at $129; ask about other discounts and specials. And if you're meeting someone, rendezvous under the "emerald" in the lobby. The Wyndham Emerald Plaza is at the Emerald-Shapery Center (between Columbia and State), 400 W. Broadway, tel. (619) 239-4500, www.wyndham.com. For reservations, call toll-free (800) 996-3426.

Horton Grand Hotel

Another notable downtown presence is the genteel Horton Grand Hotel in the Gaslamp Quarter, on Island Street between Third and Fourth. The ambience here is historic yet new, a neat trick achieved by building what amounts to one hotel from the old-brick bones of two time-honored neighborhood hotels otherwise doomed by redevelopment—including the original Horton Grand, which stood in the way of Horton Plaza. Rooms here are cozy, in the Victorian style, with neat touches such as gas fireplaces and TV sets cleverly tucked into the wall (behind a mirror). Premium-Luxury. Rates run $139-219, with various discounts and special packages often available. For more information, contact: Horton Grand Hotel, 311 Island Avenue (at Fourth Ave.), tel. toll-free (800) 542-1886 for reservations or (619) 544-1886, www.hortongrand.com.

Downtown Area Bed and Breakfasts

The friendly **Balboa Park Inn,** right across the street from Balboa Park, is a stylistic complement to the park's 1915 exposition architecture. All rooms at the inn—actually, four Spanish colonial homes interconnected by courtyards—are tasteful yet simple suites with either one or two bedrooms; fun "specialty" suites include the Paris in the 30s, Nob Hill, and Nouveau Ritz suites. Amenities vary (as does room décor) but include kitchens, fireplaces, patios, in-room whirlpools, and wetbars. Continental breakfast and the morning newspaper are delivered to your door. The inn is on the north end of Balboa Park, and you can walk to park attractions. Expensive-Luxury. Rates start at $95 per night. For more information, contact: Balboa Park Inn, 3402 Park Blvd., tel. toll-free (800) 938-8181 or (619) 298-0823, www.balboaparkinn.com.

Though a summertime stay often requires considerable advance booking, another great deal is the impeccably restored 1913 **Gaslamp Plaza Suites** just a block from Horton Plaza at 520 E Street (corner of 5th Ave.), tel. (619) 232-9500, or toll-free tel. (800) 874-8770, a time-share condo that also rents out rooms as available. The building itself, with a lovely lobby chiseled from marble and mosaic tiles, is San Diego's first high-rise, circa 1913, and listed on the National Register of Historic Places. The suites—larger ones feature a separate bedroom—are attractive and named famous writers including Shelley, Fitzgerald, and Emerson, with various amenities, some including microwaves, refrigerators, coffeemakers, color TV, the works. Rates range from $93-200, depending on room size and amenities, and include continental breakfast—served on the roof, weather permitting. The view is free.

Best Downtown Bets on a Budget

A comfortable downtown budget hotel, on India Street at Date, residential-style **La Pensione** is contemporary and clean. Especially appealing if you'll be staying awhile—the general ambience here, plus on-site laundry, make that an attractive idea—each cozy room (two people maximum) features a private bath, a kitchenette with microwave and refrigerator, and adequate space for spreading out work projects or tourist brochures. Moderate. Daily rates are $60-80, single or double. Ask about weekly and monthly rates. For more information, contact: La Pensione, 1700 India St., tel. (619) 236-8000, www.lapensionehotel.com. For reservations, call toll-free (800) 232-4683.

La Pacifica Hotel is another San Diego find—a well-located residential hotel with style, grace, and great rates (daily, weekly, monthly). This gem has a similar set-up to La Pensione—private baths, kitchenettes with microwaves and refrigerators, telephone, color TV with cable. Some rooms even have a harbor view. Other pluses: daily maid service, on-site laundry, bicycle storage, and nearby public parking. Moderate. In summer, rates start at $60 per day. La Pacifica is downtown on Second Ave., between Beech and Cedar. For more information, contact: La Pacifica Hotel, 1546 Second Ave., tel. (619) 236-9292.

Definitely a bargain—one of those places where you'll find a bed even when conventioneers have taken every other place in town—is the landmark **Embassy Hotel** just north of Balboa Park at 3645 Park Blvd., tel. (619) 296-3141, these days primarily a residential home for the elderly. Inexpensive. Rooms, $54 per night, are fairly basic but quiet and roomy, with private bathrooms and in-room phones. Free laundry facilities. You can even eat with the residents, in the decent cafeteria-style dining room.

HI-AYH Metropolitan Hostel

Affiliated with Hostelling International-American Youth Hostels, the Metropolitan Hostel replaces downtown's Hostel on Broadway. On the corner of Fifth Ave. and Market in the heart of the Gaslamp Quarter, the fully renovated Metropolitan features private and dorm rooms, a laundry, lockers, common kitchen, pool table, and rental bikes. Rates are $17-19 per person. For more information, contact: HI-AYH Metropolitan Hostel, 521 Market St., tel. (619) 525-1531. Groups welcome. Children (under age 18) are welcome if accompanied by an adult. Reserva-

tions are essential in summer (through September). The office is open daily 7 a.m.-midnight. For information via the Internet, the address is www.hiayh.org.

AT THE BAY AND ALONG THE COAST

Near The Embarcadero

Downtown yet on the bay, adjacent to Seaport Village and a stone's throw from the convention center, is the stylish sky-high **Hyatt Regency San Diego** just off Harbor Drive, particularly popular with businessfolk and conventioneers—definitely a great choice if someone else is picking up the tab. All rooms here have an ocean view, but the best look-see of them all is the 360-degree vista from the lounge, especially impressive at sunset. The chic but casual British men's club sensibility here is leavened with bright California sunshine and all-American room to roam, from the health club, pool, and lighted tennis courts to the marina (sailboats available for rent). Luxury. Regular room rates are $245-290, often lower on weekends. For more information, contact: Hyatt Regency San Diego, One Market Place (at Harbor Dr.), San Diego, tel. (619) 232-1234. For reservations, call toll-free (800) 233-1234.

Also along the Embarcadero and almost affordable is the **Holiday Inn on the Bay,** 1355 N. Harbor Drive (at Ash), toll-free tel. (800) 465-4329 or tel. (619) 232-3861, with large rooms and all the usual amenities. Premium-Luxury. Regular rates run $139-199, but inquire about off-season rates and other specials.

Shelter Island, Harbor Island, and Vicinity

This area naturally attracts the sailing set but also draws wannabe yachters, what with all those pretty, high-priced boats bobbing around everywhere. And the spectacular bay views attract everyone else.

Attractive Hawaii-like tropical landscape and the endless "tiki" on parade is the real appeal of **Humphrey's Half Moon Inn** on Shelter Island, making for comfortable California coastal kitsch complete with in-room refrigerators and coffeemakers. In the midst of San Diego's bustling boat harbor, Humphrey's provides a private boat dock, huge heated pool, and whirlpool spa; for tooling around, rental bikes are available; special events, such as the great outdoor jazz, folk, and easy-rock concerts in summer, keep everyone coming back. (For cool jazz—indoors—during the rest of the year, show up on Sunday and Monday nights.) Luxury. High-season rates start at $169 or $179 depending on the view, with a two-night minimum on weekends from Memorial Day through Labor Day. For more information, contact: Humphrey's Half Moon Inn and Suites, 2303 Shelter Island Dr., tel. toll-free (800) 345-9995 or (619) 224-3411, www.halfmooninn.com.

To spend substantially more, head for Harbor Island and the **Sheraton San Diego Hotel and Marina,** 1380 Harbor Island Dr., tel. (619) 291-2900 or toll-free (800) 325-3535, fax (619) 692-2337, www.sheraton.com, originally two separate Sheraton hotels, all recently redone and refashioned into one hotel. Ongoing shuttle bus service connects the two high-rise towers, lower buildings, and various services and programs. Luxury. Regular rates start at $200.

Along the Coast and Mission Bay

Mission Beach, Mission Bay, and Pacific Beach are filled to the gills with resorts and large hotels, many quite pricey and, in summer, overrun by fellow travelers. But the coastal areas also offer some nice midrange motel-style stays; a motel sitting literally above the surf, on a pier; and several hostels. For more on inexpensive hostel stays, see below.

Mission Bay's classic family getaway is the lush and lovely **San Diego Paradise Point Resort,** a 44-acre island formerly the Princess Resort owned by Princess Cruises. The endless recreation here is the real draw—including paddleboats, water sports, five swimming pools, croquet, and volleyball. Rent bikes and cruise over to the beach, an easy few miles away, with or without the kids; in summer, the organized kids' program gives grown-ups a break, too. Luxury. Rates run $245-290 in summer. For more information, contact: San Diego Paradise Point Resort, 1404 W. Vacation Rd., tel. toll-free (800) 344-2626 or (858) 274-4630, www.noblehouse-hotels.com. Also on the upscale end of family-style fun is the 18-acre **San Diego Hilton Beach and Tennis Resort,** 1775 E. Mission Bay Dr., tel. toll-free (800) 445-8667 or (619) 276-4010,

www.hilton.com, offering both bungalows and high-rise rooms recently redone in modern mission style. Luxury. Summer rates are $205-335.

One of the best values around is the **Bahia Resort Hotel,** 998 W. Mission Bay Dr., tel. toll-free (800) 576-4229 or (858) 488-0551, www.bahiahotel.com, semi-tropical and attractive, right across the street from a grassy park area and just a stroll from the beach. A bay beach and marina, where the paddlewheeler *Bahia Belle* is berthed (bay cruises, even dinner cruises, available), augment the backyard view from some rooms. Premium-Luxury. Rates are $129 and up, often discounted on a space-available basis. Also reasonable—and a reasonably good family setup, since some rooms feature kitchens or kitchenettes—is the very nice **Pacific Shores Inn** in Pacific Beach at 4802 Mission Blvd., tel. toll-free (800) 826-0715 (reservations only) or (858) 483-6300, just 100 feet from the broad sandy beach. All rooms have HBO, some have kitchenettes, and continental breakfast is included. Premium-Luxury. Rates run $144-179, lower in the off-season.

The *classic* Pacific Beach stay, though, is right in the middle of the local action—out on the Crystal Pier, at the landmark 1930s **Crystal Pier Hotel,** 4500 Ocean Blvd., tel. toll-free (800) 748-5894 or (858) 483-6983, actually a pier-long collection of motel-style cottages. The Crystal Pier Hotel features 26 white-and-blue cottages with kitchenettes and surf-view patios—nothing fancy but unique and immensely popular, a fact reflected in the price. Premium-Luxury, with rates $145-305. Make reservations well in advance for summer (three-day minimum stay in summer, two-night otherwise). Weekly and monthly rates are available in the off-season.

Budget-Travel Bonanza: Three Coastal Hostels

Most surprisingly, San Diego boasts three hostels at, or very near, the beach. Bright yellow, almost brand-new, and affiliated with the American Association of International Hostels, bustling **Beach Banana Bungalow San Diego** is right at the beach—on Reed Ave. at Mission Blvd.—and right in the middle of the way-cool, way-young Pacific Beach scene. Accommodations are dormitory style, with four to eight beds per room. Budget. Rates run $16 for dormitory rooms, $20 for semi-private rooms. Breakfast and sand volleyball are included; laundry facilities and storage lockers are available. No reservations are taken; show up by 11 a.m. to grab a bed. For more information, contact: Beach Banana Bungalow San Diego, 707 Reed Ave., tel. toll-free (800) 546-7835 or (858) 273-3060, www.bananabungalow.com.

The newest place around, though, is also the oldest—the **Ocean Beach International Backpacker Hostel,** at home in the historic Hotel Newport in Ocean Beach, on Newport Ave. between Cable and Bacon. This 80-bed hostel is just one block from the beach in San Diego's most laid-back and "local" beach community. Budget. Small but private "couples rooms," with two beds and a bathroom, cost $17-19. Most rooms are semi-private with four or six beds per room; most of these also have private bathrooms. (More bathrooms are in the hallways.) Rates are $15 per person semi-private, $17 private—including pastries for breakfast. For more information, contact: Ocean Beach International Backpacker Hostel, 4961 Newport Ave., tel. toll-free (800) 339-7263 or (619) 223-7873, e-mail obihostel@aol.com.

The **Point Loma/Elliott Hostel,** affiliated with Hostelling International-American Youth Hostels, is in a pleasant Point Loma residential neighborhood—close to the ocean but not particularly close to San Diego's other attractions. Yet this 60-bed hostel, on Udall St., off Voltaire between Warden and Poinsettia, is a reasonably good base for wanderings farther afield. Draws include full kitchen, a travel library, and baggage storage. The basic dormitory rate is $17 for non-members, $14 for members. Family rooms are also available. (Children under age 18 are welcome if accompanied by an adult.) Office hours: 8-11 a.m. and 5:30-11 p.m. For more information, contact: Point Loma/Elliott HI-AYH Hostel, 3790 Udall Street, tel. (619) 223-4778. For information on HI-AYH hostels via the Internet, the address is: www.hiayh.org.

Mission San Diego de Acalá as it appeared at the end of the 19th century

STAYING IN AND AROUND OLD TOWN

In Old Town

Old Town San Diego offers some of the best lodging bargains around, including the all-suites **Best Western Hacienda Hotel Old Town.** Once a mission-style mini-mall, it's now a multilevel hillside motel—a quite clever renovation albeit a bit baffling at first, with multiple patios, passageways, stairways, terraces, and elevators to navigate. Wheelchair-accessible rooms are reached via elevators. Once you do find your way around—and find the on-site restaurants and pleasant pool area—you're set for an enjoyable stay. The mood here is San Diego-style Southwestern, with lovely landscaping outside; some rooms open onto terraces, with partially private patios. Inside, most rooms are smallish but quite adequate, with all the usual amenities plus ceiling fans, in-room coffeemakers, microwaves, and refrigerators. Great harbor views at night, especially from upper levels. Premium-Luxury. Rates are $145 and up in summer, somewhat lower at other times, but weekdays rates can go as low as $125. Ask about packages and seasonal specials. The Hacienda Hotel Old Town is at 4041 Harney St. (just off Juan), tel. toll-free (800) 888-1991 or (619) 298-4707, www.bestwestern.com.

Depending on when you're coming—weekdays are usually the best deal any time but summer—other relative bargains in the neighborhood include the **Holiday Inn Hotel Old Town,** $118-189, right next to the freeway at 2435 Jefferson St. (exit I-5 at Old Town Ave.), tel. toll-free (800) 433-2131 or (619) 260-8500; and the **Ramada Limited Old Town,** 3900 Old Town Ave., tel. toll-free (800) 451-9846 or tel. (619) 299-7400, where rooms $129-159 include continental breakfast. Both are Premium-Luxury.

For a quick trip into Victorian San Diego, stay at the gracious two-story **Heritage Park Bed & Breakfast Inn,** the star of Heritage Park just above Old Town, 2470 Heritage Park Row, tel. (619) 299-6832, www.heritageparkinn.com. Eight rooms (some share a bath) and one suite make this 1889 Queen Anne most accommodating. Expensive-Luxury, with rates $100-235 (include breakfast and refreshments), with a two-night minimum on weekends; weekly and monthly rates are available. No smoking, no children under age 14.

Staying near Old Town: Hotel Circle and Mission Valley

"Hotel Circle" refers to the low-priced and midrange motels that flank I-8 between Old Town and Mission Valley—not a bad location given the instant freeway access, assuming you have a car and don't mind doing the freeways to get around.

Among the cheaper choices in the neighborhood is good old **Motel 6 Hotel Circle,** 2424 Hotel Circle N., San Diego, tel. (619) 296-1612, or, for reservations at any Motel 6 nationwide, toll-free (800) 466-8356, www.motel6.com. This one features a swimming pool and the usual basics for $45.99 and up. Inexpensive. A remarkable value for sporting types is the 20-acre **Quality Resort Mission Valley,** 875 Hotel Circle S., tel. toll-free (800) 362-7871 or (619) 298-8281, www.qualityresort.com. Try to land a room away from the freeway noise, and then plunge into any of the three swimming pools (one's heated) or head to the adjacent tennis, racquetball, and health club facilities. Expensive-Luxury. Rooms here start at $99 in summer.

If you can't yet swing that trip to Hawaii, consider a stay at the very pleasant **Hanalei Hotel,** 2270 Hotel Circle N., tel. toll-free (800) 882-0858 or (619) 297-1101, www.hanaleihotel.com, yet another of San Diego's Polynesian-themed sleep palaces. Since Hanalei is Hawaiian for "valley of the flowers," the lush tropical foliage fits—as do the extravagant summertime luaus staged in the courtyard and the appealing pool area. Premium-Luxury. Room rates start at $129 in summer, and $109 in the off season.

Mission Valley's top-drawer digs include the **San Diego Marriott Mission Valley,** a business traveler's hot spot at 8757 Rio San Diego Dr. (exit I-8 at Stadium Way), tel. toll-free (800) 228-9290 or (619) 692-3800, www.marriott.com, Premium-Luxury ($129-258), and the sound-proofed **San Diego Mission Valley Hilton** just off the freeway at 901 Camino del Rio S. (exit I-8 at Mission Center Rd.), tel. toll-free (800) 445-8667 or (619) 543-9000, www.hilton.com, Expensive-Luxury ($99-199).

STAYING IN LA JOLLA AND DEL MAR

Affordable In La Jolla

As you'd guess in such exclusive neighborhoods, life can get quite pricey in La Jolla and adjacent Del Mar. Because parking space is also a local luxury, many establishments charge extra for parking; be sure to inquire. **La Jolla Town Council** volunteers, tel. (858) 454-1444, can be very helpful if you'd like some personal assistance in making local lodging arrangements.

Low-rent accommodations don't exist in and around upscale, conservative La Jolla. Quite decent midrange motels are available, however, including the **Holiday Inn Express** (previously the La Jolla Palms), 6705 La Jolla Blvd., tel. toll-free (800) 451-0358 or (858) 454-7101. This place is not in the midst of the local hubbub, but that can be a plus. About five long blocks south of downtown, an easy 20-minute walk, and close to world-famous "locals only" Windansea Beach, the Holiday Inn features large rooms, recently renovated, with all the basics plus a few extras, such as in-room coffeemakers, color TV, cable, and free movies. If you plan to do some home-away-from-home home cooking, a some rooms here have full kitchens. Good shopping and great restaurants are a stroll away. Expensive-Luxury, with rates $89-149.

Nothing fancy, **La Jolla Cove Suites** is stylin' it circa the 1950s but still a sweet deal. Quite well-situated—right across the street from La Jolla Cove, as advertised—here you'll get the same views as the very rich at a much more reasonable price. You'll also get a full kitchen, so you can eat in anytime you want. Luxury. Rates run $165 and up in the summer, otherwise $125 and up. Find La Jolla Cove Suites at 1150 Coast Blvd., tel. toll-free (800) 248-2683 or (858) 459-2621, www.lajollacove.com. And if there's no room here, there may be space at the **Shell**

Beach Apartment Motel, 981 Coast Blvd., run by the same folks.

Considerably more expensive but another great deal is the smoke-free **Prospect Park Inn,** a charming contemporary small motel with European hotel style. Squeezed onto a triangular lot at 1110 Prospect next to the grand La Valencia Hotel, it's too easily missed. Nice view from the patio up on the roof. High-season rates are Luxury—$150 and up for two, continental breakfast included—but ask about off-season specials. For reservations, call toll-free (800) 433-1609 or (858) 454-0133, www.prospectparkinn.com

Affordable in Del Mar

A genuine gem in Del Mar, literally *on* the beach, is the minimalist **Del Mar Motel,** close to the racetrack and just a stroll into downtown at 1702 Coast Blvd., tel. toll-free (800) 223-8449 or (858) 755-1534. Rooms come with refrigerators, color TV, and courtesy coffee; barbecue grills available. Premium-Luxury, with rates from $130 in the high season, starting at $85 otherwise.

Another good deal, between La Jolla and Del Mar, is **The Lodge at Torrey Pines,** 11480 N. Torrey Pines Rd., tel. toll-free (800) 995-4507 or (858) 453-4420, www.lodgetorreypines.com, boasting one of the best "view" locations around and attractive motel-style rooms. Expensive-Luxury, with official rates $95-155, but look for discounts during the off-season.

Upmarket in and around La Jolla

La Jolla's oldest hotel is the still-dignified and fairly staid four-story **Grande Colonial,** close to everything downtown at 910 Prospect, tel. toll-free (800) 829-1278 or (858) 454-2181, www.the-grandecolonial.com, with pool, restaurant, and full bar. Tea is served every afternoon. Luxury, with high season rates $229-429, low season rates $179-299. Ocean-view rooms are the more expensive.

Downtown's darling, though, is the historic **La Valencia Hotel,** 1132 Prospect (at Herschel), tel. toll-free (800) 451-0772 or (858) 454-0771, www.lavalenciahotel.com. Art deco La Valencia, still pretty in pink, was one of those legendary Hollywood celebrity destinations in the 1930s and '40s—*the* place to be, in the classic style of European luxury, as La Jolla began making a name for itself. And it still is, for those who

can afford it. Luxury. Rates run $250 and up, with some of the cheaper rooms not all that stellar. The layout of this Mediterranean-style pleasure palace is stellar, however. "Street level" happens to be the fourth floor, with the floors below on the way down to the ocean, and the others above. Even the elevator—with a human being at the controls!—is straight out of an old classic movie. Three restaurants—one with a 10th-floor view—a swimming pool and gardens terraced into the hillside, and a small spa are also modern classics.

For postmodern comforts, head for La Jolla's "Golden Triangle" east of I-5 and the neoclassical 400-room **Hyatt Regency La Jolla at Aventine,** designed by architect Michael Graves. The rooms here are large and airy—but not nearly as airy as the stunning atrium—and the associated health club is one of San Diego's best. Plenty of restaurants are on-site; it's also an easy stroll from here to the University Town Center, where you'll find more dining. Luxury. Regular rates run $215 and up, but weekend specials and other discounts can drop prices to $165, based upon availability. For more information, contact: Hyatt Regency La Jolla, 3777 La Jolla Village Dr., tel. toll-free (800) 233-1234 or (858) 552-1234, www.hyatt.com.

Another best bet is the clifftop **Hilton La Jolla Torrey Pines,** 10950 N. Torrey Pines Rd., tel. toll-free (800) 774-1500 or (858) 558-1500, www.hilton.com, a subtle presence overlooking the ocean, and right next to a great municipal golf course and an excellent health club. Rooms are elegant and generous, with either a terrace or balcony and every imaginable luxury—including free Starbucks coffee, shirt press, and newspaper every morning. Luxury. Regular rates run $200 and up.

L'Auberge Del Mar Resort and Spa

Right in the middle of everything in Del Mar, this luxury resort with a hillside ocean view graces the site of the famed Hotel Del Mar, a playground for the Hollywood celebrity set from the 1920s through the 1940s. The architecture of this Victorian-style beachhouse mimics the original, and the lobby still serves as the resort's social center. Guest rooms are country French, with marble bathrooms and the usual luxury amenities. Also here: full European-style spa and fitness facilities—affordable, by separate fee, for just about anyone, if lodging at the hotel is a bit too rich—plus tennis courts, two pools, great restaurants. Best of all, it's only one block to the beach. Luxury. July, August, and September—race season at the Del Mar Race Track—is the high season, with rates $395 and up. Much lower rates are available at other times. L'Auberge Del Mar Resort and Spa is at 1540 Camino del Mar, tel. toll-free (800) 553-1336 or (858) 259-1515, www.laubergedelmar.com. To get here from I-5, head west on Del Mar Heights Rd. for one mile, then turn north onto Camino del Mar. The resort is one mile farther.

Resorts in Rancho Santa Fe

Often a real deal for a special-occasion escape is the **Inn at Rancho Santa Fe,** a San Diego classic with 20 acres of terraced gardens, vine-draped cottages, croquet courses, tennis courts, pool, exercise facilities, and on-site restaurant, with golf and horseback riding available nearby. Another perk here: daytime access to an inn-owned beach cottage in Del Mar. The inn's main building dates from 1923, and was originally built as a guesthouse for prospective real estate buyers after the Santa Fe Railroad's local experiment with eucalyptus trees failed. (Santa Fe had hoped eucalyptus would produce quality wood for railroad ties; instead, the trees grew up to produce shade for the very exclusive residential neighborhoods here.) Quiet and relaxed, it's not particularly oriented toward families though kids are welcome. Premium-Luxury, with rates $120 and up, AAA discounts and other specials often available. To get here, exit I-5 at Loma Santa Fe Dr. (Hwy. 58) and continue east four miles. For more information: Inn at Rancho Santa Fe, 5951 Linea del Cielo (at Paseo), tel. toll-free (800) 843-4661 or (858) 756-1131, www.theinnatranchosantafe.com.

Privileged sibling to La Jolla's lovely La Valencia Hotel, the contemporary Old California-style **Rancho Valencia Resort,** near Del Mar in Rancho Santa Fe, has it all—red-tiled roofs, bougainvillea-draped walkways, fountains, romantic and luxurious suites tucked into the lush landscape, 18 tennis courts, exercise facilities, championship croquet lawn, pool, jacuzzis, and sauna. You'll find an 18-hole golf course next door to this exclusive 40-acre playground. Luxury. Official rates are $425 and up, but ask about midweek and off-season specials. For more information: Rancho Valencia Resort, 5921 Valencia Circle, tel. toll-free (800) 548-3664 or (858) 756-1123, www.ranchovalencia.com.

EATING IN SAN DIEGO

IN AND AROUND DOWNTOWN

Uptown Downtown

Even for those who avoid shopping malls as a matter of principle, the **Panda Inn** at Horton Plaza, tel. (619) 233-7800, merits an exception. This wonderful Chinese restaurant is as elegant as it is inclusive, with an impressive list of Mandarin and Szechuan selections. From noodle dishes and twice-cooked pork to fresh seafood, nothing here disappoints. It's open daily 11 a.m.- 10 p.m., until 10:30 p.m. on Friday and Saturday, closed Thanksgiving and Christmas.

Just across the street from hustle-bustle Horton Plaza, the **Grant Grill** at the venerable U.S. Grant Hotel, on Broadway between Third and Fourth, tel. (619) 239-6806, is a sure bet for escaping the tourist hordes. The hotel's elegant, dignified, and historically correct decor lends a men's club sensibility to the surprisingly good food—from American standards at breakfast and good salads, sandwiches, and specials at lunch to steak and lobster dinners. Full bar. The Grant Grill is open daily 6:30-11 a.m. for breakfast, 11:30 a.m.-2 p.m. for lunch, and 5-10 p.m. for dress-up dinner (until 10:30 p.m. on weekends).

Rainwater's, 1202 Kettner (next door to the Santa Fe Depot), on the second floor, tel. (619) 233-5757, is a very uptown downtown establishment and one of the best steakhouses around. Steaks here are huge, side dishes simple but artfully selected. Grilled seafood is also prominent on the menu. If you can manage dessert—and here, that's typically a challenge— locals swear by the hot-fudge sundaes. Rainwater's is also a popular lunchtime rendezvous for the suit and tie set. It's open Mon.-Fri. 11:30 a.m.-midnight, on Saturday 5-9 p.m., on Sunday 5-11 p.m. Call for holiday schedules (they vary from year to year).

The Gaslamp Quarter

Fio's, 801 Fifth Ave. (at F St.), tel. (619) 234-3467, is tried and true among the Gaslamp Quarter's trendy Fifth Avenue restaurants—a cheery contemporary Italian place looking down on the fray from its seasoned-brick setting. Those with smaller appetites and/or the budget-minded should stick to pastas and salads—or split one of those great pizzas fresh from the wood-fired oven. This a very popular place, so reservations are advisable at dinner. It's open weekdays for lunch 11:30 a.m.-3 p.m., nightly for dinner 5-11 p.m. (until midnight on Friday and Saturday, until 10 p.m. on Sunday). Closed Thanksgiving, Christmas, and New Year's Day. Other excellent choices in the neighborhood: **Bella Luna,** with all those pretty moons, at 748 Fifth Ave. (between F and G), tel. (619) 239-3222, open daily for both lunch and dinner, and the stylish Tuscan **Trattoria La Strada,** 702 Fifth Ave. (at G), tel. (619) 239-3400, open nightly for dinner, weekdays only for lunch. More casual than its Italian neighbors, bistro-style **Osteria Panevino,** 722 Fifth Ave. (at G), tel. (619) 595-7959, open daily for lunch and dinner, serves wonderful vegetable focaccia, spinach ravioli, and pizzas.

Or, try another country. For tapas and other Spanish selections, head to very friendly **Tapas Picasso,** 3923 Fourth Ave. (between Washington and University), tel. (619) 294-3061, open nightly for dinner, Tues.-Fri. for lunch. Turn a corner and try yet another country. **Athens Market,** 109 W. F St. (at First Ave.), tel. (619) 234-1955, takes you on an ersatz sail through the Aegean—on weekend nights, an experience complete with Greek music, folk dancing, and belly dancers. Perfect for a simple dinner or—to fully sample the tastiest fare, including the specialty sausage—dive into the appetizer menu. Reservations advisable. For coffee and after-dinner sweets, adjourn to the coffeehouse next door (open late). Open daily for lunch and dinner 11:30 a.m.-10 p.m. (no lunch on Sunday), closed Thanksgiving and Christmas, sometimes open only half days on other U.S. holidays.

Another shining light in downtown's Gaslamp Quarter is **Croce's,** 802 Fifth Ave. (at F St.), tel. (619) 233-4355, a noted jazz club named in honor of the late singer Jim Croce and operated by his family. The music continues, these days with a pretty jazzy dinner menu, too, on which imaginative international riffs include pastas, salads, and seafood entrees. Best of all, Croce's is open late every night—for dinner, 5 p.m.-midnight. (Closed Thanksgiving and Christmas.) The affiliated **Croce's West** in the same block, tel. (619) 233-6945, is another eat-out possibility, open every day at 7:30 a.m. for breakfast.

Not that the good ol' U.S. of A. can't be exotic. At the **Bayou Bar and Grill,** 329 Market St. (between Third and Fourth), tel. (619) 696-8747, if you didn't know it was San Diego you'd swear you'd somehow stumbled into Louisiana, what with the ceiling fans and color scheme. Once inside, keep it simple. Whether you choose seafood gumbo, another fresh fish dish, or rice and beans accompanied by homemade sausage, do leave room for dessert. Suitably decadent selections include Cajun velvet pie (chocolate and peanut butter) and Creole pecan pie. It's open Mon.-Sat. 11:30 a.m.-3 p.m. and 5-10 p.m. (until 11 p.m. on Friday and Saturday), on Sunday 11:30 a.m.-10 p.m., closed Easter, Thanksgiving, Christmas Eve night, Christmas Day, and New Year's Day.

And there are outposts of downhome Western exotica, such as the gussied-up **Dakota Grill and Spirits,** 901 Fifth (at E St.), tel. (619) 234-5554, specializing in "cowboy steak" and other surprises, and **American Buffalo Joe's BBQ Grill and Saloon,** 600 Fifth (at F St.), tel. (619) 236-1616, where the 'cue is as good as the country-western.

Eateries on the Way to Hillcrest

Hob Nob Hill, just blocks from Balboa Park at 2271 First Ave. (at Juniper), tel. (619) 239-8176, is a long-running neighborhood favorite—serving heaping helpings of all-American favorites, such as pot roast and fried chicken, at very reasonable prices. Breakfast here is one of the best deals in town, and on Sunday everyone shows up (reservations wise).

Also beyond the typical tourist definition of downtown, look for **Little Italy** along India Street, just north of Date. The 1700 block of India is still the center of San Diego's historic Italian district, first settled more than 100 years ago by fishing families. Savory stops here include **Mimmo's Italian Village Deli & Bakery,** tel. (619) 239-3710, great for pizza; **Caffe Italia,** tel. (619) 234-6767, for sandwiches, coffee, and such; and a number of good delis and bakeries.

Farther north, in an area overrun with freeway on- and off-ramps, another section of India Street marks the turn-off to Hillcrest, with additional worthy (and inexpensive) eateries. An institution in San Diego, the original "uptown" **El Indio,** 3695 India St. (at Washington), tel. (619) 299-0333, is where locals go for Mexican. El Indio claims to have invented the term "taquito," so be sure to try a few. But save space for the killer fish tacos and cheese enchiladas, the burritos, the tostadas. Abundant vegetarian choices, everything inexpensive. And if you're in a hurry, call ahead for takeout. It's open daily 7 a.m.-9 p.m., closed Thanksgiving, Christmas, and New Year's Day. The casual **Banzai Cantina,** tel. (619) 298-6388, specializing in imaginative Japanese-Mexican fare at both lunch and dinner, is another neighborhood celebrity. Stop by **Saffron,** tel. (619) 574-0177, for takeout.

Hot Stuff in Hillcrest

The **Corvette Diner Bar and Grill** in Hillcrest at 3946 Fifth Ave. (near Washington), tel. (619) 542-1001 or (619) 542-1476, is one of San Diego's best bets for kids, a raucous rock-out joint complete with DJs and singing wait staff. They'll also like the burgers, shakes, and fries. A rollicking imitation of a 1950s-style diner, the Corvette is known, too, for its meatloaf and other baby-boomer-era comfort foods. Very popular, so expect to wait (no reservations taken). It's open daily Sun.-Thurs. 11 a.m.-11 p.m., until midnight on weekend nights, closed Thanksgiving (and on Christmas if it falls on a weekday). Another hot spot for burgers is **Hamburger Mary's,** 308 University (at Third Ave.), tel. (619) 491-0400.

Best bet for pizza is **Pizza Nova** in the Village Hillcrest, 3955 Fifth Ave. (between Washington and University), tel. (619) 296-6682. Always cheap and also good is the down-to-earth Japanese **Ichiban** in Hillcrest at 1449 University, tel. (619) 299-7203. Another great Italian, this one popular for patio dining, is **Busalacchi's,** 3683 Fifth Ave. (at Pennsylvania), tel. (619) 298-0119.

Refreshingly, San Diego still doesn't entirely cotton to the faddish and overly fancy in food, which explains the popularity of casual yet cutting edge **Kemo Sabe,** 3958 Fifth Ave. (between Washington and University), tel. (619) 220-6802, with its imaginative and witty Mexican and multiethnic cuisine—"Mad About Moo" enchiladas, for example, starring moo shu pork. Then there's **Montanas,** "an American grill" at 1421 University (between Richmond and Normal), tel. (619) 297-0722, fueled by grilled everything and some incredible desserts. More chic in the usual sense is the exceptional **California Cuisine,** 1027 University Ave. (between 10th Ave. and University), tel. (619) 543-0790, closed on Monday but otherwise serving lunch on weekdays, dinner nightly.

AT THE BAY AND ALONG THE COAST

Dining by the Bay

A local favorite is the **Fish Market,** 750 N. Harbor Dr. (near Broadway), tel. (619) 232-3474. Here, parents can enjoy good seafood—even with young children in tow—along with one of the best waterfront views in town. Most grownups go for the mesquite-grilled fish and seafood selections. Most kids are happy with fish and chips, though the children's menu also includes burgers and other American standards. There's a fish market downstairs, plus sushi and shellfish bars and a cocktail lounge. Upstairs is the dressier, more expensive **Top of the Market** dinner restaurant, tel. (619) 234-4867, also popular for self-indulgent Sunday brunch. The Fish Market is open daily 11 a.m.-9:30 p.m., until 10 p.m. on Friday and Saturday nights, closed Thanksgiving and Christmas.

Another seafood hot spot is **Anthony's,** a popular local chain. The dress-up destination is **Anthony's Star of the Sea Room,** 1360 N. Harbor (at Ash), tel. (619) 232-7408, holding its own bayside with beautiful views and an even grander international seafood selection. A better bet by far, though, is **Sally's** at the Hyatt Regency, One Market Place (at Harbor Dr.), tel. (619) 687-6080, where the seafood is served Mediterranean style.

Of course, Coronado Island has its share of bayside bounty—including the elegant French **Chez Loma** 1132 Loma (off Orange Ave.), tel. (619) 435-0661, set in an 1889 Victorian cottage and one of San Diego's most romantic restaurants in any category. For other suggestions, see Coronado: Crown of the Bay above.

Coastal Cuisine: Ocean Beach, Mission Beach, Pacific Beach

San Diego's classic beach towns have their share of classic burger and taco joints—and a few surprises, such as **Machupicchu** in Ocean Beach, 4755 Voltaire St. (at Sunset Cliffs Dr.), tel. (619) 222-2656, which introduces the foods of Peru. The classic appetizer here: the *papas rellenas,* or spicy stuffed potatoes filled with three types of finely chopped meat and vegetables. Among favorite entrees: lamb stew with cilantro sauce, fish with rice and potatoes, the beef sauté (with onions, peppers, and other vegetables), and several wonderful chicken dishes. Other crowd pleasers include the Peruvian clam chowder, the Peruvian *cerviche* (without tomatoes), and pasta with basil sauce. For smaller appetites, try a few appetizers along with the special spinach soup—the latter a big hit with kids, believe it or not. Beer and wine available. It's open Monday and Wed.-Fri. 5:30-9:30 p.m., and Sat.-Sun. 3-9 p.m. (sometimes expanded hours in summer), closed major holidays.

Also something of a surprise, and an Ocean Beach institution, is **The Belgian Lion,** a very fine dining destination at 2265 Bacon St. (near Lotus St.), tel. (619) 223-2700, specializing in traditional French fare and lighter seafood and fresh fish. It's open for dinner only, and only on Thursday, Friday, and Saturday nights. Reservations a must. For German at either lunch or dinner, head for **Kaiserhof,** 2253 Sunset Cliffs Blvd. (at West Point Loma), tel. (619) 224-0606 (closed Monday).

IN OLD TOWN

The colorful **Old Town Mexican Cafe,** 2489 San Diego Ave. (at Congress), tel. (619) 297-4330, is famous for its humongous portions of just about every Mexican standard and a popular place for locals and tourists alike. And if the kids don't know how tortillas are made, here they can watch. It's open daily for both lunch and dinner.

But **Berta's Latin American Restaurant,** 3928 Twiggs St. (at Congress), tel. (619) 295-2343, ranges far beyond predictable Old Town south-of-the-border fare. High points of this Latin American tour include pastas, stews, Peruvian chicken with chiles and feta cheese, and seafood *vatapa* from Brazil—all good opportunities for the kids to move beyond tacos and burritos. The wine list is also international. You'll be pleasantly surprised by this friendly respite from the tourist hordes. In balmy weather, the patio is perfect. Berta's is open for lunch and dinner daily, 11 a.m.-10 p.m., closed major holidays.

California-style **Cafe Pacifica,** 2414 San Diego Ave. (between Arista and Linwood), tel. (619) 291-6666, a longstanding local choice for uptown dining in Old Town, specializes in seafood. Entree choices change daily, but count on mesquite-grilled fresh fish selections served with house-made salsa, fruit chutney, or herbed sauces. For smaller appetites: fish tacos, crab cakes, and surprising salads and pastas. It's open for lunch Tues.-Fri. 11:30 a.m.-2 p.m., for dinner nightly 5:30-10 p.m.

IN LA JOLLA AND DEL MAR

Downtown La Jolla Jewels

If you're looking to pack a food-lover's picnic—a basket brimming with garden-fresh produce and fresh fruit—look no farther than **Chino's Vegetable Stand,** 6123 Calzada del Bosque, tel. (858) 756-3184. This vegetable stand supplies some of the best restaurants in California, including Berkeley's Chez Panisse. It's open Mon.-Sat. 10 a.m.-4 p.m., on Sunday 10 a.m.-1 p.m., closed Christmas Day.

If you've got teenagers in tow, you won't be able to avoid La Jolla's **Hard Rock Cafe,** 909 Prospect Ave. (at Fay), tel. (858) 454-5101, with good burger fare, the usual brain-scrambling blare, and rock memorabilia and mementos. For good coffee and a simple breakfast the place (packed on weekends) is the coffeehouse-style **Brockton Villa,** 1235 Coast Blvd. (near Prospect), tel. (858) 454-7393. Another locals' choice for a casual meal is **SamSon's** deli, 8861 Villa La Jolla Dr., tel. (858) 455-1461, where you can count on great omelettes or lox plates at breakfast, great corned beef sandwiches at lunch, stick-to-your-ribs homestyle dinners, and celebrity-kitsch decor anytime. It's open daily for breakfast, lunch, and dinner. For something more exotic, try the buffet lunch at the very good

Star of India, 1000 Prospect (at Gerard), tel. (858) 459-3355, a popular place. If you come for dinner, make reservations.

George's at the Cove, 1250 Prospect St. (near Ivanhoe), tel. (858) 454-4244, is at the top of La Jolla's seafood food chain, and as beloved for its contemporary American cuisine as for its spectacular local views. You'll have to dress up for the dining room (reservations), but not for either the **Cafe** or the **Terrace,** upstairs, which are more relaxed (no reservations taken, so be prepared for a wait). Simpler fare includes soups, salads, shellfish pastas, fish tacos, even seafood sausages. George's is open daily for lunch 11 a.m.-4 p.m. (until 2 p.m. in the fine dining room), nightly for dinner 5-10 p.m. (until 11 p.m. on Friday and Saturday nights).

For fine dining, French sets the local standard. The excellent, expensive, and somewhat staid **Top o' the Cove,** 1216 Prospect St. (near Ivanhoe), tel. (858) 454-7779, a long-running local institution, serves classic French fare and romantic ambience with a view. **The Sky Room,** nearby at La Valencia Hotel, 1132 Prospect (at Herschel), tel. (858) 454-0771, is tiny (12 tables) and specializes in contemporary French and spectacular views of both sea and sky. (La Valencia's continental **The Whaling Bar,** open for both lunch and dinner, is another option.)

Inland La Jolla Jewels

Another dine-around destination is La Jolla's "Golden Triangle," rich real estate reared on biotechnology and other high-tech enterprise wedged into the triangle created by I-5, I-805, and Highway 52. The **Hops!** microbrewery at La Jolla's University Town Center (between Broadway and Robinson's May), 4353 La Jolla Village Dr., tel. (858) 587-6677, enlivens its shopping mall setting with high-test homemade beers—Brewer's Blonde, Red Moon Raspberry, Three-Peat Wheat, and Grateful Red ales plus Triangle India Pale Ale and Superstition Stout. The Brewmaster's Special changes. The food's also quite good, imaginative but not too eclectic California-style bistro fare, wood-fired pizza and such, everything under $12. Patio dining available. It's open daily for lunch and dinner 11 a.m.-11 p.m. (until 1 a.m. on Friday and Saturday), closed major holidays.

Other culinary attractions at and near University Town Center include the continental California-style **St. James Bar & Restaurant,** jazzing up a high-rise bank building at 4370 La Jolla Village Dr. (near Executive Way), tel. (858) 453-6650, with a menu including low-fat specialties high on flavor; and the Italian **Tutto Mare,** 4365 Executive Dr. (reached via Town Center Dr., north from Jolla Village Dr.), tel. (858) 597-1188, where roasted seafood and seafood pastas star.

Center stage at the theatrical **Aventine Center** nearby, on University Center Lane, are a number of great restaurants, including the very stylish and fairly expensive **Cafe Japengo,** tel. (858) 450-3355, offering trendy Pacific Rim cuisine and sushi, and an extensive list of creative desserts.

Best Bets in and around Del Mar

Sbicca's in Del Mar, 215 15th St. (at Camino del Mar), tel. (858) 481-1001, is an inventive California bistro serving brunch—crepes, omelets, *huevos rancheros,* and eggs benedict—on weekends until 3 p.m. Count on healthy items like the free-range turkey burger, vegetable lasagna, or grilled ahi at lunch. For dinner, consider the salmon au poivre or the asian-jalapeno flat iron steak. Hours vary, so call ahead.

Other best bets in Del Mar live in the Del Mar Plaza mall at 1555 Camino del Mar (at 15th Street), including the faux-'50s **Johnny Rockets** burger joint on the first floor, tel. (858) 755-1954, where burgers, good fries, and malts make the menu. More trendy in the neighborhood, all on the third floor and all serving spectacular ocean views from their outdoor patios: **Epazote,** tel. (858) 259-9966, serving California-style Mexican and southwestern cuisine; ever-popular northern Italian **Il Fornaio,** tel. (858) 755-8876; and **Pacifica Del Mar,** tel. (858) 792-0476, serving exotic California-style Cajun, Italian, southwestern, and Pacific Rim fare. All are open daily for lunch and dinner, with dinner reservations advisable.

Downstairs from Pacifica Del Mar, the **Pacifica Breeze Café** serves breakfast, sandwiches, and dinners in the $7-10 range. And the bar draws a fun, trendy crowd on the weekends.

For dress-up dining in nearby Rancho Santa Fe, serving somewhat pricey but casual California-style American fare is **Delicias,** 6106 Paseo Delicias, tel. (858) 756-8000, open for lunch and dinner daily except Monday and major holidays. At the top of the local food chain, though, is the fancy French **Mille Fleurs** just a stroll away at 6009 Paseo Delicias, tel. (858) 756-3085, open daily for lunch and dinner.

PRACTICAL SAN DIEGO

VISITOR INFORMATION

For current visitor information, contact the multilingual **San Diego International Visitor Information Center,** 11 Horton Plaza in downtown San Diego, tel. (619) 236-1212. For information via the Internet, the address is www.sandiego.com.

If you're rolling into town on the spur of the moment, stop off at the **Mission Bay Visitor Information Center** on E. Mission Bay Drive (exit I-5 at Clairemont), tel. (619) 276-8200, open daily, where you can get enough info to get you around.

The San Diego Union-Tribune is the local newspaper of record but not all that impressive a rag, though even a cursory read will give you some sense of just how conservative this city is. The Thursday "Night and Day" section is useful for figuring out what's going on, but all in all the weekly *San Diego Reader* is a better information source, particularly for entertainment and restaurant listings. Entertaining alternative publications pop up, too; look for them in hip bookstores, music shops, and cool coffeehouses.

SAN DIEGO TRANSPORT

Getting Here by Air

Everybody calls it Lindbergh Field, but the official name is the **San Diego International Airport,** lies just three miles northwest of downtown San Diego (closer to Harbor Island) near the bay, just off Harbor Drive. Served by all major U.S. carriers—including **America West, American, Continental, Delta, Northwest, Reno Air, TWA, United,** and including the ever-popular

Southwest Airlines. The airport is also served by **Aeromexico,** and smaller commuter lines. You can't store anything at the airport (no lockers), but it is open 24 hours, with restaurants, snack stops, and ATMs. For general airport information, call (619) 231-2100.

Getting Into Town from the Airport
By Bus: San Diego's Metropolitan Transit System (MTS) Route 992 provides service from the airport and downtown San Diego with stops outside each terminal. Buses run every 10 minutes during the week and every 15 minutes on weekends, though if you're traveling on a holiday be sure to check the holiday schedule. Fare is $2; for more information call (619) 233-3004.

By Shuttle: One of the easiest ways to get where you're going is via shuttle. The 24-hour **Cloud 9 Shuttle,** tel. (858) 278-8877 or toll-free (800) 9-SHUTTLE, is the most popular shuttle, and charges $6-10 to major points in the city.

By Taxi: Taxis line up outside the terminal and charge $7-10 for the trip downtown, usually a 5-10 minute ride.

Getting Here by Train
In many ways, the most civilized way to get here is by train. San Diego is easily reached by **Amtrak,** tel. toll-free (800) 872-7245 or (619) 239-9021 for recorded information, www.amtrak.com, with daily trains coming and going from Los Angeles, Santa Barbara, and San Luis Obispo; you can also get to Solana Beach and other coastal San Diego County stops on one train or another.

The very attractive **Santa Fe Depot** downtown, 1050 Kettner Blvd. (at Broadway), is open all night; the ticket office is open daily 5 a.m.-9 p.m. The **San Diego Trolley** mass transit lines start here, too, making it quite easy to get around, at least between 5 a.m. and midnight.

Getting Here by Bus
The **Greyhound** bus station, open 24 hours, is downtown, just a few blocks east of the train station at 120 W. Broadway, tel. toll-free (800) 231-2222 or (619) 239-3266. From here, L.A. is the major destination, though you can also trek east. Since the bus station is in an unsavory neighborhood, by San Diego standards, don't plan to walk the streets late at night—and keep an eye on your luggage. (Lockers are available.)

Getting Here by Car
Most people drive here—a fact quite obvious once you're on the local freeways, where traffic is typically nightmarish. The straight shot into downtown is provided by **I-5,** which dead-ends at the Mexican border; I-5 is also the main thoroughfare for reaching San Diego beach towns, Old Town, and Coronado Island. Inland, **I-15** creates the city's de facto eastern edge; if you follow it north it'll eventually deliver you to Las Vegas. The area's major east-west freeway is **I-8,** which slithers in out of the desert and slides to a stop at Mission Bay (after crossing paths with both I-15 and I-5). Heads up. And good luck, especially when merging—or trying to merge.

Getting Around
San Diego's public **Metropolitan Transit System (MTS),** tel. (619) 685-4900 (recorded), also provides around-town bus service. Pick up a transit map at the visitor information center at Horton Plaza or call the MTS **Information Line,** tel. (619) 233-3004 or TTY/TDD (619) 234-5005 (5:30 a.m.-8:30 p.m.), to figure out which bus will get you where. Another resource is the **Transit Store,** downtown at 449 Broadway (at Fifth), tel. (619) 234-1060, where you can pick up free brochures, route maps, and schedules. This is also the place to buy a variety of passes: the **Day Tripper** pass, for example, buys all-day access to local buses, the trolley system, and the ferry to Coronado.

More fun by far is the **San Diego Trolley** mass transit system, tel. (619) 231-8549 for current route and fare information (recorded). For assistance call (619) 233-3004, (619) 234-5005 TTY/TDD. Several lines are now up and running—the **Old Town Line** from the Old Town transit center to the Santa Fe Depot; the **South Line** to the U.S./Mexico border; the **East Line** serving the east-county cities of El Cajon, Lemon Grove, and La Mesa; and the **Bayside Line** through the Gaslamp Quarter and on to the convention center and Seaport Village. The recently completed **Mission Valley** extension extends to Qualcomm Stadium, and is a handy way to get to the park on game days. Trolleys run 5 a.m.-8 p.m. at least every 15 minutes, and every half-hour until midnight, though the schedule varies somewhat from line to line; call for current information, or pick up a schedule at the Transit

Store on Broadway (see above). One-way trolley fares run $1-2, depending on how far you're going; before boarding, buy your ticket at the relevant transit center vending machines (carry exact change)—or buy a Day Tripper pass at the Transit Store.

If they didn't drive into town, to get farther faster most people "go local" and rent a car. San Diego is served by the usual car rental agencies—the visitor center can provide you with a current listing—and some allow their cars to be driven into Mexico. If you don't particularly care about appearances, save some money with **Rent-a-Wreck,** toll-free (800) 535-1391 or (619) 223-3300. Rent-a-Wreck even rents motor homes, along with new and used cars, trucks, and vans. Other options include **Avis,** toll-free tel. (800) 331-1212/(800) 331-2323 TDD, and **Payless Car Rental,** toll-free tel. (800) PAYLESS.

BOOKLIST

The virtual "publisher of record" for all things Californian is the **University of California Press,** 2120 Berkeley Way, Berkeley, CA 94720, tel. (510) 642-4247 or toll-free (800) 777-4726 and fax (800) 999-1958 for orders, www.ucpress.edu, which publishes hundreds of titles on the subject—all excellent. Stanford University's **Stanford University Press,** 521 Lomita Mall, Stanford, CA 94305, tel. (650) 723-9434, fax (650) 725-3457, www.sup.org, also offers some books of particular interest to Californiacs—especially under the subject categories of American Literature, California History, and Natural History—though in general these are books of academic interest.

Other publishers offering California titles, particularly general interest, history, hiking, and regional travel titles, include **Chronicle Books,** Division of Chronicle Publishing Co., 85 Second St., Sixth Floor, San Francisco, CA 94105, tel. (415) 537-3730 or toll-free tel. (800) 722-6657, www.chronbooks.com, and **Heyday Books,** 2054 University Ave., Ste. 400, P.O. Box 9145, Berkeley, CA 94709, tel. (510) 549-3564, fax (510) 549-1889. **Foghorn Outdoors,** Avalon Travel Publishing, 5855 Beaudry St., Emeryville, CA 95608, tel. (510) 595-3664, fax (510) 595-4228, www.foghorn.com, publishes a generous list of unusual, and unusually thorough, California outdoor guides, including Tom Stienstra's camping, fishing, and "getaways" guides.

Sierra Club Books, 85 Second St., Second Fl., San Francisco, CA 94105, tel. (415) 977-5500 or toll-free (888) 722-6657 for orders, www.sierraclub.org/books, and **Wilderness Press,** 1200 Fifth St., Berkeley, CA 94704, tel. (510) 558-1666 or toll-free (800) 443-7227 for orders, fax (510) 538-1696, www.wilderness-press.com, are the two top publishers of wilderness guides and maps for California. Among their titles are some particularly useful for exploration of the San Francisco Bay Area. Particularly useful from the Sierra Club, for example, is Peggy Wayburn's *Adventuring in the San Francisco Bay Area.* Wilderness Press publish-

es some good regional hiking guides, including *East Bay Trails* and *North Bay Trails.*

Contact these and other publishers, mentioned below, for a complete list of current titles relating to California.

The following book listings represent a fairly basic introduction to books about California history, natural history, literature, recreation, and travel, and particularly as these relate to the California coast. Interested readers can find many other titles by visiting good local bookstores and/or state and national park visitor centers. As always, the author would appreciate suggestions about other books that should be included. Send the names of new candidates—or actual books, if you're either a publisher or an unusually generous person—for *Coastal California*'s booklist, not to mention possible text additions, corrections, and suggestions, to: Kim Weir, c/o Moon Handbooks, Avalon Travel Publishing, 5855 Beaudry St., Emeryville, CA 94608.

COMPANION READING, GENERAL TRAVEL

Baldy, Marian. *The University Wine Course.* San Francisco: The Wine Appreciation Guild, 1992. Destined to be a classic and designed for both instructional and personal use, this friendly book offers a comprehensive education about wine. *The University Wine Course* explains it all, from viticulture to varietals. And the lips-on lab exercises and chapter-by-chapter examinations help even the hopelessly déclassé develop the subtle sensory awareness necessary for any deeper appreciation of the winemaker's art. Special sections and appendixes on reading (and understanding) wine labels, combining wine and food, and understanding wine terminology make it a lifelong personal library reference. Definitely "do" this book before doing the California wine country. For college wine appreciation instructors and winery personnel, the companion *Teacher's Manual for The University Wine Course* (1993) may also come in handy.

Bierce, Ambrose Gwinnet, wickedly illustrated by Gahan Wilson. *The Devil's Dictionary.* New York: Oxford University Press, 1998. According to *The Devil's Dictionary,* a saint is a "dead sinner revised and edited," and a bore is a "person who talks when you wish him to listen." The satiric aphorisms included herein earned Ambrose Bierce the nicknames Bitter Bierce and the Wickedest Man in San Francisco, though—considering his talent for heaving his witty pitchfork at any and all he happened to encounter in life—it's clear that Bierce was born way too soon. He would have a field day in contemporary California.

Bright, William O. *1,500 California Place Names: Their Origin and Meaning.* A revised version of the classic *1,000 California Place Names* by Erwin G. Gudde, first published in 1949. Berkeley: University of California Press, 1998. Though you can also get the revised edition of Gudde's original masterpiece (see below), this convenient, alphabetically arranged pocketbook—now in an expanded and updated edition—is perfect for travelers, explaining the names of mountains, rivers, and towns throughout California.

Bronson, Po. *The Nudist on the Late Shift and Other True Tales of Silicon Valley.* New York: Random House, 1999. The extent that the technological innovations and inventions now streaming out of the San Francisco Bay Area's Silicon Valley are changing U.S.—and world—societies is all but impossible to chronicle. But Po Bronson gives it a go, bravely taking his readers on a personal nonfiction tour through the silicon heart of the beast. To sample Bronson's fiction, try *Bombardiers* and *The First $20 Million Is Always the Hardest.*

Buckley, Christopher, and Gary Young, eds. *The Geography of Home: California's Poetry of Place.* Berkeley: Heyday Books, 1999. This contemporary anthology showcases the work of 76 California poets. In addition to multiple selections of each poet's work, the poets also talk about their history in California, and the state's influence on their poetry.

Cain, James. *Three Novels.* New York: Alfred A. Knopf, 1941. Los Angeles classics, all: *Double Indemnity, Mildred Pierce,* and *The Postman Always Rings Twice.*

Callenbach, Ernest. *Ecotopia.* Berkeley: Banyan Tree, 1975. Also worthwhile, from the perspective that northernmost Northern California belongs in its own utopian state, is Callenbach's *Ecotopia Emerging* (1981).

Chandler, Raymond. *The Big Sleep.* New York: Vintage Books, 1992. The first mystery writer to be initiated into the Library of America—the U.S.A.'s literary hall of fame—Raymond Chandler and his legacy have been all but put to sleep by successors in the genre, including parodies such as the film *Dead Men Don't Wear Plaid.* But if one hasn't succumbed to today's trendy nihilism—if one understands that pain hurts and life matters—then *The Big Sleep,* first published in 1939, is still spellbinding and fresh. And Philip Marlowe, Chandler's alter ego and private-eye protagonist, is still the L.A. insider's outsider. (As James Wolcott puts it, to Marlowe the rich are risen scum.) Lesser works by Chandler include *Farewell, My Lovely, The Long Goodbye,* and *The Little Sister.*

Clappe, Louise Amelia Knapp Smith, with an introduction by Marlene Smithe-Baranzini. *The Shirley Letters from the California Mines, 1851-1852.* Berkeley: Heyday Books, 1998. A classic of California gold rush-era literature, and a vivid portrait of both the exuberance and brutality of life in that time—a tale told from a woman's perspective. An absolutely superb read.

Clark, Donald Thomas. *Monterey County Place Names: A Geographical Dictionary.* Carmel Valley, CA: Kestrel Press, 1991. This marvelous resource, meticulously researched and guaranteed to enlighten all who dip into it, is a gift from the UC Santa Cruz University Librarian, Emeritus. Also well worth searching for, though out of print at last report, is the author's *Santa Cruz County Place Names* (1986).

Dana, Richard Henry, Jr. *Two Years Before the Mast.* New York: New American Library, 1990. A classic of early California literature. After recovering from a bout with the measles, young Harvard man Richard Henry Dana sailed off to complete his convalescence—not as a privileged ship passenger but as a sailor. On August 14, 1834, he boarded the *Pilgrim* in Boston Harbor and was underway on what was to be the greatest adventure of his life. This realistic depiction of life on the high seas offers an accurate firsthand account of what it was like to see the California coastline for the first time—and to tie up in San Francisco *before* the gold rush. Some of the earliest written descriptions of California—and still an exceptional read.

Duane, Daniel. *Caught Inside: A Surfer's Year on the California Coast.* San Francisco: Northpoint Press, 1997. What would it be like to shuck the jive and live instead the inspired life of a surf rat? Duane decided to find out, and in the process he took a careful look at the quirks of surf culture and shared some appreciations of the coast's natural power.

Fitzgerald, F. Scott. *The Last Tycoon.* New York: Charles Scribner's Sons, 1940. The golden boy of American letters had a heck of a time as a screenwriter in Hollywood—people still say Tinseltown did him in—but, after this (unfinished) novel, there was never any question that he knew the place as well as his own skin. In this, the barely disguised story of MGM genius Irving Thalberg, Fitzgerald demonstrates his genius and supreme talent as a writer.

Fisher, M.F.K. *The Art of Eating.* Foster City, CA: IDG Books Worldwide, 1990. Reprint ed. John Updike has called her "the poet of the appetites." According to the *Chicago Sun-Times,* "M.F.K. Fisher is to literary prose what Laurence Olivier is to acting." And that point is hard to argue. Often characterized as California's premier food writer, particularly after she settled into the Sonoma County wine country, Mary Frances Kennedy Fisher was actually a *writer*—one who understood that the fundamental human needs are food, love, and security. She wrote about them all, in more than 20 books and countless other essays, letters, and stories. Five of her most beloved book-length essays—*An Alphabet of Gourmets, Consider the Oyster, The Gastronomical Me, How to Cook a Wolf,* and *Serve It Forth*—are all included in this collection.

Gebhard, David. *The California Architecture of Frank Lloyd Wright.* San Francisco: Chronicle Books, 1997. Reprint ed. Accompanied by color photographs, architectural renderings, and floor plans, this book provides an analysis of 24 California buildings—public and private—that were designed by the noted American architect.

Gilbar, Steven, ed. *California Shorts.* Berkeley: Heyday Books, 1999. This wonderful collection of 20 short stories presents surprisingly different versions of the California experience—urban and rural, native and immigrant.

Gilbar, Steven. *Natural State: A Literary Anthology of California Nature Writing.* Berkeley: University of California Press, 1998. This hefty and dazzling collection includes many of the writers you'd expect—Gretel Ehrlich, M.F.K. Fisher, John McPhee, John Muir, Gary Snyder, and Robert Louis Stevenson—but also a few surprises, including Joan Didion, Jack Kerouac, and Henry Miller.

Gioia, Ted. *West Coast Jazz: Modern Jazz in California, 1945-1960. Berkeley: University of California Press, 1998.* Reprint edition.

Gudde, Erwin G. Edited by William O. Bright. *California Place Names: The Origin and Etymology of Current Geographical Names.* Berkeley: University of California Press, 1998. Did you know that *Siskiyou* was the Chinook word for "bobtailed horse," as borrowed from the Cree language? More truths await every time you dip into this ultimate guide to California place names (and how to pronounce them). A revised and expanded fourth edition, building upon the masterwork of Gudde, who died in 1969.

Hammett, Dashiell. *The Maltese Falcon*. New York: Vintage Books, 1992. Reissue ed. More *noir* than even Humphrey Bogart, who starred in the Hollywood version of this classic mystery, Sam Spade is Dashiell Hammett's tough-as-nails San Francisco private dick. Also central to Hammett's *The Dain Curse* and *The Glass Key*, in this story Spade attempts to unravel the enigma of the Maltese Falcon, a solid-gold statuette originally crafted as a tribute to the Holy Roman Emperor Charles IV. While trying to find the falcon, Spade's partner is murdered, the coppers blame him for it, and the bad guys are determined to get him, too. Then, of course, there's also the beautiful redhead, who appears and just as mysteriously disappears. Whodunnit? And why? Other classic Hammett reads include *The Continental Op* and *The Thin Man*.

Hansen, Gladys. *San Francisco Almanac*. Second revised ed. San Francisco: Chronicle Books, 1995. Finally back in print after a too-long hiatus, this easy-to-use source for San Francisco facts was written by the city archivist. Contains a detailed chronology, maps, and bibliography. Also fun: what some famous people have said about San Francisco. Fascinating, too, is the author's *Denial of Disaster: The Untold Story & Unpublished Photographs of the San Francisco Earthquake & Fire of 1906*, co-authored by Emmet Condon, 1989 (Cameron & Co.).

Hart, James D. *A Companion to California*. Berkeley: University of California Press. Revised and expanded, 1987 (OP). Another very worthy book for Californiacs to collect, if you can find it, with thousands of brief entries on all aspects of California as well as more in-depth pieces on subjects such as literature.

Herron, Don. *The Literary World of San Francisco and its Environs*. San Francisco: City Lights Books, 1985 (OP). A well-mapped "pocket guide" for do-it-yourself walking and driving tours to sites where literary lights shine in and around San Francisco, their homes and haunts. This is the companion guide to the excellent *Literary San Francisco* by Lawrence Ferlinghetti and Nancy J. Peters. Also by Herron: *The Dashiell Hammet Tour: A Guidebook*.

Hong Kingston, Maxine. *The Woman Warrior: Memoirs of a Girlhood Among Ghosts*. New York: Vintage Books, 1989. Reissue ed. Fictionalized memoir about growing up Chinese-American in Stockton, California. In China, ghosts are supernatural beings, but in California they become everyone who is not from China. This is an elliptical and powerful story about finding a place in American society, though still raising ire in some quarters for its representations of Chinese culture.

Houston, James D. *Californians: Searching for the Golden State*. Santa Cruz, CA: Otter B Books, 1992. 10th reprint ed. Good prose, good points in this collection of personal essays about Californians in their endless search for the meaning of their own dream.

Huxley, Aldous. *After Many a Summer Dies the Swan*. London: Chatto and Windus, 1939. As an expatriate in Southern California, Huxley never did entirely warm up to the place. But he understood it, as he so deftly demonstrated in this literary masterpiece, inspired by the larger-than-life life of William Randolph Hearst.

Jackson, Helen Hunt. *Ramona*. New York: New American Library, 1988. The author was an early activist on behalf of California's native peoples. Despairing that so few cared about the Indians' plight, Jackson decided to tell the story as a romance—an interracial romance. As she herself put it: "I am going to try to write a novel, in which will be set forth some Indian experiences in a way to move people's hearts. People will read a novel when they will not read serious books." The resulting *Ramona* was a national sensation when it was first published in 1884. It is the now official California State Play, staged since 1923 at the annual outdoor Ramona Pageant near Hemet.

Jeffers, Robinson. *Selected Poems*. New York: Random House, 1965. The poet Robinson Jeffers died in 1961 at the age of 75, on a rare day when it actually snowed in Carmel. One of California's finest poets, sophisticated yet accessible, many of his poems pay homage to the beauty of his beloved Big Sur coast. Poems collected here are selections from some of his major works, including *Be Angry at the Sun, The Beginning and the End, Hungerfield,* and *Tamar and Other Poems.*

Kadohata, Cynthia. *In the Heart of the Valley of Love.* New York: Penguin Books, 1993. A new edition is published by the University of California Press. This gritty, stunning novel envisions a future Los Angeles in which almost nothing—food, water, clean air, education—is available to the multiethnic multitudes. Yet humanity abides. A beautifully written and inspiring, if disturbing, book.

Kael, Pauline, Herman J. Mankiewicz, and Orson Welles. *The Citizen Kane Book: Raising Kane.* New York: Limelight Editions, 1984 (OP). Includes an excellent essay on the classic American film—which one can't help wanting to see again, following a tour of Hearst's San Simeon palace—plus script and stills.

Kahrl, William. *Water and Power: The Conflict over Los Angeles' Water Supply in the Owens Valley.* Berkeley: University of California Press, 1982. Perhaps the best book available for anyone who wants to understand the politics of water and power in California, and how water and political power have transformed the state's economy and land. To keep up with new twists and turns in this meandering tale, read the *Sacramento Bee* (where Kahrl is now an editor).

Kerouac, Jack. *Subterraneans.* New York: Grove Press, 1989. Considered by some to be Kerouac's masterpiece and first published in 1958, this is a Beat exploration of life on the fringes, a novel largely set in the San Francisco Bay Area. Others, however, prefer *The Dharma Bums* (1958) and *Big Sur* (1962).

Kirker, Harold. *California's Architectural Frontier.* San Marino, CA: The Huntington Library, 1970 (OP). Perhaps more useful and easier to find is Kirker's 1991 *Old Forms on a New Land: California Architecture in Perspective.*

Le Guin, Ursula K. *Always Coming Home.* Unbelievably, this book is now out of print. Ms. Le Guin gained fame as a science fiction writer, for novels including *The Left Hand of Darkness* and *The Dispossessed.* Her formal literary recognition includes the Hugo, Gandalf, Kafka, Nebula, and National Book awards. *Always Coming Home* is perhaps Le Guin's masterwork, and a special treat for those who love California—particularly Northern California, where the lay of the land happens to coincide with the geographical borders of the land she describes (and maps) in this imaginative exploration of "futuristic anthropology."

Le Guin, Ursula K. *Dancing at the Edge of the World: Thoughts on Words, Women, Places.* New York: Grove Press, 1989. This delightful collection of essays includes some rare sidelong glances into the soul of the northstate—and why not? The daughter of UC Berkeley anthropologist Alfred L. Kroeber and Ishi's biographer Theodora Kroeber, Le Guin offers a unique perspective on California as a place—then, now, and in the times to come. Particularly enjoyable in this context: "A Non-Euclidean View of California as a Cold Place to Be"; "The Fisherwoman's Daughter" (about, among other things, her mother); and "Woman/Wilderness." In addition, the foreword to *Northern California Handbook,* "World-Making," appeared here first.

London, Jack, ed. by Gerald Haslam. *Jack London's Golden State: Selected California Writings.* Berkeley: Heyday Books, 1999. The first major U.S. writer to use California as his base, Jack London has finally come home—so California can reclaim him. Included here are some of London's finest works, from *John Barleycorn: or Alcoholic Memoirs* and *Star Rover* to *Valley of the Moon,* along with journalism, short stories, and letters.

MacDonald, Ross. *The Moving Target.* New York: Alfred A. Knopf, 1967. In this, one of MacDonald's many Southern California intrigues, private dick Lew Archer encounters Los Angeles criminals at their most entertaining.

McPhee, John. *Assembling California*. New York: Noonday Press (Farrar, Straus and Giroux), 1993. If you didn't read it as excerpted in the *New Yorker*, here's your chance. The eclectic and indefatigable natural history writer here deconstructs California, tectonically speaking, as a cross-section of both human and geologic time. Who would have thought speculations about the geological underpinnings of the Golden State could be so fascinating?

Michaels, Leonard, David Reid, and Raquel Scherr, eds. *West of the West: Imagining California*. New York: HarperCollins Publishers, 1991. Though any anthology about California is destined to be incomplete, this one is exceptional—offering selections by Maya Angelou, Simone de Beauvoir, Joan Didion, Umberto Eco, Gretel Ehrlich, M.F.K. Fisher, Aldous Huxley, Jack Kerouac, Maxine Hong Kingston, Rudyard Kipling, Henry Miller, Ishmael Reed, Kenneth Rexroth, Richard Rodriguez, Randy Shilts, Gertrude Stein, John Steinbeck, Octavio Paz, Amy Tan, Gore Vidal, Walt Whitman, and Tom Wolfe.

Miller, Henry. *Big Sur and the Oranges of Hieronymus Bosch*. New York: W.W. Norton & Co., 1978. First published in 1958, the famed writer shares his impressions of art and writing along with his view of life as seen from the Big Sur coastline—the center of his personal universe in his later years, and the first real home he had ever found.

Mosley, Walter. *Devil in a Blue Dress*. New York: W.W. Norton & Co., 1990. Easy Rawlins, the reluctant private-eye hero of Walter Mosley's noir hero of Los Angeles, reveals post-World War II truths from the perspective of Watts and South-Central L.A. But beyond the plot—black detective takes job from white man to find a mysterious woman—the story of African American migration into Los Angeles is also told here, a depth of experience, and mistrust, grounded in the Deep South. Even after you've seen the movie (starring Denzel Washington as Easy Rawlins) and vicariously relived L.A.'s jazz club cultural heyday, you can follow Easy on more Los Angeles adventures in Mosley's *Black Betty, White Butterfly, A Red Death,* and *A Little Yellow Dog.*

Muscatine, Doris. *The University of California/Sotheby Book of California Wine*. Berkeley: University of California Press, 1984. A rather expensive companion but worthwhile for wine lovers.

Norris, Frank. *McTeague: A Story of San Francisco*. New York: New American Library, 1997. Reissue ed. The basis for the classic silent film *Greed,* Norris's novel is, in a way, the ultimate Western. First published in 1899, a retelling of an actual crime, *McTeague* tells the story of a dimwitted dentist and his greedy wife—all in all a bleak, low-brow tour of life in San Francisco at the turn of the 20th century, ending with McTeague stumbling off into the desert.

Olmstead, R., and T.H. Watkins. *Here Today: San Francisco Architectural Heritage*. San Francisco: Chronicle Books, 1978 (OP).

Paddison, Joshua, ed. *A World Transformed: Firsthand Accounts of California Before the Gold Rush*. Berkeley: Heyday Books, 1999. According to popular California mythology, the Golden State was "born" with the onrushing change that came with the gold rush of 1848. But this collection of earlier California writings gathers together some intriguing earlier observations—from European explorers and visitors, missionaries, and sea captains— that reveal pre-gold rush California.

Parker, T. Jefferson. *Laguna Heat*. New York: St. Martin's Press, 1985. So, who says only L.A. does down and dirty whodunits? Orange County's own T. Jefferson Parker, in his bestselling national debut, certainly did Laguna Beach proud. And when you're done untangling this tale, there's always *Little Saigon, Pacific Beat,* and *Summer of Fear,* not to mention more recent works.

Rice, Scott, ed. *It Was a Dark and Stormy Night: The Final Conflict*. New York: Penguin, 1992. An anthology of the best of bad fiction from San Jose State University's Bullwer-Lytton fiction contest.

Rodriguez, Richard. *Hunger of Memory: The Education of Richard Rodriguez*. New York:

Bantam Books, 1983. California-born Rodriguez got into all kinds of trouble by suggesting, in this book, that affirmative action and bilingual education do a disservice to children of immigrants to the United States. He uses his own experience by way of illustration. As an intellectual biography of an immensely gifted writer, a longtime editor at San Francisco's Pacific News Service and frequent essayist on PBS's *The News Hour, Hunger of Memory* chronicles his education—when he starts school in Sacramento, knowing a sparse 50 words of English, and when he completes his formal studies in the elite reading room of the British Museum. He chronicles the high costs of social assimilation, including sadness at the increasing distance from his own family, but also exemplifies the freedoms that come with the mastery and love of language. Less controversial is Rodriguez's lyrical *Days of Obligation: An Argument with My Mexican Father,* a fascinating extended essay on contemporary California—and much of the U.S.—as caught between optimism and pessimism, Protestantism and Catholicism, youth and old age.

Russack, Benjamin, ed. *Wine Country: A Literary Companion.* Berkeley: Heyday Books, 1999. This intriguing anthology includes stories from the Wappo Indians and early explorers as well as recognized literary figures—Robert Louis Stevenson, Jack London, Ambrose Bierce, Dorothy Bryant, Jessamyn West, among others—associated with the Napa and Sonoma Valleys.

Sale, Kirkpatrick. *Dwellers in the Land: The Bioregional Vision.* San Francisco: Sierra Club Books, 1985 (OP). One of the first books putting forth the bioregional philosophy, envisioning a world based not on political borders but on natural geographic regions.

See, Carolyn. *Dreaming: Hard Luck and Good Times in America.* Berkeley: University of California Press, 1996. A bittersweet reevaluation of the American dream, presented as memoir. Also by See, and well worth a read: *Golden Days,* a provocative fictional look at life in 1970s and '80s L.A., as linked to an "iffy" future, and *Mother, Daughter.*

Sinclair, Upton. *Oil!* Berkeley: University of California Press, 1997. Reprise of the original 1927 edition, in which journalist and socialist gadfly Sinclair fictionally recreates the Signal Hill oil fields of Long Beach and the Teapot Dome oil reserve scandals.

Snyder, Gary. *Turtle Island.* New York: W.W. Norton & Co., 1974. Titled with a Native American term for the entire North American continent, this Pulitzer Prize-winning 1975 poetry collection honors almost every aspect of that vast landscape. When the poem cycle *Mountains and Rivers Without End* was published in 1996, Snyder was awarded the Böllingen Poetry Prize and the *Los Angeles Times*'s Robert Kirsch Lifetime Achievement Award.

Southern, Terry. *Flash and Filigree.* New York: Grove Press, 1958. Just so you know what you're in for, Terry Southern was also the screenwriter for that hilarious cinematic celebration of apocalypse, *Dr. Strangelove: Or How I Learned to Love the Bomb.* No one else quite captures the banality of Los Angeles with such affectionate horror.

Stegner, Wallace Earle. *Angle of Repose.* New York: Penguin USA, 1992. Reprint ed. Wallace Stegner's Pulitzer Prize-winning novel, in which the disenchanted, wheelchair-bound historian Lyman Ward decides to write about the lives of his grandparents on the American frontier.

Stegner, Wallace Earle. Edited and with a preface from the author's son, Page Stegner. *Marking the Sparrow's Fall: Wallace Stegner's American West.* New York: H. Holt, 1998. This brilliant collection of Stegner's conservation writings traces his development as a Westerner—and as a Western writer—starting with his seemingly inauspicious beginnings as an avid reader, hunkered down in small-town libraries in places almost no one's ever heard of. The first collection of Stegner's work since the author's death in 1993, *Marking the Sparrow's Fall* includes 15 essays never before published, his best-known essays on the American West—including *Wilderness Letter*—and a little-known novella.

Stegner, Wallace Earle. *Where the Bluebird Sings to the Lemonade Springs: Living and Writing in the West.* New York: Penguin USA, 1993. Reprint ed. It's certainly understandable that, at the end of his days, Wallace Stegner wasn't entirely optimistic about the future of the West, bedeviled as it is, still, by development pressures and insane political decisions. In these 16 thoughtful essays, he spells out his concerns—and again pays poetic homage to the West's big sky and bigger landscapes. In the end, he remains hopeful that a new spirit of place is emerging in the West—and that within a generation or two we will "work out some sort of compromise between what must be done to earn a living and what must be done to restore health to the earth, air, and water."

Steinbeck, John. *Cannery Row.* New York: Penguin USA, 1993. Reprint ed. Here it is, a poem, a stink, a grating noise, told in the days when sardines still ruled the boardwalk on Monterey's Cannery Row. Also worth an imaginative sidetrip on a tour of the California coast is Steinbeck's *East of Eden,* first published in 1952, the Salinas Valley version of the Cain and Abel story. Steinbeck's classic California work, though, is still *The Grapes of Wrath.*

Stevenson, Robert Louis. *The Complete Short Stories of Robert Louis Stevenson: With a Selection of the Best Short Novels.* New York: Da Capo Press, 1998. It's hard to know where-to start with Stevenson, whose California journeys served to launch his literary career. Da Capo's collection is as good a place as any.

van der Zee, John, and Boyd Jacobson. *The Imagined City: San Francisco in the Minds of Its Writers.* San Francisco: California Living Books, 1980 (OP). Quotes about San Francisco pulled from the works—mostly fiction—of 37 writers, both widely known and locally celebrated. Accompanied by photos and a page-long biography of each author, as well as historical photographs.

Waugh, Evelyn. *The Loved One.* Boston: Little, Brown, 1948. Pet cemeteries and people cemeteries with that eternal touch—nobody denies death better than L.A. And nobody writes about it better than Waugh.

West, Nathanael. *The Day of the Locust.* New York: New Directions, 1962. Before West and his wife were killed in a car accident, he published this surreal novel of L.A. apocalypse. This 1939 tale of terror premieres in Hollywood, naturally, but the story is about the troublesome troupes no longer needed by the silver screen.

WPA Guide to California: The Federal Writers Project Guide to 1930s California. New York: Pantheon Press (an imprint of Random House), 1984. The classic travel guide to California, first published during the Depression, is somewhat dated as far as contemporary sights but excellent as a companion volume and background information source.

HISTORY AND PEOPLE

Atherton, Gertrude. *My San Francisco, A Wayward Biography.* Indianapolis and New York: The Bobbs-Merrill Company, 1946. The 56th book—written at the age of 90—by the woman Kevin Starr has called "the daughter of the elite" whose career of historical fiction "document[ed] . . . itself . . . in a careless but vivid output. . . ." A delightfully chatty browse through the past, filled with dropped names and accounts of Atherton's own meetings with historic figures.

Barlett, Donald L., and James B. Steele. *Empire: The Life, Legend and Madness of Howard Hughes.* New York: W.W. Norton & Co., 1979. He of obsessive habits and unclipped fingernails wasn't always a madman. Earlier, Hughes was a noted Hollywood gadfly cum empire builder. This is the definitive work on the man and his mission.

Bean, Lowell John, and Lisa J. Bourgeault. *The Cahuilla.* New York: Chelsea House Publishers, 1989. Part of Chelsea's Indians of North America Series, this book explores the culture and history of the native peoples near Palm Springs. From rock art, pottery, and other details of daily life to contemporary history, *The Cahuilla* is a good, very readable introduction.

Bonadio, Felice. *A.P. Giannini: Banker of America.* Berkeley: University of California Press, 1994. Fascinating biography of Amadeo Peter Giannini, son of Italian immigrants, ruthless financial genius, friend of "the people," and founder of San Francisco's own (at least at one time) Bank of America. This is the story of the man who was the first to extend credit to working stiffs, and who also shared the bank's wealth with bank employees.

Brady, Frank. *Citizen Welles.* New York: Scribner, 1989. One of the noted few in Hollywood's genius genre, even Orson Welles had a tough time of it in Tinseltown.

Bronson, William. *The Earth Shook, The Sky Burned: A Photographic Record of the 1906 San Francisco Earthquake & Fire.* San Francisco: Chronicle Books, 1997. Originally published by Doubleday, 1959. A San Francisco classic—just the book to tote home as a memento of your San Francisco vacation. This moving story of the city's devastating 1906 earthquake and the four-day fire that followed includes more than 400 on-the-scene photographs.

Carnes, Mark C., ed. *Past Imperfect: History According to the Movies.* New York: Henry Holt & Co., 1995. Published under the aegis of the Society of American Historians, this historical peek into Hollywood's version of reality is offered via eclectic essays from about 60 writers, including Frances Fitzgerald, Stephen J. Gould, Antonia Fraser, Anthony Lewis, and Gore Vidal. *Past Imperfect* is as entertaining as it is educational.

Cleland, Robert Glass. *A History of California: The American Period.* Westport, CT: Greenwood Press, 1975. Originally published in 1922.

Cleland, Robert Glass. *From Wilderness to Empire: A History of California.* New York: Alfred A. Knopf, 1944 (OP).

Cole, Tom. *A Short History of San Francisco.* Lagunitas, CA: Lexikos, 1986. Very accessible, thoroughly entertaining overview, with clean design and some great old photos and illustrations.

Dalton, David. *James Dean: The Mutant King.* San Francisco: Straight Arrow Books, 1974. Dean's cult has grown larger and more disaffected since the actor's violent death on the highway after completing only three films for Hollywood. This pulpy bio digs into the Dean legend.

Davis, Margaret Leslie. *Rivers in the Desert: William Mulholland and the Inventing of Los Angeles.* New York: HarperCollins, 1993 (published in paperback by Harper Perennial). The astonishing and meticulously researched story of how self-taught water engineer William Mulholland masterminded massive water supplies for present-day Los Angeles, told with admiration and respect. Davis sidesteps the temptation to demonize Mulholland with 20/20 hindsight, though she does acknowledge more pointed current criticisms. In her epilogue she also takes care to exonerate Mulholland for the grievous sins history had tarred him with—the St. Francis Dam Disaster and the multitude of lives lost.

Davis, Mike. *City of Quartz: Excavating the Future in Los Angeles.* With photos by Robert Morrow. New York: Vintage Books, 1992. Something of a surprise bestseller in Southern California, as historical dust-up *City of Quartz* takes issue with the idea of California as an innocent and sunny paradise lost. From the book's prologue: "The pattern or urbanization here is what design critic Peter Plagens once called 'the ecology of evil.' Developers don't grow homes in the desert—this isn't Marrakesh or even Tucson—they just clear, grade and pave, hook up some pipes to the artificial river (the federally subsidized California Aqueduct), build a security wall, and plug in the 'product.' With generations of experience in uprooting the citrus gardens of Orange County and the San Fernando Valley, the developers . . . regard the desert as simply another abstraction of dirt and dollar signs." And with that, he's just warming up. A must-read for anyone who loves Los Angeles—or even the idea of Los Angeles.

Dreyer, Peter. *A Gardener Touched with Genius: The Life of Luther Burbank.* Berkeley: University of California Press, 1985.

Ellison, William Henry. *A Self-Governing Dominion, California 1849-1860.* Berkeley: University of California Press, 1978.

Farquhar, Francis P., ed. *Up and Down California in 1860-1864: The Journal of William H. Brewer.* Berkeley: University of California Press, 1974. Reprint of 1966 edition.

Fogelson, Robert M. *The Fragmented Metropolis: Los Angeles, 1850-1930.* With a new foreword by Robert Fishman. Berkeley: University of California Press, 1993. This new UC Press edition of an urban history classic includes a new preface and updated bibliography.

Frémont, John Charles. *Memoirs of My Life.* New York: Penguin, 1984. Originally published in Chicago, 1887. The old Bearflagger himself tells the story of early California—at least some of it.

Gutiérrez, Ramon A., and Richard J. Orsi, eds. *Contested Eden: California Before the Gold Rush.* Berkeley: University of California Press, 1998. In this first volume of a projected four-part series, essays explore California before the gold rush.

Harlow, Neal. *California Conquered: The Annexation of a Mexican Province, 1846-1850.* Berkeley: University of California Press, 1982.

Harte, Bret. *The Writings of Bret Harte.* New York: AMS Press, 1903.

Heizer, Robert F. *The Destruction of the California Indians.* Utah: Gibbs Smith Publishing, 1974.

Heizer, Robert F., and Albert B. Elsasser. *The Natural World of the California Indians.* Berkeley: University of California Press, 1980. As an adjunct to the rest of Heizer's work, this fact-packed volume provides the setting—the natural environment, the village environment—for California's native peoples.

Heizer, Robert F., and M.A. Whipple. *The California Indians.* Berkeley: University of California Press, 1971. A worthwhile collection of essays about California's native peoples, covering general, regional, and specific topics— a good supplement to the work of A.L. Kroeber (who also contributed to this volume).

Hine, Robert V. *California's Utopian Colonies.* Berkeley: University of California Press, 1983.

Holiday, James. *The World Rushed In: The California Gold Rush Experience: An Eyewitness Account of a Nation Heading West.* New York: Simon and Schuster, 1981. Reprint of a classic history, made while new Californians were busy making up the myth.

Horton, Tom. *Super Span: The Golden Gate Bridge.* San Francisco: Chronicle Books, 1983. How the Golden Gate Bridge came to be, illustrated with anecdotes and photographs—a very compelling history of an inanimate object.

Houston, James, and Jeanne Houston. *Farewell to Manzanar.* New York: Bantam Books, 1983. A good goodbye to California's World War II internment of Japanese immigrants and American citizens of Japanese descent, a nightmarish experience that lives on in the cultural memory of Southern California's large population of Japanese Americans.

Hutchinson, W.H. *California: The Golden Shore by the Sundown Sea.* Belmont, CA: Star Publishing Company, 1988. The late author, a professor emeritus of history at CSU Chico known as Old Hutch to former students, presents a dizzying amount of historical, economic, and political detail from his own unique perspective in this analysis of California's past and present. Hutchinson saw the state from many sides during a lifetime spent as "a horse wrangler, cowboy, miner, boiler fireman, merchant seaman, corporate bureaucrat, rodeo and horse show announcer, and freelance writer."

Irons, Peter. *Justice at War: The Story of the Japanese-American Internment Cases.* Berkeley: University of California Press, 1993. Irons examines the internment of Japanese Americans and noncitizen immigrants in World War II "relocation" camps as historical travesty in a brilliantly researched, beautifully written book.

Jackson, Mrs. Helen Hunt. *Century of Dishonor: A Sketch of the US Government's Dealings (with some of the Indian tribes).* Temecula, CA: Reprint Services, 1988. Originally published in Boston, 1881.

Kroeber, Alfred L. *Handbook of the Indians of California.* New York: Dover Publications, 1976 (unabridged facsimile version of the original work, Bulletin 78 of the Bureau of American Ethnology of the Smithsonian Institution, published by the U.S. Government Printing Office). The classic compendium of observed facts about California's native peoples by the noted UC Berkeley anthropologist who befriended Ishi—but also betrayed him, posthumously, by allowing his body to be autopsied (in violation of Ishi's beliefs) then shipping his brain to the Smithsonian Institution.

Kroeber, Theodora. *Ishi in Two Worlds: A Biography of the Last Wild Indian in North America.* Berkeley: University of California Press, 1961. The classic biography of Ishi, an incredible 20th-century story—illustrating California's location at the edge of the wilderness well into the 20th century—well-told by A.L. Kroeber's widow and also available in an illustrated edition. Also very worthwhile by Kroeber: Inland Whale: California Indian Legends, and, co-written with Robert F. Heizer, Ishi the Last Yahi: A Documentary History. That Ishi may not have been the last Yahi after all just makes the story all the more intriguing.

Lennon, Nigey. *Mark Twain in California.* San Francisco: Chronicle Books, 1982. An entertaining, enlightened, easy-reading biography from a true lover of Samuel Clemens's writings as Mark Twain.

Lewis, Oscar. *The Big Four.* Sausalito, CA: Comstock Editions, 1982. Originally published in New York, 1938.

Margolin, Malcolm. *The Way We Lived.* Berkeley: Heyday Books, 1981. A wonderful collection of California native peoples' reminiscences, stories, and songs. Also by Margolin: The Ohlone Way, about the life of California's first residents of the San Francisco-Monterey Bay Area.

McDonald, Linda, and Carol Cullen. *California Historical Landmarks.* Sacramento, CA: California Department of Parks and Recreation, 1997. Revised ed. Originally compiled in response to the National Historic Preservation Act of 1966, directing all states to identify all properties "possessing historical, architectural, archaeological, and cultural value," this updated edition covers more than 1,000 California Registered Historical Landmarks, organized by category—sites of aboriginal, economic, or government interest, for example—and indexed by county. A wide variety of other publications is available from the Department of Parks and Recreation. To order, call toll-free (800) 777-0369.

McWilliams, Carey, with a foreword by Lewis H. Lapham. *California, the Great Exception.* Berkeley: University of California Press, 1999. Historian, journalist, and lawyer Carey McWilliams, editor of The Nation from 1955 to 1975, stepped back from his other tasks in 1949 to assess the state of the Golden State at the end of its first 100 years. And while he acknowledged the state's prodigious productivity even then, he also noted the brutality with which the great nation-state of California dealt with "the Indian problem," the water problem, and the agricultural labor problem—all issues of continuing relevance to California today. McWilliams' classic work on the essence of California, reprinted with a new foreword by the editor of Harper's magazine, is a must-read for all Californians.

McWilliams, Carey. *Southern California Country: An Island Upon the Land.* New York: Duell, Sloan & Pierce, 1946. The classic of pre-World

War II L.A. history, still the best in terms of placing the city's seeming peculiarities in their proper contexts.

Milosz, Czeslaw. *Visions from San Francisco Bay*. New York: Farrar, Straus & Giroux, 1982. Essays on emigration from the Nobel Prize winner in literature. Originally published in Polish, 1969.

Monroy, Douglas. *Thrown Among Strangers: The Making of Mexican Culture in Frontier California*. Berkeley: University of California Press, 1990.

Nadeau, Remi. *City-Makers*. Garden City, NY: Doubleday, 1948. Hey, Chinatown fans. Here's the dark side of L.A. history in book form—the tale of the boosters, promoters, and sleazy business deals that together created present-day L.A., much to the detriment of the place and its people.

Perry, Charles. *The Haight-Ashbury: A History*. New York: Rolling Stone Press (an imprint of Random House), 1984. A detailed chronicle of events that began in 1965 and led up to the Summer of Love, with research, writing, and some pointed observations by the author, a Rolling Stone editor.

Pitt, Leonard. *Decline of the Californios: A Social History of the Spanish-Speaking Californians, 1846-1890*. Berkeley: University of California Press, 1966.

Powers, Stephen. *Tribes of California*. Berkeley: University of California Press, 1977.

Reisner, Marc. *Cadillac Desert: The American West and Its Disappearing Water*. New York: Penguin Books, 1993. Revised ed. Inspiration for the four-part PBS documentary of the same name, first broadcast in 1997, this is the contemporary yet classic tale of water and the unromantic West—a drama of unquenchable thirst and reluctant conservation, political intrigue and corruption, and economic and ecological disasters. How Los Angeles got its water figures prominently—the histories of

William Mulholland and the Owens Valley as well as the Colorado River. A must-read book.

Ridge, John. *The Life and Adventures of Joaquin Murrieta*. Norman, OK: University of Oklahoma Press, 1986.

Robinson, W.W. *Land in California: The Story of Mission Lands, Ranchos, Squatters, Mining Claims, Railroad Grants, Land Scrip, Homesteads*. Berkeley: University of California Press, 1979.

Royce, Josiah. *California from the Conquest in 1846 to the Second Vigilance Committee in San Francisco 1856*. New York: AMS Press. Originally published in Boston, 1886.

Santa Barbara Museum of Natural History. *California's Chumash Indians*. San Luis Obispo, CA: EZ Nature Books, 1988. A fascinating overview of Chumash culture, innovation, trade, and tradition.

St. Pierre, Brian. *John Steinbeck: The California Years*. San Francisco: Chronicle Books, 1983 (OP).

Saunders, Richard. *Ambrose Bierce: The Making of a Misanthrope*. San Francisco: Chronicle Books, 1984 (OP).

Sinclair, Upton. *American Outpost: A Book of Reminiscences*. Temecula, CA: Reprint Services, 1992.

Sinclair, Upton. *I, Candidate for Governor: And How I Got Licked*. Berkeley: University of California Press, 1994. Reprint of the original edition. This is a genuine treasure of California history—a first-person account of California's liveliest and most notorious gubernatorial race, in which California business employed Hollywood's tools to defeat muckraking journalist and socialist Democratic candidate Sinclair in the too-close-to-call 1934 campaign. Sinclair's platform was EPIC—End Poverty in California—and he almost got the chance to try. Though it's hard to imagine at the turn of this century, at other times in its history—certainly during the Great Depression—California as place got seriously agitated over issues of social justice, giving the good ol' boys quite a scare.

Starr, Kevin. *Americans and the California Dream: 1850-1915.* New York: Oxford University Press, 1973. A cultural history, written by a native San Franciscan, former newspaper columnist, onetime head of the city's library system, professor and historian, and current California State Librarian. The focus on Northern California taps an impressively varied body of sources as it seeks to "suggest the poetry and the moral drama of social experience" from California's first days of statehood through the Panama-Pacific Exposition of 1915 when, in the author's opinion, "California came of age." Starr's 1985 *Inventing the Dream: California Through the Progressive Era,* second in his California history series, and *Material Dreams: Southern California Through the 1920s,* his third, primarily tell the southstate story. Annotations in all three suggest rich possibilities for further reading.

Starr, Kevin. *The Dream Endures: California Enters the 1940s.* New York: Oxford University Press, 1997. This, the fifth volume in Kevin Starr's impressive California history series, traces the history of the California good life—in architecture, fiction, film, and leisure pursuits—and how it came to define American culture and society. Chosen Outstanding Academic Book of 1997 by *Choice,* and one of the best 100 books of 1997 by the *Los Angeles Times Book Review.*

Starr, Kevin. *Endangered Dreams: The Great Depression in California.* New York: Oxford University Press, 1996. "California," Wallace Stegner has noted, "is like the rest of the United States, only more so." And so begins the fourth volume of Starr's imaginative and immense California history, in which the author delves into the Golden State's dark past—a period in which strikes and unions were forcibly suppressed, soup kitchens became social institutions, and both socialism and fascism had their day. The "therapy" that finally cured California involved massive transfu-

sions of public capital in the form of public works projects. Yet some things don't change: San Francisco is still a strong union town, and Los Angeles barely tolerates unionism.

Starr, Kevin. *Inventing the Dream: California Through the Progressive Era.* New York: Oxford University Press, 1985. Second in Starr's projected five-part series on California history, *Inventing the Dream* addresses Southern California's ascendancy in the late 19th and early 20th centuries.

Starr, Kevin. *Material Dreams: Southern California Through the 1920s.* New York: Oxford University Press, 1990. The third book in Starr's lively symbolic celebration of California history chronicles the most compelling period of explosive growth in Los Angeles—which the author affectionately calls "the Great Gatsby of American cities"—made possible by the arrival of water.

Steinbeck, John. *Working Days: The Journals of the Grapes of Wrath 1938-1941.* New York: Penguin, 1989. Less an explanation for *The Grapes of Wrath* than a portrait of a writer possessed—and therefore quite interesting.

Stevenson, Robert Louis. *From Scotland to Silverado.* Cambridge, MA: The Belknap Press of Harvard University Press, 1966. An annotated collection of the sickly and lovelorn young Stevenson's travel essays, including his first impressions of Monterey and San Francisco, and the works that have come to be known as *The Silverado Squatters.* Contains considerable text—marked therein—that the author's family and friends had removed from previous editions. A useful introduction by James D. Hart details the journeys and relationships behind the essays.

Stone, Irving. *Jack London: Sailor on Horseback.* New York: Doubleday, 1986. Originally published in Boston, 1938.

Stone, Irving. *Men to Match My Mountains.* New York: Berkeley Publishers, 1987. A classic California history, originally published in 1956.

Stryker, Susan, and Jim Van Buskirk. *Gay by the Bay: A History of Queer Culture in the San Francisco Bay Area*. San Francisco: Chronicle Books, 1996. Chronicling the origin and evolution of lesbian, gay, bisexual, and transgender culture in San Francisco and environs, this book was published to coincide with the opening of the Gay and Lesbian Center—the first of its kind in this country—in the new San Francisco Public Library.

Walton, John. *Western Times and Water Wars: State, Culture, and Rebellion in California*. Berkeley: University of California Press, 1992. Winner of both the Robert Park and J.S. Holliday Awards, Walton's compelling chronicle of the water wars between Los Angeles and the farmers and ranchers of the Owens Valley is a masterpiece of California history.

NATURE AND NATURAL HISTORY

Alden, Peter. *National Audubon Society Field Guide to California*. New York: Alfred A. Knopf, 1998. A wonderful field guide to some 1,000 of the state's native inhabitants, from the world's smallest butterfly—the Western Pygmy Blue—to its oldest, largest, and tallest trees. Well illustrated with striking color photography.

Alt, David, and Donald Hyndman. *Roadside Geology of Northern & Central California*. Missoula, MT: Mountain Press, 1999. Second edition. The classic glovebox companion guide to the northstate landscape is now revised—and expanded to include central regions.

Bailey, Harry P. *The Weather of Southern California*. Berkeley: University of California Press, 1966.

Bakker, Elna. *An Island Called California: An Ecological Introduction to Its Natural Communities*. Berkeley: University of California Press, 1985. Expanded revised ed. An excellent, time-honored introduction to the characteristics of, and relationships between, California's natural communities. New chapters on Southern California, added in this edition, make *An Island* more helpful statewide.

Balls, Edward K. *Early Uses of California Plants*. Berkeley: University of California Press, 1962.

Barbour, Michael, Bruce Pavlik, Susan Lindstrom, and Frank Drysdale, with a foreword by Pulitzer Prize-winning California poet Gary Snyder. *California's Changing Landscapes: Diversity and Conservation of California Vegetation*. Sacramento: California Native Plant Society Press, 1993. Finalist for the Publishers Marketing Association's 1994 Benjamin Franklin Award in the Nature category, this well-illustrated, well-indexed lay guide to California's astonishing botanical variety is an excellent introduction. For more in-depth personal study, the society also publishes some excellent regional floras and plant keys.

Belzer, Thomas J. *Roadside Plants of Southern California*. Missoula, MT: Mountain Press, 1984. If as a nature lover you rarely venture far from the family car, this is the plant guide for you. From trees to cacti and wildflowers, the most likely roadside specimens are described in reasonable detail and illustrated with full-color photos.

Berry, William, and Elizabeth Berry. *Mammals of the San Francisco Bay Region*. Berkeley: University of California Press, 1959. Among other regional titles available: *Evolution of the Landscapes of the San Francisco Bay Region*, by Arthur David Howard; *Introduction to the Natural History of the San Francisco Bay Region*, by Arthur Smith; *Native Shrubs of the San Francisco Bay Region*, by Roxana S. Ferris; *Native Trees of the San Francisco Bay Region*, by Woodbridge Metcalf; *Rocks and Minerals of the San Francisco Bay Region*, by Oliver E. Bowen Jr.; *Spring Wildflowers of the San Francisco Bay Region*, by Helen Sharsmith; and *Weather of the San Francisco Bay Region*, by Harold Gilliam.

California Coastal Commission, State of California. *California Coastal Resource Guide*. Berkeley: University of California Press, 1997. This is the revised and expanded fifth edition of the California coast lover's bible, the indispensable guide to the Pacific coast and its wonders—the land, marine geology, biology—as well as parks, landmarks, and amusements. But for practical travel purposes, get the commission's *The California Coastal Access Guide,* listed under Enjoying the Outdoors below.

Clarke, Charlotte Bringle. *Edible and Useful Plants of California.* Berkeley: University of California Press, 1977. With this book in hand, almost anyone can manage to make a meal in the wilderness—or whip up a spring salad from the vacant lot next door.

Cogswell, Howard. *Water Birds of California.* Berkeley: University of California Press, 1977.

Collier, Michael. *A Land in Motion: California's San Andreas Fault.* Berkeley: University of California Press, 1999. An intriguing geologic tour of the world's most famous fault, which runs the entire length of western California—and right through the San Francisco Bay Area. Wonderful photographs.

Crampton, Beecher. *Grasses in California.* Berkeley: University of California Press, 1974.

Dale, Nancy. *Flowering Plants of the Santa Monica Mountains: Coastal and Chaparral Regions of Southern California.* Santa Barbara: Capra Press, 1986. With 214 color photos, dozens of illustrations and maps, and suggested wildflower walks, this is an invaluable book to tuck into the daypack for anyone spending serious time in the Santa Monicas.

Dawson, E. Yale. *Cacti of California.* Berkeley: University of California Press, 1966.

Dawson, E. Yale, and Michael Foster. *Seashore Plants of California.* Berkeley: University of California Press, 1982.

DeSante, David, and Peter Pyle. *Distributional Checklist to North American Birds.* The most accurate and up-to-date information ever assembled on the abundance and status of birds north of Mexico—indispensable to serious birders—but hard to find.

Duremberger, Robert. *Elements of California Geography.* Out of print but worth searching for. This is the classic work on California geography.

Ewing, Susan, and Elizabeth Grossman, eds. *Shadow Cat: Encountering the American Mountain Lion.* Seattle, WA: Sasquatch Books, 1999. This engaging, highly partisan collection of essays explores the uneasy coexistence we humans have with *Felis concolor,* now that cougars are increasing in numbers and populating almost every area remaining to them.

Farrand, John Jr. *Western Birds: An Audubon Handbook.* New York: McGraw-Hill Book Co., 1988. This birding guide includes color photographs instead of artwork for illustrations; conveniently included with descriptive listings. Though the book contains no range maps, the "Similar Species" listing helps eliminate birds with similar features.

Fitch, John. *Tidepool and Nearshore Fishes of California.* Berkeley: University of California Press, 1975.

Fitch, John E., and Robert J. Lavenberg. *California Marine Food and Game Fishes.* Berkeley: University of California Press, 1971.

Fradkin, Philip L. *The Seven States of California: A Natural and Human History.* New York: Henry Holt & Co., 1995; subsequently published in paperback by the University of California Press. Both personal and historical exploration of California.

Fuller, Thomas C., and Elizabeth McClintock. *Poisonous Plants of California.* Berkeley: University of California Press, 1987.

Garth, John S., and J.W. Tilden. *California Butterflies.* Berkeley: University of California Press, 1986. At long last, the definitive field guide and key to California butterflies (in both the larval and adult stages) is available, and in paperback; compact and fairly convenient to tote around.

Geologic Society of the Oregon Country. *Roadside Geology of the Eastern Sierra Nevada.* Informative pamphlet-sized book including Devil's Postpile, Mono Lake, the White Mountains, and Yosemite, at last report available from the Mono Lake Committee.

Grillos, Steve. *Fern and Fern Allies of California.* Berkeley: University of California Press, 1966.

Grinnell, Joseph, and Alden Miller. *The Distribution of the Birds of California.* Out of print but worth looking for (try the Mono Lake Committee; see The Sierra Nevada chapter), this is the definitive California birder's guide—for those interested in serious study.

Hale, Mason, and Mariette Cole. *Lichens of California.* Berkeley: University of California Press, 1988.

Hedgpeth, Joel W. *Introduction to Seashore Life of the San Francisco Bay Region and the Coast of Northern California.* Berkeley: University of California Press, 1969.

Hickman, Jim, ed. *The Jepson Manual: Higher Plants of California.* Berkeley: University of California Press (with cooperation and support from the California Native Plant Society and the Jepson Herbarium), 1993. Hot off the presses but at least 10 years in the making, *The Jepson Manual* is already considered the bible of California botany. The brainchild of both Jim Hickman and Larry Heckard, curator of the Jepson Herbarium, this book is a cumulative picture of the extraordinary flora of California, and the first comprehensive attempt to fit it all into one volume since the Munz *A California Flora* was published in 1959. The best work of almost 200 botanist-authors has been collected here, along with exceptional line drawings and illustrations (absent from the Munz flora) that make it easier to identify and compare plant species. This book is the botanical reference book for a California lifetime—a hefty investment for a hefty tome, especially essential for serious ecologists and botanists, amateur and otherwise.

Hill, Mary. *California Landscape: Origin and Evolution.* Berkeley: University of California Press, 1984. An emphasis on the most recent history of California landforms. Also by Hill: *Geology of the Sierra Nevada.*

Hinton, Sam. *Seashore Life of Southern California.* Berkeley: University of California Press, 1988. Revised and expanded.

Houk, Walter, Sue Irwin, and Richard A. Lovett. *A Visitor's Guide to California's State Parks,* Sacramento, CA: California Department of Parks and Recreation, 1990. This large-format, very pretty book includes abundant full-color photography and brief, accessible basic information about the features and facilities of the state's parks and recreation areas. *A Visitor's Guide* is available at retail and online bookstores and at the state parks themselves.

Jaeger, Edmund C., and Arthur C. Smith. *Introduction to the Natural History of Southern California.* Berkeley: University of California Press, 1966. A must-have for the southstate naturalist's bookshelf.

Johnston, Verna R. *California Forests and Woodlands: A Natural History.* Berkeley: University of California Press, 1994. For beginning botany students, a very helpful general introduction to the plants, animals, and ecological relationships within California's varied types of forests.

Kaufman, Kenn. *Lives of North American Birds.* New York: Houghton Mifflin Co., 1997. Sponsored by the Roger Tory Peterson Institute. A bit bulky for a field guide but already considered a classic, this 674-page hardbound tome focuses less on identifying features and names and more on observing and understanding birds within the contexts of their own lives. Now, there's a concept.

Klauber, Laurence. *Rattlesnakes.* Berkeley: University of California Press, 1982.

Leatherwood, Stephen, and Randall Reeves. *The Sierra Club Handbook of Whales and*

Dolphins. San Francisco: Sierra Club Books, 1983.

Le Boeuf, Burney J., and Stephanie Kaza. *The Natural History of Año Nuevo.* Santa Cruz, CA: Otter B Books, 1985. Reprint ed. An excellent, very comprehensive guide to the natural features of the Año Nuevo area just north of Santa Cruz.

Lederer, Roger. *Pacific Coast Bird Finder.* Berkeley: Nature Study Guild, 1977. A handy, hippocket-sized guide to birding for beginners. Also available: *Pacific Coast Tree Finder* by Tom Watts, among similar titles. All "Finder" titles are now available through Wilderness Press.

McCauley, Jane, and the National Geographic Society staff. *National Geographic Society Field Guide to the Birds of North America.* Washington, D.C.: National Geographic Society, 1993. One of the best guides to bird identification available.

McConnaughey, Bayard H., and Evelyn McConnaughey. *Pacific Coast.* New York: Alfred A. Knopf, 1986. One of the Audubon Society Nature Guides. More than 600 color plates, keyed to region and habitat type, make it easy to identify marine mammals, shorebirds, seashells, and other inhabitants and features of the West Coast, from Alaska to California.

McGinnis, Samuel. *Freshwater Fishes of California.* Berkeley: University of California Press, 1985. Including a simple but effective method of identifying fish, this guide also offers fisherfolk help in developing better angling strategies, since it indicates when and where a species feeds and what its food preferences are.

McMinn, Howard. *An Illustrated Manual of California Shrubs.* Berkeley: University of California Press, 1939. Reprint ed. An aid in getting to know about 800 California shrubs, this classic manual includes keys, descriptions of flowering, elevations, and geographic distributions. For the serious amateur botanist, another title for the permanent library.

Miller, Crane S., and Richard S. Hyslop. *California: The Geography of Diversity.* Palo Alto, CA: Mayfield Publishing Company, 1999. Second ed.

Munz, Philip A. *A Flora of Southern California.* Berkeley: University of California Press, 1974. This hefty hardcover tome, 1,086 pages, should be more than enough to help any plant lover explore every square inch of unpaved Southern California.

Munz, Phillip A., and David D. Keck. *A California Flora and Supplement.* Berkeley: University of California Press, 1968. Until quite recently this was it, the California botanist's bible—a complete descriptive "key" to every plant known to grow in California—but quite hefty to tote around on pleasure trips. More useful for amateur botanists are Munz's *California Mountain Wildflowers, Shore Wildflowers,* and *California Desert Wildflowers,* as well as other illustrated plant guides published by UC Press. Serious amateur and professional botanists and ecologists are more than ecstatic these days about the recent publication of the *new* California plant bible: *The Jepson Manual,* edited by Jim Hickman. (For more information, see above.)

Niesen, Thomas M. *Beachcomber's Guide to California Marine Life.* Houston: Gulf Publishing Co, 1994.

Nilsson, Karen B. *A Wildflower by Any Other Name.* Yosemite National Park: Yosemite Association, 1994. This engaging book tells the story of pioneering Western naturalists whose names—Eschscholtz and Chamisso, for example—often define either genus or species in the Latin names of many native plants. In an age of mass-marketed information, this is a gold mine for serious botany students and trivia buffs alike.

Ornduff, Robert. *Introduction to California Plant Life.* Berkeley: University of California Press, 1974. An essential for native plant libraries, this classic offers a marvelous introduction to California's botanical abundance.

Orr, Robert T., and Roger Helm. *Marine Mammals of California*. Berkeley: University of California Press, 1989. Revised ed. A handy guide for identifying marine mammals along the California coast—with practical tips on the best places to observe them.

Orr, R.T., and D.B. Orr. *Mushrooms of Western North America*. Berkeley: University of California Press, 1979.

Pavlik, Bruce, Pamela Muick, Sharon Johnson, and Marjorie Popper. *Oaks of California*. Santa Barbara: Cachuma Press, 1991. In ancient European times, oaks were considered spiritual beings, the sacred inspiration of artists, healers, and writers since these particular trees were thought to court the lightning flash. Time spent with this stunning book will soon convince anyone that this truth lives on. Packed with photos and lovely watercolor illustrations, maps, even an oak lover's travel guide, this book celebrates the many species of California oaks.

Peterson, Roger Tory. *A Field Guide to Western Birds*. Boston: Houghton Mifflin Co., 1990. The third edition of this birding classic has striking new features, including full-color illustrations (including juveniles, females, and in-flight birds) facing the written descriptions. The only thing you'll have to flip around for are the range maps, tucked away in the back. Among other intriguing titles in the Peterson Field Guide series: *A Field Guide to Western Birds' Nests* by Hal Harrison.

Powell, Jerry. *California Insects*. Berkeley: University of California Press, 1980.

Raven, Peter H. *Native Shrubs of California*. Berkeley: University of California Press, 1966.

Raven, Peter H., and Daniel Axelrod. *Origin and Relationships of the California Flora*. Sacramento: California Native Plant Society Press, 1995. Reprint of the 1978 original, another title most appropriate for serious students of botany.

Robbins, Chandler, et al. *Birds of North America*. New York: Golden Books Publishing Co., 1983. A good field guide for California bird-watching.

Roos-Collins, Margit. *The Flavors of Home: A Guide to the Wild Edible Plants of the San Francisco Bay Area*. Berkeley: Heyday Books, 1990. Just the thing to help you whip up a fresh trailside salad, a botanical essay, field guide, and cookbook all in one.

Schmitz, Marjorie. *Growing California Native Plants*. Berkeley: University of California Press, 1980. A handy guide for those interested in planting, growing, and otherwise supporting the success of California's beleaguered native plants.

Schoenherr, Allan A. *A Natural History of California*. Berkeley: University of California Press, 1992. With introductory chapters on ecology and geology, *A Natural History* covers California's climate, geology, soil, plant life, and animals based on distinct bioregions, with almost 300 photographs and numerous illustrations and tables. An exceptionally readable and well-illustrated introduction to California's astounding natural diversity and drama written by an ecology professor from CSU Fullerton, this 700-some page reference belongs on any Californiac's library shelf.

Starker, Leopold A. *The California Quail*. Berkeley: University of California Press, 1985. This is the definitive book on the California quail, its history and biology.

Stebbins, Robert. *California Amphibians and Reptiles*. Berkeley: University of California Press, 1972.

Wiltens, James. *Thistle Greens and Mistletoe: Edible and Poisonous Plants of Northern California*. Berkeley: Wilderness Press, 1988 (OP). How to eat cactus and pine cones and make gourmet weed salads are just a few of the fascinating and practical facts shared here about common northstate plants.

ENJOYING THE OUTDOORS: RECREATION, TOURS, TRAVEL

Bakalinsky, Adah. *Stairway Walks in San Francisco.* Berkeley: Wilderness Press, 1998. Third revised ed. This updated San Francisco classic offers 27 neighborhood walks connecting San Francisco's 200-plus stairways, choreographed by a veteran city walker and walking tour guide.

Blue, Anthony Dias, ed. *Zagat San Francisco Bay Area Restaurant Survey.* New York: Zagat Survey. This annually updated collection, a compilation of "people's reviews" of regional restaurants, is a fairly reliable guide to what's hot and what's not in San Francisco and surrounding Bay Area destinations.

Brant, Michelle. *Timeless Walks in San Francisco: A Historical Walking Guide.* Berkeley: Brant, 1996.

California Coastal Commission, State of California. *The California Coastal Access Guide.* Berkeley: University of California Press, 1997. Fifth revised ed. According to the *Oakland Tribune,* this is "no doubt the most comprehensive look at California's coastline published to date." A must-have for serious Californiacs.

California Coastal Conservancy, State of California. *San Francisco Bay Shoreline Guide.* Berkeley: University of California Press, 1995. This is it, the definitive guide to the entire 400-mile Bay Trail shoreline route, from its piers to its paths and parks. Comprehensive and user-friendly, with full-color maps and illustrations.

Cassady, Jim, and Fryar Calhoun. *California White Water: A Guide to the Rivers.* Berkeley: North Fork Press, 1995. Third revised ed. Also available: *California River Maps* and *White Water Guides.*

Clark, Jeanne L. *California Wildlife Viewing Guide.* Helena, MT: Falcon Press, 1996. Second ed. This revised and expanded guide tells you where to go for a good look at native wildlife, and what to do once you're there. Color photos, overview maps.

Collins, Andrew. *Fodor's Gay Guide to Los Angeles and Southern California.* New York: Fodor's, 1997.

Culliney, John, and Edward Crockett. *Exploring Underwater.* San Francisco: Sierra Club Books, 1980.

Dirksen, Diane J. *Recreation Lakes of California.* Port Angeles, WA: Recreation Sales Publishing, 1999. 12th ed. A very useful guide to the multitude of recreation lakes in California, complete with general maps (not to scale) and local contact addresses and phones. A worthwhile investment for boaters and fisherfolk.

Doss, Margot Patterson. *New San Francisco at Your Feet.* New York: Grove-Atlantic Press, 1990. One of a series of popular Bay Area walking guides by the same author, including: *The Bay Area at Your Feet,* 1987 (Lexicos); *There, There: East San Francisco Bay at Your Feet* (OP); and *A Walker's Yearbook: 52 Seasonal Walks in the San Francisco Bay Area,* 1989 (Lexicos).

Fein, Art. *L.A. Musical History Tour: A Guide to the Rock and Roll Landmarks of Los Angeles.* London: Faber and Faber, 1990.

Fong-Torres, Shirley. *San Francisco Chinatown: A Walking Tour.* San Francisco: China Books, 1991. Definitely an insider's guide to Chinatown, escorting visitors through the neighborhood almost step by step while filling in fascinating details about the history and culture of the Chinese in California. Fong-Torres also includes a culinary education, even abundant recipes for simple and authentic Chinese cuisine. For information on "Wok Wiz" culinary tours led by the author and her staff, see this book's San Francisco chapter. And buy *In the Chinese Kitchen with Shirley Fong-Torres,* 1993 (Pacific View Press).

Forée, Rebecca Poole, et al., eds. *Northern California Best Places.* Seattle, WA: Sasquatch

Books, 1998. Third ed. Though this reviewer also contributed to the first edition of *Best Places* and therefore isn't entirely objective, this massive compilation of detailed restaurant and accommodation reviews offers some entertaining insights as well as good local guidance in most price categories—always a plus.

Foster, Lynne. *Adventuring in the California Desert: The Sierra Club Travel Guide to the Great Basin, Mojave, and Colorado Desert Regions of California.* San Francisco: Sierra Club Books, 1997. Revised and updated edition. So, you wanna do the desert? This book is the best overall guide for figuring out where to go, when, and how. Out-there desert hikes are the book's obvious strength. But along with such sage advice you'll also find out plenty about desert history and natural history.

Gayot, André, ed. *The Best of Los Angeles and Southern California.* Los Angeles: Gault Millau, 1998. Sixth ed. Updated every three to four years. The bible for what to see and do, where to shop, and where to eat in L.A. and Southern California. Even Angelenos always have a copy on hand.

Gebhard, David, and Robert Winter. *Los Angeles: An Architectural Guide.* Layton, UT: Gibbs Smith, 1994. This is the Baedeker for devotees of Los Angeles architecture, encyclopedic in scope, though you may find the error quotient a bit high, even by everything-always-changes L.A. standards. Also worth it, from the same authors, with a broader reach: *A Guide to Architecture in Los Angeles and Southern California.*

Gersg-Young, Marjorie. *Hot Springs and Hot Pools of the Southwest.* Berkeley: Aqua Thermal Access (distributed by Wilderness Press), 1998. Revised and updated ed. A useful guide to California's commercial as well as unimproved (natural) yet accessible hot springs, including those in Arizona, Nevada, New Mexico, Texas, and Baja Mexico.

Greenwald, John A. *Saddleback Sightseeing in California: A Guide to Rental Horses, Trail Rides, and Guest Ranches.* Baldwin Park,

CA: Gem Guides Book Co., 1992. For modern-day dudes and dudettes, everything from hourly rental riding opportunities to guest ranch riding and pack trips is included here.

Hart, John. *Walking Softly in the Wilderness: The Sierra Club Guide to Backpacking.* San Francisco: Sierra Club Books, 1998. Third reprint ed. Also by Hart: *Hiking the Bigfoot Country* and *Hiking the Great Basin.*

Hosler, Ray. *Bay Area Bike Rides.* San Francisco: Chronicle Books, 1994. Second ed. More than 50 bike rides throughout the greater Bay Area—all the way to Napa and Sonoma Counties—useful for both mountain bikers and touring cyclists.

Jeneid, Michael. *Adventure Kayaking: Trips from the Russian River to Monterey.* Berkeley: Wilderness Press, 1998. Tired of fighting that freeway traffic around the Bay Area? Try a kayak. Under decent weather conditions—and with an experienced kayaker to clue you in—you can get just about everywhere. If you'll be shoving off a bit farther south, try *Adventure Kayaking: Trips from Big Sur to San Diego,* by Robert Mohle (1998).

Keator, Glenn. *Complete Garden Guide to the Native Shrubs of California.* San Francisco: Chronicle Books, 1994. California's native plants are under siege just about everywhere in the Golden State—so help nature out by stashing some natural biological diversity in your own backyard. More than 500 native shrub species are listed here, some beautifully represented by turn-of-the-century line drawings.

Kegan, Stephanie, and Elizabeth Pomada. *Fun Places to go with Children in Southern California.* San Francisco: Chronicle Books, 1997. Sixth ed. As important as finding a place to eat with kids is finding appropriate places to take them before and after meals.

Kirkendall, Tom, and Vicky Springs. *Bicycling the Pacific Coast.* Seattle: The Mountaineers, 1998. Third ed. A very good, very practical mile-by-mile guide to the tricky business of cycling along the California coast (and north).

Koenig, David. *Mouse Tales: A Behind-the-Ears Look at Disneyland.* Irvine, CA: Bonaventure Press, 1994. Disneyland is still one of Koenig's happiest places on earth, but that doesn't mean there aren't unofficial tales to tell—unsavory stories such as labor and discrimination disputes, gang fights, stabbings, shootings, a full-tilt riot, accidents, and of course lawsuits. And then there was the time the Yippies—Youth International Party anti-war activists—flew the Viet Cong flag over Tom Sawyer Island and turned Monsanto's Adventure through Inner Space into a pot-smoking den of druggy iniquity. Too much like real life, sure, and more than the average reader would care to know about Disneyland, but a good read nonetheless.

Lorentzen, Bob. *The Hiker's Hip Pocket Guide to the Mendocino Coast.* Mendocino, CA: Bored Feet Publications, 1998. Third ed. One of the stars in Lorentzen's excellent hiking series, this best-selling, easy-to-follow hiking guide now includes 100 more miles of trails. Coverage includes all Mendocino area state parks, Jackson State Forest, Sinkyone Wilderness State Park, and little-known coastal access points. Also by Lorentzen: *The Hiker's Hip Pocket Guide to the Humboldt Coast* (1996) and *The Hiker's Hip Pocket Guide to Sonoma County* (1995).

Lorentzen, Bob. *The Hiker's Hip Pocket Guide to the Mendocino Highlands.* Mendocino, CA: Bored Feet Publications, 1992. Updated ed. Another very good hiking guide, this one selects day hikes and overnight trips in inland Mendocino and Lake counties, including the Yolla Bolly-Middle Eel and Snow Mountain wildernesses. And Lorentzen's guides really *do* fit in your pocket—quite handy.

Lorentzen, Bob. *Mendocino Coast Bike Rides: Road & Trail Rides from Easy to Advanced.* Mendocino, CA: Bored Feet Publications, 1996.

Lorentzen, Bob, and Richard Nichols. *Hiking the California Coastal Trail, Volume One: Oregon to Monterey.* Mendocino, CA: Bored Feet Publications, 1998. The first comprehensive guide to the work-in-progress California Coastal Trail, America's newest and most diverse long-distance trail. Published in conjunction with Coastwalk—which receives a hefty percentage of the proceeds, to support its efforts to complete the trail—this accessible guide describes 85 sections of the California Coastal Trail's northern reach. Keep an eye out, too, for *Hiking the California Coastal Trail, Volume Two: Monterey to Mexico,* tentatively scheduled for publication in 1999.

Margolin, Malcolm. *East Bay Out.* Berkeley: Heyday Books, 1988. Second revised ed. Published with the cooperation and sponsorship of the East Bay Regional Parks District, this excellent guide focuses as much on the *feeling* as the facts of the East Bay's remaining wildlands, also urban parks and diversions. Highly recommended.

McConnell, Doug, with Jerry Emory and Stacy Gelken. *Bay Area Backroads.* San Francisco: Chronicle Books, 1993. Day trips and more throughout the greater Bay Area—and beyond—brought to you by the host of the San Francisco Bay Area's most popular local television show.

McKinney, John. *Coast Walks: 150 Adventures Along the California Coast.* Santa Barbara: Olympus Press, 1998. The new edition of McKinney's coast hiking classic contains plenty of new adventures, from Border Field State Park at the Mexican Border north to Damnation Creek and Pelican Bay. Along the way, you'll also learn about local lore, history, and natural history—a bargain no matter how you hike it. Maps and illustrations.

McKinney, John. *Day Hiker's Guide to California State Parks.* Santa Barbara: Olympus Press, 1997. All you need to know to stretch your legs *and* see the sights in the Golden State's hikable parks and recreation areas.

McKinney, John. *Day Hiker's Guide to Southern California,* Vols. I and II. Santa Barbara: Olympus Press, 1997. Second eds. Out in new, updated form in 1997, McKinney's Southern California hiking guides cover it all, from beach to desert badlands. As in the original editions,

Vol. I covers the author's favorite day hikes, from the Santa Barbara and Santa Monica Mountains to the vast inland deserts and San Diego backcountry. And you have to have Vol. II, which covers the same basic territory but includes instead everyone else's favorite hikes. Helpful maps (to scale) and black-and-white photos. If you can find it, also pick up *Walk Santa Barbara* by McKinney and Cheri Rae, for some nice city strolls.

McMillon, Bill, and Kevin McMillon. *Best Hikes With Children: San Francisco's North Bay.* Seattle: The Mountaineers, 1992. Also consider the McMillons' hiking guides to the South Bay and Sacramento.

Mitchell, Linda, and Allen Mitchell. *California Parks Access.* Berkeley: Cougar Pass Publications, 1992 (distributed by Wilderness Press). A very useful guide to national and state parks in California for visitors with limited mobility. Both challenges and wheelchair-accessible features are listed. Informationally accessible appendixes are helpful, too.

National Register of Historic Places, *Early History of the California Coast.* Washington, D.C.: National Conference of State Historic Preservation Officers, 1997. Map. This fold-out introduction to the California coast serves as a travel itinerary with 45 stops illustrating the coast's earliest settlement and culture.

Ostertag, Rhonda, and George Ostertag. *California State Parks: A Complete Recreation Guide.* Seattle: The Mountaineers, 1995. Moving from north to south, this readable companion serves as a good general introduction to the state parks—and guide to what to do while you're there, with an emphasis on hikes. Here California is divided into six regions. Helpful maps, some entertaining photos.

Parr, Barry. *San Francisco and the Bay Area.* Oakland: Compass American Guides, 1996. Fourth ed. With its dazzling prose and impressive intellectual intimacy, Parr's general guide to The City and vicinity is one of the best available, enjoyable, too, even for California natives, as companion reading.

Perry, John, and Jane Greverus Perry. *The Sierra Club Guide to the Natural Areas of California.* San Francisco: Sierra Club Books, 1997. Second ed. A just-the-facts yet very useful guide to California's public lands and parks— a book to tuck into the glovebox. Organized by regions, also indexed for easy access.

Pomada, Elizabeth. *Fun Places to Go with Children in Northern California.* San Francisco: Chronicle Books, 1997. Eighth ed. This long-running guide is based on the premise that, as important as it is to find a comfortable place to eat with kids, equally important is finding appropriate places to take them before and after meals. For aficionados of California's Victorian homes and buildings, the author's *Painted Ladies* series, co-authored with Michael Larsen, is also quite charming.

Rusmore, Jean. *The Bay Area Ridge Trail: Ridgetop Adventures Above San Francisco Bay.* San Francisco: Wilderness Press, 1998. This update of the original edition offers abundant adventures for hikers, bikers, and horseback riders, along 38 completed segments of this in-progress trail. Includes area maps, trailhead directions, and complete trail descriptions.

Rusmore, Jean, et al. *Peninsula Trails: Outdoor Adventures on the San Francisco Peninsula.* Berkeley: Wilderness Press, 1999. This updated third edition covers all parks and open-space preserves from Fort Funston south to Saratoga Gap. Also by Rusmore, and Frances Spangle: *South Bay Trails: Outdoor Adventures Around the Santa Clara Valley.*

Schad, Jerry. *Afoot and Afield in San Diego County.* Berkeley: Wilderness Press, 1992. Revised ed. Well-written, informative hiking guide offering a wide variety of hikes (rated for difficulty) along the coast and inland both in mountainous areas and desert. Also by Jerry Schad: *Afoot and Afield in Los Angeles County* (1990) and *Afoot and Afield in Orange County* (1988).

Schaffer, Jeffrey. *Hiking the Big Sur Country: The Ventana Wilderness.* Berkeley: Wilderness Press, 1988.

Schindler, Merrill, and Karen Berk, eds. *Zagat Survey:* Los Angeles/Southern California Restaurants. New York: Zagat Survey. Updated edition published annually. As in Zagat's guides to New York, San Francisco, and other cities, this compilation of "people's reviews" of regional restaurants is a fairly reliable guide to what's hot and what's not. It also includes some restaurants in Orange County, San Diego, and Santa Barbara.

Silverman, Goldie. *Backpacking with Babies and Small Children.* Berkeley: Wilderness Press, 1998. Third ed. Everything adventurous parents need to know, or consider, before heading to the woods with youngsters in tow.

Soares, Marc J. *Best Coast Hikes of Northern California: A Guide to the Top Trails from Bug Sur to the Oregon Border.* San Francisco: Sierra Club Books, 1998. There's something for everyone here—75 scenic trails, organized north to south, suited for all skill levels (including mention of those that allow dogs).

Socolich, Sally. *Bargain Hunting in the Bay Area.* San Francisco: Chronicle Books, 2000. The ultimate shop-til-you-drop guide, now in its 13th edition, including discount stores, outlets, flea markets, and the year's best sales.

Stevens, Barbara, and Nancy Conner. *Where on Earth: A Guide to Specialty Nurseries and Other Resources for California Gardeners.* Berkeley: Heyday Books, 1997. Ever wondered where to get that unusual color of iris or that exotic azalea, or where to find the state's best native plant nurseries? Wonder no more. California gardeners won't be able to live for long without *this* essential resource.

Stienstra, Tom. *California Camping: The Complete Guide.* Emeryville, CA: Foghorn Outdoors, 1999. Eleventh ed. This is undoubtedly the ultimate reference to California camping and campgrounds, public and private. Every single one is in here. Also included here are Stienstra's "Secret Campgrounds," an invaluable list when the aim is to truly get away from it all. In addition to a thorough practical introduction to the basics of California camping—

and reviews of the latest high-tech gear, for hiking and camping comfort and safety—this guidebook is meticulously organized by area, starting with the general subdivisions of Northern, Central, and Southern California. Even accidental outdoorspeople should carry this one along at all times.

Stienstra, Tom. *California Fishing: The Complete Guide.* Emeryville, CA: Foghorn Outdoors, 1999. This is it, *the* guide for people who think finding God has something to do with strapping on rubber waders or climbing into a tiny boat; making educated fish-eyed guesses about lures, ripples, or lake depths; and generally observing a strict code of silence in the outdoors. As besieged as California's fisheries have been by the state's 30 million-plus population and the attendant devastations and distractions of modern times, fisherfolk can still enjoy some world-class sport in California. This tome contains just about everything novices and masters need to know to figure out what to do as well as where and when to do it.

Stienstra, Tom. *Easy Camping in Northern California.* Emeryville: Foghorn Outdoors, 1999. Second ed. A great guide for beginning campers, detailing 100 easily accessible campgrounds and cabin getaways.

Unterman, Patricia, *Patricia Unterman's Food Lover's Guide to San Francisco.* San Francisco: Chronicle Books, 1997. Now out in an updated second edition, this is a marvelous guide to gustatory bliss by the Bay—written by the *San Francisco Examiner* food critic, also owner of the Hayes Street Grill—includes cheese shops, coffee emporiums, and favorites cafés and restaurants.

Wach, Bonnie. *San Francisco as You Like It: 20 Tailor-Made Tours for Culture Vultures, Shopaholics, Neo-Bohemians, Fitness Freaks, Savvy Natives, and Everyone Else.* San Francisco: Chronicle Books, 1998. A hefty helping of more than the usual tourist fare, from The Politically Correct and Avant-Garde Aunts tours to Current and Former Hippies, and Queer and Curious. And a good time will be had by all.

Wayburn, Peggy. *Adventuring in the San Francisco Bay Area*. San Francisco: Sierra Club Books, 1995. Revised ed. A fine guide to outdoor activities in the nine Bay Area counties, as well as the islands of the bay. Appendixes list frequent and occasional bird visitors, as well as California state parks, environmental organizations, and nature classes, all with addresses and phones.

Weintraub, David. *North Bay Trails: Outdoor Adventures in Marin, Napa, and Sonoma Counties*. Berkeley: Wilderness Press, 1999. Once you get there, this substantial guide to North Bay trails will help you get around.

Whitnah, Dorothy L. *Point Reyes*. Berkeley: Wilderness Press, 1997. Third revised ed. A very good and comprehensive guide (with an introduction by John Carroll) including trails, campgrounds, and picnic areas.

Winnett, Thomas, and Melanie Findling. *Backpacking Basics*. Berkeley: Wilderness Press, 1994. Fourth ed. Everything you need to know about going the distance on foot—with an emphasis on getting (and staying) in shape, the principles of low-impact camping, and how to save money on just about everything needed.

Zilly, John. *Wild Pigs: The Mountain Bike Adventure Guide to the Pacific Coast*. A personal tour of 47 spectacular trails and rides between Santa Barbara and British Columbia, with useful tips on making your own West Coast mountain bike adventures—responsibly.

INDEX

Outrigger Championships 368;
California Rodeo: 272; Cross-
Country Kinetic Sculpture Race
63, 64; Del Mar National
Horseshow 572; Formula One
International Motorcycle Races
294; Fortuna Rodeo 74, 77;
Gasquet Raft Race 58; Hang
Gliding Festival 367; Heavy
Wind Surfing Championships
351; Kinetic Sculpture Race 76;
Kinetic Sculpture Race at
Ventura 385; National Amateur
Horse Show 368; National
Horse Show 368; Ojai Valley
Tennis Tournament 382; Orick
Rodeo 74; Pacific Coast Open
Polo Tournament 368; San
Diego Crew Classic 572; San
Diego International Triathlon
572; San Diego Marathon 572;
Santa Cruz to Capitola Wharf to
Wharf Race 264-265; Tour of
the Unknown Coast Bicycle
Ride 76; Toyota Grand Prix of
Long Beach 462; U.S. Open of
Surfing 479, 486; Valley of the
Flowers Half-Marathon 351;
Visa Sports Car Championships
295
attitude: 30
Audubon Canyon Ranch: 131
automobiles: 40-43
Avalon: 470
Avenue of the Giants: 80
aviation: 539
Avila Beach: 344
Avila Hot Springs: 344
A.W. Way County Park: 89
Azalea State Reserve: 64

B
Bach Dancing & Dynamite
Society: 237
Backbone Trail: 449
Backesto Building: 556
Bahia Belle: 563
Bailey House: 441
Baker Beach: 147, 151
Balboa Beach: 494
Balboa Ferry: 494, 495
Balboa Island: 495
Balboa Park: 543-550
Balboa Pavilion: 494

Balboa Pier: 494
Balconies Trail: 174
Ballard: 355
Ballet Pacifica: 512
Ballona Wetlands: 429
Balmy Alley: 168
Bank of California building: 163
Banning Residence Museum: 460
Barbary Coast Trail: 193

Barbra Streisand Center for
Conservancy Studies: 448
Bargetto Winery: 278
Bark Park: 514
Barnstorming Adventures Ltd.:
574
baseball: 176, 402, 574
basketball: 402
Batiquitos Lagoon: 530

ART AND THEATER FESTIVALS

Art-A-Fair: 479, 511-512
Art & Wine Festival: 265
Art in the Gardens: 109
Art in the Park: 559
Art Walk: 479
Art Walk Lunch: 512
Beach Arts and Crafts Show: 369
Carmel Shakespeare Festival: 312
Catalina Festival of Art: 469
Downtown ArtWalk: 572
Festival of Animation: 572
Festival of Arts: 479
Festival of the Arts: 511
Films in the Forest: 312
Gualala Arts Studio Tour: 109
Half Moon Bay Art and Pumpkin Festival: 238
Humboldt Arts Festival: 74
I Madonnari Italian Street Painting Festival: 367
Julian Weed Show and Art Mart: 568
Mendocino Shakespeare Festival: 110
Monterey Bay Theatrefest: 295
Ojai International Film Festival: 382
Old Globe Festival: 547
Old Globe Shakespeare Festival: 571
Old Mission Art Festival: 368
Pageant of the Masters: 479, 511
San Francisco International Film Festival: 156
San Francisco International Lesbian and Gay Film Festival: 156
Santa Barbara Art Walk: 368
Santa Barbara Arts & Crafts Show: 367
Santa Barbara International Film Festival: 367, 368
Sawdust Festival: 479, 511
Shakespeare at Benbow Lake: 83
Shakespeare Santa Cruz: 264
Silent Film Festival: 469
Summer Art Fair: 109
Summer Arts Fair: 83
Summer Theaterfest: 353
Thanksgiving Art Festival: 109
Venice Art Walk: 428

DIVING/SCUBA

KID STUFF

SURFING

WHALEWATCHING

ABOUT THE AUTHOR

Kim Weir is a California native. She is also a journalist and writer. A curious generalist by nature, Weir is most happy when turning over rocks—literally and figuratively—or poking into this and that to discover what usually goes unnoticed. She lives in Northern California.

Weir's formal study of environmental issues began at the University of California at Santa Barbara and continued at California State University, Chico, where she studied biology and obtained a bachelor's degree in environmental studies and analysis. Since all things are interconnected, as a journalist Weir covered the political environment and the natural and unnatural antics of politicians. Before signing on with Moon Publications, she also held an editorial post with a scholarly publishing company.

Weir is a member of the Society of American Travel Writers (SATW). Her award-winning essay on ecotourism was published in the 1993 international *American Express Annual Review of Travel.* She is also a graduate student, a member of the initial class of the new California State University consortium MFA in Creative Writing program.

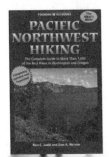

FOR TRAVELERS WITH
SPECIAL INTERESTS

GUIDES

The 100 Best Small Art Towns in America • Asia in New York City
The Big Book of Adventure Travel • Cities to Go
Cross-Country Ski Vacations • Gene Kilgore's Ranch Vacations
Great American Motorcycle Tours • Healing Centers and Retreats
Indian America • Into the Heart of Jerusalem
The People's Guide to Mexico • The Practical Nomad
Saddle Up! • Staying Healthy in Asia, Africa, and Latin America
Steppin' Out • Travel Unlimited • Understanding Europeans
Watch It Made in the U.S.A. • The Way of the Traveler
Work Worldwide • The World Awaits
The Top Retirement Havens • Yoga Vacations

SERIES

Adventures in Nature
The Dog Lover's Companion
Kidding Around
Live Well

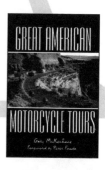

MOON HANDBOOKS

provide comprehensive coverage of a region's arts, history, land, people, and social issues in addition to detailed practical listings for accommodations, food, outdoor recreation, and entertainment. Moon Handbooks allow complete immersion in a region's culture—ideal for travelers who want to combine sightseeing with insight for an extraordinary travel experience.

USA

Alaska-Yukon • Arizona • Big Island of Hawaii • Boston
Coastal California • Colorado • Connecticut • Georgia
Grand Canyon • Hawaii • Honolulu-Waikiki • Idaho • Kauai
Los Angeles • Maine • Massachusetts • Maui • Michigan
Montana • Nevada • New Hampshire • New Mexico
New York City • New York State • North Carolina
Northern California • Ohio • Oregon • Pennsylvania
San Francisco • Santa Fe-Taos • Silicon Valley
South Carolina • Southern California • Tahoe • Tennessee
Texas • Utah • Virginia • Washington • Wisconsin
Wyoming • Yellowstone-Grand Teton

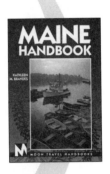

INTERNATIONAL

Alberta and the Northwest Territories • Archaeological Mexico
Atlantic Canada • Australia • Baja • Bangkok • Bali • Belize
British Columbia • Cabo • Canadian Rockies • Cancún
Caribbean Vacations • Colonial Mexico • Costa Rica • Cuba
Dominican Republic • Ecuador • Fiji • Havana • Honduras
Hong Kong • Indonesia • Jamaica • Mexico City • Mexico
Micronesia • The Moon • Nepal • New Zealand • Northern Mexico
Oaxaca • Pacific Mexico • Pakistan • Philippines • Puerto Vallarta
Singapore • South Korea • South Pacific • Southeast Asia • Tahiti
Thailand • Tonga-Samoa • Vancouver • Vietnam, Cambodia and Laos
Virgin Islands • Yucatán Peninsula

www.moon.com

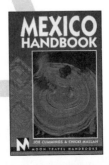

Rick Steves shows you where to travel and how to travel—all while getting the most value for your dollar. His Back Door travel philosophy is about making friends, having fun, and avoiding tourist rip-offs.

Rick's been traveling to Europe for more than 25 years and is the author of 22 guidebooks, which have sold more than a million copies. He also hosts the award-winning public television series Travels in Europe with Rick Steves.

RICK STEVES' COUNTRY & CITY GUIDES
Best of Europe
France, Belgium & the Netherlands
Germany, Austria & Switzerland
Great Britain & Ireland
Italy • London • Paris • Rome • Scandinavia • Spain & Portugal

RICK STEVES' PHRASE BOOKS
French • German • Italian • French, Italian & German
Spanish & Portuguese

MORE EUROPE FROM RICK STEVES
Europe 101
Europe Through the Back Door
Mona Winks
Postcards from Europe

WWW.RICKSTEVES.COM

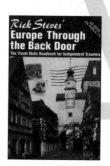

ROAD TRIP USA

Getting there is half the fun, and Road Trip USA guides are your ticket to driving adventure. Taking you off the interstates and onto less-traveled, two-lane highways, each guide is filled with fascinating trivia, historical information, photographs, facts about regional writers, and details on where to sleep and eat—all contributing to your exploration of the American road.

"Books so full of the pleasures of the American road, you can smell the upholstery."
~ BBC radio

THE ORIGINAL CLASSIC GUIDE
Road Trip USA

ROAD TRIP USA REGIONAL GUIDE
Road Trip USA: California and the Southwest

ROAD TRIP USA GETAWAYS
Road Trip USA Getaways: Chicago
Road Trip USA Getaways: New Orleans
Road Trip USA Getaways: San Francisco
Road Trip USA Getaways: Seattle

www.roadtripusa.com

TRAVEL ✦ SMART® guidebooks are accessible, route-based driving guides. Special interest tours provide the most practical routes for family fun, outdoor activities, or regional history for a trip of anywhere from two to 22 days. Travel Smarts take the guesswork out of planning a trip by recommending only the most interesting places to eat, stay, and visit.

"One of the few travel series that rates sightseeing attractions. That's a handy feature. It helps to have some guidance so that every minute counts."
~ San Diego Union-Tribune

TRAVEL SMART REGIONS

Alaska
American Southwest
Arizona
Carolinas
Colorado
Deep South
Eastern Canada
Florida Gulf Coast
Florida
Georgia
Hawaii
Illinois/Indiana
Iowa/Nebraska
Kentucky/Tennessee
Maryland/Delaware
Michigan
Minnesota/Wisconsin
Montana/Wyoming/Idaho
Nevada
New England
New Mexico
New York State

Northern California
Ohio
Oregon
Pacific Northwest
Pennsylvania/New Jersey
South Florida and the Keys
Southern California
Texas
Utah
Virginias
Western Canada

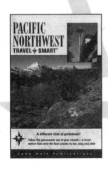

Foghorn Outdoors

guides are for campers, hikers, boaters, anglers, bikers, and golfers of all levels of daring and skill. Each guide contains site descriptions and ratings, driving directions, facilities and fees information, and easy-to-read maps that leave only the task of deciding where to go.

"Foghorn Outdoors has established an ecological conservation standard unmatched by any other publisher."
~ Sierra Club

CAMPING Arizona and New Mexico Camping
Baja Camping • California Camping
Camper's Companion • Colorado Camping
Easy Camping in Northern California
Easy Camping in Southern California
Florida Camping • New England Camping
Pacific Northwest Camping
Utah and Nevada Camping

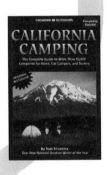

HIKING 101 Great Hikes of the San Francisco Bay Area
California Hiking • Day-Hiking California's National Parks
Easy Hiking in Northern California
Easy Hiking in Southern California
New England Hiking
Pacific Northwest Hiking • Utah Hiking

FISHING Alaska Fishing • California Fishing
Washington Fishing

BOATING California Recreational Lakes and Rivers
Washington Boating and Water Sports

OTHER OUTDOOR RECREATION California Beaches
California Golf • California Waterfalls • California Wildlife
Easy Biking in Northern California • Florida Beaches
The Outdoor Getaway Guide For Southern California
Tom Stienstra's Outdoor Getaway Guide: Northern California

WWW.FOGHORN.COM

CiTY·SMaRT™

The best way to enjoy a city is to get advice from someone who lives there—and that's exactly what City Smart guidebooks offer. City Smarts are written by local authors with hometown perspectives who have personally selected the best places to eat, shop, sightsee, and simply hang out. The honest, lively, and opinionated advice is perfect for business travelers looking to relax with the locals or for longtime residents looking for something new to do Saturday night.

A portion of sales from each title
benefits a non-profit literacy organization in that city.

CITY SMART CITIES

Albuquerque	Anchorage
Austin	Baltimore
Berkeley/Oakland	Boston
Calgary	Charlotte
Chicago	Cincinnati
Cleveland	Dallas/Ft. Worth
Denver	Indianapolis
Kansas City	Memphis
Milwaukee	Minneapolis/St. Paul
Nashville	Pittsburgh
Portland	Richmond
San Francisco	Sacramento
St. Louis	Salt Lake City
San Antonio	San Diego
Tampa/St. Petersburg	Toronto
Tucson	Vancouver

www.travelmatters.com

User-friendly, informative, and fun:
Because travel _matters_.

**Visit our newly launched web site and explore the variety
of titles and travel information available online, featuring
an interactive _Road Trip USA_ exhibit.**

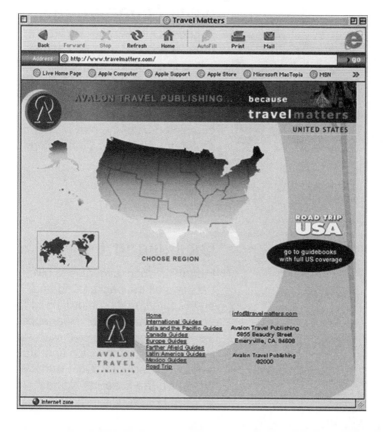

www.ricksteves.com

The Rick Steves web site is bursting with information to boost your travel I.Q. and liven up your European adventure. Including:

- The latest from Rick on what's hot in Europe
- Excerpts from Rick's books
- Rick's comprehensive Guide to European Railpasses

www.foghorn.com

Foghorn Outdoors guides are the premier source for United States outdoor recreation information. Visit the Foghorn Outdoors web site for more information on these activity-based travel guides, including the complete text of the handy *Foghorn Outdoors: Camper's Companion*.

www.moon.com

Moon Handbooks' goal is to give travelers all the background and practical information they'll need for an extraordinary travel experience. Visit the Moon Handbooks web site for interesting information and practical advice, including Q&A with the author of *The Practical Nomad*, Edward Hasbrouck.

U.S.~METRIC CONVERSION

1 inch = 2.54 centimeters (cm)
1 foot = .3048 meters (m)
1 yard = 0.914 meters
1 mile = 1.6093 kilometers (km)
1 km = .6214 miles
1 fathom = 1.8288 m
1 chain = 20.1168 m
1 furlong = 201.168 m
1 acre = .4047 hectares
1 sq km = 100 hectares
1 sq mile = 2.59 square km
1 ounce = 28.35 grams
1 pound = .4536 kilograms
1 short ton = .90718 metric ton
1 short ton = 2000 pounds
1 long ton = 1.016 metric tons
1 long ton = 2240 pounds
1 metric ton = 1000 kilograms
1 quart = .94635 liters
1 US gallon = 3.7854 liters
1 Imperial gallon = 4.5459 liters
1 nautical mile = 1.852 km

To compute celsius temperatures, subtract 32 from Fahrenheit and divide by 1.8. To go the other way, multiply celsius by 1.8 and add 32.

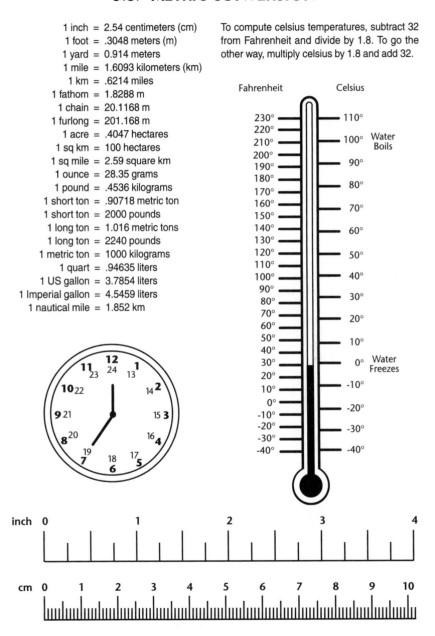

Next time, make your *own* hotel arrangements.

Yahoo! Travel

Do You Yahoo!?